STRANGE TALES #129
WRITER: DON RICO
ILLUSTRATOR: STEVE DITKO
LETTERER: SAM ROSEN

STRANGE TALES #130
WRITER: STAN LEE
ILLUSTRATOR: STEVE DITKO
LETTERER: ART SIMEK

STRANGE TALES #131
WRITER: STAN LEE
ILLUSTRATOR: STEVE DITKO
LETTERER: ART SIMEK

STRANGE TALES #132
WRITER: STAN LEE
ILLUSTRATOR: STEVE DITKO
LETTERER: ART SIMEK

STRANGE TALES #133
WRITER: STAN LEE
ILLUSTRATOR: STEVE DITKO
LETTERER: SAM ROSEN

STRANGE TALES #134
WRITER: STAN LEE
ILLUSTRATOR: STEVE DITKO
LETTERER: ART SIMEK

STRANGE TALES #135
WRITER: STAN LEE
ILLUSTRATOR: STEVE DITKO
LETTERER: SAM ROSEN

STRANGE TALES #136
WRITER: STAN LEE
ILLUSTRATOR: STEVE DITKO
LETTERER: ART SIMEK

STRANGE TALES #137
WRITER: STAN LEE
ILLUSTRATOR: STEVE DITKO
LETTERER: ART SIMEK

STRANGE TALES #138
WRITER: STAN LEE
ILLUSTRATOR: STEVE DITKO
LETTERER: SAM ROSEN

STRANGE TALES #139
WRITER: STAN LEE
ILLUSTRATOR: STEVE DITKO
LETTERER: ART SIMEK

STRANGE TALES #140
WRITER: STAN LEE
ILLUSTRATOR: STEVE DITKO
LETTERER: SAM ROSEN

STRANGE TALES #141
WRITER: STAN LEE
ILLUSTRATOR: STEVE DITKO
LETTERER: ART SIMEK

STRANGE TALES #142
WRITER: STAN LEE
ILLUSTRATOR: STEVE DITKO
LETTERER: ART SIMEK

STRANGE TALES #143
WRITER: ROY THOMAS
ILLUSTRATOR: STEVE DITKO
LETTERER: ART SIMEK

STRANGE TALES #144
WRITER: ROY THOMAS
ILLUSTRATOR: STEVE DITKO
LETTERER: ART SIMEK

STRANGE TALES #145
WRITER: DENNIS O'NEIL
ILLUSTRATOR: STEVE DITKO
LETTERER: ART SIMEK

STRANGE TALES #146
WRITER: DENNIS O'NEIL
ILLUSTRATOR: STEVE DITKO
LETTERER: ART SIMEK

STRANGE TALES #147
WRITERS: STAN LEE & DENNIS O'NEIL
ILLUSTRATOR: BILL EVERETT
LETTERER: SAM ROSEN

STRANGE TALES #148
WRITER: DENNIS O'NEIL
ILLUSTRATOR: BILL EVERETT
LETTERER: ART SIMEK

STRANGE TALES #149
WRITER: DENNIS O'NEIL
ILLUSTRATOR: BILL EVERETT
LETTERER: SAM ROSEN

STRANGE TALES #150
WRITER: ROY THOMAS
ILLUSTRATOR: BILL EVERETT
LETTERER: ART SIMEK

STRANGE TALES #151
WRITER: STAN LEE
ILLUSTRATOR: BILL EVERETT
LETTERER: ART SIMEK

STRANGE TALES #152
WRITER: STAN LEE
ILLUSTRATOR: BILL EVERETT
LETTERER: ART SIMEK

STRANGE TALES #153
WRITER: STAN LEE
ILLUSTRATOR: MARIE SEVERIN
LETTERER: SAM ROSEN

STRANGE TALES #154
WRITER: STAN LEE
ILLUSTRATOR: MARIE SEVERIN
LETTERER: SAM ROSEN

STRANGE TALES #155
WRITER: STAN LEE
ILLUSTRATOR: MARIE SEVERIN
LETTERER: ART SIMEK

STRANGE TALES #156
WRITER: STAN LEE
ILLUSTRATOR: MARIE SEVERIN
LETTERER: ART SIMEK

STRANGE TALES #157
WRITER: STAN LEE
PENCILER: MARIE SEVERIN
INKER: HERB TRIMPE
LETTERER: ART SIMEK

STRANGE TALES #158
WRITER: ROY THOMAS
PENCILER: MARIE SEVERIN
INKER: HERB TRIMPE
LETTERER: ART SIMEK

STRANGE TALES #159
WRITER: ROY THOMAS
PENCILER: MARIE SEVERIN
INKER: HERB TRIMPE
LETTERER: AL KURZROK

STRANGE TALES #160
WRITER: RAMOND MARAIS
PENCILER: MARIE SEVERIN
INKER: HERB TRIMPE
LETTERER: AL KURZROK

STRANGE TALES #161
WRITER: RAMOND MARAIS
ILLUSTRATOR: DAN ADKINS
LETTERER: AL KURZROK

STRANGE TALES #162
WRITER: JIM LAWRENCE
ILLUSTRATOR: DAN ADKINS
LETTERER: SAM ROSEN

STRANGE TALES #163

WRITER: JIM LAWRENCE
ILLUSTRATOR: DAN ADKINS
LETTERER: AL KURZROK

STRANGE TALES #164

WRITER: JIM LAWRENCE
ILLUSTRATOR: DAN ADKINS
LETTERER: AL KURZROK

STRANGE TALES #165

WRITER: JIM LAWRENCE
ILLUSTRATOR: DAN ADKINS
LETTERER: AL KURZROK

STRANGE TALES #166

WRITER: JIM LAWRENCE
PENCILER: GEORGE TUSKA
INKER: DAN ADKINS
LETTERER: ART SIMEK

STRANGE TALES #167

WRITER: DENNY O'NEIL
ILLUSTRATOR: DAN ADKINS
LETTERER: SAM ROSEN

STRANGE TALES #168

WRITER: DENNY O'NEIL
ILLUSTRATOR: DAN ADKINS
LETTERER: SAM ROSEN

REPRINT CREDITS

COVER ART
STEVE DITKO

COVER COLORS
TOMMY CHU

COVER & INTERIOR DESIGN
JOHN 'JG' ROSHELL OF COMICRAFT

PRODUCTION ASSISTANT
CORY SEDLMEIER

ASSISTANT EDITOR
MIKE FARAH

COLLECTIONS EDITOR
MATTY RYAN

MANUFACTURING REPRESENTATIVE
FENTON ENG

DIRECTOR-PUBLISHING OPERATIONS
BOB GREENBERGER

EDITOR IN CHIEF
JOE QUESADA

PRESIDENT & COO PUBLISHING, CONSUMER PRODUCTS & NEW MEDIA
BILL JEMAS

ESSENTIAL DR. STRANGE ® VOL 1. Contains material originally published in magazine form as STRANGE TALES #110-111, 114-168. First printing, December 2001. ISBN# 0-7851-0816-5. GST. #R127032852. Published by MARVEL COMICS, a division of MARVEL ENTERTAINMENT GROUP, INC. OFFICE OF PUBLICATION: 10 EAST 40th STREET, NEW YORK, NY 10016. Printed in Canada. PETER CUNEO, Chief Executive Officer; AVI ARAD, Chief Creative Officer; GUI KARYO, Chief Information Officer; BOB GREENBERGER, Director – Publishing Operations; STAN LEE, Chairman Emeritus.

10 9 8 7 6 5 4 3 2 1

ESSENTIAL

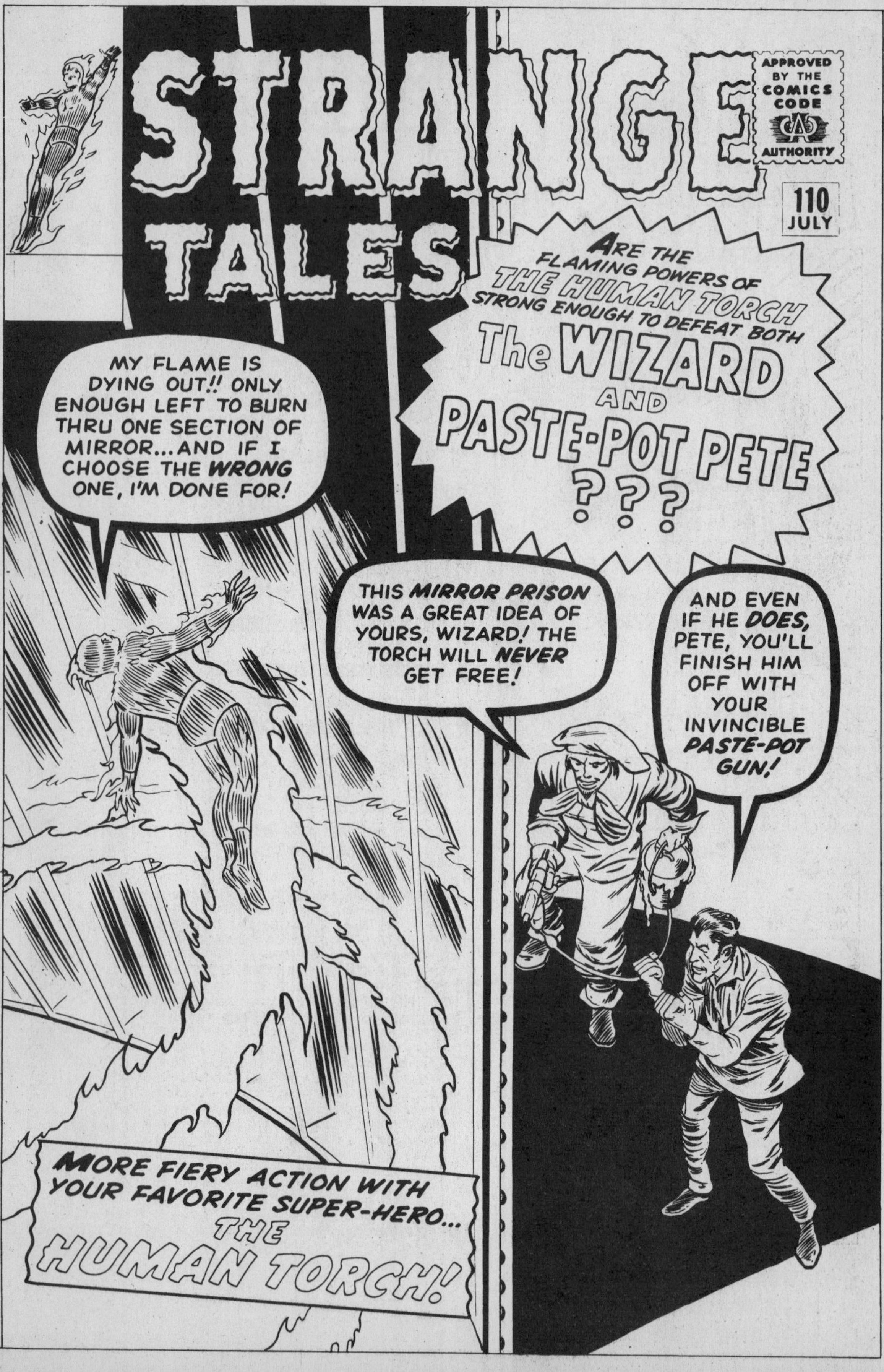

STRANGE TALES
APPROVED BY THE COMICS CODE AUTHORITY
110 JULY
ARE THE FLAMING POWERS OF THE HUMAN TORCH STRONG ENOUGH TO DEFEAT BOTH The WIZARD AND PASTE-POT PETE ???
MY FLAME IS DYING OUT!! ONLY ENOUGH LEFT TO BURN THRU ONE SECTION OF MIRROR...AND IF I CHOOSE THE WRONG ONE, I'M DONE FOR!
THIS MIRROR PRISON WAS A GREAT IDEA OF YOURS, WIZARD! THE TORCH WILL NEVER GET FREE!
AND EVEN IF HE DOES, PETE, YOU'LL FINISH HIM OFF WITH YOUR INVINCIBLE PASTE-POT GUN!
MORE FIERY ACTION WITH YOUR FAVORITE SUPER-HERO... THE HUMAN TORCH!

"Dr. STRANGE MASTER of BLACK MAGIC!"

MEN CALL HIM *DR. STRANGE!* NEVER HAVE YOU KNOWN HIS LIKE! IT IS A GREAT PLEASURE AND PRIVILEGE FOR THE EDITORS OF *STRANGE TALES* TO PRESENT, QUIETLY AND WITHOUT FANFARE, THE FIRST OF A NEW SERIES, BASED UPON A *DIFFERENT* KIND OF SUPER HERO--

DR. STRANGE MASTER OF BLACK MAGIC!

STORY:	STAN LEE
ART:	STEVE DITKO
LETTERING:	TERRY SZENICS

SOMEWHERE IN THE CITY, BETWEEN DARKNESS AND DAWN, A TORTURED MAN TOSSES FITFULLY IN HIS BED, VAINLY SEEKING PEACE THAT WILL NOT COME...

NO! NO!! GO AWAY! PLEASE-- *PLEASE GO AWAY!*

IT'S NO USE! I CAN'T SLEEP! I *DARE* NOT SLEEP! IT'S THAT SAME DREAM! EVERY NIGHT THE SAME! BUT *WHY?* WHAT CAN IT *MEAN??*

I CAN'T FIGHT IT ALONE! I NEED HELP! I'VE HEARD A NAME--- SPOKEN IN WHISPERS--- *DR. STRANGE!* HE DABBLES IN BLACK MAGIC! PERHAPS *HE* CAN HELP ME!

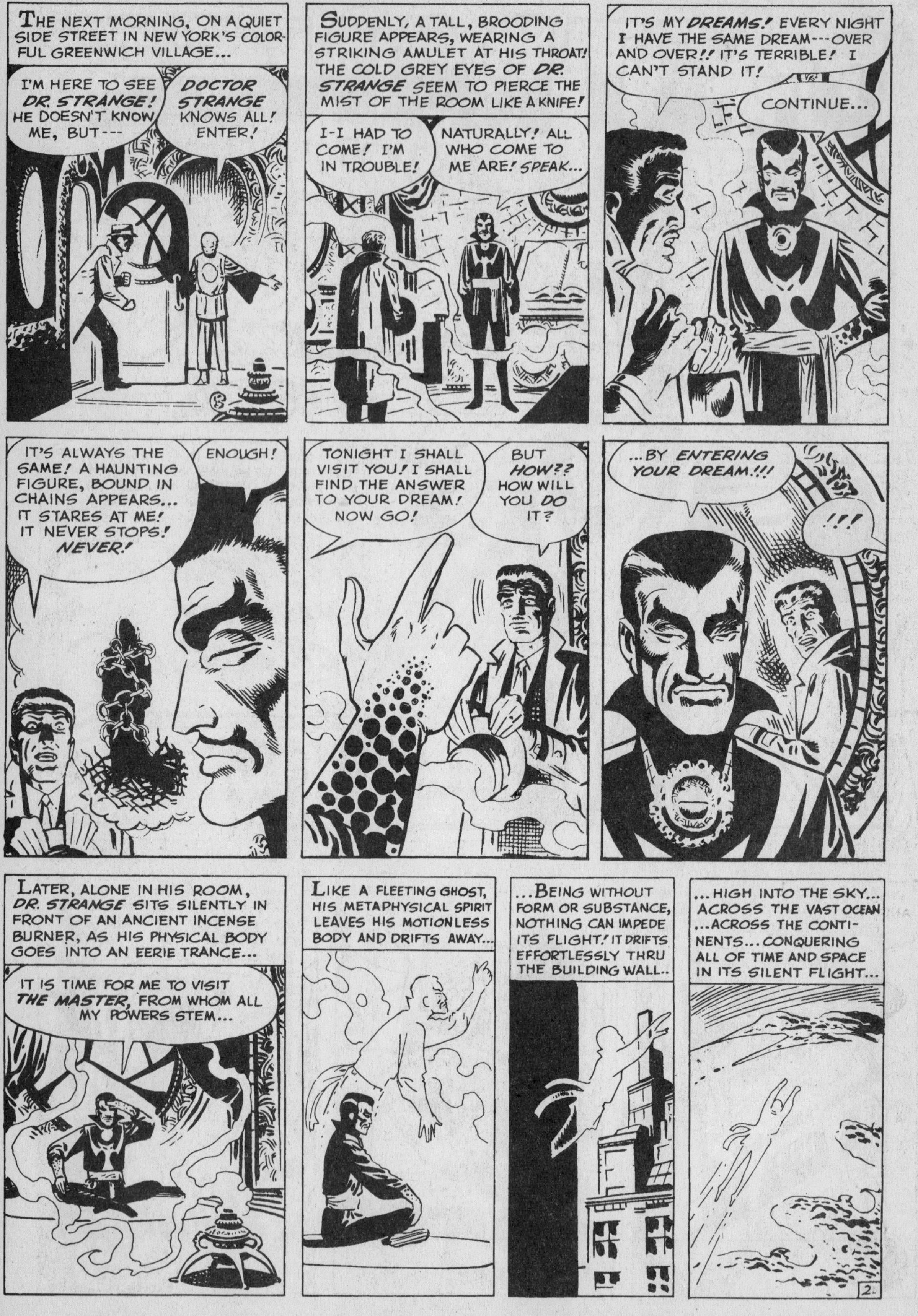
THE NEXT MORNING, ON A QUIET SIDE STREET IN NEW YORK'S COLORFUL GREENWICH VILLAGE...
I'M HERE TO SEE DR. STRANGE! HE DOESN'T KNOW ME, BUT---
DOCTOR STRANGE KNOWS ALL! ENTER!
SUDDENLY, A TALL, BROODING FIGURE APPEARS, WEARING A STRIKING AMULET AT HIS THROAT! THE COLD GREY EYES OF DR. STRANGE SEEM TO PIERCE THE MIST OF THE ROOM LIKE A KNIFE!
I-I HAD TO COME! I'M IN TROUBLE!
NATURALLY! ALL WHO COME TO ME ARE! SPEAK...
IT'S MY DREAMS! EVERY NIGHT I HAVE THE SAME DREAM---OVER AND OVER!! IT'S TERRIBLE! I CAN'T STAND IT!
CONTINUE...
IT'S ALWAYS THE SAME! A HAUNTING FIGURE, BOUND IN CHAINS APPEARS... IT STARES AT ME! IT NEVER STOPS! NEVER!
ENOUGH!
TONIGHT I SHALL VISIT YOU! I SHALL FIND THE ANSWER TO YOUR DREAM! NOW GO!
BUT HOW?? HOW WILL YOU DO IT?
...BY ENTERING YOUR DREAM!!!
!!!
LATER, ALONE IN HIS ROOM, DR. STRANGE SITS SILENTLY IN FRONT OF AN ANCIENT INCENSE BURNER, AS HIS PHYSICAL BODY GOES INTO AN EERIE TRANCE...
IT IS TIME FOR ME TO VISIT THE MASTER, FROM WHOM ALL MY POWERS STEM...
LIKE A FLEETING GHOST, HIS METAPHYSICAL SPIRIT LEAVES HIS MOTIONLESS BODY AND DRIFTS AWAY...
...BEING WITHOUT FORM OR SUBSTANCE, NOTHING CAN IMPEDE ITS FLIGHT! IT DRIFTS EFFORTLESSLY THRU THE BUILDING WALL..
...HIGH INTO THE SKY... ACROSS THE VAST OCEAN ...ACROSS THE CONTINENTS... CONQUERING ALL OF TIME AND SPACE IN ITS SILENT FLIGHT...
2.

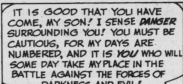
...UNTIL FINALLY, AT A HIDDEN TEMPLE SOMEWHERE IN THE REMOTE VASTNESS OF ASIA...

IT IS GOOD THAT YOU HAVE COME, MY SON! I SENSE *DANGER* SURROUNDING YOU! YOU MUST BE CAUTIOUS, FOR MY DAYS ARE NUMBERED, AND IT IS *YOU* WHO WILL SOME DAY TAKE MY PLACE IN THE BATTLE AGAINST THE FORCES OF DARKNESS AND EVIL!

I SHALL HEED YOUR WORDS, RESPECTED MASTER! I SHALL TRY TO PROVE WORTHY OF YOUR TRUST IN ME!

SO BE IT! NOW GO, FOR I AM WEARY! BUT MARK YOU WELL---SHOULD DANGER THREATEN, DEPEND UPON YOUR MAGIC AMULET!

THAT NIGHT, THOUSANDS OF MILES TO THE WEST, *DR. STRANGE*, IN HIS MORTAL FORM AGAIN, VISITS THE MAN WHO HAS SOUGHT HIS HELP!

YOU MUST SLEEP NOW--- AND HAVE NO FEAR! I SHALL BE NEARBY!

I DON'T KNOW WHAT THERE IS ABOUT YOU, BUT IT GIVES A MAN A FEELING OF--- CONFIDENCE!

MINUTES LATER...

SLEEP HAS OVERCOME HIM! HE BEGINS TO DREAM! IT IS TIME FOR ME TO ENTER MY TRANCE!

AND, AS HIS BODY GOES RIGID AND COLD, THE METAPHYSICAL SPIRIT OF *DR. STRANGE* DRIFTS UPWARD, INTO THE VERY DREAM ITSELF WHICH UNFURLS BEFORE IT!

IT IS DESOLATE HERE--LONELY AND FORBODING! WAIT! SOMEONE BEGINS TO APPEAR!

NO! NO!! STAY AWAY! PLEASE--- STAY AWAY!

YOU! WHOEVER--- WHATEVER YOU ARE--- WHY DO YOU TORMENT HIM SO??

HE WELL KNOWS THE REASON WHY!

3.

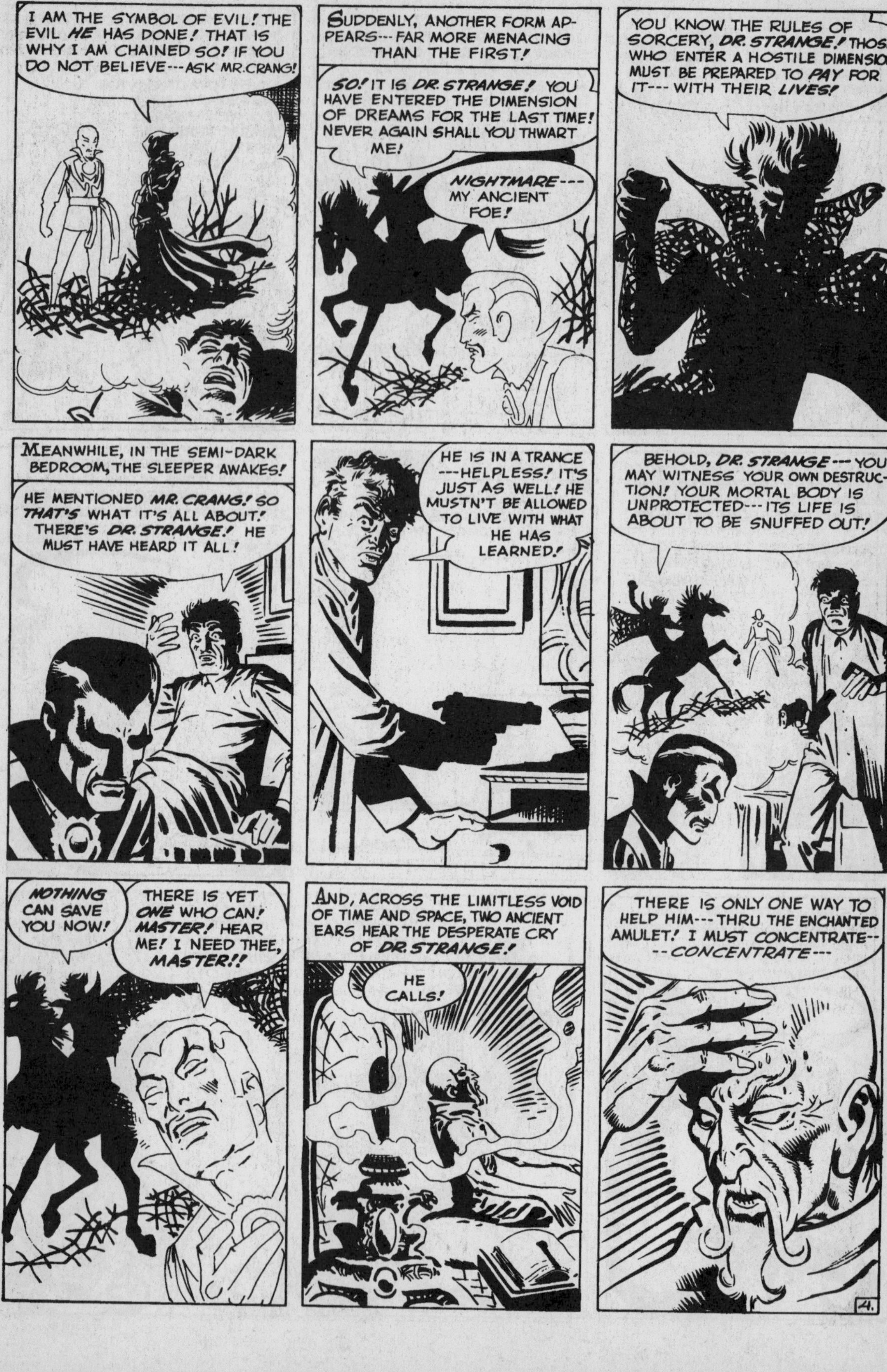
I AM THE SYMBOL OF EVIL! THE EVIL HE HAS DONE! THAT IS WHY I AM CHAINED SO! IF YOU DO NOT BELIEVE---ASK MR. CRANG!
SUDDENLY, ANOTHER FORM APPEARS---FAR MORE MENACING THAN THE FIRST!
SO! IT IS DR. STRANGE! YOU HAVE ENTERED THE DIMENSION OF DREAMS FOR THE LAST TIME! NEVER AGAIN SHALL YOU THWART ME!
NIGHTMARE--- MY ANCIENT FOE!
YOU KNOW THE RULES OF SORCERY, DR. STRANGE! THOSE WHO ENTER A HOSTILE DIMENSION MUST BE PREPARED TO PAY FOR IT--- WITH THEIR LIVES!
MEANWHILE, IN THE SEMI-DARK BEDROOM, THE SLEEPER AWAKES!
HE MENTIONED MR. CRANG! SO THAT'S WHAT IT'S ALL ABOUT! THERE'S DR. STRANGE! HE MUST HAVE HEARD IT ALL!
HE IS IN A TRANCE ---HELPLESS! IT'S JUST AS WELL! HE MUSTN'T BE ALLOWED TO LIVE WITH WHAT HE HAS LEARNED!
BEHOLD, DR. STRANGE--- YOU MAY WITNESS YOUR OWN DESTRUCTION! YOUR MORTAL BODY IS UNPROTECTED--- ITS LIFE IS ABOUT TO BE SNUFFED OUT!
NOTHING CAN SAVE YOU NOW!
THERE IS YET ONE WHO CAN! MASTER! HEAR ME! I NEED THEE, MASTER!!
AND, ACROSS THE LIMITLESS VOID OF TIME AND SPACE, TWO ANCIENT EARS HEAR THE DESPERATE CRY OF DR. STRANGE!
HE CALLS!
THERE IS ONLY ONE WAY TO HELP HIM--- THRU THE ENCHANTED AMULET! I MUST CONCENTRATE-- --CONCENTRATE---
4.

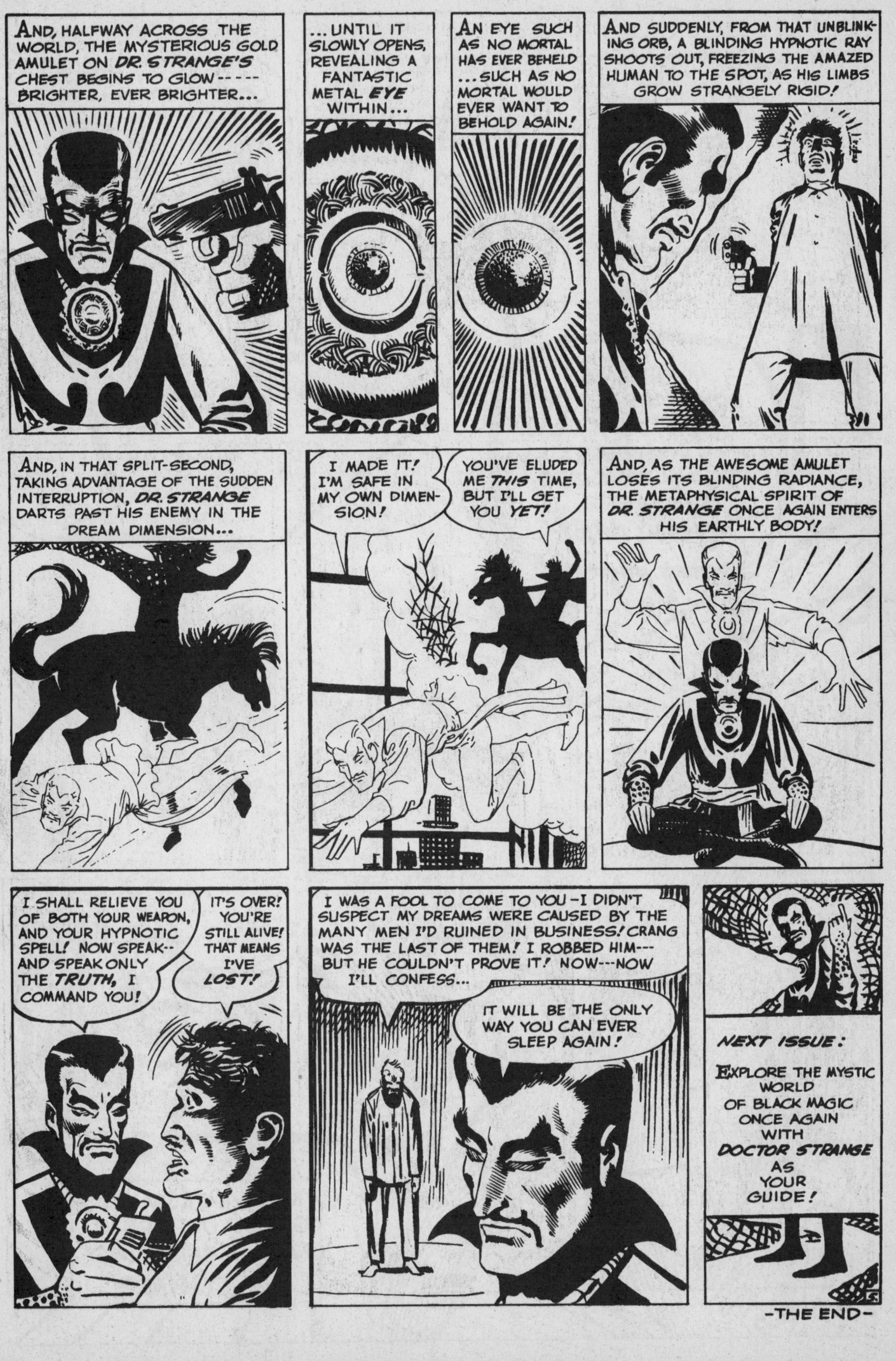
AND, HALFWAY ACROSS THE WORLD, THE MYSTERIOUS GOLD AMULET ON DR. STRANGE'S CHEST BEGINS TO GLOW----- BRIGHTER, EVER BRIGHTER...
...UNTIL IT SLOWLY OPENS, REVEALING A FANTASTIC METAL EYE WITHIN...
AN EYE SUCH AS NO MORTAL HAS EVER BEHELD ...SUCH AS NO MORTAL WOULD EVER WANT TO BEHOLD AGAIN!
AND SUDDENLY, FROM THAT UNBLINKING ORB, A BLINDING HYPNOTIC RAY SHOOTS OUT, FREEZING THE AMAZED HUMAN TO THE SPOT, AS HIS LIMBS GROW STRANGELY RIGID!
AND, IN THAT SPLIT-SECOND, TAKING ADVANTAGE OF THE SUDDEN INTERRUPTION, DR. STRANGE DARTS PAST HIS ENEMY IN THE DREAM DIMENSION...
I MADE IT! I'M SAFE IN MY OWN DIMENSION!
YOU'VE ELUDED ME THIS TIME, BUT I'LL GET YOU YET!
AND, AS THE AWESOME AMULET LOSES ITS BLINDING RADIANCE, THE METAPHYSICAL SPIRIT OF DR. STRANGE ONCE AGAIN ENTERS HIS EARTHLY BODY!
I SHALL RELIEVE YOU OF BOTH YOUR WEAPON, AND YOUR HYPNOTIC SPELL! NOW SPEAK-- AND SPEAK ONLY THE TRUTH, I COMMAND YOU!
IT'S OVER! YOU'RE STILL ALIVE! THAT MEANS I'VE LOST!
I WAS A FOOL TO COME TO YOU - I DIDN'T SUSPECT MY DREAMS WERE CAUSED BY THE MANY MEN I'D RUINED IN BUSINESS! CRANG WAS THE LAST OF THEM! I ROBBED HIM--- BUT HE COULDN'T PROVE IT! NOW---NOW I'LL CONFESS...
IT WILL BE THE ONLY WAY YOU CAN EVER SLEEP AGAIN!
NEXT ISSUE:
EXPLORE THE MYSTIC WORLD OF BLACK MAGIC ONCE AGAIN WITH DOCTOR STRANGE AS YOUR GUIDE!
-THE END-

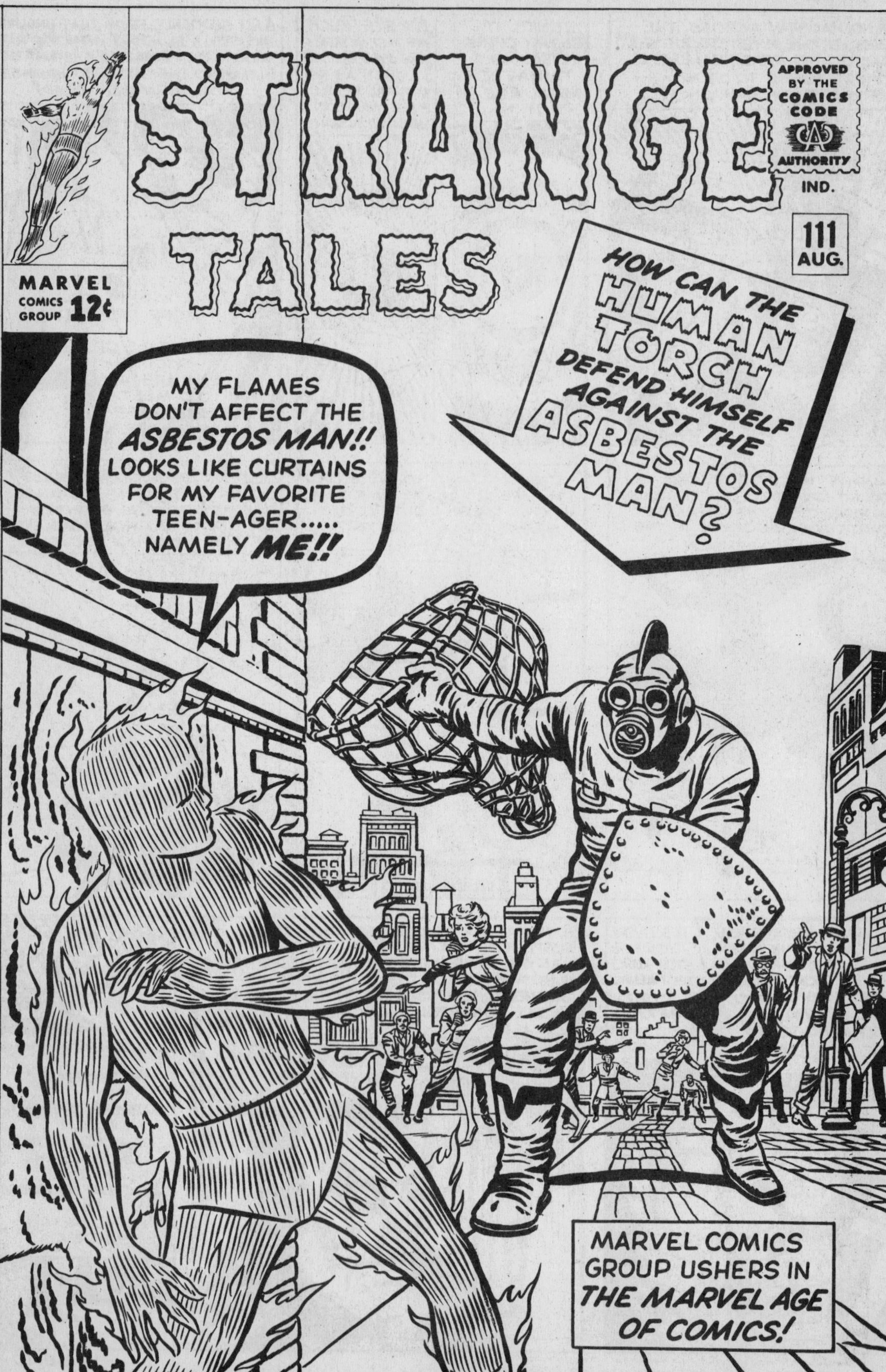
STRANGE TALES
APPROVED BY THE COMICS CODE AUTHORITY
IND.
111 AUG.
MARVEL COMICS GROUP 12¢
HOW CAN THE HUMAN TORCH DEFEND HIMSELF AGAINST THE ASBESTOS MAN?
MY FLAMES DON'T AFFECT THE ASBESTOS MAN!! LOOKS LIKE CURTAINS FOR MY FAVORITE TEEN-AGER..... NAMELY ME!!
MARVEL COMICS GROUP USHERS IN THE MARVEL AGE OF COMICS!

Dr. STRANGE MASTER OF--- BLACK MAGIC

Story —— STAN LEE
Art —— STEVE DITKO
Lettering— TERRY SZENICS

MEN CALL HIM *DR. STRANGE*, AND SPEAK HIS NAME IN WHISPERS! BUT THERE IS *ANOTHER*--- ONE WHO IS STILL MORE DREADED!

IN THIS TALE OF THE OCCULT YOU ARE ABOUT TO MEET *DR. STRANGE'S* ARCH-FOE, THE DREADED *BARON MORDO* !!

"FACE-TO-FACE WITH THE MAGIC OF BARON MORDO!"

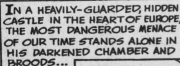

IN A HEAVILY-GUARDED, HIDDEN CASTLE IN THE HEART OF EUROPE, THE MOST DANGEROUS MENACE OF OUR TIME STANDS ALONE IN HIS DARKENED CHAMBER AND BROODS...

ONLY *ONE* MAN KNOWS MORE SECRETS OF BLACK MAGIC THAN *I* DO! AND HE IS THE ONE WHO *TAUGHT* ME YEARS AGO --- HE IS *THE MASTER!!*

BUT THE TIME HAS COME FOR ME TO WREST THOSE SECRETS FROM HIM! FOR IT IS I, *BARON MORDO*, WHO MUST BE THE MOST POWERFUL MAGICIAN OF ALL!

ONCE I HAVE CONQUERED THE *MASTER*, THEN I NEED NEVER AGAIN FEAR THE WRATH OF MY ARCH-FOE, *DR. STRANGE!* FOR I SHALL BE *STRONGER* THAN HE!

AND SO, IT IS TIME FOR ME TO ENTER A TRANCE ONCE AGAIN...

LATER, THOUSANDS OF MILES AWAY, IN THE *MASTER'S* STUDY, SOMEWHERE IN TIBET...

AHH, GOOD! HE IS TOO DEEP IN THOUGHT TO SENSE MY PRESENCE!

MY SPIRIT IMAGE IS FREE TO ROAM ABOUT UNTIL I CAN FIND---

---AHH, THE ONE I SEEK ---HIS SERVANT, PREPARING THE *MASTER'S* MEAL!

HE IS POWERLESS TO RESIST MY MENTAL COMMANDS! HE *MUST* OBEY THE ORDERS OF *BARON MORDO!*

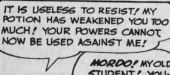

I-MUST-PREPARE-POWERFUL-POTION---PUT-IN-*MASTER'S* -FOOD---

I CANNOT FAIL! I SHALL ACHIEVE THE IMPOSSIBLE! VICTORY OVER THE *MASTER!*

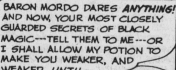

MINUTES LATER...

SO! IT IS DONE!

I HAVE BEEN *BETRAYED!* MY FOOD WAS TAMPERED WITH!

TOO LATE, *MASTER!* BARON MORDO HAS BEATEN YOU!

IT IS USELESS TO RESIST! MY POTION HAS WEAKENED YOU TOO MUCH! YOUR POWERS CANNOT NOW BE USED AGAINST ME!

MORDO! MY OLD STUDENT! YOU---YOU *DARE* DO THIS ??!

BARON MORDO DARES *ANYTHING!* AND NOW, YOUR MOST CLOSELY GUARDED SECRETS OF BLACK MAGIC---TELL THEM TO ME---OR I SHALL ALLOW MY POTION TO MAKE YOU WEAKER, AND WEAKER, *UNTIL*--

NO! NO! *NEVER!*

YOU *MUST!* UNLESS YOU DO AS I SAY, MY POTION WILL DRAIN AWAY ALL YOUR STRENGTH ---YOUR VERY *LIFE* ITSELF! *SPEAK*---WHILE THERE IS STILL TIME!

NEVER...

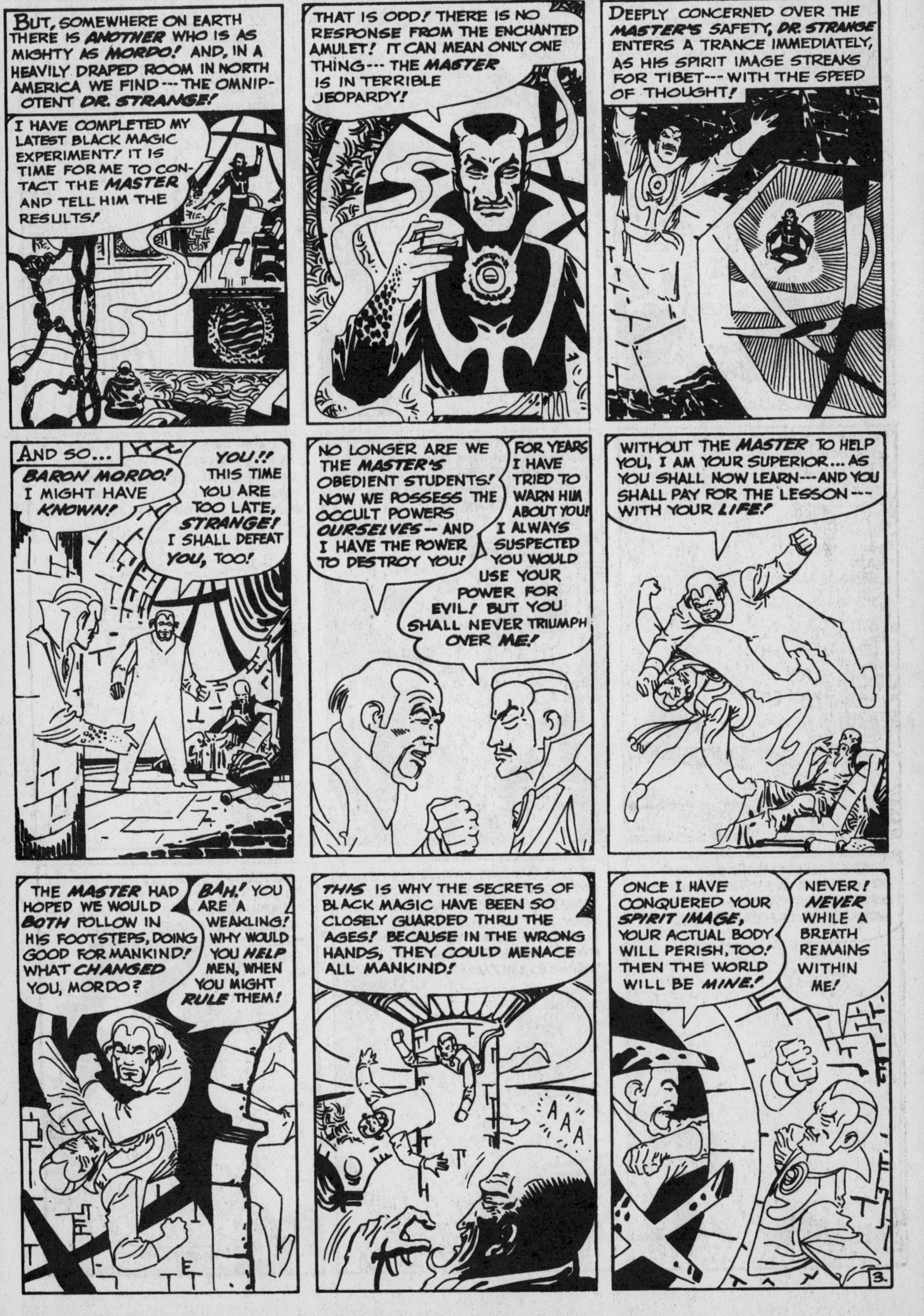
BUT, SOMEWHERE ON EARTH THERE IS ANOTHER WHO IS AS MIGHTY AS MORDO! AND, IN A HEAVILY DRAPED ROOM IN NORTH AMERICA WE FIND --- THE OMNIPOTENT DR. STRANGE!
I HAVE COMPLETED MY LATEST BLACK MAGIC EXPERIMENT! IT IS TIME FOR ME TO CONTACT THE MASTER AND TELL HIM THE RESULTS!
THAT IS ODD! THERE IS NO RESPONSE FROM THE ENCHANTED AMULET! IT CAN MEAN ONLY ONE THING--- THE MASTER IS IN TERRIBLE JEOPARDY!
DEEPLY CONCERNED OVER THE MASTER'S SAFETY, DR. STRANGE ENTERS A TRANCE IMMEDIATELY, AS HIS SPIRIT IMAGE STREAKS FOR TIBET--- WITH THE SPEED OF THOUGHT!
AND SO...
BARON MORDO! I MIGHT HAVE KNOWN!
YOU!! THIS TIME YOU ARE TOO LATE, STRANGE! I SHALL DEFEAT YOU, TOO!
NO LONGER ARE WE THE MASTER'S OBEDIENT STUDENTS! NOW WE POSSESS THE OCCULT POWERS OURSELVES -- AND I HAVE THE POWER TO DESTROY YOU!
FOR YEARS I HAVE TRIED TO WARN HIM ABOUT YOU! I ALWAYS SUSPECTED YOU WOULD USE YOUR POWER FOR EVIL! BUT YOU SHALL NEVER TRIUMPH OVER ME!
WITHOUT THE MASTER TO HELP YOU, I AM YOUR SUPERIOR... AS YOU SHALL NOW LEARN---AND YOU SHALL PAY FOR THE LESSON--- WITH YOUR LIFE!
THE MASTER HAD HOPED WE WOULD BOTH FOLLOW IN HIS FOOTSTEPS, DOING GOOD FOR MANKIND! WHAT CHANGED YOU, MORDO?
BAH! YOU ARE A WEAKLING! WHY WOULD YOU HELP MEN, WHEN YOU MIGHT RULE THEM!
THIS IS WHY THE SECRETS OF BLACK MAGIC HAVE BEEN SO CLOSELY GUARDED THRU THE AGES! BECAUSE IN THE WRONG HANDS, THEY COULD MENACE ALL MANKIND!
AAA
ONCE I HAVE CONQUERED YOUR SPIRIT IMAGE, YOUR ACTUAL BODY WILL PERISH, TOO! THEN THE WORLD WILL BE MINE!
NEVER! NEVER WHILE A BREATH REMAINS WITHIN ME!
3.

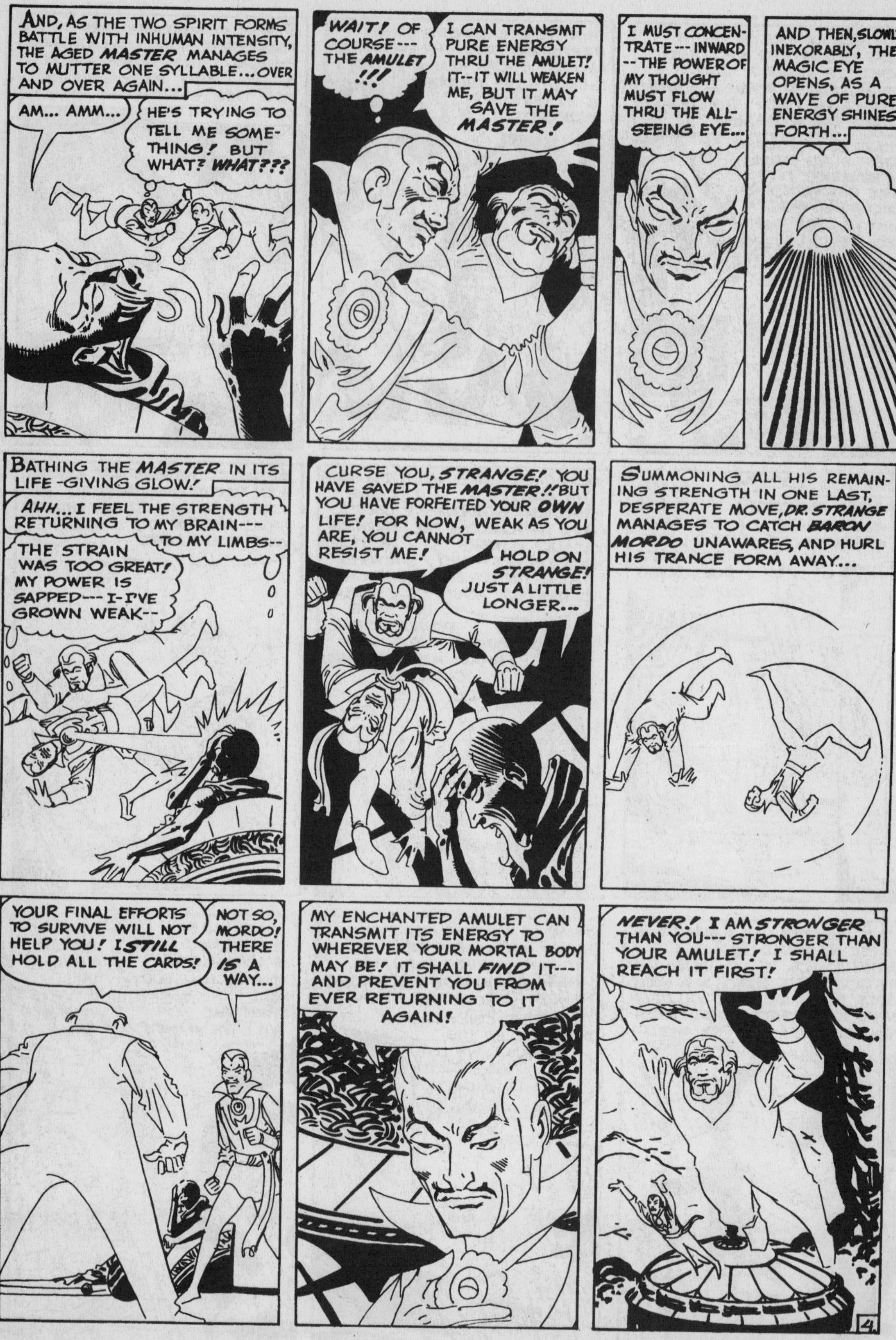
AND, AS THE TWO SPIRIT FORMS BATTLE WITH INHUMAN INTENSITY, THE AGED MASTER MANAGES TO MUTTER ONE SYLLABLE...OVER AND OVER AGAIN...
AM... AMM...
HE'S TRYING TO TELL ME SOMETHING! BUT WHAT? WHAT???
WAIT! OF COURSE--- THE AMULET !!!
I CAN TRANSMIT PURE ENERGY THRU THE AMULET! IT--IT WILL WEAKEN ME, BUT IT MAY SAVE THE MASTER!
I MUST CONCENTRATE--- INWARD --THE POWER OF MY THOUGHT MUST FLOW THRU THE ALL-SEEING EYE...
AND THEN, SLOWLY, INEXORABLY, THE MAGIC EYE OPENS, AS A WAVE OF PURE ENERGY SHINES FORTH...
BATHING THE MASTER IN ITS LIFE-GIVING GLOW!
AHH... I FEEL THE STRENGTH RETURNING TO MY BRAIN--- TO MY LIMBS--
THE STRAIN WAS TOO GREAT! MY POWER IS SAPPED--- I-I'VE GROWN WEAK--
CURSE YOU, STRANGE! YOU HAVE SAVED THE MASTER!! BUT YOU HAVE FORFEITED YOUR OWN LIFE! FOR NOW, WEAK AS YOU ARE, YOU CANNOT RESIST ME!
HOLD ON STRANGE! JUST A LITTLE LONGER...
SUMMONING ALL HIS REMAINING STRENGTH IN ONE LAST, DESPERATE MOVE, DR. STRANGE MANAGES TO CATCH BARON MORDO UNAWARES, AND HURL HIS TRANCE FORM AWAY...
YOUR FINAL EFFORTS TO SURVIVE WILL NOT HELP YOU! I STILL HOLD ALL THE CARDS!
NOT SO, MORDO! THERE IS A WAY...
MY ENCHANTED AMULET CAN TRANSMIT ITS ENERGY TO WHEREVER YOUR MORTAL BODY MAY BE! IT SHALL FIND IT--- AND PREVENT YOU FROM EVER RETURNING TO IT AGAIN!
NEVER! I AM STRONGER THAN YOU--- STRONGER THAN YOUR AMULET! I SHALL REACH IT FIRST!
4

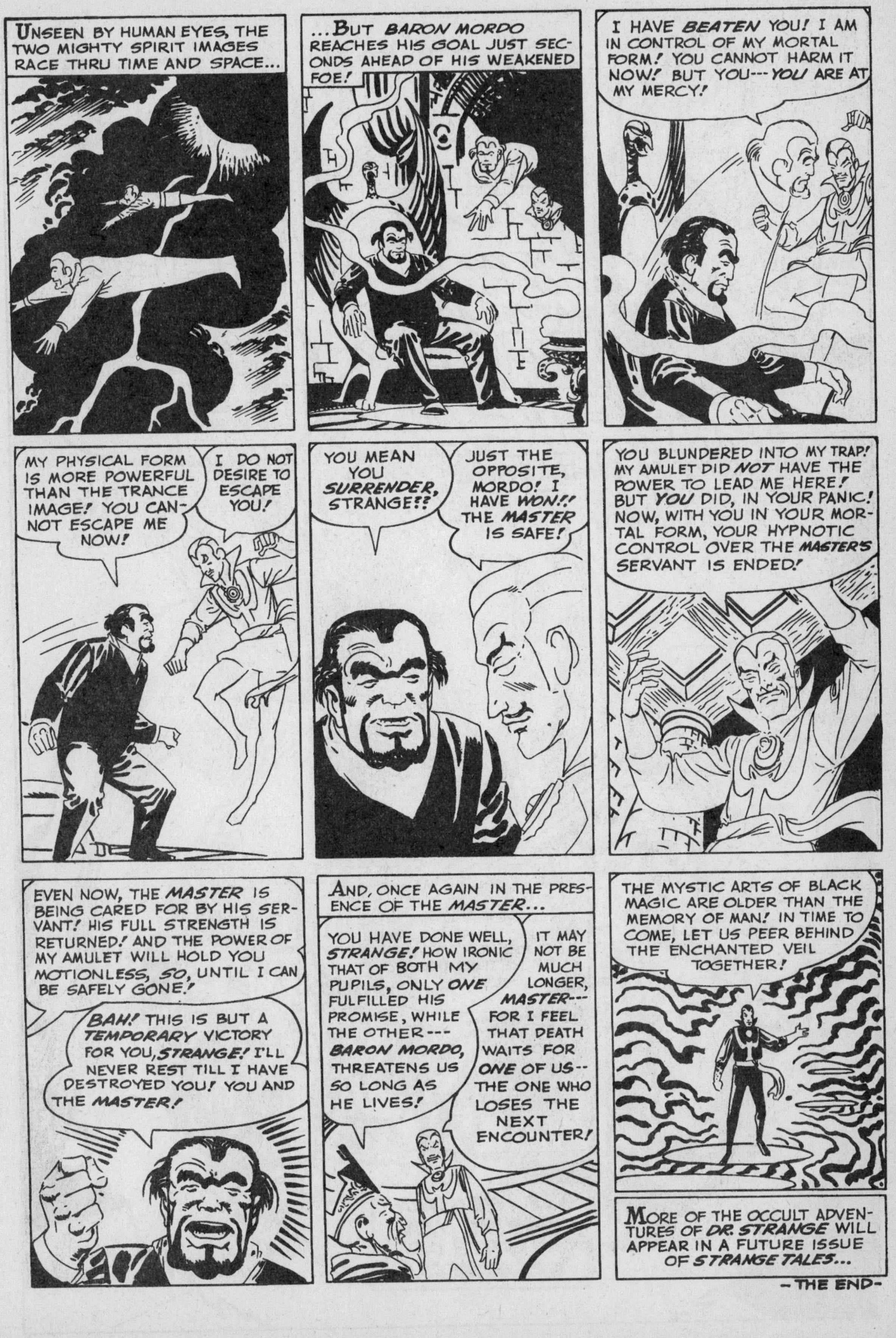
UNSEEN BY HUMAN EYES, THE TWO MIGHTY SPIRIT IMAGES RACE THRU TIME AND SPACE...
...BUT BARON MORDO REACHES HIS GOAL JUST SECONDS AHEAD OF HIS WEAKENED FOE!
I HAVE BEATEN YOU! I AM IN CONTROL OF MY MORTAL FORM! YOU CANNOT HARM IT NOW! BUT YOU---YOU ARE AT MY MERCY!
MY PHYSICAL FORM IS MORE POWERFUL THAN THE TRANCE IMAGE! YOU CANNOT ESCAPE ME NOW!
I DO NOT DESIRE TO ESCAPE YOU!
YOU MEAN YOU SURRENDER, STRANGE!?
JUST THE OPPOSITE, MORDO! I HAVE WON!! THE MASTER IS SAFE!
YOU BLUNDERED INTO MY TRAP! MY AMULET DID NOT HAVE THE POWER TO LEAD ME HERE! BUT YOU DID, IN YOUR PANIC! NOW, WITH YOU IN YOUR MORTAL FORM, YOUR HYPNOTIC CONTROL OVER THE MASTER'S SERVANT IS ENDED!
EVEN NOW, THE MASTER IS BEING CARED FOR BY HIS SERVANT! HIS FULL STRENGTH IS RETURNED! AND THE POWER OF MY AMULET WILL HOLD YOU MOTIONLESS, SO, UNTIL I CAN BE SAFELY GONE!
BAH! THIS IS BUT A TEMPORARY VICTORY FOR YOU, STRANGE! I'LL NEVER REST TILL I HAVE DESTROYED YOU! YOU AND THE MASTER!
AND, ONCE AGAIN IN THE PRESENCE OF THE MASTER...
YOU HAVE DONE WELL, STRANGE! HOW IRONIC THAT OF BOTH MY PUPILS, ONLY ONE FULFILLED HIS PROMISE, WHILE THE OTHER---BARON MORDO, THREATENS US SO LONG AS HE LIVES!
IT MAY NOT BE MUCH LONGER, MASTER---FOR I FEEL THAT DEATH WAITS FOR ONE OF US--THE ONE WHO LOSES THE NEXT ENCOUNTER!
THE MYSTIC ARTS OF BLACK MAGIC ARE OLDER THAN THE MEMORY OF MAN! IN TIME TO COME, LET US PEER BEHIND THE ENCHANTED VEIL TOGETHER!
MORE OF THE OCCULT ADVENTURES OF DR. STRANGE WILL APPEAR IN A FUTURE ISSUE OF STRANGE TALES...
-THE END-

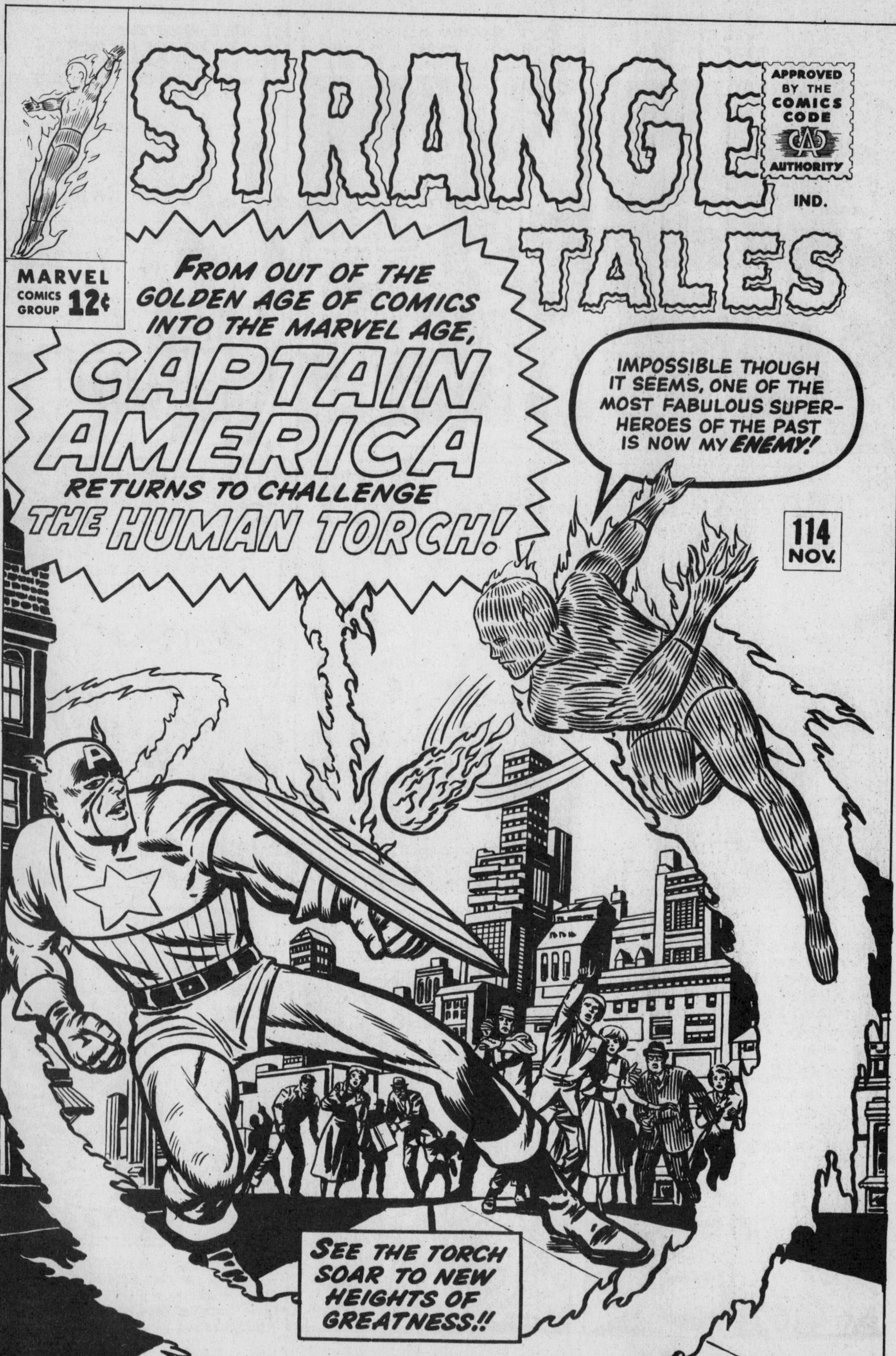

STRANGE TALES
APPROVED BY THE COMICS CODE AUTHORITY
IND.
MARVEL COMICS GROUP 12¢
FROM OUT OF THE GOLDEN AGE OF COMICS INTO THE MARVEL AGE,
CAPTAIN AMERICA
RETURNS TO CHALLENGE
THE HUMAN TORCH!
IMPOSSIBLE THOUGH IT SEEMS, ONE OF THE MOST FABULOUS SUPER-HEROES OF THE PAST IS NOW MY ENEMY!
114 NOV.
SEE THE TORCH SOAR TO NEW HEIGHTS OF GREATNESS!!

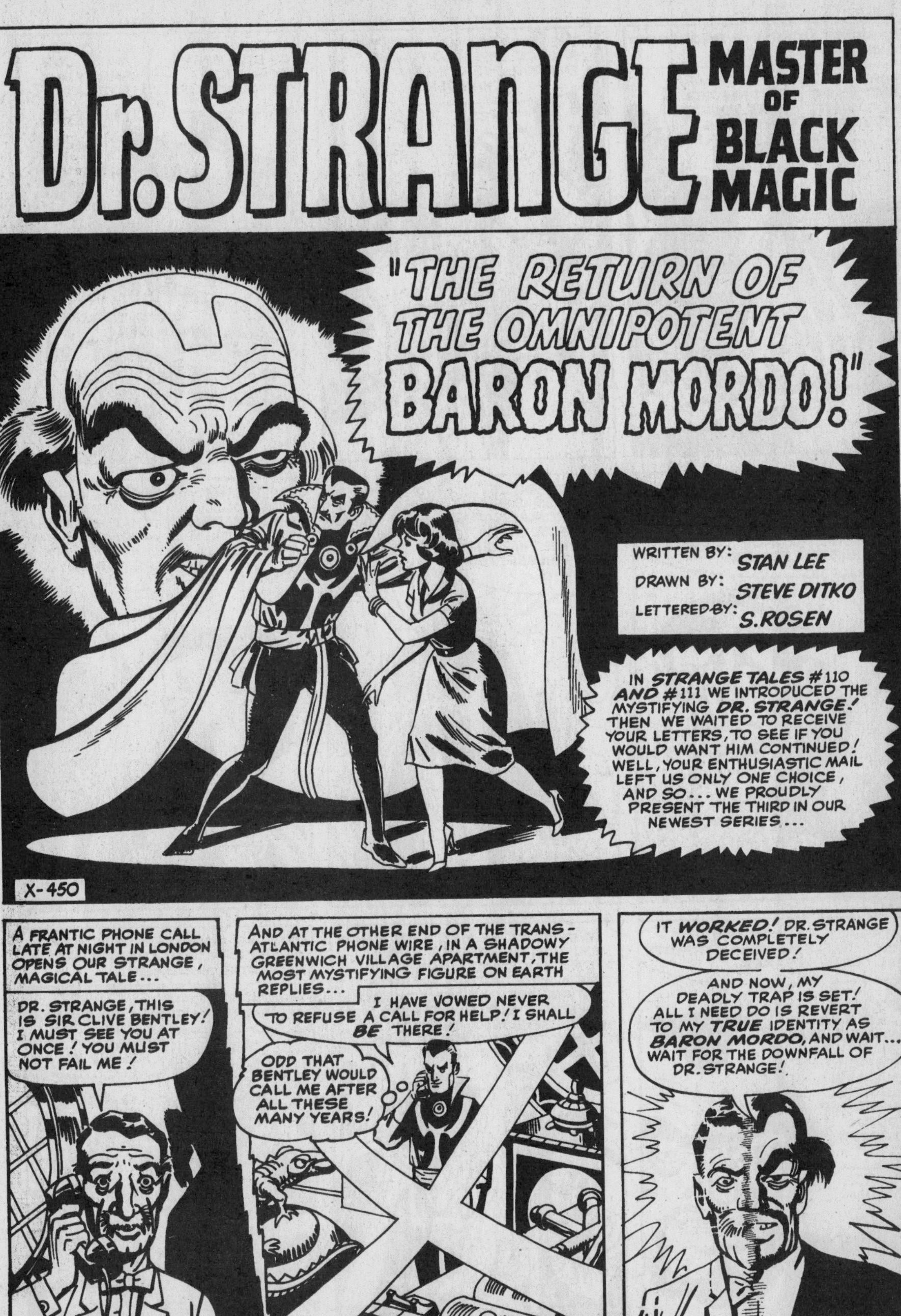

Dr. STRANGE MASTER OF BLACK MAGIC
"THE RETURN OF THE OMNIPOTENT BARON MORDO!"
WRITTEN BY: STAN LEE
DRAWN BY: STEVE DITKO
LETTERED BY: S.ROSEN
IN STRANGE TALES #110 AND #111 WE INTRODUCED THE MYSTIFYING DR. STRANGE! THEN WE WAITED TO RECEIVE YOUR LETTERS, TO SEE IF YOU WOULD WANT HIM CONTINUED! WELL, YOUR ENTHUSIASTIC MAIL LEFT US ONLY ONE CHOICE, AND SO... WE PROUDLY PRESENT THE THIRD IN OUR NEWEST SERIES...
X-450
A FRANTIC PHONE CALL LATE AT NIGHT IN LONDON OPENS OUR STRANGE, MAGICAL TALE...
DR. STRANGE, THIS IS SIR CLIVE BENTLEY! I MUST SEE YOU AT ONCE! YOU MUST NOT FAIL ME!
AND AT THE OTHER END OF THE TRANS-ATLANTIC PHONE WIRE, IN A SHADOWY GREENWICH VILLAGE APARTMENT, THE MOST MYSTIFYING FIGURE ON EARTH REPLIES...
I HAVE VOWED NEVER TO REFUSE A CALL FOR HELP! I SHALL BE THERE!
ODD THAT BENTLEY WOULD CALL ME AFTER ALL THESE MANY YEARS!
IT WORKED! DR. STRANGE WAS COMPLETELY DECEIVED!
AND NOW, MY DEADLY TRAP IS SET! ALL I NEED DO IS REVERT TO MY TRUE IDENTITY AS BARON MORDO, AND WAIT... WAIT FOR THE DOWNFALL OF DR. STRANGE!

SOMETIME LATER, IN A DARK, FOGGY LONDON STREET...

SURE YOU DON'T WANT ME TO WAIT, GUV'NOR?

NO! LEAVE ME! ALL I NEEDED WERE YOUR DIRECTIONS TO SIR BENTLEY'S CASTLE!

THE DOOR IS UNLOCKED! THE SILENCE LIES HEAVY AS A SHROUD OVER THE ENTIRE CHAMBER!

THE ENTIRE CASTLE SEEMS DESERTED... DEVOID OF LIFE!

CAN IT BE THAT I HAVE ARRIVED... TOO LATE ??

ALTHOUGH I CAN HEAR AND SEE NOTHING, STILL I SENSE A TERRIBLE DANGER! I DETECT THE PRESENCE OF SOME AWESOME MENACE... SOME SINISTER POWER!

THAT CANDLE... IT GIVES OFF AN UNNATURAL VAPOR... A VAPOR WHICH GROWS THICKER! MY SENSES TELL ME IT IS...

I CANNOT MOVE! THE VAPOR HAS PARALYZED ME!

ONLY ONE MAN COULD HAVE TRAPPED ME SO! ONLY THE EVIL...

YOU ARE RIGHT, DR. STRANGE! IT IS I, BARON MORDO! I HAVE MADE YOU MY PRISONER!

WITH EACH FLICKER OF THE CANDLE'S FLAME YOUR STRENGTH WILL GROW WEAKER!

UNTIL THE CANDLE HAS FINALLY BURNED ITSELF OUT... AT WHICH TIME YOUR LIFE ALSO WILL BE SNUFFED OUT... FOREVER!

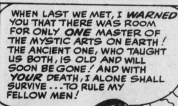

WHEN LAST WE MET, I WARNED YOU THAT THERE WAS ROOM FOR ONLY ONE MASTER OF THE MYSTIC ARTS ON EARTH! THE ANCIENT ONE, WHO TAUGHT US BOTH, IS OLD AND WILL SOON BE GONE! AND WITH YOUR DEATH, I ALONE SHALL SURVIVE... TO RULE MY FELLOW MEN!

BUT, AS MORDO LEAVES, THE ALL-SEEING ANCIENT ONE PROJECTS A MENTAL MESSAGE...

PERHAPS I CAN HELP YOU, MY SON!

NO! VENERABLE, ONE... YOU MUST NOT! I FORBID IT!

2.

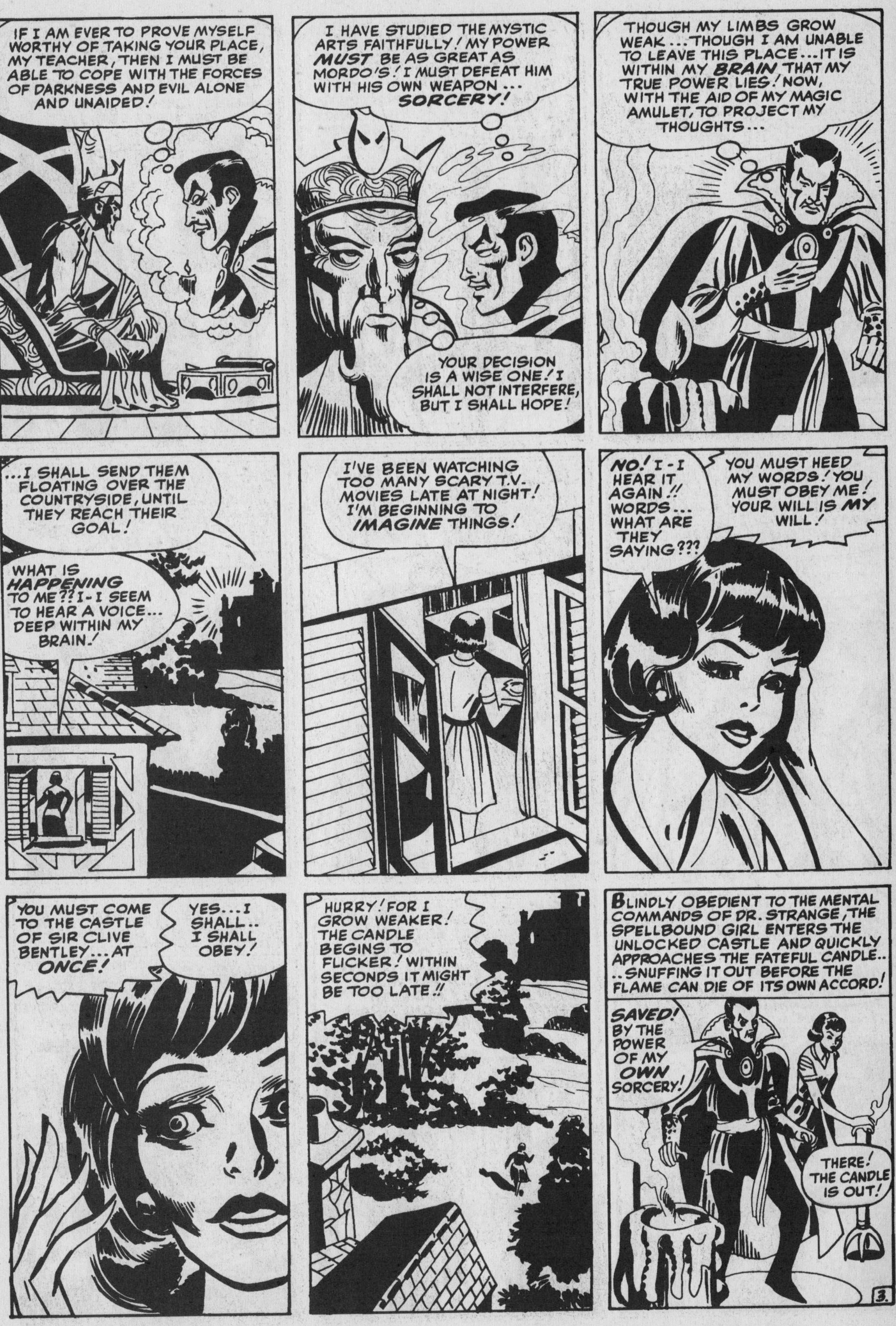
IF I AM EVER TO PROVE MYSELF WORTHY OF TAKING YOUR PLACE, MY TEACHER, THEN I MUST BE ABLE TO COPE WITH THE FORCES OF DARKNESS AND EVIL ALONE AND UNAIDED!
I HAVE STUDIED THE MYSTIC ARTS FAITHFULLY! MY POWER MUST BE AS GREAT AS MORDO'S! I MUST DEFEAT HIM WITH HIS OWN WEAPON ... SORCERY!
YOUR DECISION IS A WISE ONE! I SHALL NOT INTERFERE, BUT I SHALL HOPE!
THOUGH MY LIMBS GROW WEAK ... THOUGH I AM UNABLE TO LEAVE THIS PLACE ... IT IS WITHIN MY BRAIN THAT MY TRUE POWER LIES! NOW, WITH THE AID OF MY MAGIC AMULET, TO PROJECT MY THOUGHTS ...
... I SHALL SEND THEM FLOATING OVER THE COUNTRYSIDE, UNTIL THEY REACH THEIR GOAL!
WHAT IS HAPPENING TO ME?? I-I SEEM TO HEAR A VOICE ... DEEP WITHIN MY BRAIN!
I'VE BEEN WATCHING TOO MANY SCARY T.V. MOVIES LATE AT NIGHT! I'M BEGINNING TO IMAGINE THINGS!
NO! I-I HEAR IT AGAIN!! WORDS ... WHAT ARE THEY SAYING???
YOU MUST HEED MY WORDS! YOU MUST OBEY ME! YOUR WILL IS MY WILL!
YOU MUST COME TO THE CASTLE OF SIR CLIVE BENTLEY ... AT ONCE!
YES ... I SHALL .. I SHALL OBEY!
HURRY! FOR I GROW WEAKER! THE CANDLE BEGINS TO FLICKER! WITHIN SECONDS IT MIGHT BE TOO LATE!!
BLINDLY OBEDIENT TO THE MENTAL COMMANDS OF DR. STRANGE, THE SPELLBOUND GIRL ENTERS THE UNLOCKED CASTLE AND QUICKLY APPROACHES THE FATEFUL CANDLE .. .. SNUFFING IT OUT BEFORE THE FLAME CAN DIE OF ITS OWN ACCORD!
SAVED! BY THE POWER OF MY OWN SORCERY!
THERE! THE CANDLE IS OUT!
3.

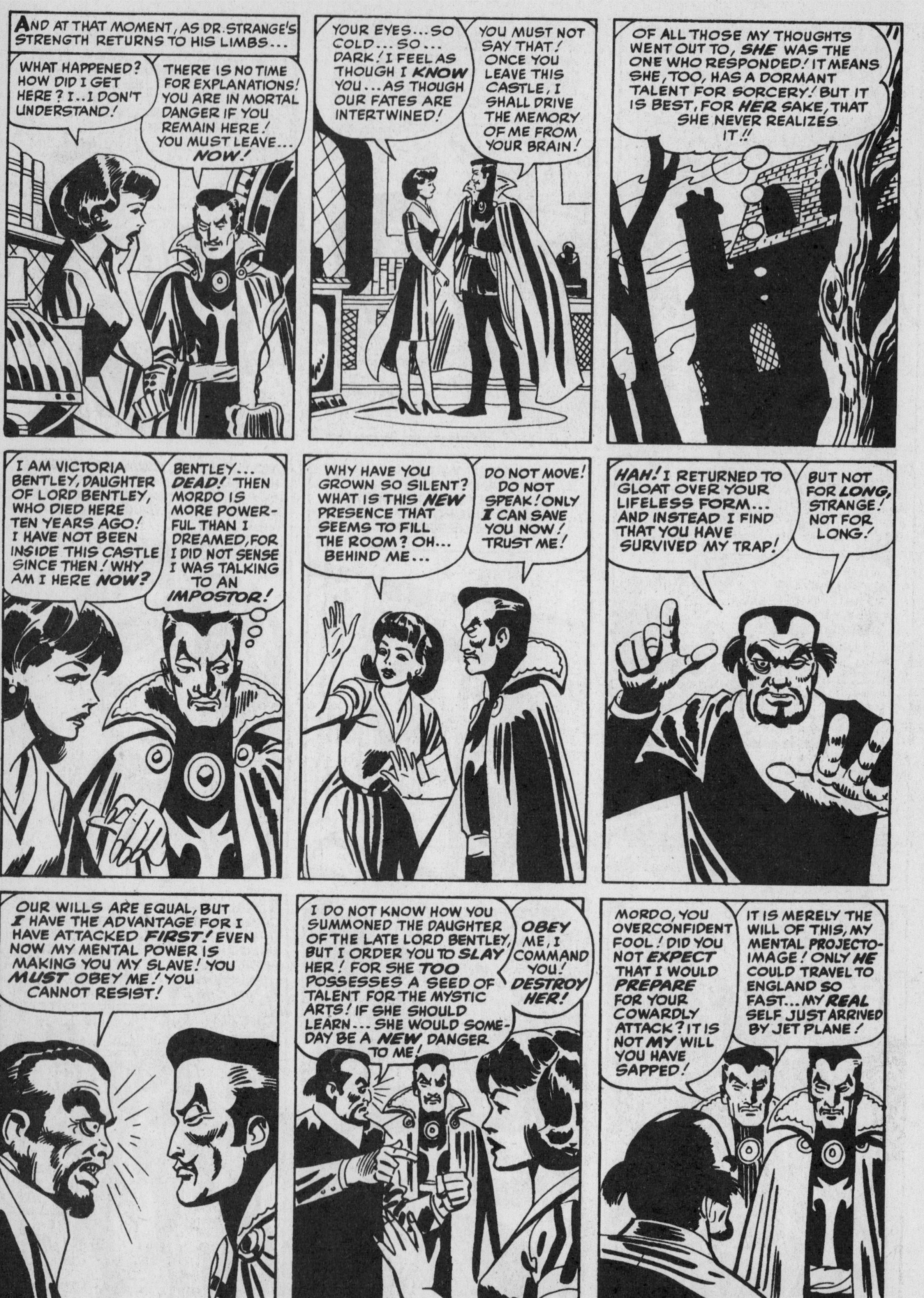
AND AT THAT MOMENT, AS DR. STRANGE'S STRENGTH RETURNS TO HIS LIMBS...
WHAT HAPPENED? HOW DID I GET HERE? I..I DON'T UNDERSTAND!
THERE IS NO TIME FOR EXPLANATIONS! YOU ARE IN MORTAL DANGER IF YOU REMAIN HERE! YOU MUST LEAVE... NOW!
YOUR EYES... SO COLD... SO... DARK! I FEEL AS THOUGH I KNOW YOU... AS THOUGH OUR FATES ARE INTERTWINED!
YOU MUST NOT SAY THAT! ONCE YOU LEAVE THIS CASTLE, I SHALL DRIVE THE MEMORY OF ME FROM YOUR BRAIN!
OF ALL THOSE MY THOUGHTS WENT OUT TO, SHE WAS THE ONE WHO RESPONDED! IT MEANS SHE, TOO, HAS A DORMANT TALENT FOR SORCERY! BUT IT IS BEST, FOR HER SAKE, THAT SHE NEVER REALIZES IT!!
I AM VICTORIA BENTLEY, DAUGHTER OF LORD BENTLEY, WHO DIED HERE TEN YEARS AGO! I HAVE NOT BEEN INSIDE THIS CASTLE SINCE THEN! WHY AM I HERE NOW?
BENTLEY... DEAD! THEN MORDO IS MORE POWER-FUL THAN I DREAMED, FOR I DID NOT SENSE I WAS TALKING TO AN IMPOSTOR!
WHY HAVE YOU GROWN SO SILENT? WHAT IS THIS NEW PRESENCE THAT SEEMS TO FILL THE ROOM? OH... BEHIND ME...
DO NOT MOVE! DO NOT SPEAK! ONLY I CAN SAVE YOU NOW! TRUST ME!
HAH! I RETURNED TO GLOAT OVER YOUR LIFELESS FORM... AND INSTEAD I FIND THAT YOU HAVE SURVIVED MY TRAP!
BUT NOT FOR LONG, STRANGE! NOT FOR LONG!
OUR WILLS ARE EQUAL, BUT I HAVE THE ADVANTAGE FOR I HAVE ATTACKED FIRST! EVEN NOW MY MENTAL POWER IS MAKING YOU MY SLAVE! YOU MUST OBEY ME! YOU CANNOT RESIST!
I DO NOT KNOW HOW YOU SUMMONED THE DAUGHTER OF THE LATE LORD BENTLEY, BUT I ORDER YOU TO SLAY HER! FOR SHE TOO POSSESSES A SEED OF TALENT FOR THE MYSTIC ARTS! IF SHE SHOULD LEARN... SHE WOULD SOME-DAY BE A NEW DANGER TO ME!
OBEY ME, I COMMAND YOU! DESTROY HER!
MORDO, YOU OVERCONFIDENT FOOL! DID YOU NOT EXPECT THAT I WOULD PREPARE FOR YOUR COWARDLY ATTACK? IT IS NOT MY WILL YOU HAVE SAPPED!
IT IS MERELY THE WILL OF THIS, MY MENTAL PROJECTO-IMAGE! ONLY HE COULD TRAVEL TO ENGLAND SO FAST... MY REAL SELF JUST ARRIVED BY JET PLANE!
4.

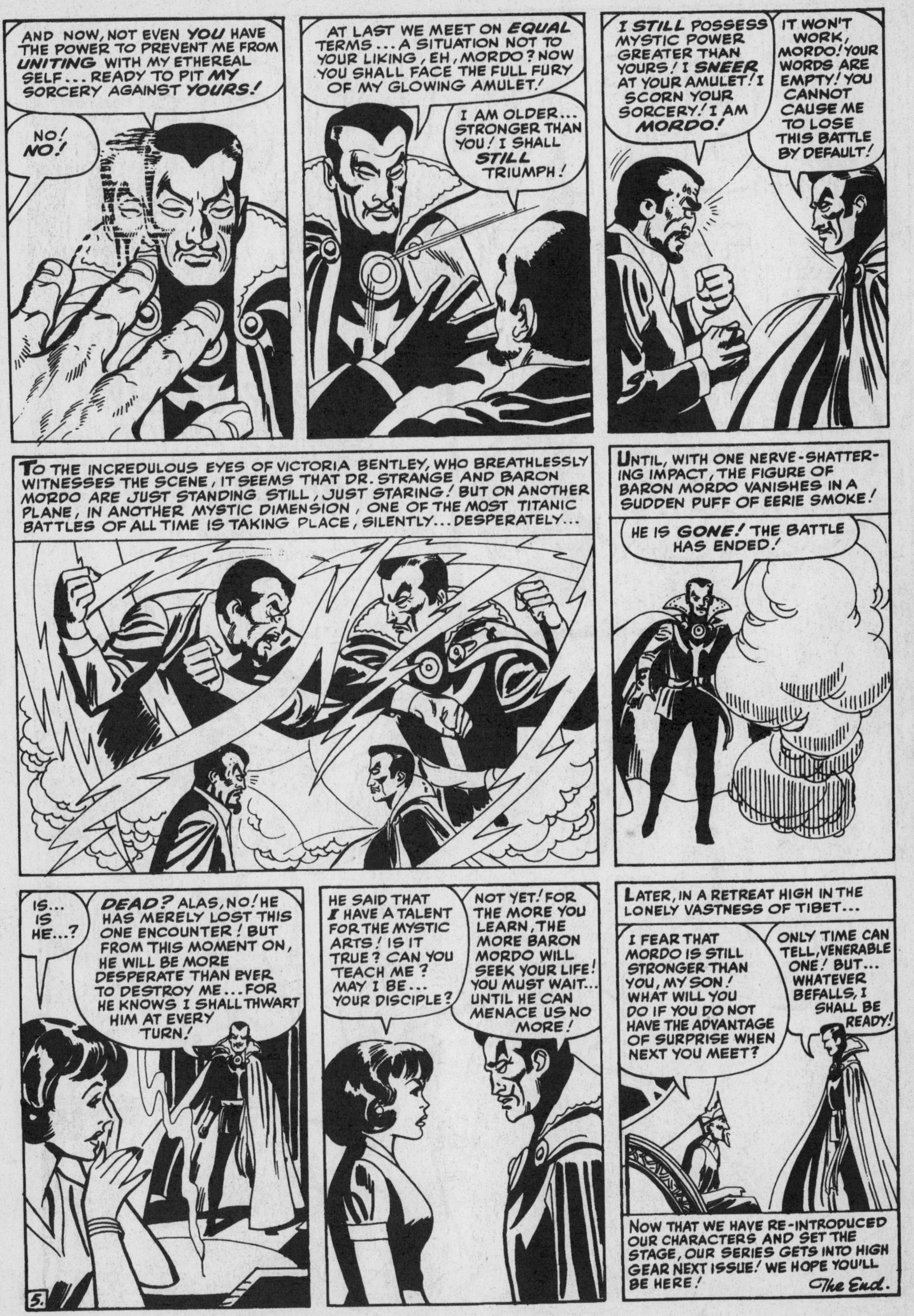

AND NOW, NOT EVEN YOU HAVE THE POWER TO PREVENT ME FROM UNITING WITH MY ETHEREAL SELF... READY TO PIT MY SORCERY AGAINST YOURS!
NO! NO!
AT LAST WE MEET ON EQUAL TERMS... A SITUATION NOT TO YOUR LIKING, EH, MORDO? NOW YOU SHALL FACE THE FULL FURY OF MY GLOWING AMULET!
I AM OLDER... STRONGER THAN YOU! I SHALL STILL TRIUMPH!
I STILL POSSESS MYSTIC POWER GREATER THAN YOURS! I SNEER AT YOUR AMULET! I SCORN YOUR SORCERY! I AM MORDO!
IT WON'T WORK, MORDO! YOUR WORDS ARE EMPTY! YOU CANNOT CAUSE ME TO LOSE THIS BATTLE BY DEFAULT!
TO THE INCREDULOUS EYES OF VICTORIA BENTLEY, WHO BREATHLESSLY WITNESSES THE SCENE, IT SEEMS THAT DR. STRANGE AND BARON MORDO ARE JUST STANDING STILL, JUST STARING! BUT ON ANOTHER PLANE, IN ANOTHER MYSTIC DIMENSION, ONE OF THE MOST TITANIC BATTLES OF ALL TIME IS TAKING PLACE, SILENTLY... DESPERATELY...
UNTIL, WITH ONE NERVE-SHATTERING IMPACT, THE FIGURE OF BARON MORDO VANISHES IN A SUDDEN PUFF OF EERIE SMOKE!
HE IS GONE! THE BATTLE HAS ENDED!
IS... IS HE...?
DEAD? ALAS, NO! HE HAS MERELY LOST THIS ONE ENCOUNTER! BUT FROM THIS MOMENT ON, HE WILL BE MORE DESPERATE THAN EVER TO DESTROY ME... FOR HE KNOWS I SHALL THWART HIM AT EVERY TURN!
HE SAID THAT I HAVE A TALENT FOR THE MYSTIC ARTS! IS IT TRUE? CAN YOU TEACH ME? MAY I BE... YOUR DISCIPLE?
NOT YET! FOR THE MORE YOU LEARN, THE MORE BARON MORDO WILL SEEK YOUR LIFE! YOU MUST WAIT... UNTIL HE CAN MENACE US NO MORE!
LATER, IN A RETREAT HIGH IN THE LONELY VASTNESS OF TIBET...
I FEAR THAT MORDO IS STILL STRONGER THAN YOU, MY SON! WHAT WILL YOU DO IF YOU DO NOT HAVE THE ADVANTAGE OF SURPRISE WHEN NEXT YOU MEET?
ONLY TIME CAN TELL, VENERABLE ONE! BUT... WHATEVER BEFALLS, I SHALL BE READY!
NOW THAT WE HAVE RE-INTRODUCED OUR CHARACTERS AND SET THE STAGE, OUR SERIES GETS INTO HIGH GEAR NEXT ISSUE! WE HOPE YOU'LL BE HERE!
The End.
5.

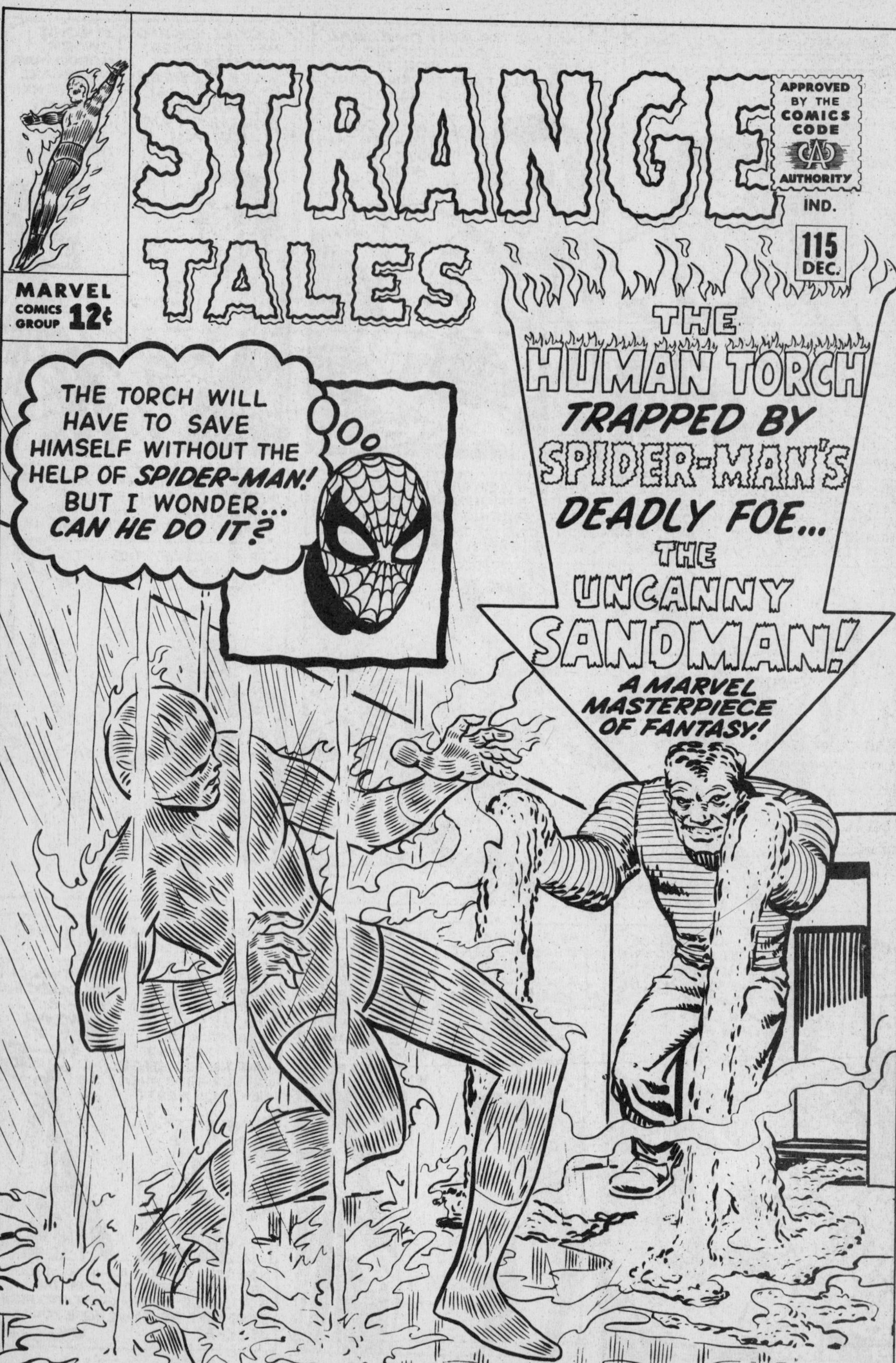

STRANGE TALES
MARVEL COMICS GROUP 12¢
APPROVED BY THE COMICS CODE AUTHORITY
IND.
115 DEC.
THE TORCH WILL HAVE TO SAVE HIMSELF WITHOUT THE HELP OF SPIDER-MAN! BUT I WONDER... CAN HE DO IT?
THE HUMAN TORCH TRAPPED BY SPIDER-MAN'S DEADLY FOE... THE UNCANNY SANDMAN!
A MARVEL MASTERPIECE OF FANTASY!

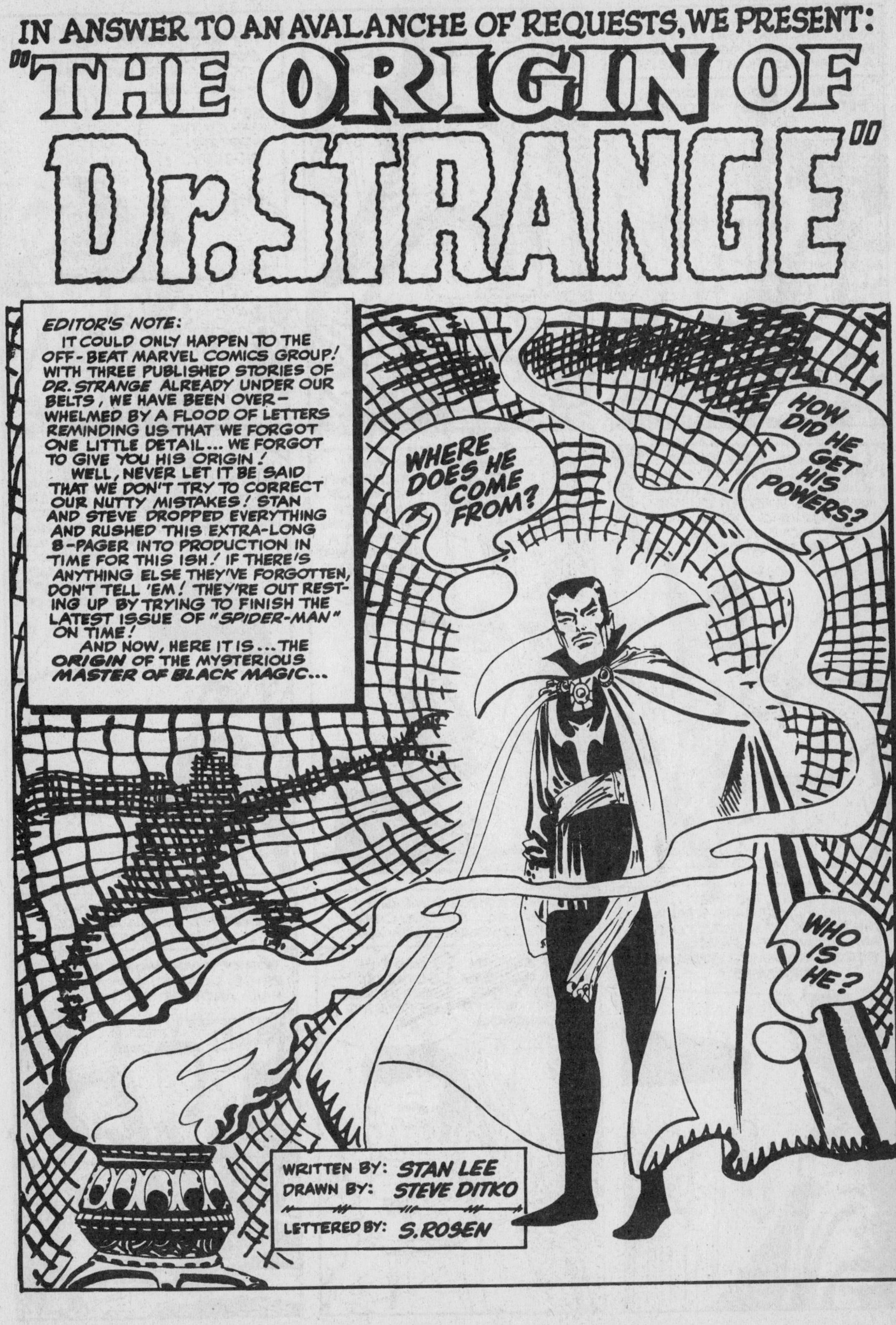
IN ANSWER TO AN AVALANCHE OF REQUESTS, WE PRESENT:
"THE ORIGIN OF Dr. STRANGE"
EDITOR'S NOTE:
IT COULD ONLY HAPPEN TO THE OFF-BEAT MARVEL COMICS GROUP! WITH THREE PUBLISHED STORIES OF DR. STRANGE ALREADY UNDER OUR BELTS, WE HAVE BEEN OVER-WHELMED BY A FLOOD OF LETTERS REMINDING US THAT WE FORGOT ONE LITTLE DETAIL... WE FORGOT TO GIVE YOU HIS ORIGIN!
WELL, NEVER LET IT BE SAID THAT WE DON'T TRY TO CORRECT OUR NUTTY MISTAKES! STAN AND STEVE DROPPED EVERYTHING AND RUSHED THIS EXTRA-LONG 8-PAGER INTO PRODUCTION IN TIME FOR THIS ISH! IF THERE'S ANYTHING ELSE THEY'VE FORGOTTEN, DON'T TELL 'EM! THEY'RE OUT RESTING UP BY TRYING TO FINISH THE LATEST ISSUE OF "SPIDER-MAN" ON TIME!
AND NOW, HERE IT IS... THE ORIGIN OF THE MYSTERIOUS MASTER OF BLACK MAGIC...
WHERE DOES HE COME FROM?
HOW DID HE GET HIS POWERS?
WHO IS HE?
WRITTEN BY: STAN LEE
DRAWN BY: STEVE DITKO
LETTERED BY: S. ROSEN

COME WITH US TO INDIA, LAND OF MYSTIC ENCHANTMENT, WHERE WE FIND A HAGGARD FIGURE ENTERING A STRANGELY SILENT CHAMBER...

I'VE SEARCHED FOR MONTHS, BUT NOW AT LAST MY QUEST IS ENDED!

YOU! OLD MAN! ARE YOU THE ONE I SEEK? ARE YOU CALLED "THE ANCIENT ONE?"

I AM THE ANCIENT ONE!

THEN YOU'RE THE ONE WITH THE MAGIC HEALING POWER! I NEED YOU! YOU HAVE TO HELP ME!

BE PATIENT, MAN OF THE WESTERN WORLD!

I HEAL NONE SAVE THOSE WHO DESERVE IT! THE POWER OF MY MAGIC MUST NEVER BE WASTED ON THE UNDESERVING! FIRST, YOU MUST PROVE YOU ARE WORTHY!

YOU CAN'T REFUSE ME! I WON'T LET YOU! I'VE TRAVELED TOO FAR...WAITED TOO LONG...

STOP! I WILL PERMIT NO ACT OF VIOLENCE HERE! NONE MAY LIFT A HAND AGAINST THE ANCIENT ONE!

OH!! WHA--?

HE...HE IS HOLDING ME MOTIONLESS ABOVE THE GROUND... JUST BY A GESTURE! IT'S UNCANNY!

AND NOW I SHALL PEER INTO YOUR BRAIN ...INTO YOUR MEMORY... AND LEARN THE TRUTH ABOUT YOU!

I SEE YOU IN THE PAST...IN AMERICA...YOU ARE WEARING THE FROCK OF A DOCTOR! AHH, YOU WERE A FAMOUS SURGEON NAMED STEPHEN STRANGE!

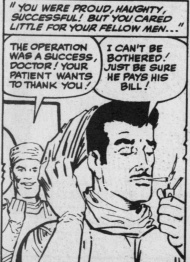

"YOU WERE PROUD, HAUGHTY, SUCCESSFUL! BUT YOU CARED LITTLE FOR YOUR FELLOW MEN..."

THE OPERATION WAS A SUCCESS, DOCTOR! YOUR PATIENT WANTS TO THANK YOU!

I CAN'T BE BOTHERED! JUST BE SURE HE PAYS HIS BILL!

"MONEY...THAT WAS ALL THAT INTERESTED YOU... ALL YOU CARED ABOUT..."

SORRY, IF YOU WON'T PAY MY PRICE, I CAN'T HELP YOU! FIND ANOTHER DOCTOR!

2.

Panel 1:
"TO YOU THE PROBLEMS OF OTHERS MEANT LESS THAN NOTHING!"

DR. STRANGE, WE NEED YOUR HELP ON OUR NEW MEDICAL RESEARCH PROJECT!

SORRY! I AM NOT INTERESTED IN CHARITY WORK!

Panel 2:
BUT WITH YOUR SKILL, YOUR KNOWLEDGE, WE MIGHT BE ABLE TO FIND A CURE FOR... WAIT!! COME BACK!

WHEN YOU'RE WILLING TO PAY ME FOR MY TALENT, I WILL LISTEN! NOT UNTIL THEN! GOOD DAY!

Panel 3:
"BUT WHAT IS THIS? THE SCENE NOW CHANGES! I SEE AN AUTO ACCIDENT, ON A LONELY ROAD! THE VICTIM IS ALIVE, BUT INJURED! THE VICTIM IS... YOU!!"

WE GOT HERE JUST IN TIME, JOE! CALL FOR AN AMBULANCE!

Panel 4:
"YOU RECOVERED IN DUE TIME! YOUR LIFE WAS SPARED, BUT YOU SUFFERED A TERRIBLE BLOW..."

I DON'T KNOW HOW TO TELL YOU THIS...

SPEAK UP, MAN! I CAN TAKE IT! WHAT DO THE X-RAYS SHOW?

Panel 5:
ALTHOUGH YOUR HANDS SEEM TO BE ALL RIGHT, THE NERVES HAVE BEEN SEVERELY DAMAGED!

YOU... YOU... MEAN...?

Panel 6:
YES! YOU WILL NEVER BE ABLE TO PERFORM AN OPERATION AGAIN!

NO! NO!

I DON'T BELIEVE YOU! YOU'RE LYING! YOU MUST BE LYING!

Panel 7:
"OTHERS TRIED TO HELP YOU, BUT YOU WERE TOO BITTER... TOO FULL OF PENT-UP SELF-PITY!"

EVEN THOUGH YOU CAN'T OPERATE, YOU CAN WORK AS A CONSULTANT.. AS MY ASSISTANT!

STEPHEN STRANGE ASSISTS NOBODY!

Panel 8:
"AND SO YOU WENT INTO SECLUSION ...YOU SPENT YOUR DAYS BROODING, AS BITTERNESS FILLED YOUR SOUL!"

I MUST BE THE BEST... THE GREATEST!!! OR ELSE... NOTHING!

I'LL NEVER CONSENT TO WORK FOR ANYONE ELSE!

Panel 9:
"YOU LOST TRACK OF TIME... YOU BECAME A DRIFTER... LITTLE MORE THAN A HUMAN DERELICT! AND THEN, ONE DAY, ON THE DOCKS, YOU OVERHEARD TWO SAILORS!"

YEAH, I HEARD OF THE ANCIENT ONE, ALSO! THEY SAY HE CAN CURE ANYTHING... BY SOME MAGIC POWER!

IF YOU ASK ME, HE'S JUST A LEGEND!

3.

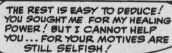

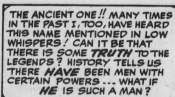

THE ANCIENT ONE!! MANY TIMES IN THE PAST I, TOO, HAVE HEARD THIS NAME MENTIONED IN LOW WHISPERS! CAN IT BE THAT THERE IS SOME *TRUTH* TO THE LEGENDS? HISTORY TELLS US THERE *HAVE* BEEN MEN WITH CERTAIN POWERS... WHAT IF *HE* IS SUCH A MAN?

THE REST IS EASY TO DEDUCE! YOU SOUGHT ME FOR MY HEALING POWER! BUT I CANNOT HELP YOU... FOR YOUR MOTIVES ARE STILL SELFISH!

AND YET, I SEEM TO SEE A SPARK WITHIN YOU... A SPARK OF DECENCY... OF GOODNESS.. WHICH I MIGHT BE ABLE TO FAN INTO A FLAME!

IF YOU WILL STAY HERE... STUDY WITH ME... PERHAPS YOU WILL FIND WITHIN YOURSELF THE CURE YOU SEEK!

I SHOULD HAVE *KNOWN!* IT WAS JUST A WASTE OF TIME! YOU'RE NOTHING BUT AN OLD FRAUD!

YOUR LITTLE PARLOR TRICKS DON'T IMPRESS *ME!* I'M LEAVING! SAY... WHERE DID THAT *SNOW* COME FROM?! IT WASN'T THERE BEFORE!! I COULD NEVER MAKE IT DOWN THE PASS NOW!

NO!...YOU WILL HAVE TO REMAIN UNTIL IT THAWS!

THAT SNOW ISN'T *YOUR* DOING, IS IT?? AW, WHAT AM I SAYING? PRETTY SOON, I'LL CONVINCE MYSELF YOU *DO* HAVE MAGIC POWERS!

NATURALLY, MAN OF THE WESTERN WORLD, YOU MUST NOT ALLOW YOURSELF TO BELIEVE IN MAGIC! IT WOULD BE... UNSEEMLY!

AND NOW, INASMUCH AS YOU MUST REMAIN HERE UNTIL THE SNOW THAWS, MY PUPIL, MORDO, WILL SHOW YOU TO YOUR CHAMBER!

MORDO! WHAT A CREEPY-LOOKING CHARACTER!

ALL HE DOES IS STUDY THOSE MEANINGLESS SCROLLS AND RECITE HIS EMPTY DIRGES! WHAT A WASTE OF TIME!

I NEVER SHOULD HAVE COME HERE IN THE FIRST PLACE!

I'LL ASK THE OLD MAN IF HE KNOWS HOW LONG IT TAKES THE SNOW TO MELT AROUND HERE! HMM....LOOKS LIKE HE'S ASLEEP! SAY, WHAT'S THAT VAPOR SWIRLING AROUND HIM?

THE VAPORS OF VALTORR!! I AM BEING ATTACKED BY AN UNSEEN ENEMY!

THE VAPORS WERE SPAWNED BY BLACK MAGIC, AND ONLY BY BLACK MAGIC CAN THEY BE DISPELLED!

4.

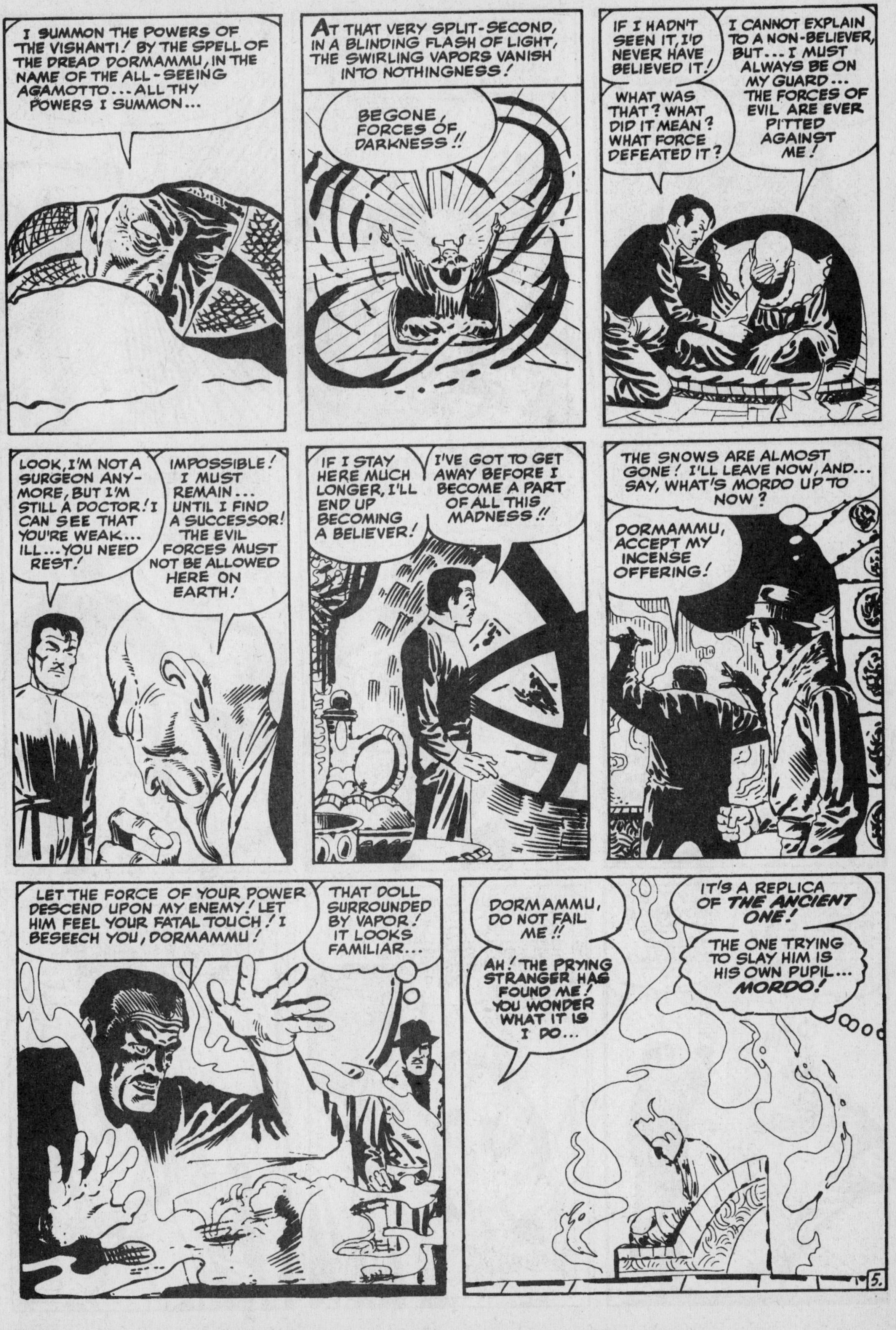
I SUMMON THE POWERS OF THE VISHANTI! BY THE SPELL OF THE DREAD DORMAMMU, IN THE NAME OF THE ALL-SEEING AGAMOTTO... ALL THY POWERS I SUMMON...
AT THAT VERY SPLIT-SECOND, IN A BLINDING FLASH OF LIGHT, THE SWIRLING VAPORS VANISH INTO NOTHINGNESS!
BEGONE, FORCES OF DARKNESS!!
IF I HADN'T SEEN IT, I'D NEVER HAVE BELIEVED IT!
WHAT WAS THAT? WHAT DID IT MEAN? WHAT FORCE DEFEATED IT?
I CANNOT EXPLAIN TO A NON-BELIEVER, BUT... I MUST ALWAYS BE ON MY GUARD... THE FORCES OF EVIL ARE EVER PITTED AGAINST ME!
LOOK, I'M NOT A SURGEON ANYMORE, BUT I'M STILL A DOCTOR! I CAN SEE THAT YOU'RE WEAK... ILL... YOU NEED REST!
IMPOSSIBLE! I MUST REMAIN... UNTIL I FIND A SUCCESSOR! THE EVIL FORCES MUST NOT BE ALLOWED HERE ON EARTH!
IF I STAY HERE MUCH LONGER, I'LL END UP BECOMING A BELIEVER!
I'VE GOT TO GET AWAY BEFORE I BECOME A PART OF ALL THIS MADNESS!!
THE SNOWS ARE ALMOST GONE! I'LL LEAVE NOW, AND... SAY, WHAT'S MORDO UP TO NOW?
DORMAMMU, ACCEPT MY INCENSE OFFERING!
LET THE FORCE OF YOUR POWER DESCEND UPON MY ENEMY! LET HIM FEEL YOUR FATAL TOUCH! I BESEECH YOU, DORMAMMU!
THAT DOLL SURROUNDED BY VAPOR! IT LOOKS FAMILIAR...
DORMAMMU, DO NOT FAIL ME!!
AH! THE PRYING STRANGER HAS FOUND ME! YOU WONDER WHAT IT IS I DO...
IT'S A REPLICA OF THE ANCIENT ONE!
THE ONE TRYING TO SLAY HIM IS HIS OWN PUPIL... MORDO!
5.

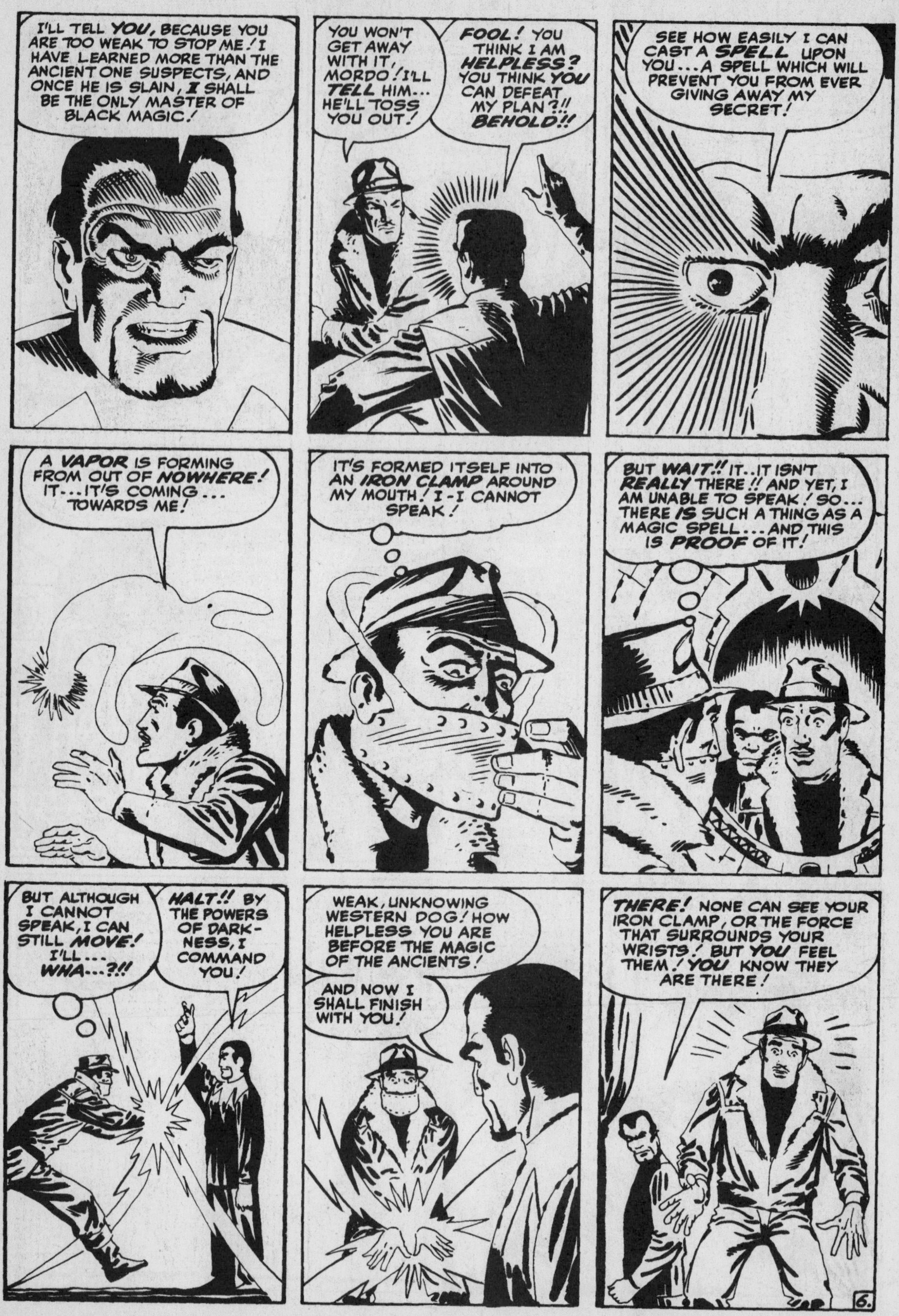
I'LL TELL YOU, BECAUSE YOU ARE TOO WEAK TO STOP ME! I HAVE LEARNED MORE THAN THE ANCIENT ONE SUSPECTS, AND ONCE HE IS SLAIN, I SHALL BE THE ONLY MASTER OF BLACK MAGIC!
YOU WON'T GET AWAY WITH IT, MORDO! I'LL TELL HIM... HE'LL TOSS YOU OUT!
FOOL! YOU THINK I AM HELPLESS? YOU THINK YOU CAN DEFEAT MY PLAN?!! BEHOLD!!
SEE HOW EASILY I CAN CAST A SPELL UPON YOU... A SPELL WHICH WILL PREVENT YOU FROM EVER GIVING AWAY MY SECRET!
A VAPOR IS FORMING FROM OUT OF NOWHERE! IT...IT'S COMING... TOWARDS ME!
IT'S FORMED ITSELF INTO AN IRON CLAMP AROUND MY MOUTH! I-I CANNOT SPEAK!
BUT WAIT!! IT..IT ISN'T REALLY THERE!! AND YET, I AM UNABLE TO SPEAK! SO... THERE IS SUCH A THING AS A MAGIC SPELL... AND THIS IS PROOF OF IT!
BUT ALTHOUGH I CANNOT SPEAK, I CAN STILL MOVE! I'LL... WHA...?!!
HALT!! BY THE POWERS OF DARK-NESS, I COMMAND YOU!
WEAK, UNKNOWING WESTERN DOG! HOW HELPLESS YOU ARE BEFORE THE MAGIC OF THE ANCIENTS!
AND NOW I SHALL FINISH WITH YOU!
THERE! NONE CAN SEE YOUR IRON CLAMP, OR THE FORCE THAT SURROUNDS YOUR WRISTS! BUT YOU FEEL THEM! YOU KNOW THEY ARE THERE!
6.

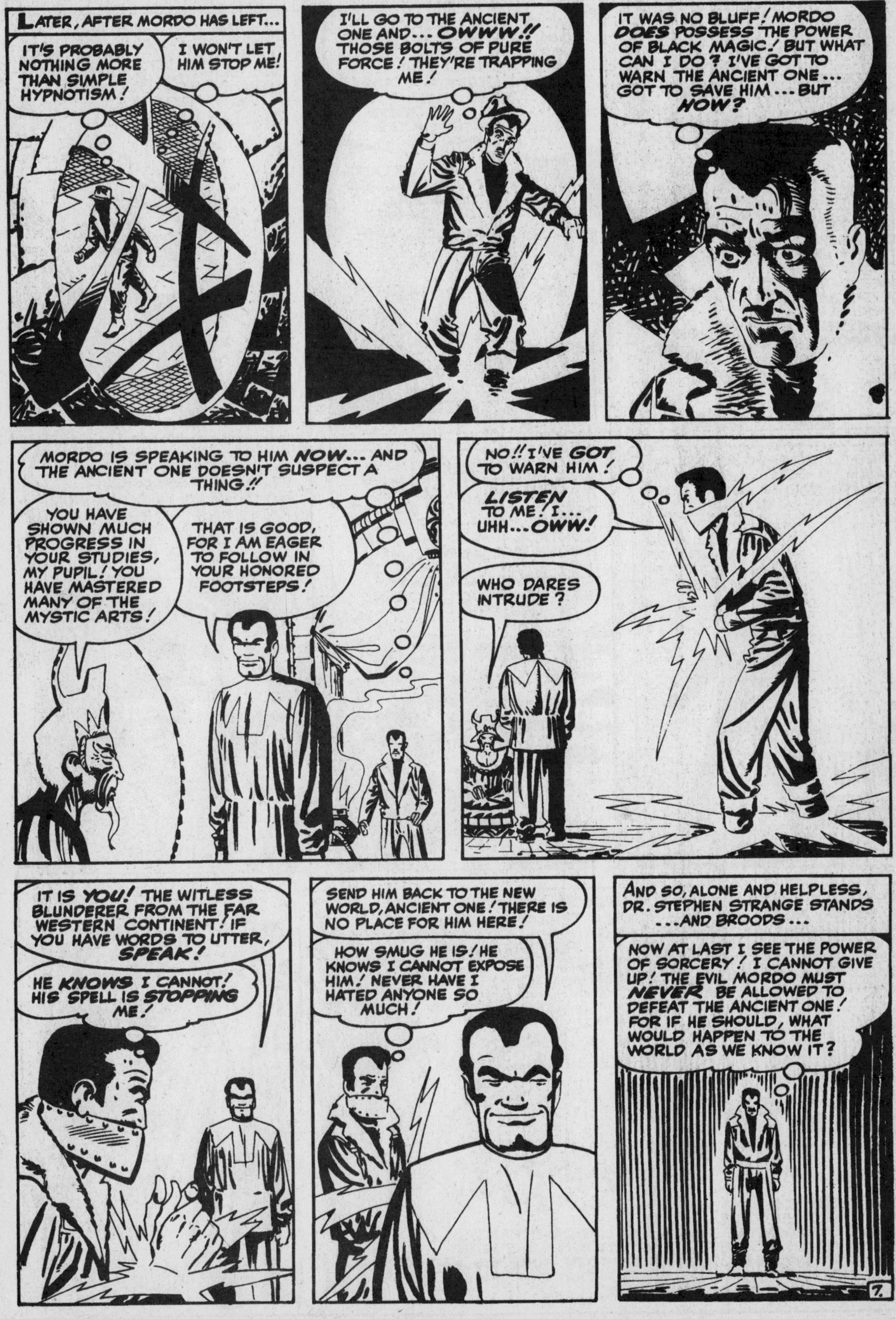

LATER, AFTER MORDO HAS LEFT...
IT'S PROBABLY NOTHING MORE THAN SIMPLE HYPNOTISM!
I WON'T LET HIM STOP ME!
I'LL GO TO THE ANCIENT ONE AND... OWWW!! THOSE BOLTS OF PURE FORCE! THEY'RE TRAPPING ME!
IT WAS NO BLUFF! MORDO DOES POSSESS THE POWER OF BLACK MAGIC! BUT WHAT CAN I DO? I'VE GOT TO WARN THE ANCIENT ONE... GOT TO SAVE HIM... BUT HOW?
MORDO IS SPEAKING TO HIM NOW... AND THE ANCIENT ONE DOESN'T SUSPECT A THING!!
YOU HAVE SHOWN MUCH PROGRESS IN YOUR STUDIES, MY PUPIL! YOU HAVE MASTERED MANY OF THE MYSTIC ARTS!
THAT IS GOOD, FOR I AM EAGER TO FOLLOW IN YOUR HONORED FOOTSTEPS!
NO!! I'VE GOT TO WARN HIM!
LISTEN TO ME! I... UHH... OWW!
WHO DARES INTRUDE?
IT IS YOU! THE WITLESS BLUNDERER FROM THE FAR WESTERN CONTINENT! IF YOU HAVE WORDS TO UTTER, SPEAK!
HE KNOWS I CANNOT! HIS SPELL IS STOPPING ME!
SEND HIM BACK TO THE NEW WORLD, ANCIENT ONE! THERE IS NO PLACE FOR HIM HERE!
HOW SMUG HE IS! HE KNOWS I CANNOT EXPOSE HIM! NEVER HAVE I HATED ANYONE SO MUCH!
AND SO, ALONE AND HELPLESS, DR. STEPHEN STRANGE STANDS ...AND BROODS...
NOW AT LAST I SEE THE POWER OF SORCERY! I CANNOT GIVE UP! THE EVIL MORDO MUST NEVER BE ALLOWED TO DEFEAT THE ANCIENT ONE! FOR IF HE SHOULD, WHAT WOULD HAPPEN TO THE WORLD AS WE KNOW IT?
7.

I AM ONLY SUBJECT TO MORDO'S SPELL IF I TRY TO *WARN* THE ANCIENT ONE! YET, I AM ABLE TO SPEAK OF *OTHER* MATTERS...SO THERE IS STILL ONE HOPE!

IF *I, TOO,* CAN LEARN THE SECRETS OF BLACK MAGIC, THEN *I* CAN BATTLE MORDO WITH HIS OWN WEAPONS!

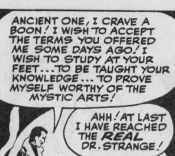

ANCIENT ONE, I CRAVE A BOON! I WISH TO ACCEPT THE TERMS YOU OFFERED ME SOME DAYS AGO! I WISH TO STUDY AT YOUR FEET...TO BE TAUGHT YOUR KNOWLEDGE...TO PROVE MYSELF WORTHY OF THE MYSTIC ARTS!

AHH! AT LAST I HAVE REACHED THE *REAL* DR. STRANGE!

I KNEW THAT THERE WAS *GOOD* WITHIN YOU...IF I COULD BUT BRING IT TO THE SURFACE! I *ACCEPT* YOU, MY SON! YOU SHALL BE MY DISCIPLE!

FIRST, I RELEASE YOU FROM MORDO'S SPELL...*SO!* NOW YOU ARE FREE TO SPEAK, TO ACT, EVEN AS BEFORE!

YOU...YOU *KNEW* OF MORDO'S SPELL?!!

OF COURSE! THE PUPIL CAN HAVE NO SECRETS FROM HIS MASTER! BUT, ALTHOUGH HE IS EVIL, I PREFER TO KEEP MORDO *HERE* WHERE I CAN CONTROL HIM, RATHER THAN BANISH HIM! ONE DAY, MY SON, WHEN I AM GONE, IT WILL BE *YOUR* TASK TO BATTLE MORDO...TO THE FINISH!

YOU HAVE BEEN TESTED, AND YOU HAVE PASSED YOUR BAPTISM OF FIRE! BUT THE PATH AHEAD OF YOU WILL BE DIFFICULT, AND FRAUGHT WITH DANGER! DO YOU STILL WISH TO CONTINUE?

I DO, ANCIENT ONE!

AND SO IT BEGAN! THE DAYS TURNED TO WEEKS, TO MONTHS, TO YEARS, AS DR. STRANGE STUDIED THE LONG-DEAD MYSTIC ARTS! SLOWLY HE CHANGED...SLOWLY HIS LIFE TOOK ON A NEW DEEPER MEANING...SLOWLY HE PREPARED HIMSELF FOR THE EPIC BATTLES AHEAD, THE BATTLES WHICH COULD ONLY BE WON BY DR. STRANGE, MASTER OF BLACK MAGIC!

AND THERE YOU HAVE IT! IT HAS TAKEN FOUR ISSUES FOR US TO REACH THIS POINT, BUT, LIKE DR. STRANGE, WE ARE READY AT LAST...READY TO BEGIN THE MOST MYSTIC ADVENTURES OF ALL TIME! SO BE SURE YOU ARE WITH US NEXT ISSUE AND SEE FOR YOURSELF THAT OUR TALES-TO-COME WERE WELL WORTH WAITING FOR!

The End

8

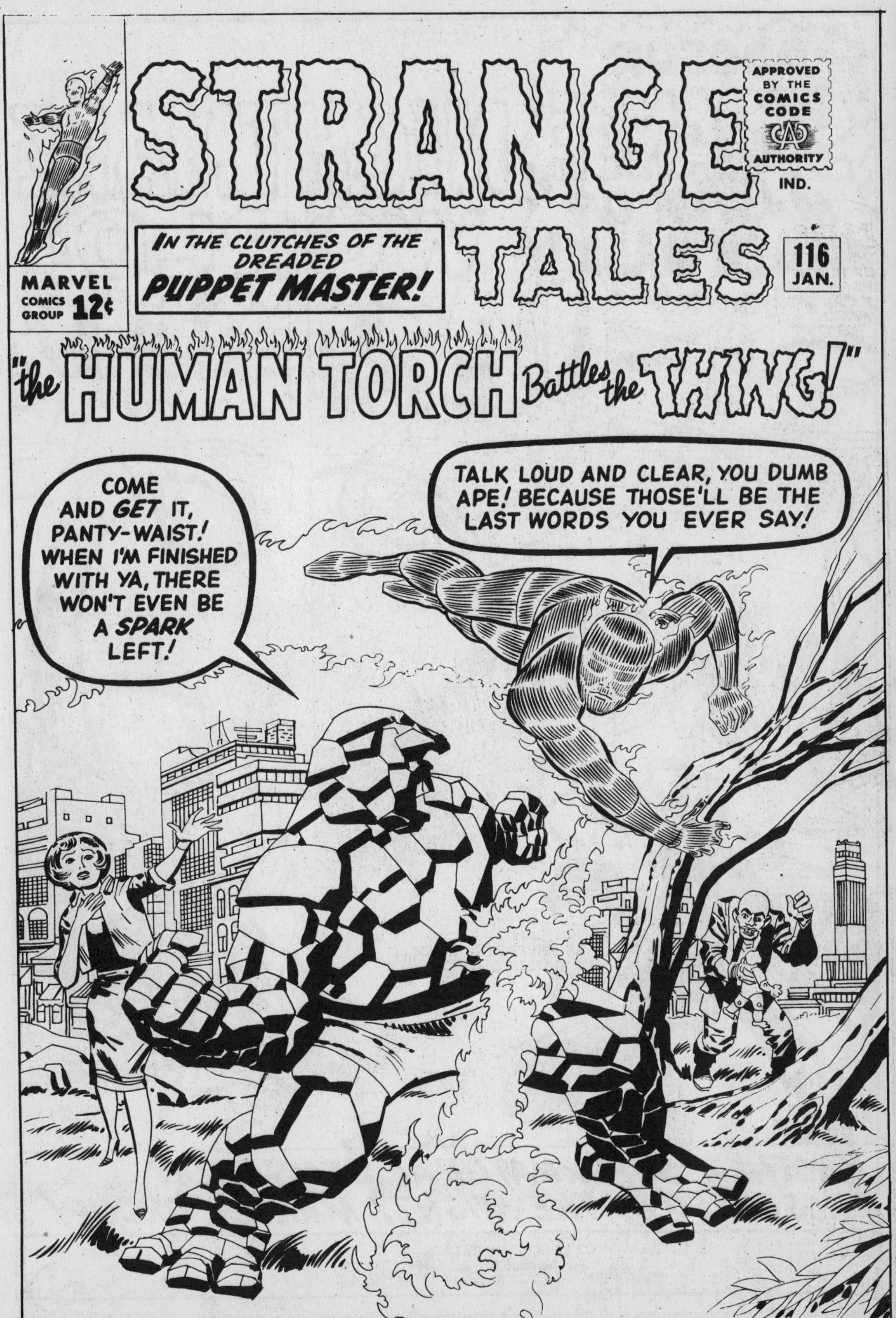
STRANGE TALES
APPROVED BY THE COMICS CODE AUTHORITY
IND.
MARVEL COMICS GROUP 12¢
IN THE CLUTCHES OF THE DREADED PUPPET MASTER!
116 JAN.
"the HUMAN TORCH Battles the THING!"
COME AND GET IT, PANTY-WAIST! WHEN I'M FINISHED WITH YA, THERE WON'T EVEN BE A SPARK LEFT!
TALK LOUD AND CLEAR, YOU DUMB APE! BECAUSE THOSE'LL BE THE LAST WORDS YOU EVER SAY!

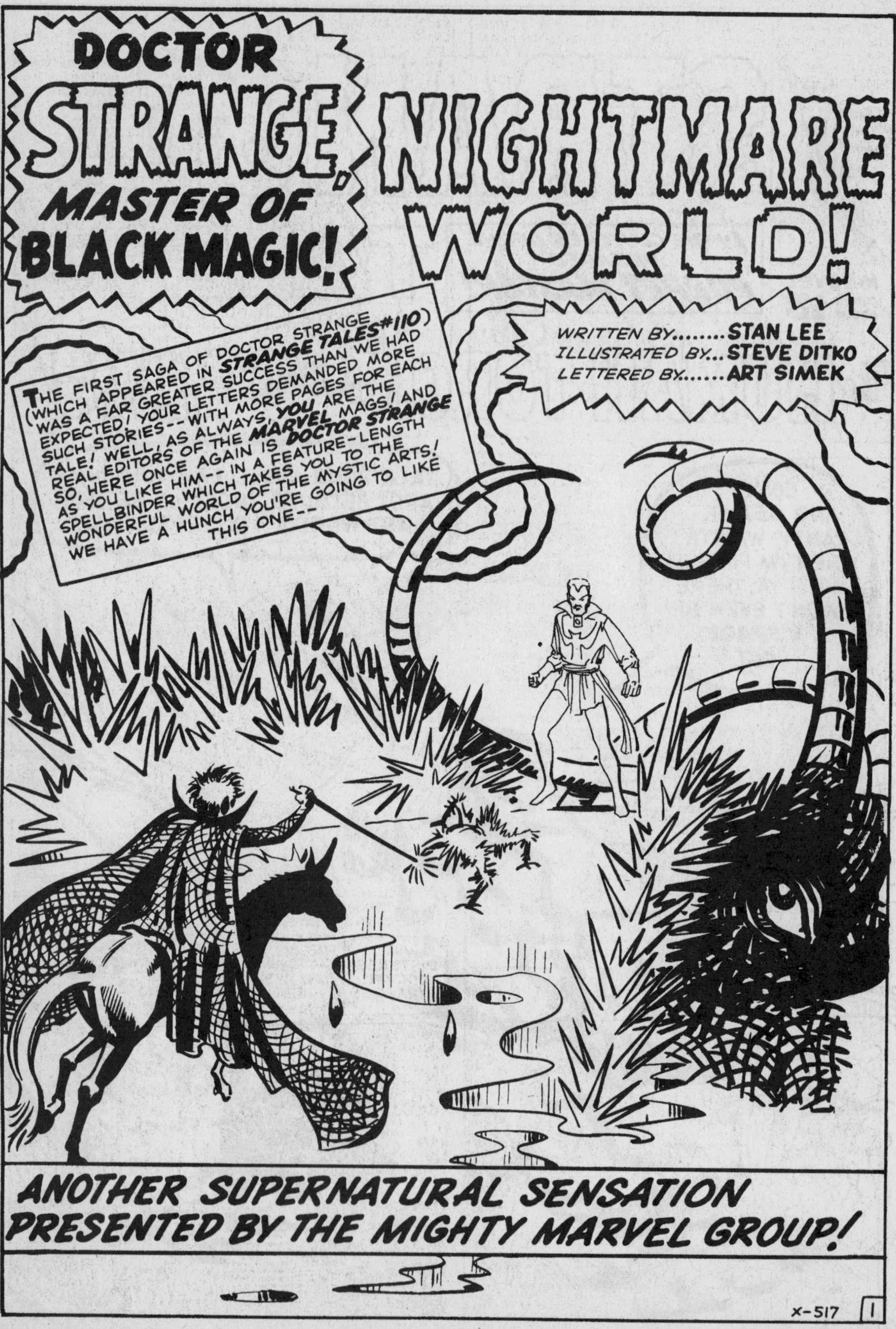
DOCTOR STRANGE, MASTER OF BLACK MAGIC!
NIGHTMARE WORLD!
THE FIRST SAGA OF DOCTOR STRANGE (WHICH APPEARED IN STRANGE TALES#110) WAS A FAR GREATER SUCCESS THAN WE HAD EXPECTED! YOUR LETTERS DEMANDED MORE SUCH STORIES--WITH MORE PAGES FOR EACH TALE! WELL, AS ALWAYS, YOU ARE THE REAL EDITORS OF THE MARVEL MAGS! AND SO, HERE ONCE AGAIN IS DOCTOR STRANGE AS YOU LIKE HIM-- IN A FEATURE-LENGTH SPELLBINDER WHICH TAKES YOU TO THE WONDERFUL WORLD OF THE MYSTIC ARTS! WE HAVE A HUNCH YOU'RE GOING TO LIKE THIS ONE--
WRITTEN BY........STAN LEE
ILLUSTRATED BY...STEVE DITKO
LETTERED BY......ART SIMEK
ANOTHER SUPERNATURAL SENSATION PRESENTED BY THE MIGHTY MARVEL GROUP!
X-517

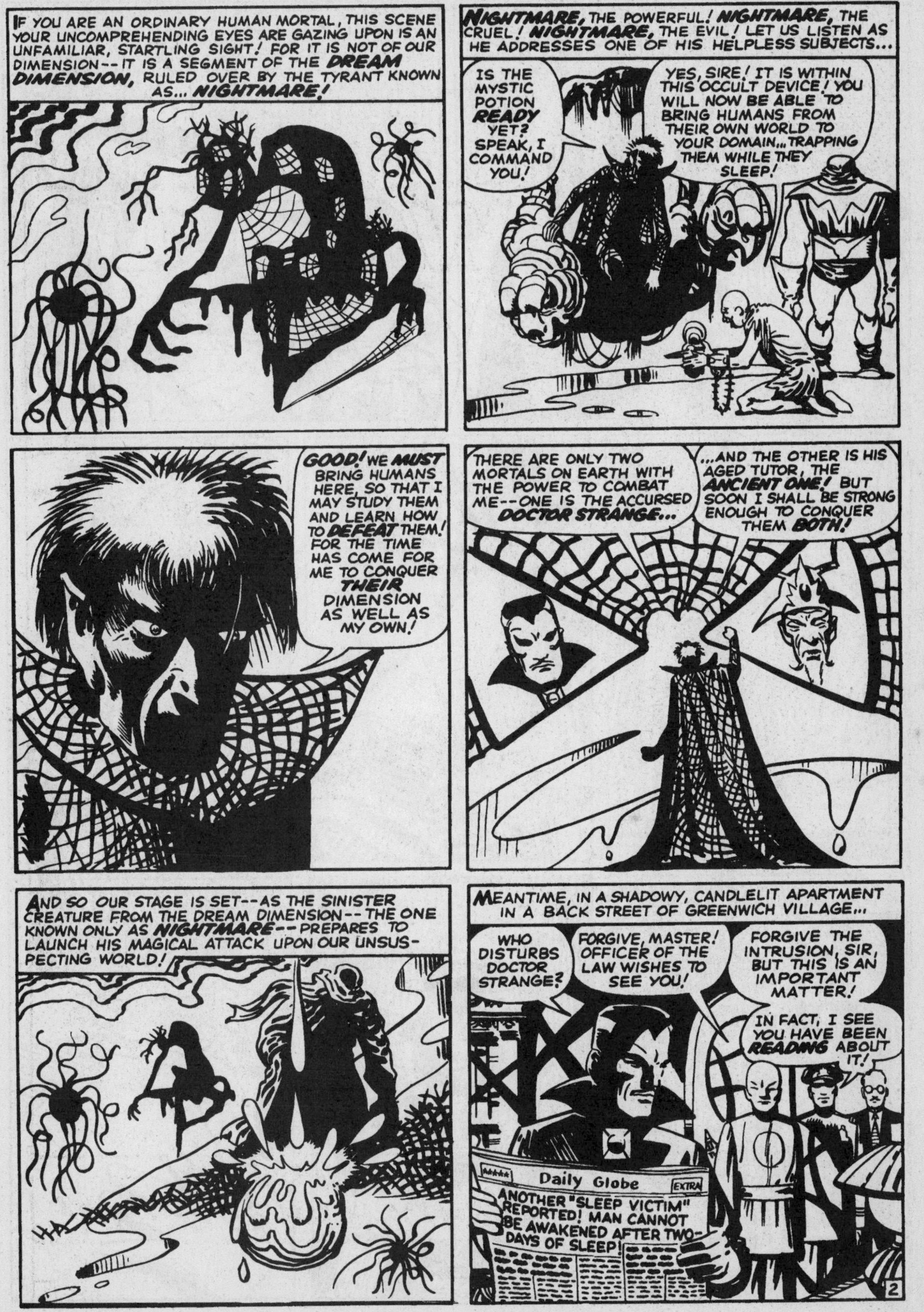

IF YOU ARE AN ORDINARY HUMAN MORTAL, THIS SCENE YOUR UNCOMPREHENDING EYES ARE GAZING UPON IS AN UNFAMILIAR, STARTLING SIGHT! FOR IT IS NOT OF OUR DIMENSION--IT IS A SEGMENT OF THE DREAM DIMENSION, RULED OVER BY THE TYRANT KNOWN AS... NIGHTMARE!
NIGHTMARE, THE POWERFUL! NIGHTMARE, THE CRUEL! NIGHTMARE, THE EVIL! LET US LISTEN AS HE ADDRESSES ONE OF HIS HELPLESS SUBJECTS...
IS THE MYSTIC POTION READY YET? SPEAK, I COMMAND YOU!
YES, SIRE! IT IS WITHIN THIS OCCULT DEVICE! YOU WILL NOW BE ABLE TO BRING HUMANS FROM THEIR OWN WORLD TO YOUR DOMAIN... TRAPPING THEM WHILE THEY SLEEP!
GOOD! WE MUST BRING HUMANS HERE, SO THAT I MAY STUDY THEM AND LEARN HOW TO DEFEAT THEM! FOR THE TIME HAS COME FOR ME TO CONQUER THEIR DIMENSION AS WELL AS MY OWN!
THERE ARE ONLY TWO MORTALS ON EARTH WITH THE POWER TO COMBAT ME--ONE IS THE ACCURSED DOCTOR STRANGE...
...AND THE OTHER IS HIS AGED TUTOR, THE ANCIENT ONE! BUT SOON I SHALL BE STRONG ENOUGH TO CONQUER THEM BOTH!
AND SO OUR STAGE IS SET--AS THE SINISTER CREATURE FROM THE DREAM DIMENSION--THE ONE KNOWN ONLY AS NIGHTMARE--PREPARES TO LAUNCH HIS MAGICAL ATTACK UPON OUR UNSUSPECTING WORLD!
MEANTIME, IN A SHADOWY, CANDLELIT APARTMENT IN A BACK STREET OF GREENWICH VILLAGE...
WHO DISTURBS DOCTOR STRANGE?
FORGIVE, MASTER! OFFICER OF THE LAW WISHES TO SEE YOU!
FORGIVE THE INTRUSION, SIR, BUT THIS IS AN IMPORTANT MATTER!
IN FACT, I SEE YOU HAVE BEEN READING ABOUT IT!
Daily Globe
EXTRA
ANOTHER "SLEEP VICTIM" REPORTED! MAN CANNOT BE AWAKENED AFTER TWO-DAYS OF SLEEP!
2

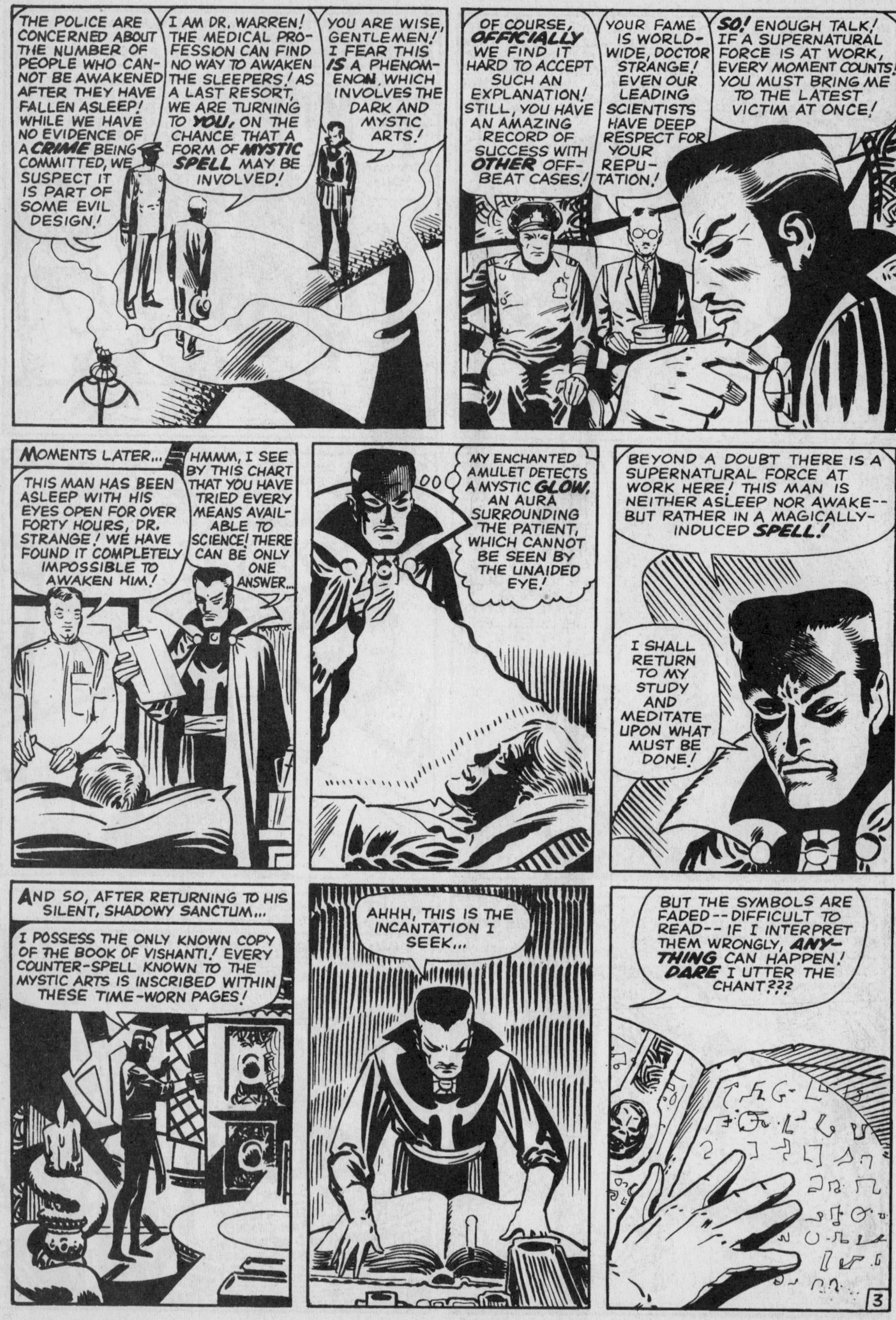
THE POLICE ARE CONCERNED ABOUT THE NUMBER OF PEOPLE WHO CANNOT BE AWAKENED AFTER THEY HAVE FALLEN ASLEEP! WHILE WE HAVE NO EVIDENCE OF A CRIME BEING COMMITTED, WE SUSPECT IT IS PART OF SOME EVIL DESIGN!
I AM DR. WARREN! THE MEDICAL PROFESSION CAN FIND NO WAY TO AWAKEN THE SLEEPERS! AS A LAST RESORT, WE ARE TURNING TO YOU, ON THE CHANCE THAT A FORM OF MYSTIC SPELL MAY BE INVOLVED!
YOU ARE WISE, GENTLEMEN! I FEAR THIS IS A PHENOMENON, WHICH INVOLVES THE DARK AND MYSTIC ARTS!
OF COURSE, OFFICIALLY WE FIND IT HARD TO ACCEPT SUCH AN EXPLANATION! STILL, YOU HAVE AN AMAZING RECORD OF SUCCESS WITH OTHER OFF-BEAT CASES!
YOUR FAME IS WORLD-WIDE, DOCTOR STRANGE! EVEN OUR LEADING SCIENTISTS HAVE DEEP RESPECT FOR YOUR REPUTATION!
SO! ENOUGH TALK! IF A SUPERNATURAL FORCE IS AT WORK, EVERY MOMENT COUNTS! YOU MUST BRING ME TO THE LATEST VICTIM AT ONCE!
MOMENTS LATER...
THIS MAN HAS BEEN ASLEEP WITH HIS EYES OPEN FOR OVER FORTY HOURS, DR. STRANGE! WE HAVE FOUND IT COMPLETELY IMPOSSIBLE TO AWAKEN HIM!
HMMM, I SEE BY THIS CHART THAT YOU HAVE TRIED EVERY MEANS AVAILABLE TO SCIENCE! THERE CAN BE ONLY ONE ANSWER...
MY ENCHANTED AMULET DETECTS A MYSTIC GLOW, AN AURA SURROUNDING THE PATIENT, WHICH CANNOT BE SEEN BY THE UNAIDED EYE!
BEYOND A DOUBT THERE IS A SUPERNATURAL FORCE AT WORK HERE! THIS MAN IS NEITHER ASLEEP NOR AWAKE-- BUT RATHER IN A MAGICALLY-INDUCED SPELL!
I SHALL RETURN TO MY STUDY AND MEDITATE UPON WHAT MUST BE DONE!
AND SO, AFTER RETURNING TO HIS SILENT, SHADOWY SANCTUM...
I POSSESS THE ONLY KNOWN COPY OF THE BOOK OF VISHANTI! EVERY COUNTER-SPELL KNOWN TO THE MYSTIC ARTS IS INSCRIBED WITHIN THESE TIME-WORN PAGES!
AHHH, THIS IS THE INCANTATION I SEEK...
BUT THE SYMBOLS ARE FADED -- DIFFICULT TO READ -- IF I INTERPRET THEM WRONGLY, ANYTHING CAN HAPPEN! DARE I UTTER THE CHANT???
3

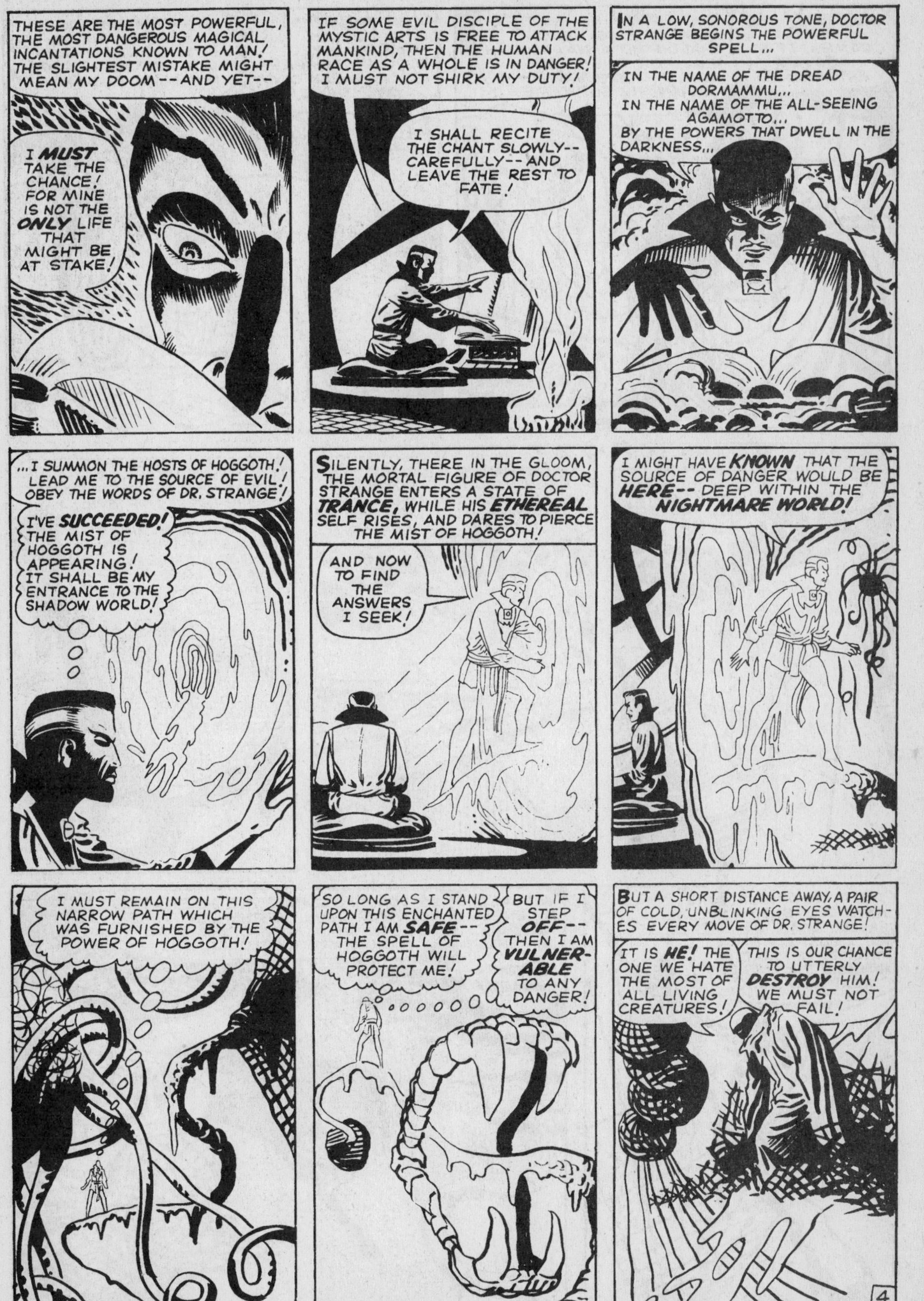
THESE ARE THE MOST POWERFUL, THE MOST DANGEROUS MAGICAL INCANTATIONS KNOWN TO MAN! THE SLIGHTEST MISTAKE MIGHT MEAN MY DOOM -- AND YET--
I MUST TAKE THE CHANCE! FOR MINE IS NOT THE ONLY LIFE THAT MIGHT BE AT STAKE!
IF SOME EVIL DISCIPLE OF THE MYSTIC ARTS IS FREE TO ATTACK MANKIND, THEN THE HUMAN RACE AS A WHOLE IS IN DANGER! I MUST NOT SHIRK MY DUTY!
I SHALL RECITE THE CHANT SLOWLY-- CAREFULLY-- AND LEAVE THE REST TO FATE!
IN A LOW, SONOROUS TONE, DOCTOR STRANGE BEGINS THE POWERFUL SPELL...
IN THE NAME OF THE DREAD DORMAMMU... IN THE NAME OF THE ALL-SEEING AGAMOTTO... BY THE POWERS THAT DWELL IN THE DARKNESS...
...I SUMMON THE HOSTS OF HOGGOTH! LEAD ME TO THE SOURCE OF EVIL! OBEY THE WORDS OF DR. STRANGE!
I'VE SUCCEEDED! THE MIST OF HOGGOTH IS APPEARING! IT SHALL BE MY ENTRANCE TO THE SHADOW WORLD!
SILENTLY, THERE IN THE GLOOM, THE MORTAL FIGURE OF DOCTOR STRANGE ENTERS A STATE OF TRANCE, WHILE HIS ETHEREAL SELF RISES, AND DARES TO PIERCE THE MIST OF HOGGOTH!
AND NOW TO FIND THE ANSWERS I SEEK!
I MIGHT HAVE KNOWN THAT THE SOURCE OF DANGER WOULD BE HERE-- DEEP WITHIN THE NIGHTMARE WORLD!
I MUST REMAIN ON THIS NARROW PATH WHICH WAS FURNISHED BY THE POWER OF HOGGOTH!
SO LONG AS I STAND UPON THIS ENCHANTED PATH I AM SAFE-- THE SPELL OF HOGGOTH WILL PROTECT ME!
BUT IF I STEP OFF-- THEN I AM VULNERABLE TO ANY DANGER!
BUT A SHORT DISTANCE AWAY, A PAIR OF COLD, UNBLINKING EYES WATCHES EVERY MOVE OF DR. STRANGE!
IT IS HE! THE ONE WE HATE THE MOST OF ALL LIVING CREATURES!
THIS IS OUR CHANCE TO UTTERLY DESTROY HIM! WE MUST NOT FAIL!
4

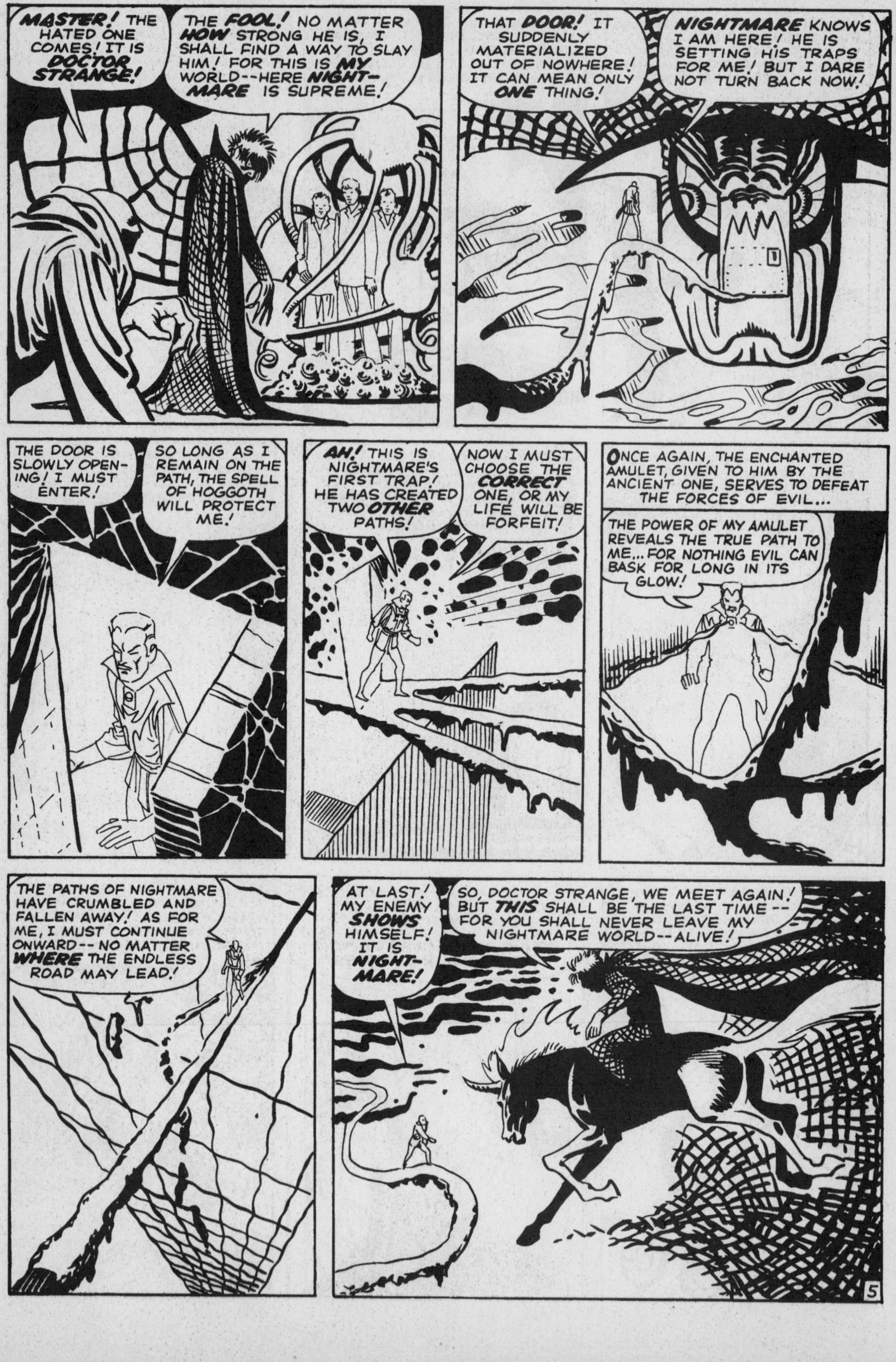
MASTER! THE HATED ONE COMES! IT IS DOCTOR STRANGE!
THE FOOL! NO MATTER HOW STRONG HE IS, I SHALL FIND A WAY TO SLAY HIM! FOR THIS IS MY WORLD--HERE NIGHT-MARE IS SUPREME!
THAT DOOR! IT SUDDENLY MATERIALIZED OUT OF NOWHERE! IT CAN MEAN ONLY ONE THING!
NIGHTMARE KNOWS I AM HERE! HE IS SETTING HIS TRAPS FOR ME! BUT I DARE NOT TURN BACK NOW!
THE DOOR IS SLOWLY OPEN-ING! I MUST ENTER!
SO LONG AS I REMAIN ON THE PATH, THE SPELL OF HOGGOTH WILL PROTECT ME!
AH! THIS IS NIGHTMARE'S FIRST TRAP! HE HAS CREATED TWO OTHER PATHS!
NOW I MUST CHOOSE THE CORRECT ONE, OR MY LIFE WILL BE FORFEIT!
ONCE AGAIN, THE ENCHANTED AMULET, GIVEN TO HIM BY THE ANCIENT ONE, SERVES TO DEFEAT THE FORCES OF EVIL...
THE POWER OF MY AMULET REVEALS THE TRUE PATH TO ME... FOR NOTHING EVIL CAN BASK FOR LONG IN ITS GLOW!
THE PATHS OF NIGHTMARE HAVE CRUMBLED AND FALLEN AWAY! AS FOR ME, I MUST CONTINUE ONWARD-- NO MATTER WHERE THE ENDLESS ROAD MAY LEAD!
AT LAST! MY ENEMY SHOWS HIMSELF! IT IS NIGHT-MARE!
SO, DOCTOR STRANGE, WE MEET AGAIN! BUT THIS SHALL BE THE LAST TIME -- FOR YOU SHALL NEVER LEAVE MY NIGHTMARE WORLD--ALIVE!
5

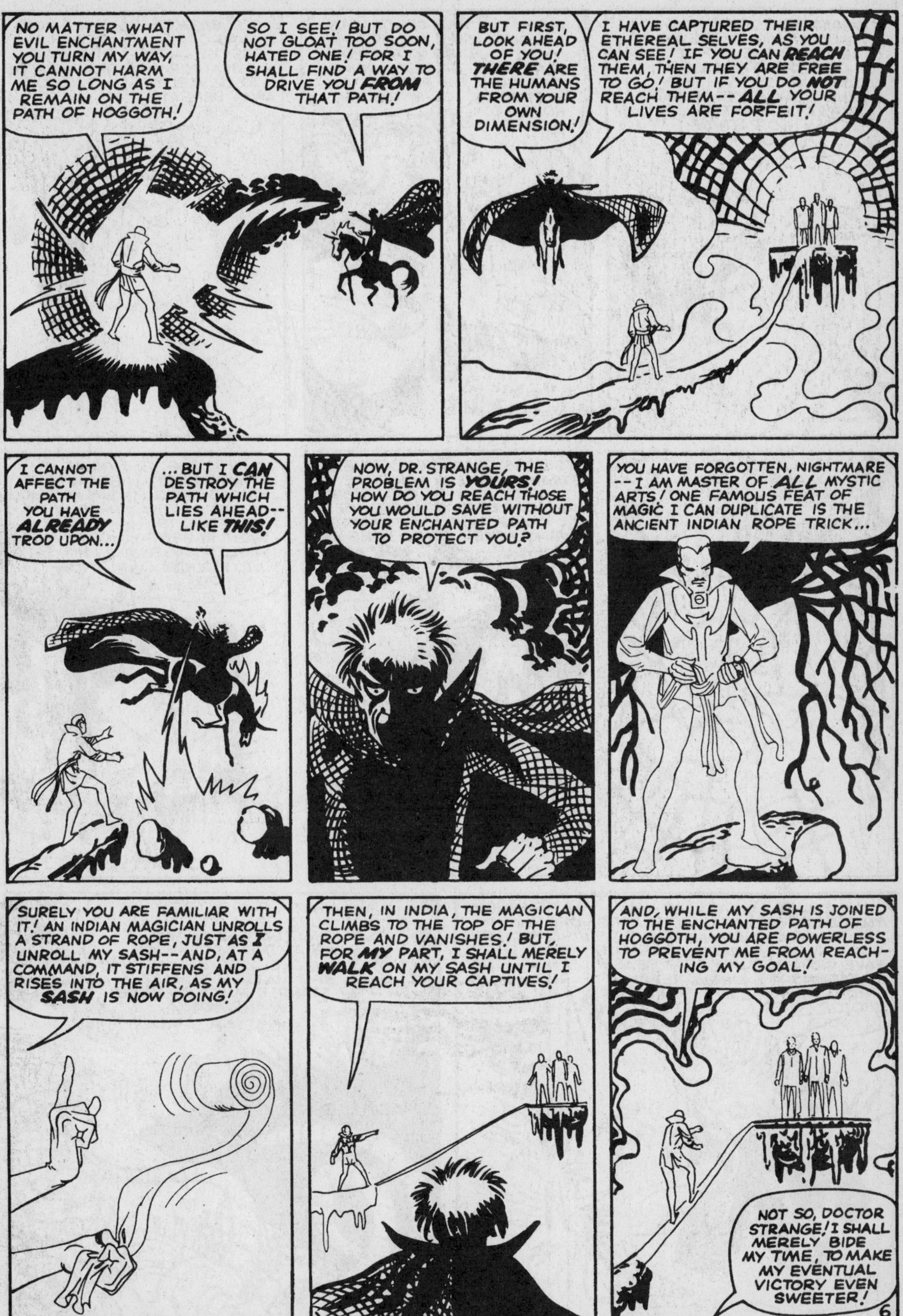
NO MATTER WHAT EVIL ENCHANTMENT YOU TURN MY WAY, IT CANNOT HARM ME SO LONG AS I REMAIN ON THE PATH OF HOGGOTH!
SO I SEE! BUT DO NOT GLOAT TOO SOON, HATED ONE! FOR I SHALL FIND A WAY TO DRIVE YOU FROM THAT PATH!
BUT FIRST, LOOK AHEAD OF YOU! THERE ARE THE HUMANS FROM YOUR OWN DIMENSION!
I HAVE CAPTURED THEIR ETHEREAL SELVES, AS YOU CAN SEE! IF YOU CAN REACH THEM, THEN THEY ARE FREE TO GO! BUT IF YOU DO NOT REACH THEM--ALL YOUR LIVES ARE FORFEIT!
I CANNOT AFFECT THE PATH YOU HAVE ALREADY TROD UPON...
...BUT I CAN DESTROY THE PATH WHICH LIES AHEAD--LIKE THIS!
NOW, DR. STRANGE, THE PROBLEM IS YOURS! HOW DO YOU REACH THOSE YOU WOULD SAVE WITHOUT YOUR ENCHANTED PATH TO PROTECT YOU?
YOU HAVE FORGOTTEN, NIGHTMARE --I AM MASTER OF ALL MYSTIC ARTS! ONE FAMOUS FEAT OF MAGIC I CAN DUPLICATE IS THE ANCIENT INDIAN ROPE TRICK...
SURELY YOU ARE FAMILIAR WITH IT! AN INDIAN MAGICIAN UNROLLS A STRAND OF ROPE, JUST AS I UNROLL MY SASH--AND, AT A COMMAND, IT STIFFENS AND RISES INTO THE AIR, AS MY SASH IS NOW DOING!
THEN, IN INDIA, THE MAGICIAN CLIMBS TO THE TOP OF THE ROPE AND VANISHES! BUT, FOR MY PART, I SHALL MERELY WALK ON MY SASH UNTIL I REACH YOUR CAPTIVES!
AND, WHILE MY SASH IS JOINED TO THE ENCHANTED PATH OF HOGGOTH, YOU ARE POWERLESS TO PREVENT ME FROM REACHING MY GOAL!
NOT SO, DOCTOR STRANGE! I SHALL MERELY BIDE MY TIME, TO MAKE MY EVENTUAL VICTORY EVEN SWEETER!
6

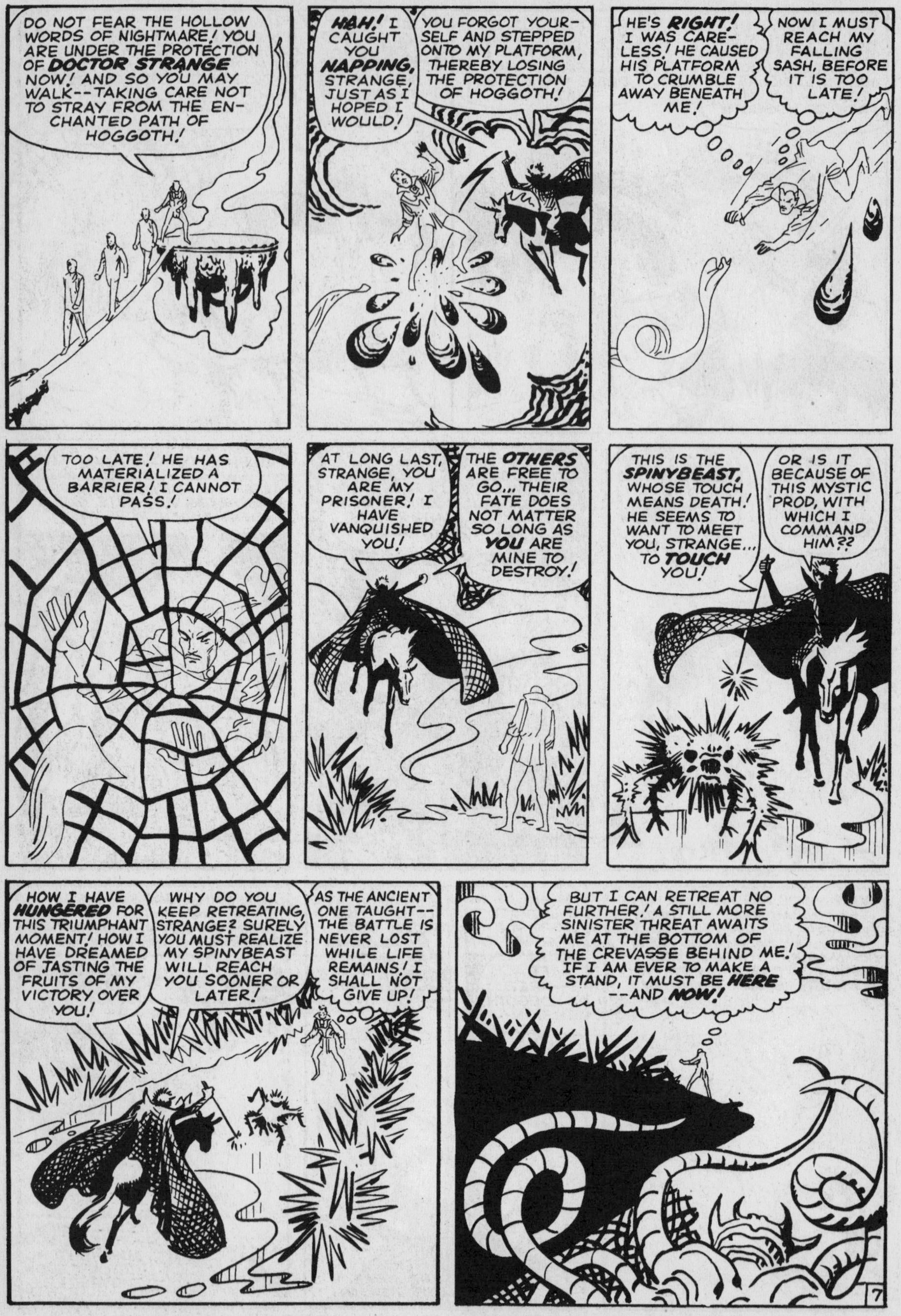
DO NOT FEAR THE HOLLOW WORDS OF NIGHTMARE! YOU ARE UNDER THE PROTECTION OF DOCTOR STRANGE NOW! AND SO YOU MAY WALK--TAKING CARE NOT TO STRAY FROM THE ENCHANTED PATH OF HOGGOTH!
HAH! I CAUGHT YOU NAPPING, STRANGE, JUST AS I HOPED I WOULD!
YOU FORGOT YOURSELF AND STEPPED ONTO MY PLATFORM, THEREBY LOSING THE PROTECTION OF HOGGOTH!
HE'S RIGHT! I WAS CARELESS! HE CAUSED HIS PLATFORM TO CRUMBLE AWAY BENEATH ME!
NOW I MUST REACH MY FALLING SASH, BEFORE IT IS TOO LATE!
TOO LATE! HE HAS MATERIALIZED A BARRIER! I CANNOT PASS!
AT LONG LAST, STRANGE, YOU ARE MY PRISONER! I HAVE VANQUISHED YOU!
THE OTHERS ARE FREE TO GO... THEIR FATE DOES NOT MATTER SO LONG AS YOU ARE MINE TO DESTROY!
THIS IS THE SPINYBEAST, WHOSE TOUCH MEANS DEATH! HE SEEMS TO WANT TO MEET YOU, STRANGE... TO TOUCH YOU!
OR IS IT BECAUSE OF THIS MYSTIC PROD, WITH WHICH I COMMAND HIM??
HOW I HAVE HUNGERED FOR THIS TRIUMPHANT MOMENT! HOW I HAVE DREAMED OF TASTING THE FRUITS OF MY VICTORY OVER YOU!
WHY DO YOU KEEP RETREATING, STRANGE? SURELY YOU MUST REALIZE MY SPINYBEAST WILL REACH YOU SOONER OR LATER!
AS THE ANCIENT ONE TAUGHT-- THE BATTLE IS NEVER LOST WHILE LIFE REMAINS! I SHALL NOT GIVE UP!
BUT I CAN RETREAT NO FURTHER! A STILL MORE SINISTER THREAT AWAITS ME AT THE BOTTOM OF THE CREVASSE BEHIND ME! IF I AM EVER TO MAKE A STAND, IT MUST BE HERE --AND NOW!
7

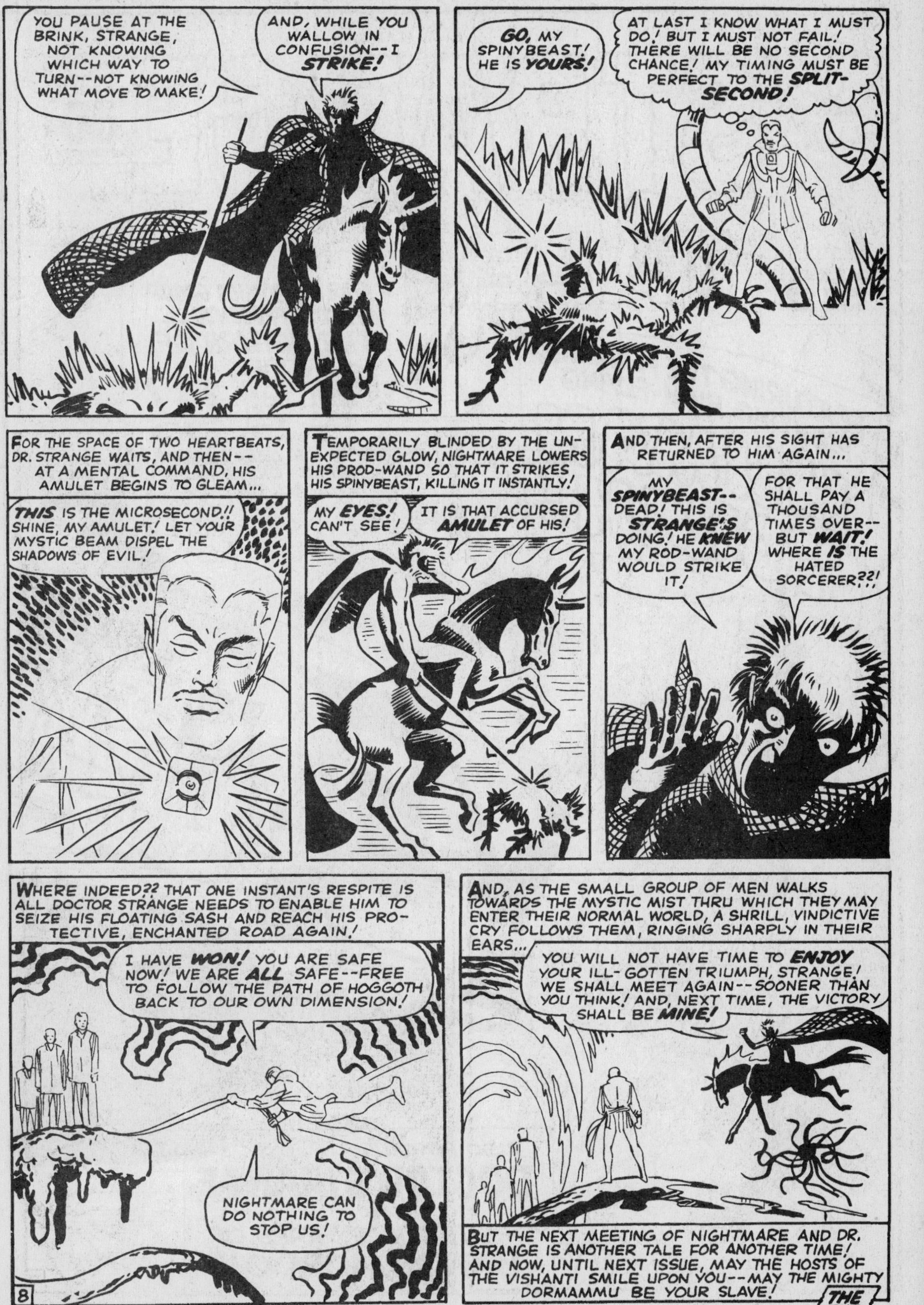
YOU PAUSE AT THE BRINK, STRANGE, NOT KNOWING WHICH WAY TO TURN--NOT KNOWING WHAT MOVE TO MAKE!
AND, WHILE YOU WALLOW IN CONFUSION--I STRIKE!
GO, MY SPINYBEAST! HE IS YOURS!
AT LAST I KNOW WHAT I MUST DO! BUT I MUST NOT FAIL! THERE WILL BE NO SECOND CHANCE! MY TIMING MUST BE PERFECT TO THE SPLIT-SECOND!
FOR THE SPACE OF TWO HEARTBEATS, DR. STRANGE WAITS, AND THEN-- AT A MENTAL COMMAND, HIS AMULET BEGINS TO GLEAM...
THIS IS THE MICROSECOND!! SHINE, MY AMULET! LET YOUR MYSTIC BEAM DISPEL THE SHADOWS OF EVIL!
TEMPORARILY BLINDED BY THE UNEXPECTED GLOW, NIGHTMARE LOWERS HIS PROD-WAND SO THAT IT STRIKES HIS SPINYBEAST, KILLING IT INSTANTLY!
MY EYES! CAN'T SEE!
IT IS THAT ACCURSED AMULET OF HIS!
AND THEN, AFTER HIS SIGHT HAS RETURNED TO HIM AGAIN...
MY SPINYBEAST-- DEAD! THIS IS STRANGE'S DOING! HE KNEW MY ROD-WAND WOULD STRIKE IT!
FOR THAT HE SHALL PAY A THOUSAND TIMES OVER-- BUT WAIT! WHERE IS THE HATED SORCERER??!
WHERE INDEED?? THAT ONE INSTANT'S RESPITE IS ALL DOCTOR STRANGE NEEDS TO ENABLE HIM TO SEIZE HIS FLOATING SASH AND REACH HIS PROTECTIVE, ENCHANTED ROAD AGAIN!
I HAVE WON! YOU ARE SAFE NOW! WE ARE ALL SAFE--FREE TO FOLLOW THE PATH OF HOGGOTH BACK TO OUR OWN DIMENSION!
NIGHTMARE CAN DO NOTHING TO STOP US!
8
AND, AS THE SMALL GROUP OF MEN WALKS TOWARDS THE MYSTIC MIST THRU WHICH THEY MAY ENTER THEIR NORMAL WORLD, A SHRILL, VINDICTIVE CRY FOLLOWS THEM, RINGING SHARPLY IN THEIR EARS...
YOU WILL NOT HAVE TIME TO ENJOY YOUR ILL-GOTTEN TRIUMPH, STRANGE! WE SHALL MEET AGAIN--SOONER THAN YOU THINK! AND, NEXT TIME, THE VICTORY SHALL BE MINE!
BUT THE NEXT MEETING OF NIGHTMARE AND DR. STRANGE IS ANOTHER TALE FOR ANOTHER TIME! AND NOW, UNTIL NEXT ISSUE, MAY THE HOSTS OF THE VISHANTI SMILE UPON YOU--MAY THE MIGHTY DORMAMMU BE YOUR SLAVE!
THE END

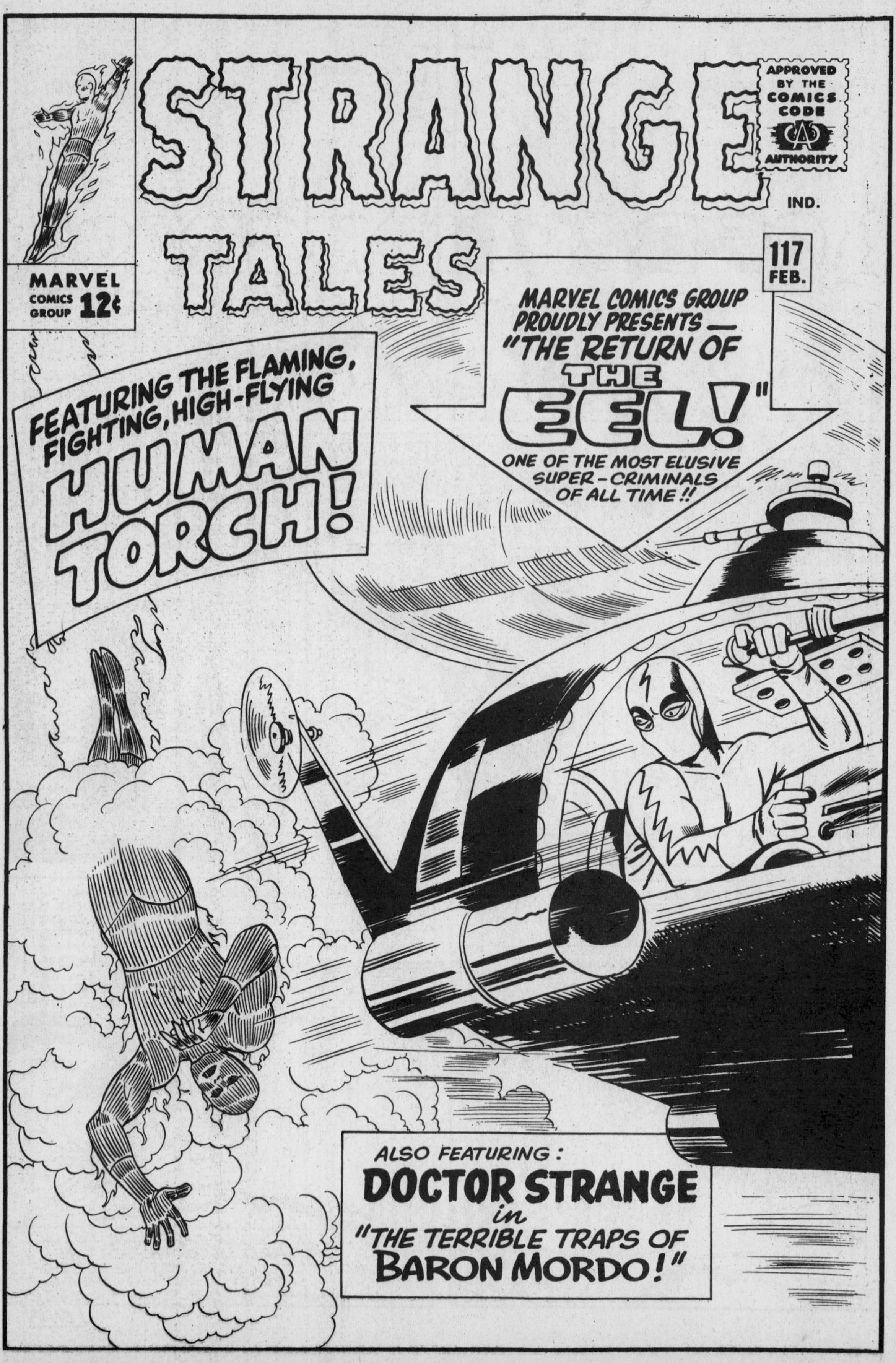
STRANGE TALES
MARVEL COMICS GROUP 12¢
APPROVED BY THE COMICS CODE AUTHORITY
IND.
117 FEB.
FEATURING THE FLAMING, FIGHTING, HIGH-FLYING HUMAN TORCH!
MARVEL COMICS GROUP PROUDLY PRESENTS — "THE RETURN OF THE EEL!"
ONE OF THE MOST ELUSIVE SUPER-CRIMINALS OF ALL TIME!!
ALSO FEATURING :
DOCTOR STRANGE
in
"THE TERRIBLE TRAPS OF BARON MORDO!"

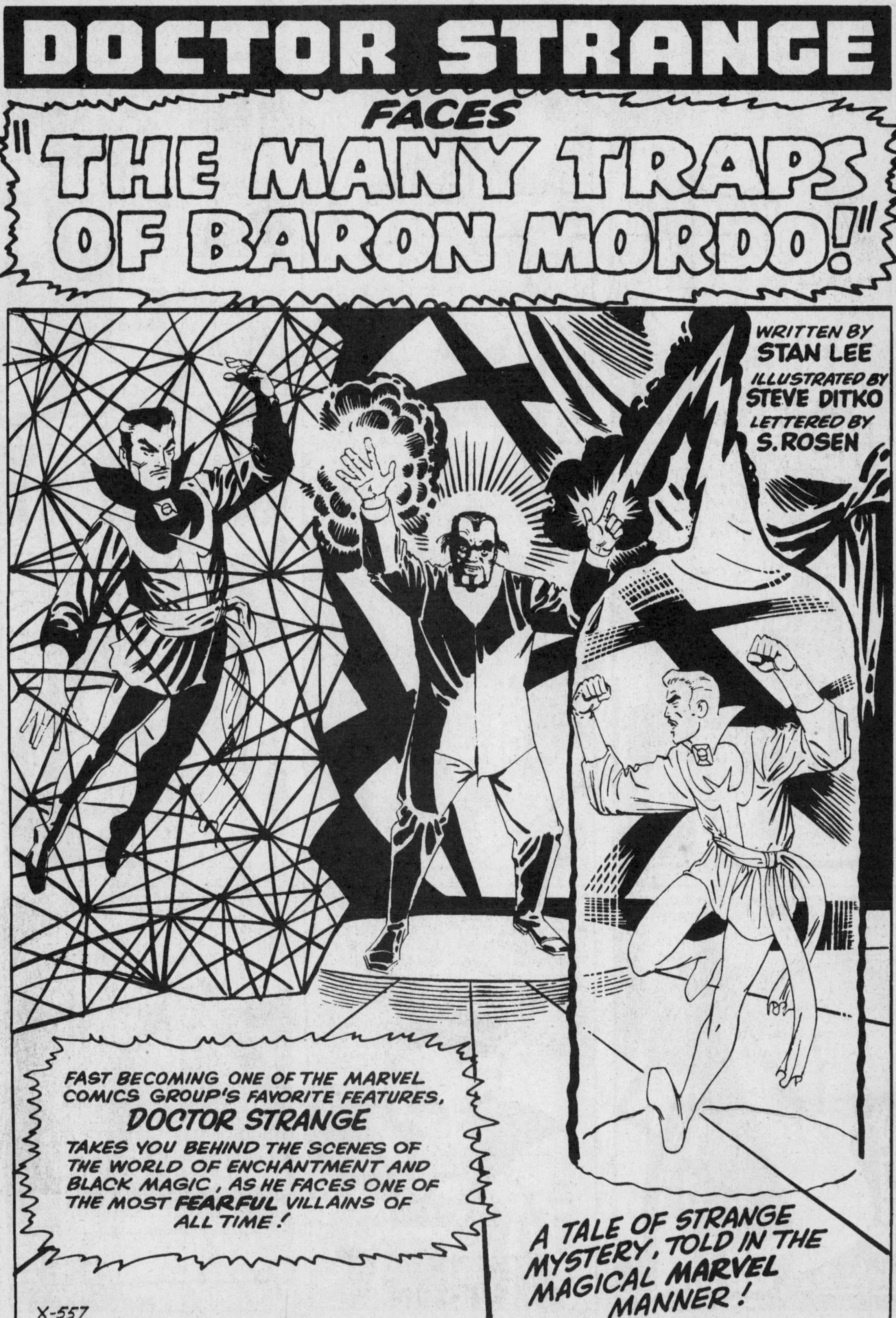
DOCTOR STRANGE
FACES
"THE MANY TRAPS OF BARON MORDO!"
WRITTEN BY STAN LEE
ILLUSTRATED BY STEVE DITKO
LETTERED BY S. ROSEN
FAST BECOMING ONE OF THE MARVEL COMICS GROUP'S FAVORITE FEATURES, DOCTOR STRANGE TAKES YOU BEHIND THE SCENES OF THE WORLD OF ENCHANTMENT AND BLACK MAGIC, AS HE FACES ONE OF THE MOST FEARFUL VILLAINS OF ALL TIME!
A TALE OF STRANGE MYSTERY, TOLD IN THE MAGICAL MARVEL MANNER!
X-557

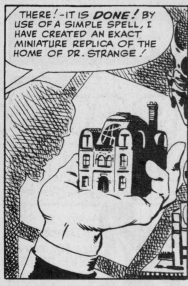

THERE! —IT IS **DONE**! BY USE OF A SIMPLE SPELL, I HAVE CREATED AN EXACT MINIATURE REPLICA OF THE HOME OF DR. STRANGE!

AND NOW, WHEN I **REPEAT** THE SPELL, SAYING IT SLOWLY... A MAGICAL MIST COVERS MY PRECIOUS MODEL!

THEN, AT THE NEXT COMMAND OF **BARON MORDO**, MY ENCHANTED MIST DRIFTS OUT OF MY WINDOW... AND INTO THE SKY!

....WHERE IT SETTLES OVER THE REAL-LIFE HOUSE OF THE ACCURSED DR. STRANGE!

...SLOWLY, SILENTLY, THE MIST PENETRATES EVERY BRICK, EVERY PIECE OF STONE AND WOOD AND MORTAR, UNTIL IT BECOMES PART OF THE HOUSE ITSELF!

AND SO IT IS **DONE**! MY TRAP IS SET! THE HOME OF DR. STRANGE IS UNDER MY SPELL...THE SPELL OF **BARON MORDO**!

LATER, A TALL STATELY FIGURE WALKS THROUGH THE STREETS OF THE CITY...

IT IS THE IMPOSING FIGURE OF **DR. STRANGE**, MASTER OF BLACK MAGIC!! LOST IN THOUGHT, THE SILENT MAN HAS NO SUSPICION OF WHAT AWAITS HIM...

...WHILE HIS ARCH-ENEMY WATCHES HIS EVERY MOVE WITH SINISTER GLEE...

HE IS ENTERING HIS HOUSE! HE HAS DOOMED HIMSELF! I'VE **BEATEN** HIM!

2.

THEN, AS THE DOOR CREAKS SHUT BEHIND DR. STRANGE...

...AND THE LIGHTS GO ON WITHIN THE SHROUDED BUILDING...

...THE ENTIRE BUILDING BEGINS TO SHUDDER... TO WAVER... TO FADE FROM SIGHT...

..UNTIL, SECONDS LATER, THE HOME OF DR. STRANGE, AND ALL IT CONTAINS IS GONE... VANISHED, AS THOUGH FROM THE FACE OF THE EARTH!

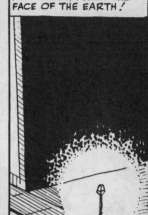

HOW *EASY* IT WAS! HE SUSPECTED NOTHING! AND NOW, HE CAN NEVER ESCAPE ME AGAIN!

MEANTIME, THE ENCHANTED HOUSE REAPPEARS AGAIN... BUT *THIS* TIME IT IS ALONE... IN THE SHIMMERING VASTNESS OF AN UNKNOWN DIMENSION!

AND WITHIN THE BUILDING'S WALLS...

A POWERFUL SPELL IS AT WORK HERE! I HAVE BEEN TRANSPORTED TO A STRANGE DIMENSION, WHERE I FIND MYSELF WEIGHTLESS AND HELPLESS!

NO! NOT QUITE HELPLESS! FOR I STILL HAVE THE POWER OF MY MAGIC *AMULET* TO AID ME!

THE SPELL I AM UNDER IS TOO STRONG TO BE BROKEN BY MY PHYSICAL SELF! BUT I STILL HAVE A CHANCE! BY THE POWER OF MY AMULET, I SHALL CHANGE TO MY *ETHEREAL* SELF...

...AND MY ENCHANTED GEM WILL UNERRINGLY GUIDE ME TO THE *SOURCE* OF THIS OMINOUS OCCURRENCE.

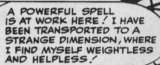

3

AHH, I SHOULD HAVE KNOWN! IT IS *BARON MORDO*, MY ARCH-ENEMY, WHO IS RESPONSIBLE!

BEFORE HE IS AWARE OF MY PRESENCE, PERHAPS I CAN FIND A CLUE TO THE TYPE OF SPELL HE CAST WHICH TRAPPED MY PHYSICAL SELF IN THAT DARK DIMENSION!

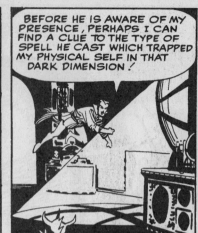

WHAT IS *THIS?* AN ETHEREAL CYLINDER HAS DROPPED FROM ABOVE, IMPRISONING MY SPIRIT FORM!

NOW I AM *DOUBLY* TRAPPED!

IT IS USELESS TO STRUGGLE, STRANGE! MY ENCHANTED CYLINDER IS *ESCAPE-PROOF!*

MY TRAPS HAVE SUCCEEDED BETTER THAN I DARED HOPE!

WHAT IS YOUR *PURPOSE*, EVIL ONE? WHAT SINISTER GOAL DO YOU SEEK?

SURELY YOU CAN *IMAGINE* WHAT I AM AFTER, STRANGE!

ONLY *ONE MAN* KNOWS MORE THAN I OF THE MYSTIC ARTS... AND HE IS THE *ANCIENT ONE*... OUR MASTER!

YOU HAVE ALWAYS PROTECTED HIM FROM ME, BUT *NOW* HE WILL BE AT MY MERCY!

AND WHEN THE ANCIENT ONE IS GONE, I SHALL RETURN TO DISPOSE OF YOU AT WILL! THEN I, *BARON MORDO*, WILL BE MASTER OF BLACK MAGIC!

I *MUST* ESCAPE! HE MUST NOT HARM THE ANCIENT ONE!

BUT MORDO'S SPELL IS TOO STRONG! EVEN MY AMULET CANNOT SET ME FREE!

BUT I SHALL NOT GIVE UP! SOMEWHERE, SOMEHOW, I SHALL FIND THE WAY... FOR IT IS WRITTEN THAT *GOOD* MUST ALWAYS TRIUMPH OVER EVIL!

4.

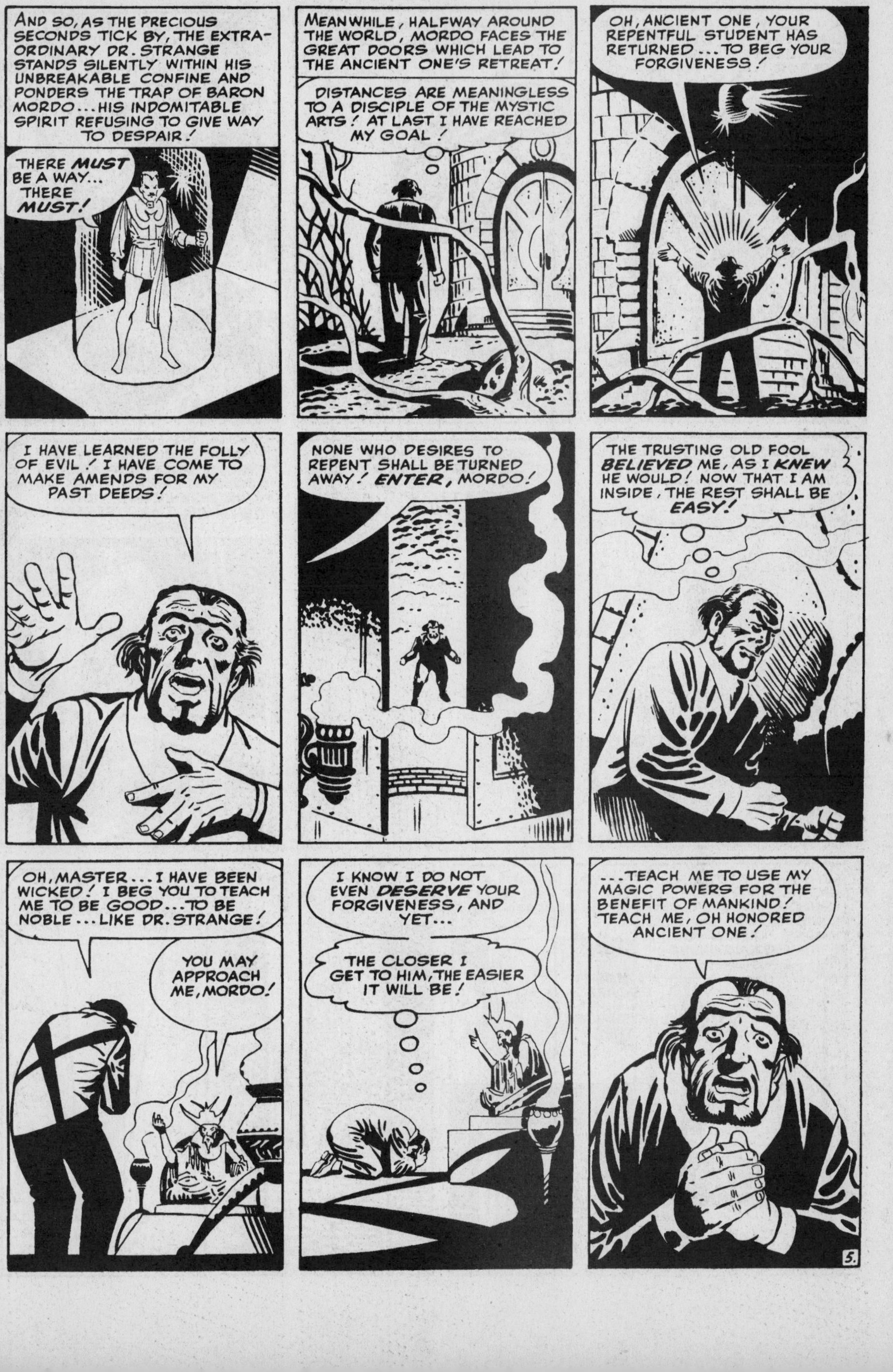
AND SO, AS THE PRECIOUS SECONDS TICK BY, THE EXTRA-ORDINARY DR. STRANGE STANDS SILENTLY WITHIN HIS UNBREAKABLE CONFINE AND PONDERS THE TRAP OF BARON MORDO... HIS INDOMITABLE SPIRIT REFUSING TO GIVE WAY TO DESPAIR!
THERE MUST BE A WAY... THERE MUST!
MEANWHILE, HALFWAY AROUND THE WORLD, MORDO FACES THE GREAT DOORS WHICH LEAD TO THE ANCIENT ONE'S RETREAT!
DISTANCES ARE MEANINGLESS TO A DISCIPLE OF THE MYSTIC ARTS! AT LAST I HAVE REACHED MY GOAL!
OH, ANCIENT ONE, YOUR REPENTFUL STUDENT HAS RETURNED... TO BEG YOUR FORGIVENESS!
I HAVE LEARNED THE FOLLY OF EVIL! I HAVE COME TO MAKE AMENDS FOR MY PAST DEEDS!
NONE WHO DESIRES TO REPENT SHALL BE TURNED AWAY! ENTER, MORDO!
THE TRUSTING OLD FOOL BELIEVED ME, AS I KNEW HE WOULD! NOW THAT I AM INSIDE, THE REST SHALL BE EASY!
OH, MASTER... I HAVE BEEN WICKED! I BEG YOU TO TEACH ME TO BE GOOD... TO BE NOBLE... LIKE DR. STRANGE!
YOU MAY APPROACH ME, MORDO!
I KNOW I DO NOT EVEN DESERVE YOUR FORGIVENESS, AND YET...
THE CLOSER I GET TO HIM, THE EASIER IT WILL BE!
...TEACH ME TO USE MY MAGIC POWERS FOR THE BENEFIT OF MANKIND! TEACH ME, OH HONORED ANCIENT ONE!
5.

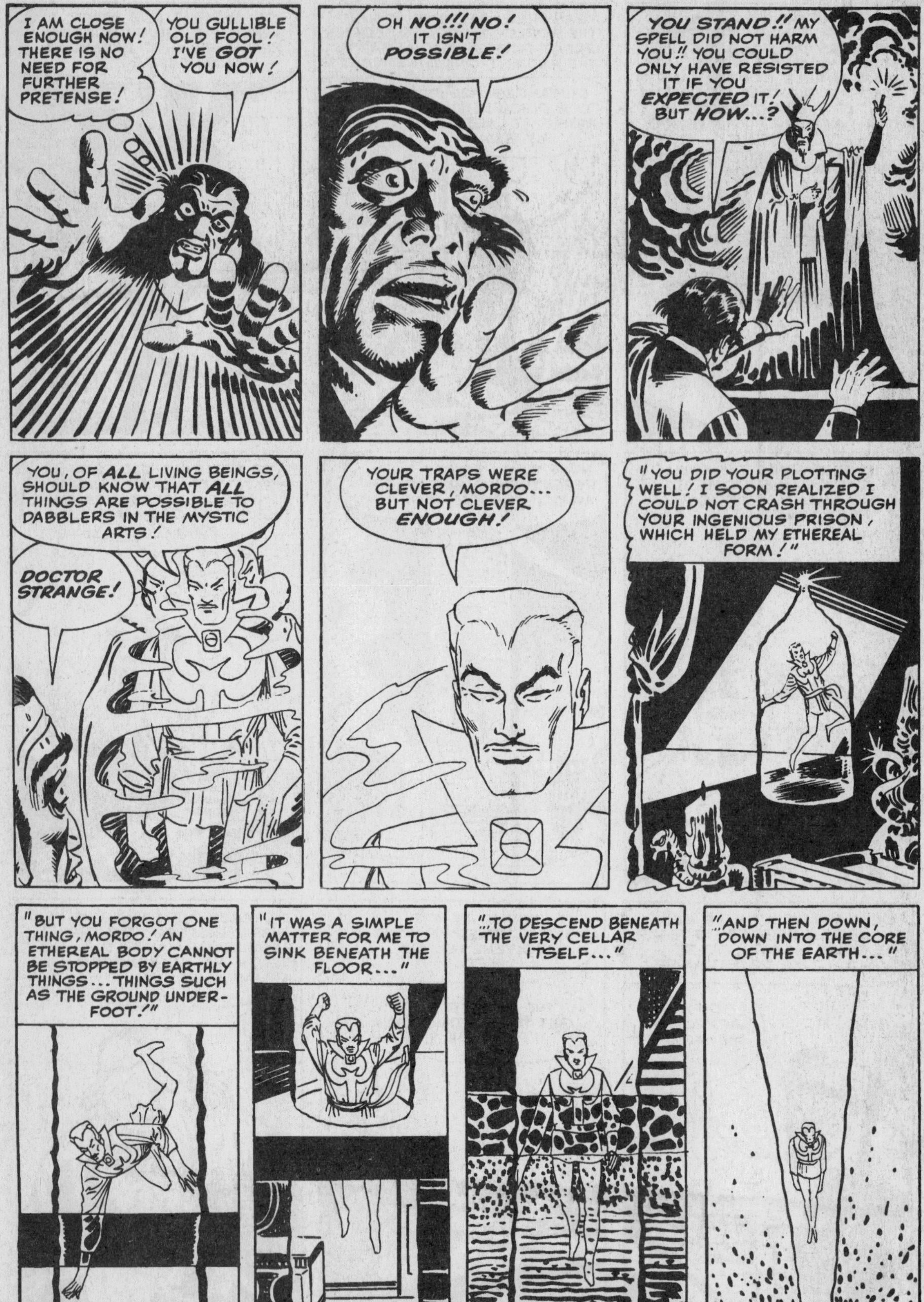
I AM CLOSE ENOUGH NOW! THERE IS NO NEED FOR FURTHER PRETENSE!
YOU GULLIBLE OLD FOOL! I'VE GOT YOU NOW!
OH NO!!! NO! IT ISN'T POSSIBLE!
YOU STAND!! MY SPELL DID NOT HARM YOU!! YOU COULD ONLY HAVE RESISTED IT IF YOU EXPECTED IT! BUT HOW...?
YOU, OF ALL LIVING BEINGS, SHOULD KNOW THAT ALL THINGS ARE POSSIBLE TO DABBLERS IN THE MYSTIC ARTS!
DOCTOR STRANGE!
YOUR TRAPS WERE CLEVER, MORDO... BUT NOT CLEVER ENOUGH!
"YOU DID YOUR PLOTTING WELL! I SOON REALIZED I COULD NOT CRASH THROUGH YOUR INGENIOUS PRISON, WHICH HELD MY ETHEREAL FORM!"
"BUT YOU FORGOT ONE THING, MORDO! AN ETHEREAL BODY CANNOT BE STOPPED BY EARTHLY THINGS... THINGS SUCH AS THE GROUND UNDER-FOOT!"
"IT WAS A SIMPLE MATTER FOR ME TO SINK BENEATH THE FLOOR..."
"...TO DESCEND BENEATH THE VERY CELLAR ITSELF..."
"...AND THEN DOWN, DOWN INTO THE CORE OF THE EARTH..."
6.

"YOU NEVER EXPECTED THAT I WOULD DO SUCH A THING, AND THE FURTHER DOWN I WENT, THE WEAKER YOUR SPELL BECAME... UNTIL AT LAST I EMERGED AT THE OTHER SIDE OF THE GLOBE, FREE OF YOUR ETHEREAL TRAP!"

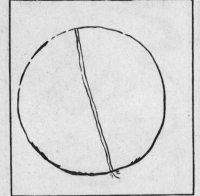

"AND THUS I WAS ABLE TO REACH THE ANCIENT ONE BEFORE YOU!"

DR. STRANGE!

"WITHIN SECONDS I HAD EXPLAINED HIS DANGER..."

I CAME TO WARN YOU, MASTER! IN MY ETHEREAL FORM, I CANNOT BATTLE MORDO, AND YET... SOMETHING MUST BE DONE!

YOUR WORDS HAVE THE RING OF TRUTH, MY SON!

AND, IN RETURN, I PRESENT YOU WITH *THIS* RING...WHICH WILL ENABLE YOU TO DO EVERYTHING YOU MIGHT DO IN YOUR REAL-LIFE FORM... SO THAT YOU MAY BATTLE MORDO!

AS FOR *ME*, I AM OLD AND WEARY! BUT I SHALL PERMIT *YOU* TO TRANSFORM YOUR-SELF TO RESEMBLE ME, FOR YOU SHALL BATTLE MORDO IN MY PLACE!

YOU WERE A *FOOL* TO TELL ME, STRANGE! NOW THAT I KNOW WHAT HAPPENED, I KNOW I CAN *STILL* DEFEAT YOU!

I CALL UPON ALL THE SHADOWY SHAPES, ALL THE DREAD POWERS OF THE MIGHTY DORMAMMU TO COME TO MY AID!!

AND *I* CALL UPON MY ENCHANTED RING TO SHIELD ME FROM WHATEVER HOSTS OF EVIL YOU CONJURE FORTH!

BY THE POWER OF THE VISHANTI...IN THE NAME OF THE ALL-SEEING ANCIENT ONE...I SUMMON ALL THE FORCES OF GOOD...AND FOCUS THEIR BLINDING POWER UPON YOU, THROUGH THE FACETS OF THIS RING!

NO! *NO!* I CANNOT BEAR TO LOOK AT IT!

7.

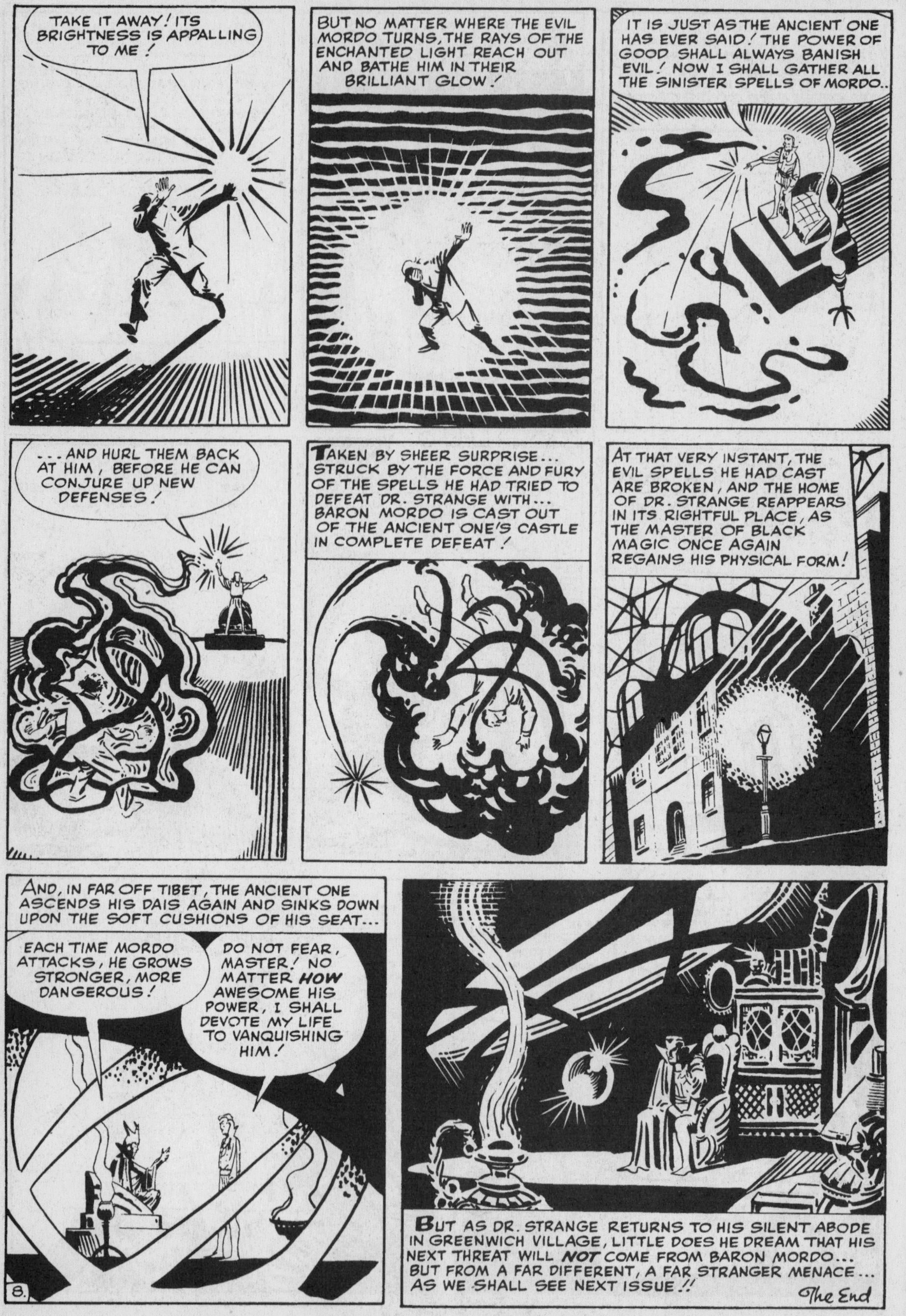
TAKE IT AWAY! ITS BRIGHTNESS IS APPALLING TO ME!
BUT NO MATTER WHERE THE EVIL MORDO TURNS, THE RAYS OF THE ENCHANTED LIGHT REACH OUT AND BATHE HIM IN THEIR BRILLIANT GLOW!
IT IS JUST AS THE ANCIENT ONE HAS EVER SAID! THE POWER OF GOOD SHALL ALWAYS BANISH EVIL! NOW I SHALL GATHER ALL THE SINISTER SPELLS OF MORDO..
...AND HURL THEM BACK AT HIM, BEFORE HE CAN CONJURE UP NEW DEFENSES!
TAKEN BY SHEER SURPRISE... STRUCK BY THE FORCE AND FURY OF THE SPELLS HE HAD TRIED TO DEFEAT DR. STRANGE WITH... BARON MORDO IS CAST OUT OF THE ANCIENT ONE'S CASTLE IN COMPLETE DEFEAT!
AT THAT VERY INSTANT, THE EVIL SPELLS HE HAD CAST ARE BROKEN, AND THE HOME OF DR. STRANGE REAPPEARS IN ITS RIGHTFUL PLACE, AS THE MASTER OF BLACK MAGIC ONCE AGAIN REGAINS HIS PHYSICAL FORM!
AND, IN FAR OFF TIBET, THE ANCIENT ONE ASCENDS HIS DAIS AGAIN AND SINKS DOWN UPON THE SOFT CUSHIONS OF HIS SEAT...
EACH TIME MORDO ATTACKS, HE GROWS STRONGER, MORE DANGEROUS!
DO NOT FEAR, MASTER! NO MATTER HOW AWESOME HIS POWER, I SHALL DEVOTE MY LIFE TO VANQUISHING HIM!
8.
BUT AS DR. STRANGE RETURNS TO HIS SILENT ABODE IN GREENWICH VILLAGE, LITTLE DOES HE DREAM THAT HIS NEXT THREAT WILL NOT COME FROM BARON MORDO... BUT FROM A FAR DIFFERENT, A FAR STRANGER MENACE... AS WE SHALL SEE NEXT ISSUE!!
The End

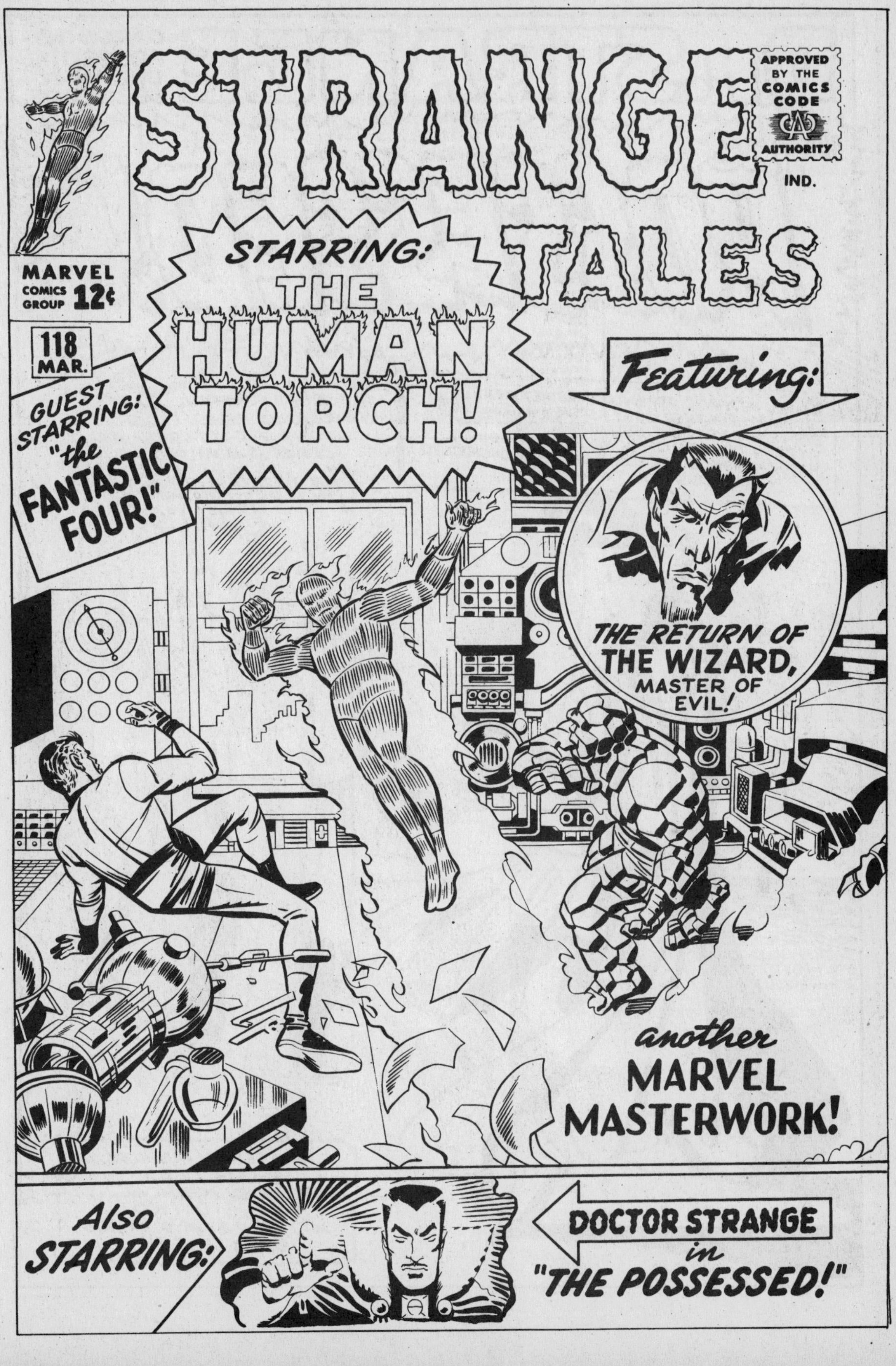
STRANGE TALES
APPROVED BY THE COMICS CODE AUTHORITY
IND.
MARVEL COMICS GROUP 12¢
118 MAR.
STARRING: THE HUMAN TORCH!
GUEST STARRING: "the FANTASTIC FOUR!"
Featuring:
THE RETURN OF THE WIZARD, MASTER OF EVIL!
another MARVEL MASTERWORK!
Also STARRING:
DOCTOR STRANGE in "THE POSSESSED!"

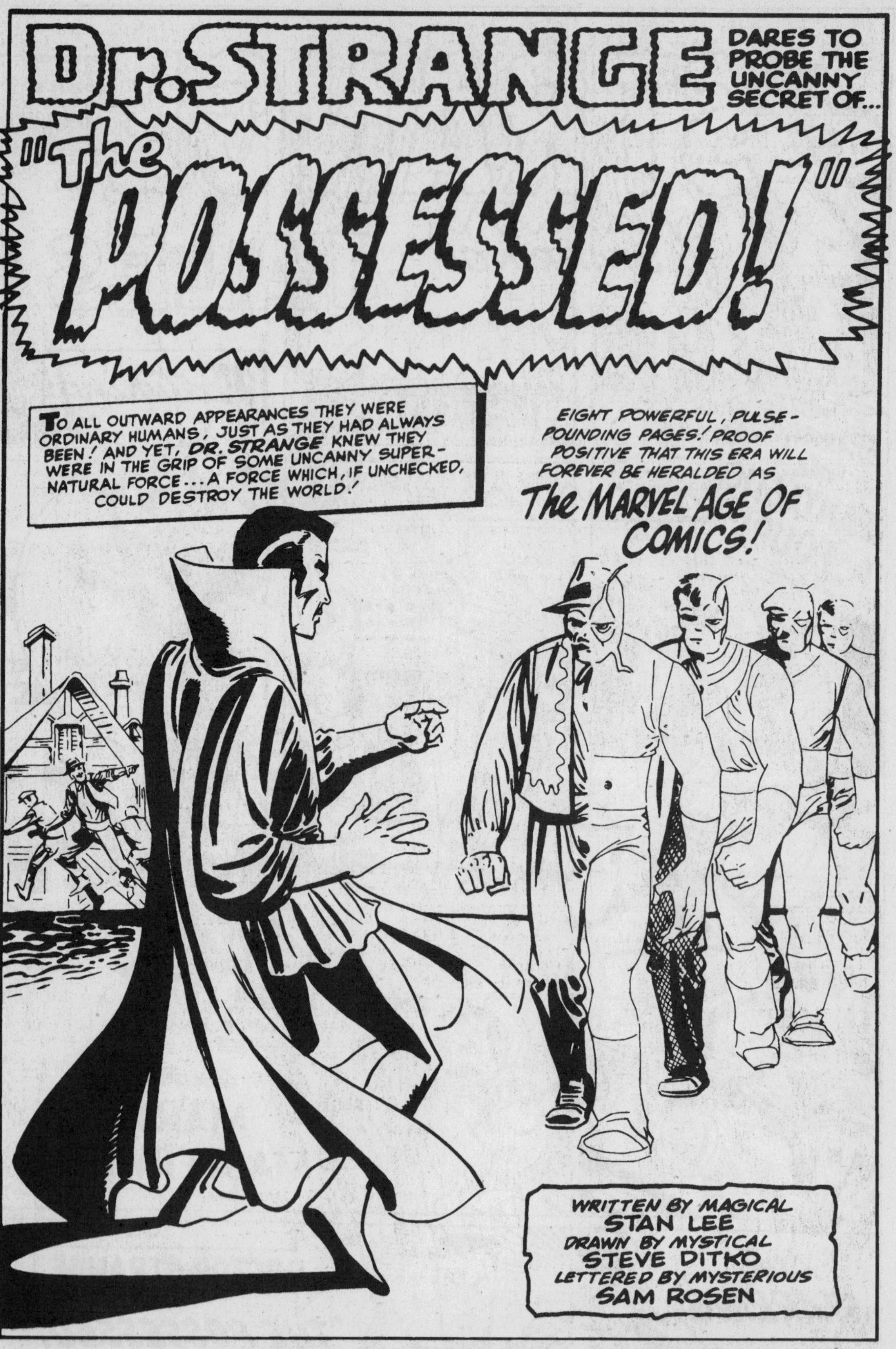
Dr. STRANGE DARES TO PROBE THE UNCANNY SECRET OF...
"The POSSESSED!"
TO ALL OUTWARD APPEARANCES THEY WERE ORDINARY HUMANS, JUST AS THEY HAD ALWAYS BEEN! AND YET, DR. STRANGE KNEW THEY WERE IN THE GRIP OF SOME UNCANNY SUPER-NATURAL FORCE... A FORCE WHICH, IF UNCHECKED, COULD DESTROY THE WORLD!
EIGHT POWERFUL, PULSE-POUNDING PAGES! PROOF POSITIVE THAT THIS ERA WILL FOREVER BE HERALDED AS The MARVEL AGE OF COMICS!
WRITTEN BY MAGICAL STAN LEE
DRAWN BY MYSTICAL STEVE DITKO
LETTERED BY MYSTERIOUS SAM ROSEN

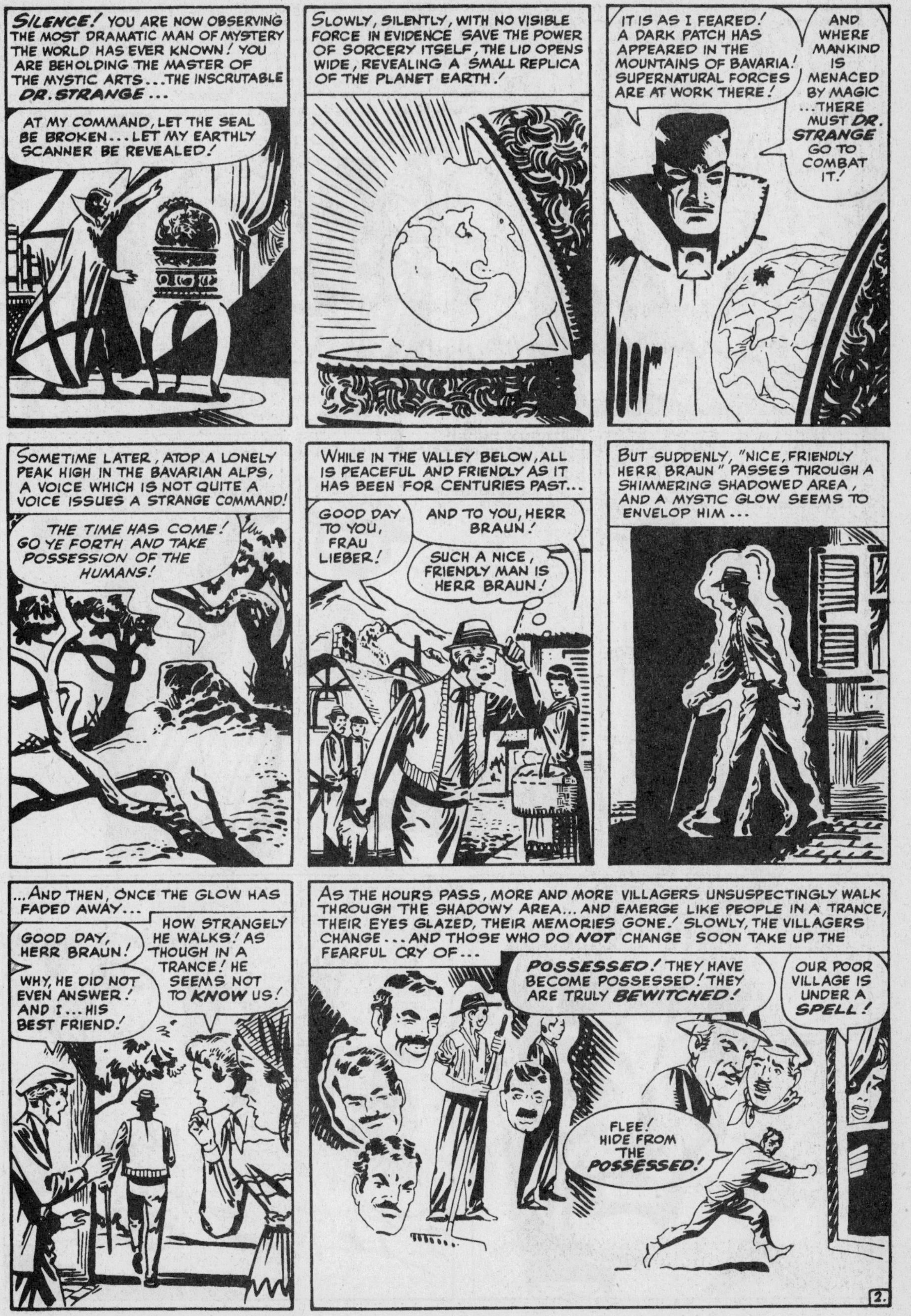
SILENCE! YOU ARE NOW OBSERVING THE MOST DRAMATIC MAN OF MYSTERY THE WORLD HAS EVER KNOWN! YOU ARE BEHOLDING THE MASTER OF THE MYSTIC ARTS... THE INSCRUTABLE DR. STRANGE...
AT MY COMMAND, LET THE SEAL BE BROKEN... LET MY EARTHLY SCANNER BE REVEALED!
SLOWLY, SILENTLY, WITH NO VISIBLE FORCE IN EVIDENCE SAVE THE POWER OF SORCERY ITSELF, THE LID OPENS WIDE, REVEALING A SMALL REPLICA OF THE PLANET EARTH!
IT IS AS I FEARED! A DARK PATCH HAS APPEARED IN THE MOUNTAINS OF BAVARIA! SUPERNATURAL FORCES ARE AT WORK THERE!
AND WHERE MANKIND IS MENACED BY MAGIC ...THERE MUST DR. STRANGE GO TO COMBAT IT!
SOMETIME LATER, ATOP A LONELY PEAK HIGH IN THE BAVARIAN ALPS, A VOICE WHICH IS NOT QUITE A VOICE ISSUES A STRANGE COMMAND!
THE TIME HAS COME! GO YE FORTH AND TAKE POSSESSION OF THE HUMANS!
WHILE IN THE VALLEY BELOW, ALL IS PEACEFUL AND FRIENDLY AS IT HAS BEEN FOR CENTURIES PAST...
GOOD DAY TO YOU, FRAU LIEBER!
AND TO YOU, HERR BRAUN!
SUCH A NICE, FRIENDLY MAN IS HERR BRAUN!
BUT SUDDENLY, "NICE, FRIENDLY HERR BRAUN" PASSES THROUGH A SHIMMERING SHADOWED AREA, AND A MYSTIC GLOW SEEMS TO ENVELOP HIM...
...AND THEN, ONCE THE GLOW HAS FADED AWAY...
GOOD DAY, HERR BRAUN!
HOW STRANGELY HE WALKS! AS THOUGH IN A TRANCE! HE SEEMS NOT TO KNOW US!
WHY, HE DID NOT EVEN ANSWER! AND I... HIS BEST FRIEND!
AS THE HOURS PASS, MORE AND MORE VILLAGERS UNSUSPECTINGLY WALK THROUGH THE SHADOWY AREA... AND EMERGE LIKE PEOPLE IN A TRANCE, THEIR EYES GLAZED, THEIR MEMORIES GONE! SLOWLY, THE VILLAGERS CHANGE... AND THOSE WHO DO NOT CHANGE SOON TAKE UP THE FEARFUL CRY OF...
POSSESSED! THEY HAVE BECOME POSSESSED! THEY ARE TRULY BEWITCHED!
OUR POOR VILLAGE IS UNDER A SPELL!
FLEE! HIDE FROM THE POSSESSED!
2.

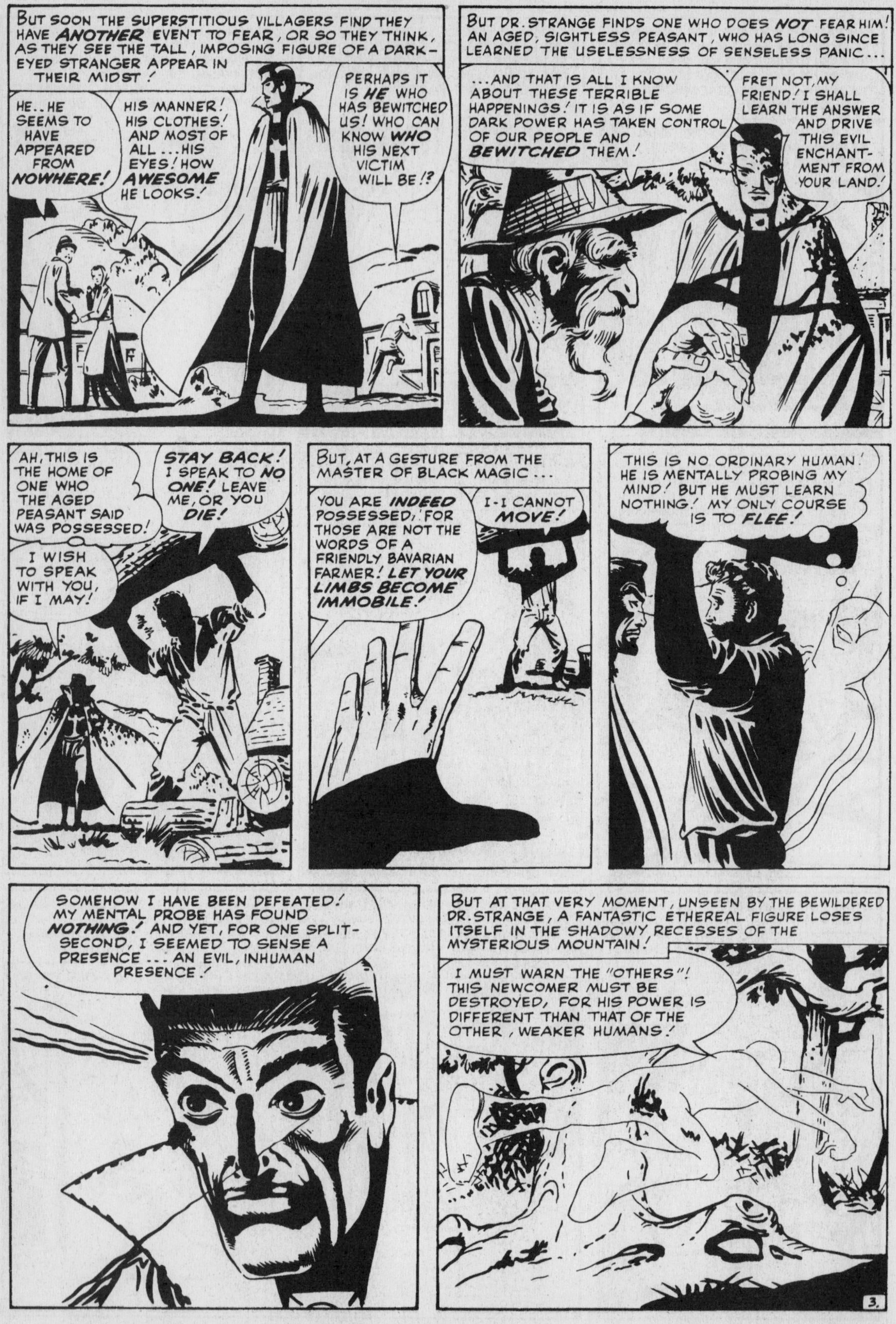

BUT SOON THE SUPERSTITIOUS VILLAGERS FIND THEY HAVE **ANOTHER** EVENT TO FEAR, OR SO THEY THINK, AS THEY SEE THE TALL, IMPOSING FIGURE OF A DARK-EYED STRANGER APPEAR IN THEIR MIDST!
HE..HE SEEMS TO HAVE APPEARED FROM **NOWHERE!**
HIS MANNER! HIS CLOTHES! AND MOST OF ALL...HIS EYES! HOW **AWESOME** HE LOOKS!
PERHAPS IT IS **HE** WHO HAS BEWITCHED US! WHO CAN KNOW **WHO** HIS NEXT VICTIM WILL BE!?
BUT DR. STRANGE FINDS ONE WHO DOES **NOT** FEAR HIM! AN AGED, SIGHTLESS PEASANT, WHO HAS LONG SINCE LEARNED THE USELESSNESS OF SENSELESS PANIC...
...AND THAT IS ALL I KNOW ABOUT THESE TERRIBLE HAPPENINGS! IT IS AS IF SOME DARK POWER HAS TAKEN CONTROL OF OUR PEOPLE AND **BEWITCHED** THEM!
FRET NOT, MY FRIEND! I SHALL LEARN THE ANSWER AND DRIVE THIS EVIL ENCHANTMENT FROM YOUR LAND!
AH, THIS IS THE HOME OF ONE WHO THE AGED PEASANT SAID WAS POSSESSED!
STAY BACK! I SPEAK TO **NO ONE!** LEAVE ME, OR YOU **DIE!**
I WISH TO SPEAK WITH YOU, IF I MAY!
BUT, AT A GESTURE FROM THE MASTER OF BLACK MAGIC...
YOU ARE **INDEED** POSSESSED, FOR THOSE ARE NOT THE WORDS OF A FRIENDLY BAVARIAN FARMER! **LET YOUR LIMBS BECOME IMMOBILE!**
I-I CANNOT **MOVE!**
THIS IS NO ORDINARY HUMAN! HE IS MENTALLY PROBING MY MIND! BUT HE MUST LEARN NOTHING! MY ONLY COURSE IS TO **FLEE!**
SOMEHOW I HAVE BEEN DEFEATED! MY MENTAL PROBE HAS FOUND **NOTHING!** AND YET, FOR ONE SPLIT-SECOND, I SEEMED TO SENSE A PRESENCE... AN EVIL, INHUMAN PRESENCE!
BUT AT THAT VERY MOMENT, UNSEEN BY THE BEWILDERED DR. STRANGE, A FANTASTIC ETHEREAL FIGURE LOSES ITSELF IN THE SHADOWY RECESSES OF THE MYSTERIOUS MOUNTAIN!
I MUST WARN THE "OTHERS"! THIS NEWCOMER MUST BE DESTROYED, FOR HIS POWER IS DIFFERENT THAN THAT OF THE OTHER, WEAKER HUMANS!
3.

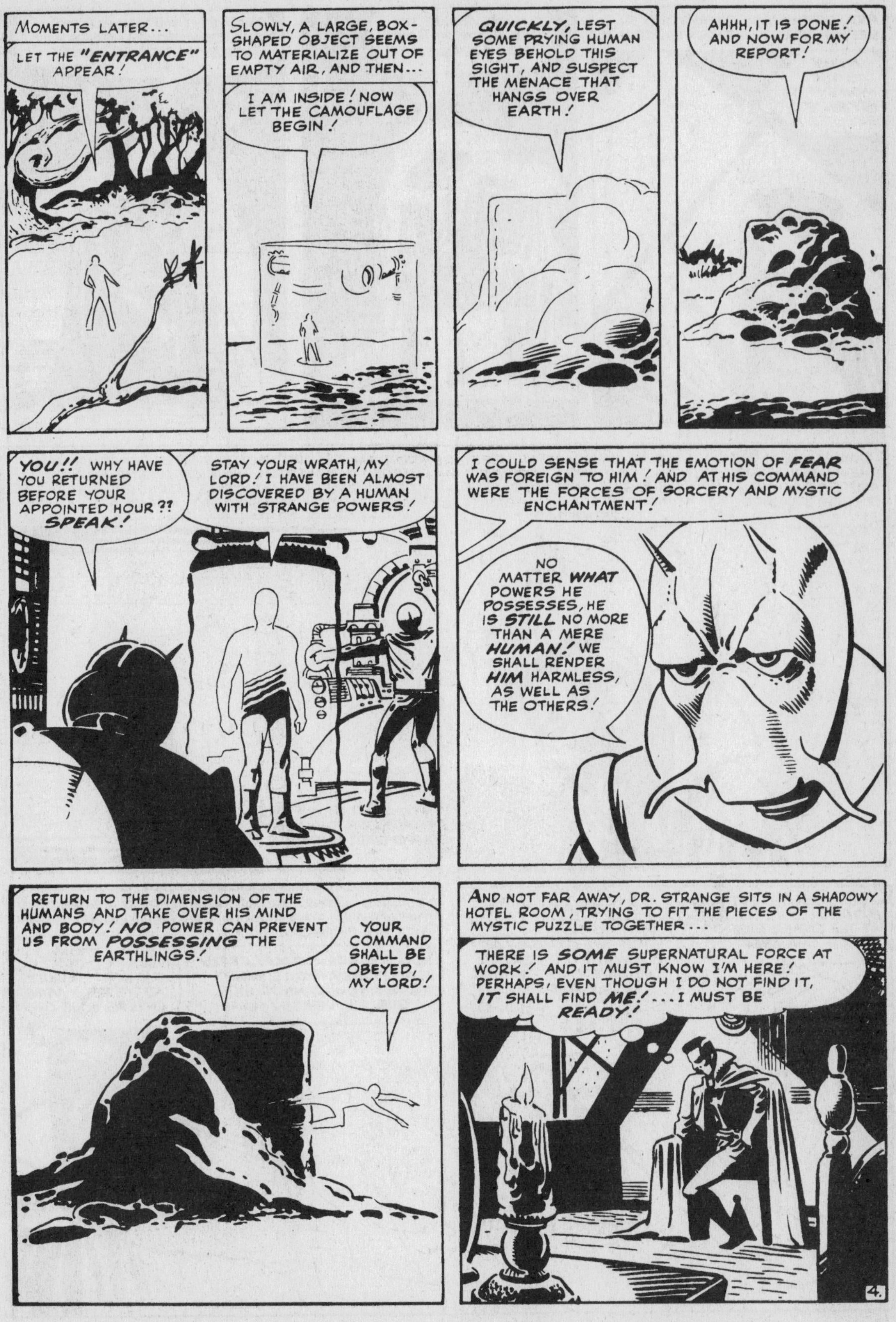
MOMENTS LATER...
LET THE "ENTRANCE" APPEAR!
SLOWLY, A LARGE, BOX-SHAPED OBJECT SEEMS TO MATERIALIZE OUT OF EMPTY AIR, AND THEN...
I AM INSIDE! NOW LET THE CAMOUFLAGE BEGIN!
QUICKLY, LEST SOME PRYING HUMAN EYES BEHOLD THIS SIGHT, AND SUSPECT THE MENACE THAT HANGS OVER EARTH!
AHHH, IT IS DONE! AND NOW FOR MY REPORT!
YOU!! WHY HAVE YOU RETURNED BEFORE YOUR APPOINTED HOUR?? SPEAK!
STAY YOUR WRATH, MY LORD! I HAVE BEEN ALMOST DISCOVERED BY A HUMAN WITH STRANGE POWERS!
I COULD SENSE THAT THE EMOTION OF FEAR WAS FOREIGN TO HIM! AND AT HIS COMMAND WERE THE FORCES OF SORCERY AND MYSTIC ENCHANTMENT!
NO MATTER WHAT POWERS HE POSSESSES, HE IS STILL NO MORE THAN A MERE HUMAN! WE SHALL RENDER HIM HARMLESS, AS WELL AS THE OTHERS!
RETURN TO THE DIMENSION OF THE HUMANS AND TAKE OVER HIS MIND AND BODY! NO POWER CAN PREVENT US FROM POSSESSING THE EARTHLINGS!
YOUR COMMAND SHALL BE OBEYED, MY LORD!
AND NOT FAR AWAY, DR. STRANGE SITS IN A SHADOWY HOTEL ROOM, TRYING TO FIT THE PIECES OF THE MYSTIC PUZZLE TOGETHER...
THERE IS SOME SUPERNATURAL FORCE AT WORK! AND IT MUST KNOW I'M HERE! PERHAPS, EVEN THOUGH I DO NOT FIND IT, IT SHALL FIND ME! ...I MUST BE READY!
4.

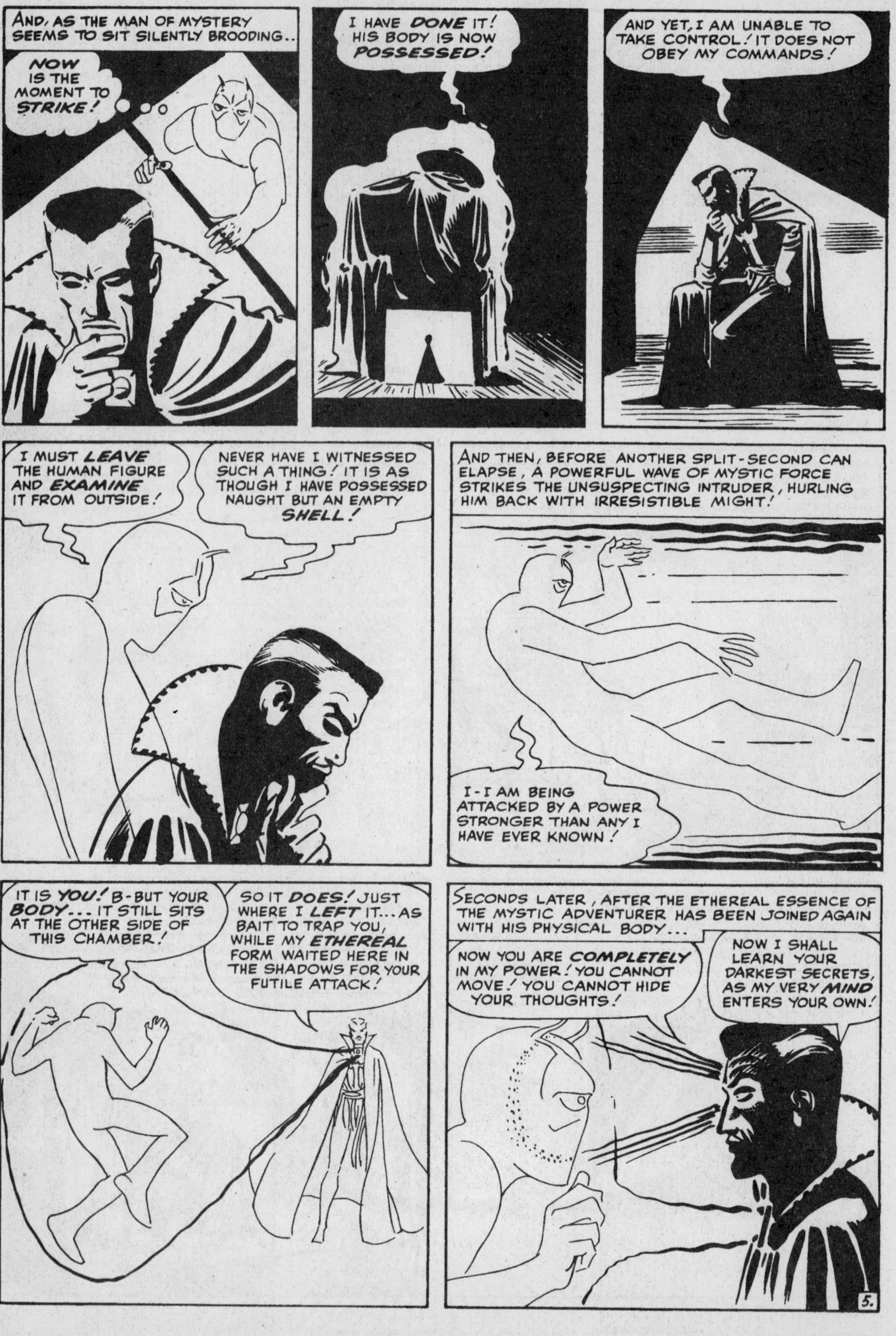
AND, AS THE MAN OF MYSTERY SEEMS TO SIT SILENTLY BROODING..
NOW IS THE MOMENT TO STRIKE!
I HAVE DONE IT! HIS BODY IS NOW POSSESSED!
AND YET, I AM UNABLE TO TAKE CONTROL! IT DOES NOT OBEY MY COMMANDS!
I MUST LEAVE THE HUMAN FIGURE AND EXAMINE IT FROM OUTSIDE!
NEVER HAVE I WITNESSED SUCH A THING! IT IS AS THOUGH I HAVE POSSESSED NAUGHT BUT AN EMPTY SHELL!
AND THEN, BEFORE ANOTHER SPLIT-SECOND CAN ELAPSE, A POWERFUL WAVE OF MYSTIC FORCE STRIKES THE UNSUSPECTING INTRUDER, HURLING HIM BACK WITH IRRESISTIBLE MIGHT!
I-I AM BEING ATTACKED BY A POWER STRONGER THAN ANY I HAVE EVER KNOWN!
IT IS YOU! B-BUT YOUR BODY... IT STILL SITS AT THE OTHER SIDE OF THIS CHAMBER!
SO IT DOES! JUST WHERE I LEFT IT... AS BAIT TO TRAP YOU, WHILE MY ETHEREAL FORM WAITED HERE IN THE SHADOWS FOR YOUR FUTILE ATTACK!
SECONDS LATER, AFTER THE ETHEREAL ESSENCE OF THE MYSTIC ADVENTURER HAS BEEN JOINED AGAIN WITH HIS PHYSICAL BODY...
NOW YOU ARE COMPLETELY IN MY POWER! YOU CANNOT MOVE! YOU CANNOT HIDE YOUR THOUGHTS!
NOW I SHALL LEARN YOUR DARKEST SECRETS, AS MY VERY MIND ENTERS YOUR OWN!
5.

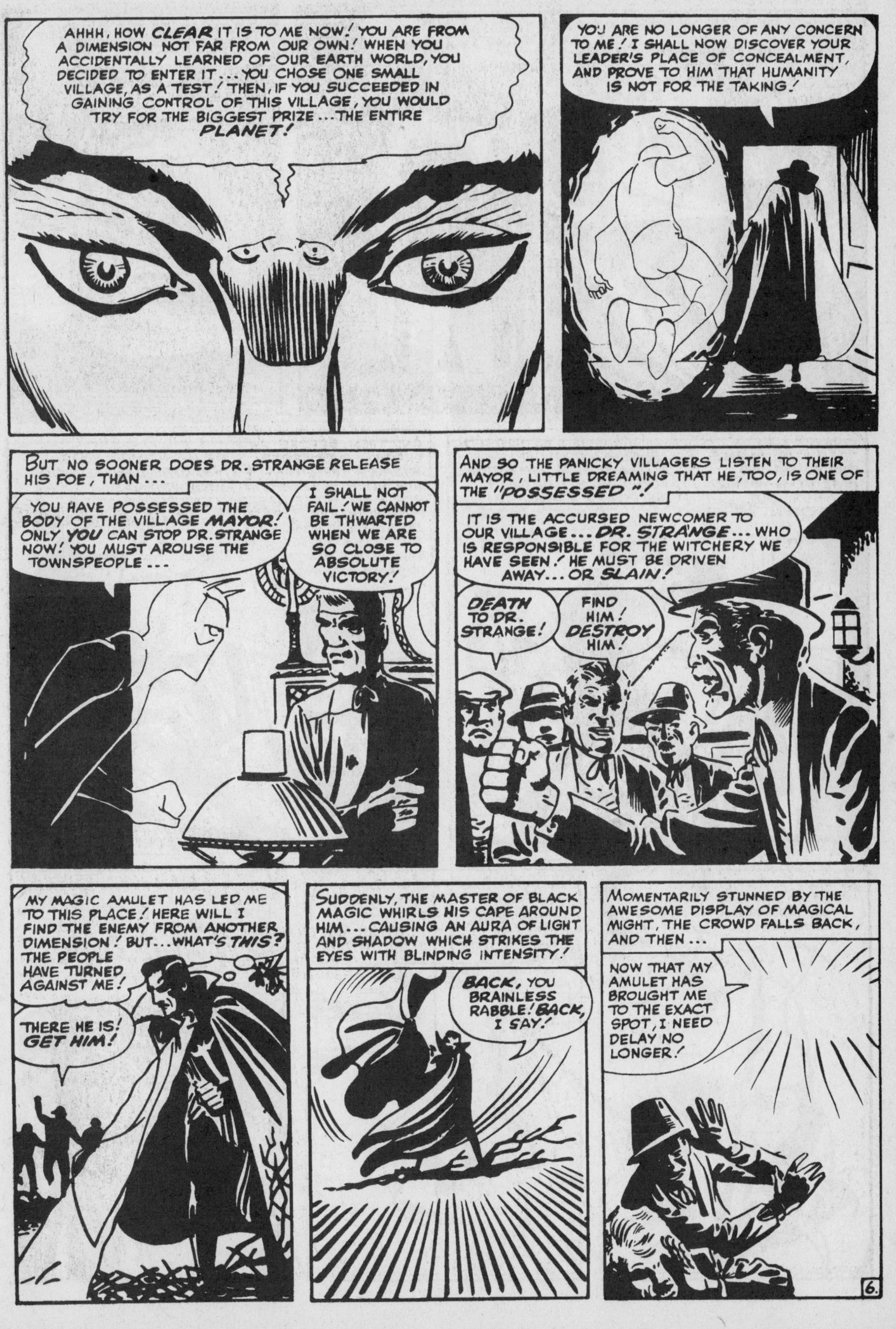

AHHH, HOW CLEAR IT IS TO ME NOW! YOU ARE FROM A DIMENSION NOT FAR FROM OUR OWN! WHEN YOU ACCIDENTALLY LEARNED OF OUR EARTH WORLD, YOU DECIDED TO ENTER IT... YOU CHOSE ONE SMALL VILLAGE, AS A TEST! THEN, IF YOU SUCCEEDED IN GAINING CONTROL OF THIS VILLAGE, YOU WOULD TRY FOR THE BIGGEST PRIZE... THE ENTIRE PLANET!
YOU ARE NO LONGER OF ANY CONCERN TO ME! I SHALL NOW DISCOVER YOUR LEADER'S PLACE OF CONCEALMENT, AND PROVE TO HIM THAT HUMANITY IS NOT FOR THE TAKING!
BUT NO SOONER DOES DR. STRANGE RELEASE HIS FOE, THAN...
YOU HAVE POSSESSED THE BODY OF THE VILLAGE MAYOR! ONLY YOU CAN STOP DR. STRANGE NOW! YOU MUST AROUSE THE TOWNSPEOPLE...
I SHALL NOT FAIL! WE CANNOT BE THWARTED WHEN WE ARE SO CLOSE TO ABSOLUTE VICTORY!
AND SO THE PANICKY VILLAGERS LISTEN TO THEIR MAYOR, LITTLE DREAMING THAT HE, TOO, IS ONE OF THE "POSSESSED"!
IT IS THE ACCURSED NEWCOMER TO OUR VILLAGE... DR. STRANGE... WHO IS RESPONSIBLE FOR THE WITCHERY WE HAVE SEEN! HE MUST BE DRIVEN AWAY... OR SLAIN!
DEATH TO DR. STRANGE!
FIND HIM! DESTROY HIM!
MY MAGIC AMULET HAS LED ME TO THIS PLACE! HERE WILL I FIND THE ENEMY FROM ANOTHER DIMENSION! BUT... WHAT'S THIS? THE PEOPLE HAVE TURNED AGAINST ME!
THERE HE IS! GET HIM!
SUDDENLY, THE MASTER OF BLACK MAGIC WHIRLS HIS CAPE AROUND HIM... CAUSING AN AURA OF LIGHT AND SHADOW WHICH STRIKES THE EYES WITH BLINDING INTENSITY!
BACK, YOU BRAINLESS RABBLE! BACK, I SAY!
MOMENTARILY STUNNED BY THE AWESOME DISPLAY OF MAGICAL MIGHT, THE CROWD FALLS BACK, AND THEN...
NOW THAT MY AMULET HAS BROUGHT ME TO THE EXACT SPOT, I NEED DELAY NO LONGER!
6.

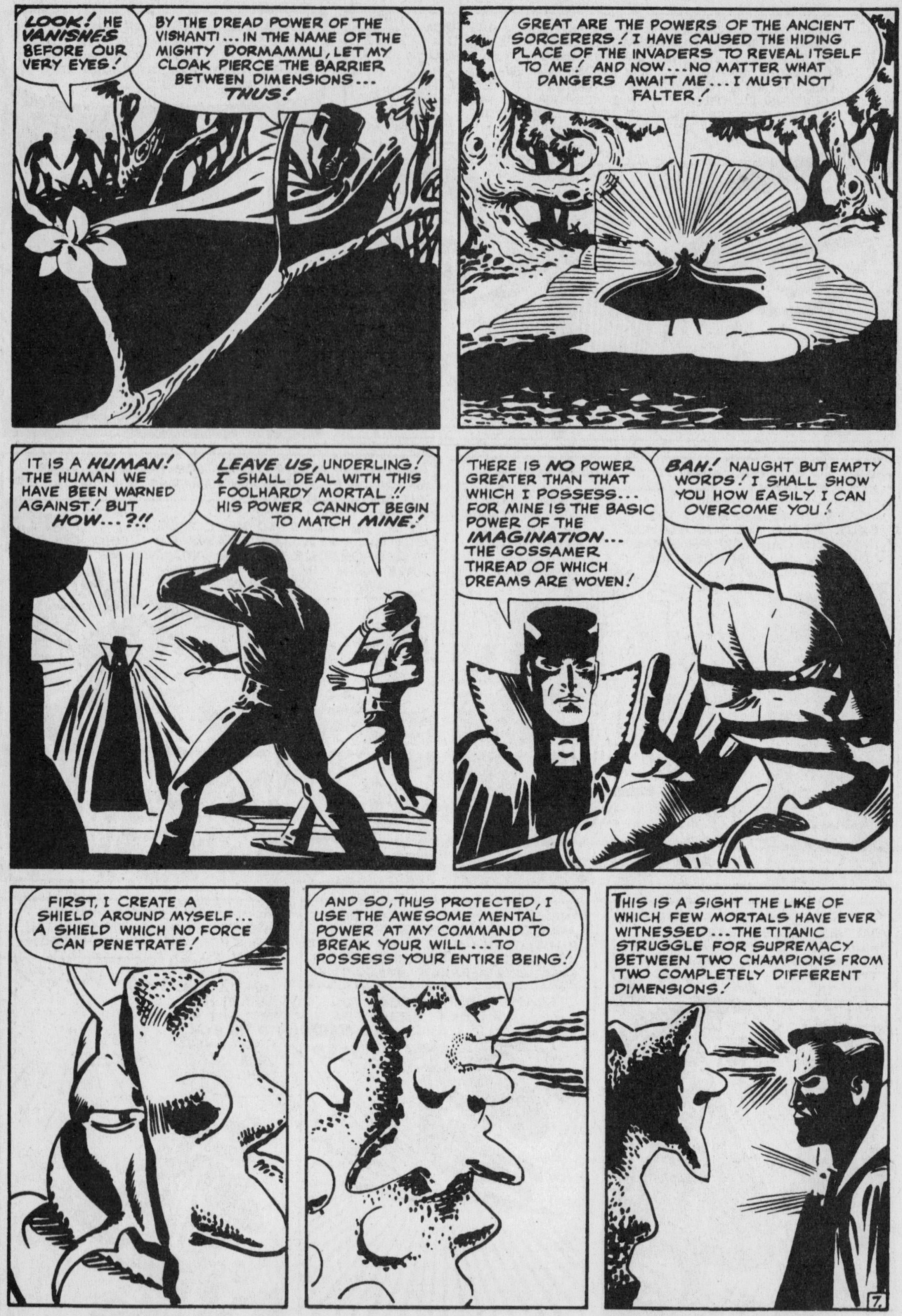
LOOK! HE VANISHES BEFORE OUR VERY EYES!
BY THE DREAD POWER OF THE VISHANTI... IN THE NAME OF THE MIGHTY DORMAMMU, LET MY CLOAK PIERCE THE BARRIER BETWEEN DIMENSIONS... THUS!
GREAT ARE THE POWERS OF THE ANCIENT SORCERERS! I HAVE CAUSED THE HIDING PLACE OF THE INVADERS TO REVEAL ITSELF TO ME! AND NOW... NO MATTER WHAT DANGERS AWAIT ME... I MUST NOT FALTER!
IT IS A HUMAN! THE HUMAN WE HAVE BEEN WARNED AGAINST! BUT HOW...?!!
LEAVE US, UNDERLING! I SHALL DEAL WITH THIS FOOLHARDY MORTAL!! HIS POWER CANNOT BEGIN TO MATCH MINE!
THERE IS NO POWER GREATER THAN THAT WHICH I POSSESS... FOR MINE IS THE BASIC POWER OF THE IMAGINATION... THE GOSSAMER THREAD OF WHICH DREAMS ARE WOVEN!
BAH! NAUGHT BUT EMPTY WORDS! I SHALL SHOW YOU HOW EASILY I CAN OVERCOME YOU!
FIRST, I CREATE A SHIELD AROUND MYSELF... A SHIELD WHICH NO FORCE CAN PENETRATE!
AND SO, THUS PROTECTED, I USE THE AWESOME MENTAL POWER AT MY COMMAND TO BREAK YOUR WILL... TO POSSESS YOUR ENTIRE BEING!
THIS IS A SIGHT THE LIKE OF WHICH FEW MORTALS HAVE EVER WITNESSED... THE TITANIC STRUGGLE FOR SUPREMACY BETWEEN TWO CHAMPIONS FROM TWO COMPLETELY DIFFERENT DIMENSIONS!
7.

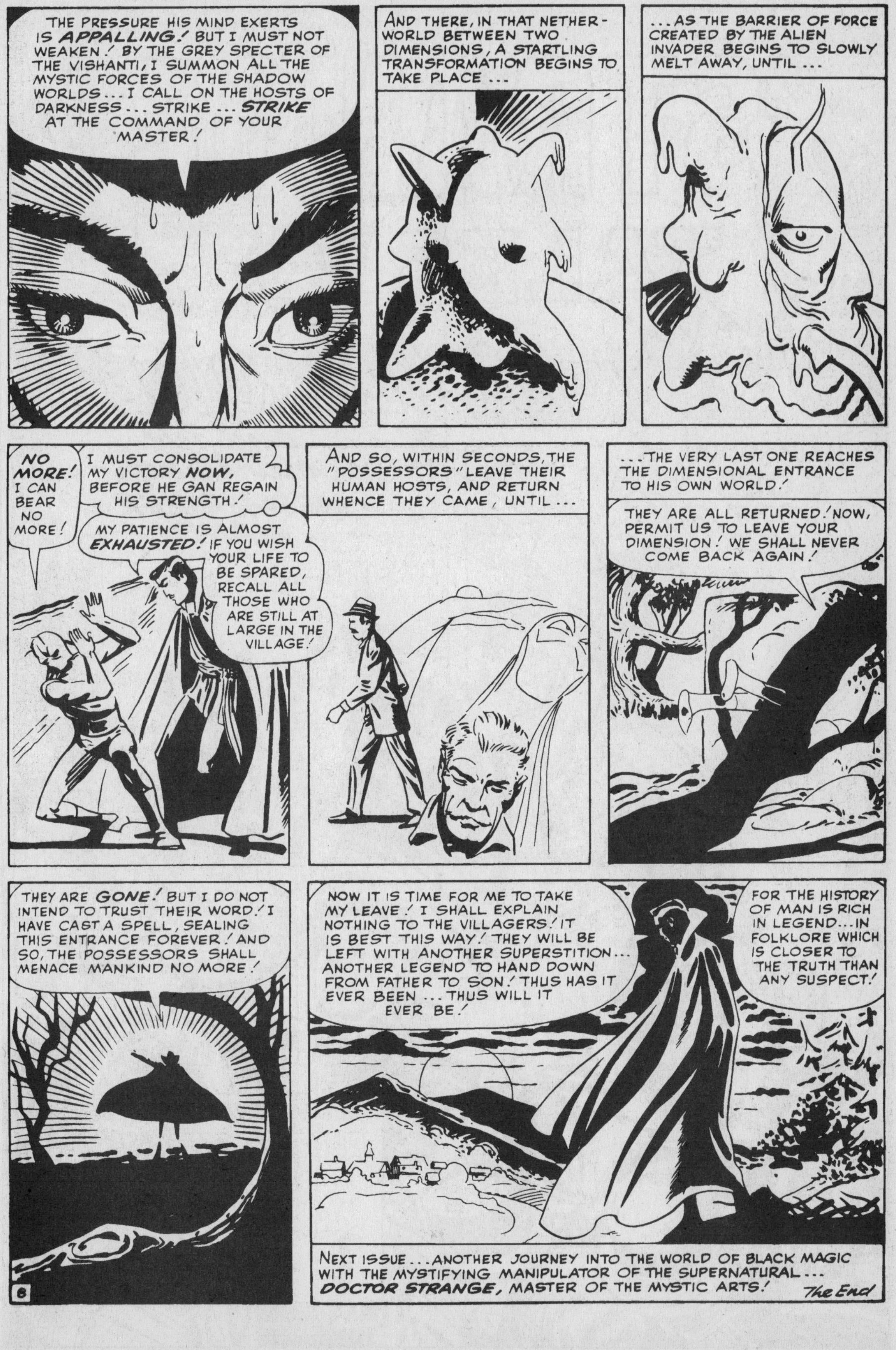

THE PRESSURE HIS MIND EXERTS IS APPALLING! BUT I MUST NOT WEAKEN! BY THE GREY SPECTER OF THE VISHANTI, I SUMMON ALL THE MYSTIC FORCES OF THE SHADOW WORLDS... I CALL ON THE HOSTS OF DARKNESS... STRIKE... STRIKE AT THE COMMAND OF YOUR MASTER!
AND THERE, IN THAT NETHER-WORLD BETWEEN TWO DIMENSIONS, A STARTLING TRANSFORMATION BEGINS TO TAKE PLACE...
...AS THE BARRIER OF FORCE CREATED BY THE ALIEN INVADER BEGINS TO SLOWLY MELT AWAY, UNTIL...
NO MORE! I CAN BEAR NO MORE!
I MUST CONSOLIDATE MY VICTORY NOW, BEFORE HE CAN REGAIN HIS STRENGTH!
MY PATIENCE IS ALMOST EXHAUSTED! IF YOU WISH YOUR LIFE TO BE SPARED, RECALL ALL THOSE WHO ARE STILL AT LARGE IN THE VILLAGE!
AND SO, WITHIN SECONDS, THE "POSSESSORS" LEAVE THEIR HUMAN HOSTS, AND RETURN WHENCE THEY CAME, UNTIL...
...THE VERY LAST ONE REACHES THE DIMENSIONAL ENTRANCE TO HIS OWN WORLD!
THEY ARE ALL RETURNED! NOW, PERMIT US TO LEAVE YOUR DIMENSION! WE SHALL NEVER COME BACK AGAIN!
THEY ARE GONE! BUT I DO NOT INTEND TO TRUST THEIR WORD! I HAVE CAST A SPELL, SEALING THIS ENTRANCE FOREVER! AND SO, THE POSSESSORS SHALL MENACE MANKIND NO MORE!
NOW IT IS TIME FOR ME TO TAKE MY LEAVE! I SHALL EXPLAIN NOTHING TO THE VILLAGERS! IT IS BEST THIS WAY! THEY WILL BE LEFT WITH ANOTHER SUPERSTITION... ANOTHER LEGEND TO HAND DOWN FROM FATHER TO SON! THUS HAS IT EVER BEEN... THUS WILL IT EVER BE!
FOR THE HISTORY OF MAN IS RICH IN LEGEND... IN FOLKLORE WHICH IS CLOSER TO THE TRUTH THAN ANY SUSPECT!
NEXT ISSUE... ANOTHER JOURNEY INTO THE WORLD OF BLACK MAGIC WITH THE MYSTIFYING MANIPULATOR OF THE SUPERNATURAL... DOCTOR STRANGE, MASTER OF THE MYSTIC ARTS!
The End

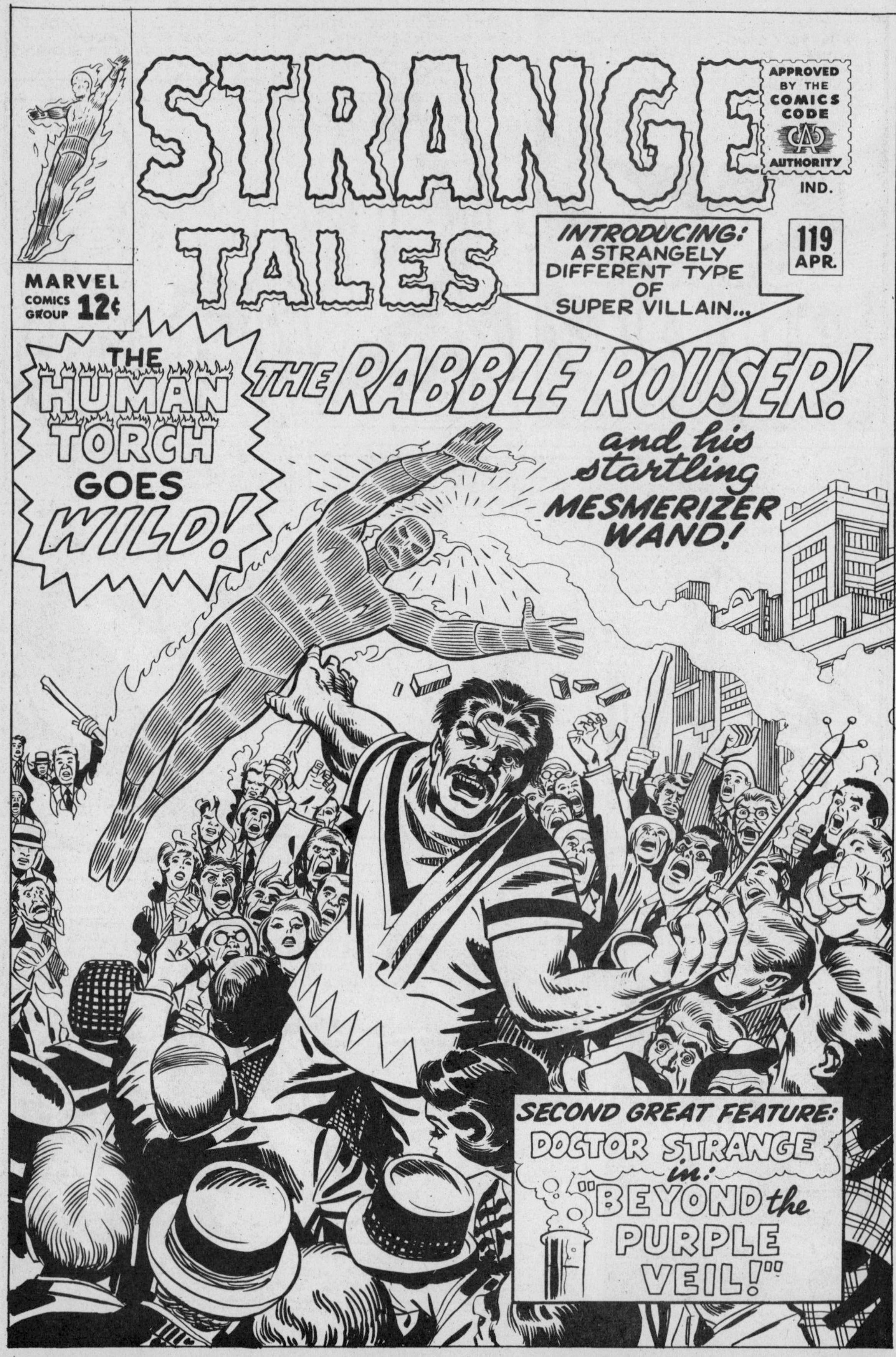
STRANGE TALES
APPROVED BY THE COMICS CODE AUTHORITY
IND.
MARVEL COMICS GROUP 12¢
119 APR.
INTRODUCING: A STRANGELY DIFFERENT TYPE OF SUPER VILLAIN...
THE HUMAN TORCH GOES WILD!
THE RABBLE ROUSER!
and his startling MESMERIZER WAND!
SECOND GREAT FEATURE: DOCTOR STRANGE in: "BEYOND the PURPLE VEIL!"

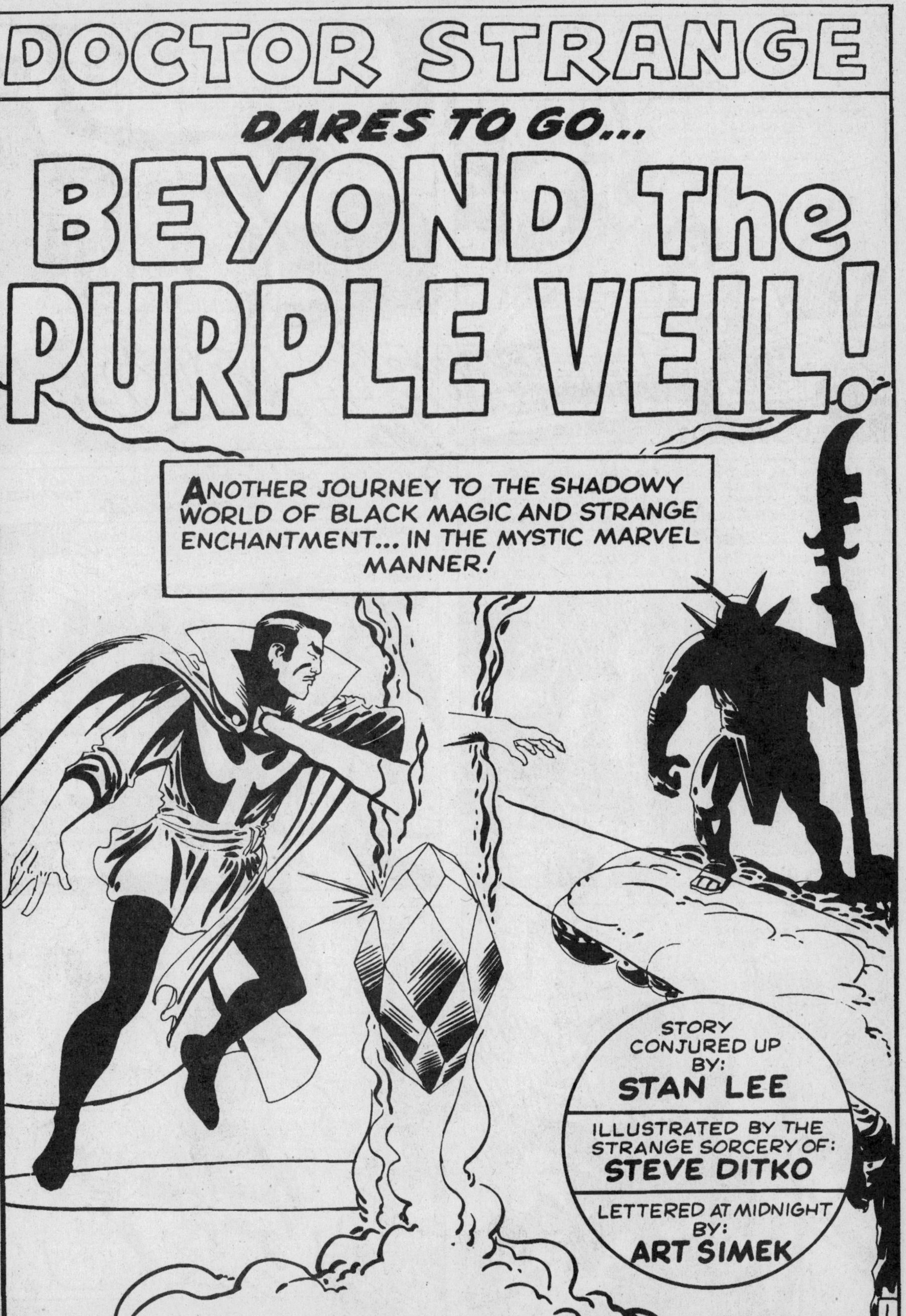
DOCTOR STRANGE
DARES TO GO...
BEYOND THE PURPLE VEIL!
ANOTHER JOURNEY TO THE SHADOWY WORLD OF BLACK MAGIC AND STRANGE ENCHANTMENT... IN THE MYSTIC MARVEL MANNER!
STORY CONJURED UP BY: STAN LEE
ILLUSTRATED BY THE STRANGE SORCERY OF: STEVE DITKO
LETTERED AT MIDNIGHT BY: ART SIMEK
1

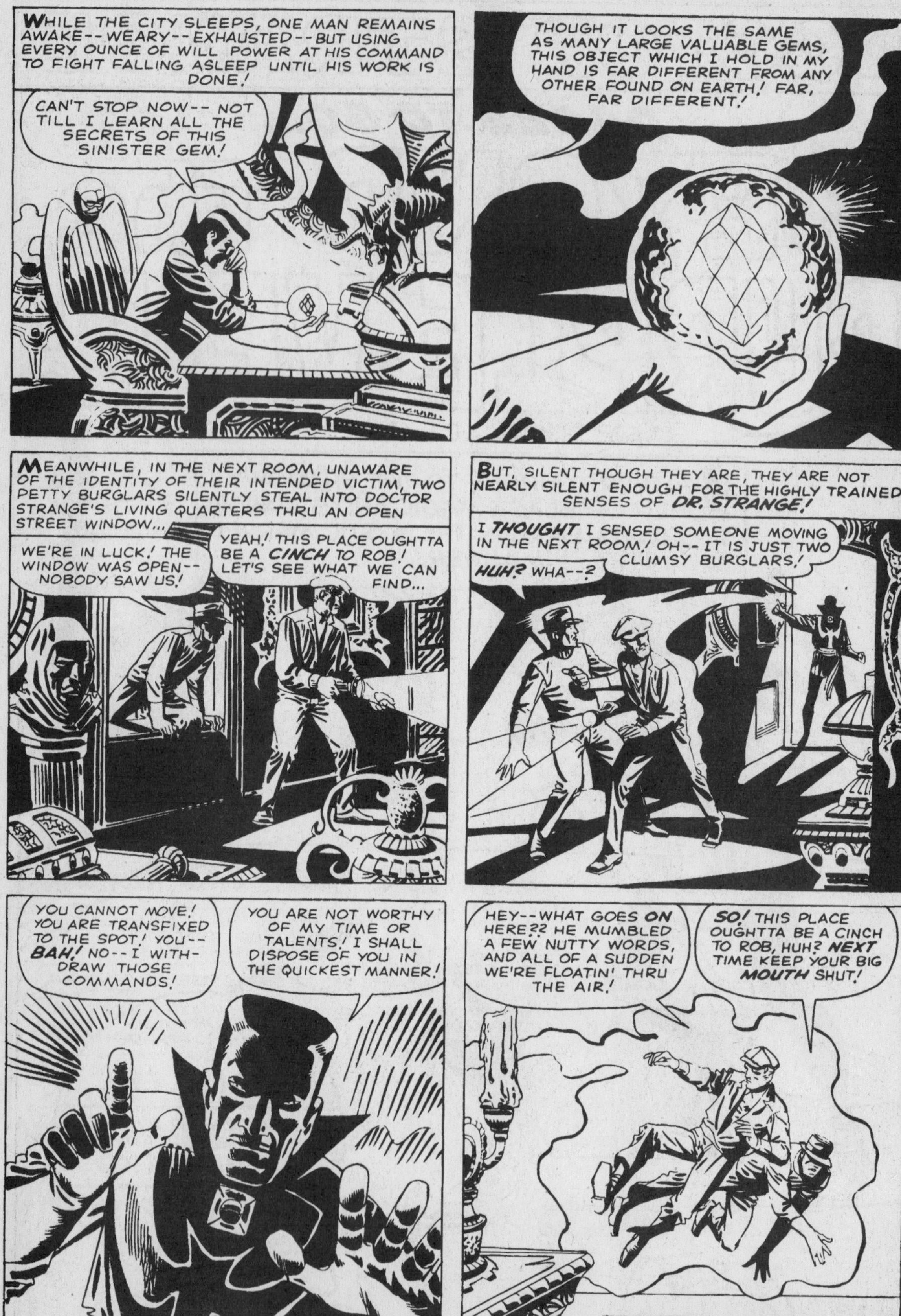
WHILE THE CITY SLEEPS, ONE MAN REMAINS AWAKE--WEARY--EXHAUSTED--BUT USING EVERY OUNCE OF WILL POWER AT HIS COMMAND TO FIGHT FALLING ASLEEP UNTIL HIS WORK IS DONE!
CAN'T STOP NOW-- NOT TILL I LEARN ALL THE SECRETS OF THIS SINISTER GEM!
THOUGH IT LOOKS THE SAME AS MANY LARGE VALUABLE GEMS, THIS OBJECT WHICH I HOLD IN MY HAND IS FAR DIFFERENT FROM ANY OTHER FOUND ON EARTH! FAR, FAR DIFFERENT!
MEANWHILE, IN THE NEXT ROOM, UNAWARE OF THE IDENTITY OF THEIR INTENDED VICTIM, TWO PETTY BURGLARS SILENTLY STEAL INTO DOCTOR STRANGE'S LIVING QUARTERS THRU AN OPEN STREET WINDOW...
WE'RE IN LUCK! THE WINDOW WAS OPEN-- NOBODY SAW US!
YEAH! THIS PLACE OUGHTTA BE A CINCH TO ROB! LET'S SEE WHAT WE CAN FIND...
BUT, SILENT THOUGH THEY ARE, THEY ARE NOT NEARLY SILENT ENOUGH FOR THE HIGHLY TRAINED SENSES OF DR. STRANGE!
I THOUGHT I SENSED SOMEONE MOVING IN THE NEXT ROOM! OH-- IT IS JUST TWO CLUMSY BURGLARS!
HUH? WHA--?
YOU CANNOT MOVE! YOU ARE TRANSFIXED TO THE SPOT! YOU-- BAH! NO--I WITHDRAW THOSE COMMANDS!
YOU ARE NOT WORTHY OF MY TIME OR TALENTS! I SHALL DISPOSE OF YOU IN THE QUICKEST MANNER!
HEY--WHAT GOES ON HERE?? HE MUMBLED A FEW NUTTY WORDS, AND ALL OF A SUDDEN WE'RE FLOATIN' THRU THE AIR!
SO! THIS PLACE OUGHTTA BE A CINCH TO ROB, HUH? NEXT TIME KEEP YOUR BIG MOUTH SHUT!
2

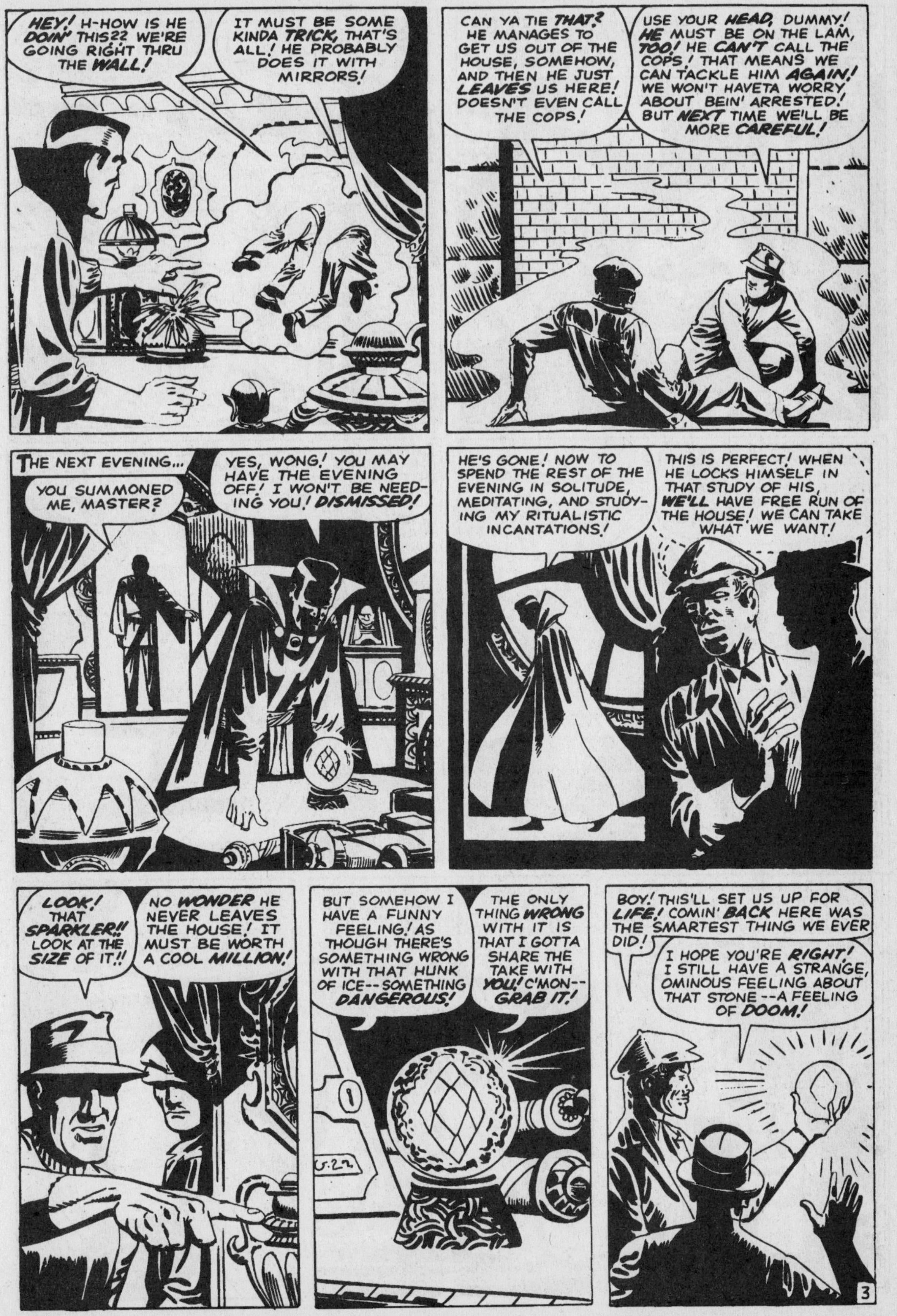
HEY! H-HOW IS HE DOIN' THIS?? WE'RE GOING RIGHT THRU THE WALL!
IT MUST BE SOME KINDA TRICK, THAT'S ALL! HE PROBABLY DOES IT WITH MIRRORS!
CAN YA TIE THAT? HE MANAGES TO GET US OUT OF THE HOUSE, SOMEHOW, AND THEN HE JUST LEAVES US HERE! DOESN'T EVEN CALL THE COPS!
USE YOUR HEAD, DUMMY! HE MUST BE ON THE LAM, TOO! HE CAN'T CALL THE COPS! THAT MEANS WE CAN TACKLE HIM AGAIN! WE WON'T HAVETA WORRY ABOUT BEIN' ARRESTED! BUT NEXT TIME WE'LL BE MORE CAREFUL!
THE NEXT EVENING...
YOU SUMMONED ME, MASTER?
YES, WONG! YOU MAY HAVE THE EVENING OFF! I WON'T BE NEEDING YOU! DISMISSED!
HE'S GONE! NOW TO SPEND THE REST OF THE EVENING IN SOLITUDE, MEDITATING, AND STUDYING MY RITUALISTIC INCANTATIONS!
THIS IS PERFECT! WHEN HE LOCKS HIMSELF IN THAT STUDY OF HIS, WE'LL HAVE FREE RUN OF THE HOUSE! WE CAN TAKE WHAT WE WANT!
LOOK! THAT SPARKLER!! LOOK AT THE SIZE OF IT!!
NO WONDER HE NEVER LEAVES THE HOUSE! IT MUST BE WORTH A COOL MILLION!
BUT SOMEHOW I HAVE A FUNNY FEELING! AS THOUGH THERE'S SOMETHING WRONG WITH THAT HUNK OF ICE--SOMETHING DANGEROUS!
THE ONLY THING WRONG WITH IT IS THAT I GOTTA SHARE THE TAKE WITH YOU! C'MON--GRAB IT!
BOY! THIS'LL SET US UP FOR LIFE! COMIN' BACK HERE WAS THE SMARTEST THING WE EVER DID!
I HOPE YOU'RE RIGHT! I STILL HAVE A STRANGE, OMINOUS FEELING ABOUT THAT STONE --A FEELING OF DOOM!
3

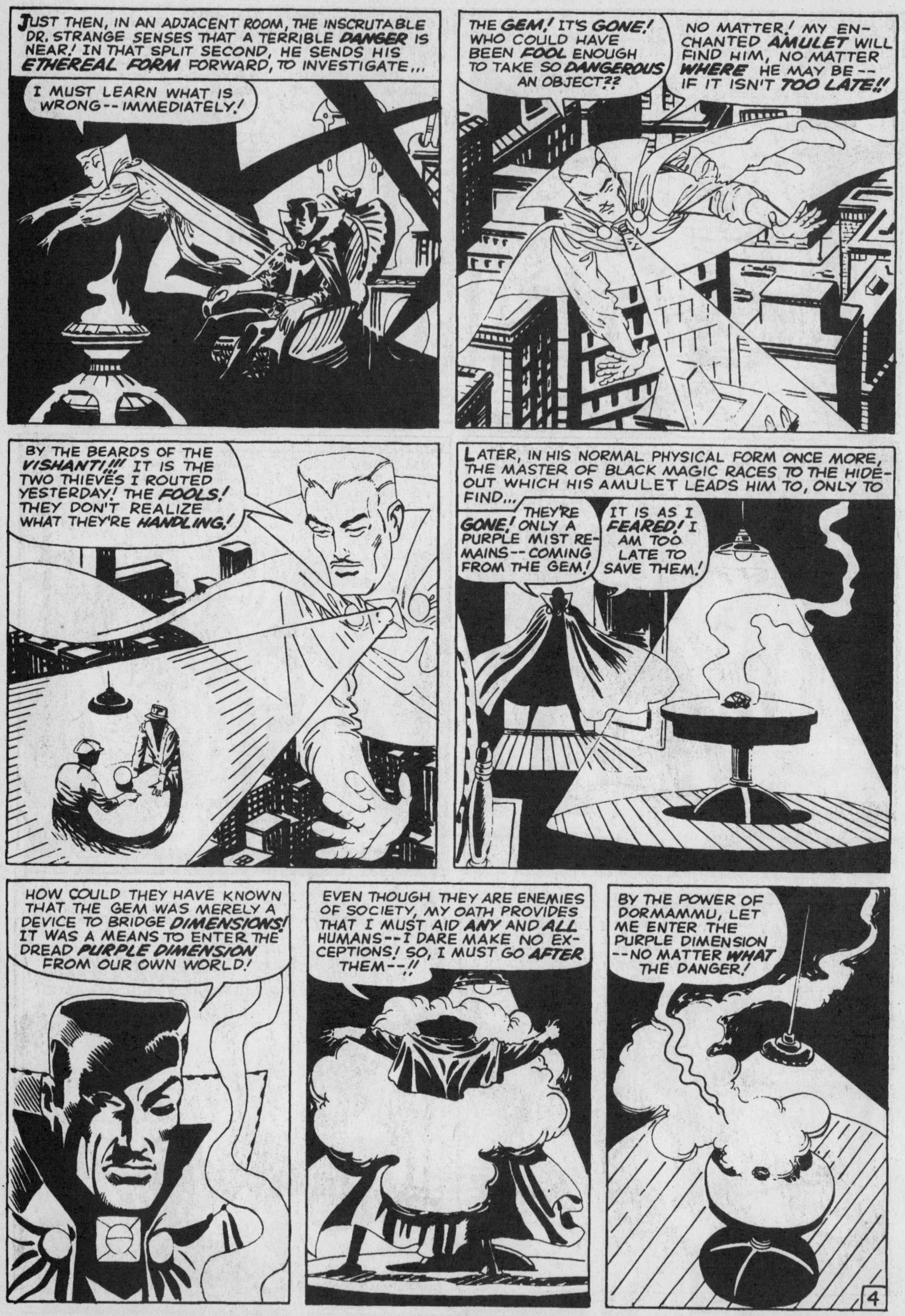
JUST THEN, IN AN ADJACENT ROOM, THE INSCRUTABLE DR. STRANGE SENSES THAT A TERRIBLE DANGER IS NEAR! IN THAT SPLIT SECOND, HE SENDS HIS ETHEREAL FORM FORWARD, TO INVESTIGATE...
I MUST LEARN WHAT IS WRONG--IMMEDIATELY!
THE GEM! IT'S GONE! WHO COULD HAVE BEEN FOOL ENOUGH TO TAKE SO DANGEROUS AN OBJECT??
NO MATTER! MY ENCHANTED AMULET WILL FIND HIM, NO MATTER WHERE HE MAY BE--IF IT ISN'T TOO LATE!!
BY THE BEARDS OF THE VISHANTI!!! IT IS THE TWO THIEVES I ROUTED YESTERDAY! THE FOOLS! THEY DON'T REALIZE WHAT THEY'RE HANDLING!
LATER, IN HIS NORMAL PHYSICAL FORM ONCE MORE, THE MASTER OF BLACK MAGIC RACES TO THE HIDE-OUT WHICH HIS AMULET LEADS HIM TO, ONLY TO FIND...
THEY'RE GONE! ONLY A PURPLE MIST REMAINS--COMING FROM THE GEM!
IT IS AS I FEARED! I AM TOO LATE TO SAVE THEM!
HOW COULD THEY HAVE KNOWN THAT THE GEM WAS MERELY A DEVICE TO BRIDGE DIMENSIONS! IT WAS A MEANS TO ENTER THE DREAD PURPLE DIMENSION FROM OUR OWN WORLD!
EVEN THOUGH THEY ARE ENEMIES OF SOCIETY, MY OATH PROVIDES THAT I MUST AID ANY AND ALL HUMANS--I DARE MAKE NO EXCEPTIONS! SO, I MUST GO AFTER THEM--!!
BY THE POWER OF DORMAMMU, LET ME ENTER THE PURPLE DIMENSION--NO MATTER WHAT THE DANGER!
4

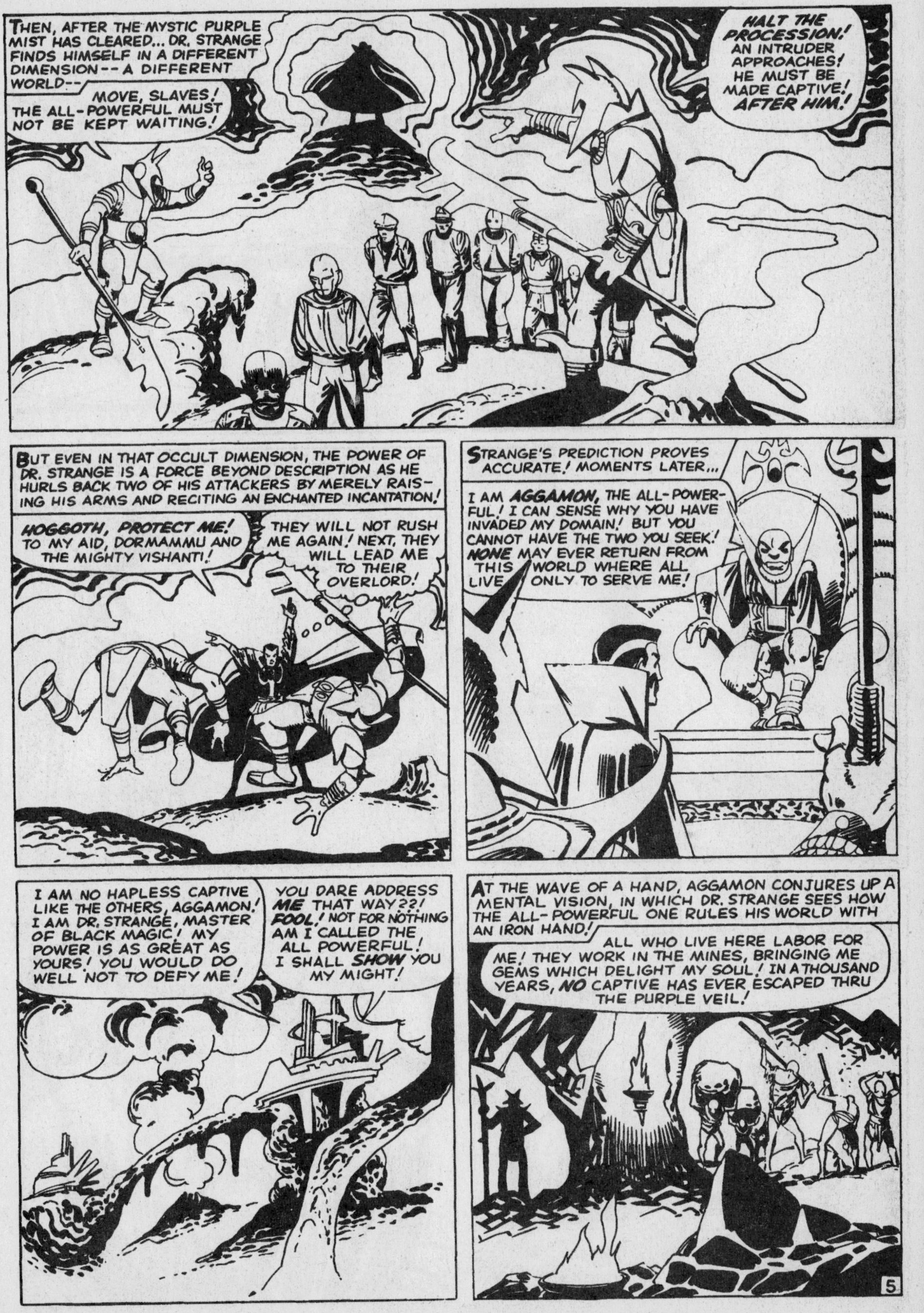
THEN, AFTER THE MYSTIC PURPLE MIST HAS CLEARED... DR. STRANGE FINDS HIMSELF IN A DIFFERENT DIMENSION-- A DIFFERENT WORLD--
MOVE, SLAVES! THE ALL-POWERFUL MUST NOT BE KEPT WAITING!
HALT THE PROCESSION! AN INTRUDER APPROACHES! HE MUST BE MADE CAPTIVE! AFTER HIM!
BUT EVEN IN THAT OCCULT DIMENSION, THE POWER OF DR. STRANGE IS A FORCE BEYOND DESCRIPTION AS HE HURLS BACK TWO OF HIS ATTACKERS BY MERELY RAISING HIS ARMS AND RECITING AN ENCHANTED INCANTATION!
HOGGOTH, PROTECT ME! TO MY AID, DORMAMMU AND THE MIGHTY VISHANTI!
THEY WILL NOT RUSH ME AGAIN! NEXT, THEY WILL LEAD ME TO THEIR OVERLORD!
STRANGE'S PREDICTION PROVES ACCURATE! MOMENTS LATER...
I AM AGGAMON, THE ALL-POWERFUL! I CAN SENSE WHY YOU HAVE INVADED MY DOMAIN! BUT YOU CANNOT HAVE THE TWO YOU SEEK! NONE MAY EVER RETURN FROM THIS WORLD WHERE ALL LIVE ONLY TO SERVE ME!
I AM NO HAPLESS CAPTIVE LIKE THE OTHERS, AGGAMON! I AM DR. STRANGE, MASTER OF BLACK MAGIC! MY POWER IS AS GREAT AS YOURS! YOU WOULD DO WELL NOT TO DEFY ME!
YOU DARE ADDRESS ME THAT WAY??! FOOL! NOT FOR NOTHING AM I CALLED THE ALL POWERFUL! I SHALL SHOW YOU MY MIGHT!
AT THE WAVE OF A HAND, AGGAMON CONJURES UP A MENTAL VISION, IN WHICH DR. STRANGE SEES HOW THE ALL-POWERFUL ONE RULES HIS WORLD WITH AN IRON HAND!
ALL WHO LIVE HERE LABOR FOR ME! THEY WORK IN THE MINES, BRINGING ME GEMS WHICH DELIGHT MY SOUL! IN A THOUSAND YEARS, NO CAPTIVE HAS EVER ESCAPED THRU THE PURPLE VEIL!
5

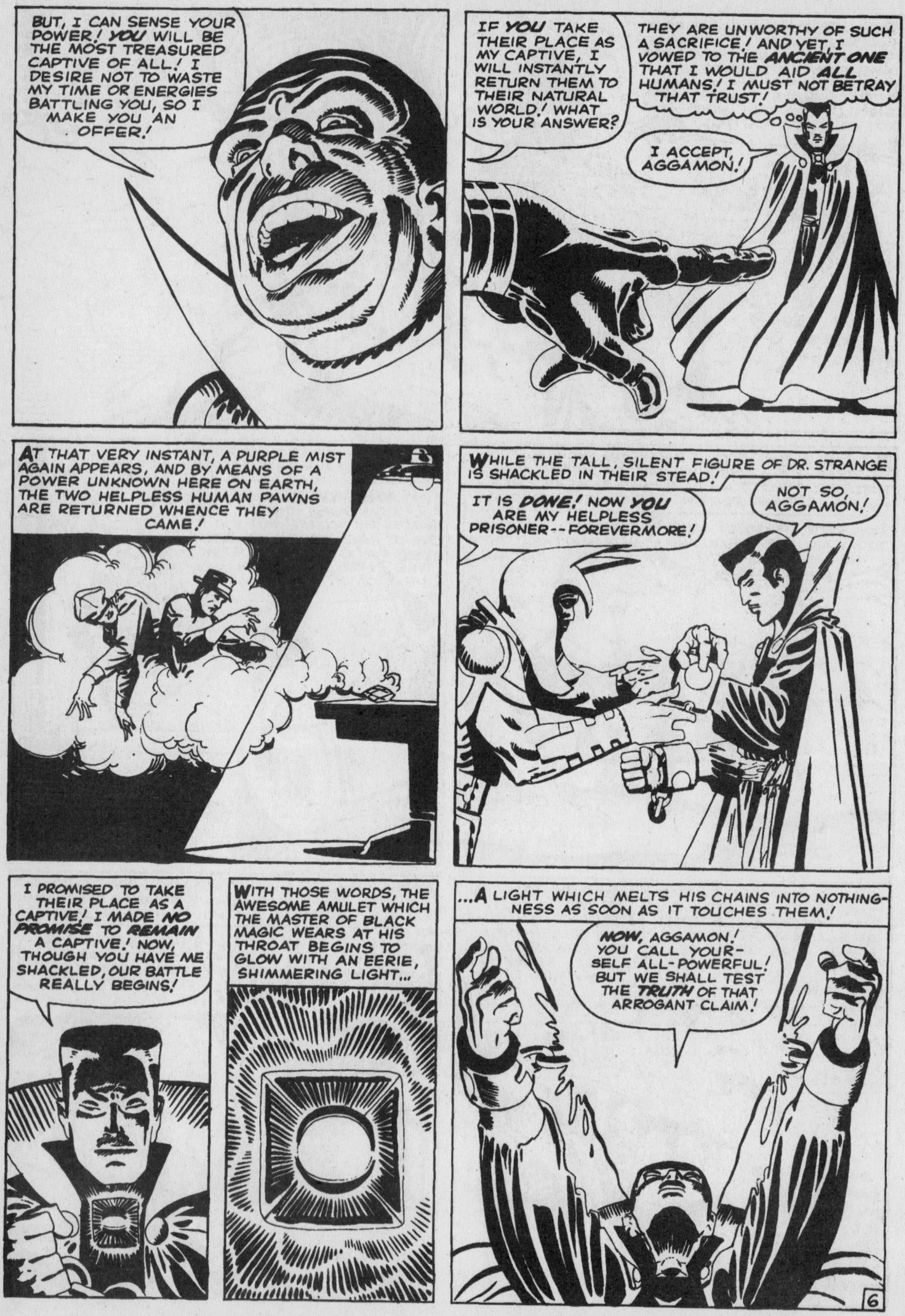
BUT, I CAN SENSE YOUR POWER! YOU WILL BE THE MOST TREASURED CAPTIVE OF ALL! I DESIRE NOT TO WASTE MY TIME OR ENERGIES BATTLING YOU, SO I MAKE YOU AN OFFER!
IF YOU TAKE THEIR PLACE AS MY CAPTIVE, I WILL INSTANTLY RETURN THEM TO THEIR NATURAL WORLD! WHAT IS YOUR ANSWER?
THEY ARE UNWORTHY OF SUCH A SACRIFICE! AND YET, I VOWED TO THE ANCIENT ONE THAT I WOULD AID ALL HUMANS! I MUST NOT BETRAY THAT TRUST!
I ACCEPT, AGGAMON!
AT THAT VERY INSTANT, A PURPLE MIST AGAIN APPEARS, AND BY MEANS OF A POWER UNKNOWN HERE ON EARTH, THE TWO HELPLESS HUMAN PAWNS ARE RETURNED WHENCE THEY CAME!
WHILE THE TALL, SILENT FIGURE OF DR. STRANGE IS SHACKLED IN THEIR STEAD!
IT IS DONE! NOW YOU ARE MY HELPLESS PRISONER--FOREVERMORE!
NOT SO, AGGAMON!
I PROMISED TO TAKE THEIR PLACE AS A CAPTIVE! I MADE NO PROMISE TO REMAIN A CAPTIVE! NOW, THOUGH YOU HAVE ME SHACKLED, OUR BATTLE REALLY BEGINS!
WITH THOSE WORDS, THE AWESOME AMULET WHICH THE MASTER OF BLACK MAGIC WEARS AT HIS THROAT BEGINS TO GLOW WITH AN EERIE, SHIMMERING LIGHT...
...A LIGHT WHICH MELTS HIS CHAINS INTO NOTHINGNESS AS SOON AS IT TOUCHES THEM!
NOW, AGGAMON! YOU CALL YOURSELF ALL-POWERFUL! BUT WE SHALL TEST THE TRUTH OF THAT ARROGANT CLAIM!
6

AT ANOTHER GESTURE FROM DR. STRANGE, AGGAMON'S GUARDS, WHO POSSESS NO MAGIC POWERS OF THEMSELVES, ARE SCATTERED AS SEEDS BEFORE THE WIND...

NONE WILL AID YOU, AGGAMON! WE MUST BATTLE *ALONE!*

SO BE IT, MAN OF EARTH! THOUGH YOUR POWER IS GREAT, *MINE* IS STILL THE GREATER!

NOTHING THAT LIVES CAN WITHSTAND THE FORCE OF MY JEWELED DEMOLISHER BEAM! YOU WILL HAVE *FOUND* YOUR FREEDOM, DR. STRANGE, BUT ONLY IN *DEATH!*

BUT THE FATAL BEAM NEVER REACHES THE MIGHTY MAN OF MYSTERY! FOR, IN MIDAIR, IT IS COUNTERED BY THE EQUALLY POWERFUL BEAM OF DR. STRANGE'S MAGIC AMULET!

THE LONG MINUTES TICK ON, AS DEMOLISHER AND AMULET CONTEND WITH EACH OTHER, WHILE AGGAMON AND DR. STRANGE GROW STEADILY WEAKER IN THE GRIM, SILENT BATTLE!

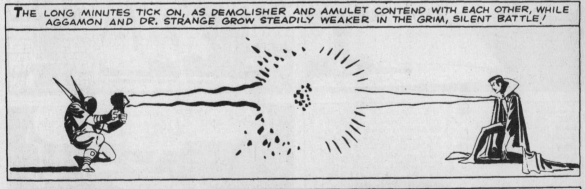

AS THE HOURS CREEP BY, BOTH ANTAGONISTS FEEL THE VERY LIFE ESSENCE DRAINING FROM THEIR BODIES, AS THEY REALIZE THAT THEY *BOTH* ARE DOOMED, UNLESS ONE SURRENDERS FIRST! FOR NOTHING THAT LIVES CAN LONG WITHSTAND THE MIND-STAGGERING PRESSURE TO WHICH THEY ARE SUBJECTED!

SURRENDER, YOU MORTAL FOOL! YOU HAVE NO OTHER CHOICE-- EXCEPT CERTAIN DEATH!

THE CHOICE IS *YOURS* AS WELL, AGGAMON! I DO NOT FEAR DEATH--LET US SEE IF *YOU* CAN FACE IT AS UNFLINCHINGLY AS I!!

7

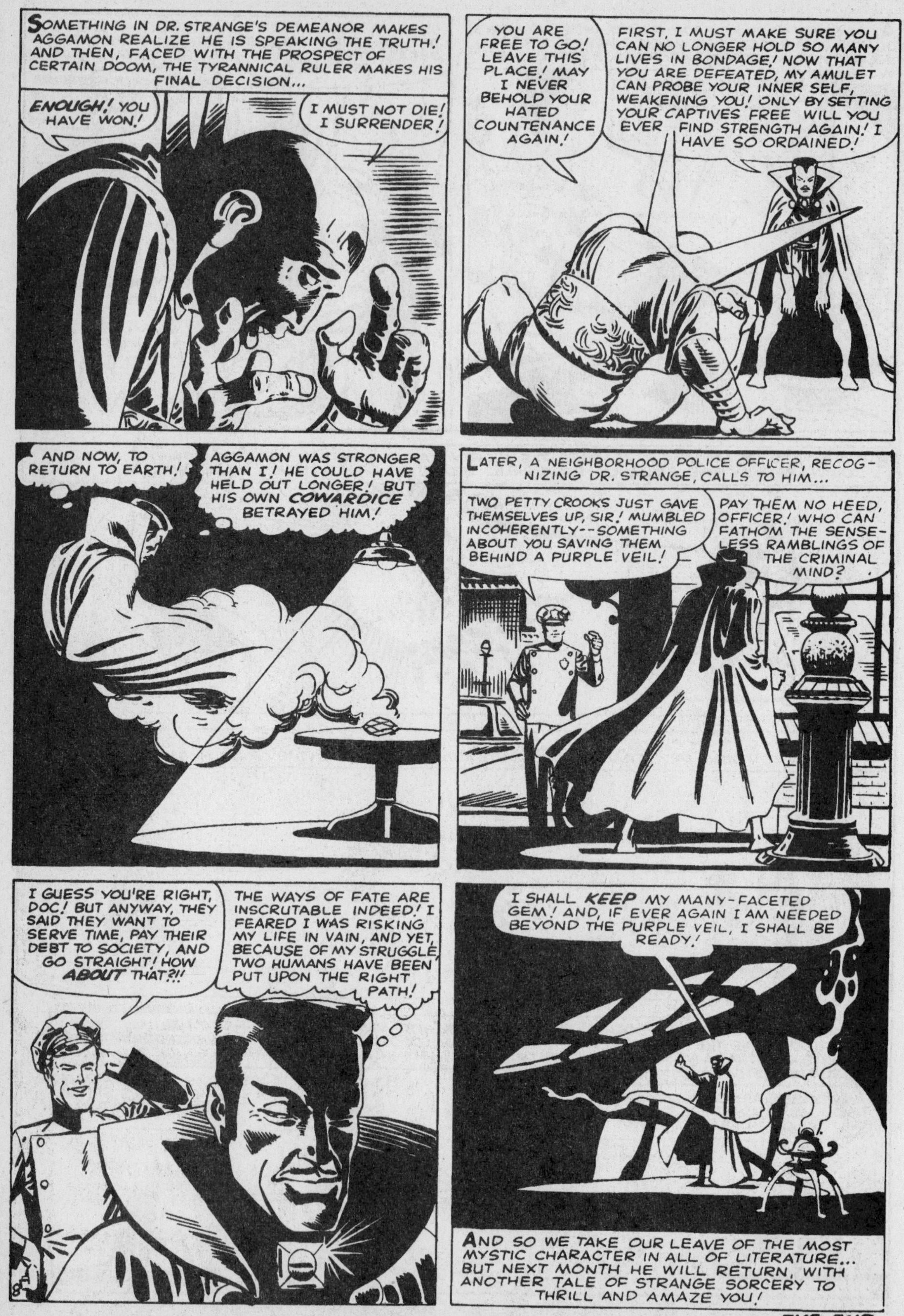
SOMETHING IN DR. STRANGE'S DEMEANOR MAKES AGGAMON REALIZE HE IS SPEAKING THE TRUTH! AND THEN, FACED WITH THE PROSPECT OF CERTAIN DOOM, THE TYRANNICAL RULER MAKES HIS FINAL DECISION...
ENOUGH! YOU HAVE WON!
I MUST NOT DIE! I SURRENDER!
YOU ARE FREE TO GO! LEAVE THIS PLACE! MAY I NEVER BEHOLD YOUR HATED COUNTENANCE AGAIN!
FIRST, I MUST MAKE SURE YOU CAN NO LONGER HOLD SO MANY LIVES IN BONDAGE! NOW THAT YOU ARE DEFEATED, MY AMULET CAN PROBE YOUR INNER SELF, WEAKENING YOU! ONLY BY SETTING YOUR CAPTIVES FREE WILL YOU EVER FIND STRENGTH AGAIN! I HAVE SO ORDAINED!
AND NOW, TO RETURN TO EARTH!
AGGAMON WAS STRONGER THAN I! HE COULD HAVE HELD OUT LONGER! BUT HIS OWN COWARDICE BETRAYED HIM!
LATER, A NEIGHBORHOOD POLICE OFFICER, RECOGNIZING DR. STRANGE, CALLS TO HIM...
TWO PETTY CROOKS JUST GAVE THEMSELVES UP, SIR! MUMBLED INCOHERENTLY--SOMETHING ABOUT YOU SAVING THEM BEHIND A PURPLE VEIL!
PAY THEM NO HEED, OFFICER! WHO CAN FATHOM THE SENSELESS RAMBLINGS OF THE CRIMINAL MIND?
I GUESS YOU'RE RIGHT, DOC! BUT ANYWAY, THEY SAID THEY WANT TO SERVE TIME, PAY THEIR DEBT TO SOCIETY, AND GO STRAIGHT! HOW ABOUT THAT?!!
THE WAYS OF FATE ARE INSCRUTABLE INDEED! I FEARED I WAS RISKING MY LIFE IN VAIN, AND YET, BECAUSE OF MY STRUGGLE, TWO HUMANS HAVE BEEN PUT UPON THE RIGHT PATH!
8
I SHALL KEEP MY MANY-FACETED GEM! AND, IF EVER AGAIN I AM NEEDED BEYOND THE PURPLE VEIL, I SHALL BE READY!
AND SO WE TAKE OUR LEAVE OF THE MOST MYSTIC CHARACTER IN ALL OF LITERATURE... BUT NEXT MONTH HE WILL RETURN, WITH ANOTHER TALE OF STRANGE SORCERY TO THRILL AND AMAZE YOU!

THE END

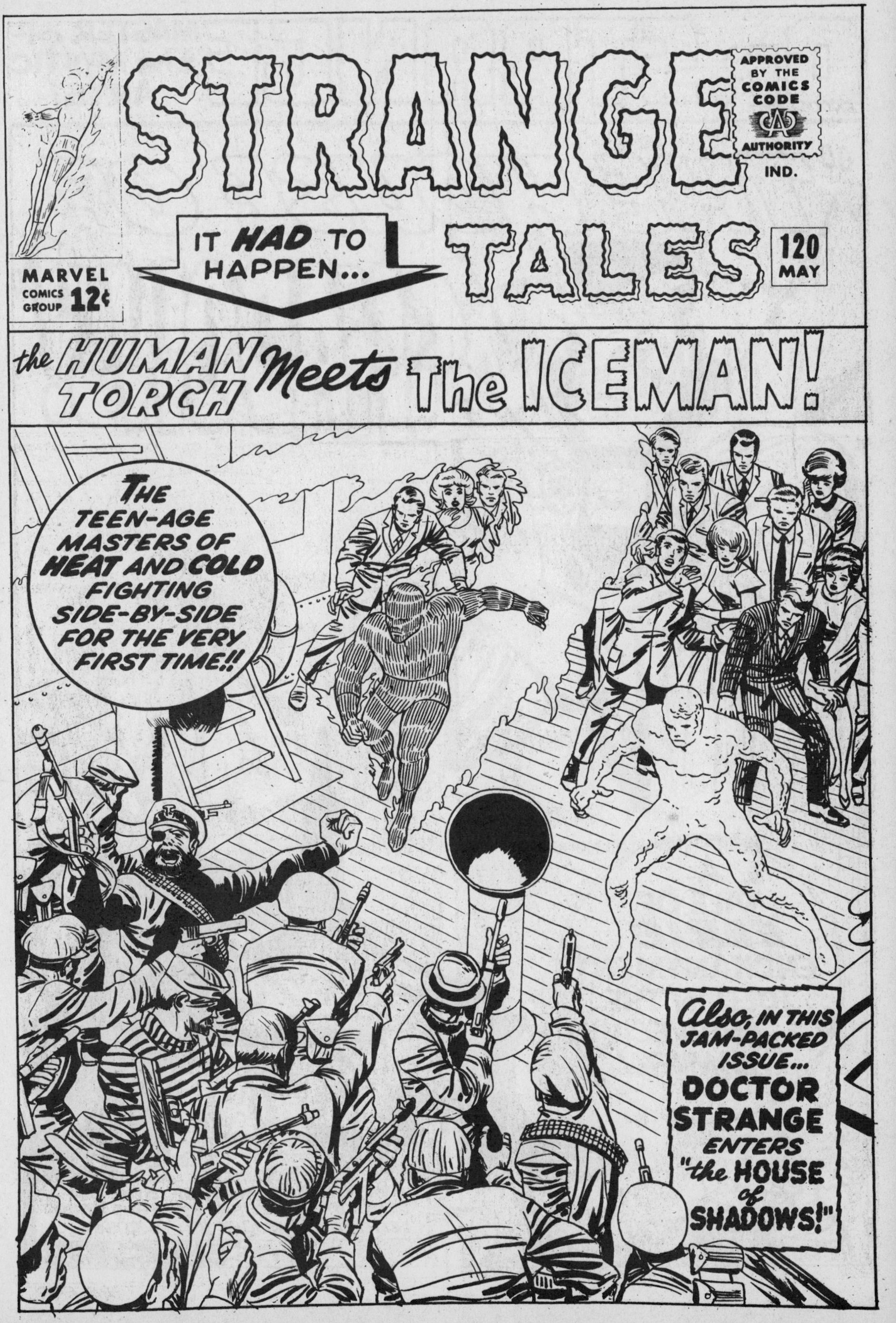
STRANGE TALES
APPROVED BY THE COMICS CODE AUTHORITY
IND.
IT HAD TO HAPPEN...
120 MAY
MARVEL COMICS GROUP 12¢
the HUMAN TORCH Meets The ICEMAN!
THE TEEN-AGE MASTERS OF HEAT AND COLD FIGHTING SIDE-BY-SIDE FOR THE VERY FIRST TIME!!
Also, IN THIS JAM-PACKED ISSUE... DOCTOR STRANGE ENTERS "the HOUSE of SHADOWS!"

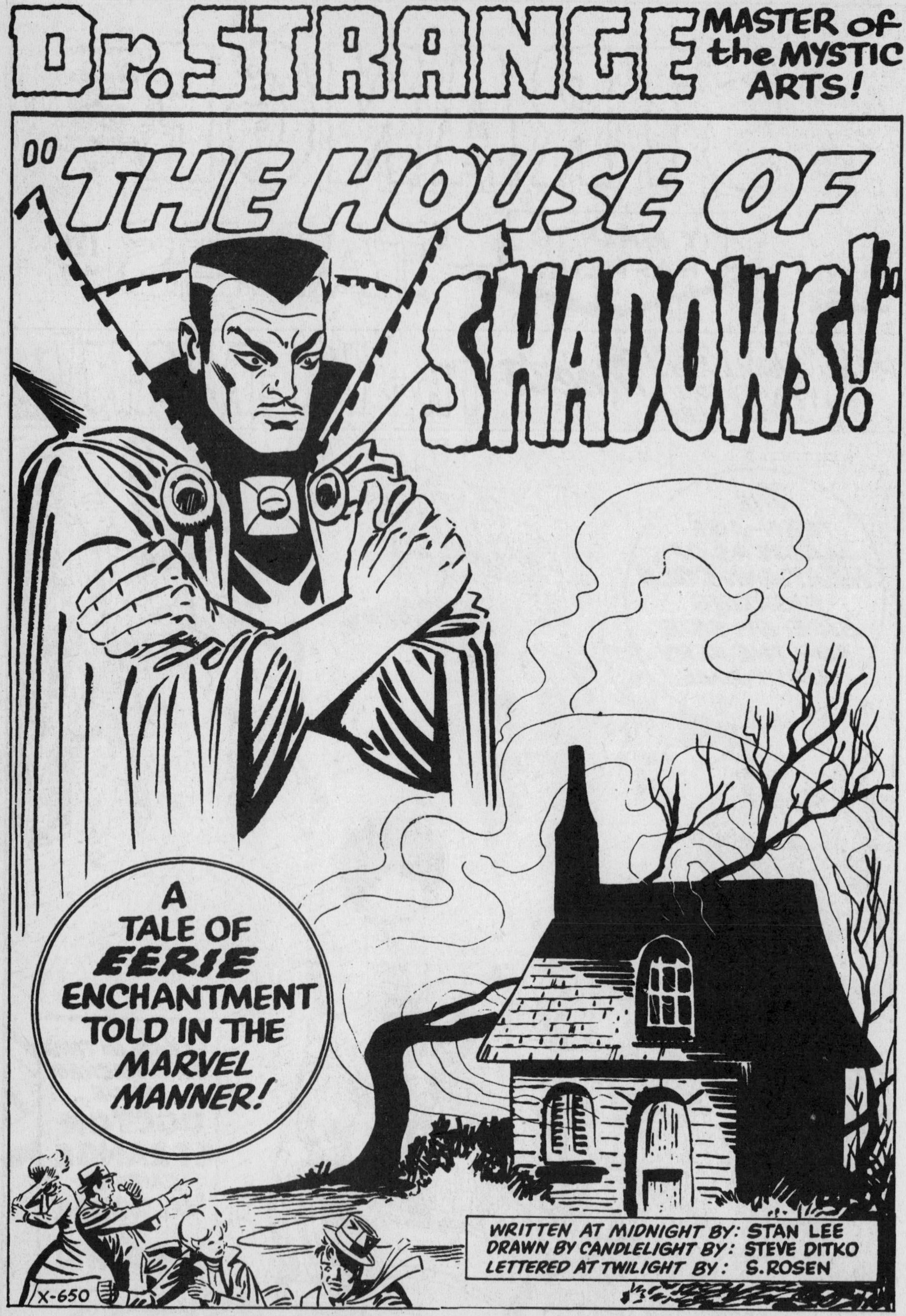
Dr. STRANGE
MASTER of the MYSTIC ARTS!
"THE HOUSE OF SHADOWS!"
A TALE OF EERIE ENCHANTMENT TOLD IN THE MARVEL MANNER!
WRITTEN AT MIDNIGHT BY: STAN LEE
DRAWN BY CANDLELIGHT BY: STEVE DITKO
LETTERED AT TWILIGHT BY: S. ROSEN
X-650

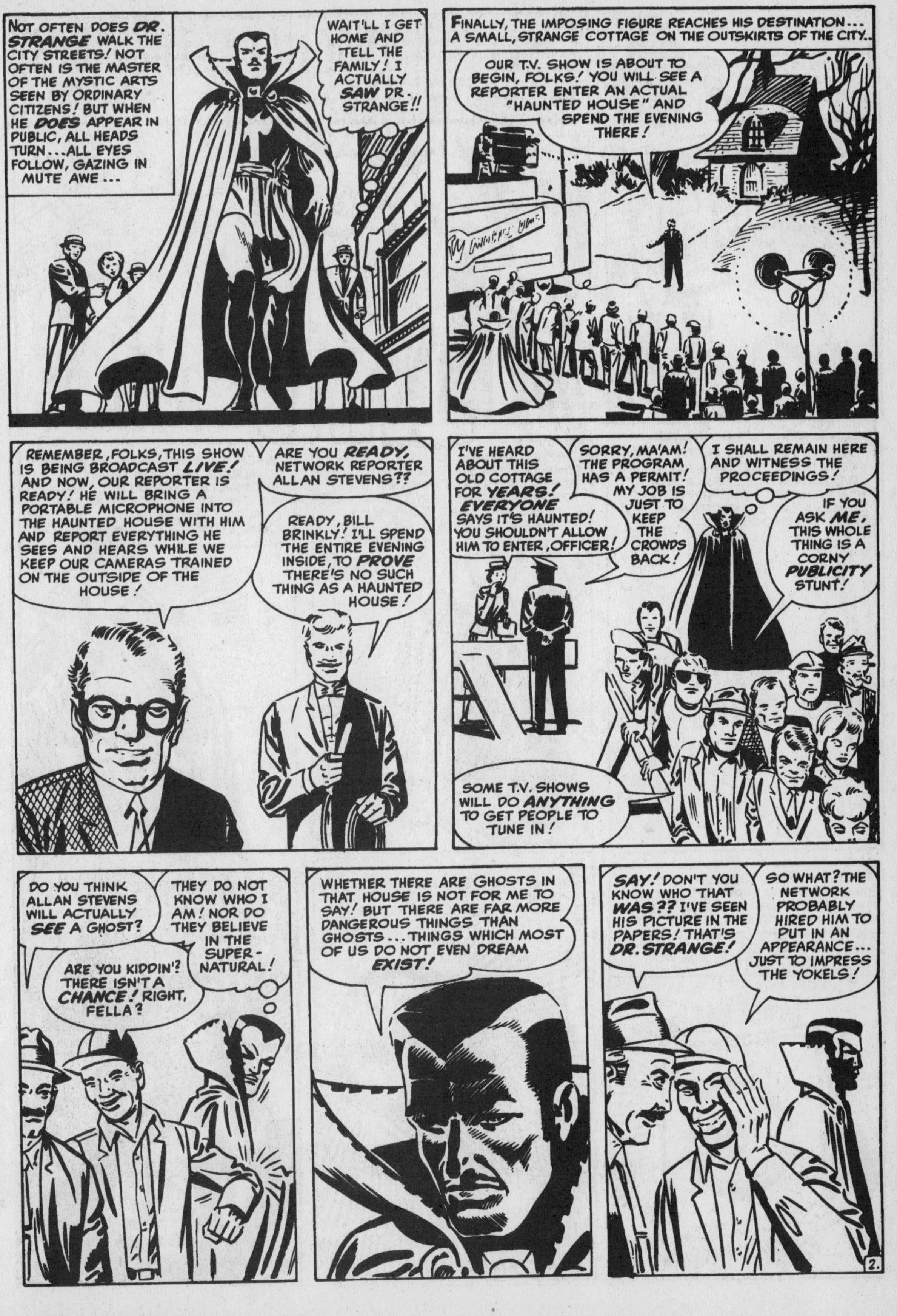

NOT OFTEN DOES DR. STRANGE WALK THE CITY STREETS! NOT OFTEN IS THE MASTER OF THE MYSTIC ARTS SEEN BY ORDINARY CITIZENS! BUT WHEN HE DOES APPEAR IN PUBLIC, ALL HEADS TURN... ALL EYES FOLLOW, GAZING IN MUTE AWE...
WAIT'LL I GET HOME AND TELL THE FAMILY! I ACTUALLY SAW DR. STRANGE!!
FINALLY, THE IMPOSING FIGURE REACHES HIS DESTINATION... A SMALL, STRANGE COTTAGE ON THE OUTSKIRTS OF THE CITY...
OUR T.V. SHOW IS ABOUT TO BEGIN, FOLKS! YOU WILL SEE A REPORTER ENTER AN ACTUAL "HAUNTED HOUSE" AND SPEND THE EVENING THERE!
REMEMBER, FOLKS, THIS SHOW IS BEING BROADCAST LIVE! AND NOW, OUR REPORTER IS READY! HE WILL BRING A PORTABLE MICROPHONE INTO THE HAUNTED HOUSE WITH HIM AND REPORT EVERYTHING HE SEES AND HEARS WHILE WE KEEP OUR CAMERAS TRAINED ON THE OUTSIDE OF THE HOUSE!
ARE YOU READY, NETWORK REPORTER ALLAN STEVENS??
READY, BILL BRINKLY! I'LL SPEND THE ENTIRE EVENING INSIDE, TO PROVE THERE'S NO SUCH THING AS A HAUNTED HOUSE!
I'VE HEARD ABOUT THIS OLD COTTAGE FOR YEARS! EVERYONE SAYS IT'S HAUNTED! YOU SHOULDN'T ALLOW HIM TO ENTER, OFFICER!
SORRY, MA'AM! THE PROGRAM HAS A PERMIT! MY JOB IS JUST TO KEEP THE CROWDS BACK!
I SHALL REMAIN HERE AND WITNESS THE PROCEEDINGS!
IF YOU ASK ME, THIS WHOLE THING IS A CORNY PUBLICITY STUNT!
SOME T.V. SHOWS WILL DO ANYTHING TO GET PEOPLE TO TUNE IN!
DO YOU THINK ALLAN STEVENS WILL ACTUALLY SEE A GHOST?
ARE YOU KIDDIN'? THERE ISN'T A CHANCE! RIGHT, FELLA?
THEY DO NOT KNOW WHO I AM! NOR DO THEY BELIEVE IN THE SUPER-NATURAL!
WHETHER THERE ARE GHOSTS IN THAT HOUSE IS NOT FOR ME TO SAY! BUT THERE ARE FAR MORE DANGEROUS THINGS THAN GHOSTS... THINGS WHICH MOST OF US DO NOT EVEN DREAM EXIST!
SAY! DON'T YOU KNOW WHO THAT WAS?? I'VE SEEN HIS PICTURE IN THE PAPERS! THAT'S DR. STRANGE!
SO WHAT? THE NETWORK PROBABLY HIRED HIM TO PUT IN AN APPEARANCE... JUST TO IMPRESS THE YOKELS!
2.

THERE HE *GOES*, FOLKS! OUR FEARLESS, INTREPID REPORTER, ALLAN STEVENS, IS ABOUT TO ENTER THE HAUNTED HOUSE!

AND AT THAT MOMENT, HIDDEN IN THE SHADOWS, DR. STRANGE LEAVES HIS MATERIAL SELF STANDING NEAR A TREE, AS...

IN MY UNPHYSICAL ECTOPLASMIC FORM, I'LL BE ABLE TO ENTER THE HOUSE *WITH* HIM, UNSEEN BY ANY HUMAN EYES!

SOMETHING IS *AMISS* HERE! I CANNOT ENTER... EVEN THOUGH I AM NOT IN A SOLID FORM!

TRY AS I MAY, I CANNOT PENETRATE THE INVISIBLE BARRIER WHICH SURROUNDS THIS HOUSE! IT IS HOPELESS! I MUST TRY *ANOTHER* METHOD!

I SHALL RETURN TO MY PHYSICAL SELF! IT IS MOST FORTUNATE THAT I DECIDED TO OBSERVE THIS EVENT! I AM CERTAIN NOW THAT *SUPER-NATURAL FORCES* ARE TRULY INVOLVED!

WHEN ALL ELSE FAILS, MY MOST POWERFUL WEAPON IS MY ENCHANTED *AMULET!* AND SO I MUST CALL ON IT AGAIN! I MUST CONCENTRATE... CONCENTRATE...

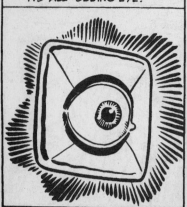

AS THE POTENT THOUGHT WAVES EMITTED BY DR. STRANGE STRIKE THE AMULET AT HIS COLLAR, THE ENCHANTED OBJECT SEEMS TO GLOW WITH AN UNEARTHLY LIGHT AS IT OPENS WIDE, REVEALING ITS ALL-SEEING EYE!

SLOWLY, THE "EYE," WHICH IS ACTUALLY A FOCAL POINT FOR HIS MYSTIC POWER, SEEMS TO LEAVE THE AMULET AND SILENTLY RISE...

...UNTIL IT COMES TO REST ON THE BROW OF THE MASTER OF THE MYSTIC ARTS!!

AND NOW I AM *READY* ONCE AGAIN!

3.

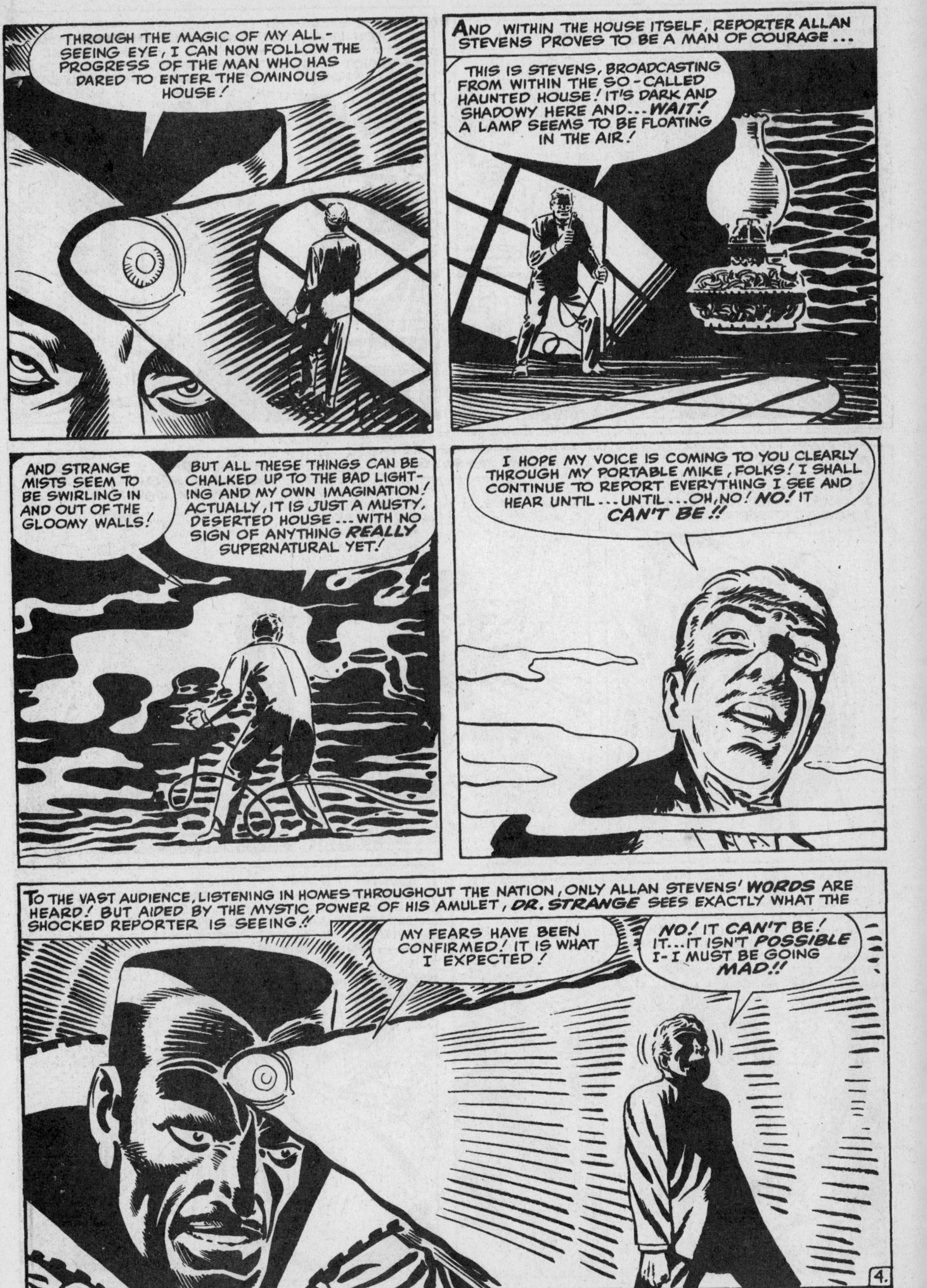
THROUGH THE MAGIC OF MY ALL-SEEING EYE, I CAN NOW FOLLOW THE PROGRESS OF THE MAN WHO HAS DARED TO ENTER THE OMINOUS HOUSE!
AND WITHIN THE HOUSE ITSELF, REPORTER ALLAN STEVENS PROVES TO BE A MAN OF COURAGE...
THIS IS STEVENS, BROADCASTING FROM WITHIN THE SO-CALLED HAUNTED HOUSE! IT'S DARK AND SHADOWY HERE AND...WAIT! A LAMP SEEMS TO BE FLOATING IN THE AIR!
AND STRANGE MISTS SEEM TO BE SWIRLING IN AND OUT OF THE GLOOMY WALLS!
BUT ALL THESE THINGS CAN BE CHALKED UP TO THE BAD LIGHTING AND MY OWN IMAGINATION! ACTUALLY, IT IS JUST A MUSTY, DESERTED HOUSE...WITH NO SIGN OF ANYTHING REALLY SUPERNATURAL YET!
I HOPE MY VOICE IS COMING TO YOU CLEARLY THROUGH MY PORTABLE MIKE, FOLKS! I SHALL CONTINUE TO REPORT EVERYTHING I SEE AND HEAR UNTIL...UNTIL...OH, NO! NO! IT CAN'T BE!!
TO THE VAST AUDIENCE, LISTENING IN HOMES THROUGHOUT THE NATION, ONLY ALLAN STEVENS' WORDS ARE HEARD! BUT AIDED BY THE MYSTIC POWER OF HIS AMULET, DR. STRANGE SEES EXACTLY WHAT THE SHOCKED REPORTER IS SEEING!!
MY FEARS HAVE BEEN CONFIRMED! IT IS WHAT I EXPECTED!
NO! IT CAN'T BE! IT...IT ISN'T POSSIBLE I-I MUST BE GOING MAD!!
4.

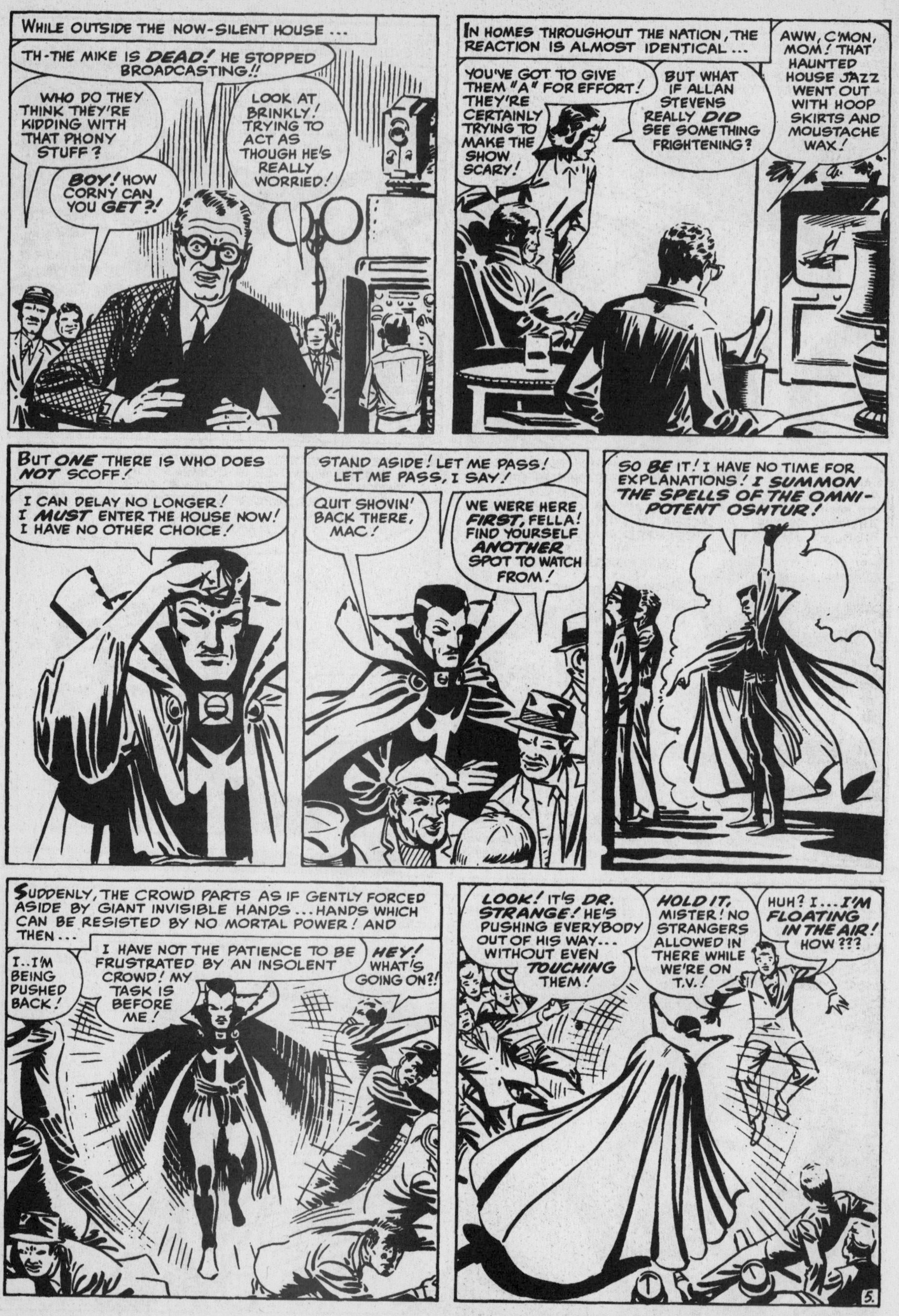

WHILE OUTSIDE THE NOW-SILENT HOUSE ...
TH-THE MIKE IS DEAD! HE STOPPED BROADCASTING!!
WHO DO THEY THINK THEY'RE KIDDING WITH THAT PHONY STUFF?
BOY! HOW CORNY CAN YOU GET?!
LOOK AT BRINKLY! TRYING TO ACT AS THOUGH HE'S REALLY WORRIED!
IN HOMES THROUGHOUT THE NATION, THE REACTION IS ALMOST IDENTICAL ...
YOU'VE GOT TO GIVE THEM "A" FOR EFFORT! THEY'RE CERTAINLY TRYING TO MAKE THE SHOW SCARY!
BUT WHAT IF ALLAN STEVENS REALLY DID SEE SOMETHING FRIGHTENING?
AWW, C'MON, MOM! THAT HAUNTED HOUSE JAZZ WENT OUT WITH HOOP SKIRTS AND MOUSTACHE WAX!
BUT ONE THERE IS WHO DOES NOT SCOFF!
I CAN DELAY NO LONGER! I MUST ENTER THE HOUSE NOW! I HAVE NO OTHER CHOICE!
STAND ASIDE! LET ME PASS! LET ME PASS, I SAY!
QUIT SHOVIN' BACK THERE, MAC!
WE WERE HERE FIRST, FELLA! FIND YOURSELF ANOTHER SPOT TO WATCH FROM!
SO BE IT! I HAVE NO TIME FOR EXPLANATIONS! I SUMMON THE SPELLS OF THE OMNI-POTENT OSHTUR!
SUDDENLY, THE CROWD PARTS AS IF GENTLY FORCED ASIDE BY GIANT INVISIBLE HANDS ... HANDS WHICH CAN BE RESISTED BY NO MORTAL POWER! AND THEN ...
I..I'M BEING PUSHED BACK!
I HAVE NOT THE PATIENCE TO BE FRUSTRATED BY AN INSOLENT CROWD! MY TASK IS BEFORE ME!
HEY! WHAT'S GOING ON?!
LOOK! IT'S DR. STRANGE! HE'S PUSHING EVERYBODY OUT OF HIS WAY... WITHOUT EVEN TOUCHING THEM!
HOLD IT, MISTER! NO STRANGERS ALLOWED IN THERE WHILE WE'RE ON T.V.!
HUH? I... I'M FLOATING IN THE AIR! HOW???
5.

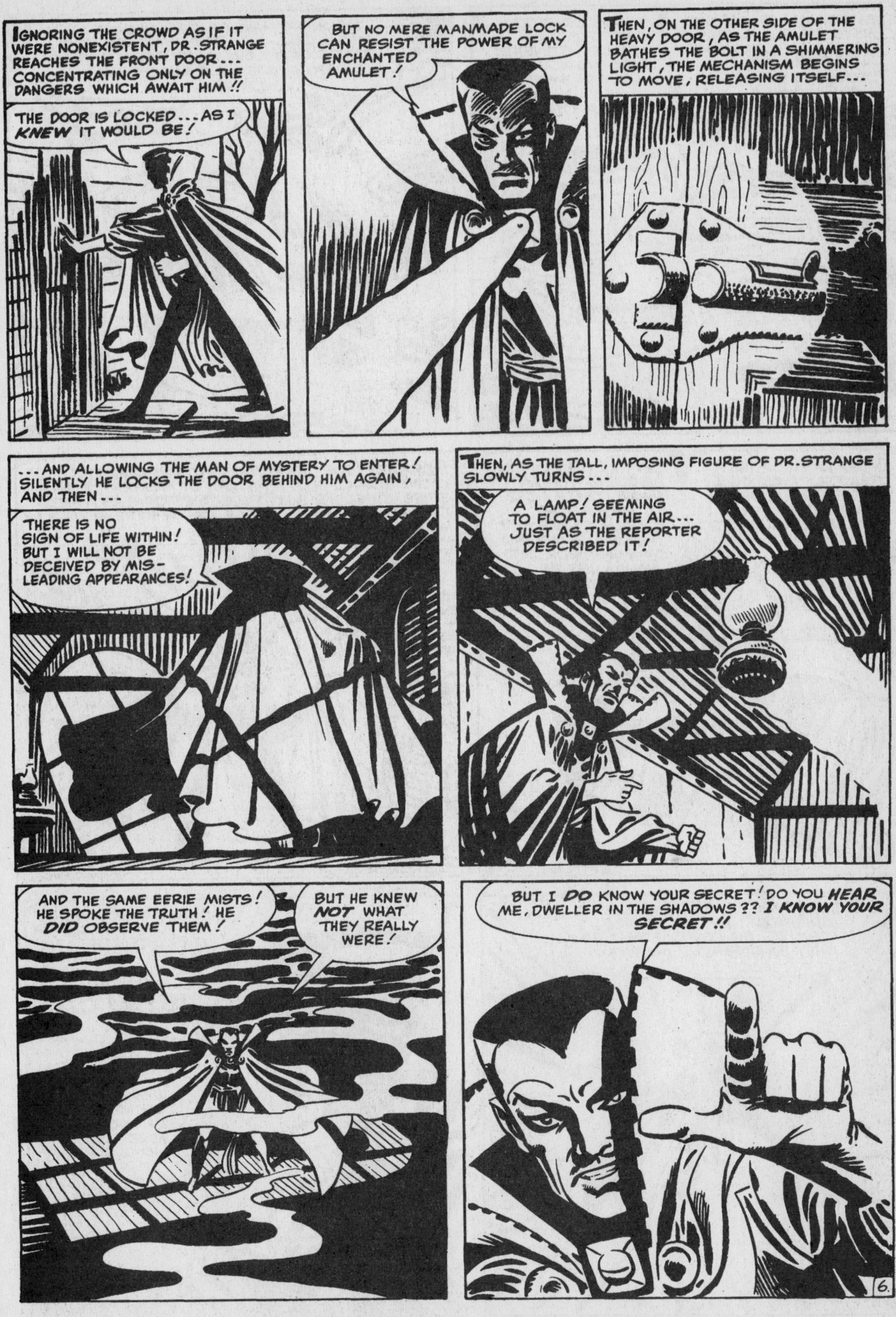
IGNORING THE CROWD AS IF IT WERE NONEXISTENT, DR. STRANGE REACHES THE FRONT DOOR... CONCENTRATING ONLY ON THE DANGERS WHICH AWAIT HIM!!
THE DOOR IS LOCKED... AS I KNEW IT WOULD BE!
BUT NO MERE MANMADE LOCK CAN RESIST THE POWER OF MY ENCHANTED AMULET!
THEN, ON THE OTHER SIDE OF THE HEAVY DOOR, AS THE AMULET BATHES THE BOLT IN A SHIMMERING LIGHT, THE MECHANISM BEGINS TO MOVE, RELEASING ITSELF...
...AND ALLOWING THE MAN OF MYSTERY TO ENTER! SILENTLY HE LOCKS THE DOOR BEHIND HIM AGAIN, AND THEN...
THERE IS NO SIGN OF LIFE WITHIN! BUT I WILL NOT BE DECEIVED BY MIS-LEADING APPEARANCES!
THEN, AS THE TALL, IMPOSING FIGURE OF DR. STRANGE SLOWLY TURNS...
A LAMP! SEEMING TO FLOAT IN THE AIR... JUST AS THE REPORTER DESCRIBED IT!
AND THE SAME EERIE MISTS! HE SPOKE THE TRUTH! HE DID OBSERVE THEM!
BUT HE KNEW NOT WHAT THEY REALLY WERE!
BUT I DO KNOW YOUR SECRET! DO YOU HEAR ME, DWELLER IN THE SHADOWS?? I KNOW YOUR SECRET!!
6.

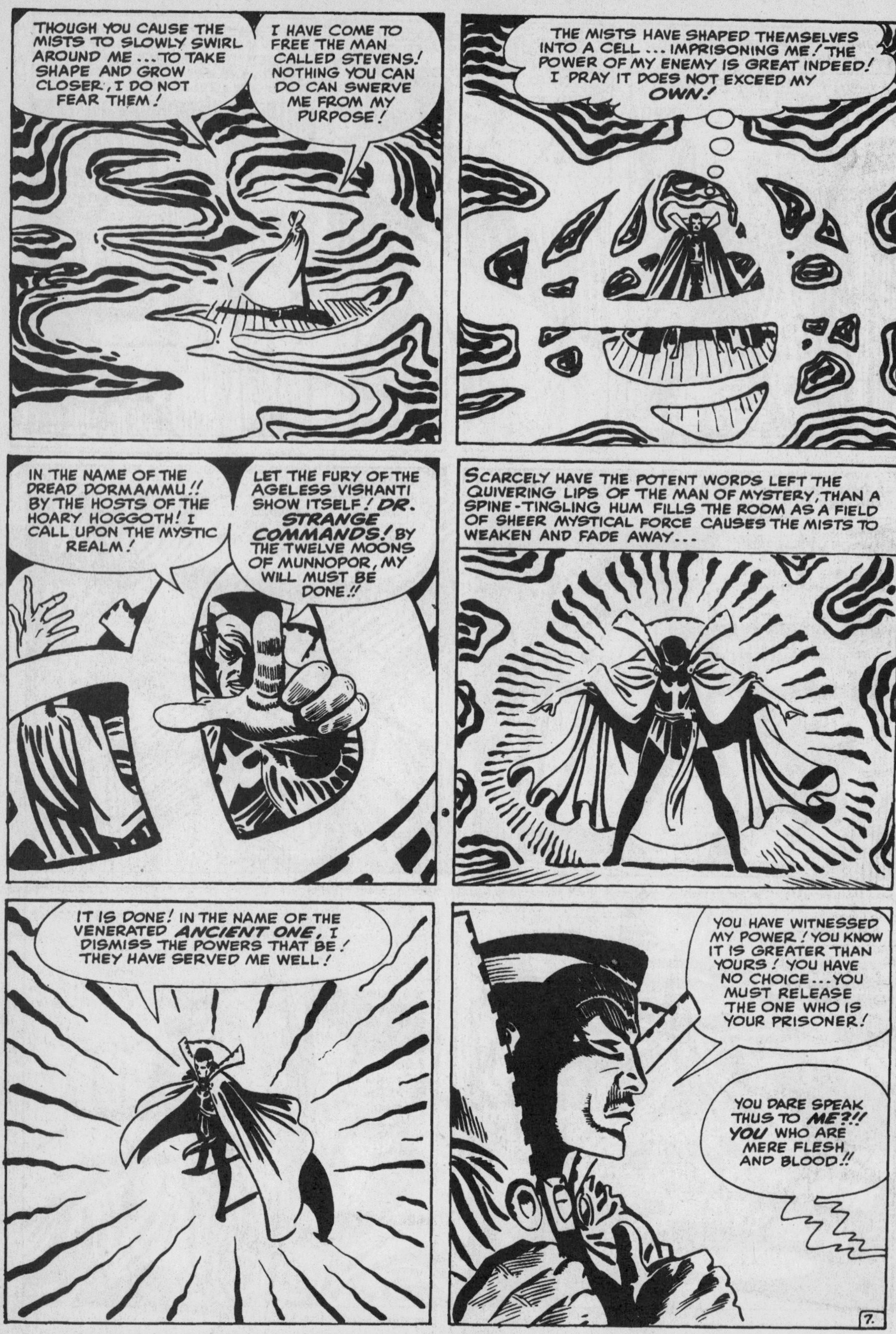
THOUGH YOU CAUSE THE MISTS TO SLOWLY SWIRL AROUND ME ... TO TAKE SHAPE AND GROW CLOSER, I DO NOT FEAR THEM!
I HAVE COME TO FREE THE MAN CALLED STEVENS! NOTHING YOU CAN DO CAN SWERVE ME FROM MY PURPOSE!
THE MISTS HAVE SHAPED THEMSELVES INTO A CELL ... IMPRISONING ME! THE POWER OF MY ENEMY IS GREAT INDEED! I PRAY IT DOES NOT EXCEED MY OWN!
IN THE NAME OF THE DREAD DORMAMMU!! BY THE HOSTS OF THE HOARY HOGGOTH! I CALL UPON THE MYSTIC REALM!
LET THE FURY OF THE AGELESS VISHANTI SHOW ITSELF! DR. STRANGE COMMANDS! BY THE TWELVE MOONS OF MUNNOPOR, MY WILL MUST BE DONE!!
SCARCELY HAVE THE POTENT WORDS LEFT THE QUIVERING LIPS OF THE MAN OF MYSTERY, THAN A SPINE-TINGLING HUM FILLS THE ROOM AS A FIELD OF SHEER MYSTICAL FORCE CAUSES THE MISTS TO WEAKEN AND FADE AWAY...
IT IS DONE! IN THE NAME OF THE VENERATED ANCIENT ONE, I DISMISS THE POWERS THAT BE! THEY HAVE SERVED ME WELL!
YOU HAVE WITNESSED MY POWER! YOU KNOW IT IS GREATER THAN YOURS! YOU HAVE NO CHOICE...YOU MUST RELEASE THE ONE WHO IS YOUR PRISONER!
YOU DARE SPEAK THUS TO ME?!! YOU WHO ARE MERE FLESH AND BLOOD!!
7.

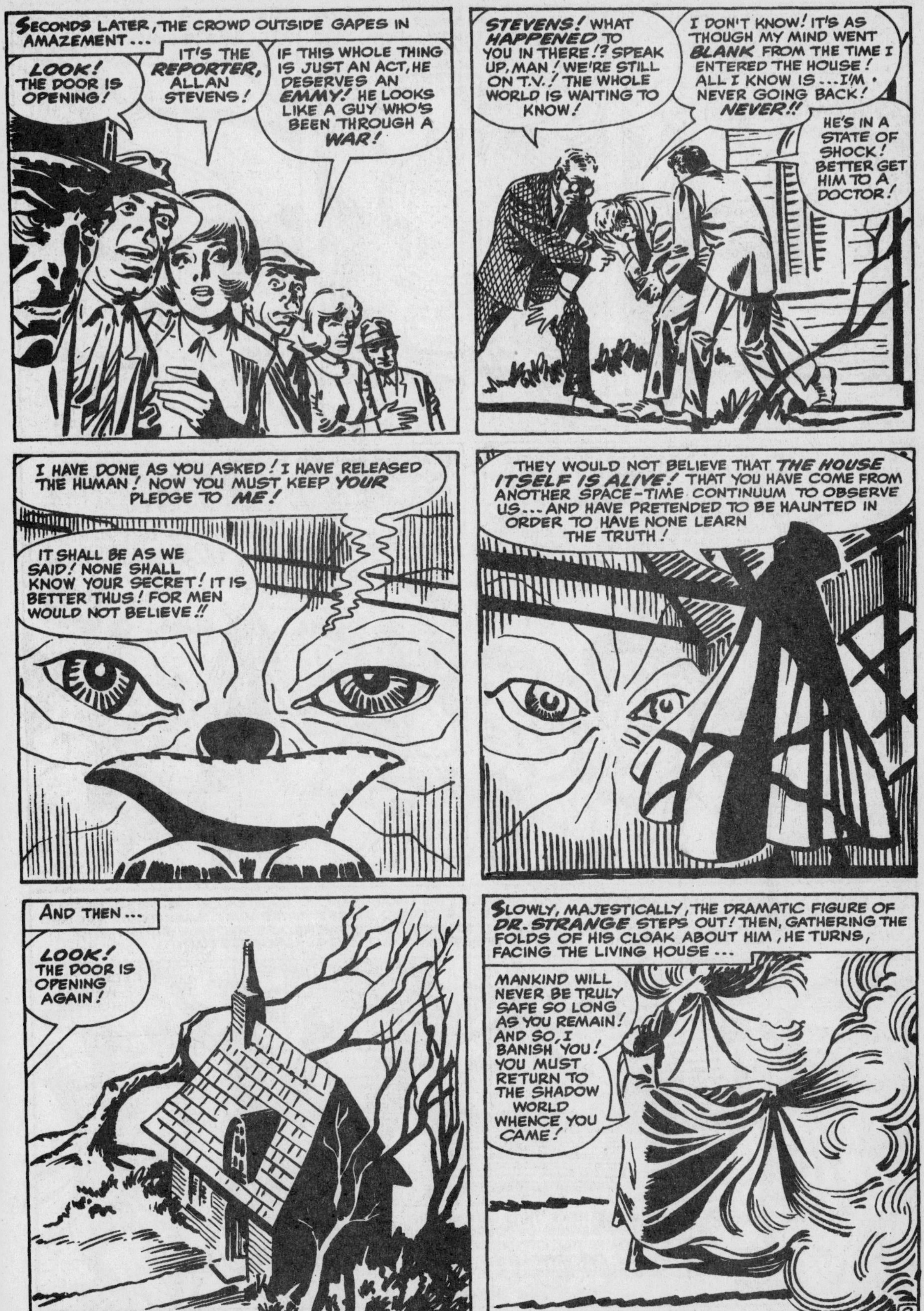
SECONDS LATER, THE CROWD OUTSIDE GAPES IN AMAZEMENT...
LOOK! THE DOOR IS OPENING!
IT'S THE REPORTER, ALLAN STEVENS!
IF THIS WHOLE THING IS JUST AN ACT, HE DESERVES AN EMMY! HE LOOKS LIKE A GUY WHO'S BEEN THROUGH A WAR!
STEVENS! WHAT HAPPENED TO YOU IN THERE!? SPEAK UP, MAN! WE'RE STILL ON T.V.! THE WHOLE WORLD IS WAITING TO KNOW!
I DON'T KNOW! IT'S AS THOUGH MY MIND WENT BLANK FROM THE TIME I ENTERED THE HOUSE! ALL I KNOW IS...I'M NEVER GOING BACK! NEVER!!
HE'S IN A STATE OF SHOCK! BETTER GET HIM TO A DOCTOR!
I HAVE DONE AS YOU ASKED! I HAVE RELEASED THE HUMAN! NOW YOU MUST KEEP YOUR PLEDGE TO ME!
IT SHALL BE AS WE SAID! NONE SHALL KNOW YOUR SECRET! IT IS BETTER THUS! FOR MEN WOULD NOT BELIEVE!!
THEY WOULD NOT BELIEVE THAT THE HOUSE ITSELF IS ALIVE! THAT YOU HAVE COME FROM ANOTHER SPACE-TIME CONTINUUM TO OBSERVE US...AND HAVE PRETENDED TO BE HAUNTED IN ORDER TO HAVE NONE LEARN THE TRUTH!
AND THEN...
LOOK! THE DOOR IS OPENING AGAIN!
SLOWLY, MAJESTICALLY, THE DRAMATIC FIGURE OF DR. STRANGE STEPS OUT! THEN, GATHERING THE FOLDS OF HIS CLOAK ABOUT HIM, HE TURNS, FACING THE LIVING HOUSE...
MANKIND WILL NEVER BE TRULY SAFE SO LONG AS YOU REMAIN! AND SO, I BANISH YOU! YOU MUST RETURN TO THE SHADOW WORLD WHENCE YOU CAME!
8

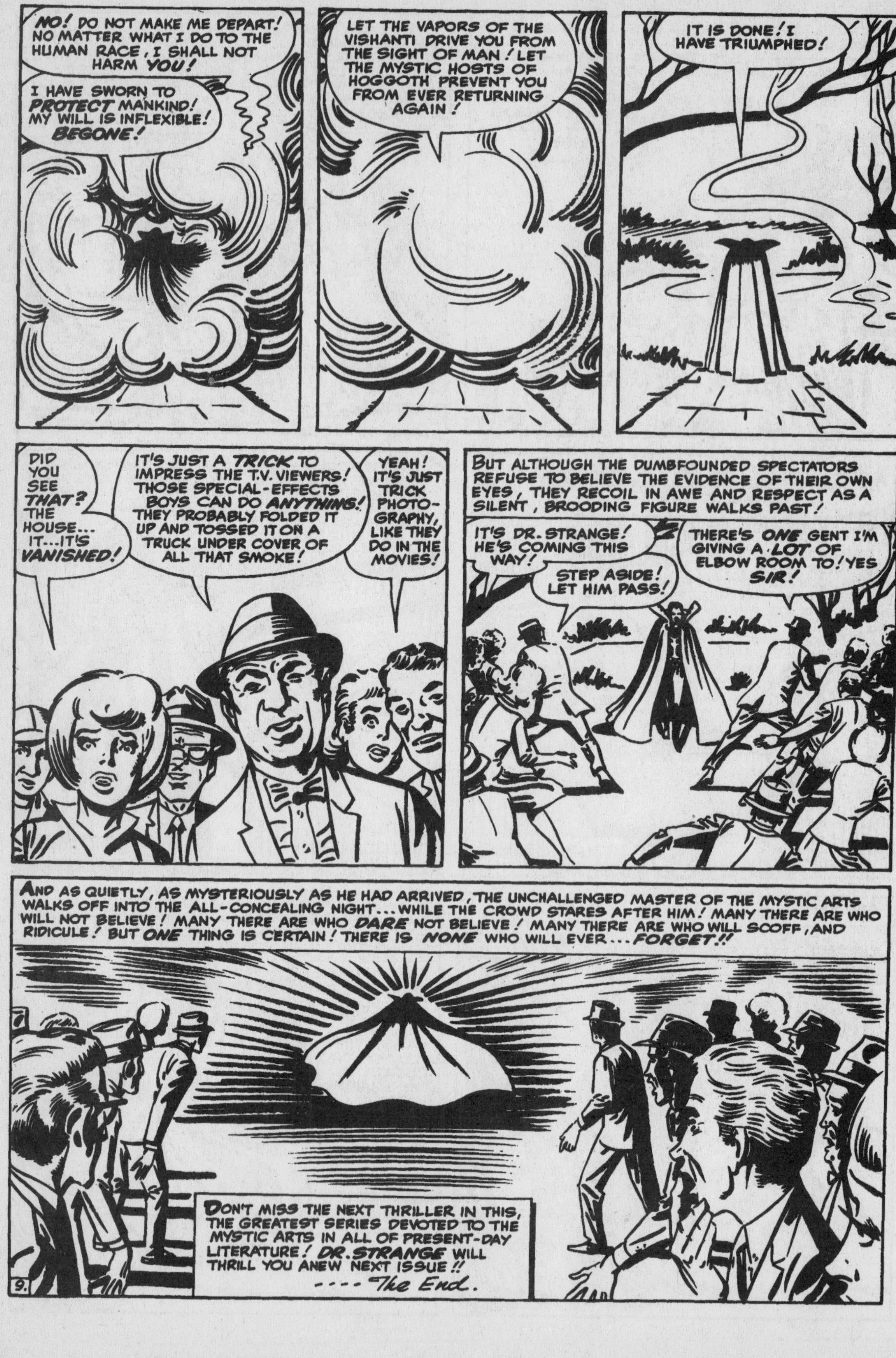
NO! DO NOT MAKE ME DEPART! NO MATTER WHAT I DO TO THE HUMAN RACE, I SHALL NOT HARM YOU!
I HAVE SWORN TO PROTECT MANKIND! MY WILL IS INFLEXIBLE! BEGONE!
LET THE VAPORS OF THE VISHANTI DRIVE YOU FROM THE SIGHT OF MAN! LET THE MYSTIC HOSTS OF HOGGOTH PREVENT YOU FROM EVER RETURNING AGAIN!
IT IS DONE! I HAVE TRIUMPHED!
DID YOU SEE THAT? THE HOUSE... IT...IT'S VANISHED!
IT'S JUST A TRICK TO IMPRESS THE T.V. VIEWERS! THOSE SPECIAL-EFFECTS BOYS CAN DO ANYTHING! THEY PROBABLY FOLDED IT UP AND TOSSED IT ON A TRUCK UNDER COVER OF ALL THAT SMOKE!
YEAH! IT'S JUST TRICK PHOTOGRAPHY, LIKE THEY DO IN THE MOVIES!
BUT ALTHOUGH THE DUMBFOUNDED SPECTATORS REFUSE TO BELIEVE THE EVIDENCE OF THEIR OWN EYES, THEY RECOIL IN AWE AND RESPECT AS A SILENT, BROODING FIGURE WALKS PAST!
IT'S DR. STRANGE! HE'S COMING THIS WAY!
STEP ASIDE! LET HIM PASS!
THERE'S ONE GENT I'M GIVING A LOT OF ELBOW ROOM TO! YES SIR!
AND AS QUIETLY, AS MYSTERIOUSLY AS HE HAD ARRIVED, THE UNCHALLENGED MASTER OF THE MYSTIC ARTS WALKS OFF INTO THE ALL-CONCEALING NIGHT... WHILE THE CROWD STARES AFTER HIM! MANY THERE ARE WHO WILL NOT BELIEVE! MANY THERE ARE WHO DARE NOT BELIEVE! MANY THERE ARE WHO WILL SCOFF, AND RIDICULE! BUT ONE THING IS CERTAIN! THERE IS NONE WHO WILL EVER... FORGET!!
DON'T MISS THE NEXT THRILLER IN THIS, THE GREATEST SERIES DEVOTED TO THE MYSTIC ARTS IN ALL OF PRESENT-DAY LITERATURE! DR. STRANGE WILL THRILL YOU ANEW NEXT ISSUE!!
---- The End.
9.

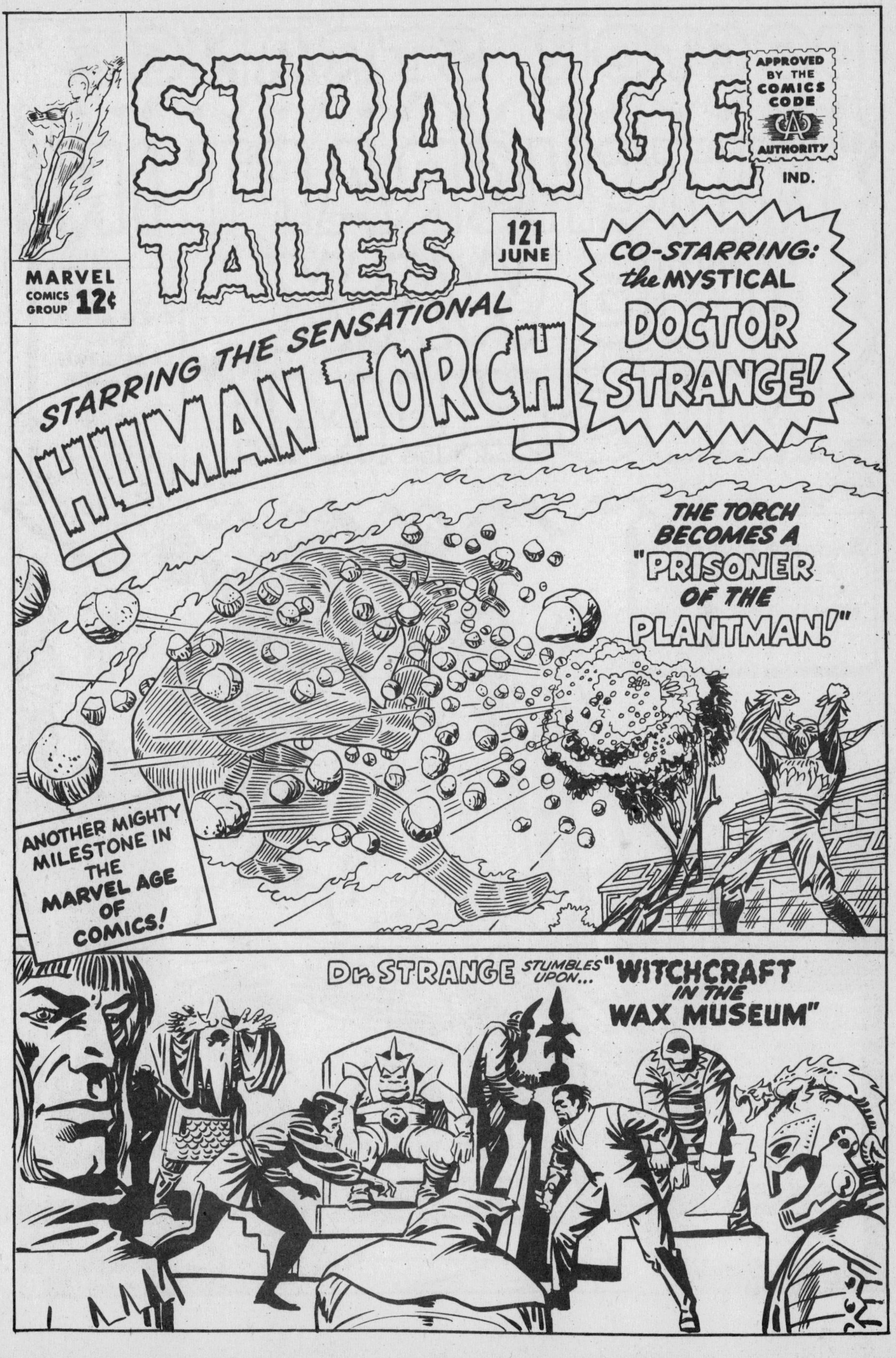

STRANGE TALES
APPROVED BY THE COMICS CODE AUTHORITY
IND.
121
JUNE
MARVEL COMICS GROUP 12¢
STARRING THE SENSATIONAL
HUMAN TORCH
CO-STARRING: the MYSTICAL DOCTOR STRANGE!
THE TORCH BECOMES A "PRISONER OF THE PLANTMAN!"
ANOTHER MIGHTY MILESTONE IN THE MARVEL AGE OF COMICS!
Dr. STRANGE STUMBLES UPON... "WITCHCRAFT IN THE WAX MUSEUM"

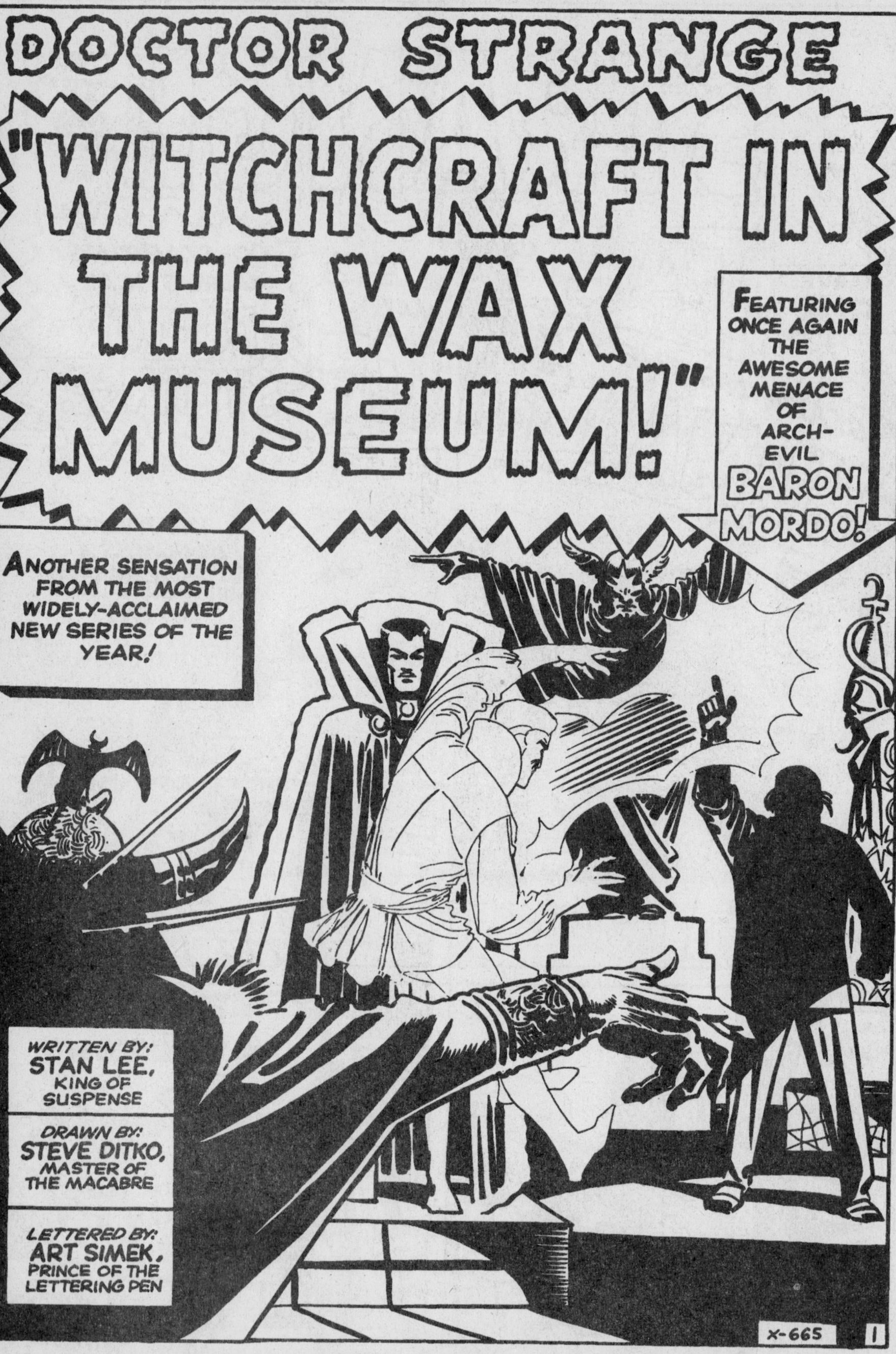
DOCTOR STRANGE
"WITCHCRAFT IN THE WAX MUSEUM!"
FEATURING ONCE AGAIN THE AWESOME MENACE OF ARCH-EVIL BARON MORDO!
ANOTHER SENSATION FROM THE MOST WIDELY-ACCLAIMED NEW SERIES OF THE YEAR!
WRITTEN BY: STAN LEE, KING OF SUSPENSE
DRAWN BY: STEVE DITKO, MASTER OF THE MACABRE
LETTERED BY: ART SIMEK, PRINCE OF THE LETTERING PEN
X-665
1

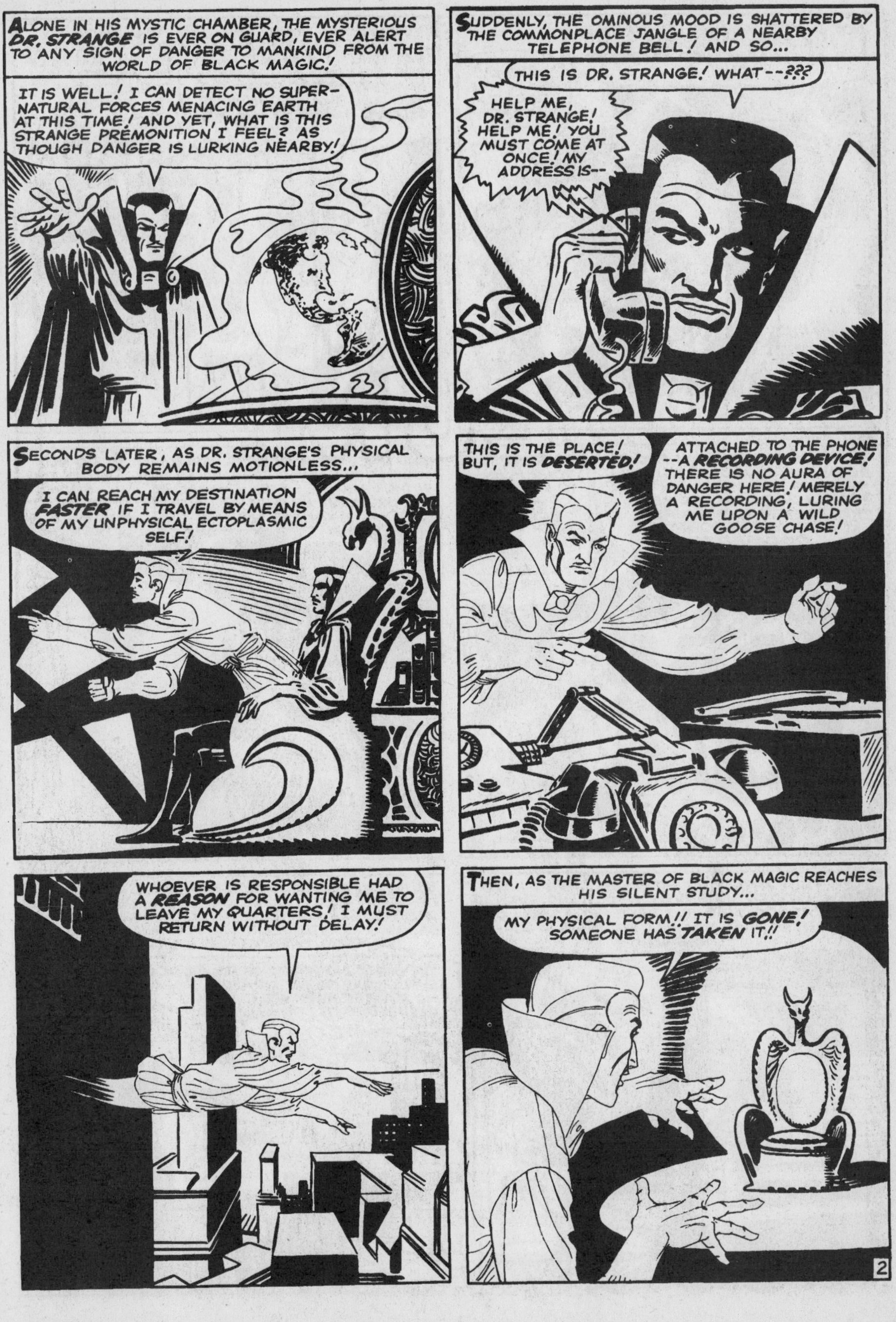
ALONE IN HIS MYSTIC CHAMBER, THE MYSTERIOUS DR. STRANGE IS EVER ON GUARD, EVER ALERT TO ANY SIGN OF DANGER TO MANKIND FROM THE WORLD OF BLACK MAGIC!
IT IS WELL! I CAN DETECT NO SUPER-NATURAL FORCES MENACING EARTH AT THIS TIME! AND YET, WHAT IS THIS STRANGE PREMONITION I FEEL? AS THOUGH DANGER IS LURKING NEARBY!
SUDDENLY, THE OMINOUS MOOD IS SHATTERED BY THE COMMONPLACE JANGLE OF A NEARBY TELEPHONE BELL! AND SO...
THIS IS DR. STRANGE! WHAT--???
HELP ME, DR. STRANGE! HELP ME! YOU MUST COME AT ONCE! MY ADDRESS IS--
SECONDS LATER, AS DR. STRANGE'S PHYSICAL BODY REMAINS MOTIONLESS...
I CAN REACH MY DESTINATION FASTER IF I TRAVEL BY MEANS OF MY UNPHYSICAL ECTOPLASMIC SELF!
THIS IS THE PLACE! BUT, IT IS DESERTED!
ATTACHED TO THE PHONE --A RECORDING DEVICE! THERE IS NO AURA OF DANGER HERE! MERELY A RECORDING, LURING ME UPON A WILD GOOSE CHASE!
WHOEVER IS RESPONSIBLE HAD A REASON FOR WANTING ME TO LEAVE MY QUARTERS! I MUST RETURN WITHOUT DELAY!
THEN, AS THE MASTER OF BLACK MAGIC REACHES HIS SILENT STUDY...
MY PHYSICAL FORM!! IT IS GONE! SOMEONE HAS TAKEN IT!!
2

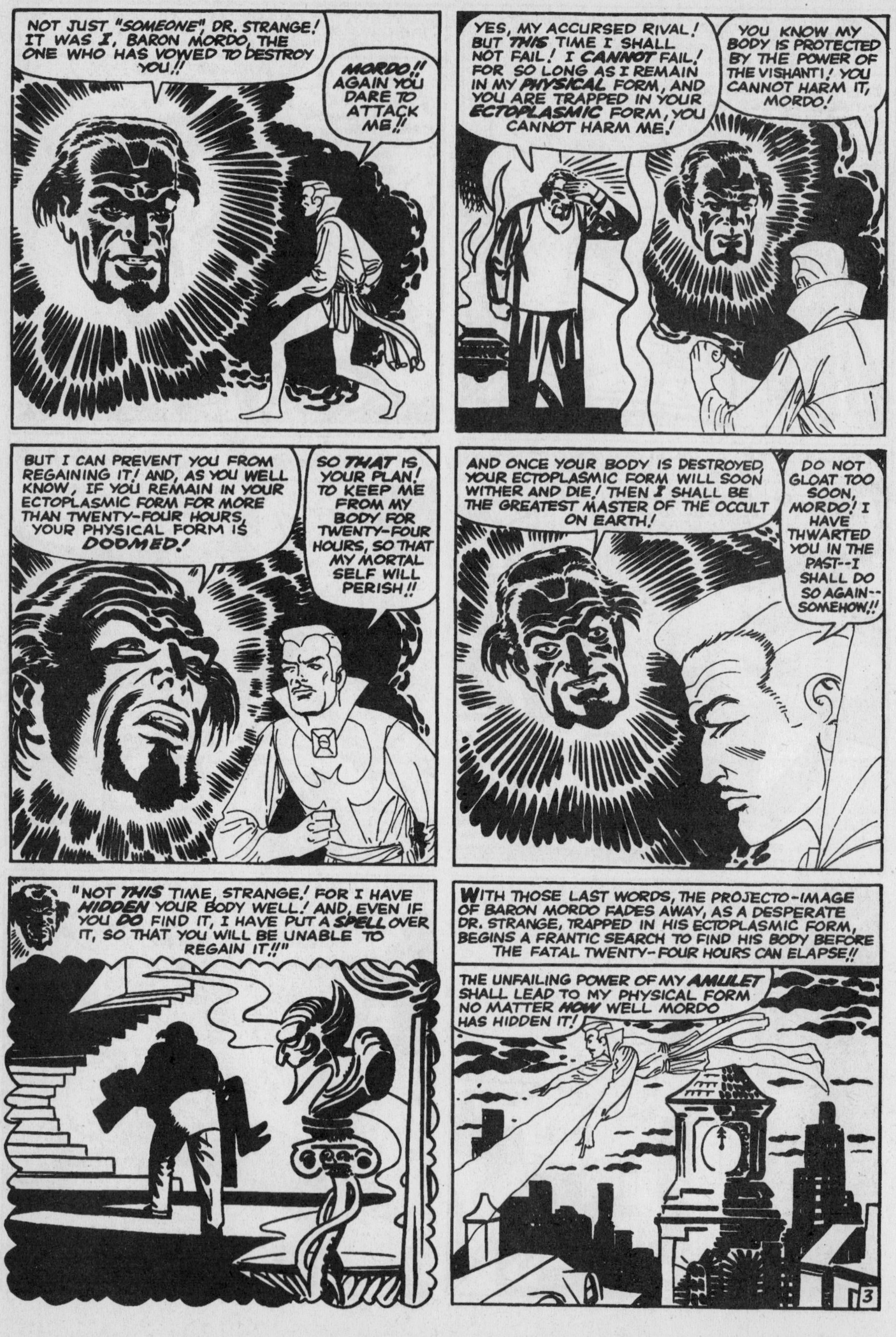
NOT JUST "SOMEONE", DR. STRANGE! IT WAS I, BARON MORDO, THE ONE WHO HAS VOWED TO DESTROY YOU!!
MORDO!! AGAIN YOU DARE TO ATTACK ME!!
YES, MY ACCURSED RIVAL! BUT THIS TIME I SHALL NOT FAIL! I CANNOT FAIL! FOR SO LONG AS I REMAIN IN MY PHYSICAL FORM, AND YOU ARE TRAPPED IN YOUR ECTOPLASMIC FORM, YOU CANNOT HARM ME!
YOU KNOW MY BODY IS PROTECTED BY THE POWER OF THE VISHANTI! YOU CANNOT HARM IT, MORDO!
BUT I CAN PREVENT YOU FROM REGAINING IT! AND, AS YOU WELL KNOW, IF YOU REMAIN IN YOUR ECTOPLASMIC FORM FOR MORE THAN TWENTY-FOUR HOURS, YOUR PHYSICAL FORM IS DOOMED!
SO THAT IS YOUR PLAN! TO KEEP ME FROM MY BODY FOR TWENTY-FOUR HOURS, SO THAT MY MORTAL SELF WILL PERISH!!
AND ONCE YOUR BODY IS DESTROYED, YOUR ECTOPLASMIC FORM WILL SOON WITHER AND DIE! THEN I SHALL BE THE GREATEST MASTER OF THE OCCULT ON EARTH!
DO NOT GLOAT TOO SOON, MORDO! I HAVE THWARTED YOU IN THE PAST--I SHALL DO SO AGAIN--SOMEHOW!!
"NOT THIS TIME, STRANGE! FOR I HAVE HIDDEN YOUR BODY WELL! AND, EVEN IF YOU DO FIND IT, I HAVE PUT A SPELL OVER IT, SO THAT YOU WILL BE UNABLE TO REGAIN IT!!"
WITH THOSE LAST WORDS, THE PROJECTO-IMAGE OF BARON MORDO FADES AWAY, AS A DESPERATE DR. STRANGE, TRAPPED IN HIS ECTOPLASMIC FORM, BEGINS A FRANTIC SEARCH TO FIND HIS BODY BEFORE THE FATAL TWENTY-FOUR HOURS CAN ELAPSE!!
THE UNFAILING POWER OF MY AMULET SHALL LEAD TO MY PHYSICAL FORM NO MATTER HOW WELL MORDO HAS HIDDEN IT!
3

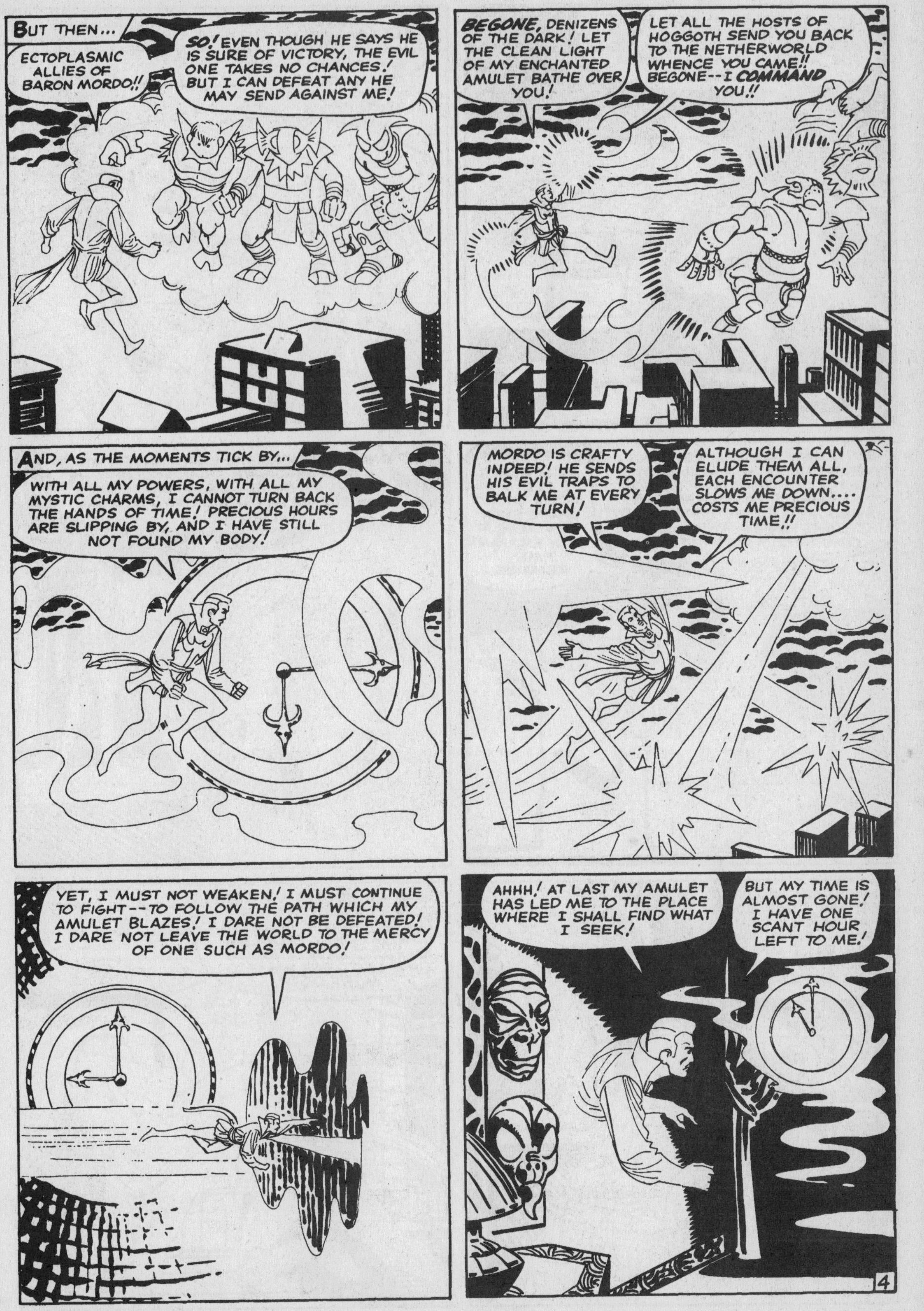
BUT THEN...
ECTOPLASMIC ALLIES OF BARON MORDO!!
SO! EVEN THOUGH HE SAYS HE IS SURE OF VICTORY, THE EVIL ONE TAKES NO CHANCES! BUT I CAN DEFEAT ANY HE MAY SEND AGAINST ME!
BEGONE, DENIZENS OF THE DARK! LET THE CLEAN LIGHT OF MY ENCHANTED AMULET BATHE OVER YOU!
LET ALL THE HOSTS OF HOGGOTH SEND YOU BACK TO THE NETHERWORLD WHENCE YOU CAME!! BEGONE--I COMMAND YOU!!
AND, AS THE MOMENTS TICK BY...
WITH ALL MY POWERS, WITH ALL MY MYSTIC CHARMS, I CANNOT TURN BACK THE HANDS OF TIME! PRECIOUS HOURS ARE SLIPPING BY, AND I HAVE STILL NOT FOUND MY BODY!
MORDO IS CRAFTY INDEED! HE SENDS HIS EVIL TRAPS TO BALK ME AT EVERY TURN!
ALTHOUGH I CAN ELUDE THEM ALL, EACH ENCOUNTER SLOWS ME DOWN.... COSTS ME PRECIOUS TIME!!
YET, I MUST NOT WEAKEN! I MUST CONTINUE TO FIGHT--TO FOLLOW THE PATH WHICH MY AMULET BLAZES! I DARE NOT BE DEFEATED! I DARE NOT LEAVE THE WORLD TO THE MERCY OF ONE SUCH AS MORDO!
AHHH! AT LAST MY AMULET HAS LED ME TO THE PLACE WHERE I SHALL FIND WHAT I SEEK!
BUT MY TIME IS ALMOST GONE! I HAVE ONE SCANT HOUR LEFT TO ME!
4

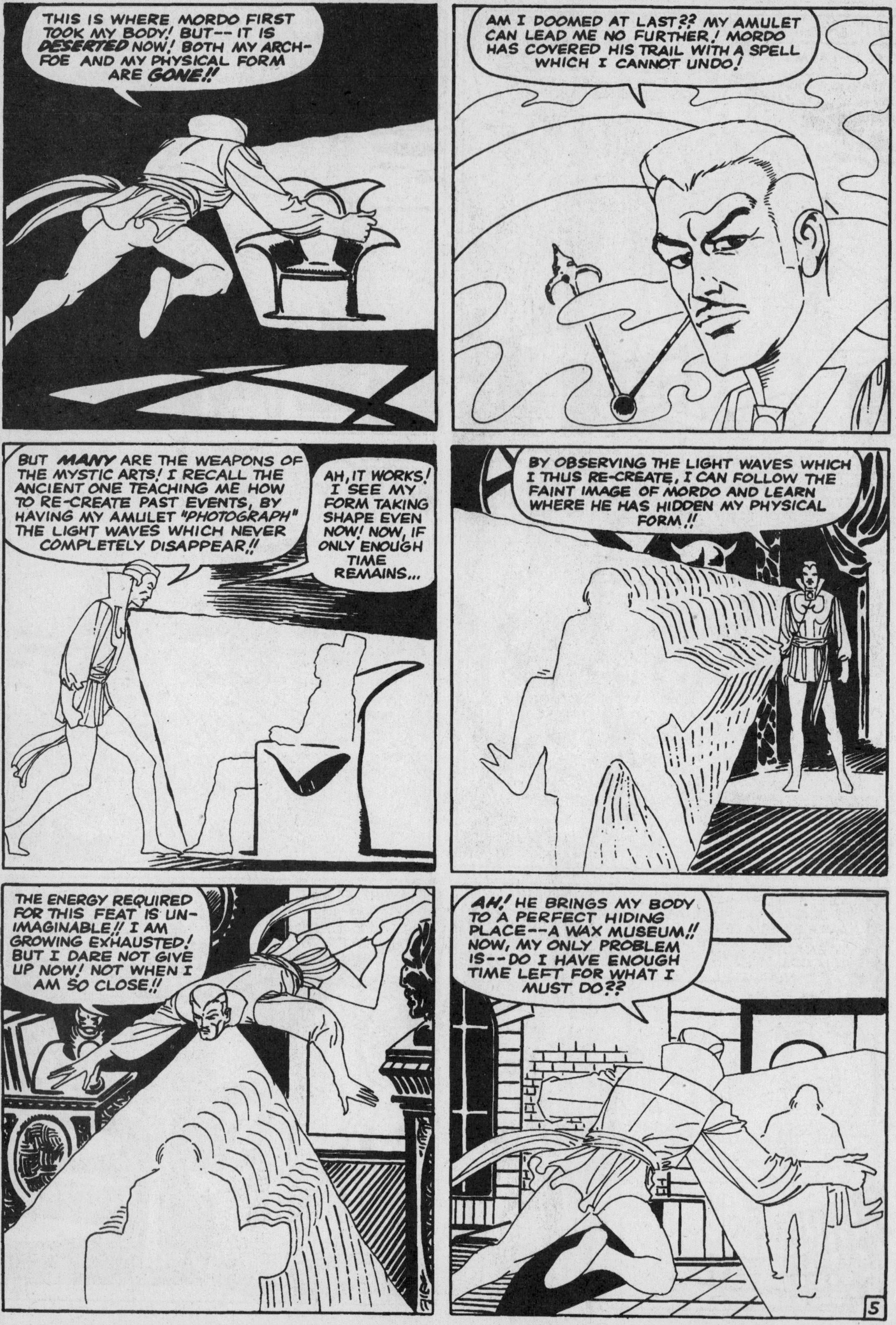
THIS IS WHERE MORDO FIRST TOOK MY BODY! BUT-- IT IS DESERTED NOW! BOTH MY ARCH-FOE AND MY PHYSICAL FORM ARE GONE!!
AM I DOOMED AT LAST?? MY AMULET CAN LEAD ME NO FURTHER! MORDO HAS COVERED HIS TRAIL WITH A SPELL WHICH I CANNOT UNDO!
BUT MANY ARE THE WEAPONS OF THE MYSTIC ARTS! I RECALL THE ANCIENT ONE TEACHING ME HOW TO RE-CREATE PAST EVENTS, BY HAVING MY AMULET "PHOTOGRAPH" THE LIGHT WAVES WHICH NEVER COMPLETELY DISAPPEAR!!
AH, IT WORKS! I SEE MY FORM TAKING SHAPE EVEN NOW! NOW, IF ONLY ENOUGH TIME REMAINS...
BY OBSERVING THE LIGHT WAVES WHICH I THUS RE-CREATE, I CAN FOLLOW THE FAINT IMAGE OF MORDO AND LEARN WHERE HE HAS HIDDEN MY PHYSICAL FORM!!
THE ENERGY REQUIRED FOR THIS FEAT IS UN-IMAGINABLE!! I AM GROWING EXHAUSTED! BUT I DARE NOT GIVE UP NOW! NOT WHEN I AM SO CLOSE!!
AH! HE BRINGS MY BODY TO A PERFECT HIDING PLACE--A WAX MUSEUM!! NOW, MY ONLY PROBLEM IS--DO I HAVE ENOUGH TIME LEFT FOR WHAT I MUST DO??

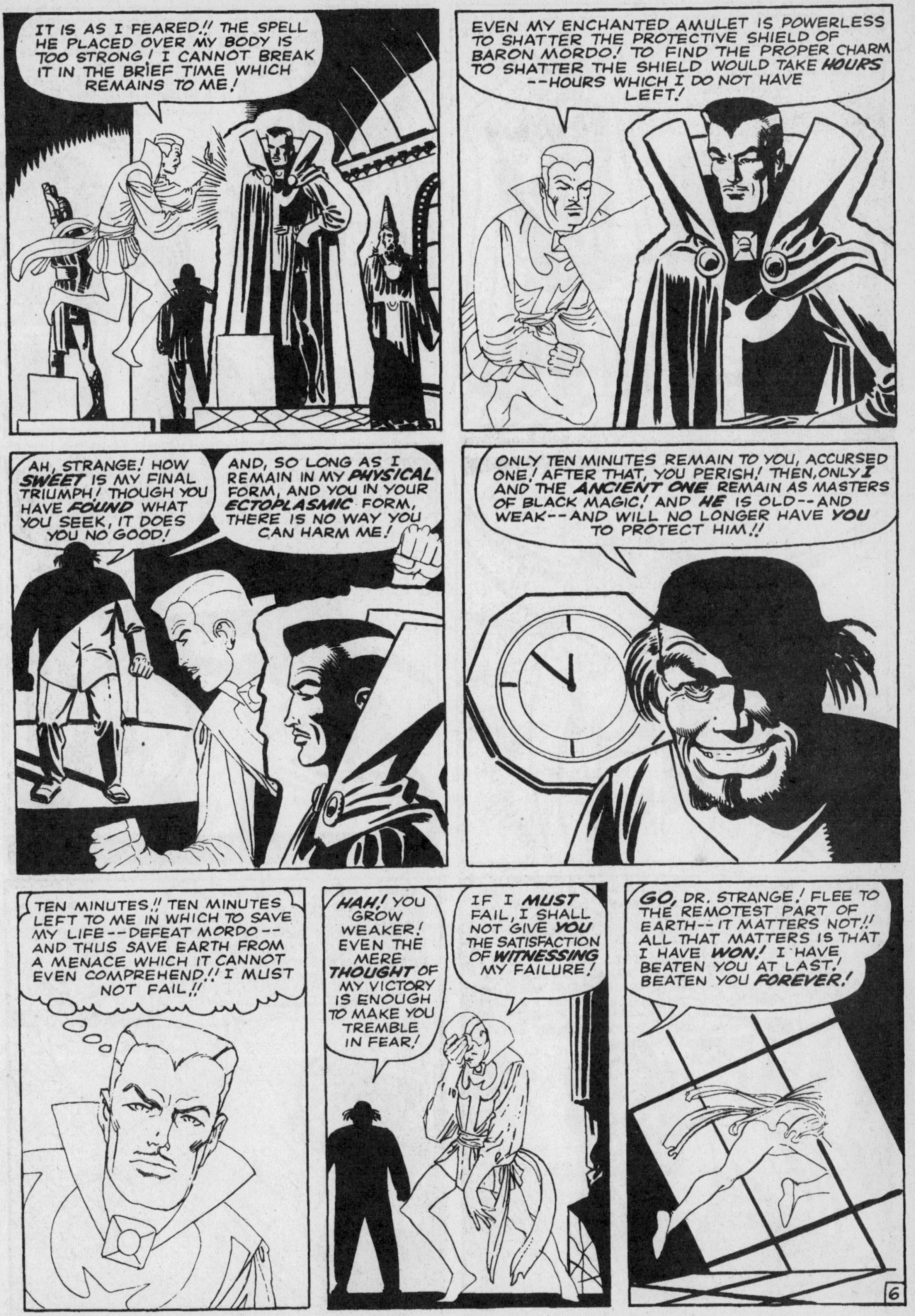

IT IS AS I FEARED!! THE SPELL HE PLACED OVER MY BODY IS TOO STRONG! I CANNOT BREAK IT IN THE BRIEF TIME WHICH REMAINS TO ME!
EVEN MY ENCHANTED AMULET IS POWERLESS TO SHATTER THE PROTECTIVE SHIELD OF BARON MORDO! TO FIND THE PROPER CHARM TO SHATTER THE SHIELD WOULD TAKE HOURS --HOURS WHICH I DO NOT HAVE LEFT!
AH, STRANGE! HOW SWEET IS MY FINAL TRIUMPH! THOUGH YOU HAVE FOUND WHAT YOU SEEK, IT DOES YOU NO GOOD!
AND, SO LONG AS I REMAIN IN MY PHYSICAL FORM, AND YOU IN YOUR ECTOPLASMIC FORM, THERE IS NO WAY YOU CAN HARM ME!
ONLY TEN MINUTES REMAIN TO YOU, ACCURSED ONE! AFTER THAT, YOU PERISH! THEN, ONLY I AND THE ANCIENT ONE REMAIN AS MASTERS OF BLACK MAGIC! AND HE IS OLD--AND WEAK--AND WILL NO LONGER HAVE YOU TO PROTECT HIM!!
TEN MINUTES!! TEN MINUTES LEFT TO ME IN WHICH TO SAVE MY LIFE--DEFEAT MORDO--AND THUS SAVE EARTH FROM A MENACE WHICH IT CANNOT EVEN COMPREHEND!! I MUST NOT FAIL!!
HAH! YOU GROW WEAKER! EVEN THE MERE THOUGHT OF MY VICTORY IS ENOUGH TO MAKE YOU TREMBLE IN FEAR!
IF I MUST FAIL, I SHALL NOT GIVE YOU THE SATISFACTION OF WITNESSING MY FAILURE!
GO, DR. STRANGE! FLEE TO THE REMOTEST PART OF EARTH--IT MATTERS NOT!! ALL THAT MATTERS IS THAT I HAVE WON! I HAVE BEATEN YOU AT LAST! BEATEN YOU FOREVER!
6

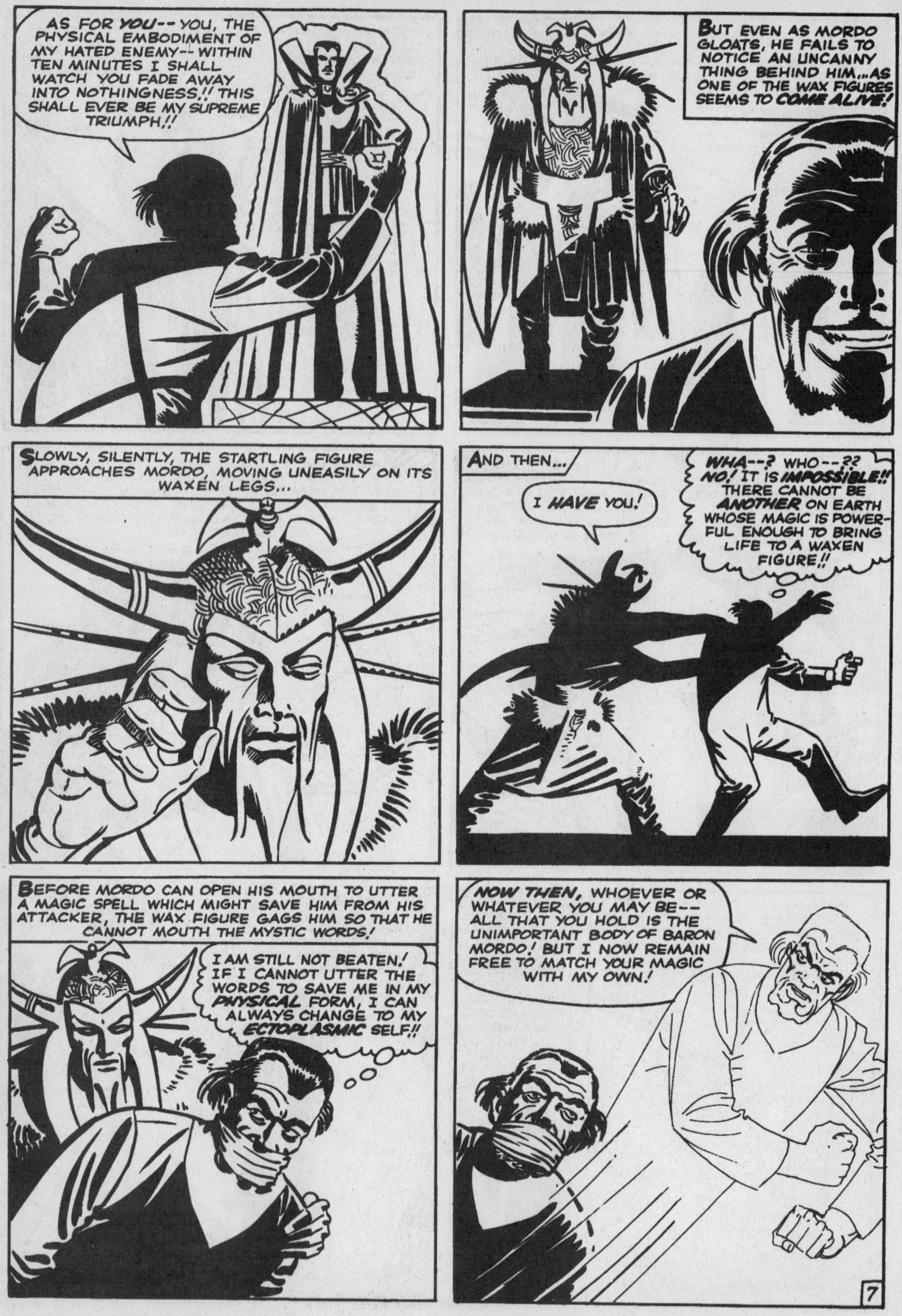
AS FOR YOU-- YOU, THE PHYSICAL EMBODIMENT OF MY HATED ENEMY-- WITHIN TEN MINUTES I SHALL WATCH YOU FADE AWAY INTO NOTHINGNESS!! THIS SHALL EVER BE MY SUPREME TRIUMPH!!
BUT EVEN AS MORDO GLOATS, HE FAILS TO NOTICE AN UNCANNY THING BEHIND HIM...AS ONE OF THE WAX FIGURES SEEMS TO COME ALIVE!
SLOWLY, SILENTLY, THE STARTLING FIGURE APPROACHES MORDO, MOVING UNEASILY ON ITS WAXEN LEGS...
AND THEN...
I HAVE YOU!
WHA--? WHO--?? NO! IT IS IMPOSSIBLE!! THERE CANNOT BE ANOTHER ON EARTH WHOSE MAGIC IS POWERFUL ENOUGH TO BRING LIFE TO A WAXEN FIGURE!!
BEFORE MORDO CAN OPEN HIS MOUTH TO UTTER A MAGIC SPELL WHICH MIGHT SAVE HIM FROM HIS ATTACKER, THE WAX FIGURE GAGS HIM SO THAT HE CANNOT MOUTH THE MYSTIC WORDS!
I AM STILL NOT BEATEN! IF I CANNOT UTTER THE WORDS TO SAVE ME IN MY PHYSICAL FORM, I CAN ALWAYS CHANGE TO MY ECTOPLASMIC SELF!!
NOW THEN, WHOEVER OR WHATEVER YOU MAY BE-- ALL THAT YOU HOLD IS THE UNIMPORTANT BODY OF BARON MORDO! BUT I NOW REMAIN FREE TO MATCH YOUR MAGIC WITH MY OWN!
7

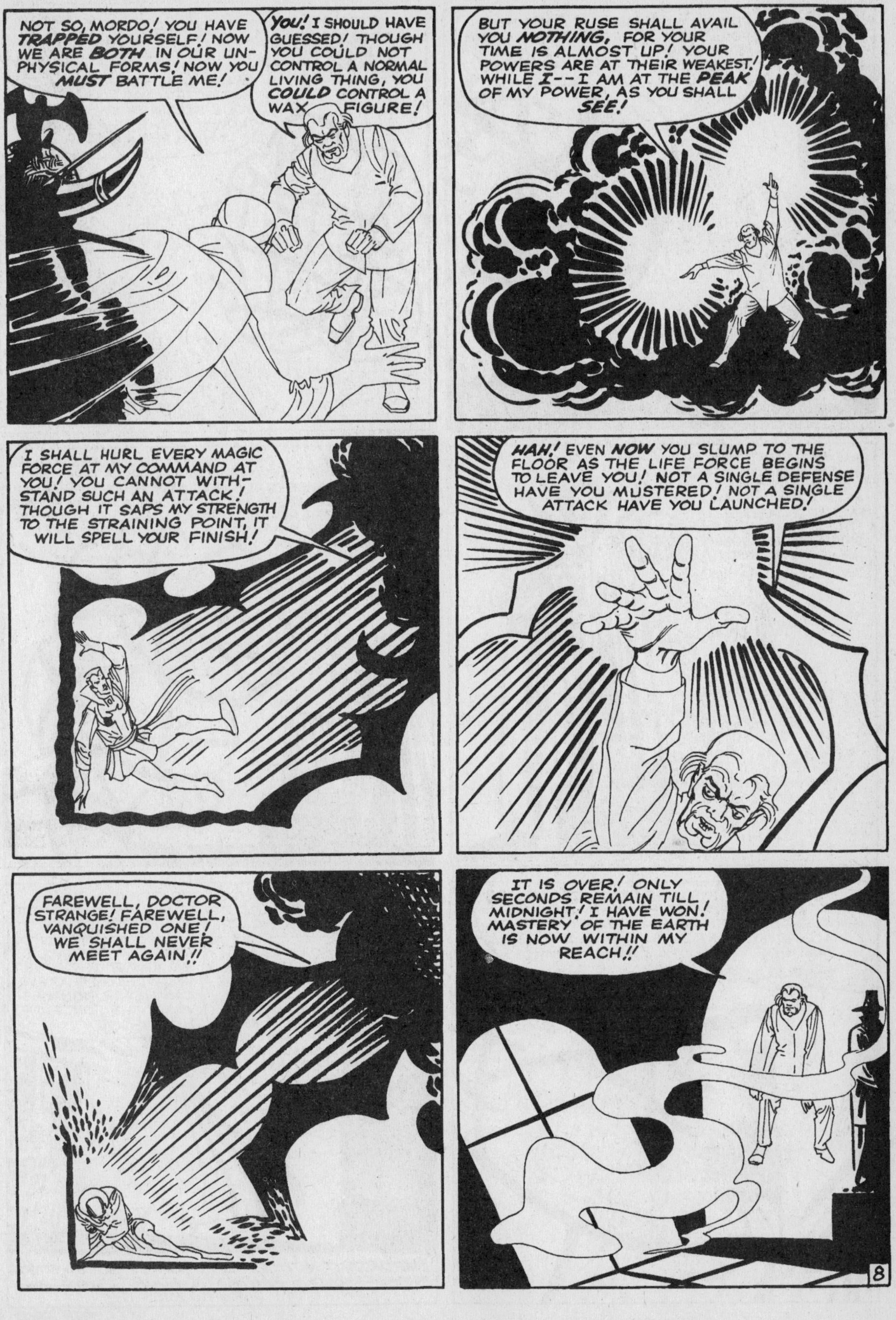
NOT SO, MORDO! YOU HAVE TRAPPED YOURSELF! NOW WE ARE BOTH IN OUR UN-PHYSICAL FORMS! NOW YOU MUST BATTLE ME!
YOU! I SHOULD HAVE GUESSED! THOUGH YOU COULD NOT CONTROL A NORMAL LIVING THING, YOU COULD CONTROL A WAX FIGURE!
BUT YOUR RUSE SHALL AVAIL YOU NOTHING, FOR YOUR TIME IS ALMOST UP! YOUR POWERS ARE AT THEIR WEAKEST! WHILE I-- I AM AT THE PEAK OF MY POWER, AS YOU SHALL SEE!
I SHALL HURL EVERY MAGIC FORCE AT MY COMMAND AT YOU! YOU CANNOT WITH-STAND SUCH AN ATTACK! THOUGH IT SAPS MY STRENGTH TO THE STRAINING POINT, IT WILL SPELL YOUR FINISH!
HAH! EVEN NOW YOU SLUMP TO THE FLOOR AS THE LIFE FORCE BEGINS TO LEAVE YOU! NOT A SINGLE DEFENSE HAVE YOU MUSTERED! NOT A SINGLE ATTACK HAVE YOU LAUNCHED!
FAREWELL, DOCTOR STRANGE! FAREWELL, VANQUISHED ONE! WE SHALL NEVER MEET AGAIN!!
IT IS OVER! ONLY SECONDS REMAIN TILL MIDNIGHT! I HAVE WON! MASTERY OF THE EARTH IS NOW WITHIN MY REACH!!
8

NOW, I MUST RETURN TO MY PHYSICAL FORM! I MUST REST-- FEEL WEAK-- I VENTED ALL MY POWER ON THAT FATAL ATTACK!

WHA--? SOMETHING PREVENTS ME FROM MOVING!! I CANNOT REACH MY FORM!

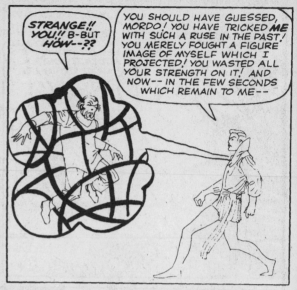

STRANGE!! YOU!! B-BUT HOW--??

YOU SHOULD HAVE GUESSED, MORDO! YOU HAVE TRICKED ME WITH SUCH A RUSE IN THE PAST! YOU MERELY FOUGHT A FIGURE IMAGE OF MYSELF WHICH I PROJECTED! YOU WASTED ALL YOUR STRENGTH ON IT! AND NOW-- IN THE FEW SECONDS WHICH REMAIN TO ME--

--I RETURN TO MY OWN BODY! FOR, WITH YOU HELD AT BAY BY MY ENCHANTED AMULET, THE SPELL WHICH SHIELDED MY FORM IS NOW VANISHED!

AS FOR YOU, EVIL ONE, I MUST ALLOW YOU TO LIVE --FOR I HAVE VOWED NEVER TO TAKE A LIFE, NO MATTER HOW DESERVING IT MAY BE OF DEATH! BUT I SHALL KEEP YOU FROM YOUR BODY FOR TWENTY-THREE HOURS, WHILE YOU PONDER ON THE USELESSNESS OF AN EVIL LIFE!

YOU ARE A FOOL, STRANGE! YOUR REFUSAL TO FINISH ME WILL PROVE TO BE YOUR UNDOING! FOR I SHALL NEVER STOP ATTACKING YOU! I SHALL NEVER REST UNTIL I HAVE RID THE EARTH OF YOU-- UNTIL I AM SUPREME!

9

AND, AS THE MOON BATHES THE CITY IN A SILENT GLOW, A TALL, DRAMATIC FIGURE SLOWLY WALKS FROM THE WAX MUSEUM, WRAPPED IN HIS OWN SOBER THOUGHTS...

SO LONG AS LIFE EXISTS, THE RIGHTEOUS MUST ALWAYS GUARD AGAINST THE WICKED!! I SHALL BE VIGILANT! NO MATTER WHERE, OR HOW MORDO MAY STRIKE-- I SHALL BE READY FOR HIM!

AND ALWAYS SHALL I BE ARMED WITH THE KNOWLEDGE THAT EVIL CAN NEVER TRIUMPH OVER THE FORCE OF GOOD!

IMPORTANT NOTICE: DR. STRANGE GUEST-STARS IN THE FABULOUS FANTASTIC FOUR #27, ON SALE NOW!! DON'T DARE TO MISS IT!!

THE END

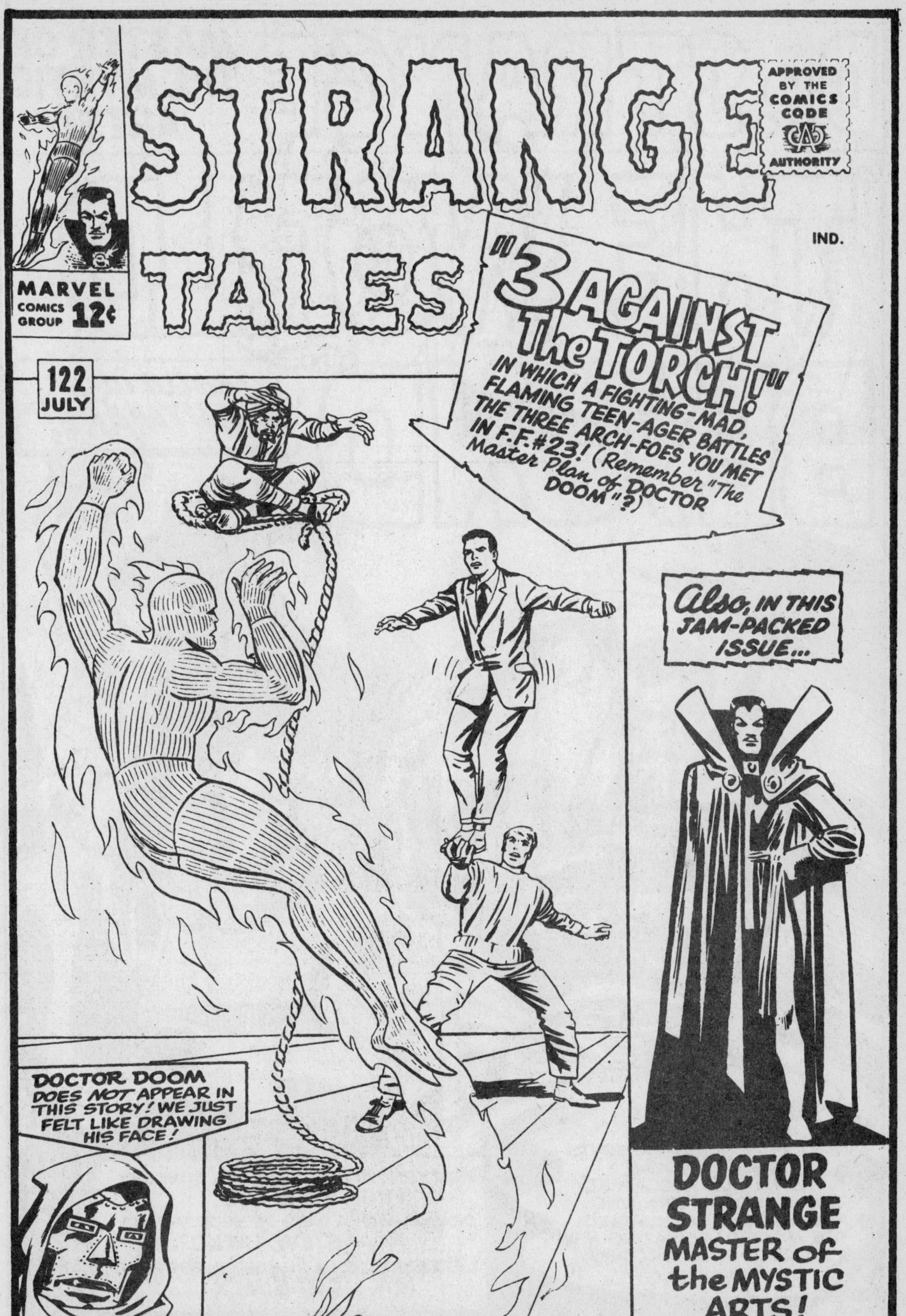
STRANGE TALES
APPROVED BY THE COMICS CODE AUTHORITY
MARVEL COMICS GROUP 12¢
IND.
122 JULY
"3 AGAINST The TORCH!"
IN WHICH A FIGHTING-MAD, FLAMING TEEN-AGER BATTLES THE THREE ARCH-FOES YOU MET IN F.F. #23! (Remember "The Master Plan of DOCTOR DOOM"?)
Also, IN THIS JAM-PACKED ISSUE...
DOCTOR STRANGE MASTER of the MYSTIC ARTS!
DOCTOR DOOM DOES NOT APPEAR IN THIS STORY! WE JUST FELT LIKE DRAWING HIS FACE!

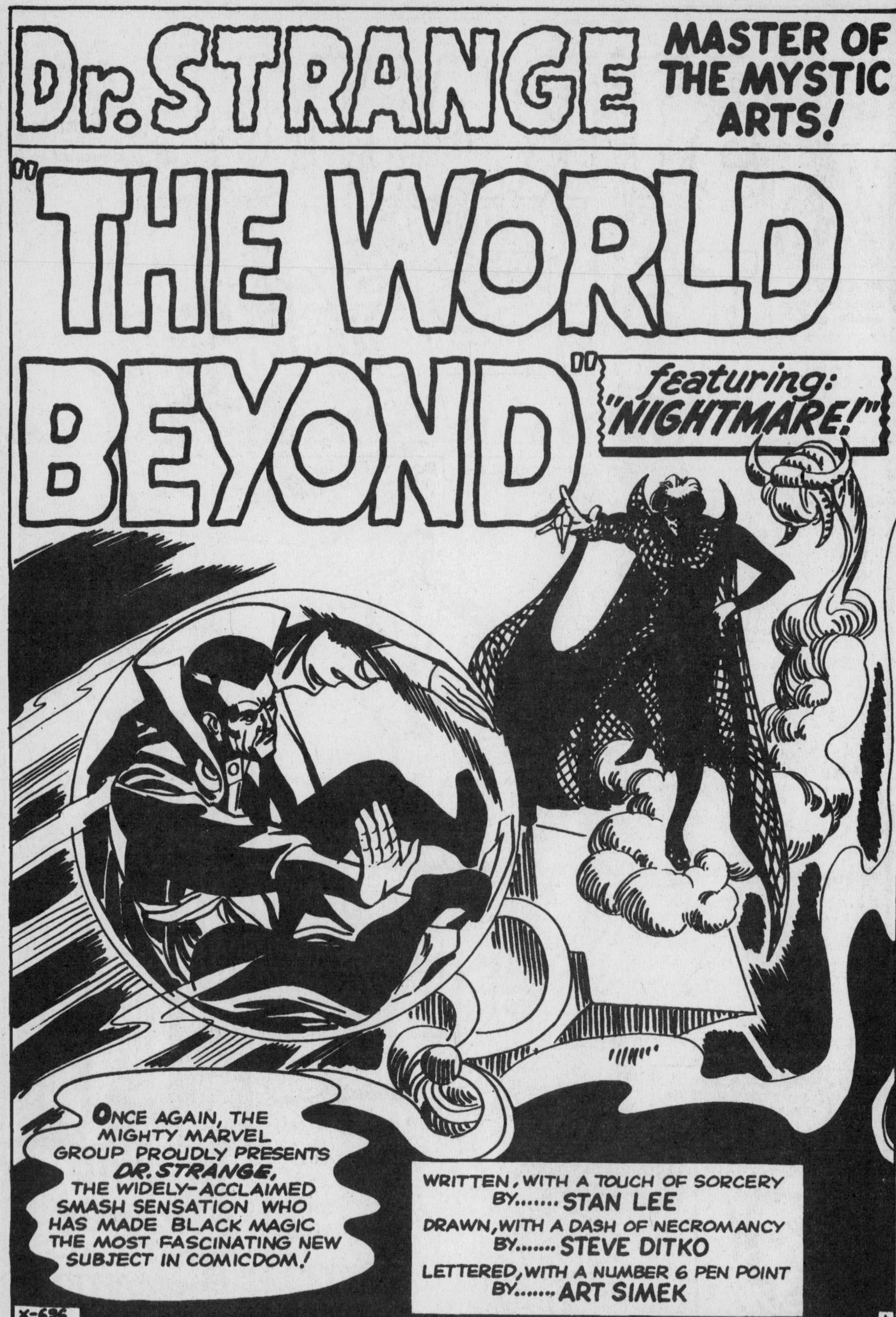

Dr. STRANGE
MASTER OF THE MYSTIC ARTS!
"THE WORLD BEYOND"
featuring: "NIGHTMARE!"
ONCE AGAIN, THE MIGHTY MARVEL GROUP PROUDLY PRESENTS DR. STRANGE, THE WIDELY-ACCLAIMED SMASH SENSATION WHO HAS MADE BLACK MAGIC THE MOST FASCINATING NEW SUBJECT IN COMICDOM!
WRITTEN, WITH A TOUCH OF SORCERY BY....... STAN LEE
DRAWN, WITH A DASH OF NECROMANCY BY....... STEVE DITKO
LETTERED, WITH A NUMBER 6 PEN POINT BY....... ART SIMEK
X-696
1

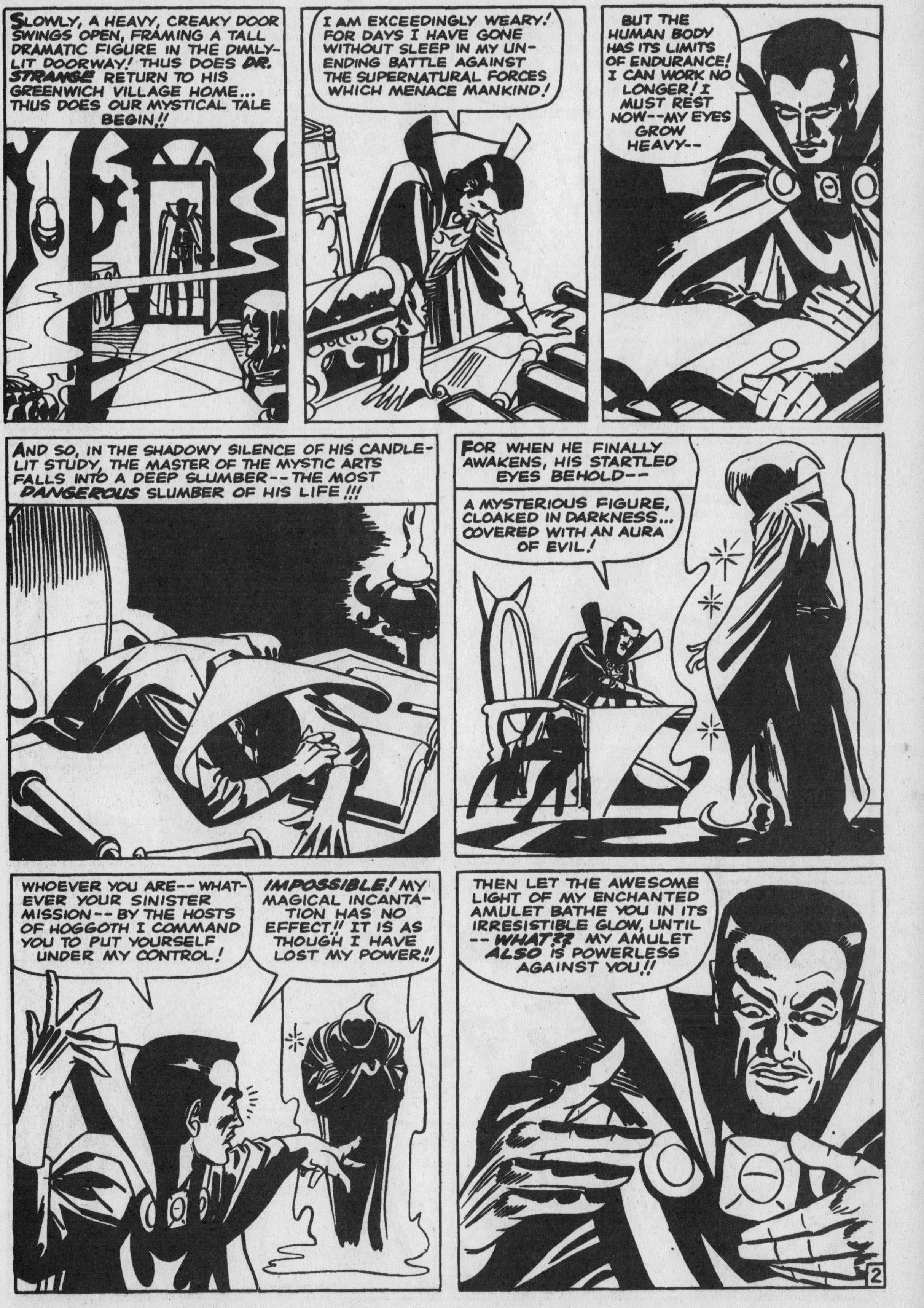
SLOWLY, A HEAVY, CREAKY DOOR SWINGS OPEN, FRAMING A TALL DRAMATIC FIGURE IN THE DIMLY-LIT DOORWAY! THUS DOES DR. STRANGE RETURN TO HIS GREENWICH VILLAGE HOME... THUS DOES OUR MYSTICAL TALE BEGIN!!
I AM EXCEEDINGLY WEARY! FOR DAYS I HAVE GONE WITHOUT SLEEP IN MY UN-ENDING BATTLE AGAINST THE SUPERNATURAL FORCES WHICH MENACE MANKIND!
BUT THE HUMAN BODY HAS ITS LIMITS OF ENDURANCE! I CAN WORK NO LONGER! I MUST REST NOW--MY EYES GROW HEAVY--
AND SO, IN THE SHADOWY SILENCE OF HIS CANDLE-LIT STUDY, THE MASTER OF THE MYSTIC ARTS FALLS INTO A DEEP SLUMBER--THE MOST DANGEROUS SLUMBER OF HIS LIFE!!!
FOR WHEN HE FINALLY AWAKENS, HIS STARTLED EYES BEHOLD--
A MYSTERIOUS FIGURE, CLOAKED IN DARKNESS... COVERED WITH AN AURA OF EVIL!
WHOEVER YOU ARE--WHAT-EVER YOUR SINISTER MISSION--BY THE HOSTS OF HOGGOTH I COMMAND YOU TO PUT YOURSELF UNDER MY CONTROL!
IMPOSSIBLE! MY MAGICAL INCANTA-TION HAS NO EFFECT!! IT IS AS THOUGH I HAVE LOST MY POWER!!
THEN LET THE AWESOME LIGHT OF MY ENCHANTED AMULET BATHE YOU IN ITS IRRESISTIBLE GLOW, UNTIL --WHAT?? MY AMULET ALSO IS POWERLESS AGAINST YOU!!
2

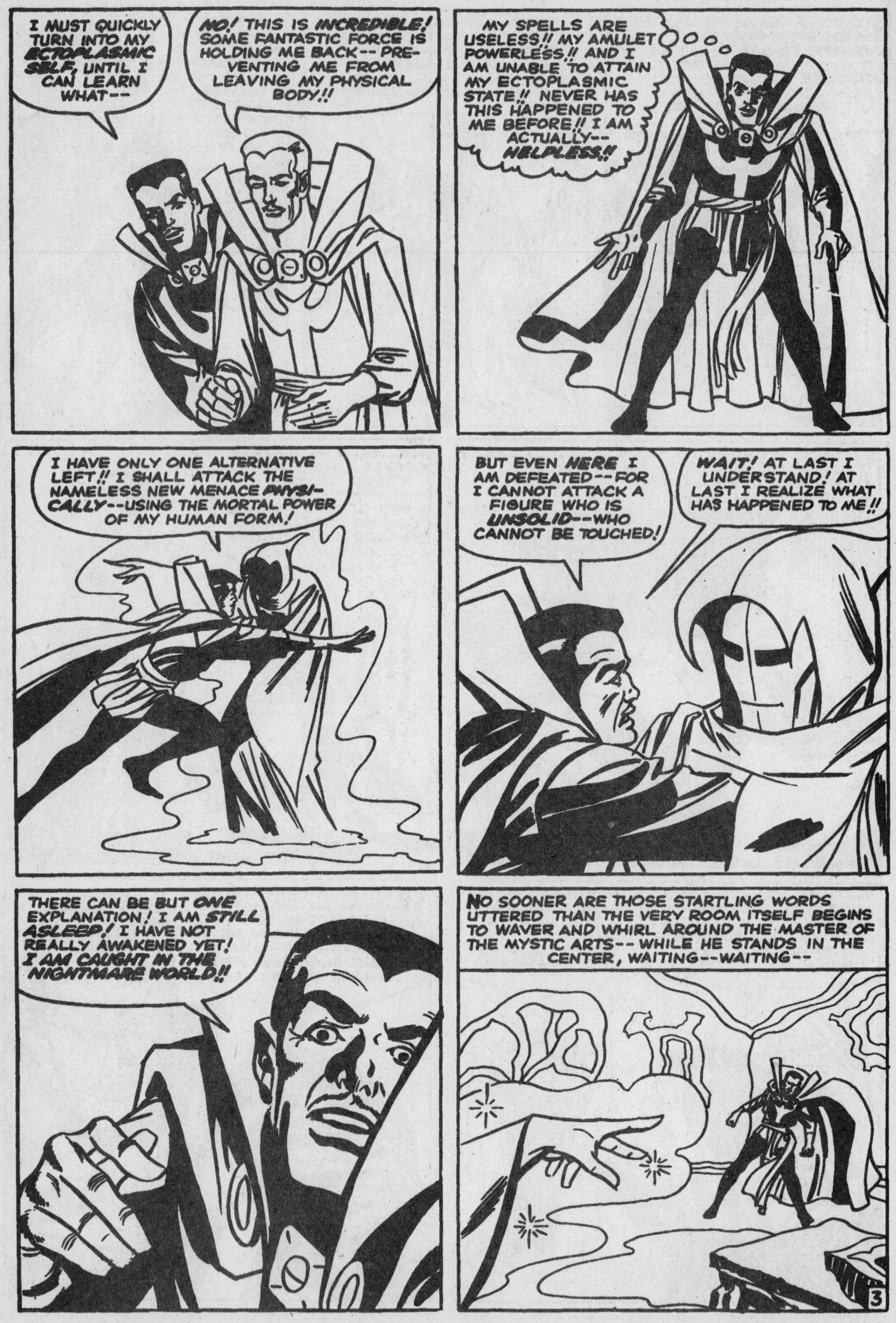
I MUST QUICKLY TURN INTO MY ECTOPLASMIC SELF, UNTIL I CAN LEARN WHAT--
NO! THIS IS INCREDIBLE! SOME FANTASTIC FORCE IS HOLDING ME BACK--PREVENTING ME FROM LEAVING MY PHYSICAL BODY!!
MY SPELLS ARE USELESS!! MY AMULET POWERLESS!! AND I AM UNABLE TO ATTAIN MY ECTOPLASMIC STATE!! NEVER HAS THIS HAPPENED TO ME BEFORE!! I AM ACTUALLY--HELPLESS!!
I HAVE ONLY ONE ALTERNATIVE LEFT!! I SHALL ATTACK THE NAMELESS NEW MENACE PHYSICALLY--USING THE MORTAL POWER OF MY HUMAN FORM!
BUT EVEN HERE I AM DEFEATED--FOR I CANNOT ATTACK A FIGURE WHO IS UNSOLID--WHO CANNOT BE TOUCHED!
WAIT! AT LAST I UNDERSTAND! AT LAST I REALIZE WHAT HAS HAPPENED TO ME!!
THERE CAN BE BUT ONE EXPLANATION! I AM STILL ASLEEP! I HAVE NOT REALLY AWAKENED YET! I AM CAUGHT IN THE NIGHTMARE WORLD!!
NO SOONER ARE THOSE STARTLING WORDS UTTERED THAN THE VERY ROOM ITSELF BEGINS TO WAVER AND WHIRL AROUND THE MASTER OF THE MYSTIC ARTS--WHILE HE STANDS IN THE CENTER, WAITING--WAITING--
3

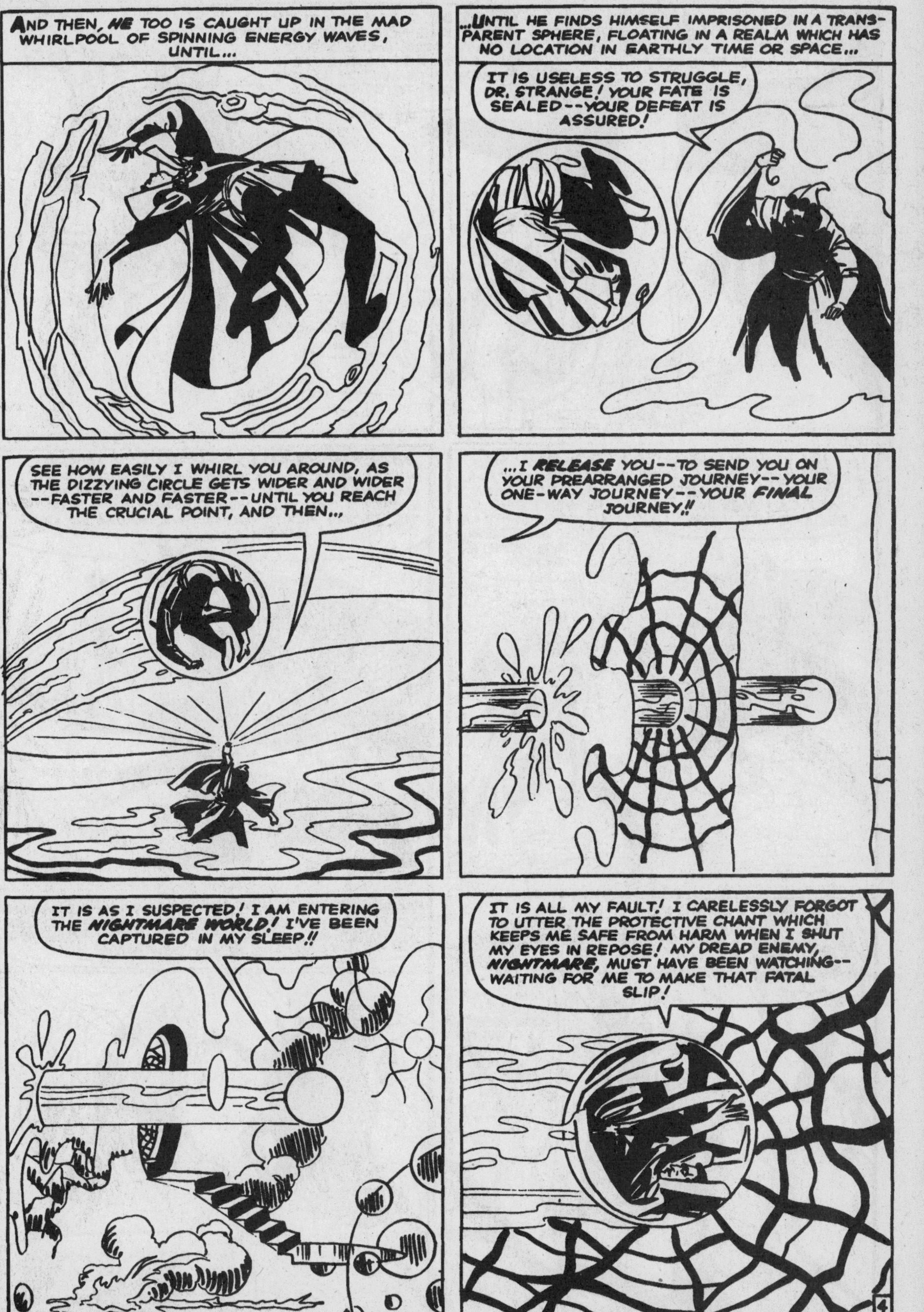
AND THEN, HE TOO IS CAUGHT UP IN THE MAD WHIRLPOOL OF SPINNING ENERGY WAVES, UNTIL...
...UNTIL HE FINDS HIMSELF IMPRISONED IN A TRANSPARENT SPHERE, FLOATING IN A REALM WHICH HAS NO LOCATION IN EARTHLY TIME OR SPACE...
IT IS USELESS TO STRUGGLE, DR. STRANGE! YOUR FATE IS SEALED--YOUR DEFEAT IS ASSURED!
SEE HOW EASILY I WHIRL YOU AROUND, AS THE DIZZYING CIRCLE GETS WIDER AND WIDER --FASTER AND FASTER--UNTIL YOU REACH THE CRUCIAL POINT, AND THEN...,
...I RELEASE YOU--TO SEND YOU ON YOUR PREARRANGED JOURNEY--YOUR ONE-WAY JOURNEY--YOUR FINAL JOURNEY!!
IT IS AS I SUSPECTED! I AM ENTERING THE NIGHTMARE WORLD! I'VE BEEN CAPTURED IN MY SLEEP!!
IT IS ALL MY FAULT! I CARELESSLY FORGOT TO UTTER THE PROTECTIVE CHANT WHICH KEEPS ME SAFE FROM HARM WHEN I SHUT MY EYES IN REPOSE! MY DREAD ENEMY, NIGHTMARE, MUST HAVE BEEN WATCHING--WAITING FOR ME TO MAKE THAT FATAL SLIP!
4

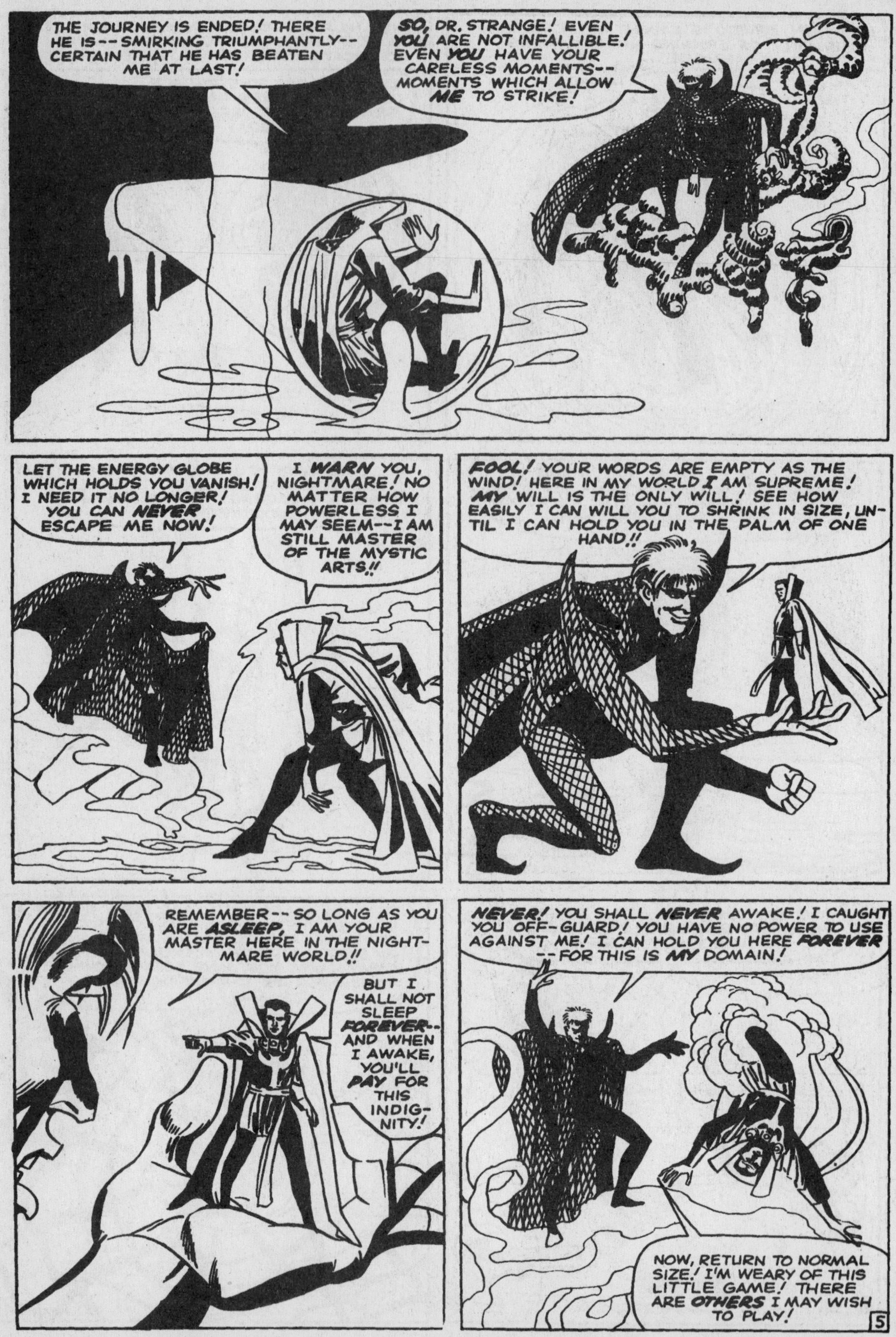
THE JOURNEY IS ENDED! THERE HE IS--SMIRKING TRIUMPHANTLY--CERTAIN THAT HE HAS BEATEN ME AT LAST!
SO, DR. STRANGE! EVEN YOU ARE NOT INFALLIBLE! EVEN YOU HAVE YOUR CARELESS MOMENTS--MOMENTS WHICH ALLOW ME TO STRIKE!
LET THE ENERGY GLOBE WHICH HOLDS YOU VANISH! I NEED IT NO LONGER! YOU CAN NEVER ESCAPE ME NOW!
I WARN YOU, NIGHTMARE! NO MATTER HOW POWERLESS I MAY SEEM--I AM STILL MASTER OF THE MYSTIC ARTS!!
FOOL! YOUR WORDS ARE EMPTY AS THE WIND! HERE IN MY WORLD I AM SUPREME! MY WILL IS THE ONLY WILL! SEE HOW EASILY I CAN WILL YOU TO SHRINK IN SIZE, UNTIL I CAN HOLD YOU IN THE PALM OF ONE HAND!!
REMEMBER--SO LONG AS YOU ARE ASLEEP, I AM YOUR MASTER HERE IN THE NIGHTMARE WORLD!!
BUT I SHALL NOT SLEEP FOREVER--AND WHEN I AWAKE, YOU'LL PAY FOR THIS INDIGNITY!
NEVER! YOU SHALL NEVER AWAKE! I CAUGHT YOU OFF-GUARD! YOU HAVE NO POWER TO USE AGAINST ME! I CAN HOLD YOU HERE FOREVER--FOR THIS IS MY DOMAIN!
NOW, RETURN TO NORMAL SIZE! I'M WEARY OF THIS LITTLE GAME! THERE ARE OTHERS I MAY WISH TO PLAY!
5

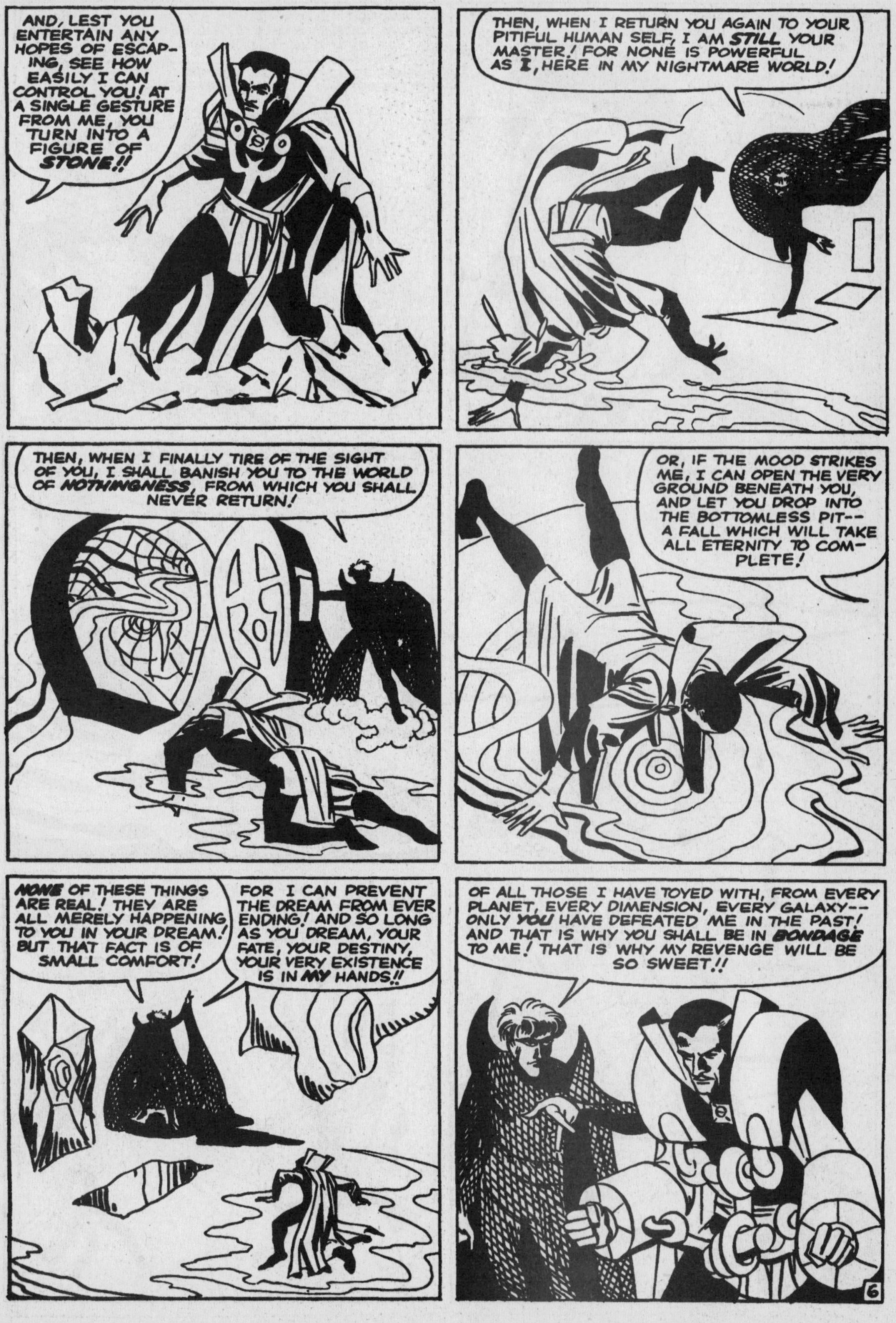
AND, LEST YOU ENTERTAIN ANY HOPES OF ESCAPING, SEE HOW EASILY I CAN CONTROL YOU! AT A SINGLE GESTURE FROM ME, YOU TURN INTO A FIGURE OF STONE!!
THEN, WHEN I RETURN YOU AGAIN TO YOUR PITIFUL HUMAN SELF, I AM STILL YOUR MASTER! FOR NONE IS POWERFUL AS I, HERE IN MY NIGHTMARE WORLD!
THEN, WHEN I FINALLY TIRE OF THE SIGHT OF YOU, I SHALL BANISH YOU TO THE WORLD OF NOTHINGNESS, FROM WHICH YOU SHALL NEVER RETURN!
OR, IF THE MOOD STRIKES ME, I CAN OPEN THE VERY GROUND BENEATH YOU, AND LET YOU DROP INTO THE BOTTOMLESS PIT-- A FALL WHICH WILL TAKE ALL ETERNITY TO COMPLETE!
NONE OF THESE THINGS ARE REAL! THEY ARE ALL MERELY HAPPENING TO YOU IN YOUR DREAM! BUT THAT FACT IS OF SMALL COMFORT!
FOR I CAN PREVENT THE DREAM FROM EVER ENDING! AND SO LONG AS YOU DREAM, YOUR FATE, YOUR DESTINY, YOUR VERY EXISTENCE IS IN MY HANDS!!
OF ALL THOSE I HAVE TOYED WITH, FROM EVERY PLANET, EVERY DIMENSION, EVERY GALAXY-- ONLY YOU HAVE DEFEATED ME IN THE PAST! AND THAT IS WHY YOU SHALL BE IN BONDAGE TO ME! THAT IS WHY MY REVENGE WILL BE SO SWEET!!
6

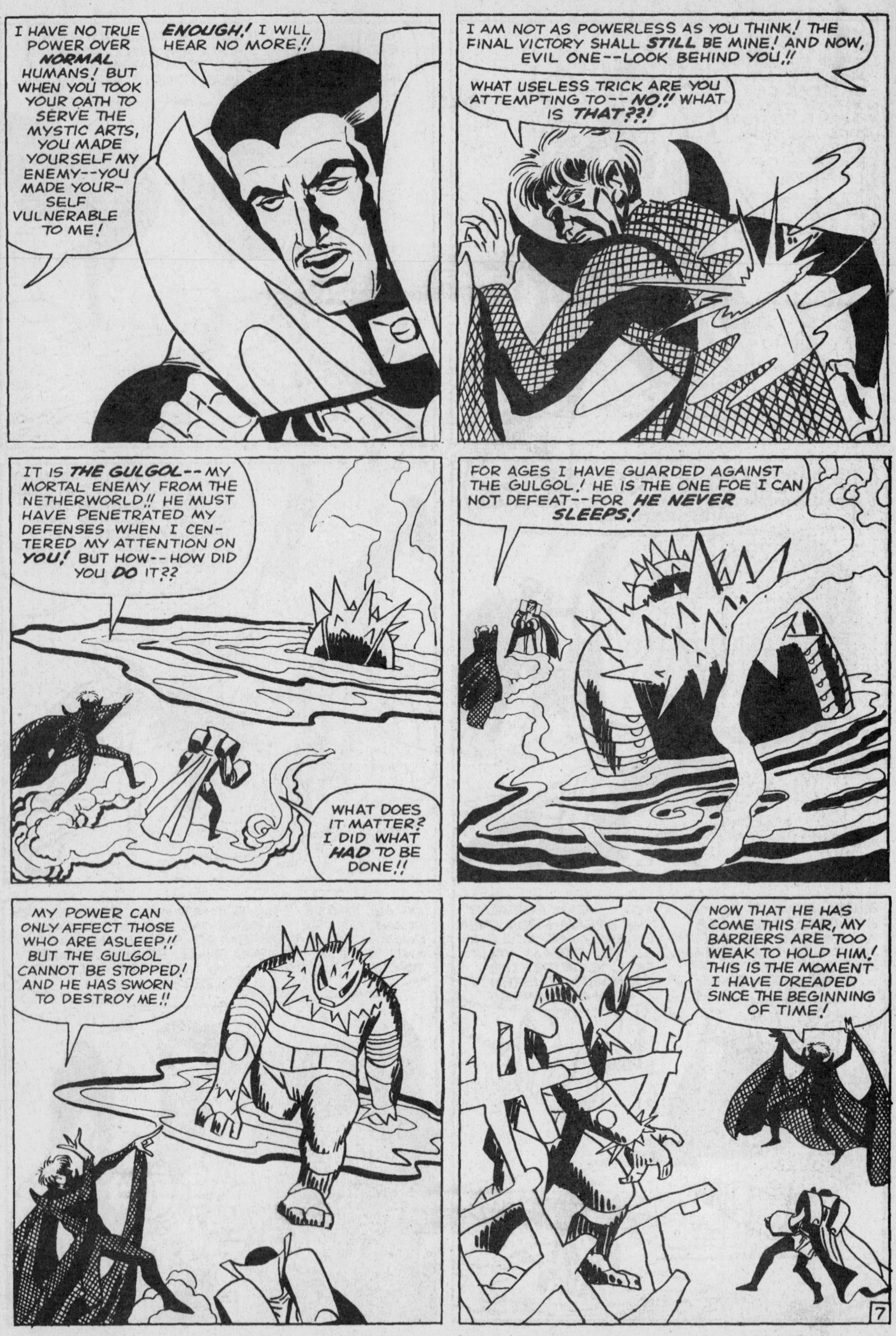

I HAVE NO TRUE POWER OVER NORMAL HUMANS! BUT WHEN YOU TOOK YOUR OATH TO SERVE THE MYSTIC ARTS, YOU MADE YOURSELF MY ENEMY--YOU MADE YOURSELF VULNERABLE TO ME!
ENOUGH! I WILL HEAR NO MORE!!
I AM NOT AS POWERLESS AS YOU THINK! THE FINAL VICTORY SHALL STILL BE MINE! AND NOW, EVIL ONE--LOOK BEHIND YOU!!
WHAT USELESS TRICK ARE YOU ATTEMPTING TO--NO!! WHAT IS THAT??!
IT IS THE GULGOL--MY MORTAL ENEMY FROM THE NETHERWORLD!! HE MUST HAVE PENETRATED MY DEFENSES WHEN I CENTERED MY ATTENTION ON YOU! BUT HOW--HOW DID YOU DO IT??
WHAT DOES IT MATTER? I DID WHAT HAD TO BE DONE!!
FOR AGES I HAVE GUARDED AGAINST THE GULGOL! HE IS THE ONE FOE I CAN NOT DEFEAT--FOR HE NEVER SLEEPS!
MY POWER CAN ONLY AFFECT THOSE WHO ARE ASLEEP!! BUT THE GULGOL CANNOT BE STOPPED! AND HE HAS SWORN TO DESTROY ME!!
NOW THAT HE HAS COME THIS FAR, MY BARRIERS ARE TOO WEAK TO HOLD HIM! THIS IS THE MOMENT I HAVE DREADED SINCE THE BEGINNING OF TIME!

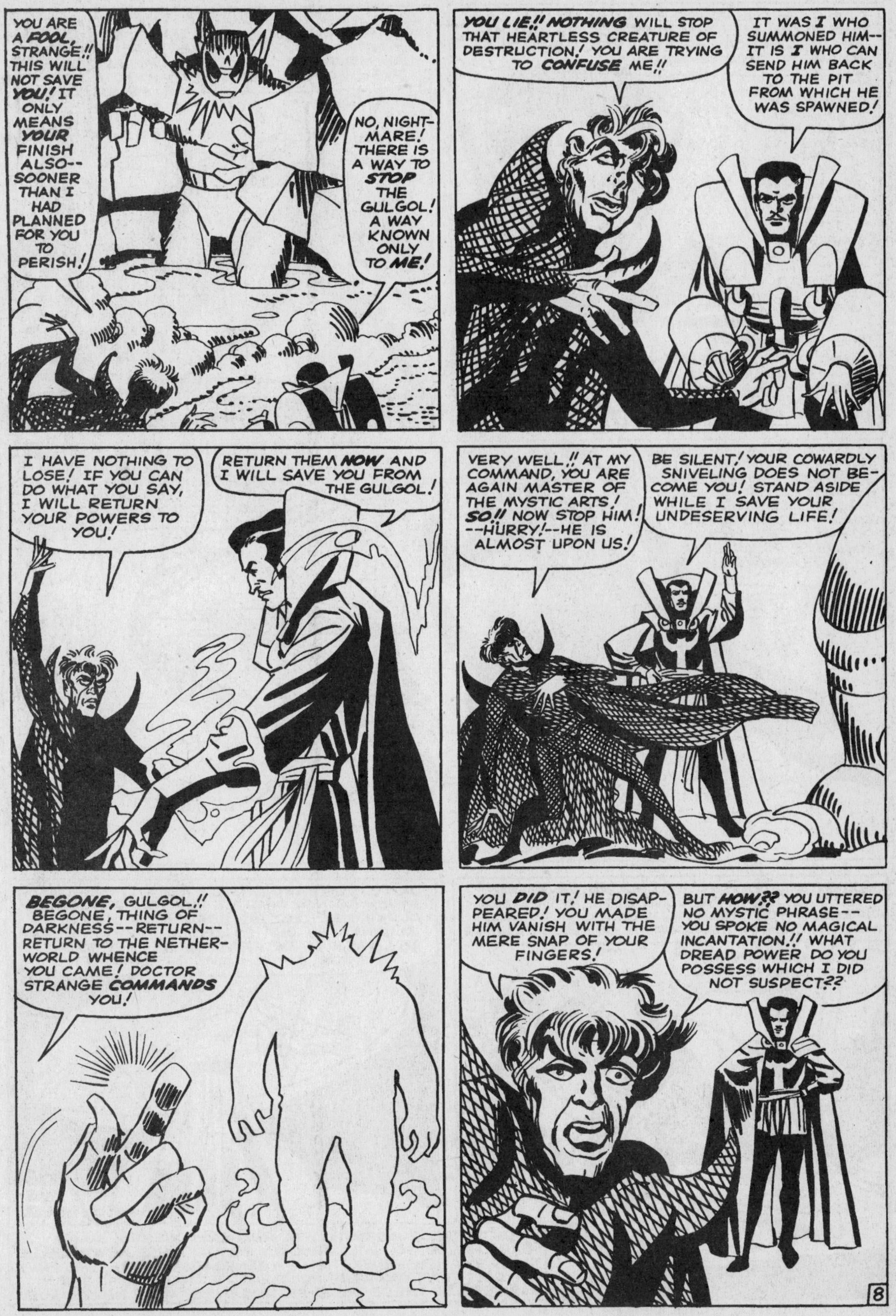
YOU ARE A FOOL, STRANGE!! THIS WILL NOT SAVE YOU! IT ONLY MEANS YOUR FINISH ALSO-- SOONER THAN I HAD PLANNED FOR YOU TO PERISH!
NO, NIGHT-MARE! THERE IS A WAY TO STOP THE GULGOL! A WAY KNOWN ONLY TO ME!
YOU LIE!! NOTHING WILL STOP THAT HEARTLESS CREATURE OF DESTRUCTION! YOU ARE TRYING TO CONFUSE ME!!
IT WAS I WHO SUMMONED HIM-- IT IS I WHO CAN SEND HIM BACK TO THE PIT FROM WHICH HE WAS SPAWNED!
I HAVE NOTHING TO LOSE! IF YOU CAN DO WHAT YOU SAY, I WILL RETURN YOUR POWERS TO YOU!
RETURN THEM NOW AND I WILL SAVE YOU FROM THE GULGOL!
VERY WELL!! AT MY COMMAND, YOU ARE AGAIN MASTER OF THE MYSTIC ARTS! SO!! NOW STOP HIM! --HURRY!--HE IS ALMOST UPON US!
BE SILENT! YOUR COWARDLY SNIVELING DOES NOT BE-COME YOU! STAND ASIDE WHILE I SAVE YOUR UNDESERVING LIFE!
BEGONE, GULGOL!! BEGONE, THING OF DARKNESS--RETURN-- RETURN TO THE NETHER-WORLD WHENCE YOU CAME! DOCTOR STRANGE COMMANDS YOU!
YOU DID IT! HE DISAP-PEARED! YOU MADE HIM VANISH WITH THE MERE SNAP OF YOUR FINGERS!
BUT HOW?? YOU UTTERED NO MYSTIC PHRASE-- YOU SPOKE NO MAGICAL INCANTATION!! WHAT DREAD POWER DO YOU POSSESS WHICH I DID NOT SUSPECT??

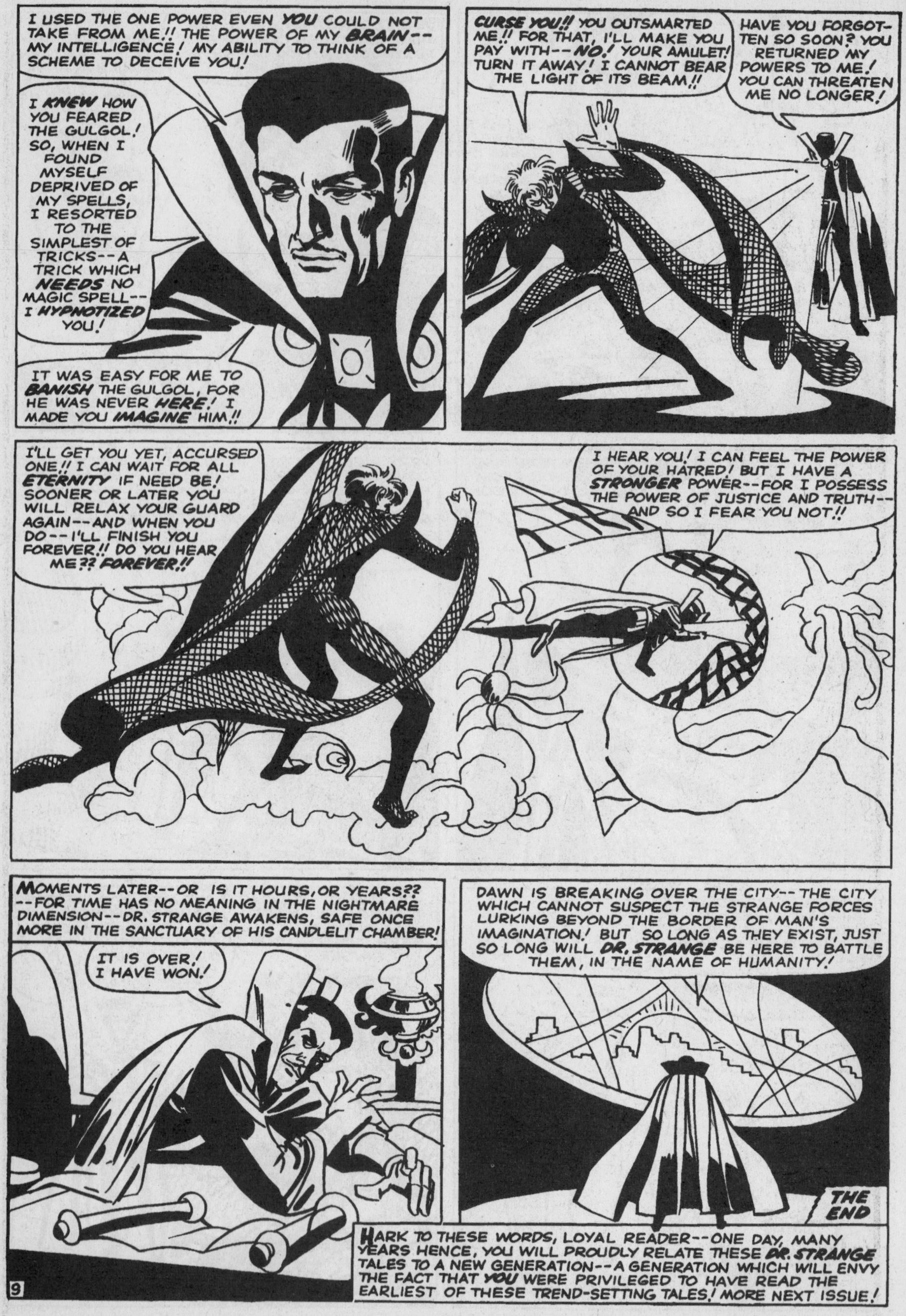
I USED THE ONE POWER EVEN YOU COULD NOT TAKE FROM ME!! THE POWER OF MY BRAIN-- MY INTELLIGENCE! MY ABILITY TO THINK OF A SCHEME TO DECEIVE YOU!
I KNEW HOW YOU FEARED THE GULGOL! SO, WHEN I FOUND MYSELF DEPRIVED OF MY SPELLS, I RESORTED TO THE SIMPLEST OF TRICKS--A TRICK WHICH NEEDS NO MAGIC SPELL-- I HYPNOTIZED YOU!
IT WAS EASY FOR ME TO BANISH THE GULGOL, FOR HE WAS NEVER HERE! I MADE YOU IMAGINE HIM!!
CURSE YOU!! YOU OUTSMARTED ME!! FOR THAT, I'LL MAKE YOU PAY WITH--NO! YOUR AMULET! TURN IT AWAY! I CANNOT BEAR THE LIGHT OF ITS BEAM!!
HAVE YOU FORGOTTEN SO SOON? YOU RETURNED MY POWERS TO ME! YOU CAN THREATEN ME NO LONGER!
I'LL GET YOU YET, ACCURSED ONE!! I CAN WAIT FOR ALL ETERNITY IF NEED BE! SOONER OR LATER YOU WILL RELAX YOUR GUARD AGAIN--AND WHEN YOU DO--I'LL FINISH YOU FOREVER!! DO YOU HEAR ME?? FOREVER!!
I HEAR YOU! I CAN FEEL THE POWER OF YOUR HATRED! BUT I HAVE A STRONGER POWER--FOR I POSSESS THE POWER OF JUSTICE AND TRUTH-- AND SO I FEAR YOU NOT!!
MOMENTS LATER--OR IS IT HOURS, OR YEARS?? --FOR TIME HAS NO MEANING IN THE NIGHTMARE DIMENSION--DR. STRANGE AWAKENS, SAFE ONCE MORE IN THE SANCTUARY OF HIS CANDLELIT CHAMBER!
IT IS OVER! I HAVE WON!
DAWN IS BREAKING OVER THE CITY--THE CITY WHICH CANNOT SUSPECT THE STRANGE FORCES LURKING BEYOND THE BORDER OF MAN'S IMAGINATION! BUT SO LONG AS THEY EXIST, JUST SO LONG WILL DR. STRANGE BE HERE TO BATTLE THEM, IN THE NAME OF HUMANITY!
THE END
HARK TO THESE WORDS, LOYAL READER--ONE DAY, MANY YEARS HENCE, YOU WILL PROUDLY RELATE THESE DR. STRANGE TALES TO A NEW GENERATION--A GENERATION WHICH WILL ENVY THE FACT THAT YOU WERE PRIVILEGED TO HAVE READ THE EARLIEST OF THESE TREND-SETTING TALES! MORE NEXT ISSUE!
9

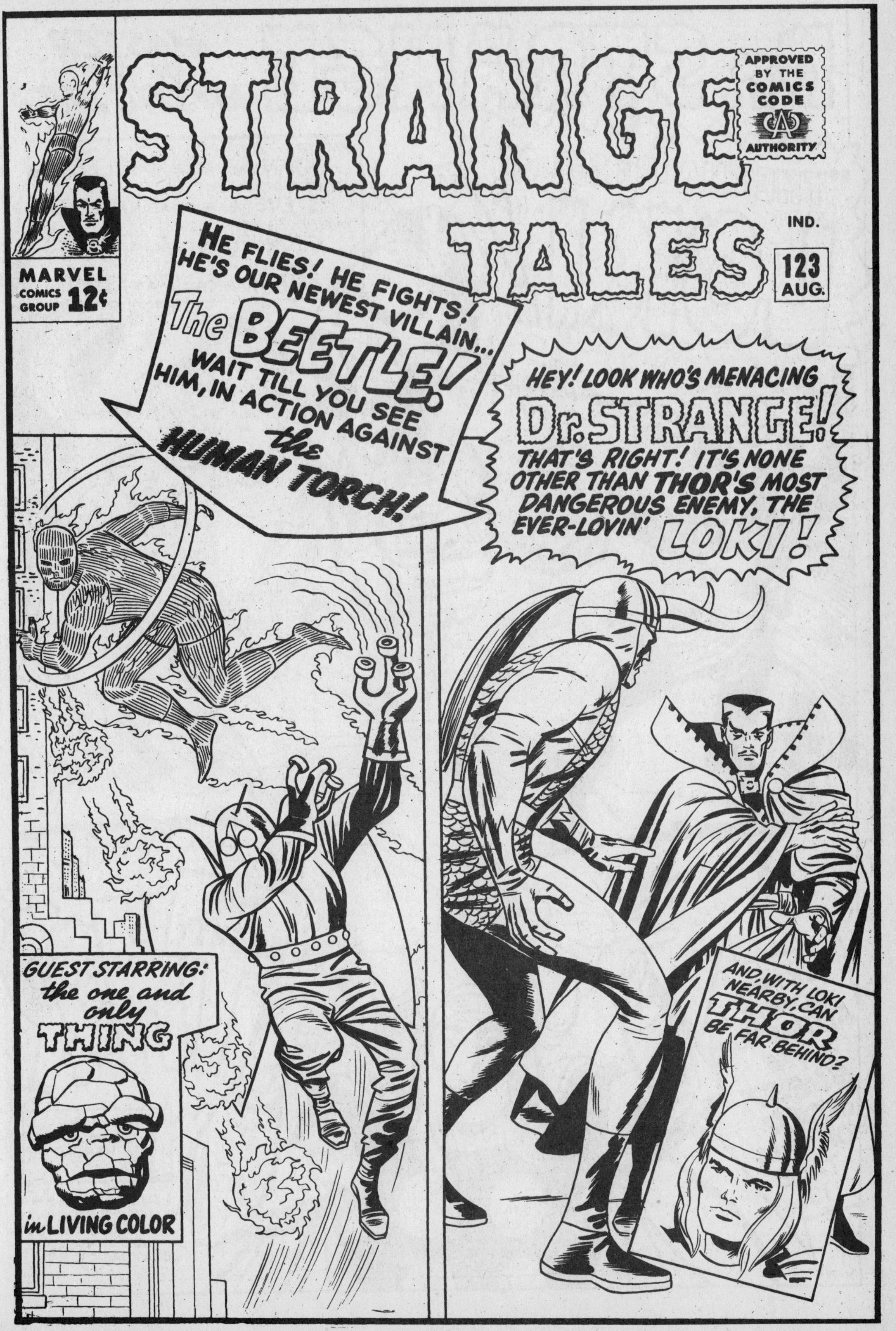
STRANGE TALES
APPROVED BY THE COMICS CODE AUTHORITY
IND.
123 AUG.
MARVEL COMICS GROUP 12¢
HE FLIES! HE FIGHTS! HE'S OUR NEWEST VILLAIN... The BEETLE! WAIT TILL YOU SEE HIM, IN ACTION AGAINST the HUMAN TORCH!
HEY! LOOK WHO'S MENACING Dr. STRANGE! THAT'S RIGHT! IT'S NONE OTHER THAN THOR'S MOST DANGEROUS ENEMY, THE EVER-LOVIN' LOKI!
GUEST STARRING: the one and only THING in LIVING COLOR
AND, WITH LOKI NEARBY, CAN THOR BE FAR BEHIND?

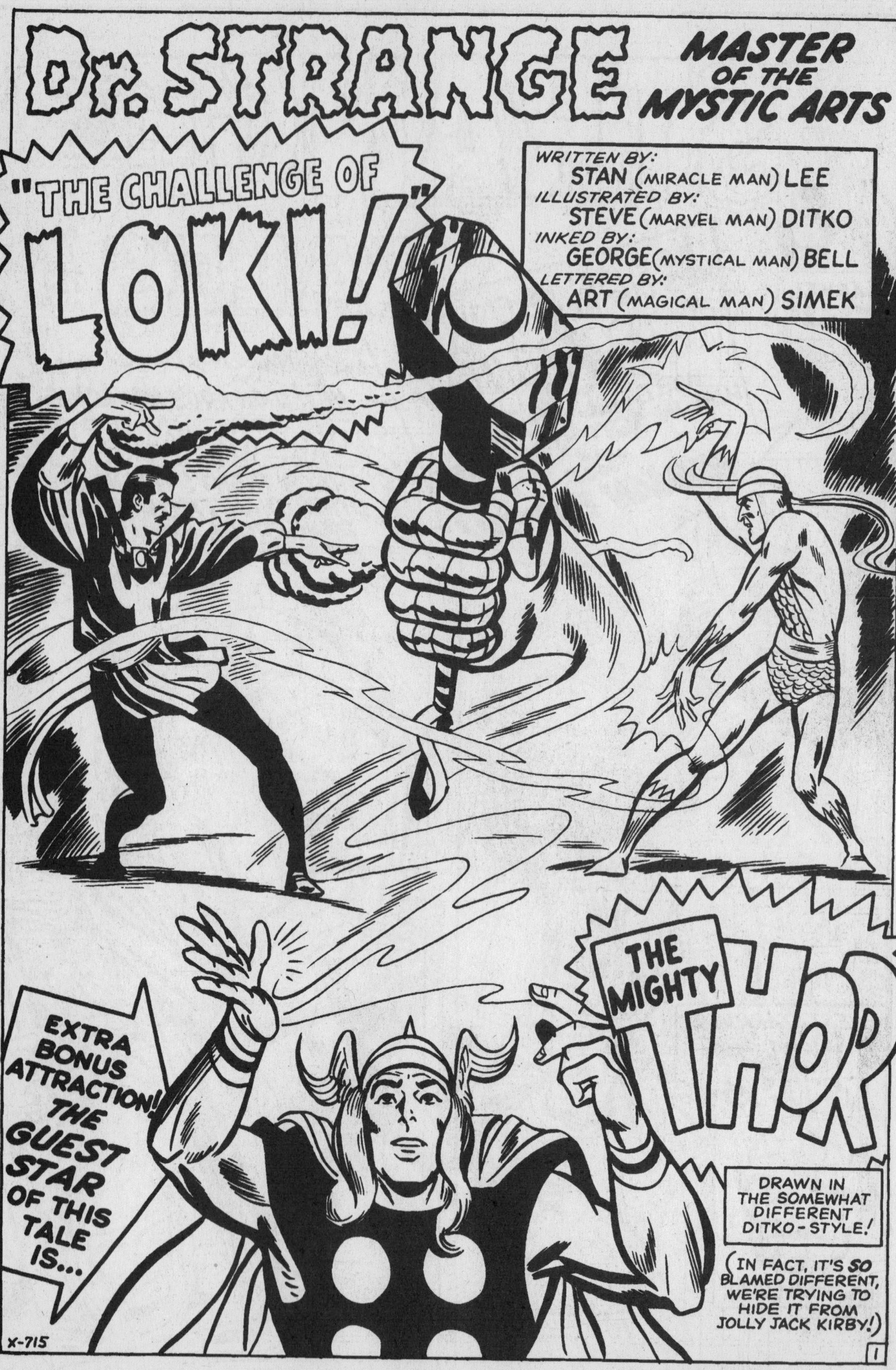
Dr. STRANGE
MASTER OF THE MYSTIC ARTS
"THE CHALLENGE OF LOKI!"
WRITTEN BY: STAN (MIRACLE MAN) LEE
ILLUSTRATED BY: STEVE (MARVEL MAN) DITKO
INKED BY: GEORGE (MYSTICAL MAN) BELL
LETTERED BY: ART (MAGICAL MAN) SIMEK
EXTRA BONUS ATTRACTION! THE GUEST STAR OF THIS TALE IS...
THE MIGHTY THOR
DRAWN IN THE SOMEWHAT DIFFERENT DITKO-STYLE!
(IN FACT, IT'S SO BLAMED DIFFERENT, WE'RE TRYING TO HIDE IT FROM JOLLY JACK KIRBY!)
X-715
1

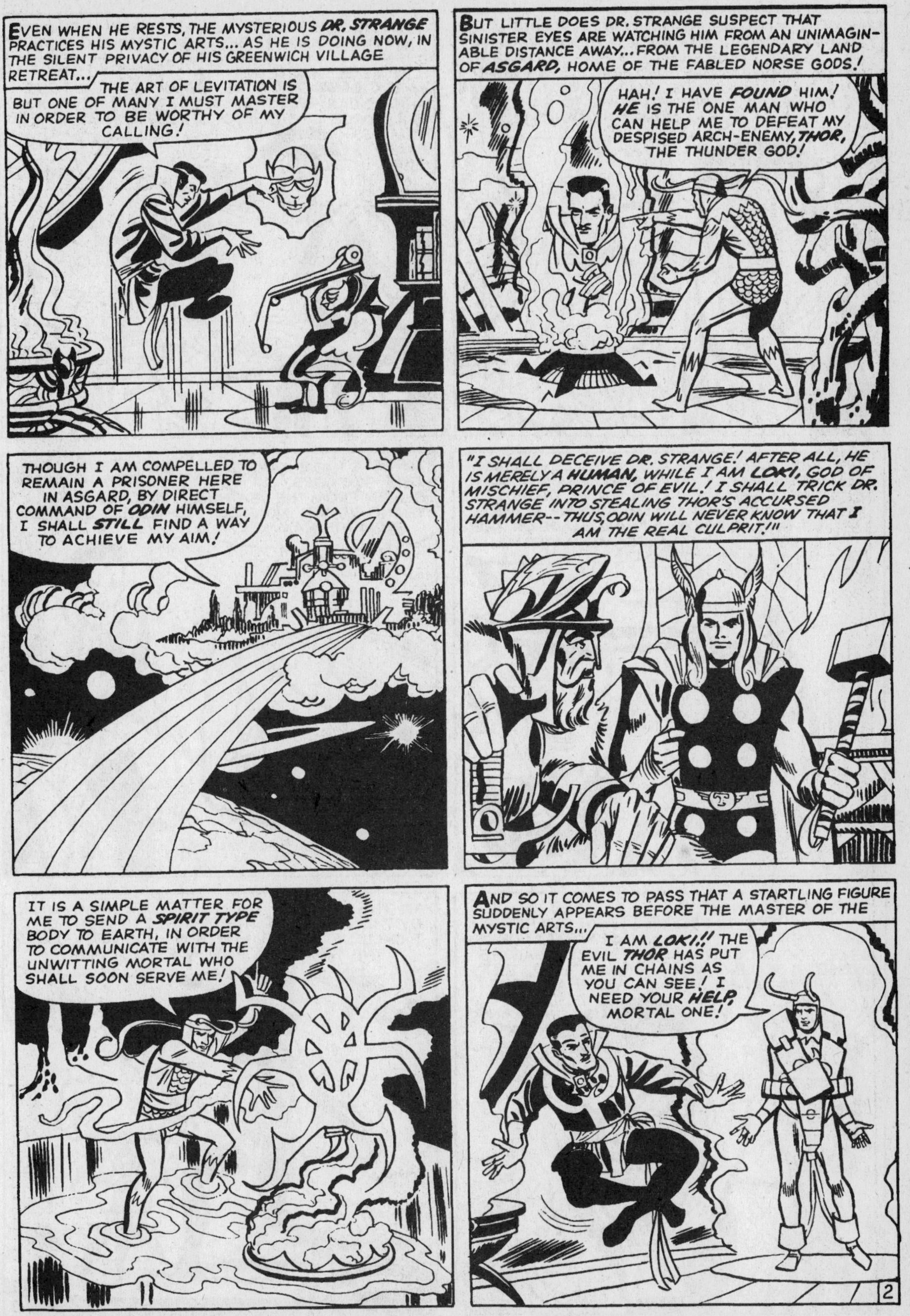
EVEN WHEN HE RESTS, THE MYSTERIOUS DR. STRANGE PRACTICES HIS MYSTIC ARTS... AS HE IS DOING NOW, IN THE SILENT PRIVACY OF HIS GREENWICH VILLAGE RETREAT...
THE ART OF LEVITATION IS BUT ONE OF MANY I MUST MASTER IN ORDER TO BE WORTHY OF MY CALLING!
BUT LITTLE DOES DR. STRANGE SUSPECT THAT SINISTER EYES ARE WATCHING HIM FROM AN UNIMAGINABLE DISTANCE AWAY... FROM THE LEGENDARY LAND OF ASGARD, HOME OF THE FABLED NORSE GODS!
HAH! I HAVE FOUND HIM! HE IS THE ONE MAN WHO CAN HELP ME TO DEFEAT MY DESPISED ARCH-ENEMY, THOR, THE THUNDER GOD!
THOUGH I AM COMPELLED TO REMAIN A PRISONER HERE IN ASGARD, BY DIRECT COMMAND OF ODIN HIMSELF, I SHALL STILL FIND A WAY TO ACHIEVE MY AIM!
"I SHALL DECEIVE DR. STRANGE! AFTER ALL, HE IS MERELY A HUMAN, WHILE I AM LOKI, GOD OF MISCHIEF, PRINCE OF EVIL! I SHALL TRICK DR. STRANGE INTO STEALING THOR'S ACCURSED HAMMER--THUS, ODIN WILL NEVER KNOW THAT I AM THE REAL CULPRIT!"
IT IS A SIMPLE MATTER FOR ME TO SEND A SPIRIT TYPE BODY TO EARTH, IN ORDER TO COMMUNICATE WITH THE UNWITTING MORTAL WHO SHALL SOON SERVE ME!
AND SO IT COMES TO PASS THAT A STARTLING FIGURE SUDDENLY APPEARS BEFORE THE MASTER OF THE MYSTIC ARTS...
I AM LOKI!! THE EVIL THOR HAS PUT ME IN CHAINS AS YOU CAN SEE! I NEED YOUR HELP, MORTAL ONE!
2

THOR? BUT--I THOUGHT THAT HE FOUGHT ONLY FOR RIGHT AND JUSTICE!

NO! HE HAS DECEIVED THE HUMAN RACE, EVEN AS HE NOW DECEIVES HIS FATHER, ODIN! HE PLANS TO CONQUER MANKIND--AND HE CHAINED ME THUS WHEN I TRIED TO COME TO EARTH TO WARN HUMANITY!

BUT I ESCAPED, AND I CAME TO YOU-- THE ONE HUMAN WHO MIGHT BELIEVE--WHO MIGHT HELP!

LET ME SEE WHAT MY MAGIC AMULET REVEALS! AHH-- I CAN FEEL THE EVIL FORCE OF THOSE CHAINS! THEY WILL NOT BREAK!

GOOD! HE DOESN'T SUSPECT THAT THE EVIL HE SENSES IS IN MY HEART!

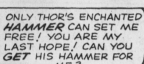

ONLY THOR'S ENCHANTED HAMMER CAN SET ME FREE! YOU ARE MY LAST HOPE! CAN YOU GET HIS HAMMER FOR ME?

MY SPELLS WILL NOT WORK AGAINST SO ALIEN AN OBJECT! IF ONLY I HAD SOMETHING MADE OF THE SAME MATERIAL...

HERE! I HAVE CARRIED THIS FOR AGES! IT IS A SLIVER FROM THE LEATHER THONG WHICH DANGLES FROM HIS HAMMER!

GOOD! THAT IS ALL I NEED IN ORDER TO CAST A SPELL!

I KNEW IT! I KNEW IT WOULD BE EASY TO DECEIVE HIM! MORTALS ARE ALL ALIKE-- SO TRUSTING-- SO UNUSED TO DEALING WITH ONE WHO IS THOROUGHLY EVIL!

I CAN SENSE THAT THERE IS MORE TO LOKI'S STORY THAN HE HAS TOLD! BUT I SHALL SEE WHAT HAPPENS NEXT...

IN THE NAME OF THE DREAD DORMAMMU... BY THE POWER OF THE DEATHLESS VISHANTI... I CALL UPON THE HOSTS OF HOGGOTH! HEED THE WORDS OF THY MORTAL SERVANT!

3

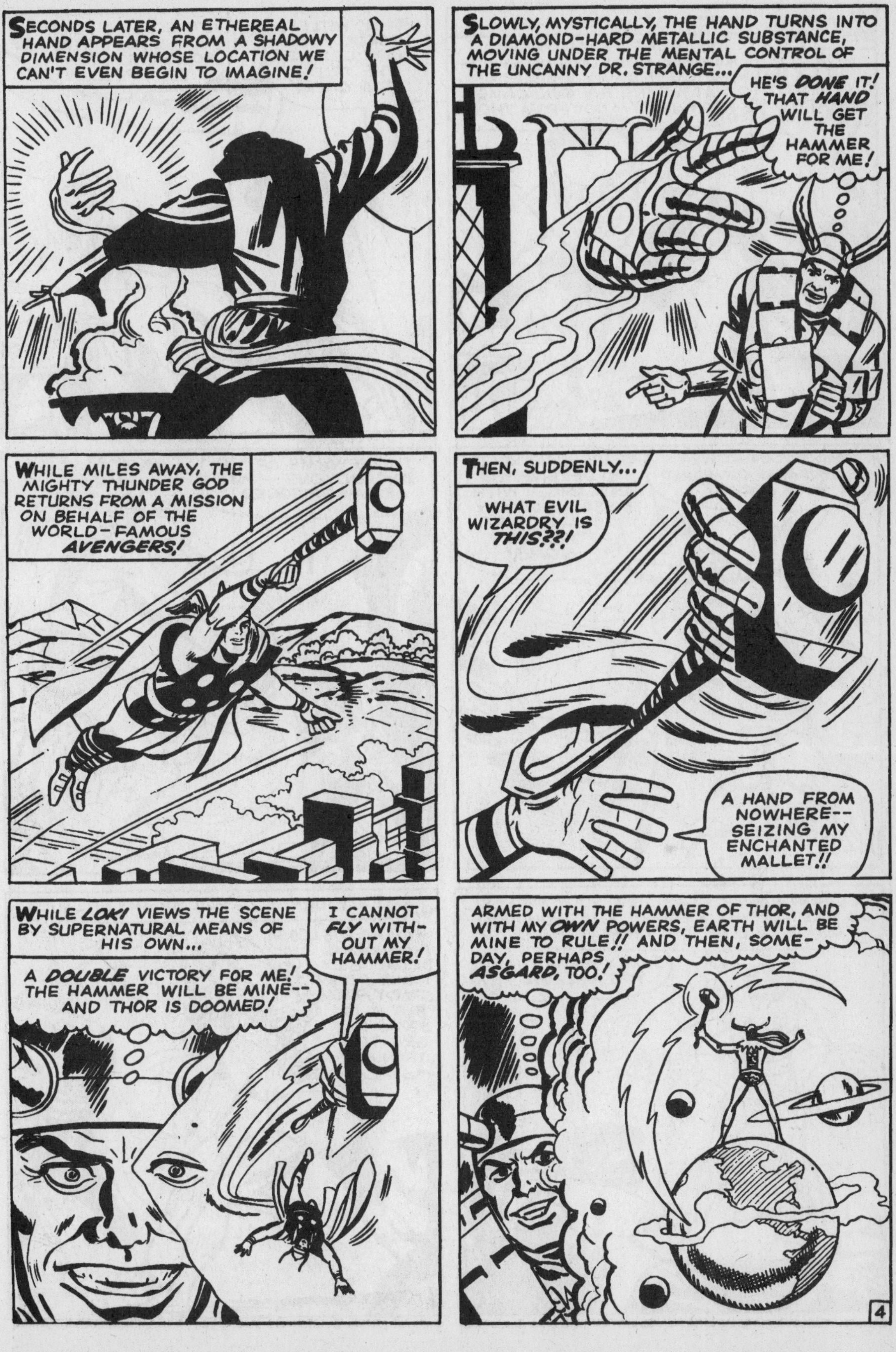
SECONDS LATER, AN ETHEREAL HAND APPEARS FROM A SHADOWY DIMENSION WHOSE LOCATION WE CAN'T EVEN BEGIN TO IMAGINE!
SLOWLY, MYSTICALLY, THE HAND TURNS INTO A DIAMOND-HARD METALLIC SUBSTANCE, MOVING UNDER THE MENTAL CONTROL OF THE UNCANNY DR. STRANGE...
HE'S DONE IT! THAT HAND WILL GET THE HAMMER FOR ME!
WHILE MILES AWAY, THE MIGHTY THUNDER GOD RETURNS FROM A MISSION ON BEHALF OF THE WORLD-FAMOUS AVENGERS!
THEN, SUDDENLY...
WHAT EVIL WIZARDRY IS THIS??!
A HAND FROM NOWHERE-- SEIZING MY ENCHANTED MALLET!!
WHILE LOKI VIEWS THE SCENE BY SUPERNATURAL MEANS OF HIS OWN...
I CANNOT FLY WITH-OUT MY HAMMER!
A DOUBLE VICTORY FOR ME! THE HAMMER WILL BE MINE-- AND THOR IS DOOMED!
ARMED WITH THE HAMMER OF THOR, AND WITH MY OWN POWERS, EARTH WILL BE MINE TO RULE!! AND THEN, SOME-DAY, PERHAPS ASGARD, TOO!
4

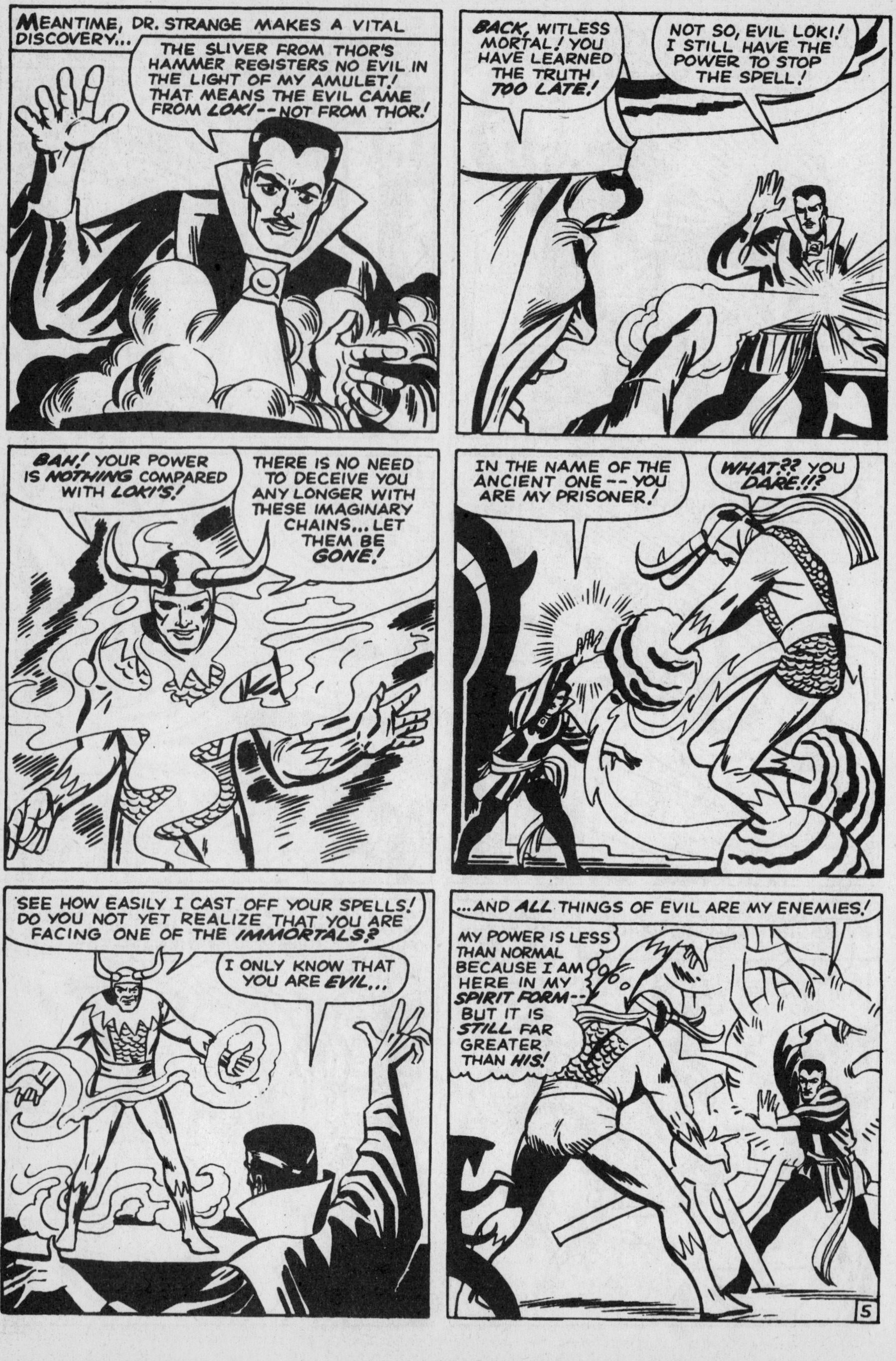
MEANTIME, DR. STRANGE MAKES A VITAL DISCOVERY...
THE SLIVER FROM THOR'S HAMMER REGISTERS NO EVIL IN THE LIGHT OF MY AMULET! THAT MEANS THE EVIL CAME FROM LOKI!--NOT FROM THOR!
BACK, WITLESS MORTAL! YOU HAVE LEARNED THE TRUTH TOO LATE!
NOT SO, EVIL LOKI! I STILL HAVE THE POWER TO STOP THE SPELL!
BAH! YOUR POWER IS NOTHING COMPARED WITH LOKI'S!
THERE IS NO NEED TO DECEIVE YOU ANY LONGER WITH THESE IMAGINARY CHAINS... LET THEM BE GONE!
IN THE NAME OF THE ANCIENT ONE -- YOU ARE MY PRISONER!
WHAT?? YOU DARE!!?
SEE HOW EASILY I CAST OFF YOUR SPELLS! DO YOU NOT YET REALIZE THAT YOU ARE FACING ONE OF THE IMMORTALS?
I ONLY KNOW THAT YOU ARE EVIL...
...AND ALL THINGS OF EVIL ARE MY ENEMIES!
MY POWER IS LESS THAN NORMAL BECAUSE I AM HERE IN MY SPIRIT FORM-- BUT IT IS STILL FAR GREATER THAN HIS!
5

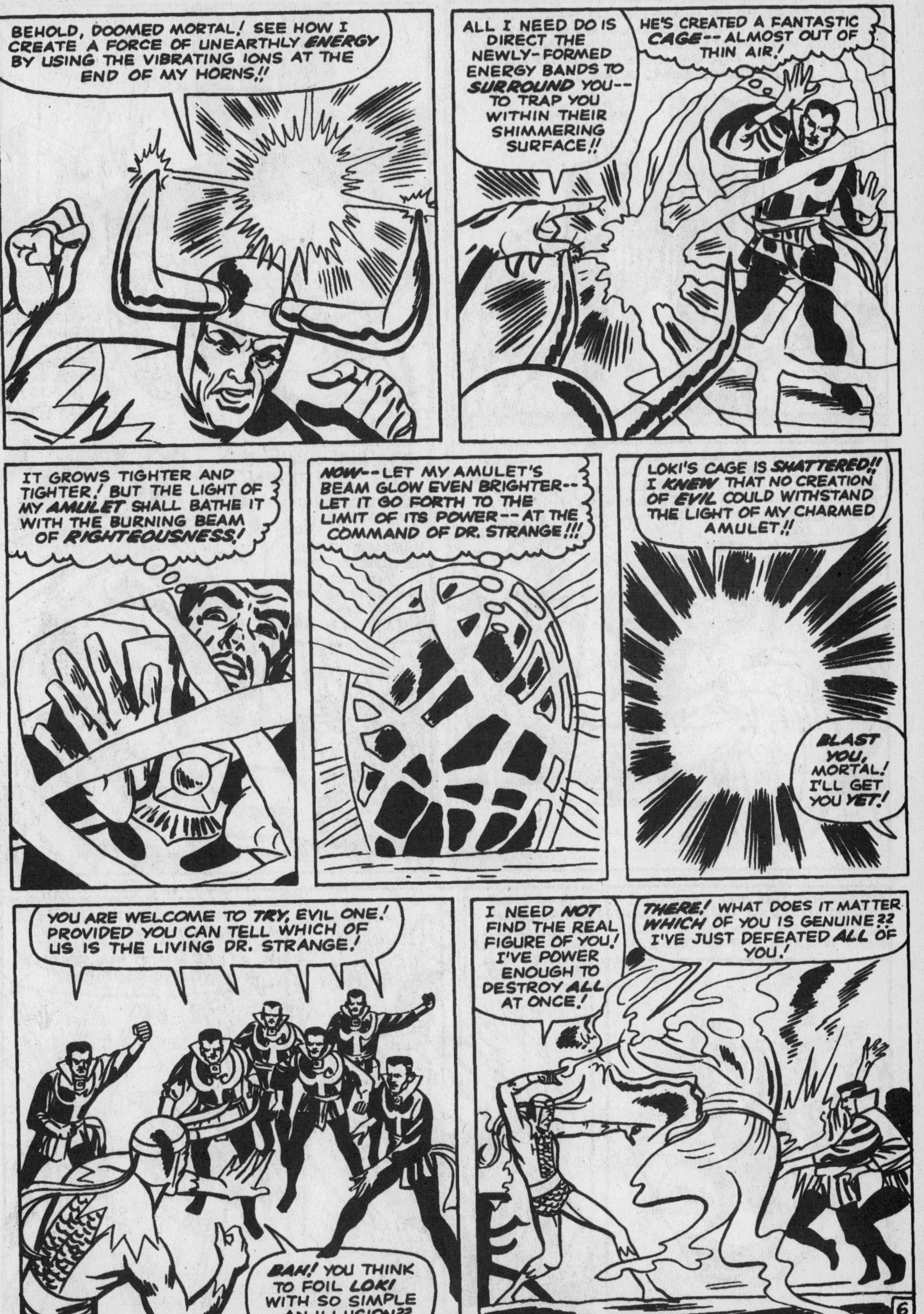
BEHOLD, DOOMED MORTAL! SEE HOW I CREATE A FORCE OF UNEARTHLY ENERGY BY USING THE VIBRATING IONS AT THE END OF MY HORNS!!
ALL I NEED DO IS DIRECT THE NEWLY-FORMED ENERGY BANDS TO SURROUND YOU-- TO TRAP YOU WITHIN THEIR SHIMMERING SURFACE!!
HE'S CREATED A FANTASTIC CAGE-- ALMOST OUT OF THIN AIR!
IT GROWS TIGHTER AND TIGHTER! BUT THE LIGHT OF MY AMULET SHALL BATHE IT WITH THE BURNING BEAM OF RIGHTEOUSNESS!
NOW--LET MY AMULET'S BEAM GLOW EVEN BRIGHTER-- LET IT GO FORTH TO THE LIMIT OF ITS POWER--AT THE COMMAND OF DR. STRANGE!!!
LOKI'S CAGE IS SHATTERED!! I KNEW THAT NO CREATION OF EVIL COULD WITHSTAND THE LIGHT OF MY CHARMED AMULET!!
BLAST YOU, MORTAL! I'LL GET YOU YET!
YOU ARE WELCOME TO TRY, EVIL ONE! PROVIDED YOU CAN TELL WHICH OF US IS THE LIVING DR. STRANGE!
BAH! YOU THINK TO FOIL LOKI WITH SO SIMPLE AN ILLUSION??
I NEED NOT FIND THE REAL FIGURE OF YOU! I'VE POWER ENOUGH TO DESTROY ALL AT ONCE!
THERE! WHAT DOES IT MATTER WHICH OF YOU IS GENUINE?? I'VE JUST DEFEATED ALL OF YOU!
6

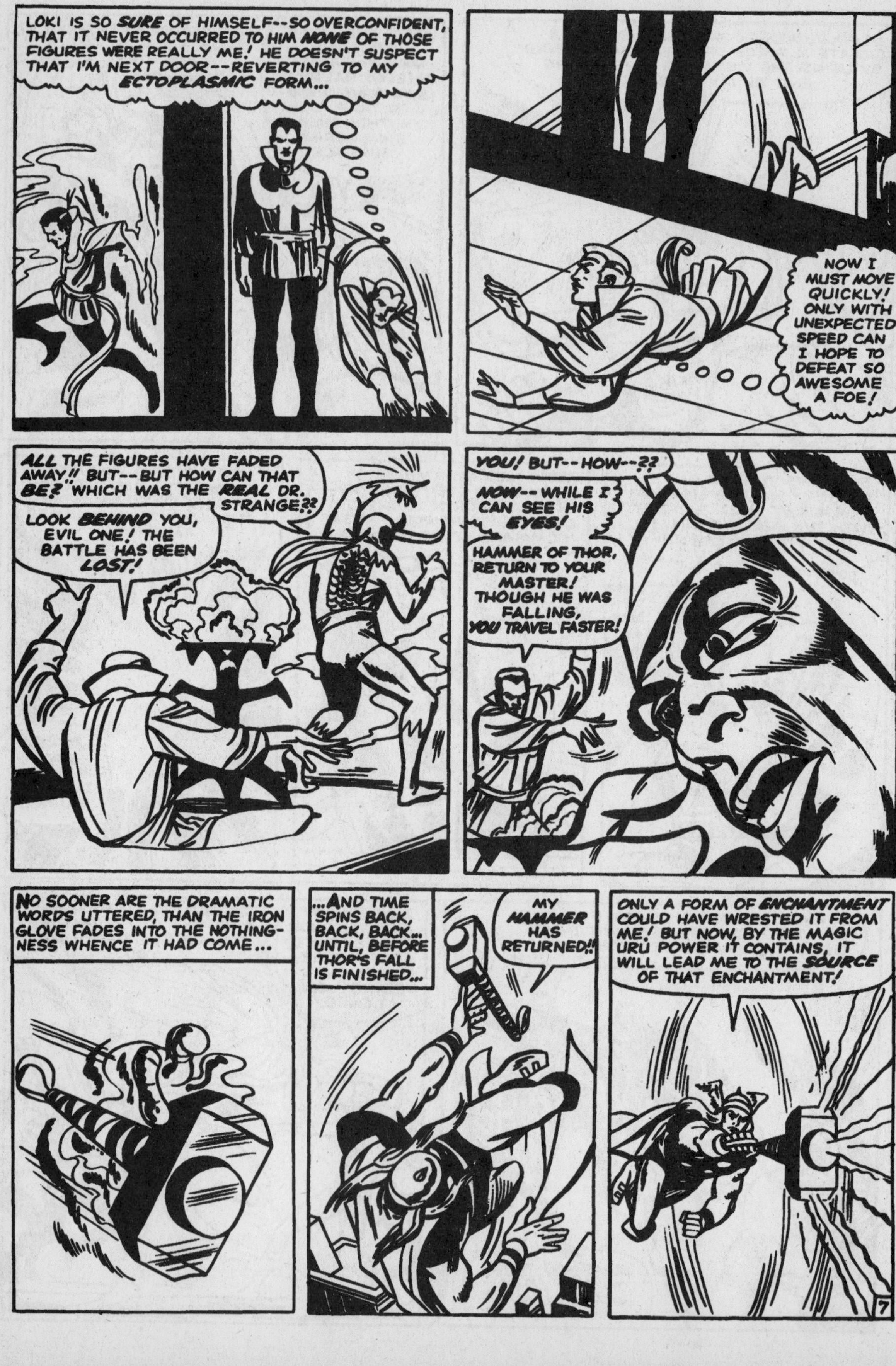
LOKI IS SO SURE OF HIMSELF--SO OVERCONFIDENT, THAT IT NEVER OCCURRED TO HIM NONE OF THOSE FIGURES WERE REALLY ME! HE DOESN'T SUSPECT THAT I'M NEXT DOOR--REVERTING TO MY ECTOPLASMIC FORM...
NOW I MUST MOVE QUICKLY! ONLY WITH UNEXPECTED SPEED CAN I HOPE TO DEFEAT SO AWESOME A FOE!
ALL THE FIGURES HAVE FADED AWAY!! BUT--BUT HOW CAN THAT BE? WHICH WAS THE REAL DR. STRANGE??
LOOK BEHIND YOU, EVIL ONE! THE BATTLE HAS BEEN LOST!
YOU! BUT--HOW--??
NOW--WHILE I CAN SEE HIS EYES!
HAMMER OF THOR, RETURN TO YOUR MASTER! THOUGH HE WAS FALLING, YOU TRAVEL FASTER!
NO SOONER ARE THE DRAMATIC WORDS UTTERED, THAN THE IRON GLOVE FADES INTO THE NOTHINGNESS WHENCE IT HAD COME...
...AND TIME SPINS BACK, BACK, BACK... UNTIL, BEFORE THOR'S FALL IS FINISHED...
MY HAMMER HAS RETURNED!!
ONLY A FORM OF ENCHANTMENT COULD HAVE WRESTED IT FROM ME! BUT NOW, BY THE MAGIC URU POWER IT CONTAINS, IT WILL LEAD ME TO THE SOURCE OF THAT ENCHANTMENT!
7

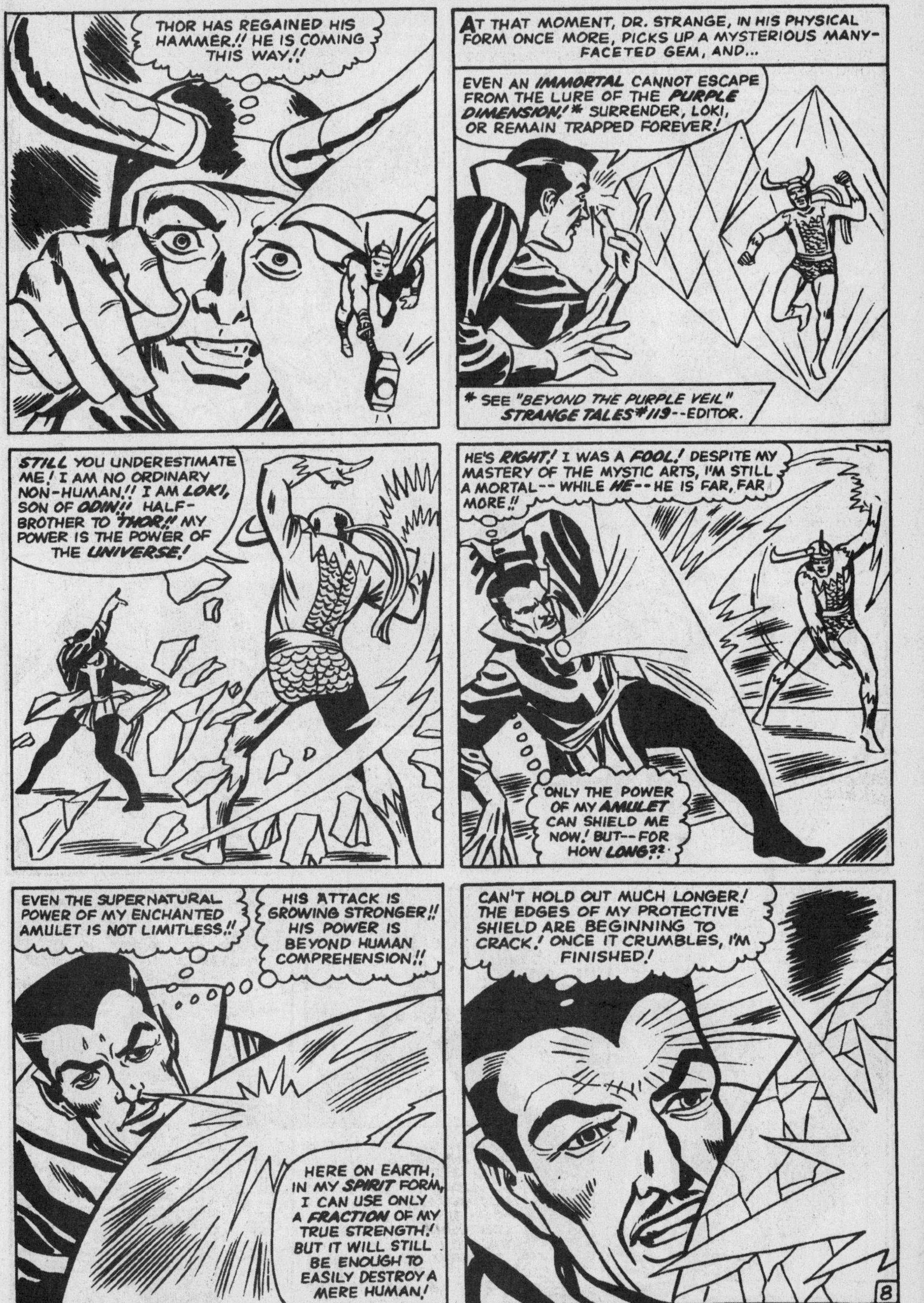
THOR HAS REGAINED HIS HAMMER!! HE IS COMING THIS WAY!!
AT THAT MOMENT, DR. STRANGE, IN HIS PHYSICAL FORM ONCE MORE, PICKS UP A MYSTERIOUS MANY-FACETED GEM, AND...
EVEN AN IMMORTAL CANNOT ESCAPE FROM THE LURE OF THE PURPLE DIMENSION!* SURRENDER, LOKI, OR REMAIN TRAPPED FOREVER!
* SEE "BEYOND THE PURPLE VEIL" STRANGE TALES #119--EDITOR.
STILL YOU UNDERESTIMATE ME! I AM NO ORDINARY NON-HUMAN!! I AM LOKI, SON OF ODIN!! HALF-BROTHER TO "THOR!" MY POWER IS THE POWER OF THE UNIVERSE!
HE'S RIGHT! I WAS A FOOL! DESPITE MY MASTERY OF THE MYSTIC ARTS, I'M STILL A MORTAL-- WHILE HE-- HE IS FAR, FAR MORE!!
ONLY THE POWER OF MY AMULET CAN SHIELD ME NOW! BUT--FOR HOW LONG??
EVEN THE SUPERNATURAL POWER OF MY ENCHANTED AMULET IS NOT LIMITLESS!!
HIS ATTACK IS GROWING STRONGER!! HIS POWER IS BEYOND HUMAN COMPREHENSION!!
HERE ON EARTH, IN MY SPIRIT FORM, I CAN USE ONLY A FRACTION OF MY TRUE STRENGTH! BUT IT WILL STILL BE ENOUGH TO EASILY DESTROY A MERE HUMAN!
CAN'T HOLD OUT MUCH LONGER! THE EDGES OF MY PROTECTIVE SHIELD ARE BEGINNING TO CRACK! ONCE IT CRUMBLES, I'M FINISHED!
8

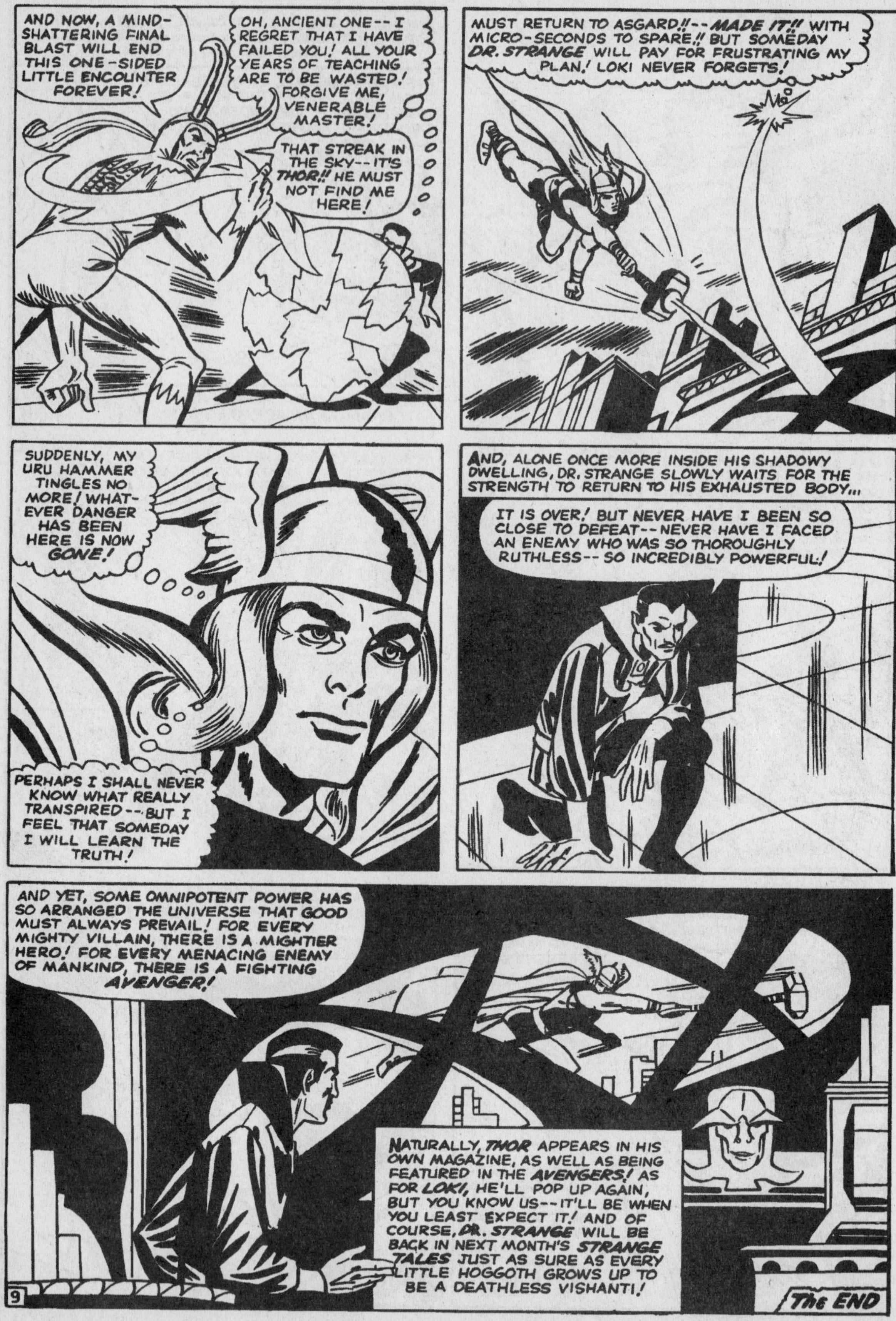
AND NOW, A MIND-SHATTERING FINAL BLAST WILL END THIS ONE-SIDED LITTLE ENCOUNTER FOREVER!
OH, ANCIENT ONE-- I REGRET THAT I HAVE FAILED YOU! ALL YOUR YEARS OF TEACHING ARE TO BE WASTED! FORGIVE ME, VENERABLE MASTER!
THAT STREAK IN THE SKY--IT'S THOR!! HE MUST NOT FIND ME HERE!
MUST RETURN TO ASGARD!!--MADE IT!! WITH MICRO-SECONDS TO SPARE!! BUT SOMEDAY DR. STRANGE WILL PAY FOR FRUSTRATING MY PLAN! LOKI NEVER FORGETS!
SUDDENLY, MY URU HAMMER TINGLES NO MORE! WHAT-EVER DANGER HAS BEEN HERE IS NOW GONE!
PERHAPS I SHALL NEVER KNOW WHAT REALLY TRANSPIRED--BUT I FEEL THAT SOMEDAY I WILL LEARN THE TRUTH!
AND, ALONE ONCE MORE INSIDE HIS SHADOWY DWELLING, DR. STRANGE SLOWLY WAITS FOR THE STRENGTH TO RETURN TO HIS EXHAUSTED BODY...
IT IS OVER! BUT NEVER HAVE I BEEN SO CLOSE TO DEFEAT--NEVER HAVE I FACED AN ENEMY WHO WAS SO THOROUGHLY RUTHLESS-- SO INCREDIBLY POWERFUL!
AND YET, SOME OMNIPOTENT POWER HAS SO ARRANGED THE UNIVERSE THAT GOOD MUST ALWAYS PREVAIL! FOR EVERY MIGHTY VILLAIN, THERE IS A MIGHTIER HERO! FOR EVERY MENACING ENEMY OF MANKIND, THERE IS A FIGHTING AVENGER!
NATURALLY, THOR APPEARS IN HIS OWN MAGAZINE, AS WELL AS BEING FEATURED IN THE AVENGERS! AS FOR LOKI, HE'LL POP UP AGAIN, BUT YOU KNOW US--IT'LL BE WHEN YOU LEAST EXPECT IT! AND OF COURSE, DR. STRANGE WILL BE BACK IN NEXT MONTH'S STRANGE TALES JUST AS SURE AS EVERY LITTLE HOGGOTH GROWS UP TO BE A DEATHLESS VISHANTI!
9
The END

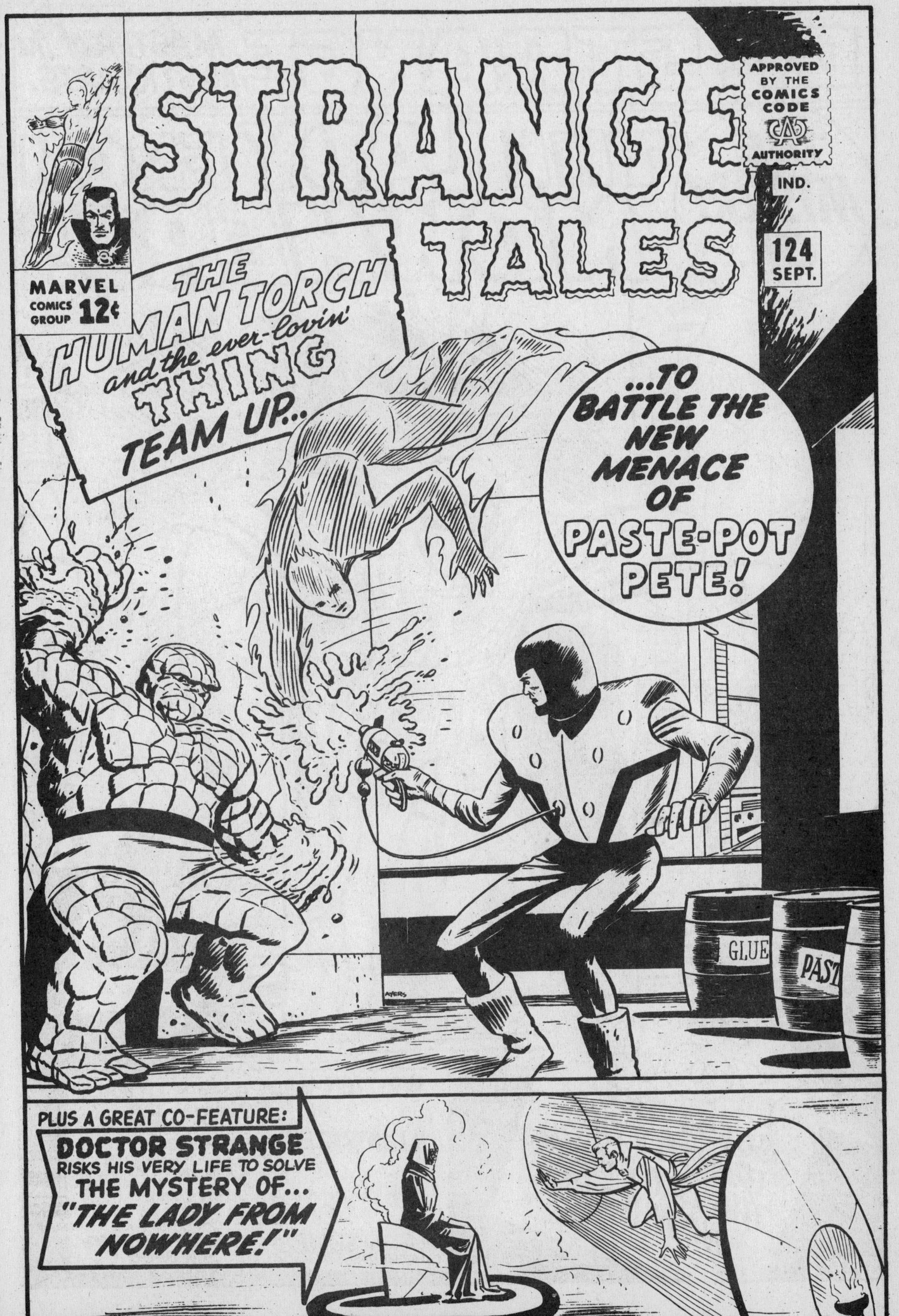

STRANGE TALES
APPROVED BY THE COMICS CODE AUTHORITY
IND.
124
SEPT.
MARVEL COMICS GROUP 12¢
THE HUMAN TORCH and the ever-lovin' THING TEAM UP...
...TO BATTLE THE NEW MENACE OF PASTE-POT PETE!
GLUE
PAST
AYERS
PLUS A GREAT CO-FEATURE:
DOCTOR STRANGE RISKS HIS VERY LIFE TO SOLVE THE MYSTERY OF... "THE LADY FROM NOWHERE!"

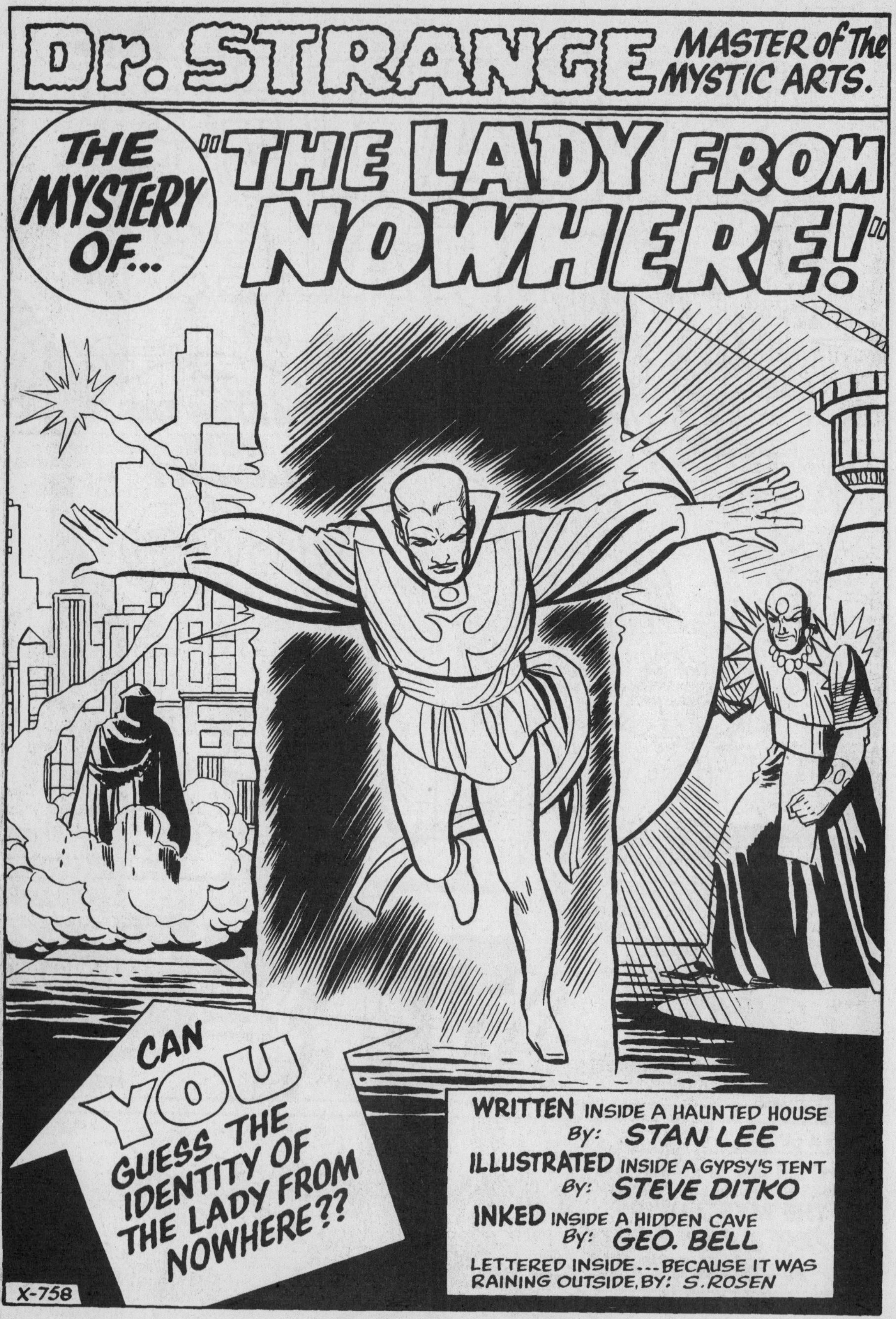

Dr. STRANGE MASTER of The MYSTIC ARTS.
THE MYSTERY OF...
"THE LADY FROM NOWHERE!"
CAN YOU GUESS THE IDENTITY OF THE LADY FROM NOWHERE??
WRITTEN INSIDE A HAUNTED HOUSE By: STAN LEE
ILLUSTRATED INSIDE A GYPSY'S TENT By: STEVE DITKO
INKED INSIDE A HIDDEN CAVE By: GEO. BELL
LETTERED INSIDE...BECAUSE IT WAS RAINING OUTSIDE, BY: S. ROSEN
X-758

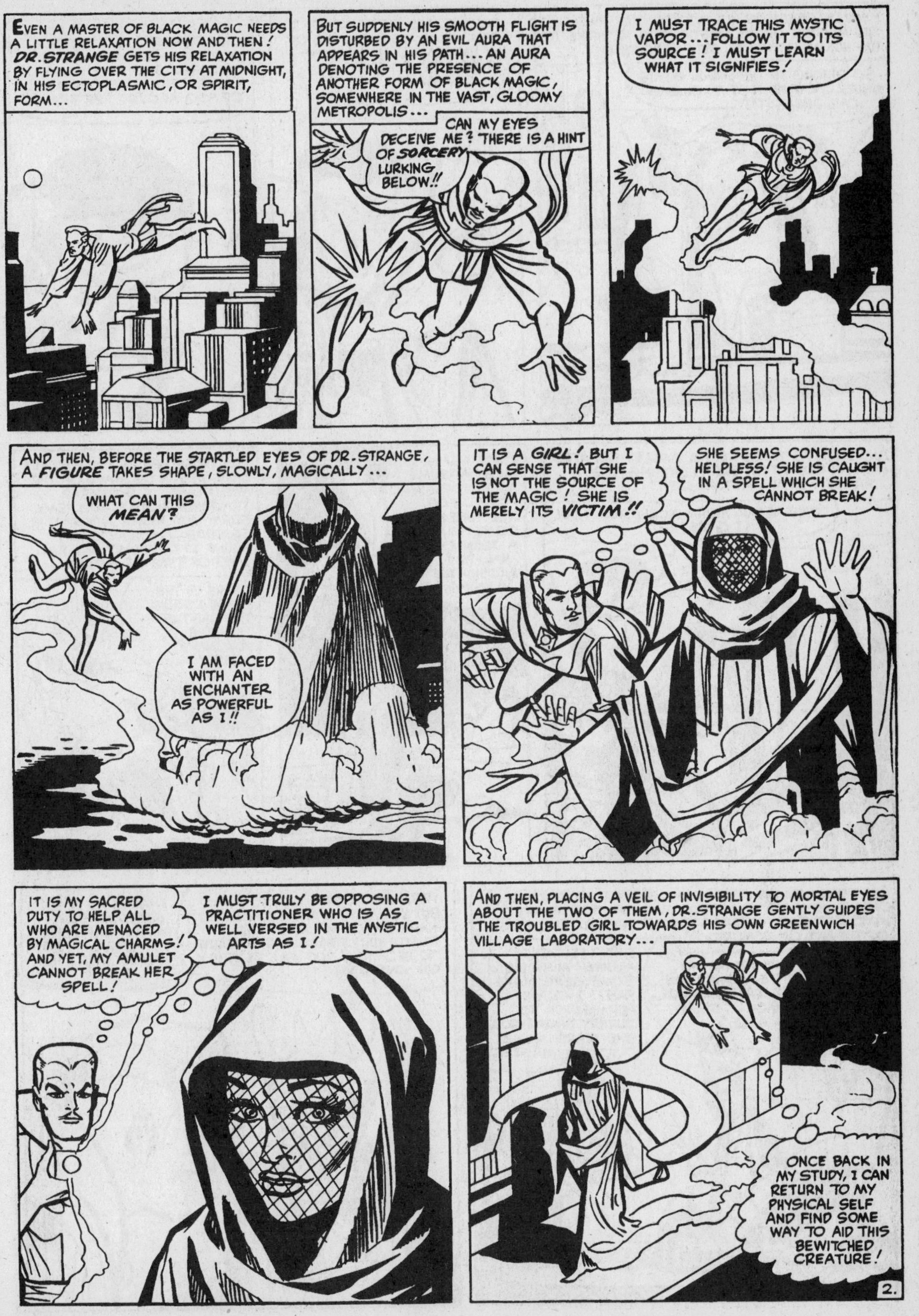
EVEN A MASTER OF BLACK MAGIC NEEDS A LITTLE RELAXATION NOW AND THEN! DR. STRANGE GETS HIS RELAXATION BY FLYING OVER THE CITY AT MIDNIGHT, IN HIS ECTOPLASMIC, OR SPIRIT, FORM...
BUT SUDDENLY HIS SMOOTH FLIGHT IS DISTURBED BY AN EVIL AURA THAT APPEARS IN HIS PATH... AN AURA DENOTING THE PRESENCE OF ANOTHER FORM OF BLACK MAGIC, SOMEWHERE IN THE VAST, GLOOMY METROPOLIS...
CAN MY EYES DECEIVE ME? THERE IS A HINT OF SORCERY LURKING BELOW!!
I MUST TRACE THIS MYSTIC VAPOR... FOLLOW IT TO ITS SOURCE! I MUST LEARN WHAT IT SIGNIFIES!
AND THEN, BEFORE THE STARTLED EYES OF DR. STRANGE, A FIGURE TAKES SHAPE, SLOWLY, MAGICALLY...
WHAT CAN THIS MEAN?
I AM FACED WITH AN ENCHANTER AS POWERFUL AS I!!
IT IS A GIRL! BUT I CAN SENSE THAT SHE IS NOT THE SOURCE OF THE MAGIC! SHE IS MERELY ITS VICTIM!!
SHE SEEMS CONFUSED... HELPLESS! SHE IS CAUGHT IN A SPELL WHICH SHE CANNOT BREAK!
IT IS MY SACRED DUTY TO HELP ALL WHO ARE MENACED BY MAGICAL CHARMS! AND YET, MY AMULET CANNOT BREAK HER SPELL!
I MUST TRULY BE OPPOSING A PRACTITIONER WHO IS AS WELL VERSED IN THE MYSTIC ARTS AS I!
AND THEN, PLACING A VEIL OF INVISIBILITY TO MORTAL EYES ABOUT THE TWO OF THEM, DR. STRANGE GENTLY GUIDES THE TROUBLED GIRL TOWARDS HIS OWN GREENWICH VILLAGE LABORATORY...
ONCE BACK IN MY STUDY, I CAN RETURN TO MY PHYSICAL SELF AND FIND SOME WAY TO AID THIS BEWITCHED CREATURE!
2.

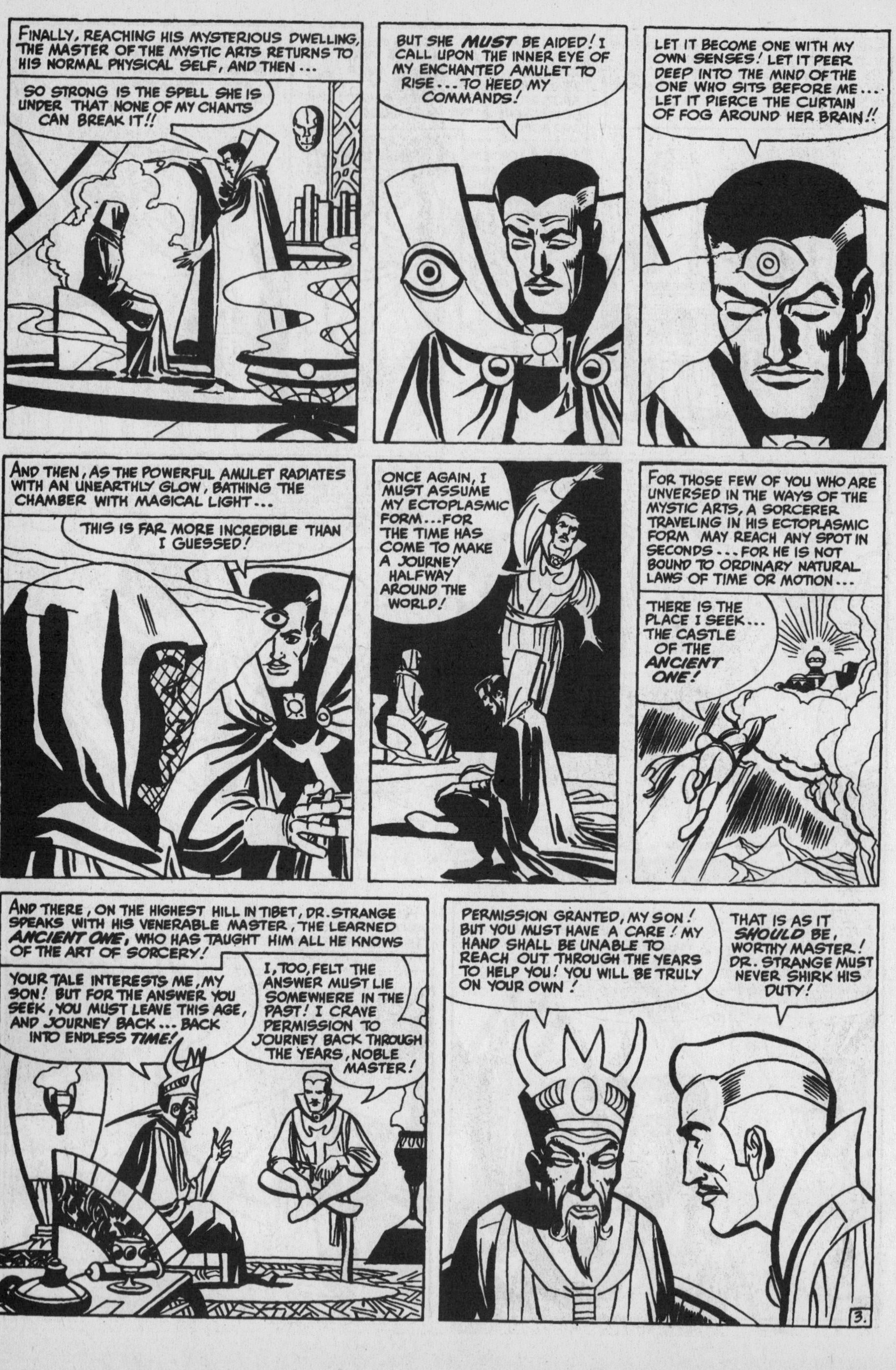
FINALLY, REACHING HIS MYSTERIOUS DWELLING, THE MASTER OF THE MYSTIC ARTS RETURNS TO HIS NORMAL PHYSICAL SELF, AND THEN...
SO STRONG IS THE SPELL SHE IS UNDER THAT NONE OF MY CHANTS CAN BREAK IT!!
BUT SHE MUST BE AIDED! I CALL UPON THE INNER EYE OF MY ENCHANTED AMULET TO RISE... TO HEED MY COMMANDS!
LET IT BECOME ONE WITH MY OWN SENSES! LET IT PEER DEEP INTO THE MIND OF THE ONE WHO SITS BEFORE ME... LET IT PIERCE THE CURTAIN OF FOG AROUND HER BRAIN!!
AND THEN, AS THE POWERFUL AMULET RADIATES WITH AN UNEARTHLY GLOW, BATHING THE CHAMBER WITH MAGICAL LIGHT...
THIS IS FAR MORE INCREDIBLE THAN I GUESSED!
ONCE AGAIN, I MUST ASSUME MY ECTOPLASMIC FORM... FOR THE TIME HAS COME TO MAKE A JOURNEY HALFWAY AROUND THE WORLD!
FOR THOSE FEW OF YOU WHO ARE UNVERSED IN THE WAYS OF THE MYSTIC ARTS, A SORCERER TRAVELING IN HIS ECTOPLASMIC FORM MAY REACH ANY SPOT IN SECONDS... FOR HE IS NOT BOUND TO ORDINARY NATURAL LAWS OF TIME OR MOTION...
THERE IS THE PLACE I SEEK... THE CASTLE OF THE ANCIENT ONE!
AND THERE, ON THE HIGHEST HILL IN TIBET, DR. STRANGE SPEAKS WITH HIS VENERABLE MASTER, THE LEARNED ANCIENT ONE, WHO HAS TAUGHT HIM ALL HE KNOWS OF THE ART OF SORCERY!
YOUR TALE INTERESTS ME, MY SON! BUT FOR THE ANSWER YOU SEEK, YOU MUST LEAVE THIS AGE, AND JOURNEY BACK... BACK INTO ENDLESS TIME!
I, TOO, FELT THE ANSWER MUST LIE SOMEWHERE IN THE PAST! I CRAVE PERMISSION TO JOURNEY BACK THROUGH THE YEARS, NOBLE MASTER!
PERMISSION GRANTED, MY SON! BUT YOU MUST HAVE A CARE! MY HAND SHALL BE UNABLE TO REACH OUT THROUGH THE YEARS TO HELP YOU! YOU WILL BE TRULY ON YOUR OWN!
THAT IS AS IT SHOULD BE, WORTHY MASTER! DR. STRANGE MUST NEVER SHIRK HIS DUTY!
3.

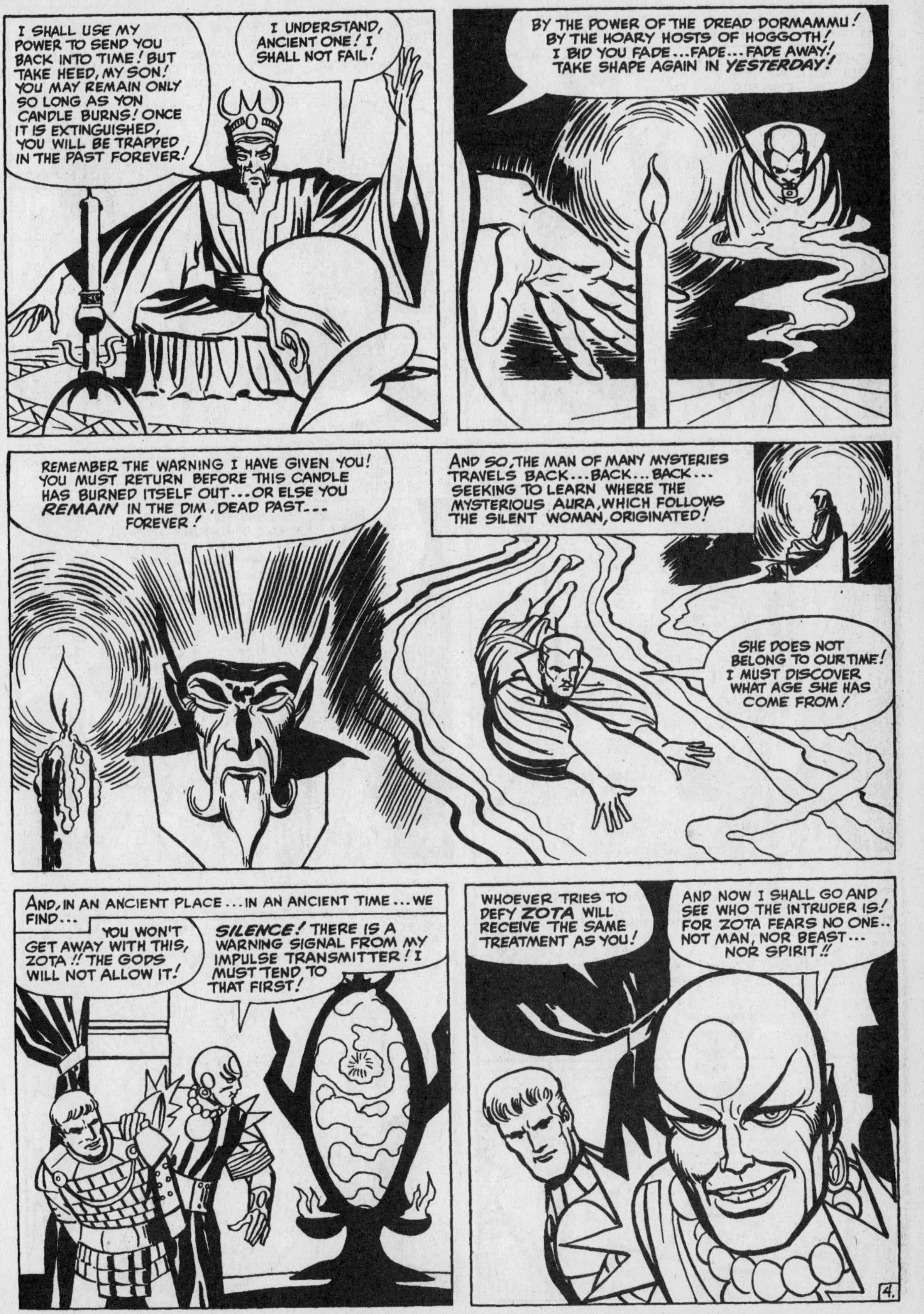
I SHALL USE MY POWER TO SEND YOU BACK INTO TIME! BUT TAKE HEED, MY SON! YOU MAY REMAIN ONLY SO LONG AS YON CANDLE BURNS! ONCE IT IS EXTINGUISHED, YOU WILL BE TRAPPED IN THE PAST FOREVER!
I UNDERSTAND, ANCIENT ONE! I SHALL NOT FAIL!
BY THE POWER OF THE DREAD DORMAMMU! BY THE HOARY HOSTS OF HOGGOTH! I BID YOU FADE...FADE...FADE AWAY! TAKE SHAPE AGAIN IN YESTERDAY!
REMEMBER THE WARNING I HAVE GIVEN YOU! YOU MUST RETURN BEFORE THIS CANDLE HAS BURNED ITSELF OUT...OR ELSE YOU REMAIN IN THE DIM, DEAD PAST... FOREVER!
AND SO, THE MAN OF MANY MYSTERIES TRAVELS BACK...BACK...BACK... SEEKING TO LEARN WHERE THE MYSTERIOUS AURA, WHICH FOLLOWS THE SILENT WOMAN, ORIGINATED!
SHE DOES NOT BELONG TO OUR TIME! I MUST DISCOVER WHAT AGE SHE HAS COME FROM!
AND, IN AN ANCIENT PLACE...IN AN ANCIENT TIME...WE FIND...
YOU WON'T GET AWAY WITH THIS, ZOTA!! THE GODS WILL NOT ALLOW IT!
SILENCE! THERE IS A WARNING SIGNAL FROM MY IMPULSE TRANSMITTER! I MUST TEND TO THAT FIRST!
WHOEVER TRIES TO DEFY ZOTA WILL RECEIVE THE SAME TREATMENT AS YOU!
AND NOW I SHALL GO AND SEE WHO THE INTRUDER IS! FOR ZOTA FEARS NO ONE.. NOT MAN, NOR BEAST... NOR SPIRIT!!
4.

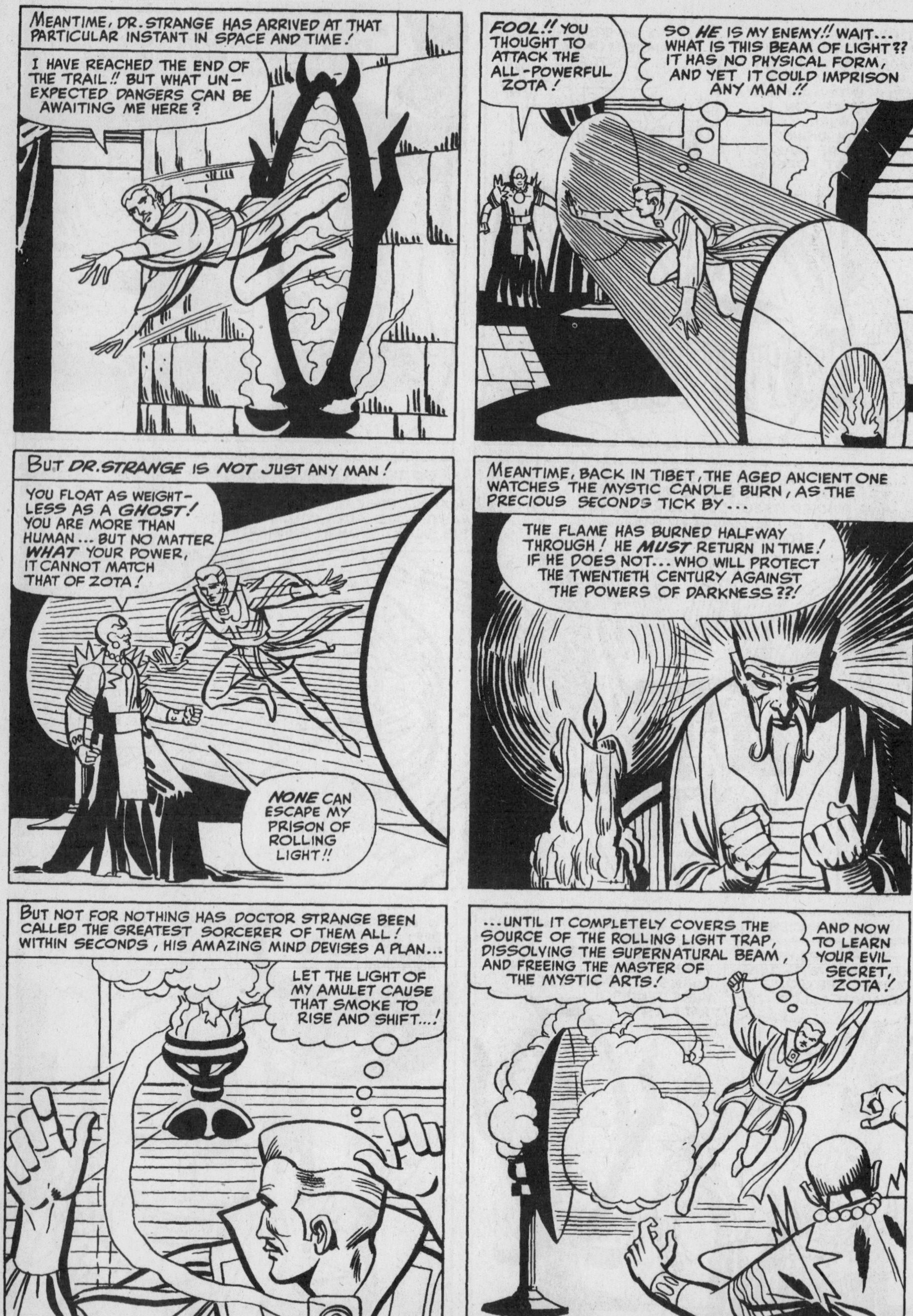
MEANTIME, DR. STRANGE HAS ARRIVED AT THAT PARTICULAR INSTANT IN SPACE AND TIME!
I HAVE REACHED THE END OF THE TRAIL!! BUT WHAT UN-EXPECTED DANGERS CAN BE AWAITING ME HERE?
FOOL!! YOU THOUGHT TO ATTACK THE ALL-POWERFUL ZOTA!
SO HE IS MY ENEMY!! WAIT... WHAT IS THIS BEAM OF LIGHT?? IT HAS NO PHYSICAL FORM, AND YET IT COULD IMPRISON ANY MAN!!
BUT DR. STRANGE IS NOT JUST ANY MAN!
YOU FLOAT AS WEIGHT-LESS AS A GHOST! YOU ARE MORE THAN HUMAN... BUT NO MATTER WHAT YOUR POWER, IT CANNOT MATCH THAT OF ZOTA!
NONE CAN ESCAPE MY PRISON OF ROLLING LIGHT!!
MEANTIME, BACK IN TIBET, THE AGED ANCIENT ONE WATCHES THE MYSTIC CANDLE BURN, AS THE PRECIOUS SECONDS TICK BY...
THE FLAME HAS BURNED HALFWAY THROUGH! HE MUST RETURN IN TIME! IF HE DOES NOT... WHO WILL PROTECT THE TWENTIETH CENTURY AGAINST THE POWERS OF DARKNESS??!
BUT NOT FOR NOTHING HAS DOCTOR STRANGE BEEN CALLED THE GREATEST SORCERER OF THEM ALL! WITHIN SECONDS, HIS AMAZING MIND DEVISES A PLAN...
LET THE LIGHT OF MY AMULET CAUSE THAT SMOKE TO RISE AND SHIFT...!
...UNTIL IT COMPLETELY COVERS THE SOURCE OF THE ROLLING LIGHT TRAP, DISSOLVING THE SUPERNATURAL BEAM, AND FREEING THE MASTER OF THE MYSTIC ARTS!
AND NOW TO LEARN YOUR EVIL SECRET, ZOTA!
5.

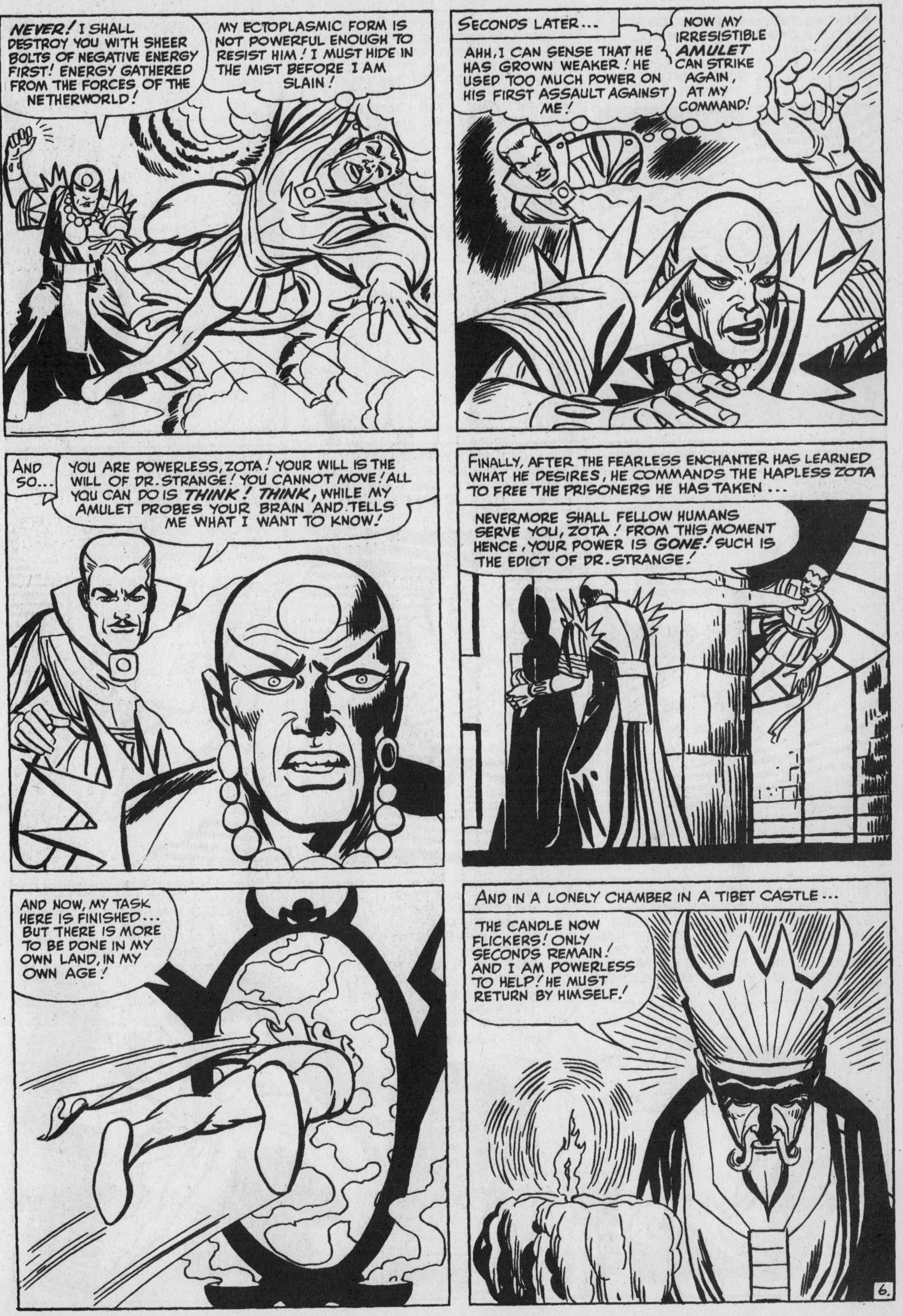
NEVER! I SHALL DESTROY YOU WITH SHEER BOLTS OF NEGATIVE ENERGY FIRST! ENERGY GATHERED FROM THE FORCES OF THE NETHERWORLD!
MY ECTOPLASMIC FORM IS NOT POWERFUL ENOUGH TO RESIST HIM! I MUST HIDE IN THE MIST BEFORE I AM SLAIN!
SECONDS LATER...
AHH, I CAN SENSE THAT HE HAS GROWN WEAKER! HE USED TOO MUCH POWER ON HIS FIRST ASSAULT AGAINST ME!
NOW MY IRRESISTIBLE AMULET CAN STRIKE AGAIN, AT MY COMMAND!
AND SO...
YOU ARE POWERLESS, ZOTA! YOUR WILL IS THE WILL OF DR. STRANGE! YOU CANNOT MOVE! ALL YOU CAN DO IS THINK! THINK, WHILE MY AMULET PROBES YOUR BRAIN AND TELLS ME WHAT I WANT TO KNOW!
FINALLY, AFTER THE FEARLESS ENCHANTER HAS LEARNED WHAT HE DESIRES, HE COMMANDS THE HAPLESS ZOTA TO FREE THE PRISONERS HE HAS TAKEN ...
NEVERMORE SHALL FELLOW HUMANS SERVE YOU, ZOTA! FROM THIS MOMENT HENCE, YOUR POWER IS GONE! SUCH IS THE EDICT OF DR. STRANGE!
AND NOW, MY TASK HERE IS FINISHED... BUT THERE IS MORE TO BE DONE IN MY OWN LAND, IN MY OWN AGE!
AND IN A LONELY CHAMBER IN A TIBET CASTLE...
THE CANDLE NOW FLICKERS! ONLY SECONDS REMAIN! AND I AM POWERLESS TO HELP! HE MUST RETURN BY HIMSELF!
6.

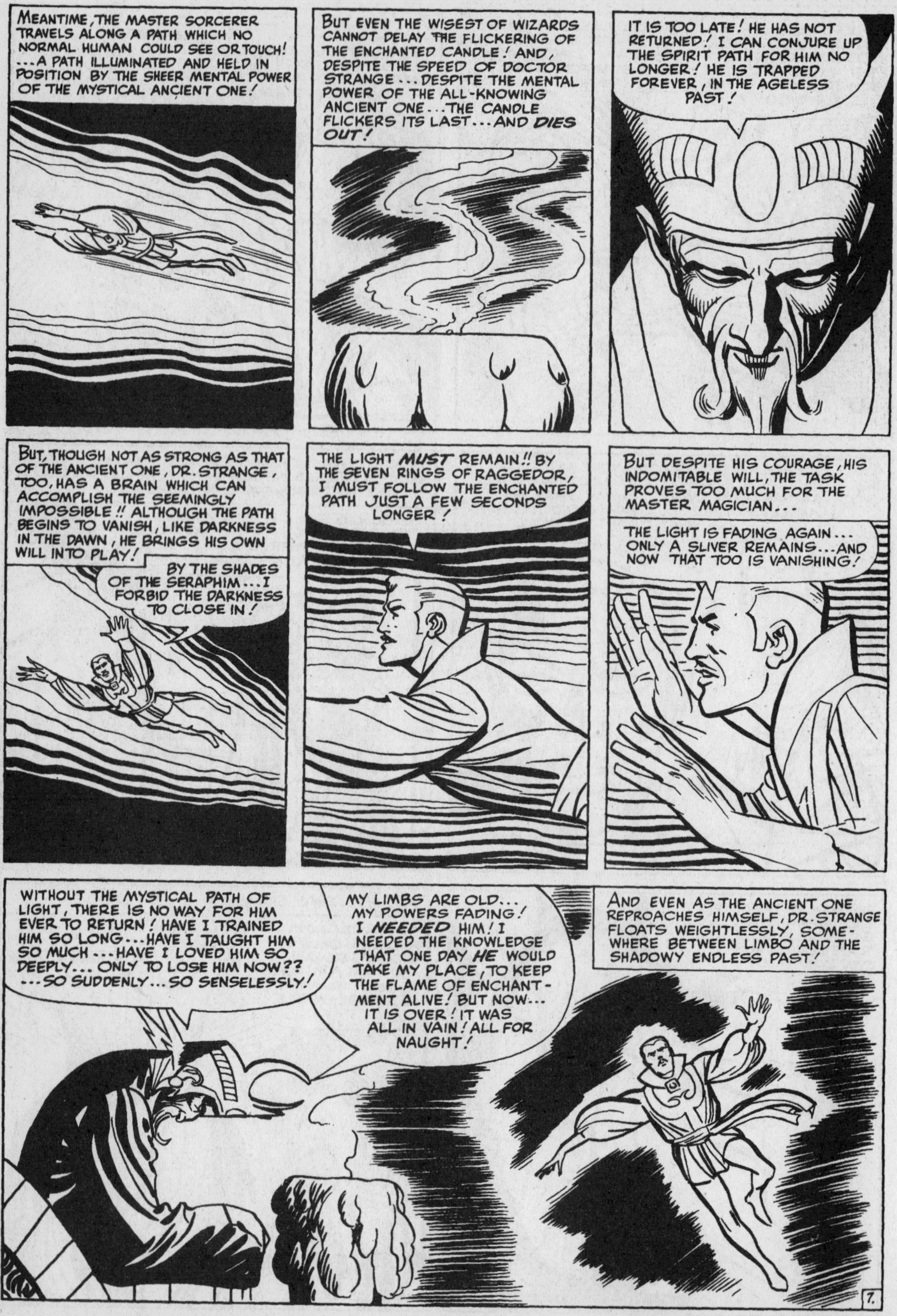
MEANTIME, THE MASTER SORCERER TRAVELS ALONG A PATH WHICH NO NORMAL HUMAN COULD SEE OR TOUCH! ...A PATH ILLUMINATED AND HELD IN POSITION BY THE SHEER MENTAL POWER OF THE MYSTICAL ANCIENT ONE!
BUT EVEN THE WISEST OF WIZARDS CANNOT DELAY THE FLICKERING OF THE ENCHANTED CANDLE! AND, DESPITE THE SPEED OF DOCTOR STRANGE ... DESPITE THE MENTAL POWER OF THE ALL-KNOWING ANCIENT ONE... THE CANDLE FLICKERS ITS LAST... AND DIES OUT!
IT IS TOO LATE! HE HAS NOT RETURNED! I CAN CONJURE UP THE SPIRIT PATH FOR HIM NO LONGER! HE IS TRAPPED FOREVER, IN THE AGELESS PAST!
BUT, THOUGH NOT AS STRONG AS THAT OF THE ANCIENT ONE, DR. STRANGE, TOO, HAS A BRAIN WHICH CAN ACCOMPLISH THE SEEMINGLY IMPOSSIBLE!! ALTHOUGH THE PATH BEGINS TO VANISH, LIKE DARKNESS IN THE DAWN, HE BRINGS HIS OWN WILL INTO PLAY!
BY THE SHADES OF THE SERAPHIM... I FORBID THE DARKNESS TO CLOSE IN!
THE LIGHT MUST REMAIN!! BY THE SEVEN RINGS OF RAGGEDOR, I MUST FOLLOW THE ENCHANTED PATH JUST A FEW SECONDS LONGER!
BUT DESPITE HIS COURAGE, HIS INDOMITABLE WILL, THE TASK PROVES TOO MUCH FOR THE MASTER MAGICIAN...
THE LIGHT IS FADING AGAIN... ONLY A SLIVER REMAINS... AND NOW THAT TOO IS VANISHING!
WITHOUT THE MYSTICAL PATH OF LIGHT, THERE IS NO WAY FOR HIM EVER TO RETURN! HAVE I TRAINED HIM SO LONG... HAVE I TAUGHT HIM SO MUCH ... HAVE I LOVED HIM SO DEEPLY... ONLY TO LOSE HIM NOW?? ...SO SUDDENLY... SO SENSELESSLY!
MY LIMBS ARE OLD... MY POWERS FADING! I NEEDED HIM! I NEEDED THE KNOWLEDGE THAT ONE DAY HE WOULD TAKE MY PLACE, TO KEEP THE FLAME OF ENCHANT-MENT ALIVE! BUT NOW... IT IS OVER! IT WAS ALL IN VAIN! ALL FOR NAUGHT!
AND EVEN AS THE ANCIENT ONE REPROACHES HIMSELF, DR. STRANGE FLOATS WEIGHTLESSLY, SOME-WHERE BETWEEN LIMBO AND THE SHADOWY ENDLESS PAST!
7.

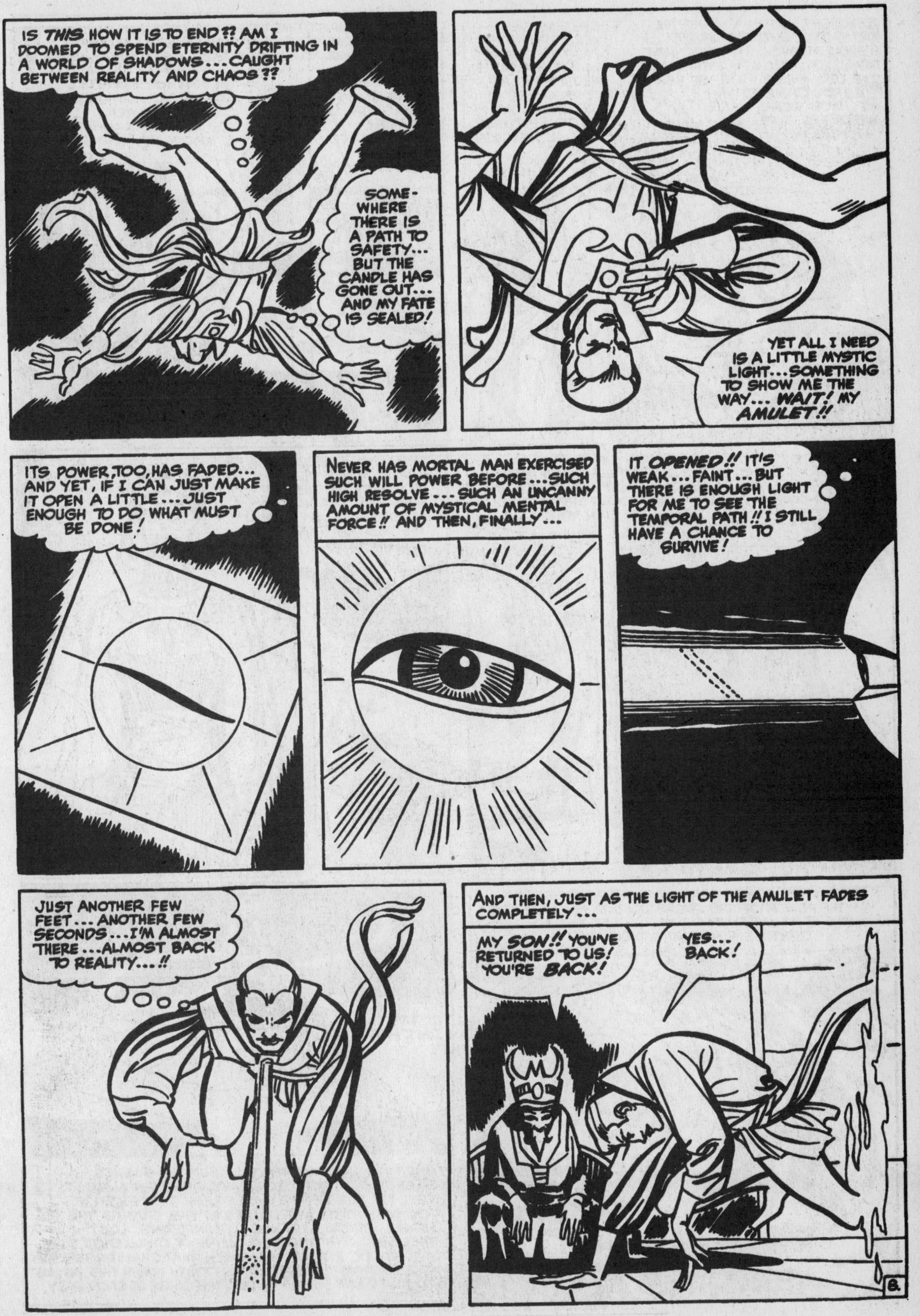
IS THIS HOW IT IS TO END?? AM I DOOMED TO SPEND ETERNITY DRIFTING IN A WORLD OF SHADOWS...CAUGHT BETWEEN REALITY AND CHAOS??
SOME-WHERE THERE IS A PATH TO SAFETY... BUT THE CANDLE HAS GONE OUT... AND MY FATE IS SEALED!
YET ALL I NEED IS A LITTLE MYSTIC LIGHT...SOMETHING TO SHOW ME THE WAY... WAIT! MY AMULET!!
ITS POWER, TOO, HAS FADED... AND YET, IF I CAN JUST MAKE IT OPEN A LITTLE...JUST ENOUGH TO DO WHAT MUST BE DONE!
NEVER HAS MORTAL MAN EXERCISED SUCH WILL POWER BEFORE...SUCH HIGH RESOLVE...SUCH AN UNCANNY AMOUNT OF MYSTICAL MENTAL FORCE!! AND THEN, FINALLY...
IT OPENED!! IT'S WEAK...FAINT...BUT THERE IS ENOUGH LIGHT FOR ME TO SEE THE TEMPORAL PATH!! I STILL HAVE A CHANCE TO SURVIVE!
JUST ANOTHER FEW FEET...ANOTHER FEW SECONDS...I'M ALMOST THERE...ALMOST BACK TO REALITY...!!
AND THEN, JUST AS THE LIGHT OF THE AMULET FADES COMPLETELY...
MY SON!! YOU'VE RETURNED TO US! YOU'RE BACK!
YES... BACK!
8.

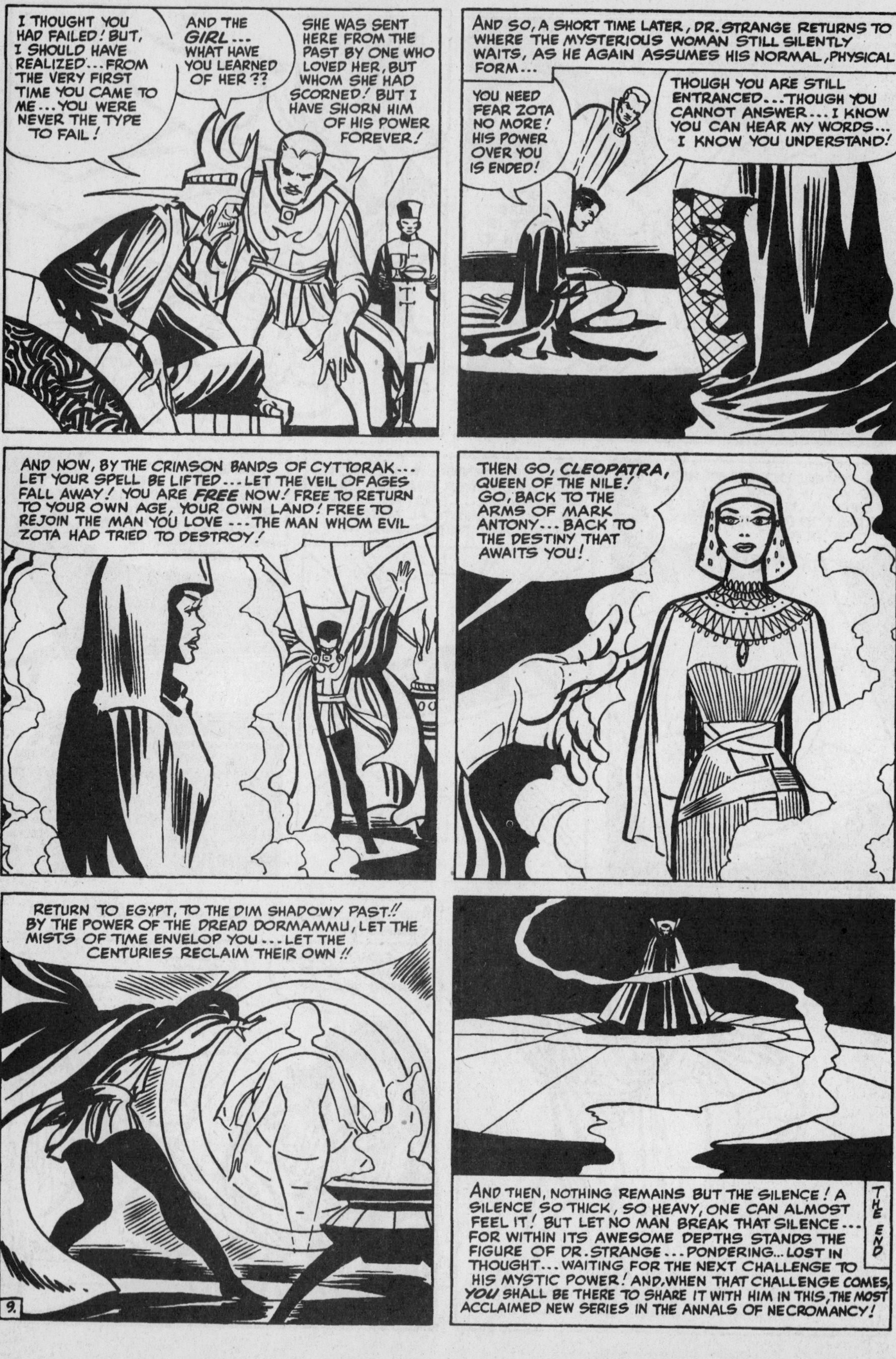
I THOUGHT YOU HAD FAILED! BUT, I SHOULD HAVE REALIZED... FROM THE VERY FIRST TIME YOU CAME TO ME... YOU WERE NEVER THE TYPE TO FAIL!
AND THE GIRL... WHAT HAVE YOU LEARNED OF HER??
SHE WAS SENT HERE FROM THE PAST BY ONE WHO LOVED HER, BUT WHOM SHE HAD SCORNED! BUT I HAVE SHORN HIM OF HIS POWER FOREVER!
AND SO, A SHORT TIME LATER, DR. STRANGE RETURNS TO WHERE THE MYSTERIOUS WOMAN STILL SILENTLY WAITS, AS HE AGAIN ASSUMES HIS NORMAL, PHYSICAL FORM...
YOU NEED FEAR ZOTA NO MORE! HIS POWER OVER YOU IS ENDED!
THOUGH YOU ARE STILL ENTRANCED... THOUGH YOU CANNOT ANSWER... I KNOW YOU CAN HEAR MY WORDS... I KNOW YOU UNDERSTAND!
AND NOW, BY THE CRIMSON BANDS OF CYTTORAK... LET YOUR SPELL BE LIFTED... LET THE VEIL OF AGES FALL AWAY! YOU ARE FREE NOW! FREE TO RETURN TO YOUR OWN AGE, YOUR OWN LAND! FREE TO REJOIN THE MAN YOU LOVE --- THE MAN WHOM EVIL ZOTA HAD TRIED TO DESTROY!
THEN GO, CLEOPATRA, QUEEN OF THE NILE! GO, BACK TO THE ARMS OF MARK ANTONY... BACK TO THE DESTINY THAT AWAITS YOU!
RETURN TO EGYPT, TO THE DIM SHADOWY PAST!! BY THE POWER OF THE DREAD DORMAMMU, LET THE MISTS OF TIME ENVELOP YOU... LET THE CENTURIES RECLAIM THEIR OWN!!
9.
AND THEN, NOTHING REMAINS BUT THE SILENCE! A SILENCE SO THICK, SO HEAVY, ONE CAN ALMOST FEEL IT! BUT LET NO MAN BREAK THAT SILENCE... FOR WITHIN ITS AWESOME DEPTHS STANDS THE FIGURE OF DR. STRANGE... PONDERING... LOST IN THOUGHT... WAITING FOR THE NEXT CHALLENGE TO HIS MYSTIC POWER! AND, WHEN THAT CHALLENGE COMES, YOU SHALL BE THERE TO SHARE IT WITH HIM IN THIS, THE MOST ACCLAIMED NEW SERIES IN THE ANNALS OF NECROMANCY!
THE END

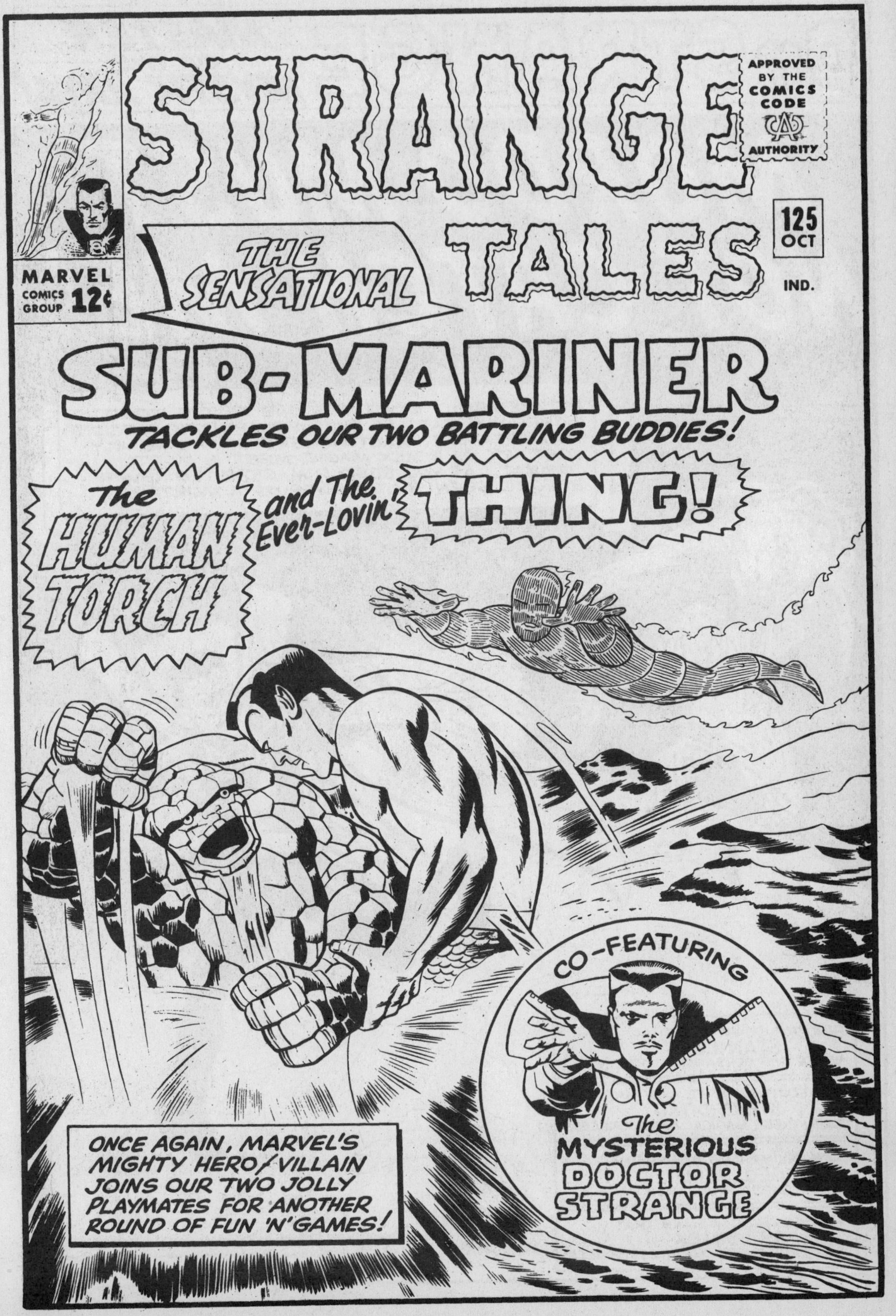
STRANGE TALES
APPROVED BY THE COMICS CODE AUTHORITY
125 OCT
IND.
MARVEL COMICS GROUP 12¢
THE SENSATIONAL
SUB-MARINER
TACKLES OUR TWO BATTLING BUDDIES!
The HUMAN TORCH
and The Ever-Lovin'
THING!
ONCE AGAIN, MARVEL'S MIGHTY HERO/VILLAIN JOINS OUR TWO JOLLY PLAYMATES FOR ANOTHER ROUND OF FUN 'N' GAMES!
CO-FEATURING
The MYSTERIOUS DOCTOR STRANGE

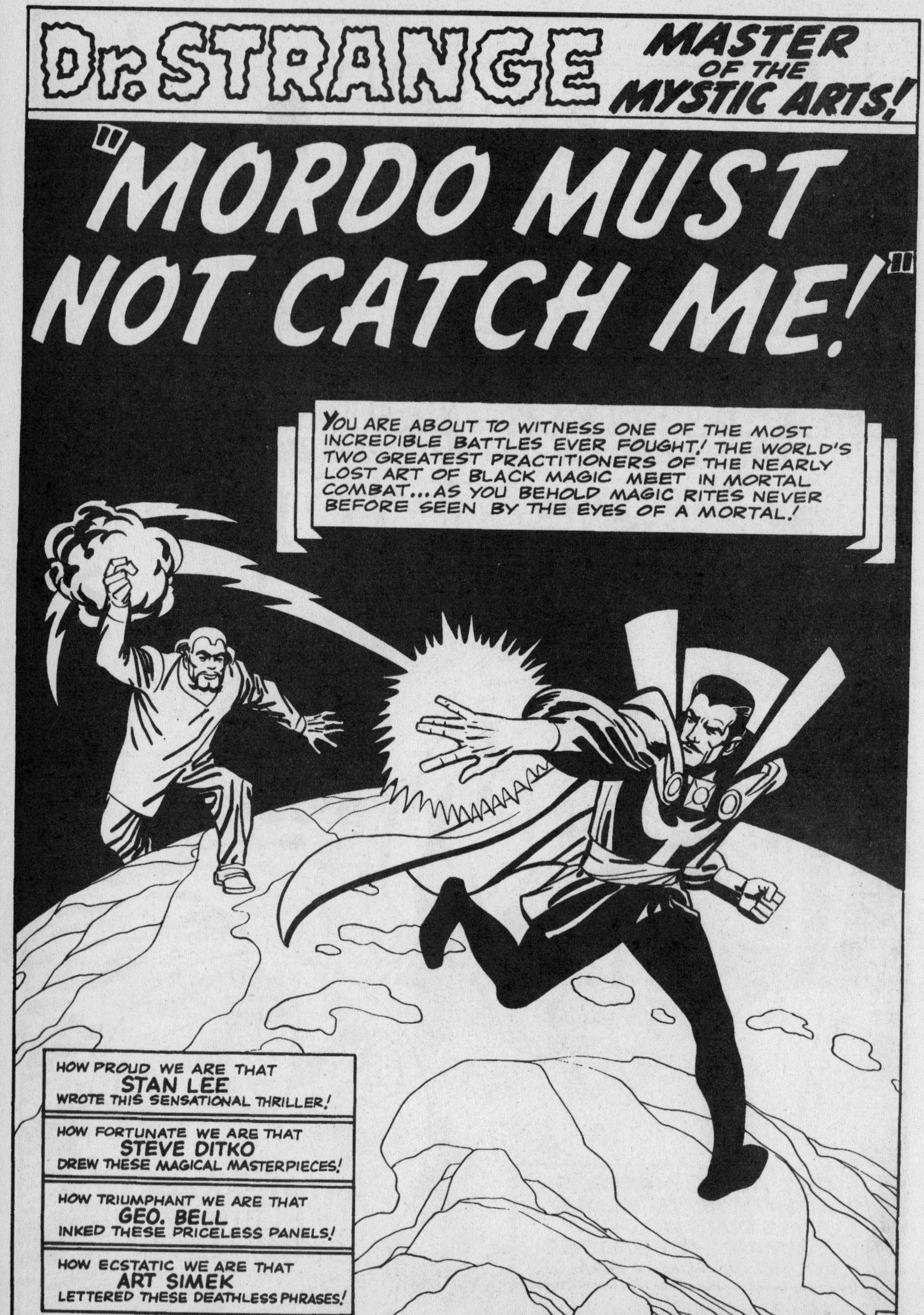
Dr. STRANGE
MASTER OF THE MYSTIC ARTS!
"MORDO MUST NOT CATCH ME!"
YOU ARE ABOUT TO WITNESS ONE OF THE MOST INCREDIBLE BATTLES EVER FOUGHT! THE WORLD'S TWO GREATEST PRACTITIONERS OF THE NEARLY LOST ART OF BLACK MAGIC MEET IN MORTAL COMBAT...AS YOU BEHOLD MAGIC RITES NEVER BEFORE SEEN BY THE EYES OF A MORTAL!
HOW PROUD WE ARE THAT STAN LEE WROTE THIS SENSATIONAL THRILLER!
HOW FORTUNATE WE ARE THAT STEVE DITKO DREW THESE MAGICAL MASTERPIECES!
HOW TRIUMPHANT WE ARE THAT GEO. BELL INKED THESE PRICELESS PANELS!
HOW ECSTATIC WE ARE THAT ART SIMEK LETTERED THESE DEATHLESS PHRASES!
X-773
1

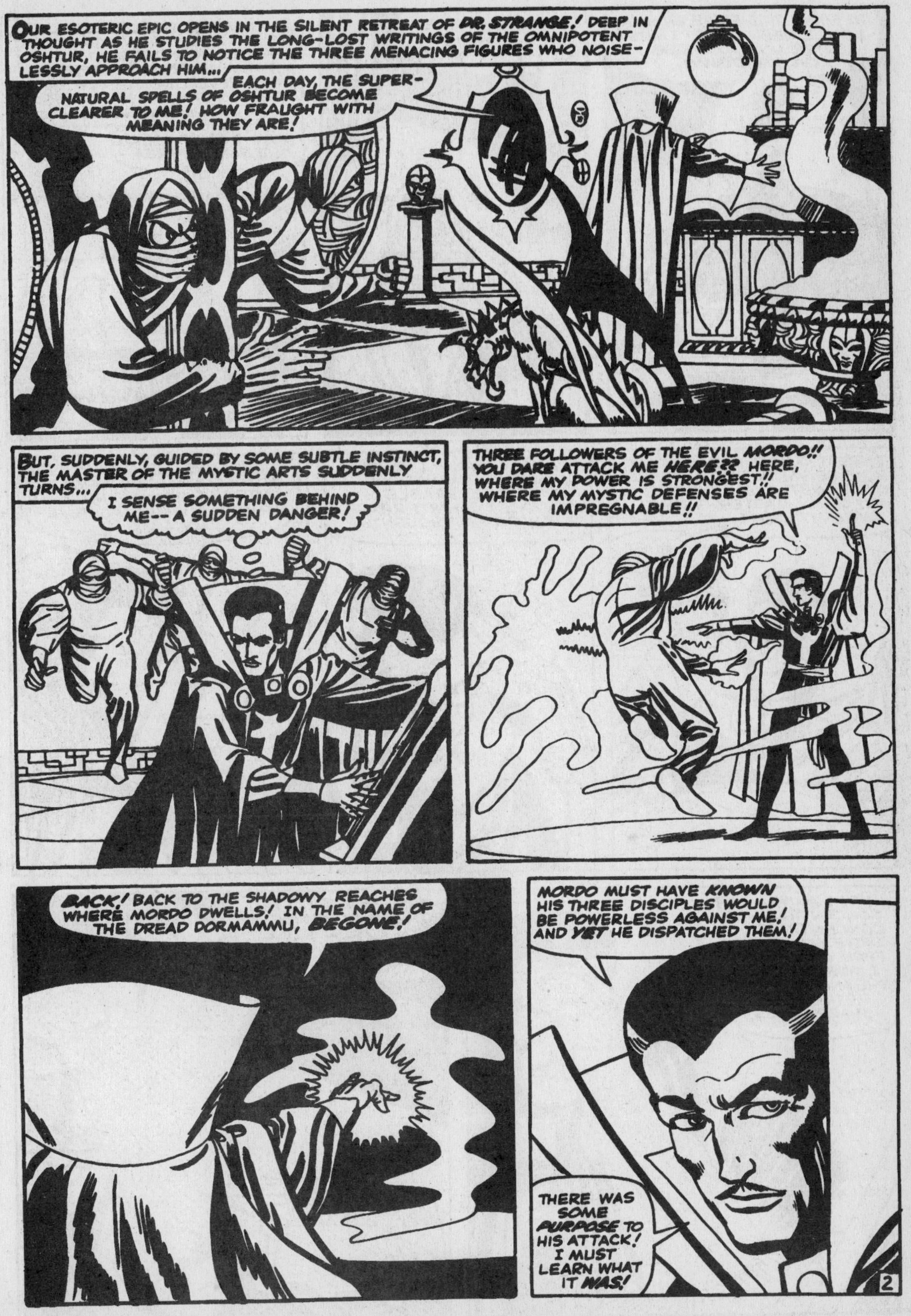
OUR ESOTERIC EPIC OPENS IN THE SILENT RETREAT OF DR. STRANGE! DEEP IN THOUGHT AS HE STUDIES THE LONG-LOST WRITINGS OF THE OMNIPOTENT OSHTUR, HE FAILS TO NOTICE THE THREE MENACING FIGURES WHO NOISE-LESSLY APPROACH HIM...
EACH DAY, THE SUPER-NATURAL SPELLS OF OSHTUR BECOME CLEARER TO ME! HOW FRAUGHT WITH MEANING THEY ARE!
BUT, SUDDENLY, GUIDED BY SOME SUBTLE INSTINCT, THE MASTER OF THE MYSTIC ARTS SUDDENLY TURNS...
I SENSE SOMETHING BEHIND ME-- A SUDDEN DANGER!
THREE FOLLOWERS OF THE EVIL MORDO!! YOU DARE ATTACK ME HERE?? HERE, WHERE MY POWER IS STRONGEST!! WHERE MY MYSTIC DEFENSES ARE IMPREGNABLE!!
BACK! BACK TO THE SHADOWY REACHES WHERE MORDO DWELLS! IN THE NAME OF THE DREAD DORMAMMU, BEGONE!
MORDO MUST HAVE KNOWN HIS THREE DISCIPLES WOULD BE POWERLESS AGAINST ME! AND YET HE DISPATCHED THEM!
THERE WAS SOME PURPOSE TO HIS ATTACK! I MUST LEARN WHAT IT WAS!
2

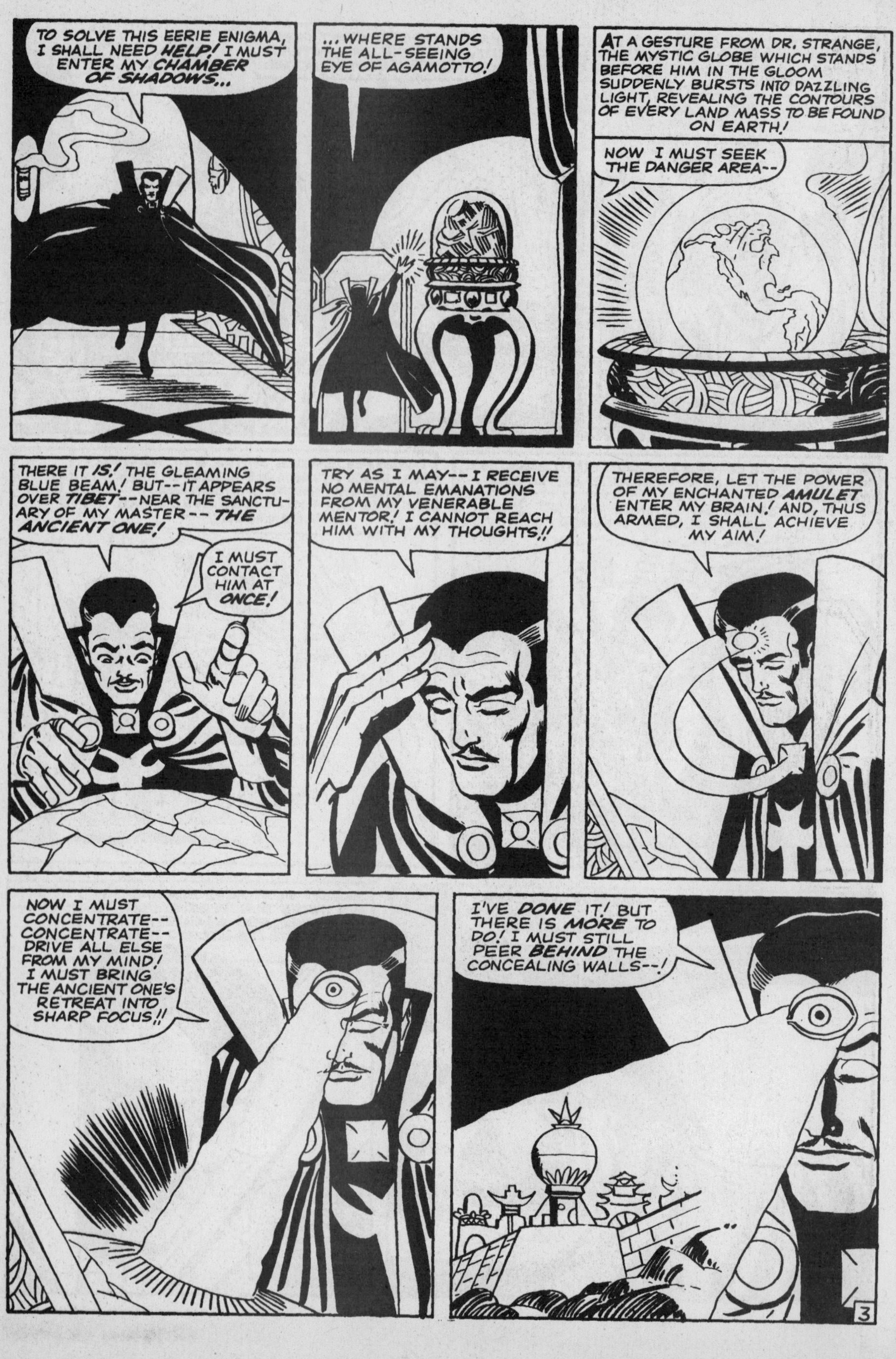

TO SOLVE THIS EERIE ENIGMA, I SHALL NEED HELP! I MUST ENTER MY CHAMBER OF SHADOWS...
...WHERE STANDS THE ALL-SEEING EYE OF AGAMOTTO!
AT A GESTURE FROM DR. STRANGE, THE MYSTIC GLOBE WHICH STANDS BEFORE HIM IN THE GLOOM SUDDENLY BURSTS INTO DAZZLING LIGHT, REVEALING THE CONTOURS OF EVERY LAND MASS TO BE FOUND ON EARTH!
NOW I MUST SEEK THE DANGER AREA--
THERE IT IS! THE GLEAMING BLUE BEAM! BUT--IT APPEARS OVER TIBET--NEAR THE SANCTUARY OF MY MASTER--THE ANCIENT ONE!
I MUST CONTACT HIM AT ONCE!
TRY AS I MAY--I RECEIVE NO MENTAL EMANATIONS FROM MY VENERABLE MENTOR! I CANNOT REACH HIM WITH MY THOUGHTS!!
THEREFORE, LET THE POWER OF MY ENCHANTED AMULET ENTER MY BRAIN! AND, THUS ARMED, I SHALL ACHIEVE MY AIM!
NOW I MUST CONCENTRATE--CONCENTRATE--DRIVE ALL ELSE FROM MY MIND! I MUST BRING THE ANCIENT ONE'S RETREAT INTO SHARP FOCUS!!
I'VE DONE IT! BUT THERE IS MORE TO DO! I MUST STILL PEER BEHIND THE CONCEALING WALLS--!
3

SLOWLY, THE WALLS SEEM TO MELT AWAY AS DR. STRANGE'S ENCHANTED AMULET BRINGS THE INTERIOR OF THE HIDDEN SANCTUARY INTO VIEW...

...BUT, WHEN THE MASTER OF BLACK MAGIC FINALLY REACHES HIS OBJECTIVE, THE UNIQUE CHAIR WHICH STANDS IN THE CENTER OF THE CHAMBER, HE FINDS IT-- *EMPTY!*

THE ANCIENT ONE IS *GONE!!* BUT THAT CAN-NOT BE.!! HE *NEVER* LEAVES HIS CHAMBER.!!

NEVER-- UNTIL *NOW!!* FOR I HAVE *CHANGED* THINGS, STRANGE!

MORDO.!! HERE IN MY OWN SANCTUM SANCTORUM.!!

YES, STRANGE-- IT IS I, BARON MORDO! I, WHO FEAR YOU *NO LONGER!*

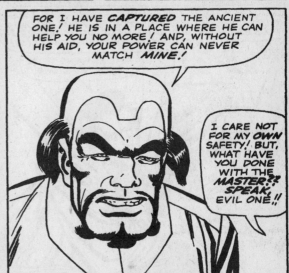

FOR I HAVE *CAPTURED* THE ANCIENT ONE! HE IS IN A PLACE WHERE HE CAN HELP YOU NO MORE! AND, WITHOUT HIS AID, YOUR POWER CAN NEVER MATCH *MINE!*

I CARE NOT FOR MY *OWN* SAFETY! BUT, WHAT HAVE YOU DONE WITH THE *MASTER??* SPEAK, EVIL ONE.!!

NO NEED FOR *WORDS*-- WHEN I CAN *SHOW* YOU THE ONE I HAVE OVER-COME! *BEHOLD*-- MY PRISONER!

IT IS *TRUE!* MORDO HAS CAPTURED HIM! AND IF HE CAN OVERCOME *ME*, TOO-- THEN ALL MANKIND WILL BE AT HIS MERCY!!

4

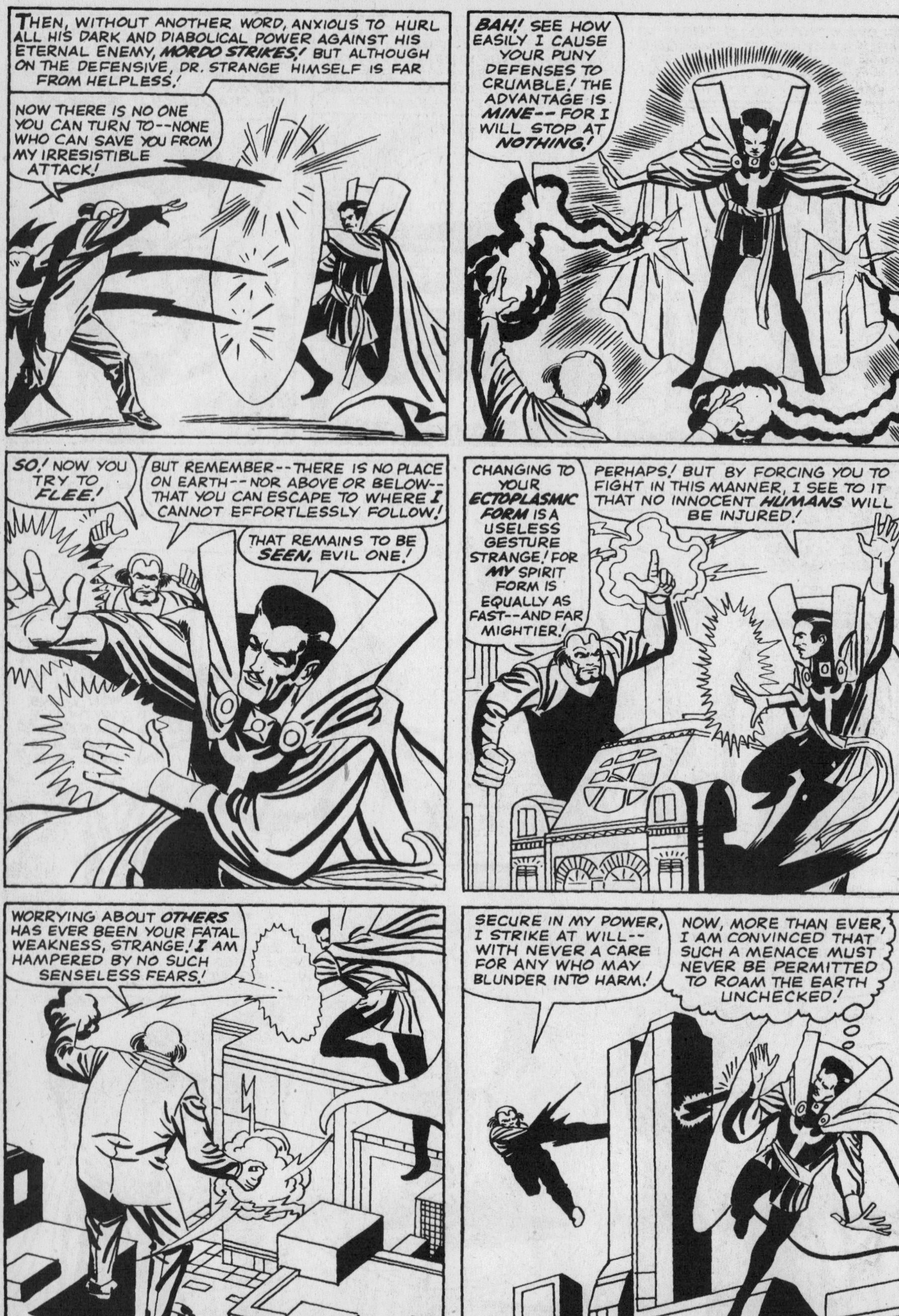
THEN, WITHOUT ANOTHER WORD, ANXIOUS TO HURL ALL HIS DARK AND DIABOLICAL POWER AGAINST HIS ETERNAL ENEMY, MORDO STRIKES! BUT ALTHOUGH ON THE DEFENSIVE, DR. STRANGE HIMSELF IS FAR FROM HELPLESS!
NOW THERE IS NO ONE YOU CAN TURN TO--NONE WHO CAN SAVE YOU FROM MY IRRESISTIBLE ATTACK!
BAH! SEE HOW EASILY I CAUSE YOUR PUNY DEFENSES TO CRUMBLE! THE ADVANTAGE IS MINE--FOR I WILL STOP AT NOTHING!
SO! NOW YOU TRY TO FLEE!
BUT REMEMBER--THERE IS NO PLACE ON EARTH--NOR ABOVE OR BELOW--THAT YOU CAN ESCAPE TO WHERE I CANNOT EFFORTLESSLY FOLLOW!
THAT REMAINS TO BE SEEN, EVIL ONE!
CHANGING TO YOUR ECTOPLASMIC FORM IS A USELESS GESTURE STRANGE! FOR MY SPIRIT FORM IS EQUALLY AS FAST--AND FAR MIGHTIER!
PERHAPS! BUT BY FORCING YOU TO FIGHT IN THIS MANNER, I SEE TO IT THAT NO INNOCENT HUMANS WILL BE INJURED!
WORRYING ABOUT OTHERS HAS EVER BEEN YOUR FATAL WEAKNESS, STRANGE! I AM HAMPERED BY NO SUCH SENSELESS FEARS!
SECURE IN MY POWER, I STRIKE AT WILL--WITH NEVER A CARE FOR ANY WHO MAY BLUNDER INTO HARM!
NOW, MORE THAN EVER, I AM CONVINCED THAT SUCH A MENACE MUST NEVER BE PERMITTED TO ROAM THE EARTH UNCHECKED!
5

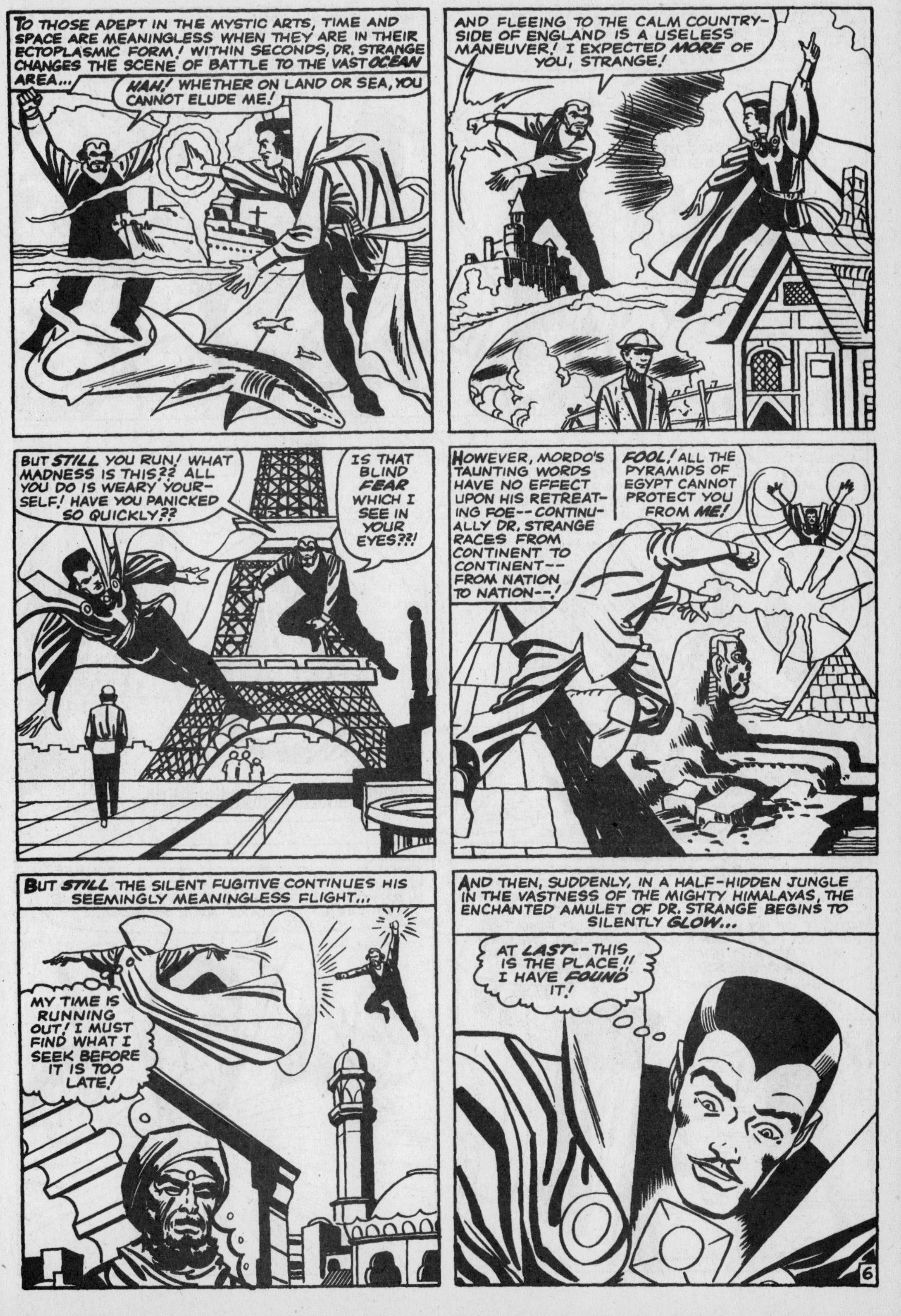
TO THOSE ADEPT IN THE MYSTIC ARTS, TIME AND SPACE ARE MEANINGLESS WHEN THEY ARE IN THEIR ECTOPLASMIC FORM! WITHIN SECONDS, DR. STRANGE CHANGES THE SCENE OF BATTLE TO THE VAST OCEAN AREA...
HAH! WHETHER ON LAND OR SEA, YOU CANNOT ELUDE ME!
AND FLEEING TO THE CALM COUNTRY-SIDE OF ENGLAND IS A USELESS MANEUVER! I EXPECTED MORE OF YOU, STRANGE!
BUT STILL YOU RUN! WHAT MADNESS IS THIS?? ALL YOU DO IS WEARY YOUR-SELF! HAVE YOU PANICKED SO QUICKLY??
IS THAT BLIND FEAR WHICH I SEE IN YOUR EYES??!
HOWEVER, MORDO'S TAUNTING WORDS HAVE NO EFFECT UPON HIS RETREATING FOE--CONTINUALLY DR. STRANGE RACES FROM CONTINENT TO CONTINENT--FROM NATION TO NATION--!
FOOL! ALL THE PYRAMIDS OF EGYPT CANNOT PROTECT YOU FROM ME!
BUT STILL THE SILENT FUGITIVE CONTINUES HIS SEEMINGLY MEANINGLESS FLIGHT...
MY TIME IS RUNNING OUT! I MUST FIND WHAT I SEEK BEFORE IT IS TOO LATE!
AND THEN, SUDDENLY, IN A HALF-HIDDEN JUNGLE IN THE VASTNESS OF THE MIGHTY HIMALAYAS, THE ENCHANTED AMULET OF DR. STRANGE BEGINS TO SILENTLY GLOW...
AT LAST--THIS IS THE PLACE!! I HAVE FOUND IT!
6

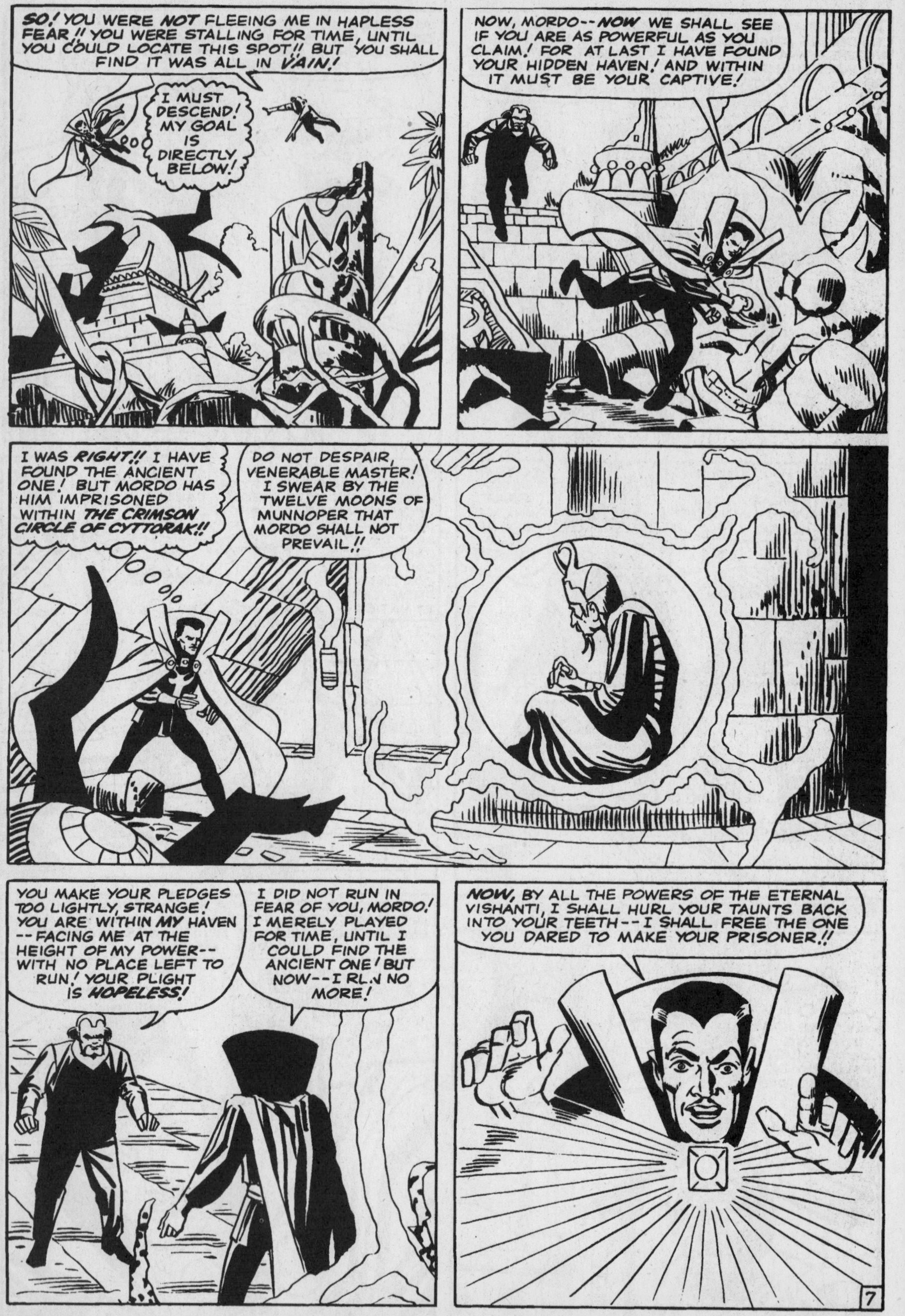
SO! YOU WERE NOT FLEEING ME IN HAPLESS FEAR!! YOU WERE STALLING FOR TIME, UNTIL YOU COULD LOCATE THIS SPOT!! BUT YOU SHALL FIND IT WAS ALL IN VAIN!
I MUST DESCEND! MY GOAL IS DIRECTLY BELOW!
NOW, MORDO--NOW WE SHALL SEE IF YOU ARE AS POWERFUL AS YOU CLAIM! FOR AT LAST I HAVE FOUND YOUR HIDDEN HAVEN! AND WITHIN IT MUST BE YOUR CAPTIVE!
I WAS RIGHT!! I HAVE FOUND THE ANCIENT ONE! BUT MORDO HAS HIM IMPRISONED WITHIN THE CRIMSON CIRCLE OF CYTTORAK!!
DO NOT DESPAIR, VENERABLE MASTER! I SWEAR BY THE TWELVE MOONS OF MUNNOPER THAT MORDO SHALL NOT PREVAIL!!
YOU MAKE YOUR PLEDGES TOO LIGHTLY, STRANGE! YOU ARE WITHIN MY HAVEN --FACING ME AT THE HEIGHT OF MY POWER-- WITH NO PLACE LEFT TO RUN! YOUR PLIGHT IS HOPELESS!
I DID NOT RUN IN FEAR OF YOU, MORDO! I MERELY PLAYED FOR TIME, UNTIL I COULD FIND THE ANCIENT ONE! BUT NOW--I RUN NO MORE!
NOW, BY ALL THE POWERS OF THE ETERNAL VISHANTI, I SHALL HURL YOUR TAUNTS BACK INTO YOUR TEETH--I SHALL FREE THE ONE YOU DARED TO MAKE YOUR PRISONER!!
7

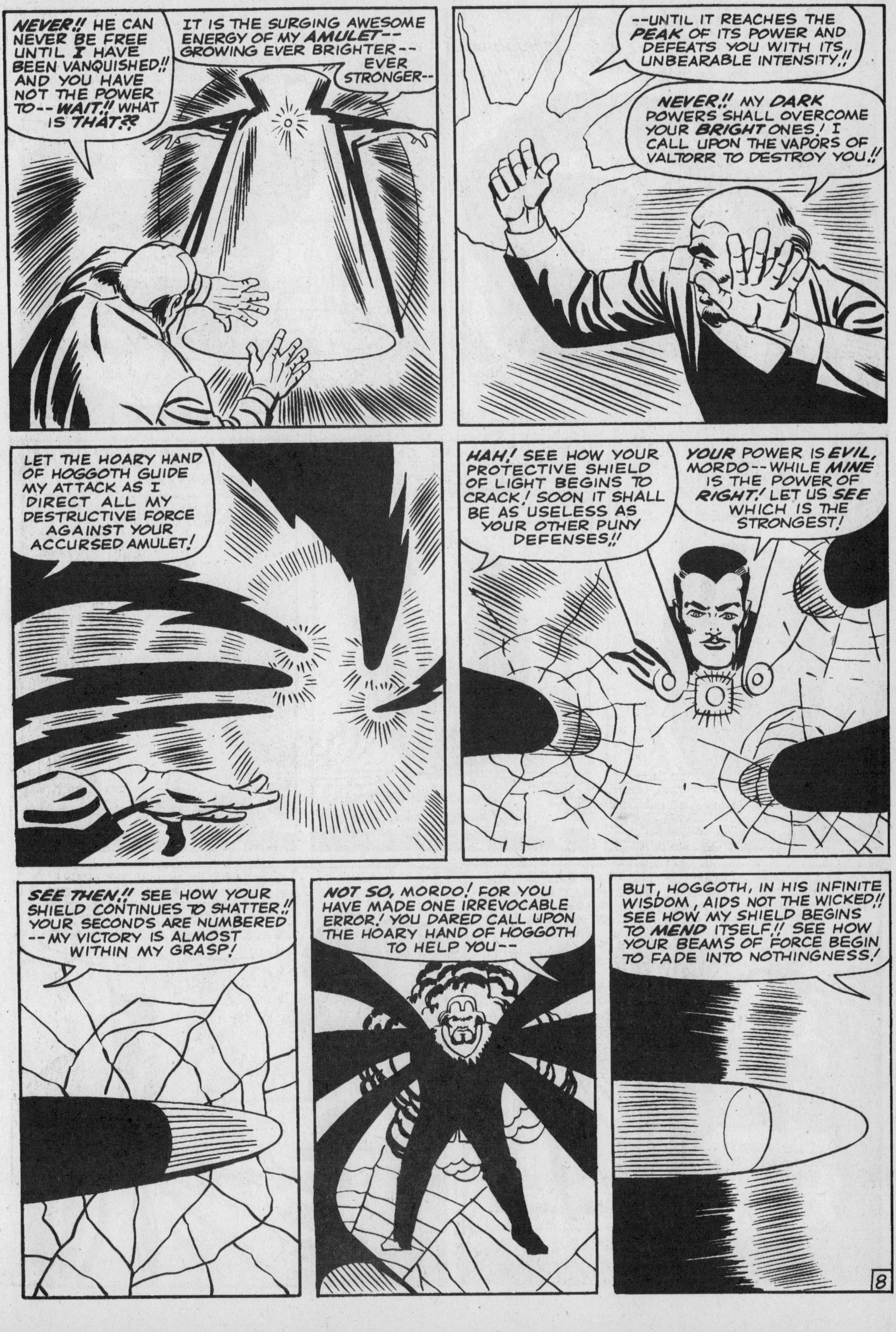
NEVER!! HE CAN NEVER BE FREE UNTIL I HAVE BEEN VANQUISHED!! AND YOU HAVE NOT THE POWER TO-- WAIT!! WHAT IS THAT??
IT IS THE SURGING AWESOME ENERGY OF MY AMULET-- GROWING EVER BRIGHTER-- EVER STRONGER--
--UNTIL IT REACHES THE PEAK OF ITS POWER AND DEFEATS YOU WITH ITS UNBEARABLE INTENSITY!!
NEVER!! MY DARK POWERS SHALL OVERCOME YOUR BRIGHT ONES! I CALL UPON THE VAPORS OF VALTORR TO DESTROY YOU!!
LET THE HOARY HAND OF HOGGOTH GUIDE MY ATTACK AS I DIRECT ALL MY DESTRUCTIVE FORCE AGAINST YOUR ACCURSED AMULET!
HAH! SEE HOW YOUR PROTECTIVE SHIELD OF LIGHT BEGINS TO CRACK! SOON IT SHALL BE AS USELESS AS YOUR OTHER PUNY DEFENSES!!
YOUR POWER IS EVIL, MORDO-- WHILE MINE IS THE POWER OF RIGHT! LET US SEE WHICH IS THE STRONGEST!
SEE THEN!! SEE HOW YOUR SHIELD CONTINUES TO SHATTER!! YOUR SECONDS ARE NUMBERED --MY VICTORY IS ALMOST WITHIN MY GRASP!
NOT SO, MORDO! FOR YOU HAVE MADE ONE IRREVOCABLE ERROR! YOU DARED CALL UPON THE HOARY HAND OF HOGGOTH TO HELP YOU--
BUT, HOGGOTH, IN HIS INFINITE WISDOM, AIDS NOT THE WICKED!! SEE HOW MY SHIELD BEGINS TO MEND ITSELF!! SEE HOW YOUR BEAMS OF FORCE BEGIN TO FADE INTO NOTHINGNESS!

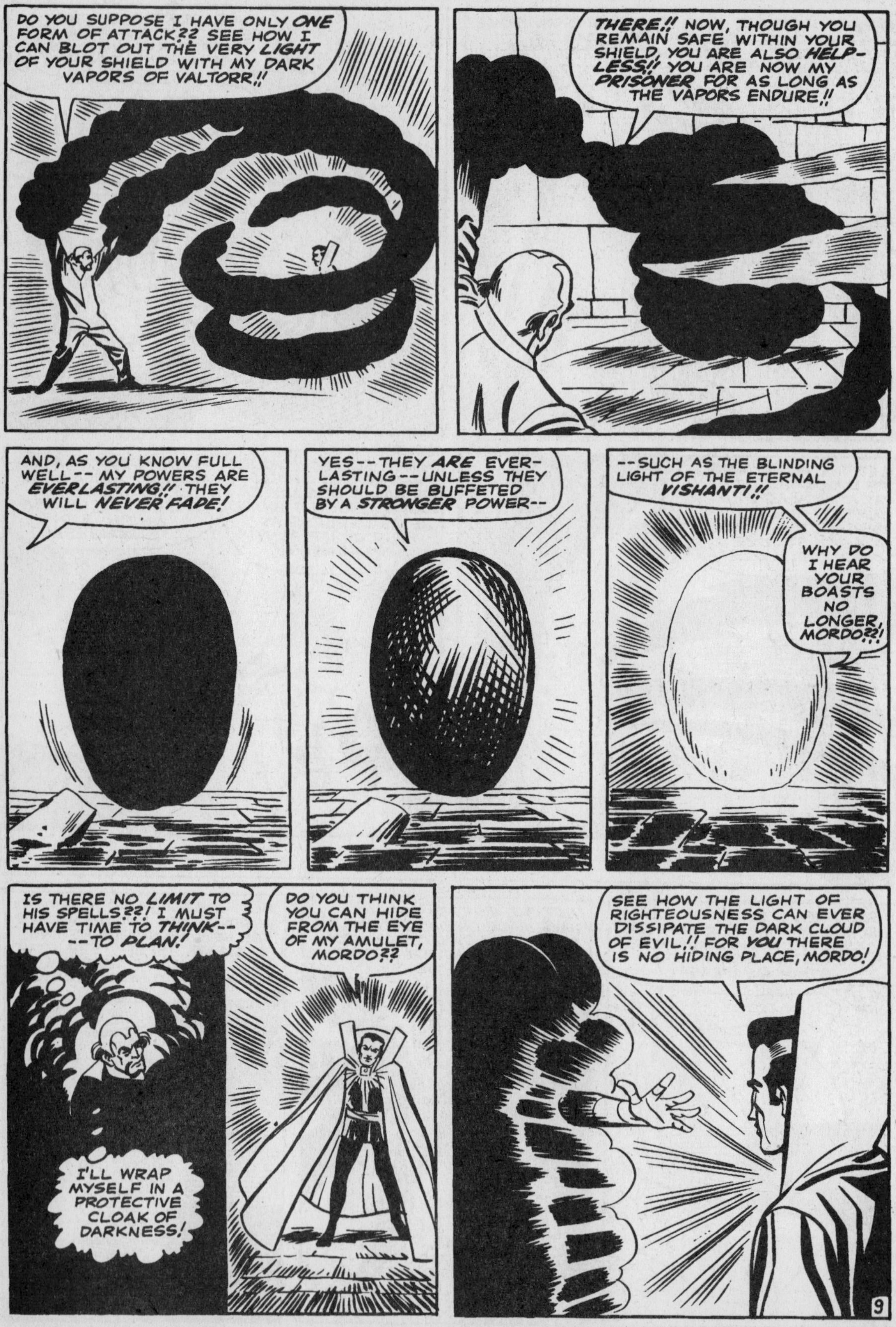
DO YOU SUPPOSE I HAVE ONLY ONE FORM OF ATTACK?? SEE HOW I CAN BLOT OUT THE VERY LIGHT OF YOUR SHIELD WITH MY DARK VAPORS OF VALTORR!!
THERE!! NOW, THOUGH YOU REMAIN SAFE WITHIN YOUR SHIELD, YOU ARE ALSO HELPLESS!! YOU ARE NOW MY PRISONER FOR AS LONG AS THE VAPORS ENDURE!!
AND, AS YOU KNOW FULL WELL-- MY POWERS ARE EVERLASTING!! THEY WILL NEVER FADE!
YES--THEY ARE EVERLASTING--UNLESS THEY SHOULD BE BUFFETED BY A STRONGER POWER--
--SUCH AS THE BLINDING LIGHT OF THE ETERNAL VISHANTI!!
WHY DO I HEAR YOUR BOASTS NO LONGER, MORDO??!
IS THERE NO LIMIT TO HIS SPELLS??! I MUST HAVE TIME TO THINK-- --TO PLAN!
I'LL WRAP MYSELF IN A PROTECTIVE CLOAK OF DARKNESS!
DO YOU THINK YOU CAN HIDE FROM THE EYE OF MY AMULET, MORDO??
SEE HOW THE LIGHT OF RIGHTEOUSNESS CAN EVER DISSIPATE THE DARK CLOUD OF EVIL!! FOR YOU THERE IS NO HIDING PLACE, MORDO!
9

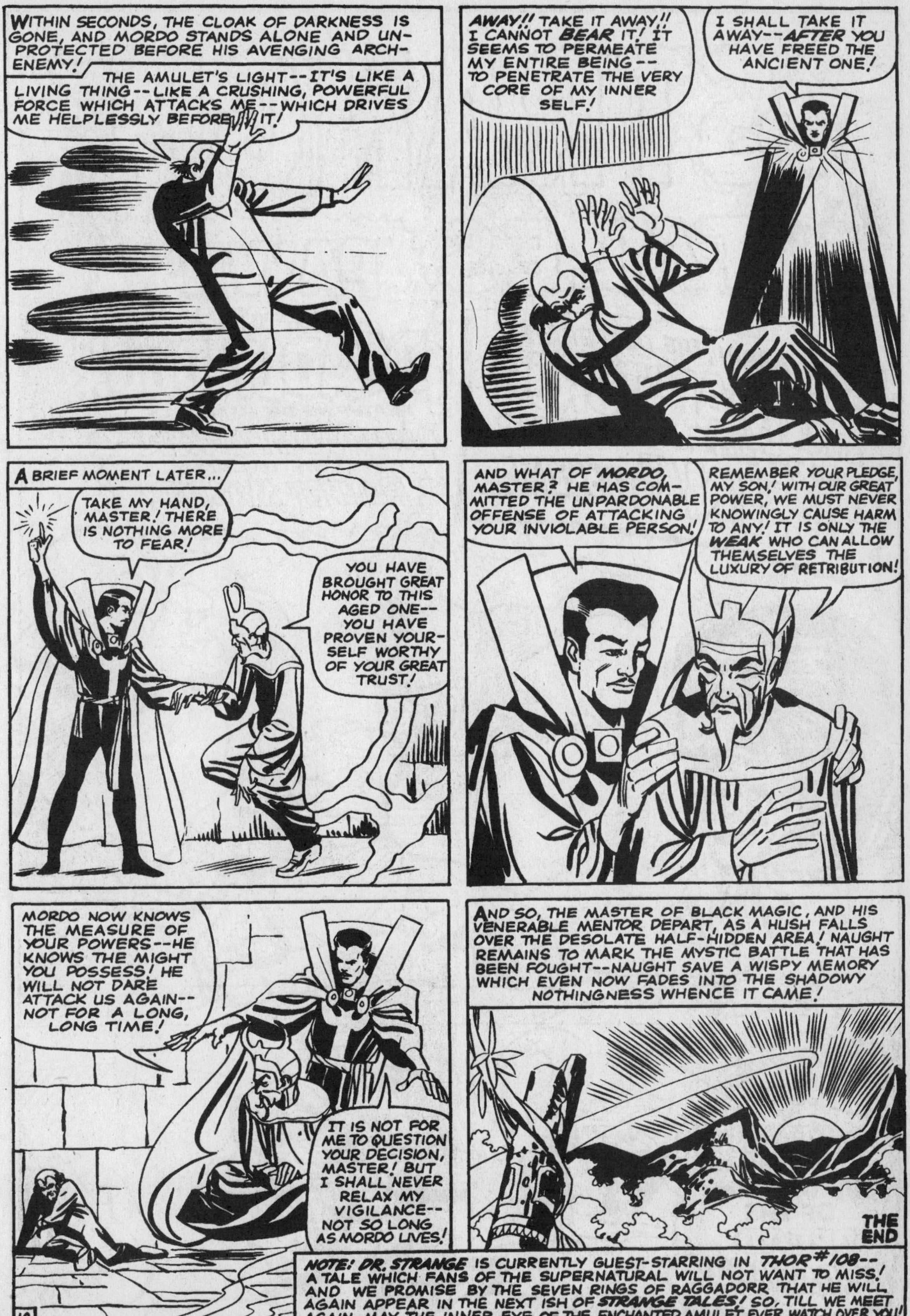
WITHIN SECONDS, THE CLOAK OF DARKNESS IS GONE, AND MORDO STANDS ALONE AND UNPROTECTED BEFORE HIS AVENGING ARCH-ENEMY!
THE AMULET'S LIGHT--IT'S LIKE A LIVING THING--LIKE A CRUSHING, POWERFUL FORCE WHICH ATTACKS ME--WHICH DRIVES ME HELPLESSLY BEFORE IT!
AWAY!! TAKE IT AWAY!! I CANNOT BEAR IT! IT SEEMS TO PERMEATE MY ENTIRE BEING--TO PENETRATE THE VERY CORE OF MY INNER SELF!
I SHALL TAKE IT AWAY--AFTER YOU HAVE FREED THE ANCIENT ONE!
A BRIEF MOMENT LATER...
TAKE MY HAND, MASTER! THERE IS NOTHING MORE TO FEAR!
YOU HAVE BROUGHT GREAT HONOR TO THIS AGED ONE--YOU HAVE PROVEN YOURSELF WORTHY OF YOUR GREAT TRUST!
AND WHAT OF MORDO, MASTER? HE HAS COMMITTED THE UNPARDONABLE OFFENSE OF ATTACKING YOUR INVIOLABLE PERSON!
REMEMBER YOUR PLEDGE, MY SON! WITH OUR GREAT POWER, WE MUST NEVER KNOWINGLY CAUSE HARM TO ANY! IT IS ONLY THE WEAK WHO CAN ALLOW THEMSELVES THE LUXURY OF RETRIBUTION!
MORDO NOW KNOWS THE MEASURE OF YOUR POWERS--HE KNOWS THE MIGHT YOU POSSESS! HE WILL NOT DARE ATTACK US AGAIN--NOT FOR A LONG, LONG TIME!
IT IS NOT FOR ME TO QUESTION YOUR DECISION, MASTER! BUT I SHALL NEVER RELAX MY VIGILANCE--NOT SO LONG AS MORDO LIVES!
AND SO, THE MASTER OF BLACK MAGIC, AND HIS VENERABLE MENTOR DEPART, AS A HUSH FALLS OVER THE DESOLATE HALF-HIDDEN AREA! NAUGHT REMAINS TO MARK THE MYSTIC BATTLE THAT HAS BEEN FOUGHT--NAUGHT SAVE A WISPY MEMORY WHICH EVEN NOW FADES INTO THE SHADOWY NOTHINGNESS WHENCE IT CAME!
THE END
NOTE: DR. STRANGE IS CURRENTLY GUEST-STARRING IN THOR #108--A TALE WHICH FANS OF THE SUPERNATURAL WILL NOT WANT TO MISS! AND WE PROMISE BY THE SEVEN RINGS OF RAGGADORR THAT HE WILL AGAIN APPEAR IN THE NEXT ISH OF STRANGE TALES! SO, TILL WE MEET AGAIN, MAY THE INNER EYE OF THE ENCHANTED AMULET EVER WATCH OVER YOU!
10

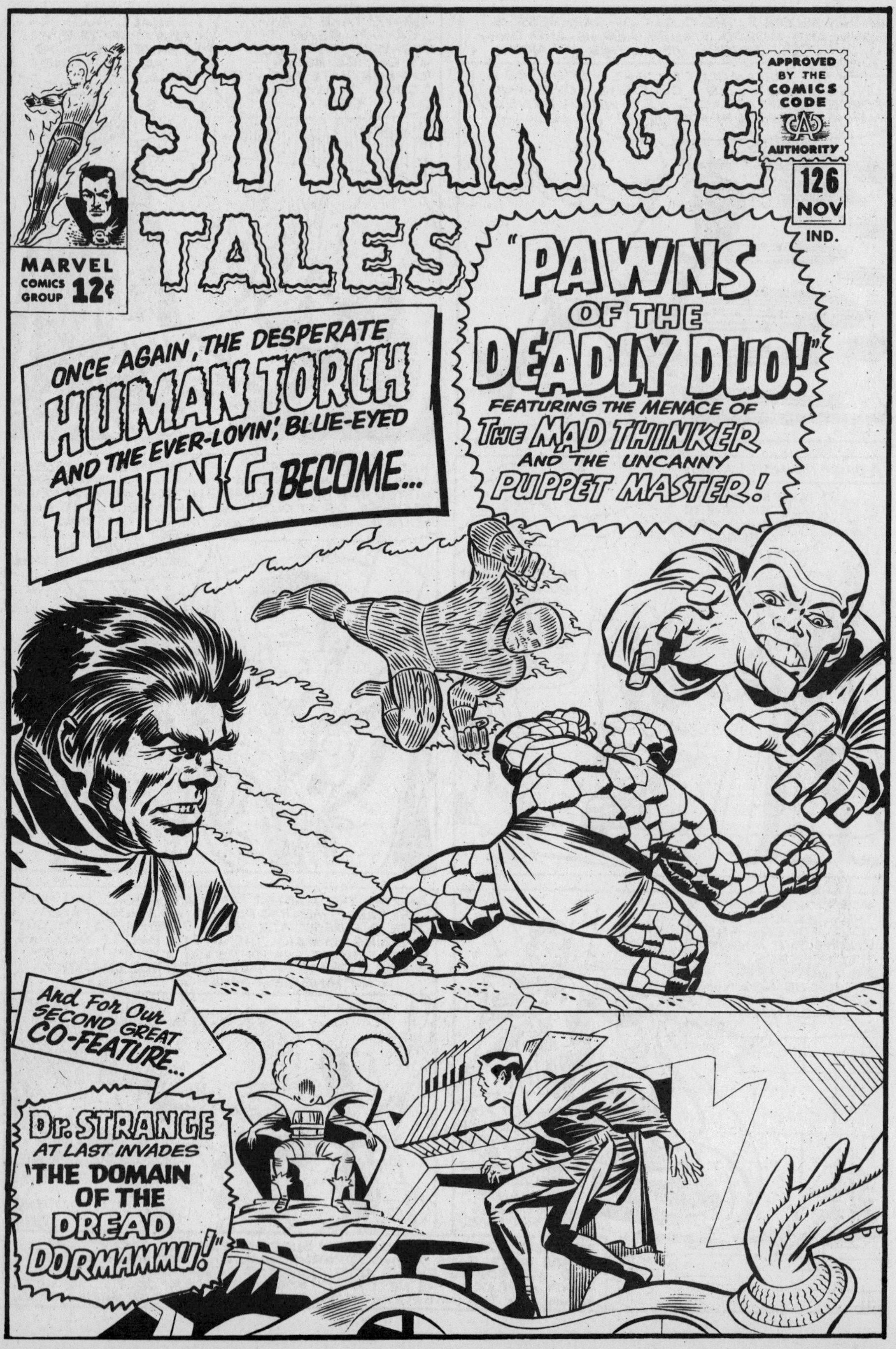

STRANGE TALES
APPROVED BY THE COMICS CODE AUTHORITY
126
NOV
IND.
MARVEL COMICS GROUP 12¢
"PAWNS OF THE DEADLY DUO!"
FEATURING THE MENACE OF THE MAD THINKER AND THE UNCANNY PUPPET MASTER!
ONCE AGAIN, THE DESPERATE HUMAN TORCH AND THE EVER-LOVIN', BLUE-EYED THING BECOME...
And For Our SECOND GREAT CO-FEATURE...
Dr. STRANGE AT LAST INVADES "THE DOMAIN OF THE DREAD DORMAMMU!"

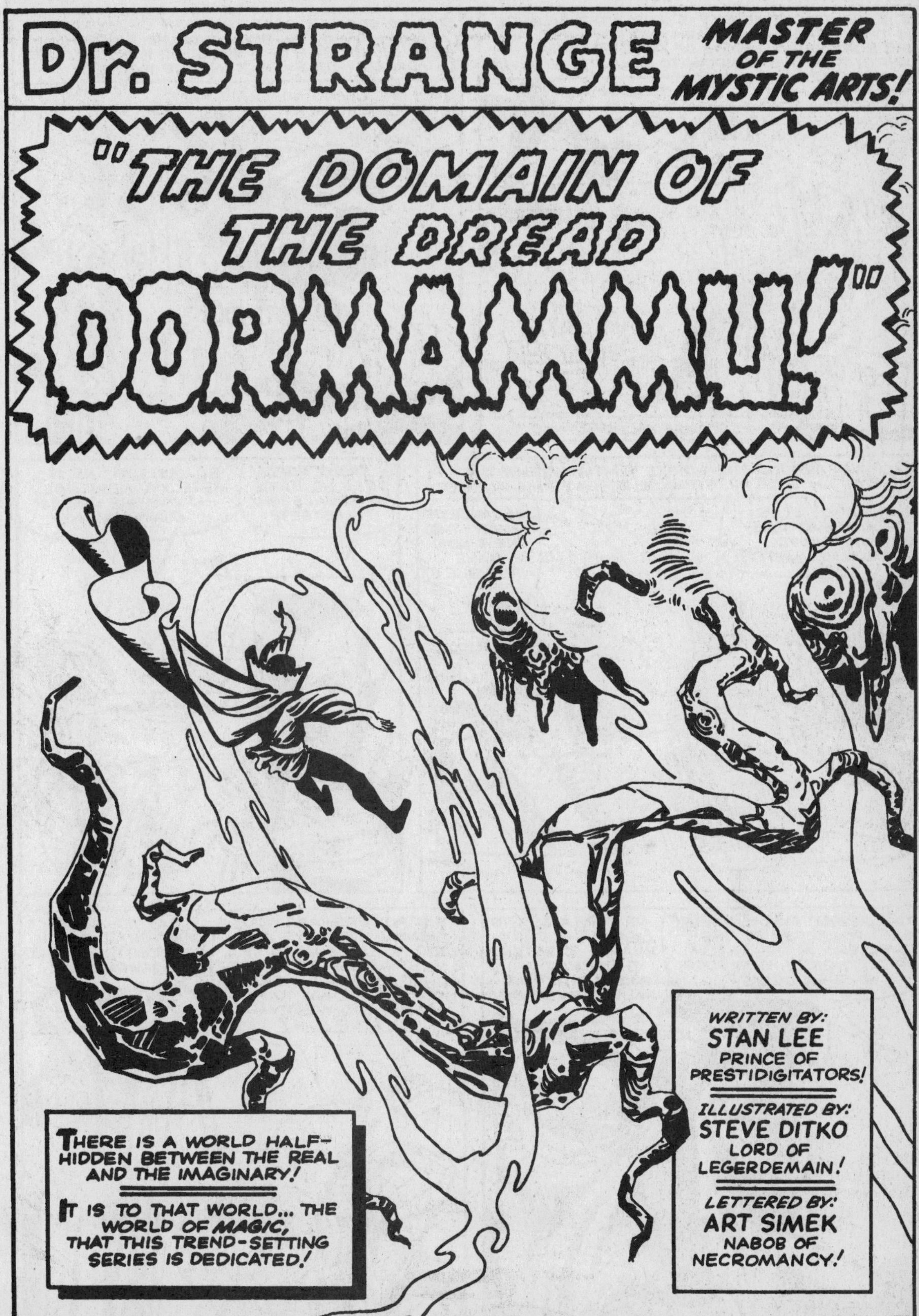
Dr. STRANGE
MASTER OF THE MYSTIC ARTS!
"THE DOMAIN OF THE DREAD DORMAMMU!"
THERE IS A WORLD HALF-HIDDEN BETWEEN THE REAL AND THE IMAGINARY!
IT IS TO THAT WORLD... THE WORLD OF MAGIC, THAT THIS TREND-SETTING SERIES IS DEDICATED!
WRITTEN BY: STAN LEE PRINCE OF PRESTIDIGITATORS!
ILLUSTRATED BY: STEVE DITKO LORD OF LEGERDEMAIN!
LETTERED BY: ART SIMEK NABOB OF NECROMANCY!
X-796
1

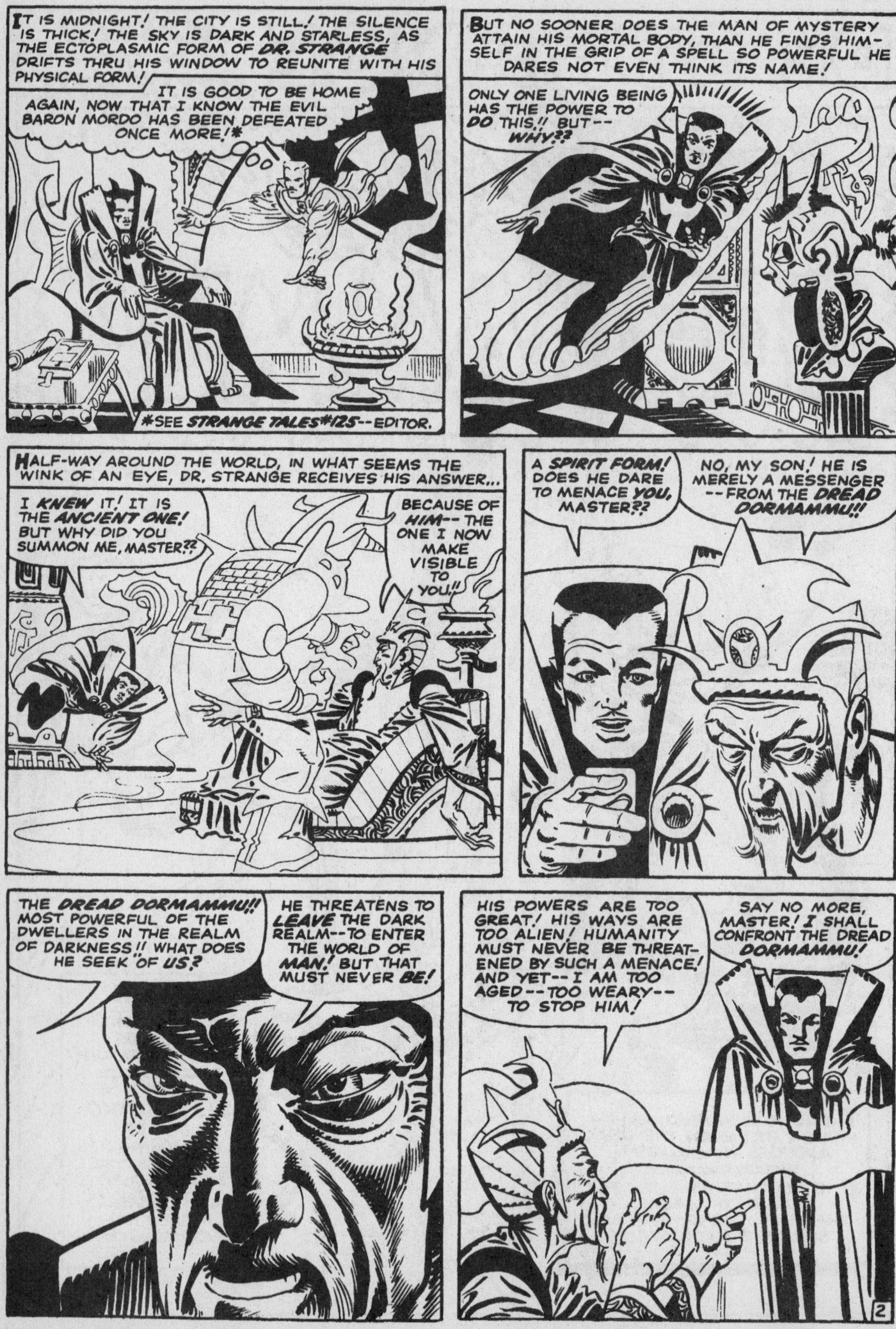

IT IS MIDNIGHT! THE CITY IS STILL! THE SILENCE IS THICK! THE SKY IS DARK AND STARLESS, AS THE ECTOPLASMIC FORM OF DR. STRANGE DRIFTS THRU HIS WINDOW TO REUNITE WITH HIS PHYSICAL FORM!
IT IS GOOD TO BE HOME AGAIN, NOW THAT I KNOW THE EVIL BARON MORDO HAS BEEN DEFEATED ONCE MORE!*
*SEE STRANGE TALES #125--EDITOR.
BUT NO SOONER DOES THE MAN OF MYSTERY ATTAIN HIS MORTAL BODY, THAN HE FINDS HIMSELF IN THE GRIP OF A SPELL SO POWERFUL HE DARES NOT EVEN THINK ITS NAME!
ONLY ONE LIVING BEING HAS THE POWER TO DO THIS!! BUT-- WHY??
HALF-WAY AROUND THE WORLD, IN WHAT SEEMS THE WINK OF AN EYE, DR. STRANGE RECEIVES HIS ANSWER...
I KNEW IT! IT IS THE ANCIENT ONE! BUT WHY DID YOU SUMMON ME, MASTER??
BECAUSE OF HIM-- THE ONE I NOW MAKE VISIBLE TO YOU!!
A SPIRIT FORM! DOES HE DARE TO MENACE YOU, MASTER??
NO, MY SON! HE IS MERELY A MESSENGER --FROM THE DREAD DORMAMMU!!
THE DREAD DORMAMMU!! MOST POWERFUL OF THE DWELLERS IN THE REALM OF DARKNESS!! WHAT DOES HE SEEK OF US?
HE THREATENS TO LEAVE THE DARK REALM--TO ENTER THE WORLD OF MAN! BUT THAT MUST NEVER BE!
HIS POWERS ARE TOO GREAT! HIS WAYS ARE TOO ALIEN! HUMANITY MUST NEVER BE THREATENED BY SUCH A MENACE! AND YET-- I AM TOO AGED--TOO WEARY-- TO STOP HIM!
SAY NO MORE, MASTER! I SHALL CONFRONT THE DREAD DORMAMMU!
2

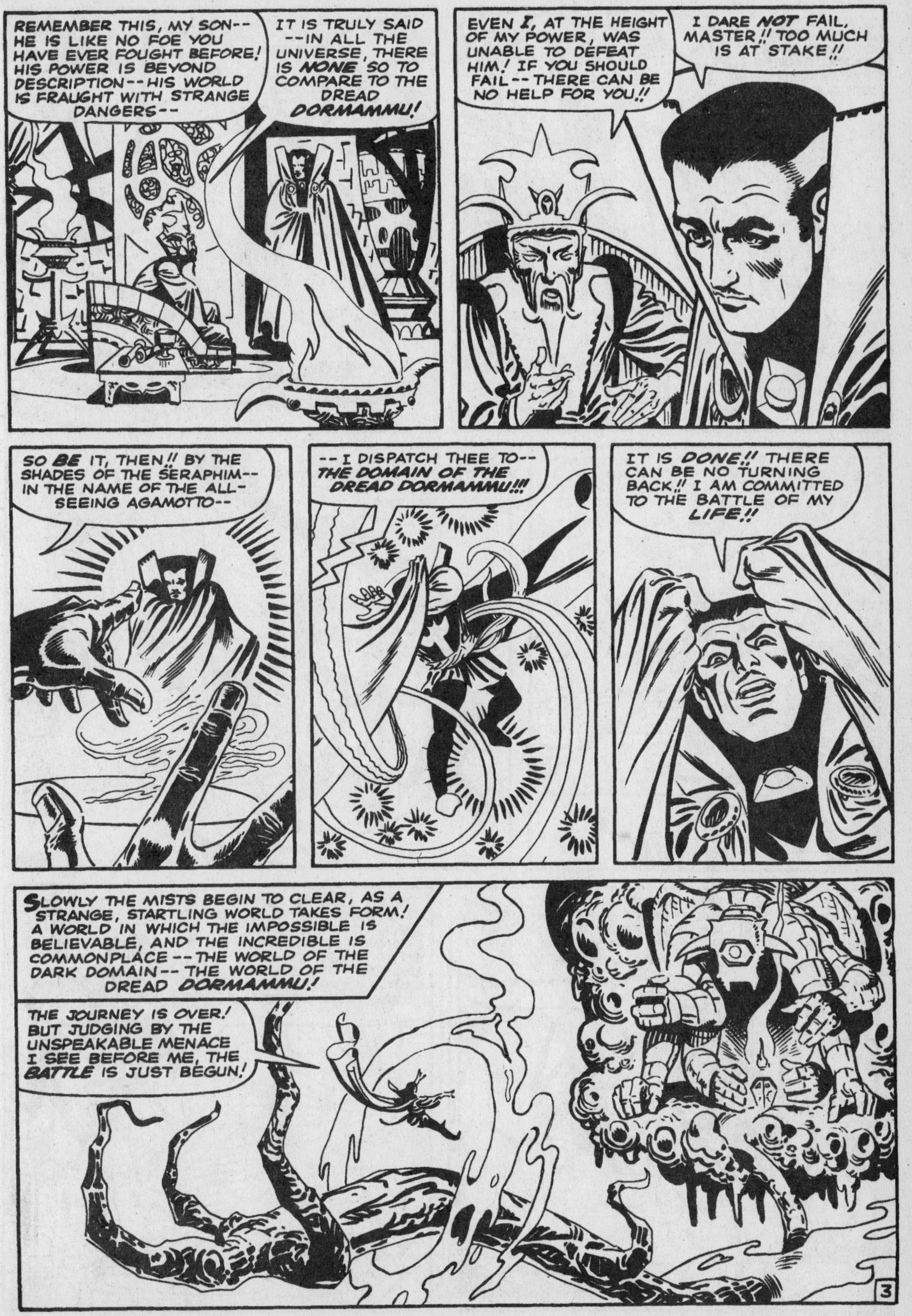
REMEMBER THIS, MY SON-- HE IS LIKE NO FOE YOU HAVE EVER FOUGHT BEFORE! HIS POWER IS BEYOND DESCRIPTION--HIS WORLD IS FRAUGHT WITH STRANGE DANGERS--
IT IS TRULY SAID --IN ALL THE UNIVERSE, THERE IS NONE SO TO COMPARE TO THE DREAD DORMAMMU!
EVEN I, AT THE HEIGHT OF MY POWER, WAS UNABLE TO DEFEAT HIM! IF YOU SHOULD FAIL--THERE CAN BE NO HELP FOR YOU!!
I DARE NOT FAIL, MASTER!! TOO MUCH IS AT STAKE!!
SO BE IT, THEN!! BY THE SHADES OF THE SERAPHIM-- IN THE NAME OF THE ALL-SEEING AGAMOTTO--
--I DISPATCH THEE TO-- THE DOMAIN OF THE DREAD DORMAMMU!!!
IT IS DONE!! THERE CAN BE NO TURNING BACK!! I AM COMMITTED TO THE BATTLE OF MY LIFE!!
SLOWLY THE MISTS BEGIN TO CLEAR, AS A STRANGE, STARTLING WORLD TAKES FORM! A WORLD IN WHICH THE IMPOSSIBLE IS BELIEVABLE, AND THE INCREDIBLE IS COMMONPLACE--THE WORLD OF THE DARK DOMAIN--THE WORLD OF THE DREAD DORMAMMU!
THE JOURNEY IS OVER! BUT JUDGING BY THE UNSPEAKABLE MENACE I SEE BEFORE ME, THE BATTLE IS JUST BEGUN!
3

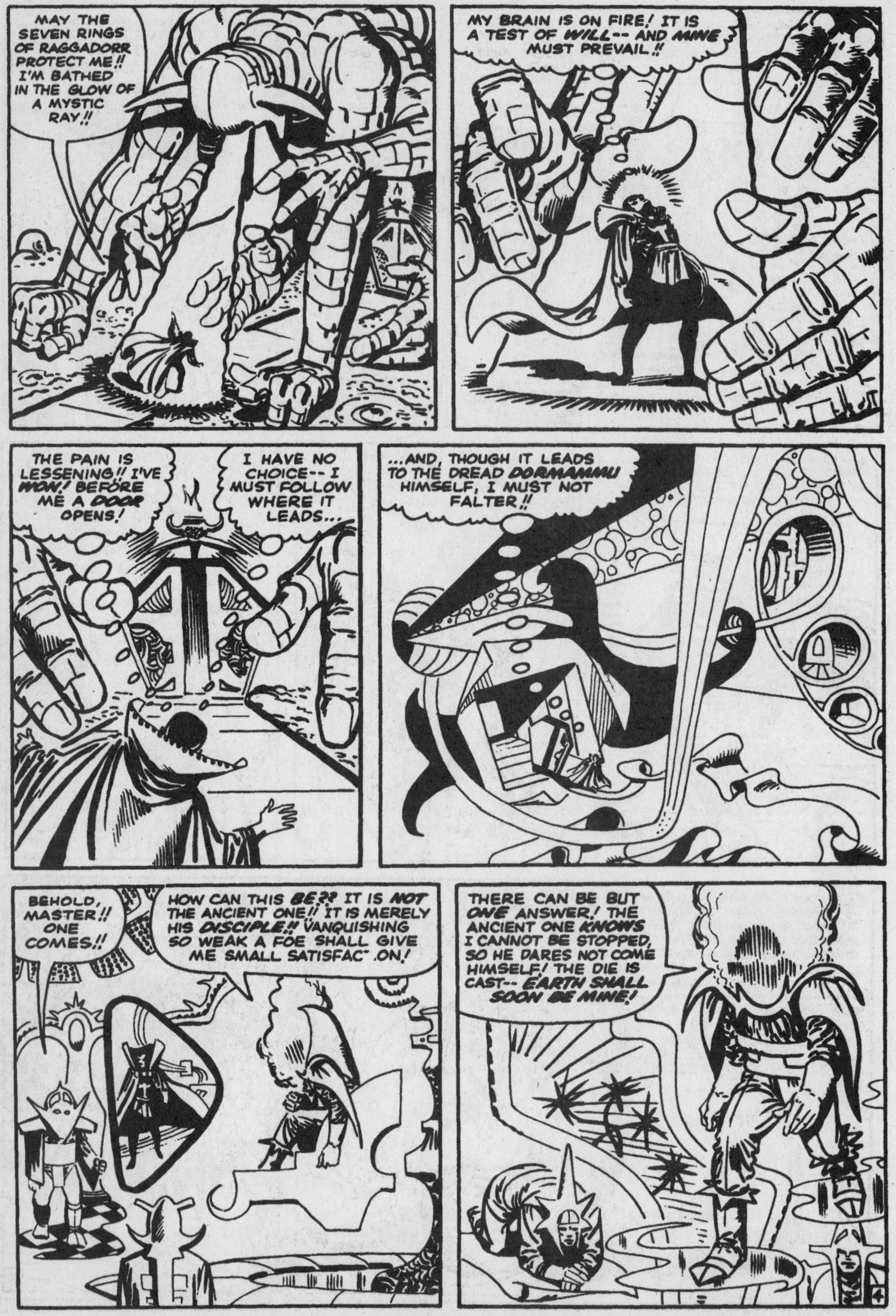
MAY THE SEVEN RINGS OF RAGGADORR PROTECT ME!! I'M BATHED IN THE GLOW OF A MYSTIC RAY!!
MY BRAIN IS ON FIRE! IT IS A TEST OF WILL-- AND MINE MUST PREVAIL!!
THE PAIN IS LESSENING!! I'VE WON! BEFORE ME A DOOR OPENS!
I HAVE NO CHOICE-- I MUST FOLLOW WHERE IT LEADS...
...AND, THOUGH IT LEADS TO THE DREAD DORMAMMU HIMSELF, I MUST NOT FALTER!!
BEHOLD, MASTER!! ONE COMES!!
HOW CAN THIS BE?? IT IS NOT THE ANCIENT ONE!! IT IS MERELY HIS DISCIPLE!! VANQUISHING SO WEAK A FOE SHALL GIVE ME SMALL SATISFAC .ON!
THERE CAN BE BUT ONE ANSWER! THE ANCIENT ONE KNOWS I CANNOT BE STOPPED, SO HE DARES NOT COME HIMSELF! THE DIE IS CAST-- EARTH SHALL SOON BE MINE!
4

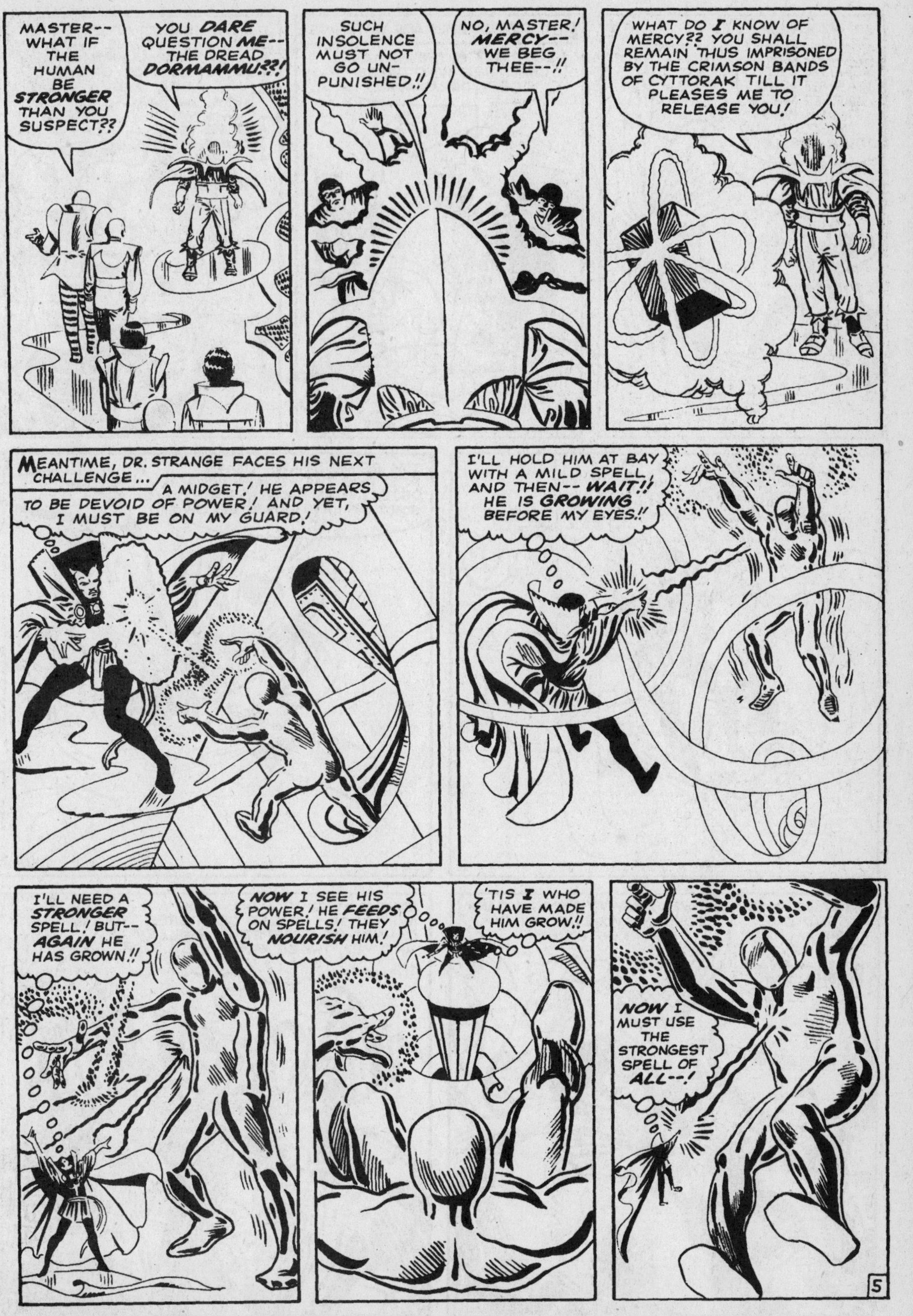

MASTER-- WHAT IF THE HUMAN BE STRONGER THAN YOU SUSPECT??
YOU DARE QUESTION ME-- THE DREAD DORMAMMU??!
SUCH INSOLENCE MUST NOT GO UN-PUNISHED!!
NO, MASTER! MERCY-- WE BEG THEE--!!
WHAT DO I KNOW OF MERCY?? YOU SHALL REMAIN THUS IMPRISONED BY THE CRIMSON BANDS OF CYTTORAK TILL IT PLEASES ME TO RELEASE YOU!
MEANTIME, DR. STRANGE FACES HIS NEXT CHALLENGE...
A MIDGET! HE APPEARS TO BE DEVOID OF POWER! AND YET, I MUST BE ON MY GUARD!
I'LL HOLD HIM AT BAY WITH A MILD SPELL, AND THEN-- WAIT!! HE IS GROWING BEFORE MY EYES!!
I'LL NEED A STRONGER SPELL! BUT-- AGAIN HE HAS GROWN!!
NOW I SEE HIS POWER! HE FEEDS ON SPELLS! THEY NOURISH HIM!
'TIS I WHO HAVE MADE HIM GROW!!
NOW I MUST USE THE STRONGEST SPELL OF ALL--!
5

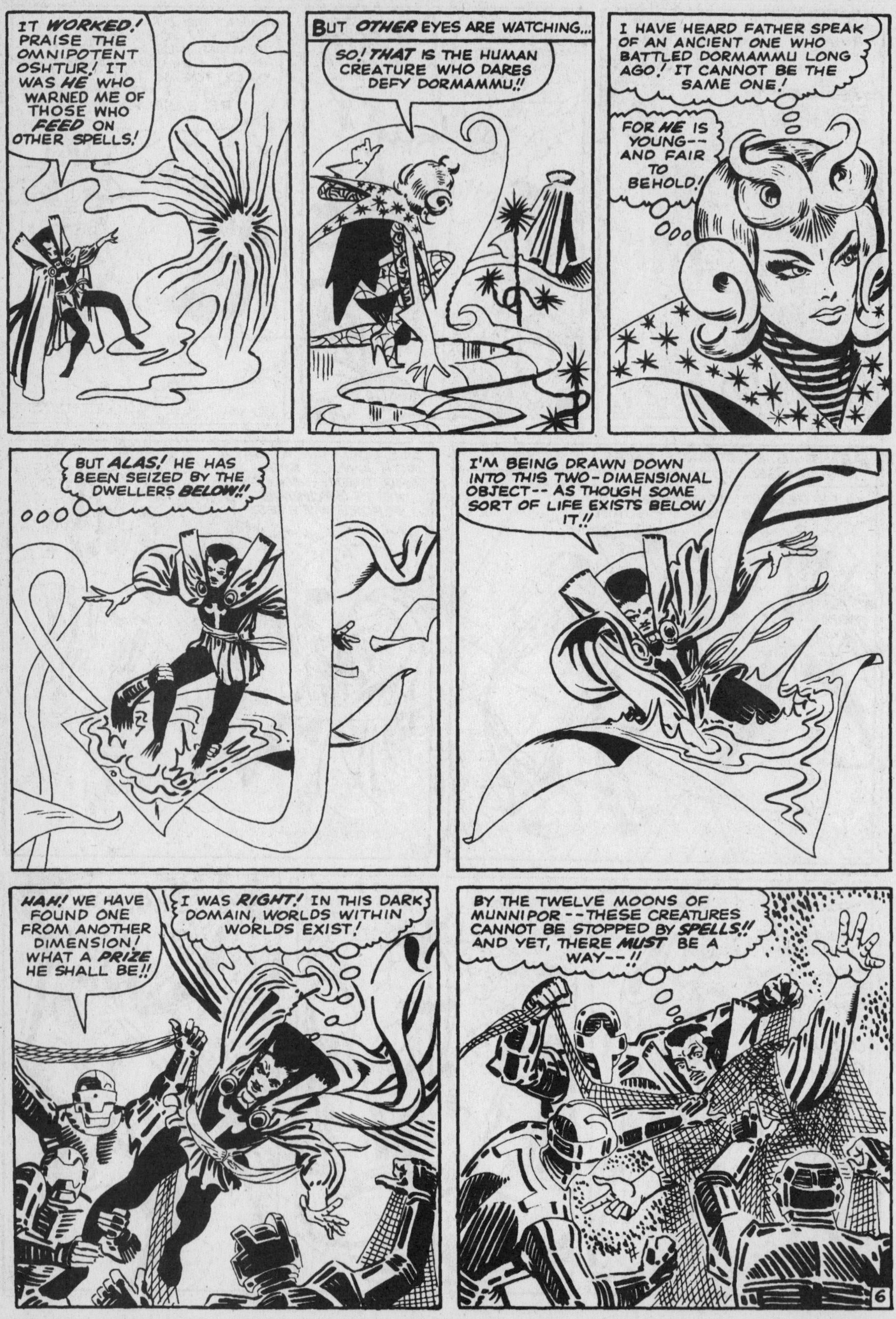
IT WORKED! PRAISE THE OMNIPOTENT OSHTUR! IT WAS HE WHO WARNED ME OF THOSE WHO FEED ON OTHER SPELLS!
BUT OTHER EYES ARE WATCHING...
SO! THAT IS THE HUMAN CREATURE WHO DARES DEFY DORMAMMU!!
I HAVE HEARD FATHER SPEAK OF AN ANCIENT ONE WHO BATTLED DORMAMMU LONG AGO! IT CANNOT BE THE SAME ONE!
FOR HE IS YOUNG-- AND FAIR TO BEHOLD!
BUT ALAS! HE HAS BEEN SEIZED BY THE DWELLERS BELOW!!
I'M BEING DRAWN DOWN INTO THIS TWO-DIMENSIONAL OBJECT-- AS THOUGH SOME SORT OF LIFE EXISTS BELOW IT!!
HAH! WE HAVE FOUND ONE FROM ANOTHER DIMENSION! WHAT A PRIZE HE SHALL BE!!
I WAS RIGHT! IN THIS DARK DOMAIN, WORLDS WITHIN WORLDS EXIST!
BY THE TWELVE MOONS OF MUNNIPOR--THESE CREATURES CANNOT BE STOPPED BY SPELLS!! AND YET, THERE MUST BE A WAY--!!
6

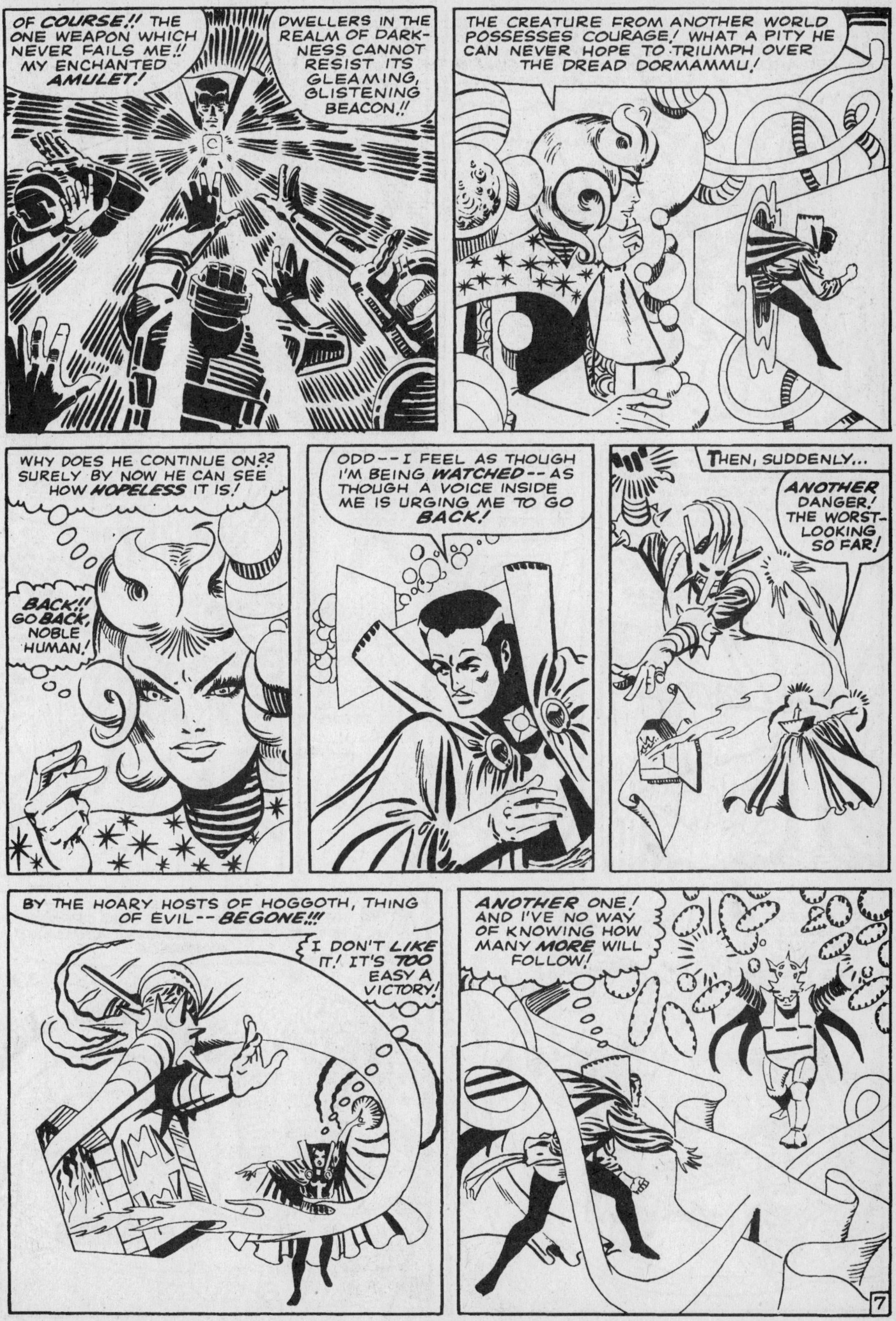
OF COURSE!! THE ONE WEAPON WHICH NEVER FAILS ME!! MY ENCHANTED AMULET!
DWELLERS IN THE REALM OF DARKNESS CANNOT RESIST ITS GLEAMING, GLISTENING BEACON!!
THE CREATURE FROM ANOTHER WORLD POSSESSES COURAGE! WHAT A PITY HE CAN NEVER HOPE TO TRIUMPH OVER THE DREAD DORMAMMU!
WHY DOES HE CONTINUE ON?? SURELY BY NOW HE CAN SEE HOW HOPELESS IT IS!
BACK!! GO BACK, NOBLE HUMAN!
ODD--I FEEL AS THOUGH I'M BEING WATCHED--AS THOUGH A VOICE INSIDE ME IS URGING ME TO GO BACK!
THEN, SUDDENLY...
ANOTHER DANGER! THE WORST-LOOKING SO FAR!
BY THE HOARY HOSTS OF HOGGOTH, THING OF EVIL--BEGONE!!!
I DON'T LIKE IT! IT'S TOO EASY A VICTORY!
ANOTHER ONE! AND I'VE NO WAY OF KNOWING HOW MANY MORE WILL FOLLOW!
7

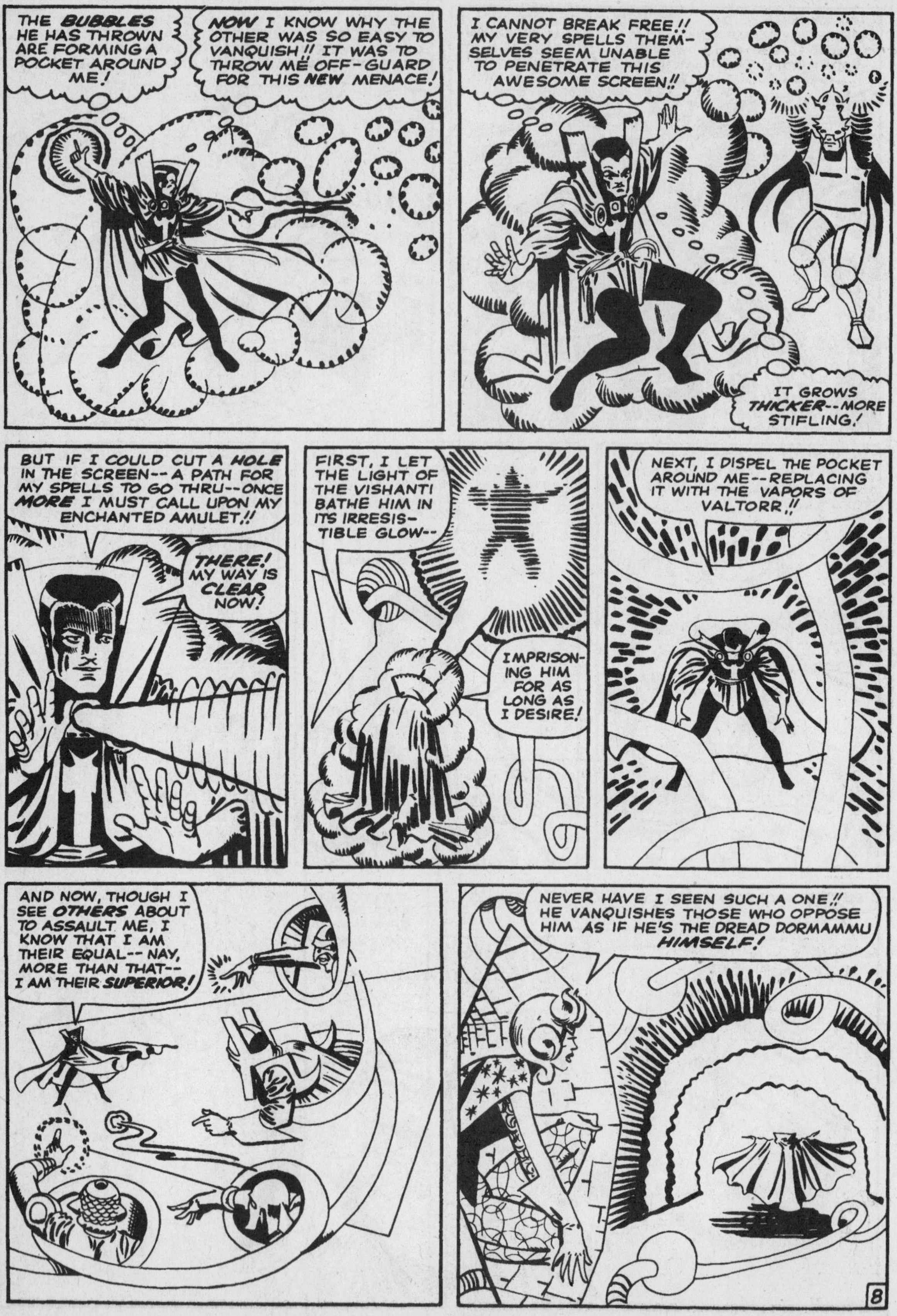
THE BUBBLES HE HAS THROWN ARE FORMING A POCKET AROUND ME!
NOW I KNOW WHY THE OTHER WAS SO EASY TO VANQUISH!! IT WAS TO THROW ME OFF-GUARD FOR THIS NEW MENACE!
I CANNOT BREAK FREE!! MY VERY SPELLS THEMSELVES SEEM UNABLE TO PENETRATE THIS AWESOME SCREEN!!
IT GROWS THICKER--MORE STIFLING!
BUT IF I COULD CUT A HOLE IN THE SCREEN--A PATH FOR MY SPELLS TO GO THRU--ONCE MORE I MUST CALL UPON MY ENCHANTED AMULET!!
THERE! MY WAY IS CLEAR NOW!
FIRST, I LET THE LIGHT OF THE VISHANTI BATHE HIM IN ITS IRRESISTIBLE GLOW--
IMPRISONING HIM FOR AS LONG AS I DESIRE!
NEXT, I DISPEL THE POCKET AROUND ME--REPLACING IT WITH THE VAPORS OF VALTORR!!
AND NOW, THOUGH I SEE OTHERS ABOUT TO ASSAULT ME, I KNOW THAT I AM THEIR EQUAL--NAY, MORE THAN THAT--I AM THEIR SUPERIOR!
NEVER HAVE I SEEN SUCH A ONE!! HE VANQUISHES THOSE WHO OPPOSE HIM AS IF HE'S THE DREAD DORMAMMU HIMSELF!
8

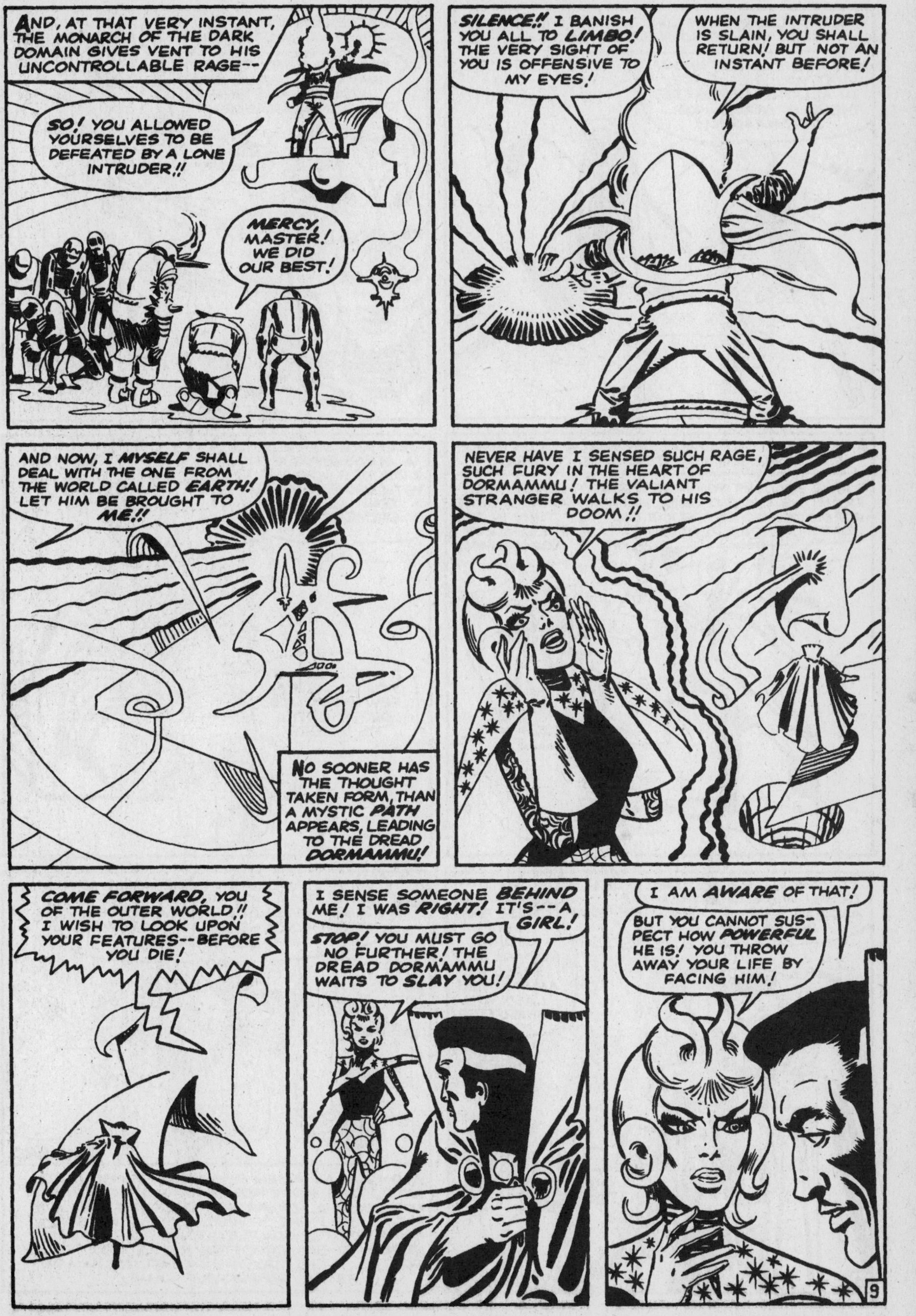
AND, AT THAT VERY INSTANT, THE MONARCH OF THE DARK DOMAIN GIVES VENT TO HIS UNCONTROLLABLE RAGE--
SO! YOU ALLOWED YOURSELVES TO BE DEFEATED BY A LONE INTRUDER!!
MERCY, MASTER! WE DID OUR BEST!
SILENCE!! I BANISH YOU ALL TO LIMBO! THE VERY SIGHT OF YOU IS OFFENSIVE TO MY EYES!
WHEN THE INTRUDER IS SLAIN, YOU SHALL RETURN! BUT NOT AN INSTANT BEFORE!
AND NOW, I MYSELF SHALL DEAL WITH THE ONE FROM THE WORLD CALLED EARTH! LET HIM BE BROUGHT TO ME!!
NO SOONER HAS THE THOUGHT TAKEN FORM, THAN A MYSTIC PATH APPEARS, LEADING TO THE DREAD DORMAMMU!
NEVER HAVE I SENSED SUCH RAGE, SUCH FURY IN THE HEART OF DORMAMMU! THE VALIANT STRANGER WALKS TO HIS DOOM!!
COME FORWARD, YOU OF THE OUTER WORLD!! I WISH TO LOOK UPON YOUR FEATURES--BEFORE YOU DIE!
I SENSE SOMEONE BEHIND ME! I WAS RIGHT! IT'S--A GIRL!
STOP! YOU MUST GO NO FURTHER! THE DREAD DORMAMMU WAITS TO SLAY YOU!
I AM AWARE OF THAT!
BUT YOU CANNOT SUSPECT HOW POWERFUL HE IS! YOU THROW AWAY YOUR LIFE BY FACING HIM!
9

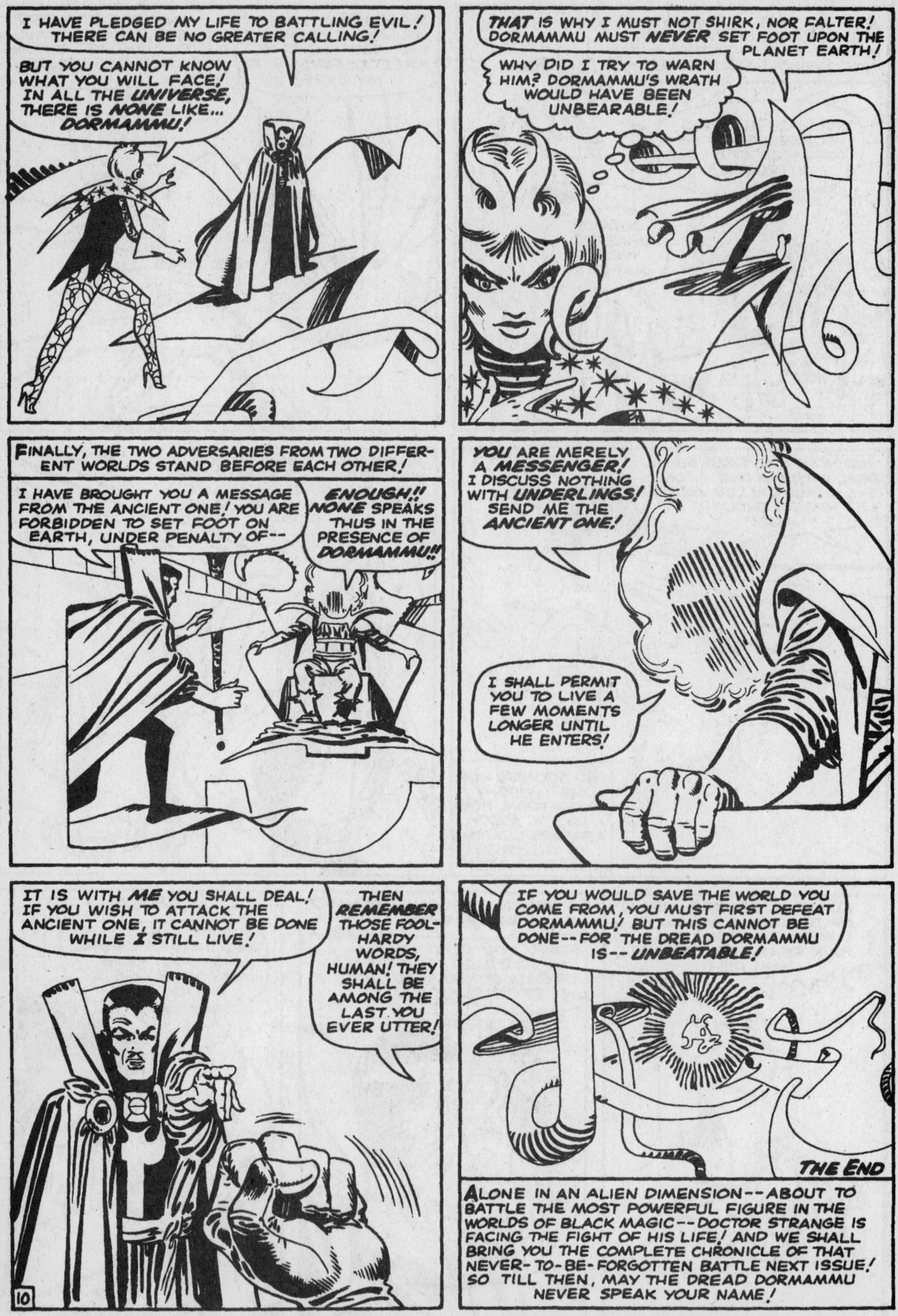
I HAVE PLEDGED MY LIFE TO BATTLING EVIL! THERE CAN BE NO GREATER CALLING!
BUT YOU CANNOT KNOW WHAT YOU WILL FACE! IN ALL THE UNIVERSE, THERE IS NONE LIKE... DORMAMMU!
THAT IS WHY I MUST NOT SHIRK, NOR FALTER! DORMAMMU MUST NEVER SET FOOT UPON THE PLANET EARTH!
WHY DID I TRY TO WARN HIM? DORMAMMU'S WRATH WOULD HAVE BEEN UNBEARABLE!
FINALLY, THE TWO ADVERSARIES FROM TWO DIFFERENT WORLDS STAND BEFORE EACH OTHER!
I HAVE BROUGHT YOU A MESSAGE FROM THE ANCIENT ONE! YOU ARE FORBIDDEN TO SET FOOT ON EARTH, UNDER PENALTY OF--
ENOUGH!! NONE SPEAKS THUS IN THE PRESENCE OF DORMAMMU!!
YOU ARE MERELY A MESSENGER! I DISCUSS NOTHING WITH UNDERLINGS! SEND ME THE ANCIENT ONE!
I SHALL PERMIT YOU TO LIVE A FEW MOMENTS LONGER UNTIL HE ENTERS!
IT IS WITH ME YOU SHALL DEAL! IF YOU WISH TO ATTACK THE ANCIENT ONE, IT CANNOT BE DONE WHILE I STILL LIVE!
THEN REMEMBER THOSE FOOL-HARDY WORDS, HUMAN! THEY SHALL BE AMONG THE LAST YOU EVER UTTER!
10
IF YOU WOULD SAVE THE WORLD YOU COME FROM, YOU MUST FIRST DEFEAT DORMAMMU! BUT THIS CANNOT BE DONE--FOR THE DREAD DORMAMMU IS--UNBEATABLE!
THE END
ALONE IN AN ALIEN DIMENSION--ABOUT TO BATTLE THE MOST POWERFUL FIGURE IN THE WORLDS OF BLACK MAGIC--DOCTOR STRANGE IS FACING THE FIGHT OF HIS LIFE! AND WE SHALL BRING YOU THE COMPLETE CHRONICLE OF THAT NEVER-TO-BE-FORGOTTEN BATTLE NEXT ISSUE! SO TILL THEN, MAY THE DREAD DORMAMMU NEVER SPEAK YOUR NAME!

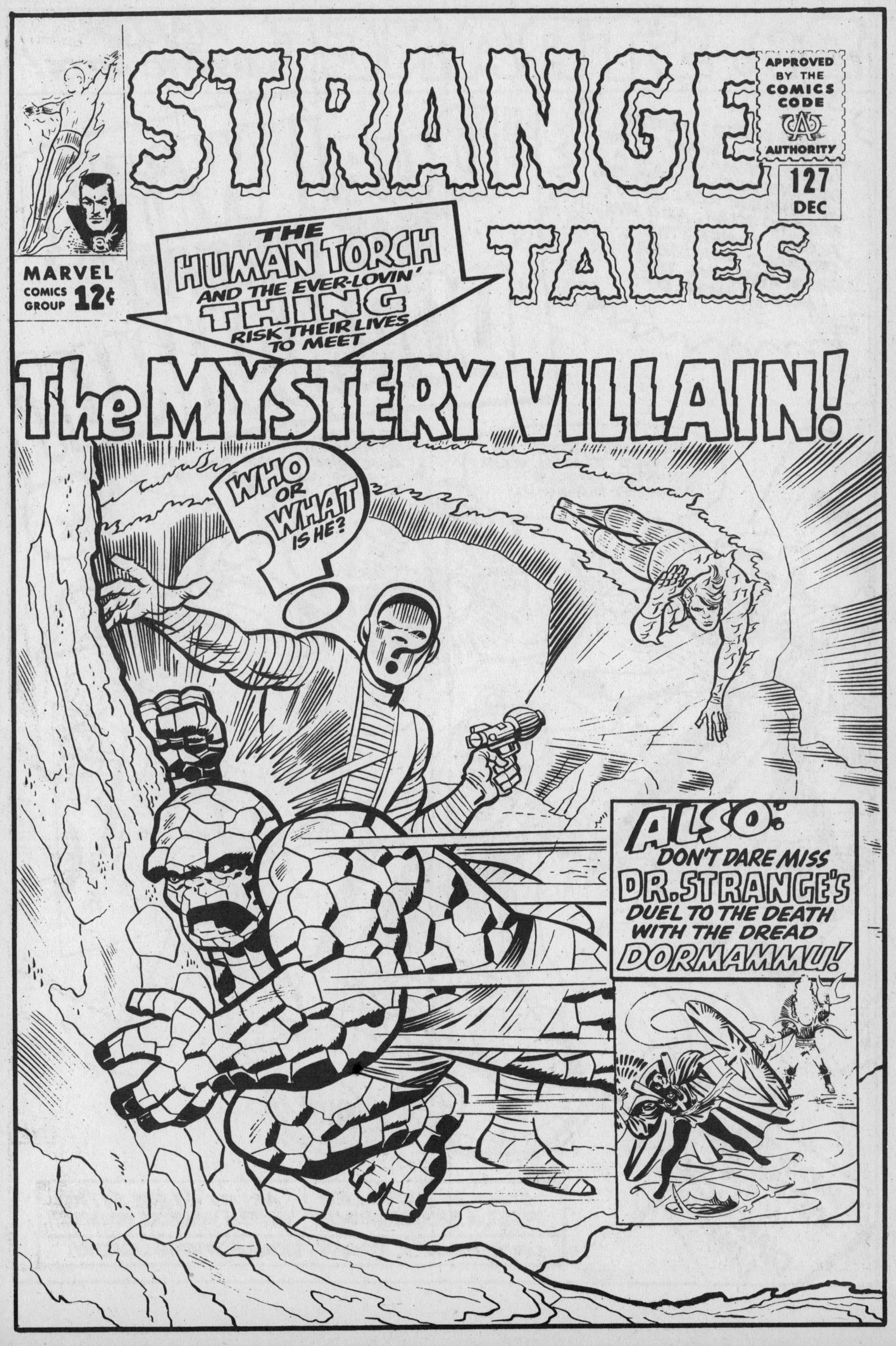
STRANGE TALES
APPROVED BY THE COMICS CODE AUTHORITY
127 DEC
MARVEL COMICS GROUP 12¢
THE HUMAN TORCH AND THE EVER-LOVIN' THING RISK THEIR LIVES TO MEET
The MYSTERY VILLAIN!
WHO OR WHAT IS HE?
ALSO: DON'T DARE MISS DR. STRANGE'S DUEL TO THE DEATH WITH THE DREAD DORMAMMU!

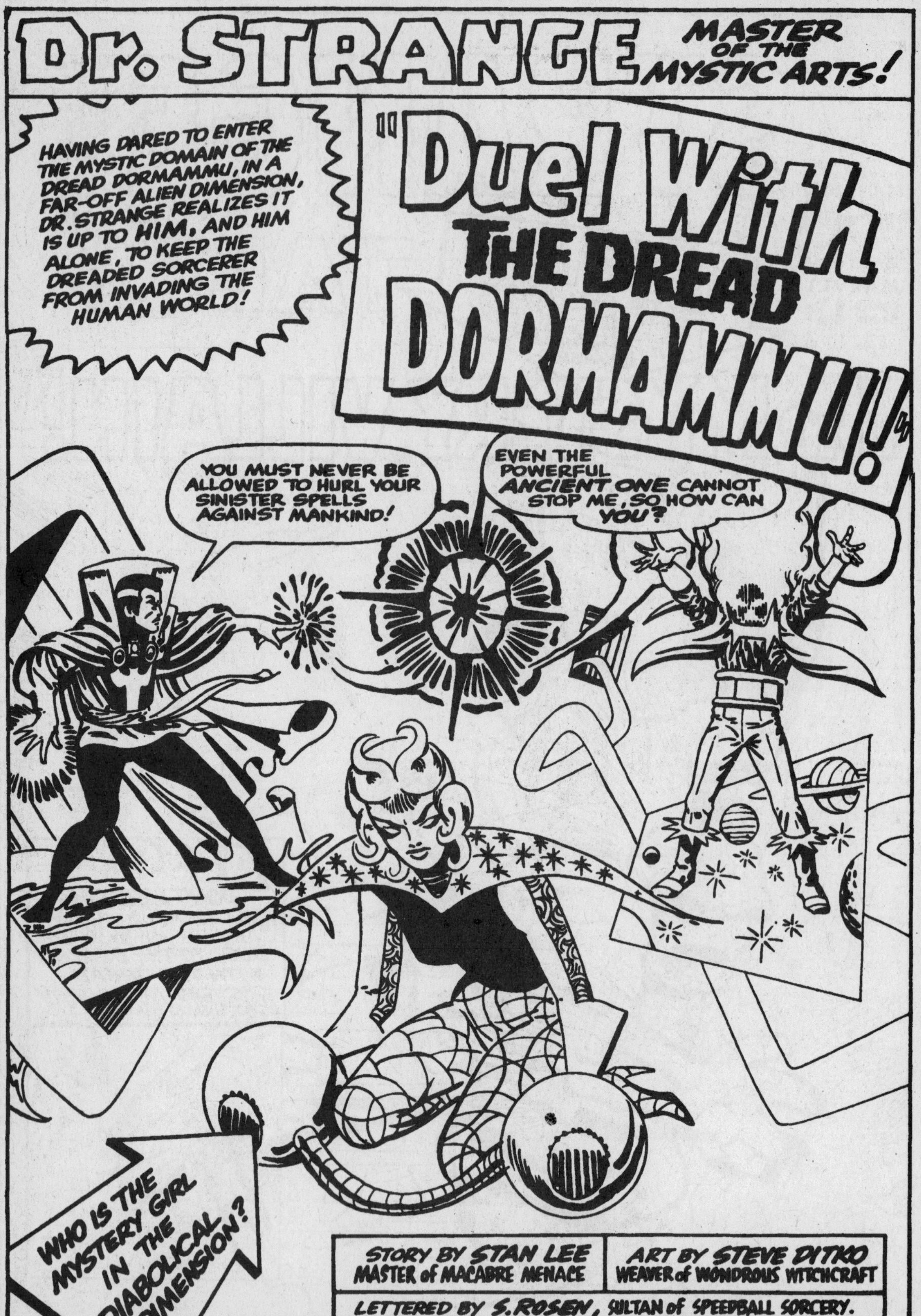
Dr. STRANGE MASTER OF THE MYSTIC ARTS!
HAVING DARED TO ENTER THE MYSTIC DOMAIN OF THE DREAD DORMAMMU, IN A FAR-OFF ALIEN DIMENSION, DR. STRANGE REALIZES IT IS UP TO HIM, AND HIM ALONE, TO KEEP THE DREADED SORCERER FROM INVADING THE HUMAN WORLD!
"Duel With THE DREAD DORMAMMU!"
YOU MUST NEVER BE ALLOWED TO HURL YOUR SINISTER SPELLS AGAINST MANKIND!
EVEN THE POWERFUL ANCIENT ONE CANNOT STOP ME, SO HOW CAN YOU?
WHO IS THE MYSTERY GIRL IN THE DIABOLICAL DIMENSION?
STORY BY STAN LEE MASTER of MACABRE MENACE
ART BY STEVE DITKO WEAVER of WONDROUS WITCHCRAFT
LETTERED BY S. ROSEN, SULTAN of SPEEDBALL SORCERY.
X-813

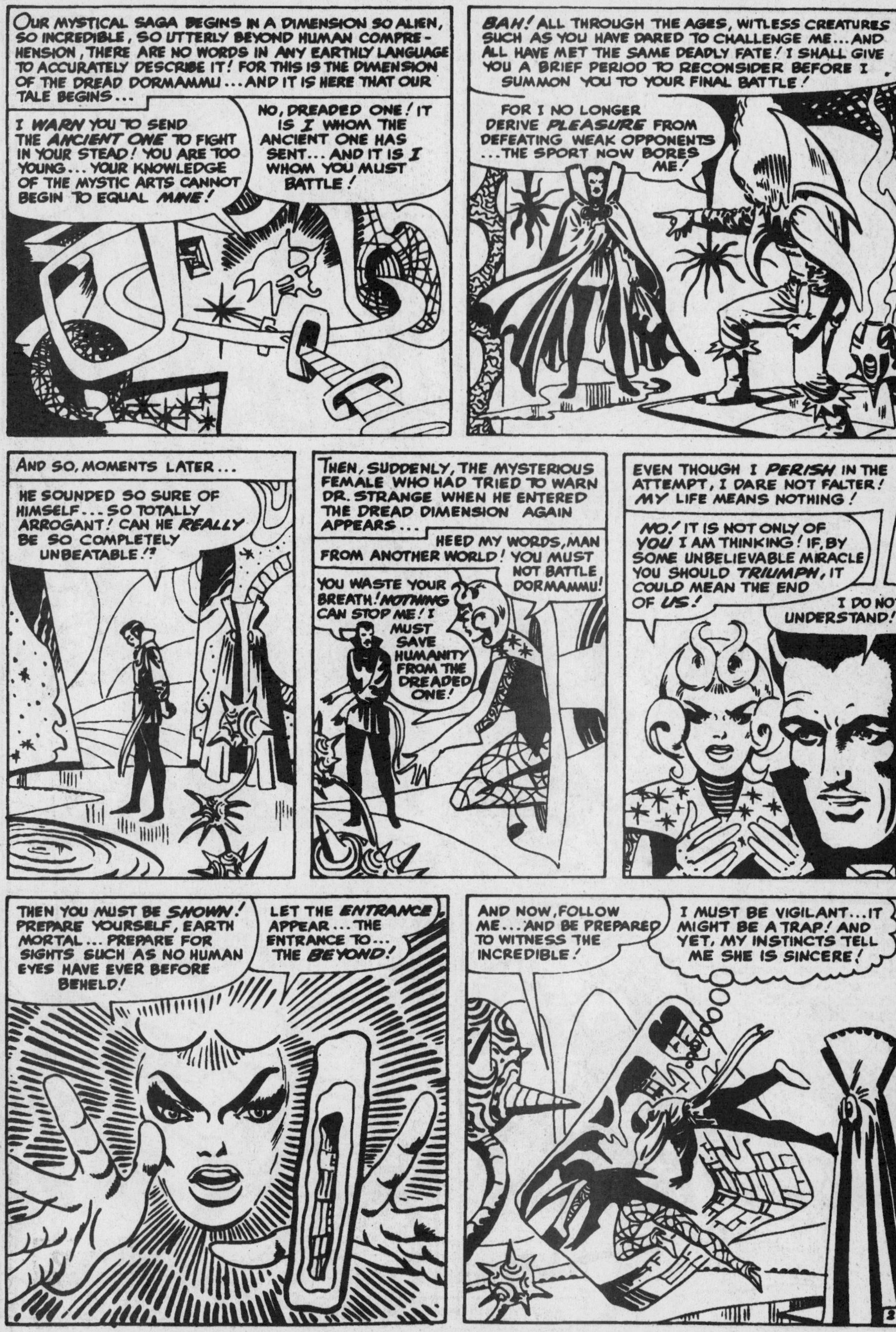

OUR MYSTICAL SAGA BEGINS IN A DIMENSION SO ALIEN, SO INCREDIBLE, SO UTTERLY BEYOND HUMAN COMPREHENSION, THERE ARE NO WORDS IN ANY EARTHLY LANGUAGE TO ACCURATELY DESCRIBE IT! FOR THIS IS THE DIMENSION OF THE DREAD DORMAMMU... AND IT IS HERE THAT OUR TALE BEGINS...
I WARN YOU TO SEND THE ANCIENT ONE TO FIGHT IN YOUR STEAD! YOU ARE TOO YOUNG... YOUR KNOWLEDGE OF THE MYSTIC ARTS CANNOT BEGIN TO EQUAL MINE!
NO, DREADED ONE! IT IS I WHOM THE ANCIENT ONE HAS SENT... AND IT IS I WHOM YOU MUST BATTLE!
BAH! ALL THROUGH THE AGES, WITLESS CREATURES SUCH AS YOU HAVE DARED TO CHALLENGE ME... AND ALL HAVE MET THE SAME DEADLY FATE! I SHALL GIVE YOU A BRIEF PERIOD TO RECONSIDER BEFORE I SUMMON YOU TO YOUR FINAL BATTLE!
FOR I NO LONGER DERIVE PLEASURE FROM DEFEATING WEAK OPPONENTS ...THE SPORT NOW BORES ME!
AND SO, MOMENTS LATER...
HE SOUNDED SO SURE OF HIMSELF... SO TOTALLY ARROGANT! CAN HE REALLY BE SO COMPLETELY UNBEATABLE!?
THEN, SUDDENLY, THE MYSTERIOUS FEMALE WHO HAD TRIED TO WARN DR. STRANGE WHEN HE ENTERED THE DREAD DIMENSION AGAIN APPEARS...
HEED MY WORDS, MAN FROM ANOTHER WORLD! YOU MUST NOT BATTLE DORMAMMU!
YOU WASTE YOUR BREATH! NOTHING CAN STOP ME! I MUST SAVE HUMANITY FROM THE DREADED ONE!
EVEN THOUGH I PERISH IN THE ATTEMPT, I DARE NOT FALTER! MY LIFE MEANS NOTHING!
NO! IT IS NOT ONLY OF YOU I AM THINKING! IF, BY SOME UNBELIEVABLE MIRACLE YOU SHOULD TRIUMPH, IT COULD MEAN THE END OF US!
I DO NOT UNDERSTAND!
THEN YOU MUST BE SHOWN! PREPARE YOURSELF, EARTH MORTAL... PREPARE FOR SIGHTS SUCH AS NO HUMAN EYES HAVE EVER BEFORE BEHELD!
LET THE ENTRANCE APPEAR... THE ENTRANCE TO... THE BEYOND!
AND NOW, FOLLOW ME... AND BE PREPARED TO WITNESS THE INCREDIBLE!
I MUST BE VIGILANT... IT MIGHT BE A TRAP! AND YET, MY INSTINCTS TELL ME SHE IS SINCERE!
2.

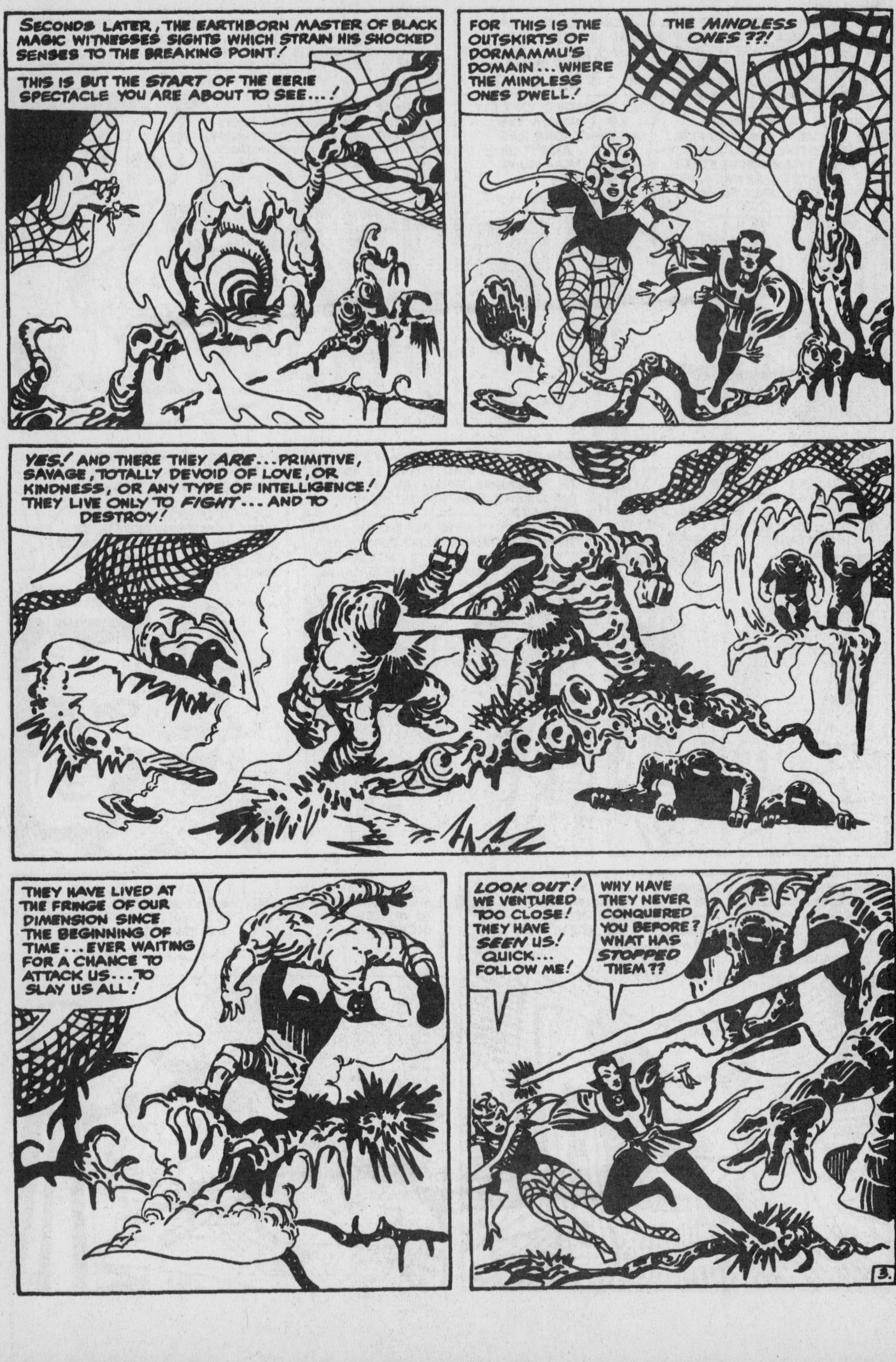
SECONDS LATER, THE EARTHBORN MASTER OF BLACK MAGIC WITNESSES SIGHTS WHICH STRAIN HIS SHOCKED SENSES TO THE BREAKING POINT!
THIS IS BUT THE START OF THE EERIE SPECTACLE YOU ARE ABOUT TO SEE...!
FOR THIS IS THE OUTSKIRTS OF DORMAMMU'S DOMAIN... WHERE THE MINDLESS ONES DWELL!
THE MINDLESS ONES ??!
YES! AND THERE THEY ARE... PRIMITIVE, SAVAGE, TOTALLY DEVOID OF LOVE, OR KINDNESS, OR ANY TYPE OF INTELLIGENCE! THEY LIVE ONLY TO FIGHT... AND TO DESTROY!
THEY HAVE LIVED AT THE FRINGE OF OUR DIMENSION SINCE THE BEGINNING OF TIME... EVER WAITING FOR A CHANCE TO ATTACK US... TO SLAY US ALL!
LOOK OUT! WE VENTURED TOO CLOSE! THEY HAVE SEEN US! QUICK... FOLLOW ME!
WHY HAVE THEY NEVER CONQUERED YOU BEFORE? WHAT HAS STOPPED THEM??
3.

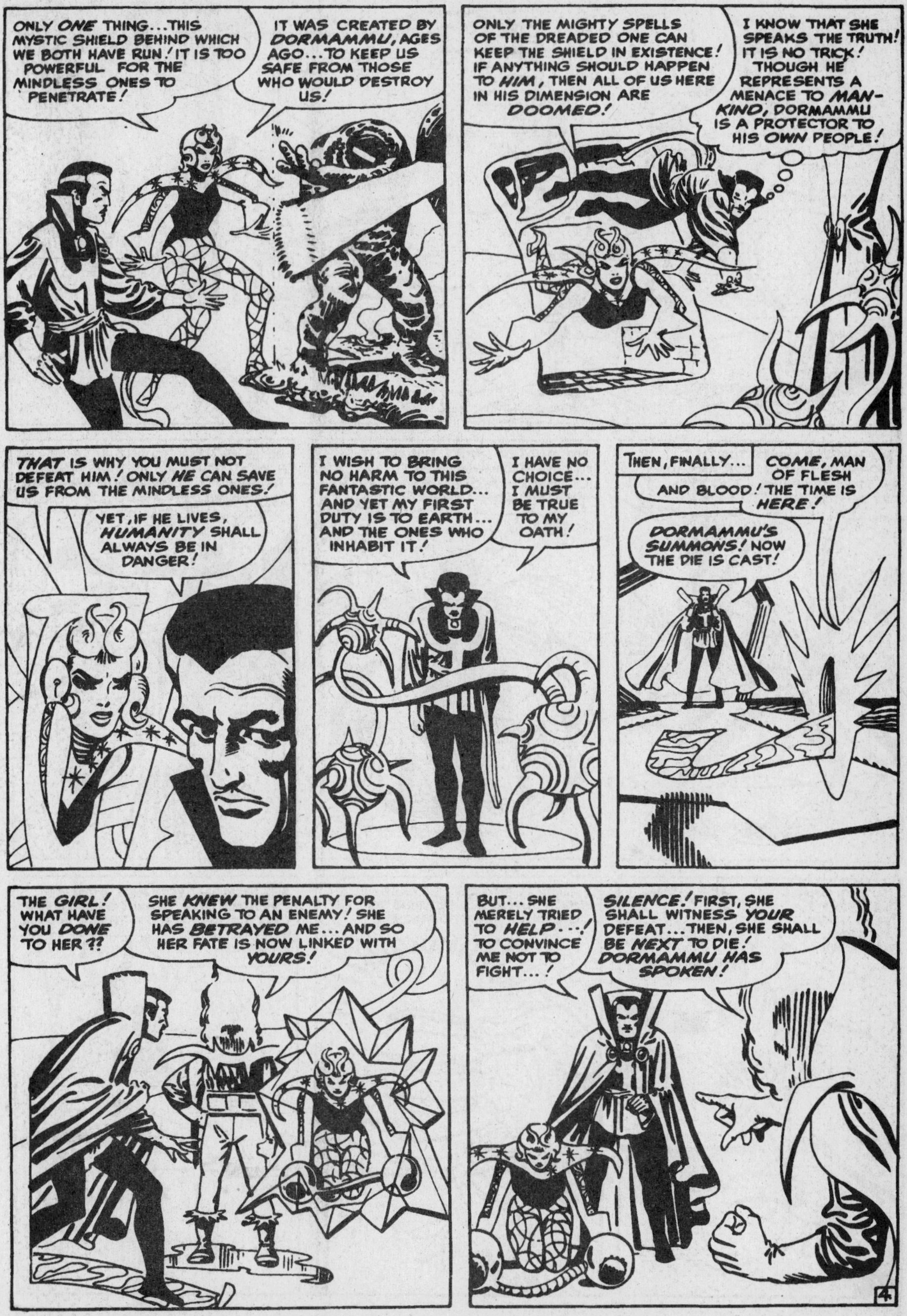
ONLY ONE THING... THIS MYSTIC SHIELD BEHIND WHICH WE BOTH HAVE RUN! IT IS TOO POWERFUL FOR THE MINDLESS ONES TO PENETRATE!
IT WAS CREATED BY DORMAMMU, AGES AGO... TO KEEP US SAFE FROM THOSE WHO WOULD DESTROY US!
ONLY THE MIGHTY SPELLS OF THE DREADED ONE CAN KEEP THE SHIELD IN EXISTENCE! IF ANYTHING SHOULD HAPPEN TO HIM, THEN ALL OF US HERE IN HIS DIMENSION ARE DOOMED!
I KNOW THAT SHE SPEAKS THE TRUTH! IT IS NO TRICK! THOUGH HE REPRESENTS A MENACE TO MAN-KIND, DORMAMMU IS A PROTECTOR TO HIS OWN PEOPLE!
THAT IS WHY YOU MUST NOT DEFEAT HIM! ONLY HE CAN SAVE US FROM THE MINDLESS ONES!
YET, IF HE LIVES, HUMANITY SHALL ALWAYS BE IN DANGER!
I WISH TO BRING NO HARM TO THIS FANTASTIC WORLD... AND YET MY FIRST DUTY IS TO EARTH... AND THE ONES WHO INHABIT IT!
I HAVE NO CHOICE... I MUST BE TRUE TO MY OATH!
THEN, FINALLY...
COME, MAN OF FLESH AND BLOOD! THE TIME IS HERE!
DORMAMMU'S SUMMONS! NOW THE DIE IS CAST!
THE GIRL! WHAT HAVE YOU DONE TO HER??
SHE KNEW THE PENALTY FOR SPEAKING TO AN ENEMY! SHE HAS BETRAYED ME... AND SO HER FATE IS NOW LINKED WITH YOURS!
BUT... SHE MERELY TRIED TO HELP...! TO CONVINCE ME NOT TO FIGHT...!
SILENCE! FIRST, SHE SHALL WITNESS YOUR DEFEAT... THEN, SHE SHALL BE NEXT TO DIE! DORMAMMU HAS SPOKEN!
4

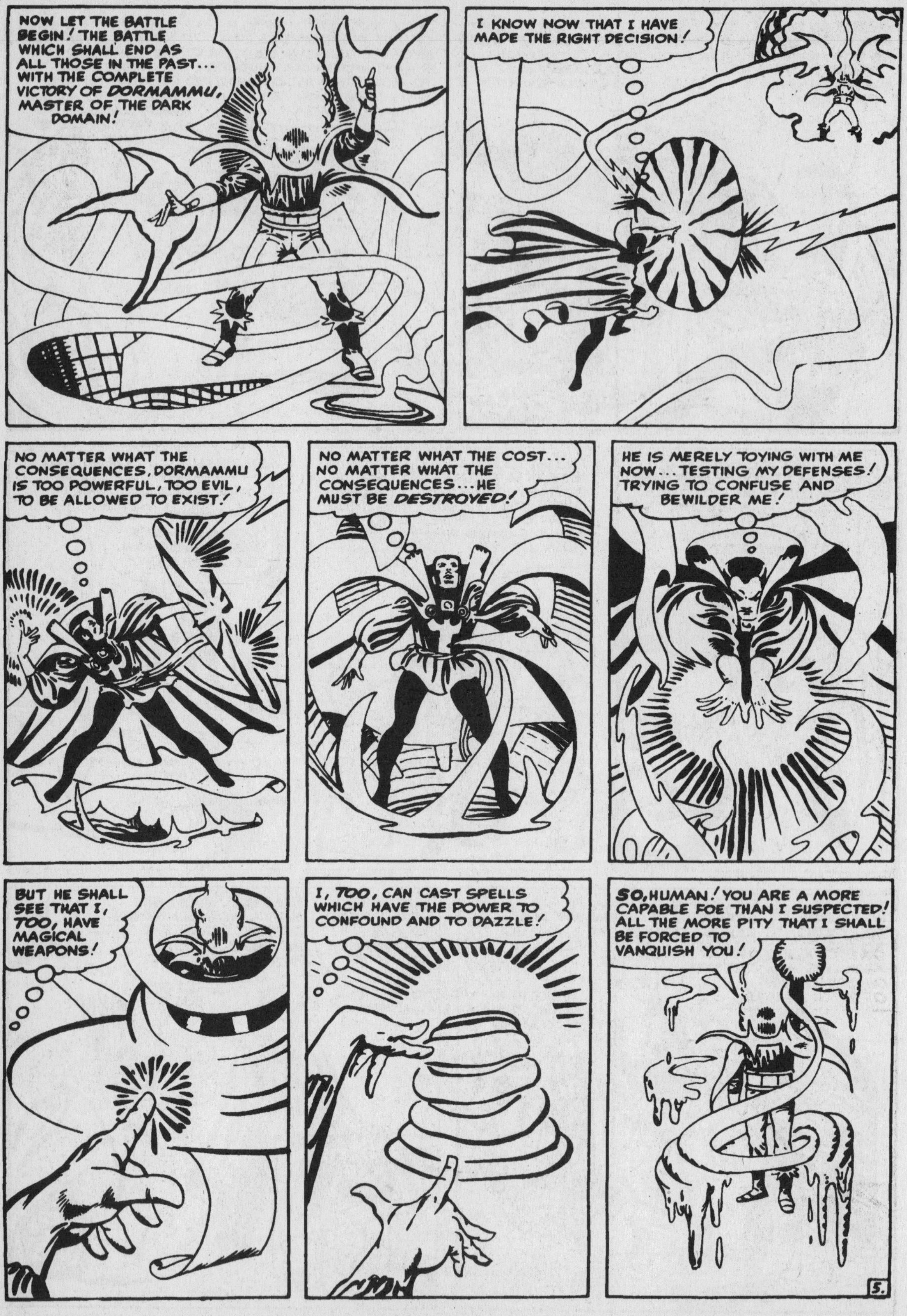
NOW LET THE BATTLE BEGIN! THE BATTLE WHICH SHALL END AS ALL THOSE IN THE PAST... WITH THE COMPLETE VICTORY OF DORMAMMU, MASTER OF THE DARK DOMAIN!
I KNOW NOW THAT I HAVE MADE THE RIGHT DECISION!
NO MATTER WHAT THE CONSEQUENCES, DORMAMMU IS TOO POWERFUL, TOO EVIL, TO BE ALLOWED TO EXIST!
NO MATTER WHAT THE COST... NO MATTER WHAT THE CONSEQUENCES... HE MUST BE DESTROYED!
HE IS MERELY TOYING WITH ME NOW... TESTING MY DEFENSES! TRYING TO CONFUSE AND BEWILDER ME!
BUT HE SHALL SEE THAT I, TOO, HAVE MAGICAL WEAPONS!
I, TOO, CAN CAST SPELLS WHICH HAVE THE POWER TO CONFOUND AND TO DAZZLE!
SO, HUMAN! YOU ARE A MORE CAPABLE FOE THAN I SUSPECTED! ALL THE MORE PITY THAT I SHALL BE FORCED TO VANQUISH YOU!
5.

OBSERVE, HELPLESS MORTAL, HOW I CAN MAKE YOU SLOWLY FADE AWAY TO SHEER NOTHINGNESS!

WITHIN A FEW BRIEF SECONDS YOU SHALL BE GONE... FOREVER!

NEVER, DORMAMMU! NOT WHILE THE HOARY HOSTS OF HOGGOTH ARE MINE TO COMMAND!

FOR, THOUGH YOU MOCK THE EARTHLY POWERS I POSSESS, THEY STILL SHALL PROVE EQUAL TO THE TASK OF DEFEATING YOU!

I SEE YOU ARE SURPRISED TO SEE ME SHRUG OFF YOUR FATAL SPELL! WELL, HERE IS YET ANOTHER SURPRISE FOR YOU...!

BAH! A MERE CONJURER'S CONE! I DABBLED WITH SUCH PUNY TRICKS WHEN I WAS BUT A CHILD!

YOU STILL CANNOT EVEN BEGIN TO COMPREHEND THE SCOPE AND EXTENT OF MY ALMOST LIMITLESS POWERS!

AND SO THE BATTLE RAGES... A BATTLE BETWEEN TWO TOTALLY ALIEN FOES... FOES WITH ONLY ONE THING IS COMMON... AN AWESOME MASTERY OF THE POWERS OF BLACK MAGIC!

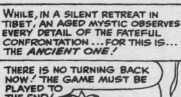

WHILE, IN A SILENT RETREAT IN TIBET, AN AGED MYSTIC OBSERVES EVERY DETAIL OF THE FATEFUL CONFRONTATION... FOR THIS IS... THE ANCIENT ONE!

THERE IS NO TURNING BACK NOW! THE GAME MUST BE PLAYED TO THE END!

MAY THE LIGHT OF THE VISHANTI SHINE UPON DR. STRANGE... AND MAY THE OMNIPOTENT OSHTUR GRANT HIM WISDOM AND STRENGTH!

6.

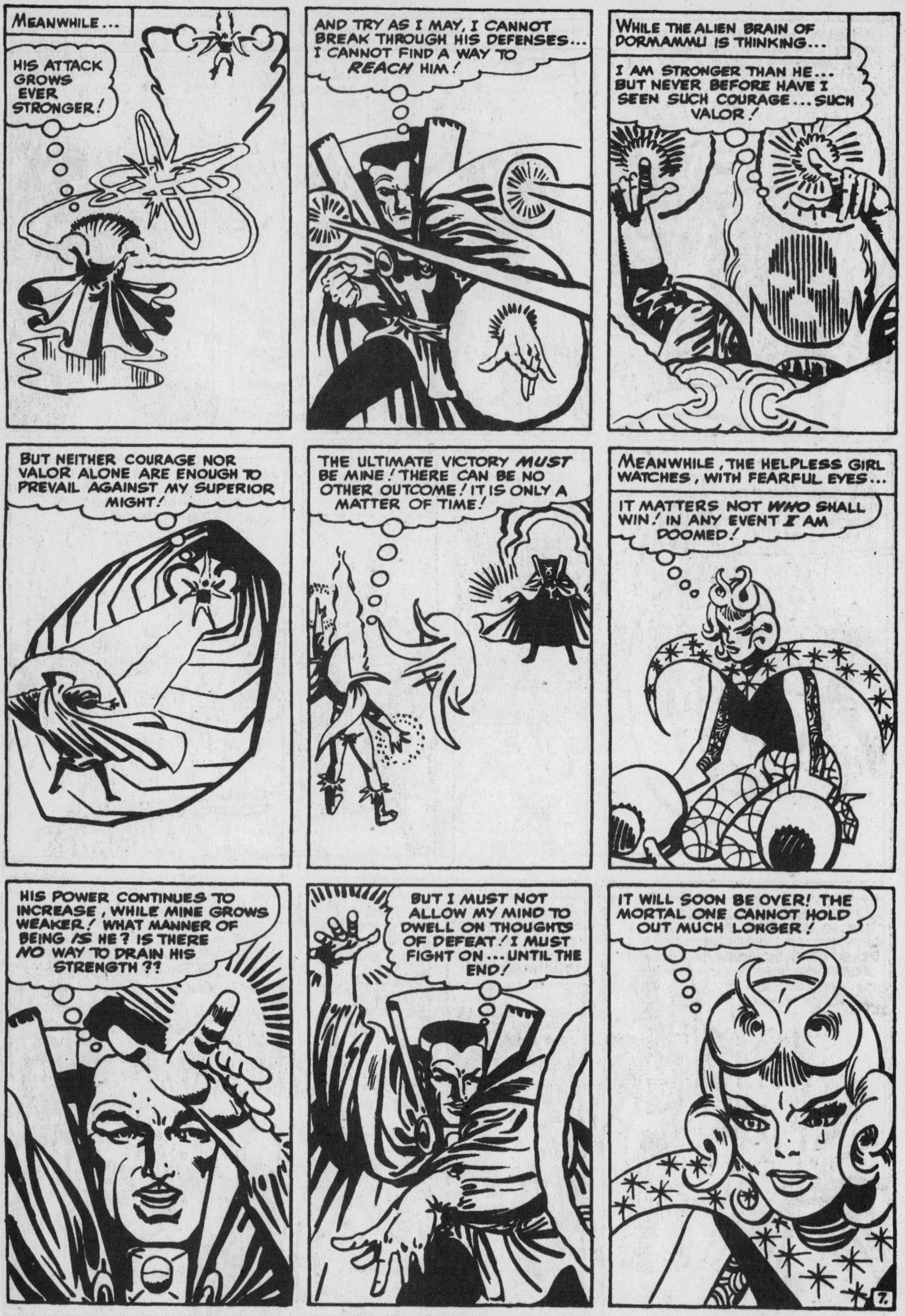
MEANWHILE...
HIS ATTACK GROWS EVER STRONGER!
AND TRY AS I MAY, I CANNOT BREAK THROUGH HIS DEFENSES... I CANNOT FIND A WAY TO REACH HIM!
WHILE THE ALIEN BRAIN OF DORMAMMU IS THINKING...
I AM STRONGER THAN HE... BUT NEVER BEFORE HAVE I SEEN SUCH COURAGE... SUCH VALOR!
BUT NEITHER COURAGE NOR VALOR ALONE ARE ENOUGH TO PREVAIL AGAINST MY SUPERIOR MIGHT!
THE ULTIMATE VICTORY MUST BE MINE! THERE CAN BE NO OTHER OUTCOME! IT IS ONLY A MATTER OF TIME!
MEANWHILE, THE HELPLESS GIRL WATCHES, WITH FEARFUL EYES...
IT MATTERS NOT WHO SHALL WIN! IN ANY EVENT I AM DOOMED!
HIS POWER CONTINUES TO INCREASE, WHILE MINE GROWS WEAKER! WHAT MANNER OF BEING IS HE? IS THERE NO WAY TO DRAIN HIS STRENGTH??
BUT I MUST NOT ALLOW MY MIND TO DWELL ON THOUGHTS OF DEFEAT! I MUST FIGHT ON... UNTIL THE END!
IT WILL SOON BE OVER! THE MORTAL ONE CANNOT HOLD OUT MUCH LONGER!
7.

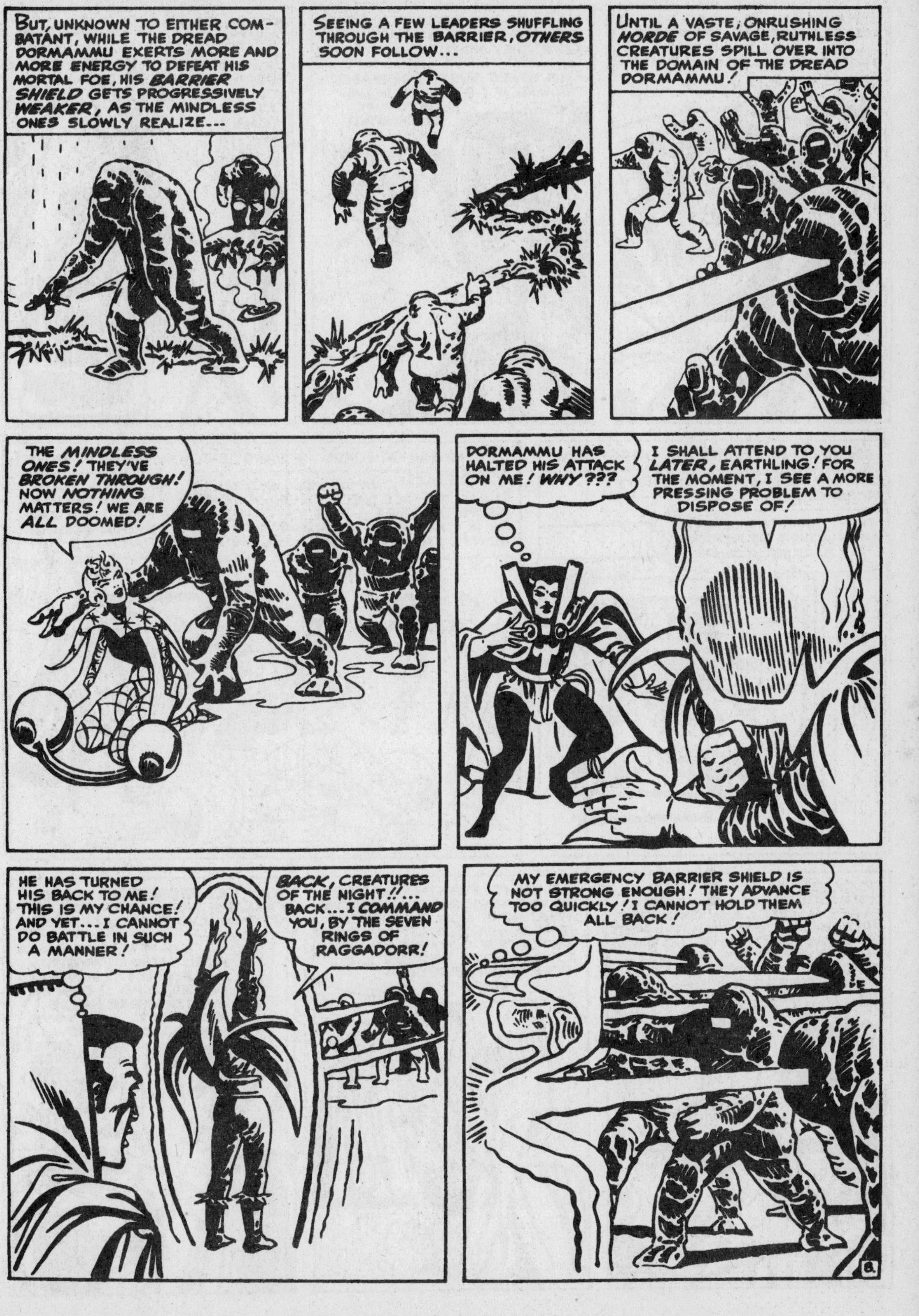

BUT, UNKNOWN TO EITHER COMBATANT, WHILE THE DREAD DORMAMMU EXERTS MORE AND MORE ENERGY TO DEFEAT HIS MORTAL FOE, HIS BARRIER SHIELD GETS PROGRESSIVELY WEAKER, AS THE MINDLESS ONES SLOWLY REALIZE...
SEEING A FEW LEADERS SHUFFLING THROUGH THE BARRIER, OTHERS SOON FOLLOW...
UNTIL A VASTE, ONRUSHING HORDE OF SAVAGE, RUTHLESS CREATURES SPILL OVER INTO THE DOMAIN OF THE DREAD DORMAMMU!
THE MINDLESS ONES! THEY'VE BROKEN THROUGH! NOW NOTHING MATTERS! WE ARE ALL DOOMED!
DORMAMMU HAS HALTED HIS ATTACK ON ME! WHY???
I SHALL ATTEND TO YOU LATER, EARTHLING! FOR THE MOMENT, I SEE A MORE PRESSING PROBLEM TO DISPOSE OF!
HE HAS TURNED HIS BACK TO ME! THIS IS MY CHANCE! AND YET... I CANNOT DO BATTLE IN SUCH A MANNER!
BACK, CREATURES OF THE NIGHT!!... BACK... I COMMAND YOU, BY THE SEVEN RINGS OF RAGGADORR!
MY EMERGENCY BARRIER SHIELD IS NOT STRONG ENOUGH! THEY ADVANCE TOO QUICKLY! I CANNOT HOLD THEM ALL BACK!
8

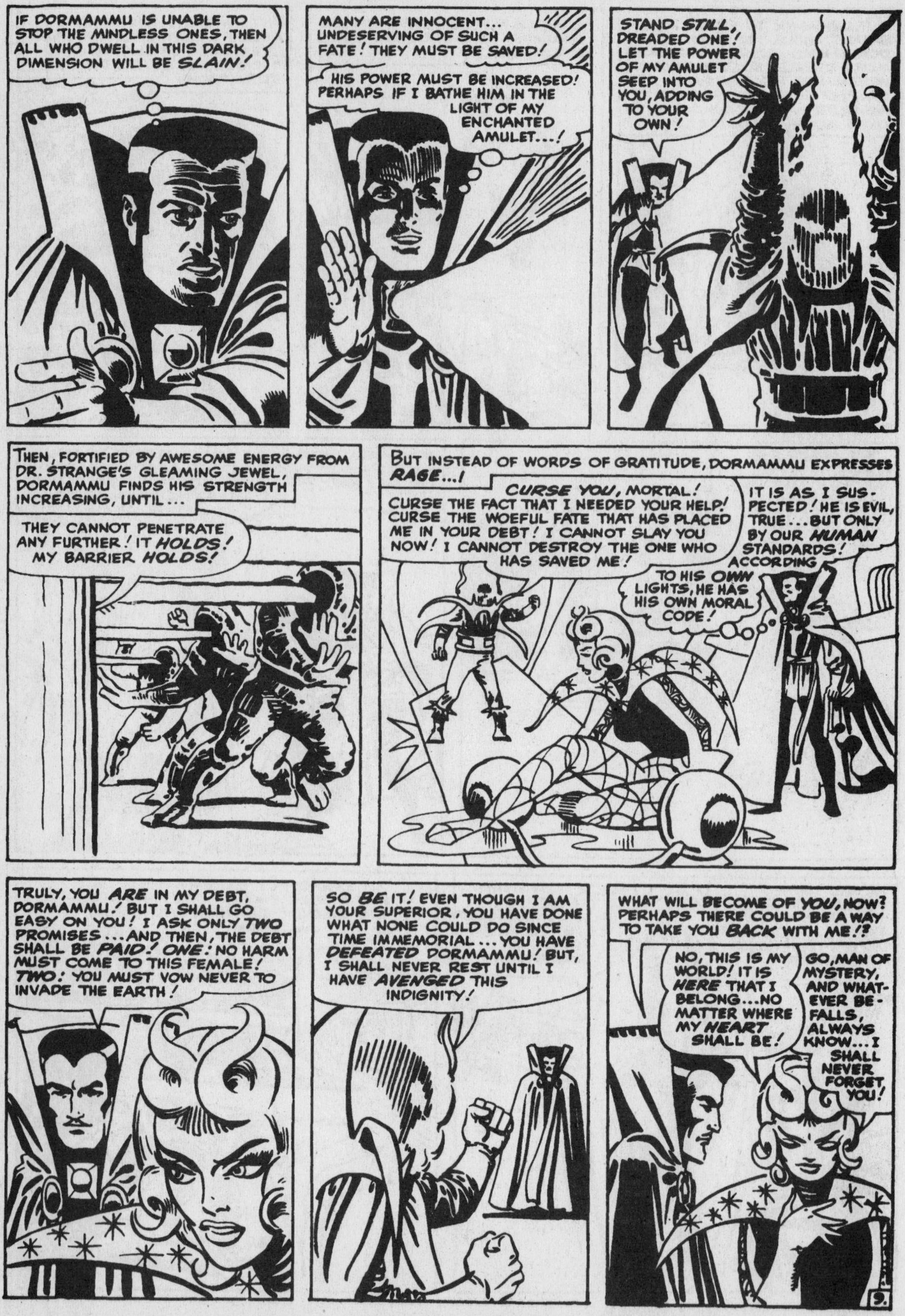

IF DORMAMMU IS UNABLE TO STOP THE MINDLESS ONES, THEN ALL WHO DWELL IN THIS DARK DIMENSION WILL BE SLAIN!
MANY ARE INNOCENT... UNDESERVING OF SUCH A FATE! THEY MUST BE SAVED!
HIS POWER MUST BE INCREASED! PERHAPS IF I BATHE HIM IN THE LIGHT OF MY ENCHANTED AMULET...!
STAND STILL, DREADED ONE! LET THE POWER OF MY AMULET SEEP INTO YOU, ADDING TO YOUR OWN!
THEN, FORTIFIED BY AWESOME ENERGY FROM DR. STRANGE'S GLEAMING JEWEL, DORMAMMU FINDS HIS STRENGTH INCREASING, UNTIL...
THEY CANNOT PENETRATE ANY FURTHER! IT HOLDS! MY BARRIER HOLDS!
BUT INSTEAD OF WORDS OF GRATITUDE, DORMAMMU EXPRESSES RAGE...!
CURSE YOU, MORTAL! CURSE THE FACT THAT I NEEDED YOUR HELP! CURSE THE WOEFUL FATE THAT HAS PLACED ME IN YOUR DEBT! I CANNOT SLAY YOU NOW! I CANNOT DESTROY THE ONE WHO HAS SAVED ME!
IT IS AS I SUSPECTED! HE IS EVIL, TRUE... BUT ONLY BY OUR HUMAN STANDARDS! ACCORDING
TO HIS OWN LIGHTS, HE HAS HIS OWN MORAL CODE!
TRULY, YOU ARE IN MY DEBT, DORMAMMU! BUT I SHALL GO EASY ON YOU! I ASK ONLY TWO PROMISES... AND THEN, THE DEBT SHALL BE PAID! ONE: NO HARM MUST COME TO THIS FEMALE! TWO: YOU MUST VOW NEVER TO INVADE THE EARTH!
SO BE IT! EVEN THOUGH I AM YOUR SUPERIOR, YOU HAVE DONE WHAT NONE COULD DO SINCE TIME IMMEMORIAL... YOU HAVE DEFEATED DORMAMMU! BUT, I SHALL NEVER REST UNTIL I HAVE AVENGED THIS INDIGNITY!
WHAT WILL BECOME OF YOU, NOW? PERHAPS THERE COULD BE A WAY TO TAKE YOU BACK WITH ME!?
NO, THIS IS MY WORLD! IT IS HERE THAT I BELONG... NO MATTER WHERE MY HEART SHALL BE!
GO, MAN OF MYSTERY, AND WHATEVER BEFALLS, ALWAYS KNOW... I SHALL NEVER FORGET YOU!
9.

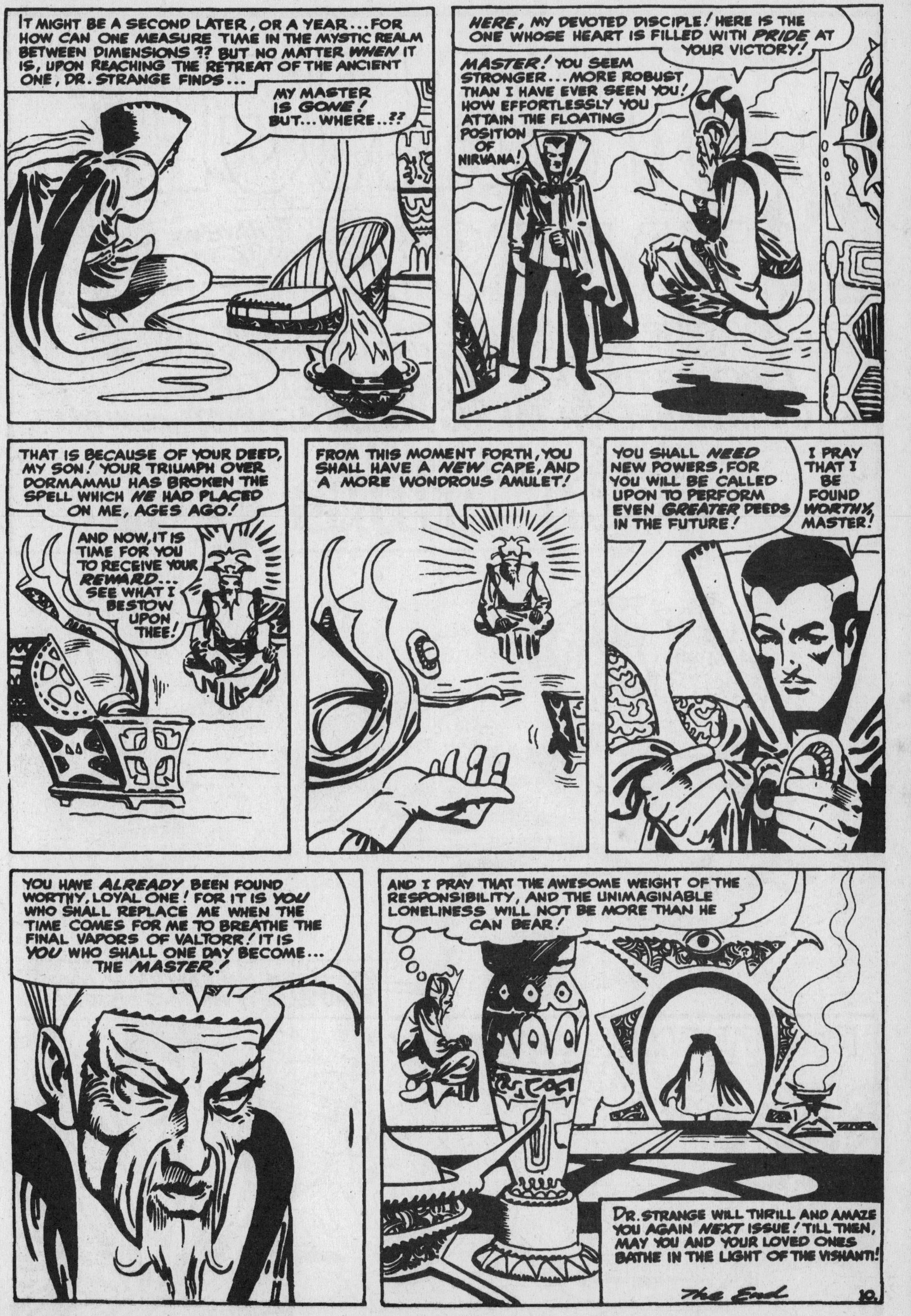
IT MIGHT BE A SECOND LATER, OR A YEAR... FOR HOW CAN ONE MEASURE TIME IN THE MYSTIC REALM BETWEEN DIMENSIONS ?? BUT NO MATTER WHEN IT IS, UPON REACHING THE RETREAT OF THE ANCIENT ONE, DR. STRANGE FINDS...
MY MASTER IS GONE! BUT... WHERE..??
HERE, MY DEVOTED DISCIPLE! HERE IS THE ONE WHOSE HEART IS FILLED WITH PRIDE AT YOUR VICTORY!
MASTER! YOU SEEM STRONGER... MORE ROBUST THAN I HAVE EVER SEEN YOU! HOW EFFORTLESSLY YOU ATTAIN THE FLOATING POSITION OF NIRVANA!
THAT IS BECAUSE OF YOUR DEED, MY SON! YOUR TRIUMPH OVER DORMAMMU HAS BROKEN THE SPELL WHICH HE HAD PLACED ON ME, AGES AGO!
AND NOW, IT IS TIME FOR YOU TO RECEIVE YOUR REWARD... SEE WHAT I BESTOW UPON THEE!
FROM THIS MOMENT FORTH, YOU SHALL HAVE A NEW CAPE, AND A MORE WONDROUS AMULET!
YOU SHALL NEED NEW POWERS, FOR YOU WILL BE CALLED UPON TO PERFORM EVEN GREATER DEEDS IN THE FUTURE!
I PRAY THAT I BE FOUND WORTHY, MASTER!
YOU HAVE ALREADY BEEN FOUND WORTHY, LOYAL ONE! FOR IT IS YOU WHO SHALL REPLACE ME WHEN THE TIME COMES FOR ME TO BREATHE THE FINAL VAPORS OF VALTORR! IT IS YOU WHO SHALL ONE DAY BECOME... THE MASTER!
AND I PRAY THAT THE AWESOME WEIGHT OF THE RESPONSIBILITY, AND THE UNIMAGINABLE LONELINESS WILL NOT BE MORE THAN HE CAN BEAR!
DR. STRANGE WILL THRILL AND AMAZE YOU AGAIN NEXT ISSUE! TILL THEN, MAY YOU AND YOUR LOVED ONES BATHE IN THE LIGHT OF THE VISHANTI!
The End
10.

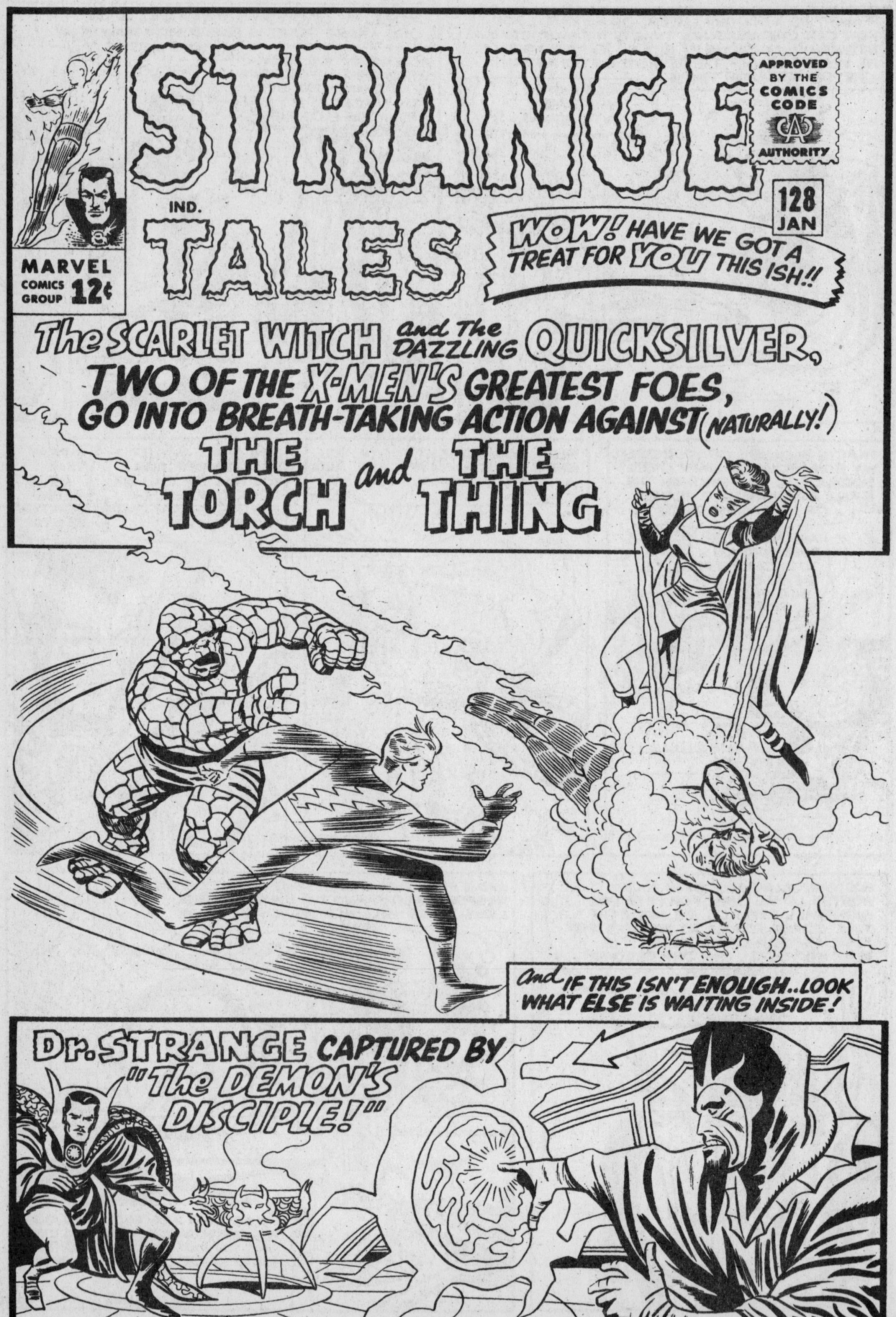

MARVEL COMICS GROUP 12¢
STRANGE TALES
IND.
APPROVED BY THE COMICS CODE AUTHORITY
128 JAN
WOW! HAVE WE GOT A TREAT FOR YOU THIS ISH!!
The SCARLET WITCH and the DAZZLING QUICKSILVER,
TWO OF THE X-MEN'S GREATEST FOES,
GO INTO BREATH-TAKING ACTION AGAINST (NATURALLY!)
THE TORCH and THE THING
and IF THIS ISN'T ENOUGH..LOOK WHAT ELSE IS WAITING INSIDE!
Dr. STRANGE CAPTURED BY "The DEMON'S DISCIPLE!"

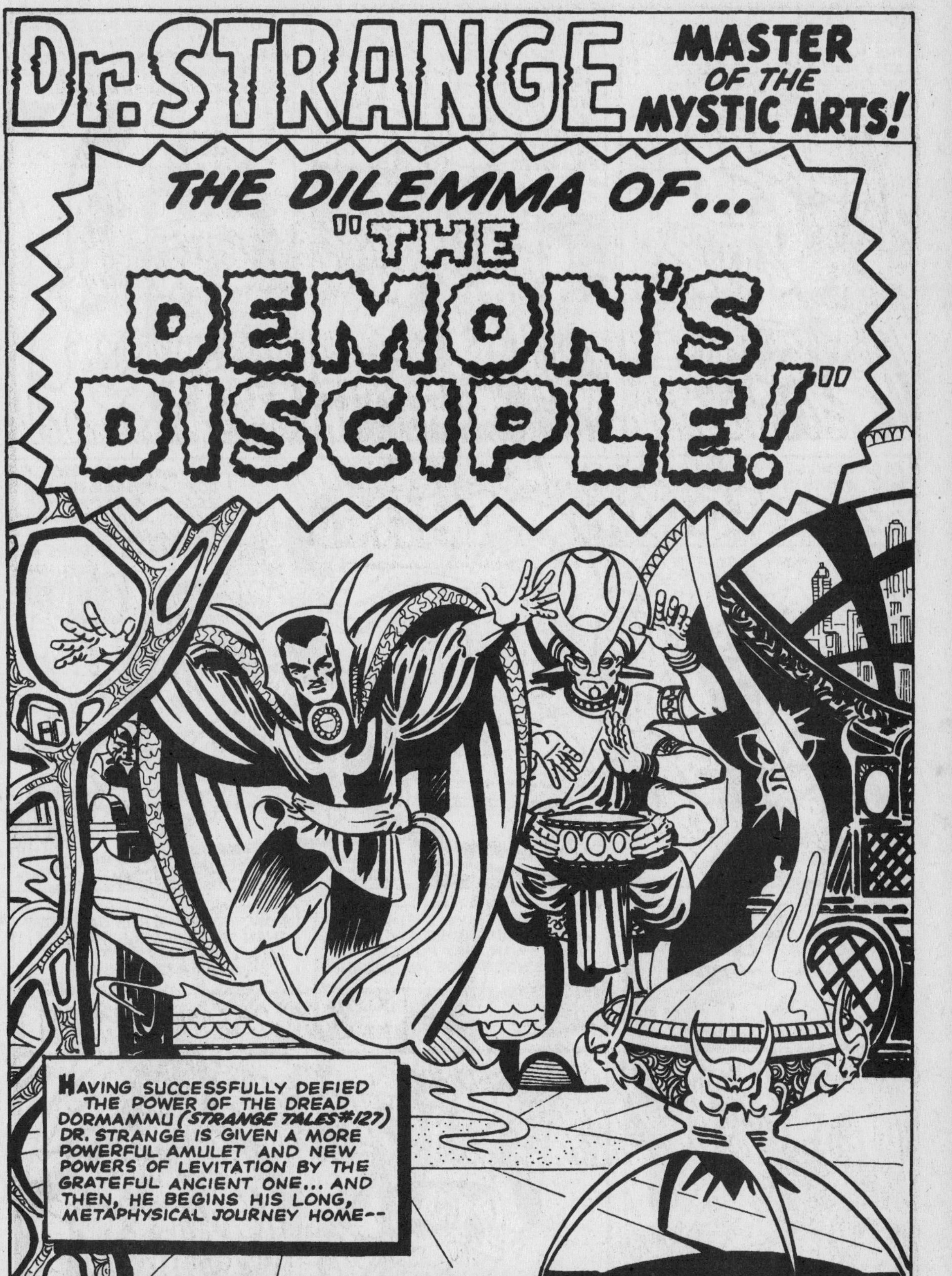

Dr. STRANGE
MASTER OF THE MYSTIC ARTS!
THE DILEMMA OF... "THE DEMON'S DISCIPLE!"
HAVING SUCCESSFULLY DEFIED THE POWER OF THE DREAD DORMAMMU (STRANGE TALES #127) DR. STRANGE IS GIVEN A MORE POWERFUL AMULET AND NEW POWERS OF LEVITATION BY THE GRATEFUL ANCIENT ONE... AND THEN, HE BEGINS HIS LONG, METAPHYSICAL JOURNEY HOME--
WRITTEN BY STAN LEE-- UNCHALLENGED MASTER OF THE DRAMATIC WORD!
DRAWN BY STEVE DITKO-- UNQUESTIONED INNOVATOR OF THE OCCULT ILLUSTRATION!
LETTERED BY ARTIE SIMEK UNABASHED PURVEYOR OF THE CAPTIVATING CAPTION!
1

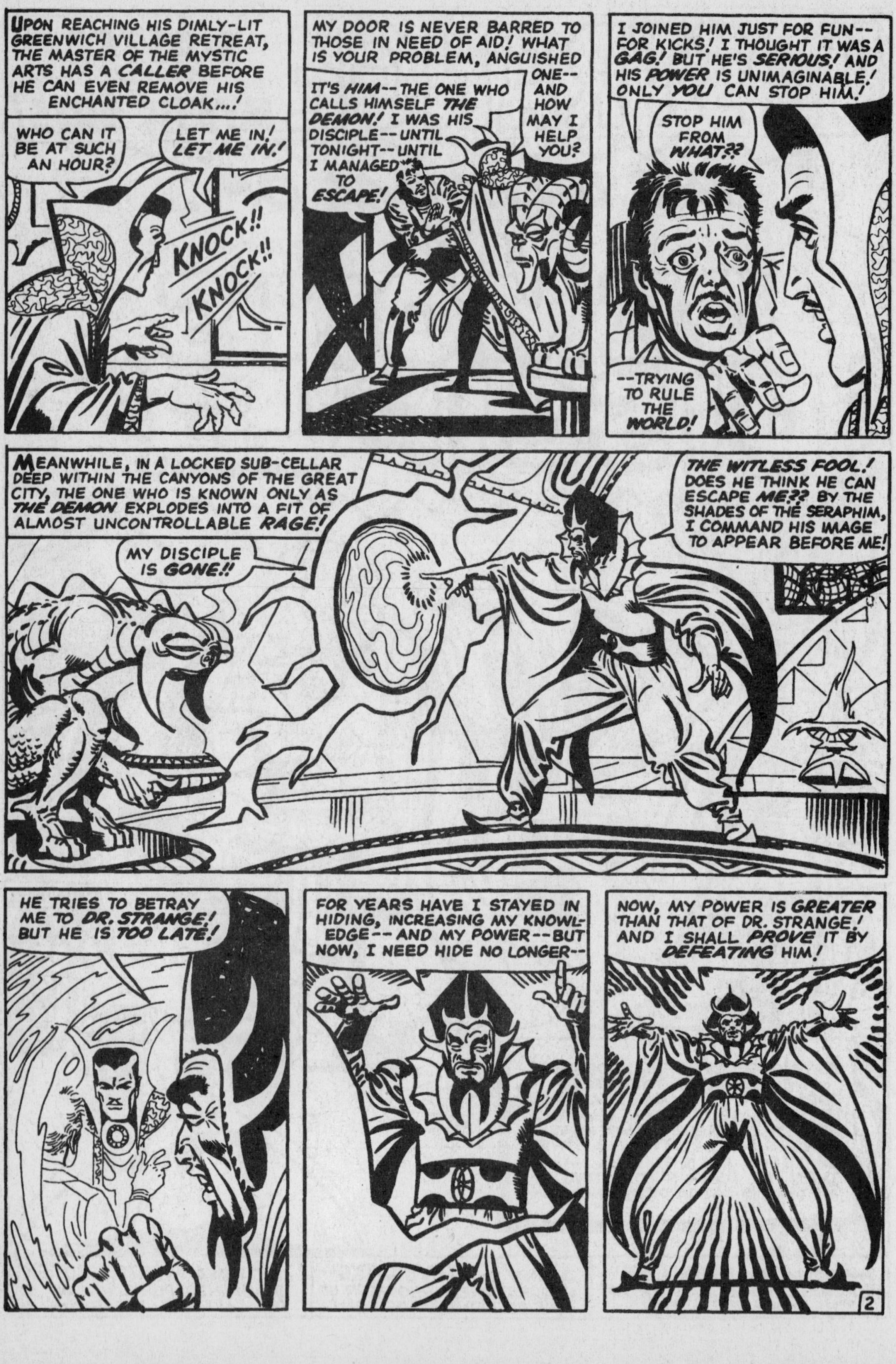

UPON REACHING HIS DIMLY-LIT GREENWICH VILLAGE RETREAT, THE MASTER OF THE MYSTIC ARTS HAS A CALLER BEFORE HE CAN EVEN REMOVE HIS ENCHANTED CLOAK...!
WHO CAN IT BE AT SUCH AN HOUR?
LET ME IN! LET ME IN!
KNOCK!! KNOCK!!
MY DOOR IS NEVER BARRED TO THOSE IN NEED OF AID! WHAT IS YOUR PROBLEM, ANGUISHED ONE--AND HOW MAY I HELP YOU?
IT'S HIM--THE ONE WHO CALLS HIMSELF THE DEMON! I WAS HIS DISCIPLE--UNTIL TONIGHT--UNTIL I MANAGED TO ESCAPE!
I JOINED HIM JUST FOR FUN--FOR KICKS! I THOUGHT IT WAS A GAG! BUT HE'S SERIOUS! AND HIS POWER IS UNIMAGINABLE! ONLY YOU CAN STOP HIM!
STOP HIM FROM WHAT??
--TRYING TO RULE THE WORLD!
MEANWHILE, IN A LOCKED SUB-CELLAR DEEP WITHIN THE CANYONS OF THE GREAT CITY, THE ONE WHO IS KNOWN ONLY AS THE DEMON EXPLODES INTO A FIT OF ALMOST UNCONTROLLABLE RAGE!
MY DISCIPLE IS GONE!!
THE WITLESS FOOL! DOES HE THINK HE CAN ESCAPE ME?? BY THE SHADES OF THE SERAPHIM, I COMMAND HIS IMAGE TO APPEAR BEFORE ME!
HE TRIES TO BETRAY ME TO DR. STRANGE! BUT HE IS TOO LATE!
FOR YEARS HAVE I STAYED IN HIDING, INCREASING MY KNOWLEDGE--AND MY POWER--BUT NOW, I NEED HIDE NO LONGER--
NOW, MY POWER IS GREATER THAN THAT OF DR. STRANGE! AND I SHALL PROVE IT BY DEFEATING HIM!
2

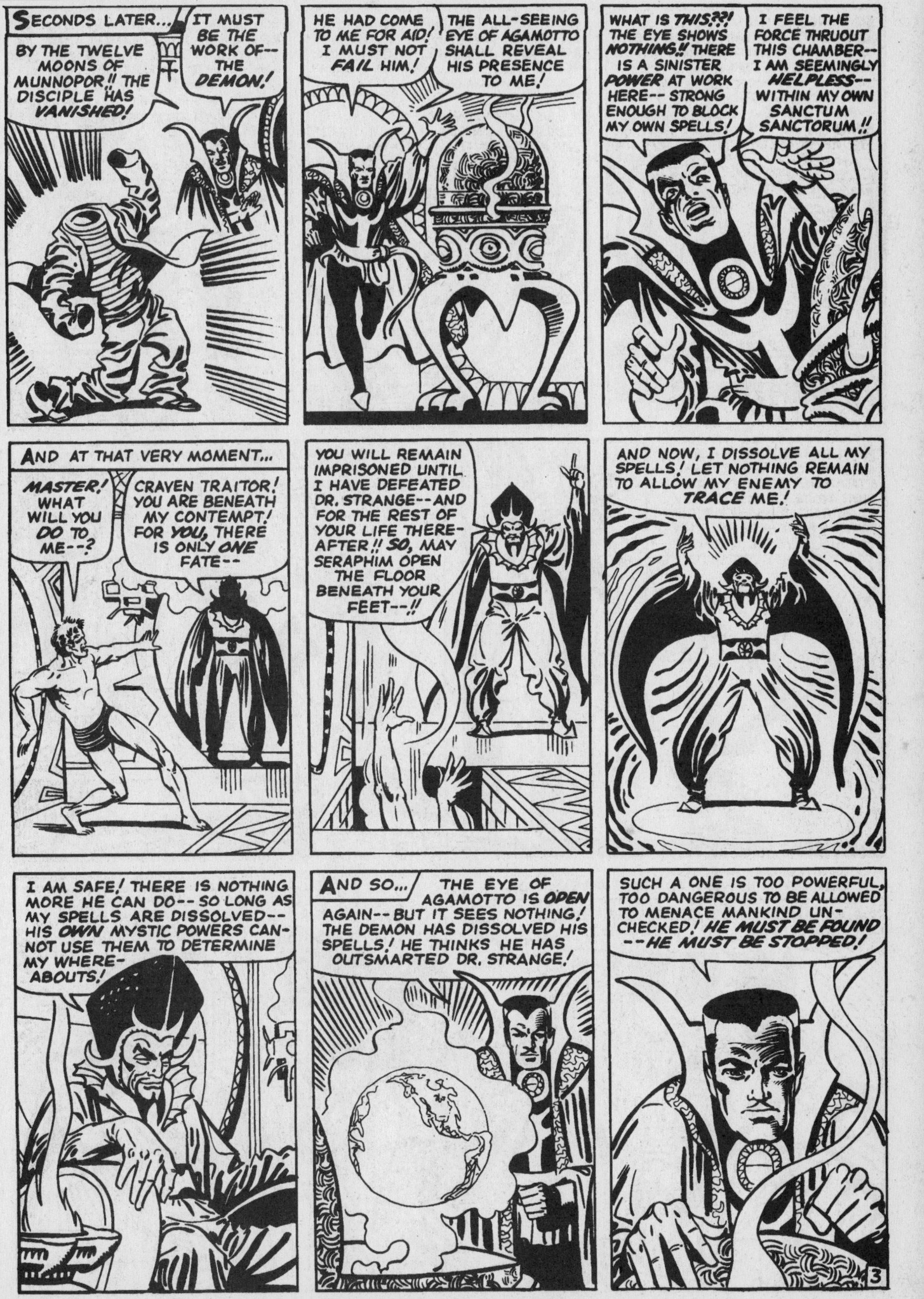
SECONDS LATER...
BY THE TWELVE MOONS OF MUNNOPOR!! THE DISCIPLE HAS VANISHED!
IT MUST BE THE WORK OF-- THE DEMON!
HE HAD COME TO ME FOR AID! I MUST NOT FAIL HIM!
THE ALL-SEEING EYE OF AGAMOTTO SHALL REVEAL HIS PRESENCE TO ME!
WHAT IS THIS??! THE EYE SHOWS NOTHING!! THERE IS A SINISTER POWER AT WORK HERE-- STRONG ENOUGH TO BLOCK MY OWN SPELLS!
I FEEL THE FORCE THRUOUT THIS CHAMBER-- I AM SEEMINGLY HELPLESS-- WITHIN MY OWN SANCTUM SANCTORUM!!
AND AT THAT VERY MOMENT...
MASTER! WHAT WILL YOU DO TO ME--?
CRAVEN TRAITOR! YOU ARE BENEATH MY CONTEMPT! FOR YOU, THERE IS ONLY ONE FATE--
YOU WILL REMAIN IMPRISONED UNTIL I HAVE DEFEATED DR. STRANGE--AND FOR THE REST OF YOUR LIFE THERE-AFTER!! SO, MAY SERAPHIM OPEN THE FLOOR BENEATH YOUR FEET--!!
AND NOW, I DISSOLVE ALL MY SPELLS! LET NOTHING REMAIN TO ALLOW MY ENEMY TO TRACE ME!
I AM SAFE! THERE IS NOTHING MORE HE CAN DO-- SO LONG AS MY SPELLS ARE DISSOLVED-- HIS OWN MYSTIC POWERS CAN-NOT USE THEM TO DETERMINE MY WHERE-ABOUTS!
AND SO...
THE EYE OF AGAMOTTO IS OPEN AGAIN-- BUT IT SEES NOTHING! THE DEMON HAS DISSOLVED HIS SPELLS! HE THINKS HE HAS OUTSMARTED DR. STRANGE!
SUCH A ONE IS TOO POWERFUL, TOO DANGEROUS TO BE ALLOWED TO MENACE MANKIND UN-CHECKED! HE MUST BE FOUND --HE MUST BE STOPPED!
3

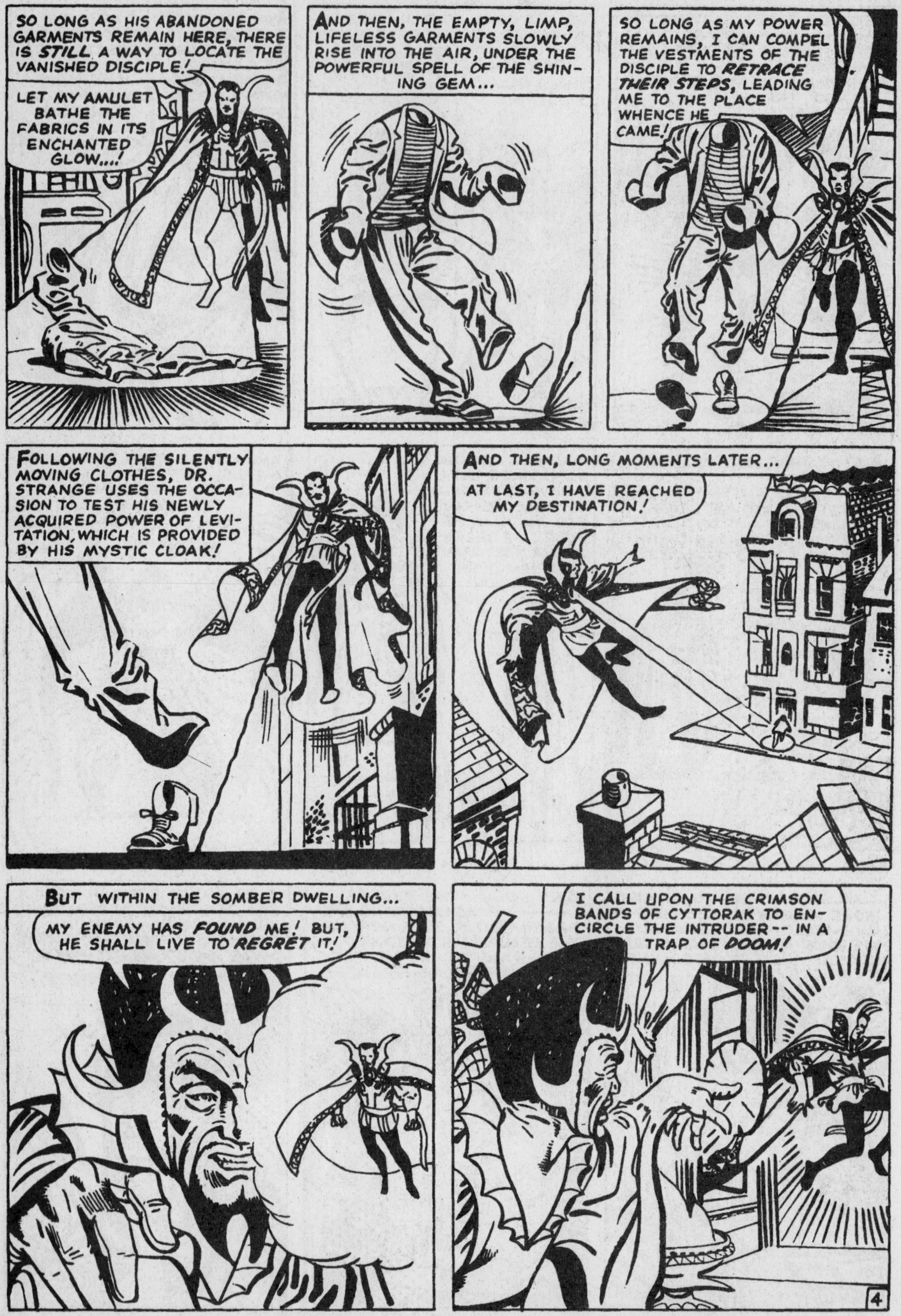
SO LONG AS HIS ABANDONED GARMENTS REMAIN HERE, THERE IS STILL A WAY TO LOCATE THE VANISHED DISCIPLE!
LET MY AMULET BATHE THE FABRICS IN ITS ENCHANTED GLOW...!
AND THEN, THE EMPTY, LIMP, LIFELESS GARMENTS SLOWLY RISE INTO THE AIR, UNDER THE POWERFUL SPELL OF THE SHINING GEM...
SO LONG AS MY POWER REMAINS, I CAN COMPEL THE VESTMENTS OF THE DISCIPLE TO RETRACE THEIR STEPS, LEADING ME TO THE PLACE WHENCE HE CAME!
FOLLOWING THE SILENTLY MOVING CLOTHES, DR. STRANGE USES THE OCCASION TO TEST HIS NEWLY ACQUIRED POWER OF LEVITATION, WHICH IS PROVIDED BY HIS MYSTIC CLOAK!
AND THEN, LONG MOMENTS LATER...
AT LAST, I HAVE REACHED MY DESTINATION!
BUT WITHIN THE SOMBER DWELLING...
MY ENEMY HAS FOUND ME! BUT, HE SHALL LIVE TO REGRET IT!
I CALL UPON THE CRIMSON BANDS OF CYTTORAK TO ENCIRCLE THE INTRUDER-- IN A TRAP OF DOOM!

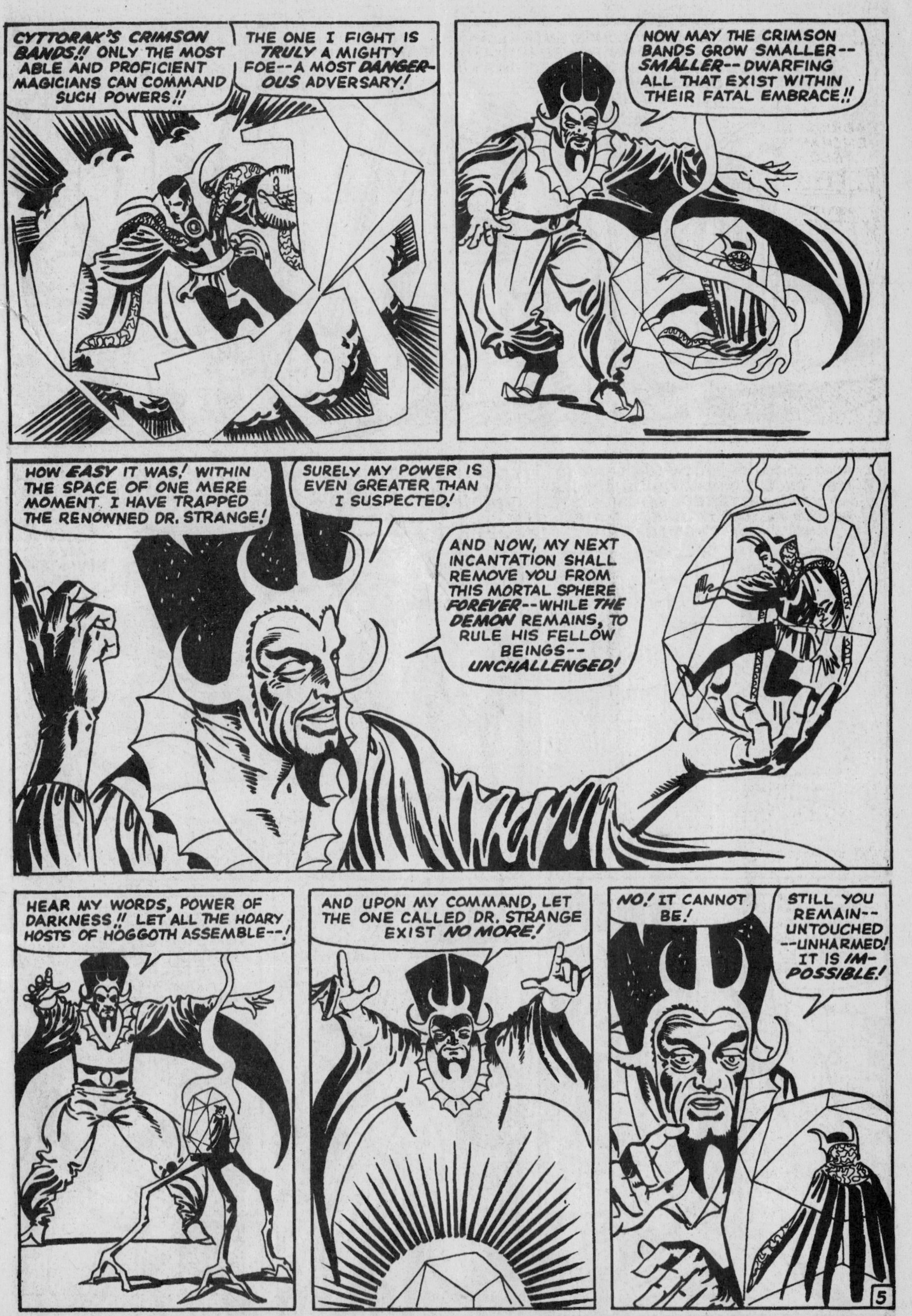
CYTTORAK'S CRIMSON BANDS!! ONLY THE MOST ABLE AND PROFICIENT MAGICIANS CAN COMMAND SUCH POWERS!!
THE ONE I FIGHT IS TRULY A MIGHTY FOE--A MOST DANGEROUS ADVERSARY!
NOW MAY THE CRIMSON BANDS GROW SMALLER--SMALLER--DWARFING ALL THAT EXIST WITHIN THEIR FATAL EMBRACE!!
HOW EASY IT WAS! WITHIN THE SPACE OF ONE MERE MOMENT I HAVE TRAPPED THE RENOWNED DR. STRANGE!
SURELY MY POWER IS EVEN GREATER THAN I SUSPECTED!
AND NOW, MY NEXT INCANTATION SHALL REMOVE YOU FROM THIS MORTAL SPHERE FOREVER--WHILE THE DEMON REMAINS, TO RULE HIS FELLOW BEINGS--UNCHALLENGED!
HEAR MY WORDS, POWER OF DARKNESS!! LET ALL THE HOARY HOSTS OF HÖGGOTH ASSEMBLE--!
AND UPON MY COMMAND, LET THE ONE CALLED DR. STRANGE EXIST NO MORE!
NO! IT CANNOT BE!
STILL YOU REMAIN--UNTOUCHED--UNHARMED! IT IS IMPOSSIBLE!
5

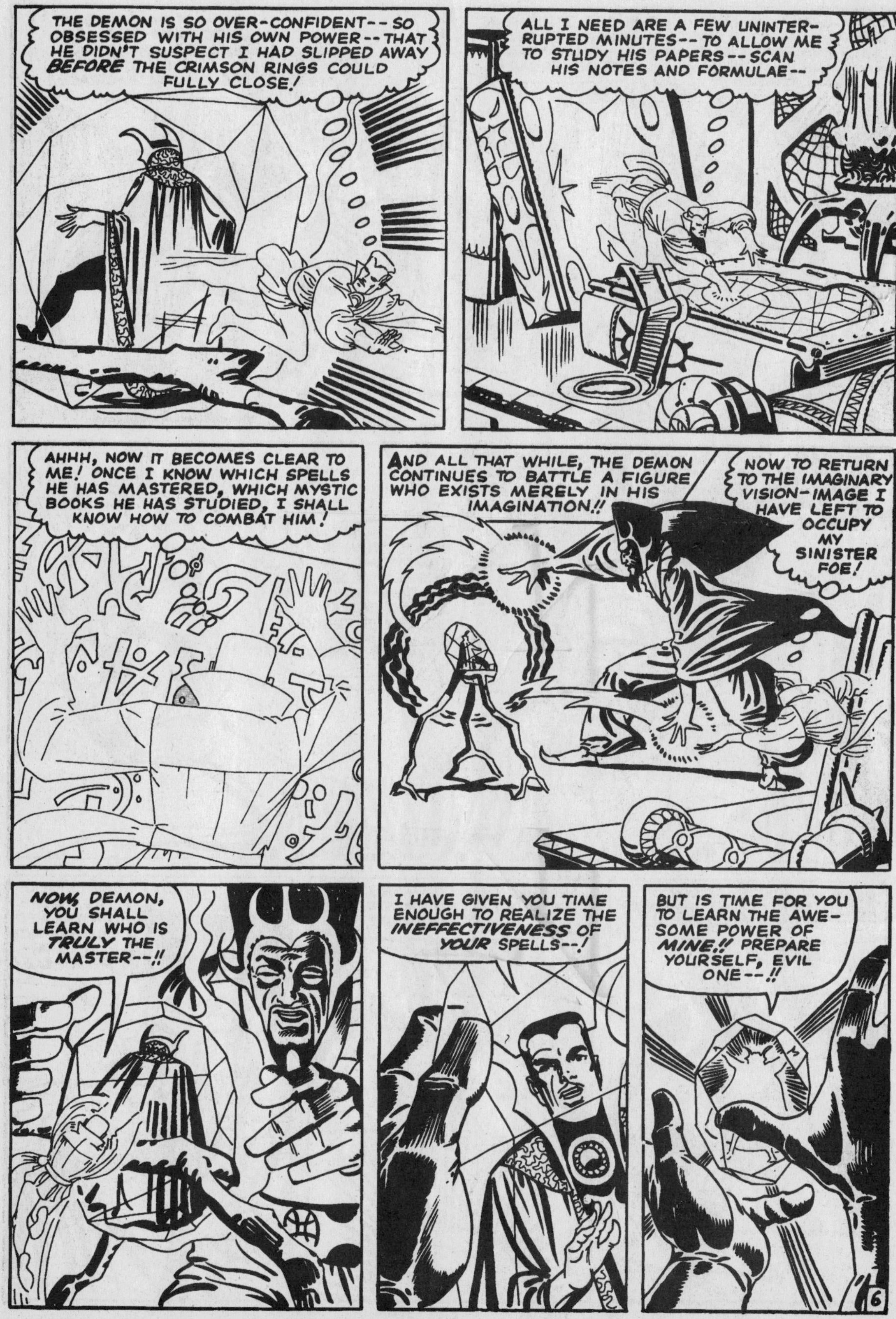
THE DEMON IS SO OVER-CONFIDENT--SO OBSESSED WITH HIS OWN POWER--THAT HE DIDN'T SUSPECT I HAD SLIPPED AWAY BEFORE THE CRIMSON RINGS COULD FULLY CLOSE!
ALL I NEED ARE A FEW UNINTERRUPTED MINUTES--TO ALLOW ME TO STUDY HIS PAPERS--SCAN HIS NOTES AND FORMULAE--
AHHH, NOW IT BECOMES CLEAR TO ME! ONCE I KNOW WHICH SPELLS HE HAS MASTERED, WHICH MYSTIC BOOKS HE HAS STUDIED, I SHALL KNOW HOW TO COMBAT HIM!
AND ALL THAT WHILE, THE DEMON CONTINUES TO BATTLE A FIGURE WHO EXISTS MERELY IN HIS IMAGINATION!!
NOW TO RETURN TO THE IMAGINARY VISION-IMAGE I HAVE LEFT TO OCCUPY MY SINISTER FOE!
NOW, DEMON, YOU SHALL LEARN WHO IS TRULY THE MASTER--!!
I HAVE GIVEN YOU TIME ENOUGH TO REALIZE THE INEFFECTIVENESS OF YOUR SPELLS--!
BUT IS TIME FOR YOU TO LEARN THE AWESOME POWER OF MINE!! PREPARE YOURSELF, EVIL ONE--!!
6

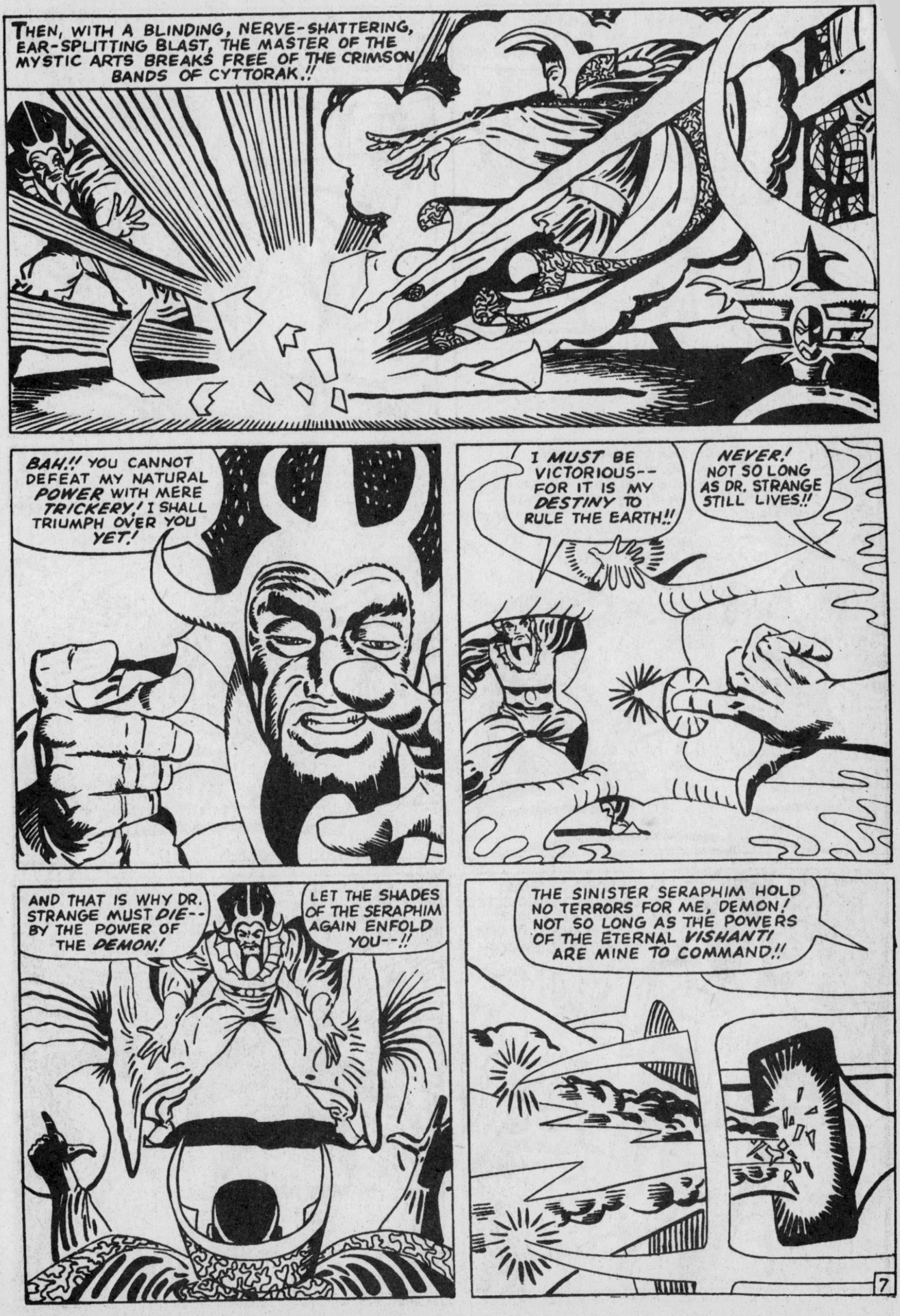
THEN, WITH A BLINDING, NERVE-SHATTERING, EAR-SPLITTING BLAST, THE MASTER OF THE MYSTIC ARTS BREAKS FREE OF THE CRIMSON BANDS OF CYTTORAK.!!
BAH!! YOU CANNOT DEFEAT MY NATURAL POWER WITH MERE TRICKERY! I SHALL TRIUMPH OVER YOU YET!
I MUST BE VICTORIOUS-- FOR IT IS MY DESTINY TO RULE THE EARTH!!
NEVER! NOT SO LONG AS DR. STRANGE STILL LIVES!!
AND THAT IS WHY DR. STRANGE MUST DIE-- BY THE POWER OF THE DEMON!
LET THE SHADES OF THE SERAPHIM AGAIN ENFOLD YOU--!!
THE SINISTER SERAPHIM HOLD NO TERRORS FOR ME, DEMON! NOT SO LONG AS THE POWERS OF THE ETERNAL VISHANTI ARE MINE TO COMMAND!!
7

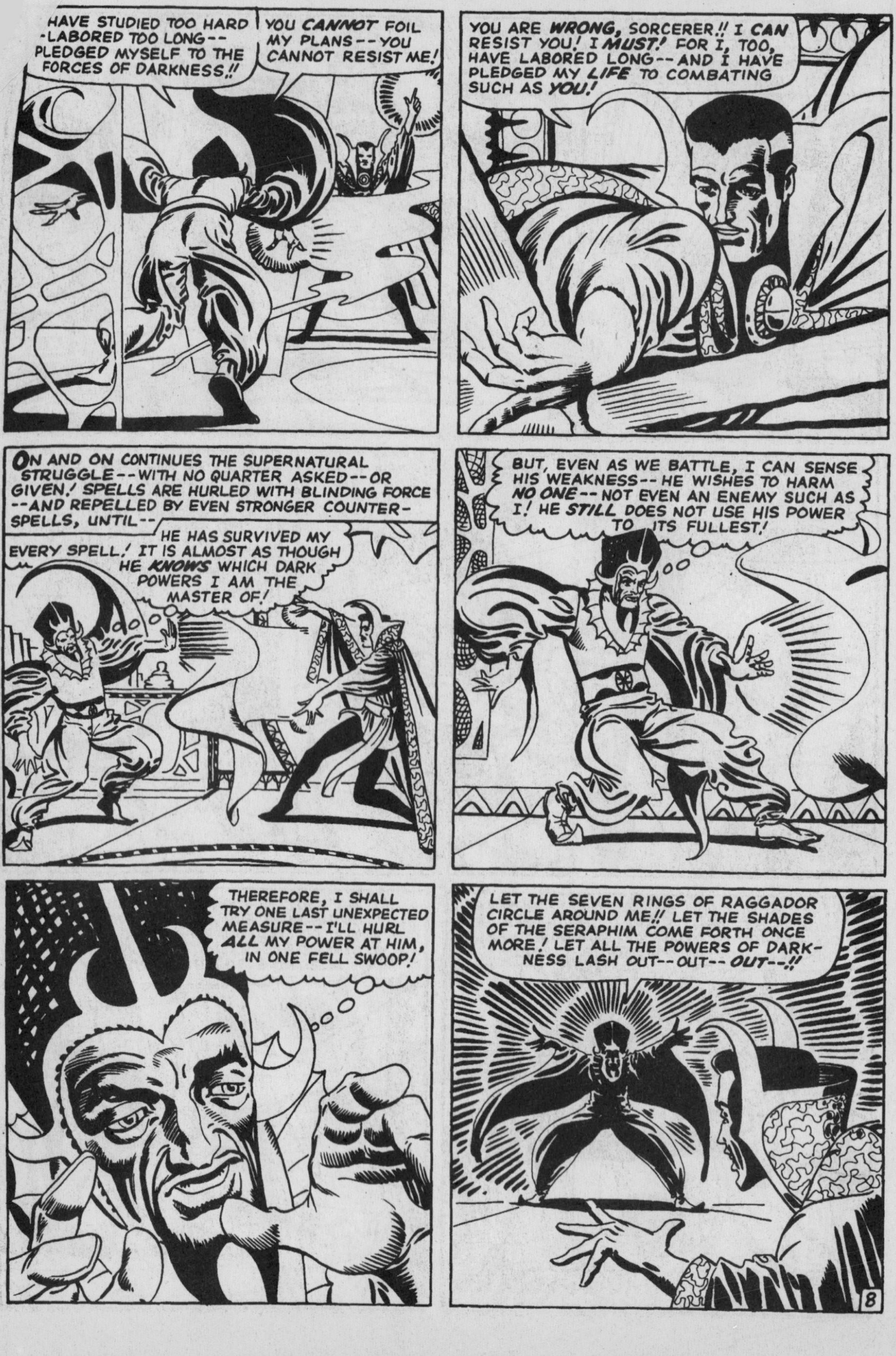

HAVE STUDIED TOO HARD -LABORED TOO LONG-- PLEDGED MYSELF TO THE FORCES OF DARKNESS.!!
YOU CANNOT FOIL MY PLANS--YOU CANNOT RESIST ME!
YOU ARE WRONG, SORCERER!! I CAN RESIST YOU! I MUST! FOR I, TOO, HAVE LABORED LONG--AND I HAVE PLEDGED MY LIFE TO COMBATING SUCH AS YOU!
ON AND ON CONTINUES THE SUPERNATURAL STRUGGLE--WITH NO QUARTER ASKED--OR GIVEN! SPELLS ARE HURLED WITH BLINDING FORCE --AND REPELLED BY EVEN STRONGER COUNTER-SPELLS, UNTIL--
HE HAS SURVIVED MY EVERY SPELL! IT IS ALMOST AS THOUGH HE KNOWS WHICH DARK POWERS I AM THE MASTER OF!
BUT, EVEN AS WE BATTLE, I CAN SENSE HIS WEAKNESS--HE WISHES TO HARM NO ONE--NOT EVEN AN ENEMY SUCH AS I! HE STILL DOES NOT USE HIS POWER TO ITS FULLEST!
THEREFORE, I SHALL TRY ONE LAST UNEXPECTED MEASURE--I'LL HURL ALL MY POWER AT HIM, IN ONE FELL SWOOP!
LET THE SEVEN RINGS OF RAGGADOR CIRCLE AROUND ME!! LET THE SHADES OF THE SERAPHIM COME FORTH ONCE MORE! LET ALL THE POWERS OF DARK-NESS LASH OUT--OUT--OUT--!!

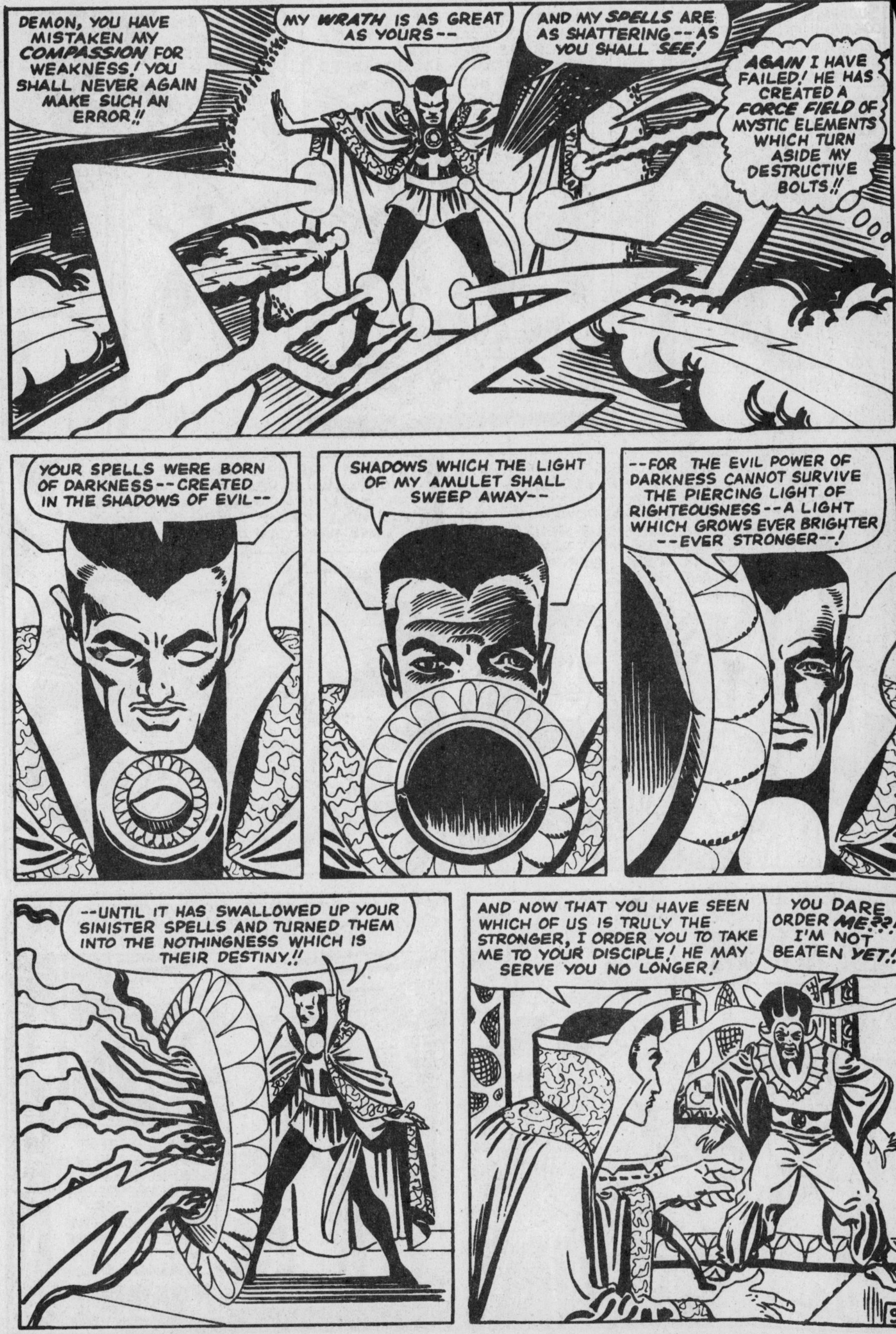
DEMON, YOU HAVE MISTAKEN MY COMPASSION FOR WEAKNESS! YOU SHALL NEVER AGAIN MAKE SUCH AN ERROR!!
MY WRATH IS AS GREAT AS YOURS--
AND MY SPELLS ARE AS SHATTERING--AS YOU SHALL SEE!
AGAIN I HAVE FAILED! HE HAS CREATED A FORCE FIELD OF MYSTIC ELEMENTS WHICH TURN ASIDE MY DESTRUCTIVE BOLTS!!
YOUR SPELLS WERE BORN OF DARKNESS--CREATED IN THE SHADOWS OF EVIL--
SHADOWS WHICH THE LIGHT OF MY AMULET SHALL SWEEP AWAY--
--FOR THE EVIL POWER OF DARKNESS CANNOT SURVIVE THE PIERCING LIGHT OF RIGHTEOUSNESS--A LIGHT WHICH GROWS EVER BRIGHTER --EVER STRONGER--!
--UNTIL IT HAS SWALLOWED UP YOUR SINISTER SPELLS AND TURNED THEM INTO THE NOTHINGNESS WHICH IS THEIR DESTINY!!
AND NOW THAT YOU HAVE SEEN WHICH OF US IS TRULY THE STRONGER, I ORDER YOU TO TAKE ME TO YOUR DISCIPLE! HE MAY SERVE YOU NO LONGER!
YOU DARE ORDER ME??! I'M NOT BEATEN YET!!
9

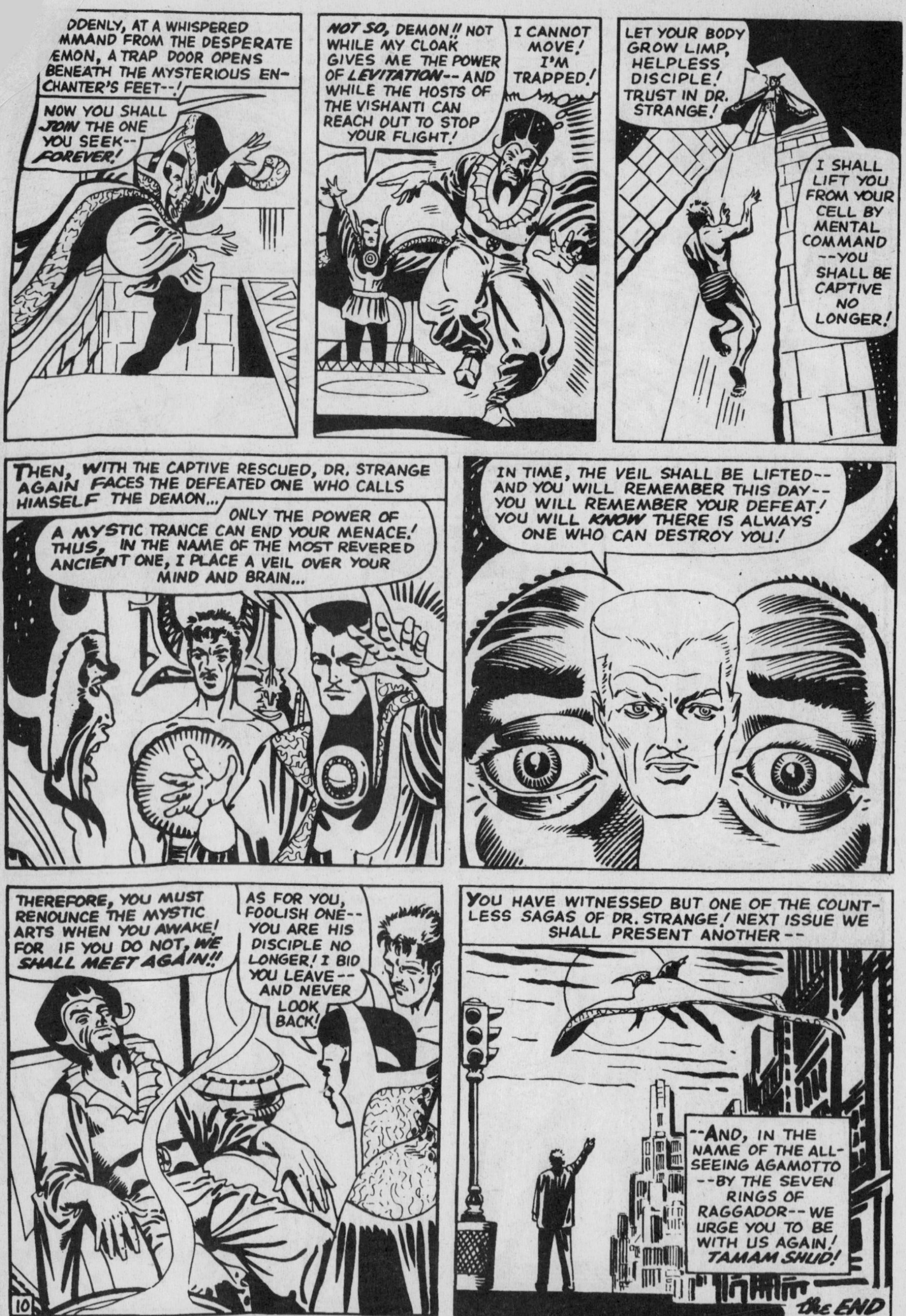

ODDENLY, AT A WHISPERED MMAND FROM THE DESPERATE EMON, A TRAP DOOR OPENS BENEATH THE MYSTERIOUS ENCHANTER'S FEET--!
NOW YOU SHALL JOIN THE ONE YOU SEEK-- FOREVER!
NOT SO, DEMON!! NOT WHILE MY CLOAK GIVES ME THE POWER OF LEVITATION-- AND WHILE THE HOSTS OF THE VISHANTI CAN REACH OUT TO STOP YOUR FLIGHT!
I CANNOT MOVE! I'M TRAPPED!
LET YOUR BODY GROW LIMP, HELPLESS DISCIPLE! TRUST IN DR. STRANGE!
I SHALL LIFT YOU FROM YOUR CELL BY MENTAL COMMAND --YOU SHALL BE CAPTIVE NO LONGER!
THEN, WITH THE CAPTIVE RESCUED, DR. STRANGE AGAIN FACES THE DEFEATED ONE WHO CALLS HIMSELF THE DEMON...
ONLY THE POWER OF A MYSTIC TRANCE CAN END YOUR MENACE! THUS, IN THE NAME OF THE MOST REVERED ANCIENT ONE, I PLACE A VEIL OVER YOUR MIND AND BRAIN...
IN TIME, THE VEIL SHALL BE LIFTED-- AND YOU WILL REMEMBER THIS DAY-- YOU WILL REMEMBER YOUR DEFEAT! YOU WILL KNOW THERE IS ALWAYS ONE WHO CAN DESTROY YOU!
THEREFORE, YOU MUST RENOUNCE THE MYSTIC ARTS WHEN YOU AWAKE! FOR IF YOU DO NOT, WE SHALL MEET AGAIN!!
AS FOR YOU, FOOLISH ONE-- YOU ARE HIS DISCIPLE NO LONGER! I BID YOU LEAVE-- AND NEVER LOOK BACK!
10
YOU HAVE WITNESSED BUT ONE OF THE COUNTLESS SAGAS OF DR. STRANGE! NEXT ISSUE WE SHALL PRESENT ANOTHER--
--AND, IN THE NAME OF THE ALL-SEEING AGAMOTTO --BY THE SEVEN RINGS OF RAGGADOR-- WE URGE YOU TO BE WITH US AGAIN! TAMAM SHUD!
THE END

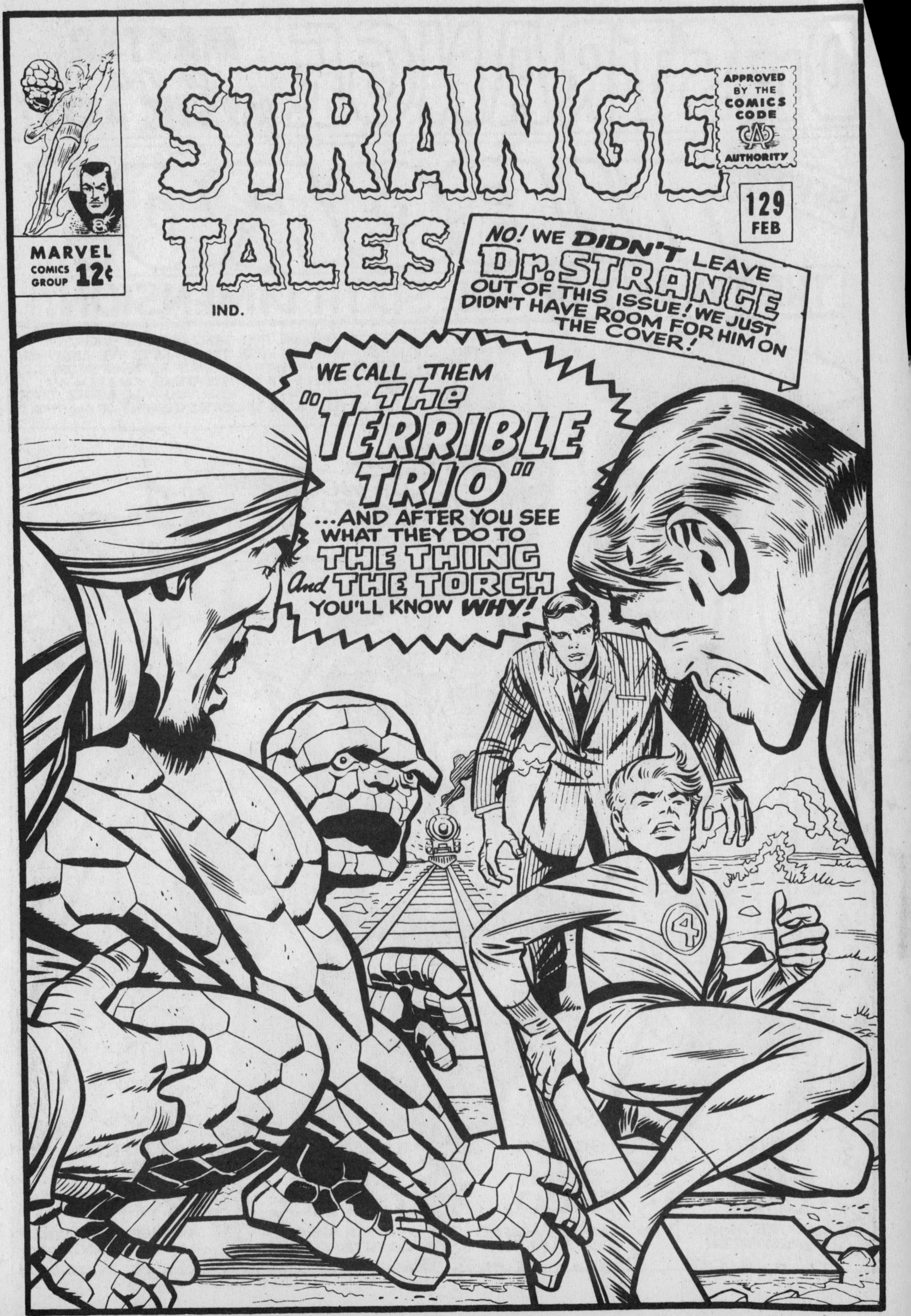
STRANGE TALES
APPROVED BY THE COMICS CODE AUTHORITY
129 FEB
MARVEL COMICS GROUP 12¢
IND.
NO! WE DIDN'T LEAVE Dr. STRANGE OUT OF THIS ISSUE! WE JUST DIDN'T HAVE ROOM FOR HIM ON THE COVER!
WE CALL THEM "The TERRIBLE TRIO" ...AND AFTER YOU SEE WHAT THEY DO TO THE THING and THE TORCH YOU'LL KNOW WHY!
4

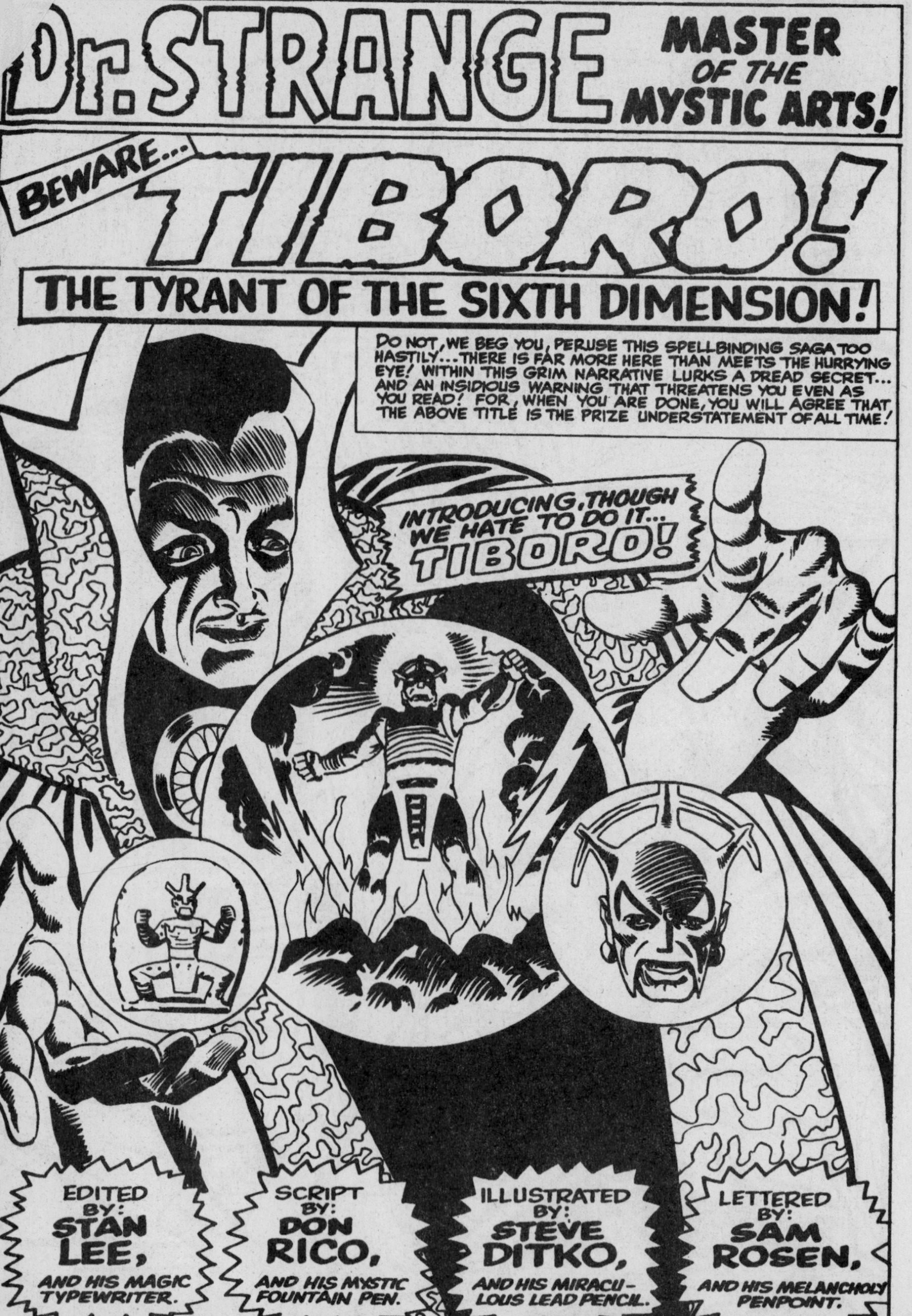
Dr. STRANGE
MASTER OF THE MYSTIC ARTS!
BEWARE... TIBORO!
THE TYRANT OF THE SIXTH DIMENSION!
DO NOT, WE BEG YOU, PERUSE THIS SPELLBINDING SAGA TOO HASTILY... THERE IS FAR MORE HERE THAN MEETS THE HURRYING EYE! WITHIN THIS GRIM NARRATIVE LURKS A DREAD SECRET... AND AN INSIDIOUS WARNING THAT THREATENS YOU EVEN AS YOU READ! FOR, WHEN YOU ARE DONE, YOU WILL AGREE THAT THE ABOVE TITLE IS THE PRIZE UNDERSTATEMENT OF ALL TIME!
INTRODUCING, THOUGH WE HATE TO DO IT... TIBORO!
EDITED BY: STAN LEE, AND HIS MAGIC TYPEWRITER.
SCRIPT BY: DON RICO, AND HIS MYSTIC FOUNTAIN PEN.
ILLUSTRATED BY: STEVE DITKO, AND HIS MIRACULOUS LEAD PENCIL.
LETTERED BY: SAM ROSEN, AND HIS MELANCHOLY PENPOINT.

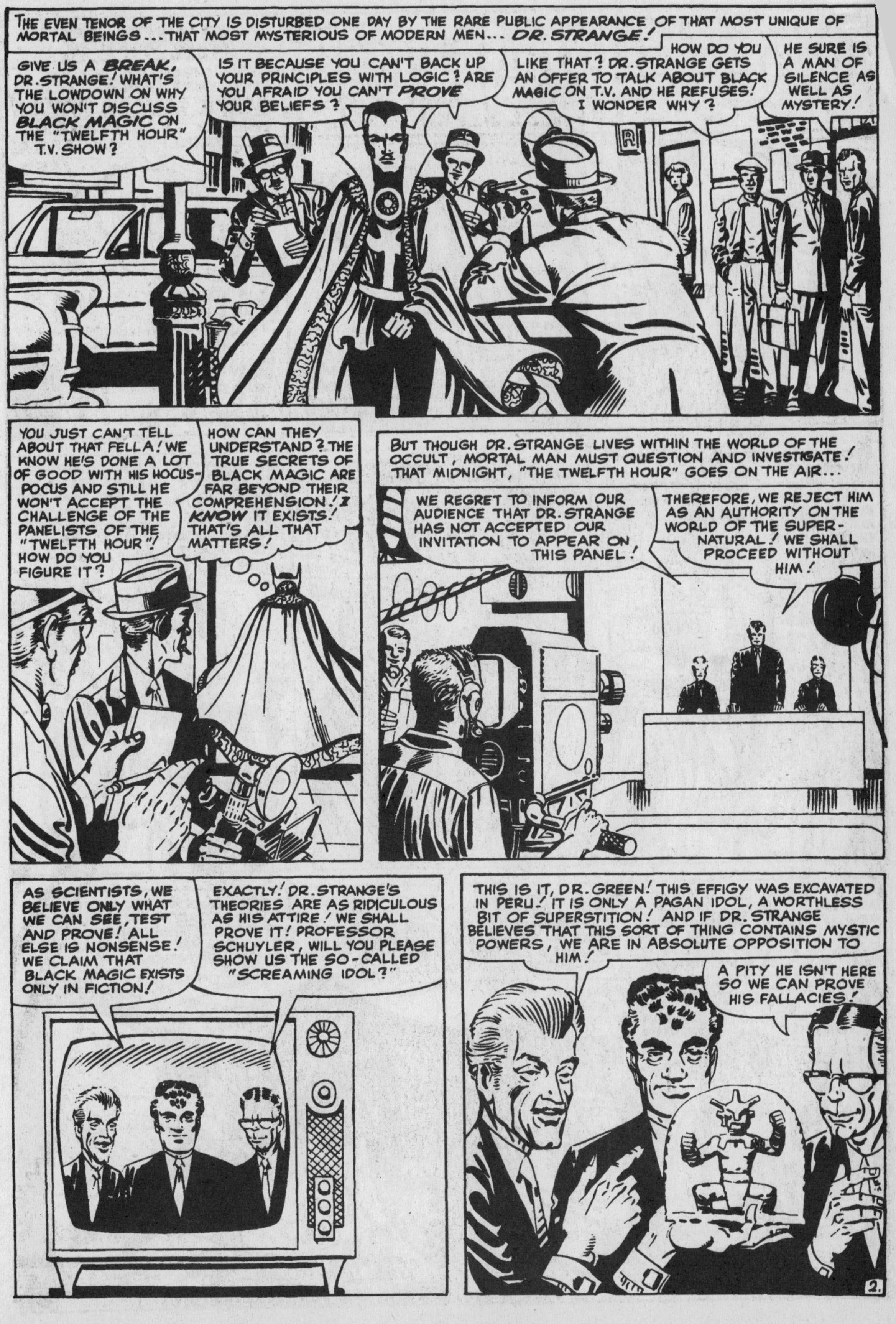

THE EVEN TENOR OF THE CITY IS DISTURBED ONE DAY BY THE RARE PUBLIC APPEARANCE OF THAT MOST UNIQUE OF MORTAL BEINGS... THAT MOST MYSTERIOUS OF MODERN MEN... DR. STRANGE!
GIVE US A BREAK, DR. STRANGE! WHAT'S THE LOWDOWN ON WHY YOU WON'T DISCUSS BLACK MAGIC ON THE "TWELFTH HOUR" T.V. SHOW?
IS IT BECAUSE YOU CAN'T BACK UP YOUR PRINCIPLES WITH LOGIC? ARE YOU AFRAID YOU CAN'T PROVE YOUR BELIEFS?
HOW DO YOU LIKE THAT? DR. STRANGE GETS AN OFFER TO TALK ABOUT BLACK MAGIC ON T.V. AND HE REFUSES! I WONDER WHY?
HE SURE IS A MAN OF SILENCE AS WELL AS MYSTERY!
YOU JUST CAN'T TELL ABOUT THAT FELLA! WE KNOW HE'S DONE A LOT OF GOOD WITH HIS HOCUS-POCUS AND STILL HE WON'T ACCEPT THE CHALLENGE OF THE PANELISTS OF THE "TWELFTH HOUR"! HOW DO YOU FIGURE IT?
HOW CAN THEY UNDERSTAND? THE TRUE SECRETS OF BLACK MAGIC ARE FAR BEYOND THEIR COMPREHENSION! I KNOW IT EXISTS! THAT'S ALL THAT MATTERS!
BUT THOUGH DR. STRANGE LIVES WITHIN THE WORLD OF THE OCCULT, MORTAL MAN MUST QUESTION AND INVESTIGATE! THAT MIDNIGHT, "THE TWELFTH HOUR" GOES ON THE AIR...
WE REGRET TO INFORM OUR AUDIENCE THAT DR. STRANGE HAS NOT ACCEPTED OUR INVITATION TO APPEAR ON THIS PANEL!
THEREFORE, WE REJECT HIM AS AN AUTHORITY ON THE WORLD OF THE SUPER-NATURAL! WE SHALL PROCEED WITHOUT HIM!
AS SCIENTISTS, WE BELIEVE ONLY WHAT WE CAN SEE, TEST AND PROVE! ALL ELSE IS NONSENSE! WE CLAIM THAT BLACK MAGIC EXISTS ONLY IN FICTION!
EXACTLY! DR. STRANGE'S THEORIES ARE AS RIDICULOUS AS HIS ATTIRE! WE SHALL PROVE IT! PROFESSOR SCHUYLER, WILL YOU PLEASE SHOW US THE SO-CALLED "SCREAMING IDOL?"
THIS IS IT, DR. GREEN! THIS EFFIGY WAS EXCAVATED IN PERU! IT IS ONLY A PAGAN IDOL, A WORTHLESS BIT OF SUPERSTITION! AND IF DR. STRANGE BELIEVES THAT THIS SORT OF THING CONTAINS MYSTIC POWERS, WE ARE IN ABSOLUTE OPPOSITION TO HIM!
A PITY HE ISN'T HERE SO WE CAN PROVE HIS FALLACIES!
2.

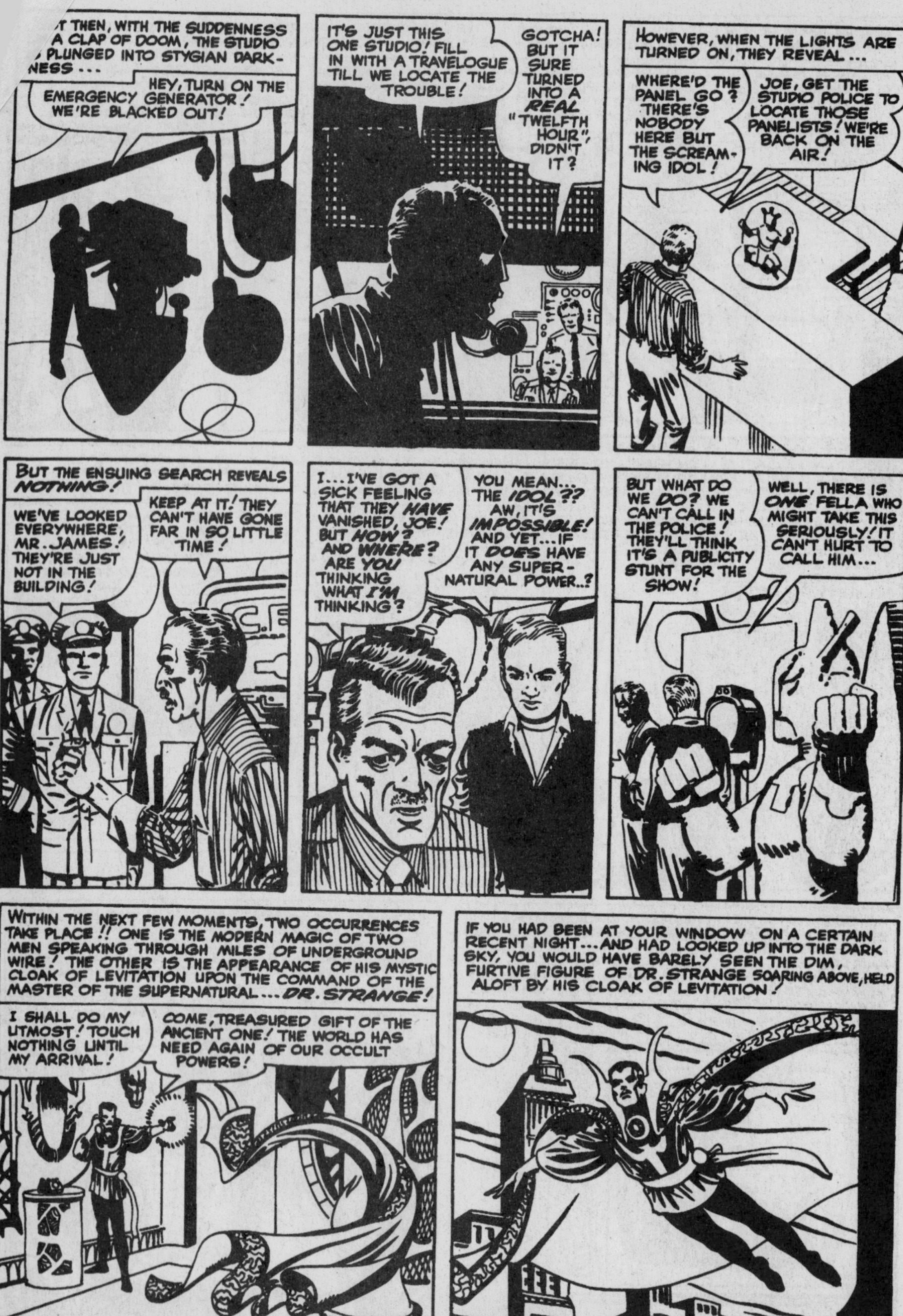

...T THEN, WITH THE SUDDENNESS ...A CLAP OF DOOM, THE STUDIO ...PLUNGED INTO STYGIAN DARK-...NESS...
HEY, TURN ON THE EMERGENCY GENERATOR! WE'RE BLACKED OUT!
IT'S JUST THIS ONE STUDIO! FILL IN WITH A TRAVELOGUE TILL WE LOCATE THE TROUBLE!
GOTCHA! BUT IT SURE TURNED INTO A REAL "TWELFTH HOUR", DIDN'T IT?
HOWEVER, WHEN THE LIGHTS ARE TURNED ON, THEY REVEAL...
WHERE'D THE PANEL GO? THERE'S NOBODY HERE BUT THE SCREAMING IDOL!
JOE, GET THE STUDIO POLICE TO LOCATE THOSE PANELISTS! WE'RE BACK ON THE AIR!
BUT THE ENSUING SEARCH REVEALS NOTHING!
WE'VE LOOKED EVERYWHERE, MR. JAMES! THEY'RE JUST NOT IN THE BUILDING!
KEEP AT IT! THEY CAN'T HAVE GONE FAR IN SO LITTLE TIME!
I... I'VE GOT A SICK FEELING THAT THEY HAVE VANISHED, JOE! BUT HOW? AND WHERE? ARE YOU THINKING WHAT I'M THINKING?
YOU MEAN... THE IDOL?? AW, IT'S IMPOSSIBLE! AND YET... IF IT DOES HAVE ANY SUPER-NATURAL POWER..?
BUT WHAT DO WE DO? WE CAN'T CALL IN THE POLICE! THEY'LL THINK IT'S A PUBLICITY STUNT FOR THE SHOW!
WELL, THERE IS ONE FELLA WHO MIGHT TAKE THIS SERIOUSLY! IT CAN'T HURT TO CALL HIM...
WITHIN THE NEXT FEW MOMENTS, TWO OCCURRENCES TAKE PLACE!! ONE IS THE MODERN MAGIC OF TWO MEN SPEAKING THROUGH MILES OF UNDERGROUND WIRE! THE OTHER IS THE APPEARANCE OF HIS MYSTIC CLOAK OF LEVITATION UPON THE COMMAND OF THE MASTER OF THE SUPERNATURAL... DR. STRANGE!
I SHALL DO MY UTMOST! TOUCH NOTHING UNTIL MY ARRIVAL!
COME, TREASURED GIFT OF THE ANCIENT ONE! THE WORLD HAS NEED AGAIN OF OUR OCCULT POWERS!
IF YOU HAD BEEN AT YOUR WINDOW ON A CERTAIN RECENT NIGHT... AND HAD LOOKED UP INTO THE DARK SKY, YOU WOULD HAVE BARELY SEEN THE DIM, FURTIVE FIGURE OF DR. STRANGE SOARING ABOVE, HELD ALOFT BY HIS CLOAK OF LEVITATION!
3

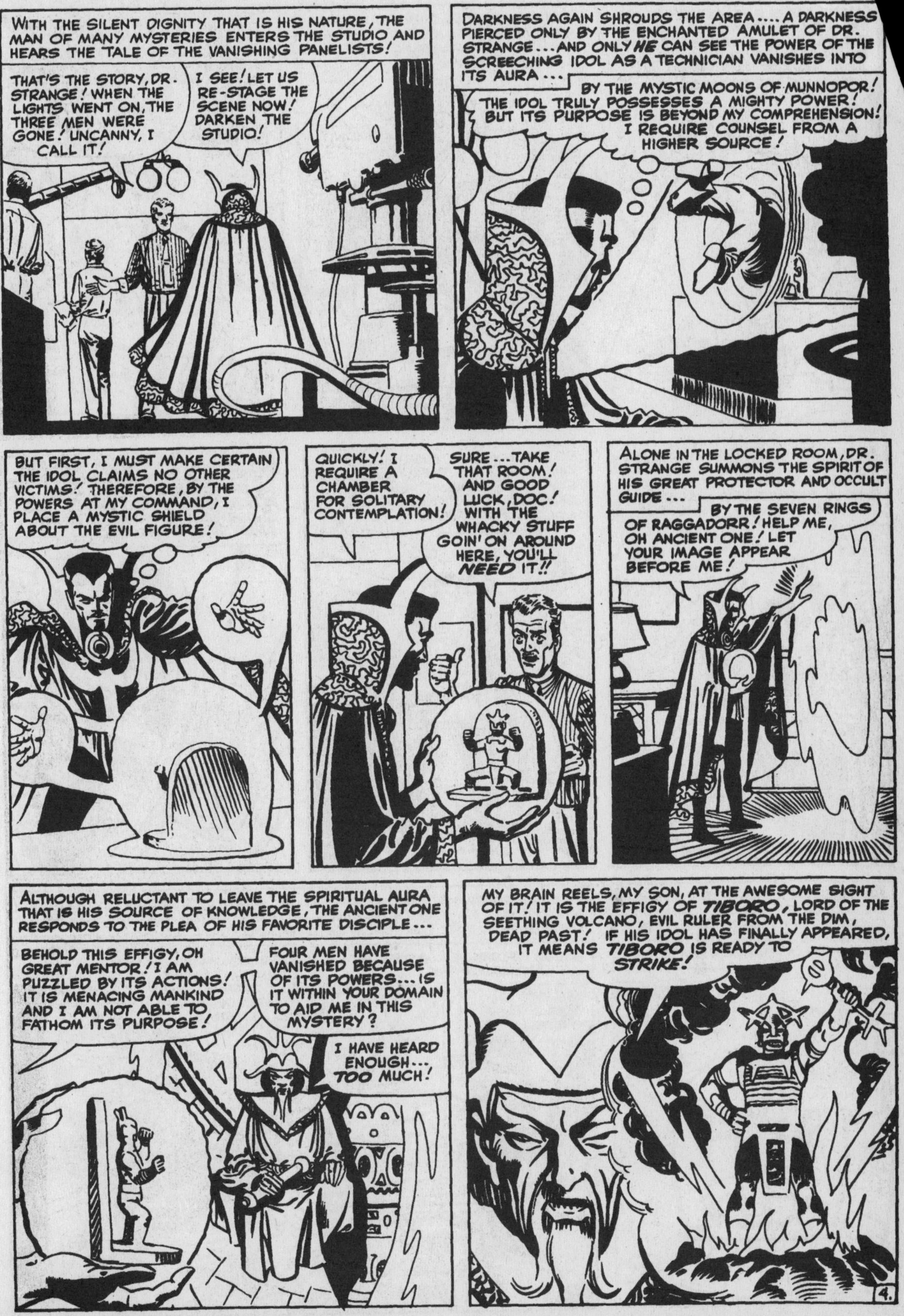
WITH THE SILENT DIGNITY THAT IS HIS NATURE, THE MAN OF MANY MYSTERIES ENTERS THE STUDIO AND HEARS THE TALE OF THE VANISHING PANELISTS!
THAT'S THE STORY, DR. STRANGE! WHEN THE LIGHTS WENT ON, THE THREE MEN WERE GONE! UNCANNY, I CALL IT!
I SEE! LET US RE-STAGE THE SCENE NOW! DARKEN THE STUDIO!
DARKNESS AGAIN SHROUDS THE AREA.... A DARKNESS PIERCED ONLY BY THE ENCHANTED AMULET OF DR. STRANGE... AND ONLY HE CAN SEE THE POWER OF THE SCREECHING IDOL AS A TECHNICIAN VANISHES INTO ITS AURA...
BY THE MYSTIC MOONS OF MUNNOPOR! THE IDOL TRULY POSSESSES A MIGHTY POWER! BUT ITS PURPOSE IS BEYOND MY COMPREHENSION! I REQUIRE COUNSEL FROM A HIGHER SOURCE!
BUT FIRST, I MUST MAKE CERTAIN THE IDOL CLAIMS NO OTHER VICTIMS! THEREFORE, BY THE POWERS AT MY COMMAND, I PLACE A MYSTIC SHIELD ABOUT THE EVIL FIGURE!
QUICKLY! I REQUIRE A CHAMBER FOR SOLITARY CONTEMPLATION!
SURE... TAKE THAT ROOM! AND GOOD LUCK, DOC! WITH THE WHACKY STUFF GOIN' ON AROUND HERE, YOU'LL NEED IT!!
ALONE IN THE LOCKED ROOM, DR. STRANGE SUMMONS THE SPIRIT OF HIS GREAT PROTECTOR AND OCCULT GUIDE...
BY THE SEVEN RINGS OF RAGGADORR! HELP ME, OH ANCIENT ONE! LET YOUR IMAGE APPEAR BEFORE ME!
ALTHOUGH RELUCTANT TO LEAVE THE SPIRITUAL AURA THAT IS HIS SOURCE OF KNOWLEDGE, THE ANCIENT ONE RESPONDS TO THE PLEA OF HIS FAVORITE DISCIPLE...
BEHOLD THIS EFFIGY, OH GREAT MENTOR! I AM PUZZLED BY ITS ACTIONS! IT IS MENACING MANKIND AND I AM NOT ABLE TO FATHOM ITS PURPOSE!
FOUR MEN HAVE VANISHED BECAUSE OF ITS POWERS... IS IT WITHIN YOUR DOMAIN TO AID ME IN THIS MYSTERY?
I HAVE HEARD ENOUGH... TOO MUCH!
MY BRAIN REELS, MY SON, AT THE AWESOME SIGHT OF IT! IT IS THE EFFIGY OF TIBORO, LORD OF THE SEETHING VOLCANO, EVIL RULER FROM THE DIM, DEAD PAST! IF HIS IDOL HAS FINALLY APPEARED, IT MEANS TIBORO IS READY TO STRIKE!
4.

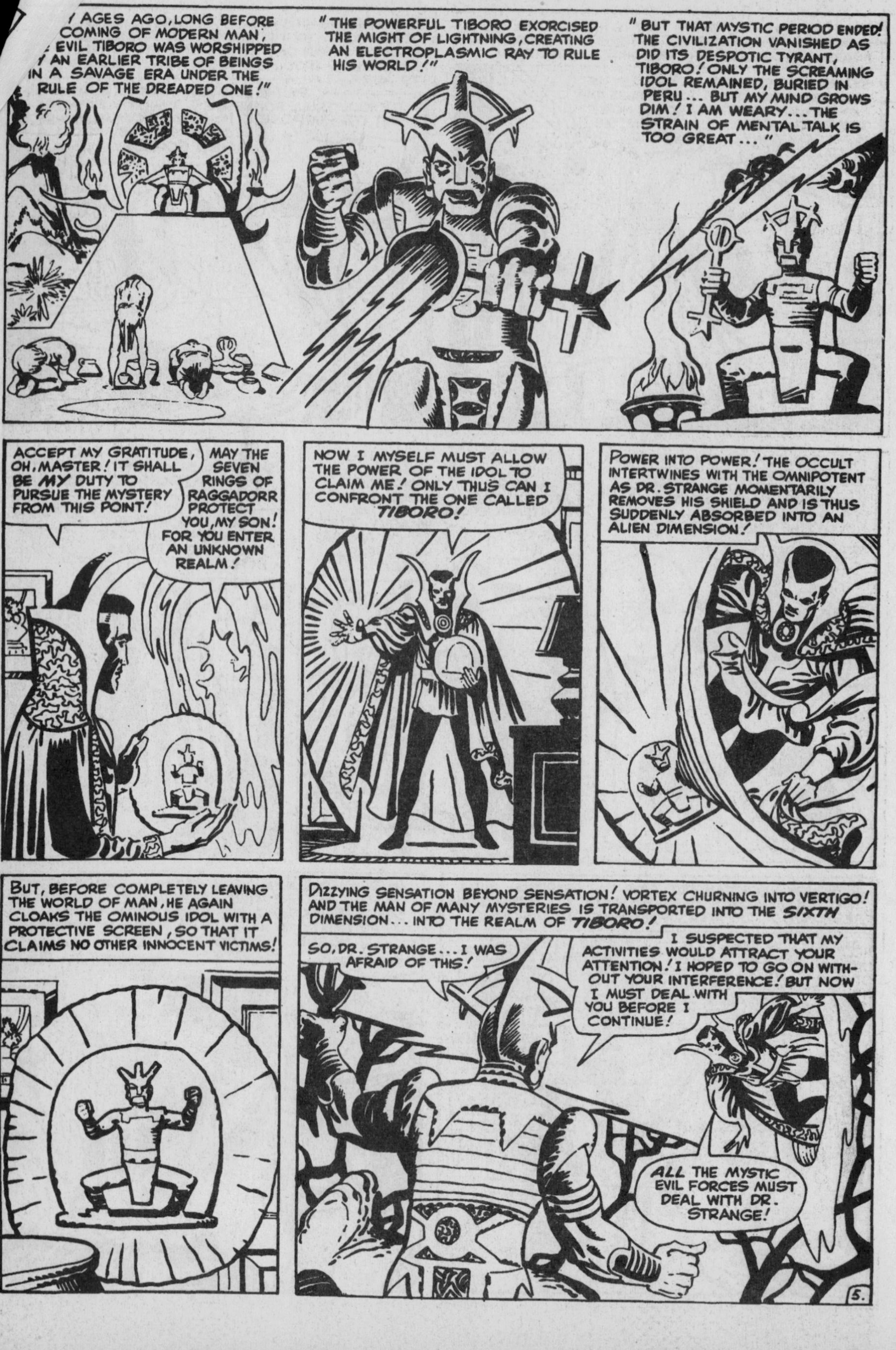

...Y AGES AGO, LONG BEFORE ... COMING OF MODERN MAN, ... EVIL TIBORO WAS WORSHIPPED ... AN EARLIER TRIBE OF BEINGS IN A SAVAGE ERA UNDER THE RULE OF THE DREADED ONE!"
"THE POWERFUL TIBORO EXORCISED THE MIGHT OF LIGHTNING, CREATING AN ELECTROPLASMIC RAY TO RULE HIS WORLD!"
"BUT THAT MYSTIC PERIOD ENDED! THE CIVILIZATION VANISHED AS DID ITS DESPOTIC TYRANT, TIBORO! ONLY THE SCREAMING IDOL REMAINED, BURIED IN PERU... BUT MY MIND GROWS DIM! I AM WEARY... THE STRAIN OF MENTAL TALK IS TOO GREAT..."
ACCEPT MY GRATITUDE, OH, MASTER! IT SHALL BE MY DUTY TO PURSUE THE MYSTERY FROM THIS POINT!
MAY THE SEVEN RINGS OF RAGGADORR PROTECT YOU, MY SON! FOR YOU ENTER AN UNKNOWN REALM!
NOW I MYSELF MUST ALLOW THE POWER OF THE IDOL TO CLAIM ME! ONLY THUS CAN I CONFRONT THE ONE CALLED TIBORO!
POWER INTO POWER! THE OCCULT INTERTWINES WITH THE OMNIPOTENT AS DR. STRANGE MOMENTARILY REMOVES HIS SHIELD AND IS THUS SUDDENLY ABSORBED INTO AN ALIEN DIMENSION!
BUT, BEFORE COMPLETELY LEAVING THE WORLD OF MAN, HE AGAIN CLOAKS THE OMINOUS IDOL WITH A PROTECTIVE SCREEN, SO THAT IT CLAIMS NO OTHER INNOCENT VICTIMS!
DIZZYING SENSATION BEYOND SENSATION! VORTEX CHURNING INTO VERTIGO! AND THE MAN OF MANY MYSTERIES IS TRANSPORTED INTO THE SIXTH DIMENSION... INTO THE REALM OF TIBORO!
SO, DR. STRANGE... I WAS AFRAID OF THIS!
I SUSPECTED THAT MY ACTIVITIES WOULD ATTRACT YOUR ATTENTION! I HOPED TO GO ON WITHOUT YOUR INTERFERENCE! BUT NOW I MUST DEAL WITH YOU BEFORE I CONTINUE!
ALL THE MYSTIC EVIL FORCES MUST DEAL WITH DR. STRANGE!
5.

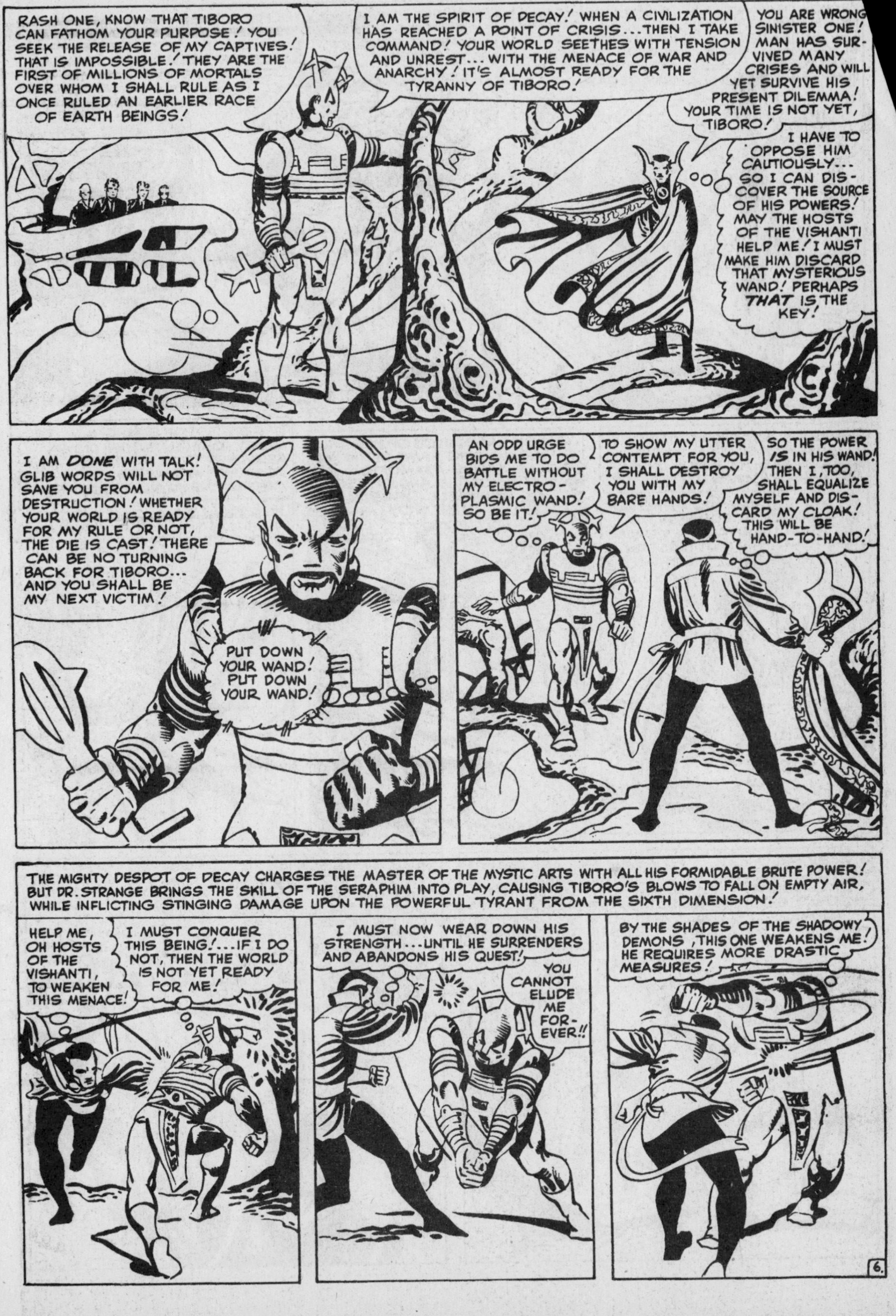

RASH ONE, KNOW THAT TIBORO CAN FATHOM YOUR PURPOSE! YOU SEEK THE RELEASE OF MY CAPTIVES! THAT IS IMPOSSIBLE! THEY ARE THE FIRST OF MILLIONS OF MORTALS OVER WHOM I SHALL RULE AS I ONCE RULED AN EARLIER RACE OF EARTH BEINGS!
I AM THE SPIRIT OF DECAY! WHEN A CIVILIZATION HAS REACHED A POINT OF CRISIS...THEN I TAKE COMMAND! YOUR WORLD SEETHES WITH TENSION AND UNREST...WITH THE MENACE OF WAR AND ANARCHY! IT'S ALMOST READY FOR THE TYRANNY OF TIBORO!
YOU ARE WRONG SINISTER ONE! MAN HAS SURVIVED MANY CRISES AND WILL YET SURVIVE HIS PRESENT DILEMMA! YOUR TIME IS NOT YET, TIBORO!
I HAVE TO OPPOSE HIM CAUTIOUSLY... SO I CAN DISCOVER THE SOURCE OF HIS POWERS! MAY THE HOSTS OF THE VISHANTI HELP ME! I MUST MAKE HIM DISCARD THAT MYSTERIOUS WAND! PERHAPS THAT IS THE KEY!
I AM DONE WITH TALK! GLIB WORDS WILL NOT SAVE YOU FROM DESTRUCTION! WHETHER YOUR WORLD IS READY FOR MY RULE OR NOT, THE DIE IS CAST! THERE CAN BE NO TURNING BACK FOR TIBORO... AND YOU SHALL BE MY NEXT VICTIM!
PUT DOWN YOUR WAND! PUT DOWN YOUR WAND!
AN ODD URGE BIDS ME TO DO BATTLE WITHOUT MY ELECTRO-PLASMIC WAND! SO BE IT!
TO SHOW MY UTTER CONTEMPT FOR YOU, I SHALL DESTROY YOU WITH MY BARE HANDS!
SO THE POWER IS IN HIS WAND! THEN I, TOO, SHALL EQUALIZE MYSELF AND DISCARD MY CLOAK! THIS WILL BE HAND-TO-HAND!
THE MIGHTY DESPOT OF DECAY CHARGES THE MASTER OF THE MYSTIC ARTS WITH ALL HIS FORMIDABLE BRUTE POWER! BUT DR. STRANGE BRINGS THE SKILL OF THE SERAPHIM INTO PLAY, CAUSING TIBORO'S BLOWS TO FALL ON EMPTY AIR, WHILE INFLICTING STINGING DAMAGE UPON THE POWERFUL TYRANT FROM THE SIXTH DIMENSION!
HELP ME, OH HOSTS OF THE VISHANTI, TO WEAKEN THIS MENACE!
I MUST CONQUER THIS BEING!...IF I DO NOT, THEN THE WORLD IS NOT YET READY FOR ME!
I MUST NOW WEAR DOWN HIS STRENGTH...UNTIL HE SURRENDERS AND ABANDONS HIS QUEST!
YOU CANNOT ELUDE ME FOREVER!!
BY THE SHADES OF THE SHADOWY DEMONS, THIS ONE WEAKENS ME! HE REQUIRES MORE DRASTIC MEASURES!
6.

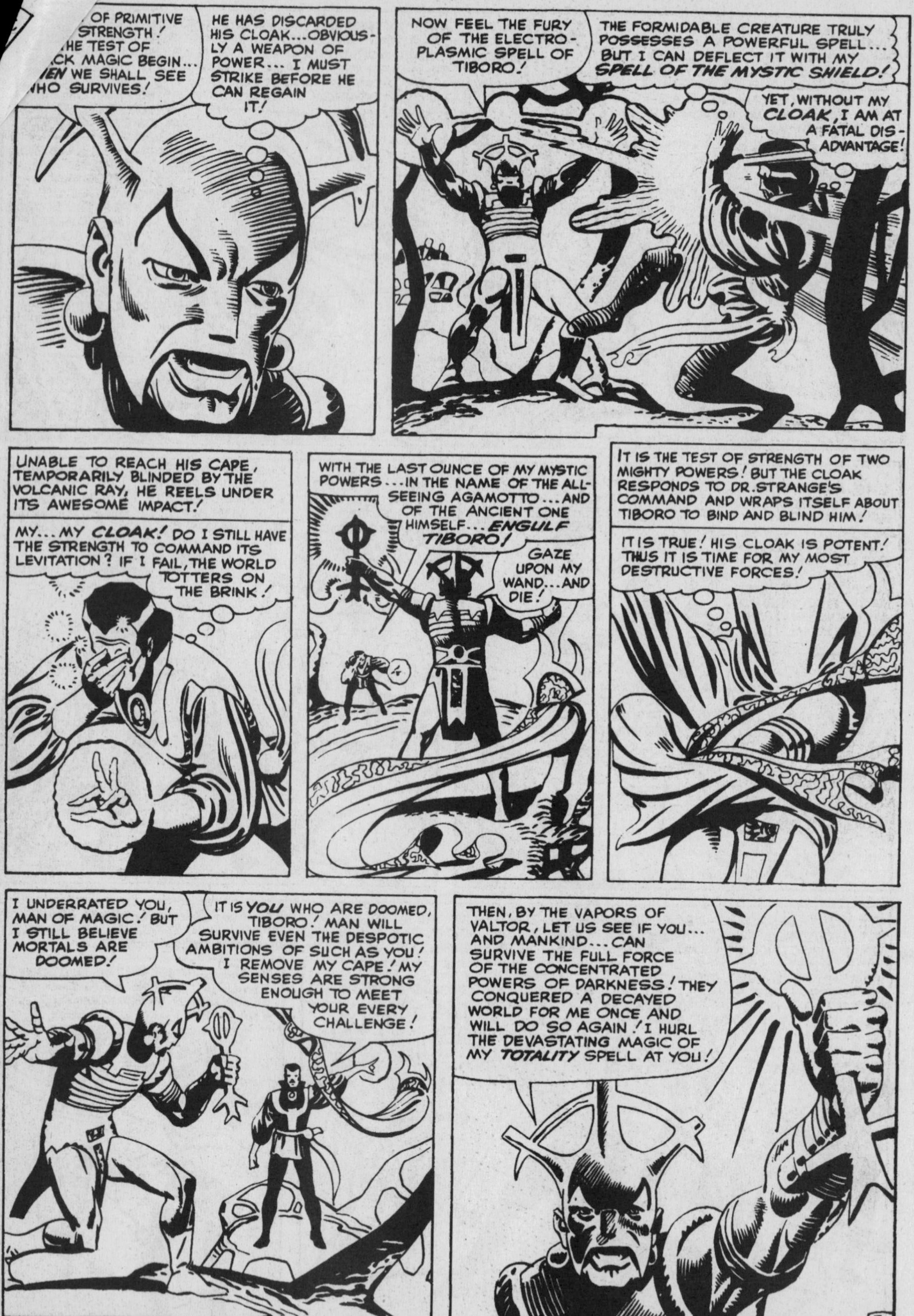
OF PRIMITIVE STRENGTH! THE TEST OF CK MAGIC BEGIN... HEN WE SHALL SEE HO SURVIVES!
HE HAS DISCARDED HIS CLOAK...OBVIOUSLY A WEAPON OF POWER... I MUST STRIKE BEFORE HE CAN REGAIN IT!
NOW FEEL THE FURY OF THE ELECTRO-PLASMIC SPELL OF TIBORO!
THE FORMIDABLE CREATURE TRULY POSSESSES A POWERFUL SPELL... BUT I CAN DEFLECT IT WITH MY SPELL OF THE MYSTIC SHIELD!
YET, WITHOUT MY CLOAK, I AM AT A FATAL DIS-ADVANTAGE!
UNABLE TO REACH HIS CAPE, TEMPORARILY BLINDED BY THE VOLCANIC RAY, HE REELS UNDER ITS AWESOME IMPACT!
MY... MY CLOAK! DO I STILL HAVE THE STRENGTH TO COMMAND ITS LEVITATION? IF I FAIL, THE WORLD TOTTERS ON THE BRINK!
WITH THE LAST OUNCE OF MY MYSTIC POWERS... IN THE NAME OF THE ALL-SEEING AGAMOTTO... AND OF THE ANCIENT ONE HIMSELF... ENGULF TIBORO!
GAZE UPON MY WAND... AND DIE!
IT IS THE TEST OF STRENGTH OF TWO MIGHTY POWERS! BUT THE CLOAK RESPONDS TO DR. STRANGE'S COMMAND AND WRAPS ITSELF ABOUT TIBORO TO BIND AND BLIND HIM!
IT IS TRUE! HIS CLOAK IS POTENT! THUS IT IS TIME FOR MY MOST DESTRUCTIVE FORCES!
I UNDERRATED YOU, MAN OF MAGIC! BUT I STILL BELIEVE MORTALS ARE DOOMED!
IT IS YOU WHO ARE DOOMED, TIBORO! MAN WILL SURVIVE EVEN THE DESPOTIC AMBITIONS OF SUCH AS YOU! I REMOVE MY CAPE! MY SENSES ARE STRONG ENOUGH TO MEET YOUR EVERY CHALLENGE!
THEN, BY THE VAPORS OF VALTOR, LET US SEE IF YOU... AND MANKIND... CAN SURVIVE THE FULL FORCE OF THE CONCENTRATED POWERS OF DARKNESS! THEY CONQUERED A DECAYED WORLD FOR ME ONCE AND WILL DO SO AGAIN! I HURL THE DEVASTATING MAGIC OF MY TOTALITY SPELL AT YOU!
7.

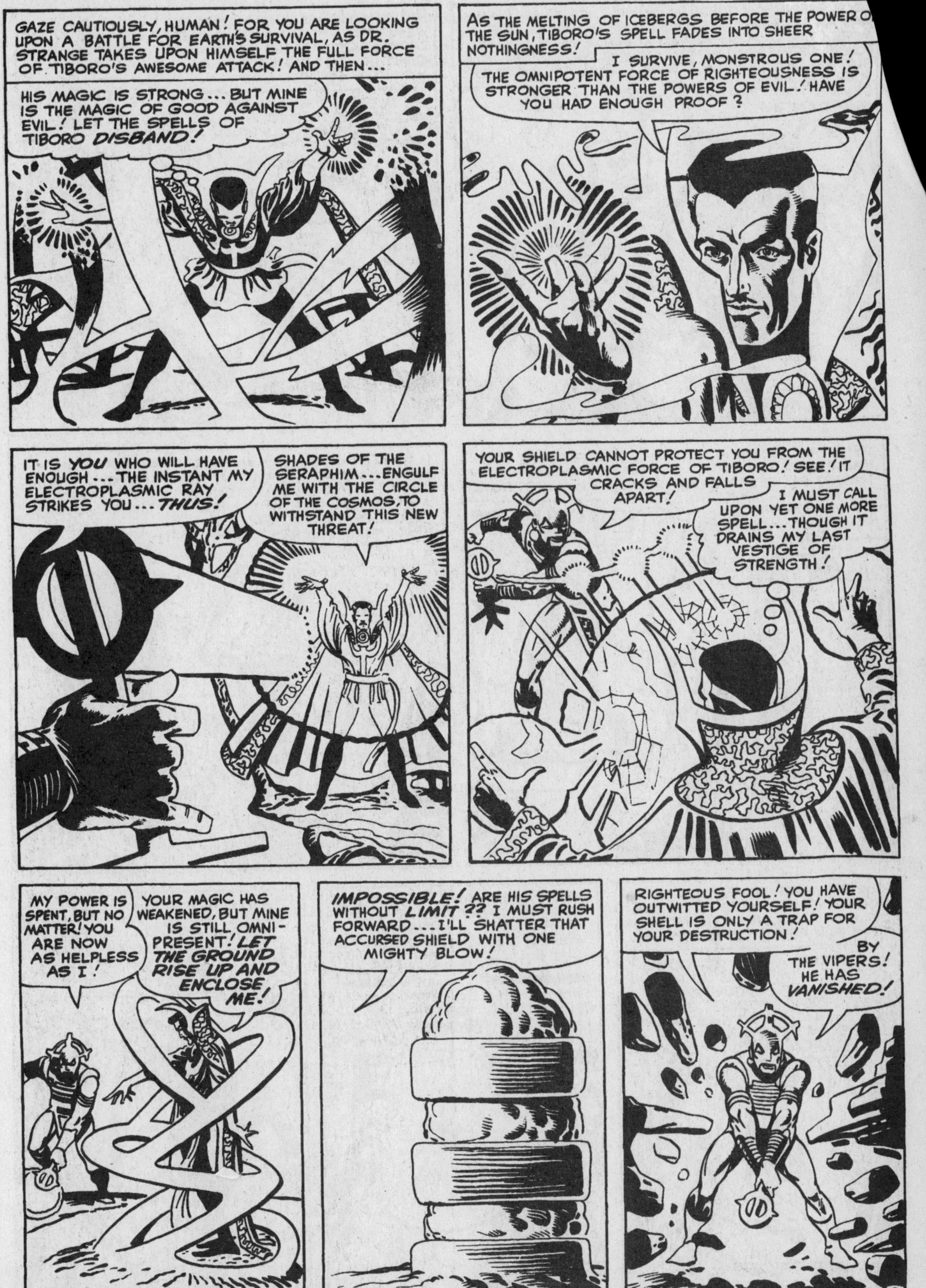
GAZE CAUTIOUSLY, HUMAN! FOR YOU ARE LOOKING UPON A BATTLE FOR EARTH'S SURVIVAL, AS DR. STRANGE TAKES UPON HIMSELF THE FULL FORCE OF TIBORO'S AWESOME ATTACK! AND THEN...
HIS MAGIC IS STRONG... BUT MINE IS THE MAGIC OF GOOD AGAINST EVIL! LET THE SPELLS OF TIBORO DISBAND!
AS THE MELTING OF ICEBERGS BEFORE THE POWER OF THE SUN, TIBORO'S SPELL FADES INTO SHEER NOTHINGNESS!
I SURVIVE, MONSTROUS ONE! THE OMNIPOTENT FORCE OF RIGHTEOUSNESS IS STRONGER THAN THE POWERS OF EVIL! HAVE YOU HAD ENOUGH PROOF?
IT IS YOU WHO WILL HAVE ENOUGH... THE INSTANT MY ELECTROPLASMIC RAY STRIKES YOU... THUS!
SHADES OF THE SERAPHIM... ENGULF ME WITH THE CIRCLE OF THE COSMOS, TO WITHSTAND THIS NEW THREAT!
YOUR SHIELD CANNOT PROTECT YOU FROM THE ELECTROPLASMIC FORCE OF TIBORO! SEE! IT CRACKS AND FALLS APART!
I MUST CALL UPON YET ONE MORE SPELL... THOUGH IT DRAINS MY LAST VESTIGE OF STRENGTH!
MY POWER IS SPENT, BUT NO MATTER! YOU ARE NOW AS HELPLESS AS I!
YOUR MAGIC HAS WEAKENED, BUT MINE IS STILL OMNI-PRESENT! LET THE GROUND RISE UP AND ENCLOSE ME!
IMPOSSIBLE! ARE HIS SPELLS WITHOUT LIMIT?? I MUST RUSH FORWARD... I'LL SHATTER THAT ACCURSED SHIELD WITH ONE MIGHTY BLOW!
RIGHTEOUS FOOL! YOU HAVE OUTWITTED YOURSELF! YOUR SHELL IS ONLY A TRAP FOR YOUR DESTRUCTION!
BY THE VIPERS! HE HAS VANISHED!
8.

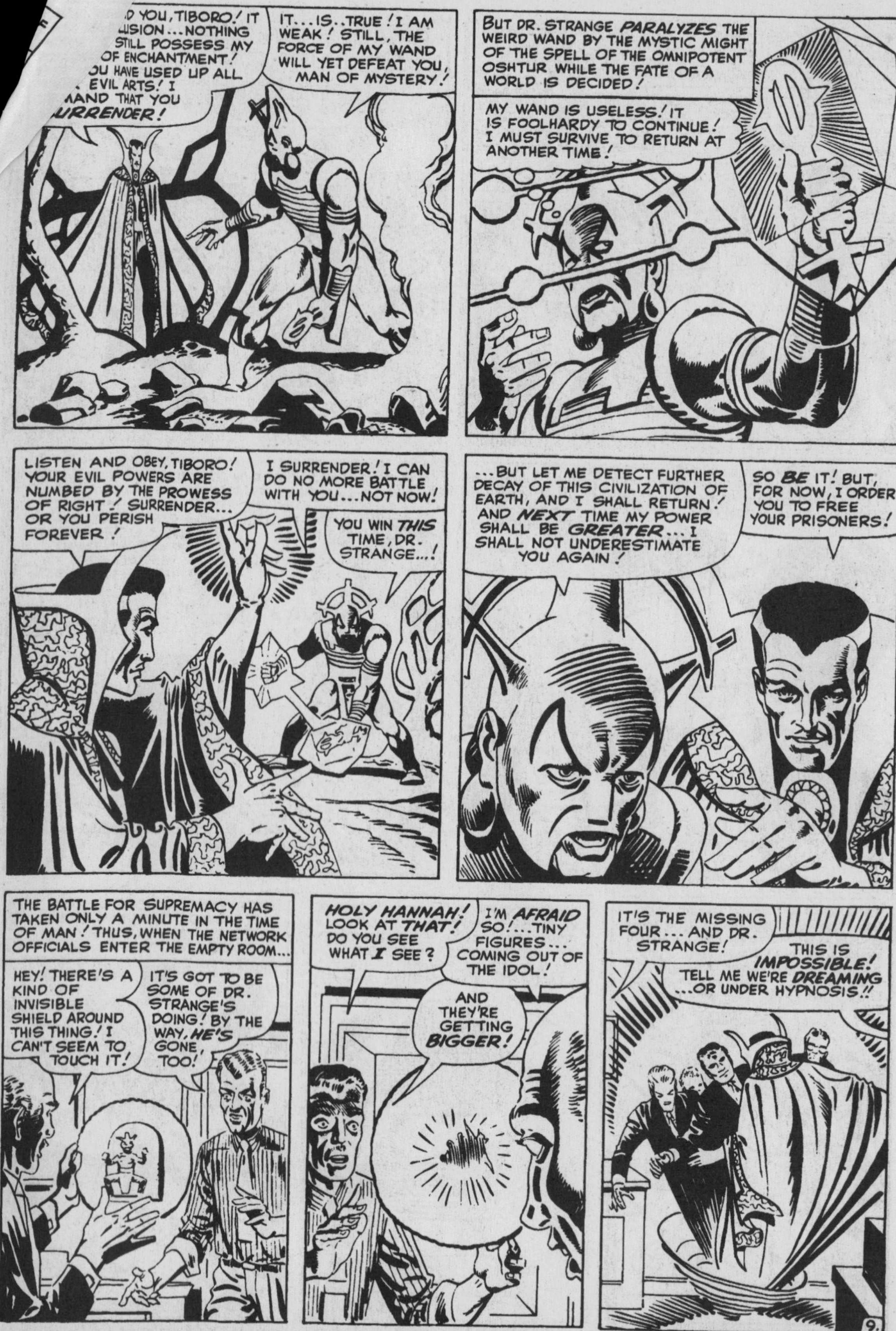
D YOU, TIBORO! IT LUSION... NOTHING STILL POSSESS MY OF ENCHANTMENT! OU HAVE USED UP ALL EVIL ARTS! I MAND THAT YOU URRENDER!
IT... IS.. TRUE! I AM WEAK! STILL, THE FORCE OF MY WAND WILL YET DEFEAT YOU, MAN OF MYSTERY!
BUT DR. STRANGE PARALYZES THE WEIRD WAND BY THE MYSTIC MIGHT OF THE SPELL OF THE OMNIPOTENT OSHTUR WHILE THE FATE OF A WORLD IS DECIDED!
MY WAND IS USELESS! IT IS FOOLHARDY TO CONTINUE! I MUST SURVIVE TO RETURN AT ANOTHER TIME!
LISTEN AND OBEY, TIBORO! YOUR EVIL POWERS ARE NUMBED BY THE PROWESS OF RIGHT! SURRENDER... OR YOU PERISH FOREVER!
I SURRENDER! I CAN DO NO MORE BATTLE WITH YOU... NOT NOW!
YOU WIN THIS TIME, DR. STRANGE...!
...BUT LET ME DETECT FURTHER DECAY OF THIS CIVILIZATION OF EARTH, AND I SHALL RETURN! AND NEXT TIME MY POWER SHALL BE GREATER... I SHALL NOT UNDERESTIMATE YOU AGAIN!
SO BE IT! BUT, FOR NOW, I ORDER YOU TO FREE YOUR PRISONERS!
THE BATTLE FOR SUPREMACY HAS TAKEN ONLY A MINUTE IN THE TIME OF MAN! THUS, WHEN THE NETWORK OFFICIALS ENTER THE EMPTY ROOM...
HEY! THERE'S A KIND OF INVISIBLE SHIELD AROUND THIS THING! I CAN'T SEEM TO TOUCH IT!
IT'S GOT TO BE SOME OF DR. STRANGE'S DOING! BY THE WAY, HE'S GONE, TOO!
HOLY HANNAH! LOOK AT THAT! DO YOU SEE WHAT I SEE?
I'M AFRAID SO!... TINY FIGURES... COMING OUT OF THE IDOL!
AND THEY'RE GETTING BIGGER!
IT'S THE MISSING FOUR... AND DR. STRANGE!
THIS IS IMPOSSIBLE! TELL ME WE'RE DREAMING ...OR UNDER HYPNOSIS!!

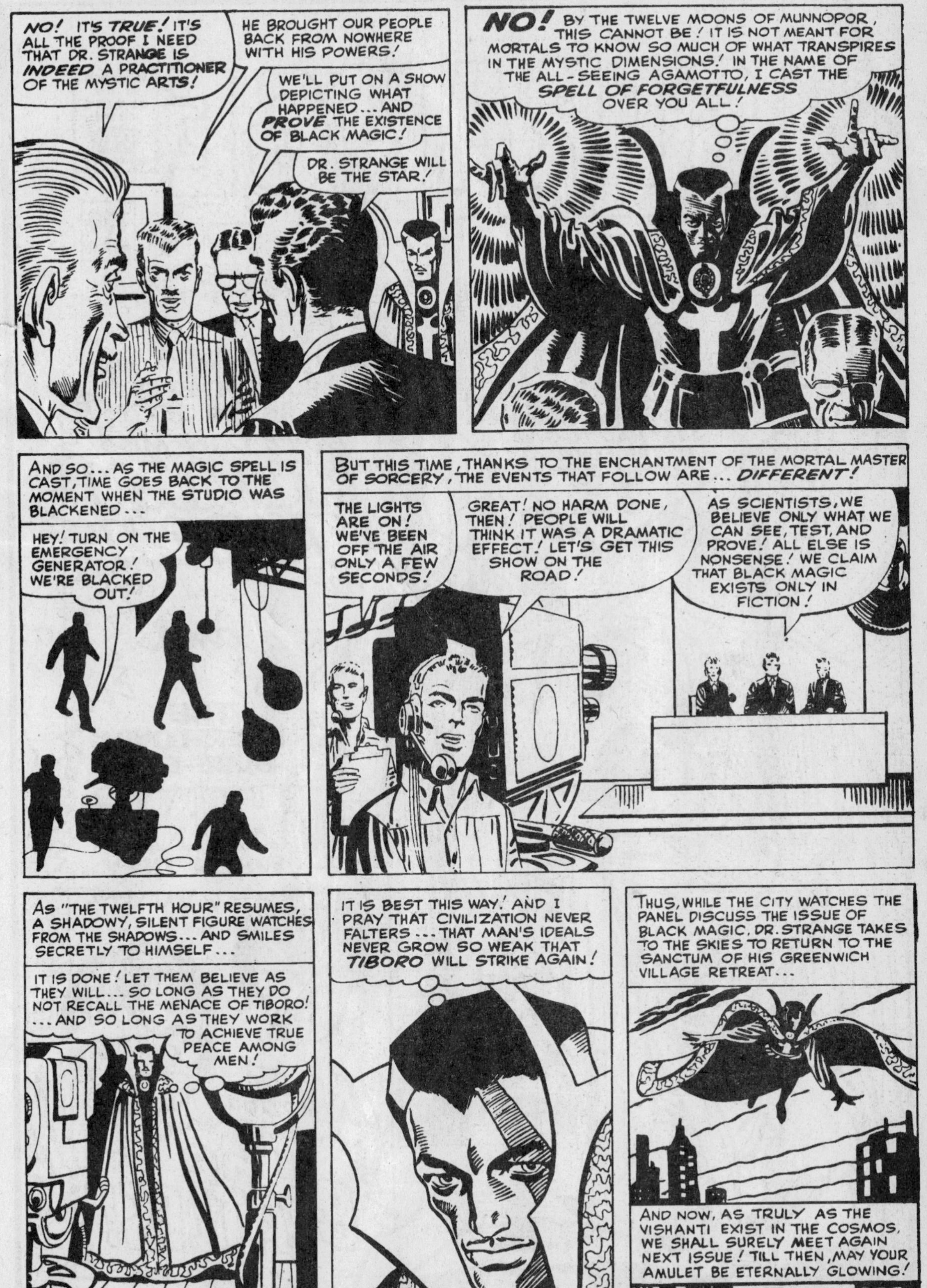
NO! IT'S TRUE! IT'S ALL THE PROOF I NEED THAT DR. STRANGE IS INDEED A PRACTITIONER OF THE MYSTIC ARTS!
HE BROUGHT OUR PEOPLE BACK FROM NOWHERE WITH HIS POWERS!
WE'LL PUT ON A SHOW DEPICTING WHAT HAPPENED... AND PROVE THE EXISTENCE OF BLACK MAGIC!
DR. STRANGE WILL BE THE STAR!
NO! BY THE TWELVE MOONS OF MUNNOPOR, THIS CANNOT BE! IT IS NOT MEANT FOR MORTALS TO KNOW SO MUCH OF WHAT TRANSPIRES IN THE MYSTIC DIMENSIONS! IN THE NAME OF THE ALL-SEEING AGAMOTTO, I CAST THE SPELL OF FORGETFULNESS OVER YOU ALL!
AND SO... AS THE MAGIC SPELL IS CAST, TIME GOES BACK TO THE MOMENT WHEN THE STUDIO WAS BLACKENED...
HEY! TURN ON THE EMERGENCY GENERATOR! WE'RE BLACKED OUT!
BUT THIS TIME, THANKS TO THE ENCHANTMENT OF THE MORTAL MASTER OF SORCERY, THE EVENTS THAT FOLLOW ARE... DIFFERENT!
THE LIGHTS ARE ON! WE'VE BEEN OFF THE AIR ONLY A FEW SECONDS!
GREAT! NO HARM DONE, THEN! PEOPLE WILL THINK IT WAS A DRAMATIC EFFECT! LET'S GET THIS SHOW ON THE ROAD!
AS SCIENTISTS, WE BELIEVE ONLY WHAT WE CAN SEE, TEST, AND PROVE! ALL ELSE IS NONSENSE! WE CLAIM THAT BLACK MAGIC EXISTS ONLY IN FICTION!
AS "THE TWELFTH HOUR" RESUMES, A SHADOWY, SILENT FIGURE WATCHES FROM THE SHADOWS... AND SMILES SECRETLY TO HIMSELF...
IT IS DONE! LET THEM BELIEVE AS THEY WILL... SO LONG AS THEY DO NOT RECALL THE MENACE OF TIBORO! ...AND SO LONG AS THEY WORK TO ACHIEVE TRUE PEACE AMONG MEN!
IT IS BEST THIS WAY! AND I PRAY THAT CIVILIZATION NEVER FALTERS... THAT MAN'S IDEALS NEVER GROW SO WEAK THAT TIBORO WILL STRIKE AGAIN!
THUS, WHILE THE CITY WATCHES THE PANEL DISCUSS THE ISSUE OF BLACK MAGIC, DR. STRANGE TAKES TO THE SKIES TO RETURN TO THE SANCTUM OF HIS GREENWICH VILLAGE RETREAT...
AND NOW, AS TRULY AS THE VISHANTI EXIST IN THE COSMOS, WE SHALL SURELY MEET AGAIN NEXT ISSUE! TILL THEN, MAY YOUR AMULET BE ETERNALLY GLOWING!
10

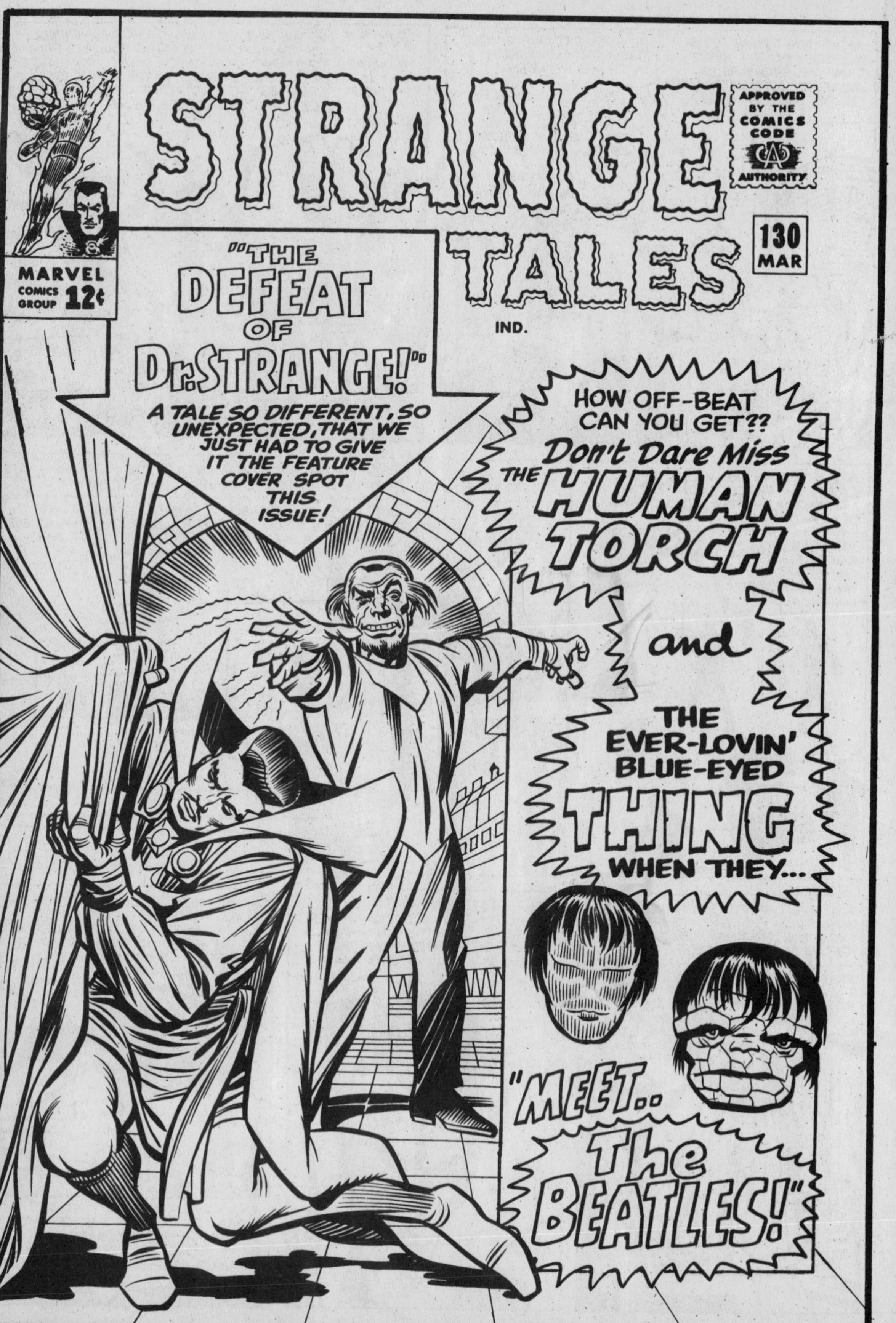
MARVEL COMICS GROUP 12¢
STRANGE TALES
APPROVED BY THE COMICS CODE AUTHORITY
130 MAR
IND.
"THE DEFEAT OF Dr. STRANGE!"
A TALE SO DIFFERENT, SO UNEXPECTED, THAT WE JUST HAD TO GIVE IT THE FEATURE COVER SPOT THIS ISSUE!
HOW OFF-BEAT CAN YOU GET??
Don't Dare Miss THE HUMAN TORCH
and
THE EVER-LOVIN' BLUE-EYED THING WHEN THEY...
"MEET.. The BEATLES!"

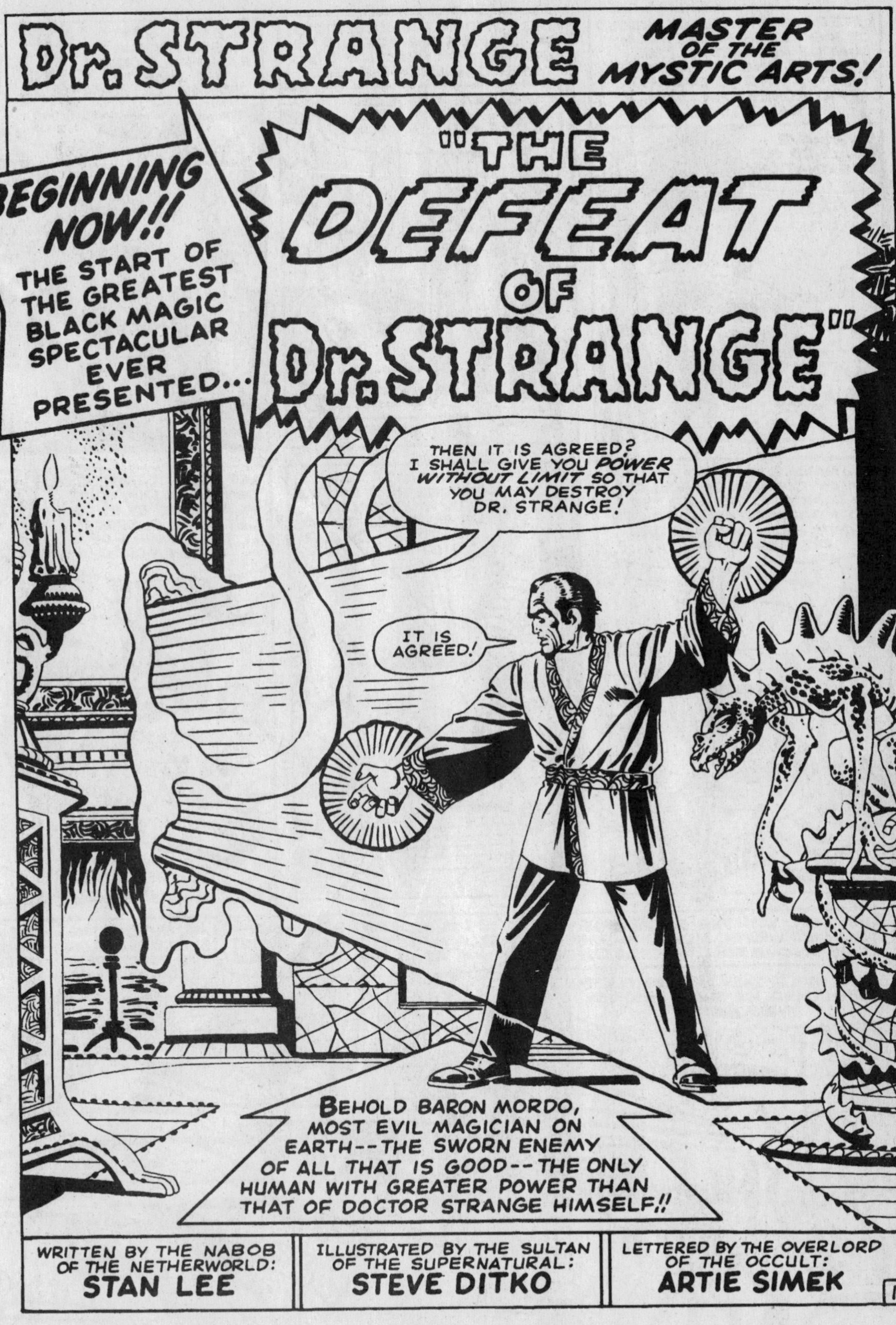
Dr. STRANGE
MASTER OF THE MYSTIC ARTS!
BEGINNING NOW!! THE START OF THE GREATEST BLACK MAGIC SPECTACULAR EVER PRESENTED...
"THE DEFEAT OF Dr. STRANGE"
THEN IT IS AGREED? I SHALL GIVE YOU POWER WITHOUT LIMIT SO THAT YOU MAY DESTROY DR. STRANGE!
IT IS AGREED!
BEHOLD BARON MORDO, MOST EVIL MAGICIAN ON EARTH--THE SWORN ENEMY OF ALL THAT IS GOOD--THE ONLY HUMAN WITH GREATER POWER THAN THAT OF DOCTOR STRANGE HIMSELF!!
WRITTEN BY THE NABOB OF THE NETHERWORLD: STAN LEE
ILLUSTRATED BY THE SULTAN OF THE SUPERNATURAL: STEVE DITKO
LETTERED BY THE OVERLORD OF THE OCCULT: ARTIE SIMEK
1

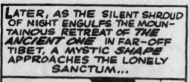

LATER, AS THE SILENT SHROUD OF NIGHT ENGULFS THE MOUNTAINOUS RETREAT OF *THE ANCIENT ONE* IN FAR-OFF TIBET, A MYSTIC *SHAPE* APPROACHES THE LONELY SANCTUM...

WE HAVE REACHED OUR DESTINATION!

WHILE, WITHIN THE COLD, STONE WALLS, *DR. STRANGE* AND HIS AGED MENTOR PRACTICE THEIR MYSTIC, AWESOME RITES...

YOU HAVE MASTERED THE SHADOWY ARTS QUITE WELL, MY SON....!

AND, OUTSIDE AGAIN

LET US NOW ASSUME OUR RIGHTFUL FORMS! THE TIME TO *STRIKE* HAS COME!

YOU WILL BOTH OBEY MY EVERY COMMAND-- FOLLOW MY ORDERS TO THE LETTER! WITH THE ADDITIONAL POWER I HAVE BEEN GIVEN, I CAN DO *ANYTHING!*

HOW EASILY I CAN CONJURE UP A SIMPLE SPELL WHICH CAUSES OUR PRESENCE TO GO UNNOTICED BY OUR VICTIMS INSIDE!

LET EVERY PROTECTIVE DEVICE WITHIN THIS PLACE BE SILENCED! LET NONE SUSPECT THE COMING OF BARON MORDO!

AND THEN, WITH THE SUDDEN FURY OF A DEMON'S WRATH, MORDO AND HIS TWO FEARSOME FOLLOWERS *ATTACK!*

NOW, WHILE THEY ARE COMPLETELY OFF-GUARD, WE SHALL DESTROY THEM *BOTH!*

IT IS *MORDO!* SAVE YOUR-SELF, MY SON! I SHALL RESIST HIM AS LONG AS I AM ABLE!

NO, ANCIENT ONE! YOUR SHIELD IS USELESS AGAINST THE POWER OF HIS ATTACK! I CANNOT LEAVE YOU!

2

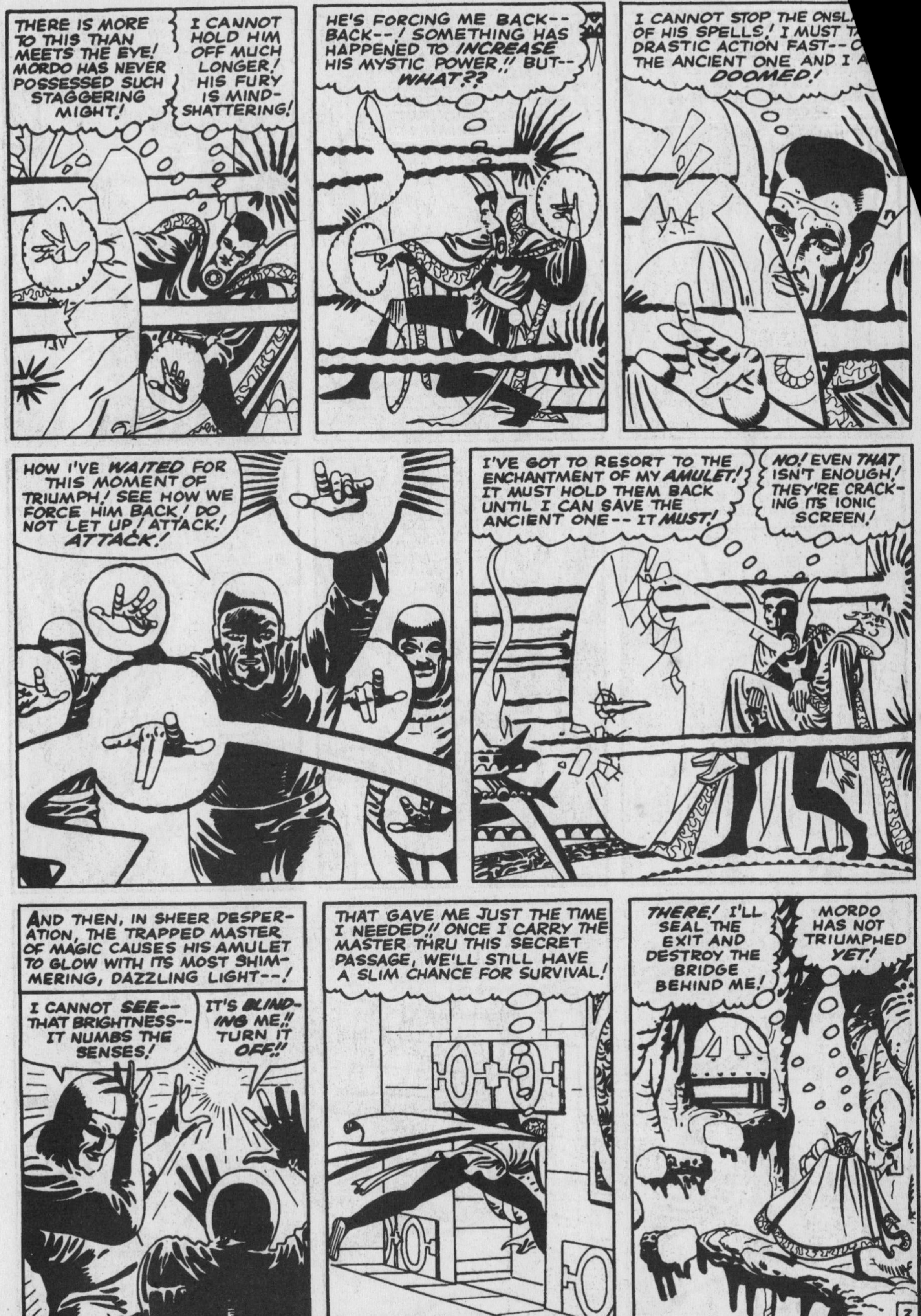
THERE IS MORE TO THIS THAN MEETS THE EYE! MORDO HAS NEVER POSSESSED SUCH STAGGERING MIGHT!
I CANNOT HOLD HIM OFF MUCH LONGER! HIS FURY IS MIND-SHATTERING!
HE'S FORCING ME BACK--BACK--! SOMETHING HAS HAPPENED TO INCREASE HIS MYSTIC POWER!! BUT--WHAT??
I CANNOT STOP THE ONSL OF HIS SPELLS! I MUST T DRASTIC ACTION FAST--O THE ANCIENT ONE AND I A DOOMED!
HOW I'VE WAITED FOR THIS MOMENT OF TRIUMPH! SEE HOW WE FORCE HIM BACK! DO NOT LET UP! ATTACK! ATTACK!
I'VE GOT TO RESORT TO THE ENCHANTMENT OF MY AMULET! IT MUST HOLD THEM BACK UNTIL I CAN SAVE THE ANCIENT ONE-- IT MUST!
NO! EVEN THAT ISN'T ENOUGH! THEY'RE CRACKING ITS IONIC SCREEN!
AND THEN, IN SHEER DESPERATION, THE TRAPPED MASTER OF MAGIC CAUSES HIS AMULET TO GLOW WITH ITS MOST SHIMMERING, DAZZLING LIGHT--!
I CANNOT SEE-- THAT BRIGHTNESS-- IT NUMBS THE SENSES!
IT'S BLINDING ME!! TURN IT OFF!!
THAT GAVE ME JUST THE TIME I NEEDED!! ONCE I CARRY THE MASTER THRU THIS SECRET PASSAGE, WE'LL STILL HAVE A SLIM CHANCE FOR SURVIVAL!
THERE! I'LL SEAL THE EXIT AND DESTROY THE BRIDGE BEHIND ME!
MORDO HAS NOT TRIUMPHED YET!
3

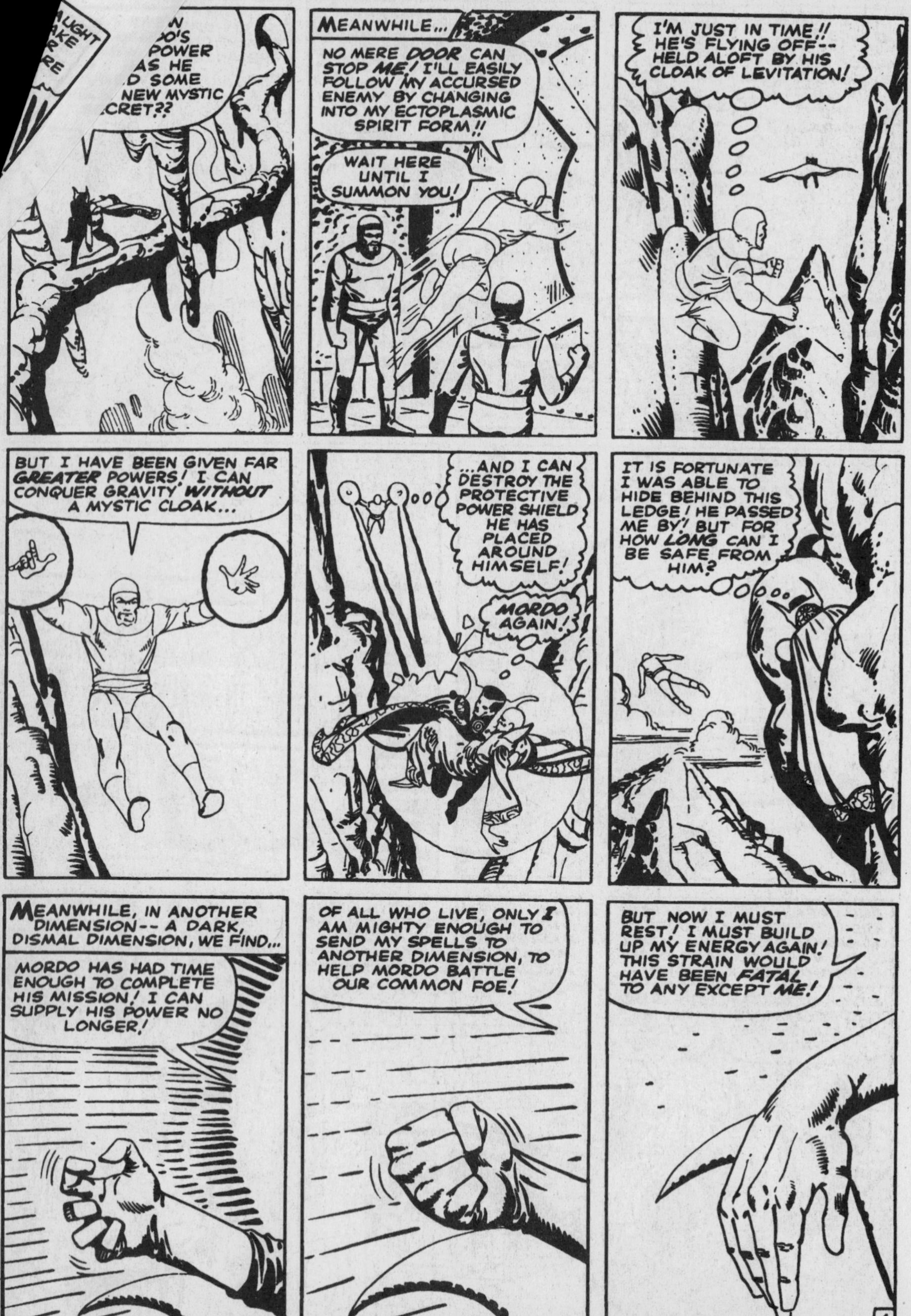
AUGHT AKE R RE
N O'S POWER AS HE D SOME NEW MYSTIC ECRET??
MEANWHILE...
NO MERE DOOR CAN STOP ME! I'LL EASILY FOLLOW MY ACCURSED ENEMY BY CHANGING INTO MY ECTOPLASMIC SPIRIT FORM!!
WAIT HERE UNTIL I SUMMON YOU!
I'M JUST IN TIME!! HE'S FLYING OFF-- HELD ALOFT BY HIS CLOAK OF LEVITATION!
BUT I HAVE BEEN GIVEN FAR GREATER POWERS! I CAN CONQUER GRAVITY WITHOUT A MYSTIC CLOAK...
...AND I CAN DESTROY THE PROTECTIVE POWER SHIELD HE HAS PLACED AROUND HIMSELF!
MORDO AGAIN!
IT IS FORTUNATE I WAS ABLE TO HIDE BEHIND THIS LEDGE! HE PASSED ME BY! BUT FOR HOW LONG CAN I BE SAFE FROM HIM?
MEANWHILE, IN ANOTHER DIMENSION-- A DARK, DISMAL DIMENSION, WE FIND...
MORDO HAS HAD TIME ENOUGH TO COMPLETE HIS MISSION! I CAN SUPPLY HIS POWER NO LONGER!
OF ALL WHO LIVE, ONLY I AM MIGHTY ENOUGH TO SEND MY SPELLS TO ANOTHER DIMENSION, TO HELP MORDO BATTLE OUR COMMON FOE!
BUT NOW I MUST REST! I MUST BUILD UP MY ENERGY AGAIN! THIS STRAIN WOULD HAVE BEEN FATAL TO ANY EXCEPT ME!
4

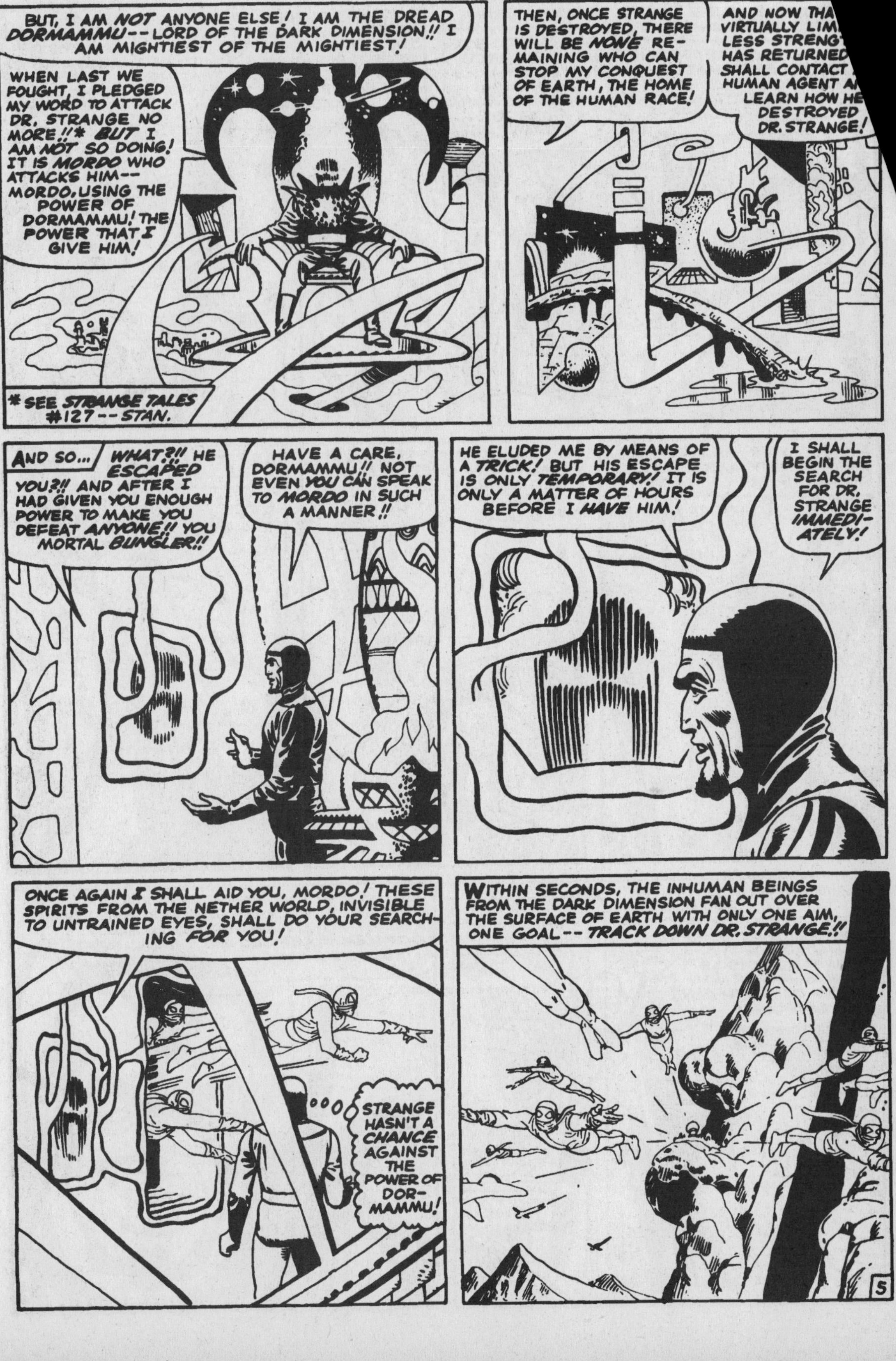
BUT, I AM NOT ANYONE ELSE! I AM THE DREAD DORMAMMU--LORD OF THE DARK DIMENSION!! I AM MIGHTIEST OF THE MIGHTIEST!
WHEN LAST WE FOUGHT, I PLEDGED MY WORD TO ATTACK DR. STRANGE NO MORE!!* BUT I AM NOT SO DOING! IT IS MORDO WHO ATTACKS HIM--MORDO, USING THE POWER OF DORMAMMU! THE POWER THAT I GIVE HIM!
* SEE STRANGE TALES #127--STAN.
THEN, ONCE STRANGE IS DESTROYED, THERE WILL BE NONE REMAINING WHO CAN STOP MY CONQUEST OF EARTH, THE HOME OF THE HUMAN RACE!
AND NOW THA
VIRTUALLY LIM
LESS STRENGT
HAS RETURNED
SHALL CONTACT
HUMAN AGENT A
LEARN HOW HE
DESTROYED
DR. STRANGE!
AND SO...
WHAT?!! HE ESCAPED YOU?!! AND AFTER I HAD GIVEN YOU ENOUGH POWER TO MAKE YOU DEFEAT ANYONE!! YOU MORTAL BUNGLER!!
HAVE A CARE, DORMAMMU!! NOT EVEN YOU CAN SPEAK TO MORDO IN SUCH A MANNER!!
HE ELUDED ME BY MEANS OF A TRICK! BUT HIS ESCAPE IS ONLY TEMPORARY! IT IS ONLY A MATTER OF HOURS BEFORE I HAVE HIM!
I SHALL BEGIN THE SEARCH FOR DR. STRANGE IMMEDIATELY!
ONCE AGAIN I SHALL AID YOU, MORDO! THESE SPIRITS FROM THE NETHER WORLD, INVISIBLE TO UNTRAINED EYES, SHALL DO YOUR SEARCHING FOR YOU!
STRANGE HASN'T A CHANCE AGAINST THE POWER OF DORMAMMU!
WITHIN SECONDS, THE INHUMAN BEINGS FROM THE DARK DIMENSION FAN OUT OVER THE SURFACE OF EARTH WITH ONLY ONE AIM, ONE GOAL--TRACK DOWN DR. STRANGE!!
5

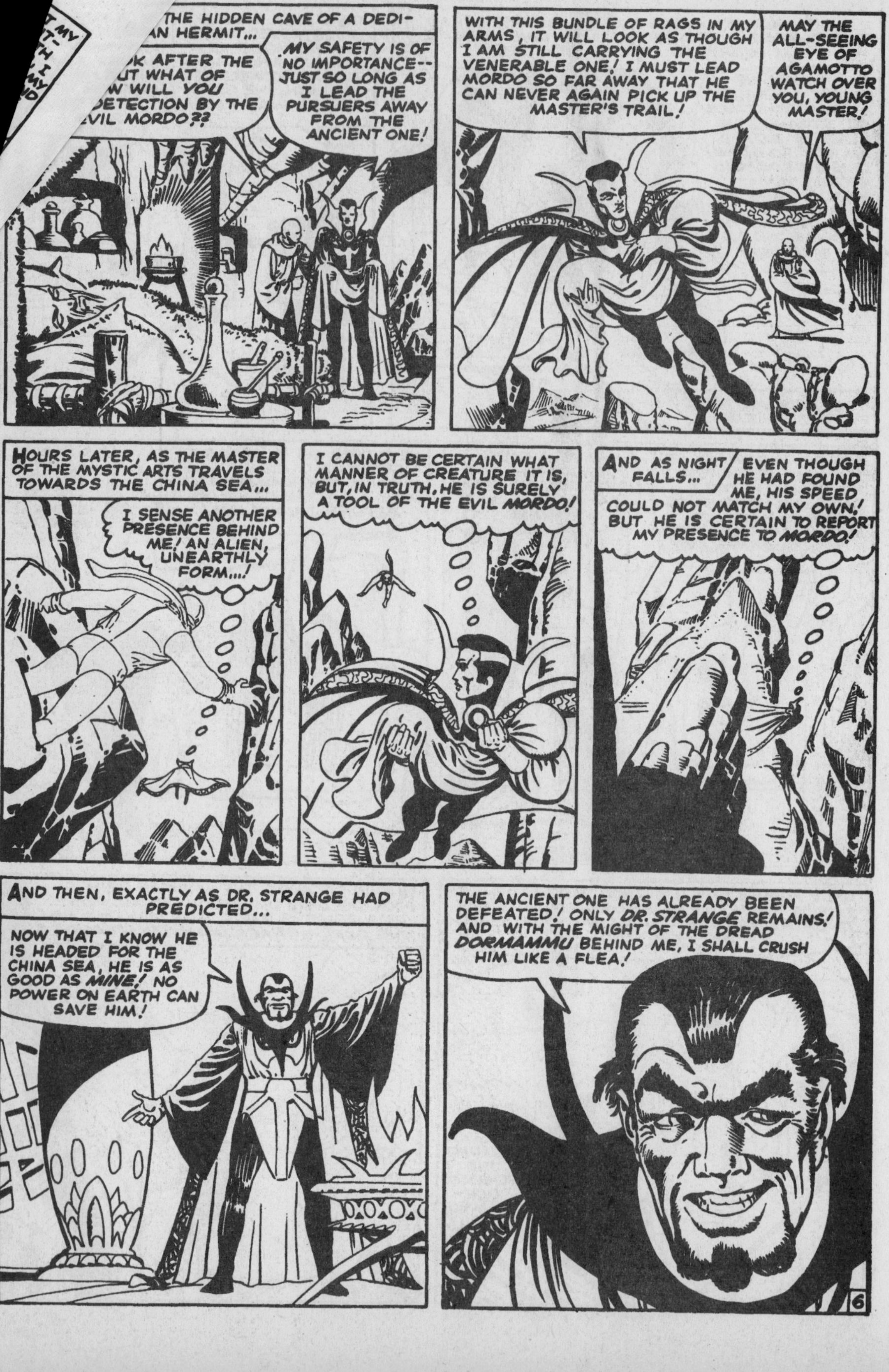
THE HIDDEN CAVE OF A DEDI-
AN HERMIT...
OK AFTER THE
UT WHAT OF
W WILL YOU
DETECTION BY THE
EVIL MORDO??
MY SAFETY IS OF NO IMPORTANCE-- JUST SO LONG AS I LEAD THE PURSUERS AWAY FROM THE ANCIENT ONE!
WITH THIS BUNDLE OF RAGS IN MY ARMS, IT WILL LOOK AS THOUGH I AM STILL CARRYING THE VENERABLE ONE! I MUST LEAD MORDO SO FAR AWAY THAT HE CAN NEVER AGAIN PICK UP THE MASTER'S TRAIL!
MAY THE ALL-SEEING EYE OF AGAMOTTO WATCH OVER YOU, YOUNG MASTER!
HOURS LATER, AS THE MASTER OF THE MYSTIC ARTS TRAVELS TOWARDS THE CHINA SEA...
I SENSE ANOTHER PRESENCE BEHIND ME! AN ALIEN, UNEARTHLY FORM...!
I CANNOT BE CERTAIN WHAT MANNER OF CREATURE IT IS, BUT, IN TRUTH, HE IS SURELY A TOOL OF THE EVIL MORDO!
AND AS NIGHT FALLS...
EVEN THOUGH HE HAD FOUND ME, HIS SPEED COULD NOT MATCH MY OWN! BUT HE IS CERTAIN TO REPORT MY PRESENCE TO MORDO!
AND THEN, EXACTLY AS DR. STRANGE HAD PREDICTED...
NOW THAT I KNOW HE IS HEADED FOR THE CHINA SEA, HE IS AS GOOD AS MINE! NO POWER ON EARTH CAN SAVE HIM!
THE ANCIENT ONE HAS ALREADY BEEN DEFEATED! ONLY DR. STRANGE REMAINS! AND WITH THE MIGHT OF THE DREAD DORMAMMU BEHIND ME, I SHALL CRUSH HIM LIKE A FLEA!
6

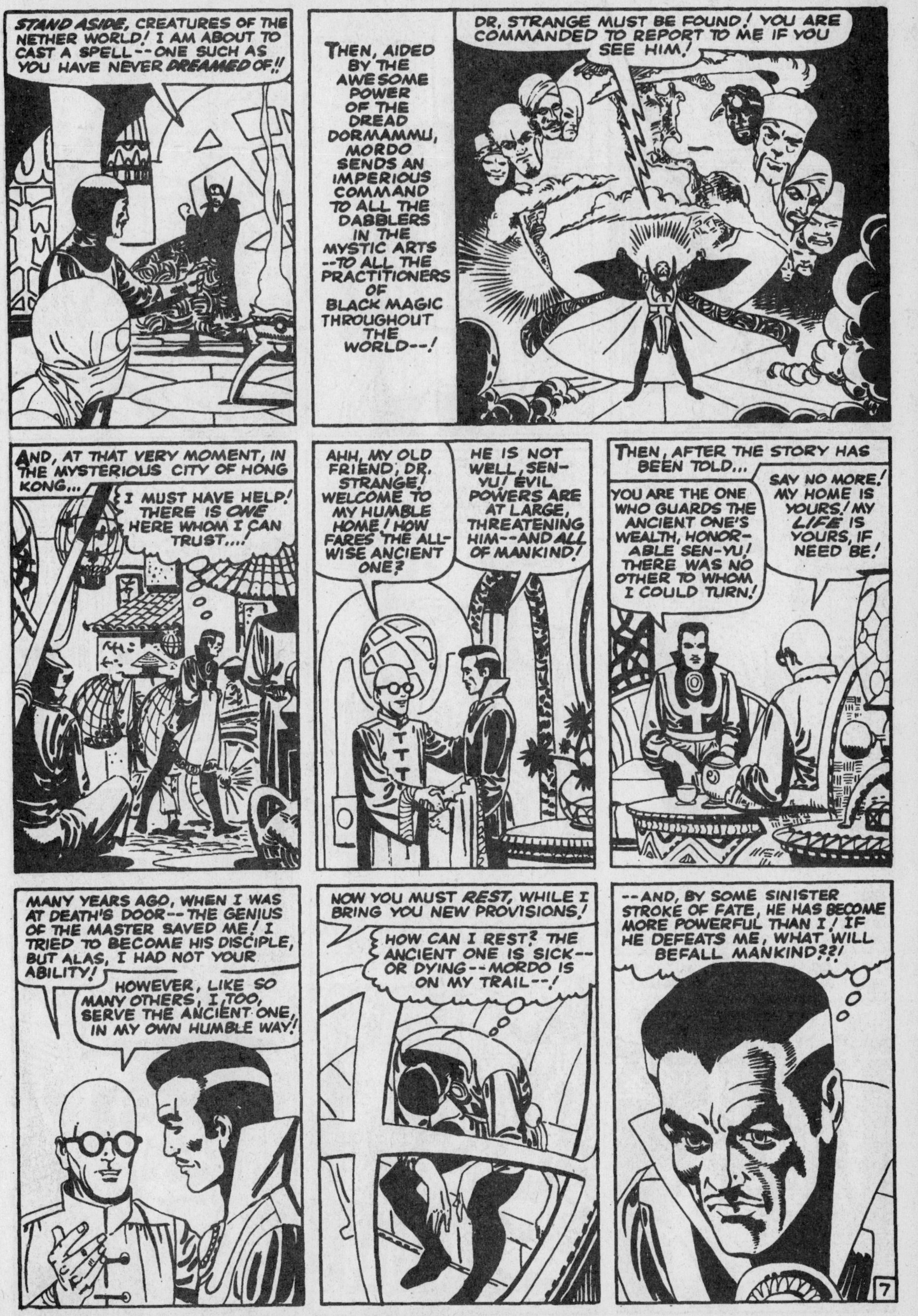
STAND ASIDE, CREATURES OF THE NETHER WORLD! I AM ABOUT TO CAST A SPELL--ONE SUCH AS YOU HAVE NEVER DREAMED OF!!
THEN, AIDED BY THE AWESOME POWER OF THE DREAD DORMAMMU, MORDO SENDS AN IMPERIOUS COMMAND TO ALL THE DABBLERS IN THE MYSTIC ARTS --TO ALL THE PRACTITIONERS OF BLACK MAGIC THROUGHOUT THE WORLD--!
DR. STRANGE MUST BE FOUND! YOU ARE COMMANDED TO REPORT TO ME IF YOU SEE HIM!
AND, AT THAT VERY MOMENT, IN THE MYSTERIOUS CITY OF HONG KONG...
I MUST HAVE HELP! THERE IS ONE HERE WHOM I CAN TRUST....!
AHH, MY OLD FRIEND, DR. STRANGE! WELCOME TO MY HUMBLE HOME! HOW FARES THE ALL-WISE ANCIENT ONE?
HE IS NOT WELL, SEN-YU! EVIL POWERS ARE AT LARGE, THREATENING HIM--AND ALL OF MANKIND!
THEN, AFTER THE STORY HAS BEEN TOLD...
YOU ARE THE ONE WHO GUARDS THE ANCIENT ONE'S WEALTH, HONORABLE SEN-YU! THERE WAS NO OTHER TO WHOM I COULD TURN!
SAY NO MORE! MY HOME IS YOURS! MY LIFE IS YOURS, IF NEED BE!
MANY YEARS AGO, WHEN I WAS AT DEATH'S DOOR--THE GENIUS OF THE MASTER SAVED ME! I TRIED TO BECOME HIS DISCIPLE, BUT ALAS, I HAD NOT YOUR ABILITY!
HOWEVER, LIKE SO MANY OTHERS, I TOO, SERVE THE ANCIENT ONE, IN MY OWN HUMBLE WAY!
NOW YOU MUST REST, WHILE I BRING YOU NEW PROVISIONS!
HOW CAN I REST? THE ANCIENT ONE IS SICK--OR DYING--MORDO IS ON MY TRAIL--!
--AND, BY SOME SINISTER STROKE OF FATE, HE HAS BECOME MORE POWERFUL THAN I! IF HE DEFEATS ME, WHAT WILL BEFALL MANKIND??!
7

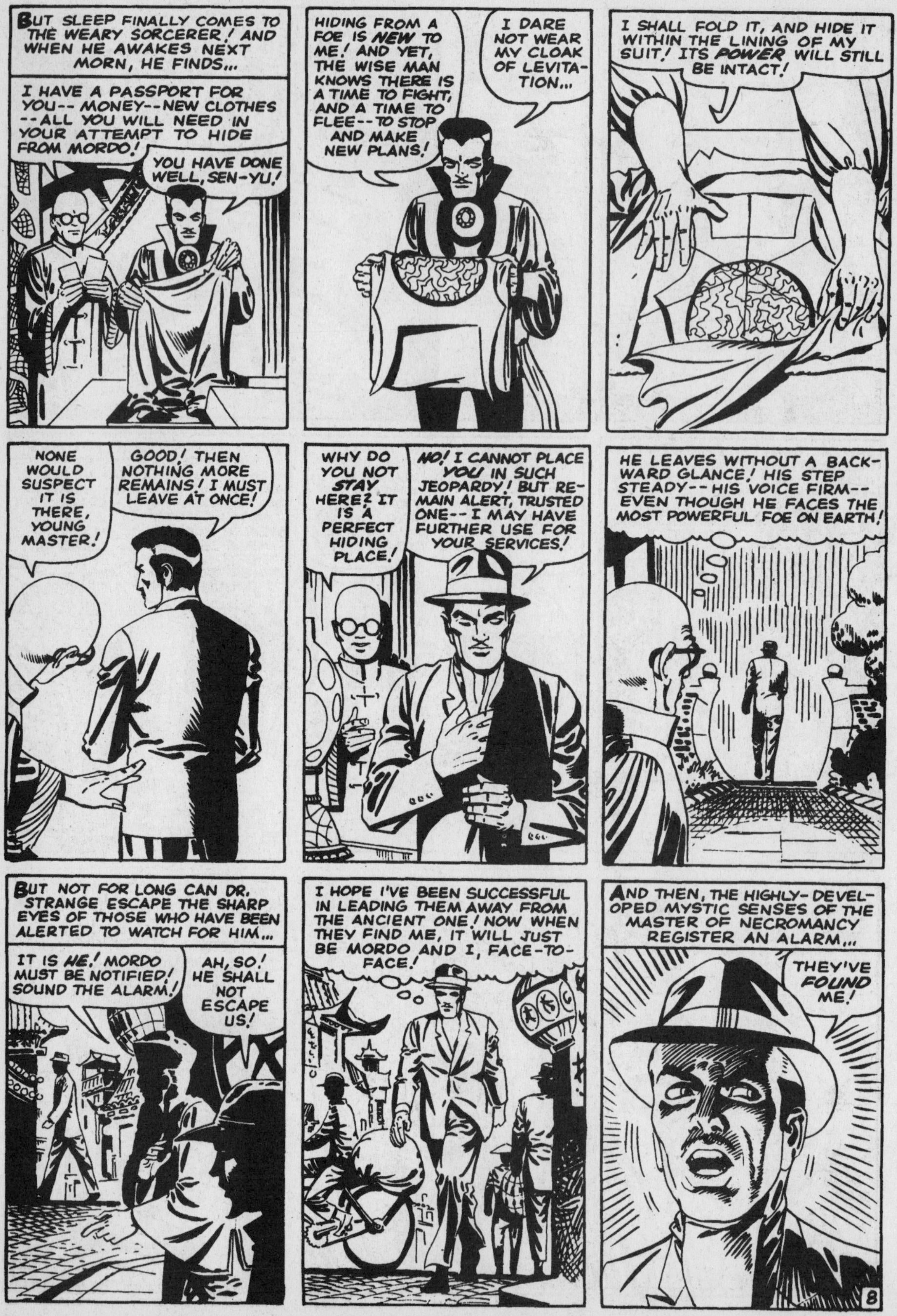
BUT SLEEP FINALLY COMES TO THE WEARY SORCERER! AND WHEN HE AWAKES NEXT MORN, HE FINDS...
I HAVE A PASSPORT FOR YOU-- MONEY--NEW CLOTHES --ALL YOU WILL NEED IN YOUR ATTEMPT TO HIDE FROM MORDO!
YOU HAVE DONE WELL, SEN-YU!
HIDING FROM A FOE IS NEW TO ME! AND YET, THE WISE MAN KNOWS THERE IS A TIME TO FIGHT, AND A TIME TO FLEE--TO STOP AND MAKE NEW PLANS!
I DARE NOT WEAR MY CLOAK OF LEVITATION...
I SHALL FOLD IT, AND HIDE IT WITHIN THE LINING OF MY SUIT! ITS POWER WILL STILL BE INTACT!
NONE WOULD SUSPECT IT IS THERE, YOUNG MASTER!
GOOD! THEN NOTHING MORE REMAINS! I MUST LEAVE AT ONCE!
WHY DO YOU NOT STAY HERE? IT IS A PERFECT HIDING PLACE!
NO! I CANNOT PLACE YOU IN SUCH JEOPARDY! BUT REMAIN ALERT, TRUSTED ONE-- I MAY HAVE FURTHER USE FOR YOUR SERVICES!
HE LEAVES WITHOUT A BACKWARD GLANCE! HIS STEP STEADY-- HIS VOICE FIRM-- EVEN THOUGH HE FACES THE MOST POWERFUL FOE ON EARTH!
BUT NOT FOR LONG CAN DR. STRANGE ESCAPE THE SHARP EYES OF THOSE WHO HAVE BEEN ALERTED TO WATCH FOR HIM...
IT IS HE! MORDO MUST BE NOTIFIED! SOUND THE ALARM!
AH, SO! HE SHALL NOT ESCAPE US!
I HOPE I'VE BEEN SUCCESSFUL IN LEADING THEM AWAY FROM THE ANCIENT ONE! NOW WHEN THEY FIND ME, IT WILL JUST BE MORDO AND I, FACE-TO-FACE!
AND THEN, THE HIGHLY-DEVELOPED MYSTIC SENSES OF THE MASTER OF NECROMANCY REGISTER AN ALARM...
THEY'VE FOUND ME!
8

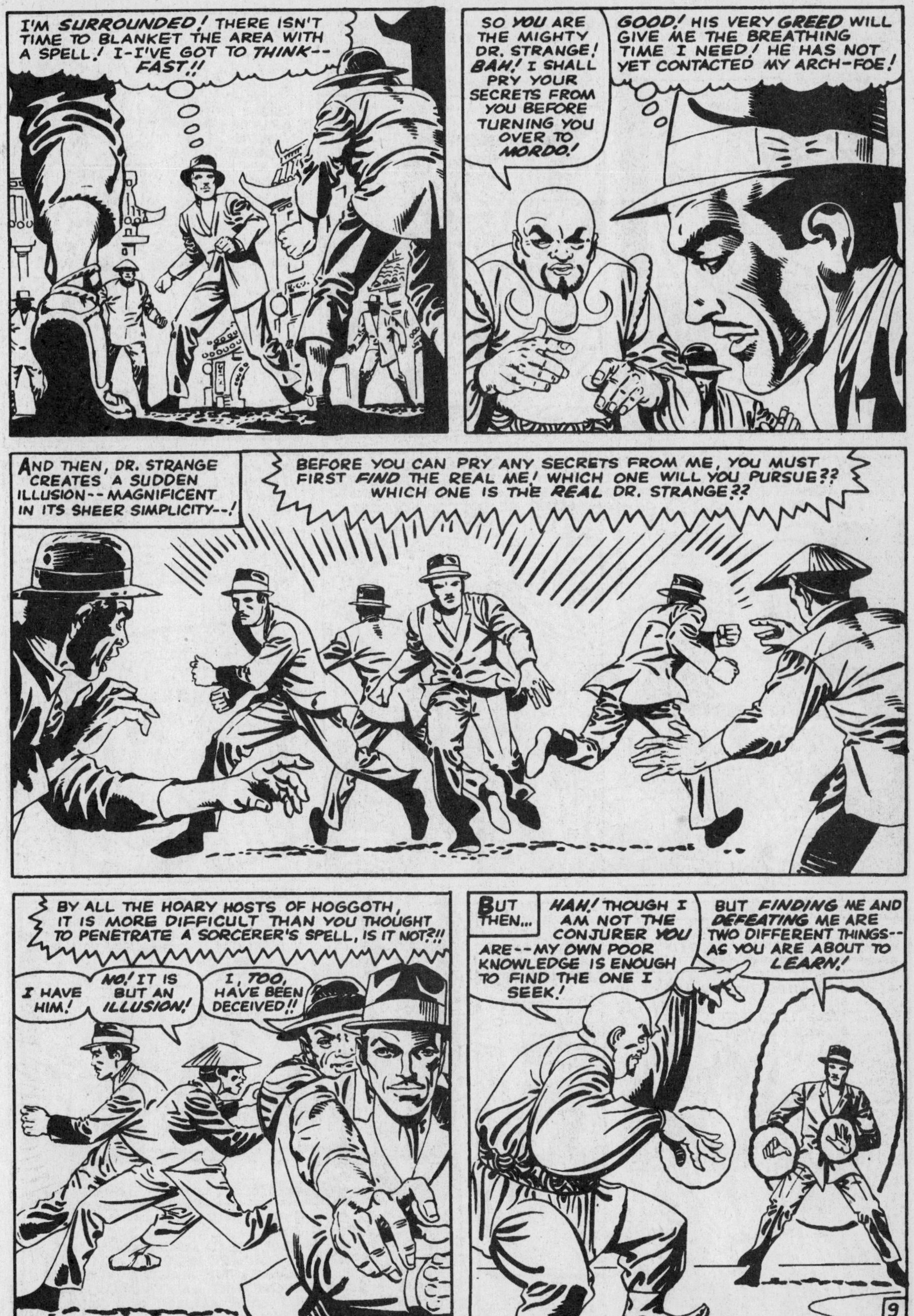
I'M SURROUNDED! THERE ISN'T TIME TO BLANKET THE AREA WITH A SPELL! I-I'VE GOT TO THINK-- FAST!!
SO YOU ARE THE MIGHTY DR. STRANGE! BAH! I SHALL PRY YOUR SECRETS FROM YOU BEFORE TURNING YOU OVER TO MORDO!
GOOD! HIS VERY GREED WILL GIVE ME THE BREATHING TIME I NEED! HE HAS NOT YET CONTACTED MY ARCH-FOE!
AND THEN, DR. STRANGE CREATES A SUDDEN ILLUSION-- MAGNIFICENT IN ITS SHEER SIMPLICITY--!
BEFORE YOU CAN PRY ANY SECRETS FROM ME, YOU MUST FIRST FIND THE REAL ME! WHICH ONE WILL YOU PURSUE?? WHICH ONE IS THE REAL DR. STRANGE??
BY ALL THE HOARY HOSTS OF HOGGOTH, IT IS MORE DIFFICULT THAN YOU THOUGHT TO PENETRATE A SORCERER'S SPELL, IS IT NOT?!!
I HAVE HIM!
NO! IT IS BUT AN ILLUSION!
I, TOO, HAVE BEEN DECEIVED!!
BUT THEN...
HAH! THOUGH I AM NOT THE CONJURER YOU ARE-- MY OWN POOR KNOWLEDGE IS ENOUGH TO FIND THE ONE I SEEK!
BUT FINDING ME AND DEFEATING ME ARE TWO DIFFERENT THINGS-- AS YOU ARE ABOUT TO LEARN!
9

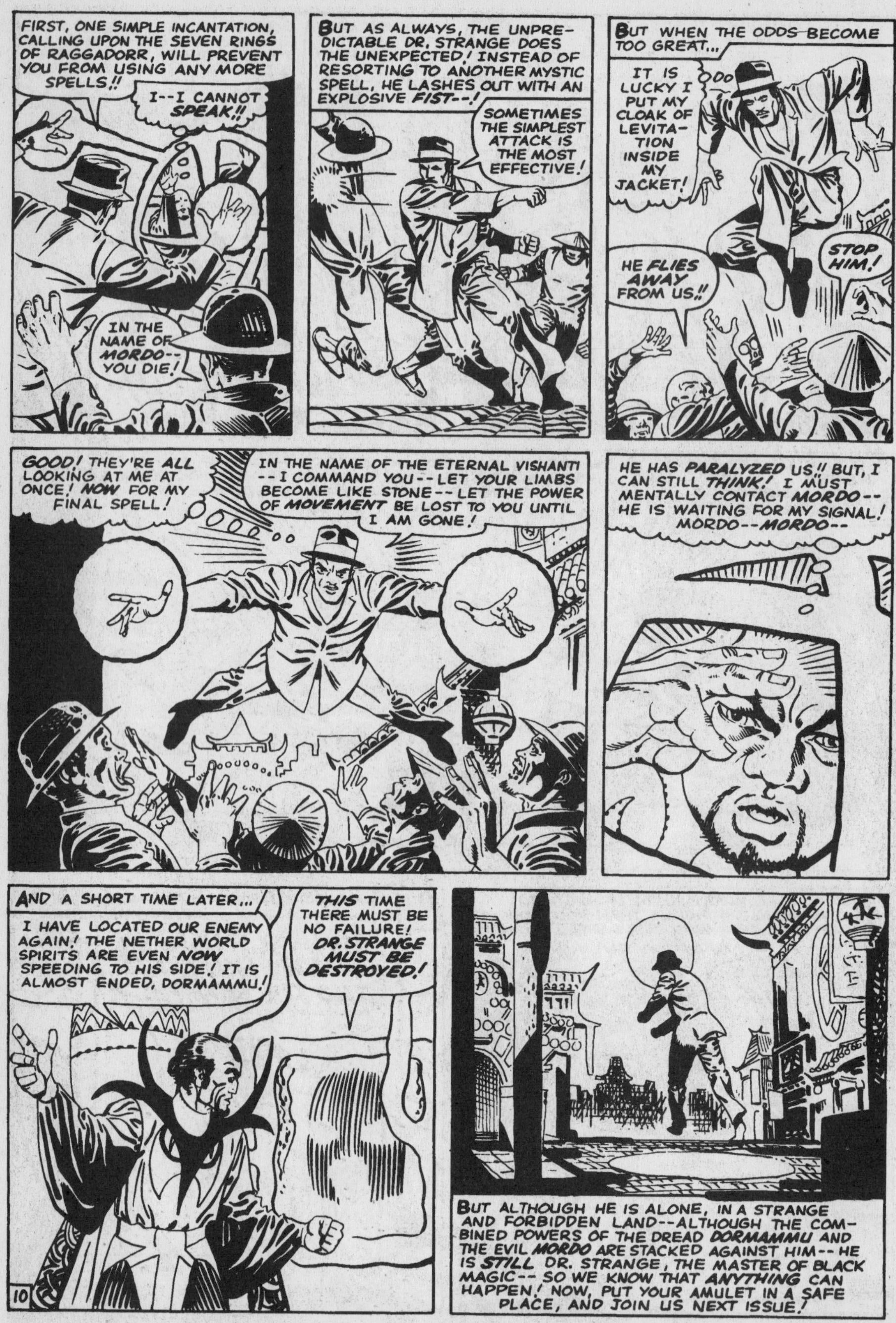

FIRST, ONE SIMPLE INCANTATION, CALLING UPON THE SEVEN RINGS OF RAGGADORR, WILL PREVENT YOU FROM USING ANY MORE SPELLS!!
I--I CANNOT SPEAK!!
IN THE NAME OF MORDO-- YOU DIE!
BUT AS ALWAYS, THE UNPREDICTABLE DR. STRANGE DOES THE UNEXPECTED! INSTEAD OF RESORTING TO ANOTHER MYSTIC SPELL, HE LASHES OUT WITH AN EXPLOSIVE FIST--!
SOMETIMES THE SIMPLEST ATTACK IS THE MOST EFFECTIVE!
BUT WHEN THE ODDS BECOME TOO GREAT...
IT IS LUCKY I PUT MY CLOAK OF LEVITATION INSIDE MY JACKET!
HE FLIES AWAY FROM US!!
STOP HIM!
GOOD! THEY'RE ALL LOOKING AT ME AT ONCE! NOW FOR MY FINAL SPELL!
IN THE NAME OF THE ETERNAL VISHANTI -- I COMMAND YOU -- LET YOUR LIMBS BECOME LIKE STONE -- LET THE POWER OF MOVEMENT BE LOST TO YOU UNTIL I AM GONE!
HE HAS PARALYZED US!! BUT, I CAN STILL THINK! I MUST MENTALLY CONTACT MORDO -- HE IS WAITING FOR MY SIGNAL! MORDO--MORDO--
AND A SHORT TIME LATER...
I HAVE LOCATED OUR ENEMY AGAIN! THE NETHER WORLD SPIRITS ARE EVEN NOW SPEEDING TO HIS SIDE! IT IS ALMOST ENDED, DORMAMMU!
THIS TIME THERE MUST BE NO FAILURE! DR. STRANGE MUST BE DESTROYED!
BUT ALTHOUGH HE IS ALONE, IN A STRANGE AND FORBIDDEN LAND--ALTHOUGH THE COMBINED POWERS OF THE DREAD DORMAMMU AND THE EVIL MORDO ARE STACKED AGAINST HIM-- HE IS STILL DR. STRANGE, THE MASTER OF BLACK MAGIC-- SO WE KNOW THAT ANYTHING CAN HAPPEN! NOW, PUT YOUR AMULET IN A SAFE PLACE, AND JOIN US NEXT ISSUE!
10

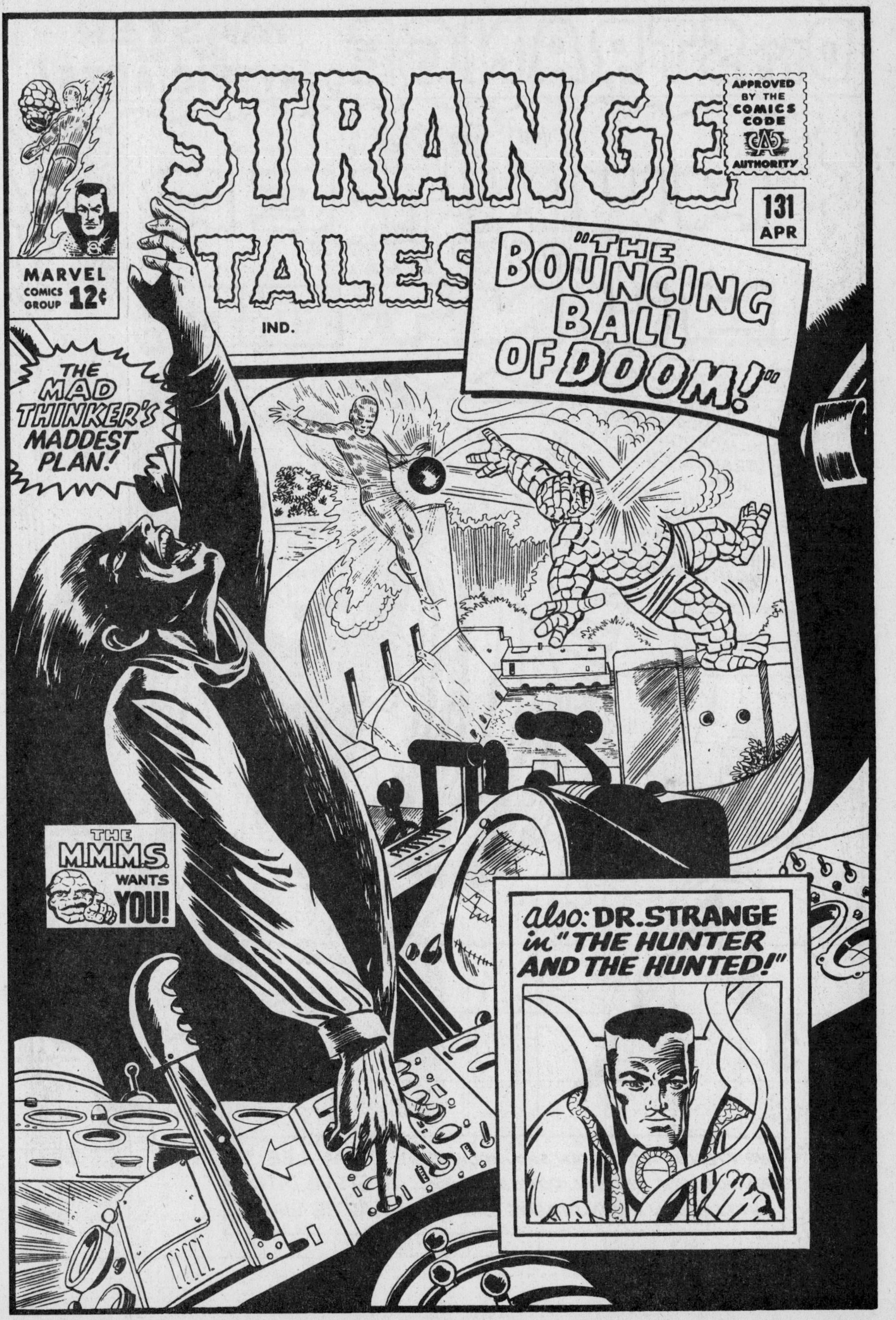
STRANGE TALES
APPROVED BY THE COMICS CODE AUTHORITY
131 APR
MARVEL COMICS GROUP 12¢
IND.
"THE BOUNCING BALL OF DOOM!"
THE MAD THINKER'S MADDEST PLAN!
THE M.M.M.S. WANTS YOU!
also: DR. STRANGE in "THE HUNTER AND THE HUNTED!"

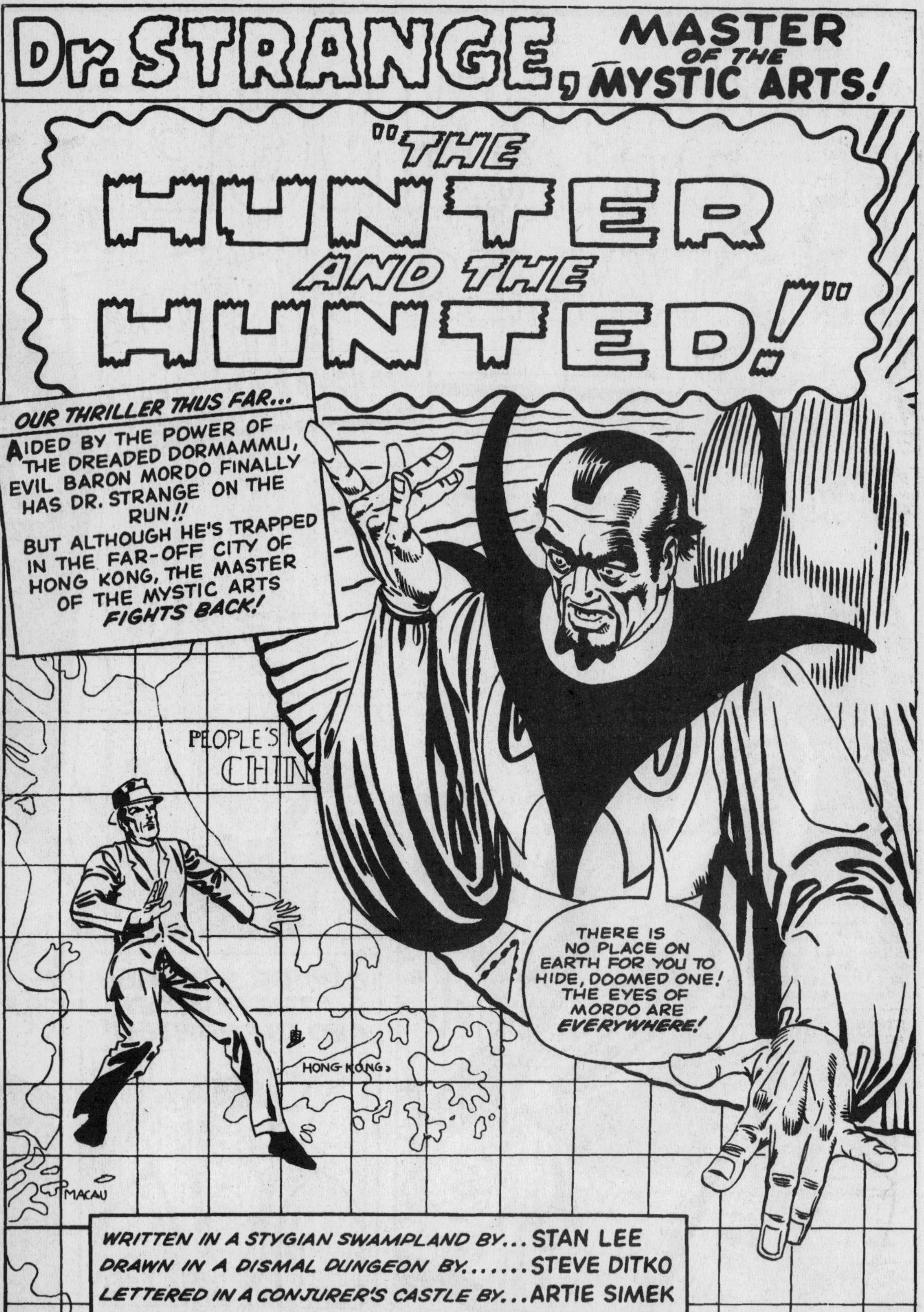

Dr. STRANGE, MASTER OF THE MYSTIC ARTS!
"THE HUNTER AND THE HUNTED!"
OUR THRILLER THUS FAR...
AIDED BY THE POWER OF THE DREADED DORMAMMU, EVIL BARON MORDO FINALLY HAS DR. STRANGE ON THE RUN!! BUT ALTHOUGH HE'S TRAPPED IN THE FAR-OFF CITY OF HONG KONG, THE MASTER OF THE MYSTIC ARTS FIGHTS BACK!
PEOPLE'S
CHIN
HONG KONG
MACAU
THERE IS NO PLACE ON EARTH FOR YOU TO HIDE, DOOMED ONE! THE EYES OF MORDO ARE EVERYWHERE!
WRITTEN IN A STYGIAN SWAMPLAND BY... STAN LEE
DRAWN IN A DISMAL DUNGEON BY...... STEVE DITKO
LETTERED IN A CONJURER'S CASTLE BY... ARTIE SIMEK
1

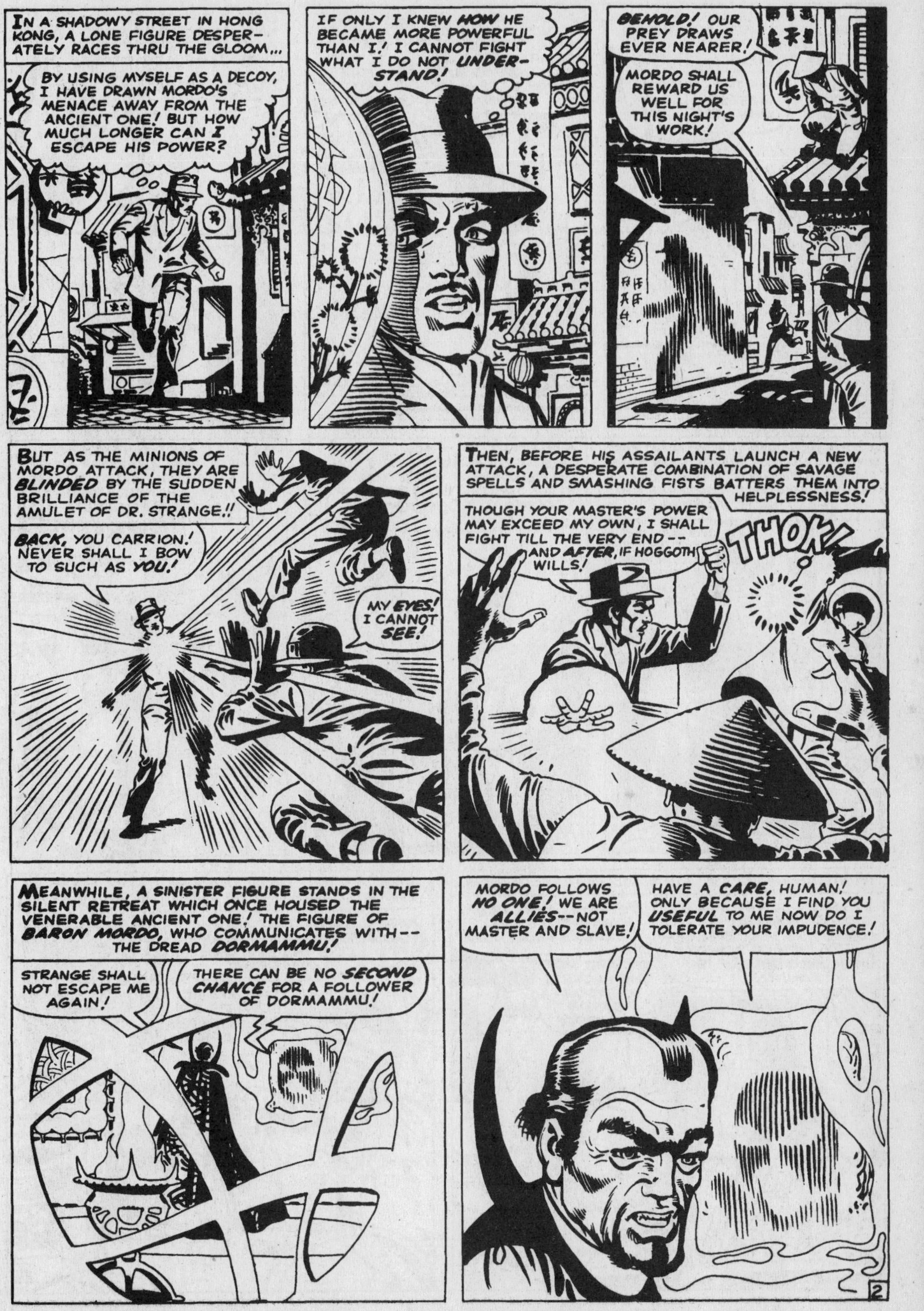
IN A SHADOWY STREET IN HONG KONG, A LONE FIGURE DESPERATELY RACES THRU THE GLOOM...
BY USING MYSELF AS A DECOY, I HAVE DRAWN MORDO'S MENACE AWAY FROM THE ANCIENT ONE! BUT HOW MUCH LONGER CAN I ESCAPE HIS POWER?
IF ONLY I KNEW HOW HE BECAME MORE POWERFUL THAN I! I CANNOT FIGHT WHAT I DO NOT UNDERSTAND!
BEHOLD! OUR PREY DRAWS EVER NEARER!
MORDO SHALL REWARD US WELL FOR THIS NIGHT'S WORK!
BUT AS THE MINIONS OF MORDO ATTACK, THEY ARE BLINDED BY THE SUDDEN BRILLIANCE OF THE AMULET OF DR. STRANGE!!
BACK, YOU CARRION! NEVER SHALL I BOW TO SUCH AS YOU!
MY EYES! I CANNOT SEE!
THEN, BEFORE HIS ASSAILANTS LAUNCH A NEW ATTACK, A DESPERATE COMBINATION OF SAVAGE SPELLS AND SMASHING FISTS BATTERS THEM INTO HELPLESSNESS!
THOUGH YOUR MASTER'S POWER MAY EXCEED MY OWN, I SHALL FIGHT TILL THE VERY END -- AND AFTER, IF HOGGOTH WILLS!
THOK!
MEANWHILE, A SINISTER FIGURE STANDS IN THE SILENT RETREAT WHICH ONCE HOUSED THE VENERABLE ANCIENT ONE! THE FIGURE OF BARON MORDO, WHO COMMUNICATES WITH -- THE DREAD DORMAMMU!
STRANGE SHALL NOT ESCAPE ME AGAIN!
THERE CAN BE NO SECOND CHANCE FOR A FOLLOWER OF DORMAMMU!
MORDO FOLLOWS NO ONE! WE ARE ALLIES--NOT MASTER AND SLAVE!
HAVE A CARE, HUMAN! ONLY BECAUSE I FIND YOU USEFUL TO ME NOW DO I TOLERATE YOUR IMPUDENCE!
2

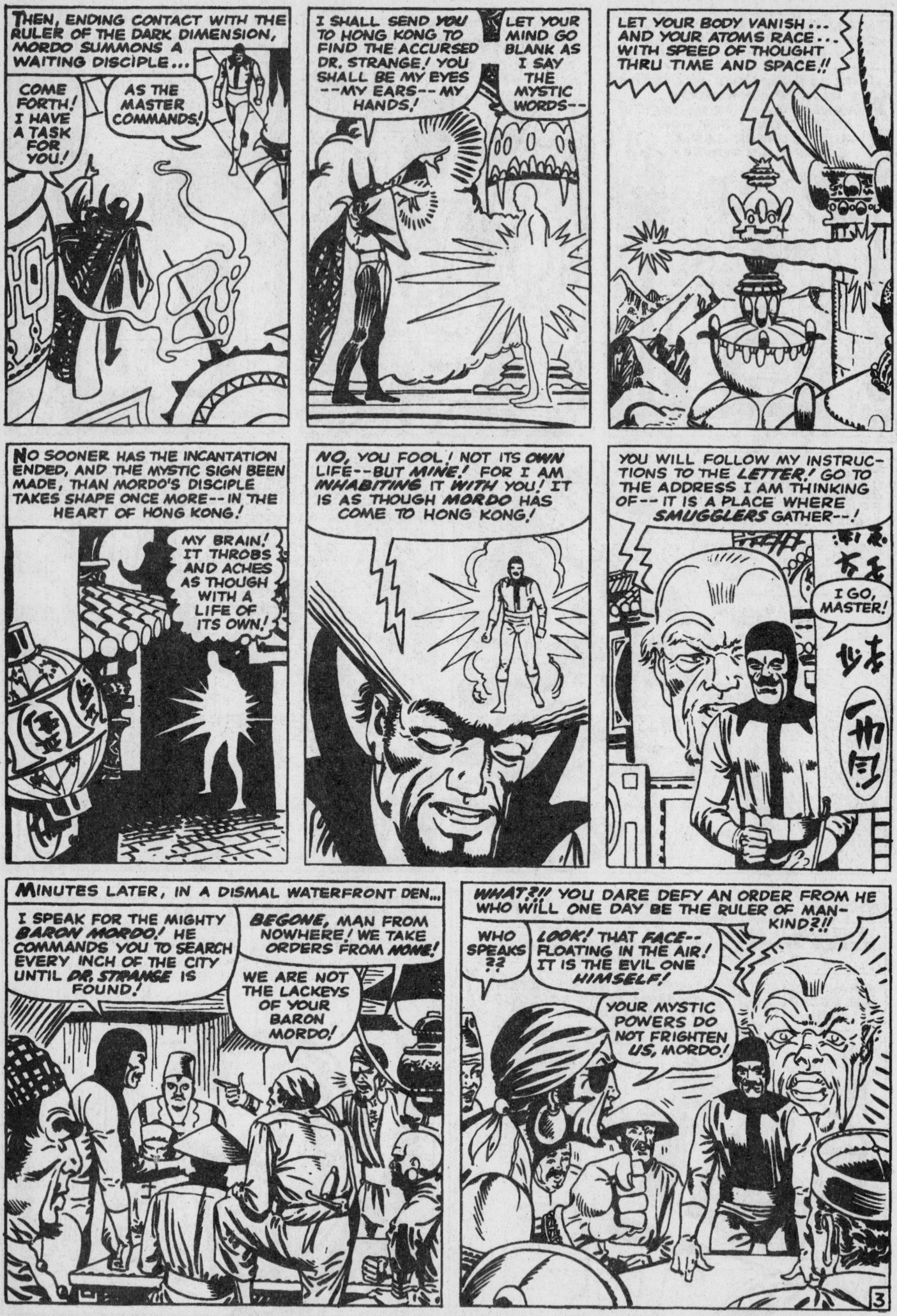
THEN, ENDING CONTACT WITH THE RULER OF THE DARK DIMENSION, MORDO SUMMONS A WAITING DISCIPLE...
COME FORTH! I HAVE A TASK FOR YOU!
AS THE MASTER COMMANDS!
I SHALL SEND YOU TO HONG KONG TO FIND THE ACCURSED DR. STRANGE! YOU SHALL BE MY EYES --MY EARS-- MY HANDS!
LET YOUR MIND GO BLANK AS I SAY THE MYSTIC WORDS--
LET YOUR BODY VANISH... AND YOUR ATOMS RACE... WITH SPEED OF THOUGHT THRU TIME AND SPACE!!
NO SOONER HAS THE INCANTATION ENDED, AND THE MYSTIC SIGN BEEN MADE, THAN MORDO'S DISCIPLE TAKES SHAPE ONCE MORE--IN THE HEART OF HONG KONG!
MY BRAIN! IT THROBS AND ACHES AS THOUGH WITH A LIFE OF ITS OWN!
NO, YOU FOOL! NOT ITS OWN LIFE--BUT MINE! FOR I AM INHABITING IT WITH YOU! IT IS AS THOUGH MORDO HAS COME TO HONG KONG!
YOU WILL FOLLOW MY INSTRUCTIONS TO THE LETTER! GO TO THE ADDRESS I AM THINKING OF-- IT IS A PLACE WHERE SMUGGLERS GATHER--!
I GO, MASTER!
MINUTES LATER, IN A DISMAL WATERFRONT DEN...
I SPEAK FOR THE MIGHTY BARON MORDO! HE COMMANDS YOU TO SEARCH EVERY INCH OF THE CITY UNTIL DR. STRANGE IS FOUND!
BEGONE, MAN FROM NOWHERE! WE TAKE ORDERS FROM NONE!
WE ARE NOT THE LACKEYS OF YOUR BARON MORDO!
WHAT?!! YOU DARE DEFY AN ORDER FROM HE WHO WILL ONE DAY BE THE RULER OF MAN-KIND?!!
WHO SPEAKS ??
LOOK! THAT FACE-- FLOATING IN THE AIR! IT IS THE EVIL ONE HIMSELF!
YOUR MYSTIC POWERS DO NOT FRIGHTEN US, MORDO!
3

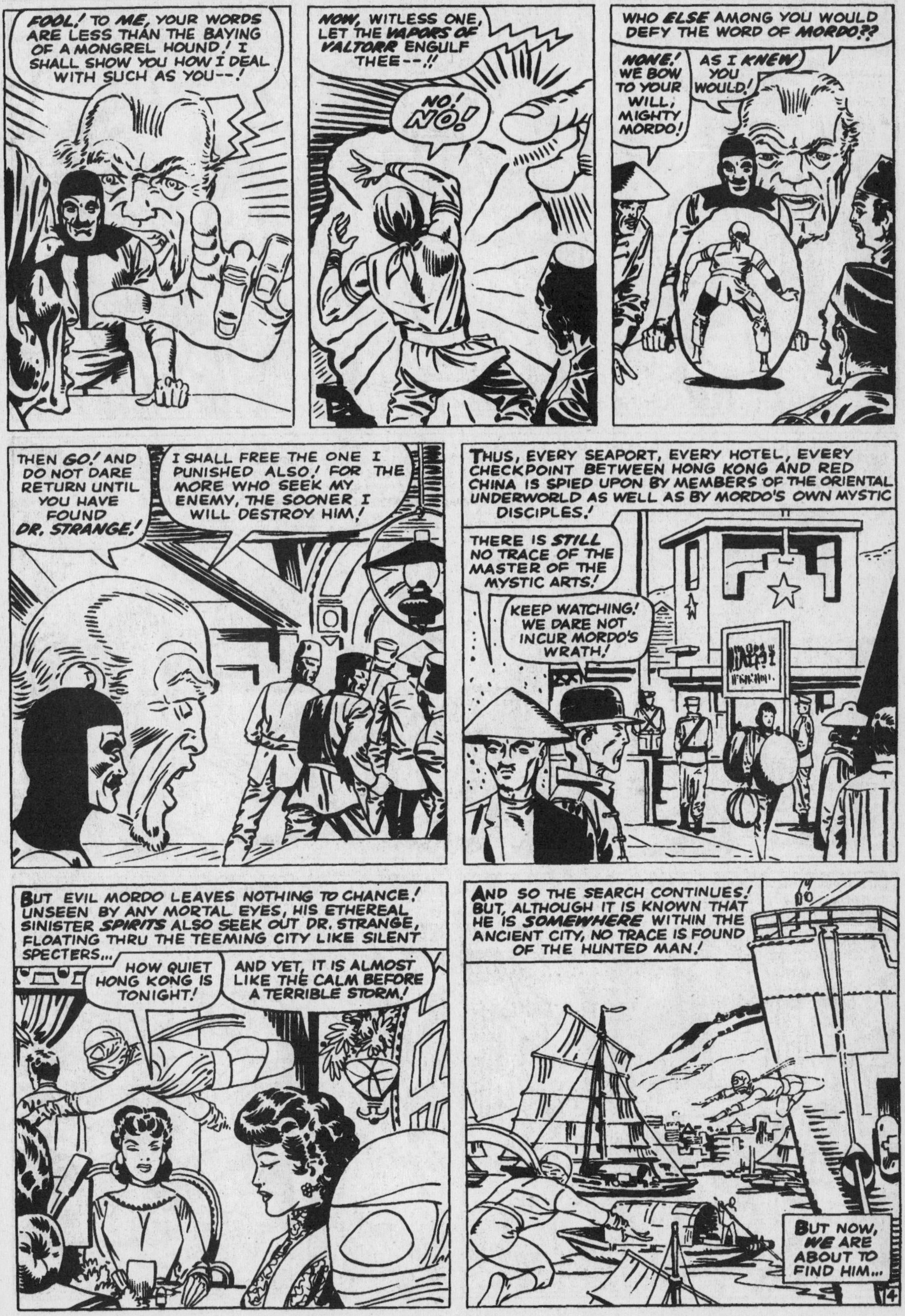
FOOL! TO ME, YOUR WORDS ARE LESS THAN THE BAYING OF A MONGREL HOUND! I SHALL SHOW YOU HOW I DEAL WITH SUCH AS YOU--!
NOW, WITLESS ONE, LET THE VAPORS OF VALTORR ENGULF THEE--!!
NO! NO!
WHO ELSE AMONG YOU WOULD DEFY THE WORD OF MORDO??
NONE! WE BOW TO YOUR WILL, MIGHTY MORDO!
AS I KNEW YOU WOULD!
THEN GO! AND DO NOT DARE RETURN UNTIL YOU HAVE FOUND DR. STRANGE!
I SHALL FREE THE ONE I PUNISHED ALSO! FOR THE MORE WHO SEEK MY ENEMY, THE SOONER I WILL DESTROY HIM!
THUS, EVERY SEAPORT, EVERY HOTEL, EVERY CHECKPOINT BETWEEN HONG KONG AND RED CHINA IS SPIED UPON BY MEMBERS OF THE ORIENTAL UNDERWORLD AS WELL AS BY MORDO'S OWN MYSTIC DISCIPLES!
THERE IS STILL NO TRACE OF THE MASTER OF THE MYSTIC ARTS!
KEEP WATCHING! WE DARE NOT INCUR MORDO'S WRATH!
BUT EVIL MORDO LEAVES NOTHING TO CHANCE! UNSEEN BY ANY MORTAL EYES, HIS ETHEREAL SINISTER SPIRITS ALSO SEEK OUT DR. STRANGE, FLOATING THRU THE TEEMING CITY LIKE SILENT SPECTERS...
HOW QUIET HONG KONG IS TONIGHT!
AND YET, IT IS ALMOST LIKE THE CALM BEFORE A TERRIBLE STORM!
AND SO THE SEARCH CONTINUES! BUT, ALTHOUGH IT IS KNOWN THAT HE IS SOMEWHERE WITHIN THE ANCIENT CITY, NO TRACE IS FOUND OF THE HUNTED MAN!
BUT NOW, WE ARE ABOUT TO FIND HIM...
4

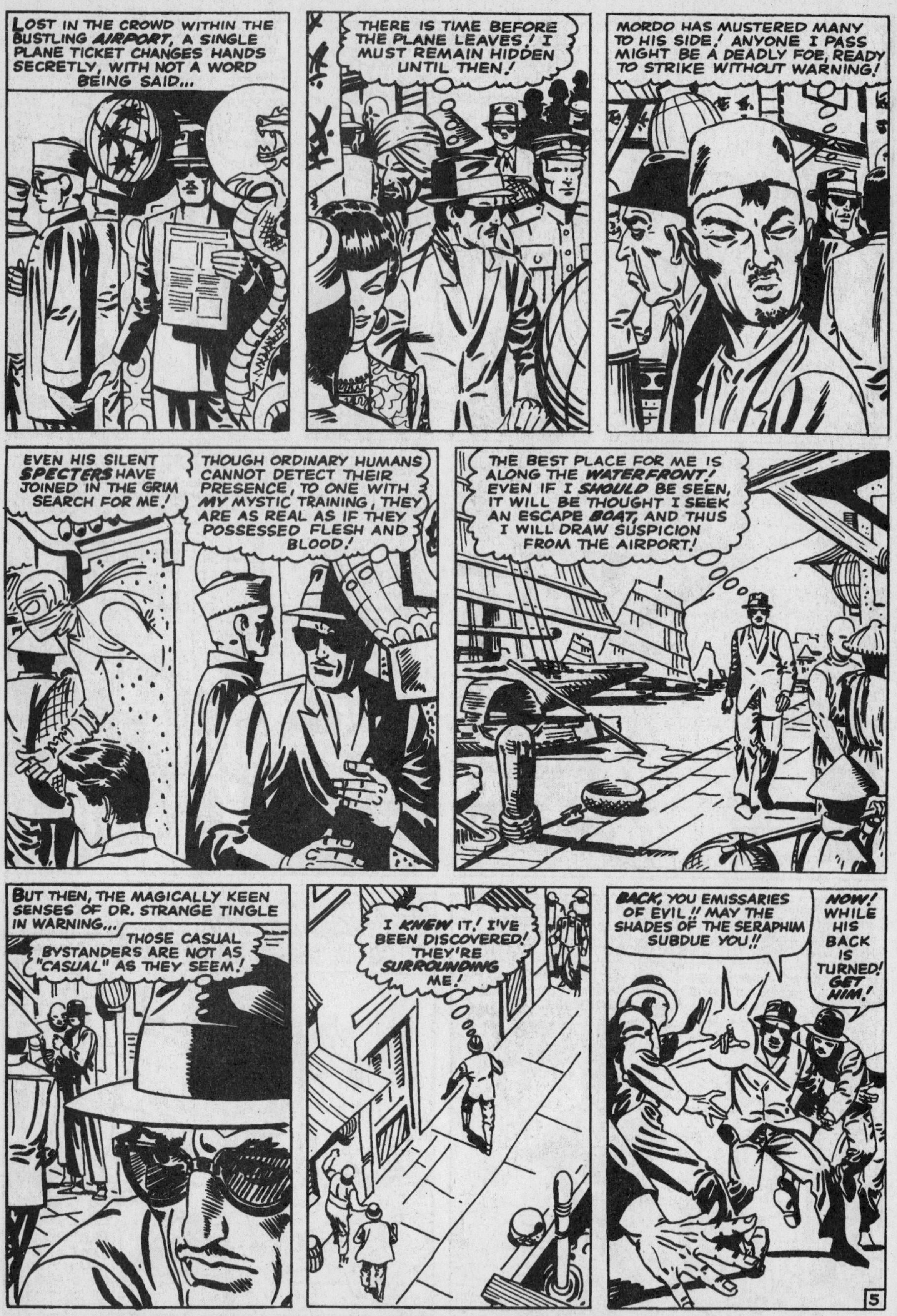
LOST IN THE CROWD WITHIN THE BUSTLING AIRPORT, A SINGLE PLANE TICKET CHANGES HANDS SECRETLY, WITH NOT A WORD BEING SAID...
THERE IS TIME BEFORE THE PLANE LEAVES! I MUST REMAIN HIDDEN UNTIL THEN!
MORDO HAS MUSTERED MANY TO HIS SIDE! ANYONE I PASS MIGHT BE A DEADLY FOE, READY TO STRIKE WITHOUT WARNING!
EVEN HIS SILENT SPECTERS HAVE JOINED IN THE GRIM SEARCH FOR ME!
THOUGH ORDINARY HUMANS CANNOT DETECT THEIR PRESENCE, TO ONE WITH MY MYSTIC TRAINING, THEY ARE AS REAL AS IF THEY POSSESSED FLESH AND BLOOD!
THE BEST PLACE FOR ME IS ALONG THE WATERFRONT! EVEN IF I SHOULD BE SEEN, IT WILL BE THOUGHT I SEEK AN ESCAPE BOAT, AND THUS I WILL DRAW SUSPICION FROM THE AIRPORT!
BUT THEN, THE MAGICALLY KEEN SENSES OF DR. STRANGE TINGLE IN WARNING...
THOSE CASUAL BYSTANDERS ARE NOT AS "CASUAL" AS THEY SEEM!
I KNEW IT! I'VE BEEN DISCOVERED! THEY'RE SURROUNDING ME!
BACK, YOU EMISSARIES OF EVIL!! MAY THE SHADES OF THE SERAPHIM SUBDUE YOU!!
NOW! WHILE HIS BACK IS TURNED! GET HIM!

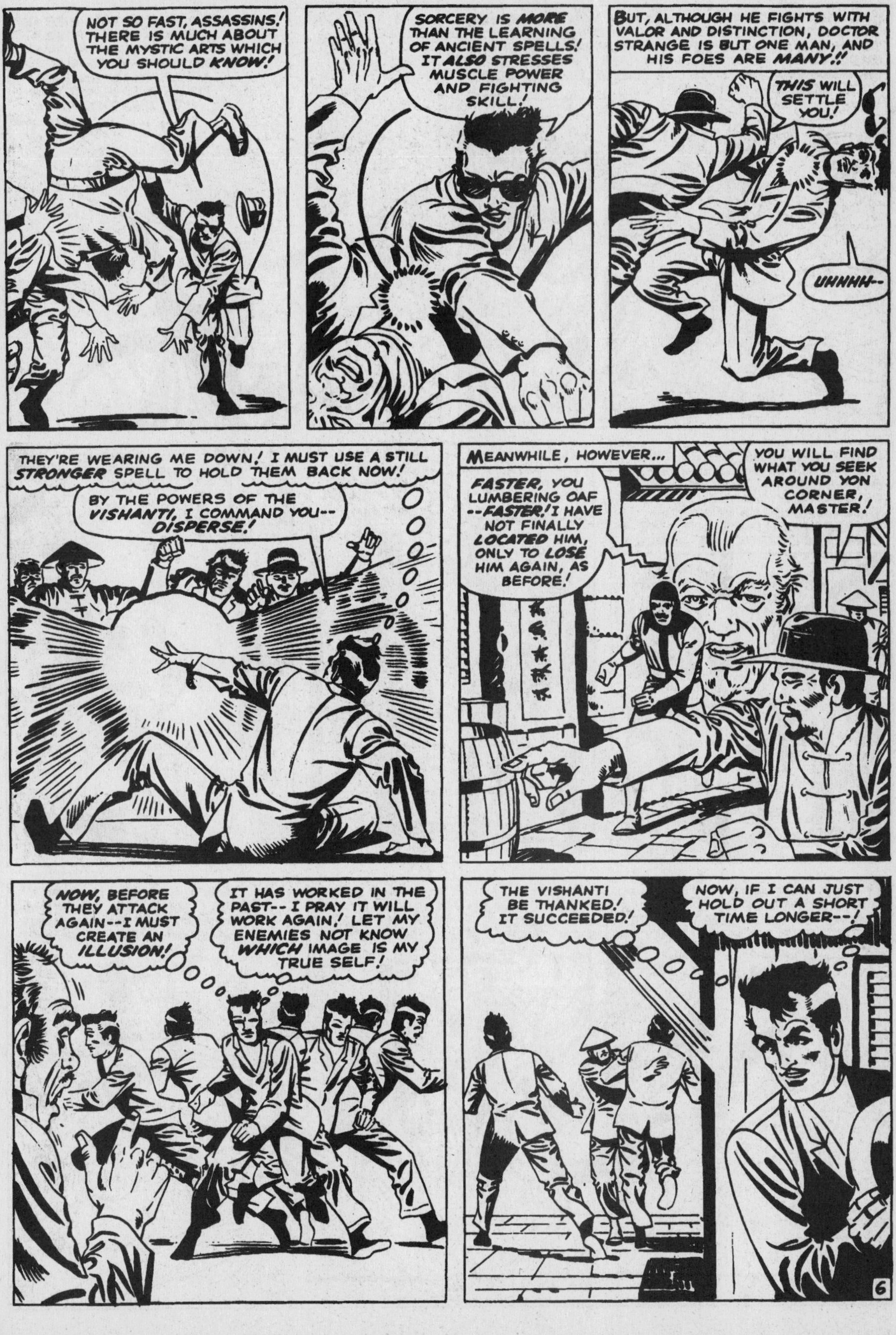
NOT SO FAST, ASSASSINS! THERE IS MUCH ABOUT THE MYSTIC ARTS WHICH YOU SHOULD KNOW!
SORCERY IS MORE THAN THE LEARNING OF ANCIENT SPELLS! IT ALSO STRESSES MUSCLE POWER AND FIGHTING SKILL!
BUT, ALTHOUGH HE FIGHTS WITH VALOR AND DISTINCTION, DOCTOR STRANGE IS BUT ONE MAN, AND HIS FOES ARE MANY!!
THIS WILL SETTLE YOU!
UHNHH--
THEY'RE WEARING ME DOWN! I MUST USE A STILL STRONGER SPELL TO HOLD THEM BACK NOW!
BY THE POWERS OF THE VISHANTI, I COMMAND YOU-- DISPERSE!
MEANWHILE, HOWEVER...
FASTER, YOU LUMBERING OAF --FASTER! I HAVE NOT FINALLY LOCATED HIM, ONLY TO LOSE HIM AGAIN, AS BEFORE!
YOU WILL FIND WHAT YOU SEEK AROUND YON CORNER, MASTER!
NOW, BEFORE THEY ATTACK AGAIN--I MUST CREATE AN ILLUSION!
IT HAS WORKED IN THE PAST-- I PRAY IT WILL WORK AGAIN! LET MY ENEMIES NOT KNOW WHICH IMAGE IS MY TRUE SELF!
THE VISHANTI BE THANKED! IT SUCCEEDED!
NOW, IF I CAN JUST HOLD OUT A SHORT TIME LONGER--!
6

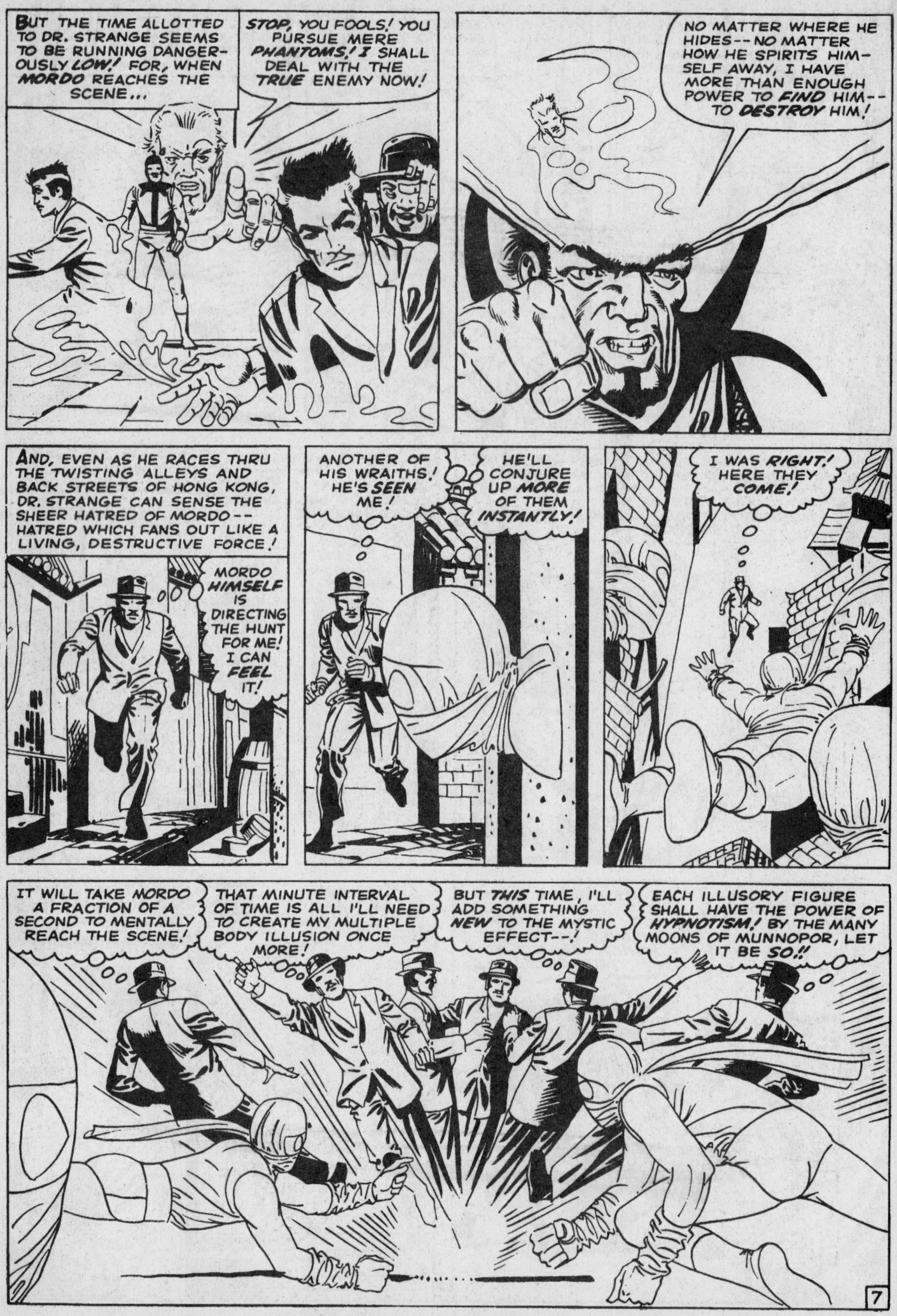

BUT THE TIME ALLOTTED TO DR. STRANGE SEEMS TO BE RUNNING DANGEROUSLY LOW! FOR, WHEN MORDO REACHES THE SCENE...
STOP, YOU FOOLS! YOU PURSUE MERE PHANTOMS! I SHALL DEAL WITH THE TRUE ENEMY NOW!
NO MATTER WHERE HE HIDES--NO MATTER HOW HE SPIRITS HIMSELF AWAY, I HAVE MORE THAN ENOUGH POWER TO FIND HIM--TO DESTROY HIM!
AND, EVEN AS HE RACES THRU THE TWISTING ALLEYS AND BACK STREETS OF HONG KONG, DR. STRANGE CAN SENSE THE SHEER HATRED OF MORDO--HATRED WHICH FANS OUT LIKE A LIVING, DESTRUCTIVE FORCE!
MORDO HIMSELF IS DIRECTING THE HUNT FOR ME! I CAN FEEL IT!
ANOTHER OF HIS WRAITHS! HE'S SEEN ME!
HE'LL CONJURE UP MORE OF THEM INSTANTLY!
I WAS RIGHT! HERE THEY COME!
IT WILL TAKE MORDO A FRACTION OF A SECOND TO MENTALLY REACH THE SCENE!
THAT MINUTE INTERVAL OF TIME IS ALL I'LL NEED TO CREATE MY MULTIPLE BODY ILLUSION ONCE MORE!
BUT THIS TIME, I'LL ADD SOMETHING NEW TO THE MYSTIC EFFECT--!
EACH ILLUSORY FIGURE SHALL HAVE THE POWER OF HYPNOTISM! BY THE MANY MOONS OF MUNNOPOR, LET IT BE SO!!

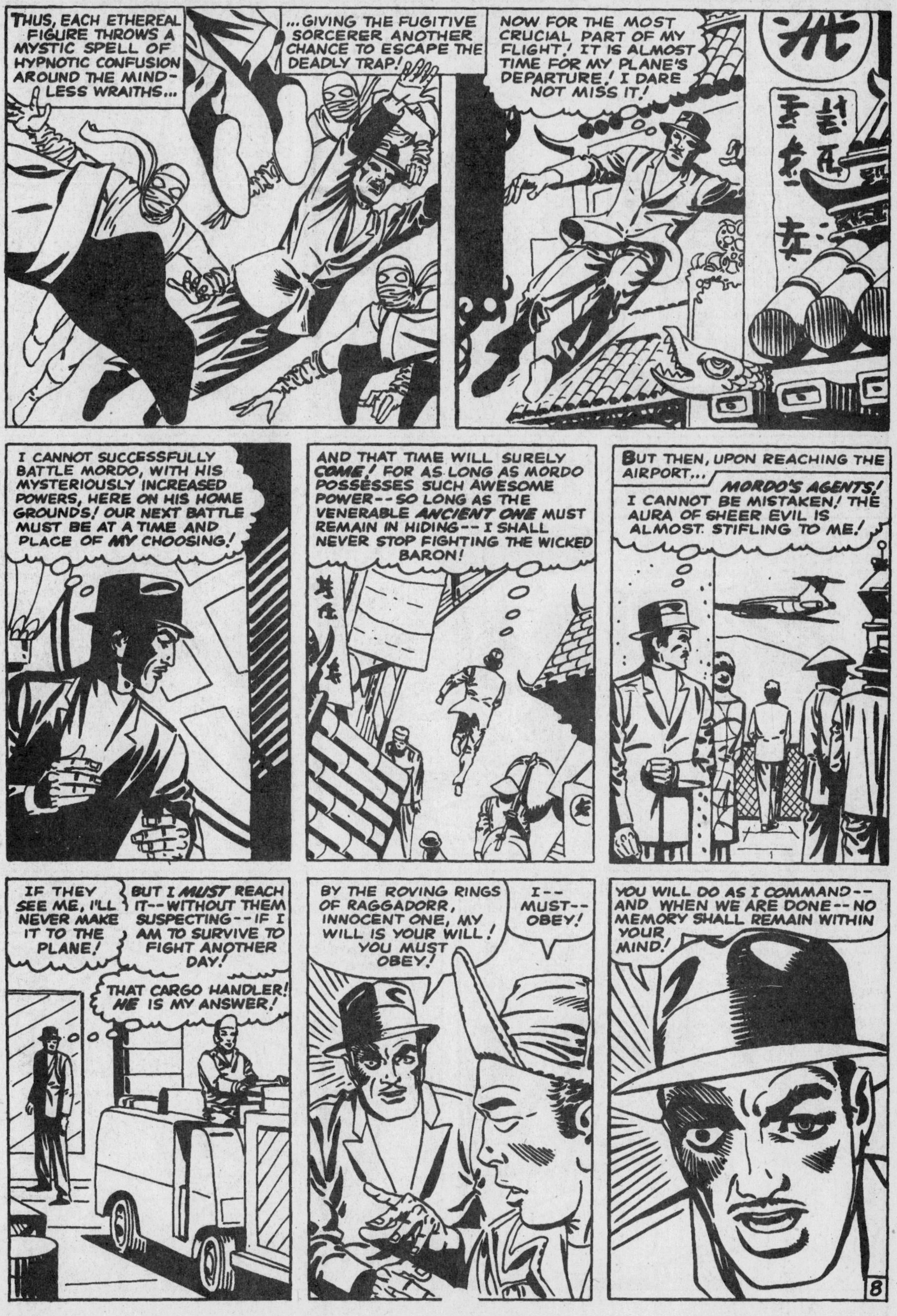
THUS, EACH ETHEREAL FIGURE THROWS A MYSTIC SPELL OF HYPNOTIC CONFUSION AROUND THE MINDLESS WRAITHS...
...GIVING THE FUGITIVE SORCERER ANOTHER CHANCE TO ESCAPE THE DEADLY TRAP!
NOW FOR THE MOST CRUCIAL PART OF MY FLIGHT! IT IS ALMOST TIME FOR MY PLANE'S DEPARTURE! I DARE NOT MISS IT!
I CANNOT SUCCESSFULLY BATTLE MORDO, WITH HIS MYSTERIOUSLY INCREASED POWERS, HERE ON HIS HOME GROUNDS! OUR NEXT BATTLE MUST BE AT A TIME AND PLACE OF MY CHOOSING!
AND THAT TIME WILL SURELY COME! FOR AS LONG AS MORDO POSSESSES SUCH AWESOME POWER--SO LONG AS THE VENERABLE ANCIENT ONE MUST REMAIN IN HIDING--I SHALL NEVER STOP FIGHTING THE WICKED BARON!
BUT THEN, UPON REACHING THE AIRPORT...
MORDO'S AGENTS! I CANNOT BE MISTAKEN! THE AURA OF SHEER EVIL IS ALMOST STIFLING TO ME!
IF THEY SEE ME, I'LL NEVER MAKE IT TO THE PLANE!
BUT I MUST REACH IT--WITHOUT THEM SUSPECTING--IF I AM TO SURVIVE TO FIGHT ANOTHER DAY!
THAT CARGO HANDLER! HE IS MY ANSWER!
BY THE ROVING RINGS OF RAGGADORR, INNOCENT ONE, MY WILL IS YOUR WILL! YOU MUST OBEY!
I--MUST--OBEY!
YOU WILL DO AS I COMMAND--AND WHEN WE ARE DONE--NO MEMORY SHALL REMAIN WITHIN YOUR MIND!
8

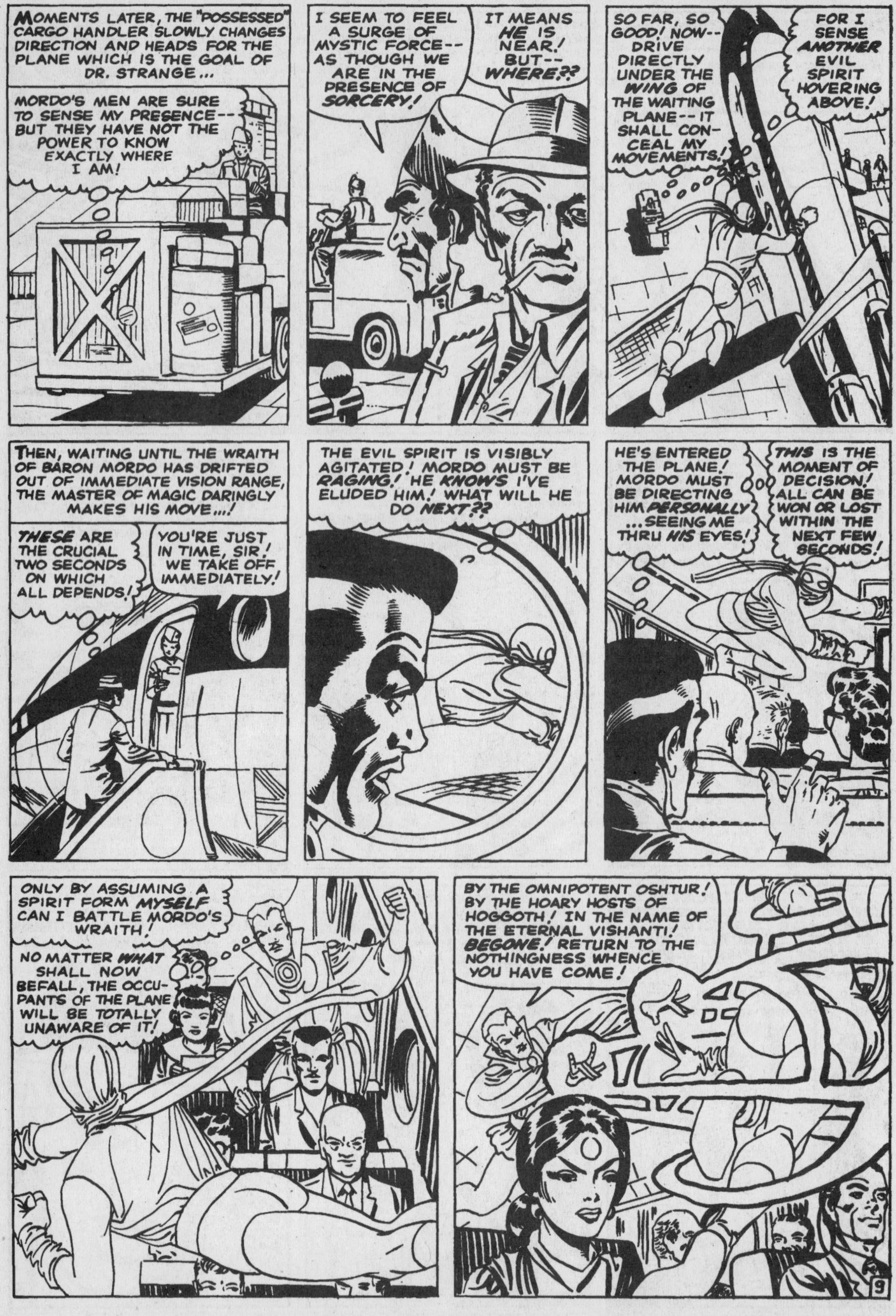
MOMENTS LATER, THE "POSSESSED" CARGO HANDLER SLOWLY CHANGES DIRECTION AND HEADS FOR THE PLANE WHICH IS THE GOAL OF DR. STRANGE...
MORDO'S MEN ARE SURE TO SENSE MY PRESENCE-- BUT THEY HAVE NOT THE POWER TO KNOW EXACTLY WHERE I AM!
I SEEM TO FEEL A SURGE OF MYSTIC FORCE-- AS THOUGH WE ARE IN THE PRESENCE OF SORCERY!
IT MEANS HE IS NEAR! BUT-- WHERE??
SO FAR, SO GOOD! NOW-- DRIVE DIRECTLY UNDER THE WING OF THE WAITING PLANE-- IT SHALL CONCEAL MY MOVEMENTS!
FOR I SENSE ANOTHER EVIL SPIRIT HOVERING ABOVE!
THEN, WAITING UNTIL THE WRAITH OF BARON MORDO HAS DRIFTED OUT OF IMMEDIATE VISION RANGE, THE MASTER OF MAGIC DARINGLY MAKES HIS MOVE...!
THESE ARE THE CRUCIAL TWO SECONDS ON WHICH ALL DEPENDS!
YOU'RE JUST IN TIME, SIR! WE TAKE OFF IMMEDIATELY!
THE EVIL SPIRIT IS VISIBLY AGITATED! MORDO MUST BE RAGING! HE KNOWS I'VE ELUDED HIM! WHAT WILL HE DO NEXT??
HE'S ENTERED THE PLANE! MORDO MUST BE DIRECTING HIM PERSONALLY ...SEEING ME THRU HIS EYES!
THIS IS THE MOMENT OF DECISION! ALL CAN BE WON OR LOST WITHIN THE NEXT FEW SECONDS!
ONLY BY ASSUMING A SPIRIT FORM MYSELF CAN I BATTLE MORDO'S WRAITH!
NO MATTER WHAT SHALL NOW BEFALL, THE OCCUPANTS OF THE PLANE WILL BE TOTALLY UNAWARE OF IT!
BY THE OMNIPOTENT OSHTUR! BY THE HOARY HOSTS OF HOGGOTH! IN THE NAME OF THE ETERNAL VISHANTI! BEGONE! RETURN TO THE NOTHINGNESS WHENCE YOU HAVE COME!
9

ONE MYSTIC MICRO-SECOND LATER...

I'VE BEEN *THWARTED!* I CAN SEE MY VICTIM NO LONGER! MY WRAITH HAS *VANISHED!* I CAN ONLY SEE THRU THE EYES OF THE *OTHERS!* AND THEY ARE TOO FAR FROM MY ENEMY!

BUT PERHAPS THERE IS STILL TIME! *FLY,* MY AVENGING WRAITHS!

FLY WITH THE SPEED OF THE TREMBLING STORM! *DEATH TO DR. STRANGE!*

THE OTHERS COME-- AS I EXPECTED!

BUT I HAVE NOW GAINED PRECIOUS *TIME!* TIME TO CONCEIVE OF A NEW *PLAN!*

IT IS BUT THE WORK OF A MOMENT TO GARB MYSELF IN THE MANNER OF MORDO'S WRAITHS!

NOW, MY FATE DEPENDS UPON SHEER *DECEPTION--* UPON THE *WITLESSNESS* OF MY SPIRIT PURSUERS!

IN MY ETHEREAL FORM, I CAN FLY AS THEY DO! BY WAVING MY ARMS, I SIGNAL THAT DR. STRANGE HAS VANISHED!

IT *WORKED!* THEY RETURN TO THEIR EVIL MASTER FOR NEW INSTRUCTIONS! THEY HAD NO REASON TO SUSPECT ONE OF THEM-- SELVES!

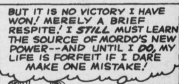

I WAS A *FOOL!* I SHOULD HAVE *KNOWN* STRANGE WOULDN'T DARE TAKE A PLANE --HE'D BE TOO VULNERABLE! HE USED AN *ILLUSION* TO LURE ME TO THE AIRPORT HE HID SOMEWHERE ELSE!

THIS WAS THE ONLY WAY! HAD I ATTEMPTED TO FLEE IN MY *ETHEREAL* FORM, MORDO WOULD HAVE FOUND ME WITH A SIMPLE SPELL! BUT HE IS NOT LIKELY TO THINK OF SEARCHING THIS PLANE AGAIN!

BUT IT IS NO VICTORY I HAVE WON! MERELY A BRIEF RESPITE! I *STILL* MUST LEARN THE SOURCE OF MORDO'S NEW POWER--AND UNTIL I *DO,* MY LIFE IS FORFEIT IF I DARE MAKE ONE MISTAKE!

BEHOLD! BY THE CRIMSON BANDS OF CYTTORAK, WE PROM-ISE YOU *THIS*-- YOUR MORTAL EYES HAVE NEVER SEEN SUCH MYSTIC ENCHANTMENT AS AWAITS YOU NEXT ISSUE! TILL THEN, MAY THE VISHANTI SPEAK YOUR NAME SOFTLY!

10

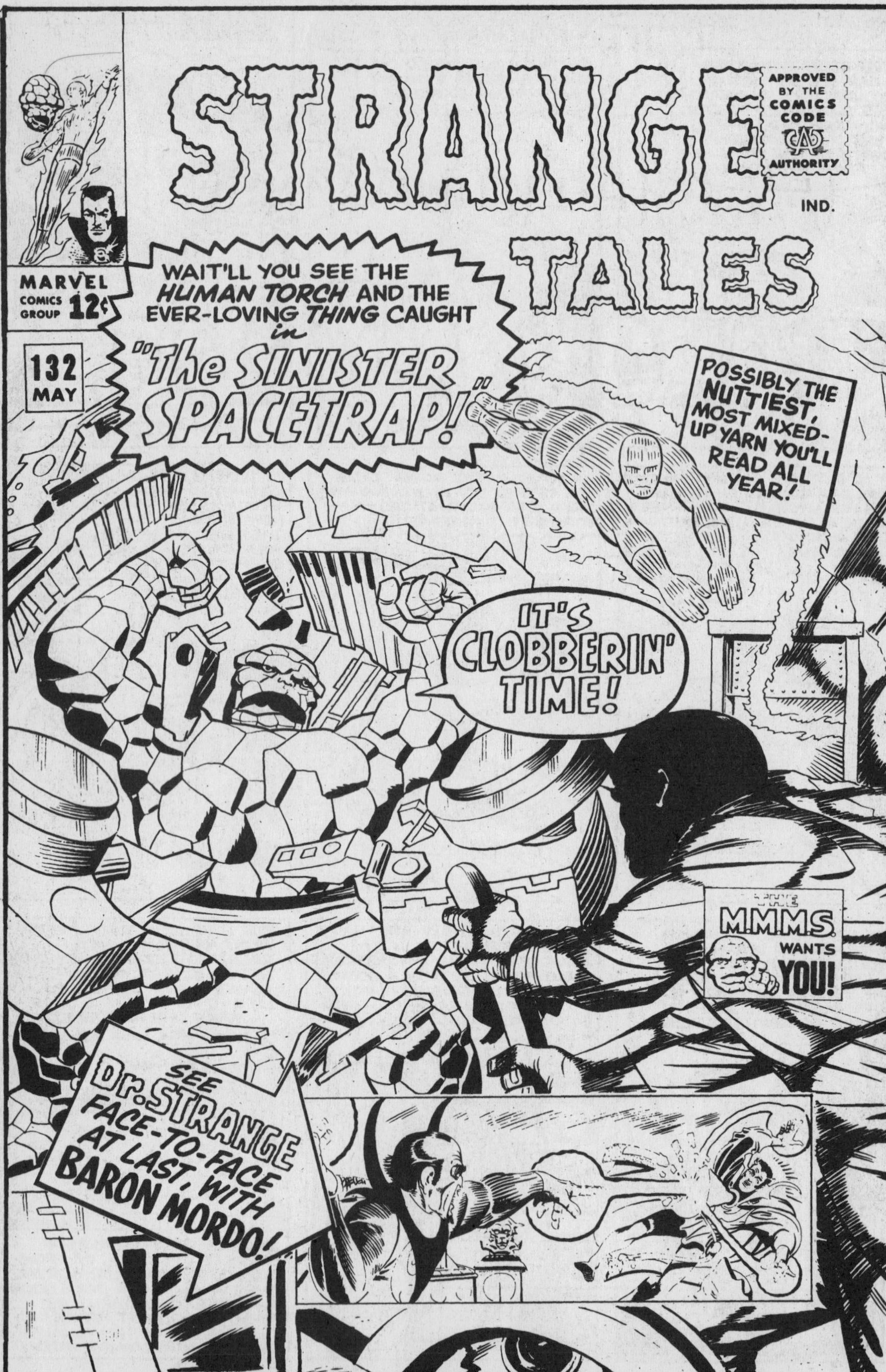

STRANGE TALES
APPROVED BY THE COMICS CODE AUTHORITY
IND.
MARVEL COMICS GROUP 12¢
132 MAY
WAIT'LL YOU SEE THE HUMAN TORCH AND THE EVER-LOVING THING CAUGHT in "The SINISTER SPACETRAP!"
POSSIBLY THE NUTTIEST, MOST MIXED-UP YARN YOU'LL READ ALL YEAR!
IT'S CLOBBERIN' TIME!
M.M.M.S. WANTS YOU!
SEE Dr. STRANGE FACE-TO-FACE AT LAST, WITH BARON MORDO!

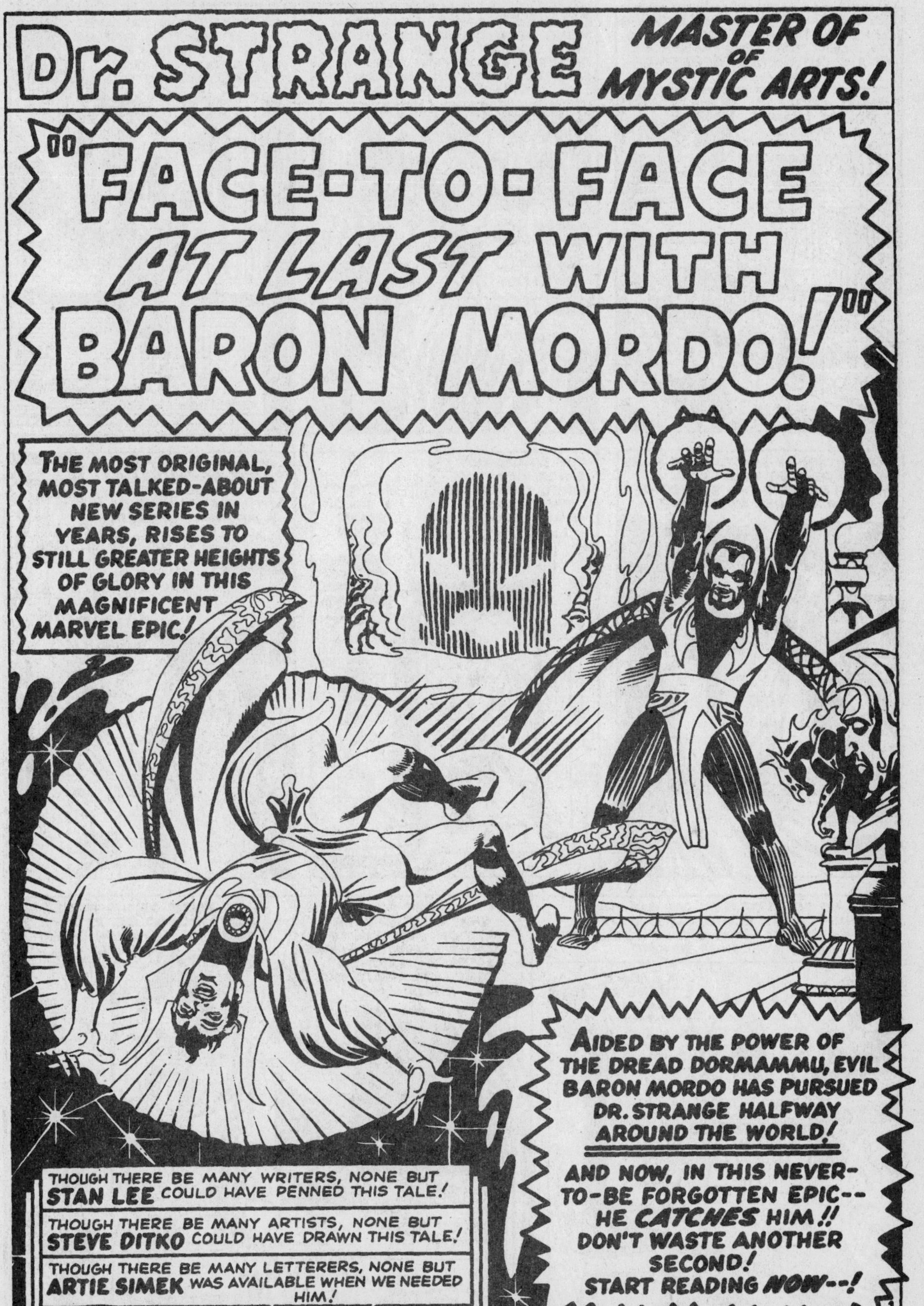

Dr. STRANGE
MASTER OF MYSTIC ARTS!
"FACE-TO-FACE AT LAST WITH BARON MORDO!"
THE MOST ORIGINAL, MOST TALKED-ABOUT NEW SERIES IN YEARS, RISES TO STILL GREATER HEIGHTS OF GLORY IN THIS MAGNIFICENT MARVEL EPIC!
AIDED BY THE POWER OF THE DREAD DORMAMMU, EVIL BARON MORDO HAS PURSUED DR. STRANGE HALFWAY AROUND THE WORLD!
AND NOW, IN THIS NEVER-TO-BE FORGOTTEN EPIC-- HE CATCHES HIM!! DON'T WASTE ANOTHER SECOND! START READING NOW--!
THOUGH THERE BE MANY WRITERS, NONE BUT STAN LEE COULD HAVE PENNED THIS TALE!
THOUGH THERE BE MANY ARTISTS, NONE BUT STEVE DITKO COULD HAVE DRAWN THIS TALE!
THOUGH THERE BE MANY LETTERERS, NONE BUT ARTIE SIMEK WAS AVAILABLE WHEN WE NEEDED HIM!
1

ON A BLEAK, RAIN-SWEPT EVENING IN NEW YORK, A TAXI DISCHARGES ITS SILENT, BROODING PASSENGER ON THE OUTSKIRTS OF GREENWICH VILLAGE...

WOW! A DOLLAR TIP! HEY, THANKS A LOT, MISTER!

HE DIDN'T ANSWER! MAYBE HE'S HARD-OF-HEARING!

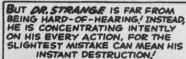

BUT *DR. STRANGE* IS FAR FROM BEING HARD-OF-HEARING! INSTEAD, HE IS CONCENTRATING INTENTLY ON HIS EVERY ACTION, FOR THE SLIGHTEST MISTAKE CAN MEAN HIS INSTANT DESTRUCTION!

MORDO WILL *NEVER* STOP SEARCHING FOR ME! I'M NO SAFER IN AMERICA THAN I WAS IN THE ORIENT!

HE IS CERTAIN TO HAVE A TRAP WAITING FOR ME AT MY GREENWICH VILLAGE RETREAT-- AND YET, I *MUST* CHANCE IT!

FOR WITHIN MY SANCTUM ARE MANY MYSTIC DEVICES WHICH WILL AID ME IN LEARNING THE SOURCE OF MORDO'S NEW STRENGTH!!

BUT I DARE NOT ENTER DIRECTLY! FIRST, I MUST SEE WHAT DANGERS AWAIT ME WITHIN!

I SHALL STAND WITHIN THE SHADOWS OF THIS DARKENED DOORWAY...

...WHILST MY INVISIBLE *SPIRIT FORM* LEAVES MY PHYSICAL BODY WITH THE SILENCE OF A MIDNIGHT BREEZE...

SINCE NO SOLID OBJECT CAN BAR THE MOVEMENT OF AN ECTOPLASMIC BODY, DR. STRANGE'S SPIRIT FORM ENTERS HIS CHAMBER WITHIN SECONDS, TO FIND...

A *LIGHT!* THERE IS SOMEONE WITHIN!!

IT IS INDEED FORTUNATE THAT I ACTED WITH CAUTION, FOR ONE OF MORDO'S MYSTIC DEMONS HAS BEEN STATIONED HERE-- TO AWAIT MY RETURN!

HOW *SURE* OF HIS POWER MUST MORDO BE, TO DARE SUCH AN INVASION OF MY DOMAIN!

2

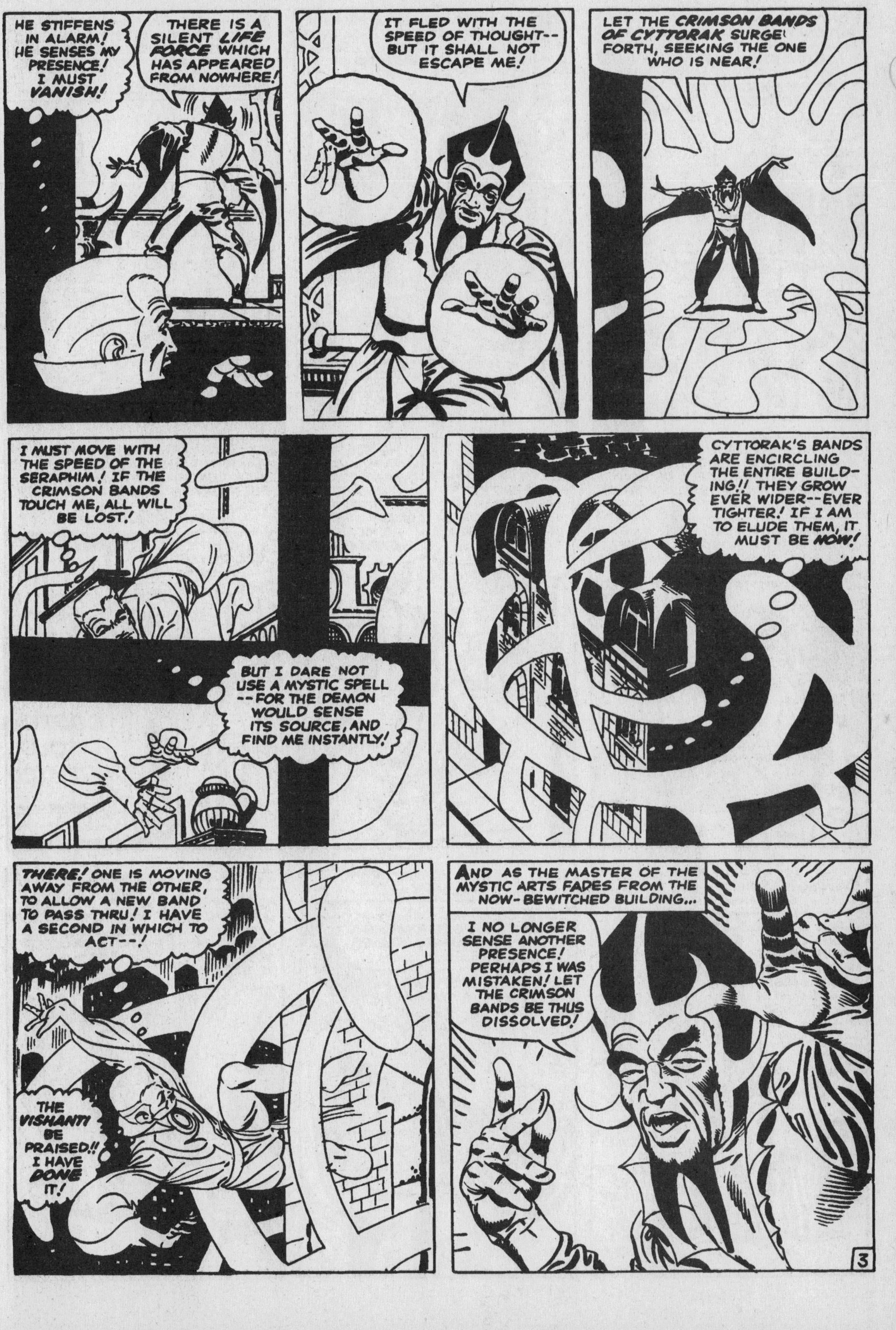
HE STIFFENS IN ALARM! HE SENSES MY PRESENCE! I MUST VANISH!
THERE IS A SILENT LIFE FORCE WHICH HAS APPEARED FROM NOWHERE!
IT FLED WITH THE SPEED OF THOUGHT-- BUT IT SHALL NOT ESCAPE ME!
LET THE CRIMSON BANDS OF CYTTORAK SURGE FORTH, SEEKING THE ONE WHO IS NEAR!
I MUST MOVE WITH THE SPEED OF THE SERAPHIM! IF THE CRIMSON BANDS TOUCH ME, ALL WILL BE LOST!
BUT I DARE NOT USE A MYSTIC SPELL --FOR THE DEMON WOULD SENSE ITS SOURCE, AND FIND ME INSTANTLY!
CYTTORAK'S BANDS ARE ENCIRCLING THE ENTIRE BUILDING!! THEY GROW EVER WIDER--EVER TIGHTER! IF I AM TO ELUDE THEM, IT MUST BE NOW!
THERE! ONE IS MOVING AWAY FROM THE OTHER, TO ALLOW A NEW BAND TO PASS THRU! I HAVE A SECOND IN WHICH TO ACT--!
THE VISHANTI BE PRAISED!! I HAVE DONE IT!
AND AS THE MASTER OF THE MYSTIC ARTS FADES FROM THE NOW-BEWITCHED BUILDING...
I NO LONGER SENSE ANOTHER PRESENCE! PERHAPS I WAS MISTAKEN! LET THE CRIMSON BANDS BE THUS DISSOLVED!
3

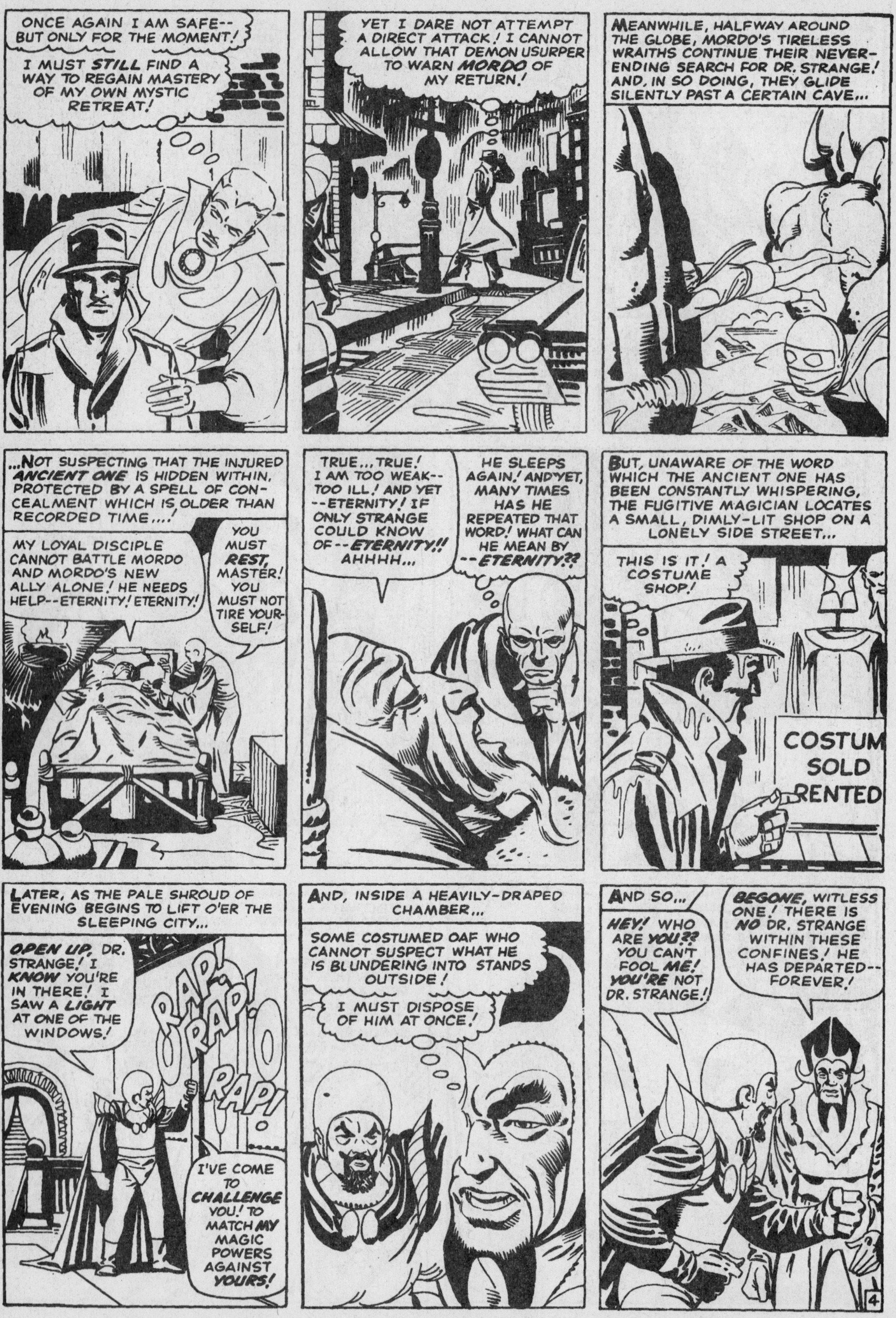

ONCE AGAIN I AM SAFE-- BUT ONLY FOR THE MOMENT!
I MUST STILL FIND A WAY TO REGAIN MASTERY OF MY OWN MYSTIC RETREAT!
YET I DARE NOT ATTEMPT A DIRECT ATTACK! I CANNOT ALLOW THAT DEMON USURPER TO WARN MORDO OF MY RETURN!
MEANWHILE, HALFWAY AROUND THE GLOBE, MORDO'S TIRELESS WRAITHS CONTINUE THEIR NEVER-ENDING SEARCH FOR DR. STRANGE! AND, IN SO DOING, THEY GLIDE SILENTLY PAST A CERTAIN CAVE...
...NOT SUSPECTING THAT THE INJURED ANCIENT ONE IS HIDDEN WITHIN, PROTECTED BY A SPELL OF CONCEALMENT WHICH IS OLDER THAN RECORDED TIME...!
MY LOYAL DISCIPLE CANNOT BATTLE MORDO AND MORDO'S NEW ALLY ALONE! HE NEEDS HELP--ETERNITY! ETERNITY!
YOU MUST REST, MASTER! YOU MUST NOT TIRE YOURSELF!
TRUE...TRUE! I AM TOO WEAK-- TOO ILL! AND YET --ETERNITY! IF ONLY STRANGE COULD KNOW OF--ETERNITY!! AHHHH...
HE SLEEPS AGAIN! AND YET, MANY TIMES HAS HE REPEATED THAT WORD! WHAT CAN HE MEAN BY --ETERNITY??
BUT, UNAWARE OF THE WORD WHICH THE ANCIENT ONE HAS BEEN CONSTANTLY WHISPERING, THE FUGITIVE MAGICIAN LOCATES A SMALL, DIMLY-LIT SHOP ON A LONELY SIDE STREET...
THIS IS IT! A COSTUME SHOP!
COSTUM SOLD RENTED
LATER, AS THE PALE SHROUD OF EVENING BEGINS TO LIFT O'ER THE SLEEPING CITY...
OPEN UP, DR. STRANGE! I KNOW YOU'RE IN THERE! I SAW A LIGHT AT ONE OF THE WINDOWS!
RAP! RAP! RAP!
I'VE COME TO CHALLENGE YOU! TO MATCH MY MAGIC POWERS AGAINST YOURS!
AND, INSIDE A HEAVILY-DRAPED CHAMBER...
SOME COSTUMED OAF WHO CANNOT SUSPECT WHAT HE IS BLUNDERING INTO STANDS OUTSIDE!
I MUST DISPOSE OF HIM AT ONCE!
AND SO...
HEY! WHO ARE YOU?? YOU CAN'T FOOL ME! YOU'RE NOT DR. STRANGE!
BEGONE, WITLESS ONE! THERE IS NO DR. STRANGE WITHIN THESE CONFINES! HE HAS DEPARTED-- FOREVER!
4

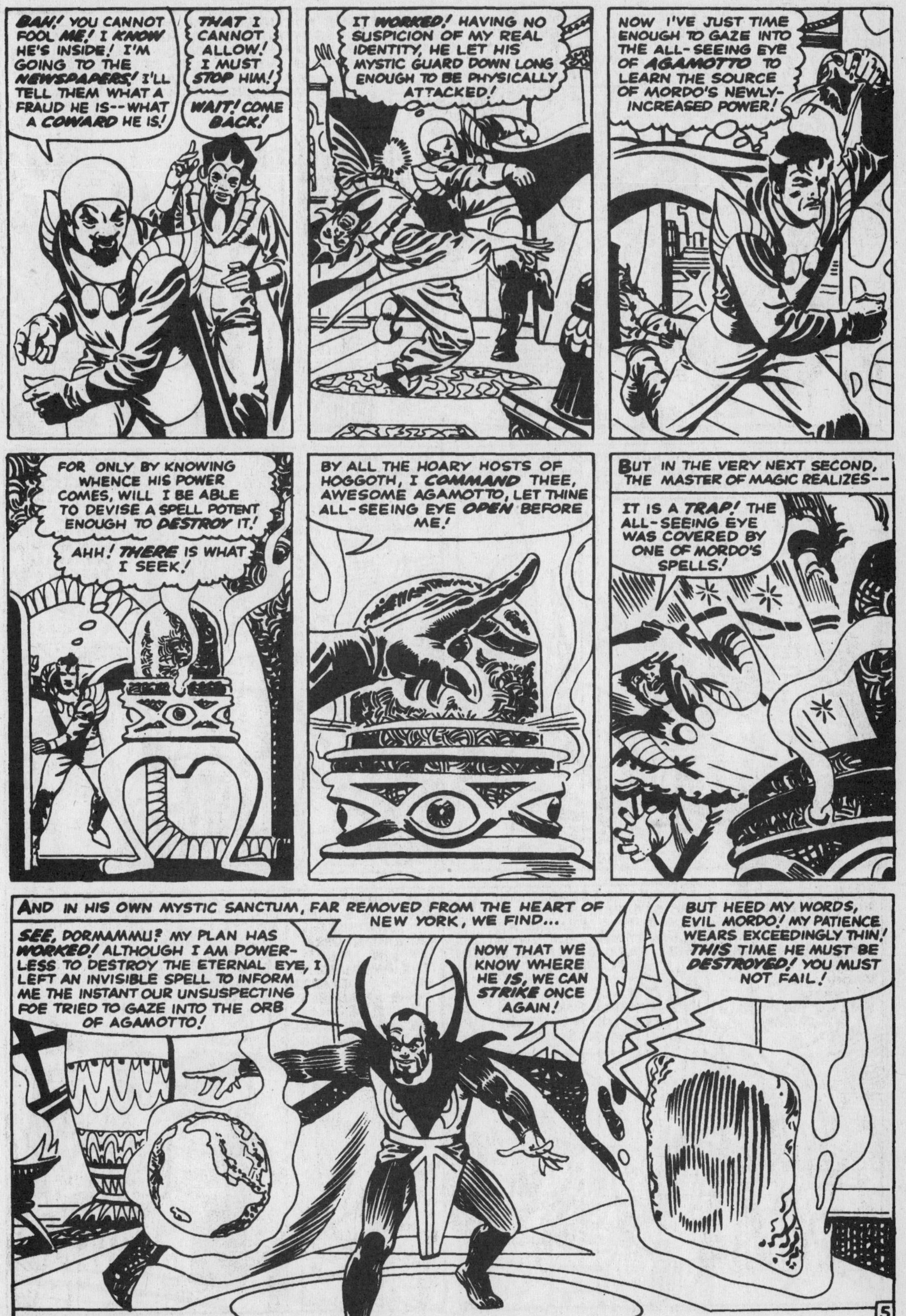
BAH! YOU CANNOT FOOL ME! I KNOW HE'S INSIDE! I'M GOING TO THE NEWSPAPERS! I'LL TELL THEM WHAT A FRAUD HE IS--WHAT A COWARD HE IS!
THAT I CANNOT ALLOW! I MUST STOP HIM!
WAIT! COME BACK!
IT WORKED! HAVING NO SUSPICION OF MY REAL IDENTITY, HE LET HIS MYSTIC GUARD DOWN LONG ENOUGH TO BE PHYSICALLY ATTACKED!
NOW I'VE JUST TIME ENOUGH TO GAZE INTO THE ALL-SEEING EYE OF AGAMOTTO TO LEARN THE SOURCE OF MORDO'S NEWLY-INCREASED POWER!
FOR ONLY BY KNOWING WHENCE HIS POWER COMES, WILL I BE ABLE TO DEVISE A SPELL POTENT ENOUGH TO DESTROY IT!
AHH! THERE IS WHAT I SEEK!
BY ALL THE HOARY HOSTS OF HOGGOTH, I COMMAND THEE, AWESOME AGAMOTTO, LET THINE ALL-SEEING EYE OPEN BEFORE ME!
BUT IN THE VERY NEXT SECOND, THE MASTER OF MAGIC REALIZES--
IT IS A TRAP! THE ALL-SEEING EYE WAS COVERED BY ONE OF MORDO'S SPELLS!
AND IN HIS OWN MYSTIC SANCTUM, FAR REMOVED FROM THE HEART OF NEW YORK, WE FIND...
SEE, DORMAMMU? MY PLAN HAS WORKED! ALTHOUGH I AM POWERLESS TO DESTROY THE ETERNAL EYE, I LEFT AN INVISIBLE SPELL TO INFORM ME THE INSTANT OUR UNSUSPECTING FOE TRIED TO GAZE INTO THE ORB OF AGAMOTTO!
NOW THAT WE KNOW WHERE HE IS, WE CAN STRIKE ONCE AGAIN!
BUT HEED MY WORDS, EVIL MORDO! MY PATIENCE WEARS EXCEEDINGLY THIN! THIS TIME HE MUST BE DESTROYED! YOU MUST NOT FAIL!
5

I **CANNOT** FAIL-- NOT NOW THAT I HAVE **YOUR** UNEARTHLY POWER ADDED TO MY OWN! AND SO, DREAD DORMAMMU, I TURN TO YOU AGAIN--

INCREASE MY POWER ONCE MORE! BATHE ME IN THE GLOW OF YOUR EERIE RADIANCE!! MORE-- **MORE**!! AHHH-- **THIS** TIME VICTORY SHALL SURELY BE OURS!

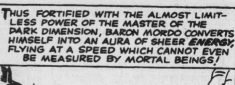

THUS FORTIFIED WITH THE ALMOST LIMIT-LESS POWER OF THE MASTER OF THE DARK DIMENSION, BARON MORDO CONVERTS HIMSELF INTO AN AURA OF SHEER **ENERGY**, FLYING AT A SPEED WHICH CANNOT EVEN BE MEASURED BY MORTAL BEINGS!

NOTHING CAN SAVE DR. STRANGE **NOW**!

WHILE THE DREAD DORMAMMU THINKS HIS OWN INHUMAN THOUGHTS --AND CREATES HIS OWN MIND-STAGGERING PLANS!

THE TIME GROWS NEARER--EVER NEARER!

ONLY THE OATH I SWORE TO DOCTOR STRANGE PREVENTS ME FROM ATTACKING THE HELPLESS DIMENSION OF HUMAN BEINGS! #

BUT ONCE STRANGE IS **DESTROYED**, I SHALL BE **FREE** OF MY OATH--AND HUMANITY WILL FALL BEFORE ME!

*STRANGE TALES #127--STAN.

EVEN **MORDO** DOES NOT SUSPECT MY **TRUE** MOTIVE FOR HELPING HIM--NOR THE EXTENT OF MY **TRUE** POWER!

FATHER, THE DREADED ONE HAS SAT THUS MOTIONLESS FOR **DAYS!** YOU ARE HIS CLOSEST **DISCIPLE!** WHAT NEW, FANTASTIC PLAN IS HE PLOTTING?

IT IS NOT SAFE TO ASK, MY CHILD! HE SHALL TELL US IN HIS OWN GOOD TIME!

ONCE BEFORE I HAD THIS SAME TERRIBLE PREMONITION! IT WAS WHEN THE MYSTERIOUS **DOCTOR STRANGE** WAS IN DANGER! CAN IT BE THAT HE **AGAIN** STANDS AT THE THRESHOLD OF-- HIS **DOOM**??

6

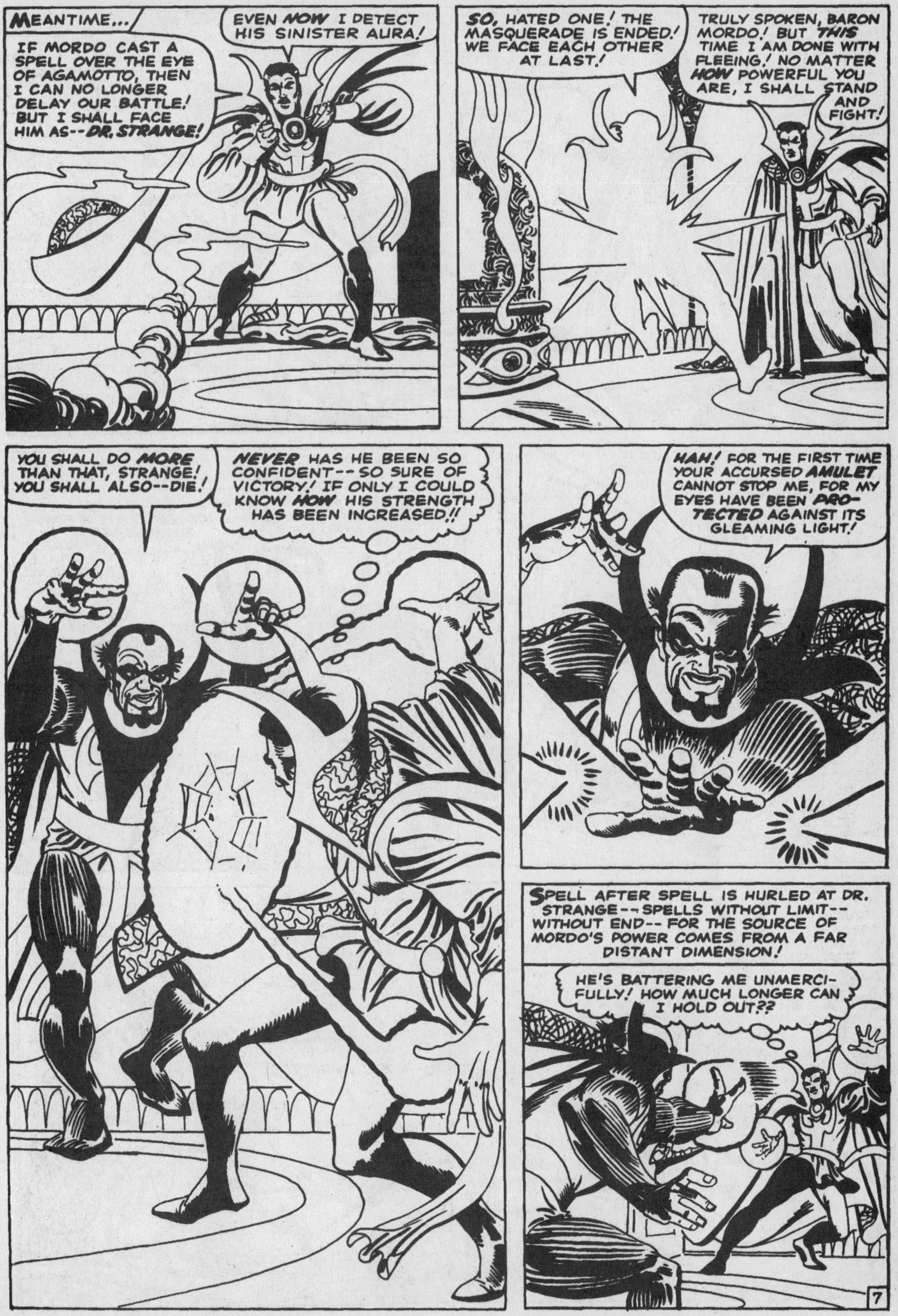
MEANTIME...
IF MORDO CAST A SPELL OVER THE EYE OF AGAMOTTO, THEN I CAN NO LONGER DELAY OUR BATTLE! BUT I SHALL FACE HIM AS--DR. STRANGE!
EVEN NOW I DETECT HIS SINISTER AURA!
SO, HATED ONE! THE MASQUERADE IS ENDED! WE FACE EACH OTHER AT LAST!
TRULY SPOKEN, BARON MORDO! BUT THIS TIME I AM DONE WITH FLEEING! NO MATTER HOW POWERFUL YOU ARE, I SHALL STAND AND FIGHT!
YOU SHALL DO MORE THAN THAT, STRANGE! YOU SHALL ALSO--DIE!
NEVER HAS HE BEEN SO CONFIDENT--SO SURE OF VICTORY! IF ONLY I COULD KNOW HOW HIS STRENGTH HAS BEEN INCREASED!!
HAH! FOR THE FIRST TIME YOUR ACCURSED AMULET CANNOT STOP ME, FOR MY EYES HAVE BEEN PROTECTED AGAINST ITS GLEAMING LIGHT!
SPELL AFTER SPELL IS HURLED AT DR. STRANGE--SPELLS WITHOUT LIMIT--WITHOUT END--FOR THE SOURCE OF MORDO'S POWER COMES FROM A FAR DISTANT DIMENSION!
HE'S BATTERING ME UNMERCIFULLY! HOW MUCH LONGER CAN I HOLD OUT??
7

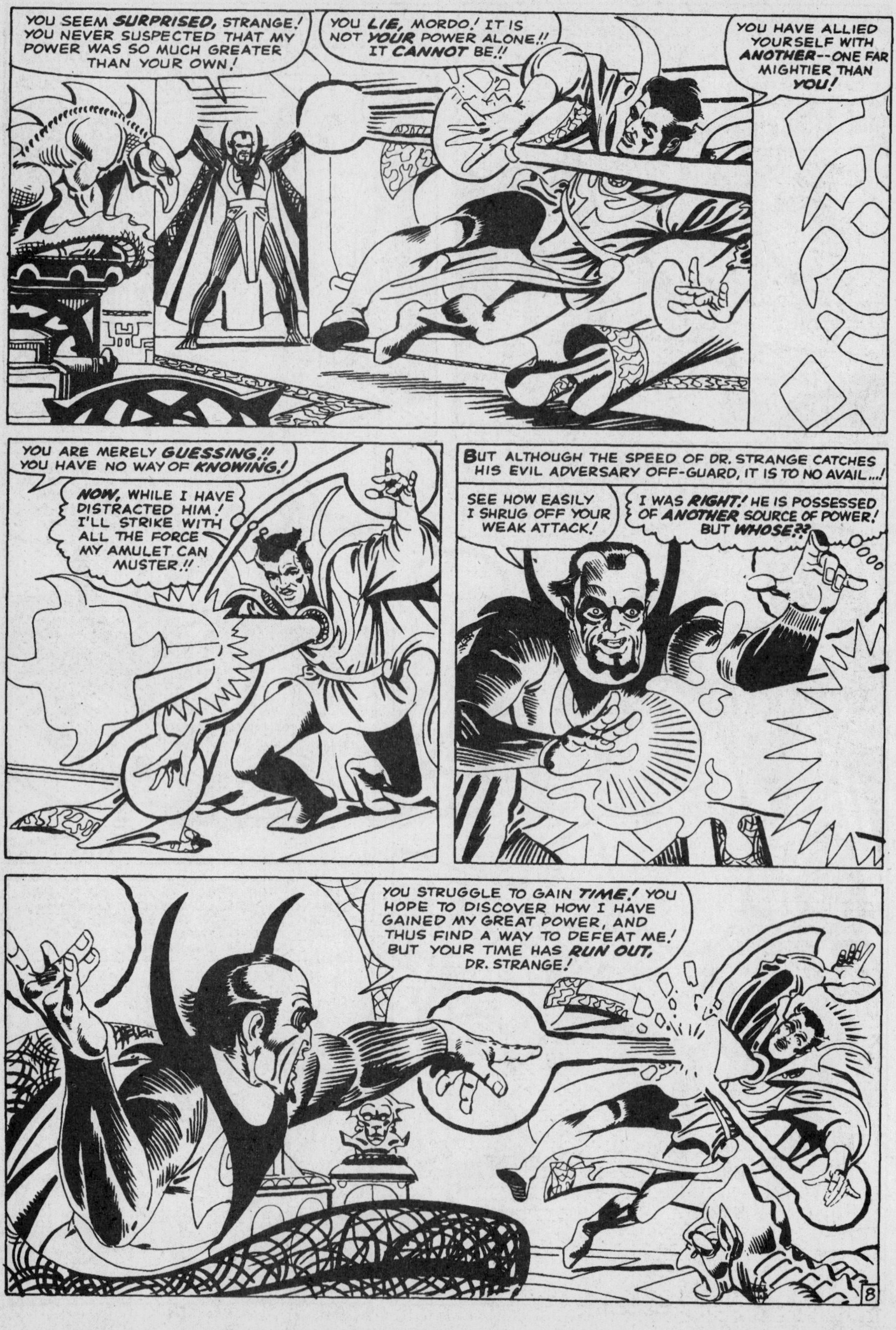
YOU SEEM SURPRISED, STRANGE! YOU NEVER SUSPECTED THAT MY POWER WAS SO MUCH GREATER THAN YOUR OWN!
YOU LIE, MORDO! IT IS NOT YOUR POWER ALONE!! IT CANNOT BE!!
YOU HAVE ALLIED YOURSELF WITH ANOTHER--ONE FAR MIGHTIER THAN YOU!
YOU ARE MERELY GUESSING!! YOU HAVE NO WAY OF KNOWING!
NOW, WHILE I HAVE DISTRACTED HIM! I'LL STRIKE WITH ALL THE FORCE MY AMULET CAN MUSTER!!
BUT ALTHOUGH THE SPEED OF DR. STRANGE CATCHES HIS EVIL ADVERSARY OFF-GUARD, IT IS TO NO AVAIL...!
SEE HOW EASILY I SHRUG OFF YOUR WEAK ATTACK!
I WAS RIGHT! HE IS POSSESSED OF ANOTHER SOURCE OF POWER! BUT WHOSE??
YOU STRUGGLE TO GAIN TIME! YOU HOPE TO DISCOVER HOW I HAVE GAINED MY GREAT POWER, AND THUS FIND A WAY TO DEFEAT ME! BUT YOUR TIME HAS RUN OUT, DR. STRANGE!
8

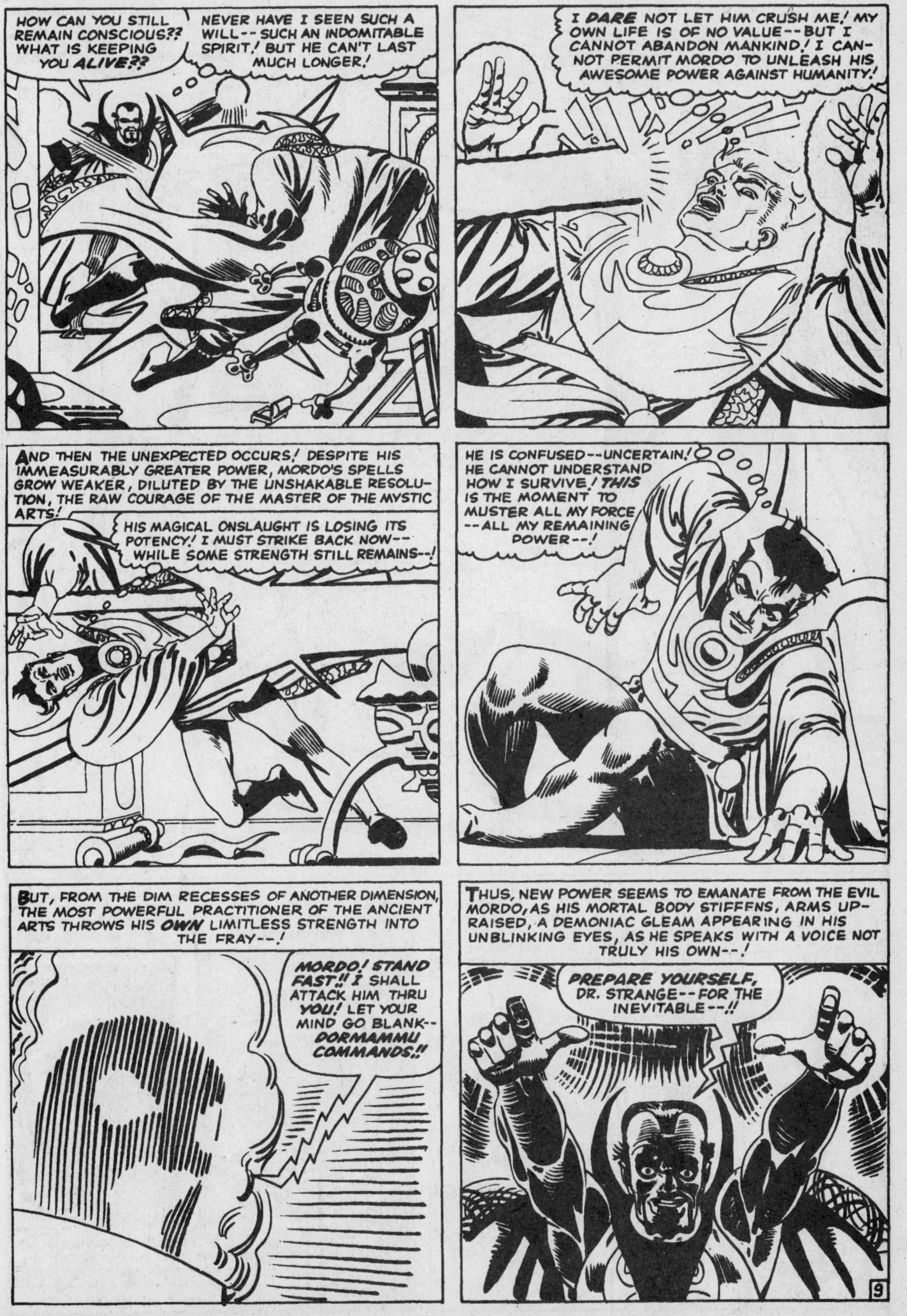
HOW CAN YOU STILL REMAIN CONSCIOUS?? WHAT IS KEEPING YOU ALIVE??
NEVER HAVE I SEEN SUCH A WILL-- SUCH AN INDOMITABLE SPIRIT! BUT HE CAN'T LAST MUCH LONGER!
I DARE NOT LET HIM CRUSH ME! MY OWN LIFE IS OF NO VALUE--BUT I CANNOT ABANDON MANKIND! I CANNOT PERMIT MORDO TO UNLEASH HIS AWESOME POWER AGAINST HUMANITY!
AND THEN THE UNEXPECTED OCCURS! DESPITE HIS IMMEASURABLY GREATER POWER, MORDO'S SPELLS GROW WEAKER, DILUTED BY THE UNSHAKABLE RESOLUTION, THE RAW COURAGE OF THE MASTER OF THE MYSTIC ARTS!
HIS MAGICAL ONSLAUGHT IS LOSING ITS POTENCY! I MUST STRIKE BACK NOW-- WHILE SOME STRENGTH STILL REMAINS--!
HE IS CONFUSED--UNCERTAIN! HE CANNOT UNDERSTAND HOW I SURVIVE! THIS IS THE MOMENT TO MUSTER ALL MY FORCE --ALL MY REMAINING POWER--!
BUT, FROM THE DIM RECESSES OF ANOTHER DIMENSION, THE MOST POWERFUL PRACTITIONER OF THE ANCIENT ARTS THROWS HIS OWN LIMITLESS STRENGTH INTO THE FRAY--!
MORDO! STAND FAST!! I SHALL ATTACK HIM THRU YOU! LET YOUR MIND GO BLANK-- DORMAMMU COMMANDS!!
THUS, NEW POWER SEEMS TO EMANATE FROM THE EVIL MORDO, AS HIS MORTAL BODY STIFFENS, ARMS UPRAISED, A DEMONIAC GLEAM APPEARING IN HIS UNBLINKING EYES, AS HE SPEAKS WITH A VOICE NOT TRULY HIS OWN--!
PREPARE YOURSELF, DR. STRANGE--FOR THE INEVITABLE--!!
9

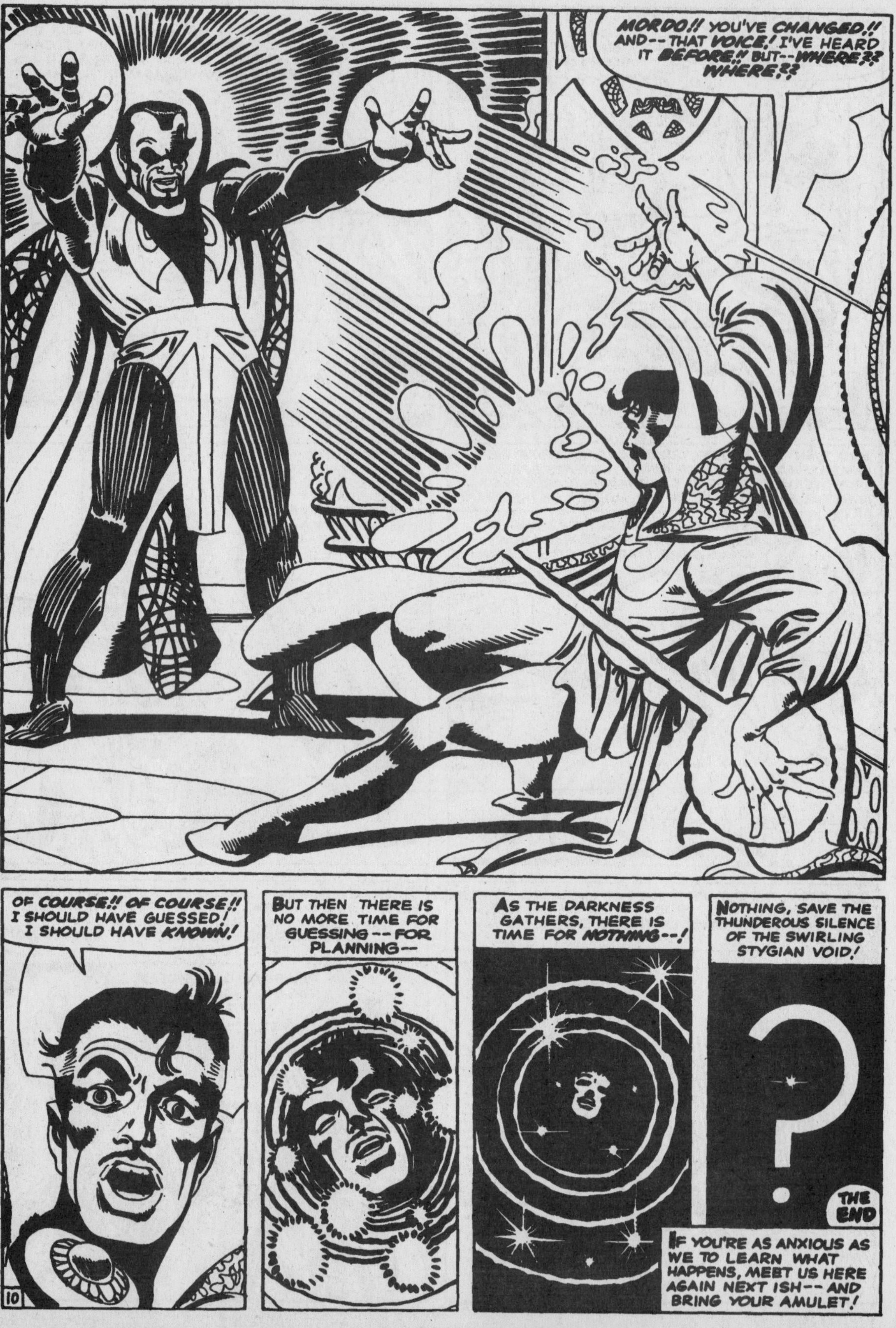
MORDO!! YOU'VE CHANGED!! AND--THAT VOICE! I'VE HEARD IT BEFORE!! BUT--WHERE?? WHERE??
OF COURSE!! OF COURSE!! I SHOULD HAVE GUESSED! I SHOULD HAVE KNOWN!
10
BUT THEN THERE IS NO MORE TIME FOR GUESSING--FOR PLANNING--
AS THE DARKNESS GATHERS, THERE IS TIME FOR NOTHING--!
NOTHING, SAVE THE THUNDEROUS SILENCE OF THE SWIRLING STYGIAN VOID!
THE END
IF YOU'RE AS ANXIOUS AS WE TO LEARN WHAT HAPPENS, MEET US HERE AGAIN NEXT ISH--AND BRING YOUR AMULET!

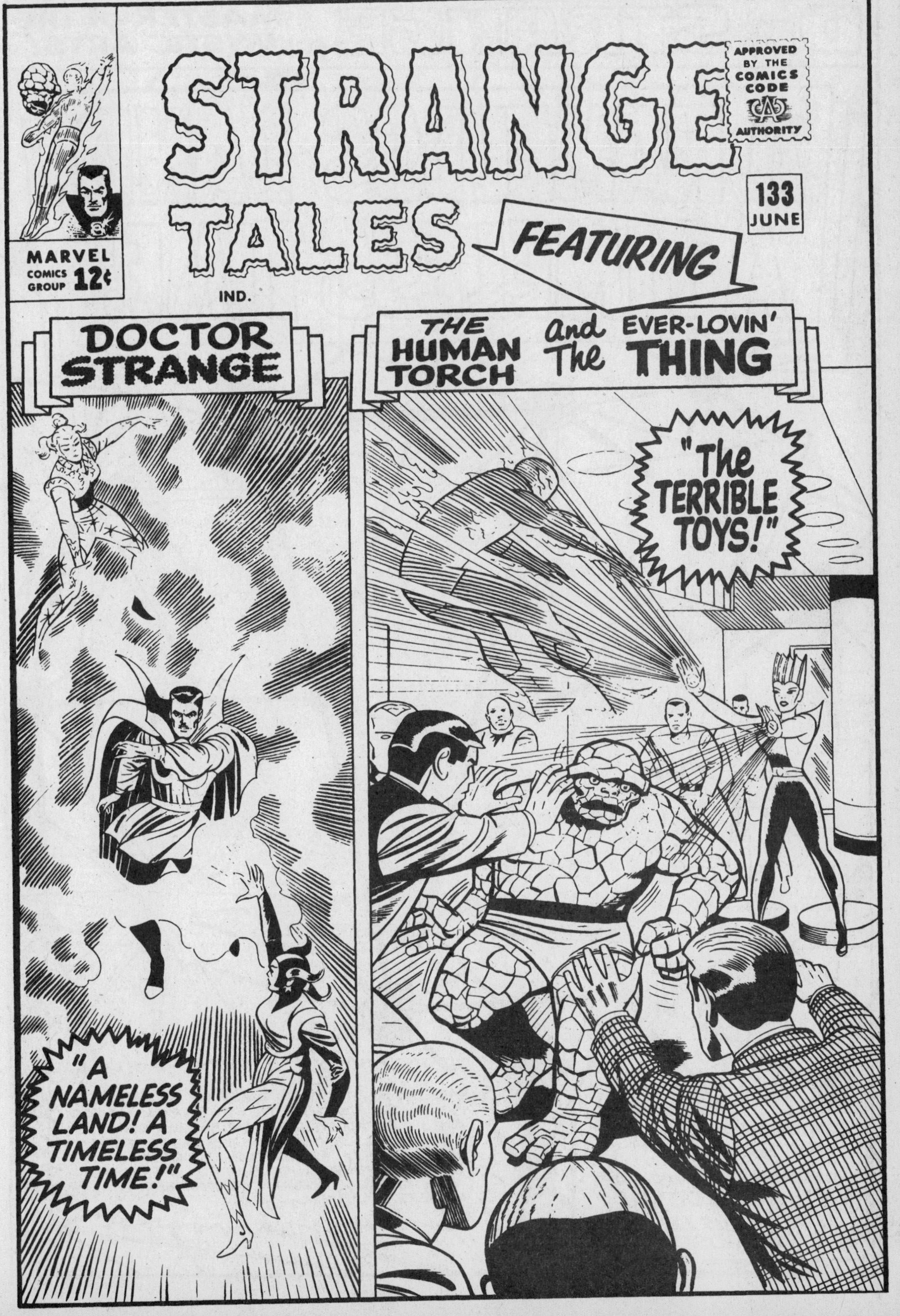
STRANGE TALES
APPROVED BY THE COMICS CODE AUTHORITY
133 JUNE
MARVEL COMICS GROUP 12¢
IND.
FEATURING
DOCTOR STRANGE
THE HUMAN TORCH and The EVER-LOVIN' THING
"The TERRIBLE TOYS!"
"A NAMELESS LAND! A TIMELESS TIME!"

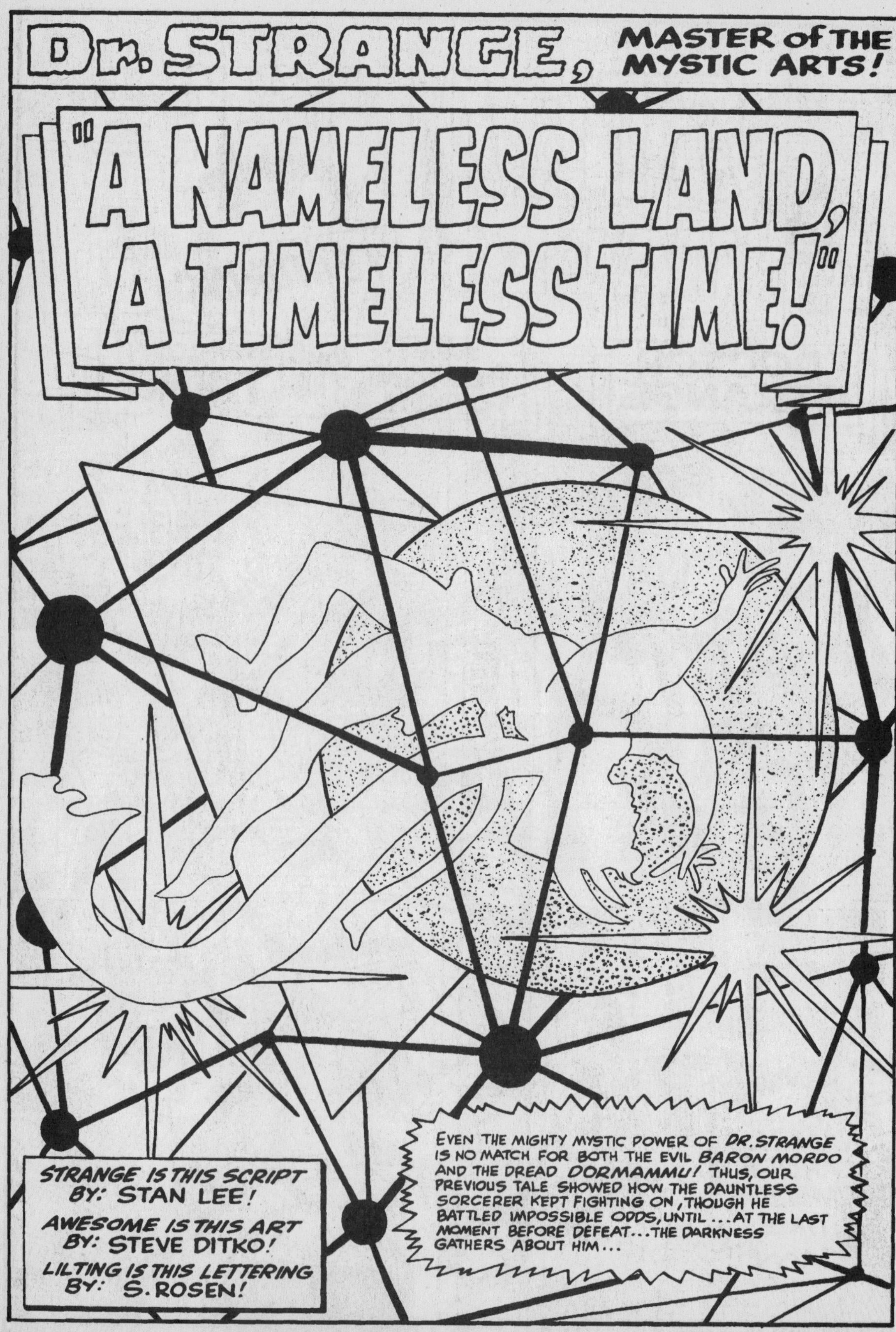
Dr. STRANGE, MASTER of THE MYSTIC ARTS!
"A NAMELESS LAND, A TIMELESS TIME!"
EVEN THE MIGHTY MYSTIC POWER OF DR. STRANGE IS NO MATCH FOR BOTH THE EVIL BARON MORDO AND THE DREAD DORMAMMU! THUS, OUR PREVIOUS TALE SHOWED HOW THE DAUNTLESS SORCERER KEPT FIGHTING ON, THOUGH HE BATTLED IMPOSSIBLE ODDS, UNTIL ... AT THE LAST MOMENT BEFORE DEFEAT ... THE DARKNESS GATHERS ABOUT HIM ...
STRANGE IS THIS SCRIPT BY: STAN LEE!
AWESOME IS THIS ART BY: STEVE DITKO!
LILTING IS THIS LETTERING BY: S. ROSEN!

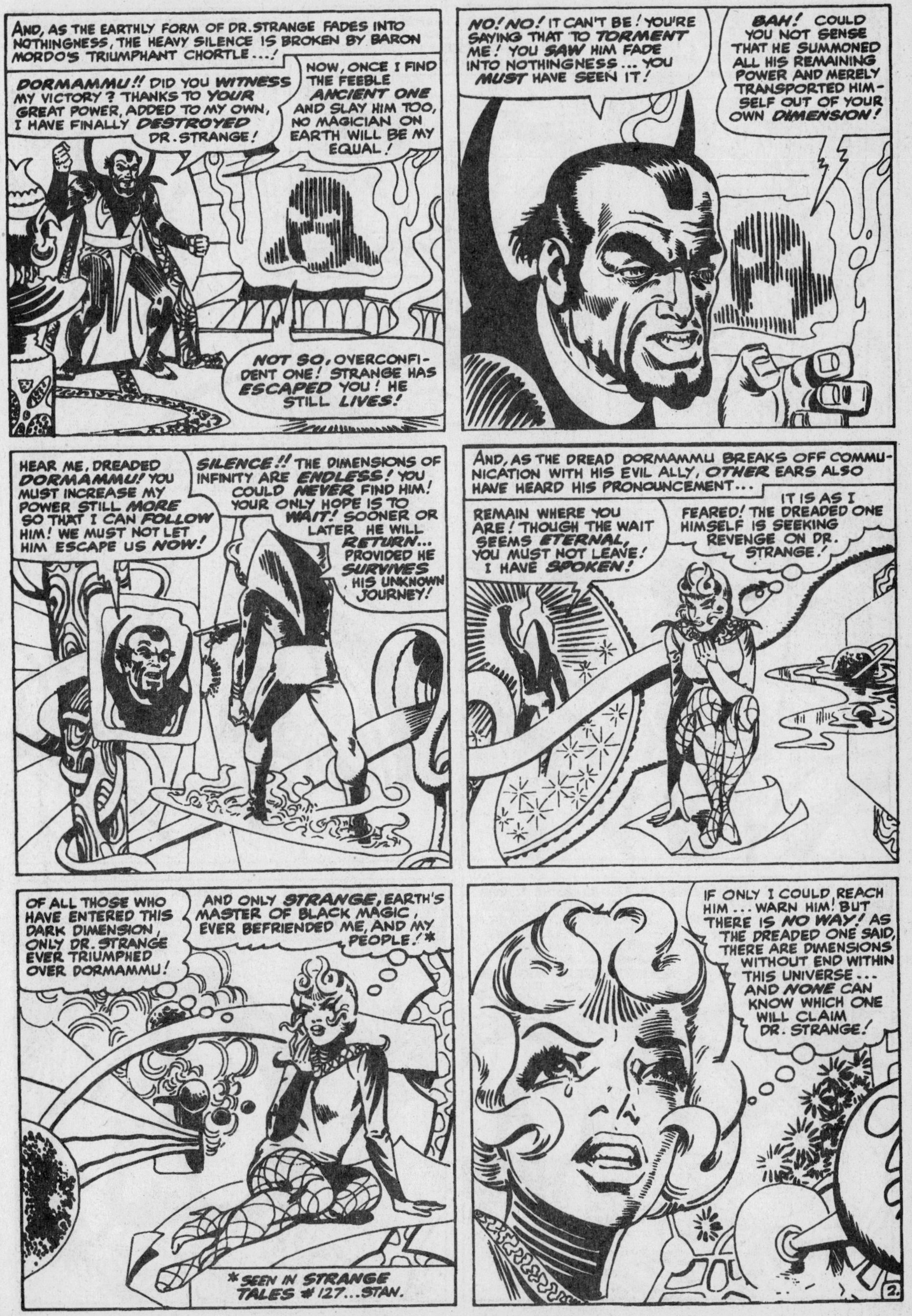

AND, AS THE EARTHLY FORM OF DR. STRANGE FADES INTO NOTHINGNESS, THE HEAVY SILENCE IS BROKEN BY BARON MORDO'S TRIUMPHANT CHORTLE ...!
DORMAMMU!! DID YOU WITNESS MY VICTORY? THANKS TO YOUR GREAT POWER, ADDED TO MY OWN, I HAVE FINALLY DESTROYED DR. STRANGE!
NOW, ONCE I FIND THE FEEBLE ANCIENT ONE AND SLAY HIM TOO, NO MAGICIAN ON EARTH WILL BE MY EQUAL!
NOT SO, OVERCONFIDENT ONE! STRANGE HAS ESCAPED YOU! HE STILL LIVES!
NO! NO! IT CAN'T BE! YOU'RE SAYING THAT TO TORMENT ME! YOU SAW HIM FADE INTO NOTHINGNESS ... YOU MUST HAVE SEEN IT!
BAH! COULD YOU NOT SENSE THAT HE SUMMONED ALL HIS REMAINING POWER AND MERELY TRANSPORTED HIMSELF OUT OF YOUR OWN DIMENSION!
HEAR ME, DREADED DORMAMMU! YOU MUST INCREASE MY POWER STILL MORE SO THAT I CAN FOLLOW HIM! WE MUST NOT LET HIM ESCAPE US NOW!
SILENCE!! THE DIMENSIONS OF INFINITY ARE ENDLESS! YOU COULD NEVER FIND HIM! YOUR ONLY HOPE IS TO WAIT! SOONER OR LATER HE WILL RETURN... PROVIDED HE SURVIVES HIS UNKNOWN JOURNEY!
AND, AS THE DREAD DORMAMMU BREAKS OFF COMMUNICATION WITH HIS EVIL ALLY, OTHER EARS ALSO HAVE HEARD HIS PRONOUNCEMENT...
REMAIN WHERE YOU ARE! THOUGH THE WAIT SEEMS ETERNAL, YOU MUST NOT LEAVE! I HAVE SPOKEN!
IT IS AS I FEARED! THE DREADED ONE HIMSELF IS SEEKING REVENGE ON DR. STRANGE!
OF ALL THOSE WHO HAVE ENTERED THIS DARK DIMENSION, ONLY DR. STRANGE EVER TRIUMPHED OVER DORMAMMU!
AND ONLY STRANGE, EARTH'S MASTER OF BLACK MAGIC, EVER BEFRIENDED ME, AND MY PEOPLE! *
* SEEN IN STRANGE TALES # 127... STAN.
IF ONLY I COULD REACH HIM ... WARN HIM! BUT THERE IS NO WAY! AS THE DREADED ONE SAID, THERE ARE DIMENSIONS WITHOUT END WITHIN THIS UNIVERSE ... AND NONE CAN KNOW WHICH ONE WILL CLAIM DR. STRANGE!
2.

AND, EVEN AS THE DISTRAUGHT FEMALE PONDERS THE FATE OF THE FLEEING MAGICIAN, A SHAPELESS FORM HURTLES THROUGH THE INFINITE AT A SPEED BEYOND HUMAN COMPREHENSION!

PASSING FROM DIMENSION TO DIMENSION, THE FORM PLUNGES ON, LOSING ITSELF IN THE MYSTIC MAZE OF INFINITY...

...PROPELLED BY A SPELL SO POWERFUL, SO IRRESISTIBLE, THAT IT SHATTERS EVERY OBSTACLE, EVERY BARRIER WHICH STANDS IN ITS WAY!

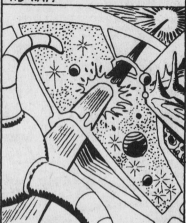

UNTIL, AT LAST, THE ENERGY OF THE SPELL IS EXHAUSTED, AND THE SPEEDING, LIVING ENTITY SLOWS ITS PACE, COMING TO REST IN A DIFFERENT DIMENSION... A NAMELESS LAND... A TIMELESS TIME!

SLOWLY, SILENTLY, THE ETHEREAL FORM BEGINS TO ASSUME A HUMAN SHAPE AS THE FLIGHT COMES TO ITS END, AN UNIMAGINABLE DISTANCE FROM THE WORLD WE KNOW AS EARTH!

AND THEN, THE JOURNEY DONE, DR. STRANGE OPENS HIS PIERCING EYES ONCE MORE...!

BY USING THE FORCE OF MORDO'S *OWN* POWER TO TRIGGER MY FINAL SPELL, I HAVE ESCAPED TO ANOTHER DIMENSION! BUT WHAT *NEW* DANGERS MIGHT BE AWAITING ME *HERE?*

SUDDENLY I SENSE ANOTHER PRESENCE NEAR ME!! BUT *WHO..??*

A *FEMALE FORM,* WITH FEAR AND ALARM SHOWING IN HER EYES!

I KNOW NOT WHO YOU ARE, NOR WHENCE YOU HAVE COME! BUT YOU MUST NOT *REMAIN!* THERE IS GREAT *DANGER* HERE!

3

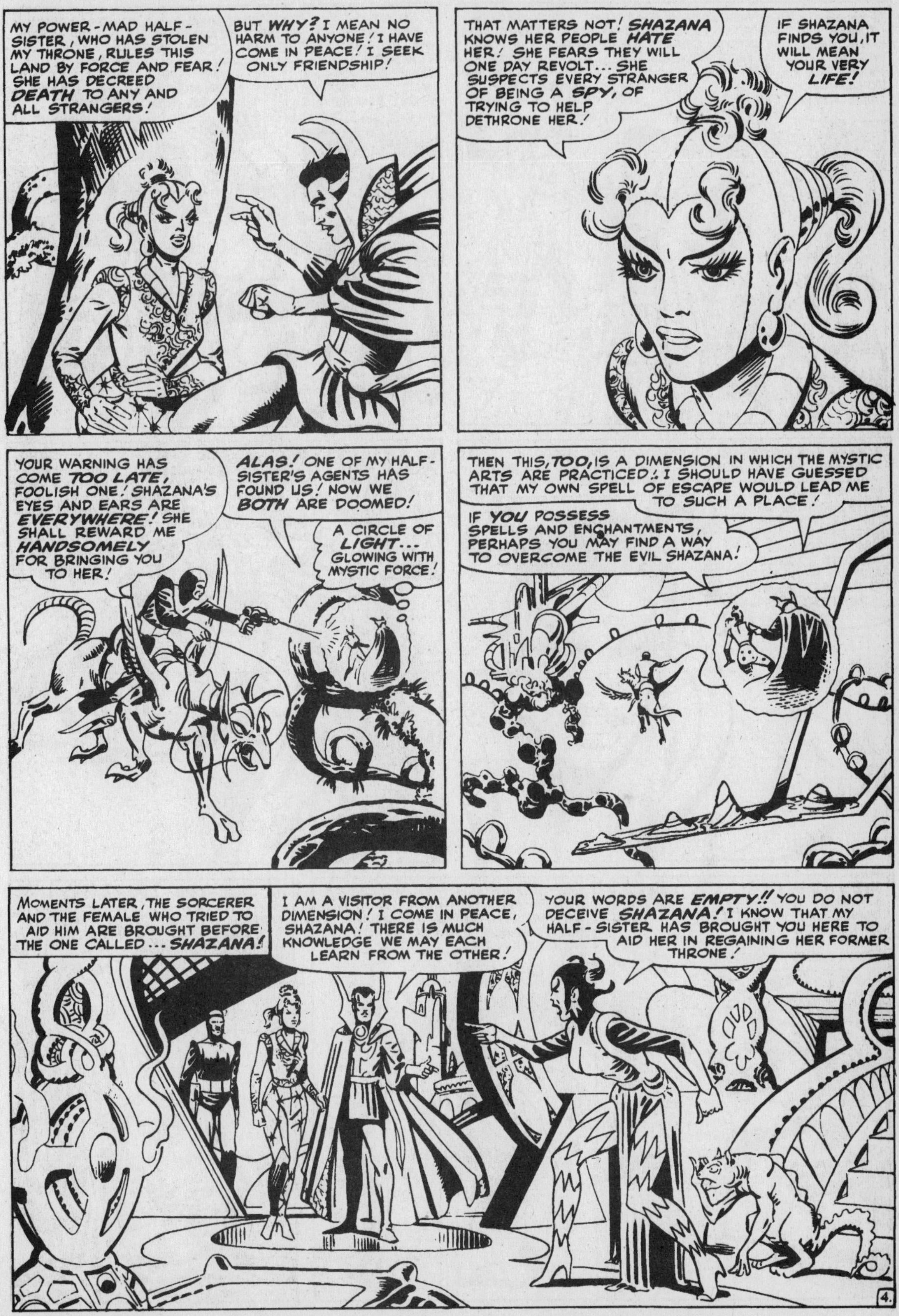
MY POWER-MAD HALF-SISTER, WHO HAS STOLEN MY THRONE, RULES THIS LAND BY FORCE AND FEAR! SHE HAS DECREED DEATH TO ANY AND ALL STRANGERS!
BUT WHY? I MEAN NO HARM TO ANYONE! I HAVE COME IN PEACE! I SEEK ONLY FRIENDSHIP!
THAT MATTERS NOT! SHAZANA KNOWS HER PEOPLE HATE HER! SHE FEARS THEY WILL ONE DAY REVOLT... SHE SUSPECTS EVERY STRANGER OF BEING A SPY, OF TRYING TO HELP DETHRONE HER!
IF SHAZANA FINDS YOU, IT WILL MEAN YOUR VERY LIFE!
YOUR WARNING HAS COME TOO LATE, FOOLISH ONE! SHAZANA'S EYES AND EARS ARE EVERYWHERE! SHE SHALL REWARD ME HANDSOMELY FOR BRINGING YOU TO HER!
ALAS! ONE OF MY HALF-SISTER'S AGENTS HAS FOUND US! NOW WE BOTH ARE DOOMED!
A CIRCLE OF LIGHT... GLOWING WITH MYSTIC FORCE!
THEN THIS, TOO, IS A DIMENSION IN WHICH THE MYSTIC ARTS ARE PRACTICED! I SHOULD HAVE GUESSED THAT MY OWN SPELL OF ESCAPE WOULD LEAD ME TO SUCH A PLACE!
IF YOU POSSESS SPELLS AND ENCHANTMENTS, PERHAPS YOU MAY FIND A WAY TO OVERCOME THE EVIL SHAZANA!
MOMENTS LATER, THE SORCERER AND THE FEMALE WHO TRIED TO AID HIM ARE BROUGHT BEFORE THE ONE CALLED... SHAZANA!
I AM A VISITOR FROM ANOTHER DIMENSION! I COME IN PEACE, SHAZANA! THERE IS MUCH KNOWLEDGE WE MAY EACH LEARN FROM THE OTHER!
YOUR WORDS ARE EMPTY!! YOU DO NOT DECEIVE SHAZANA! I KNOW THAT MY HALF-SISTER HAS BROUGHT YOU HERE TO AID HER IN REGAINING HER FORMER THRONE!
4.

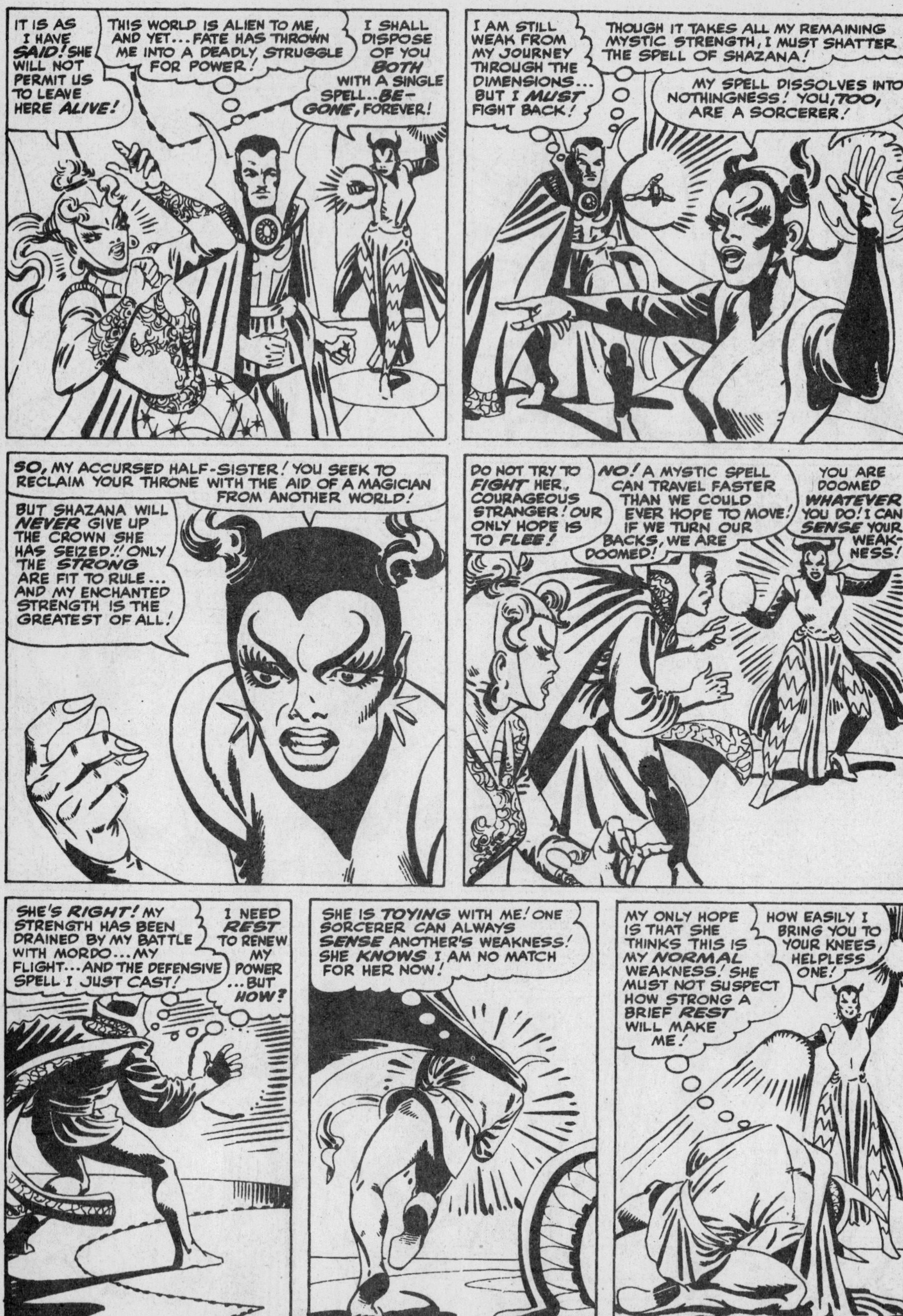
IT IS AS I HAVE SAID! SHE WILL NOT PERMIT US TO LEAVE HERE ALIVE!
THIS WORLD IS ALIEN TO ME, AND YET... FATE HAS THROWN ME INTO A DEADLY STRUGGLE FOR POWER!
I SHALL DISPOSE OF YOU BOTH WITH A SINGLE SPELL.. BE-GONE, FOREVER!
I AM STILL WEAK FROM MY JOURNEY THROUGH THE DIMENSIONS... BUT I MUST FIGHT BACK!
THOUGH IT TAKES ALL MY REMAINING MYSTIC STRENGTH, I MUST SHATTER THE SPELL OF SHAZANA!
MY SPELL DISSOLVES INTO NOTHINGNESS! YOU, TOO, ARE A SORCERER!
SO, MY ACCURSED HALF-SISTER! YOU SEEK TO RECLAIM YOUR THRONE WITH THE AID OF A MAGICIAN FROM ANOTHER WORLD!
BUT SHAZANA WILL NEVER GIVE UP THE CROWN SHE HAS SEIZED!! ONLY THE STRONG ARE FIT TO RULE... AND MY ENCHANTED STRENGTH IS THE GREATEST OF ALL!
DO NOT TRY TO FIGHT HER, COURAGEOUS STRANGER! OUR ONLY HOPE IS TO FLEE!
NO! A MYSTIC SPELL CAN TRAVEL FASTER THAN WE COULD EVER HOPE TO MOVE! IF WE TURN OUR BACKS, WE ARE DOOMED!
YOU ARE DOOMED WHATEVER YOU DO! I CAN SENSE YOUR WEAK-NESS!
SHE'S RIGHT! MY STRENGTH HAS BEEN DRAINED BY MY BATTLE WITH MORDO... MY FLIGHT... AND THE DEFENSIVE SPELL I JUST CAST!
I NEED REST TO RENEW MY POWER ...BUT HOW?
SHE IS TOYING WITH ME! ONE SORCERER CAN ALWAYS SENSE ANOTHER'S WEAKNESS! SHE KNOWS I AM NO MATCH FOR HER NOW!
MY ONLY HOPE IS THAT SHE THINKS THIS IS MY NORMAL WEAKNESS! SHE MUST NOT SUSPECT HOW STRONG A BRIEF REST WILL MAKE ME!
HOW EASILY I BRING YOU TO YOUR KNEES, HELPLESS ONE!
5.

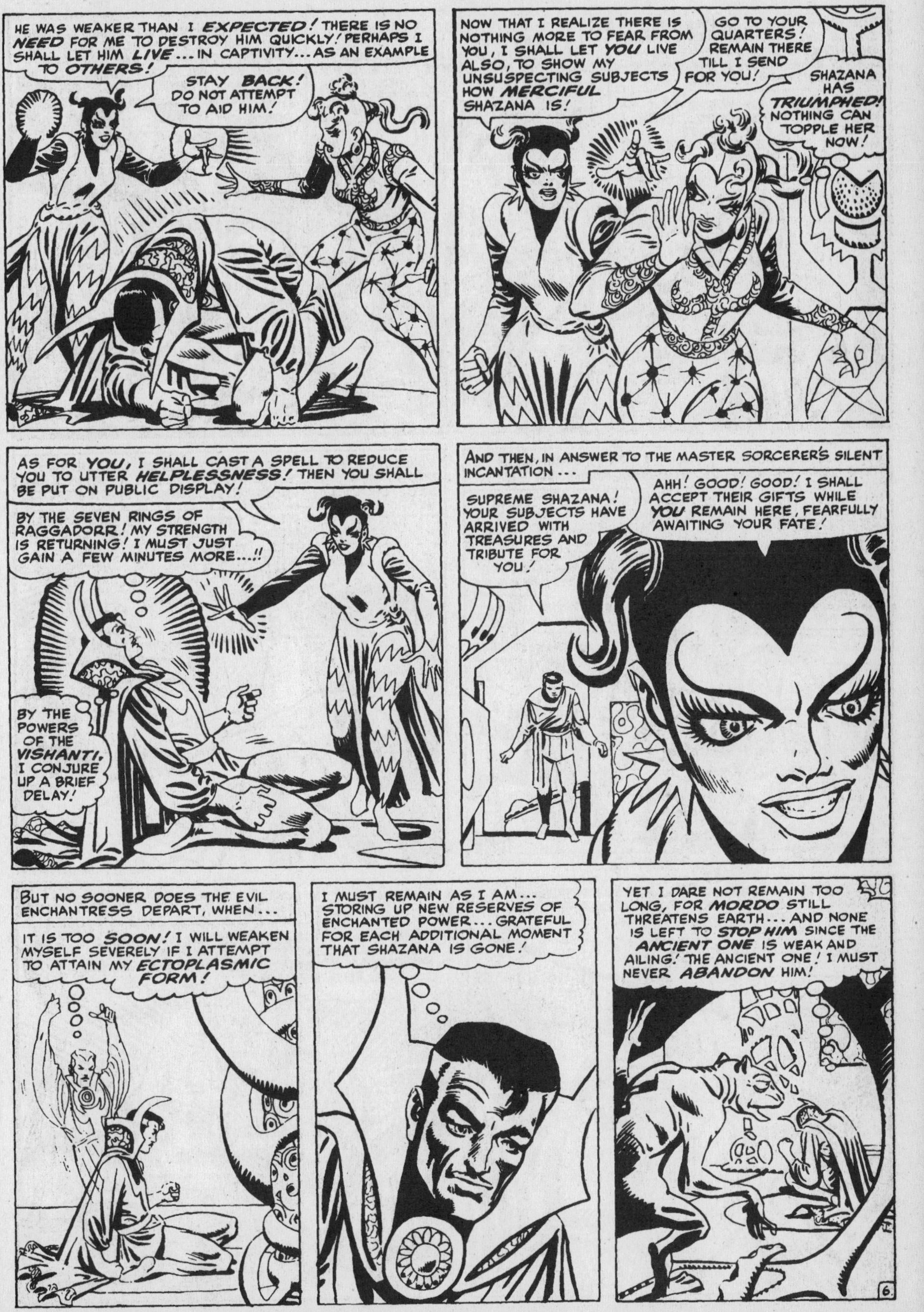

HE WAS WEAKER THAN I EXPECTED! THERE IS NO NEED FOR ME TO DESTROY HIM QUICKLY! PERHAPS I SHALL LET HIM LIVE... IN CAPTIVITY... AS AN EXAMPLE TO OTHERS!
STAY BACK! DO NOT ATTEMPT TO AID HIM!
NOW THAT I REALIZE THERE IS NOTHING MORE TO FEAR FROM YOU, I SHALL LET YOU LIVE ALSO, TO SHOW MY UNSUSPECTING SUBJECTS HOW MERCIFUL SHAZANA IS!
GO TO YOUR QUARTERS! REMAIN THERE TILL I SEND FOR YOU!
SHAZANA HAS TRIUMPHED! NOTHING CAN TOPPLE HER NOW!
AS FOR YOU, I SHALL CAST A SPELL TO REDUCE YOU TO UTTER HELPLESSNESS! THEN YOU SHALL BE PUT ON PUBLIC DISPLAY!
BY THE SEVEN RINGS OF RAGGADORR! MY STRENGTH IS RETURNING! I MUST JUST GAIN A FEW MINUTES MORE...!!
BY THE POWERS OF THE VISHANTI, I CONJURE UP A BRIEF DELAY!
AND THEN, IN ANSWER TO THE MASTER SORCERER'S SILENT INCANTATION...
SUPREME SHAZANA! YOUR SUBJECTS HAVE ARRIVED WITH TREASURES AND TRIBUTE FOR YOU!
AHH! GOOD! GOOD! I SHALL ACCEPT THEIR GIFTS WHILE YOU REMAIN HERE, FEARFULLY AWAITING YOUR FATE!
BUT NO SOONER DOES THE EVIL ENCHANTRESS DEPART, WHEN...
IT IS TOO SOON! I WILL WEAKEN MYSELF SEVERELY IF I ATTEMPT TO ATTAIN MY ECTOPLASMIC FORM!
I MUST REMAIN AS I AM... STORING UP NEW RESERVES OF ENCHANTED POWER... GRATEFUL FOR EACH ADDITIONAL MOMENT THAT SHAZANA IS GONE!
YET I DARE NOT REMAIN TOO LONG, FOR MORDO STILL THREATENS EARTH... AND NONE IS LEFT TO STOP HIM SINCE THE ANCIENT ONE IS WEAK AND AILING! THE ANCIENT ONE! I MUST NEVER ABANDON HIM!
6.

AND, EVEN AS *DR. STRANGE* THINKS OF HIS AGED MENTOR, THE ANCIENT ONE LIES HIDDEN IN A LONELY CAVE HIGH IN THE MYSTERIOUS MOUNTAINS OF TIBET...

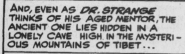

MY HEART IS HEAVY WHENEVER I MUST LEAVE THE MASTER... EVEN THOUGH IT BE FOR A BRIEF MOMENT WHILE I FETCH WATER FOR HIS DRY, PARCHED LIPS!

DOCTOR STRANGE! HE *NEEDS* ME... MY GREATEST DISCIPLE *NEEDS* ME... AND I AM TOO ILL TO AID HIM...

MASTER! DO NOT TORMENT YOURSELF! YOU NEED REST! I BEG THEE, MASTER!

HE LAPSES INTO A COMA AGAIN! HE, THE GREATEST SORCERER OF ALL! ALAS, *STRANGE* HAS VANISHED, AND EVIL *MORDO* SEEKS TO FIND HIM AND DESTROY HIM WHILE HE IS HELPLESS!

BUT IN A FAR DISTANT, FAR DIFFERENT DIMENSION, AT THAT VERY MOMENT, DR. STRANGE RESOLVES TO MAKE HIS MOVE...

THE TIME HAS *COME!* THERE IS NOTHING FURTHER TO BE GAINED BY WAITING! I MUST *USE* THE POWERS THAT HAVE RETURNED TO ME!

THIS BEAST BEFORE ME... IT IS THE *PET* OF SHAZANA! ITS BRAIN MAY HOLD THE KNOWLEDGE I NEED!

BY THE HOARY HOSTS OF HOGGOTH, I COMMAND THEE TO REMAIN *MOTIONLESS!*

NOW, LET THE MYSTIC EYE OF MY *AMULET* COME FORTH!

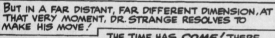

WHILE MUTTERING THE INCANTATIONS OF AGAMOTTO, DR. STRANGE WILLS HIS AMULET'S EYE TO PIERCE THE VERY BRAIN OF THE CREATURE WHO STANDS BEFORE HIM...

I MUST PROBE DEEP INTO THIS BEAST'S HIDDEN *MEMORIES* UNTIL I FIND THE FACT I SEEK! DEEPER... *DEEPER...* BY THE POWER OF AGAMOTTO!

AT LAST! AN IMAGE FORMS! A FIGURE TAKES SHAPE! IT IS THE SINISTER *SHAZANA!* BUT I MUST GO *STILL* FURTHER BACK... I CANNOT STOP NOW!

THEN, FINALLY... THROUGH A SORCERY KNOWN ONLY TO AN APPOINTED FEW, HE FINDS...

I *SEE* IT NOW! THE *SOURCE* OF SHAZANA'S POWER! SHE TEMPTED AN UNSUSPECTING *MAGICIAN* TO ENDOW HER WITH THE SECRET OF TIMELESS SPELLS!

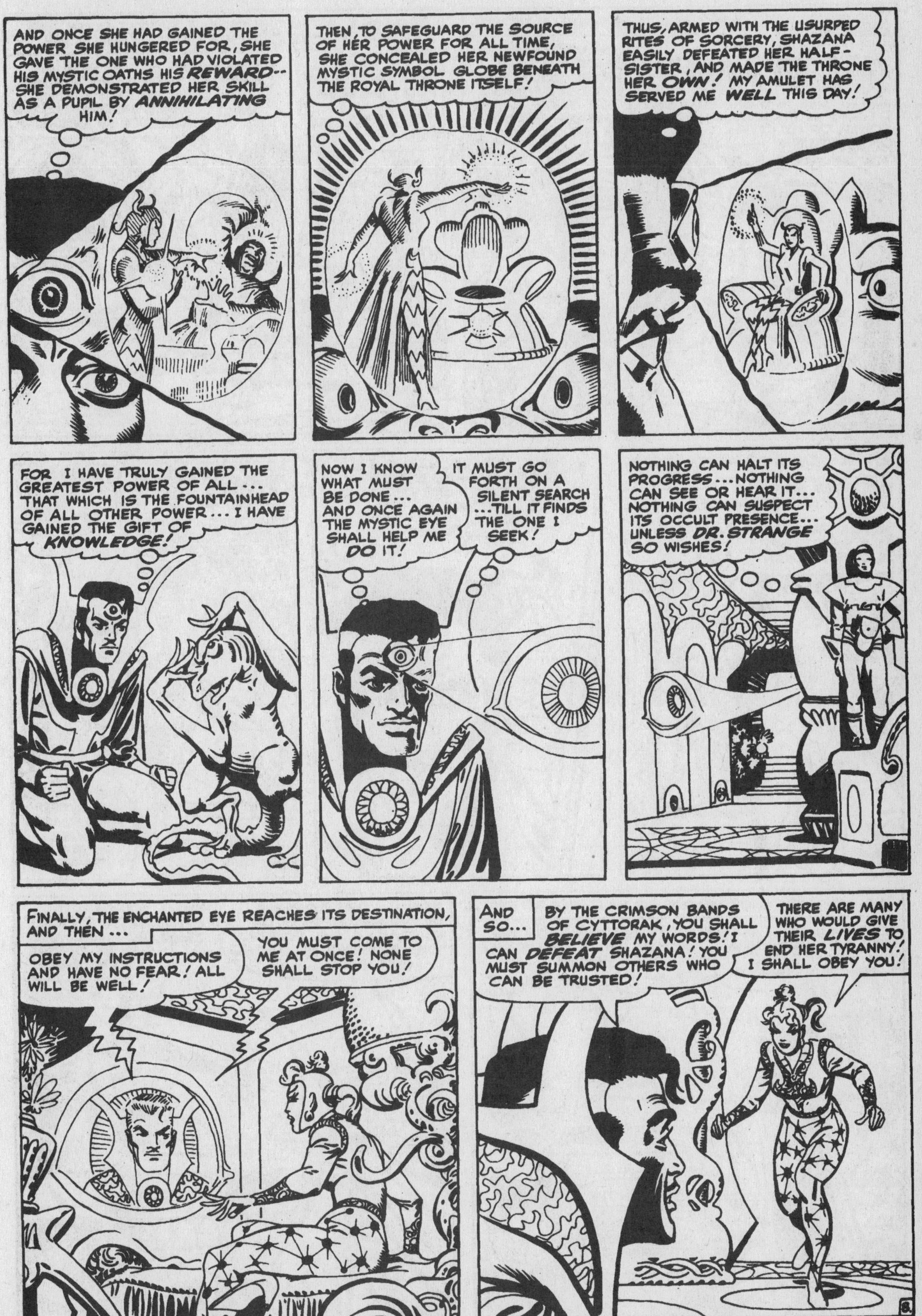

AND ONCE SHE HAD GAINED THE POWER SHE HUNGERED FOR, SHE GAVE THE ONE WHO HAD VIOLATED HIS MYSTIC OATHS HIS REWARD-- SHE DEMONSTRATED HER SKILL AS A PUPIL BY ANNIHILATING HIM!
THEN, TO SAFEGUARD THE SOURCE OF HER POWER FOR ALL TIME, SHE CONCEALED HER NEWFOUND MYSTIC SYMBOL GLOBE BENEATH THE ROYAL THRONE ITSELF!
THUS, ARMED WITH THE USURPED RITES OF SORCERY, SHAZANA EASILY DEFEATED HER HALF-SISTER, AND MADE THE THRONE HER OWN! MY AMULET HAS SERVED ME WELL THIS DAY!
FOR I HAVE TRULY GAINED THE GREATEST POWER OF ALL... THAT WHICH IS THE FOUNTAINHEAD OF ALL OTHER POWER... I HAVE GAINED THE GIFT OF KNOWLEDGE!
NOW I KNOW WHAT MUST BE DONE... AND ONCE AGAIN THE MYSTIC EYE SHALL HELP ME DO IT!
IT MUST GO FORTH ON A SILENT SEARCH ...TILL IT FINDS THE ONE I SEEK!
NOTHING CAN HALT ITS PROGRESS...NOTHING CAN SEE OR HEAR IT... NOTHING CAN SUSPECT ITS OCCULT PRESENCE... UNLESS DR. STRANGE SO WISHES!
FINALLY, THE ENCHANTED EYE REACHES ITS DESTINATION, AND THEN...
OBEY MY INSTRUCTIONS AND HAVE NO FEAR! ALL WILL BE WELL!
YOU MUST COME TO ME AT ONCE! NONE SHALL STOP YOU!
AND SO...
BY THE CRIMSON BANDS OF CYTTORAK, YOU SHALL BELIEVE MY WORDS! I CAN DEFEAT SHAZANA! YOU MUST SUMMON OTHERS WHO CAN BE TRUSTED!
THERE ARE MANY WHO WOULD GIVE THEIR LIVES TO END HER TYRANNY! I SHALL OBEY YOU!
8

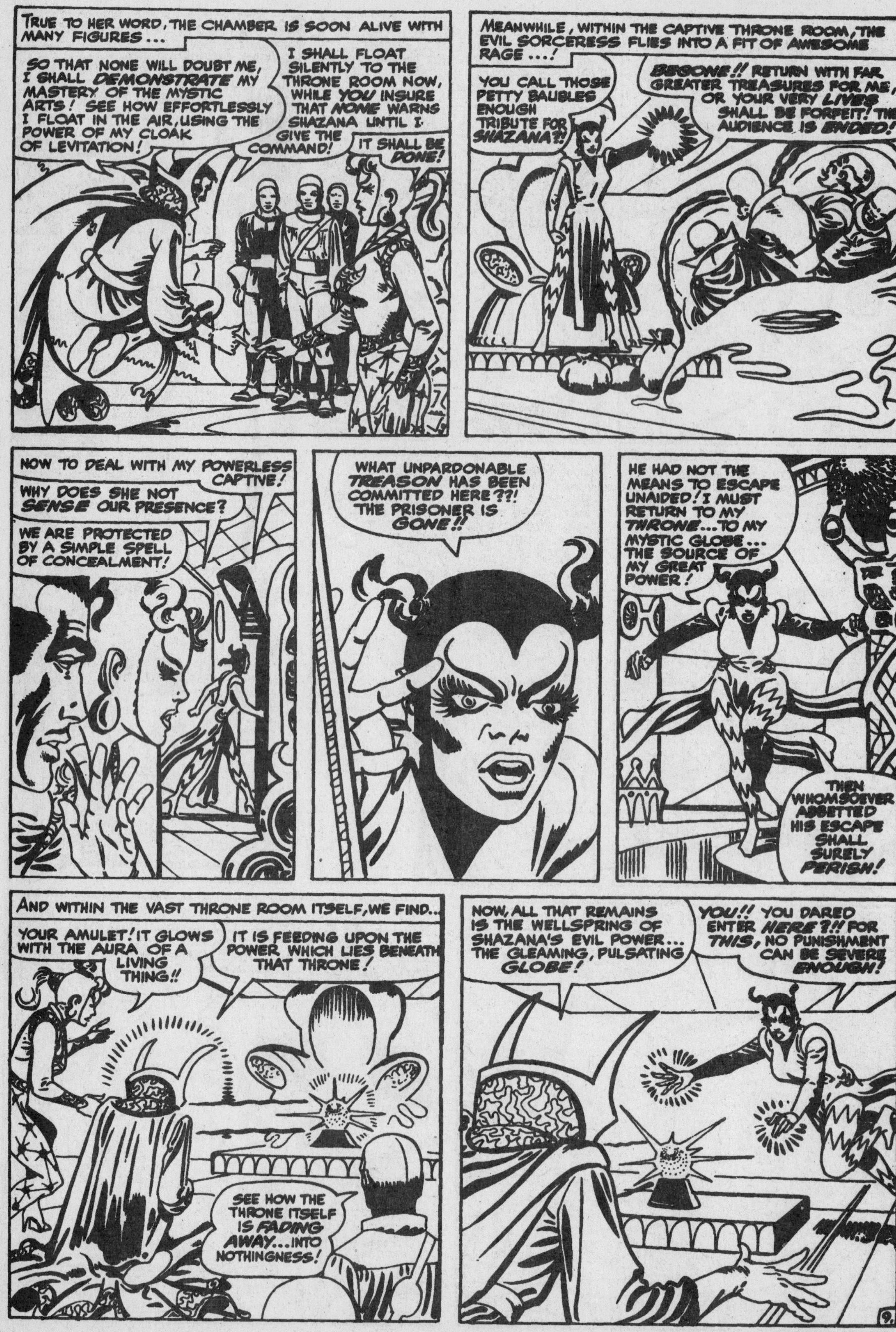
TRUE TO HER WORD, THE CHAMBER IS SOON ALIVE WITH MANY FIGURES...
SO THAT NONE WILL DOUBT ME, I SHALL DEMONSTRATE MY MASTERY OF THE MYSTIC ARTS! SEE HOW EFFORTLESSLY I FLOAT IN THE AIR, USING THE POWER OF MY CLOAK OF LEVITATION!
I SHALL FLOAT SILENTLY TO THE THRONE ROOM NOW, WHILE YOU INSURE THAT NONE WARNS SHAZANA UNTIL I GIVE THE COMMAND!
IT SHALL BE DONE!
MEANWHILE, WITHIN THE CAPTIVE THRONE ROOM, THE EVIL SORCERESS FLIES INTO A FIT OF AWESOME RAGE...!
YOU CALL THOSE PETTY BAUBLES ENOUGH TRIBUTE FOR SHAZANA?!
BEGONE!! RETURN WITH FAR GREATER TREASURES FOR ME, OR YOUR VERY LIVES SHALL BE FORFEIT! THE AUDIENCE IS ENDED!
NOW TO DEAL WITH MY POWERLESS CAPTIVE!
WHY DOES SHE NOT SENSE OUR PRESENCE?
WE ARE PROTECTED BY A SIMPLE SPELL OF CONCEALMENT!
WHAT UNPARDONABLE TREASON HAS BEEN COMMITTED HERE??! THE PRISONER IS GONE!!
HE HAD NOT THE MEANS TO ESCAPE UNAIDED! I MUST RETURN TO MY THRONE...TO MY MYSTIC GLOBE... THE SOURCE OF MY GREAT POWER!
THEN WHOMSOEVER ABETTED HIS ESCAPE SHALL SURELY PERISH!
AND WITHIN THE VAST THRONE ROOM ITSELF, WE FIND...
YOUR AMULET! IT GLOWS WITH THE AURA OF A LIVING THING!!
IT IS FEEDING UPON THE POWER WHICH LIES BENEATH THAT THRONE!
SEE HOW THE THRONE ITSELF IS FADING AWAY...INTO NOTHINGNESS!
NOW, ALL THAT REMAINS IS THE WELLSPRING OF SHAZANA'S EVIL POWER... THE GLEAMING, PULSATING GLOBE!
YOU!! YOU DARED ENTER HERE?!! FOR THIS, NO PUNISHMENT CAN BE SEVERE ENOUGH!
9.

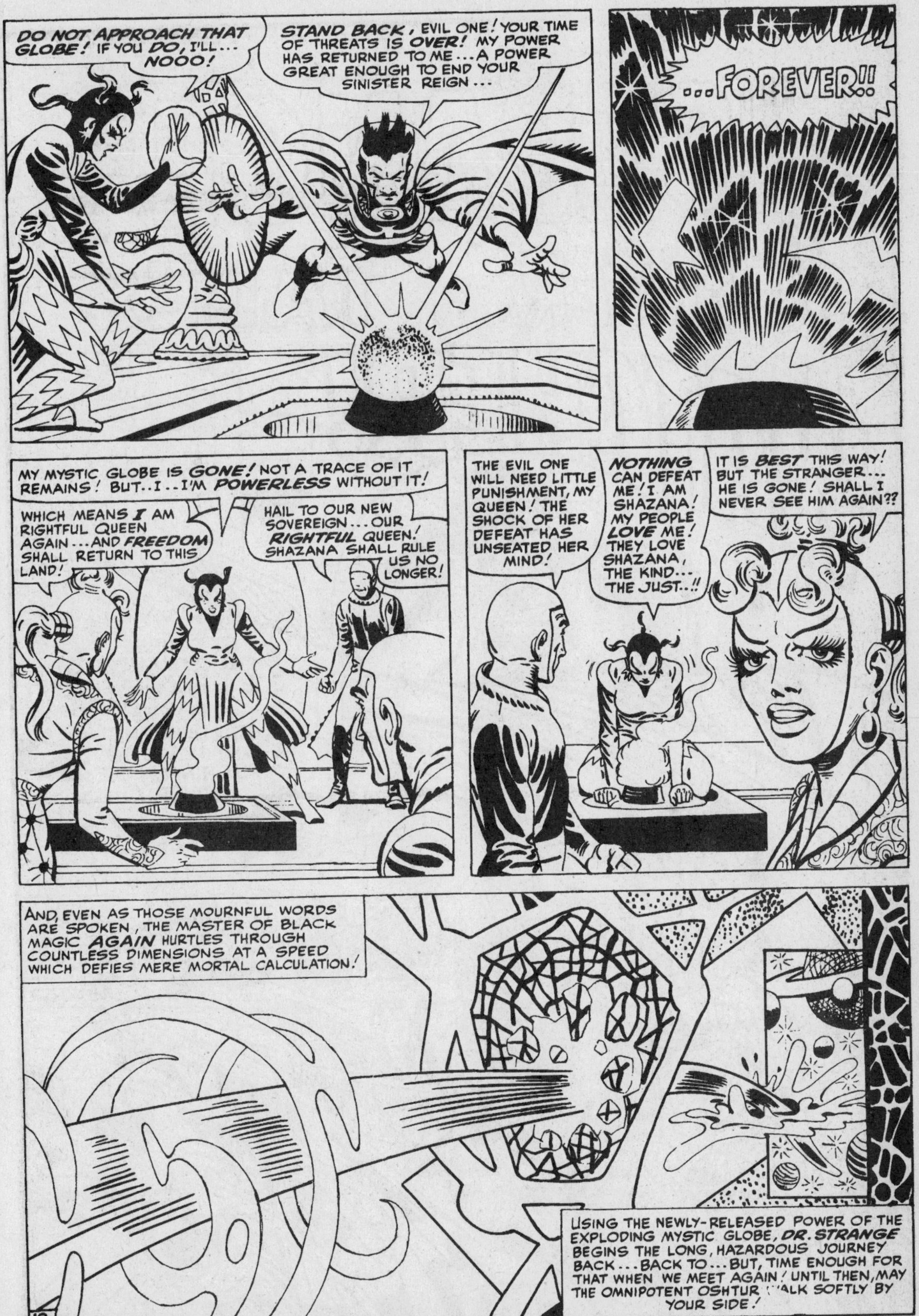

DO NOT APPROACH THAT GLOBE! IF YOU DO, I'LL... NOOO!
STAND BACK, EVIL ONE! YOUR TIME OF THREATS IS OVER! MY POWER HAS RETURNED TO ME... A POWER GREAT ENOUGH TO END YOUR SINISTER REIGN...
...FOREVER!!
MY MYSTIC GLOBE IS GONE! NOT A TRACE OF IT REMAINS! BUT..I...I'M POWERLESS WITHOUT IT!
WHICH MEANS I AM RIGHTFUL QUEEN AGAIN...AND FREEDOM SHALL RETURN TO THIS LAND!
HAIL TO OUR NEW SOVEREIGN... OUR RIGHTFUL QUEEN! SHAZANA SHALL RULE US NO LONGER!
THE EVIL ONE WILL NEED LITTLE PUNISHMENT, MY QUEEN! THE SHOCK OF HER DEFEAT HAS UNSEATED HER MIND!
NOTHING CAN DEFEAT ME! I AM SHAZANA! MY PEOPLE LOVE ME! THEY LOVE SHAZANA, THE KIND... THE JUST..!!
IT IS BEST THIS WAY! BUT THE STRANGER... HE IS GONE! SHALL I NEVER SEE HIM AGAIN??
AND, EVEN AS THOSE MOURNFUL WORDS ARE SPOKEN, THE MASTER OF BLACK MAGIC AGAIN HURTLES THROUGH COUNTLESS DIMENSIONS AT A SPEED WHICH DEFIES MERE MORTAL CALCULATION!
USING THE NEWLY-RELEASED POWER OF THE EXPLODING MYSTIC GLOBE, DR. STRANGE BEGINS THE LONG, HAZARDOUS JOURNEY BACK... BACK TO... BUT, TIME ENOUGH FOR THAT WHEN WE MEET AGAIN! UNTIL THEN, MAY THE OMNIPOTENT OSHTUR WALK SOFTLY BY YOUR SIDE!
10.

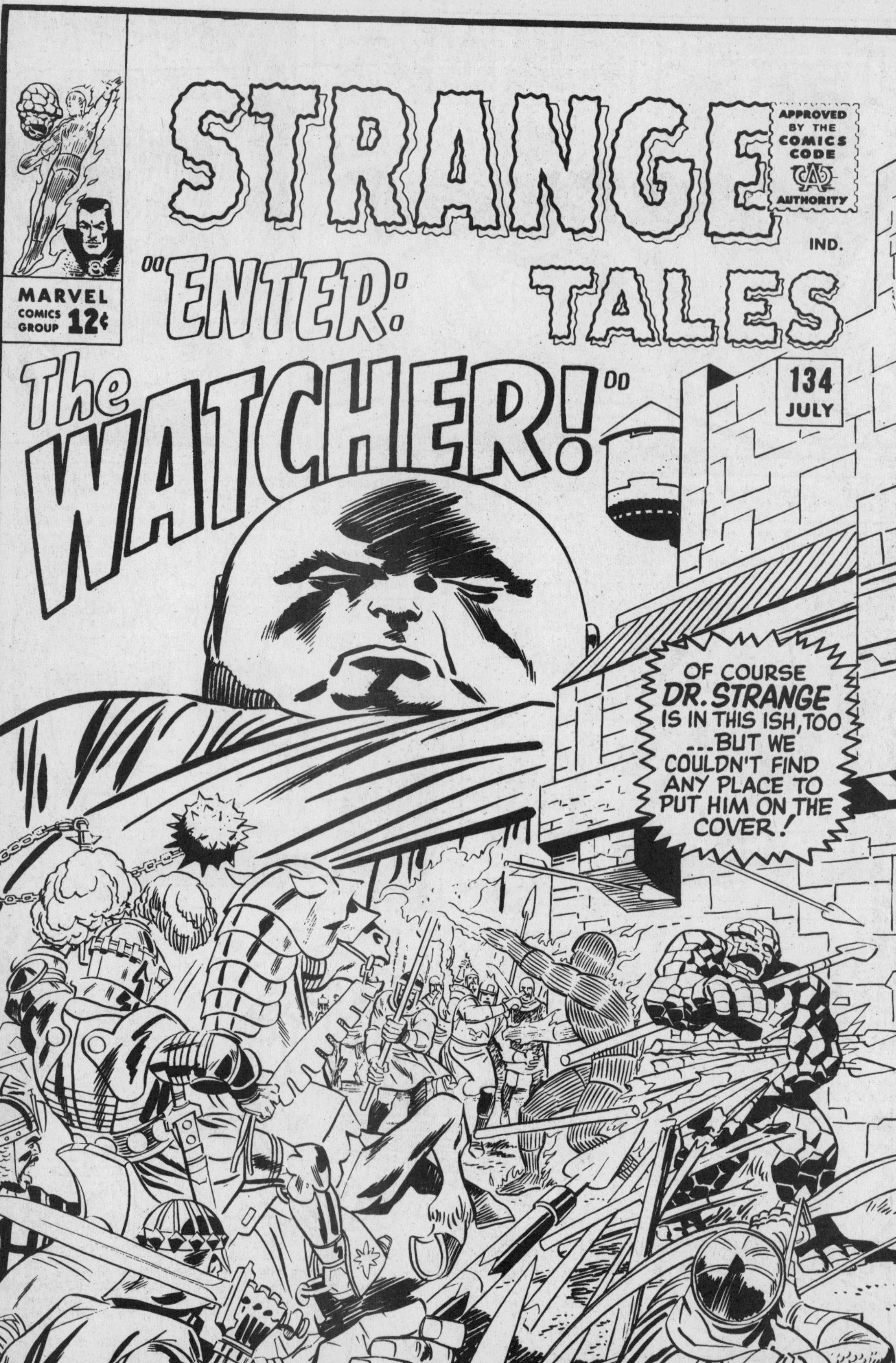
MARVEL COMICS GROUP 12¢
STRANGE TALES
APPROVED BY THE COMICS CODE AUTHORITY
IND.
"ENTER: The WATCHER!"
134 JULY
OF COURSE DR. STRANGE IS IN THIS ISH, TOO ...BUT WE COULDN'T FIND ANY PLACE TO PUT HIM ON THE COVER!

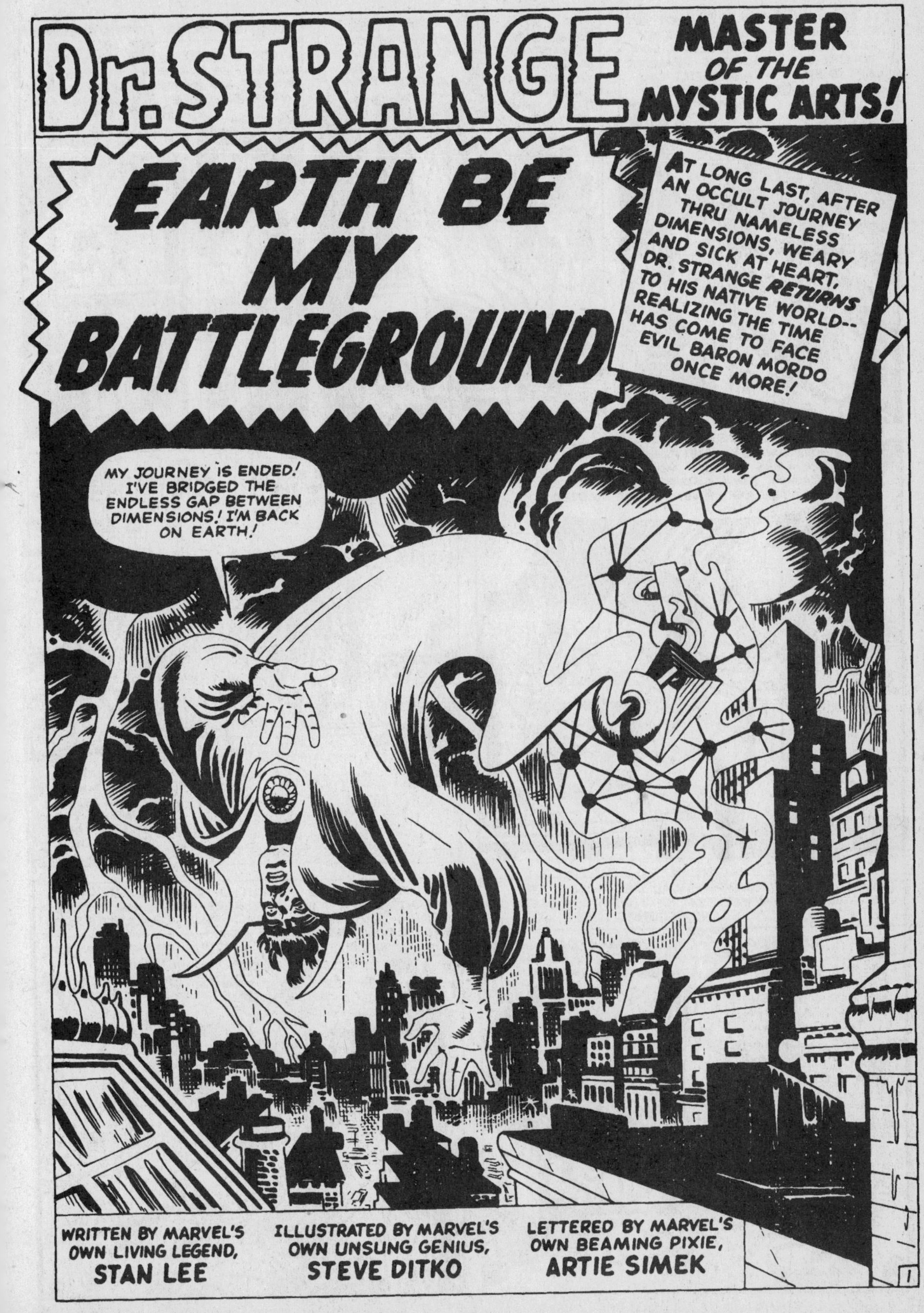
Dr. STRANGE MASTER OF THE MYSTIC ARTS!
EARTH BE MY BATTLEGROUND
AT LONG LAST, AFTER AN OCCULT JOURNEY THRU NAMELESS DIMENSIONS, WEARY AND SICK AT HEART, DR. STRANGE RETURNS TO HIS NATIVE WORLD-- REALIZING THE TIME HAS COME TO FACE EVIL BARON MORDO ONCE MORE!
MY JOURNEY IS ENDED! I'VE BRIDGED THE ENDLESS GAP BETWEEN DIMENSIONS! I'M BACK ON EARTH!
WRITTEN BY MARVEL'S OWN LIVING LEGEND, STAN LEE
ILLUSTRATED BY MARVEL'S OWN UNSUNG GENIUS, STEVE DITKO
LETTERED BY MARVEL'S OWN BEAMING PIXIE, ARTIE SIMEK
1

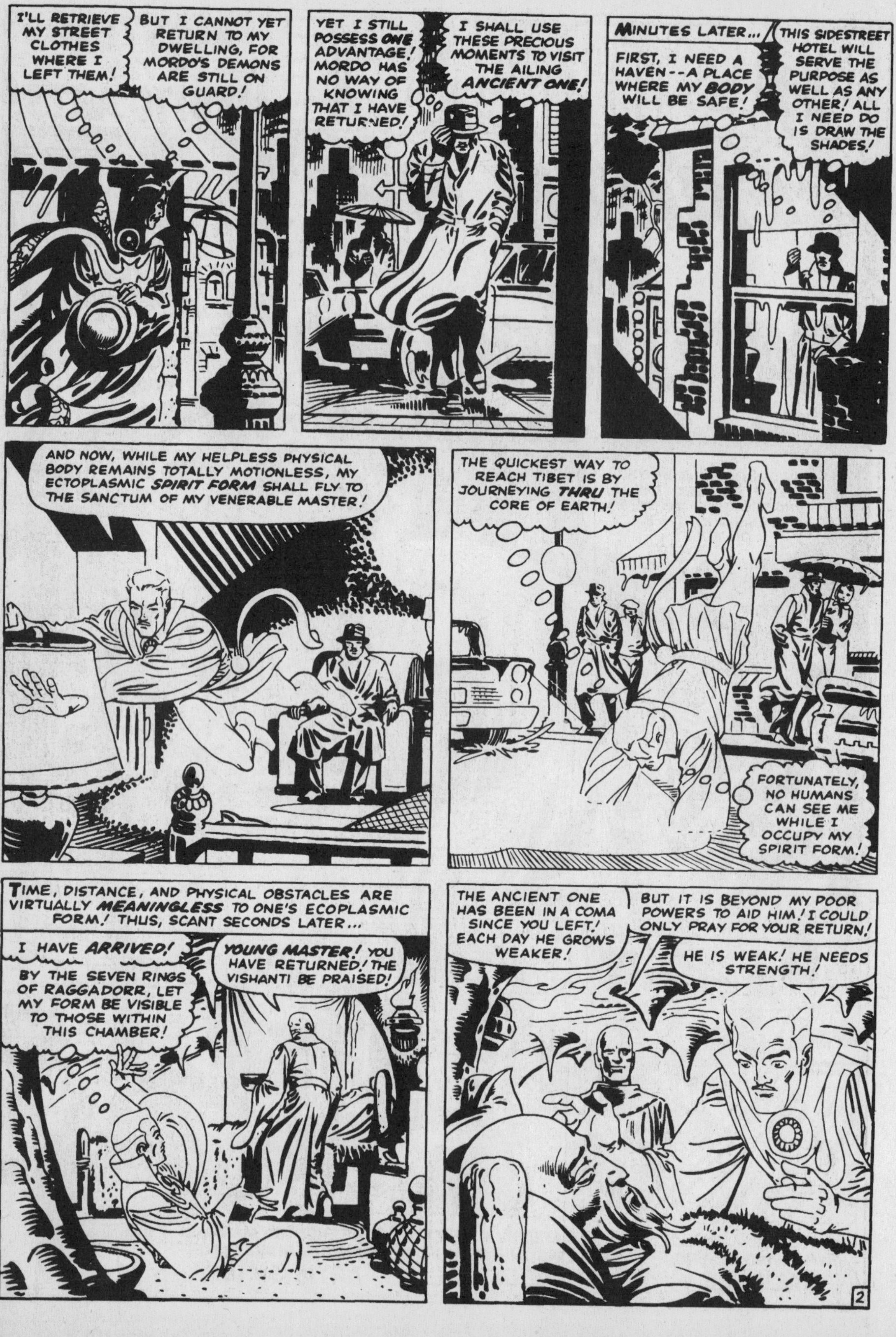

I'LL RETRIEVE MY STREET CLOTHES WHERE I LEFT THEM!
BUT I CANNOT YET RETURN TO MY DWELLING, FOR MORDO'S DEMONS ARE STILL ON GUARD!
YET I STILL POSSESS ONE ADVANTAGE! MORDO HAS NO WAY OF KNOWING THAT I HAVE RETURNED!
I SHALL USE THESE PRECIOUS MOMENTS TO VISIT THE AILING ANCIENT ONE!
MINUTES LATER...
FIRST, I NEED A HAVEN--A PLACE WHERE MY BODY WILL BE SAFE!
THIS SIDESTREET HOTEL WILL SERVE THE PURPOSE AS WELL AS ANY OTHER! ALL I NEED DO IS DRAW THE SHADES!
AND NOW, WHILE MY HELPLESS PHYSICAL BODY REMAINS TOTALLY MOTIONLESS, MY ECTOPLASMIC SPIRIT FORM SHALL FLY TO THE SANCTUM OF MY VENERABLE MASTER!
THE QUICKEST WAY TO REACH TIBET IS BY JOURNEYING THRU THE CORE OF EARTH!
FORTUNATELY, NO HUMANS CAN SEE ME WHILE I OCCUPY MY SPIRIT FORM!
TIME, DISTANCE, AND PHYSICAL OBSTACLES ARE VIRTUALLY MEANINGLESS TO ONE'S ECOPLASMIC FORM! THUS, SCANT SECONDS LATER...
I HAVE ARRIVED!
BY THE SEVEN RINGS OF RAGGADORR, LET MY FORM BE VISIBLE TO THOSE WITHIN THIS CHAMBER!
YOUNG MASTER! YOU HAVE RETURNED! THE VISHANTI BE PRAISED!
THE ANCIENT ONE HAS BEEN IN A COMA SINCE YOU LEFT! EACH DAY HE GROWS WEAKER!
BUT IT IS BEYOND MY POOR POWERS TO AID HIM! I COULD ONLY PRAY FOR YOUR RETURN!
HE IS WEAK! HE NEEDS STRENGTH!

MANY TIMES IN HIS COMA, HE MUTTERED A WORD--ONLY ONE WORD, OVER AND OVER AGAIN! THE WORD-- *ETERNITY!*

NO TIME FOR THAT NOW! I MUST REPLENISH HIS STRENGTH QUICKLY-- BEFORE IT IS TOO LATE!

LET THE POWER OF MY ENCHANTED *AMULET* BATHE THEE, VENERABLE MASTER! LET ITS STRENGTH BECOME *THY* STRENGTH!

ENOUGH! TOO STRONG A DOSE COULD PROVE *FATAL!*

I MUST *GO* NOW! I SHALL RETURN PERIODICALLY TO RE-ADMINISTER THE AMULET'S POWER!

TILL THEN, GUARD HIM WELL, FAITHFUL ONE-- WHILE I PONDER THE MEANING OF--- *ETERNITY!*

MORDO'S EVIL SPIRITS *STILL* SEARCH THE CAVERNS BENEATH THIS LAND, SEEKING THE ANCIENT ONE! MAY THE VAPORS OF VALTORR BLIND THEIR EYES!

HERE, WITHIN THE MASTER'S NOW-DESERTED RETREAT, AMONG HIS BOOKS AND PAPERS, I MAY FIND WHAT I SEEK!

MORDO HAS TOUCHED NOTHING! HE CARES NAUGHT FOR KNOWLEDGE --ONLY FOR *POWER!*

THEN, USING THE UNCANNY POWER OF HIS AMULET'S MYSTIC EYE, THE MASTER OF BLACK MAGIC SCANS EVERY VOLUME WITHOUT TOUCHING A PAGE, BUT TO NO AVAIL!

IT IS NO USE! THERE IS NO REFERENCE TO *ETERNITY!*

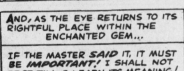

AND, AS THE EYE RETURNS TO ITS RIGHTFUL PLACE WITHIN THE ENCHANTED GEM...

IF THE MASTER *SAID* IT, IT MUST BE *IMPORTANT!* I SHALL NOT REST TILL I LEARN ITS MEANING!

BUT, AS THE SILENT ECTOPLASMIC FIGURE GLIDES THRU A WALL...

I FORGOT TO DISSOLVE THE SPELL OF VISIBILITY WHICH I CAST OVER MYSELF! ONE OF MORDO'S SPIRITS *SEES* ME!

AND AT THAT VERY INSTANT...

A *SIGNAL!* ONE OF MY SPIRITS HAS *FOUND* HIM! AT *LAST!*

3

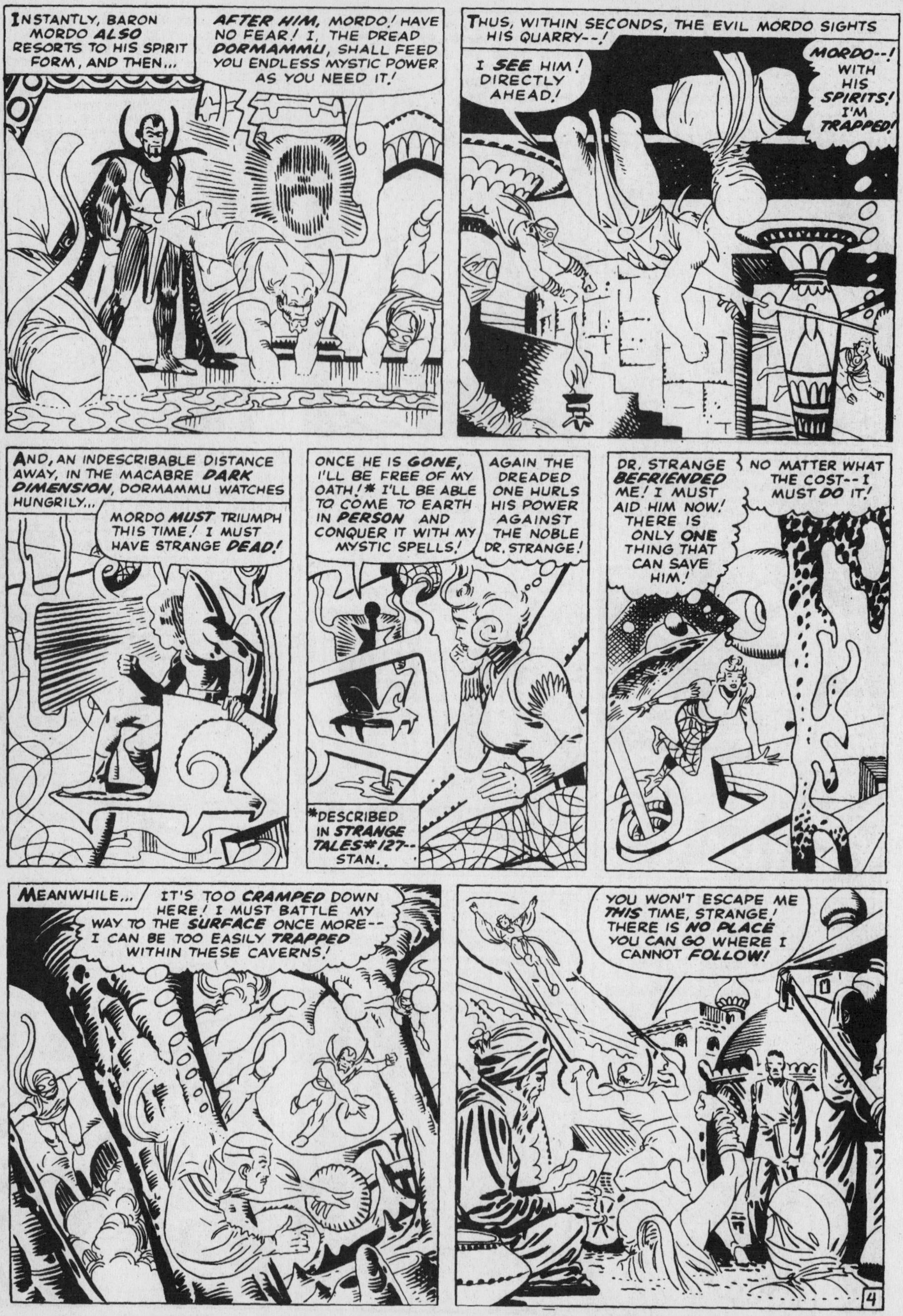
INSTANTLY, BARON MORDO ALSO RESORTS TO HIS SPIRIT FORM, AND THEN...
AFTER HIM, MORDO! HAVE NO FEAR! I, THE DREAD DORMAMMU, SHALL FEED YOU ENDLESS MYSTIC POWER AS YOU NEED IT!
THUS, WITHIN SECONDS, THE EVIL MORDO SIGHTS HIS QUARRY--!
I SEE HIM! DIRECTLY AHEAD!
MORDO--! WITH HIS SPIRITS! I'M TRAPPED!
AND, AN INDESCRIBABLE DISTANCE AWAY, IN THE MACABRE DARK DIMENSION, DORMAMMU WATCHES HUNGRILY...
MORDO MUST TRIUMPH THIS TIME! I MUST HAVE STRANGE DEAD!
ONCE HE IS GONE, I'LL BE FREE OF MY OATH!* I'LL BE ABLE TO COME TO EARTH IN PERSON AND CONQUER IT WITH MY MYSTIC SPELLS!
AGAIN THE DREADED ONE HURLS HIS POWER AGAINST THE NOBLE DR. STRANGE!
*DESCRIBED IN STRANGE TALES #127-- STAN.
DR. STRANGE BEFRIENDED ME! I MUST AID HIM NOW! THERE IS ONLY ONE THING THAT CAN SAVE HIM!
NO MATTER WHAT THE COST-- I MUST DO IT!
MEANWHILE...
IT'S TOO CRAMPED DOWN HERE! I MUST BATTLE MY WAY TO THE SURFACE ONCE MORE-- I CAN BE TOO EASILY TRAPPED WITHIN THESE CAVERNS!
YOU WON'T ESCAPE ME THIS TIME, STRANGE! THERE IS NO PLACE YOU CAN GO WHERE I CANNOT FOLLOW!
4

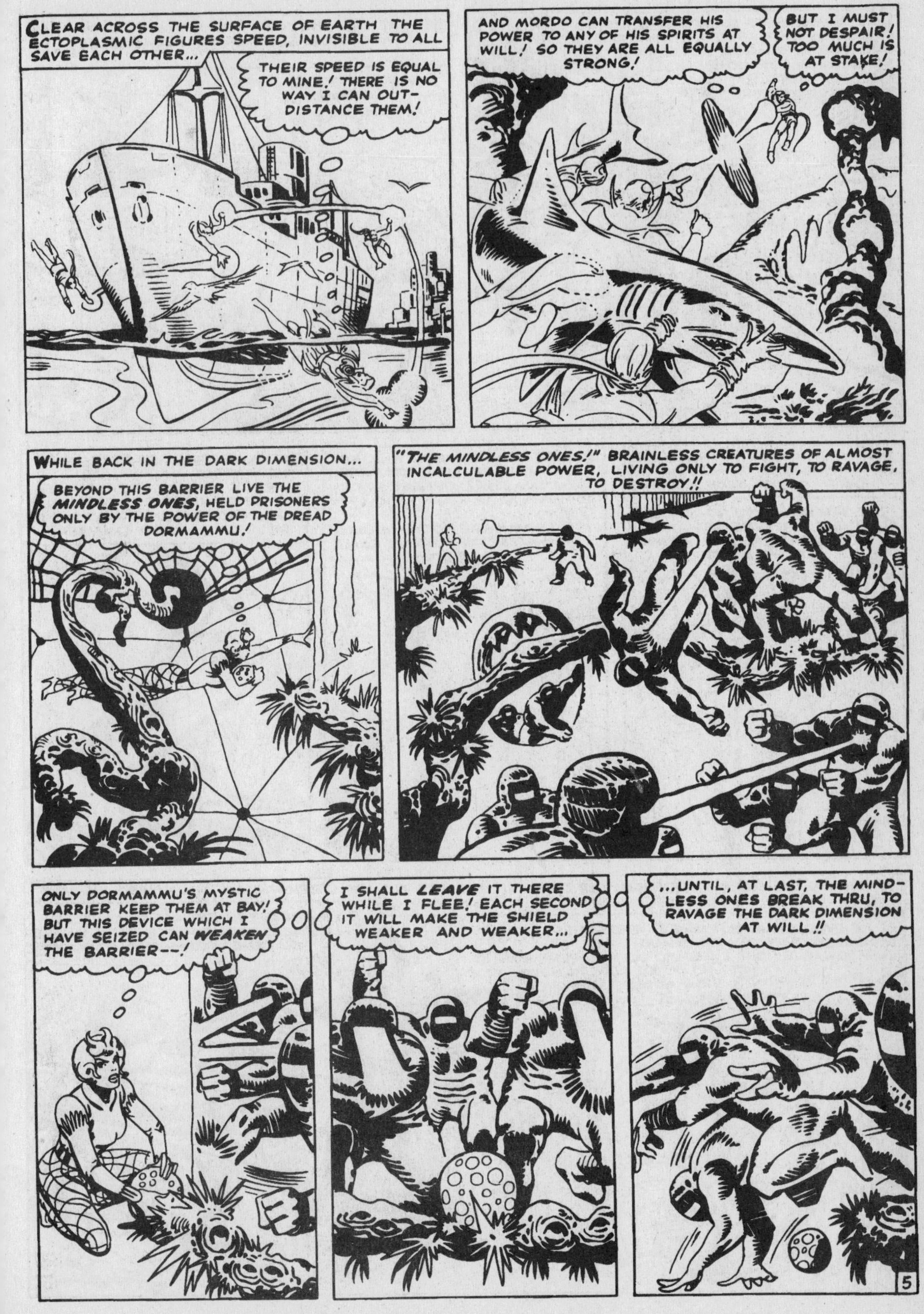
CLEAR ACROSS THE SURFACE OF EARTH THE ECTOPLASMIC FIGURES SPEED, INVISIBLE TO ALL SAVE EACH OTHER...
THEIR SPEED IS EQUAL TO MINE! THERE IS NO WAY I CAN OUT-DISTANCE THEM!
AND MORDO CAN TRANSFER HIS POWER TO ANY OF HIS SPIRITS AT WILL! SO THEY ARE ALL EQUALLY STRONG!
BUT I MUST NOT DESPAIR! TOO MUCH IS AT STAKE!
WHILE BACK IN THE DARK DIMENSION...
BEYOND THIS BARRIER LIVE THE MINDLESS ONES, HELD PRISONERS ONLY BY THE POWER OF THE DREAD DORMAMMU!
"THE MINDLESS ONES!" BRAINLESS CREATURES OF ALMOST INCALCULABLE POWER, LIVING ONLY TO FIGHT, TO RAVAGE, TO DESTROY!!
ONLY DORMAMMU'S MYSTIC BARRIER KEEP THEM AT BAY! BUT THIS DEVICE WHICH I HAVE SEIZED CAN WEAKEN THE BARRIER--!
I SHALL LEAVE IT THERE WHILE I FLEE! EACH SECOND IT WILL MAKE THE SHIELD WEAKER AND WEAKER...
...UNTIL, AT LAST, THE MIND-LESS ONES BREAK THRU, TO RAVAGE THE DARK DIMENSION AT WILL!!
5

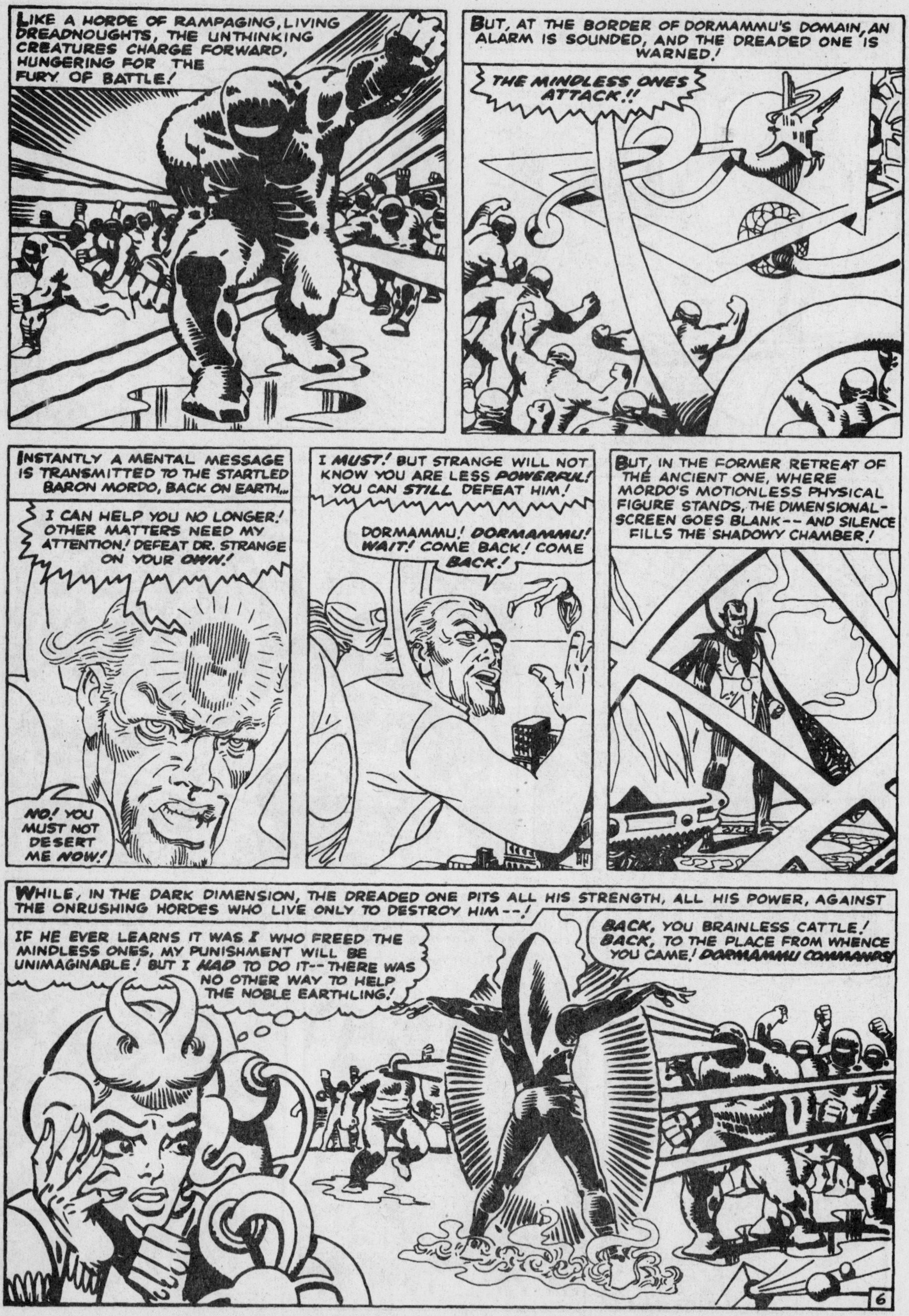
LIKE A HORDE OF RAMPAGING, LIVING DREADNOUGHTS, THE UNTHINKING CREATURES CHARGE FORWARD, HUNGERING FOR THE FURY OF BATTLE!
BUT, AT THE BORDER OF DORMAMMU'S DOMAIN, AN ALARM IS SOUNDED, AND THE DREADED ONE IS WARNED!
THE MINDLESS ONES ATTACK!!
INSTANTLY A MENTAL MESSAGE IS TRANSMITTED TO THE STARTLED BARON MORDO, BACK ON EARTH...
I CAN HELP YOU NO LONGER! OTHER MATTERS NEED MY ATTENTION! DEFEAT DR. STRANGE ON YOUR OWN!
NO! YOU MUST NOT DESERT ME NOW!
I MUST! BUT STRANGE WILL NOT KNOW YOU ARE LESS POWERFUL! YOU CAN STILL DEFEAT HIM!
DORMAMMU! DORMAMMU! WAIT! COME BACK! COME BACK!
BUT, IN THE FORMER RETREAT OF THE ANCIENT ONE, WHERE MORDO'S MOTIONLESS PHYSICAL FIGURE STANDS, THE DIMENSIONAL-SCREEN GOES BLANK-- AND SILENCE FILLS THE SHADOWY CHAMBER!
WHILE, IN THE DARK DIMENSION, THE DREADED ONE PITS ALL HIS STRENGTH, ALL HIS POWER, AGAINST THE ONRUSHING HORDES WHO LIVE ONLY TO DESTROY HIM--!
IF HE EVER LEARNS IT WAS I WHO FREED THE MINDLESS ONES, MY PUNISHMENT WILL BE UNIMAGINABLE! BUT I HAD TO DO IT-- THERE WAS NO OTHER WAY TO HELP THE NOBLE EARTHLING!
BACK, YOU BRAINLESS CATTLE! BACK, TO THE PLACE FROM WHENCE YOU CAME! DORMAMMU COMMANDS!
6

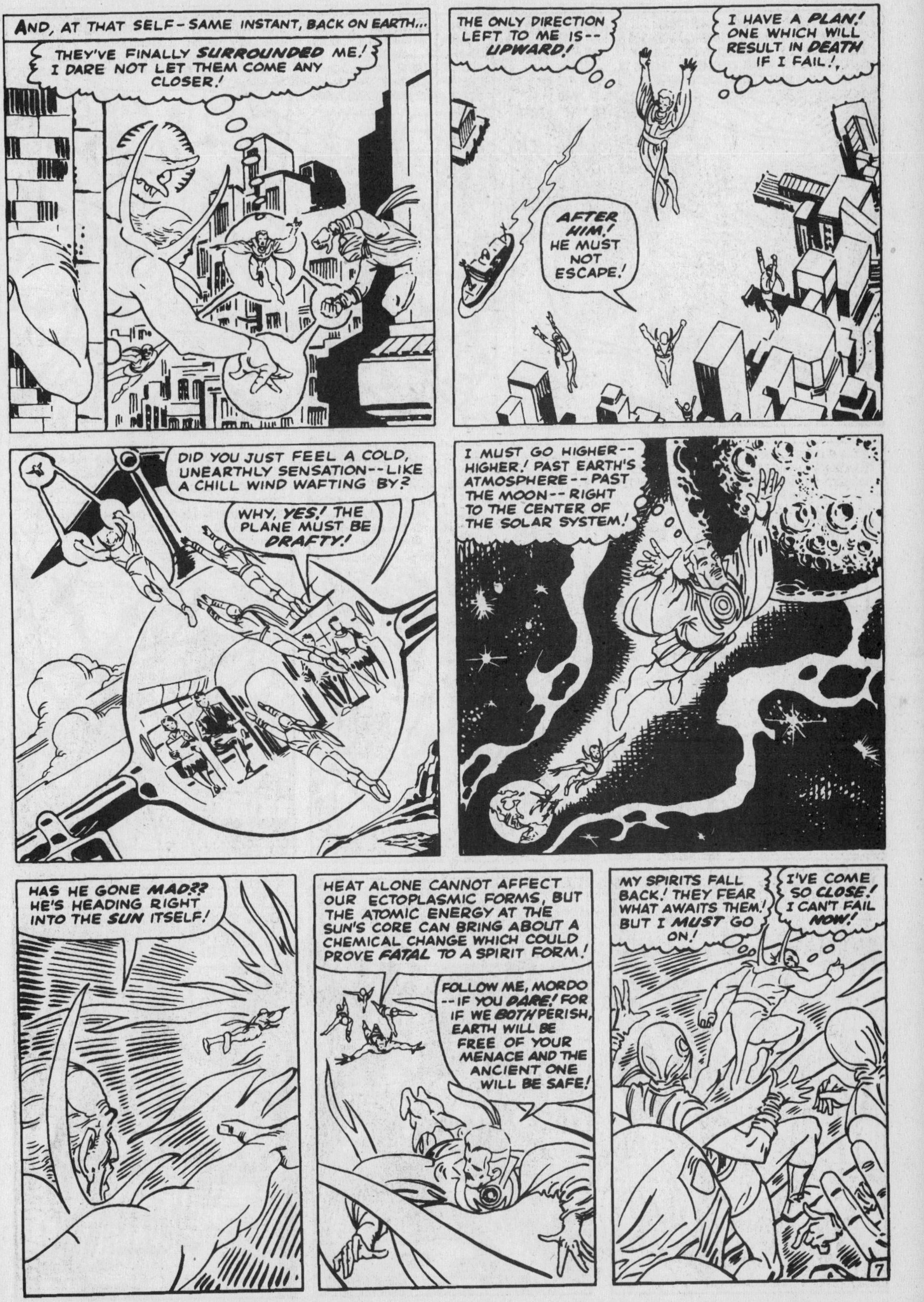
AND, AT THAT SELF-SAME INSTANT, BACK ON EARTH...
THEY'VE FINALLY SURROUNDED ME! I DARE NOT LET THEM COME ANY CLOSER!
THE ONLY DIRECTION LEFT TO ME IS-- UPWARD!
I HAVE A PLAN! ONE WHICH WILL RESULT IN DEATH IF I FAIL!
AFTER HIM! HE MUST NOT ESCAPE!
DID YOU JUST FEEL A COLD, UNEARTHLY SENSATION--LIKE A CHILL WIND WAFTING BY?
WHY, YES! THE PLANE MUST BE DRAFTY!
I MUST GO HIGHER-- HIGHER! PAST EARTH'S ATMOSPHERE-- PAST THE MOON-- RIGHT TO THE CENTER OF THE SOLAR SYSTEM!
HAS HE GONE MAD?? HE'S HEADING RIGHT INTO THE SUN ITSELF!
HEAT ALONE CANNOT AFFECT OUR ECTOPLASMIC FORMS, BUT THE ATOMIC ENERGY AT THE SUN'S CORE CAN BRING ABOUT A CHEMICAL CHANGE WHICH COULD PROVE FATAL TO A SPIRIT FORM!
FOLLOW ME, MORDO --IF YOU DARE! FOR IF WE BOTH PERISH, EARTH WILL BE FREE OF YOUR MENACE AND THE ANCIENT ONE WILL BE SAFE!
MY SPIRITS FALL BACK! THEY FEAR WHAT AWAITS THEM! BUT I MUST GO ON!
I'VE COME SO CLOSE! I CAN'T FAIL NOW!
7

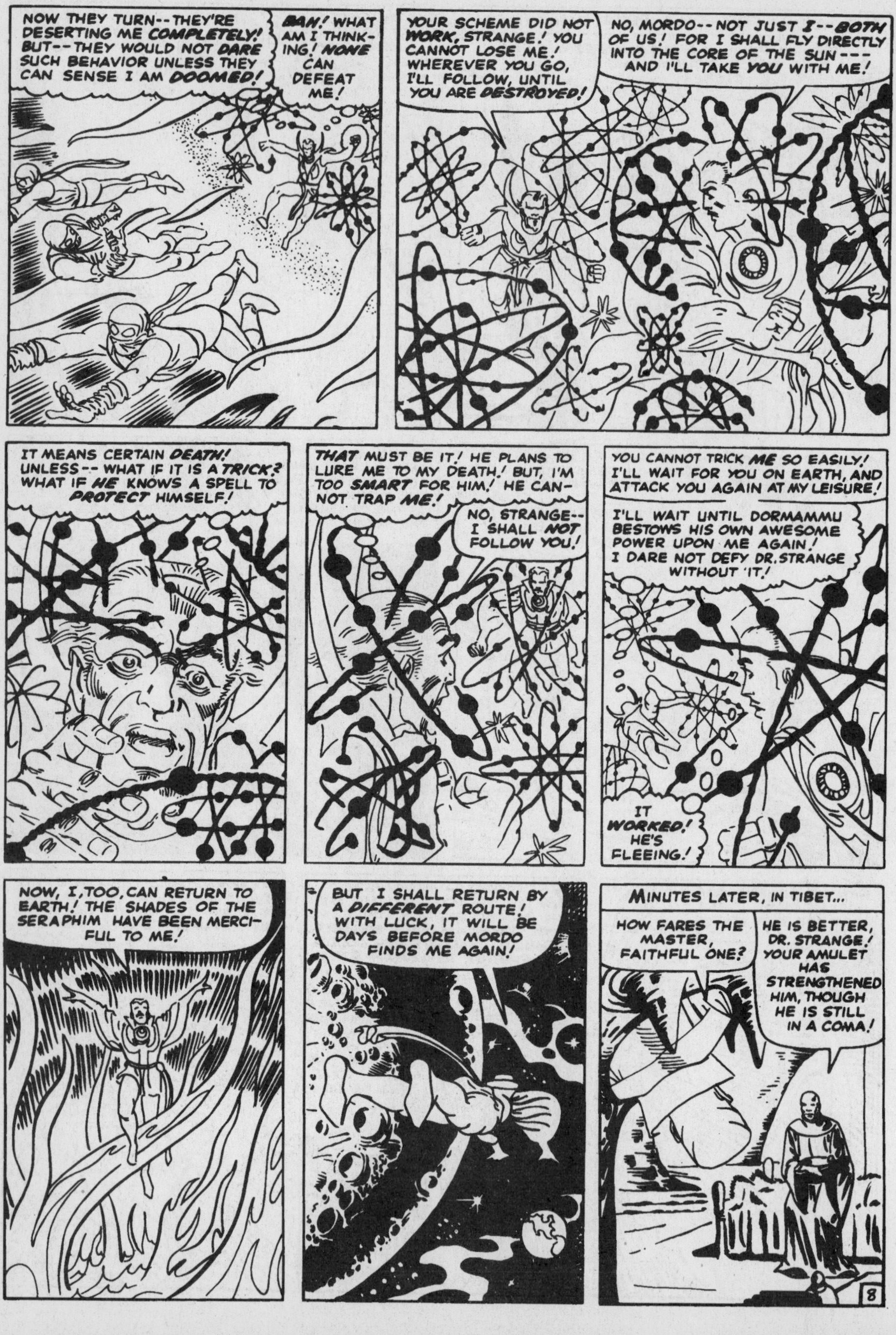
NOW THEY TURN--THEY'RE DESERTING ME COMPLETELY! BUT--THEY WOULD NOT DARE SUCH BEHAVIOR UNLESS THEY CAN SENSE I AM DOOMED!
BAH! WHAT AM I THINKING! NONE CAN DEFEAT ME!
YOUR SCHEME DID NOT WORK, STRANGE! YOU CANNOT LOSE ME! WHEREVER YOU GO, I'LL FOLLOW, UNTIL YOU ARE DESTROYED!
NO, MORDO--NOT JUST I--BOTH OF US! FOR I SHALL FLY DIRECTLY INTO THE CORE OF THE SUN--- AND I'LL TAKE YOU WITH ME!
IT MEANS CERTAIN DEATH! UNLESS--WHAT IF IT IS A TRICK? WHAT IF HE KNOWS A SPELL TO PROTECT HIMSELF!
THAT MUST BE IT! HE PLANS TO LURE ME TO MY DEATH! BUT, I'M TOO SMART FOR HIM! HE CANNOT TRAP ME!
NO, STRANGE-- I SHALL NOT FOLLOW YOU!
YOU CANNOT TRICK ME SO EASILY! I'LL WAIT FOR YOU ON EARTH, AND ATTACK YOU AGAIN AT MY LEISURE!
I'LL WAIT UNTIL DORMAMMU BESTOWS HIS OWN AWESOME POWER UPON ME AGAIN! I DARE NOT DEFY DR. STRANGE WITHOUT 'IT'!
IT WORKED! HE'S FLEEING!
NOW, I, TOO, CAN RETURN TO EARTH! THE SHADES OF THE SERAPHIM HAVE BEEN MERCIFUL TO ME!
BUT I SHALL RETURN BY A DIFFERENT ROUTE! WITH LUCK, IT WILL BE DAYS BEFORE MORDO FINDS ME AGAIN!
MINUTES LATER, IN TIBET...
HOW FARES THE MASTER, FAITHFUL ONE?
HE IS BETTER, DR. STRANGE! YOUR AMULET HAS STRENGTHENED HIM, THOUGH HE IS STILL IN A COMA!
8

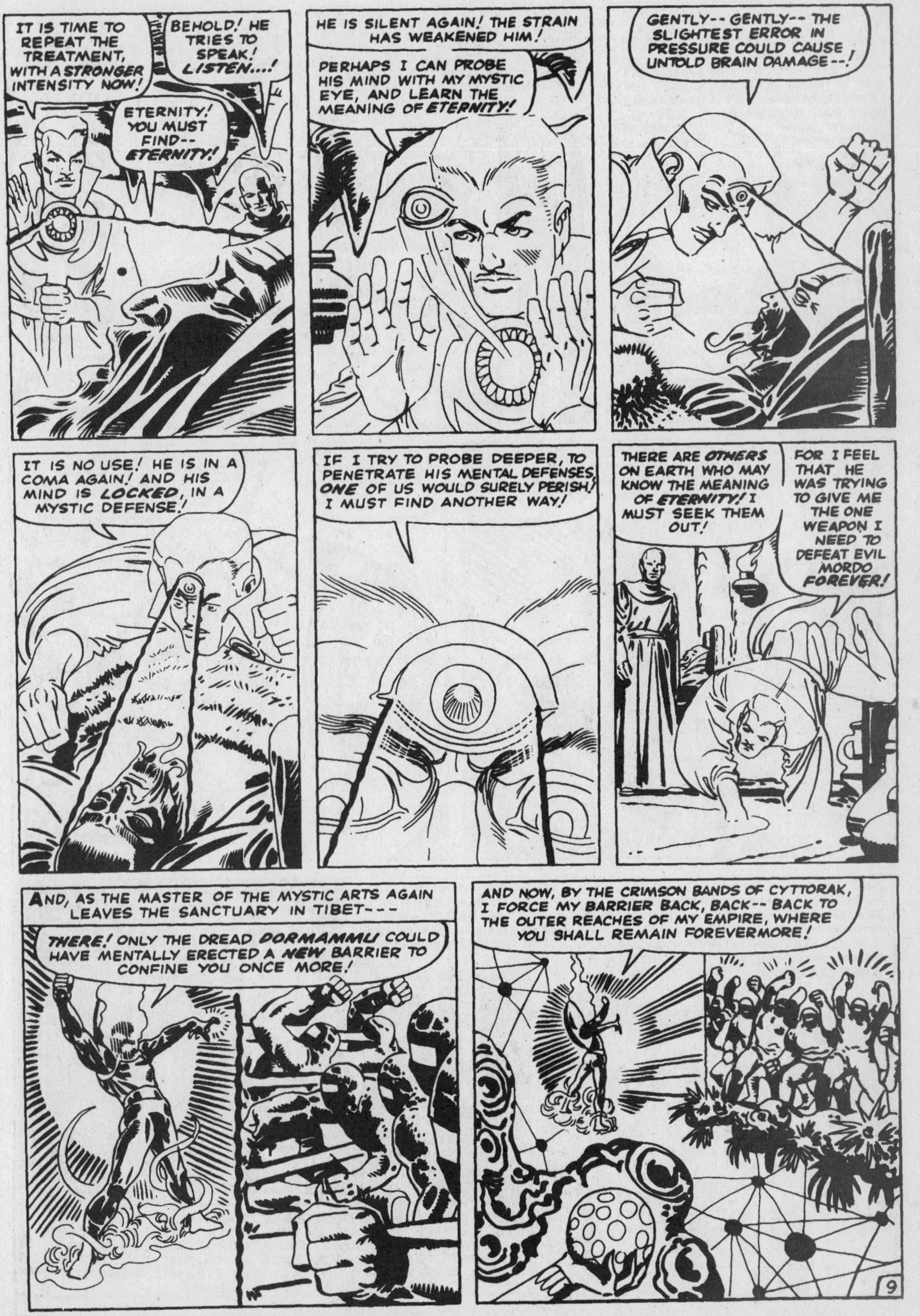
IT IS TIME TO REPEAT THE TREATMENT, WITH A STRONGER INTENSITY NOW!
BEHOLD! HE TRIES TO SPEAK! LISTEN...!
ETERNITY! YOU MUST FIND-- ETERNITY!
HE IS SILENT AGAIN! THE STRAIN HAS WEAKENED HIM!
PERHAPS I CAN PROBE HIS MIND WITH MY MYSTIC EYE, AND LEARN THE MEANING OF ETERNITY!
GENTLY-- GENTLY-- THE SLIGHTEST ERROR IN PRESSURE COULD CAUSE UNTOLD BRAIN DAMAGE--!
IT IS NO USE! HE IS IN A COMA AGAIN! AND HIS MIND IS LOCKED, IN A MYSTIC DEFENSE!
IF I TRY TO PROBE DEEPER, TO PENETRATE HIS MENTAL DEFENSES, ONE OF US WOULD SURELY PERISH! I MUST FIND ANOTHER WAY!
THERE ARE OTHERS ON EARTH WHO MAY KNOW THE MEANING OF ETERNITY! I MUST SEEK THEM OUT!
FOR I FEEL THAT HE WAS TRYING TO GIVE ME THE ONE WEAPON I NEED TO DEFEAT EVIL MORDO FOREVER!
AND, AS THE MASTER OF THE MYSTIC ARTS AGAIN LEAVES THE SANCTUARY IN TIBET---
THERE! ONLY THE DREAD DORMAMMU COULD HAVE MENTALLY ERECTED A NEW BARRIER TO CONFINE YOU ONCE MORE!
AND NOW, BY THE CRIMSON BANDS OF CYTTORAK, I FORCE MY BARRIER BACK, BACK-- BACK TO THE OUTER REACHES OF MY EMPIRE, WHERE YOU SHALL REMAIN FOREVERMORE!
9

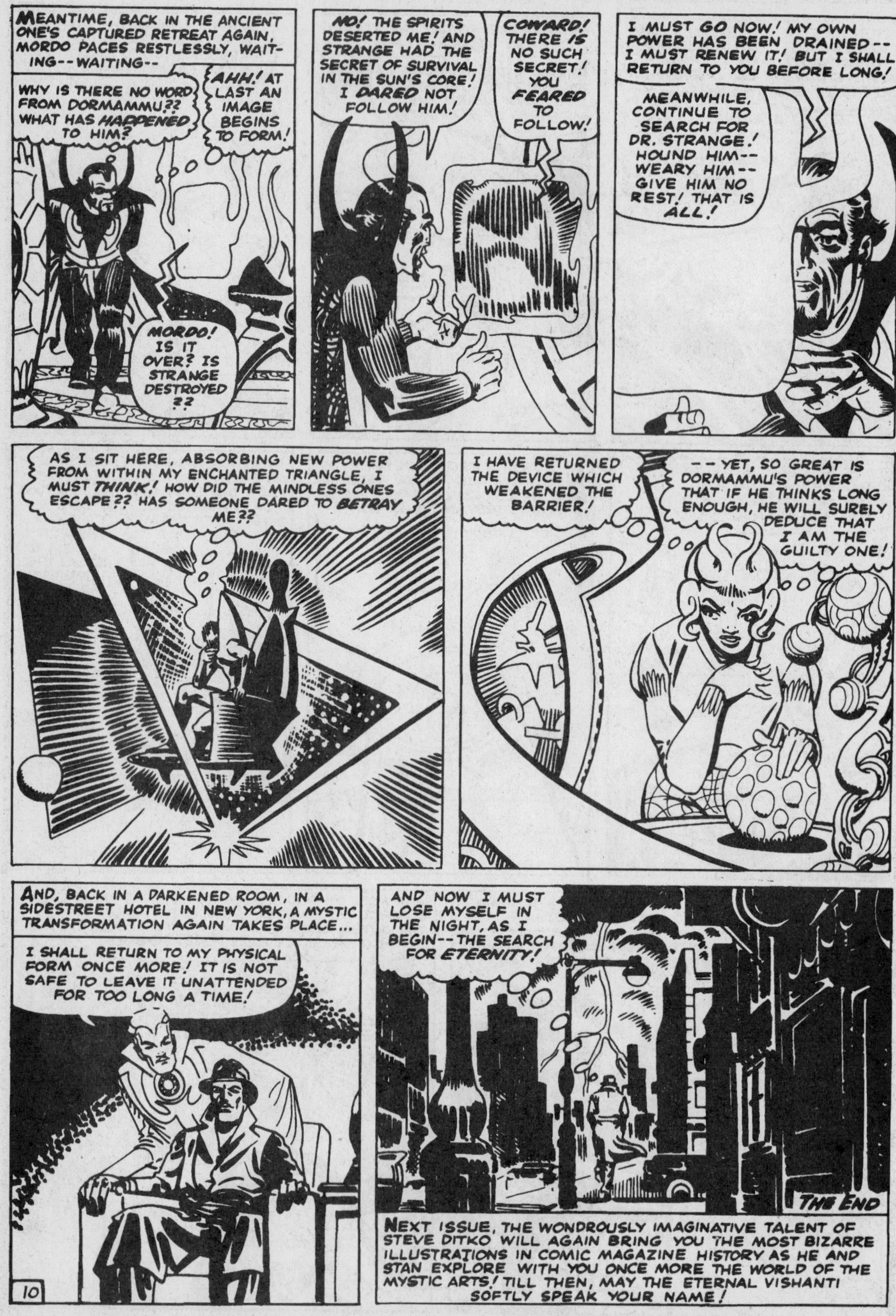
MEANTIME, BACK IN THE ANCIENT ONE'S CAPTURED RETREAT AGAIN, MORDO PACES RESTLESSLY, WAITING--WAITING--
WHY IS THERE NO WORD FROM DORMAMMU?? WHAT HAS HAPPENED TO HIM?
AHH! AT LAST AN IMAGE BEGINS TO FORM!
MORDO! IS IT OVER? IS STRANGE DESTROYED??
NO! THE SPIRITS DESERTED ME! AND STRANGE HAD THE SECRET OF SURVIVAL IN THE SUN'S CORE! I DARED NOT FOLLOW HIM!
COWARD! THERE IS NO SUCH SECRET! YOU FEARED TO FOLLOW!
I MUST GO NOW! MY OWN POWER HAS BEEN DRAINED-- I MUST RENEW IT! BUT I SHALL RETURN TO YOU BEFORE LONG!
MEANWHILE, CONTINUE TO SEARCH FOR DR. STRANGE! HOUND HIM-- WEARY HIM-- GIVE HIM NO REST! THAT IS ALL!
AS I SIT HERE, ABSORBING NEW POWER FROM WITHIN MY ENCHANTED TRIANGLE, I MUST THINK! HOW DID THE MINDLESS ONES ESCAPE?? HAS SOMEONE DARED TO BETRAY ME??
I HAVE RETURNED THE DEVICE WHICH WEAKENED THE BARRIER!
--YET, SO GREAT IS DORMAMMU'S POWER THAT IF HE THINKS LONG ENOUGH, HE WILL SURELY DEDUCE THAT I AM THE GUILTY ONE!
AND, BACK IN A DARKENED ROOM, IN A SIDESTREET HOTEL IN NEW YORK, A MYSTIC TRANSFORMATION AGAIN TAKES PLACE...
I SHALL RETURN TO MY PHYSICAL FORM ONCE MORE! IT IS NOT SAFE TO LEAVE IT UNATTENDED FOR TOO LONG A TIME!
10
AND NOW I MUST LOSE MYSELF IN THE NIGHT, AS I BEGIN--THE SEARCH FOR ETERNITY!
THE END
NEXT ISSUE, THE WONDROUSLY IMAGINATIVE TALENT OF STEVE DITKO WILL AGAIN BRING YOU THE MOST BIZARRE ILLUSTRATIONS IN COMIC MAGAZINE HISTORY AS HE AND STAN EXPLORE WITH YOU ONCE MORE THE WORLD OF THE MYSTIC ARTS! TILL THEN, MAY THE ETERNAL VISHANTI SOFTLY SPEAK YOUR NAME!

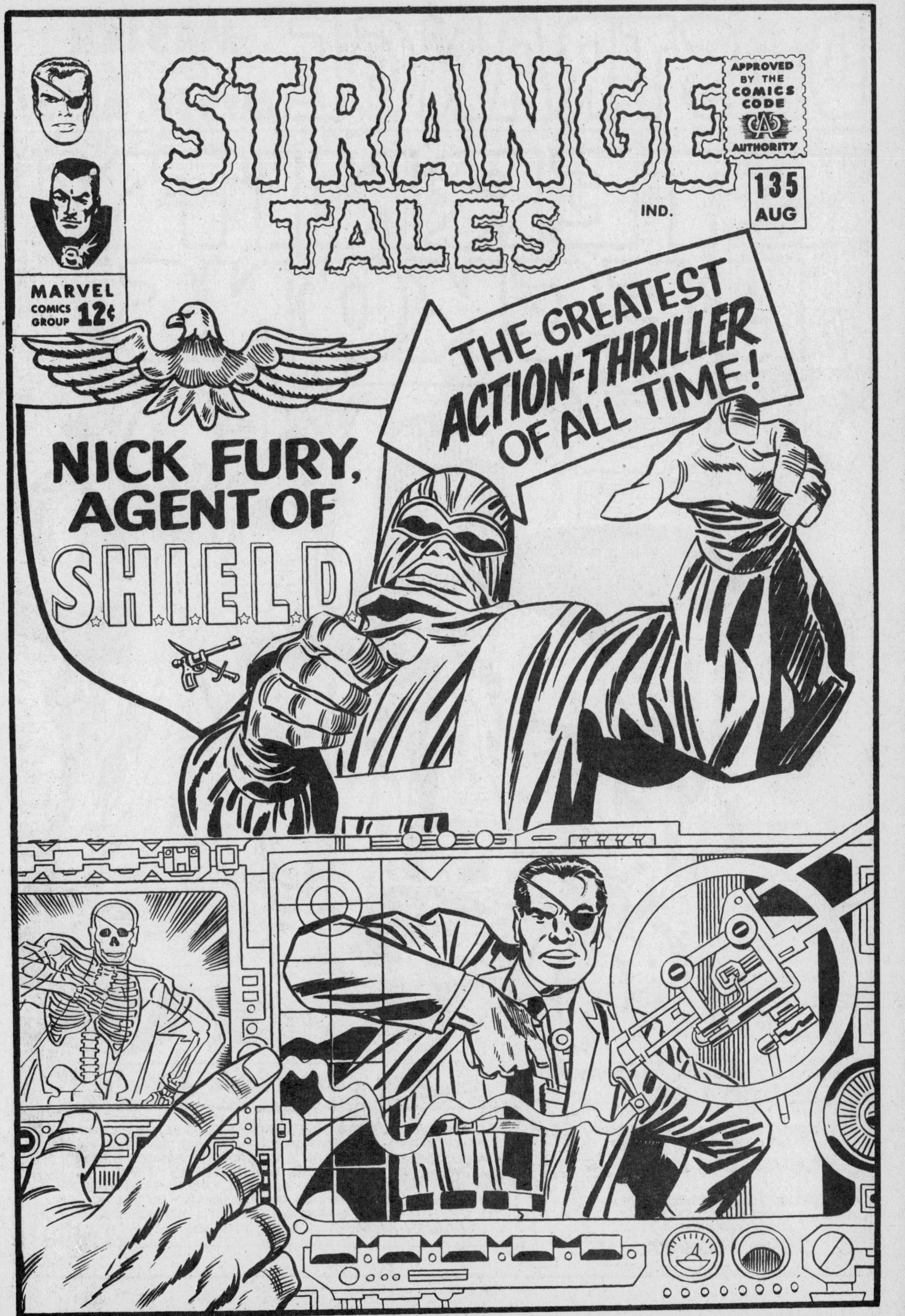
STRANGE TALES
IND.
APPROVED BY THE COMICS CODE AUTHORITY
135
AUG
MARVEL COMICS GROUP 12¢
THE GREATEST ACTION-THRILLER OF ALL TIME!
NICK FURY, AGENT OF
S.H.I.E.L.D.

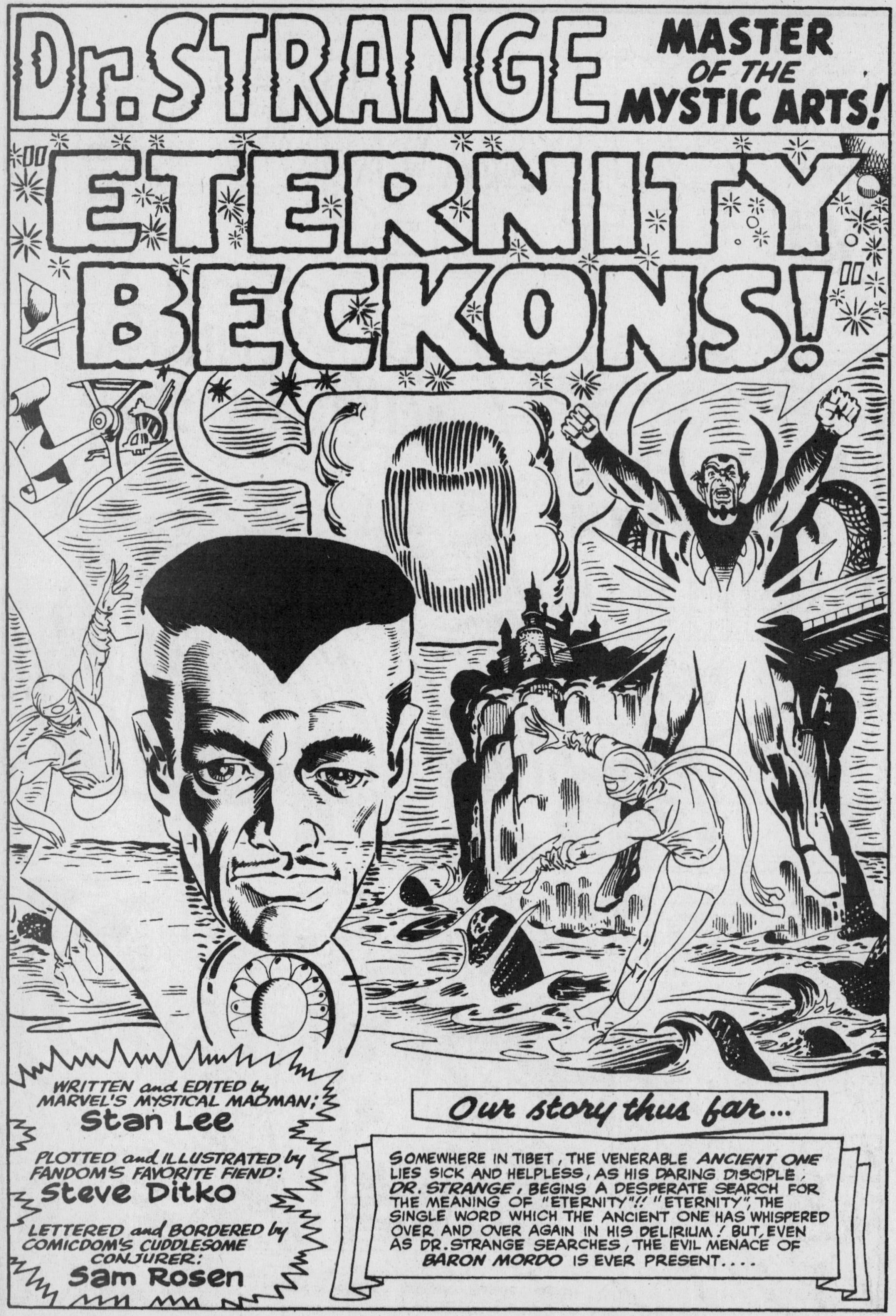
Dr. STRANGE
MASTER OF THE MYSTIC ARTS!
"ETERNITY BECKONS!"
WRITTEN and EDITED by MARVEL'S MYSTICAL MADMAN; Stan Lee
PLOTTED and ILLUSTRATED by FANDOM'S FAVORITE FIEND: Steve Ditko
LETTERED and BORDERED by COMICDOM'S CUDDLESOME CONJURER: Sam Rosen
Our story thus far...
SOMEWHERE IN TIBET, THE VENERABLE ANCIENT ONE LIES SICK AND HELPLESS, AS HIS DARING DISCIPLE, DR. STRANGE, BEGINS A DESPERATE SEARCH FOR THE MEANING OF "ETERNITY"!! "ETERNITY", THE SINGLE WORD WHICH THE ANCIENT ONE HAS WHISPERED OVER AND OVER AGAIN IN HIS DELIRIUM! BUT, EVEN AS DR. STRANGE SEARCHES, THE EVIL MENACE OF BARON MORDO IS EVER PRESENT....

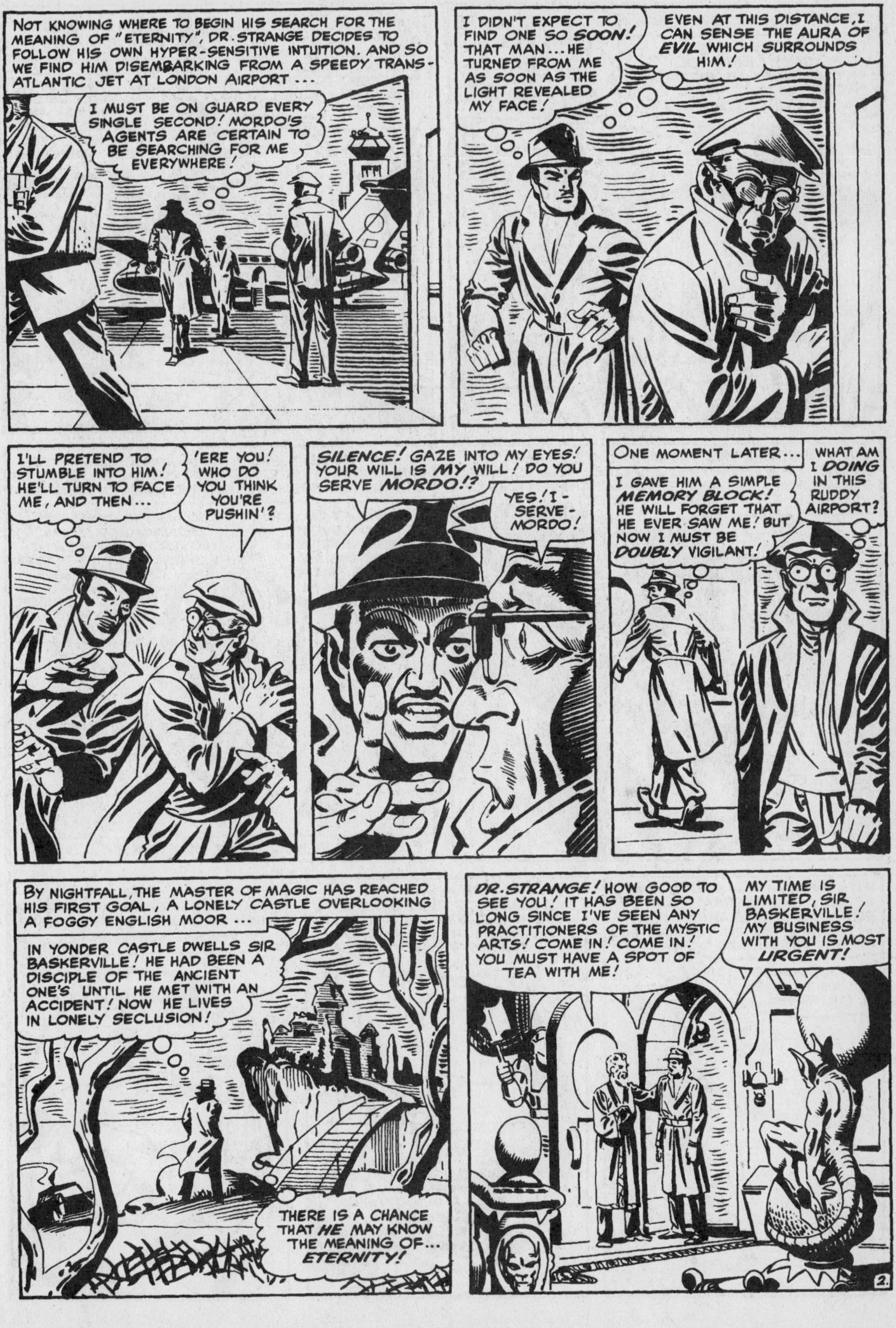
NOT KNOWING WHERE TO BEGIN HIS SEARCH FOR THE MEANING OF "ETERNITY", DR. STRANGE DECIDES TO FOLLOW HIS OWN HYPER-SENSITIVE INTUITION. AND SO WE FIND HIM DISEMBARKING FROM A SPEEDY TRANS-ATLANTIC JET AT LONDON AIRPORT...
I MUST BE ON GUARD EVERY SINGLE SECOND! MORDO'S AGENTS ARE CERTAIN TO BE SEARCHING FOR ME EVERYWHERE!
I DIDN'T EXPECT TO FIND ONE SO SOON! THAT MAN... HE TURNED FROM ME AS SOON AS THE LIGHT REVEALED MY FACE!
EVEN AT THIS DISTANCE, I CAN SENSE THE AURA OF EVIL WHICH SURROUNDS HIM!
I'LL PRETEND TO STUMBLE INTO HIM! HE'LL TURN TO FACE ME, AND THEN...
'ERE YOU! WHO DO YOU THINK YOU'RE PUSHIN'?
SILENCE! GAZE INTO MY EYES! YOUR WILL IS MY WILL! DO YOU SERVE MORDO!?
YES! I-SERVE-MORDO!
ONE MOMENT LATER...
I GAVE HIM A SIMPLE MEMORY BLOCK! HE WILL FORGET THAT HE EVER SAW ME! BUT NOW I MUST BE DOUBLY VIGILANT!
WHAT AM I DOING IN THIS RUDDY AIRPORT?
BY NIGHTFALL, THE MASTER OF MAGIC HAS REACHED HIS FIRST GOAL, A LONELY CASTLE OVERLOOKING A FOGGY ENGLISH MOOR...
IN YONDER CASTLE DWELLS SIR BASKERVILLE! HE HAD BEEN A DISCIPLE OF THE ANCIENT ONE'S UNTIL HE MET WITH AN ACCIDENT! NOW HE LIVES IN LONELY SECLUSION!
THERE IS A CHANCE THAT HE MAY KNOW THE MEANING OF... ETERNITY!
DR. STRANGE! HOW GOOD TO SEE YOU! IT HAS BEEN SO LONG SINCE I'VE SEEN ANY PRACTITIONERS OF THE MYSTIC ARTS! COME IN! COME IN! YOU MUST HAVE A SPOT OF TEA WITH ME!
MY TIME IS LIMITED, SIR BASKERVILLE! MY BUSINESS WITH YOU IS MOST URGENT!
2.

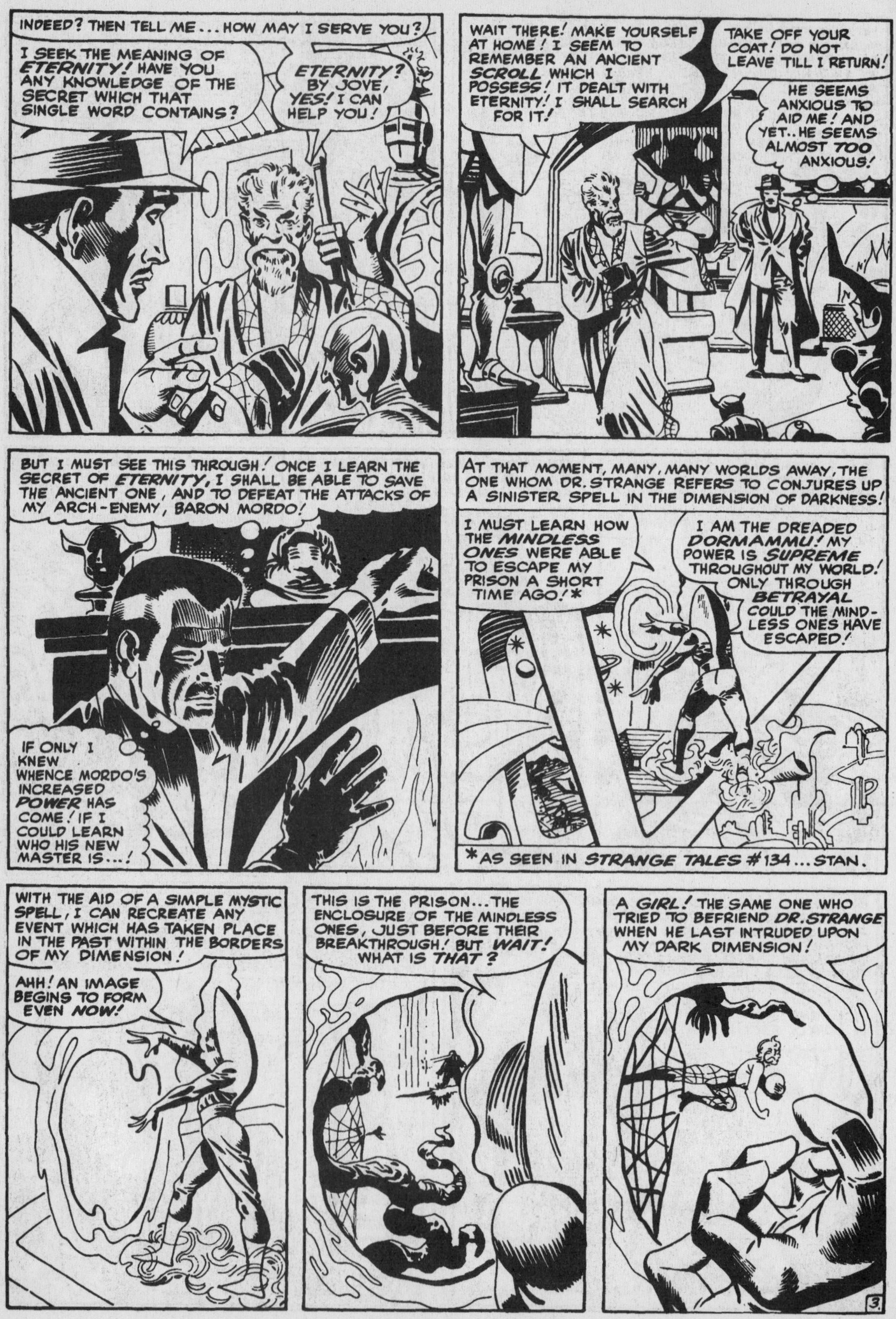
INDEED? THEN TELL ME... HOW MAY I SERVE YOU?
I SEEK THE MEANING OF ETERNITY! HAVE YOU ANY KNOWLEDGE OF THE SECRET WHICH THAT SINGLE WORD CONTAINS?
ETERNITY? BY JOVE, YES! I CAN HELP YOU!
WAIT THERE! MAKE YOURSELF AT HOME! I SEEM TO REMEMBER AN ANCIENT SCROLL WHICH I POSSESS! IT DEALT WITH ETERNITY! I SHALL SEARCH FOR IT!
TAKE OFF YOUR COAT! DO NOT LEAVE TILL I RETURN!
HE SEEMS ANXIOUS TO AID ME! AND YET.. HE SEEMS ALMOST TOO ANXIOUS!
BUT I MUST SEE THIS THROUGH! ONCE I LEARN THE SECRET OF ETERNITY, I SHALL BE ABLE TO SAVE THE ANCIENT ONE, AND TO DEFEAT THE ATTACKS OF MY ARCH-ENEMY, BARON MORDO!
IF ONLY I KNEW WHENCE MORDO'S INCREASED POWER HAS COME! IF I COULD LEARN WHO HIS NEW MASTER IS...!
AT THAT MOMENT, MANY, MANY WORLDS AWAY, THE ONE WHOM DR. STRANGE REFERS TO CONJURES UP A SINISTER SPELL IN THE DIMENSION OF DARKNESS!
I MUST LEARN HOW THE MINDLESS ONES WERE ABLE TO ESCAPE MY PRISON A SHORT TIME AGO!*
I AM THE DREADED DORMAMMU! MY POWER IS SUPREME THROUGHOUT MY WORLD! ONLY THROUGH BETRAYAL COULD THE MINDLESS ONES HAVE ESCAPED!
*AS SEEN IN STRANGE TALES #134... STAN.
WITH THE AID OF A SIMPLE MYSTIC SPELL, I CAN RECREATE ANY EVENT WHICH HAS TAKEN PLACE IN THE PAST WITHIN THE BORDERS OF MY DIMENSION!
AHH! AN IMAGE BEGINS TO FORM EVEN NOW!
THIS IS THE PRISON... THE ENCLOSURE OF THE MINDLESS ONES, JUST BEFORE THEIR BREAKTHROUGH! BUT WAIT! WHAT IS THAT?
A GIRL! THE SAME ONE WHO TRIED TO BEFRIEND DR. STRANGE WHEN HE LAST INTRUDED UPON MY DARK DIMENSION!
3

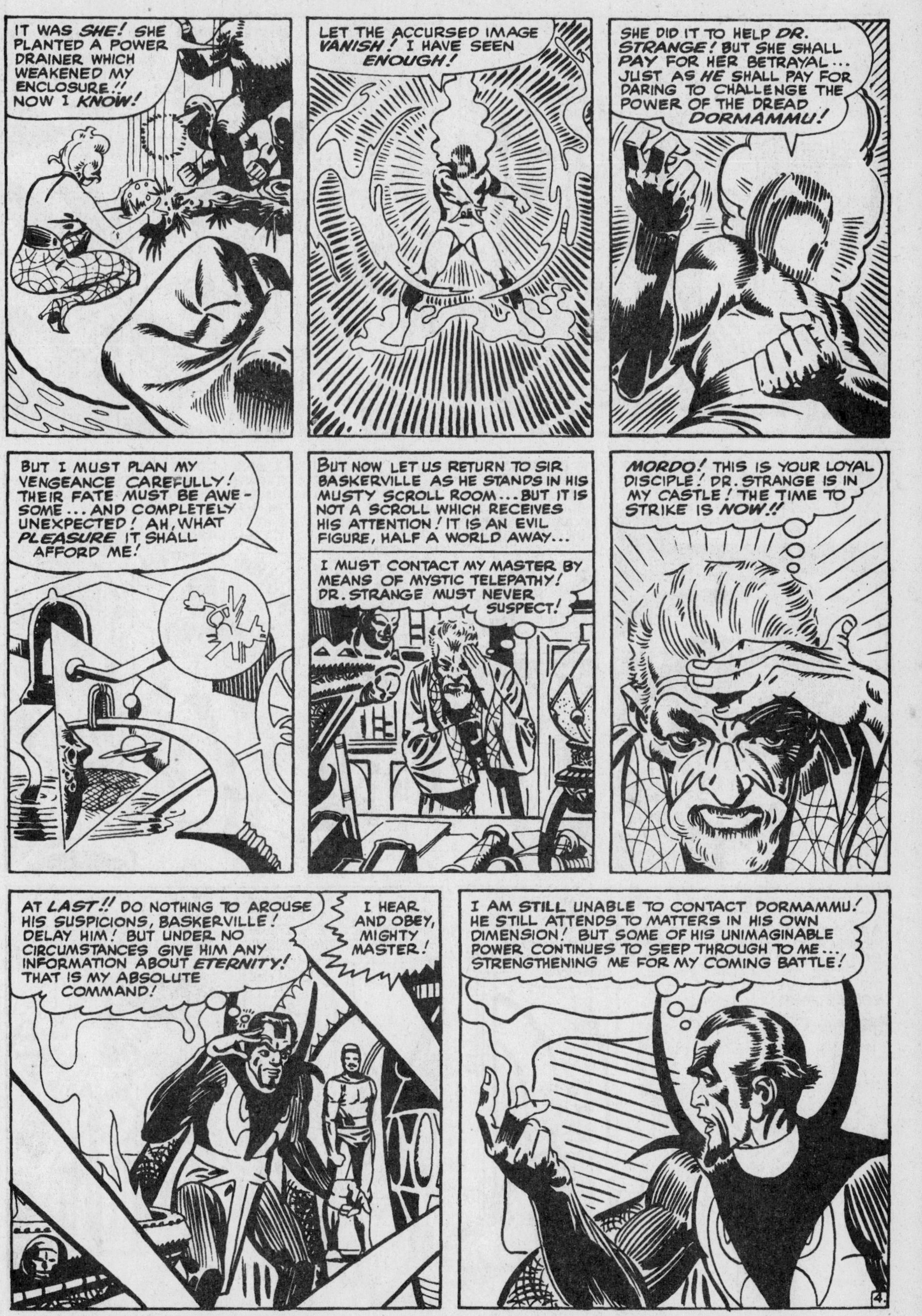

IT WAS SHE! SHE PLANTED A POWER DRAINER WHICH WEAKENED MY ENCLOSURE!! NOW I KNOW!
LET THE ACCURSED IMAGE VANISH! I HAVE SEEN ENOUGH!
SHE DID IT TO HELP DR. STRANGE! BUT SHE SHALL PAY FOR HER BETRAYAL... JUST AS HE SHALL PAY FOR DARING TO CHALLENGE THE POWER OF THE DREAD DORMAMMU!
BUT I MUST PLAN MY VENGEANCE CAREFULLY! THEIR FATE MUST BE AWE-SOME... AND COMPLETELY UNEXPECTED! AH, WHAT PLEASURE IT SHALL AFFORD ME!
BUT NOW LET US RETURN TO SIR BASKERVILLE AS HE STANDS IN HIS MUSTY SCROLL ROOM... BUT IT IS NOT A SCROLL WHICH RECEIVES HIS ATTENTION! IT IS AN EVIL FIGURE, HALF A WORLD AWAY...
I MUST CONTACT MY MASTER BY MEANS OF MYSTIC TELEPATHY! DR. STRANGE MUST NEVER SUSPECT!
MORDO! THIS IS YOUR LOYAL DISCIPLE! DR. STRANGE IS IN MY CASTLE! THE TIME TO STRIKE IS NOW!!
AT LAST!! DO NOTHING TO AROUSE HIS SUSPICIONS, BASKERVILLE! DELAY HIM! BUT UNDER NO CIRCUMSTANCES GIVE HIM ANY INFORMATION ABOUT ETERNITY! THAT IS MY ABSOLUTE COMMAND!
I HEAR AND OBEY, MIGHTY MASTER!
I AM STILL UNABLE TO CONTACT DORMAMMU! HE STILL ATTENDS TO MATTERS IN HIS OWN DIMENSION! BUT SOME OF HIS UNIMAGINABLE POWER CONTINUES TO SEEP THROUGH TO ME... STRENGTHENING ME FOR MY COMING BATTLE!
4.

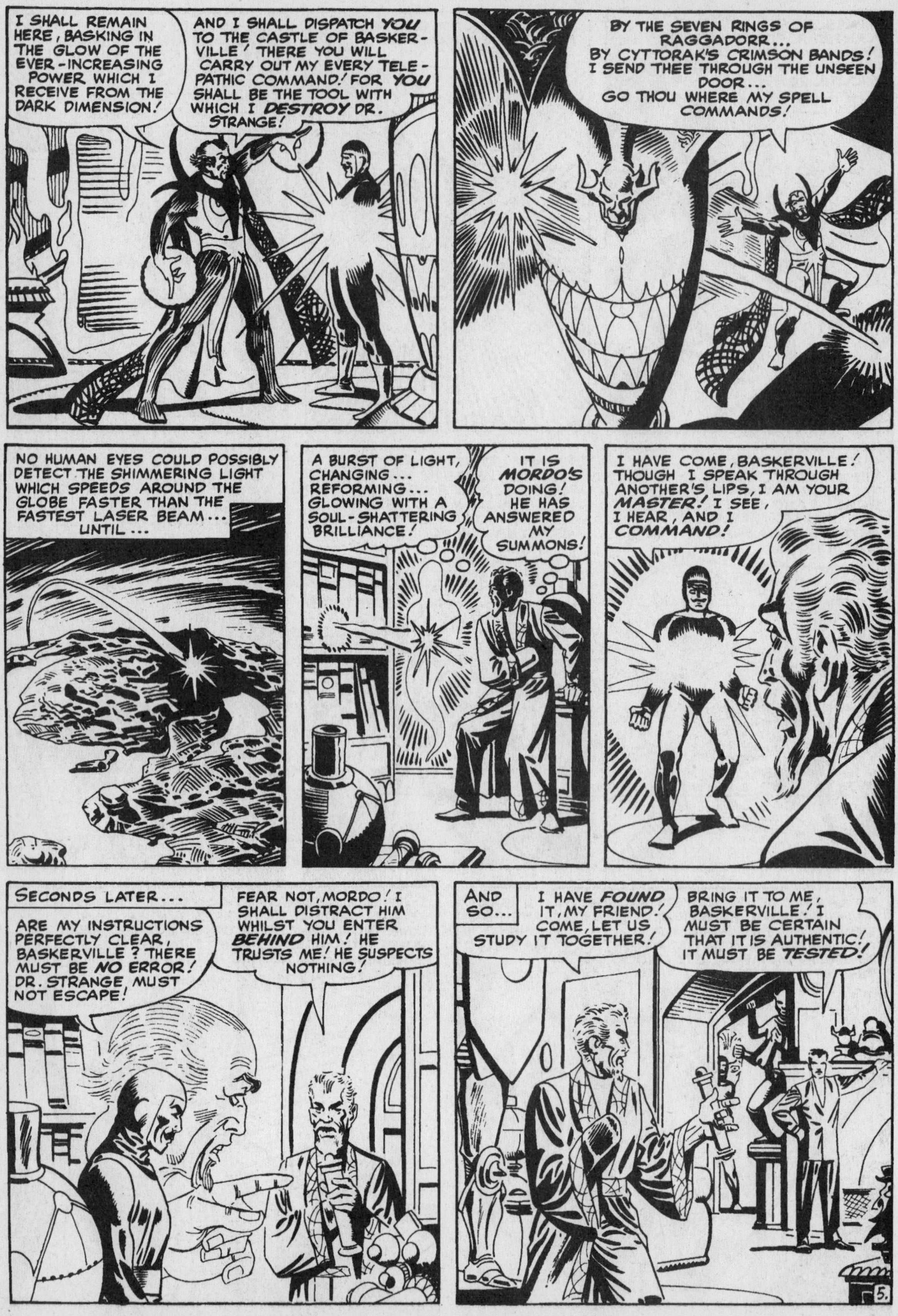
I SHALL REMAIN HERE, BASKING IN THE GLOW OF THE EVER-INCREASING POWER WHICH I RECEIVE FROM THE DARK DIMENSION!
AND I SHALL DISPATCH YOU TO THE CASTLE OF BASKERVILLE! THERE YOU WILL CARRY OUT MY EVERY TELEPATHIC COMMAND! FOR YOU SHALL BE THE TOOL WITH WHICH I DESTROY DR. STRANGE!
BY THE SEVEN RINGS OF RAGGADORR... BY CYTTORAK'S CRIMSON BANDS! I SEND THEE THROUGH THE UNSEEN DOOR... GO THOU WHERE MY SPELL COMMANDS!
NO HUMAN EYES COULD POSSIBLY DETECT THE SHIMMERING LIGHT WHICH SPEEDS AROUND THE GLOBE FASTER THAN THE FASTEST LASER BEAM... UNTIL...
A BURST OF LIGHT, CHANGING... REFORMING... GLOWING WITH A SOUL-SHATTERING BRILLIANCE!
IT IS MORDO'S DOING! HE HAS ANSWERED MY SUMMONS!
I HAVE COME, BASKERVILLE! THOUGH I SPEAK THROUGH ANOTHER'S LIPS, I AM YOUR MASTER! I SEE, I HEAR, AND I COMMAND!
SECONDS LATER...
ARE MY INSTRUCTIONS PERFECTLY CLEAR, BASKERVILLE? THERE MUST BE NO ERROR! DR. STRANGE, MUST NOT ESCAPE!
FEAR NOT, MORDO! I SHALL DISTRACT HIM WHILST YOU ENTER BEHIND HIM! HE TRUSTS ME! HE SUSPECTS NOTHING!
AND SO...
I HAVE FOUND IT, MY FRIEND! COME, LET US STUDY IT TOGETHER!
BRING IT TO ME, BASKERVILLE! I MUST BE CERTAIN THAT IT IS AUTHENTIC! IT MUST BE TESTED!
5.

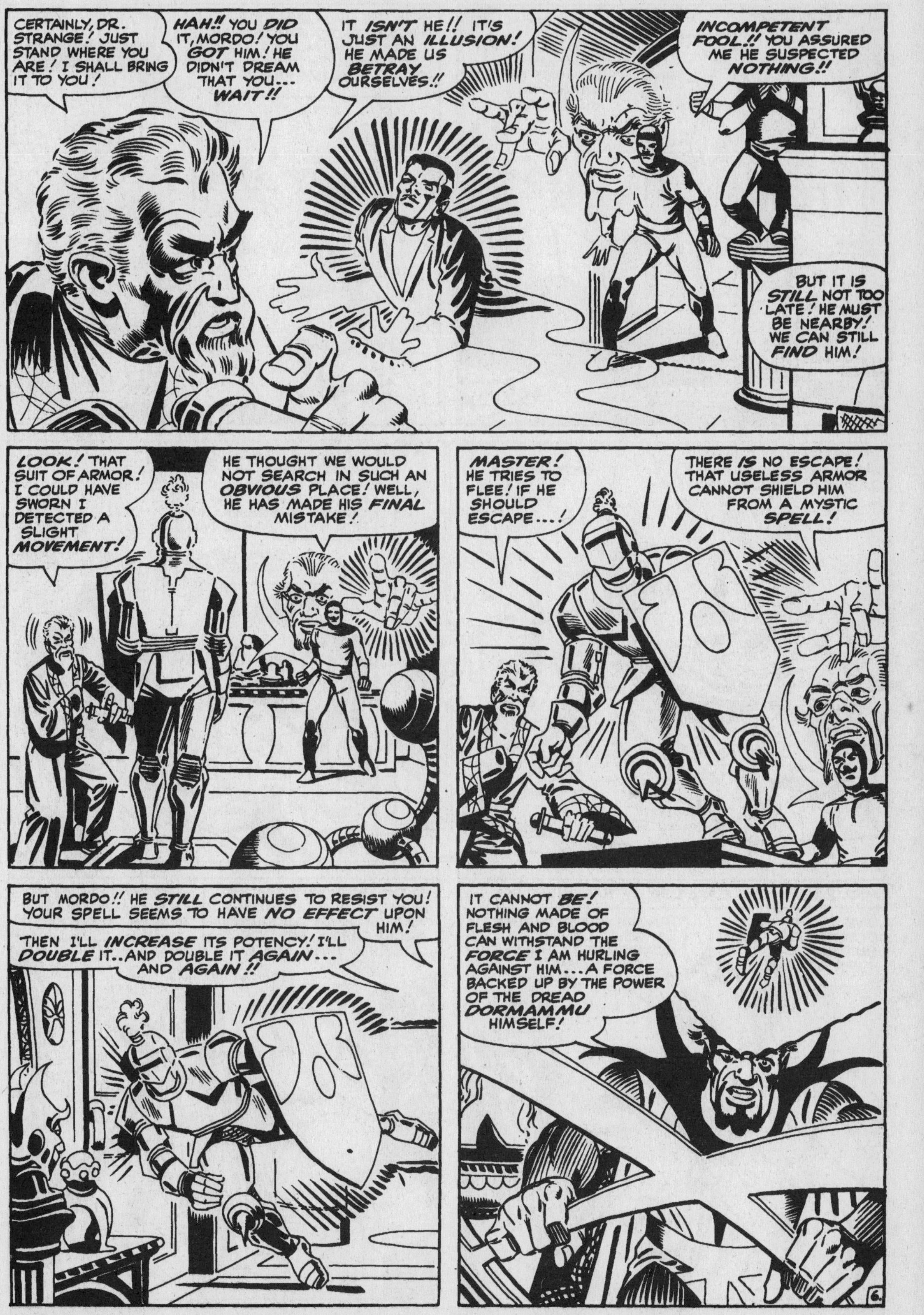

CERTAINLY, DR. STRANGE! JUST STAND WHERE YOU ARE! I SHALL BRING IT TO YOU!
HAH!! YOU DID IT, MORDO! YOU GOT HIM! HE DIDN'T DREAM THAT YOU... WAIT!!
IT ISN'T HE!! IT'S JUST AN ILLUSION! HE MADE US BETRAY OURSELVES!!
INCOMPETENT FOOL!! YOU ASSURED ME HE SUSPECTED NOTHING!!
BUT IT IS STILL NOT TOO LATE! HE MUST BE NEARBY! WE CAN STILL FIND HIM!
LOOK! THAT SUIT OF ARMOR! I COULD HAVE SWORN I DETECTED A SLIGHT MOVEMENT!
HE THOUGHT WE WOULD NOT SEARCH IN SUCH AN OBVIOUS PLACE! WELL, HE HAS MADE HIS FINAL MISTAKE!
MASTER! HE TRIES TO FLEE! IF HE SHOULD ESCAPE...!
THERE IS NO ESCAPE! THAT USELESS ARMOR CANNOT SHIELD HIM FROM A MYSTIC SPELL!
BUT MORDO!! HE STILL CONTINUES TO RESIST YOU! YOUR SPELL SEEMS TO HAVE NO EFFECT UPON HIM!
THEN I'LL INCREASE ITS POTENCY! I'LL DOUBLE IT.. AND DOUBLE IT AGAIN... AND AGAIN!!
IT CANNOT BE! NOTHING MADE OF FLESH AND BLOOD CAN WITHSTAND THE FORCE I AM HURLING AGAINST HIM... A FORCE BACKED UP BY THE POWER OF THE DREAD DORMAMMU HIMSELF!
6.

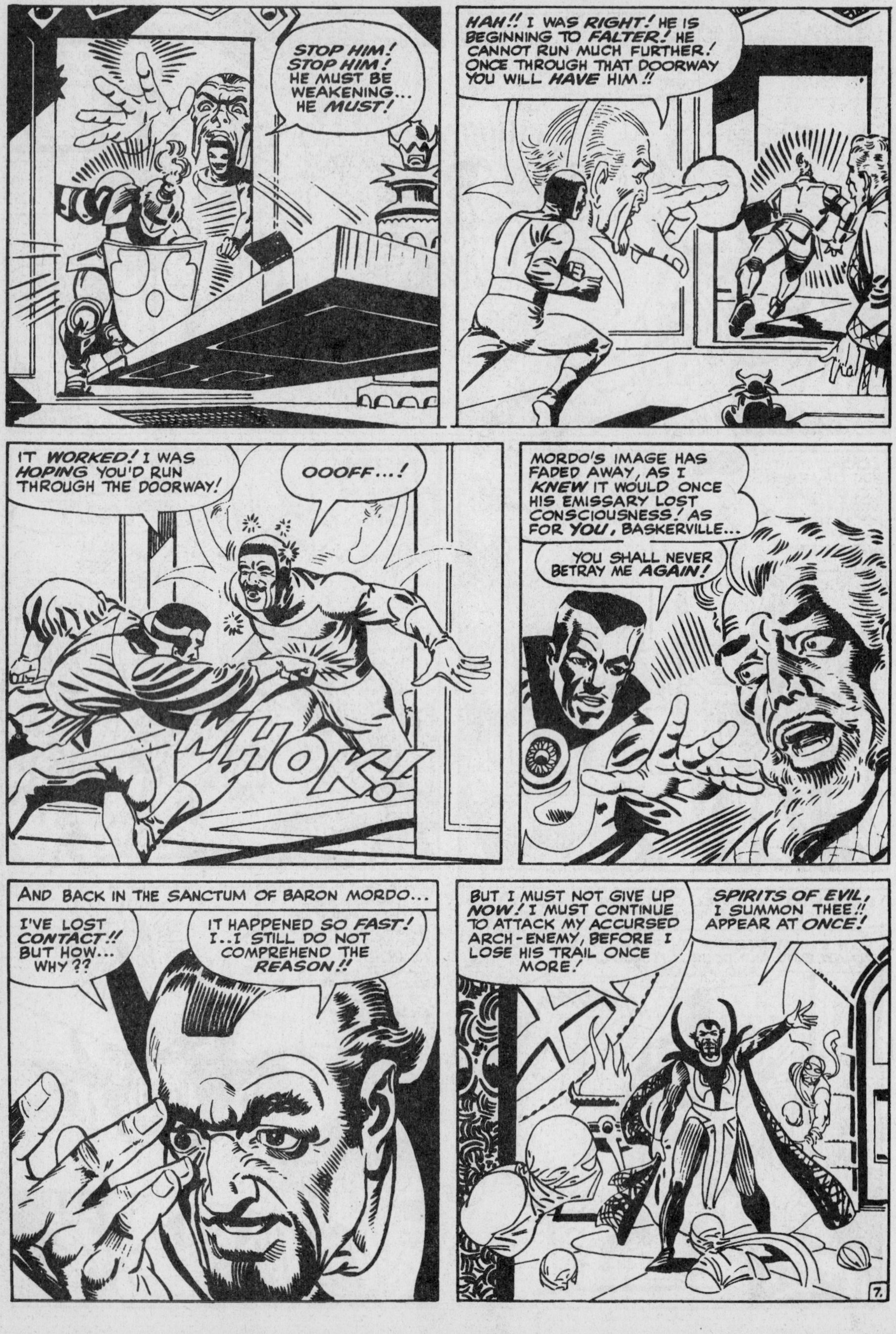
STOP HIM! STOP HIM! HE MUST BE WEAKENING... HE MUST!
HAH!! I WAS RIGHT! HE IS BEGINNING TO FALTER! HE CANNOT RUN MUCH FURTHER! ONCE THROUGH THAT DOORWAY YOU WILL HAVE HIM!!
IT WORKED! I WAS HOPING YOU'D RUN THROUGH THE DOORWAY!
OOOFF...!
WHOK!
MORDO'S IMAGE HAS FADED AWAY, AS I KNEW IT WOULD ONCE HIS EMISSARY LOST CONSCIOUSNESS! AS FOR YOU, BASKERVILLE...
YOU SHALL NEVER BETRAY ME AGAIN!
AND BACK IN THE SANCTUM OF BARON MORDO...
I'VE LOST CONTACT!! BUT HOW... WHY??
IT HAPPENED SO FAST! I..I STILL DO NOT COMPREHEND THE REASON!!
BUT I MUST NOT GIVE UP NOW! I MUST CONTINUE TO ATTACK MY ACCURSED ARCH-ENEMY, BEFORE I LOSE HIS TRAIL ONCE MORE!
SPIRITS OF EVIL, I SUMMON THEE!! APPEAR AT ONCE!
7.

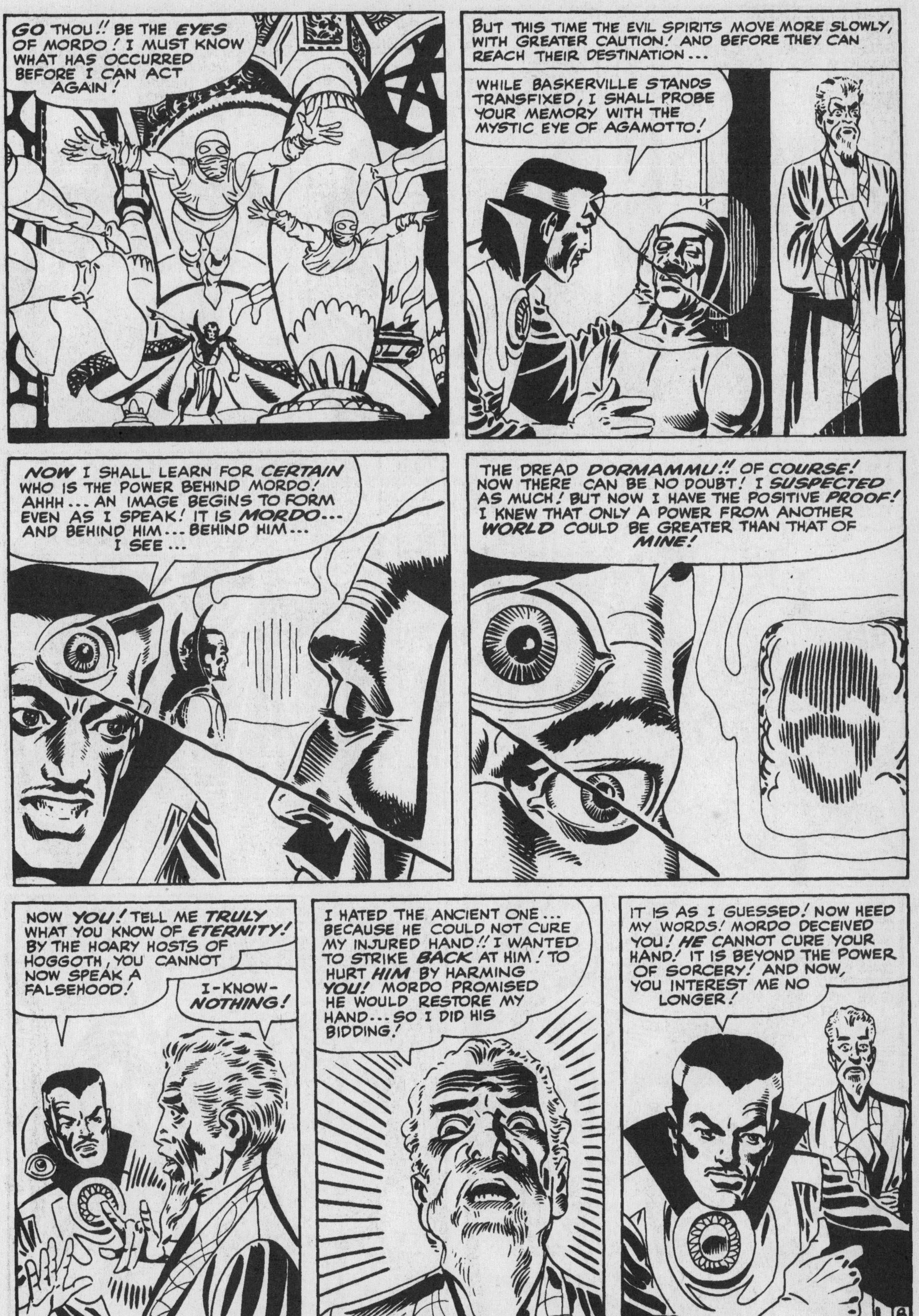
GO THOU!! BE THE EYES OF MORDO! I MUST KNOW WHAT HAS OCCURRED BEFORE I CAN ACT AGAIN!
BUT THIS TIME THE EVIL SPIRITS MOVE MORE SLOWLY, WITH GREATER CAUTION! AND BEFORE THEY CAN REACH THEIR DESTINATION...
WHILE BASKERVILLE STANDS TRANSFIXED, I SHALL PROBE YOUR MEMORY WITH THE MYSTIC EYE OF AGAMOTTO!
NOW I SHALL LEARN FOR CERTAIN WHO IS THE POWER BEHIND MORDO! AHHH... AN IMAGE BEGINS TO FORM EVEN AS I SPEAK! IT IS MORDO... AND BEHIND HIM... BEHIND HIM... I SEE...
THE DREAD DORMAMMU!! OF COURSE! NOW THERE CAN BE NO DOUBT! I SUSPECTED AS MUCH! BUT NOW I HAVE THE POSITIVE PROOF! I KNEW THAT ONLY A POWER FROM ANOTHER WORLD COULD BE GREATER THAN THAT OF MINE!
NOW YOU! TELL ME TRULY WHAT YOU KNOW OF ETERNITY! BY THE HOARY HOSTS OF HOGGOTH, YOU CANNOT NOW SPEAK A FALSEHOOD!
I-KNOW-NOTHING!
I HATED THE ANCIENT ONE... BECAUSE HE COULD NOT CURE MY INJURED HAND!! I WANTED TO STRIKE BACK AT HIM! TO HURT HIM BY HARMING YOU! MORDO PROMISED HE WOULD RESTORE MY HAND... SO I DID HIS BIDDING!
IT IS AS I GUESSED! NOW HEED MY WORDS! MORDO DECEIVED YOU! HE CANNOT CURE YOUR HAND! IT IS BEYOND THE POWER OF SORCERY! AND NOW, YOU INTEREST ME NO LONGER!
8

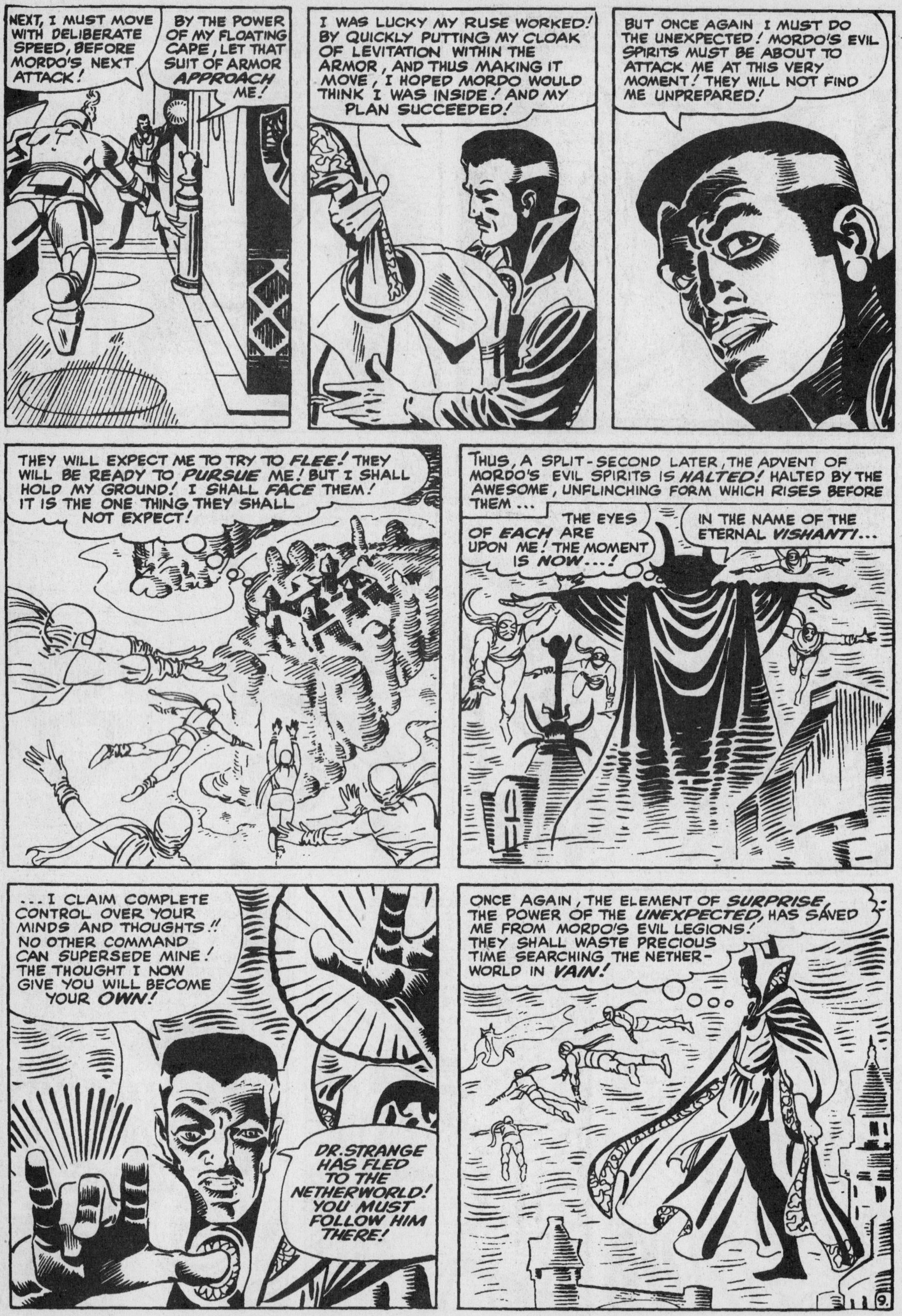
NEXT, I MUST MOVE WITH DELIBERATE SPEED, BEFORE MORDO'S NEXT ATTACK!
BY THE POWER OF MY FLOATING CAPE, LET THAT SUIT OF ARMOR APPROACH ME!
I WAS LUCKY MY RUSE WORKED! BY QUICKLY PUTTING MY CLOAK OF LEVITATION WITHIN THE ARMOR, AND THUS MAKING IT MOVE, I HOPED MORDO WOULD THINK I WAS INSIDE! AND MY PLAN SUCCEEDED!
BUT ONCE AGAIN I MUST DO THE UNEXPECTED! MORDO'S EVIL SPIRITS MUST BE ABOUT TO ATTACK ME AT THIS VERY MOMENT! THEY WILL NOT FIND ME UNPREPARED!
THEY WILL EXPECT ME TO TRY TO FLEE! THEY WILL BE READY TO PURSUE ME! BUT I SHALL HOLD MY GROUND! I SHALL FACE THEM! IT IS THE ONE THING THEY SHALL NOT EXPECT!
THUS, A SPLIT-SECOND LATER, THE ADVENT OF MORDO'S EVIL SPIRITS IS HALTED! HALTED BY THE AWESOME, UNFLINCHING FORM WHICH RISES BEFORE THEM...
THE EYES OF EACH ARE UPON ME! THE MOMENT IS NOW...!
IN THE NAME OF THE ETERNAL VISHANTI...
...I CLAIM COMPLETE CONTROL OVER YOUR MINDS AND THOUGHTS!! NO OTHER COMMAND CAN SUPERSEDE MINE! THE THOUGHT I NOW GIVE YOU WILL BECOME YOUR OWN!
DR. STRANGE HAS FLED TO THE NETHERWORLD! YOU MUST FOLLOW HIM THERE!
ONCE AGAIN, THE ELEMENT OF SURPRISE, THE POWER OF THE UNEXPECTED, HAS SAVED ME FROM MORDO'S EVIL LEGIONS! THEY SHALL WASTE PRECIOUS TIME SEARCHING THE NETHER-WORLD IN VAIN!
9.

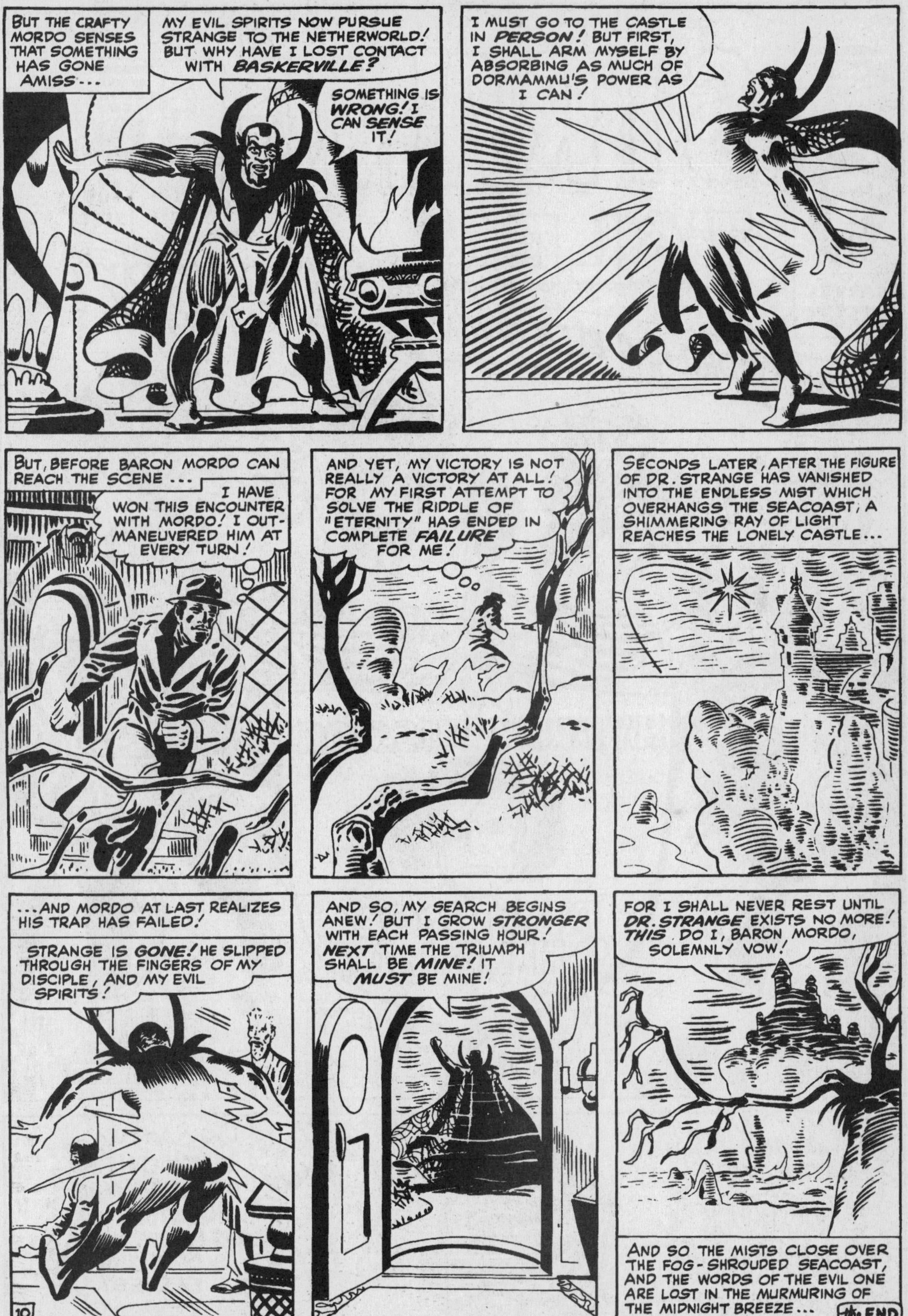
BUT THE CRAFTY MORDO SENSES THAT SOMETHING HAS GONE AMISS...
MY EVIL SPIRITS NOW PURSUE STRANGE TO THE NETHERWORLD! BUT WHY HAVE I LOST CONTACT WITH BASKERVILLE?
SOMETHING IS WRONG! I CAN SENSE IT!
I MUST GO TO THE CASTLE IN PERSON! BUT FIRST, I SHALL ARM MYSELF BY ABSORBING AS MUCH OF DORMAMMU'S POWER AS I CAN!
BUT, BEFORE BARON MORDO CAN REACH THE SCENE...
I HAVE WON THIS ENCOUNTER WITH MORDO! I OUT-MANEUVERED HIM AT EVERY TURN!
AND YET, MY VICTORY IS NOT REALLY A VICTORY AT ALL! FOR MY FIRST ATTEMPT TO SOLVE THE RIDDLE OF "ETERNITY" HAS ENDED IN COMPLETE FAILURE FOR ME!
SECONDS LATER, AFTER THE FIGURE OF DR. STRANGE HAS VANISHED INTO THE ENDLESS MIST WHICH OVERHANGS THE SEACOAST, A SHIMMERING RAY OF LIGHT REACHES THE LONELY CASTLE...
...AND MORDO AT LAST REALIZES HIS TRAP HAS FAILED!
STRANGE IS GONE! HE SLIPPED THROUGH THE FINGERS OF MY DISCIPLE, AND MY EVIL SPIRITS!
AND SO, MY SEARCH BEGINS ANEW! BUT I GROW STRONGER WITH EACH PASSING HOUR! NEXT TIME THE TRIUMPH SHALL BE MINE! IT MUST BE MINE!
FOR I SHALL NEVER REST UNTIL DR. STRANGE EXISTS NO MORE! THIS DO I, BARON MORDO, SOLEMNLY VOW!
AND SO THE MISTS CLOSE OVER THE FOG-SHROUDED SEACOAST, AND THE WORDS OF THE EVIL ONE ARE LOST IN THE MURMURING OF THE MIDNIGHT BREEZE...
the END
10

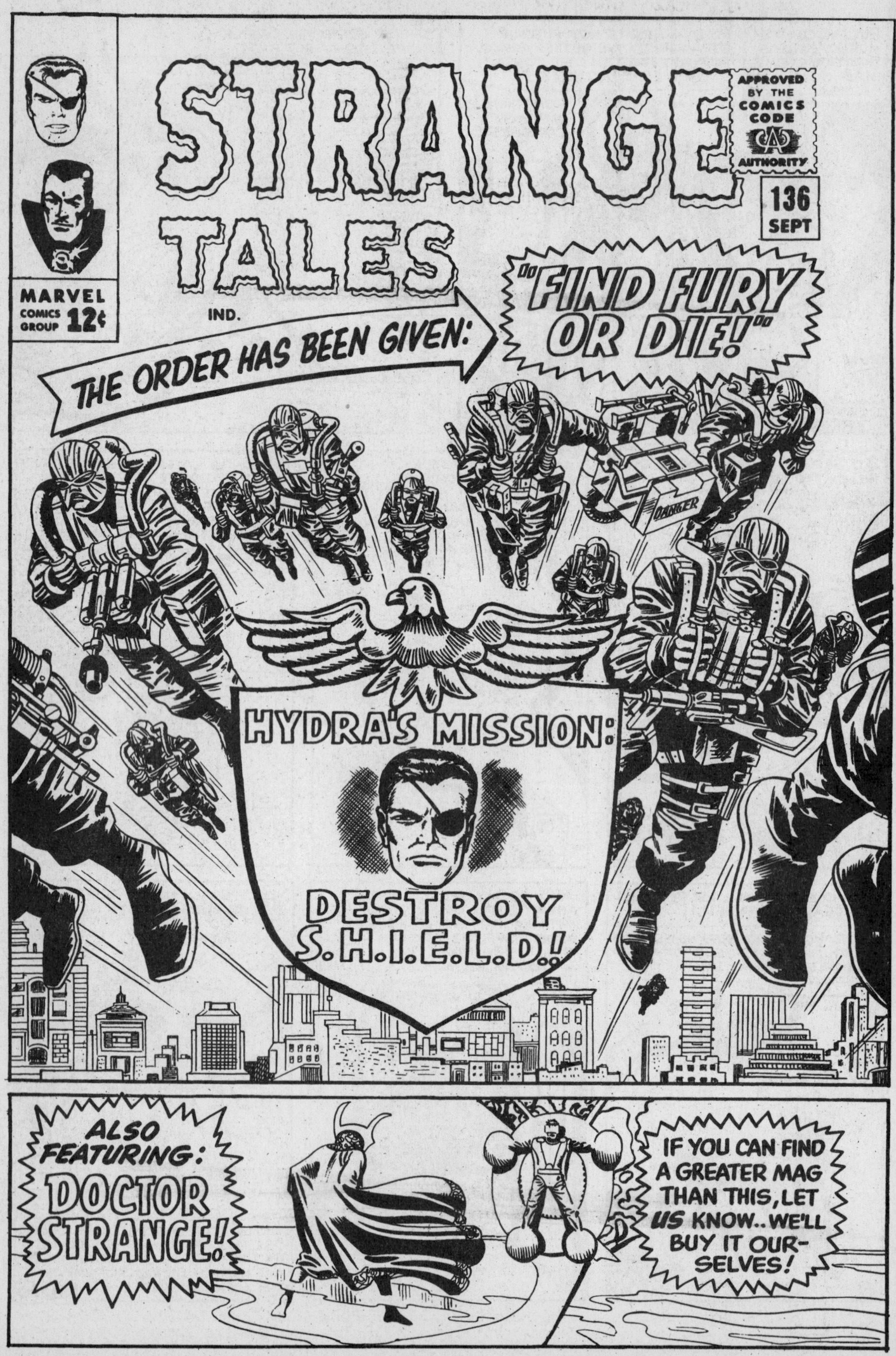

MARVEL COMICS GROUP 12¢
STRANGE TALES
IND.
APPROVED BY THE COMICS CODE AUTHORITY
136 SEPT
THE ORDER HAS BEEN GIVEN:
"FIND FURY OR DIE!"
DANGER
HYDRA'S MISSION:
DESTROY S.H.I.E.L.D.!
ALSO FEATURING:
DOCTOR STRANGE!
IF YOU CAN FIND A GREATER MAG THAN THIS, LET US KNOW.. WE'LL BUY IT OURSELVES!

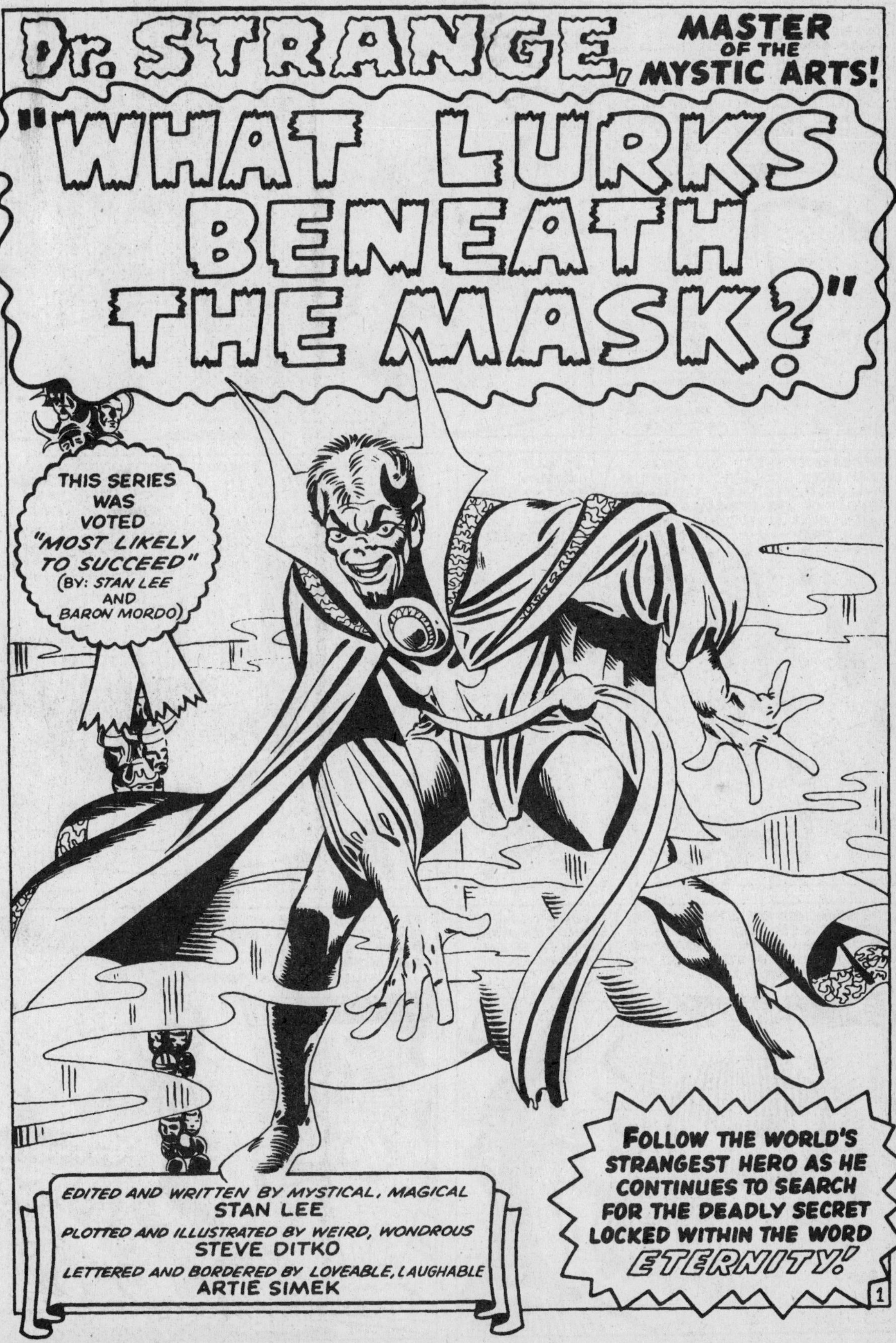

Dr. STRANGE, MASTER OF THE MYSTIC ARTS!
"WHAT LURKS BENEATH THE MASK?"
THIS SERIES WAS VOTED "MOST LIKELY TO SUCCEED" (BY: STAN LEE AND BARON MORDO)
EDITED AND WRITTEN BY MYSTICAL, MAGICAL STAN LEE
PLOTTED AND ILLUSTRATED BY WEIRD, WONDROUS STEVE DITKO
LETTERED AND BORDERED BY LOVEABLE, LAUGHABLE ARTIE SIMEK
FOLLOW THE WORLD'S STRANGEST HERO AS HE CONTINUES TO SEARCH FOR THE DEADLY SECRET LOCKED WITHIN THE WORD ETERNITY!
1

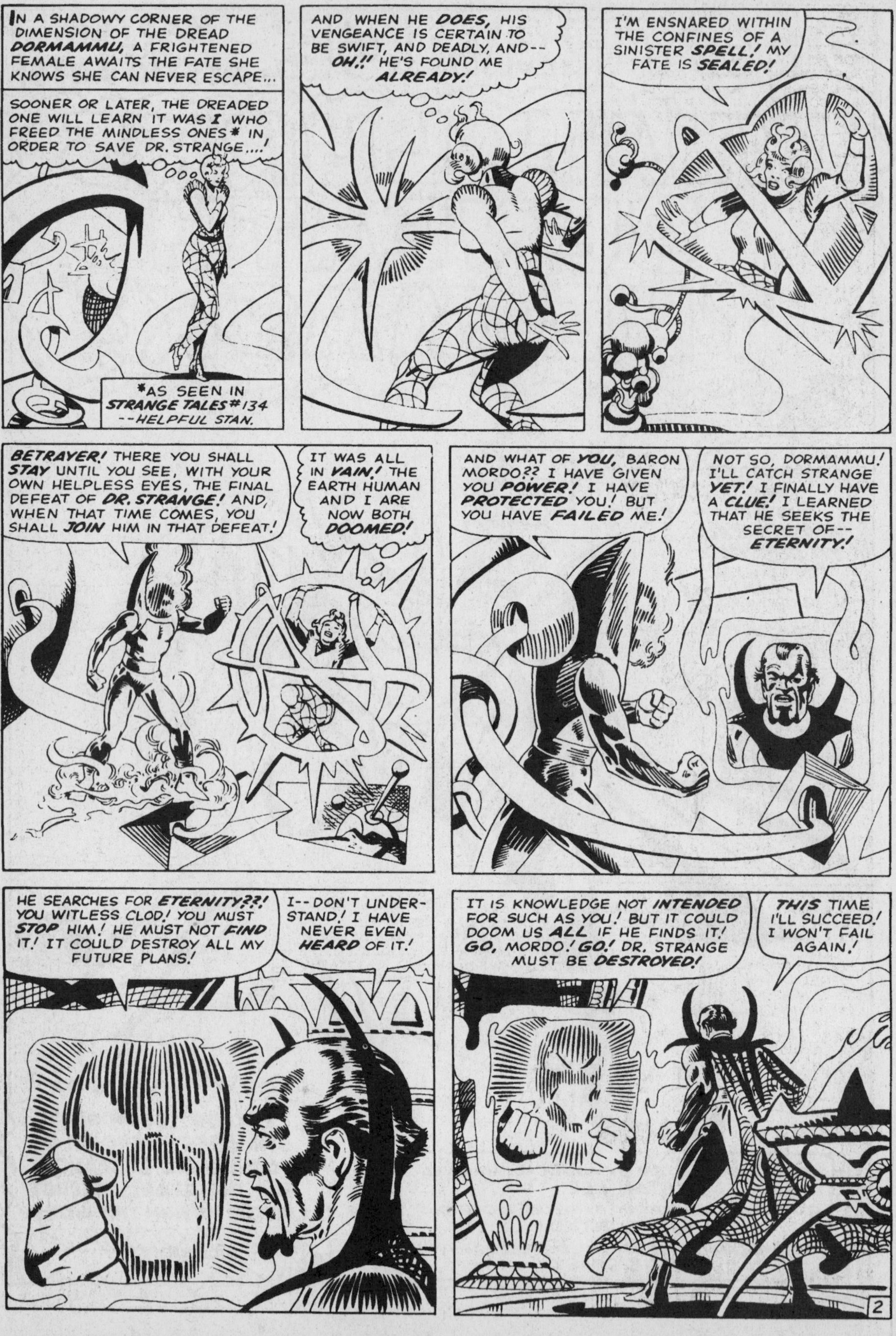
IN A SHADOWY CORNER OF THE DIMENSION OF THE DREAD DORMAMMU, A FRIGHTENED FEMALE AWAITS THE FATE SHE KNOWS SHE CAN NEVER ESCAPE...
SOONER OR LATER, THE DREADED ONE WILL LEARN IT WAS I WHO FREED THE MINDLESS ONES* IN ORDER TO SAVE DR. STRANGE....!
*AS SEEN IN STRANGE TALES #134 --HELPFUL STAN.
AND WHEN HE DOES, HIS VENGEANCE IS CERTAIN TO BE SWIFT, AND DEADLY, AND-- OH.!! HE'S FOUND ME ALREADY!
I'M ENSNARED WITHIN THE CONFINES OF A SINISTER SPELL! MY FATE IS SEALED!
BETRAYER! THERE YOU SHALL STAY UNTIL YOU SEE, WITH YOUR OWN HELPLESS EYES, THE FINAL DEFEAT OF DR. STRANGE! AND, WHEN THAT TIME COMES, YOU SHALL JOIN HIM IN THAT DEFEAT!
IT WAS ALL IN VAIN! THE EARTH HUMAN AND I ARE NOW BOTH DOOMED!
AND WHAT OF YOU, BARON MORDO?? I HAVE GIVEN YOU POWER! I HAVE PROTECTED YOU! BUT YOU HAVE FAILED ME!
NOT SO, DORMAMMU! I'LL CATCH STRANGE YET! I FINALLY HAVE A CLUE! I LEARNED THAT HE SEEKS THE SECRET OF-- ETERNITY!
HE SEARCHES FOR ETERNITY??! YOU WITLESS CLOD! YOU MUST STOP HIM! HE MUST NOT FIND IT! IT COULD DESTROY ALL MY FUTURE PLANS!
I-- DON'T UNDERSTAND! I HAVE NEVER EVEN HEARD OF IT!
IT IS KNOWLEDGE NOT INTENDED FOR SUCH AS YOU! BUT IT COULD DOOM US ALL IF HE FINDS IT! GO, MORDO! GO! DR. STRANGE MUST BE DESTROYED!
THIS TIME I'LL SUCCEED! I WON'T FAIL AGAIN!
2

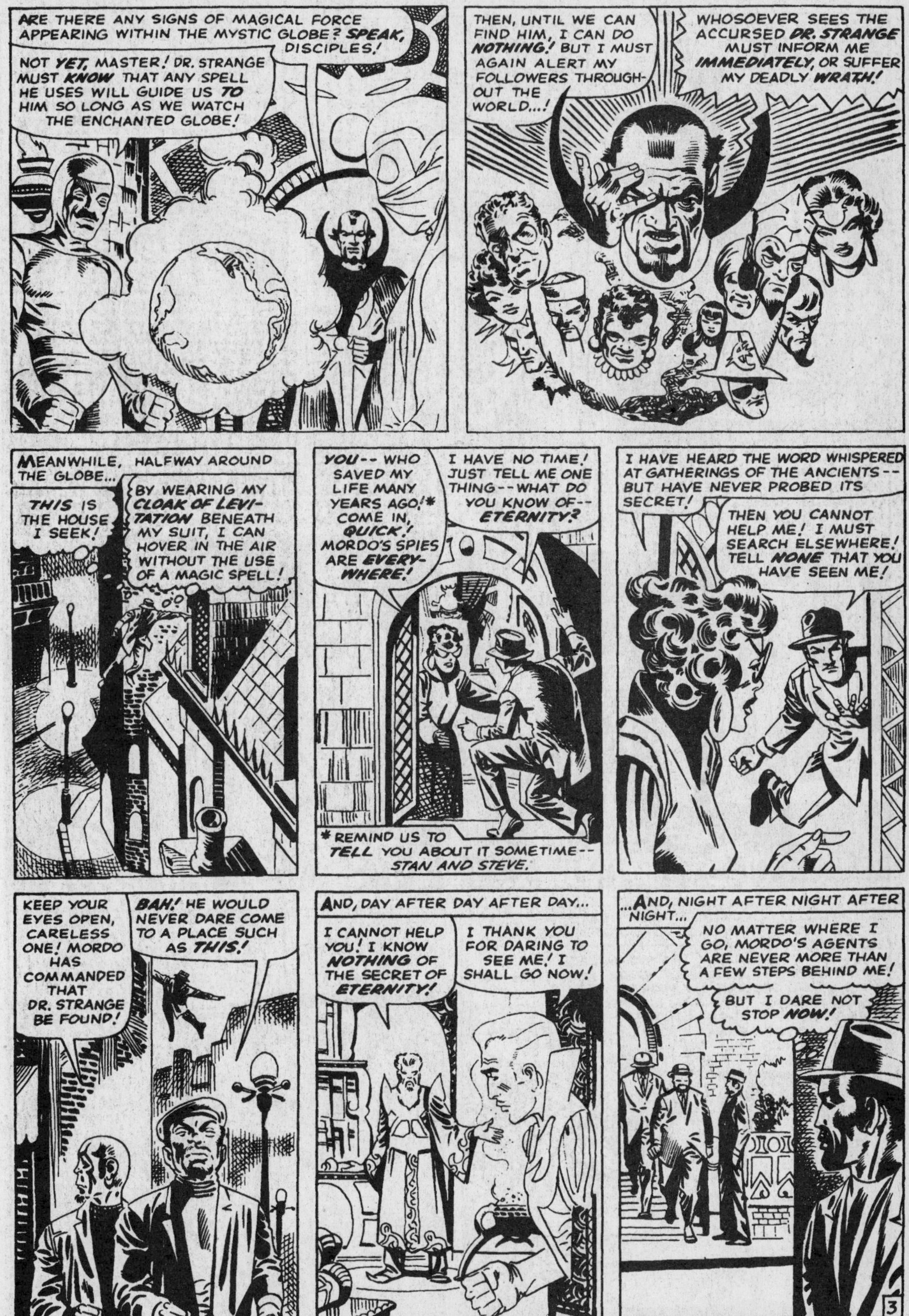

ARE THERE ANY SIGNS OF MAGICAL FORCE APPEARING WITHIN THE MYSTIC GLOBE? SPEAK, DISCIPLES!
NOT YET, MASTER! DR. STRANGE MUST KNOW THAT ANY SPELL HE USES WILL GUIDE US TO HIM SO LONG AS WE WATCH THE ENCHANTED GLOBE!
THEN, UNTIL WE CAN FIND HIM, I CAN DO NOTHING! BUT I MUST AGAIN ALERT MY FOLLOWERS THROUGH-OUT THE WORLD...!
WHOSOEVER SEES THE ACCURSED DR. STRANGE MUST INFORM ME IMMEDIATELY, OR SUFFER MY DEADLY WRATH!
MEANWHILE, HALFWAY AROUND THE GLOBE...
THIS IS THE HOUSE I SEEK!
BY WEARING MY CLOAK OF LEVI-TATION BENEATH MY SUIT, I CAN HOVER IN THE AIR WITHOUT THE USE OF A MAGIC SPELL!
YOU-- WHO SAVED MY LIFE MANY YEARS AGO!* COME IN, QUICK! MORDO'S SPIES ARE EVERY-WHERE!
I HAVE NO TIME! JUST TELL ME ONE THING--WHAT DO YOU KNOW OF-- ETERNITY?
* REMIND US TO TELL YOU ABOUT IT SOMETIME-- STAN AND STEVE.
I HAVE HEARD THE WORD WHISPERED AT GATHERINGS OF THE ANCIENTS-- BUT HAVE NEVER PROBED ITS SECRET!
THEN YOU CANNOT HELP ME! I MUST SEARCH ELSEWHERE! TELL NONE THAT YOU HAVE SEEN ME!
KEEP YOUR EYES OPEN, CARELESS ONE! MORDO HAS COMMANDED THAT DR. STRANGE BE FOUND!
BAH! HE WOULD NEVER DARE COME TO A PLACE SUCH AS THIS!
AND, DAY AFTER DAY AFTER DAY...
I CANNOT HELP YOU! I KNOW NOTHING OF THE SECRET OF ETERNITY!
I THANK YOU FOR DARING TO SEE ME! I SHALL GO NOW!
...AND, NIGHT AFTER NIGHT AFTER NIGHT...
NO MATTER WHERE I GO, MORDO'S AGENTS ARE NEVER MORE THAN A FEW STEPS BEHIND ME!
BUT I DARE NOT STOP NOW!
3

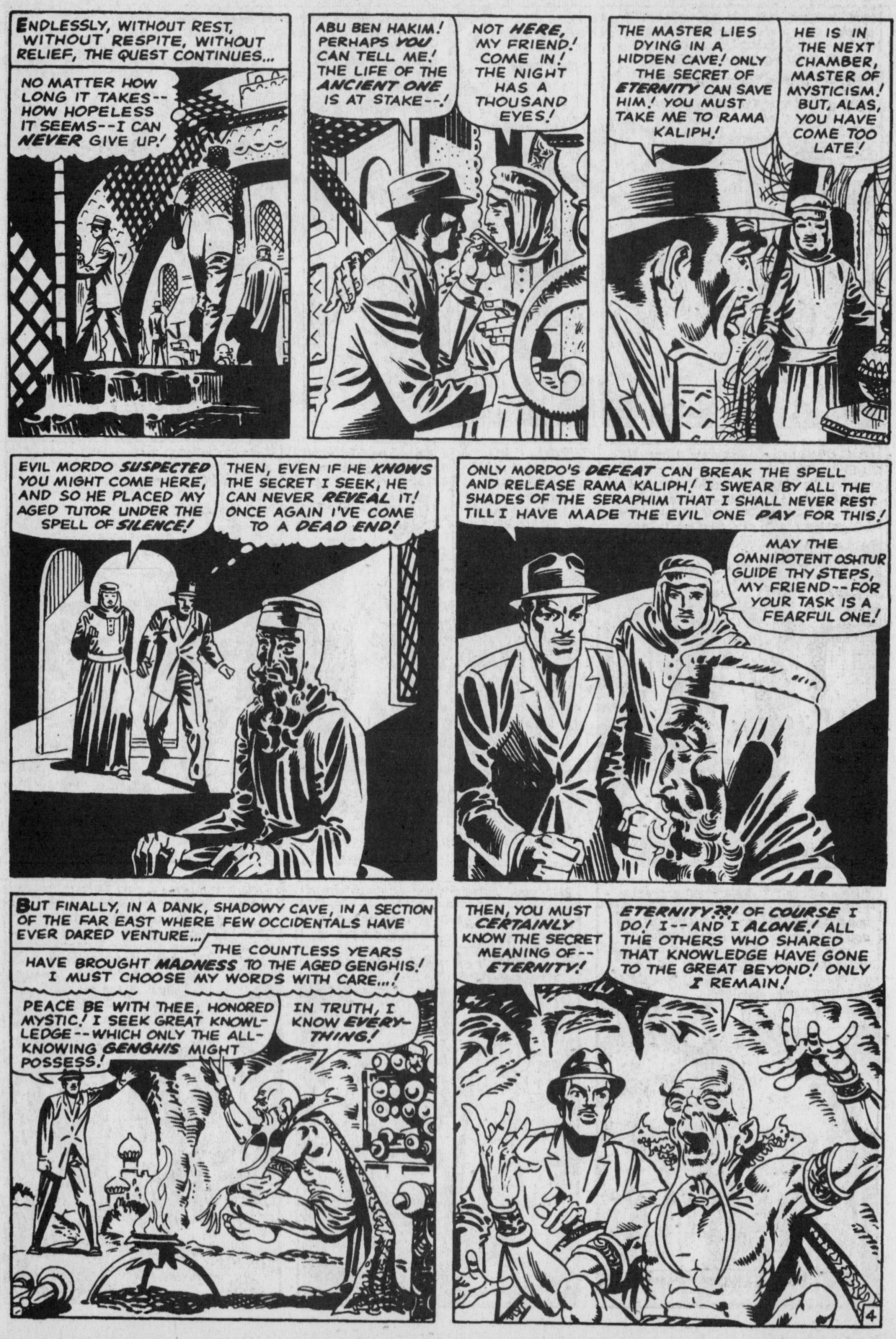
ENDLESSLY, WITHOUT REST, WITHOUT RESPITE, WITHOUT RELIEF, THE QUEST CONTINUES...
NO MATTER HOW LONG IT TAKES-- HOW HOPELESS IT SEEMS--I CAN NEVER GIVE UP!
ABU BEN HAKIM! PERHAPS YOU CAN TELL ME! THE LIFE OF THE ANCIENT ONE IS AT STAKE--!
NOT HERE, MY FRIEND! COME IN! THE NIGHT HAS A THOUSAND EYES!
THE MASTER LIES DYING IN A HIDDEN CAVE! ONLY THE SECRET OF ETERNITY CAN SAVE HIM! YOU MUST TAKE ME TO RAMA KALIPH!
HE IS IN THE NEXT CHAMBER, MASTER OF MYSTICISM! BUT, ALAS, YOU HAVE COME TOO LATE!
EVIL MORDO SUSPECTED YOU MIGHT COME HERE, AND SO HE PLACED MY AGED TUTOR UNDER THE SPELL OF SILENCE!
THEN, EVEN IF HE KNOWS THE SECRET I SEEK, HE CAN NEVER REVEAL IT! ONCE AGAIN I'VE COME TO A DEAD END!
ONLY MORDO'S DEFEAT CAN BREAK THE SPELL AND RELEASE RAMA KALIPH! I SWEAR BY ALL THE SHADES OF THE SERAPHIM THAT I SHALL NEVER REST TILL I HAVE MADE THE EVIL ONE PAY FOR THIS!
MAY THE OMNIPOTENT OSHTUR GUIDE THY STEPS, MY FRIEND--FOR YOUR TASK IS A FEARFUL ONE!
BUT FINALLY, IN A DANK, SHADOWY CAVE, IN A SECTION OF THE FAR EAST WHERE FEW OCCIDENTALS HAVE EVER DARED VENTURE...
THE COUNTLESS YEARS HAVE BROUGHT MADNESS TO THE AGED GENGHIS! I MUST CHOOSE MY WORDS WITH CARE...!
PEACE BE WITH THEE, HONORED MYSTIC! I SEEK GREAT KNOWL-LEDGE--WHICH ONLY THE ALL-KNOWING GENGHIS MIGHT POSSESS!
IN TRUTH, I KNOW EVERY-THING!
THEN, YOU MUST CERTAINLY KNOW THE SECRET MEANING OF--ETERNITY!
ETERNITY??! OF COURSE I DO! I--AND I ALONE! ALL THE OTHERS WHO SHARED THAT KNOWLEDGE HAVE GONE TO THE GREAT BEYOND! ONLY I REMAIN!
4

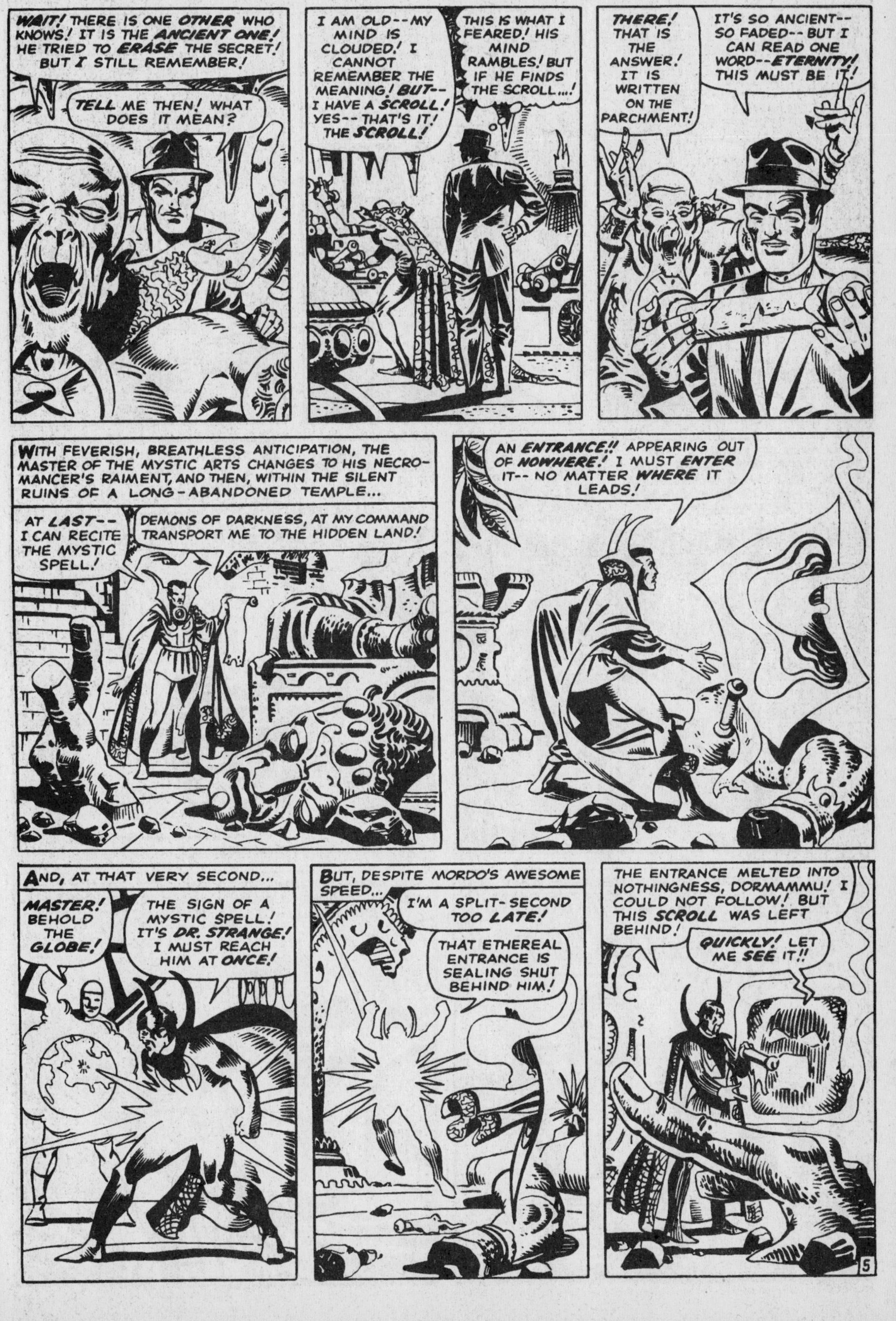
WAIT! THERE IS ONE OTHER WHO KNOWS! IT IS THE ANCIENT ONE! HE TRIED TO ERASE THE SECRET! BUT I STILL REMEMBER!
TELL ME THEN! WHAT DOES IT MEAN?
I AM OLD--MY MIND IS CLOUDED! I CANNOT REMEMBER THE MEANING! BUT--I HAVE A SCROLL! YES--THAT'S IT! THE SCROLL!
THIS IS WHAT I FEARED! HIS MIND RAMBLES! BUT IF HE FINDS THE SCROLL....!
THERE! THAT IS THE ANSWER! IT IS WRITTEN ON THE PARCHMENT!
IT'S SO ANCIENT--SO FADED--BUT I CAN READ ONE WORD--ETERNITY! THIS MUST BE IT!
WITH FEVERISH, BREATHLESS ANTICIPATION, THE MASTER OF THE MYSTIC ARTS CHANGES TO HIS NECROMANCER'S RAIMENT, AND THEN, WITHIN THE SILENT RUINS OF A LONG-ABANDONED TEMPLE...
AT LAST--I CAN RECITE THE MYSTIC SPELL!
DEMONS OF DARKNESS, AT MY COMMAND TRANSPORT ME TO THE HIDDEN LAND!
AN ENTRANCE!! APPEARING OUT OF NOWHERE! I MUST ENTER IT-- NO MATTER WHERE IT LEADS!
AND, AT THAT VERY SECOND...
MASTER! BEHOLD THE GLOBE!
THE SIGN OF A MYSTIC SPELL! IT'S DR. STRANGE! I MUST REACH HIM AT ONCE!
BUT, DESPITE MORDO'S AWESOME SPEED...
I'M A SPLIT-SECOND TOO LATE!
THAT ETHEREAL ENTRANCE IS SEALING SHUT BEHIND HIM!
THE ENTRANCE MELTED INTO NOTHINGNESS, DORMAMMU! I COULD NOT FOLLOW! BUT THIS SCROLL WAS LEFT BEHIND!
QUICKLY! LET ME SEE IT!!
5

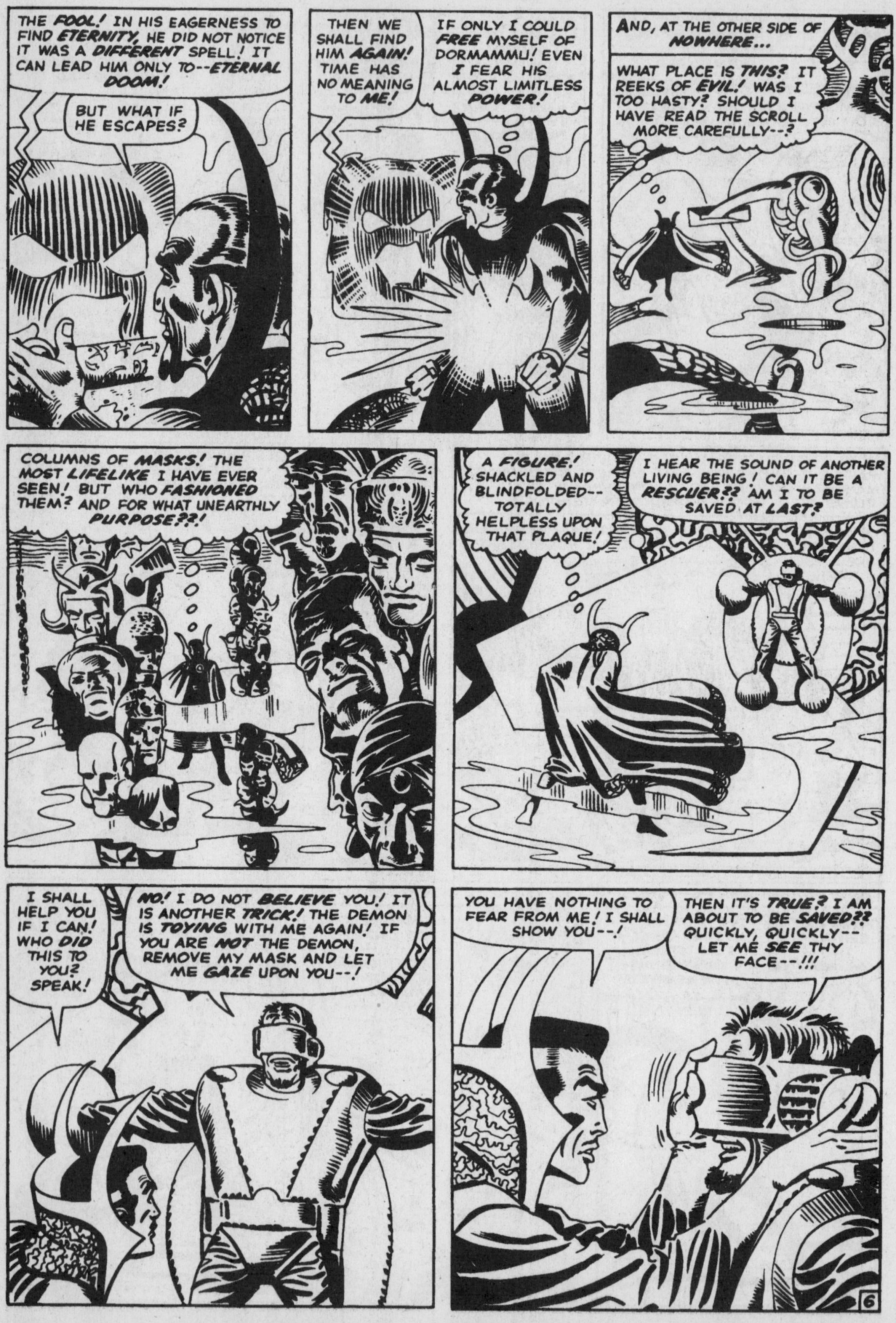

THE FOOL! IN HIS EAGERNESS TO FIND ETERNITY, HE DID NOT NOTICE IT WAS A DIFFERENT SPELL! IT CAN LEAD HIM ONLY TO--ETERNAL DOOM!
BUT WHAT IF HE ESCAPES?
THEN WE SHALL FIND HIM AGAIN! TIME HAS NO MEANING TO ME!
IF ONLY I COULD FREE MYSELF OF DORMAMMU! EVEN I FEAR HIS ALMOST LIMITLESS POWER!
AND, AT THE OTHER SIDE OF NOWHERE...
WHAT PLACE IS THIS? IT REEKS OF EVIL! WAS I TOO HASTY? SHOULD I HAVE READ THE SCROLL MORE CAREFULLY--?
COLUMNS OF MASKS! THE MOST LIFELIKE I HAVE EVER SEEN! BUT WHO FASHIONED THEM? AND FOR WHAT UNEARTHLY PURPOSE??!
A FIGURE! SHACKLED AND BLINDFOLDED-- TOTALLY HELPLESS UPON THAT PLAQUE!
I HEAR THE SOUND OF ANOTHER LIVING BEING! CAN IT BE A RESCUER?? AM I TO BE SAVED AT LAST?
I SHALL HELP YOU IF I CAN! WHO DID THIS TO YOU? SPEAK!
NO! I DO NOT BELIEVE YOU! IT IS ANOTHER TRICK! THE DEMON IS TOYING WITH ME AGAIN! IF YOU ARE NOT THE DEMON, REMOVE MY MASK AND LET ME GAZE UPON YOU--!
YOU HAVE NOTHING TO FEAR FROM ME! I SHALL SHOW YOU--!
THEN IT'S TRUE? I AM ABOUT TO BE SAVED?? QUICKLY, QUICKLY-- LET ME SEE THY FACE--!!!
6

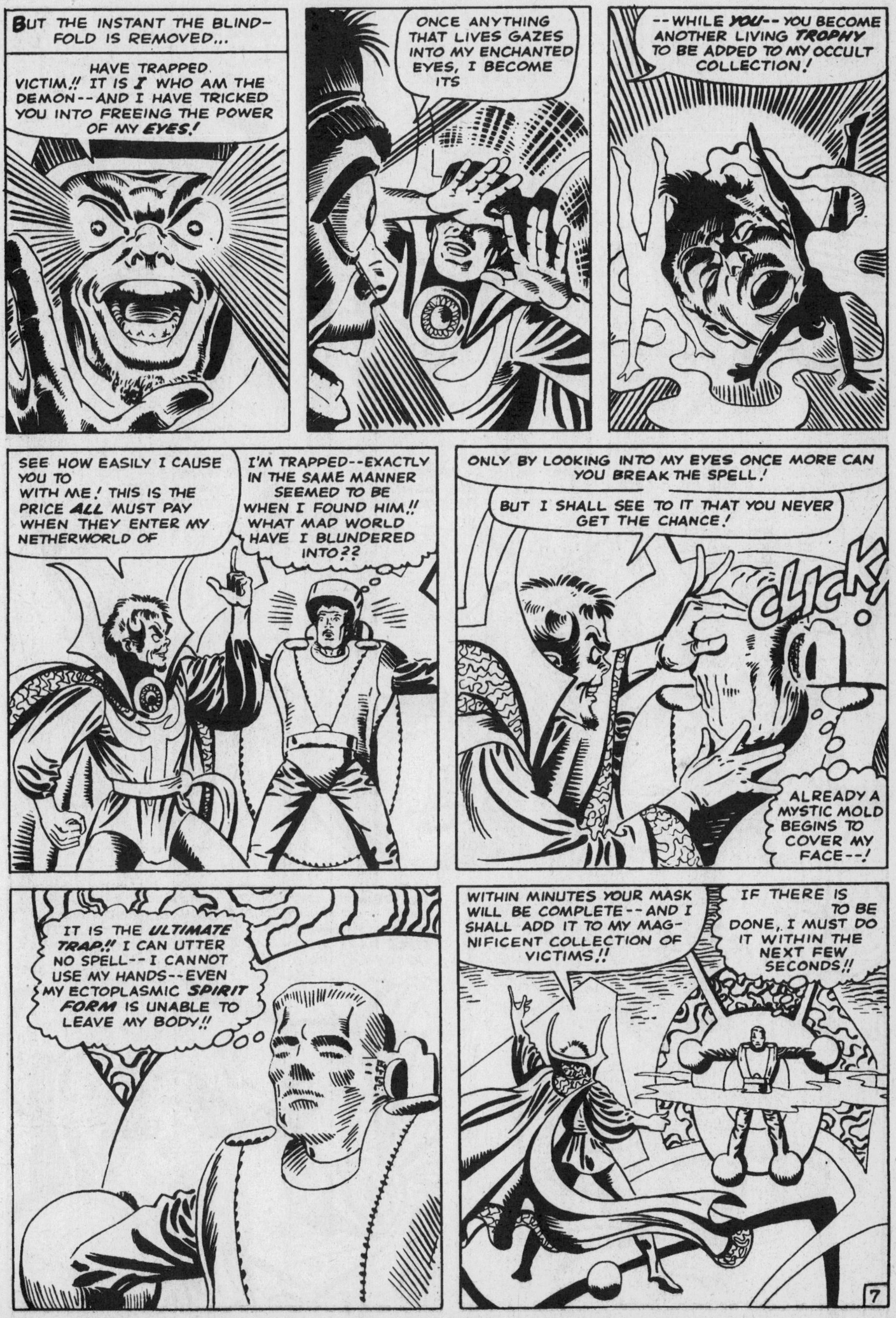

BUT THE INSTANT THE BLIND-FOLD IS REMOVED...
HAVE TRAPPED VICTIM!! IT IS I WHO AM THE DEMON--AND I HAVE TRICKED YOU INTO FREEING THE POWER OF MY EYES!
ONCE ANYTHING THAT LIVES GAZES INTO MY ENCHANTED EYES, I BECOME ITS
--WHILE YOU--YOU BECOME ANOTHER LIVING TROPHY TO BE ADDED TO MY OCCULT COLLECTION!
SEE HOW EASILY I CAUSE YOU TO WITH ME! THIS IS THE PRICE ALL MUST PAY WHEN THEY ENTER MY NETHERWORLD OF
I'M TRAPPED--EXACTLY IN THE SAME MANNER SEEMED TO BE WHEN I FOUND HIM!! WHAT MAD WORLD HAVE I BLUNDERED INTO??
ONLY BY LOOKING INTO MY EYES ONCE MORE CAN YOU BREAK THE SPELL!
BUT I SHALL SEE TO IT THAT YOU NEVER GET THE CHANCE!
CLICK!
ALREADY A MYSTIC MOLD BEGINS TO COVER MY FACE--!
IT IS THE ULTIMATE TRAP!! I CAN UTTER NO SPELL--I CANNOT USE MY HANDS--EVEN MY ECTOPLASMIC SPIRIT FORM IS UNABLE TO LEAVE MY BODY!!
WITHIN MINUTES YOUR MASK WILL BE COMPLETE--AND I SHALL ADD IT TO MY MAGNIFICENT COLLECTION OF VICTIMS!!
IF THERE IS TO BE DONE, I MUST DO IT WITHIN THE NEXT FEW SECONDS!!
7

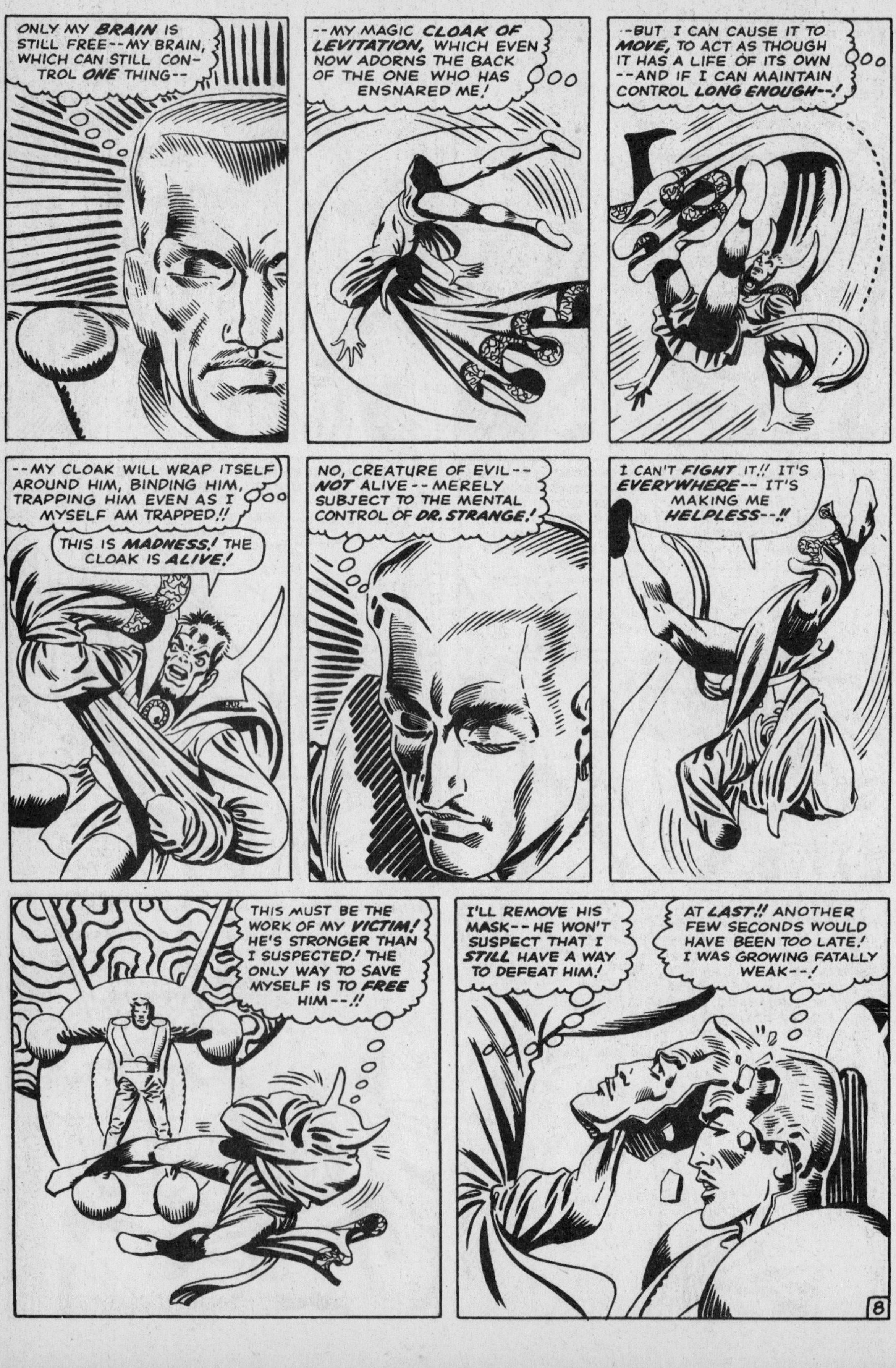
ONLY MY BRAIN IS STILL FREE--MY BRAIN, WHICH CAN STILL CON-TROL ONE THING--
--MY MAGIC CLOAK OF LEVITATION, WHICH EVEN NOW ADORNS THE BACK OF THE ONE WHO HAS ENSNARED ME!
-BUT I CAN CAUSE IT TO MOVE, TO ACT AS THOUGH IT HAS A LIFE OF ITS OWN --AND IF I CAN MAINTAIN CONTROL LONG ENOUGH--!
--MY CLOAK WILL WRAP ITSELF AROUND HIM, BINDING HIM, TRAPPING HIM EVEN AS I MYSELF AM TRAPPED!!
THIS IS MADNESS! THE CLOAK IS ALIVE!
NO, CREATURE OF EVIL-- NOT ALIVE--MERELY SUBJECT TO THE MENTAL CONTROL OF DR. STRANGE!
I CAN'T FIGHT IT!! IT'S EVERYWHERE-- IT'S MAKING ME HELPLESS--!!
THIS MUST BE THE WORK OF MY VICTIM! HE'S STRONGER THAN I SUSPECTED! THE ONLY WAY TO SAVE MYSELF IS TO FREE HIM--!!
I'LL REMOVE HIS MASK--HE WON'T SUSPECT THAT I STILL HAVE A WAY TO DEFEAT HIM!
AT LAST!! ANOTHER FEW SECONDS WOULD HAVE BEEN TOO LATE! I WAS GROWING FATALLY WEAK--!
8

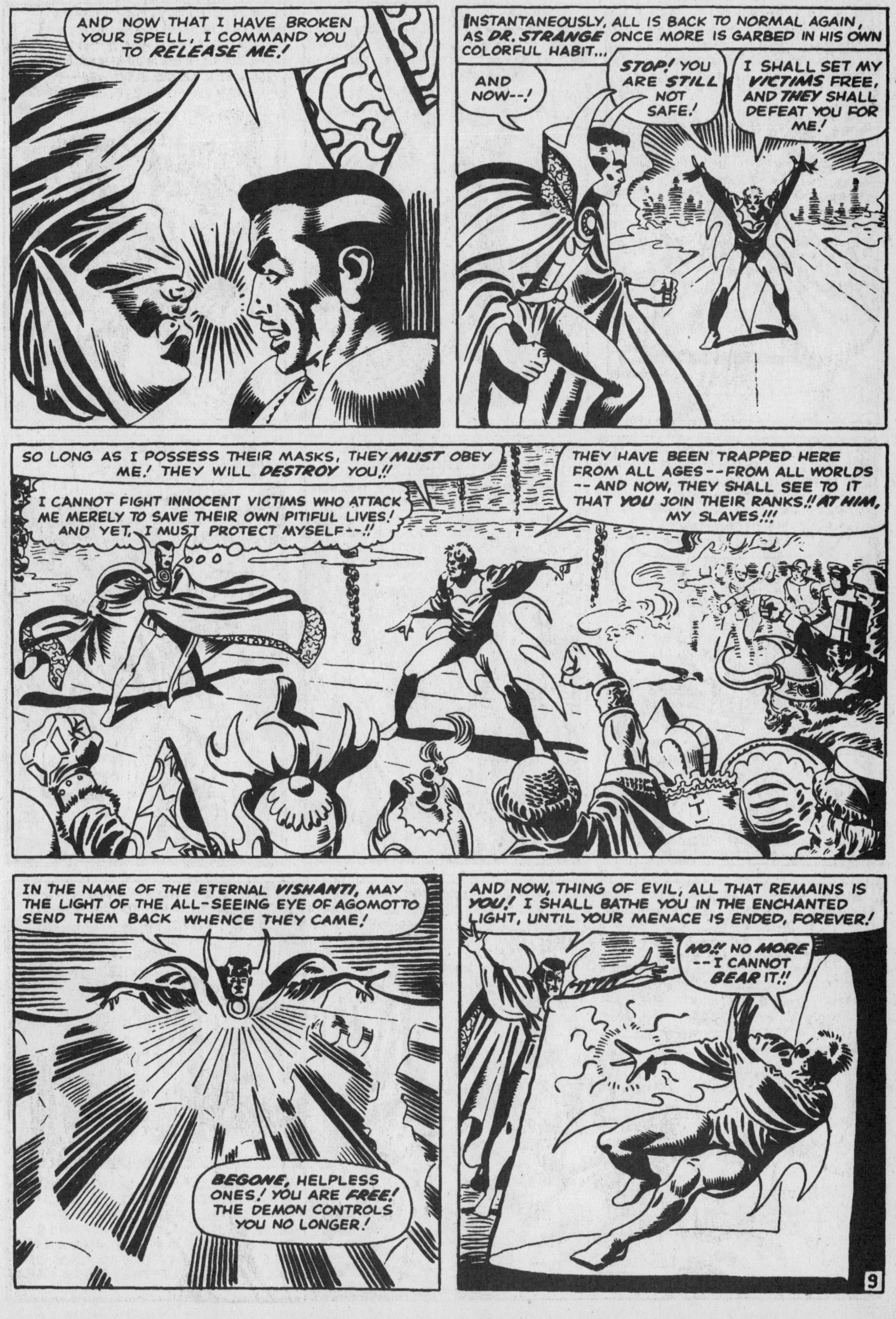
AND NOW THAT I HAVE BROKEN YOUR SPELL, I COMMAND YOU TO RELEASE ME!
INSTANTANEOUSLY, ALL IS BACK TO NORMAL AGAIN, AS DR. STRANGE ONCE MORE IS GARBED IN HIS OWN COLORFUL HABIT...
AND NOW--!
STOP! YOU ARE STILL NOT SAFE!
I SHALL SET MY VICTIMS FREE, AND THEY SHALL DEFEAT YOU FOR ME!
SO LONG AS I POSSESS THEIR MASKS, THEY MUST OBEY ME! THEY WILL DESTROY YOU!!
I CANNOT FIGHT INNOCENT VICTIMS WHO ATTACK ME MERELY TO SAVE THEIR OWN PITIFUL LIVES! AND YET, I MUST PROTECT MYSELF--!!
THEY HAVE BEEN TRAPPED HERE FROM ALL AGES--FROM ALL WORLDS --AND NOW, THEY SHALL SEE TO IT THAT YOU JOIN THEIR RANKS!! AT HIM, MY SLAVES!!!
IN THE NAME OF THE ETERNAL VISHANTI, MAY THE LIGHT OF THE ALL-SEEING EYE OF AGOMOTTO SEND THEM BACK WHENCE THEY CAME!
BEGONE, HELPLESS ONES! YOU ARE FREE! THE DEMON CONTROLS YOU NO LONGER!
AND NOW, THING OF EVIL, ALL THAT REMAINS IS YOU! I SHALL BATHE YOU IN THE ENCHANTED LIGHT, UNTIL YOUR MENACE IS ENDED, FOREVER!
NO!! NO MORE --I CANNOT BEAR IT!!
9

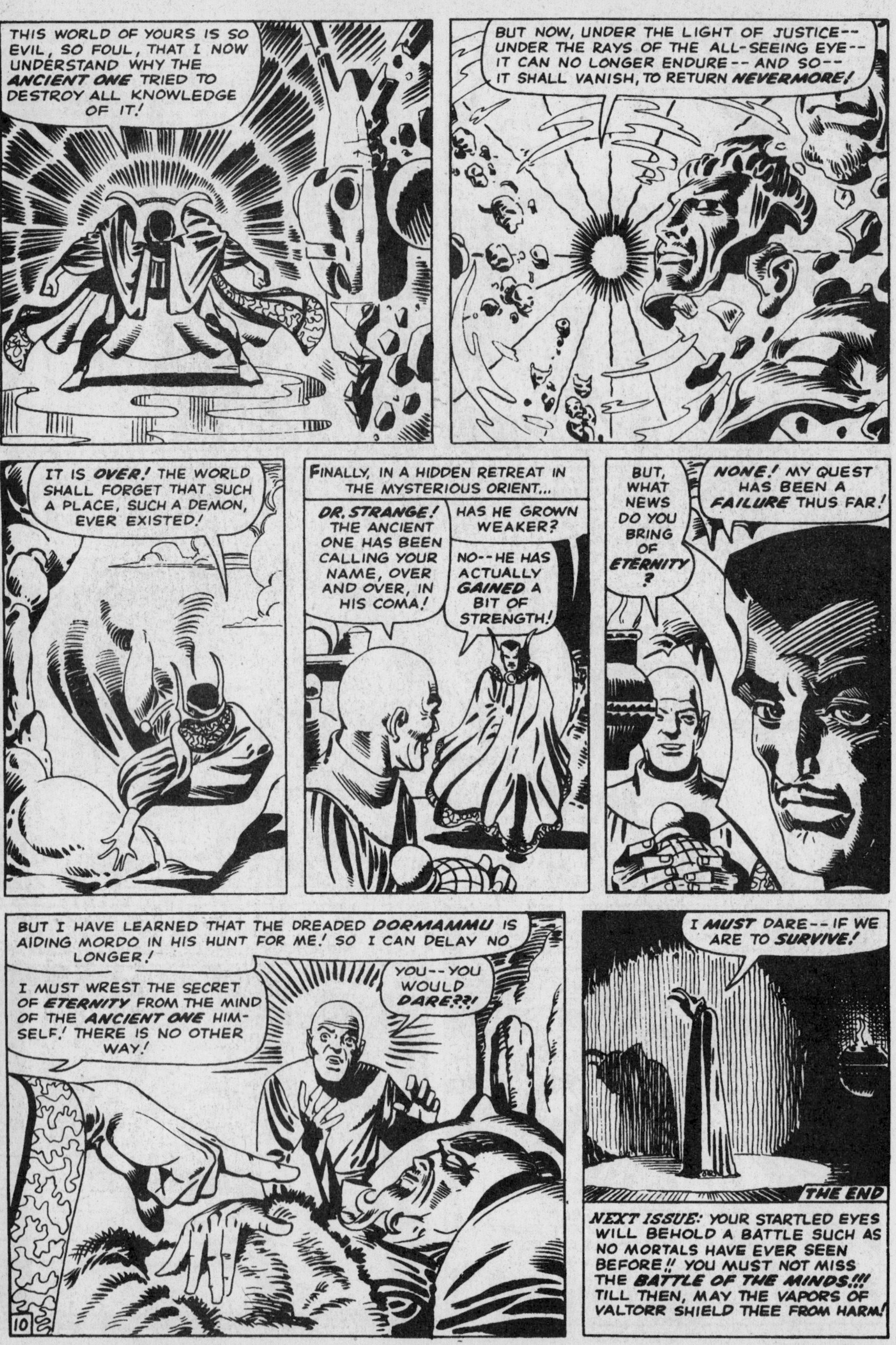

THIS WORLD OF YOURS IS SO EVIL, SO FOUL, THAT I NOW UNDERSTAND WHY THE ANCIENT ONE TRIED TO DESTROY ALL KNOWLEDGE OF IT!
BUT NOW, UNDER THE LIGHT OF JUSTICE-- UNDER THE RAYS OF THE ALL-SEEING EYE-- IT CAN NO LONGER ENDURE-- AND SO-- IT SHALL VANISH, TO RETURN NEVERMORE!
IT IS OVER! THE WORLD SHALL FORGET THAT SUCH A PLACE, SUCH A DEMON, EVER EXISTED!
FINALLY, IN A HIDDEN RETREAT IN THE MYSTERIOUS ORIENT...
DR. STRANGE! THE ANCIENT ONE HAS BEEN CALLING YOUR NAME, OVER AND OVER, IN HIS COMA!
HAS HE GROWN WEAKER?
NO--HE HAS ACTUALLY GAINED A BIT OF STRENGTH!
BUT, WHAT NEWS DO YOU BRING OF ETERNITY?
NONE! MY QUEST HAS BEEN A FAILURE THUS FAR!
BUT I HAVE LEARNED THAT THE DREADED DORMAMMU IS AIDING MORDO IN HIS HUNT FOR ME! SO I CAN DELAY NO LONGER!
I MUST WREST THE SECRET OF ETERNITY FROM THE MIND OF THE ANCIENT ONE HIMSELF! THERE IS NO OTHER WAY!
YOU--YOU WOULD DARE??!
I MUST DARE-- IF WE ARE TO SURVIVE!
THE END
NEXT ISSUE: YOUR STARTLED EYES WILL BEHOLD A BATTLE SUCH AS NO MORTALS HAVE EVER SEEN BEFORE!! YOU MUST NOT MISS THE BATTLE OF THE MINDS!!! TILL THEN, MAY THE VAPORS OF VALTORR SHIELD THEE FROM HARM!
10

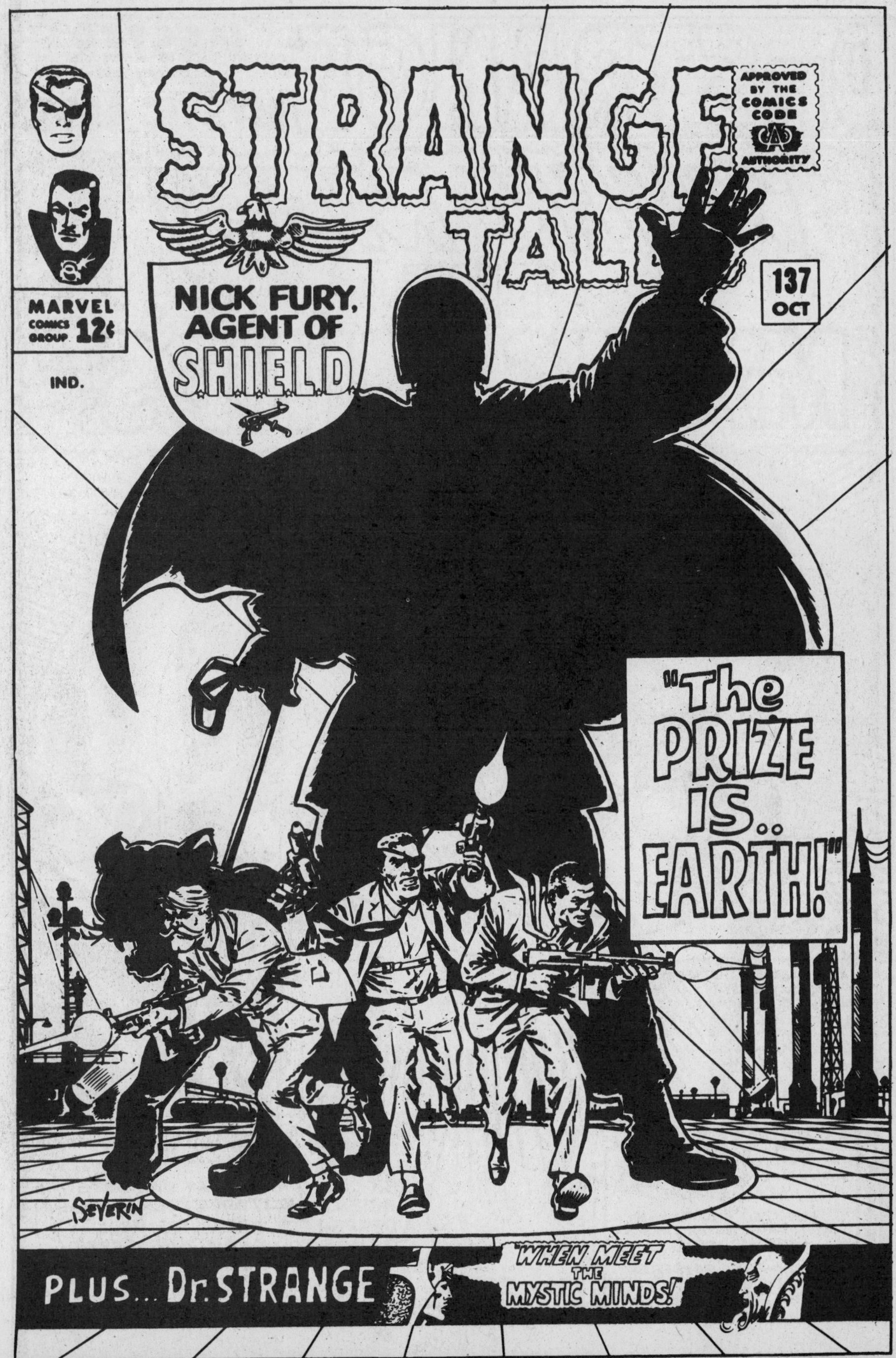
STRANGE TALES
APPROVED BY THE COMICS CODE AUTHORITY
MARVEL COMICS GROUP 12¢
IND.
137 OCT
NICK FURY, AGENT OF S.H.I.E.L.D
"The PRIZE IS.. EARTH!"
SEVERIN
PLUS... Dr. STRANGE
"WHEN MEET THE MYSTIC MINDS!"

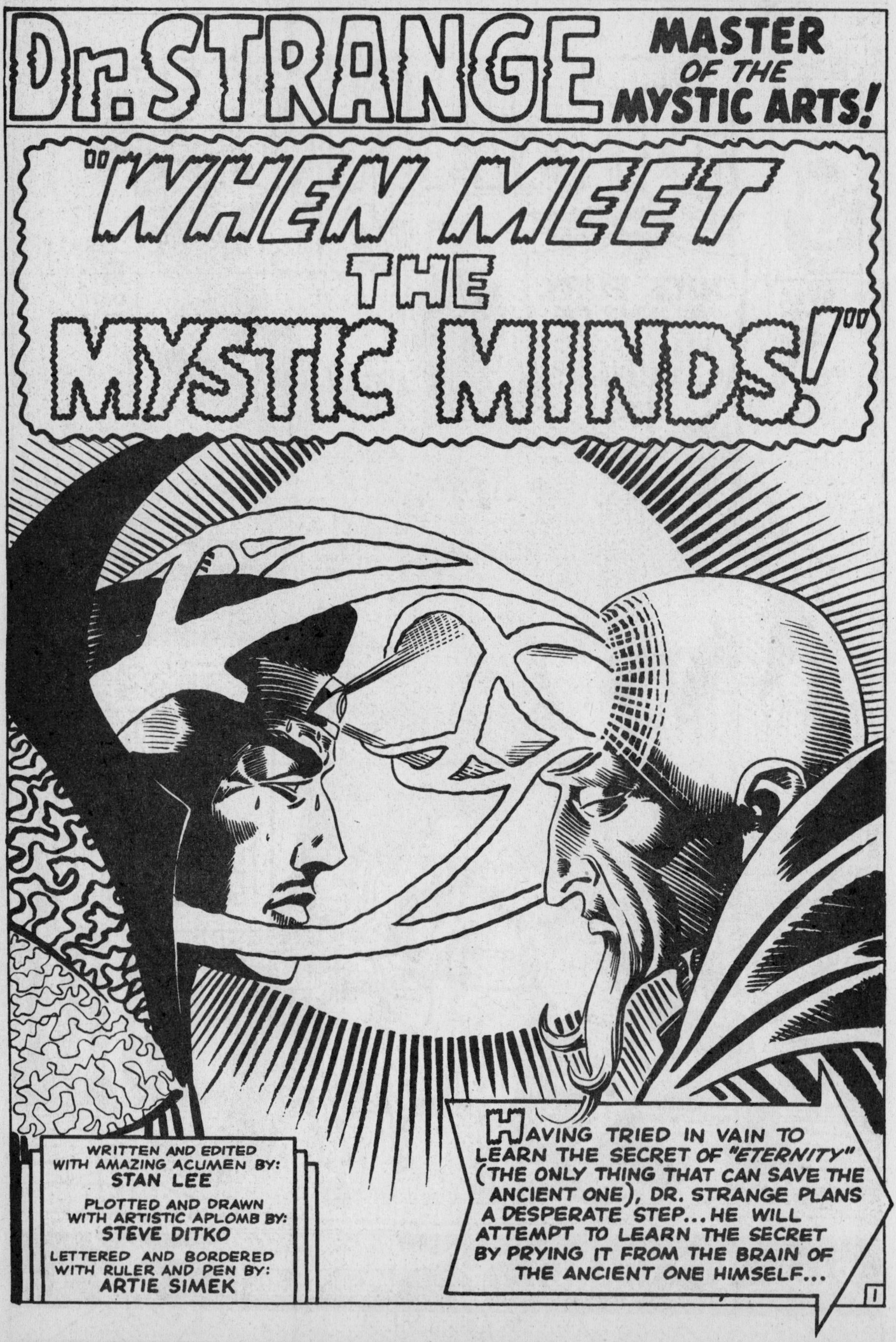

Dr. STRANGE
MASTER OF THE MYSTIC ARTS!
"WHEN MEET THE MYSTIC MINDS!"
WRITTEN AND EDITED WITH AMAZING ACUMEN BY: STAN LEE
PLOTTED AND DRAWN WITH ARTISTIC APLOMB BY: STEVE DITKO
LETTERED AND BORDERED WITH RULER AND PEN BY: ARTIE SIMEK
HAVING TRIED IN VAIN TO LEARN THE SECRET OF "ETERNITY" (THE ONLY THING THAT CAN SAVE THE ANCIENT ONE), DR. STRANGE PLANS A DESPERATE STEP... HE WILL ATTEMPT TO LEARN THE SECRET BY PRYING IT FROM THE BRAIN OF THE ANCIENT ONE HIMSELF...
1

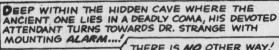

DEEP WITHIN THE HIDDEN CAVE WHERE THE ANCIENT ONE LIES IN A DEADLY COMA, HIS DEVOTED ATTENDANT TURNS TOWARDS DR. STRANGE WITH MOUNTING ALARM....!

NO! YOU MUSTN'T DO THIS! IT IS TOO DANGEROUS!

THERE IS NO OTHER WAY! THE ANCIENT ONE MUST BE CURED, AND ONLY THE SECRET OF ETERNITY WILL SAVE HIM!

BUT, HE IS SO WEAK! IF SOMETHING GOES WRONG-- THE SLIGHTEST SHOCK COULD BE FATAL!

I AM AWARE OF THAT, TRUSTED ONE! BUT, DO NOT FORGET THE DREAD DORMAMMU, AND BARON MORDO! THIS IS OUR ONLY CHANCE TO DEFEAT THEM!

AS THE ANCIENT ONE'S TRUE DISCIPLE, THE DECISION IS YOURS ALONE TO MAKE! I CAN SAY NO MORE!

THEN LEAVE US NOW! THE DEED MUST BE DONE!

FORGIVE MY TEARS, DR. STRANGE! BUT IF ANYTHING SHOULD GO WRONG--IF ANY HARM SHOULD BEFALL OUR MASTER--

I SWEAR BY THE OMNIPOTENT OSHTUR-- I SHALL GUARD HIS SAFETY WITH MY VERY LIFE!

THEN, DO WHAT YOU MUST, MASTER OF CONJURY! FOR TRULY I KNOW THAT YOU VALUE HIS WELFARE ABOVE ALL ELSE!

HE HAS BEEN MY TEACHER, MY PROTECTOR-- AND MORE THAN A FATHER!

HE CHOSE WISELY WHEN HE SELECTED YOU AS HIS FAVORED ONE! WHATEVER BEFALLS, HE SHALL KNOW THAT YOU DID YOUR BEST-- NONE COULD DO MORE!

AND SO, I LEAVE YOU TO THE MOST AWESOME TASK ANY MORTAL HAS EVER FACED! MAY THE ETERNAL VISHANTI BE EVER AT THY SIDE! SALAAM, MAN OF MYSTERY!

THE TIME IS NOW! THERE CAN BE NO TURNING BACK!

2

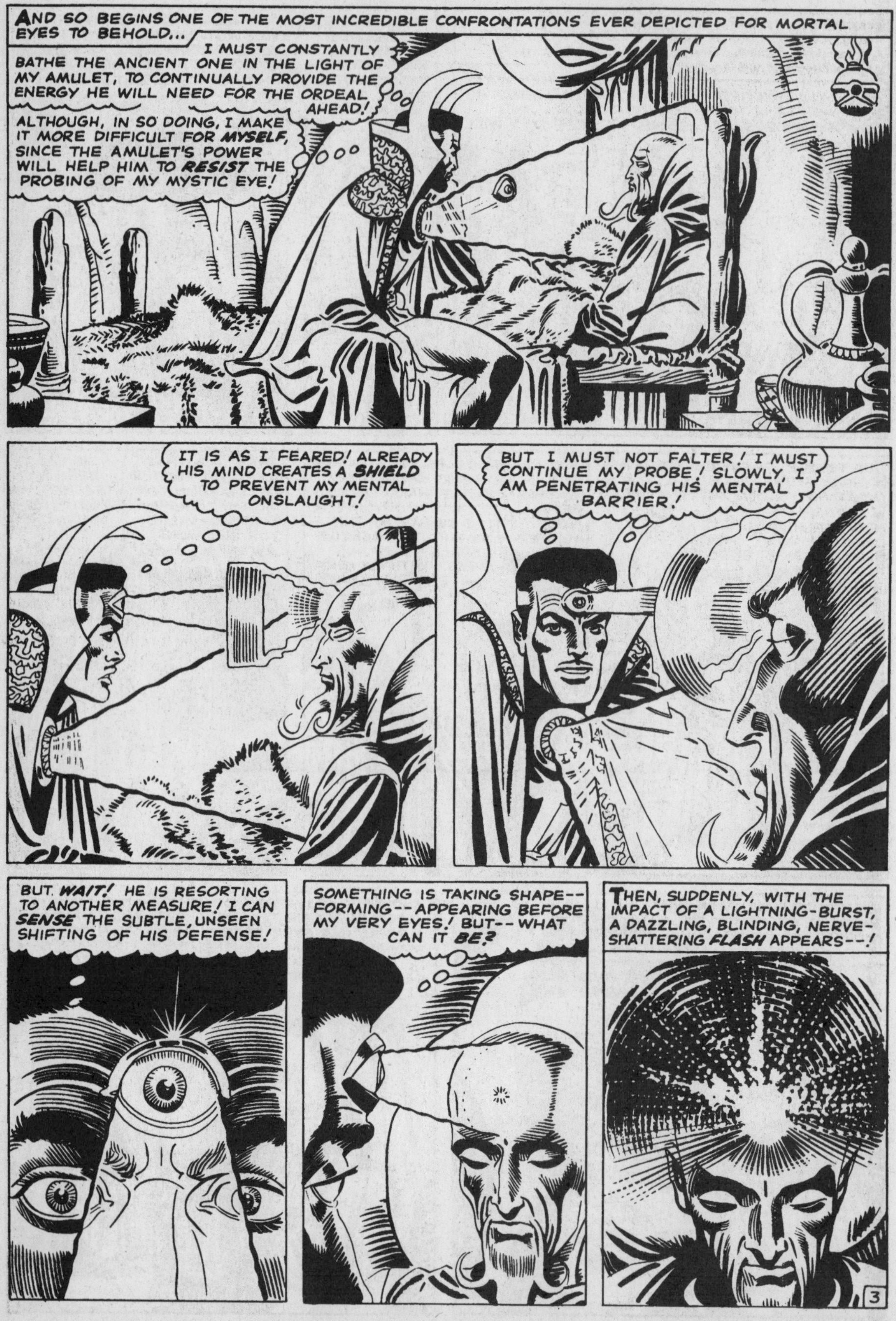
AND SO BEGINS ONE OF THE MOST INCREDIBLE CONFRONTATIONS EVER DEPICTED FOR MORTAL EYES TO BEHOLD...
I MUST CONSTANTLY BATHE THE ANCIENT ONE IN THE LIGHT OF MY AMULET, TO CONTINUALLY PROVIDE THE ENERGY HE WILL NEED FOR THE ORDEAL AHEAD!
ALTHOUGH, IN SO DOING, I MAKE IT MORE DIFFICULT FOR MYSELF, SINCE THE AMULET'S POWER WILL HELP HIM TO RESIST THE PROBING OF MY MYSTIC EYE!
IT IS AS I FEARED! ALREADY HIS MIND CREATES A SHIELD TO PREVENT MY MENTAL ONSLAUGHT!
BUT I MUST NOT FALTER! I MUST CONTINUE MY PROBE! SLOWLY, I AM PENETRATING HIS MENTAL BARRIER!
BUT WAIT! HE IS RESORTING TO ANOTHER MEASURE! I CAN SENSE THE SUBTLE, UNSEEN SHIFTING OF HIS DEFENSE!
SOMETHING IS TAKING SHAPE-- FORMING-- APPEARING BEFORE MY VERY EYES! BUT-- WHAT CAN IT BE?
THEN, SUDDENLY, WITH THE IMPACT OF A LIGHTNING-BURST, A DAZZLING, BLINDING, NERVE-SHATTERING FLASH APPEARS--!
3

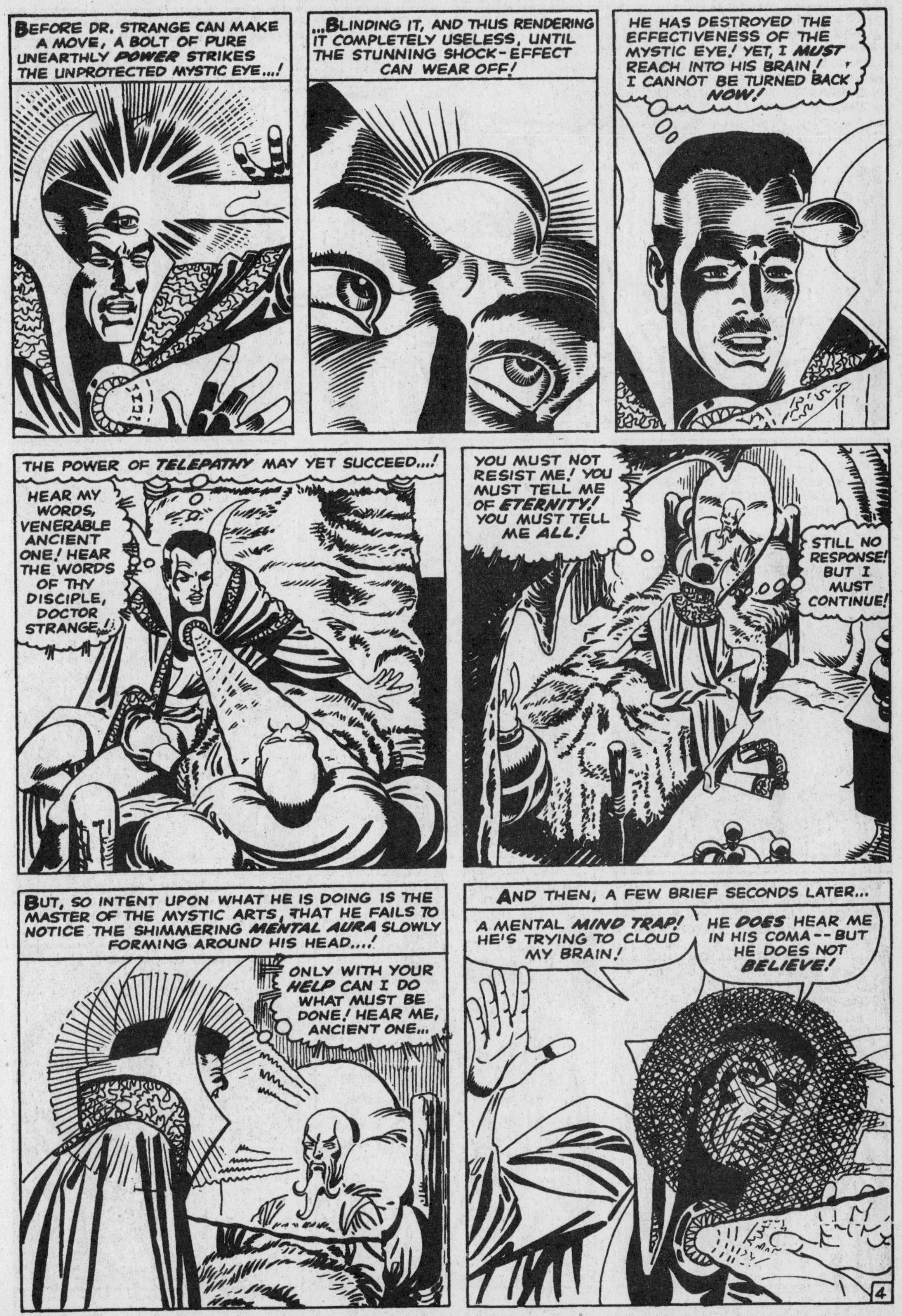
BEFORE DR. STRANGE CAN MAKE A MOVE, A BOLT OF PURE UNEARTHLY POWER STRIKES THE UNPROTECTED MYSTIC EYE...!
...BLINDING IT, AND THUS RENDERING IT COMPLETELY USELESS, UNTIL THE STUNNING SHOCK-EFFECT CAN WEAR OFF!
HE HAS DESTROYED THE EFFECTIVENESS OF THE MYSTIC EYE! YET, I MUST REACH INTO HIS BRAIN! I CANNOT BE TURNED BACK NOW!
THE POWER OF TELEPATHY MAY YET SUCCEED...!
HEAR MY WORDS, VENERABLE ANCIENT ONE! HEAR THE WORDS OF THY DISCIPLE, DOCTOR STRANGE...!
YOU MUST NOT RESIST ME! YOU MUST TELL ME OF ETERNITY! YOU MUST TELL ME ALL!
STILL NO RESPONSE! BUT I MUST CONTINUE!
BUT, SO INTENT UPON WHAT HE IS DOING IS THE MASTER OF THE MYSTIC ARTS, THAT HE FAILS TO NOTICE THE SHIMMERING MENTAL AURA SLOWLY FORMING AROUND HIS HEAD...!
ONLY WITH YOUR HELP CAN I DO WHAT MUST BE DONE! HEAR ME, ANCIENT ONE...
AND THEN, A FEW BRIEF SECONDS LATER...
A MENTAL MIND TRAP! HE'S TRYING TO CLOUD MY BRAIN!
HE DOES HEAR ME IN HIS COMA--BUT HE DOES NOT BELIEVE!
4

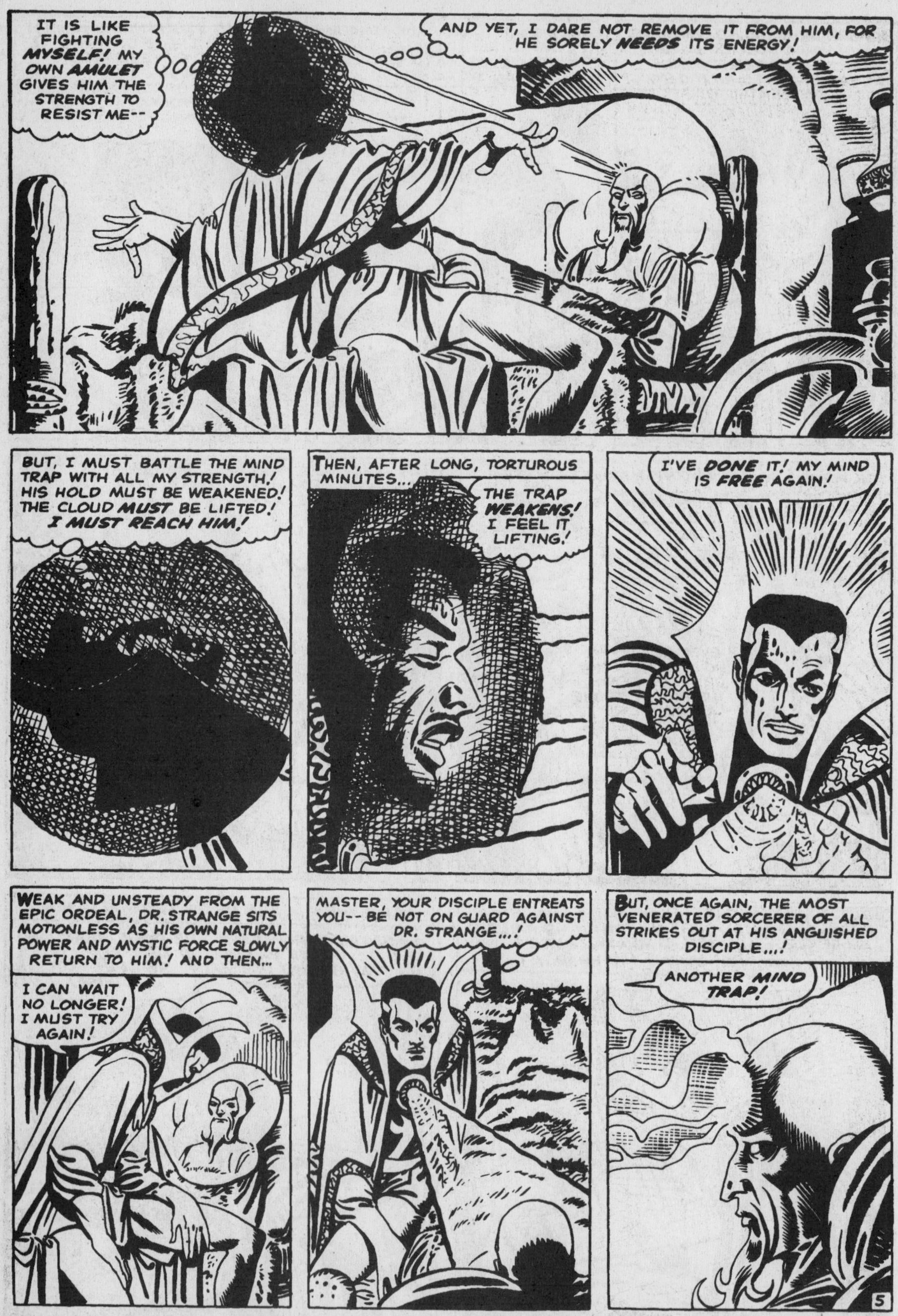
IT IS LIKE FIGHTING MYSELF! MY OWN AMULET GIVES HIM THE STRENGTH TO RESIST ME--
AND YET, I DARE NOT REMOVE IT FROM HIM, FOR HE SORELY NEEDS ITS ENERGY!
BUT, I MUST BATTLE THE MIND TRAP WITH ALL MY STRENGTH! HIS HOLD MUST BE WEAKENED! THE CLOUD MUST BE LIFTED! I MUST REACH HIM!
THEN, AFTER LONG, TORTUROUS MINUTES...
THE TRAP WEAKENS! I FEEL IT LIFTING!
I'VE DONE IT! MY MIND IS FREE AGAIN!
WEAK AND UNSTEADY FROM THE EPIC ORDEAL, DR. STRANGE SITS MOTIONLESS AS HIS OWN NATURAL POWER AND MYSTIC FORCE SLOWLY RETURN TO HIM! AND THEN...
I CAN WAIT NO LONGER! I MUST TRY AGAIN!
MASTER, YOUR DISCIPLE ENTREATS YOU-- BE NOT ON GUARD AGAINST DR. STRANGE...!
BUT, ONCE AGAIN, THE MOST VENERATED SORCERER OF ALL STRIKES OUT AT HIS ANGUISHED DISCIPLE...!
ANOTHER MIND TRAP!
5

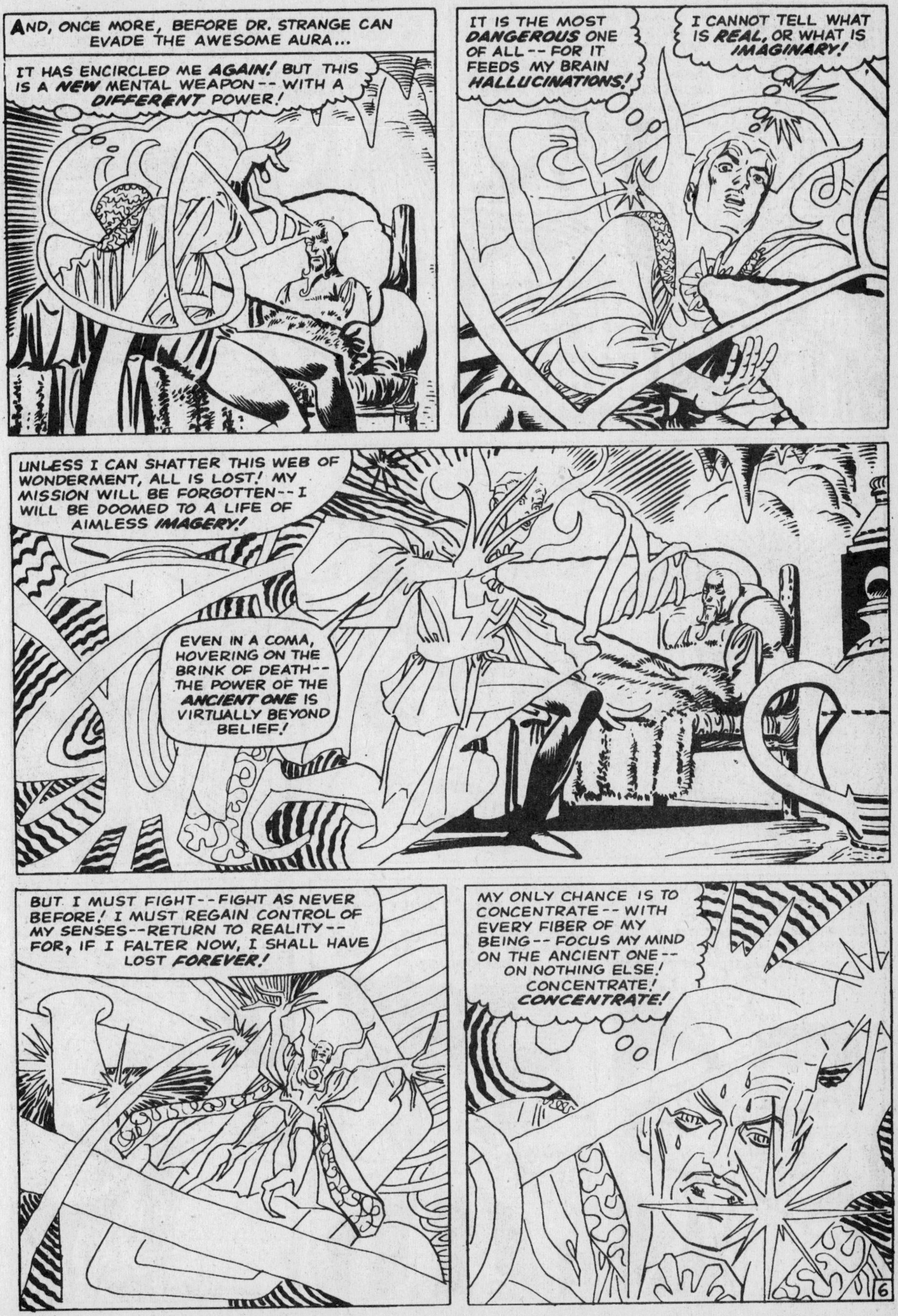
AND, ONCE MORE, BEFORE DR. STRANGE CAN EVADE THE AWESOME AURA...
IT HAS ENCIRCLED ME AGAIN! BUT THIS IS A NEW MENTAL WEAPON -- WITH A DIFFERENT POWER!
IT IS THE MOST DANGEROUS ONE OF ALL -- FOR IT FEEDS MY BRAIN HALLUCINATIONS!
I CANNOT TELL WHAT IS REAL, OR WHAT IS IMAGINARY!
UNLESS I CAN SHATTER THIS WEB OF WONDERMENT, ALL IS LOST! MY MISSION WILL BE FORGOTTEN -- I WILL BE DOOMED TO A LIFE OF AIMLESS IMAGERY!
EVEN IN A COMA, HOVERING ON THE BRINK OF DEATH -- THE POWER OF THE ANCIENT ONE IS VIRTUALLY BEYOND BELIEF!
BUT I MUST FIGHT -- FIGHT AS NEVER BEFORE! I MUST REGAIN CONTROL OF MY SENSES -- RETURN TO REALITY -- FOR, IF I FALTER NOW, I SHALL HAVE LOST FOREVER!
MY ONLY CHANCE IS TO CONCENTRATE -- WITH EVERY FIBER OF MY BEING -- FOCUS MY MIND ON THE ANCIENT ONE -- ON NOTHING ELSE! CONCENTRATE! CONCENTRATE!
6

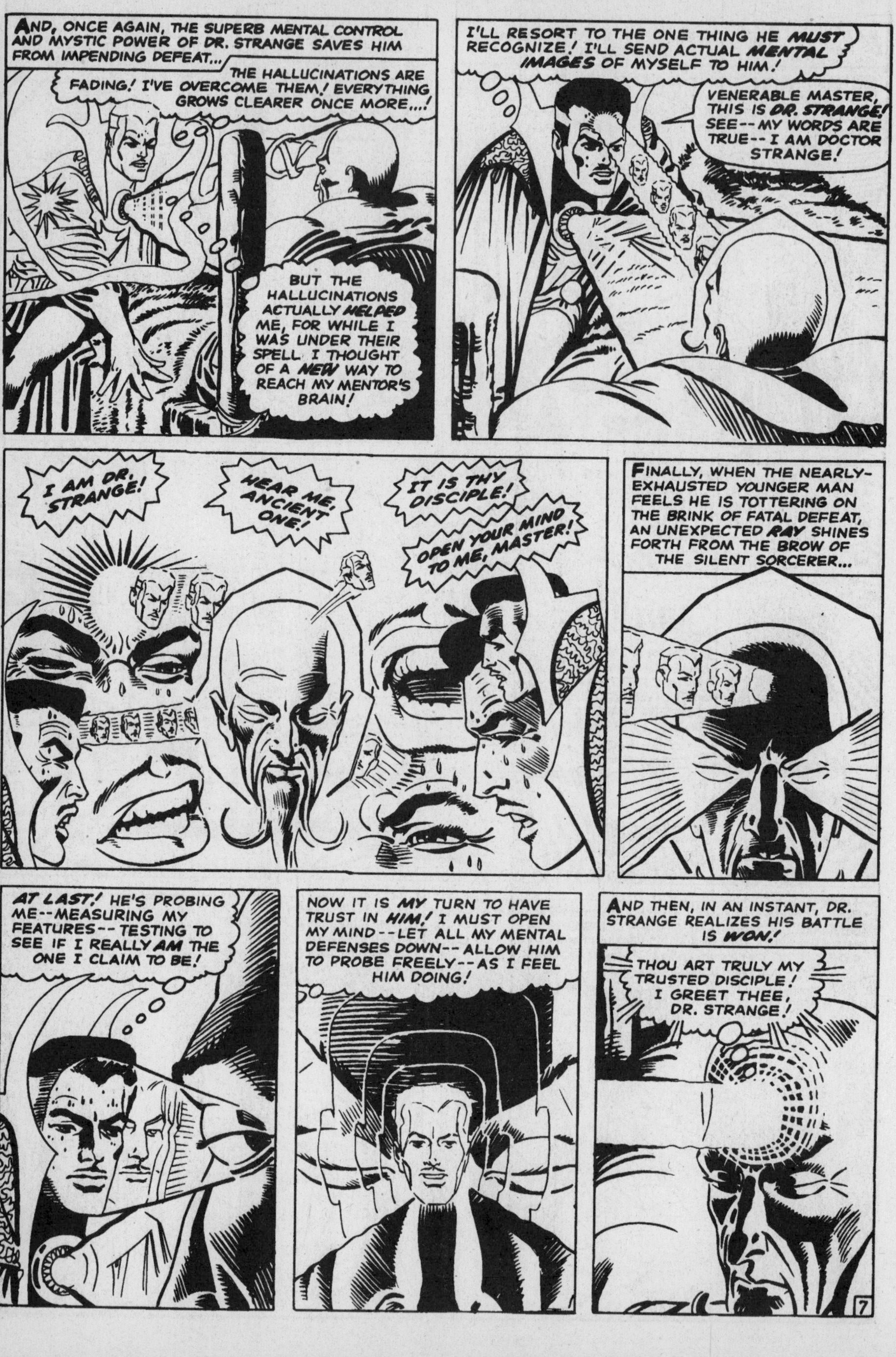

AND, ONCE AGAIN, THE SUPERB MENTAL CONTROL AND MYSTIC POWER OF DR. STRANGE SAVES HIM FROM IMPENDING DEFEAT...
THE HALLUCINATIONS ARE FADING! I'VE OVERCOME THEM! EVERYTHING GROWS CLEARER ONCE MORE...!
BUT THE HALLUCINATIONS ACTUALLY HELPED ME, FOR WHILE I WAS UNDER THEIR SPELL I THOUGHT OF A NEW WAY TO REACH MY MENTOR'S BRAIN!
I'LL RESORT TO THE ONE THING HE MUST RECOGNIZE! I'LL SEND ACTUAL MENTAL IMAGES OF MYSELF TO HIM!
VENERABLE MASTER, THIS IS DR. STRANGE! SEE--MY WORDS ARE TRUE--I AM DOCTOR STRANGE!
I AM DR. STRANGE!
HEAR ME, ANCIENT ONE!
IT IS THY DISCIPLE!
OPEN YOUR MIND TO ME, MASTER!
FINALLY, WHEN THE NEARLY-EXHAUSTED YOUNGER MAN FEELS HE IS TOTTERING ON THE BRINK OF FATAL DEFEAT, AN UNEXPECTED RAY SHINES FORTH FROM THE BROW OF THE SILENT SORCERER...
AT LAST! HE'S PROBING ME--MEASURING MY FEATURES--TESTING TO SEE IF I REALLY AM THE ONE I CLAIM TO BE!
NOW IT IS MY TURN TO HAVE TRUST IN HIM! I MUST OPEN MY MIND--LET ALL MY MENTAL DEFENSES DOWN--ALLOW HIM TO PROBE FREELY--AS I FEEL HIM DOING!
AND THEN, IN AN INSTANT, DR. STRANGE REALIZES HIS BATTLE IS WON!
THOU ART TRULY MY TRUSTED DISCIPLE! I GREET THEE, DR. STRANGE!
7

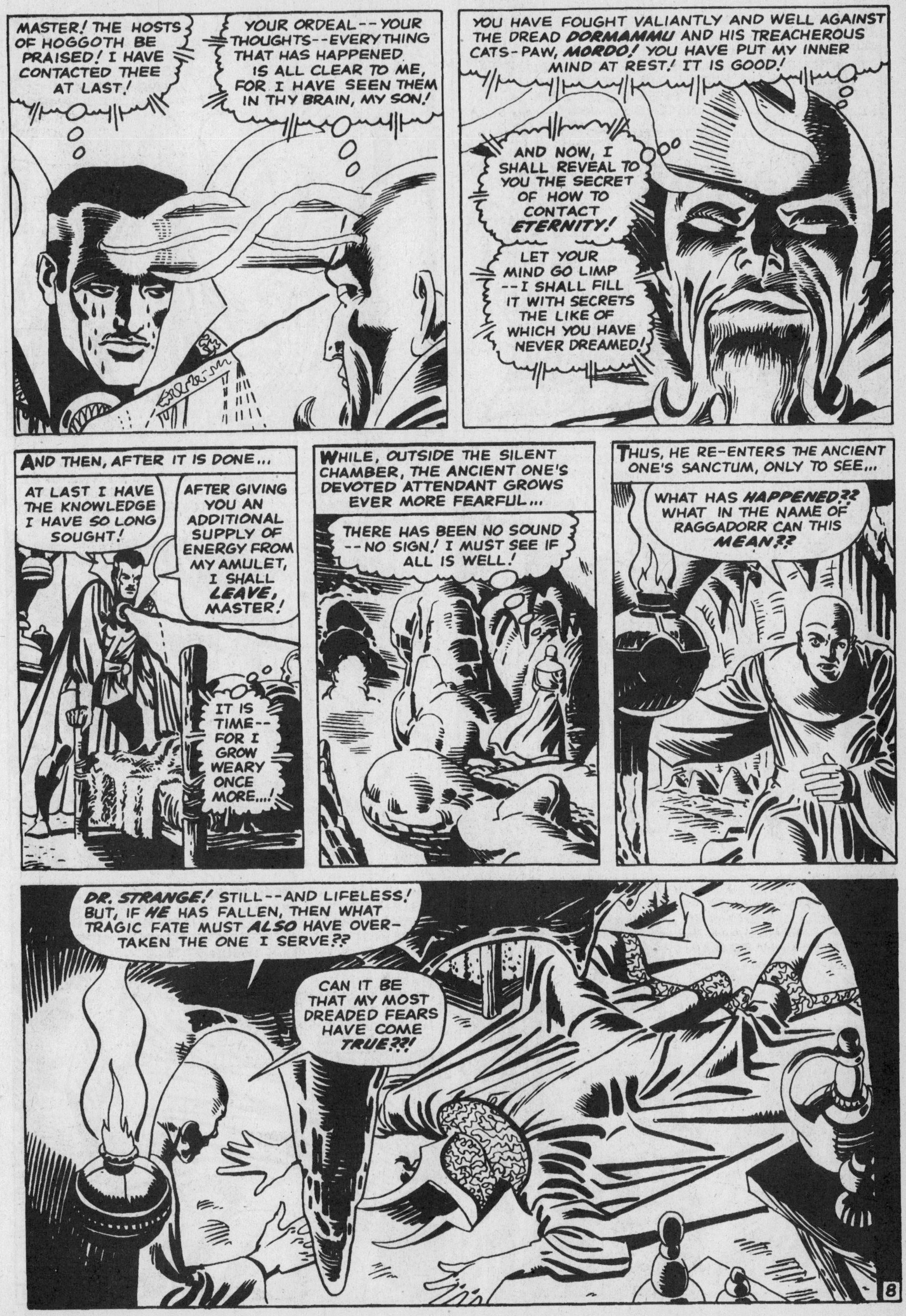

MASTER! THE HOSTS OF HOGGOTH BE PRAISED! I HAVE CONTACTED THEE AT LAST!
YOUR ORDEAL--YOUR THOUGHTS--EVERYTHING THAT HAS HAPPENED IS ALL CLEAR TO ME, FOR I HAVE SEEN THEM IN THY BRAIN, MY SON!
YOU HAVE FOUGHT VALIANTLY AND WELL AGAINST THE DREAD DORMAMMU AND HIS TREACHEROUS CATS-PAW, MORDO! YOU HAVE PUT MY INNER MIND AT REST! IT IS GOOD!
AND NOW, I SHALL REVEAL TO YOU THE SECRET OF HOW TO CONTACT ETERNITY!
LET YOUR MIND GO LIMP --I SHALL FILL IT WITH SECRETS THE LIKE OF WHICH YOU HAVE NEVER DREAMED!
AND THEN, AFTER IT IS DONE...
AT LAST I HAVE THE KNOWLEDGE I HAVE SO LONG SOUGHT!
AFTER GIVING YOU AN ADDITIONAL SUPPLY OF ENERGY FROM MY AMULET, I SHALL LEAVE, MASTER!
IT IS TIME-- FOR I GROW WEARY ONCE MORE...!
WHILE, OUTSIDE THE SILENT CHAMBER, THE ANCIENT ONE'S DEVOTED ATTENDANT GROWS EVER MORE FEARFUL...
THERE HAS BEEN NO SOUND --NO SIGN! I MUST SEE IF ALL IS WELL!
THUS, HE RE-ENTERS THE ANCIENT ONE'S SANCTUM, ONLY TO SEE...
WHAT HAS HAPPENED?? WHAT IN THE NAME OF RAGGADORR CAN THIS MEAN??
DR. STRANGE! STILL--AND LIFELESS! BUT, IF HE HAS FALLEN, THEN WHAT TRAGIC FATE MUST ALSO HAVE OVER-TAKEN THE ONE I SERVE??
CAN IT BE THAT MY MOST DREADED FEARS HAVE COME TRUE??!
8

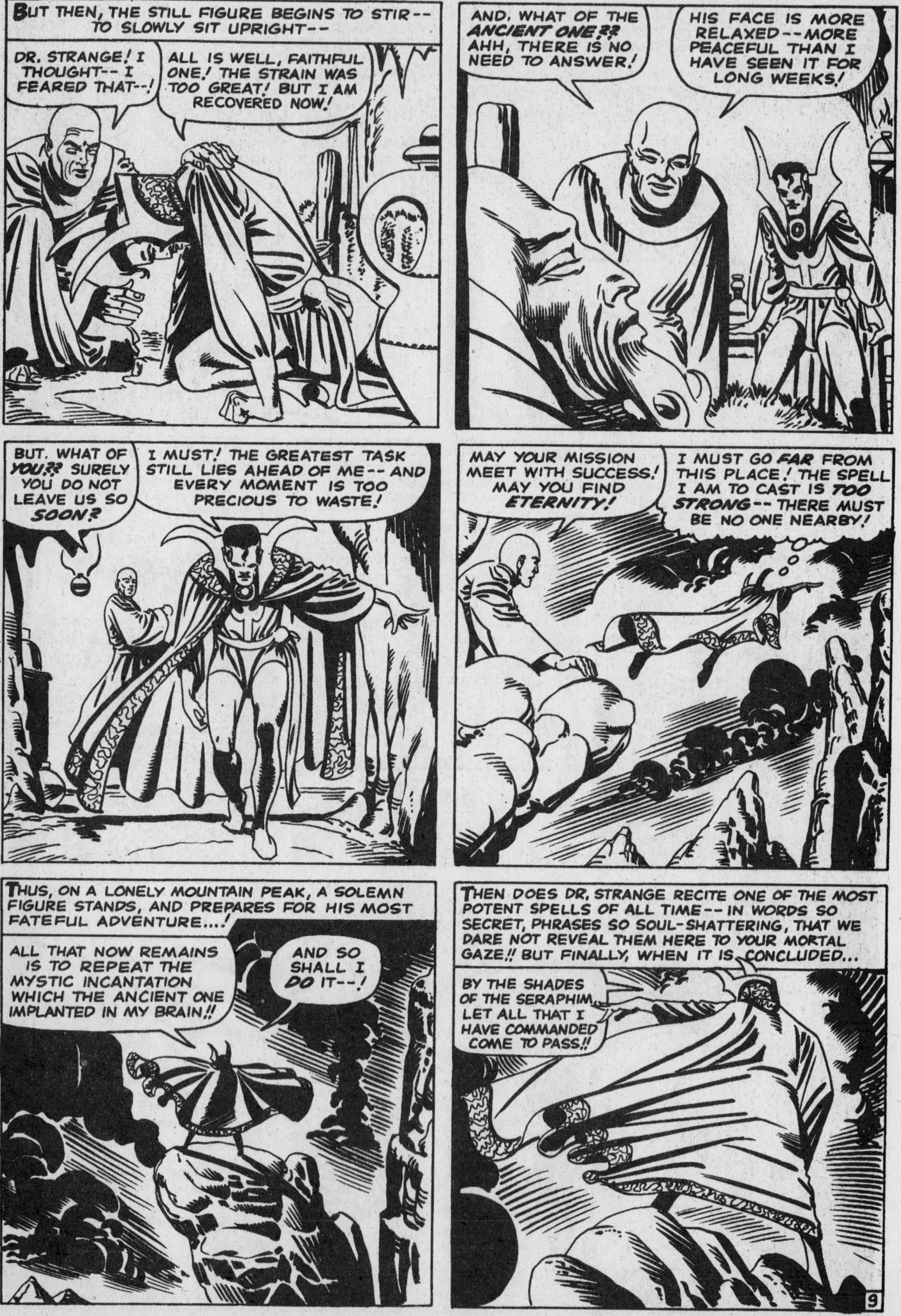
BUT THEN, THE STILL FIGURE BEGINS TO STIR-- TO SLOWLY SIT UPRIGHT--
DR. STRANGE! I THOUGHT-- I FEARED THAT--!
ALL IS WELL, FAITHFUL ONE! THE STRAIN WAS TOO GREAT! BUT I AM RECOVERED NOW!
AND, WHAT OF THE ANCIENT ONE?? AHH, THERE IS NO NEED TO ANSWER!
HIS FACE IS MORE RELAXED--MORE PEACEFUL THAN I HAVE SEEN IT FOR LONG WEEKS!
BUT, WHAT OF YOU?? SURELY YOU DO NOT LEAVE US SO SOON?
I MUST! THE GREATEST TASK STILL LIES AHEAD OF ME-- AND EVERY MOMENT IS TOO PRECIOUS TO WASTE!
MAY YOUR MISSION MEET WITH SUCCESS! MAY YOU FIND ETERNITY!
I MUST GO FAR FROM THIS PLACE! THE SPELL I AM TO CAST IS TOO STRONG-- THERE MUST BE NO ONE NEARBY!
THUS, ON A LONELY MOUNTAIN PEAK, A SOLEMN FIGURE STANDS, AND PREPARES FOR HIS MOST FATEFUL ADVENTURE....!
ALL THAT NOW REMAINS IS TO REPEAT THE MYSTIC INCANTATION WHICH THE ANCIENT ONE IMPLANTED IN MY BRAIN!!
AND SO SHALL I DO IT--!
THEN DOES DR. STRANGE RECITE ONE OF THE MOST POTENT SPELLS OF ALL TIME-- IN WORDS SO SECRET, PHRASES SO SOUL-SHATTERING, THAT WE DARE NOT REVEAL THEM HERE TO YOUR MORTAL GAZE!! BUT FINALLY, WHEN IT IS CONCLUDED...
BY THE SHADES OF THE SERAPHIM, LET ALL THAT I HAVE COMMANDED COME TO PASS!!
9

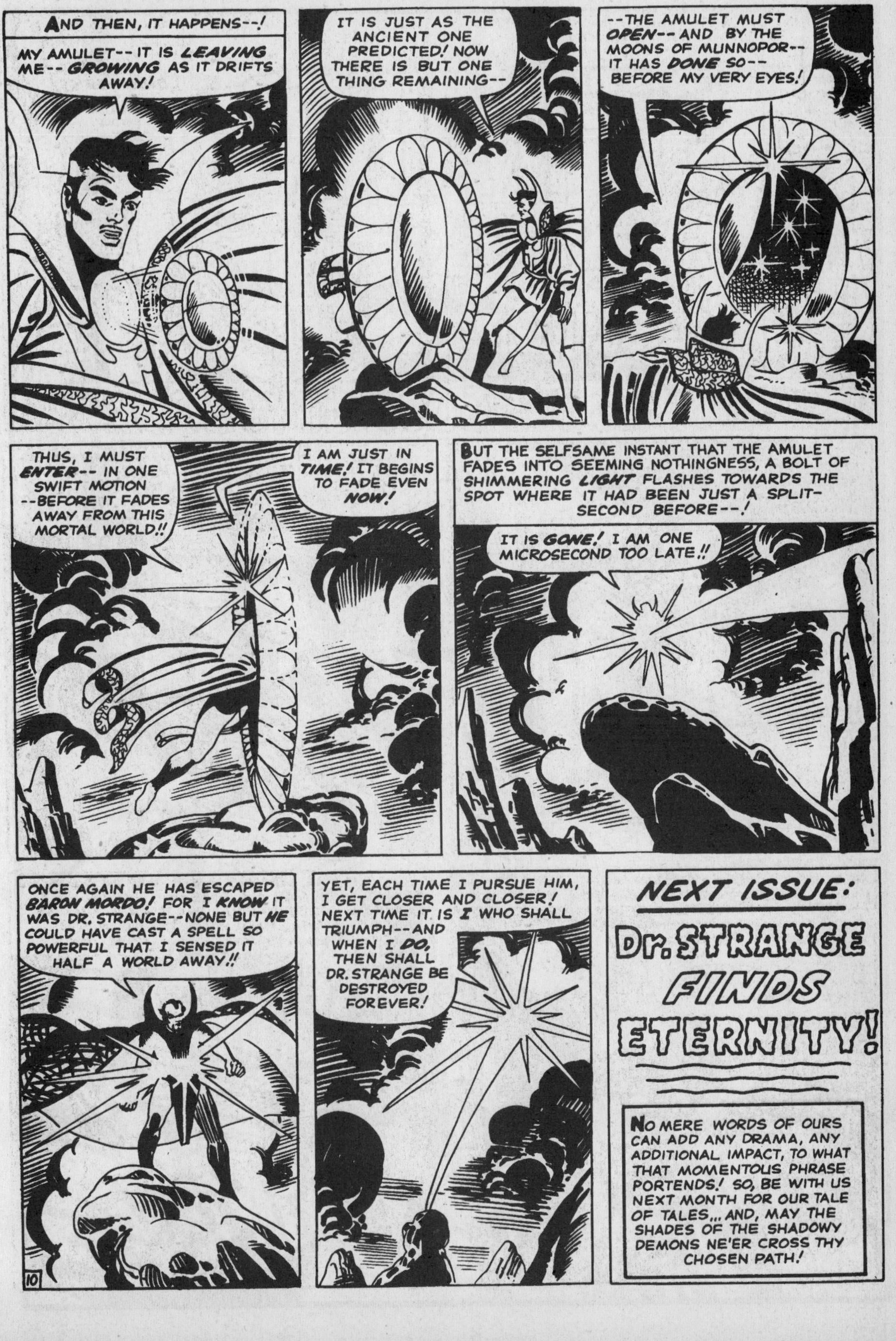

AND THEN, IT HAPPENS--!
MY AMULET-- IT IS LEAVING ME-- GROWING AS IT DRIFTS AWAY!
IT IS JUST AS THE ANCIENT ONE PREDICTED! NOW THERE IS BUT ONE THING REMAINING--
--THE AMULET MUST OPEN-- AND BY THE MOONS OF MUNNOPOR-- IT HAS DONE SO-- BEFORE MY VERY EYES!
THUS, I MUST ENTER-- IN ONE SWIFT MOTION --BEFORE IT FADES AWAY FROM THIS MORTAL WORLD!!
I AM JUST IN TIME! IT BEGINS TO FADE EVEN NOW!
BUT THE SELFSAME INSTANT THAT THE AMULET FADES INTO SEEMING NOTHINGNESS, A BOLT OF SHIMMERING LIGHT FLASHES TOWARDS THE SPOT WHERE IT HAD BEEN JUST A SPLIT-SECOND BEFORE--!
IT IS GONE! I AM ONE MICROSECOND TOO LATE!!
ONCE AGAIN HE HAS ESCAPED BARON MORDO! FOR I KNOW IT WAS DR. STRANGE--NONE BUT HE COULD HAVE CAST A SPELL SO POWERFUL THAT I SENSED IT HALF A WORLD AWAY!!
YET, EACH TIME I PURSUE HIM, I GET CLOSER AND CLOSER! NEXT TIME IT IS I WHO SHALL TRIUMPH--AND WHEN I DO, THEN SHALL DR. STRANGE BE DESTROYED FOREVER!
NEXT ISSUE:
Dr. STRANGE FINDS ETERNITY!
NO MERE WORDS OF OURS CAN ADD ANY DRAMA, ANY ADDITIONAL IMPACT, TO WHAT THAT MOMENTOUS PHRASE PORTENDS! SO, BE WITH US NEXT MONTH FOR OUR TALE OF TALES... AND, MAY THE SHADES OF THE SHADOWY DEMONS NE'ER CROSS THY CHOSEN PATH!
10

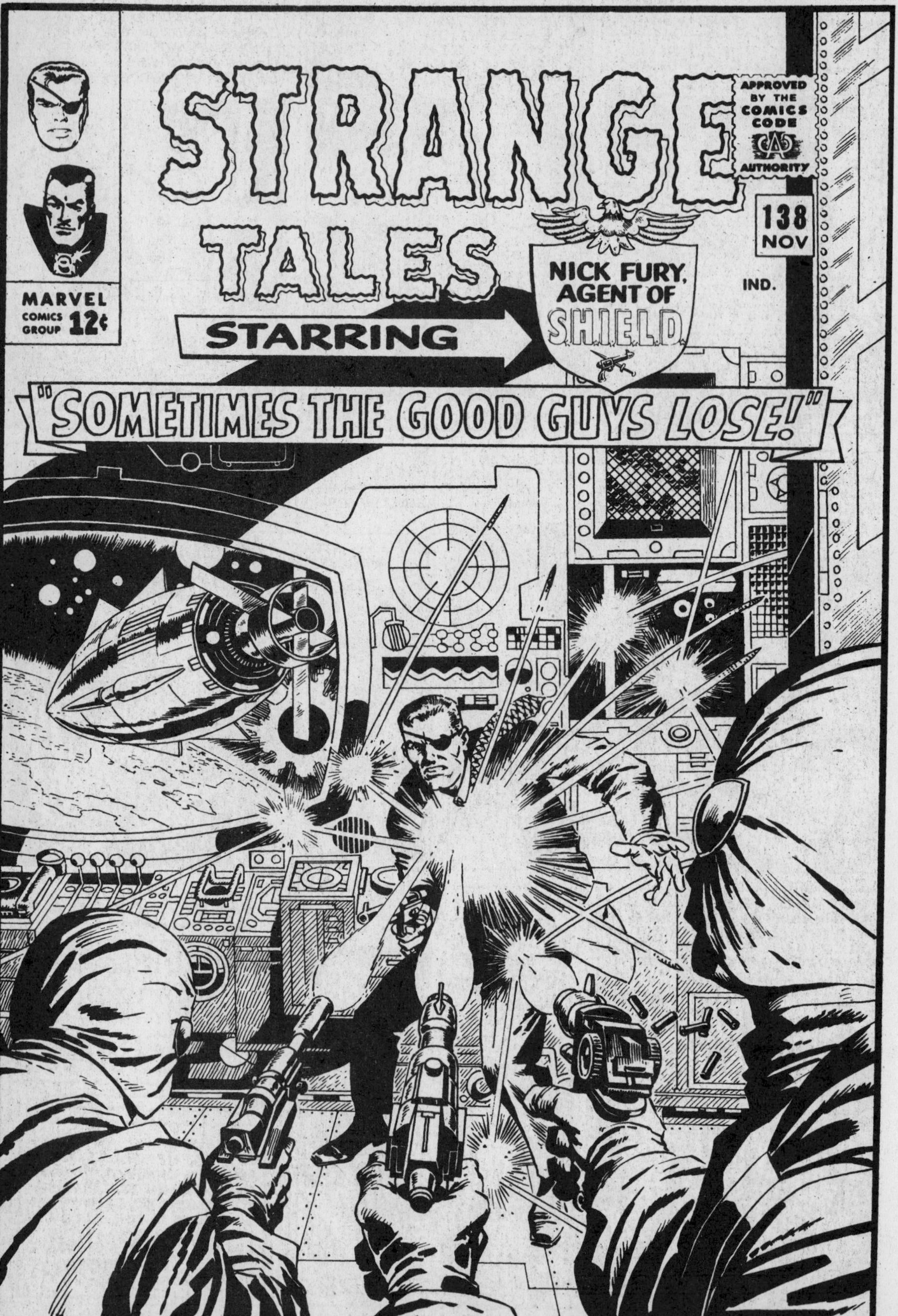

MARVEL COMICS GROUP 12¢
STRANGE TALES
APPROVED BY THE COMICS CODE AUTHORITY
138 NOV
IND.
STARRING
NICK FURY, AGENT OF S.H.I.E.L.D.
"SOMETIMES THE GOOD GUYS LOSE!"

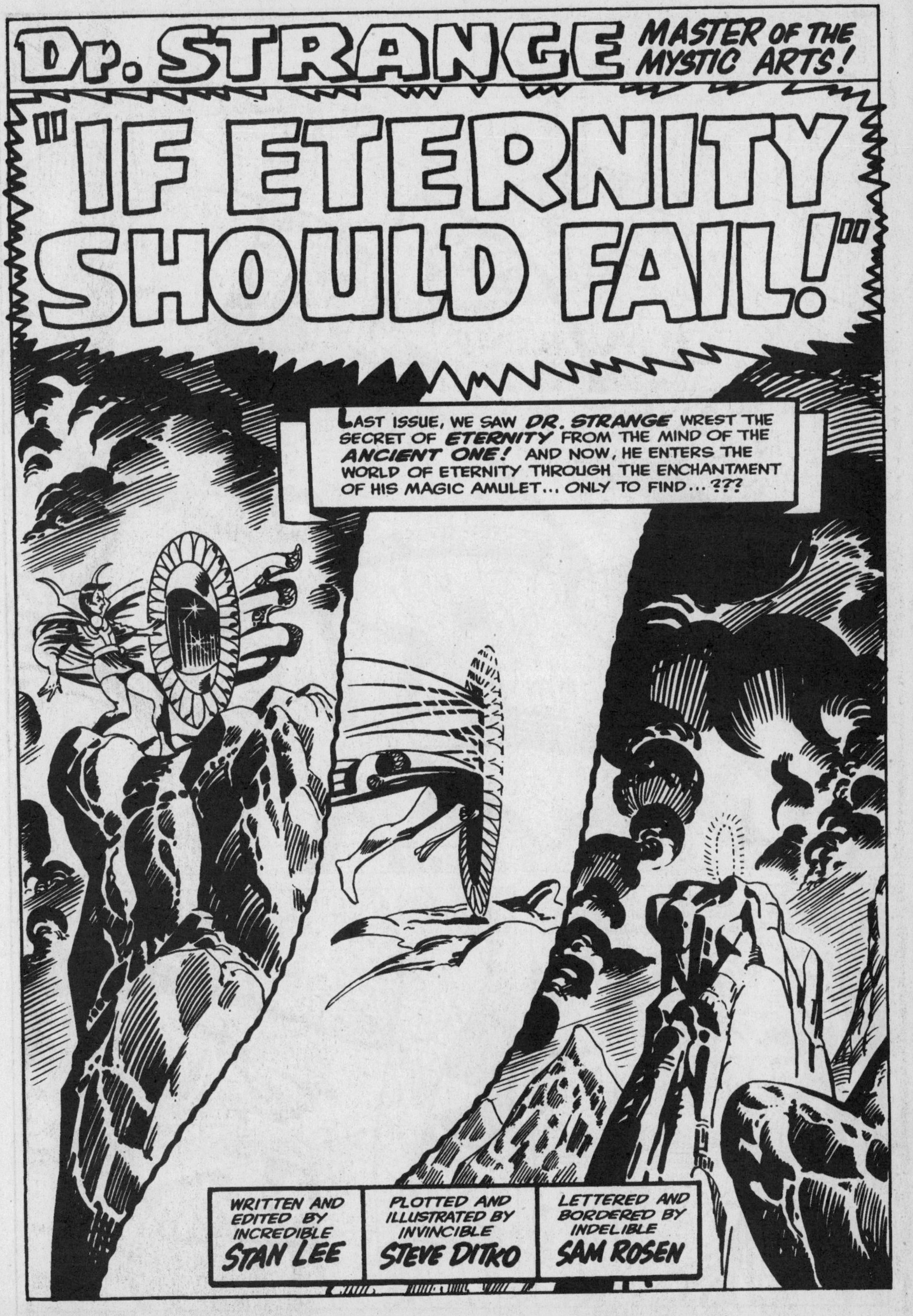
Dr. STRANGE MASTER OF THE MYSTIC ARTS!
"IF ETERNITY SHOULD FAIL!"
LAST ISSUE, WE SAW DR. STRANGE WREST THE SECRET OF ETERNITY FROM THE MIND OF THE ANCIENT ONE! AND NOW, HE ENTERS THE WORLD OF ETERNITY THROUGH THE ENCHANTMENT OF HIS MAGIC AMULET... ONLY TO FIND...???
WRITTEN AND EDITED BY INCREDIBLE STAN LEE
PLOTTED AND ILLUSTRATED BY INVINCIBLE STEVE DITKO
LETTERED AND BORDERED BY INDELIBLE SAM ROSEN

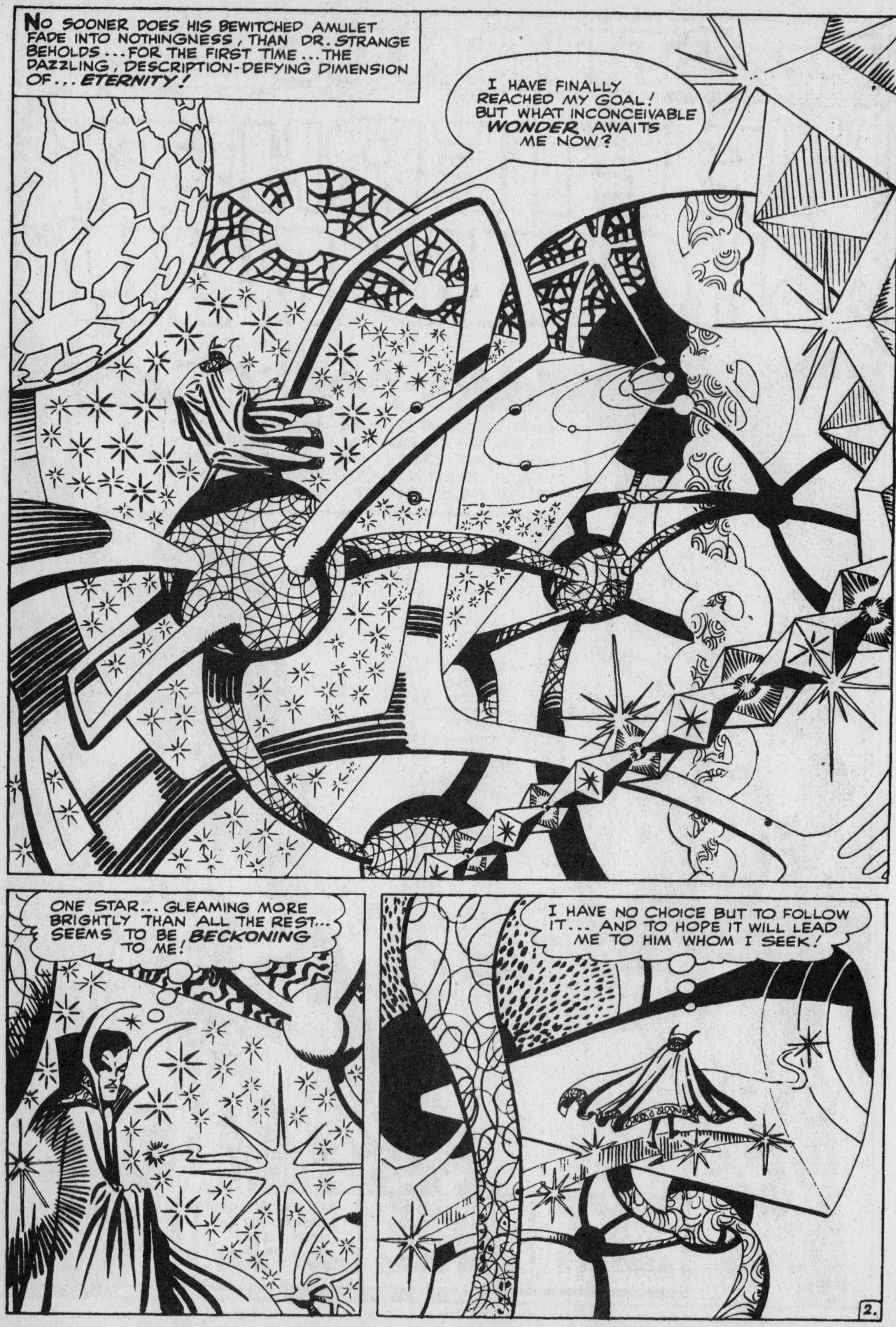
NO SOONER DOES HIS BEWITCHED AMULET FADE INTO NOTHINGNESS, THAN DR. STRANGE BEHOLDS... FOR THE FIRST TIME... THE DAZZLING, DESCRIPTION-DEFYING DIMENSION OF... ETERNITY!
I HAVE FINALLY REACHED MY GOAL! BUT WHAT INCONCEIVABLE WONDER AWAITS ME NOW?
ONE STAR... GLEAMING MORE BRIGHTLY THAN ALL THE REST... SEEMS TO BE BECKONING TO ME!
I HAVE NO CHOICE BUT TO FOLLOW IT... AND TO HOPE IT WILL LEAD ME TO HIM WHOM I SEEK!
2.

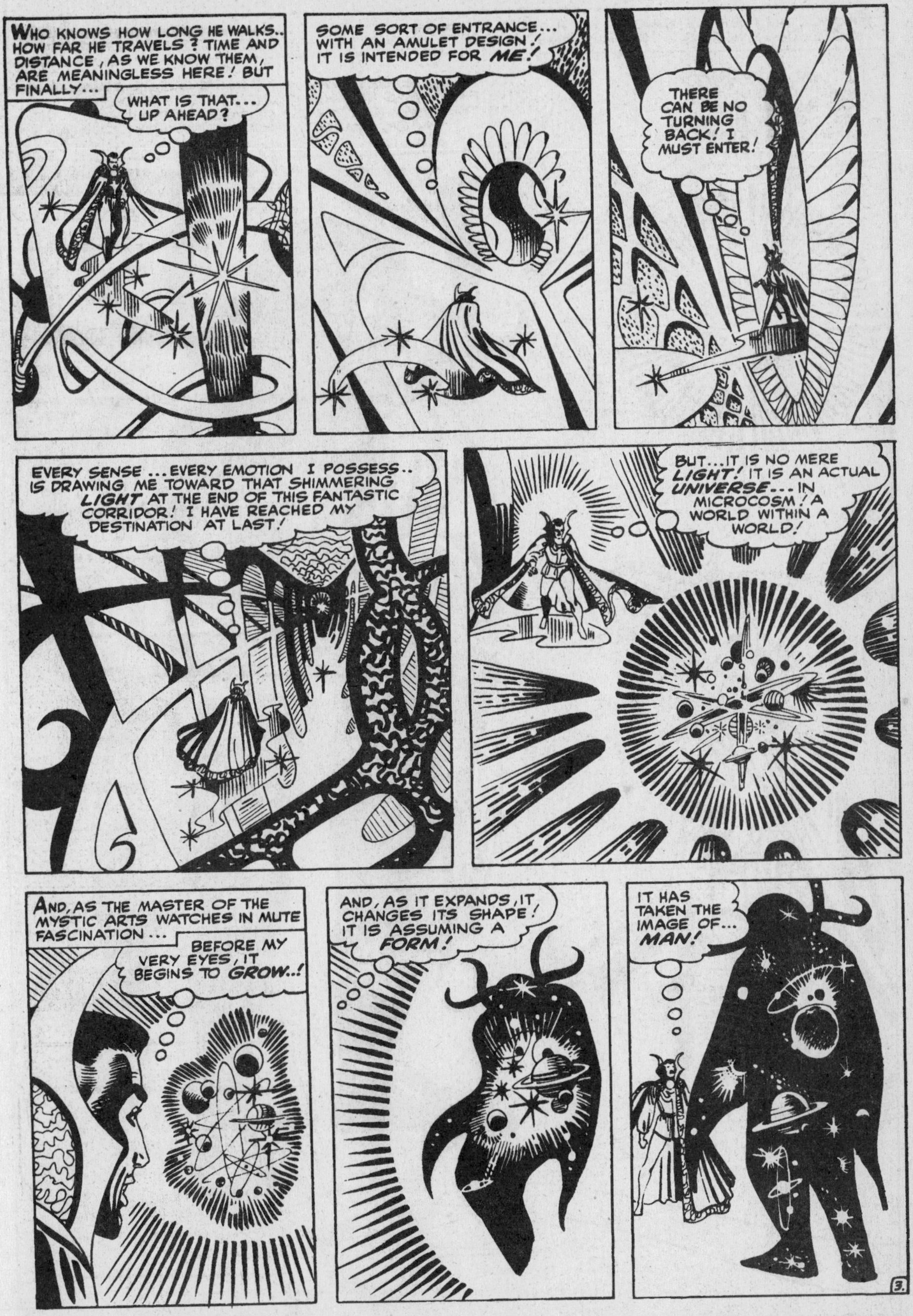
WHO KNOWS HOW LONG HE WALKS.. HOW FAR HE TRAVELS? TIME AND DISTANCE, AS WE KNOW THEM, ARE MEANINGLESS HERE! BUT FINALLY...
WHAT IS THAT... UP AHEAD?
SOME SORT OF ENTRANCE... WITH AN AMULET DESIGN! IT IS INTENDED FOR ME!
THERE CAN BE NO TURNING BACK! I MUST ENTER!
EVERY SENSE ... EVERY EMOTION I POSSESS.. IS DRAWING ME TOWARD THAT SHIMMERING LIGHT AT THE END OF THIS FANTASTIC CORRIDOR! I HAVE REACHED MY DESTINATION AT LAST!
BUT...IT IS NO MERE LIGHT! IT IS AN ACTUAL UNIVERSE... IN MICROCOSM! A WORLD WITHIN A WORLD!
AND, AS THE MASTER OF THE MYSTIC ARTS WATCHES IN MUTE FASCINATION...
BEFORE MY VERY EYES, IT BEGINS TO GROW..!
AND, AS IT EXPANDS, IT CHANGES ITS SHAPE! IT IS ASSUMING A FORM!
IT HAS TAKEN THE IMAGE OF... MAN!
3.

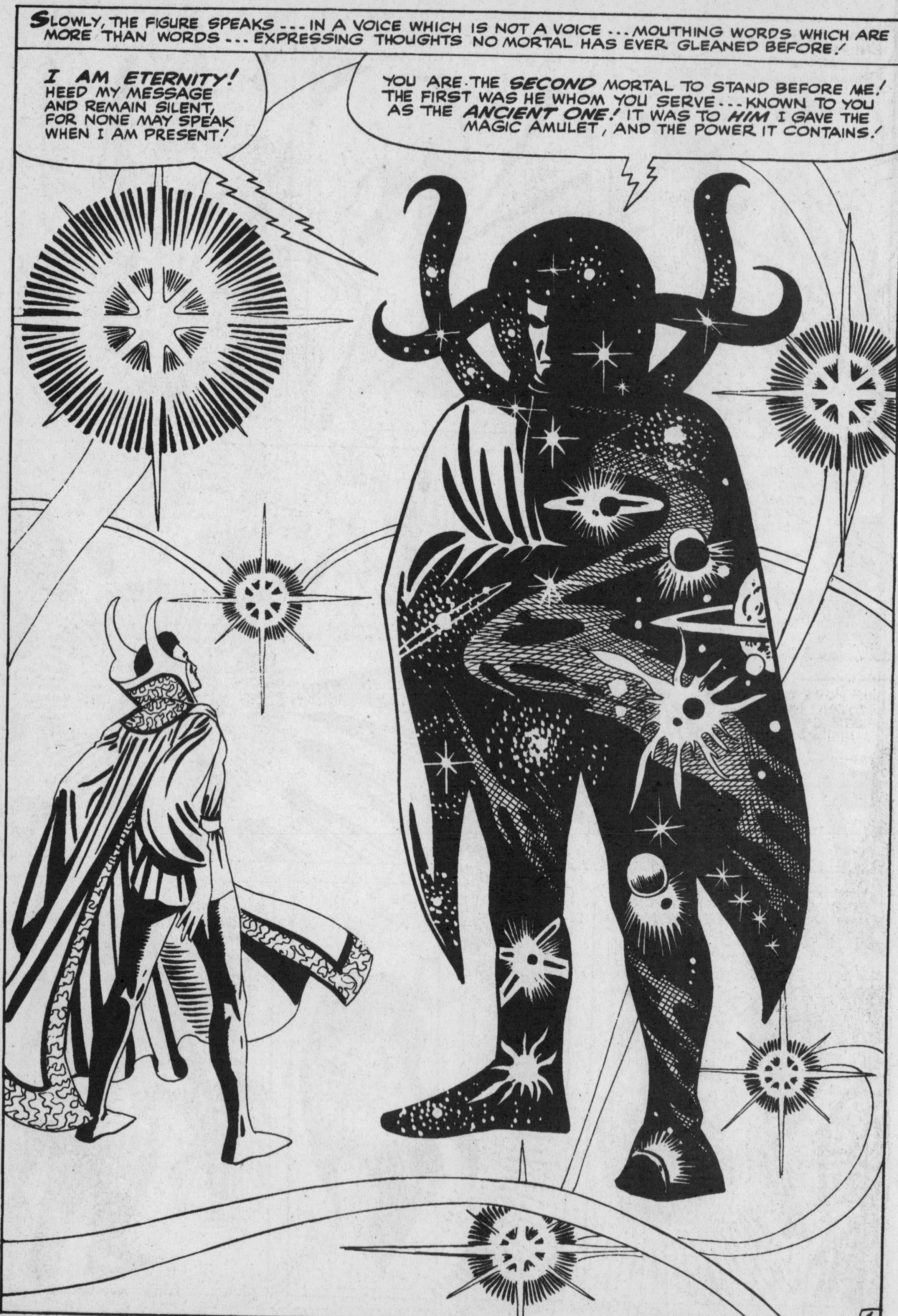
SLOWLY, THE FIGURE SPEAKS ... IN A VOICE WHICH IS NOT A VOICE ... MOUTHING WORDS WHICH ARE MORE THAN WORDS ... EXPRESSING THOUGHTS NO MORTAL HAS EVER GLEANED BEFORE!
I AM ETERNITY! HEED MY MESSAGE AND REMAIN SILENT, FOR NONE MAY SPEAK WHEN I AM PRESENT!
YOU ARE THE SECOND MORTAL TO STAND BEFORE ME! THE FIRST WAS HE WHOM YOU SERVE... KNOWN TO YOU AS THE ANCIENT ONE! IT WAS TO HIM I GAVE THE MAGIC AMULET, AND THE POWER IT CONTAINS!
4.

NONE SEEK *ETERNITY* UNLESS THEY DESIRE *POWER!* BUT, BEFORE GRANTING SUCH A BOON, I MUST LEARN IF YOU BE *WORTHY!*

REMAIN MOTIONLESS, WHILST I BATHE THEE IN THE MYSTIC GLOW OF REVEALMENT!

HIS POWER IS BEYOND MEASURE... BEYOND HUMAN *KEN!* I FEEL EVERY FIBER OF MY BEING EXPOSED TO HIS NAKED SCRUTINY!

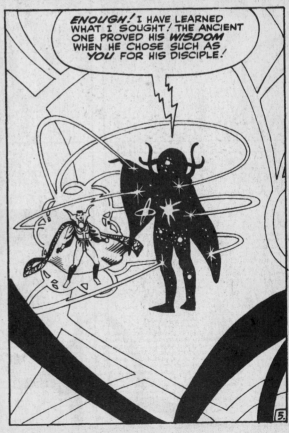

ENOUGH! I HAVE LEARNED WHAT I SOUGHT! THE ANCIENT ONE PROVED HIS *WISDOM* WHEN HE CHOSE SUCH AS *YOU* FOR HIS DISCIPLE!

5.

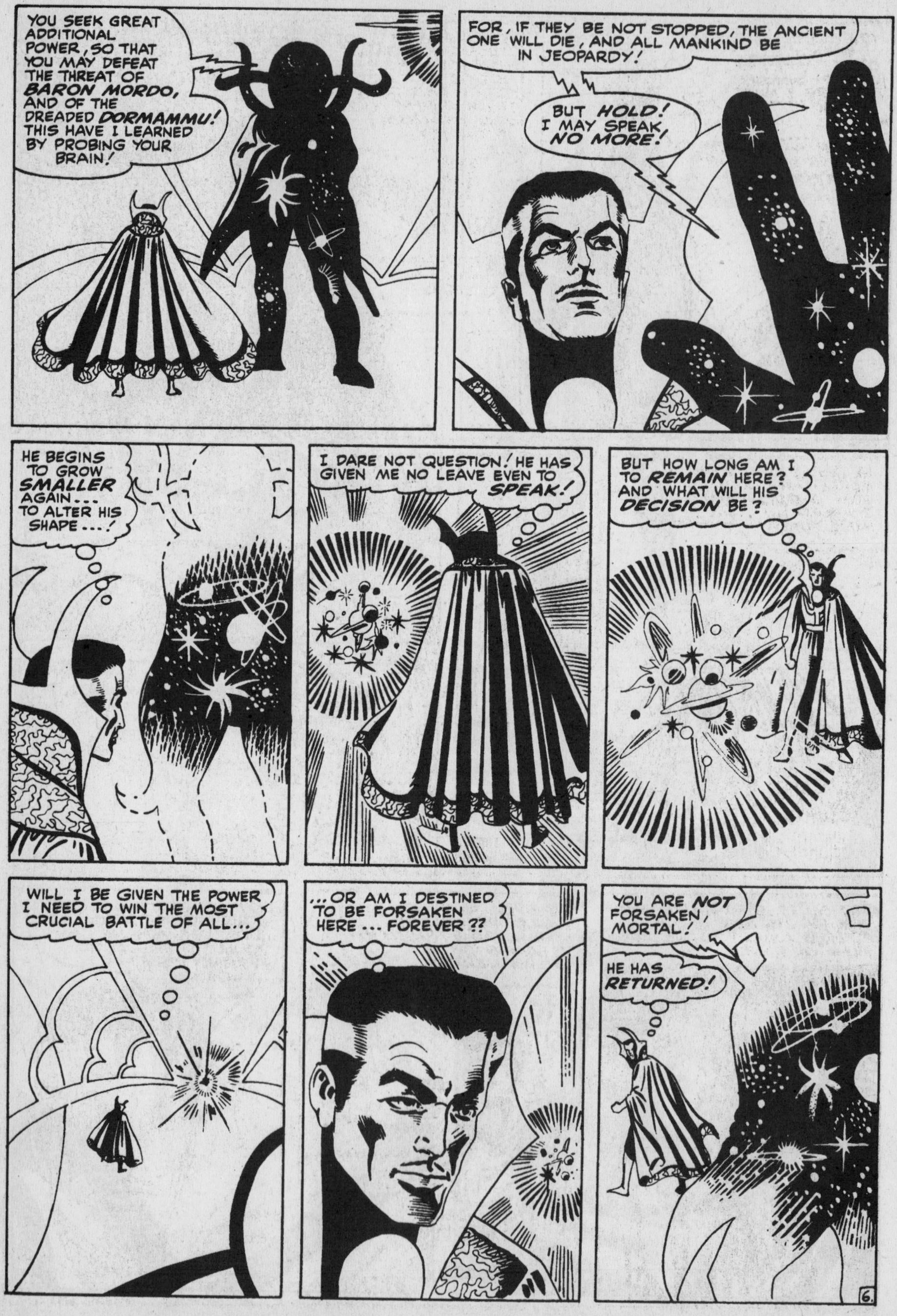
YOU SEEK GREAT ADDITIONAL POWER, SO THAT YOU MAY DEFEAT THE THREAT OF BARON MORDO, AND OF THE DREADED DORMAMMU! THIS HAVE I LEARNED BY PROBING YOUR BRAIN!
FOR, IF THEY BE NOT STOPPED, THE ANCIENT ONE WILL DIE, AND ALL MANKIND BE IN JEOPARDY!
BUT HOLD! I MAY SPEAK NO MORE!
HE BEGINS TO GROW SMALLER AGAIN... TO ALTER HIS SHAPE...!
I DARE NOT QUESTION! HE HAS GIVEN ME NO LEAVE EVEN TO SPEAK!
BUT HOW LONG AM I TO REMAIN HERE? AND WHAT WILL HIS DECISION BE?
WILL I BE GIVEN THE POWER I NEED TO WIN THE MOST CRUCIAL BATTLE OF ALL...
...OR AM I DESTINED TO BE FORSAKEN HERE ... FOREVER??
YOU ARE NOT FORSAKEN, MORTAL!
HE HAS RETURNED!
6.

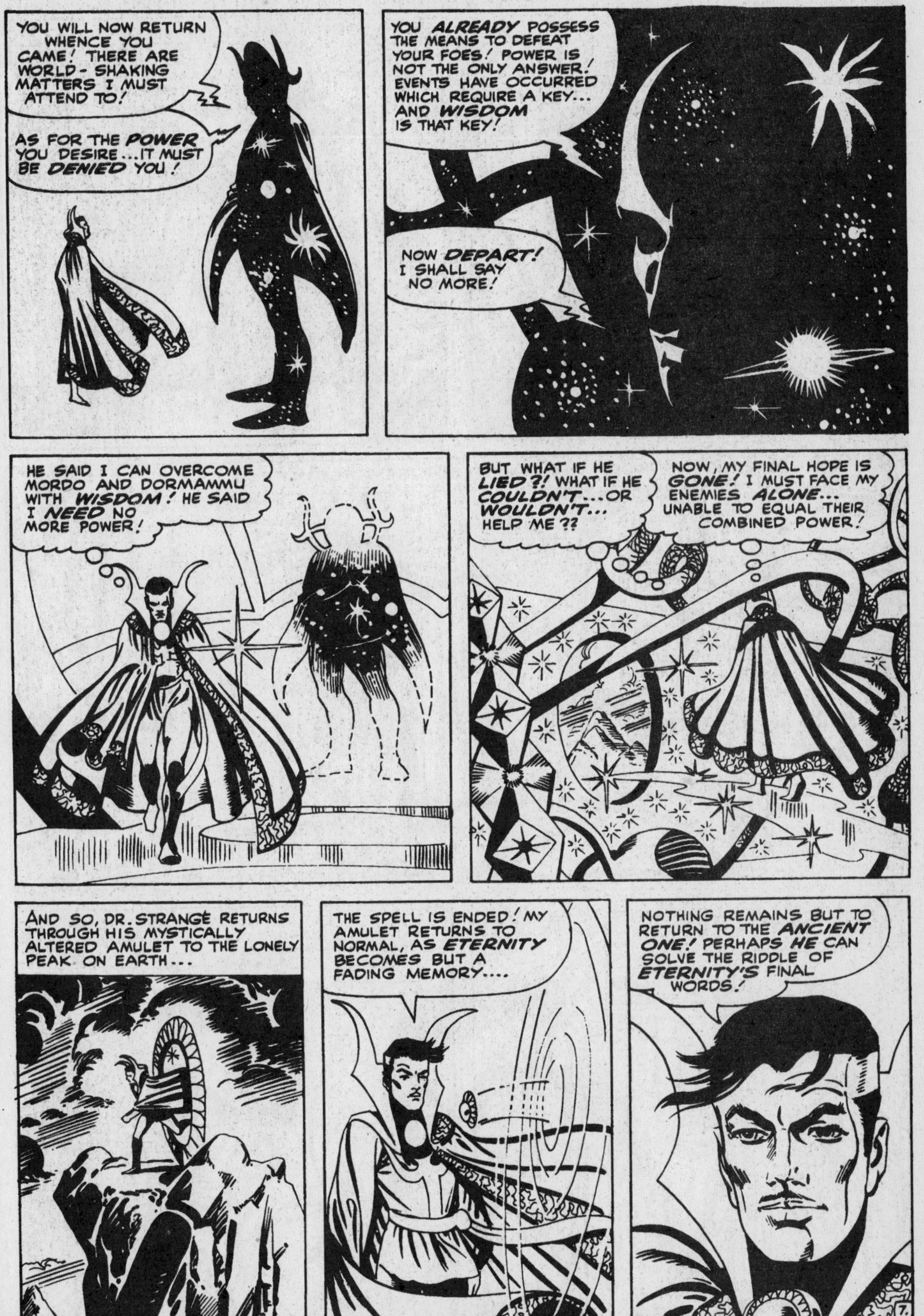
YOU WILL NOW RETURN WHENCE YOU CAME! THERE ARE WORLD-SHAKING MATTERS I MUST ATTEND TO!
AS FOR THE POWER YOU DESIRE...IT MUST BE DENIED YOU!
YOU ALREADY POSSESS THE MEANS TO DEFEAT YOUR FOES! POWER IS NOT THE ONLY ANSWER! EVENTS HAVE OCCURRED WHICH REQUIRE A KEY... AND WISDOM IS THAT KEY!
NOW DEPART! I SHALL SAY NO MORE!
HE SAID I CAN OVERCOME MORDO AND DORMAMMU WITH WISDOM! HE SAID I NEED NO MORE POWER!
BUT WHAT IF HE LIED?! WHAT IF HE COULDN'T...OR WOULDN'T... HELP ME??
NOW, MY FINAL HOPE IS GONE! I MUST FACE MY ENEMIES ALONE... UNABLE TO EQUAL THEIR COMBINED POWER!
AND SO, DR. STRANGE RETURNS THROUGH HIS MYSTICALLY ALTERED AMULET TO THE LONELY PEAK ON EARTH...
THE SPELL IS ENDED! MY AMULET RETURNS TO NORMAL, AS ETERNITY BECOMES BUT A FADING MEMORY....
NOTHING REMAINS BUT TO RETURN TO THE ANCIENT ONE! PERHAPS HE CAN SOLVE THE RIDDLE OF ETERNITY'S FINAL WORDS!
7.

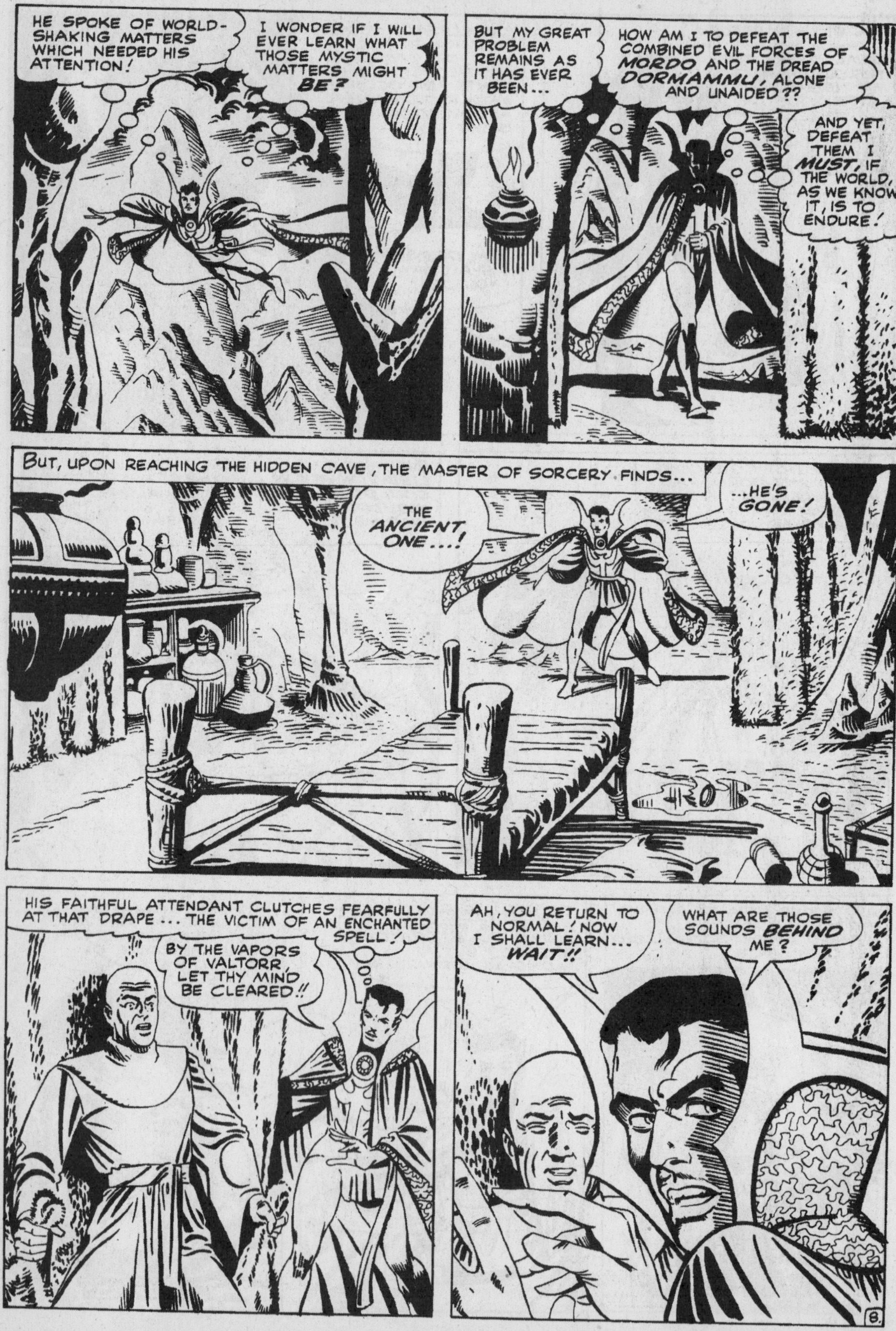

HE SPOKE OF WORLD-SHAKING MATTERS WHICH NEEDED HIS ATTENTION!
I WONDER IF I WILL EVER LEARN WHAT THOSE MYSTIC MATTERS MIGHT BE?
BUT MY GREAT PROBLEM REMAINS AS IT HAS EVER BEEN...
HOW AM I TO DEFEAT THE COMBINED EVIL FORCES OF MORDO AND THE DREAD DORMAMMU, ALONE AND UNAIDED??
AND YET, DEFEAT THEM I MUST, IF THE WORLD, AS WE KNOW IT, IS TO ENDURE!
BUT, UPON REACHING THE HIDDEN CAVE, THE MASTER OF SORCERY FINDS...
THE ANCIENT ONE...!
...HE'S GONE!
HIS FAITHFUL ATTENDANT CLUTCHES FEARFULLY AT THAT DRAPE... THE VICTIM OF AN ENCHANTED SPELL!
BY THE VAPORS OF VALTORR, LET THY MIND BE CLEARED!!
AH, YOU RETURN TO NORMAL! NOW I SHALL LEARN... WAIT!!
WHAT ARE THOSE SOUNDS BEHIND ME?
8

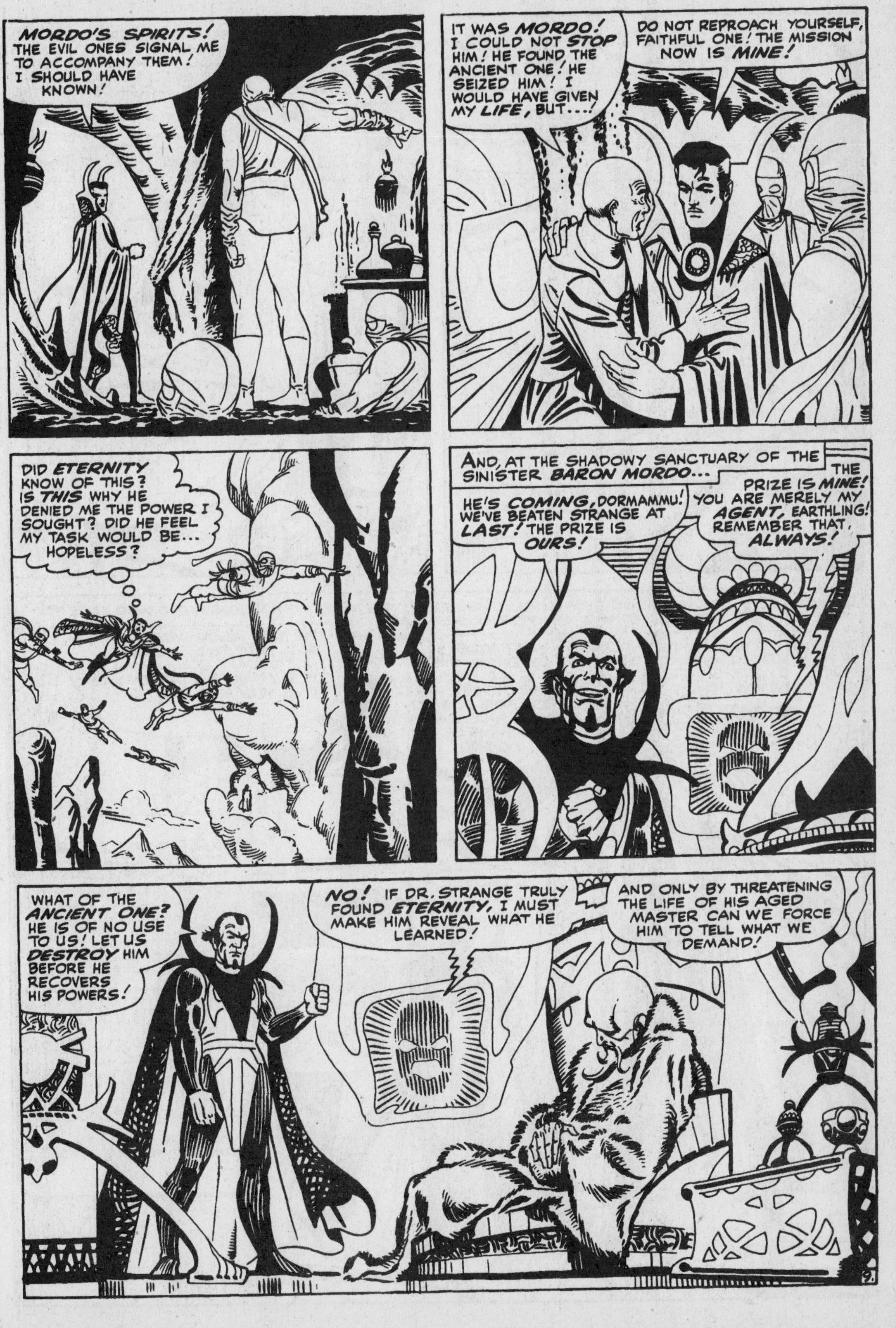
MORDO'S SPIRITS! THE EVIL ONES SIGNAL ME TO ACCOMPANY THEM! I SHOULD HAVE KNOWN!
IT WAS MORDO! I COULD NOT STOP HIM! HE FOUND THE ANCIENT ONE! HE SEIZED HIM! I WOULD HAVE GIVEN MY LIFE, BUT...!
DO NOT REPROACH YOURSELF, FAITHFUL ONE! THE MISSION NOW IS MINE!
DID ETERNITY KNOW OF THIS? IS THIS WHY HE DENIED ME THE POWER I SOUGHT? DID HE FEEL MY TASK WOULD BE... HOPELESS?
AND, AT THE SHADOWY SANCTUARY OF THE SINISTER BARON MORDO...
HE'S COMING, DORMAMMU! WE'VE BEATEN STRANGE AT LAST! THE PRIZE IS OURS!
THE PRIZE IS MINE! YOU ARE MERELY MY AGENT, EARTHLING! REMEMBER THAT, ALWAYS!
WHAT OF THE ANCIENT ONE? HE IS OF NO USE TO US! LET US DESTROY HIM BEFORE HE RECOVERS HIS POWERS!
NO! IF DR. STRANGE TRULY FOUND ETERNITY, I MUST MAKE HIM REVEAL WHAT HE LEARNED!
AND ONLY BY THREATENING THE LIFE OF HIS AGED MASTER CAN WE FORCE HIM TO TELL WHAT WE DEMAND!
9.

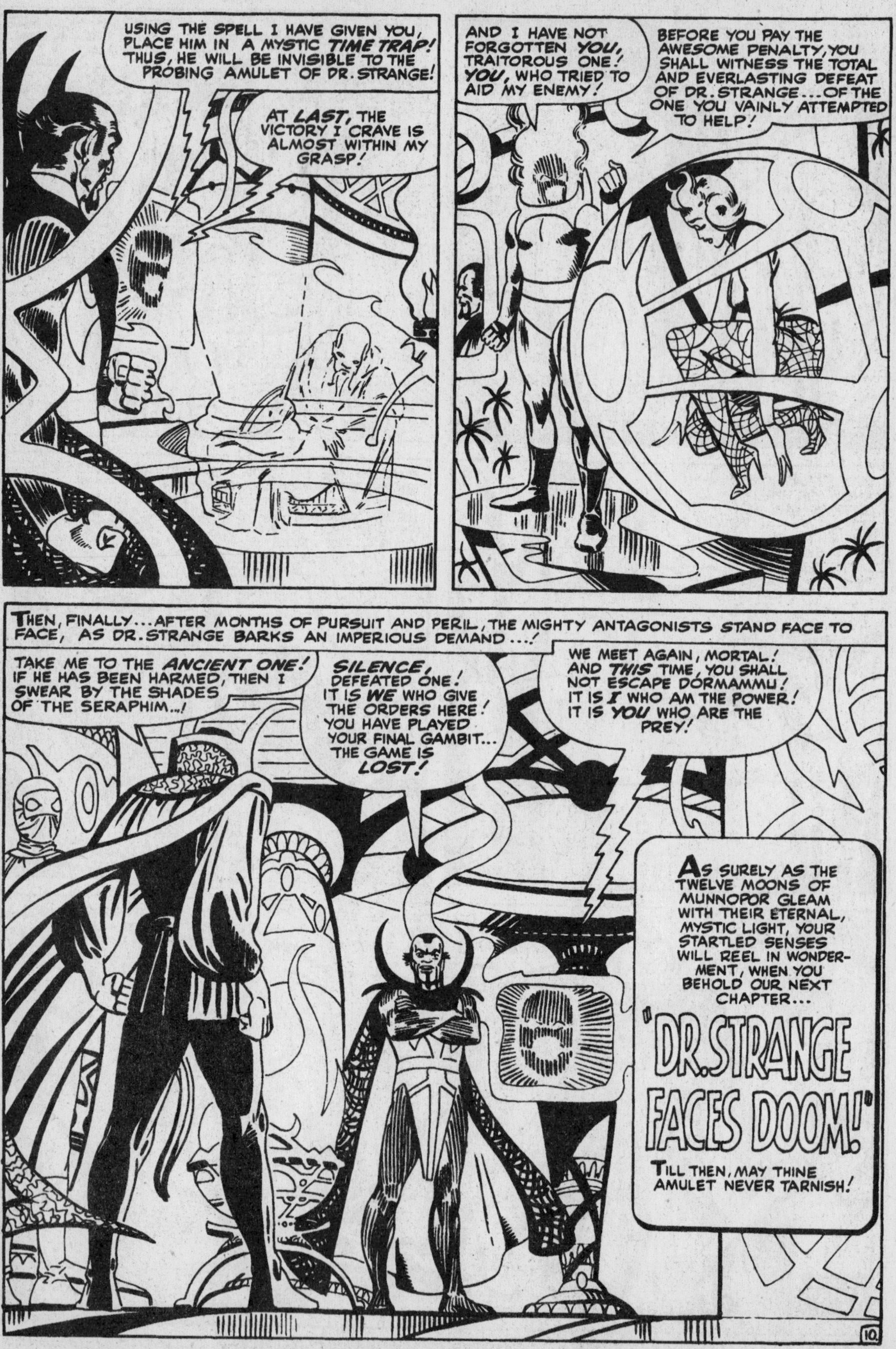
USING THE SPELL I HAVE GIVEN YOU, PLACE HIM IN A MYSTIC TIME TRAP! THUS, HE WILL BE INVISIBLE TO THE PROBING AMULET OF DR. STRANGE!
AT LAST, THE VICTORY I CRAVE IS ALMOST WITHIN MY GRASP!
AND I HAVE NOT FORGOTTEN YOU, TRAITOROUS ONE! YOU, WHO TRIED TO AID MY ENEMY!
BEFORE YOU PAY THE AWESOME PENALTY, YOU SHALL WITNESS THE TOTAL AND EVERLASTING DEFEAT OF DR. STRANGE...OF THE ONE YOU VAINLY ATTEMPTED TO HELP!
THEN, FINALLY...AFTER MONTHS OF PURSUIT AND PERIL, THE MIGHTY ANTAGONISTS STAND FACE TO FACE, AS DR. STRANGE BARKS AN IMPERIOUS DEMAND...!
TAKE ME TO THE ANCIENT ONE! IF HE HAS BEEN HARMED, THEN I SWEAR BY THE SHADES OF THE SERAPHIM...!
SILENCE, DEFEATED ONE! IT IS WE WHO GIVE THE ORDERS HERE! YOU HAVE PLAYED YOUR FINAL GAMBIT... THE GAME IS LOST!
WE MEET AGAIN, MORTAL! AND THIS TIME, YOU SHALL NOT ESCAPE DORMAMMU! IT IS I WHO AM THE POWER! IT IS YOU WHO ARE THE PREY!
AS SURELY AS THE TWELVE MOONS OF MUNNOPOR GLEAM WITH THEIR ETERNAL, MYSTIC LIGHT, YOUR STARTLED SENSES WILL REEL IN WONDERMENT, WHEN YOU BEHOLD OUR NEXT CHAPTER...
"DR. STRANGE FACES DOOM!"
TILL THEN, MAY THINE AMULET NEVER TARNISH!
10

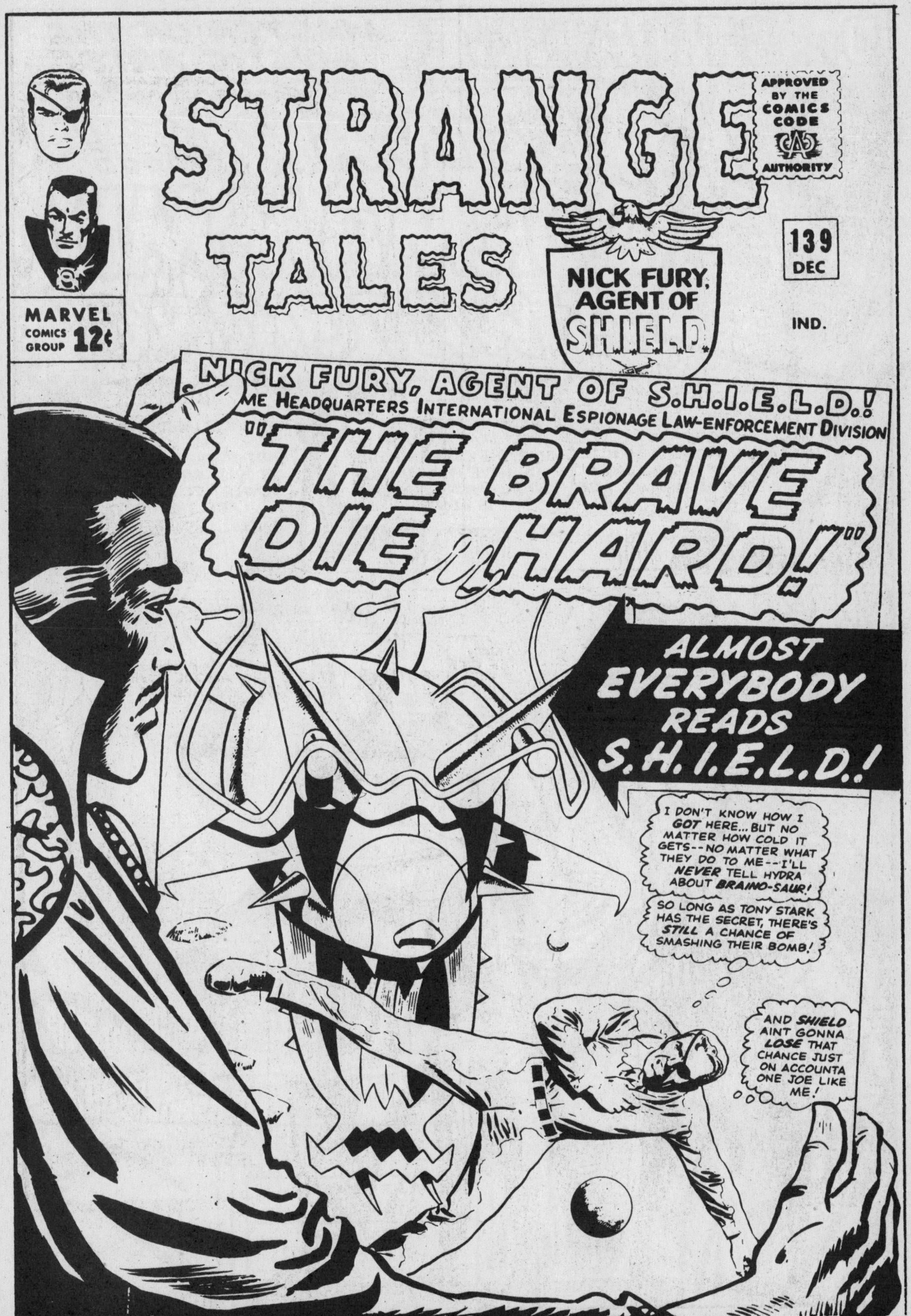
STRANGE TALES
APPROVED BY THE COMICS CODE AUTHORITY
139 DEC
IND.
NICK FURY, AGENT OF SHIELD
MARVEL COMICS GROUP 12¢
NICK FURY, AGENT OF S.H.I.E.L.D.!
ME HEADQUARTERS INTERNATIONAL ESPIONAGE LAW-ENFORCEMENT DIVISION
"THE BRAVE DIE HARD!"
ALMOST EVERYBODY READS S.H.I.E.L.D.!
I DON'T KNOW HOW I GOT HERE... BUT NO MATTER HOW COLD IT GETS--NO MATTER WHAT THEY DO TO ME--I'LL NEVER TELL HYDRA ABOUT BRAINO-SAUR!
SO LONG AS TONY STARK HAS THE SECRET, THERE'S STILL A CHANCE OF SMASHING THEIR BOMB!
AND SHIELD AINT GONNA LOSE THAT CHANCE JUST ON ACCOUNTA ONE JOE LIKE ME!

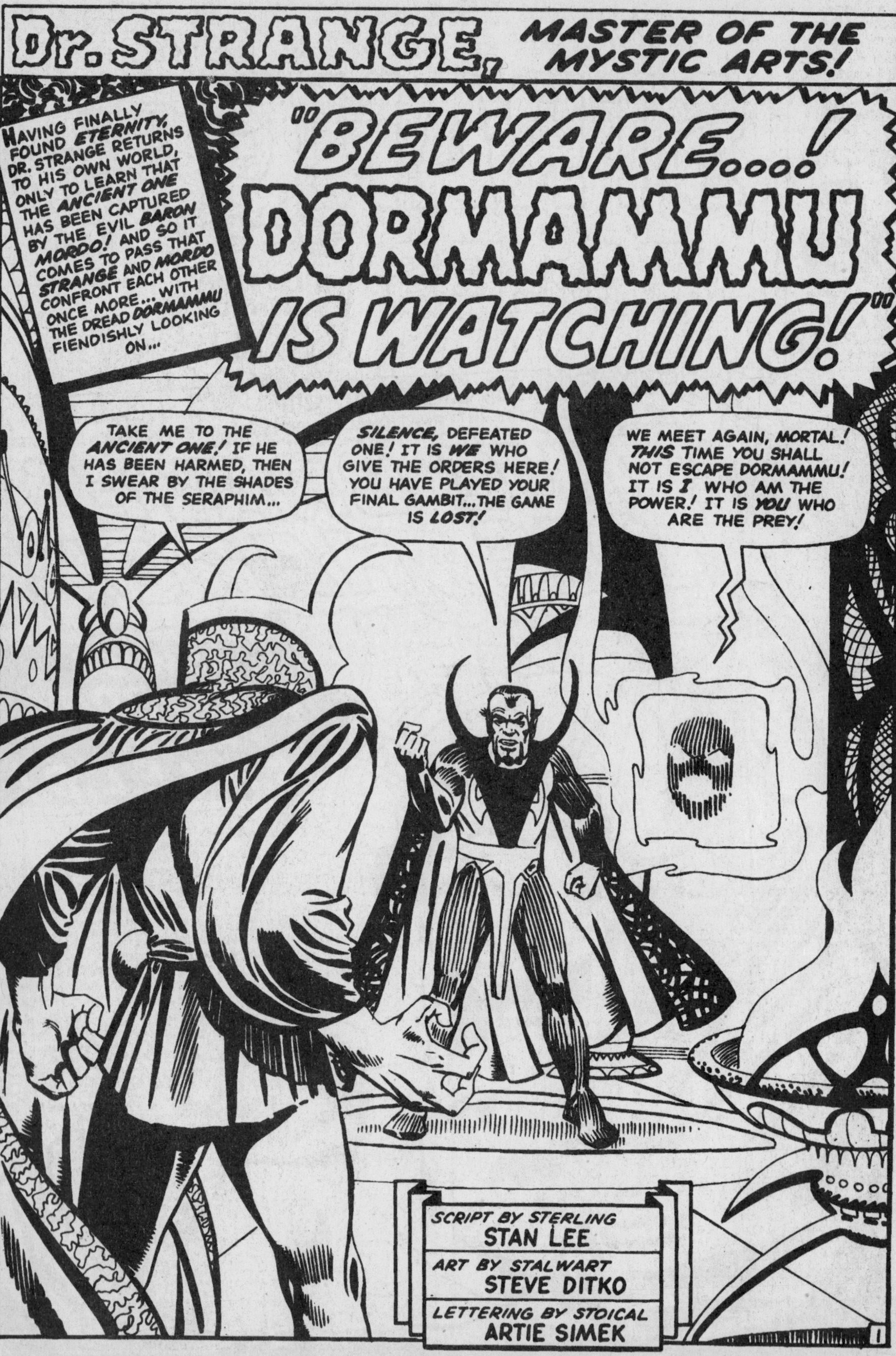

Dr. STRANGE, MASTER OF THE MYSTIC ARTS!
HAVING FINALLY FOUND ETERNITY, DR. STRANGE RETURNS TO HIS OWN WORLD, ONLY TO LEARN THAT THE ANCIENT ONE HAS BEEN CAPTURED BY THE EVIL BARON MORDO! AND SO IT COMES TO PASS THAT STRANGE AND MORDO CONFRONT EACH OTHER ONCE MORE... WITH THE DREAD DORMAMMU FIENDISHLY LOOKING ON...
"BEWARE....! DORMAMMU IS WATCHING!"
TAKE ME TO THE ANCIENT ONE! IF HE HAS BEEN HARMED, THEN I SWEAR BY THE SHADES OF THE SERAPHIM...
SILENCE, DEFEATED ONE! IT IS WE WHO GIVE THE ORDERS HERE! YOU HAVE PLAYED YOUR FINAL GAMBIT...THE GAME IS LOST!
WE MEET AGAIN, MORTAL! THIS TIME YOU SHALL NOT ESCAPE DORMAMMU! IT IS I WHO AM THE POWER! IT IS YOU WHO ARE THE PREY!
SCRIPT BY STERLING STAN LEE
ART BY STALWART STEVE DITKO
LETTERING BY STOICAL ARTIE SIMEK
1

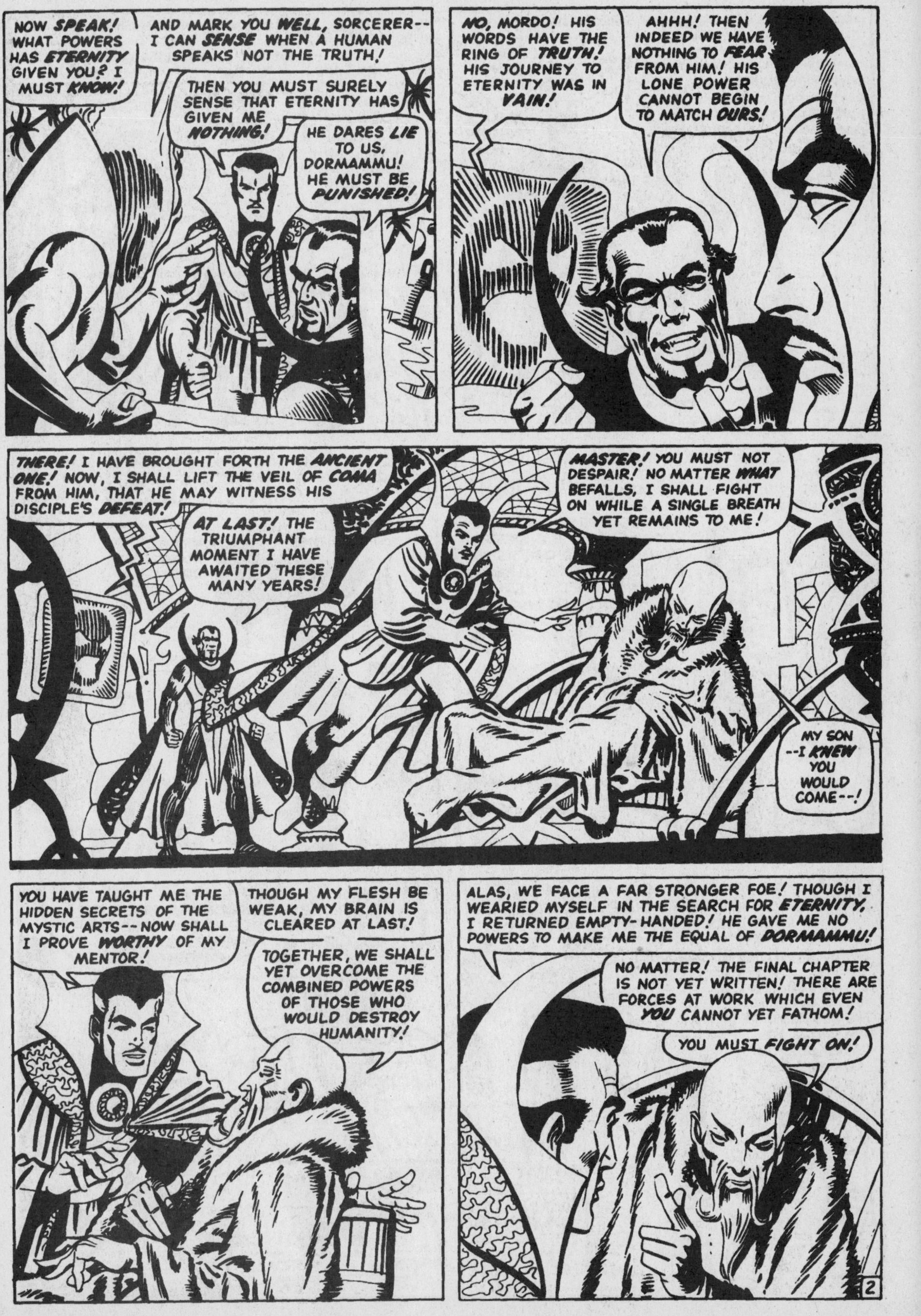

NOW SPEAK! WHAT POWERS HAS ETERNITY GIVEN YOU? I MUST KNOW!
AND MARK YOU WELL, SORCERER-- I CAN SENSE WHEN A HUMAN SPEAKS NOT THE TRUTH!
THEN YOU MUST SURELY SENSE THAT ETERNITY HAS GIVEN ME NOTHING!
HE DARES LIE TO US, DORMAMMU! HE MUST BE PUNISHED!
NO, MORDO! HIS WORDS HAVE THE RING OF TRUTH! HIS JOURNEY TO ETERNITY WAS IN VAIN!
AHHH! THEN INDEED WE HAVE NOTHING TO FEAR FROM HIM! HIS LONE POWER CANNOT BEGIN TO MATCH OURS!
THERE! I HAVE BROUGHT FORTH THE ANCIENT ONE! NOW, I SHALL LIFT THE VEIL OF COMA FROM HIM, THAT HE MAY WITNESS HIS DISCIPLE'S DEFEAT!
AT LAST! THE TRIUMPHANT MOMENT I HAVE AWAITED THESE MANY YEARS!
MASTER! YOU MUST NOT DESPAIR! NO MATTER WHAT BEFALLS, I SHALL FIGHT ON WHILE A SINGLE BREATH YET REMAINS TO ME!
MY SON --I KNEW YOU WOULD COME--!
YOU HAVE TAUGHT ME THE HIDDEN SECRETS OF THE MYSTIC ARTS--NOW SHALL I PROVE WORTHY OF MY MENTOR!
THOUGH MY FLESH BE WEAK, MY BRAIN IS CLEARED AT LAST!
TOGETHER, WE SHALL YET OVERCOME THE COMBINED POWERS OF THOSE WHO WOULD DESTROY HUMANITY!
ALAS, WE FACE A FAR STRONGER FOE! THOUGH I WEARIED MYSELF IN THE SEARCH FOR ETERNITY, I RETURNED EMPTY-HANDED! HE GAVE ME NO POWERS TO MAKE ME THE EQUAL OF DORMAMMU!
NO MATTER! THE FINAL CHAPTER IS NOT YET WRITTEN! THERE ARE FORCES AT WORK WHICH EVEN YOU CANNOT YET FATHOM!
YOU MUST FIGHT ON!
2

YOU HAVE TALKED *ENOUGH!* I GROW HUNGRY FOR THE TASTE OF *VICTORY!*

THOUGH I BE IN A FAR DISTANT DIMENSION, *MORDO* SHALL BATTLE FOR ME--WITH THE AWESOME *POWER* THAT ONLY *DORMAMMU* CAN GIVE HIM!

IT SHALL BE AS THOUGH I *MYSELF* HAVE SCORED THE ULTIMATE *TRIUMPH!*

THEN LET THE COMBAT *BEGIN!*

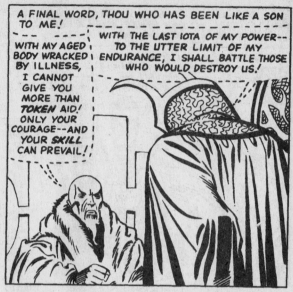

A FINAL WORD, THOU WHO HAS BEEN LIKE A SON TO ME!

WITH THE LAST IOTA OF MY POWER-- TO THE UTTER LIMIT OF MY ENDURANCE, I SHALL BATTLE THOSE WHO WOULD DESTROY US!

WITH MY AGED BODY WRACKED BY ILLNESS, I CANNOT GIVE YOU MORE THAN *TOKEN* AID! ONLY YOUR COURAGE--AND YOUR *SKILL* CAN PREVAIL!

NEVER HAS MAN BORN OF WOMAN FACED SUCH AWESOME ODDS! MORDO HAD BEEN MY DISCIPLE, EVEN AS *YOU,* BEFORE I LEARNED OF HIS BASE TREACHERY!

HE POSSESSES THE SAME KNOWLEDGE--THE SAME TRAINING AS *YOU!* AS FOR *ME,* WEAKENED BY ILLNESS, I CANNOT HOPE TO EQUAL THE POWER OF *DORMAMMU!*

WHERE THEY EMPLOY *POWER,* YOU MUST EMPLOY *WISDOM*-- THE WISDOM OF THE JUST, THE RIGHTEOUS, THE FEARLESS!

BY THE HOARY HAND OF *NOGGOTH,* I SHALL NOT FAIL THEE!

MORDO, THOU MASTER OF TREACHERY-- *I STAND READY!*

WHILE, IN THE DISTANT, DREAD DIMENSION OF *DORMAMMU,* A HELPLESS FIGURE HUDDLES IN FEAR AS SHE HEARS THE FATEFUL WORDS...

TO MY SIDE, FAITHLESS ONE! IT IS TIME FOR YOU TO WITNESS THE *UNDOING* OF HIM WHOM YOU DARED SUPPORT AGAINST *ME!*

*DURING DR. STRANGE'S LAST VISIT TO THEIR DIMENSION, REMEMBER? --STAN.

YOU WILL SEE WHAT HAPPENS TO *ALL* WHO DARE OPPOSE ME! *STRANGE MUST DIE!* AND WITH *HIM* GONE, I SHALL BE FREE TO TURN MY POWERS AGAINST *ALL OF EARTH!*

3

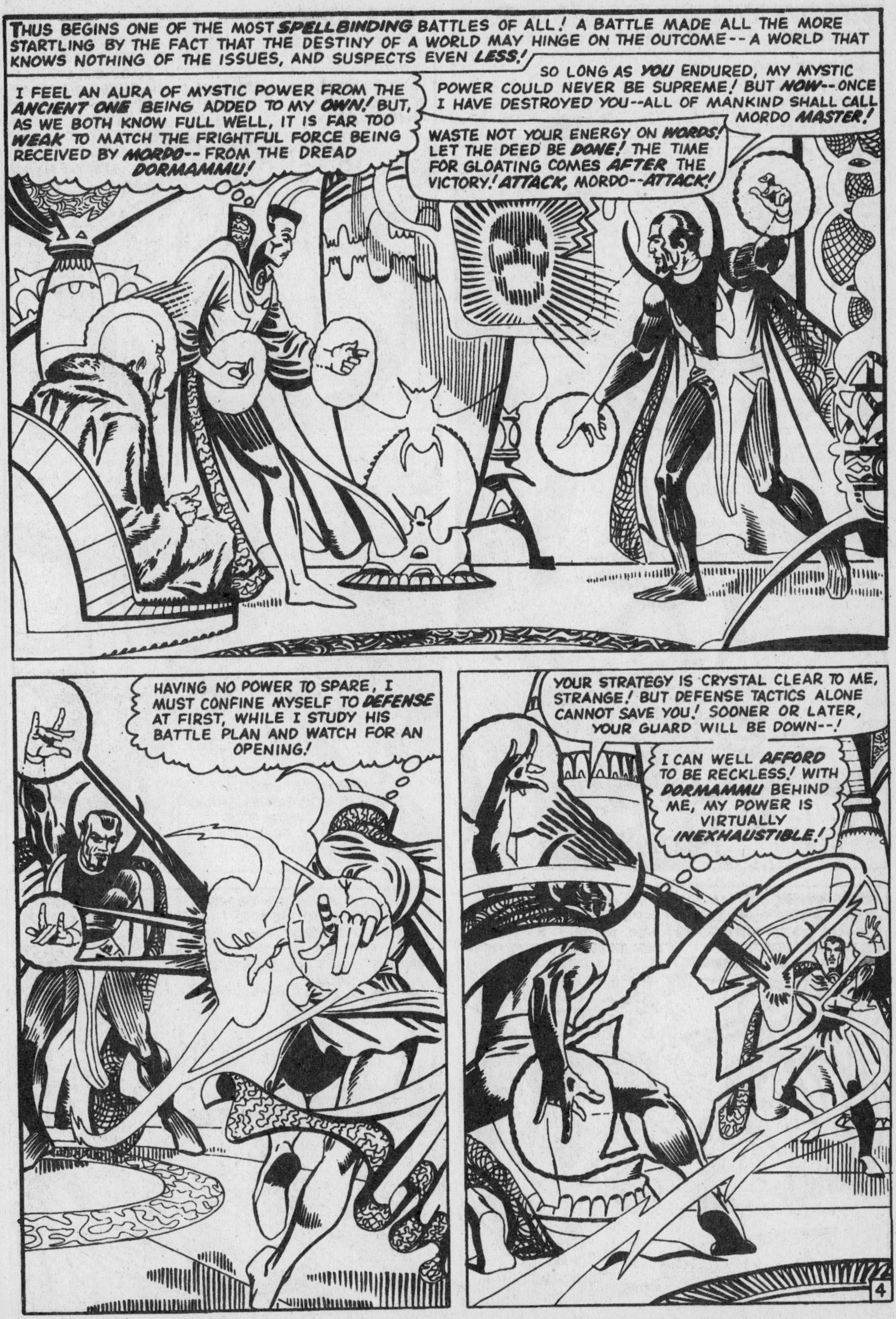
THUS BEGINS ONE OF THE MOST SPELLBINDING BATTLES OF ALL! A BATTLE MADE ALL THE MORE STARTLING BY THE FACT THAT THE DESTINY OF A WORLD MAY HINGE ON THE OUTCOME-- A WORLD THAT KNOWS NOTHING OF THE ISSUES, AND SUSPECTS EVEN LESS!
I FEEL AN AURA OF MYSTIC POWER FROM THE ANCIENT ONE BEING ADDED TO MY OWN! BUT, AS WE BOTH KNOW FULL WELL, IT IS FAR TOO WEAK TO MATCH THE FRIGHTFUL FORCE BEING RECEIVED BY MORDO-- FROM THE DREAD DORMAMMU!
SO LONG AS YOU ENDURED, MY MYSTIC POWER COULD NEVER BE SUPREME! BUT NOW--ONCE I HAVE DESTROYED YOU--ALL OF MANKIND SHALL CALL MORDO MASTER!
WASTE NOT YOUR ENERGY ON WORDS! LET THE DEED BE DONE! THE TIME FOR GLOATING COMES AFTER THE VICTORY! ATTACK, MORDO--ATTACK!
HAVING NO POWER TO SPARE, I MUST CONFINE MYSELF TO DEFENSE AT FIRST, WHILE I STUDY HIS BATTLE PLAN AND WATCH FOR AN OPENING!
YOUR STRATEGY IS CRYSTAL CLEAR TO ME, STRANGE! BUT DEFENSE TACTICS ALONE CANNOT SAVE YOU! SOONER OR LATER, YOUR GUARD WILL BE DOWN--!
I CAN WELL AFFORD TO BE RECKLESS! WITH DORMAMMU BEHIND ME, MY POWER IS VIRTUALLY INEXHAUSTIBLE!
4

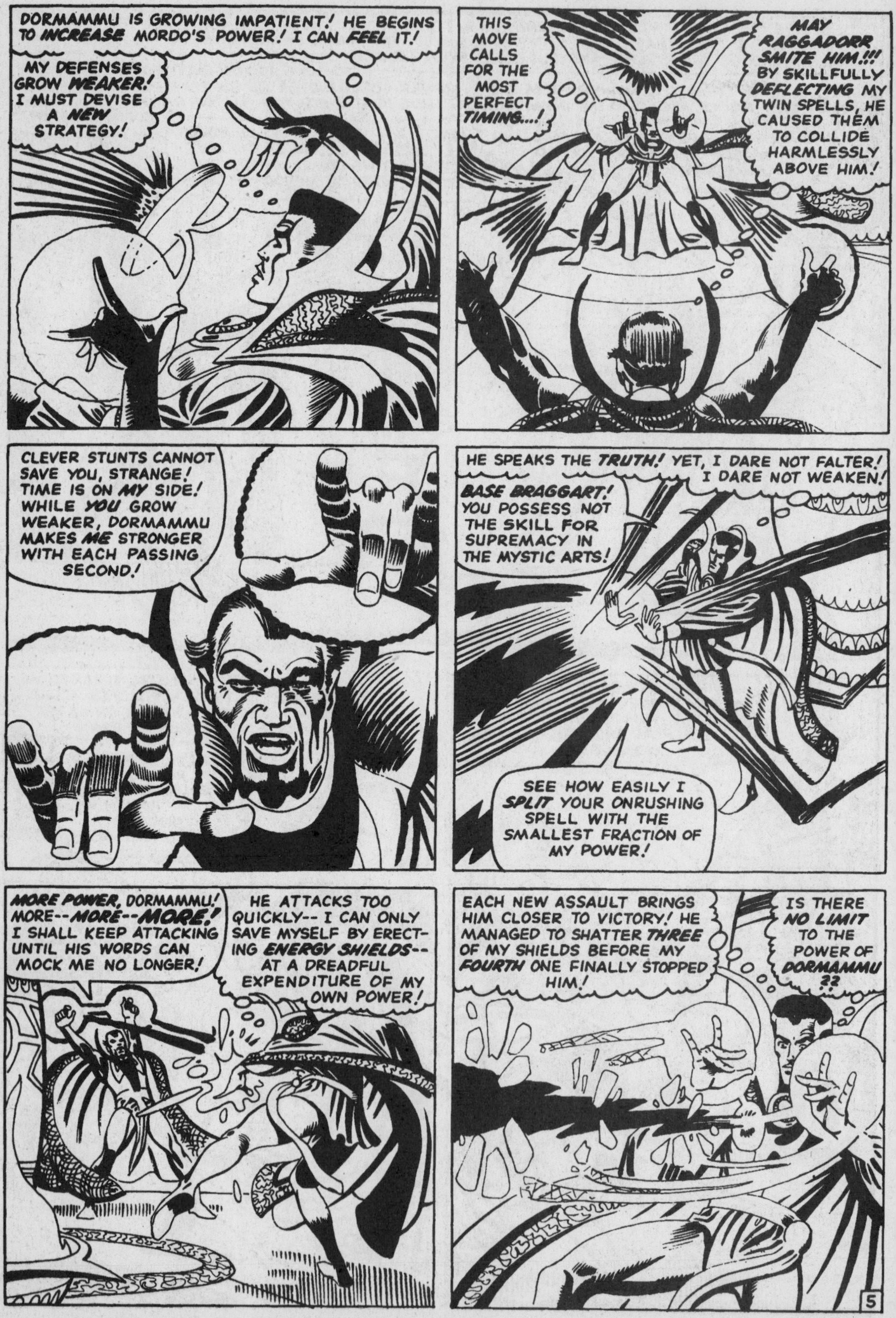
DORMAMMU IS GROWING IMPATIENT! HE BEGINS TO INCREASE MORDO'S POWER! I CAN FEEL IT!
MY DEFENSES GROW WEAKER! I MUST DEVISE A NEW STRATEGY!
THIS MOVE CALLS FOR THE MOST PERFECT TIMING...!
MAY RAGGADORR SMITE HIM!!! BY SKILLFULLY DEFLECTING MY TWIN SPELLS, HE CAUSED THEM TO COLLIDE HARMLESSLY ABOVE HIM!
CLEVER STUNTS CANNOT SAVE YOU, STRANGE! TIME IS ON MY SIDE! WHILE YOU GROW WEAKER, DORMAMMU MAKES ME STRONGER WITH EACH PASSING SECOND!
HE SPEAKS THE TRUTH! YET, I DARE NOT FALTER! I DARE NOT WEAKEN!
BASE BRAGGART! YOU POSSESS NOT THE SKILL FOR SUPREMACY IN THE MYSTIC ARTS!
SEE HOW EASILY I SPLIT YOUR ONRUSHING SPELL WITH THE SMALLEST FRACTION OF MY POWER!
MORE POWER, DORMAMMU! MORE--MORE--MORE! I SHALL KEEP ATTACKING UNTIL HIS WORDS CAN MOCK ME NO LONGER!
HE ATTACKS TOO QUICKLY-- I CAN ONLY SAVE MYSELF BY ERECTING ENERGY SHIELDS-- AT A DREADFUL EXPENDITURE OF MY OWN POWER!
EACH NEW ASSAULT BRINGS HIM CLOSER TO VICTORY! HE MANAGED TO SHATTER THREE OF MY SHIELDS BEFORE MY FOURTH ONE FINALLY STOPPED HIM!
IS THERE NO LIMIT TO THE POWER OF DORMAMMU ??
5

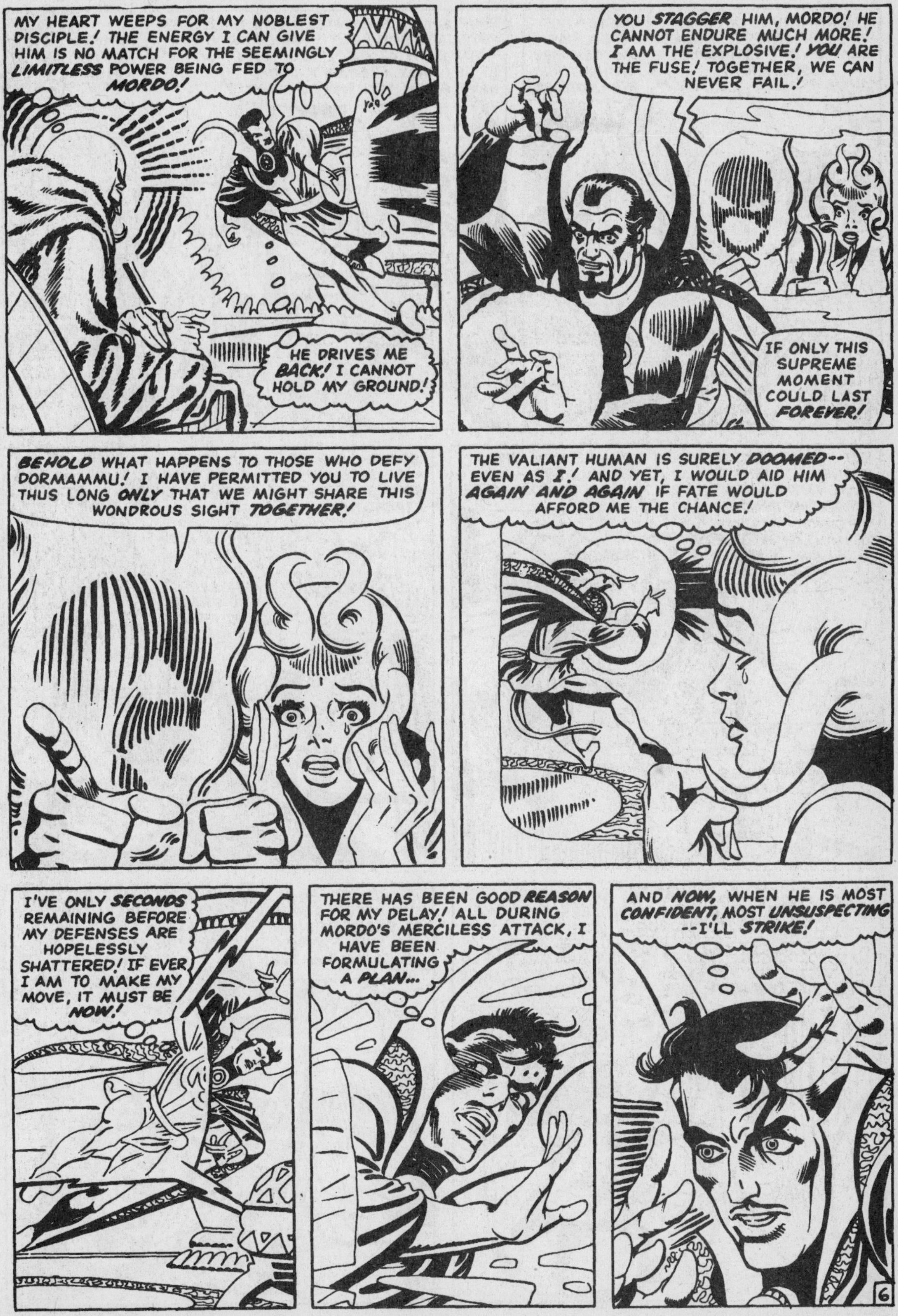
MY HEART WEEPS FOR MY NOBLEST DISCIPLE! THE ENERGY I CAN GIVE HIM IS NO MATCH FOR THE SEEMINGLY LIMITLESS POWER BEING FED TO MORDO!
HE DRIVES ME BACK! I CANNOT HOLD MY GROUND!
YOU STAGGER HIM, MORDO! HE CANNOT ENDURE MUCH MORE! I AM THE EXPLOSIVE! YOU ARE THE FUSE! TOGETHER, WE CAN NEVER FAIL!
IF ONLY THIS SUPREME MOMENT COULD LAST FOREVER!
BEHOLD WHAT HAPPENS TO THOSE WHO DEFY DORMAMMU! I HAVE PERMITTED YOU TO LIVE THUS LONG ONLY THAT WE MIGHT SHARE THIS WONDROUS SIGHT TOGETHER!
THE VALIANT HUMAN IS SURELY DOOMED-- EVEN AS I! AND YET, I WOULD AID HIM AGAIN AND AGAIN IF FATE WOULD AFFORD ME THE CHANCE!
I'VE ONLY SECONDS REMAINING BEFORE MY DEFENSES ARE HOPELESSLY SHATTERED! IF EVER I AM TO MAKE MY MOVE, IT MUST BE NOW!
THERE HAS BEEN GOOD REASON FOR MY DELAY! ALL DURING MORDO'S MERCILESS ATTACK, I HAVE BEEN FORMULATING A PLAN...
AND NOW, WHEN HE IS MOST CONFIDENT, MOST UNSUSPECTING --I'LL STRIKE!
6

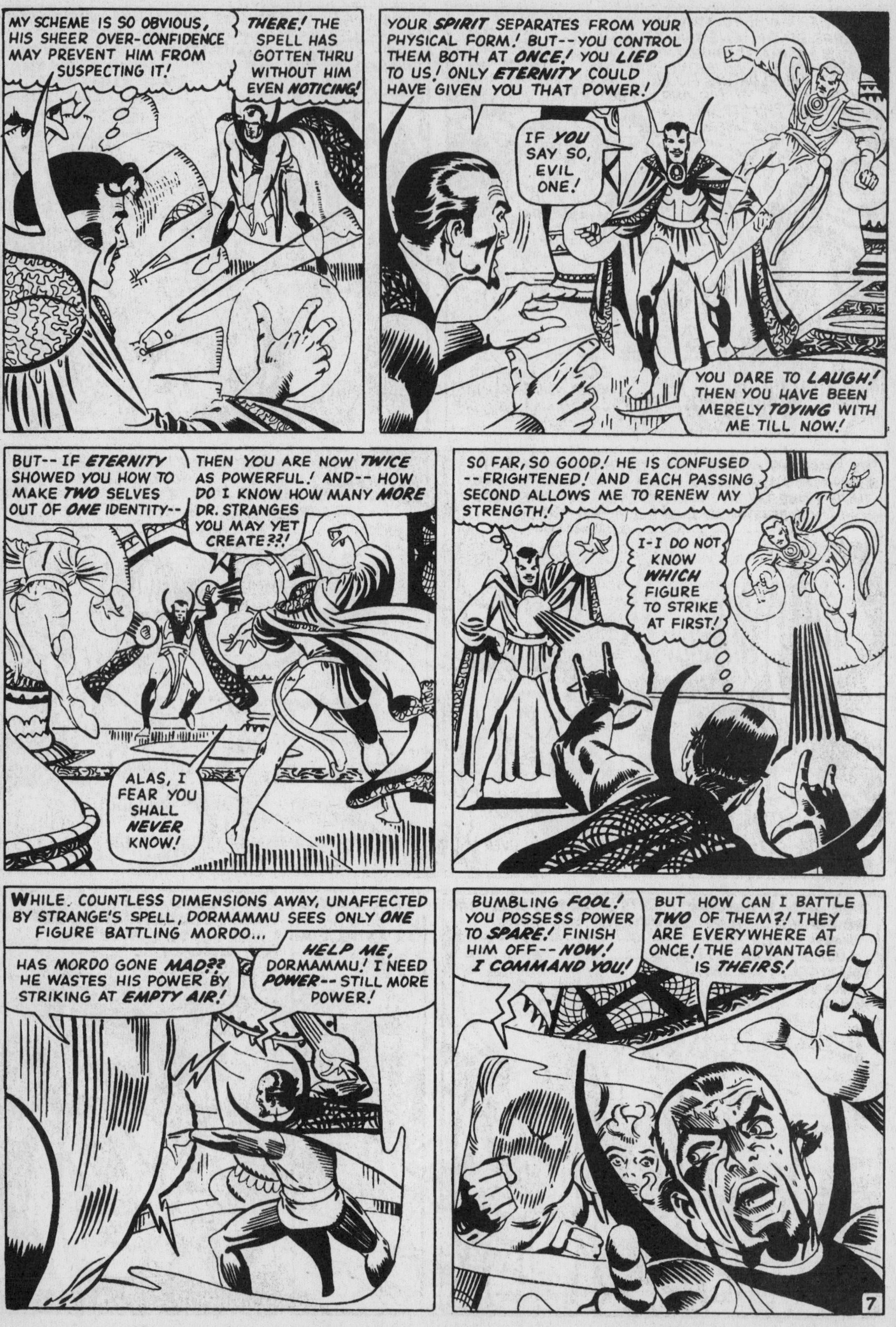
MY SCHEME IS SO OBVIOUS, HIS SHEER OVER-CONFIDENCE MAY PREVENT HIM FROM SUSPECTING IT!
THERE! THE SPELL HAS GOTTEN THRU WITHOUT HIM EVEN NOTICING!
YOUR SPIRIT SEPARATES FROM YOUR PHYSICAL FORM! BUT--YOU CONTROL THEM BOTH AT ONCE! YOU LIED TO US! ONLY ETERNITY COULD HAVE GIVEN YOU THAT POWER!
IF YOU SAY SO, EVIL ONE!
YOU DARE TO LAUGH! THEN YOU HAVE BEEN MERELY TOYING WITH ME TILL NOW!
BUT-- IF ETERNITY SHOWED YOU HOW TO MAKE TWO SELVES OUT OF ONE IDENTITY--
THEN YOU ARE NOW TWICE AS POWERFUL! AND-- HOW DO I KNOW HOW MANY MORE DR. STRANGES YOU MAY YET CREATE??!
ALAS, I FEAR YOU SHALL NEVER KNOW!
SO FAR, SO GOOD! HE IS CONFUSED --FRIGHTENED! AND EACH PASSING SECOND ALLOWS ME TO RENEW MY STRENGTH!
I-I DO NOT KNOW WHICH FIGURE TO STRIKE AT FIRST!
WHILE, COUNTLESS DIMENSIONS AWAY, UNAFFECTED BY STRANGE'S SPELL, DORMAMMU SEES ONLY ONE FIGURE BATTLING MORDO...
HAS MORDO GONE MAD?? HE WASTES HIS POWER BY STRIKING AT EMPTY AIR!
HELP ME, DORMAMMU! I NEED POWER-- STILL MORE POWER!
BUMBLING FOOL! YOU POSSESS POWER TO SPARE! FINISH HIM OFF--NOW! I COMMAND YOU!
BUT HOW CAN I BATTLE TWO OF THEM?! THEY ARE EVERYWHERE AT ONCE! THE ADVANTAGE IS THEIRS!
7

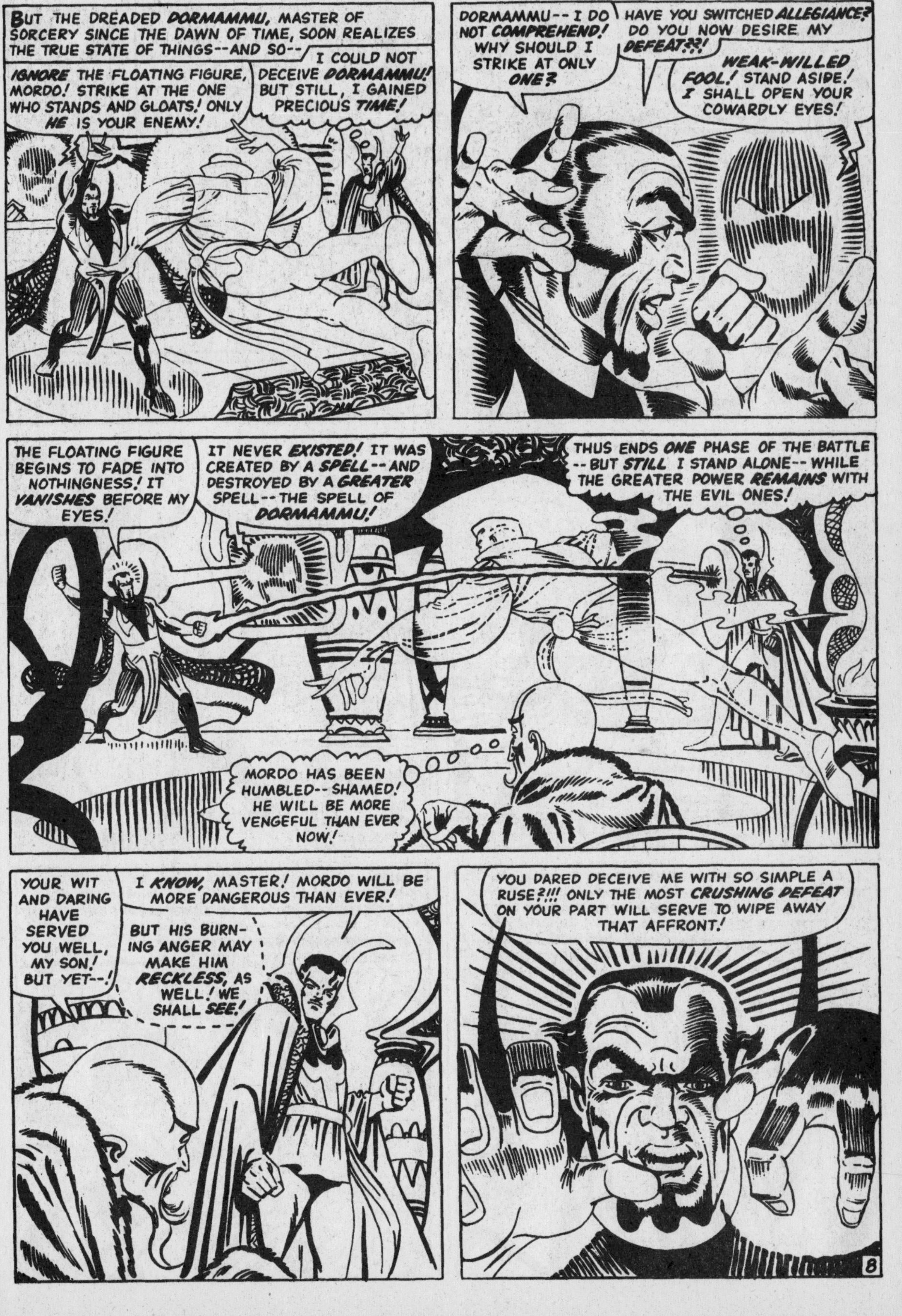

BUT THE DREADED DORMAMMU, MASTER OF SORCERY SINCE THE DAWN OF TIME, SOON REALIZES THE TRUE STATE OF THINGS--AND SO--
IGNORE THE FLOATING FIGURE, MORDO! STRIKE AT THE ONE WHO STANDS AND GLOATS! ONLY HE IS YOUR ENEMY!
I COULD NOT DECEIVE DORMAMMU! BUT STILL, I GAINED PRECIOUS TIME!
DORMAMMU-- I DO NOT COMPREHEND! WHY SHOULD I STRIKE AT ONLY ONE?
HAVE YOU SWITCHED ALLEGIANCE? DO YOU NOW DESIRE MY DEFEAT??!
WEAK-WILLED FOOL! STAND ASIDE! I SHALL OPEN YOUR COWARDLY EYES!
THE FLOATING FIGURE BEGINS TO FADE INTO NOTHINGNESS! IT VANISHES BEFORE MY EYES!
IT NEVER EXISTED! IT WAS CREATED BY A SPELL--AND DESTROYED BY A GREATER SPELL--THE SPELL OF DORMAMMU!
THUS ENDS ONE PHASE OF THE BATTLE --BUT STILL I STAND ALONE--WHILE THE GREATER POWER REMAINS WITH THE EVIL ONES!
MORDO HAS BEEN HUMBLED--SHAMED! HE WILL BE MORE VENGEFUL THAN EVER NOW!
YOUR WIT AND DARING HAVE SERVED YOU WELL, MY SON! BUT YET--!
I KNOW, MASTER! MORDO WILL BE MORE DANGEROUS THAN EVER!
BUT HIS BURN-ING ANGER MAY MAKE HIM RECKLESS, AS WELL! WE SHALL SEE!
YOU DARED DECEIVE ME WITH SO SIMPLE A RUSE?!!! ONLY THE MOST CRUSHING DEFEAT ON YOUR PART WILL SERVE TO WIPE AWAY THAT AFFRONT!

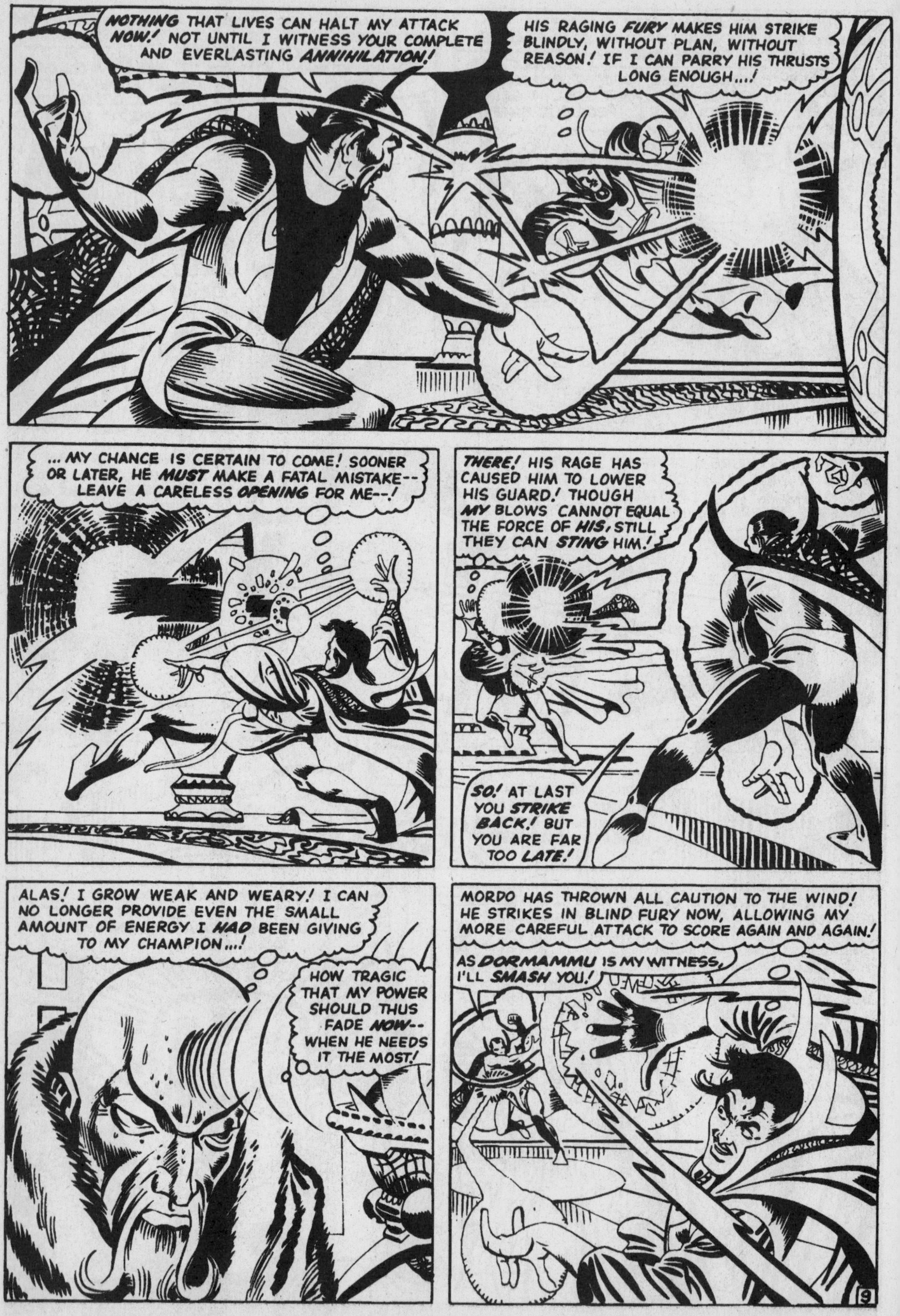

NOTHING THAT LIVES CAN HALT MY ATTACK NOW! NOT UNTIL I WITNESS YOUR COMPLETE AND EVERLASTING ANNIHILATION!
HIS RAGING FURY MAKES HIM STRIKE BLINDLY, WITHOUT PLAN, WITHOUT REASON! IF I CAN PARRY HIS THRUSTS LONG ENOUGH....!
...MY CHANCE IS CERTAIN TO COME! SOONER OR LATER, HE MUST MAKE A FATAL MISTAKE-- LEAVE A CARELESS OPENING FOR ME--!
THERE! HIS RAGE HAS CAUSED HIM TO LOWER HIS GUARD! THOUGH MY BLOWS CANNOT EQUAL THE FORCE OF HIS, STILL THEY CAN STING HIM!
SO! AT LAST YOU STRIKE BACK! BUT YOU ARE FAR TOO LATE!
ALAS! I GROW WEAK AND WEARY! I CAN NO LONGER PROVIDE EVEN THE SMALL AMOUNT OF ENERGY I HAD BEEN GIVING TO MY CHAMPION....!
HOW TRAGIC THAT MY POWER SHOULD THUS FADE NOW-- WHEN HE NEEDS IT THE MOST!
MORDO HAS THROWN ALL CAUTION TO THE WIND! HE STRIKES IN BLIND FURY NOW, ALLOWING MY MORE CAREFUL ATTACK TO SCORE AGAIN AND AGAIN!
AS DORMAMMU IS MY WITNESS, I'LL SMASH YOU!
9

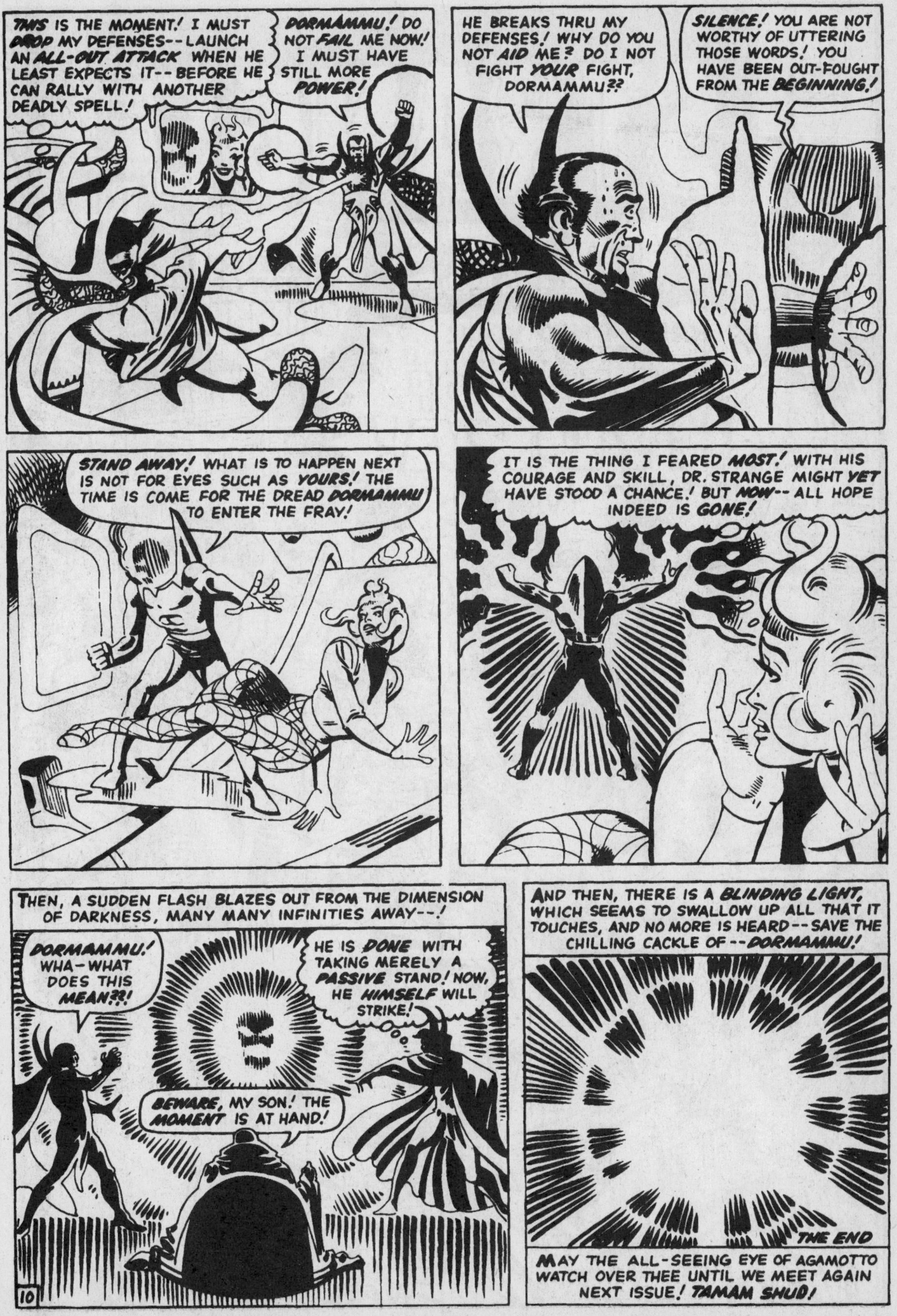
THIS IS THE MOMENT! I MUST DROP MY DEFENSES--LAUNCH AN ALL-OUT ATTACK WHEN HE LEAST EXPECTS IT--BEFORE HE CAN RALLY WITH ANOTHER DEADLY SPELL!
DORMAMMU! DO NOT FAIL ME NOW! I MUST HAVE STILL MORE POWER!
HE BREAKS THRU MY DEFENSES! WHY DO YOU NOT AID ME? DO I NOT FIGHT YOUR FIGHT, DORMAMMU??
SILENCE! YOU ARE NOT WORTHY OF UTTERING THOSE WORDS! YOU HAVE BEEN OUT-FOUGHT FROM THE BEGINNING!
STAND AWAY! WHAT IS TO HAPPEN NEXT IS NOT FOR EYES SUCH AS YOURS! THE TIME IS COME FOR THE DREAD DORMAMMU TO ENTER THE FRAY!
IT IS THE THING I FEARED MOST! WITH HIS COURAGE AND SKILL, DR. STRANGE MIGHT YET HAVE STOOD A CHANCE! BUT NOW--ALL HOPE INDEED IS GONE!
THEN, A SUDDEN FLASH BLAZES OUT FROM THE DIMENSION OF DARKNESS, MANY MANY INFINITIES AWAY--!
DORMAMMU! WHA-WHAT DOES THIS MEAN??!
HE IS DONE WITH TAKING MERELY A PASSIVE STAND! NOW, HE HIMSELF WILL STRIKE!
BEWARE, MY SON! THE MOMENT IS AT HAND!
10
AND THEN, THERE IS A BLINDING LIGHT, WHICH SEEMS TO SWALLOW UP ALL THAT IT TOUCHES, AND NO MORE IS HEARD--SAVE THE CHILLING CACKLE OF--DORMAMMU!
THE END
MAY THE ALL-SEEING EYE OF AGAMOTTO WATCH OVER THEE UNTIL WE MEET AGAIN NEXT ISSUE! TAMAM SHUD!

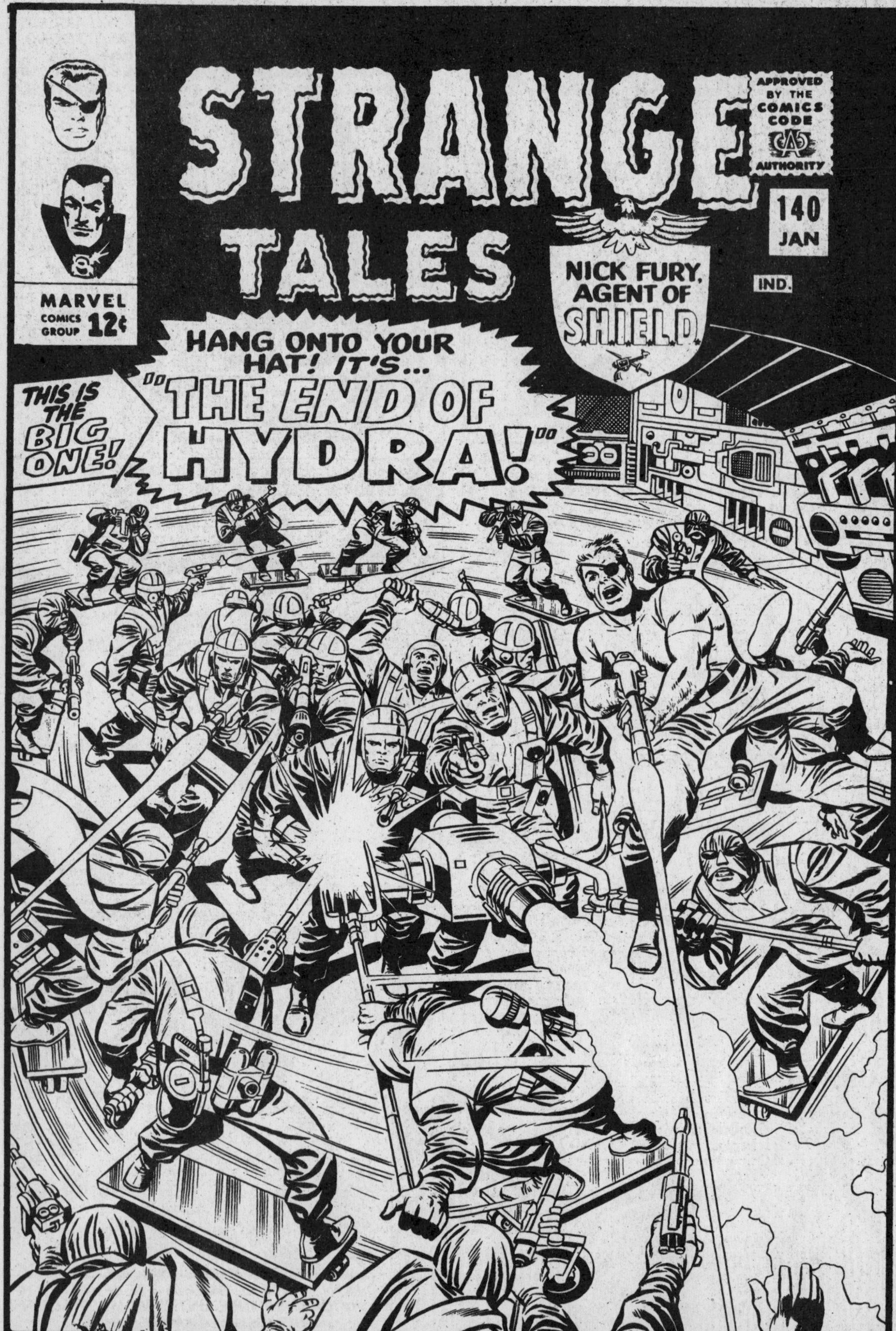

STRANGE TALES
MARVEL COMICS GROUP 12¢
APPROVED BY THE COMICS CODE AUTHORITY
140 JAN
IND.
NICK FURY, AGENT OF SHIELD
HANG ONTO YOUR HAT! IT'S... "THE END OF HYDRA!"
THIS IS THE BIG ONE!

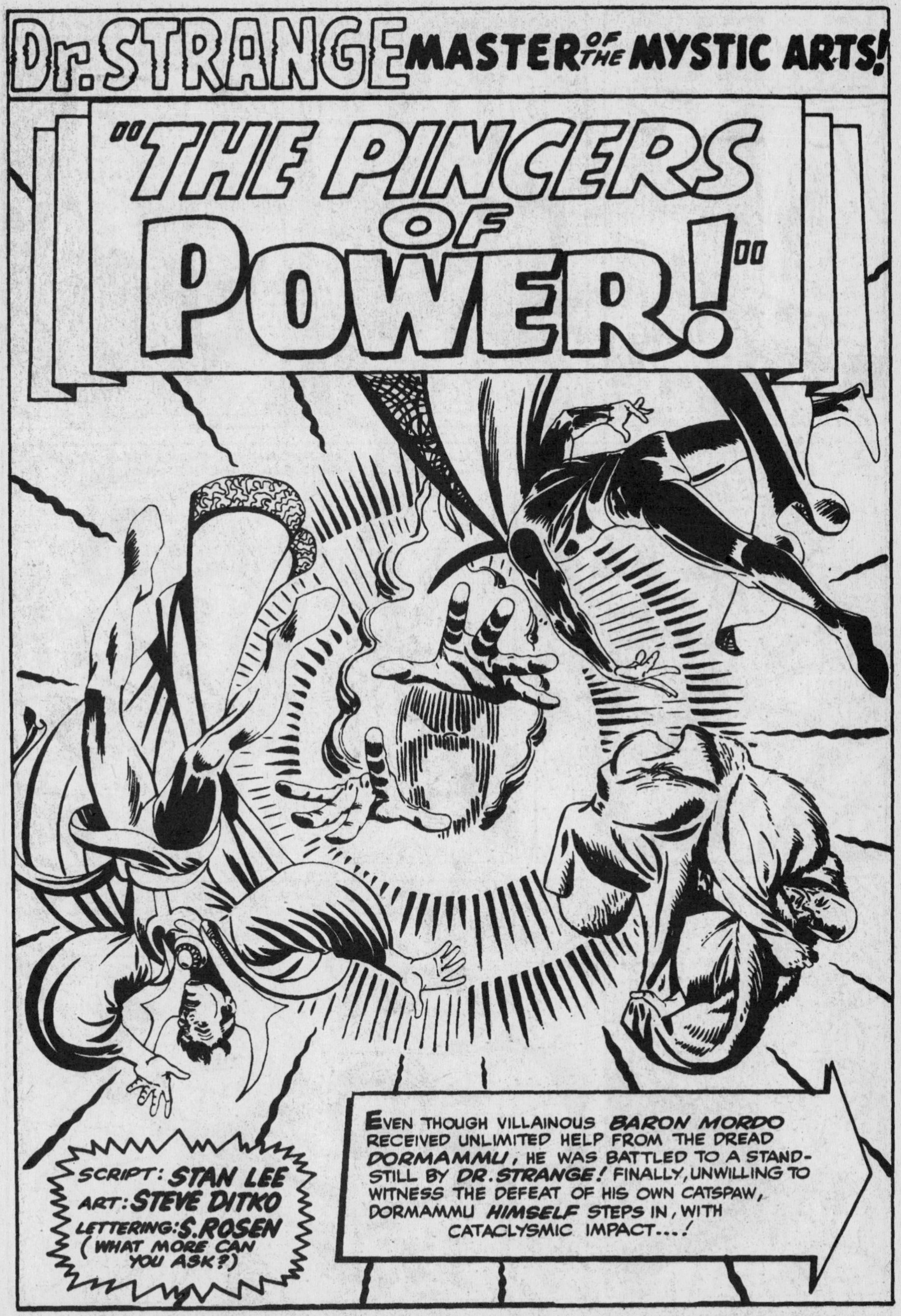
Dr. STRANGE MASTER OF THE MYSTIC ARTS!
"THE PINCERS OF POWER!"
EVEN THOUGH VILLAINOUS BARON MORDO RECEIVED UNLIMITED HELP FROM THE DREAD DORMAMMU, HE WAS BATTLED TO A STAND-STILL BY DR. STRANGE! FINALLY, UNWILLING TO WITNESS THE DEFEAT OF HIS OWN CATSPAW, DORMAMMU HIMSELF STEPS IN, WITH CATACLYSMIC IMPACT...!
SCRIPT: STAN LEE
ART: STEVE DITKO
LETTERING: S. ROSEN
(WHAT MORE CAN YOU ASK?)

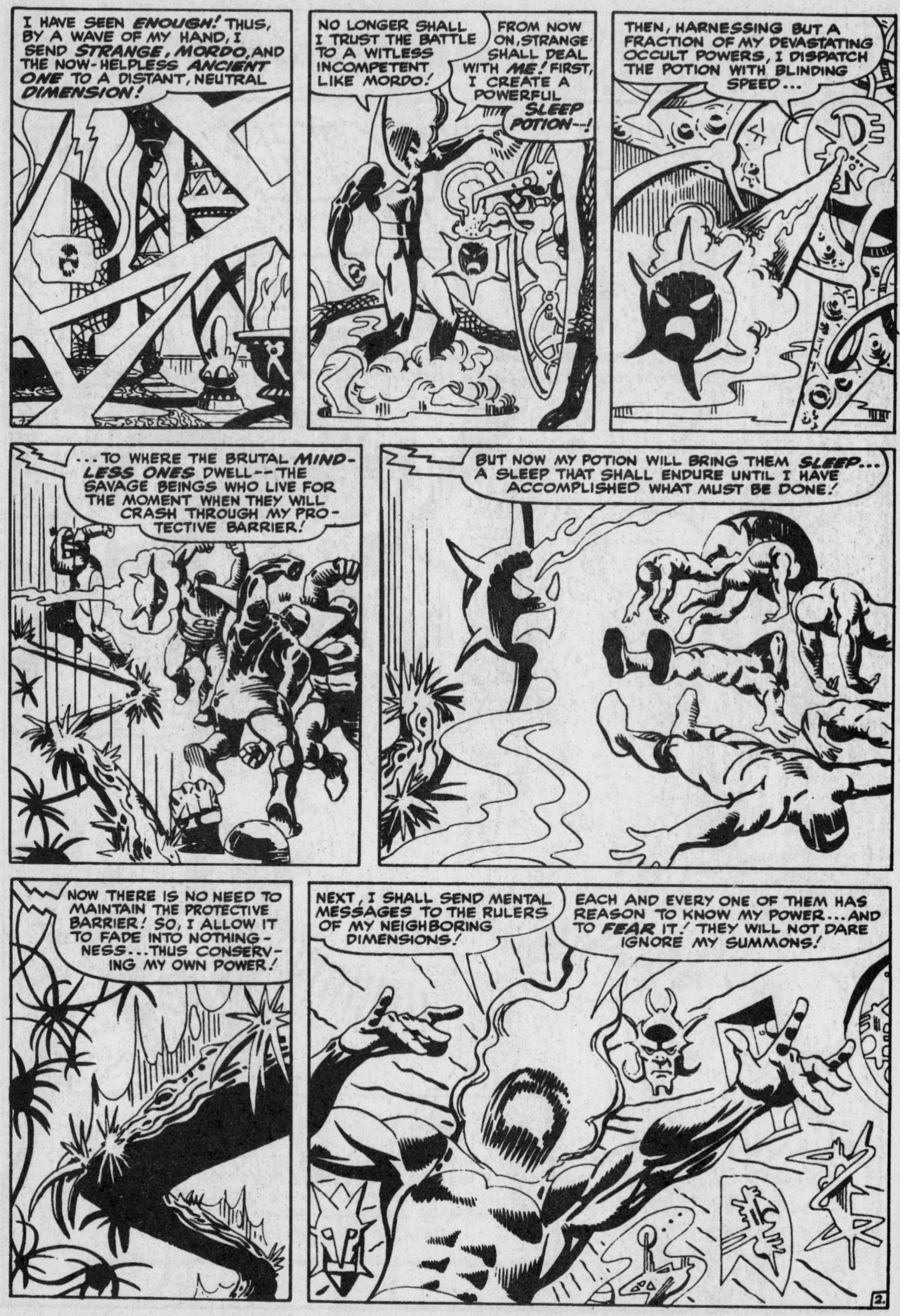
I HAVE SEEN ENOUGH! THUS, BY A WAVE OF MY HAND, I SEND STRANGE, MORDO, AND THE NOW-HELPLESS ANCIENT ONE TO A DISTANT, NEUTRAL DIMENSION!
NO LONGER SHALL I TRUST THE BATTLE TO A WITLESS INCOMPETENT LIKE MORDO!
FROM NOW ON, STRANGE SHALL DEAL WITH ME! FIRST, I CREATE A POWERFUL SLEEP POTION--!
THEN, HARNESSING BUT A FRACTION OF MY DEVASTATING OCCULT POWERS, I DISPATCH THE POTION WITH BLINDING SPEED...
...TO WHERE THE BRUTAL MINDLESS ONES DWELL--THE SAVAGE BEINGS WHO LIVE FOR THE MOMENT WHEN THEY WILL CRASH THROUGH MY PROTECTIVE BARRIER!
BUT NOW MY POTION WILL BRING THEM SLEEP... A SLEEP THAT SHALL ENDURE UNTIL I HAVE ACCOMPLISHED WHAT MUST BE DONE!
NOW THERE IS NO NEED TO MAINTAIN THE PROTECTIVE BARRIER! SO, I ALLOW IT TO FADE INTO NOTHINGNESS...THUS CONSERVING MY OWN POWER!
NEXT, I SHALL SEND MENTAL MESSAGES TO THE RULERS OF MY NEIGHBORING DIMENSIONS!
EACH AND EVERY ONE OF THEM HAS REASON TO KNOW MY POWER...AND TO FEAR IT! THEY WILL NOT DARE IGNORE MY SUMMONS!
2.

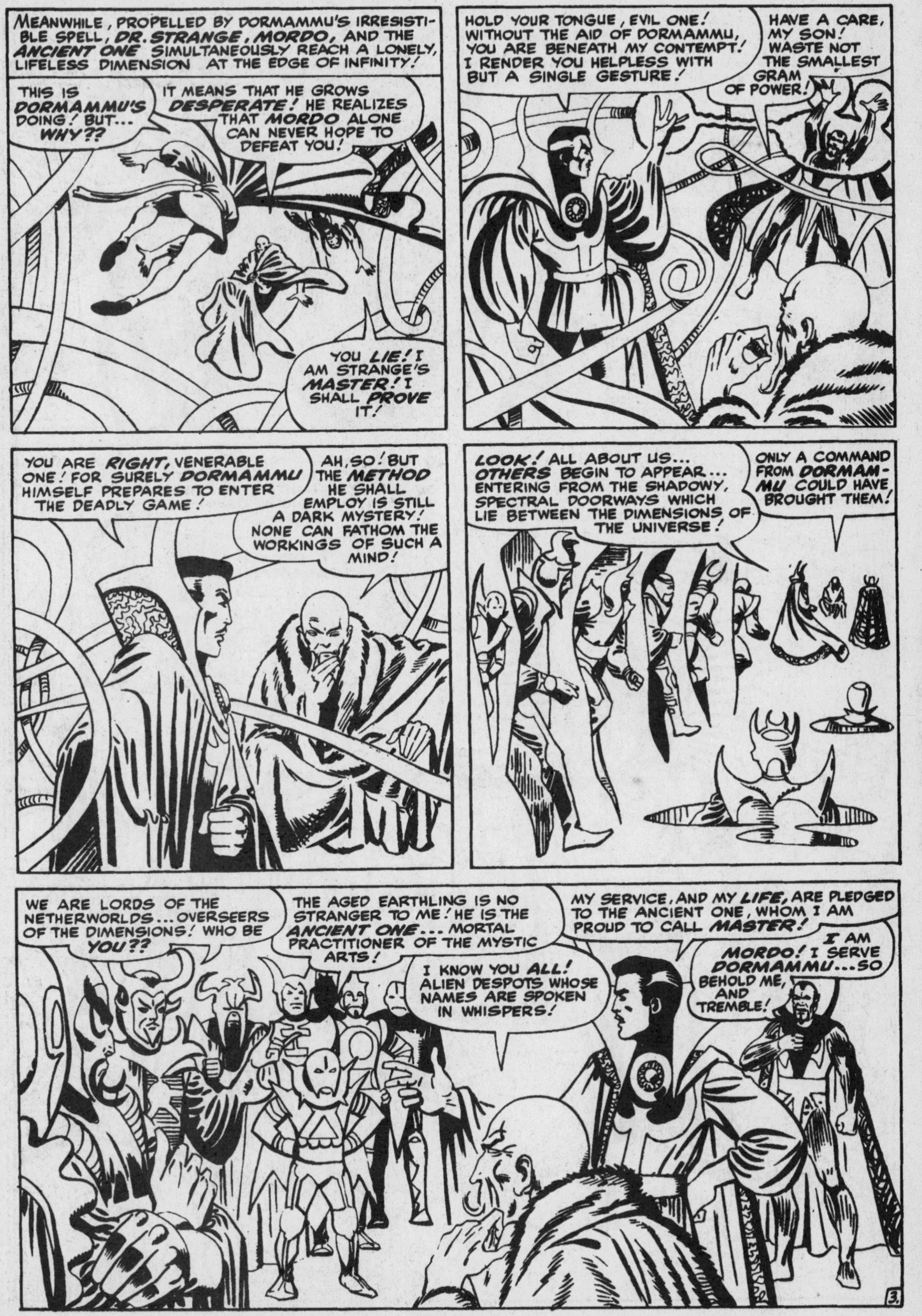
MEANWHILE, PROPELLED BY DORMAMMU'S IRRESISTIBLE SPELL, DR. STRANGE, MORDO, AND THE ANCIENT ONE SIMULTANEOUSLY REACH A LONELY, LIFELESS DIMENSION AT THE EDGE OF INFINITY!
THIS IS DORMAMMU'S DOING! BUT... WHY??
IT MEANS THAT HE GROWS DESPERATE! HE REALIZES THAT MORDO ALONE CAN NEVER HOPE TO DEFEAT YOU!
YOU LIE! I AM STRANGE'S MASTER! I SHALL PROVE IT!
HOLD YOUR TONGUE, EVIL ONE! WITHOUT THE AID OF DORMAMMU, YOU ARE BENEATH MY CONTEMPT! I RENDER YOU HELPLESS WITH BUT A SINGLE GESTURE!
HAVE A CARE, MY SON! WASTE NOT THE SMALLEST GRAM OF POWER!
YOU ARE RIGHT, VENERABLE ONE! FOR SURELY DORMAMMU HIMSELF PREPARES TO ENTER THE DEADLY GAME!
AH, SO! BUT THE METHOD HE SHALL EMPLOY IS STILL A DARK MYSTERY! NONE CAN FATHOM THE WORKINGS OF SUCH A MIND!
LOOK! ALL ABOUT US... OTHERS BEGIN TO APPEAR... ENTERING FROM THE SHADOWY, SPECTRAL DOORWAYS WHICH LIE BETWEEN THE DIMENSIONS OF THE UNIVERSE!
ONLY A COMMAND FROM DORMAMMU COULD HAVE BROUGHT THEM!
WE ARE LORDS OF THE NETHERWORLDS... OVERSEERS OF THE DIMENSIONS! WHO BE YOU??
THE AGED EARTHLING IS NO STRANGER TO ME! HE IS THE ANCIENT ONE... MORTAL PRACTITIONER OF THE MYSTIC ARTS!
I KNOW YOU ALL! ALIEN DESPOTS WHOSE NAMES ARE SPOKEN IN WHISPERS!
MY SERVICE, AND MY LIFE, ARE PLEDGED TO THE ANCIENT ONE, WHOM I AM PROUD TO CALL MASTER!
I AM MORDO! I SERVE DORMAMMU... SO BEHOLD ME, AND TREMBLE!
3.

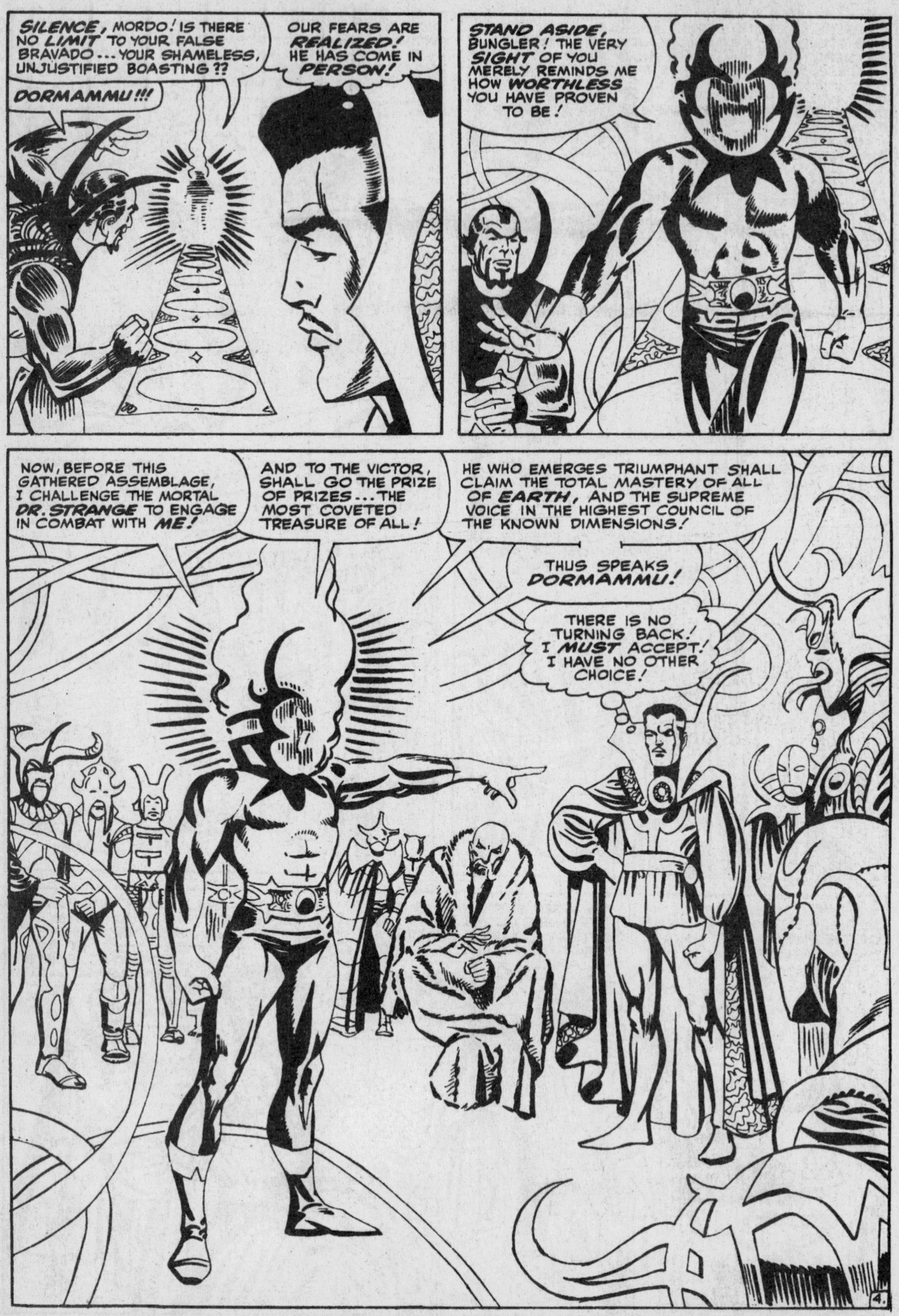
SILENCE, MORDO! IS THERE NO LIMIT TO YOUR FALSE BRAVADO... YOUR SHAMELESS, UNJUSTIFIED BOASTING??
DORMAMMU!!!
OUR FEARS ARE REALIZED! HE HAS COME IN PERSON!
STAND ASIDE, BUNGLER! THE VERY SIGHT OF YOU MERELY REMINDS ME HOW WORTHLESS YOU HAVE PROVEN TO BE!
NOW, BEFORE THIS GATHERED ASSEMBLAGE, I CHALLENGE THE MORTAL DR. STRANGE TO ENGAGE IN COMBAT WITH ME!
AND TO THE VICTOR, SHALL GO THE PRIZE OF PRIZES... THE MOST COVETED TREASURE OF ALL!
HE WHO EMERGES TRIUMPHANT SHALL CLAIM THE TOTAL MASTERY OF ALL OF EARTH, AND THE SUPREME VOICE IN THE HIGHEST COUNCIL OF THE KNOWN DIMENSIONS!
THUS SPEAKS DORMAMMU!
THERE IS NO TURNING BACK! I MUST ACCEPT! I HAVE NO OTHER CHOICE!
4.

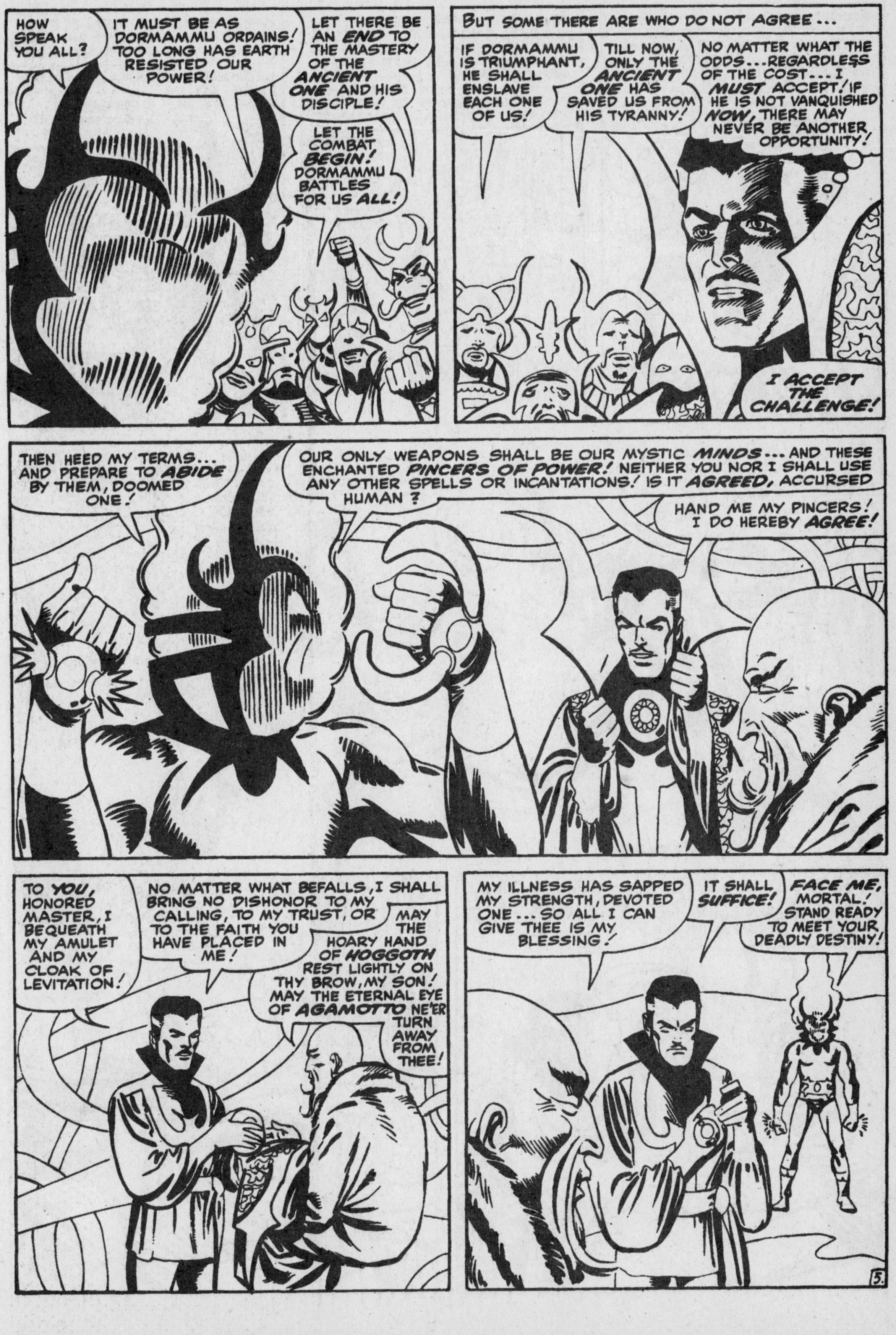
HOW SPEAK YOU ALL?
IT MUST BE AS DORMAMMU ORDAINS! TOO LONG HAS EARTH RESISTED OUR POWER!
LET THERE BE AN END TO THE MASTERY OF THE ANCIENT ONE AND HIS DISCIPLE!
LET THE COMBAT BEGIN! DORMAMMU BATTLES FOR US ALL!
BUT SOME THERE ARE WHO DO NOT AGREE...
IF DORMAMMU IS TRIUMPHANT, HE SHALL ENSLAVE EACH ONE OF US!
TILL NOW, ONLY THE ANCIENT ONE HAS SAVED US FROM HIS TYRANNY!
NO MATTER WHAT THE ODDS...REGARDLESS OF THE COST...I MUST ACCEPT! IF HE IS NOT VANQUISHED NOW, THERE MAY NEVER BE ANOTHER OPPORTUNITY!
I ACCEPT THE CHALLENGE!
THEN HEED MY TERMS... AND PREPARE TO ABIDE BY THEM, DOOMED ONE!
OUR ONLY WEAPONS SHALL BE OUR MYSTIC MINDS... AND THESE ENCHANTED PINCERS OF POWER! NEITHER YOU NOR I SHALL USE ANY OTHER SPELLS OR INCANTATIONS! IS IT AGREED, ACCURSED HUMAN?
HAND ME MY PINCERS! I DO HEREBY AGREE!
TO YOU, HONORED MASTER, I BEQUEATH MY AMULET AND MY CLOAK OF LEVITATION!
NO MATTER WHAT BEFALLS, I SHALL BRING NO DISHONOR TO MY CALLING, TO MY TRUST, OR TO THE FAITH YOU HAVE PLACED IN ME!
MAY THE HOARY HAND OF HOGGOTH REST LIGHTLY ON THY BROW, MY SON! MAY THE ETERNAL EYE OF AGAMOTTO NE'ER TURN AWAY FROM THEE!
MY ILLNESS HAS SAPPED MY STRENGTH, DEVOTED ONE... SO ALL I CAN GIVE THEE IS MY BLESSING!
IT SHALL SUFFICE!
FACE ME, MORTAL! STAND READY TO MEET YOUR DEADLY DESTINY!
5.

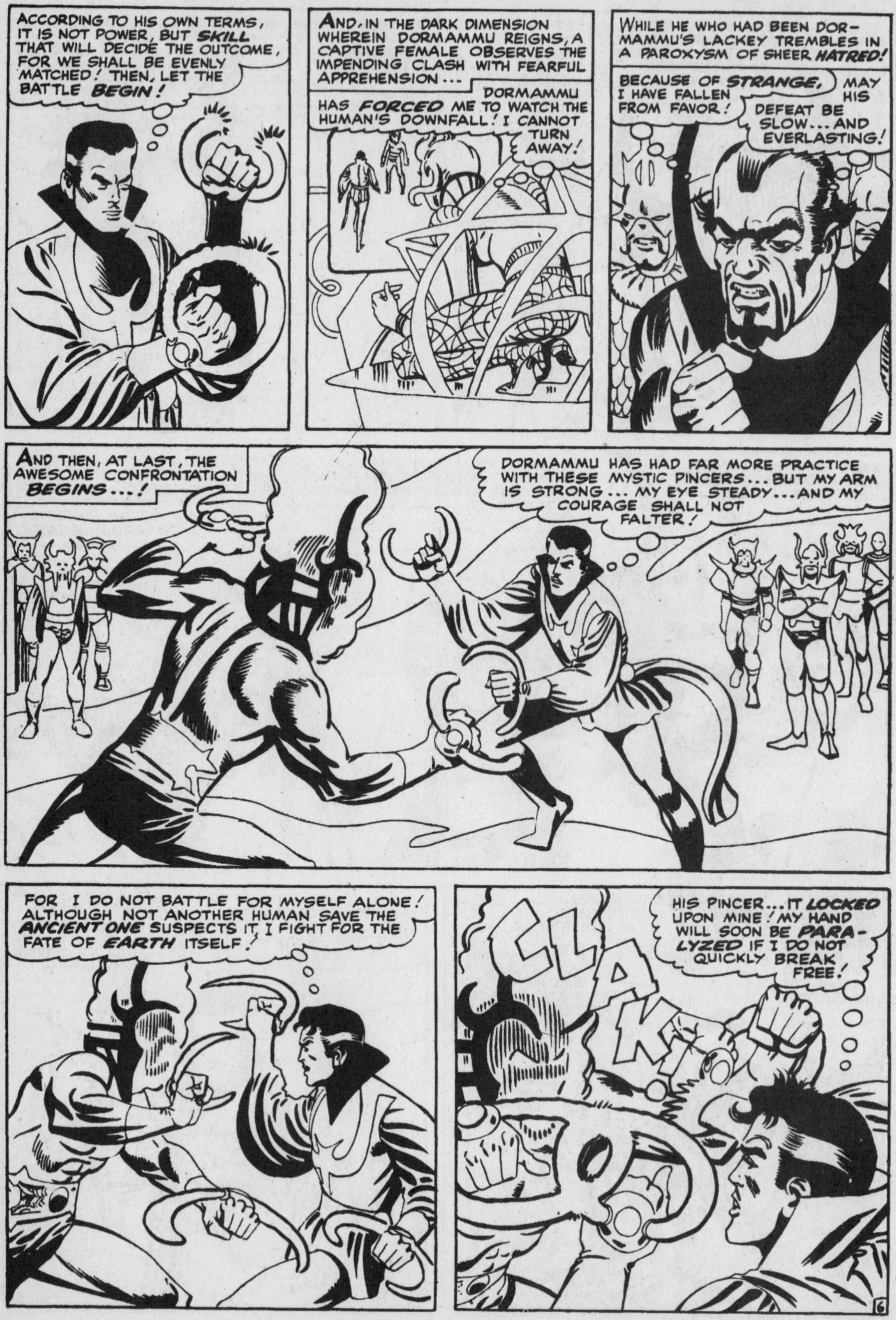
ACCORDING TO HIS OWN TERMS, IT IS NOT POWER, BUT SKILL THAT WILL DECIDE THE OUTCOME, FOR WE SHALL BE EVENLY MATCHED! THEN, LET THE BATTLE BEGIN!
AND, IN THE DARK DIMENSION WHEREIN DORMAMMU REIGNS, A CAPTIVE FEMALE OBSERVES THE IMPENDING CLASH WITH FEARFUL APPREHENSION...
DORMAMMU HAS FORCED ME TO WATCH THE HUMAN'S DOWNFALL! I CANNOT TURN AWAY!
WHILE HE WHO HAD BEEN DORMAMMU'S LACKEY TREMBLES IN A PAROXYSM OF SHEER HATRED!
BECAUSE OF STRANGE, I HAVE FALLEN FROM FAVOR!
MAY HIS DEFEAT BE SLOW... AND EVERLASTING!
AND THEN, AT LAST, THE AWESOME CONFRONTATION BEGINS...!
DORMAMMU HAS HAD FAR MORE PRACTICE WITH THESE MYSTIC PINCERS... BUT MY ARM IS STRONG... MY EYE STEADY... AND MY COURAGE SHALL NOT FALTER!
FOR I DO NOT BATTLE FOR MYSELF ALONE! ALTHOUGH NOT ANOTHER HUMAN SAVE THE ANCIENT ONE SUSPECTS IT, I FIGHT FOR THE FATE OF EARTH ITSELF!
CLAK!
HIS PINCER... IT LOCKED UPON MINE! MY HAND WILL SOON BE PARALYZED IF I DO NOT QUICKLY BREAK FREE!

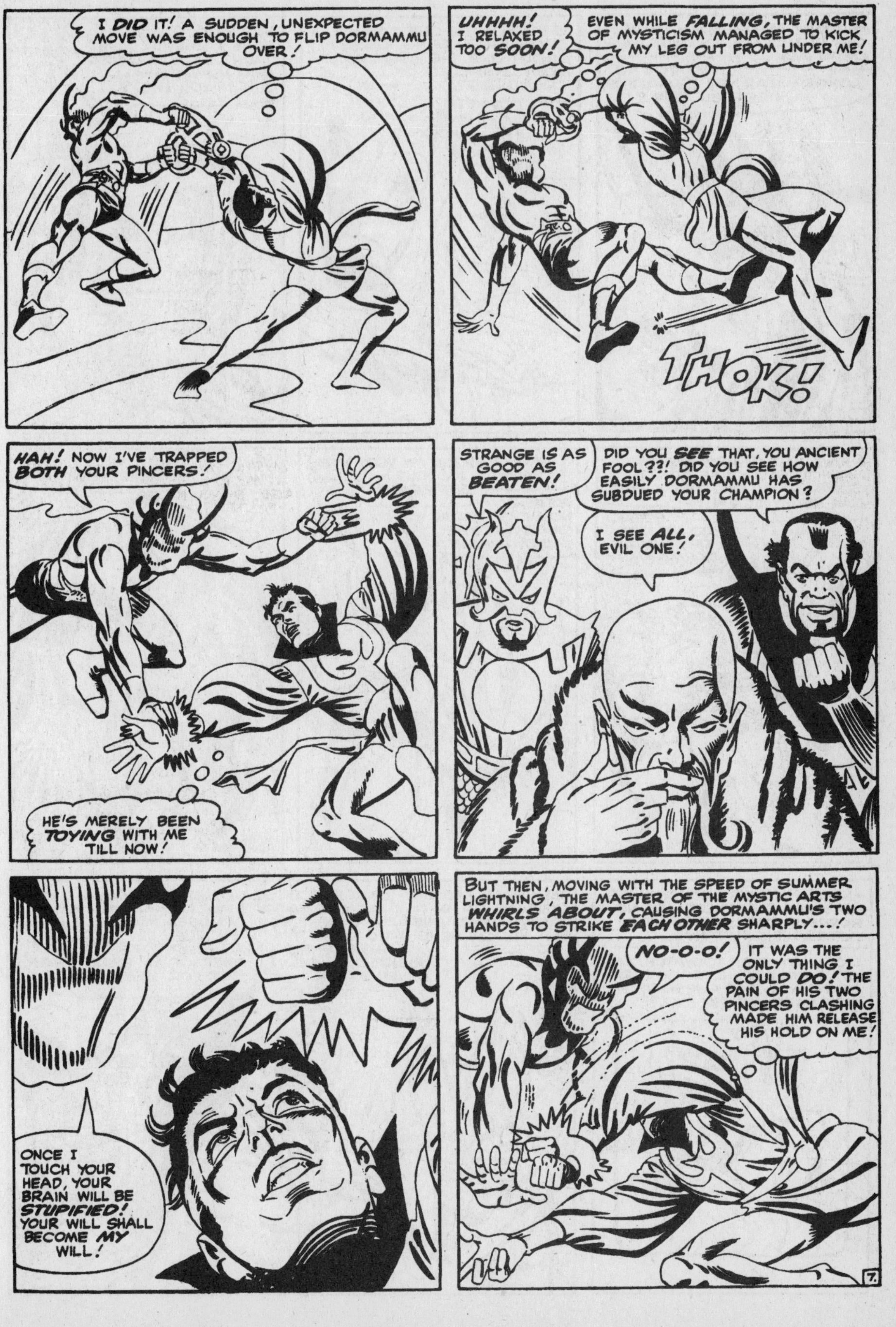

I DID IT! A SUDDEN, UNEXPECTED MOVE WAS ENOUGH TO FLIP DORMAMMU OVER!
UHHHH! I RELAXED TOO SOON!
EVEN WHILE FALLING, THE MASTER OF MYSTICISM MANAGED TO KICK MY LEG OUT FROM UNDER ME!
THOK!
HAH! NOW I'VE TRAPPED BOTH YOUR PINCERS!
HE'S MERELY BEEN TOYING WITH ME TILL NOW!
STRANGE IS AS GOOD AS BEATEN!
DID YOU SEE THAT, YOU ANCIENT FOOL??! DID YOU SEE HOW EASILY DORMAMMU HAS SUBDUED YOUR CHAMPION?
I SEE ALL, EVIL ONE!
ONCE I TOUCH YOUR HEAD, YOUR BRAIN WILL BE STUPIFIED! YOUR WILL SHALL BECOME MY WILL!
BUT THEN, MOVING WITH THE SPEED OF SUMMER LIGHTNING, THE MASTER OF THE MYSTIC ARTS WHIRLS ABOUT, CAUSING DORMAMMU'S TWO HANDS TO STRIKE EACH OTHER SHARPLY...!
NO-O-O!
IT WAS THE ONLY THING I COULD DO! THE PAIN OF HIS TWO PINCERS CLASHING MADE HIM RELEASE HIS HOLD ON ME!
7.

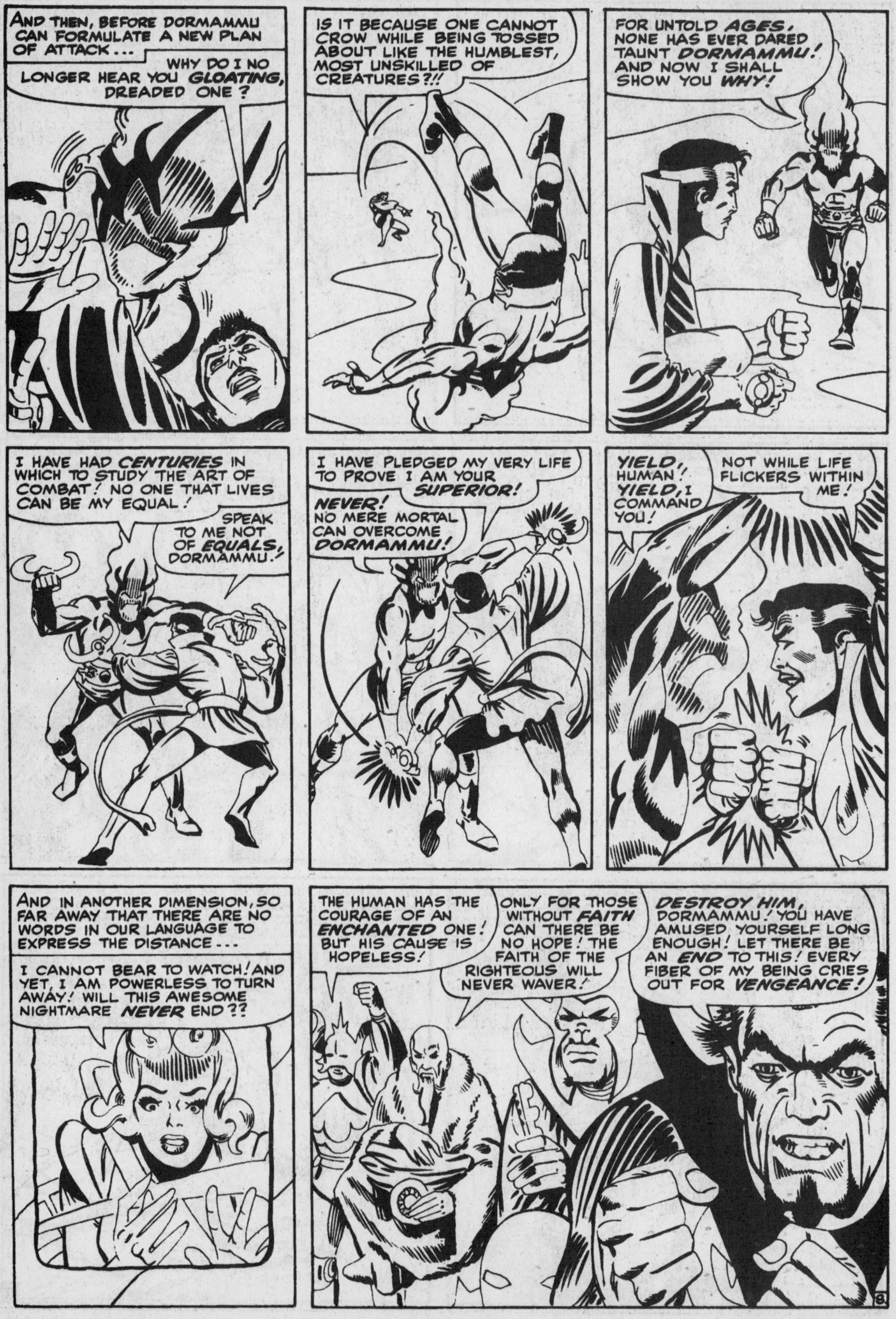
AND THEN, BEFORE DORMAMMU CAN FORMULATE A NEW PLAN OF ATTACK...
WHY DO I NO LONGER HEAR YOU GLOATING, DREADED ONE?
IS IT BECAUSE ONE CANNOT CROW WHILE BEING TOSSED ABOUT LIKE THE HUMBLEST, MOST UNSKILLED OF CREATURES?!!
FOR UNTOLD AGES, NONE HAS EVER DARED TAUNT DORMAMMU! AND NOW I SHALL SHOW YOU WHY!
I HAVE HAD CENTURIES IN WHICH TO STUDY THE ART OF COMBAT! NO ONE THAT LIVES CAN BE MY EQUAL!
SPEAK TO ME NOT OF EQUALS, DORMAMMU.!
I HAVE PLEDGED MY VERY LIFE TO PROVE I AM YOUR SUPERIOR!
NEVER! NO MERE MORTAL CAN OVERCOME DORMAMMU!
YIELD, HUMAN! YIELD, I COMMAND YOU!
NOT WHILE LIFE FLICKERS WITHIN ME!
AND IN ANOTHER DIMENSION, SO FAR AWAY THAT THERE ARE NO WORDS IN OUR LANGUAGE TO EXPRESS THE DISTANCE...
I CANNOT BEAR TO WATCH! AND YET, I AM POWERLESS TO TURN AWAY! WILL THIS AWESOME NIGHTMARE NEVER END??
THE HUMAN HAS THE COURAGE OF AN ENCHANTED ONE! BUT HIS CAUSE IS HOPELESS!
ONLY FOR THOSE WITHOUT FAITH CAN THERE BE NO HOPE! THE FAITH OF THE RIGHTEOUS WILL NEVER WAVER!
DESTROY HIM, DORMAMMU! YOU HAVE AMUSED YOURSELF LONG ENOUGH! LET THERE BE AN END TO THIS! EVERY FIBER OF MY BEING CRIES OUT FOR VENGEANCE!
8

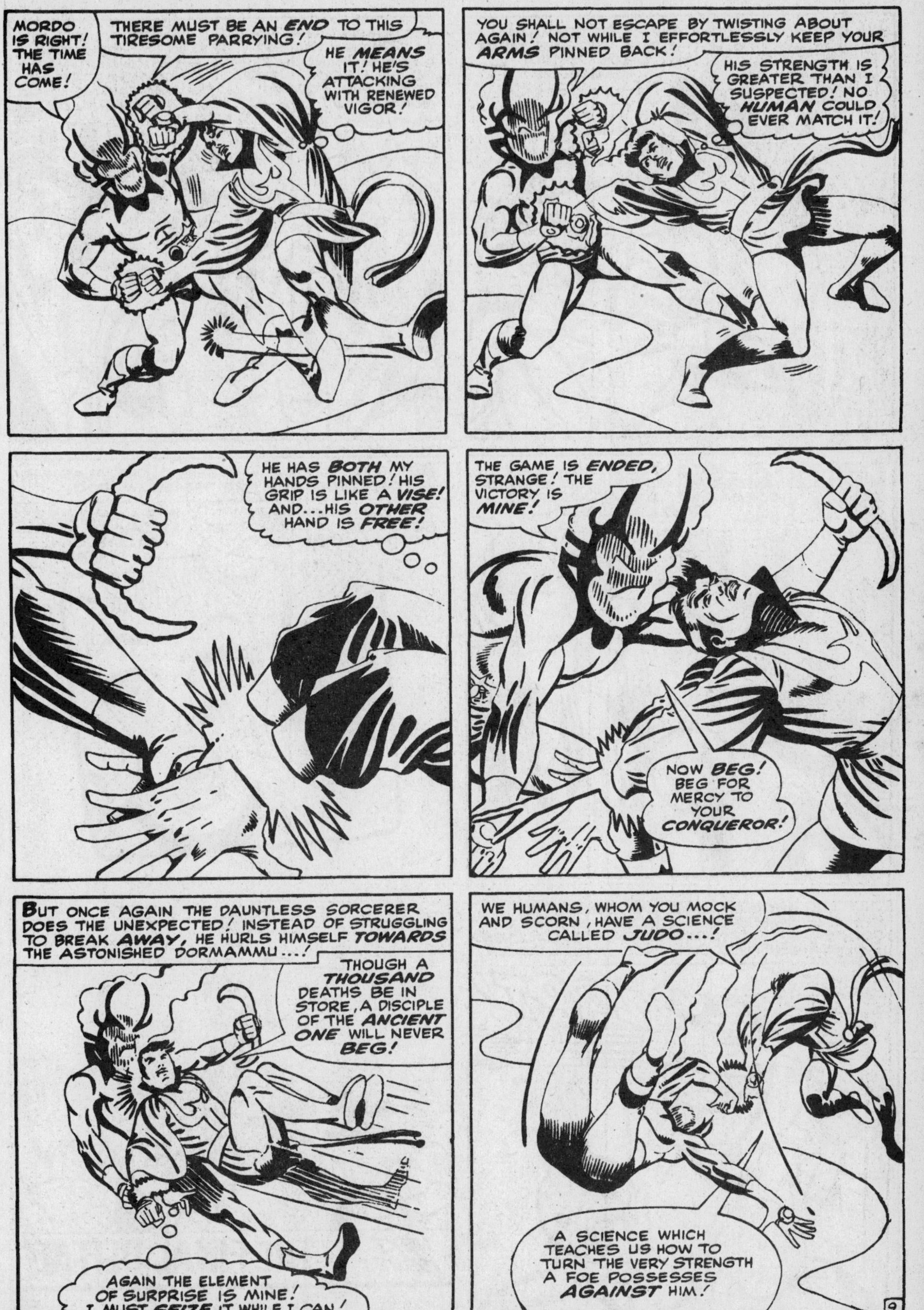
MORDO IS RIGHT! THE TIME HAS COME!
THERE MUST BE AN END TO THIS TIRESOME PARRYING!
HE MEANS IT! HE'S ATTACKING WITH RENEWED VIGOR!
YOU SHALL NOT ESCAPE BY TWISTING ABOUT AGAIN! NOT WHILE I EFFORTLESSLY KEEP YOUR ARMS PINNED BACK!
HIS STRENGTH IS GREATER THAN I SUSPECTED! NO HUMAN COULD EVER MATCH IT!
HE HAS BOTH MY HANDS PINNED! HIS GRIP IS LIKE A VISE! AND...HIS OTHER HAND IS FREE!
THE GAME IS ENDED, STRANGE! THE VICTORY IS MINE!
NOW BEG! BEG FOR MERCY TO YOUR CONQUEROR!
BUT ONCE AGAIN THE DAUNTLESS SORCERER DOES THE UNEXPECTED! INSTEAD OF STRUGGLING TO BREAK AWAY, HE HURLS HIMSELF TOWARDS THE ASTONISHED DORMAMMU...!
THOUGH A THOUSAND DEATHS BE IN STORE, A DISCIPLE OF THE ANCIENT ONE WILL NEVER BEG!
AGAIN THE ELEMENT OF SURPRISE IS MINE! I MUST SEIZE IT WHILE I CAN!
WE HUMANS, WHOM YOU MOCK AND SCORN, HAVE A SCIENCE CALLED JUDO...!
A SCIENCE WHICH TEACHES US HOW TO TURN THE VERY STRENGTH A FOE POSSESSES AGAINST HIM!
9.

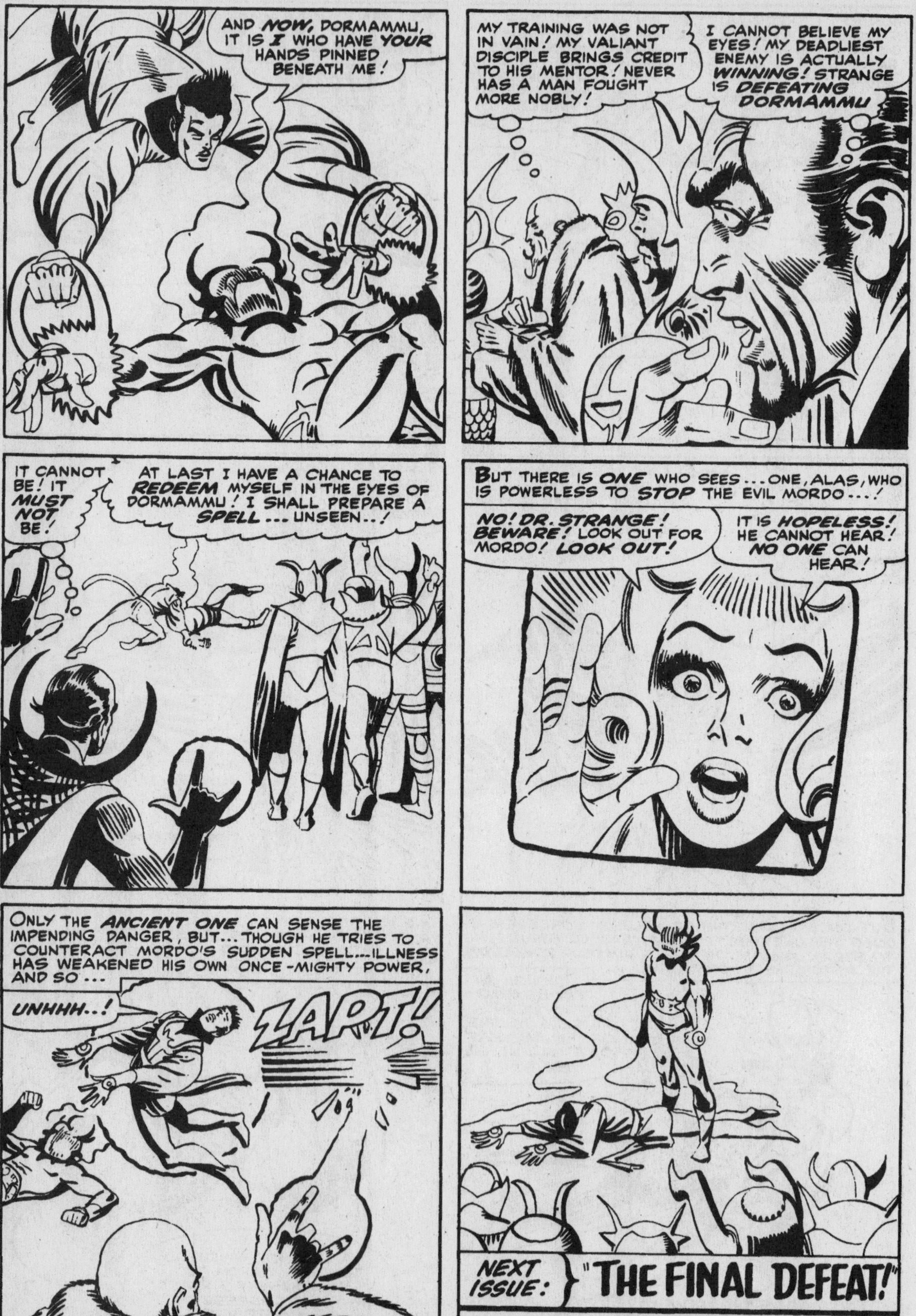
AND NOW, DORMAMMU, IT IS I WHO HAVE YOUR HANDS PINNED BENEATH ME!
MY TRAINING WAS NOT IN VAIN! MY VALIANT DISCIPLE BRINGS CREDIT TO HIS MENTOR! NEVER HAS A MAN FOUGHT MORE NOBLY!
I CANNOT BELIEVE MY EYES! MY DEADLIEST ENEMY IS ACTUALLY WINNING! STRANGE IS DEFEATING DORMAMMU!
IT CANNOT BE! IT MUST NOT BE!
AT LAST I HAVE A CHANCE TO REDEEM MYSELF IN THE EYES OF DORMAMMU! I SHALL PREPARE A SPELL... UNSEEN..!
BUT THERE IS ONE WHO SEES... ONE, ALAS, WHO IS POWERLESS TO STOP THE EVIL MORDO...!
NO! DR. STRANGE! BEWARE! LOOK OUT FOR MORDO! LOOK OUT!
IT IS HOPELESS! HE CANNOT HEAR! NO ONE CAN HEAR!
ONLY THE ANCIENT ONE CAN SENSE THE IMPENDING DANGER, BUT... THOUGH HE TRIES TO COUNTERACT MORDO'S SUDDEN SPELL... ILLNESS HAS WEAKENED HIS OWN ONCE-MIGHTY POWER, AND SO...
UNHHH..!
ZAPT!
NEXT ISSUE: "THE FINAL DEFEAT!"
10

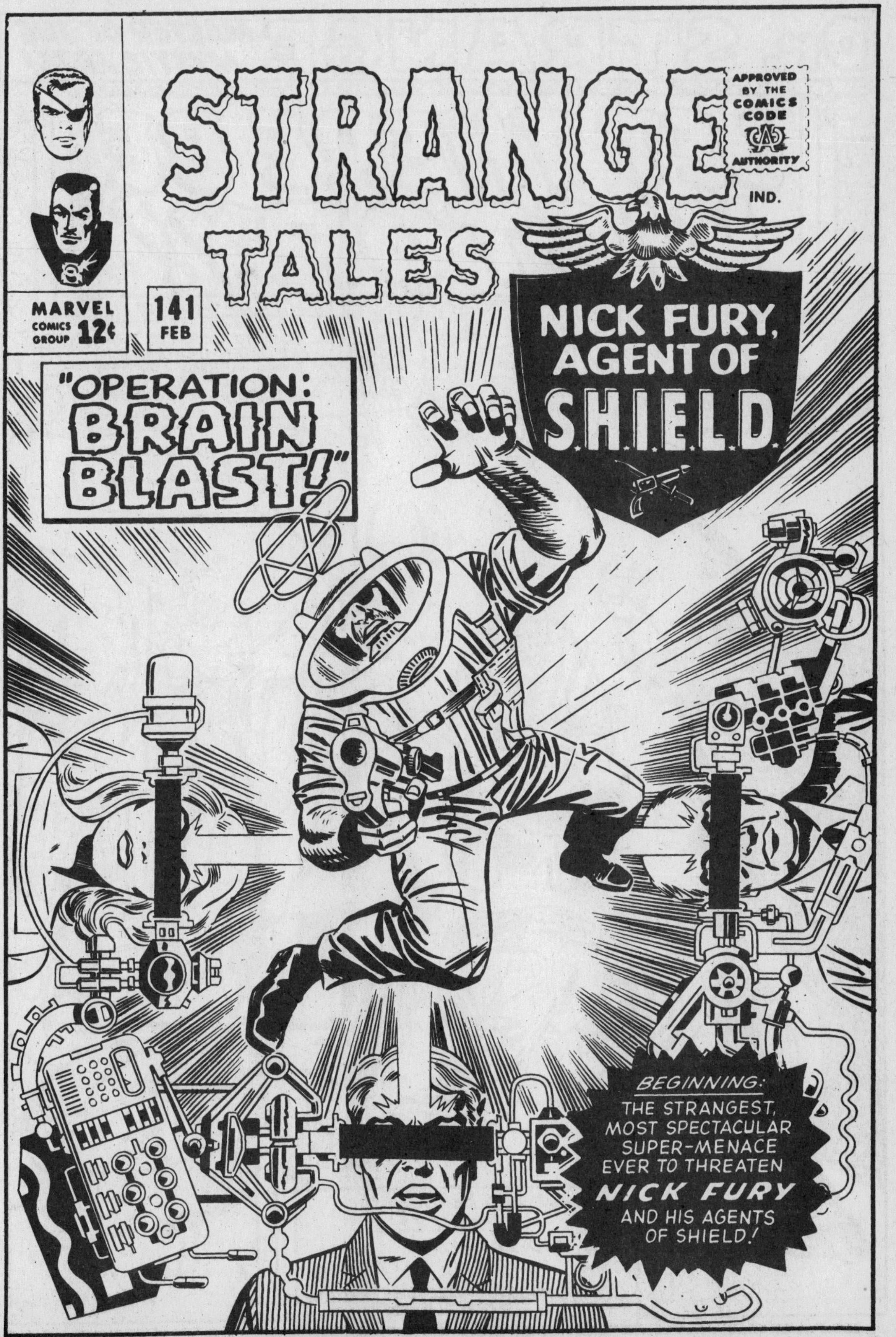
STRANGE TALES
APPROVED BY THE COMICS CODE CA AUTHORITY
IND.
MARVEL COMICS GROUP 12¢
141 FEB
NICK FURY, AGENT OF S.H.I.E.L.D.
"OPERATION: BRAIN BLAST!"
BEGINNING: THE STRANGEST, MOST SPECTACULAR SUPER-MENACE EVER TO THREATEN NICK FURY AND HIS AGENTS OF SHIELD!

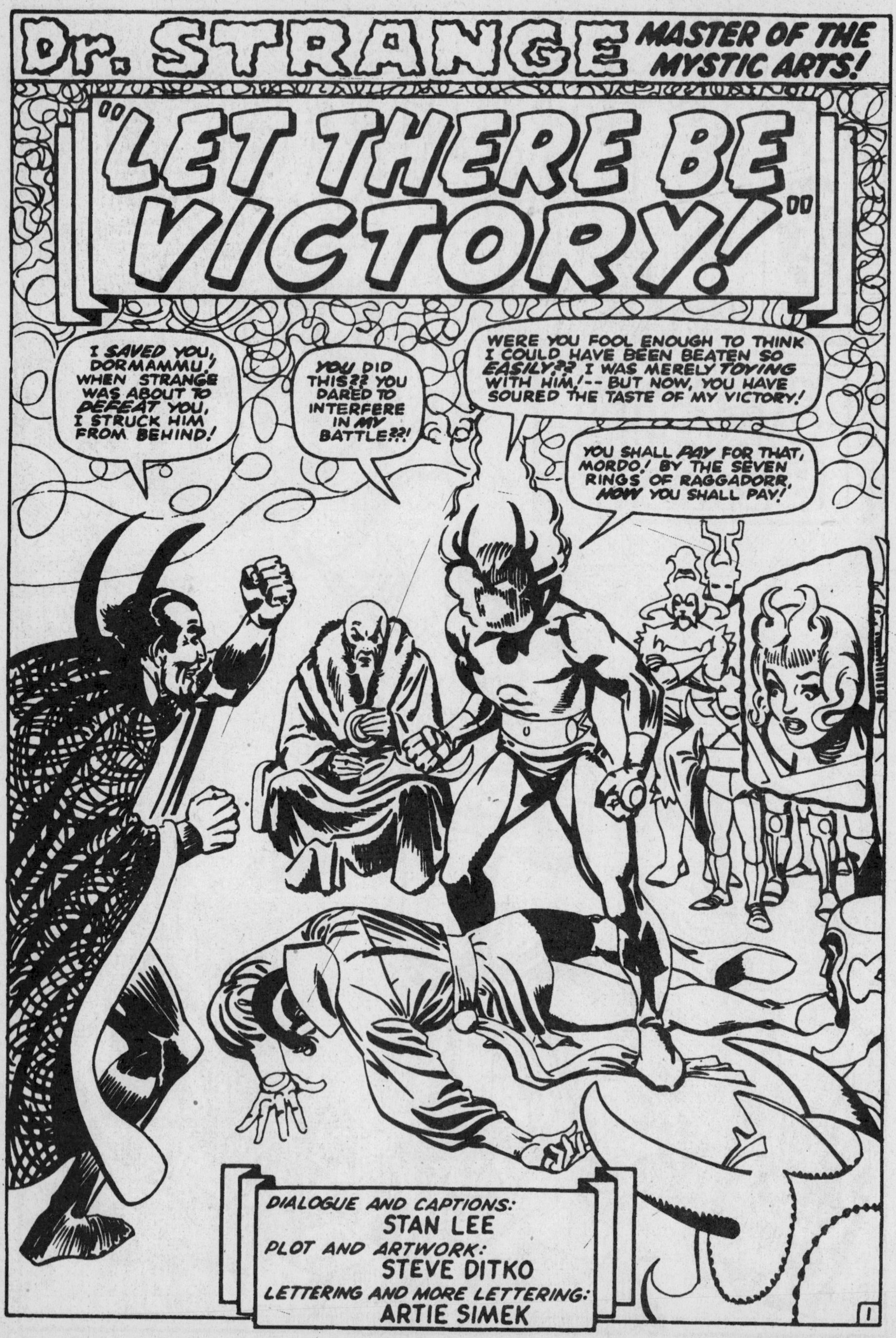
Dr. STRANGE MASTER OF THE MYSTIC ARTS!
"LET THERE BE VICTORY!"
I SAVED YOU, DORMAMMU! WHEN STRANGE WAS ABOUT TO DEFEAT YOU, I STRUCK HIM FROM BEHIND!
YOU DID THIS?? YOU DARED TO INTERFERE IN MY BATTLE??!
WERE YOU FOOL ENOUGH TO THINK I COULD HAVE BEEN BEATEN SO EASILY?? I WAS MERELY TOYING WITH HIM!-- BUT NOW, YOU HAVE SOURED THE TASTE OF MY VICTORY!
YOU SHALL PAY FOR THAT, MORDO! BY THE SEVEN RINGS OF RAGGADORR, NOW YOU SHALL PAY!
DIALOGUE AND CAPTIONS: STAN LEE
PLOT AND ARTWORK: STEVE DITKO
LETTERING AND MORE LETTERING: ARTIE SIMEK
1

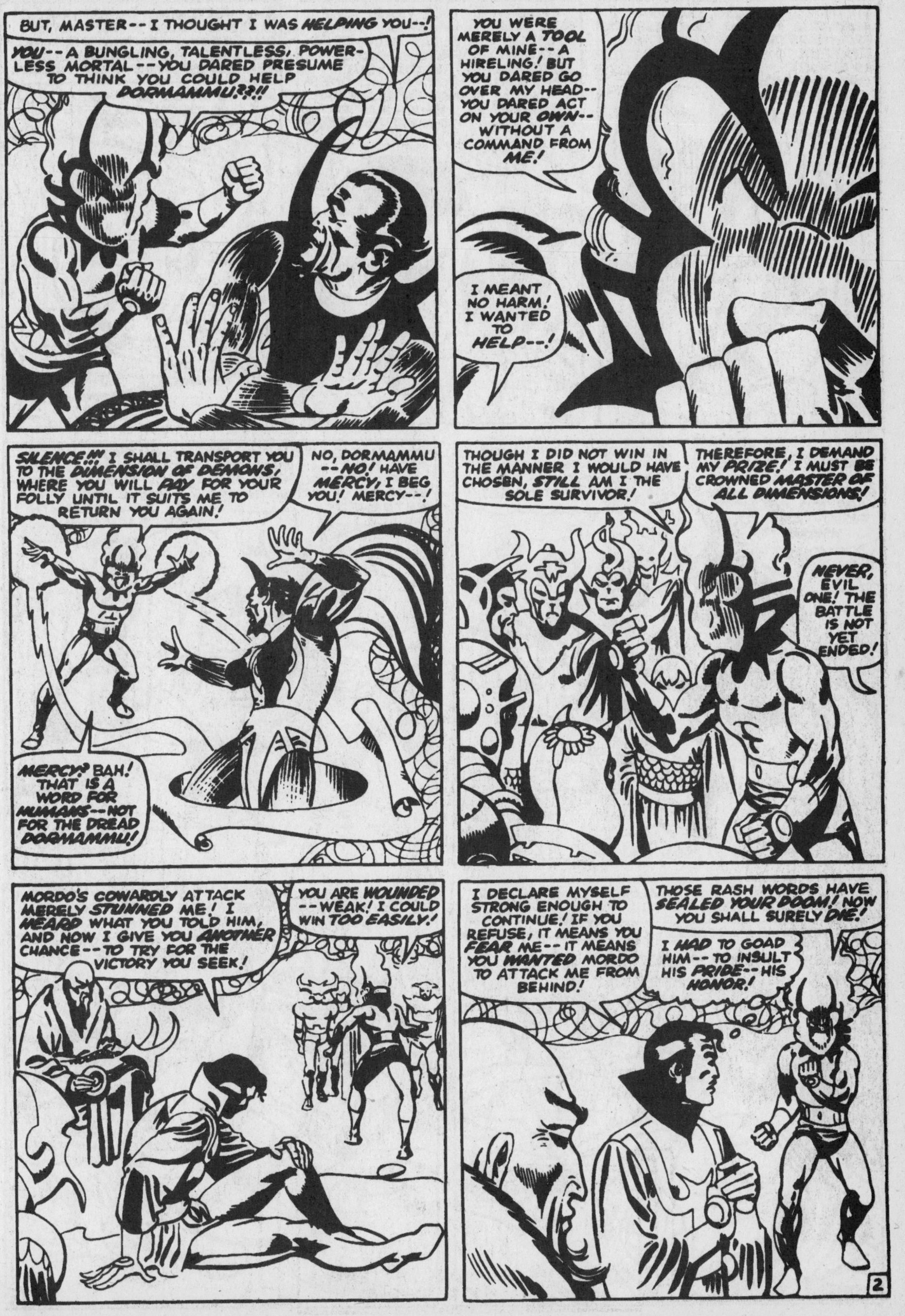
BUT, MASTER-- I THOUGHT I WAS HELPING YOU--!
YOU-- A BUNGLING, TALENTLESS, POWERLESS MORTAL--YOU DARED PRESUME TO THINK YOU COULD HELP DORMAMMU??!!
YOU WERE MERELY A TOOL OF MINE-- A HIRELING! BUT YOU DARED GO OVER MY HEAD-- YOU DARED ACT ON YOUR OWN-- WITHOUT A COMMAND FROM ME!
I MEANT NO HARM! I WANTED TO HELP--!
SILENCE!!! I SHALL TRANSPORT YOU TO THE DIMENSION OF DEMONS, WHERE YOU WILL PAY FOR YOUR FOLLY UNTIL IT SUITS ME TO RETURN YOU AGAIN!
NO, DORMAMMU --NO! HAVE MERCY, I BEG YOU! MERCY--!
MERCY? BAH! THAT IS A WORD FOR HUMANS--NOT FOR THE DREAD DORMAMMU!
THOUGH I DID NOT WIN IN THE MANNER I WOULD HAVE CHOSEN, STILL AM I THE SOLE SURVIVOR!
THEREFORE, I DEMAND MY PRIZE! I MUST BE CROWNED MASTER OF ALL DIMENSIONS!
NEVER, EVIL ONE! THE BATTLE IS NOT YET ENDED!
MORDO'S COWARDLY ATTACK MERELY STUNNED ME! I HEARD WHAT YOU TOLD HIM, AND NOW I GIVE YOU ANOTHER CHANCE--TO TRY FOR THE VICTORY YOU SEEK!
YOU ARE WOUNDED --WEAK! I COULD WIN TOO EASILY!
I DECLARE MYSELF STRONG ENOUGH TO CONTINUE! IF YOU REFUSE, IT MEANS YOU FEAR ME-- IT MEANS YOU WANTED MORDO TO ATTACK ME FROM BEHIND!
THOSE RASH WORDS HAVE SEALED YOUR DOOM! NOW YOU SHALL SURELY DIE!
I HAD TO GOAD HIM-- TO INSULT HIS PRIDE-- HIS HONOR!

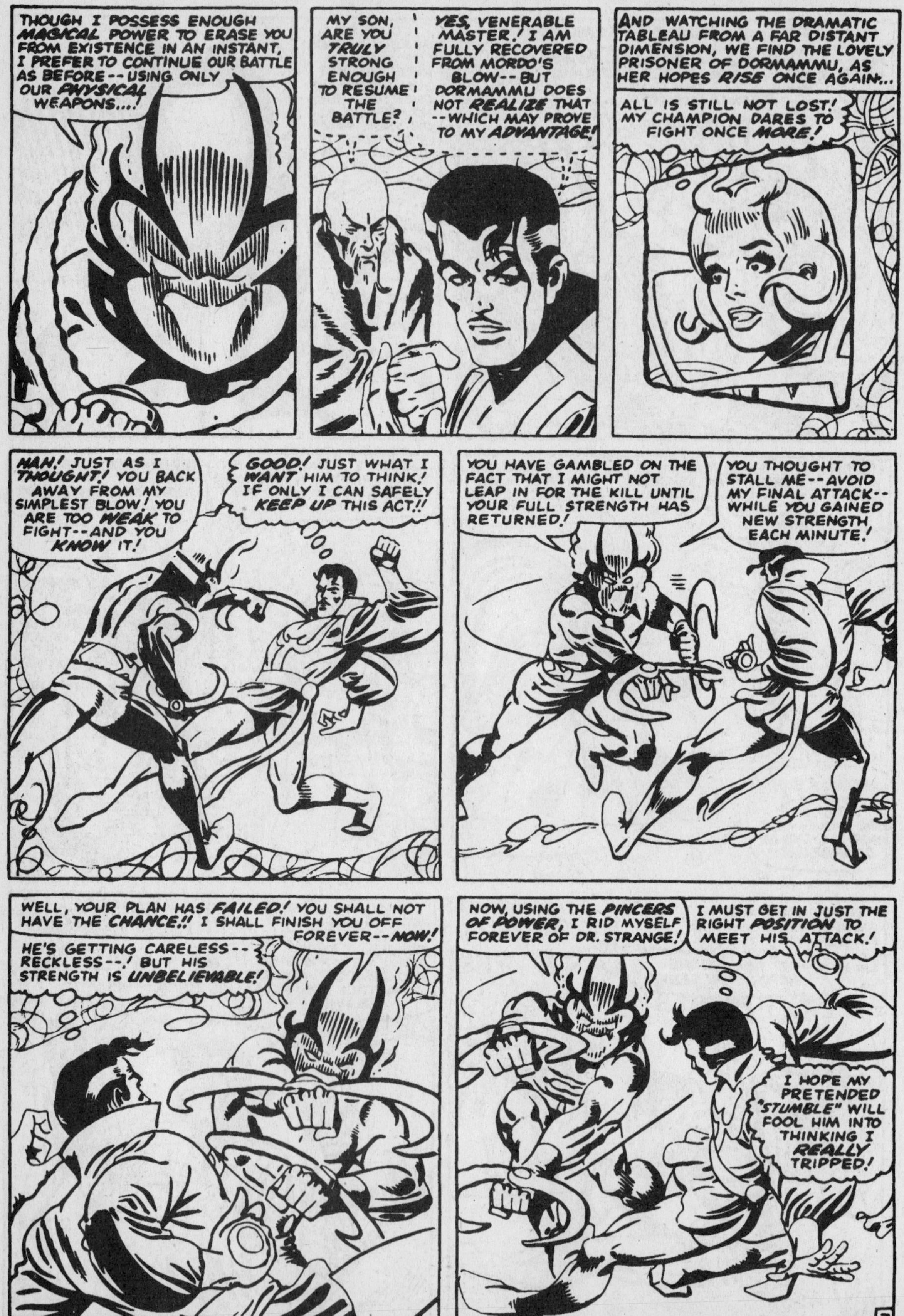
THOUGH I POSSESS ENOUGH MAGICAL POWER TO ERASE YOU FROM EXISTENCE IN AN INSTANT, I PREFER TO CONTINUE OUR BATTLE AS BEFORE--USING ONLY OUR PHYSICAL WEAPONS...!
MY SON, ARE YOU TRULY STRONG ENOUGH TO RESUME THE BATTLE?
YES, VENERABLE MASTER! I AM FULLY RECOVERED FROM MORDO'S BLOW--BUT DORMAMMU DOES NOT REALIZE THAT--WHICH MAY PROVE TO MY ADVANTAGE!
AND WATCHING THE DRAMATIC TABLEAU FROM A FAR DISTANT DIMENSION, WE FIND THE LOVELY PRISONER OF DORMAMMU, AS HER HOPES RISE ONCE AGAIN...
ALL IS STILL NOT LOST! MY CHAMPION DARES TO FIGHT ONCE MORE!
HAH! JUST AS I THOUGHT! YOU BACK AWAY FROM MY SIMPLEST BLOW! YOU ARE TOO WEAK TO FIGHT--AND YOU KNOW IT!
GOOD! JUST WHAT I WANT HIM TO THINK! IF ONLY I CAN SAFELY KEEP UP THIS ACT!!
YOU HAVE GAMBLED ON THE FACT THAT I MIGHT NOT LEAP IN FOR THE KILL UNTIL YOUR FULL STRENGTH HAS RETURNED!
YOU THOUGHT TO STALL ME--AVOID MY FINAL ATTACK--WHILE YOU GAINED NEW STRENGTH EACH MINUTE!
WELL, YOUR PLAN HAS FAILED! YOU SHALL NOT HAVE THE CHANCE!! I SHALL FINISH YOU OFF FOREVER--NOW!
HE'S GETTING CARELESS--RECKLESS--! BUT HIS STRENGTH IS UNBELIEVABLE!
NOW, USING THE PINCERS OF POWER, I RID MYSELF FOREVER OF DR. STRANGE!
I MUST GET IN JUST THE RIGHT POSITION TO MEET HIS ATTACK!
I HOPE MY PRETENDED "STUMBLE" WILL FOOL HIM INTO THINKING I REALLY TRIPPED!
3

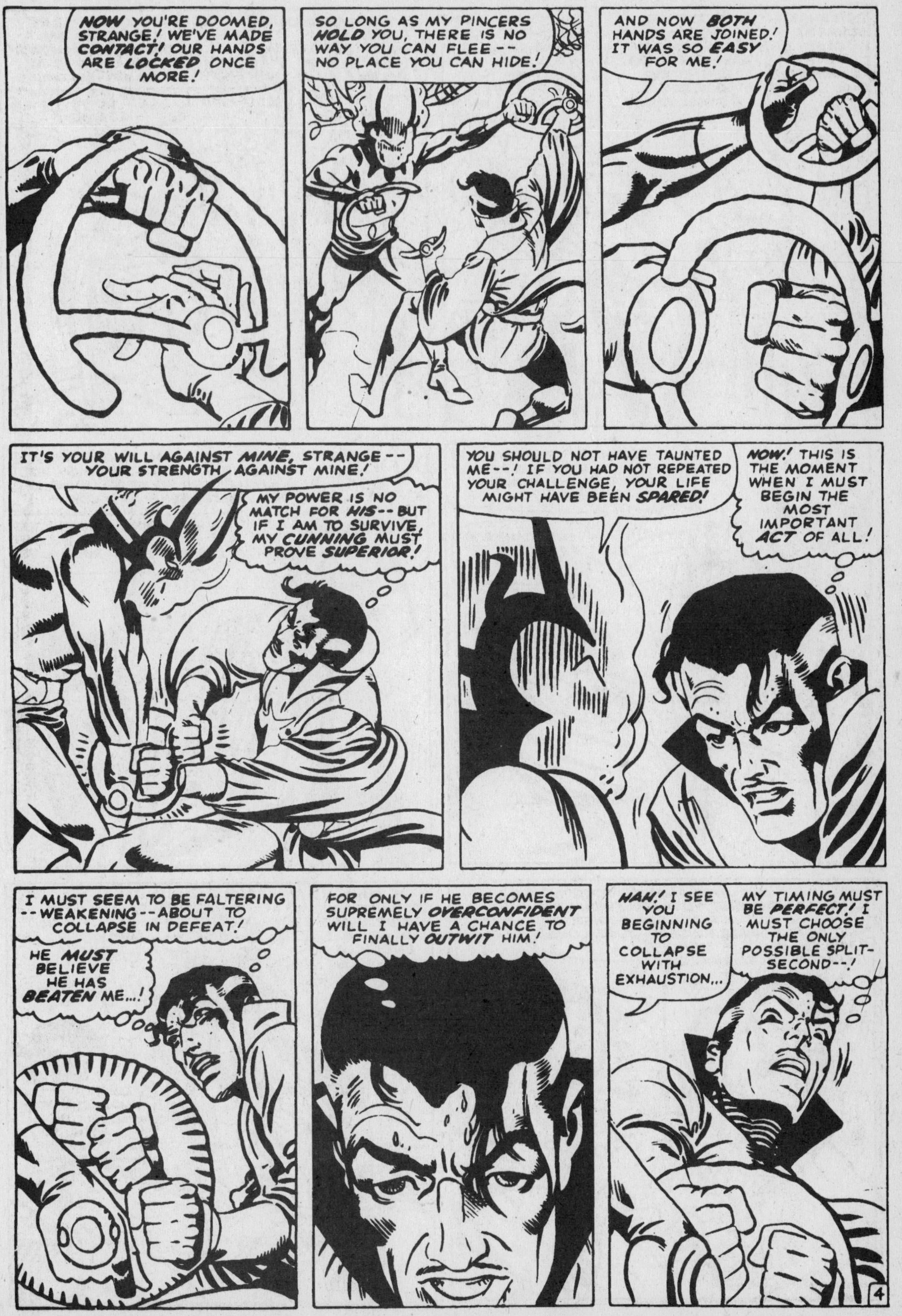
NOW YOU'RE DOOMED, STRANGE! WE'VE MADE CONTACT! OUR HANDS ARE LOCKED ONCE MORE!
SO LONG AS MY PINCERS HOLD YOU, THERE IS NO WAY YOU CAN FLEE -- NO PLACE YOU CAN HIDE!
AND NOW BOTH HANDS ARE JOINED! IT WAS SO EASY FOR ME!
IT'S YOUR WILL AGAINST MINE, STRANGE -- YOUR STRENGTH AGAINST MINE!
MY POWER IS NO MATCH FOR HIS -- BUT IF I AM TO SURVIVE, MY CUNNING MUST PROVE SUPERIOR!
YOU SHOULD NOT HAVE TAUNTED ME --! IF YOU HAD NOT REPEATED YOUR CHALLENGE, YOUR LIFE MIGHT HAVE BEEN SPARED!
NOW! THIS IS THE MOMENT WHEN I MUST BEGIN THE MOST IMPORTANT ACT OF ALL!
I MUST SEEM TO BE FALTERING -- WEAKENING -- ABOUT TO COLLAPSE IN DEFEAT!
HE MUST BELIEVE HE HAS BEATEN ME...!
FOR ONLY IF HE BECOMES SUPREMELY OVERCONFIDENT WILL I HAVE A CHANCE TO FINALLY OUTWIT HIM!
HAH! I SEE YOU BEGINNING TO COLLAPSE WITH EXHAUSTION...
MY TIMING MUST BE PERFECT! I MUST CHOOSE THE ONLY POSSIBLE SPLIT-SECOND--!
4

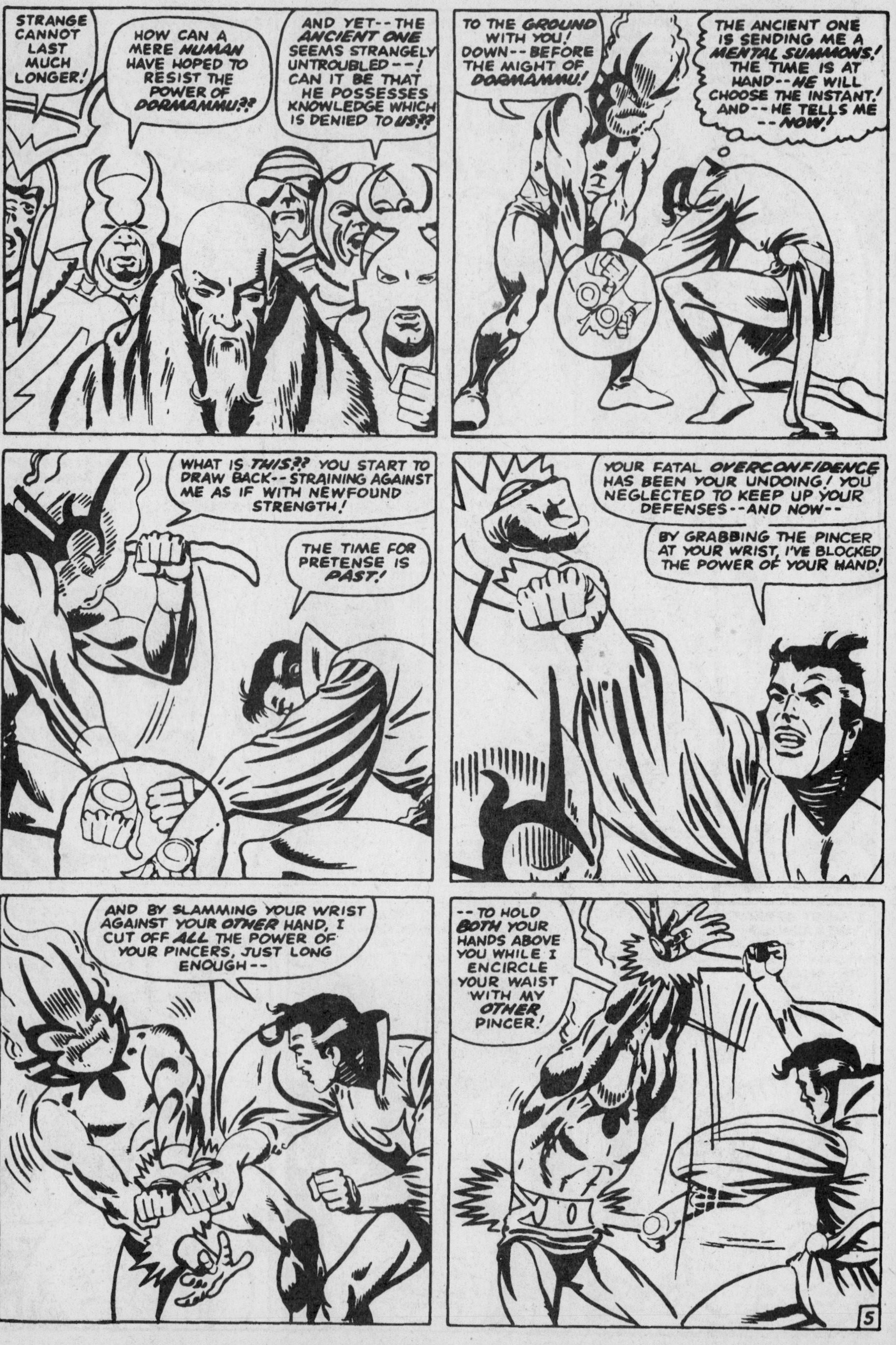
STRANGE CANNOT LAST MUCH LONGER!
HOW CAN A MERE HUMAN HAVE HOPED TO RESIST THE POWER OF DORMAMMU??
AND YET--THE ANCIENT ONE SEEMS STRANGELY UNTROUBLED--! CAN IT BE THAT HE POSSESSES KNOWLEDGE WHICH IS DENIED TO US??
TO THE GROUND WITH YOU! DOWN--BEFORE THE MIGHT OF DORMAMMU!
THE ANCIENT ONE IS SENDING ME A MENTAL SUMMONS! THE TIME IS AT HAND--HE WILL CHOOSE THE INSTANT! AND--HE TELLS ME --NOW!
WHAT IS THIS?? YOU START TO DRAW BACK--STRAINING AGAINST ME AS IF WITH NEWFOUND STRENGTH!
THE TIME FOR PRETENSE IS PAST!
YOUR FATAL OVERCONFIDENCE HAS BEEN YOUR UNDOING! YOU NEGLECTED TO KEEP UP YOUR DEFENSES--AND NOW--
BY GRABBING THE PINCER AT YOUR WRIST, I'VE BLOCKED THE POWER OF YOUR HAND!
AND BY SLAMMING YOUR WRIST AGAINST YOUR OTHER HAND, I CUT OFF ALL THE POWER OF YOUR PINCERS, JUST LONG ENOUGH--
--TO HOLD BOTH YOUR HANDS ABOVE YOU WHILE I ENCIRCLE YOUR WAIST WITH MY OTHER PINCER!
5

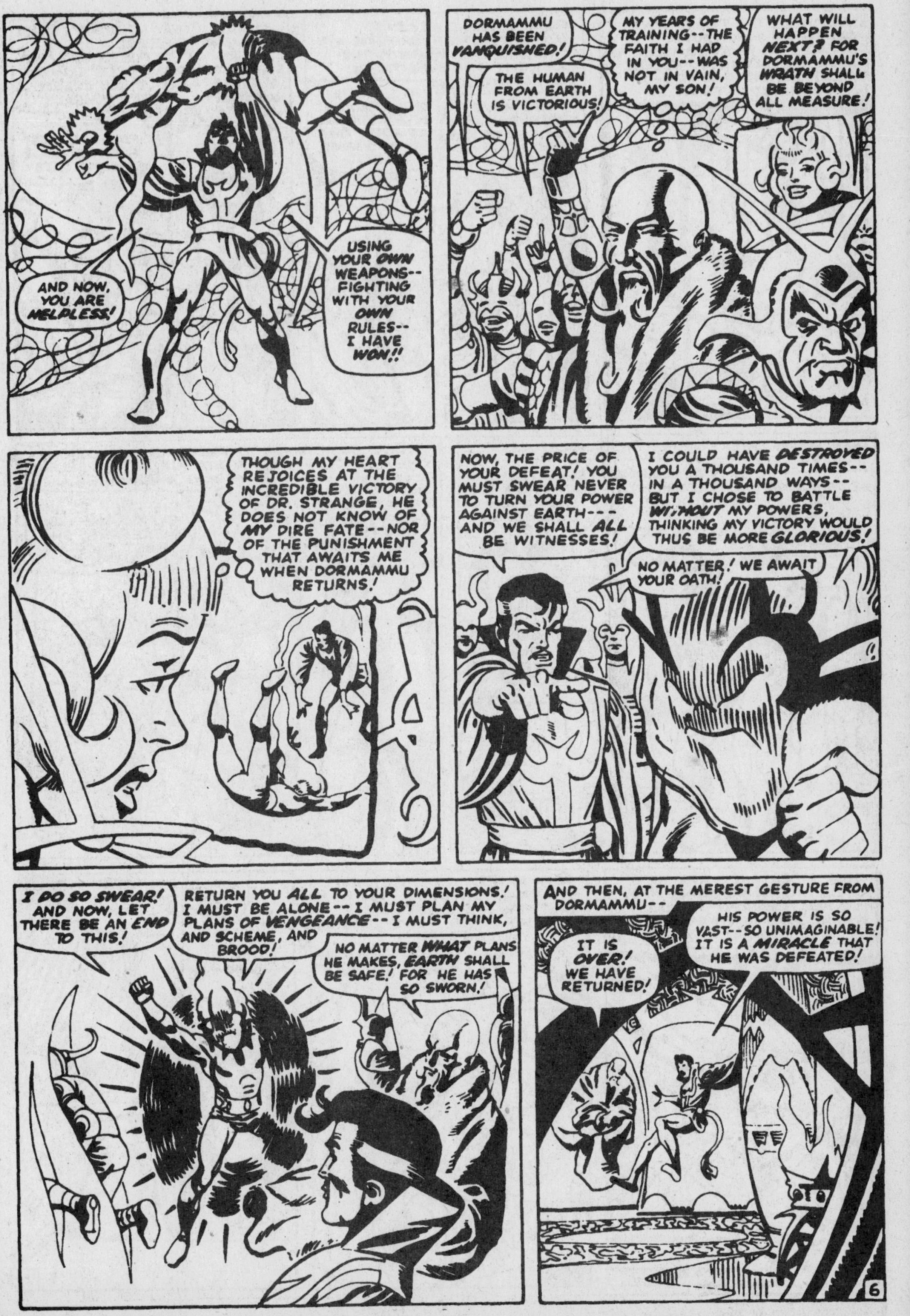
AND NOW, YOU ARE HELPLESS!
USING YOUR OWN WEAPONS-- FIGHTING WITH YOUR OWN RULES-- I HAVE WON!!
DORMAMMU HAS BEEN VANQUISHED!
THE HUMAN FROM EARTH IS VICTORIOUS!
MY YEARS OF TRAINING--THE FAITH I HAD IN YOU--WAS NOT IN VAIN, MY SON!
WHAT WILL HAPPEN NEXT? FOR DORMAMMU'S WRATH SHALL BE BEYOND ALL MEASURE!
THOUGH MY HEART REJOICES AT THE INCREDIBLE VICTORY OF DR. STRANGE, HE DOES NOT KNOW OF MY DIRE FATE--NOR OF THE PUNISHMENT THAT AWAITS ME WHEN DORMAMMU RETURNS!
NOW, THE PRICE OF YOUR DEFEAT! YOU MUST SWEAR NEVER TO TURN YOUR POWER AGAINST EARTH--- AND WE SHALL ALL BE WITNESSES!
I COULD HAVE DESTROYED YOU A THOUSAND TIMES-- IN A THOUSAND WAYS-- BUT I CHOSE TO BATTLE WITHOUT MY POWERS, THINKING MY VICTORY WOULD THUS BE MORE GLORIOUS!
NO MATTER! WE AWAIT YOUR OATH!
I DO SO SWEAR! AND NOW, LET THERE BE AN END TO THIS!
RETURN YOU ALL TO YOUR DIMENSIONS! I MUST BE ALONE--I MUST PLAN MY PLANS OF VENGEANCE--I MUST THINK, AND SCHEME, AND BROOD!
NO MATTER WHAT PLANS HE MAKES, EARTH SHALL BE SAFE! FOR HE HAS SO SWORN!
AND THEN, AT THE MEREST GESTURE FROM DORMAMMU--
IT IS OVER! WE HAVE RETURNED!
HIS POWER IS SO VAST--SO UNIMAGINABLE! IT IS A MIRACLE THAT HE WAS DEFEATED!
6

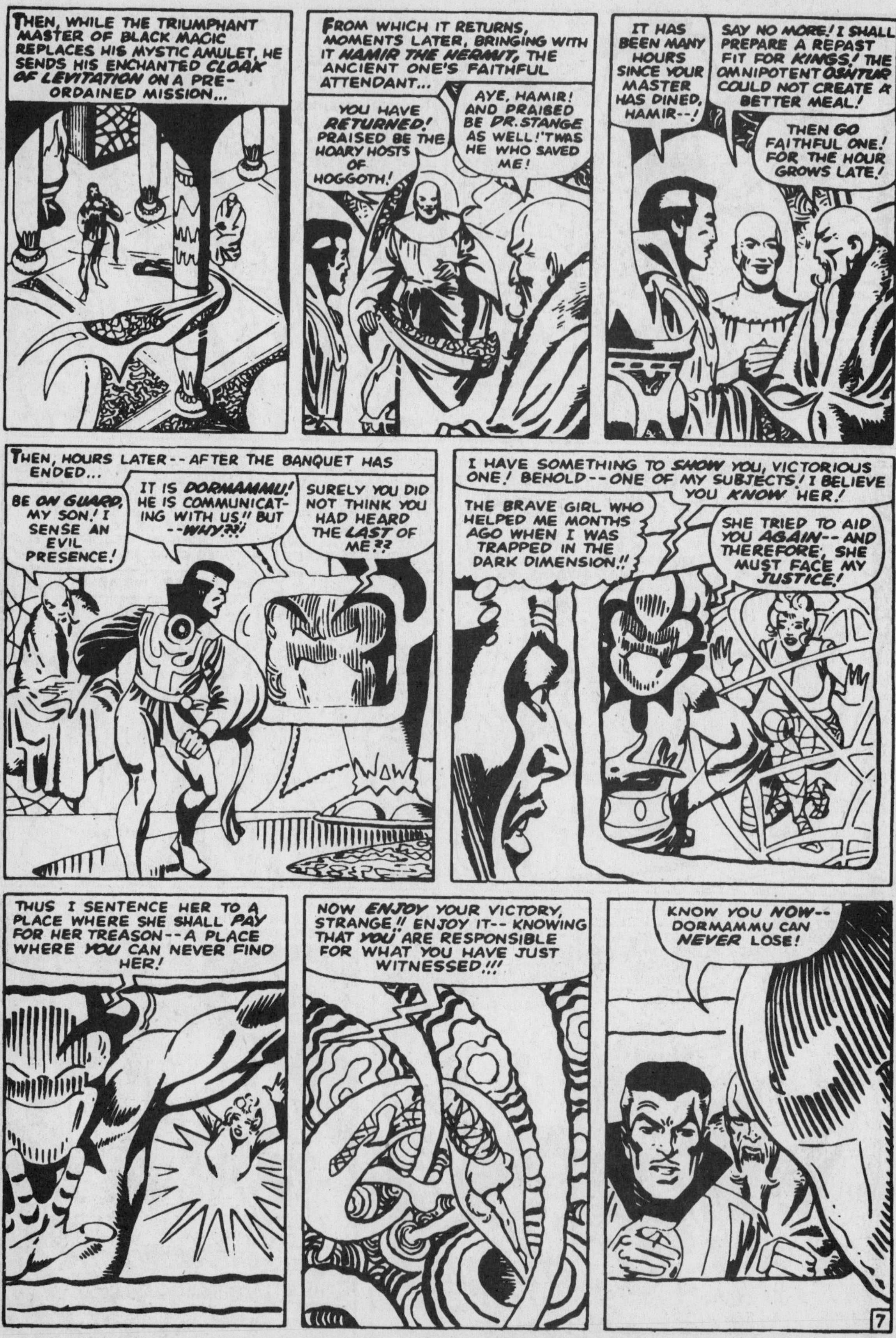
THEN, WHILE THE TRIUMPHANT MASTER OF BLACK MAGIC REPLACES HIS MYSTIC AMULET, HE SENDS HIS ENCHANTED CLOAK OF LEVITATION ON A PRE-ORDAINED MISSION...
FROM WHICH IT RETURNS, MOMENTS LATER, BRINGING WITH IT HAMIR THE HERMIT, THE ANCIENT ONE'S FAITHFUL ATTENDANT...
YOU HAVE RETURNED! PRAISED BE THE HOARY HOSTS OF HOGGOTH!
AYE, HAMIR! AND PRAISED BE DR. STANGE AS WELL! 'TWAS HE WHO SAVED ME!
IT HAS BEEN MANY HOURS SINCE YOUR MASTER HAS DINED, HAMIR--!
SAY NO MORE! I SHALL PREPARE A REPAST FIT FOR KINGS! THE OMNIPOTENT OSHTUR COULD NOT CREATE A BETTER MEAL!
THEN GO FAITHFUL ONE! FOR THE HOUR GROWS LATE!
THEN, HOURS LATER--AFTER THE BANQUET HAS ENDED...
BE ON GUARD, MY SON! I SENSE AN EVIL PRESENCE!
IT IS DORMAMMU! HE IS COMMUNICATING WITH US!! BUT --WHY??!
SURELY YOU DID NOT THINK YOU HAD HEARD THE LAST OF ME??
I HAVE SOMETHING TO SHOW YOU, VICTORIOUS ONE! BEHOLD--ONE OF MY SUBJECTS! I BELIEVE YOU KNOW HER!
THE BRAVE GIRL WHO HELPED ME MONTHS AGO WHEN I WAS TRAPPED IN THE DARK DIMENSION!!
SHE TRIED TO AID YOU AGAIN--AND THEREFORE, SHE MUST FACE MY JUSTICE!
THUS I SENTENCE HER TO A PLACE WHERE SHE SHALL PAY FOR HER TREASON--A PLACE WHERE YOU CAN NEVER FIND HER!
NOW ENJOY YOUR VICTORY, STRANGE!! ENJOY IT--KNOWING THAT YOU ARE RESPONSIBLE FOR WHAT YOU HAVE JUST WITNESSED!!!
KNOW YOU NOW--DORMAMMU CAN NEVER LOSE!
7

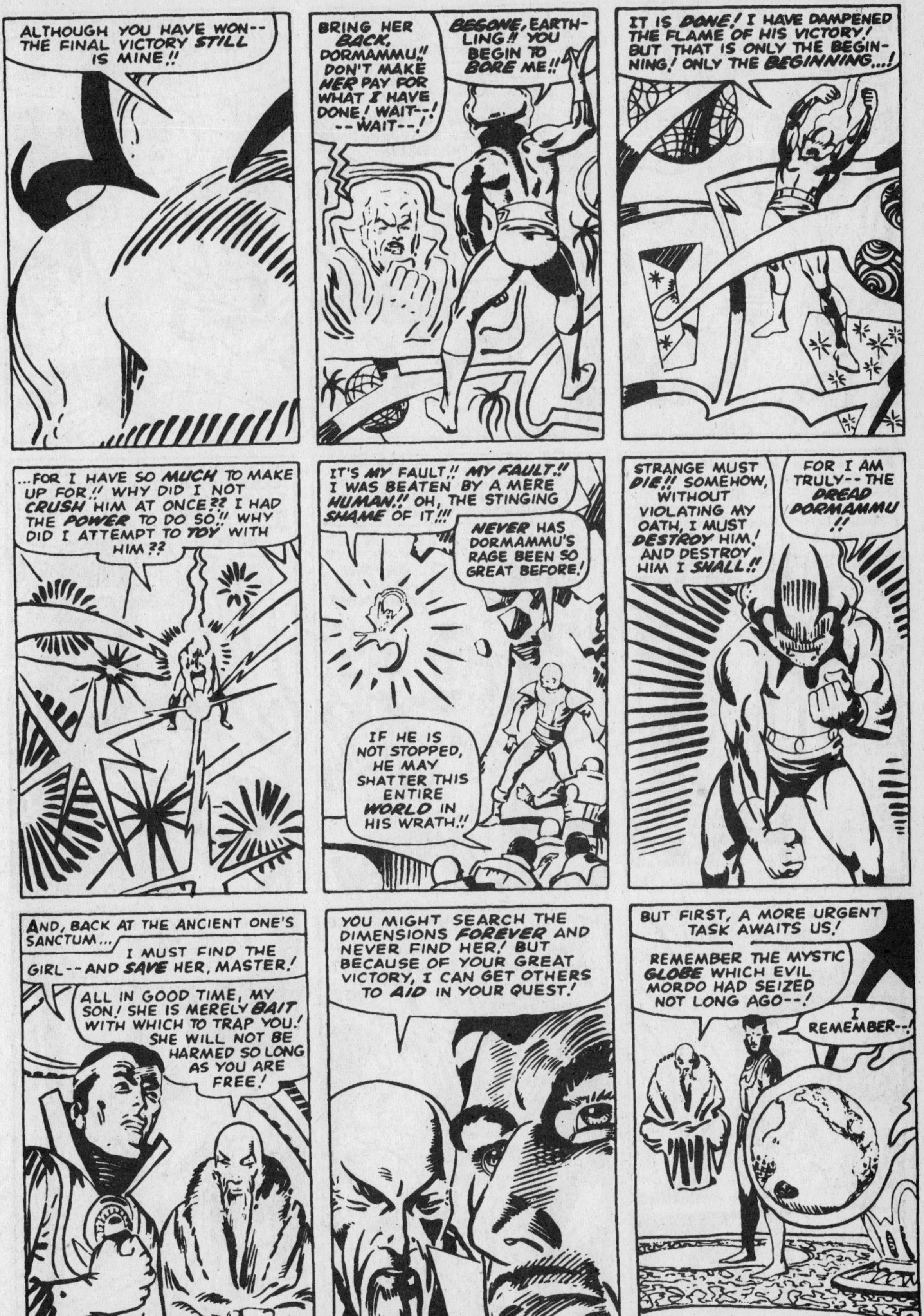
ALTHOUGH YOU HAVE WON-- THE FINAL VICTORY STILL IS MINE!!
BRING HER BACK, DORMAMMU!! DON'T MAKE HER PAY FOR WHAT I HAVE DONE! WAIT--! --WAIT--!
BEGONE, EARTHLING!! YOU BEGIN TO BORE ME!!
IT IS DONE! I HAVE DAMPENED THE FLAME OF HIS VICTORY! BUT THAT IS ONLY THE BEGINNING! ONLY THE BEGINNING...!
...FOR I HAVE SO MUCH TO MAKE UP FOR!! WHY DID I NOT CRUSH HIM AT ONCE?? I HAD THE POWER TO DO SO!! WHY DID I ATTEMPT TO TOY WITH HIM??
IT'S MY FAULT!! MY FAULT!! I WAS BEATEN BY A MERE HUMAN!! OH, THE STINGING SHAME OF IT!!!
NEVER HAS DORMAMMU'S RAGE BEEN SO GREAT BEFORE!
IF HE IS NOT STOPPED, HE MAY SHATTER THIS ENTIRE WORLD IN HIS WRATH!!
STRANGE MUST DIE!! SOMEHOW, WITHOUT VIOLATING MY OATH, I MUST DESTROY HIM! AND DESTROY HIM I SHALL!!
FOR I AM TRULY-- THE DREAD DORMAMMU!!
AND, BACK AT THE ANCIENT ONE'S SANCTUM...
I MUST FIND THE GIRL--AND SAVE HER, MASTER!
ALL IN GOOD TIME, MY SON! SHE IS MERELY BAIT WITH WHICH TO TRAP YOU! SHE WILL NOT BE HARMED SO LONG AS YOU ARE FREE!
YOU MIGHT SEARCH THE DIMENSIONS FOREVER AND NEVER FIND HER! BUT BECAUSE OF YOUR GREAT VICTORY, I CAN GET OTHERS TO AID IN YOUR QUEST!
BUT FIRST, A MORE URGENT TASK AWAITS US!
REMEMBER THE MYSTIC GLOBE WHICH EVIL MORDO HAD SEIZED NOT LONG AGO--!
I REMEMBER--!
8

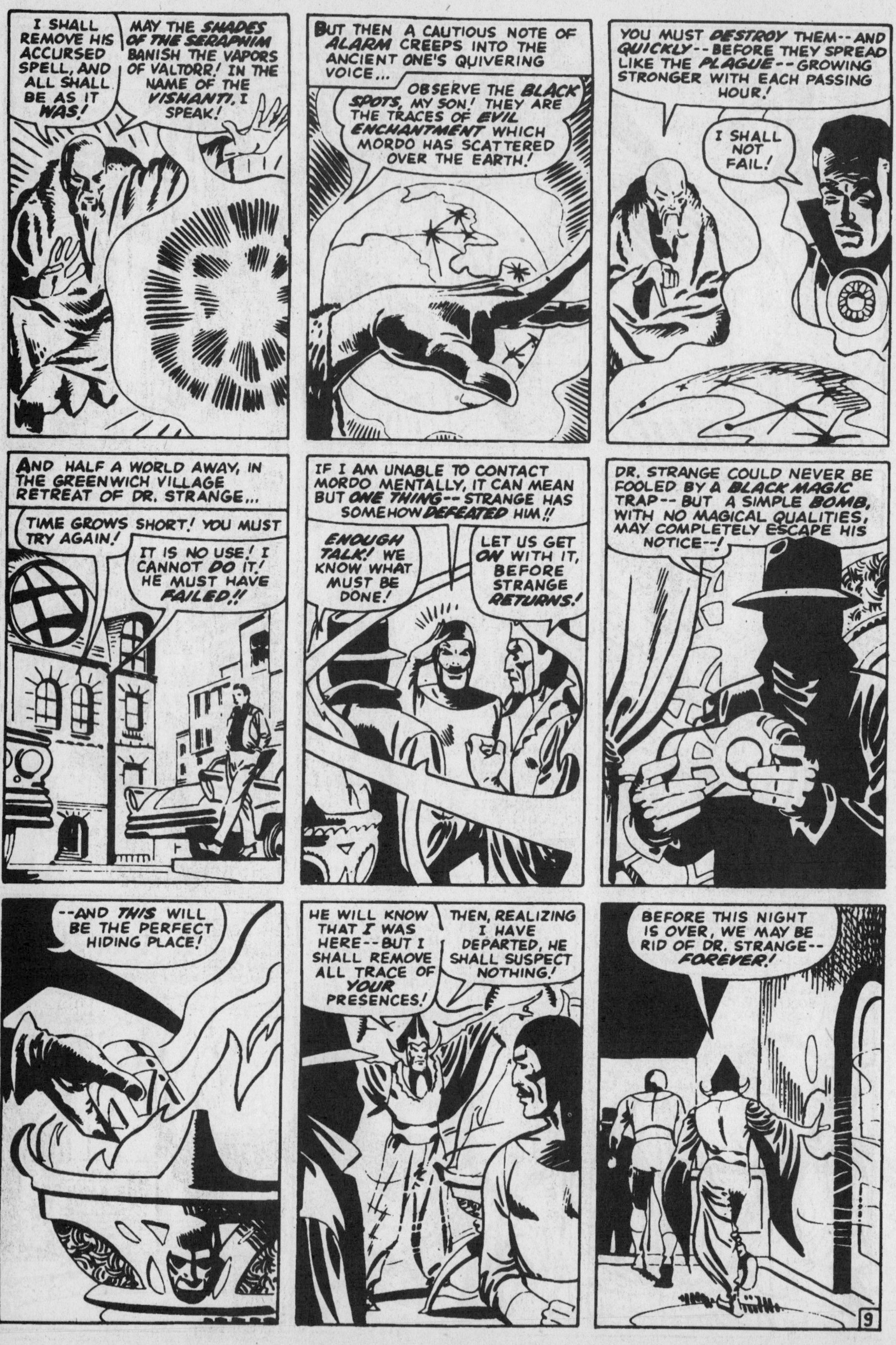
I SHALL REMOVE HIS ACCURSED SPELL, AND ALL SHALL BE AS IT WAS!
MAY THE SHADES OF THE SERAPHIM BANISH THE VAPORS OF VALTORR! IN THE NAME OF THE VISHANTI, I SPEAK!
BUT THEN A CAUTIOUS NOTE OF ALARM CREEPS INTO THE ANCIENT ONE'S QUIVERING VOICE...
OBSERVE THE BLACK SPOTS, MY SON! THEY ARE THE TRACES OF EVIL ENCHANTMENT WHICH MORDO HAS SCATTERED OVER THE EARTH!
YOU MUST DESTROY THEM--AND QUICKLY--BEFORE THEY SPREAD LIKE THE PLAGUE--GROWING STRONGER WITH EACH PASSING HOUR!
I SHALL NOT FAIL!
AND HALF A WORLD AWAY, IN THE GREENWICH VILLAGE RETREAT OF DR. STRANGE...
TIME GROWS SHORT! YOU MUST TRY AGAIN!
IT IS NO USE! I CANNOT DO IT! HE MUST HAVE FAILED!!
IF I AM UNABLE TO CONTACT MORDO MENTALLY, IT CAN MEAN BUT ONE THING--STRANGE HAS SOMEHOW DEFEATED HIM!!
ENOUGH TALK! WE KNOW WHAT MUST BE DONE!
LET US GET ON WITH IT, BEFORE STRANGE RETURNS!
DR. STRANGE COULD NEVER BE FOOLED BY A BLACK MAGIC TRAP--BUT A SIMPLE BOMB, WITH NO MAGICAL QUALITIES, MAY COMPLETELY ESCAPE HIS NOTICE--!
--AND THIS WILL BE THE PERFECT HIDING PLACE!
HE WILL KNOW THAT I WAS HERE--BUT I SHALL REMOVE ALL TRACE OF YOUR PRESENCES!
THEN, REALIZING I HAVE DEPARTED, HE SHALL SUSPECT NOTHING!
BEFORE THIS NIGHT IS OVER, WE MAY BE RID OF DR. STRANGE--FOREVER!
9

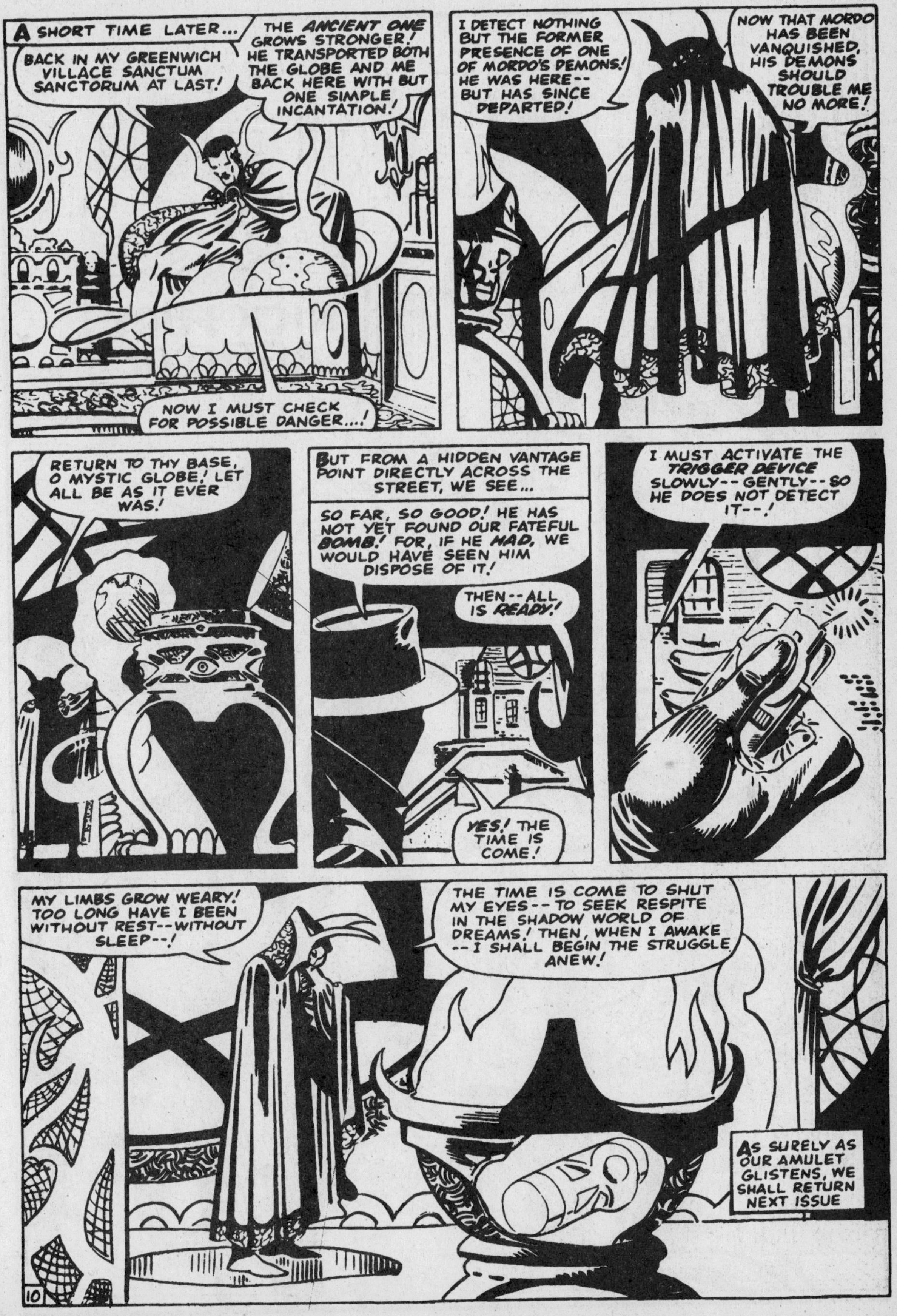

A SHORT TIME LATER...
BACK IN MY GREENWICH VILLAGE SANCTUM SANCTORUM AT LAST!
THE ANCIENT ONE GROWS STRONGER! HE TRANSPORTED BOTH THE GLOBE AND ME BACK HERE WITH BUT ONE SIMPLE INCANTATION!
NOW I MUST CHECK FOR POSSIBLE DANGER...!
I DETECT NOTHING BUT THE FORMER PRESENCE OF ONE OF MORDO'S DEMONS! HE WAS HERE-- BUT HAS SINCE DEPARTED!
NOW THAT MORDO HAS BEEN VANQUISHED, HIS DEMONS SHOULD TROUBLE ME NO MORE!
RETURN TO THY BASE, O MYSTIC GLOBE! LET ALL BE AS IT EVER WAS!
BUT FROM A HIDDEN VANTAGE POINT DIRECTLY ACROSS THE STREET, WE SEE...
SO FAR, SO GOOD! HE HAS NOT YET FOUND OUR FATEFUL BOMB! FOR, IF HE HAD, WE WOULD HAVE SEEN HIM DISPOSE OF IT!
THEN--ALL IS READY!
YES! THE TIME IS COME!
I MUST ACTIVATE THE TRIGGER DEVICE SLOWLY--GENTLY--SO HE DOES NOT DETECT IT--!
MY LIMBS GROW WEARY! TOO LONG HAVE I BEEN WITHOUT REST--WITHOUT SLEEP--!
THE TIME IS COME TO SHUT MY EYES--TO SEEK RESPITE IN THE SHADOW WORLD OF DREAMS! THEN, WHEN I AWAKE --I SHALL BEGIN THE STRUGGLE ANEW!
AS SURELY AS OUR AMULET GLISTENS, WE SHALL RETURN NEXT ISSUE
10

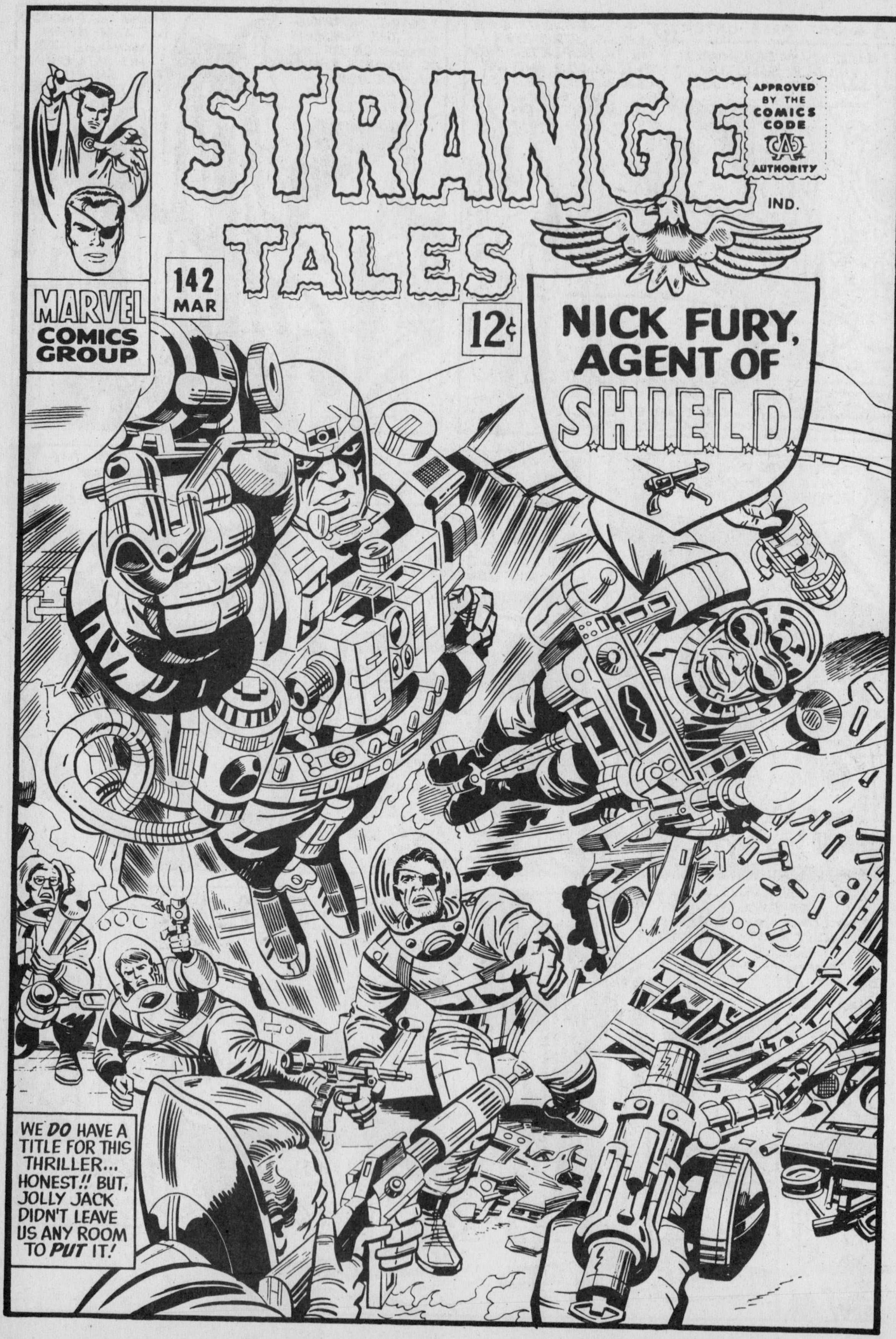
STRANGE TALES
APPROVED BY THE COMICS CODE AUTHORITY
IND.
142 MAR
MARVEL COMICS GROUP
12¢
NICK FURY, AGENT OF S.H.I.E.L.D
WE DO HAVE A TITLE FOR THIS THRILLER... HONEST!! BUT, JOLLY JACK DIDN'T LEAVE US ANY ROOM TO PUT IT!

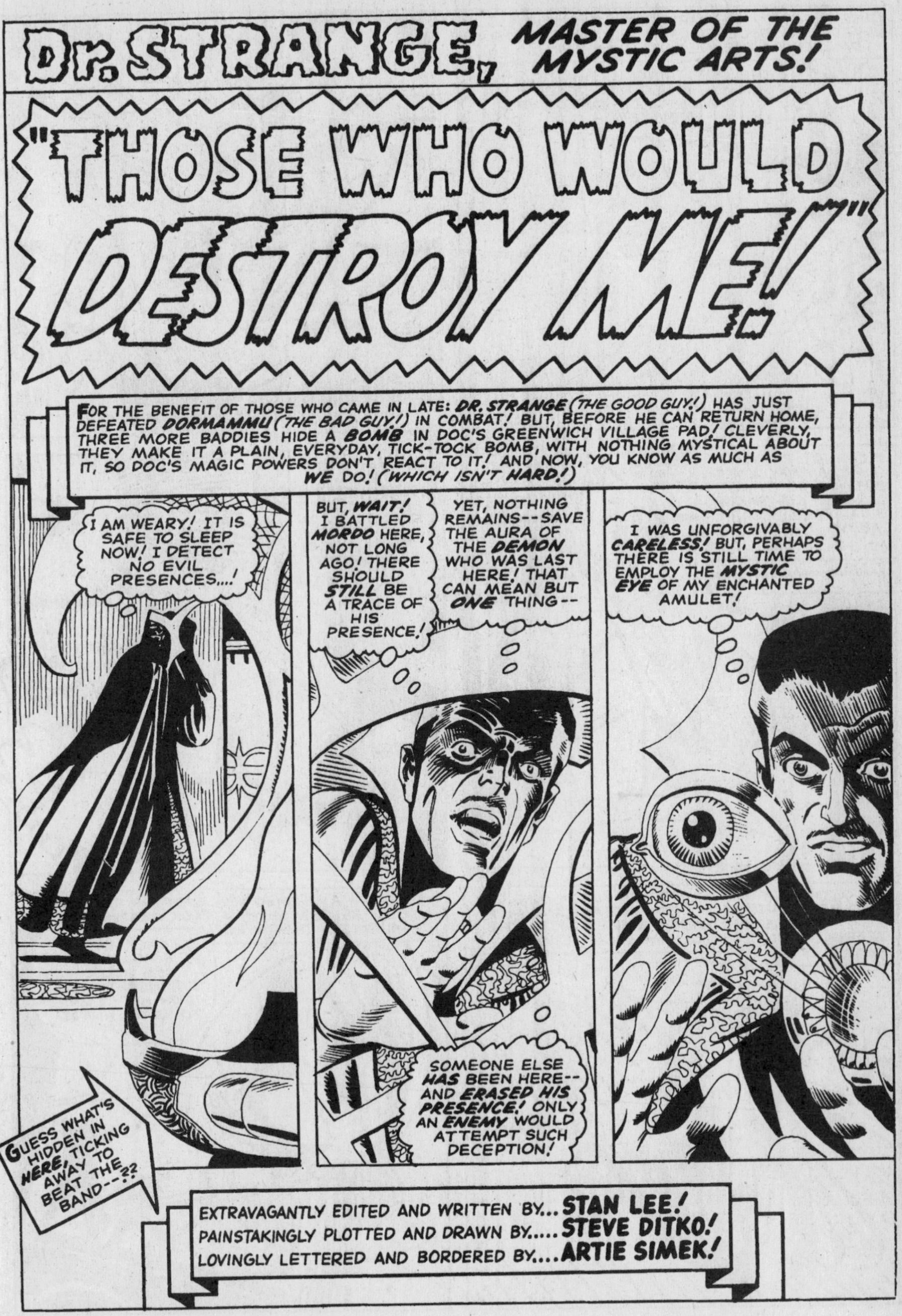
Dr. STRANGE, MASTER OF THE MYSTIC ARTS!
"THOSE WHO WOULD DESTROY ME!"
FOR THE BENEFIT OF THOSE WHO CAME IN LATE: DR. STRANGE (THE GOOD GUY!) HAS JUST DEFEATED DORMAMMU (THE BAD GUY!) IN COMBAT! BUT, BEFORE HE CAN RETURN HOME, THREE MORE BADDIES HIDE A BOMB IN DOC'S GREENWICH VILLAGE PAD! CLEVERLY, THEY MAKE IT A PLAIN, EVERYDAY, TICK-TOCK BOMB, WITH NOTHING MYSTICAL ABOUT IT, SO DOC'S MAGIC POWERS DON'T REACT TO IT! AND NOW, YOU KNOW AS MUCH AS WE DO! (WHICH ISN'T HARD!)
I AM WEARY! IT IS SAFE TO SLEEP NOW! I DETECT NO EVIL PRESENCES...!
GUESS WHAT'S HIDDEN IN HERE, TICKING AWAY TO BEAT THE BAND--??
BUT, WAIT! I BATTLED MORDO HERE, NOT LONG AGO! THERE SHOULD STILL BE A TRACE OF HIS PRESENCE!
YET, NOTHING REMAINS--SAVE THE AURA OF THE DEMON WHO WAS LAST HERE! THAT CAN MEAN BUT ONE THING--
SOMEONE ELSE HAS BEEN HERE--AND ERASED HIS PRESENCE! ONLY AN ENEMY WOULD ATTEMPT SUCH DECEPTION!
I WAS UNFORGIVABLY CARELESS! BUT, PERHAPS THERE IS STILL TIME TO EMPLOY THE MYSTIC EYE OF MY ENCHANTED AMULET!
EXTRAVAGANTLY EDITED AND WRITTEN BY... STAN LEE!
PAINSTAKINGLY PLOTTED AND DRAWN BY..... STEVE DITKO!
LOVINGLY LETTERED AND BORDERED BY.... ARTIE SIMEK!

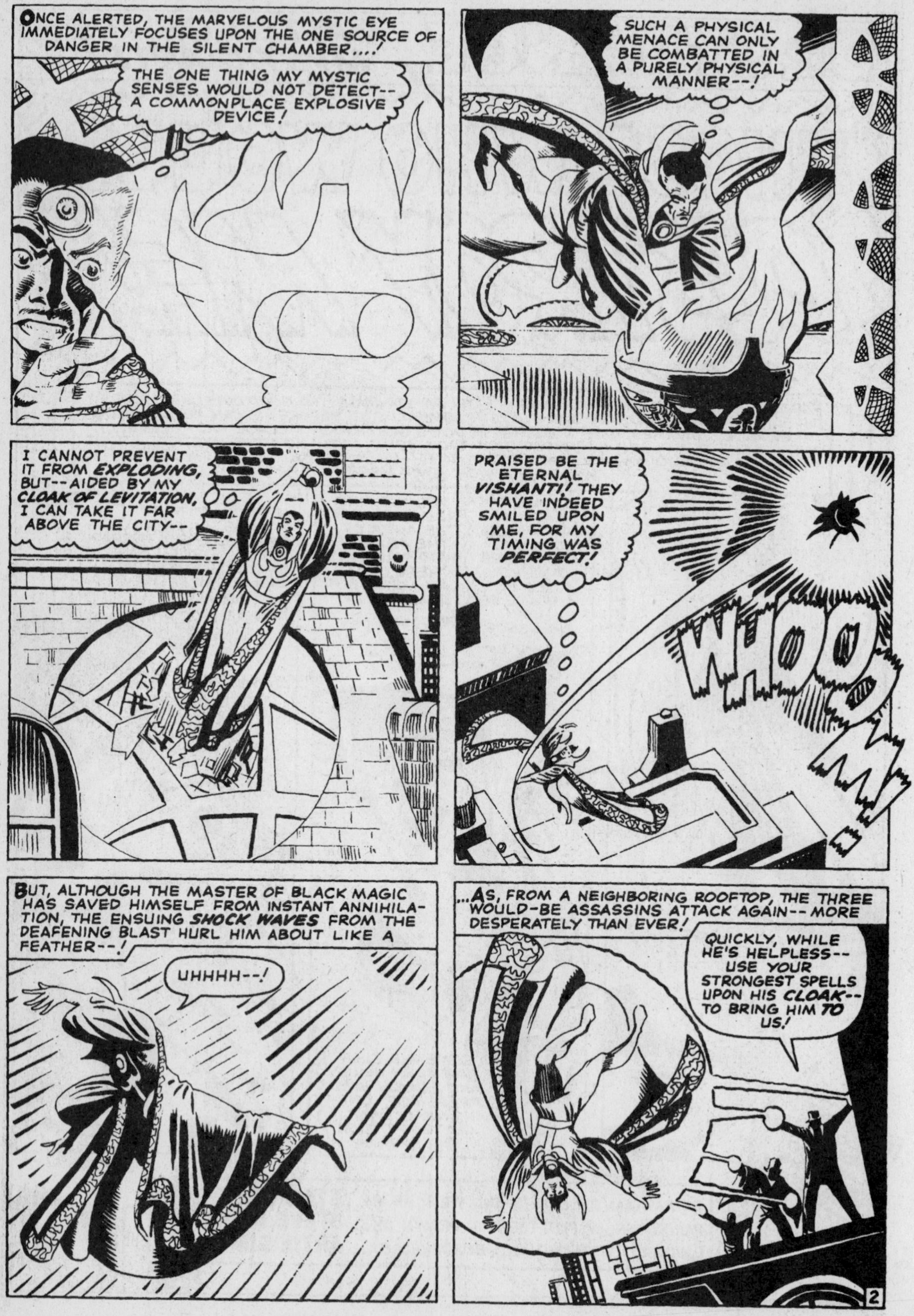
ONCE ALERTED, THE MARVELOUS MYSTIC EYE IMMEDIATELY FOCUSES UPON THE ONE SOURCE OF DANGER IN THE SILENT CHAMBER....!
THE ONE THING MY MYSTIC SENSES WOULD NOT DETECT-- A COMMONPLACE EXPLOSIVE DEVICE!
SUCH A PHYSICAL MENACE CAN ONLY BE COMBATTED IN A PURELY PHYSICAL MANNER--!
I CANNOT PREVENT IT FROM EXPLODING, BUT--AIDED BY MY CLOAK OF LEVITATION, I CAN TAKE IT FAR ABOVE THE CITY--
PRAISED BE THE ETERNAL VISHANTI! THEY HAVE INDEED SMILED UPON ME, FOR MY TIMING WAS PERFECT!
WHOOOM!
BUT, ALTHOUGH THE MASTER OF BLACK MAGIC HAS SAVED HIMSELF FROM INSTANT ANNIHILATION, THE ENSUING SHOCK WAVES FROM THE DEAFENING BLAST HURL HIM ABOUT LIKE A FEATHER--!
UHHHH--!
...AS, FROM A NEIGHBORING ROOFTOP, THE THREE WOULD-BE ASSASSINS ATTACK AGAIN-- MORE DESPERATELY THAN EVER!
QUICKLY, WHILE HE'S HELPLESS-- USE YOUR STRONGEST SPELLS UPON HIS CLOAK-- TO BRING HIM TO US!
2

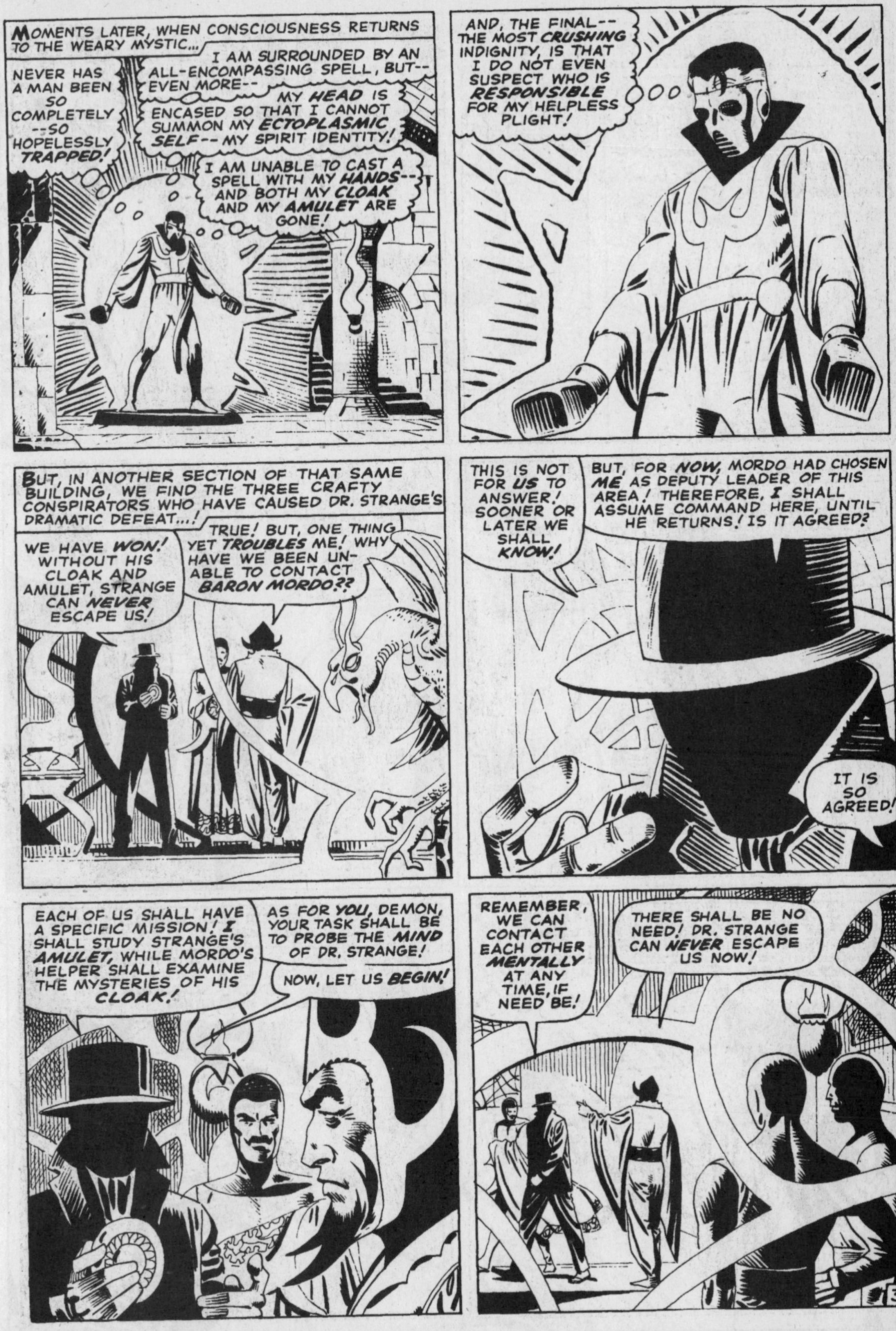
MOMENTS LATER, WHEN CONSCIOUSNESS RETURNS TO THE WEARY MYSTIC...
NEVER HAS A MAN BEEN SO COMPLETELY --SO HOPELESSLY TRAPPED!
I AM SURROUNDED BY AN ALL-ENCOMPASSING SPELL, BUT-- EVEN MORE--
MY HEAD IS ENCASED SO THAT I CANNOT SUMMON MY ECTOPLASMIC SELF-- MY SPIRIT IDENTITY!
I AM UNABLE TO CAST A SPELL WITH MY HANDS-- AND BOTH MY CLOAK AND MY AMULET ARE GONE!
AND, THE FINAL-- THE MOST CRUSHING INDIGNITY, IS THAT I DO NOT EVEN SUSPECT WHO IS RESPONSIBLE FOR MY HELPLESS PLIGHT!
BUT, IN ANOTHER SECTION OF THAT SAME BUILDING, WE FIND THE THREE CRAFTY CONSPIRATORS WHO HAVE CAUSED DR. STRANGE'S DRAMATIC DEFEAT...!
WE HAVE WON! WITHOUT HIS CLOAK AND AMULET, STRANGE CAN NEVER ESCAPE US!
TRUE! BUT, ONE THING YET TROUBLES ME! WHY HAVE WE BEEN UNABLE TO CONTACT BARON MORDO??
THIS IS NOT FOR US TO ANSWER! SOONER OR LATER WE SHALL KNOW!
BUT, FOR NOW, MORDO HAD CHOSEN ME AS DEPUTY LEADER OF THIS AREA! THEREFORE, I SHALL ASSUME COMMAND HERE, UNTIL HE RETURNS! IS IT AGREED?
IT IS SO AGREED!
EACH OF US SHALL HAVE A SPECIFIC MISSION! I SHALL STUDY STRANGE'S AMULET, WHILE MORDO'S HELPER SHALL EXAMINE THE MYSTERIES OF HIS CLOAK!
AS FOR YOU, DEMON, YOUR TASK SHALL BE TO PROBE THE MIND OF DR. STRANGE!
NOW, LET US BEGIN!
REMEMBER, WE CAN CONTACT EACH OTHER MENTALLY AT ANY TIME, IF NEED BE!
THERE SHALL BE NO NEED! DR. STRANGE CAN NEVER ESCAPE US NOW!
3

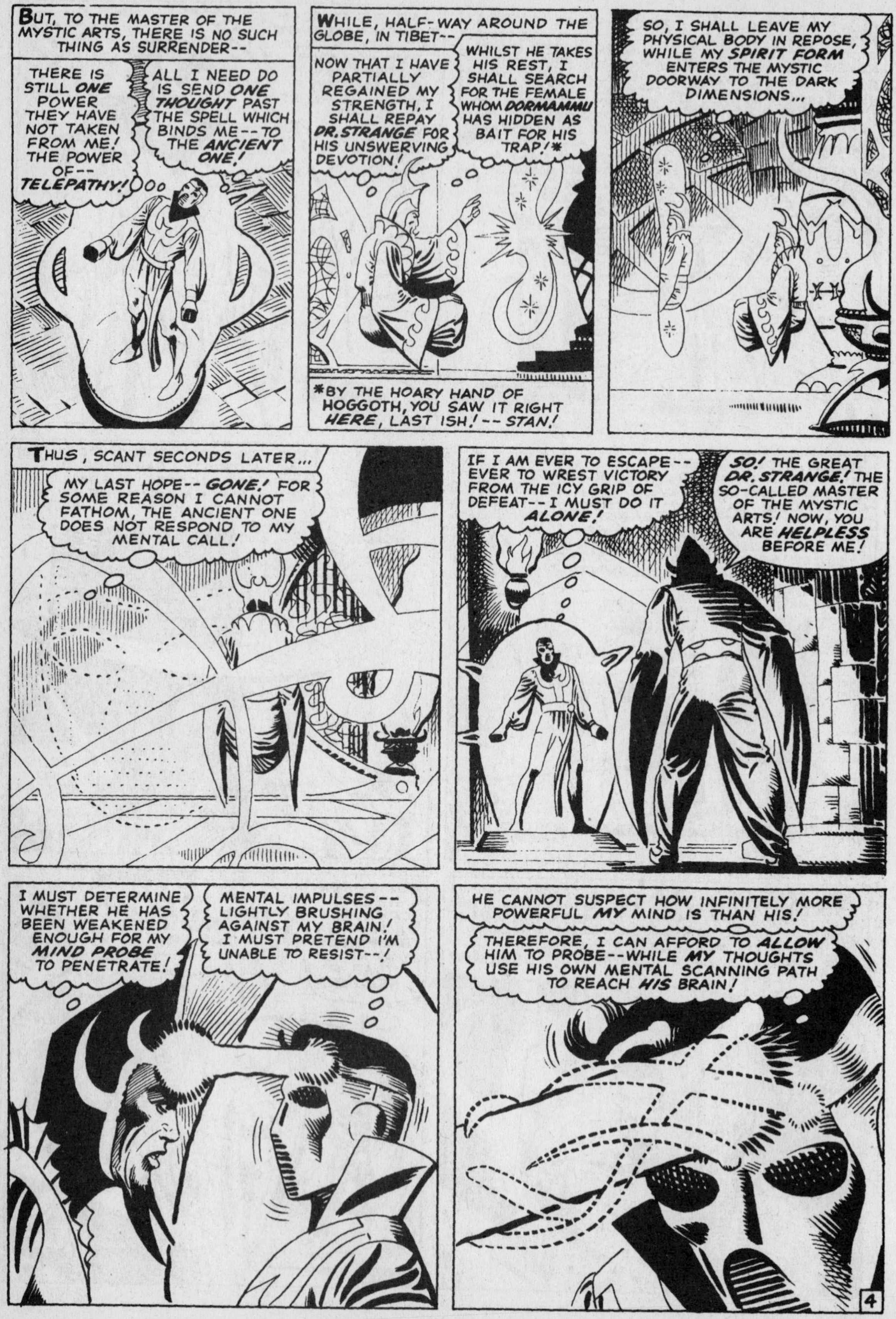

BUT, TO THE MASTER OF THE MYSTIC ARTS, THERE IS NO SUCH THING AS SURRENDER--
THERE IS STILL ONE POWER THEY HAVE NOT TAKEN FROM ME! THE POWER OF-- TELEPATHY!
ALL I NEED DO IS SEND ONE THOUGHT PAST THE SPELL WHICH BINDS ME--TO THE ANCIENT ONE!
WHILE, HALF-WAY AROUND THE GLOBE, IN TIBET--
NOW THAT I HAVE PARTIALLY REGAINED MY STRENGTH, I SHALL REPAY DR. STRANGE FOR HIS UNSWERVING DEVOTION!
WHILST HE TAKES HIS REST, I SHALL SEARCH FOR THE FEMALE WHOM DORMAMMU HAS HIDDEN AS BAIT FOR HIS TRAP!*
*BY THE HOARY HAND OF HOGGOTH, YOU SAW IT RIGHT HERE, LAST ISH!--STAN!
SO, I SHALL LEAVE MY PHYSICAL BODY IN REPOSE, WHILE MY SPIRIT FORM ENTERS THE MYSTIC DOORWAY TO THE DARK DIMENSIONS...
THUS, SCANT SECONDS LATER...
MY LAST HOPE--GONE! FOR SOME REASON I CANNOT FATHOM, THE ANCIENT ONE DOES NOT RESPOND TO MY MENTAL CALL!
IF I AM EVER TO ESCAPE--EVER TO WREST VICTORY FROM THE ICY GRIP OF DEFEAT--I MUST DO IT ALONE!
SO! THE GREAT DR. STRANGE! THE SO-CALLED MASTER OF THE MYSTIC ARTS! NOW, YOU ARE HELPLESS BEFORE ME!
I MUST DETERMINE WHETHER HE HAS BEEN WEAKENED ENOUGH FOR MY MIND PROBE TO PENETRATE!
MENTAL IMPULSES--LIGHTLY BRUSHING AGAINST MY BRAIN! I MUST PRETEND I'M UNABLE TO RESIST--!
HE CANNOT SUSPECT HOW INFINITELY MORE POWERFUL MY MIND IS THAN HIS!
THEREFORE, I CAN AFFORD TO ALLOW HIM TO PROBE--WHILE MY THOUGHTS USE HIS OWN MENTAL SCANNING PATH TO REACH HIS BRAIN!
4

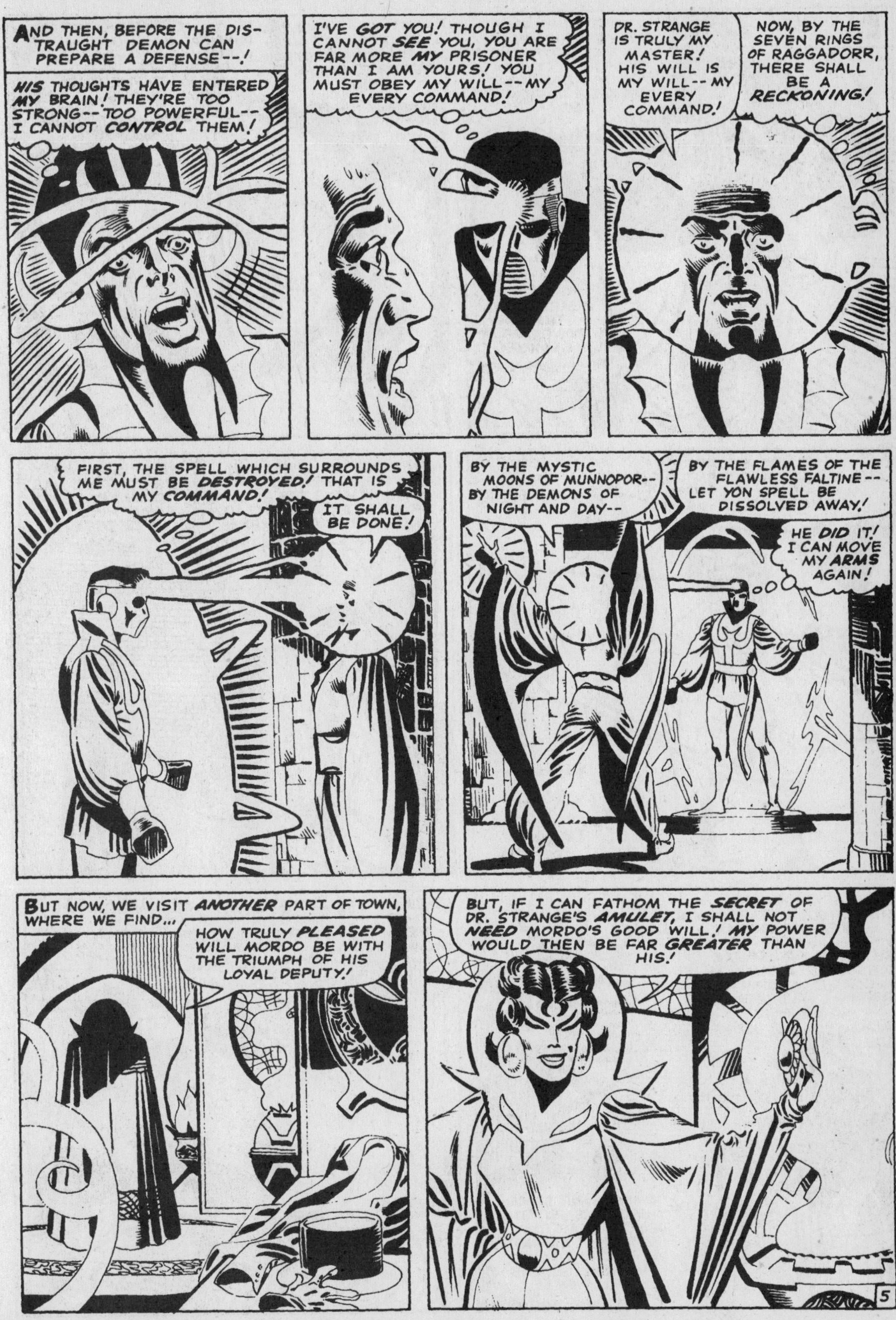

AND THEN, BEFORE THE DISTRAUGHT DEMON CAN PREPARE A DEFENSE--!
HIS THOUGHTS HAVE ENTERED MY BRAIN! THEY'RE TOO STRONG--TOO POWERFUL--I CANNOT CONTROL THEM!
I'VE GOT YOU! THOUGH I CANNOT SEE YOU, YOU ARE FAR MORE MY PRISONER THAN I AM YOURS! YOU MUST OBEY MY WILL--MY EVERY COMMAND!
DR. STRANGE IS TRULY MY MASTER! HIS WILL IS MY WILL--MY EVERY COMMAND!
NOW, BY THE SEVEN RINGS OF RAGGADORR, THERE SHALL BE A RECKONING!
FIRST, THE SPELL WHICH SURROUNDS ME MUST BE DESTROYED! THAT IS MY COMMAND!
IT SHALL BE DONE!
BY THE MYSTIC MOONS OF MUNNOPOR--BY THE DEMONS OF NIGHT AND DAY--
BY THE FLAMES OF THE FLAWLESS FALTINE--LET YON SPELL BE DISSOLVED AWAY!
HE DID IT! I CAN MOVE MY ARMS AGAIN!
BUT NOW, WE VISIT ANOTHER PART OF TOWN, WHERE WE FIND...
HOW TRULY PLEASED WILL MORDO BE WITH THE TRIUMPH OF HIS LOYAL DEPUTY!
BUT, IF I CAN FATHOM THE SECRET OF DR. STRANGE'S AMULET, I SHALL NOT NEED MORDO'S GOOD WILL! MY POWER WOULD THEN BE FAR GREATER THAN HIS!
5

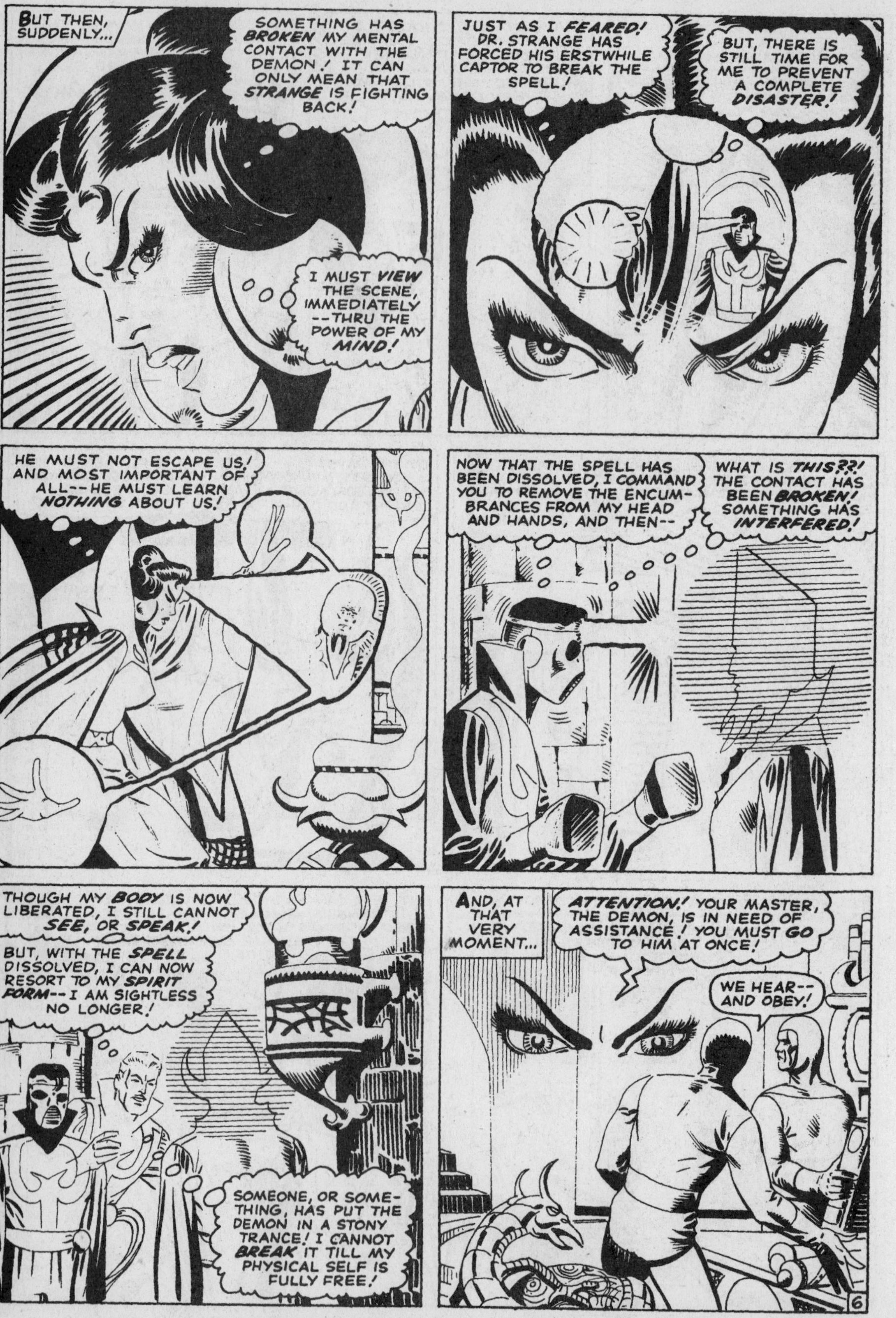
BUT THEN, SUDDENLY...
SOMETHING HAS BROKEN MY MENTAL CONTACT WITH THE DEMON! IT CAN ONLY MEAN THAT STRANGE IS FIGHTING BACK!
I MUST VIEW THE SCENE, IMMEDIATELY --THRU THE POWER OF MY MIND!
JUST AS I FEARED! DR. STRANGE HAS FORCED HIS ERSTWHILE CAPTOR TO BREAK THE SPELL!
BUT, THERE IS STILL TIME FOR ME TO PREVENT A COMPLETE DISASTER!
HE MUST NOT ESCAPE US! AND MOST IMPORTANT OF ALL--HE MUST LEARN NOTHING ABOUT US!
NOW THAT THE SPELL HAS BEEN DISSOLVED, I COMMAND YOU TO REMOVE THE ENCUM-BRANCES FROM MY HEAD AND HANDS, AND THEN--
WHAT IS THIS??! THE CONTACT HAS BEEN BROKEN! SOMETHING HAS INTERFERED!
THOUGH MY BODY IS NOW LIBERATED, I STILL CANNOT SEE, OR SPEAK!
BUT, WITH THE SPELL DISSOLVED, I CAN NOW RESORT TO MY SPIRIT FORM-- I AM SIGHTLESS NO LONGER!
SOMEONE, OR SOME-THING, HAS PUT THE DEMON IN A STONY TRANCE! I CANNOT BREAK IT TILL MY PHYSICAL SELF IS FULLY FREE!
AND, AT THAT VERY MOMENT...
ATTENTION! YOUR MASTER, THE DEMON, IS IN NEED OF ASSISTANCE! YOU MUST GO TO HIM AT ONCE!
WE HEAR-- AND OBEY!
6

THEN, SCANT SECONDS LATER...

STOP!! CEASE YOUR EXPERIMENTS WITH THE ENCHANTED CLOAK! DR. STRANGE HAS *FREED* HIMSELF! EVERY MOMENT COUNTS!

THERE! IT IS *DONE!* WITHOUT HIS MYSTIC DEVICES TO AID HIM, DR. STRANGE CANNOT ESCAPE THE OTHERS! AND SO, I CAN RETURN TO THE STUDY OF HIS AMULET!

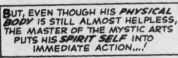

BUT, EVEN THOUGH HIS *PHYSICAL BODY* IS STILL ALMOST HELPLESS, THE MASTER OF THE MYSTIC ARTS PUTS HIS *SPIRIT SELF* INTO IMMEDIATE ACTION....!

MY FIRST TASK IS TO EXPLORE MY SURROUNDINGS AND LEARN AS MUCH AS I CAN OF THE DANGERS ABOUT ME!

IT'S ALL CLEAR SO FAR! NOW TO GUIDE MY PHYSICAL BODY BY MENTAL COMMAND--!

THOUGH I CANNOT SEE THRU THIS ENCHANTED HEAD MASK, MY *SPIRIT SELF* CAN MENTALLY DIRECT ME--!

BUT, I MUST MOVE SLOWLY-- CAREFULLY--!

SLOWLY--SLOWLY-- NOW STOP! I MUST GET MY BEARINGS! AH, THAT LOOKS LIKE AN EXIT-- STRAIGHT AHEAD!

FOOTSTEPS-- BEHIND ME! I MUST LEAVE MY BODY HERE WHILE I *INVESTIGATE!*

ONE OF MORDO'S FOLLOWERS!

IN MY SPIRIT FORM I CANNOT CAPTURE HIM--AND, IT IS TOO LATE TO HIDE!

7

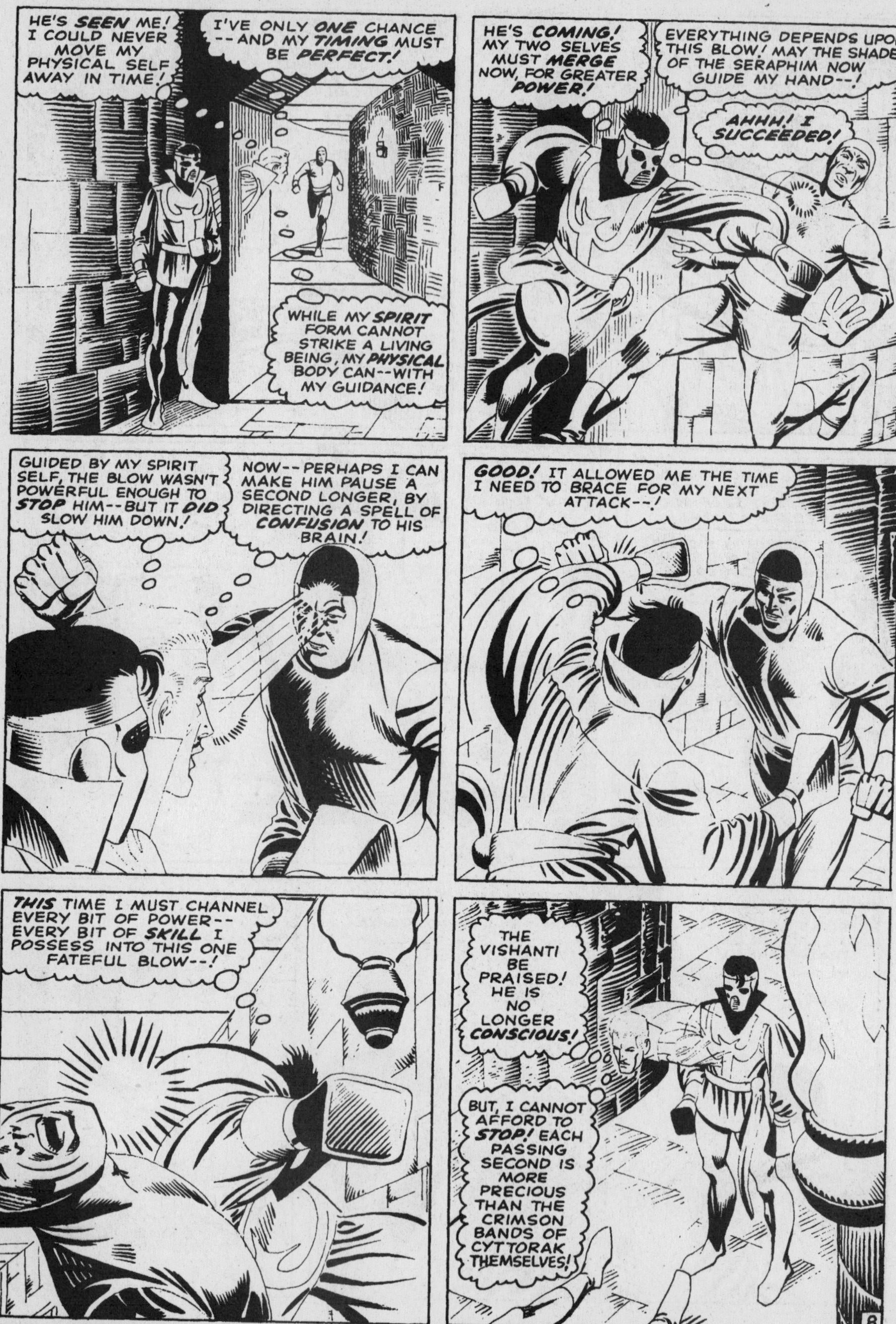
HE'S SEEN ME! I COULD NEVER MOVE MY PHYSICAL SELF AWAY IN TIME!
I'VE ONLY ONE CHANCE --AND MY TIMING MUST BE PERFECT!
WHILE MY SPIRIT FORM CANNOT STRIKE A LIVING BEING, MY PHYSICAL BODY CAN--WITH MY GUIDANCE!
HE'S COMING! MY TWO SELVES MUST MERGE NOW, FOR GREATER POWER!
EVERYTHING DEPENDS UPON THIS BLOW! MAY THE SHADES OF THE SERAPHIM NOW GUIDE MY HAND--!
AHHH! I SUCCEEDED!
GUIDED BY MY SPIRIT SELF, THE BLOW WASN'T POWERFUL ENOUGH TO STOP HIM--BUT IT DID SLOW HIM DOWN!
NOW--PERHAPS I CAN MAKE HIM PAUSE A SECOND LONGER, BY DIRECTING A SPELL OF CONFUSION TO HIS BRAIN!
GOOD! IT ALLOWED ME THE TIME I NEED TO BRACE FOR MY NEXT ATTACK--!
THIS TIME I MUST CHANNEL EVERY BIT OF POWER-- EVERY BIT OF SKILL I POSSESS INTO THIS ONE FATEFUL BLOW--!
THE VISHANTI BE PRAISED! HE IS NO LONGER CONSCIOUS!
BUT, I CANNOT AFFORD TO STOP! EACH PASSING SECOND IS MORE PRECIOUS THAN THE CRIMSON BANDS OF CYTTORAK THEMSELVES!

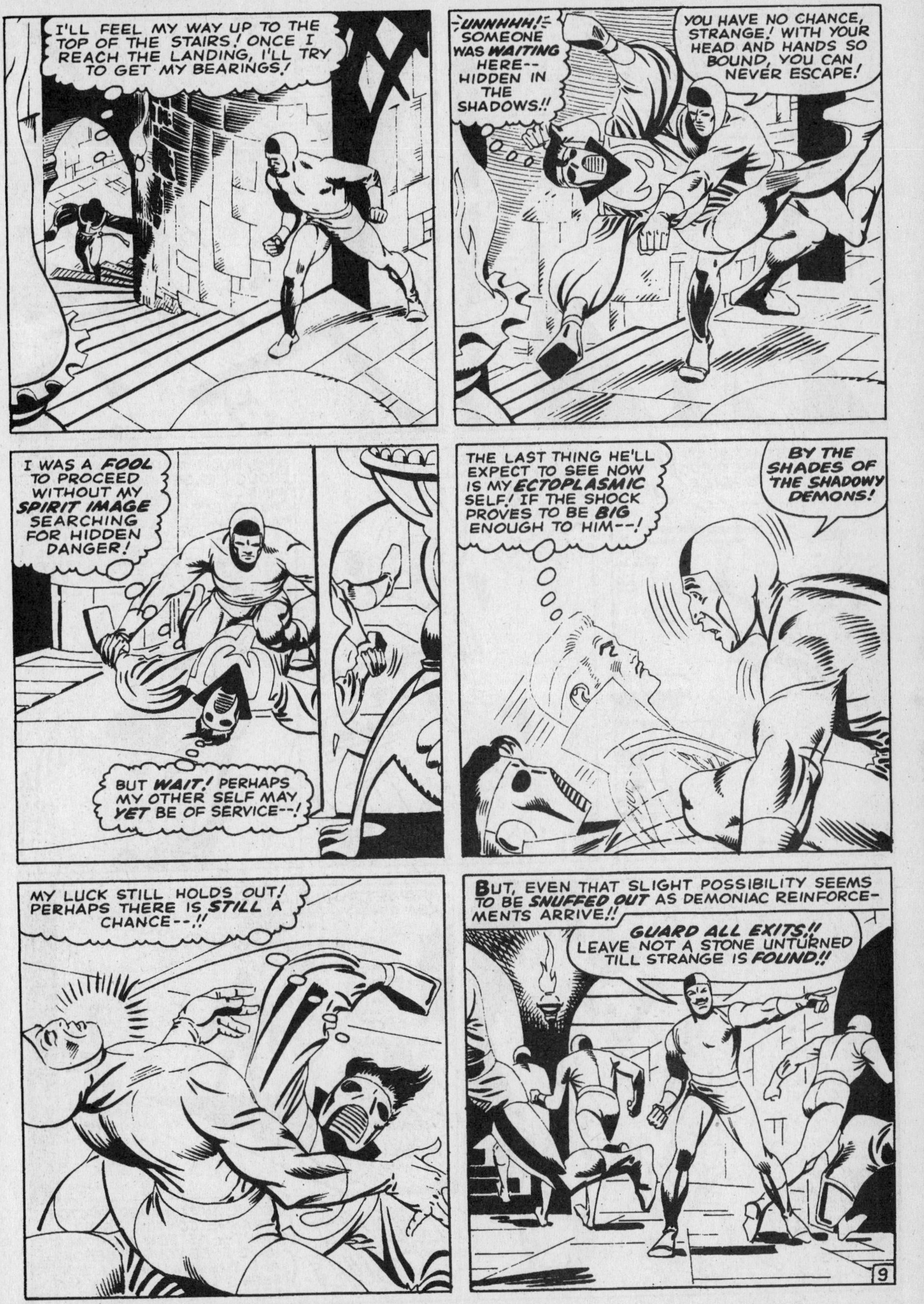
I'LL FEEL MY WAY UP TO THE TOP OF THE STAIRS! ONCE I REACH THE LANDING, I'LL TRY TO GET MY BEARINGS!
UNNHHH! SOMEONE WAS WAITING HERE-- HIDDEN IN THE SHADOWS!!
YOU HAVE NO CHANCE, STRANGE! WITH YOUR HEAD AND HANDS SO BOUND, YOU CAN NEVER ESCAPE!
I WAS A FOOL TO PROCEED WITHOUT MY SPIRIT IMAGE SEARCHING FOR HIDDEN DANGER!
BUT WAIT! PERHAPS MY OTHER SELF MAY YET BE OF SERVICE--!
THE LAST THING HE'LL EXPECT TO SEE NOW IS MY ECTOPLASMIC SELF! IF THE SHOCK PROVES TO BE BIG ENOUGH TO HIM--!
BY THE SHADES OF THE SHADOWY DEMONS!
MY LUCK STILL HOLDS OUT! PERHAPS THERE IS STILL A CHANCE--!!
BUT, EVEN THAT SLIGHT POSSIBILITY SEEMS TO BE SNUFFED OUT AS DEMONIAC REINFORCEMENTS ARRIVE!!
GUARD ALL EXITS!! LEAVE NOT A STONE UNTURNED TILL STRANGE IS FOUND!!
9

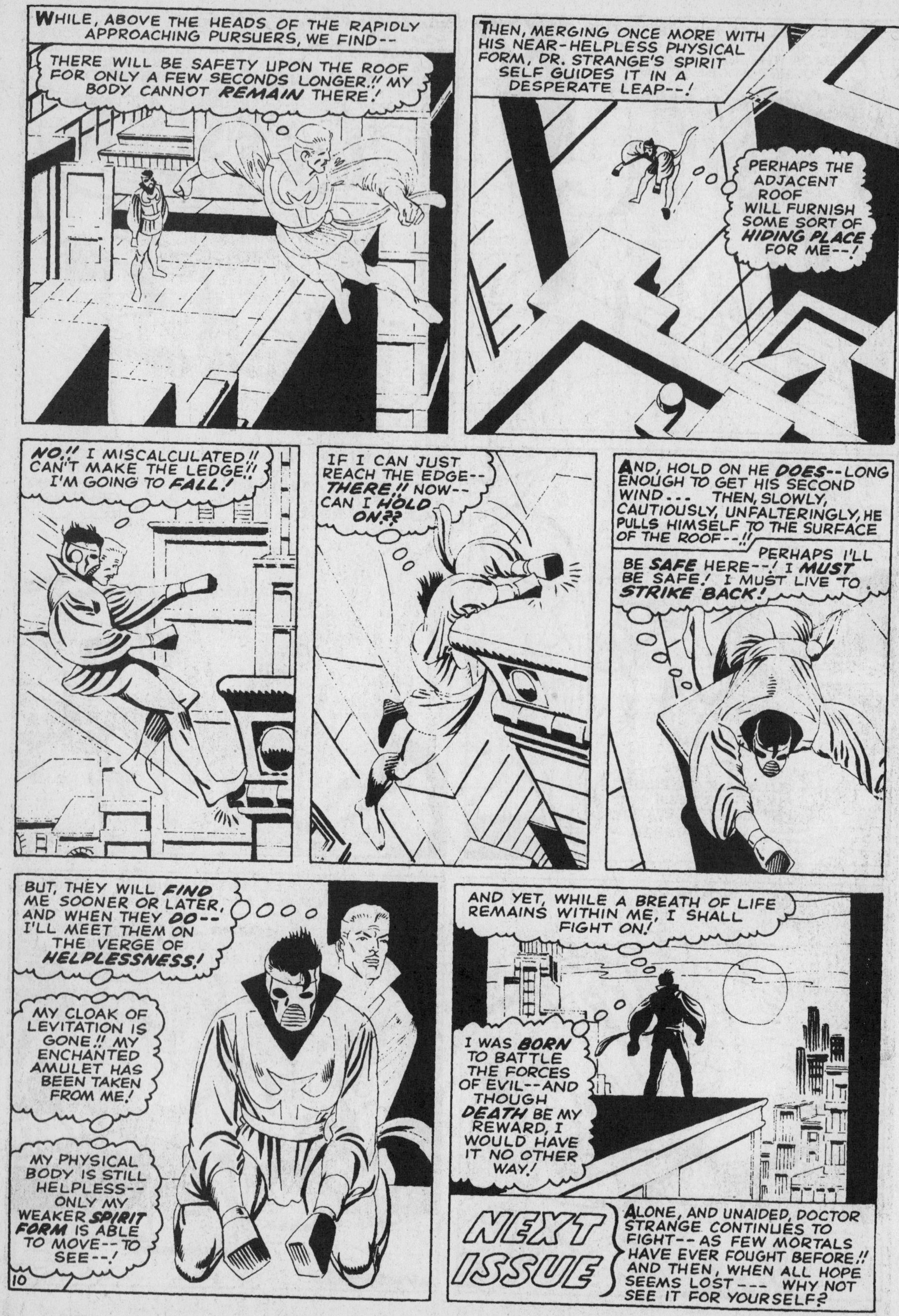

WHILE, ABOVE THE HEADS OF THE RAPIDLY APPROACHING PURSUERS, WE FIND--
THERE WILL BE SAFETY UPON THE ROOF FOR ONLY A FEW SECONDS LONGER!! MY BODY CANNOT REMAIN THERE!
THEN, MERGING ONCE MORE WITH HIS NEAR-HELPLESS PHYSICAL FORM, DR. STRANGE'S SPIRIT SELF GUIDES IT IN A DESPERATE LEAP--!
PERHAPS THE ADJACENT ROOF WILL FURNISH SOME SORT OF HIDING PLACE FOR ME--!
NO!! I MISCALCULATED!! CAN'T MAKE THE LEDGE!! I'M GOING TO FALL!
IF I CAN JUST REACH THE EDGE-- THERE!! NOW-- CAN I HOLD ON??
AND, HOLD ON HE DOES--LONG ENOUGH TO GET HIS SECOND WIND... THEN, SLOWLY, CAUTIOUSLY, UNFALTERINGLY, HE PULLS HIMSELF TO THE SURFACE OF THE ROOF--!!
PERHAPS I'LL BE SAFE HERE--! I MUST BE SAFE! I MUST LIVE TO STRIKE BACK!
BUT, THEY WILL FIND ME SOONER OR LATER, AND WHEN THEY DO-- I'LL MEET THEM ON THE VERGE OF HELPLESSNESS!
MY CLOAK OF LEVITATION IS GONE!! MY ENCHANTED AMULET HAS BEEN TAKEN FROM ME!
MY PHYSICAL BODY IS STILL HELPLESS-- ONLY MY WEAKER SPIRIT FORM IS ABLE TO MOVE--TO SEE--!
10
AND YET, WHILE A BREATH OF LIFE REMAINS WITHIN ME, I SHALL FIGHT ON!
I WAS BORN TO BATTLE THE FORCES OF EVIL--AND THOUGH DEATH BE MY REWARD, I WOULD HAVE IT NO OTHER WAY!
NEXT ISSUE
ALONE, AND UNAIDED, DOCTOR STRANGE CONTINUES TO FIGHT--AS FEW MORTALS HAVE EVER FOUGHT BEFORE!! AND THEN, WHEN ALL HOPE SEEMS LOST--- WHY NOT SEE IT FOR YOURSELF?

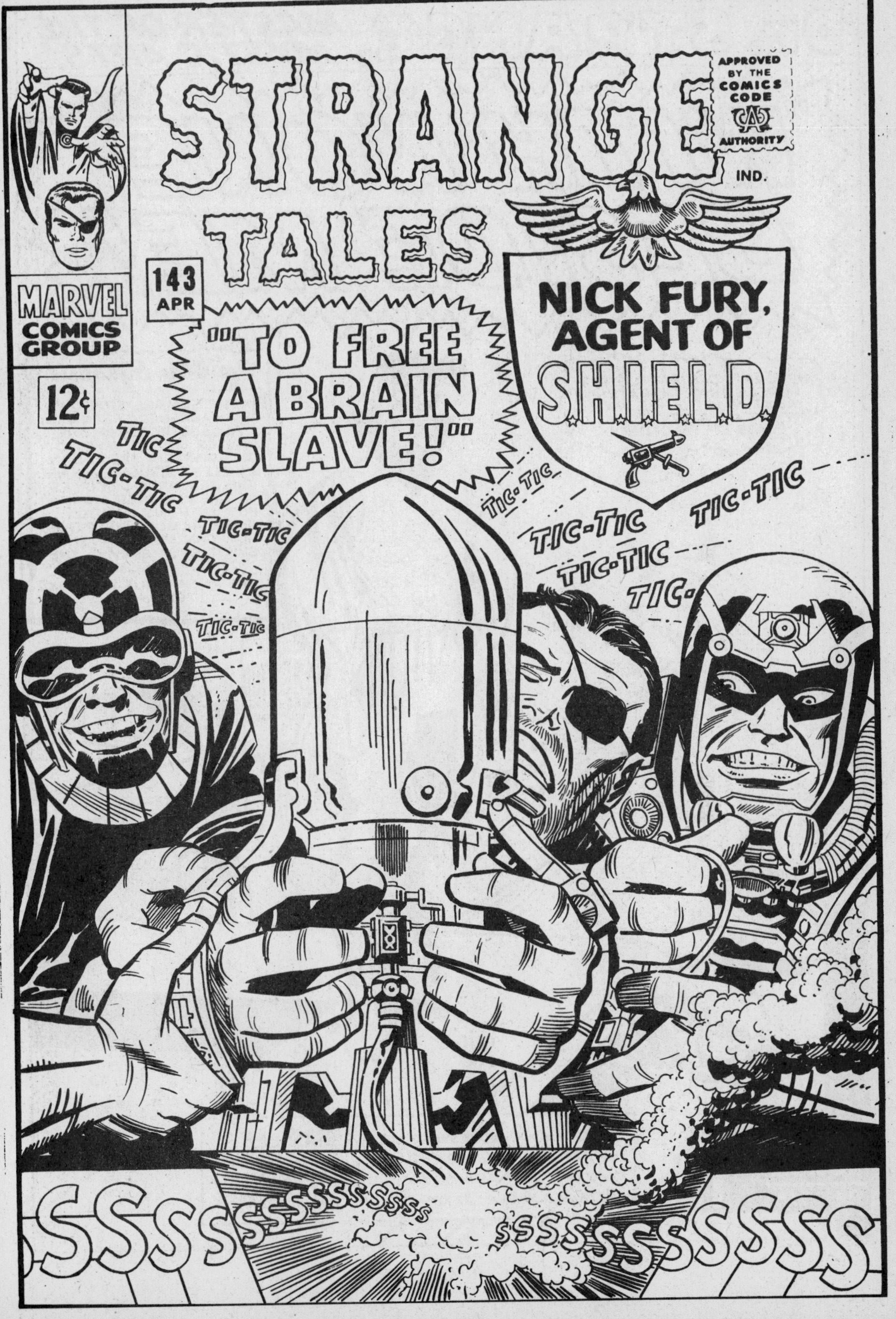
STRANGE TALES
APPROVED BY THE COMICS CODE AUTHORITY
IND.
143 APR
MARVEL COMICS GROUP
12¢
NICK FURY, AGENT OF S.H.I.E.L.D.
"TO FREE A BRAIN SLAVE!"
TIC
TIC-TIC
TIC-TIC
TIC-TIC
TIC-TIC
TIC-TIC
TIC-TIC
TIC-TIC
TIC-TIC
TIC-TIC
TIC-
SSSSSSSSSSSSSS
SSSSSSSSSSSSS

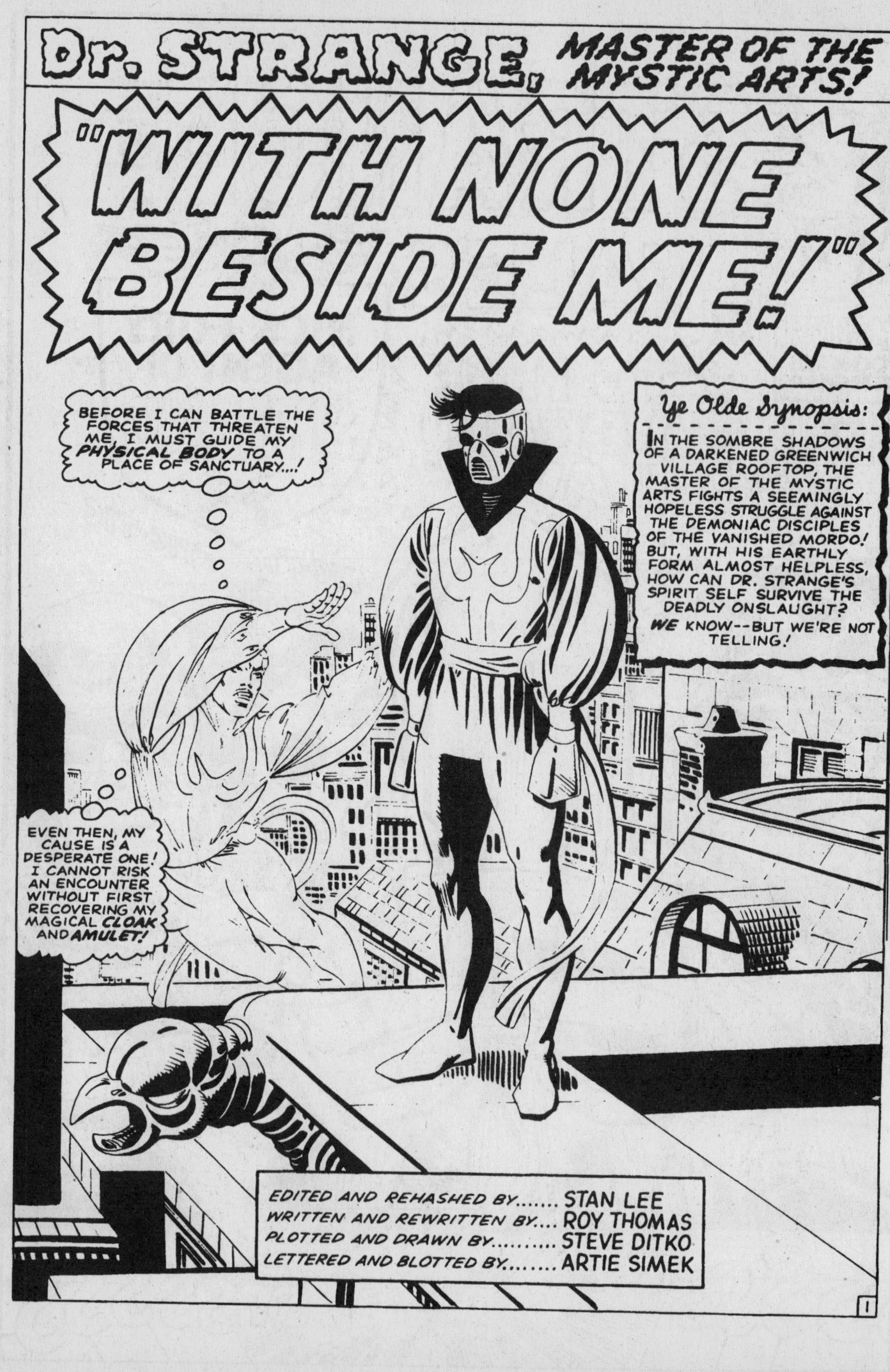

Dr. STRANGE, MASTER OF THE MYSTIC ARTS!
"WITH NONE BESIDE ME!"
BEFORE I CAN BATTLE THE FORCES THAT THREATEN ME, I MUST GUIDE MY PHYSICAL BODY TO A PLACE OF SANCTUARY...!
EVEN THEN, MY CAUSE IS A DESPERATE ONE! I CANNOT RISK AN ENCOUNTER WITHOUT FIRST RECOVERING MY MAGICAL CLOAK AND AMULET!
Ye Olde Synopsis:
IN THE SOMBRE SHADOWS OF A DARKENED GREENWICH VILLAGE ROOFTOP, THE MASTER OF THE MYSTIC ARTS FIGHTS A SEEMINGLY HOPELESS STRUGGLE AGAINST THE DEMONIAC DISCIPLES OF THE VANISHED MORDO! BUT, WITH HIS EARTHLY FORM ALMOST HELPLESS, HOW CAN DR. STRANGE'S SPIRIT SELF SURVIVE THE DEADLY ONSLAUGHT?
WE KNOW--BUT WE'RE NOT TELLING!
EDITED AND REHASHED BY....... STAN LEE
WRITTEN AND REWRITTEN BY.... ROY THOMAS
PLOTTED AND DRAWN BY.......... STEVE DITKO
LETTERED AND BLOTTED BY........ ARTIE SIMEK
1

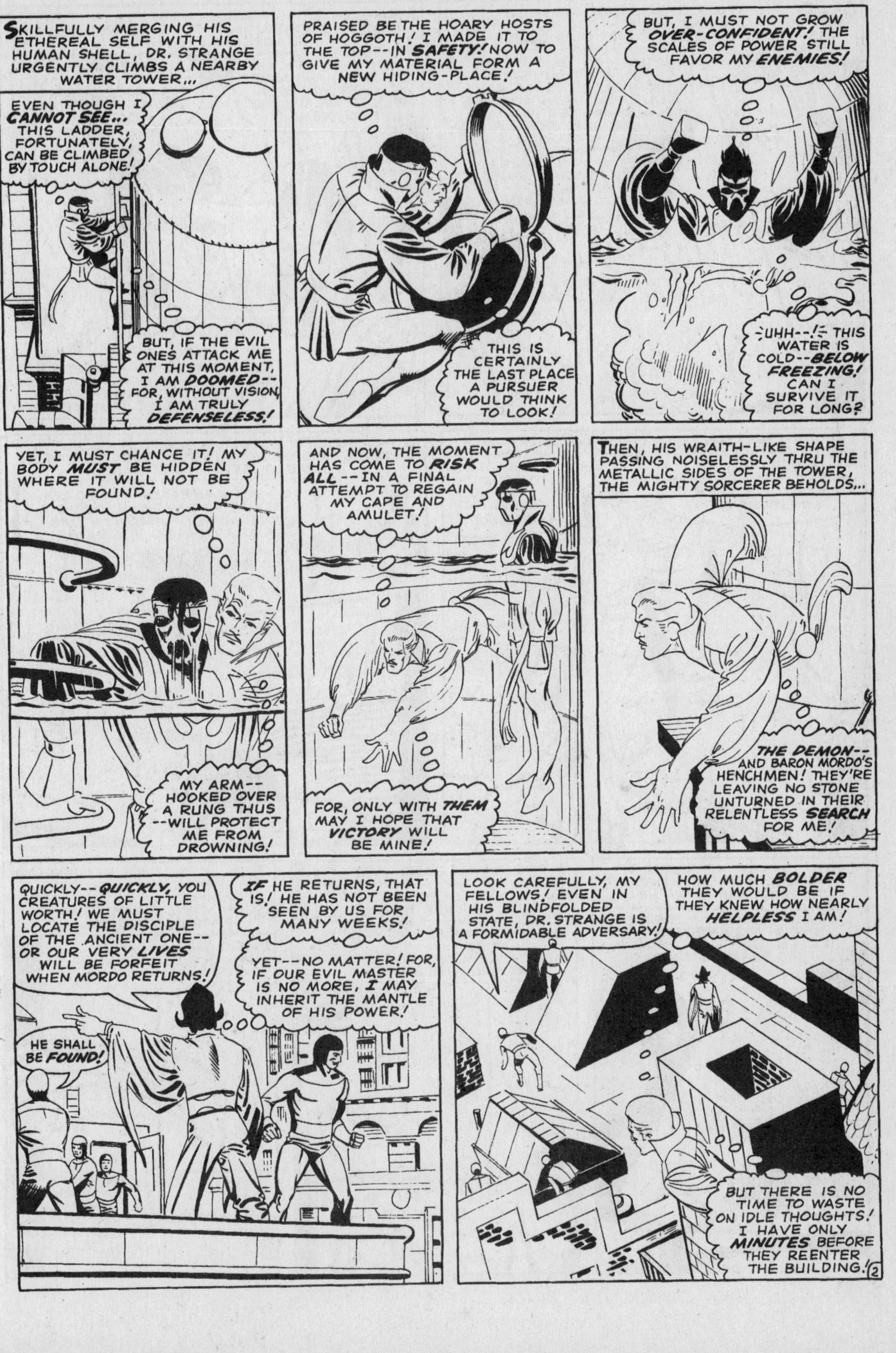
SKILLFULLY MERGING HIS ETHEREAL SELF WITH HIS HUMAN SHELL, DR. STRANGE URGENTLY CLIMBS A NEARBY WATER TOWER...
EVEN THOUGH I CANNOT SEE... THIS LADDER, FORTUNATELY, CAN BE CLIMBED BY TOUCH ALONE!
BUT, IF THE EVIL ONES ATTACK ME AT THIS MOMENT, I AM DOOMED-- FOR, WITHOUT VISION, I AM TRULY DEFENSELESS!
PRAISED BE THE HOARY HOSTS OF HOGGOTH! I MADE IT TO THE TOP--IN SAFETY! NOW TO GIVE MY MATERIAL FORM A NEW HIDING-PLACE!
THIS IS CERTAINLY THE LAST PLACE A PURSUER WOULD THINK TO LOOK!
BUT, I MUST NOT GROW OVER-CONFIDENT! THE SCALES OF POWER STILL FAVOR MY ENEMIES!
UHH--! THIS WATER IS COLD--BELOW FREEZING! CAN I SURVIVE IT FOR LONG?
YET, I MUST CHANCE IT! MY BODY MUST BE HIDDEN WHERE IT WILL NOT BE FOUND!
MY ARM-- HOOKED OVER A RUNG THUS --WILL PROTECT ME FROM DROWNING!
AND NOW, THE MOMENT HAS COME TO RISK ALL--IN A FINAL ATTEMPT TO REGAIN MY CAPE AND AMULET!
FOR, ONLY WITH THEM MAY I HOPE THAT VICTORY WILL BE MINE!
THEN, HIS WRAITH-LIKE SHAPE PASSING NOISELESSLY THRU THE METALLIC SIDES OF THE TOWER, THE MIGHTY SORCERER BEHOLDS...
THE DEMON-- AND BARON MORDO'S HENCHMEN! THEY'RE LEAVING NO STONE UNTURNED IN THEIR RELENTLESS SEARCH FOR ME!
QUICKLY--QUICKLY, YOU CREATURES OF LITTLE WORTH! WE MUST LOCATE THE DISCIPLE OF THE ANCIENT ONE-- OR OUR VERY LIVES WILL BE FORFEIT WHEN MORDO RETURNS!
IF HE RETURNS, THAT IS! HE HAS NOT BEEN SEEN BY US FOR MANY WEEKS!
YET--NO MATTER! FOR, IF OUR EVIL MASTER IS NO MORE, I MAY INHERIT THE MANTLE OF HIS POWER!
HE SHALL BE FOUND!
LOOK CAREFULLY, MY FELLOWS! EVEN IN HIS BLINDFOLDED STATE, DR. STRANGE IS A FORMIDABLE ADVERSARY!
HOW MUCH BOLDER THEY WOULD BE IF THEY KNEW HOW NEARLY HELPLESS I AM!
BUT THERE IS NO TIME TO WASTE ON IDLE THOUGHTS! I HAVE ONLY MINUTES BEFORE THEY REENTER THE BUILDING!
2

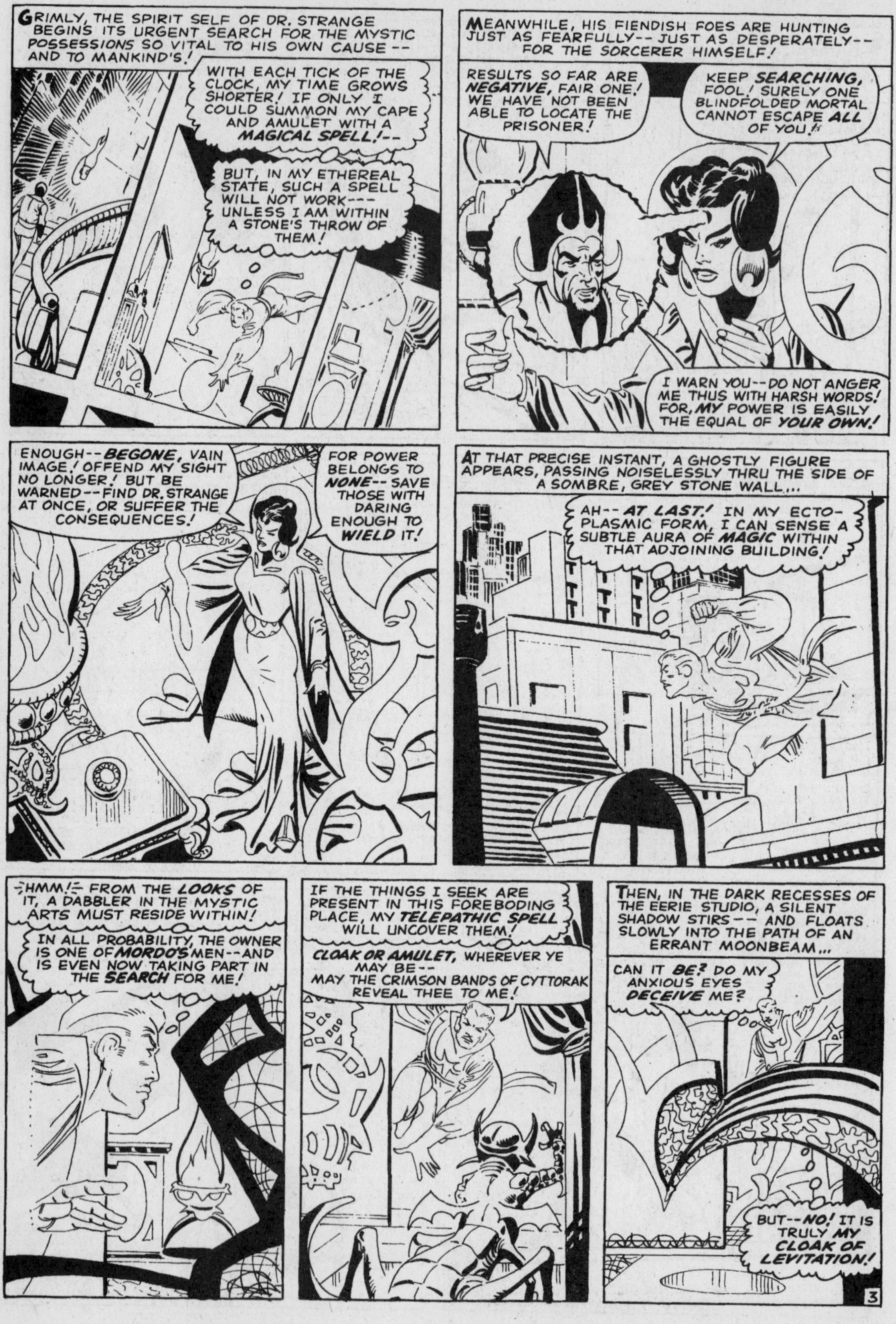
GRIMLY, THE SPIRIT SELF OF DR. STRANGE BEGINS ITS URGENT SEARCH FOR THE MYSTIC POSSESSIONS SO VITAL TO HIS OWN CAUSE -- AND TO MANKIND'S!
WITH EACH TICK OF THE CLOCK, MY TIME GROWS SHORTER! IF ONLY I COULD SUMMON MY CAPE AND AMULET WITH A MAGICAL SPELL!--
BUT, IN MY ETHEREAL STATE, SUCH A SPELL WILL NOT WORK--- UNLESS I AM WITHIN A STONE'S THROW OF THEM!
MEANWHILE, HIS FIENDISH FOES ARE HUNTING JUST AS FEARFULLY-- JUST AS DESPERATELY-- FOR THE SORCERER HIMSELF!
RESULTS SO FAR ARE NEGATIVE, FAIR ONE! WE HAVE NOT BEEN ABLE TO LOCATE THE PRISONER!
KEEP SEARCHING, FOOL! SURELY ONE BLINDFOLDED MORTAL CANNOT ESCAPE ALL OF YOU!
I WARN YOU--DO NOT ANGER ME THUS WITH HARSH WORDS! FOR, MY POWER IS EASILY THE EQUAL OF YOUR OWN!
ENOUGH--BEGONE, VAIN IMAGE! OFFEND MY SIGHT NO LONGER! BUT BE WARNED--FIND DR. STRANGE AT ONCE, OR SUFFER THE CONSEQUENCES!
FOR POWER BELONGS TO NONE-- SAVE THOSE WITH DARING ENOUGH TO WIELD IT!
AT THAT PRECISE INSTANT, A GHOSTLY FIGURE APPEARS, PASSING NOISELESSLY THRU THE SIDE OF A SOMBRE, GREY STONE WALL...
AH--AT LAST! IN MY ECTO-PLASMIC FORM, I CAN SENSE A SUBTLE AURA OF MAGIC WITHIN THAT ADJOINING BUILDING!
HMM! FROM THE LOOKS OF IT, A DABBLER IN THE MYSTIC ARTS MUST RESIDE WITHIN!
IN ALL PROBABILITY, THE OWNER IS ONE OF MORDO'S MEN--AND IS EVEN NOW TAKING PART IN THE SEARCH FOR ME!
IF THE THINGS I SEEK ARE PRESENT IN THIS FOREBODING PLACE, MY TELEPATHIC SPELL WILL UNCOVER THEM!
CLOAK OR AMULET, WHEREVER YE MAY BE-- MAY THE CRIMSON BANDS OF CYTTORAK REVEAL THEE TO ME!
THEN, IN THE DARK RECESSES OF THE EERIE STUDIO, A SILENT SHADOW STIRS-- AND FLOATS SLOWLY INTO THE PATH OF AN ERRANT MOONBEAM...
CAN IT BE? DO MY ANXIOUS EYES DECEIVE ME?
BUT--NO! IT IS TRULY MY CLOAK OF LEVITATION!
3

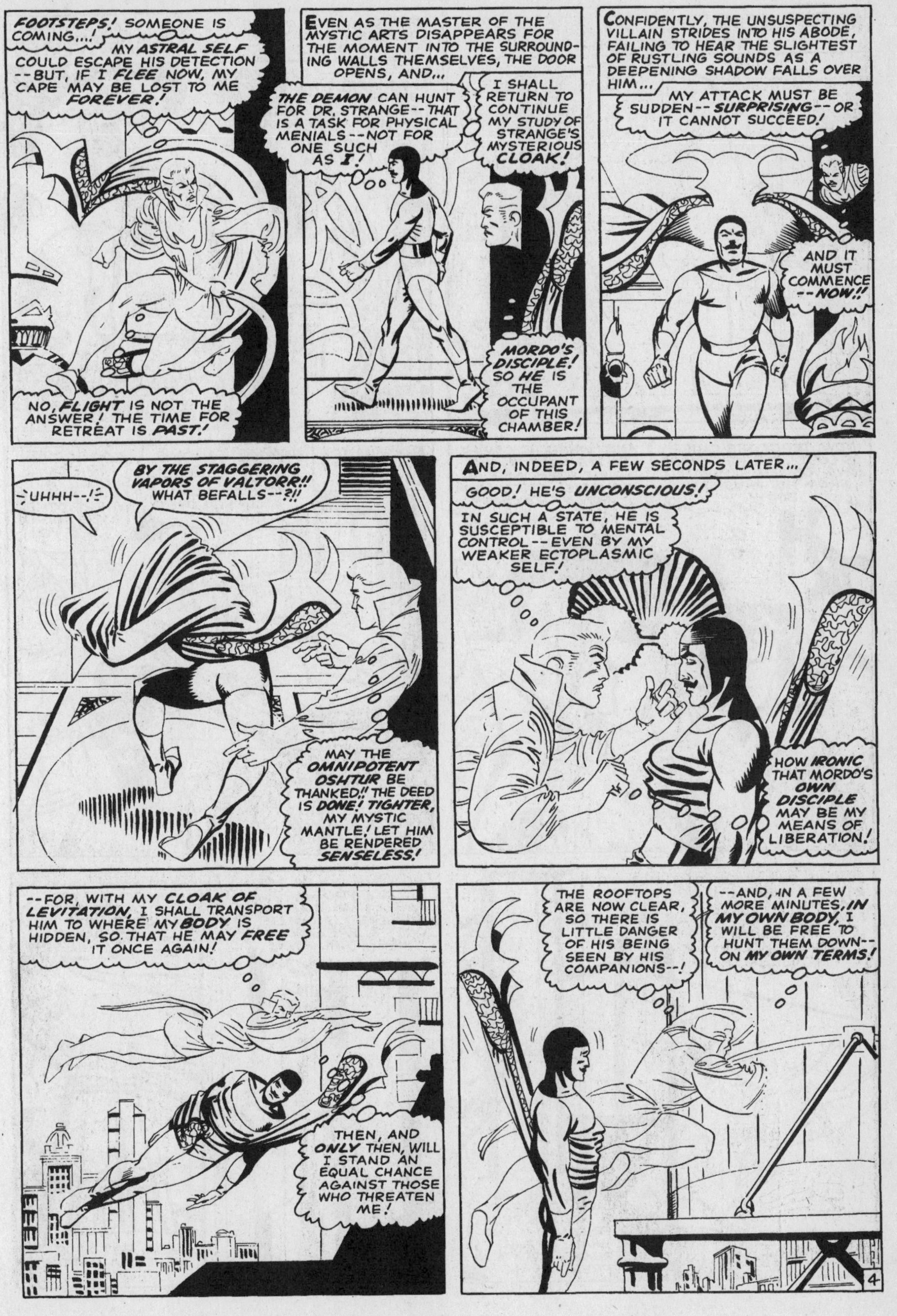
FOOTSTEPS! SOMEONE IS COMING...!
MY ASTRAL SELF COULD ESCAPE HIS DETECTION --BUT, IF I FLEE NOW, MY CAPE MAY BE LOST TO ME FOREVER!
NO, FLIGHT IS NOT THE ANSWER! THE TIME FOR RETREAT IS PAST!
EVEN AS THE MASTER OF THE MYSTIC ARTS DISAPPEARS FOR THE MOMENT INTO THE SURROUNDING WALLS THEMSELVES, THE DOOR OPENS, AND...
THE DEMON CAN HUNT FOR DR. STRANGE--THAT IS A TASK FOR PHYSICAL MENIALS--NOT FOR ONE SUCH AS I!
I SHALL RETURN TO CONTINUE MY STUDY OF STRANGE'S MYSTERIOUS CLOAK!
MORDO'S DISCIPLE! SO HE IS THE OCCUPANT OF THIS CHAMBER!
CONFIDENTLY, THE UNSUSPECTING VILLAIN STRIDES INTO HIS ABODE, FAILING TO HEAR THE SLIGHTEST OF RUSTLING SOUNDS AS A DEEPENING SHADOW FALLS OVER HIM...
MY ATTACK MUST BE SUDDEN--SURPRISING--OR IT CANNOT SUCCEED!
AND IT MUST COMMENCE --NOW!!
UHHH--!
BY THE STAGGERING VAPORS OF VALTORR!! WHAT BEFALLS--?!!
MAY THE OMNIPOTENT OSHTUR BE THANKED!! THE DEED IS DONE! TIGHTER, MY MYSTIC MANTLE! LET HIM BE RENDERED SENSELESS!
AND, INDEED, A FEW SECONDS LATER...
GOOD! HE'S UNCONSCIOUS!
IN SUCH A STATE, HE IS SUSCEPTIBLE TO MENTAL CONTROL--EVEN BY MY WEAKER ECTOPLASMIC SELF!
HOW IRONIC THAT MORDO'S OWN DISCIPLE MAY BE MY MEANS OF LIBERATION!
--FOR, WITH MY CLOAK OF LEVITATION, I SHALL TRANSPORT HIM TO WHERE MY BODY IS HIDDEN, SO THAT HE MAY FREE IT ONCE AGAIN!
THEN, AND ONLY THEN, WILL I STAND AN EQUAL CHANCE AGAINST THOSE WHO THREATEN ME!
THE ROOFTOPS ARE NOW CLEAR, SO THERE IS LITTLE DANGER OF HIS BEING SEEN BY HIS COMPANIONS--!
--AND, IN A FEW MORE MINUTES, IN MY OWN BODY, I WILL BE FREE TO HUNT THEM DOWN--ON MY OWN TERMS!

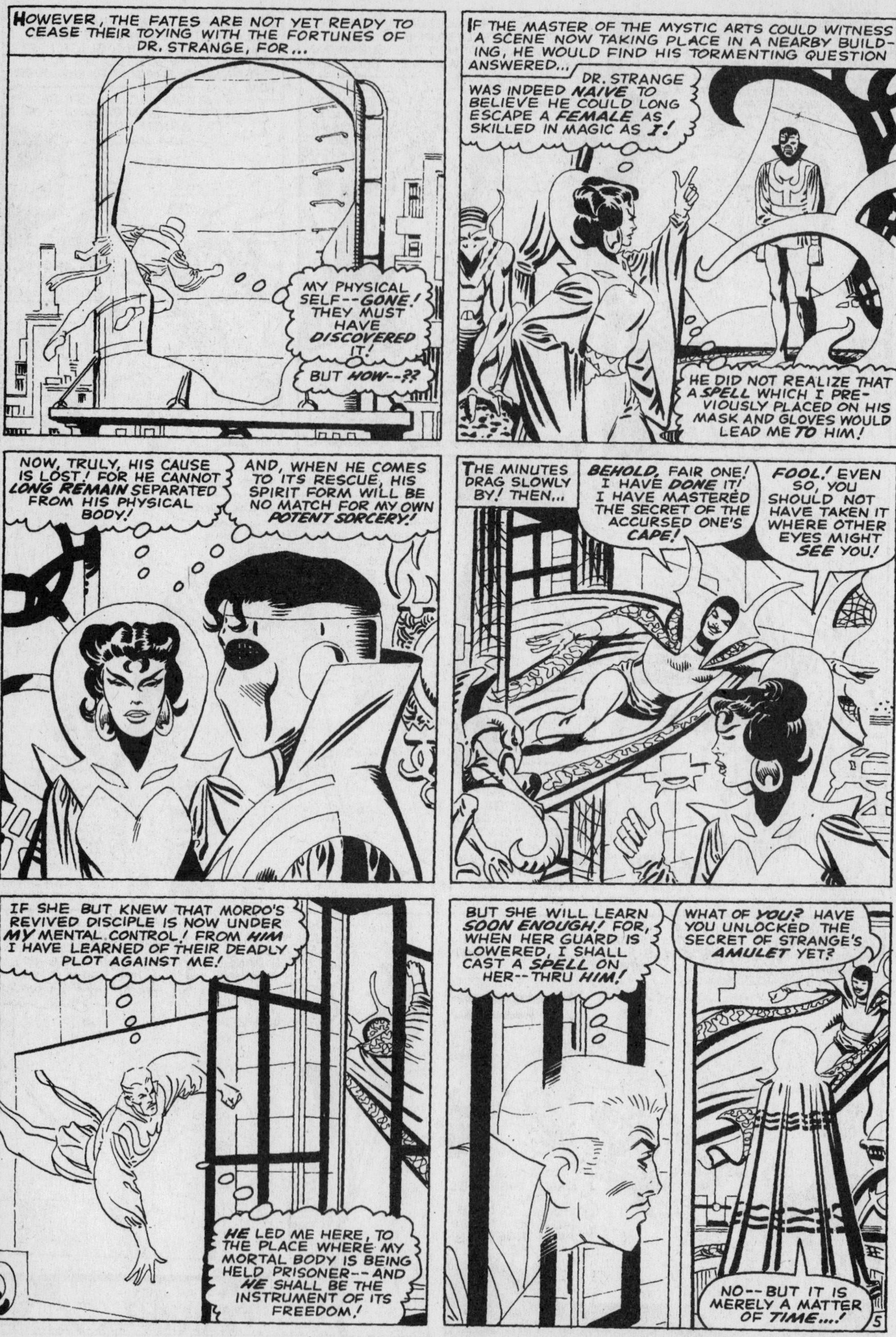
HOWEVER, THE FATES ARE NOT YET READY TO CEASE THEIR TOYING WITH THE FORTUNES OF DR. STRANGE, FOR...
MY PHYSICAL SELF--GONE! THEY MUST HAVE DISCOVERED IT!
BUT HOW--??
IF THE MASTER OF THE MYSTIC ARTS COULD WITNESS A SCENE NOW TAKING PLACE IN A NEARBY BUILDING, HE WOULD FIND HIS TORMENTING QUESTION ANSWERED...
DR. STRANGE WAS INDEED NAIVE TO BELIEVE HE COULD LONG ESCAPE A FEMALE AS SKILLED IN MAGIC AS I!
HE DID NOT REALIZE THAT A SPELL WHICH I PREVIOUSLY PLACED ON HIS MASK AND GLOVES WOULD LEAD ME TO HIM!
NOW, TRULY, HIS CAUSE IS LOST! FOR HE CANNOT LONG REMAIN SEPARATED FROM HIS PHYSICAL BODY!
AND, WHEN HE COMES TO ITS RESCUE, HIS SPIRIT FORM WILL BE NO MATCH FOR MY OWN POTENT SORCERY!
THE MINUTES DRAG SLOWLY BY! THEN...
BEHOLD, FAIR ONE! I HAVE DONE IT! I HAVE MASTERED THE SECRET OF THE ACCURSED ONE'S CAPE!
FOOL! EVEN SO, YOU SHOULD NOT HAVE TAKEN IT WHERE OTHER EYES MIGHT SEE YOU!
IF SHE BUT KNEW THAT MORDO'S REVIVED DISCIPLE IS NOW UNDER MY MENTAL CONTROL! FROM HIM I HAVE LEARNED OF THEIR DEADLY PLOT AGAINST ME!
HE LED ME HERE, TO THE PLACE WHERE MY MORTAL BODY IS BEING HELD PRISONER--AND HE SHALL BE THE INSTRUMENT OF ITS FREEDOM!
BUT SHE WILL LEARN SOON ENOUGH! FOR, WHEN HER GUARD IS LOWERED, I SHALL CAST A SPELL ON HER--THRU HIM!
WHAT OF YOU? HAVE YOU UNLOCKED THE SECRET OF STRANGE'S AMULET YET?
NO--BUT IT IS MERELY A MATTER OF TIME...!
5

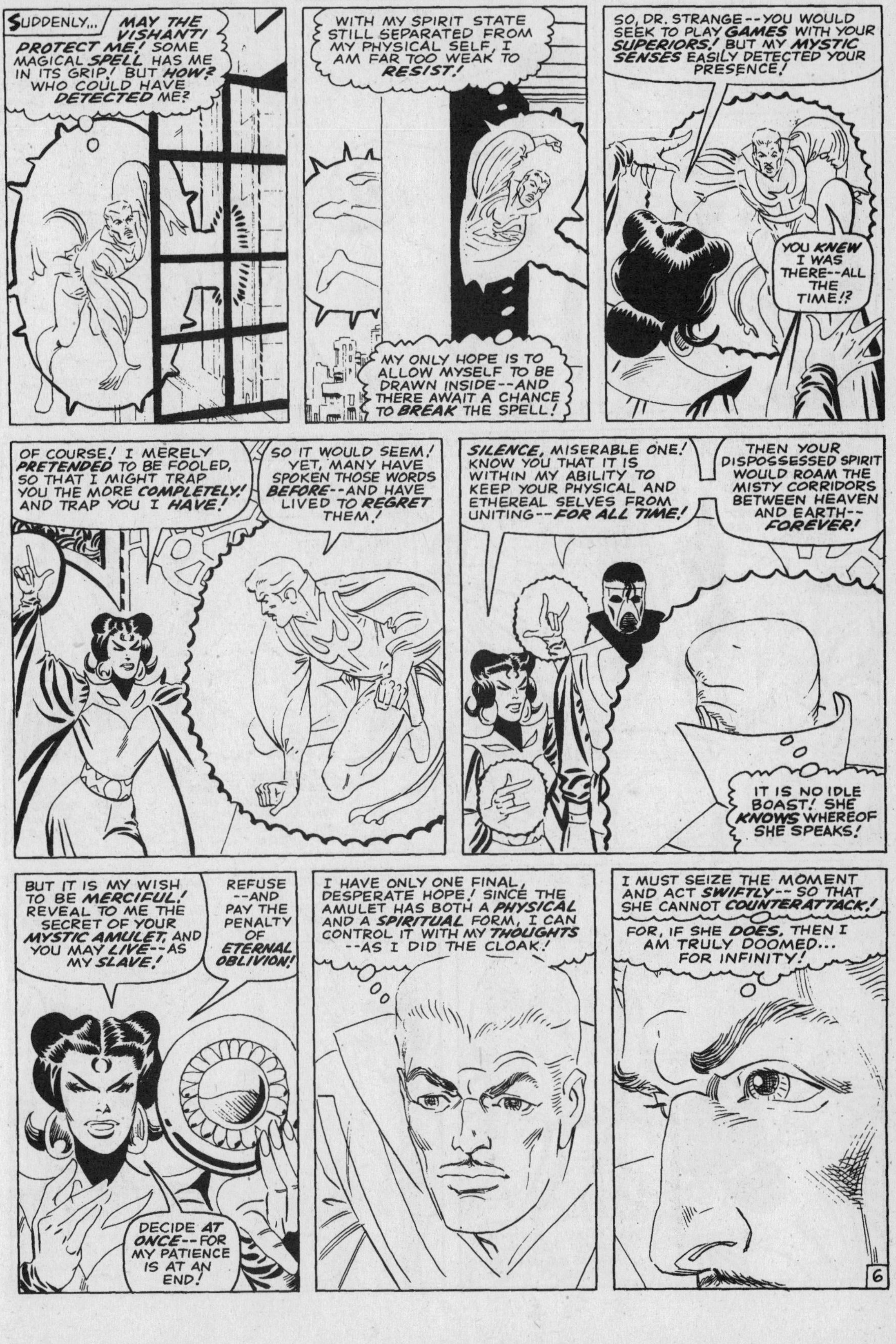
SUDDENLY...
MAY THE VISHANTI PROTECT ME! SOME MAGICAL SPELL HAS ME IN ITS GRIP! BUT HOW? WHO COULD HAVE DETECTED ME?
WITH MY SPIRIT STATE STILL SEPARATED FROM MY PHYSICAL SELF, I AM FAR TOO WEAK TO RESIST!
MY ONLY HOPE IS TO ALLOW MYSELF TO BE DRAWN INSIDE--AND THERE AWAIT A CHANCE TO BREAK THE SPELL!
SO, DR. STRANGE--YOU WOULD SEEK TO PLAY GAMES WITH YOUR SUPERIORS! BUT MY MYSTIC SENSES EASILY DETECTED YOUR PRESENCE!
YOU KNEW I WAS THERE--ALL THE TIME!?
OF COURSE! I MERELY PRETENDED TO BE FOOLED, SO THAT I MIGHT TRAP YOU THE MORE COMPLETELY! AND TRAP YOU I HAVE!
SO IT WOULD SEEM! YET, MANY HAVE SPOKEN THOSE WORDS BEFORE--AND HAVE LIVED TO REGRET THEM!
SILENCE, MISERABLE ONE! KNOW YOU THAT IT IS WITHIN MY ABILITY TO KEEP YOUR PHYSICAL AND ETHEREAL SELVES FROM UNITING--FOR ALL TIME!
THEN YOUR DISPOSSESSED SPIRIT WOULD ROAM THE MISTY CORRIDORS BETWEEN HEAVEN AND EARTH--FOREVER!
IT IS NO IDLE BOAST! SHE KNOWS WHEREOF SHE SPEAKS!
BUT IT IS MY WISH TO BE MERCIFUL! REVEAL TO ME THE SECRET OF YOUR MYSTIC AMULET, AND YOU MAY LIVE--AS MY SLAVE!
REFUSE --AND PAY THE PENALTY OF ETERNAL OBLIVION!
DECIDE AT ONCE--FOR MY PATIENCE IS AT AN END!
I HAVE ONLY ONE FINAL, DESPERATE HOPE! SINCE THE AMULET HAS BOTH A PHYSICAL AND A SPIRITUAL FORM, I CAN CONTROL IT WITH MY THOUGHTS --AS I DID THE CLOAK!
I MUST SEIZE THE MOMENT AND ACT SWIFTLY-- SO THAT SHE CANNOT COUNTERATTACK!
FOR, IF SHE DOES, THEN I AM TRULY DOOMED... FOR INFINITY!

THE NEXT INSTANT, EVEN AS THE EVIL SORCERESS HOLDS THE TALISMAN IN HER GRASP, A STARTLING PHENOMENON OCCURS!

—UHHH—!!— THAT EYE, LEAPING FROM THE AMULET ITSELF!!

IT--IT'S HYPNOTIZING ME! MY VERY WILL IS BEING SAPPED--AND I CAN DO NOTHING TO RESIST--!!

MY PLAN IS SUCCEEDING! EACH FATEFUL SECOND SHE STARES AT THE MYSTIC EYE, HER MAGIC HOLD ON ME IS DISSOLVING---!! JUST A FEW HEARTBEATS MORE, AND--

BUT, EVEN AS THE LAST REMAINING VESTIGES OF THE MAGIC SPELL FADE, THERE IS HEARD THE HEAVY, MEASURED TREAD OF SINISTER FOOTSTEPS, AND...

IT IS FORTUNATE THAT I HAPPENED TO CHOOSE THIS EXACT MOMENT TO REPORT ON OUR SEARCH!

--A BURST OF ENERGY TO INTERFERE WITH YOUR ACCURSED EYE-- AND YOUR FUTILE ATTEMPT AT HYPNOSIS IS ENDED!

AH--! AND NOW, DR. STRANGE, YOU SHALL PAY DEARLY FOR REJECTING MY TERMS!

THE DEMON! SO, I MUST BATTLE TWO FOES, EITHER OF WHOM CAN DEFEAT ME IN MY SPIRIT FORM!

BUT PERHAPS-- USING MY CONTROL OVER MORDO'S DISCIPLE, I MAY YET HAVE A CHANCE!

SHE IS AS CLEVER AS SHE IS RUTHLESS! BEFORE I COULD COMMAND MY MENTAL CAPTIVE TO AID ME, SHE RENDERED HIM POWERLESS!

UNNNHH...!

YOU SHALL NOT USE ONE OF OUR OWN NUMBER AGAINST US, IMPUDENT ONE!

IN YOUR ECTOPLASMIC STATE, YOU ARE NO MATCH FOR ONE OF US, MUCH LESS BOTH!

THAT IS NOT FOR YOU TO SAY!! I SHALL NEVER CEASE STRUGGLING-- NOT WHILE I LIVE!

THEN, WE SHALL END YOUR STRUGGLE --BY ENDING YOUR LIFE!

7

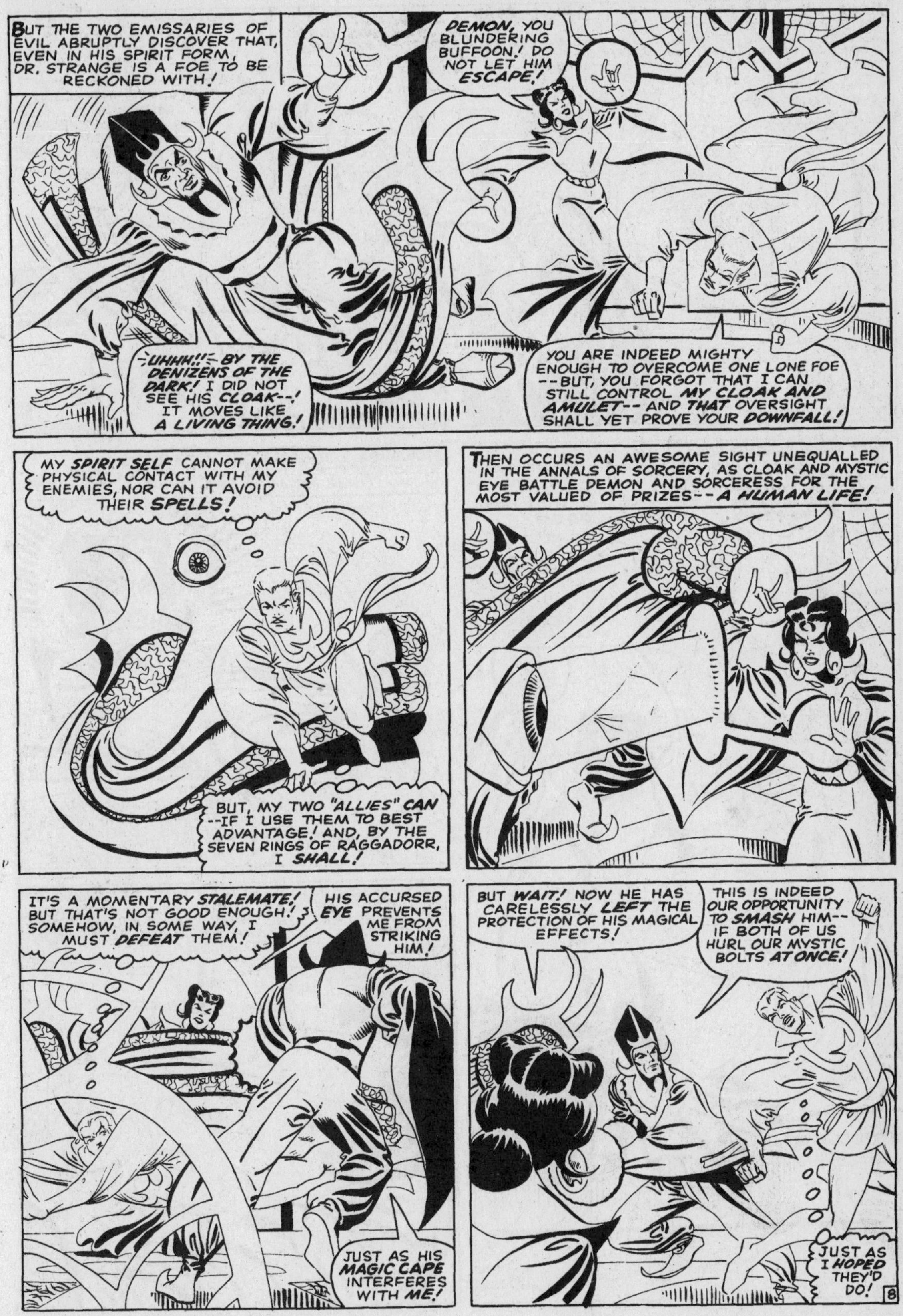
BUT THE TWO EMISSARIES OF EVIL ABRUPTLY DISCOVER THAT, EVEN IN HIS SPIRIT FORM, DR. STRANGE IS A FOE TO BE RECKONED WITH!
DEMON, YOU BLUNDERING BUFFOON! DO NOT LET HIM ESCAPE!
UHHH!!-- BY THE DENIZENS OF THE DARK! I DID NOT SEE HIS CLOAK--! IT MOVES LIKE A LIVING THING!
YOU ARE INDEED MIGHTY ENOUGH TO OVERCOME ONE LONE FOE --BUT, YOU FORGOT THAT I CAN STILL CONTROL MY CLOAK AND AMULET-- AND THAT OVERSIGHT SHALL YET PROVE YOUR DOWNFALL!
MY SPIRIT SELF CANNOT MAKE PHYSICAL CONTACT WITH MY ENEMIES, NOR CAN IT AVOID THEIR SPELLS!
BUT, MY TWO "ALLIES" CAN --IF I USE THEM TO BEST ADVANTAGE! AND, BY THE SEVEN RINGS OF RAGGADORR, I SHALL!
THEN OCCURS AN AWESOME SIGHT UNEQUALLED IN THE ANNALS OF SORCERY, AS CLOAK AND MYSTIC EYE BATTLE DEMON AND SORCERESS FOR THE MOST VALUED OF PRIZES-- A HUMAN LIFE!
IT'S A MOMENTARY STALEMATE! BUT THAT'S NOT GOOD ENOUGH! SOMEHOW, IN SOME WAY, I MUST DEFEAT THEM!
HIS ACCURSED EYE PREVENTS ME FROM STRIKING HIM!
JUST AS HIS MAGIC CAPE INTERFERES WITH ME!
BUT WAIT! NOW HE HAS CARELESSLY LEFT THE PROTECTION OF HIS MAGICAL EFFECTS!
THIS IS INDEED OUR OPPORTUNITY TO SMASH HIM-- IF BOTH OF US HURL OUR MYSTIC BOLTS AT ONCE!
JUST AS I HOPED THEY'D DO!
8

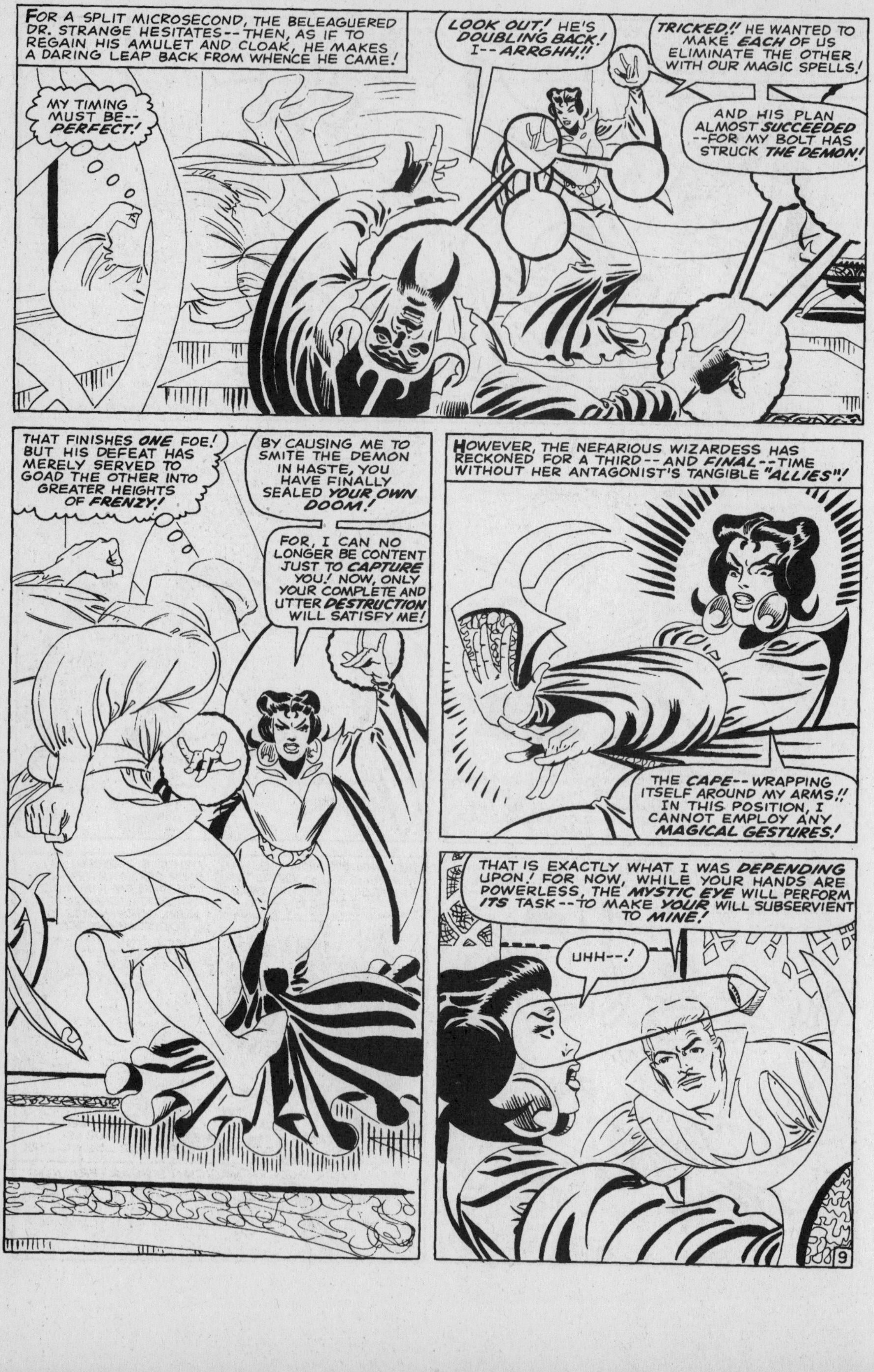
FOR A SPLIT MICROSECOND, THE BELEAGUERED DR. STRANGE HESITATES--THEN, AS IF TO REGAIN HIS AMULET AND CLOAK, HE MAKES A DARING LEAP BACK FROM WHENCE HE CAME!
LOOK OUT! HE'S DOUBLING BACK! I--ARRGHH!!
TRICKED!! HE WANTED TO MAKE EACH OF US ELIMINATE THE OTHER WITH OUR MAGIC SPELLS!
MY TIMING MUST BE--PERFECT!
AND HIS PLAN ALMOST SUCCEEDED --FOR MY BOLT HAS STRUCK THE DEMON!
THAT FINISHES ONE FOE! BUT HIS DEFEAT HAS MERELY SERVED TO GOAD THE OTHER INTO GREATER HEIGHTS OF FRENZY!
BY CAUSING ME TO SMITE THE DEMON IN HASTE, YOU HAVE FINALLY SEALED YOUR OWN DOOM!
FOR, I CAN NO LONGER BE CONTENT JUST TO CAPTURE YOU! NOW, ONLY YOUR COMPLETE AND UTTER DESTRUCTION WILL SATISFY ME!
HOWEVER, THE NEFARIOUS WIZARDESS HAS RECKONED FOR A THIRD--AND FINAL--TIME WITHOUT HER ANTAGONIST'S TANGIBLE "ALLIES"!
THE CAPE--WRAPPING ITSELF AROUND MY ARMS!! IN THIS POSITION, I CANNOT EMPLOY ANY MAGICAL GESTURES!
THAT IS EXACTLY WHAT I WAS DEPENDING UPON! FOR NOW, WHILE YOUR HANDS ARE POWERLESS, THE MYSTIC EYE WILL PERFORM ITS TASK--TO MAKE YOUR WILL SUBSERVIENT TO MINE!
UHH--!

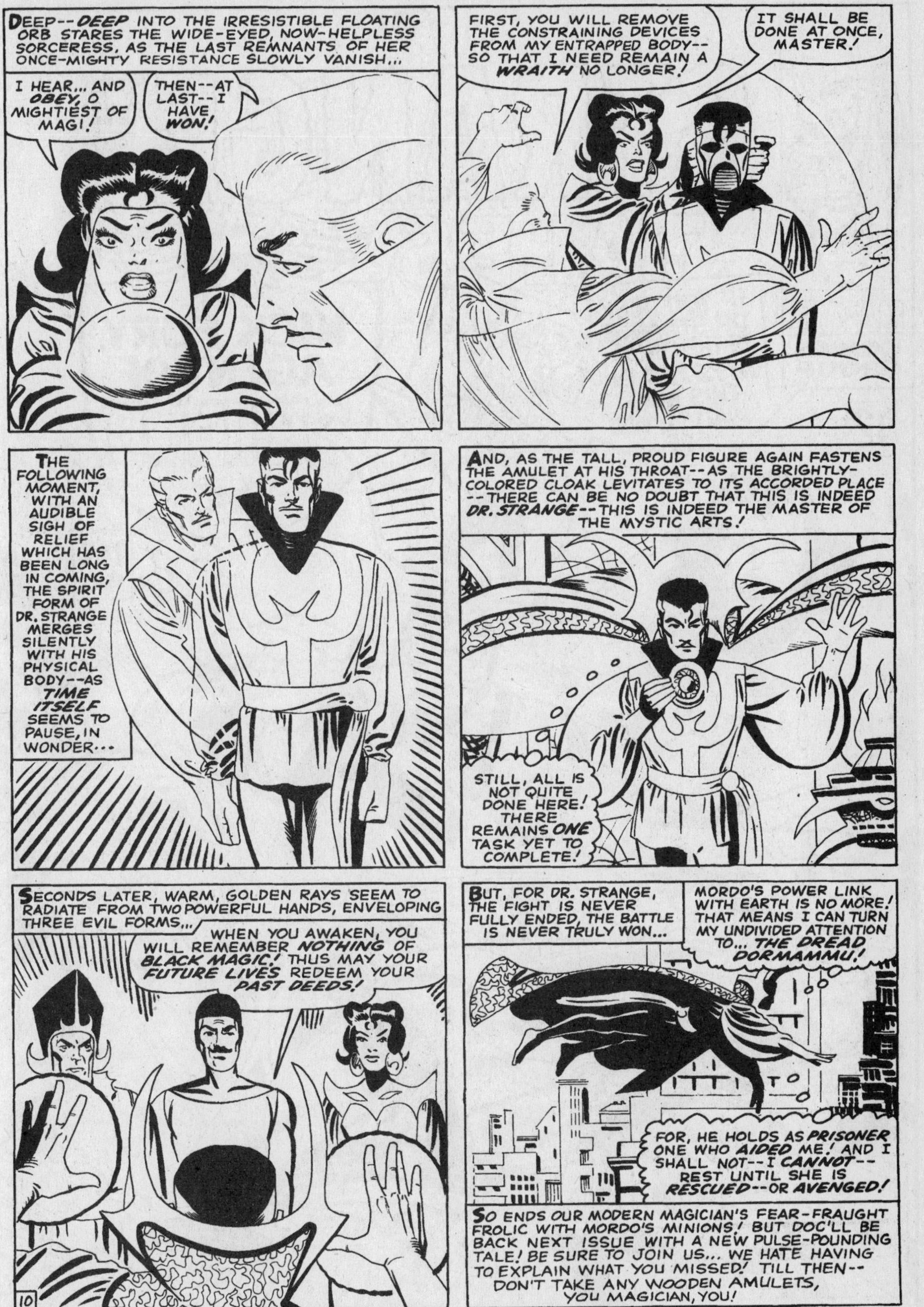
DEEP--DEEP INTO THE IRRESISTIBLE FLOATING ORB STARES THE WIDE-EYED, NOW-HELPLESS SORCERESS, AS THE LAST REMNANTS OF HER ONCE-MIGHTY RESISTANCE SLOWLY VANISH...
I HEAR... AND OBEY, O MIGHTIEST OF MAGI!
THEN--AT LAST--I HAVE WON!
FIRST, YOU WILL REMOVE THE CONSTRAINING DEVICES FROM MY ENTRAPPED BODY--SO THAT I NEED REMAIN A WRAITH NO LONGER!
IT SHALL BE DONE AT ONCE, MASTER!
THE FOLLOWING MOMENT, WITH AN AUDIBLE SIGH OF RELIEF WHICH HAS BEEN LONG IN COMING, THE SPIRIT FORM OF DR. STRANGE MERGES SILENTLY WITH HIS PHYSICAL BODY--AS TIME ITSELF SEEMS TO PAUSE, IN WONDER...
AND, AS THE TALL, PROUD FIGURE AGAIN FASTENS THE AMULET AT HIS THROAT--AS THE BRIGHTLY-COLORED CLOAK LEVITATES TO ITS ACCORDED PLACE--THERE CAN BE NO DOUBT THAT THIS IS INDEED DR. STRANGE--THIS IS INDEED THE MASTER OF THE MYSTIC ARTS!
STILL, ALL IS NOT QUITE DONE HERE! THERE REMAINS ONE TASK YET TO COMPLETE!
SECONDS LATER, WARM, GOLDEN RAYS SEEM TO RADIATE FROM TWO POWERFUL HANDS, ENVELOPING THREE EVIL FORMS...
WHEN YOU AWAKEN, YOU WILL REMEMBER NOTHING OF BLACK MAGIC! THUS MAY YOUR FUTURE LIVES REDEEM YOUR PAST DEEDS!
10
BUT, FOR DR. STRANGE, THE FIGHT IS NEVER FULLY ENDED, THE BATTLE IS NEVER TRULY WON...
MORDO'S POWER LINK WITH EARTH IS NO MORE! THAT MEANS I CAN TURN MY UNDIVIDED ATTENTION TO... THE DREAD DORMAMMU!
FOR, HE HOLDS AS PRISONER ONE WHO AIDED ME! AND I SHALL NOT--I CANNOT--REST UNTIL SHE IS RESCUED--OR AVENGED!
SO ENDS OUR MODERN MAGICIAN'S FEAR-FRAUGHT FROLIC WITH MORDO'S MINIONS! BUT DOC'LL BE BACK NEXT ISSUE WITH A NEW PULSE-POUNDING TALE! BE SURE TO JOIN US... WE HATE HAVING TO EXPLAIN WHAT YOU MISSED! TILL THEN--DON'T TAKE ANY WOODEN AMULETS, YOU MAGICIAN, YOU!

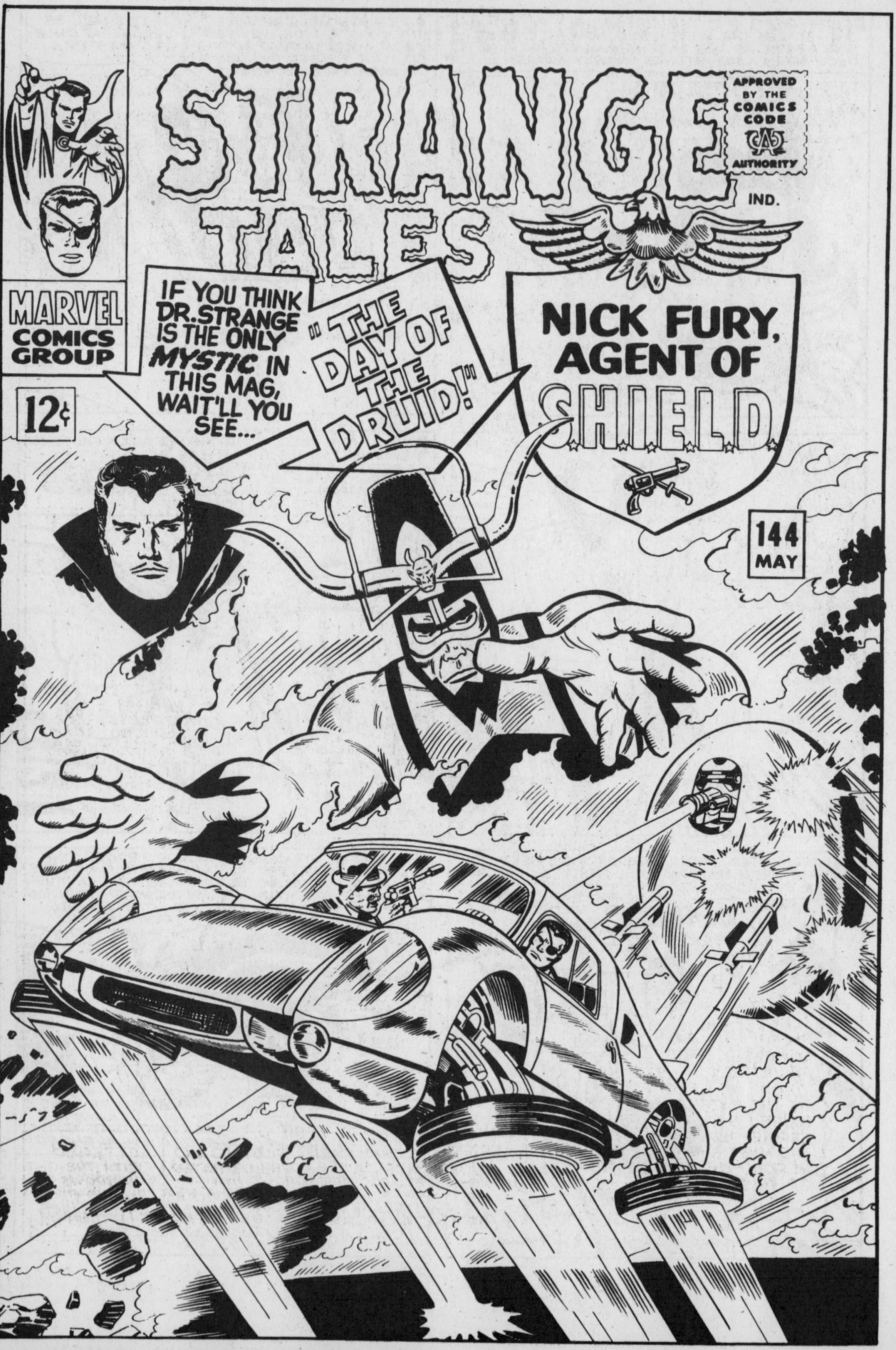

STRANGE TALES
MARVEL COMICS GROUP
12¢
APPROVED BY THE COMICS CODE AUTHORITY
IND.
IF YOU THINK DR. STRANGE IS THE ONLY MYSTIC IN THIS MAG, WAIT'LL YOU SEE...
"THE DAY OF THE DRUID!"
NICK FURY, AGENT OF S.H.I.E.L.D
144 MAY

Dr. STRANGE, MASTER OF THE MYSTIC ARTS!

"WHERE MAN HATH NEVER TROD!"

OBSERVE AND *TREMBLE*, INSOLENT MORTAL! SEE THE FATE OF THE FEMALE WHO RESCUED YOU ONCE BEFORE -- AND KNOW THAT *YOU* ARE RESPONSIBLE FOR WHAT AWAITS HER!

DORMAMMU SPEAKS THE *TRUTH*... FOR IT WAS BY AIDING *ME* THAT THE GIRL INCURRED HIS ANGER! NOW IT IS *I* WHO MUST RESCUE *HER!*

AND YET, I AM *HELPLESS* -- FOR I COULD NOT REACH HER SIDE IN TIME TO SAVE HER FROM THE FURY OF MY MALEVOLENT FOE!*

*IN CASE THIS SCENE LOOKS A BIT *FAMILIAR* TO YOU, BE IT KNOWN THAT, THRU THE GENEROSITY OF *MAGNANIMOUS MARVEL*, YOU ARE RELIVING THAT DRAMATIC MOMENT WHEN AN ENRAGED *DORMAMMU*, THWARTED IN HIS ATTEMPT TO DESTROY DR. STRANGE, TURNS HIS RAMPAGING WRATH ON THE MYSTERIOUS SILVER-HAIRED GIRL WHO HAS BEFRIENDED THE MASTER OF THE MYSTIC ARTS, AS RELATED IN *STRANGE TALES #141* -- OR WAS IT *#142*? .... FORGETFUL STAN

EDITED WITH PERSPICACITY BY:	WRITTEN WITH PRECOCITY BY:	PLOTTED AND ILLUSTRATED WITH PROFUNDITY BY:	LETTERED WITH THE WINDOWS CLOSED BY:
STAN LEE	ROY THOMAS	STEVE DITKO	ARTIE SIMEK

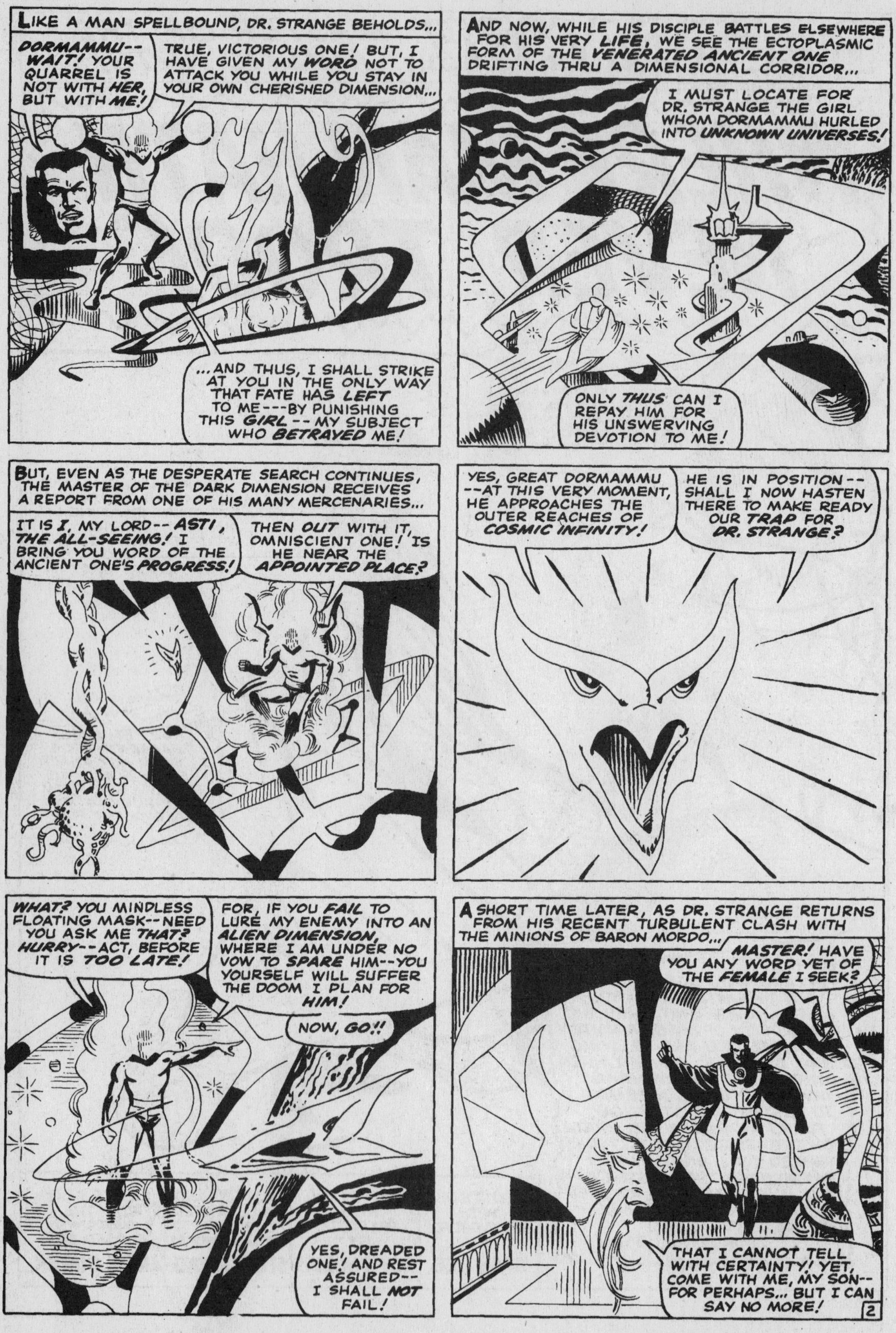
LIKE A MAN SPELLBOUND, DR. STRANGE BEHOLDS...
DORMAMMU-- WAIT! YOUR QUARREL IS NOT WITH HER, BUT WITH ME!
TRUE, VICTORIOUS ONE! BUT, I HAVE GIVEN MY WORD NOT TO ATTACK YOU WHILE YOU STAY IN YOUR OWN CHERISHED DIMENSION...
...AND THUS, I SHALL STRIKE AT YOU IN THE ONLY WAY THAT FATE HAS LEFT TO ME---BY PUNISHING THIS GIRL -- MY SUBJECT WHO BETRAYED ME!
AND NOW, WHILE HIS DISCIPLE BATTLES ELSEWHERE FOR HIS VERY LIFE, WE SEE THE ECTOPLASMIC FORM OF THE VENERATED ANCIENT ONE DRIFTING THRU A DIMENSIONAL CORRIDOR...
I MUST LOCATE FOR DR. STRANGE THE GIRL WHOM DORMAMMU HURLED INTO UNKNOWN UNIVERSES!
ONLY THUS CAN I REPAY HIM FOR HIS UNSWERVING DEVOTION TO ME!
BUT, EVEN AS THE DESPERATE SEARCH CONTINUES, THE MASTER OF THE DARK DIMENSION RECEIVES A REPORT FROM ONE OF HIS MANY MERCENARIES...
IT IS I, MY LORD-- ASTI, THE ALL-SEEING! I BRING YOU WORD OF THE ANCIENT ONE'S PROGRESS!
THEN OUT WITH IT, OMNISCIENT ONE! IS HE NEAR THE APPOINTED PLACE?
YES, GREAT DORMAMMU --AT THIS VERY MOMENT, HE APPROACHES THE OUTER REACHES OF COSMIC INFINITY!
HE IS IN POSITION-- SHALL I NOW HASTEN THERE TO MAKE READY OUR TRAP FOR DR. STRANGE?
WHAT? YOU MINDLESS FLOATING MASK--NEED YOU ASK ME THAT? HURRY--ACT, BEFORE IT IS TOO LATE!
FOR, IF YOU FAIL TO LURE MY ENEMY INTO AN ALIEN DIMENSION, WHERE I AM UNDER NO VOW TO SPARE HIM--YOU YOURSELF WILL SUFFER THE DOOM I PLAN FOR HIM!
NOW, GO!!
YES, DREADED ONE! AND REST ASSURED-- I SHALL NOT FAIL!
A SHORT TIME LATER, AS DR. STRANGE RETURNS FROM HIS RECENT TURBULENT CLASH WITH THE MINIONS OF BARON MORDO...
MASTER! HAVE YOU ANY WORD YET OF THE FEMALE I SEEK?
THAT I CANNOT TELL WITH CERTAINTY! YET, COME WITH ME, MY SON-- FOR PERHAPS... BUT I CAN SAY NO MORE!
2

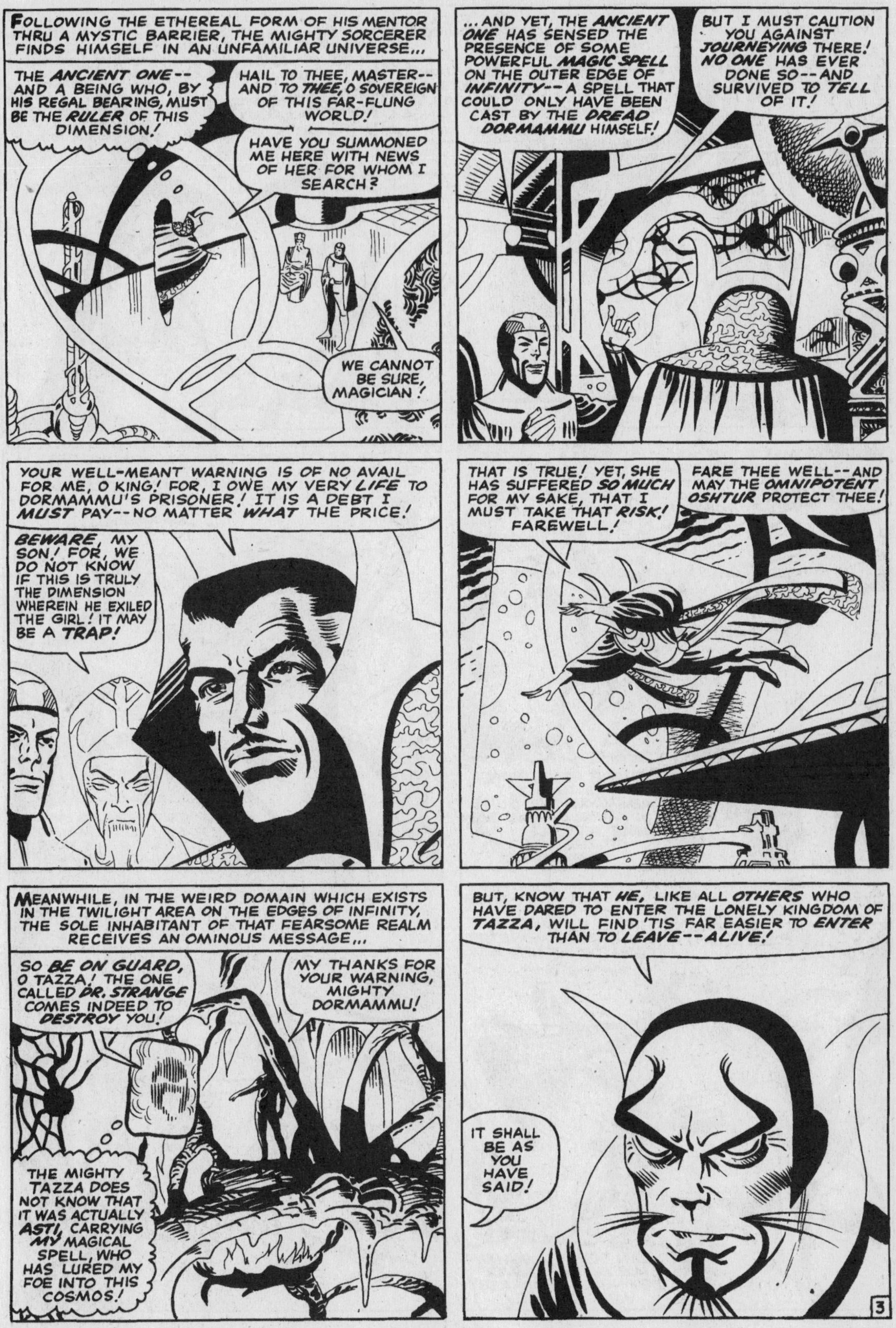
FOLLOWING THE ETHEREAL FORM OF HIS MENTOR THRU A MYSTIC BARRIER, THE MIGHTY SORCERER FINDS HIMSELF IN AN UNFAMILIAR UNIVERSE...
THE ANCIENT ONE-- AND A BEING WHO, BY HIS REGAL BEARING, MUST BE THE RULER OF THIS DIMENSION!
HAIL TO THEE, MASTER-- AND TO THEE, O SOVEREIGN OF THIS FAR-FLUNG WORLD!
HAVE YOU SUMMONED ME HERE WITH NEWS OF HER FOR WHOM I SEARCH?
WE CANNOT BE SURE, MAGICIAN!
...AND YET, THE ANCIENT ONE HAS SENSED THE PRESENCE OF SOME POWERFUL MAGIC SPELL ON THE OUTER EDGE OF INFINITY-- A SPELL THAT COULD ONLY HAVE BEEN CAST BY THE DREAD DORMAMMU HIMSELF!
BUT I MUST CAUTION YOU AGAINST JOURNEYING THERE! NO ONE HAS EVER DONE SO--AND SURVIVED TO TELL OF IT!
YOUR WELL-MEANT WARNING IS OF NO AVAIL FOR ME, O KING! FOR, I OWE MY VERY LIFE TO DORMAMMU'S PRISONER! IT IS A DEBT I MUST PAY--NO MATTER WHAT THE PRICE!
BEWARE, MY SON! FOR, WE DO NOT KNOW IF THIS IS TRULY THE DIMENSION WHEREIN HE EXILED THE GIRL! IT MAY BE A TRAP!
THAT IS TRUE! YET, SHE HAS SUFFERED SO MUCH FOR MY SAKE, THAT I MUST TAKE THAT RISK! FAREWELL!
FARE THEE WELL--AND MAY THE OMNIPOTENT OSHTUR PROTECT THEE!
MEANWHILE, IN THE WEIRD DOMAIN WHICH EXISTS IN THE TWILIGHT AREA ON THE EDGES OF INFINITY, THE SOLE INHABITANT OF THAT FEARSOME REALM RECEIVES AN OMINOUS MESSAGE...
SO BE ON GUARD, O TAZZA! THE ONE CALLED DR. STRANGE COMES INDEED TO DESTROY YOU!
MY THANKS FOR YOUR WARNING, MIGHTY DORMAMMU!
THE MIGHTY TAZZA DOES NOT KNOW THAT IT WAS ACTUALLY ASTI, CARRYING MY MAGICAL SPELL, WHO HAS LURED MY FOE INTO THIS COSMOS!
BUT, KNOW THAT HE, LIKE ALL OTHERS WHO HAVE DARED TO ENTER THE LONELY KINGDOM OF TAZZA, WILL FIND 'TIS FAR EASIER TO ENTER THAN TO LEAVE--ALIVE!
IT SHALL BE AS YOU HAVE SAID!
3

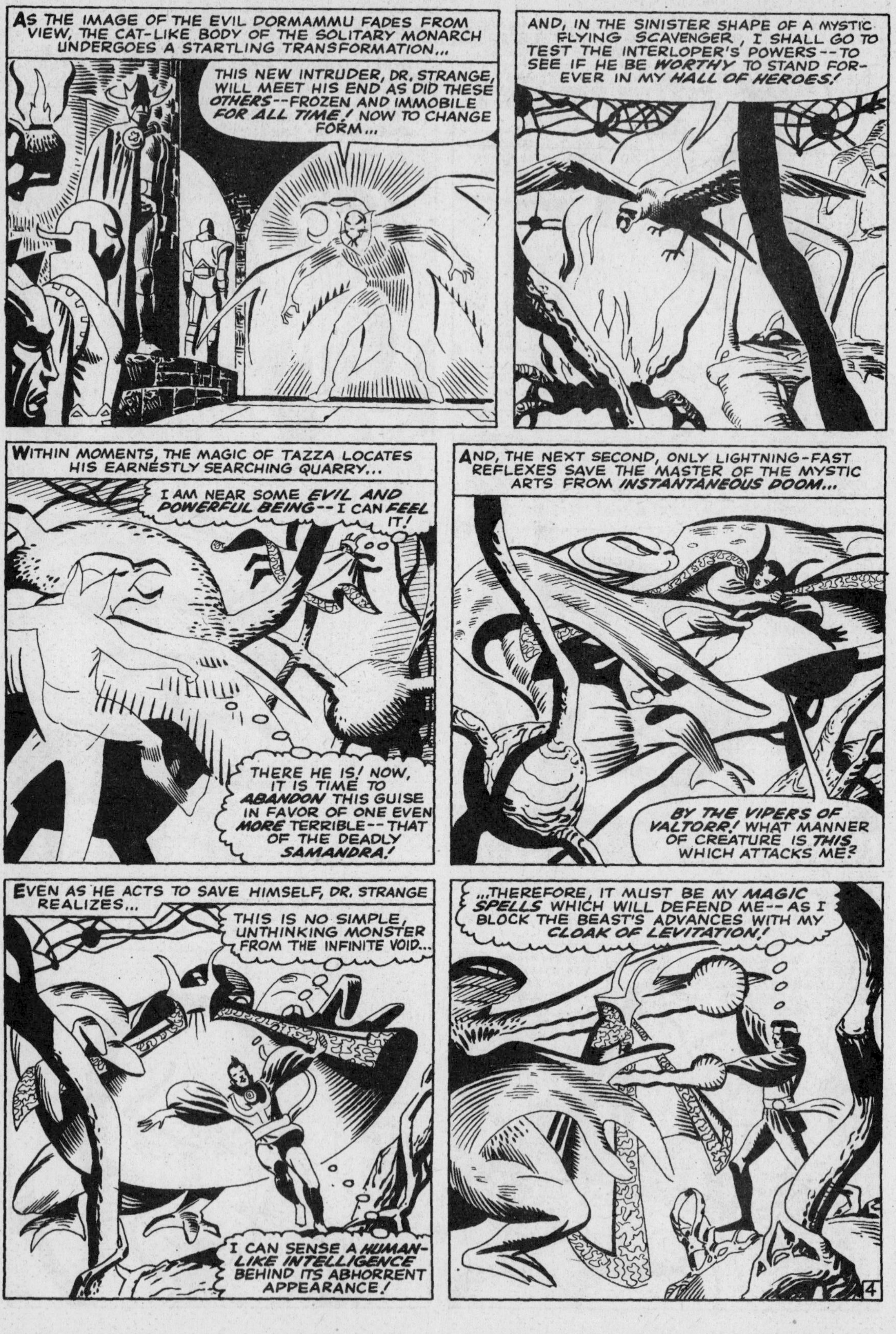
AS THE IMAGE OF THE EVIL DORMAMMU FADES FROM VIEW, THE CAT-LIKE BODY OF THE SOLITARY MONARCH UNDERGOES A STARTLING TRANSFORMATION...
THIS NEW INTRUDER, DR. STRANGE, WILL MEET HIS END AS DID THESE OTHERS--FROZEN AND IMMOBILE FOR ALL TIME! NOW TO CHANGE FORM...
AND, IN THE SINISTER SHAPE OF A MYSTIC FLYING SCAVENGER, I SHALL GO TO TEST THE INTERLOPER'S POWERS--TO SEE IF HE BE WORTHY TO STAND FOREVER IN MY HALL OF HEROES!
WITHIN MOMENTS, THE MAGIC OF TAZZA LOCATES HIS EARNESTLY SEARCHING QUARRY...
I AM NEAR SOME EVIL AND POWERFUL BEING--I CAN FEEL IT!
THERE HE IS! NOW, IT IS TIME TO ABANDON THIS GUISE IN FAVOR OF ONE EVEN MORE TERRIBLE--THAT OF THE DEADLY SAMANDRA!
AND, THE NEXT SECOND, ONLY LIGHTNING-FAST REFLEXES SAVE THE MASTER OF THE MYSTIC ARTS FROM INSTANTANEOUS DOOM...
BY THE VIPERS OF VALTORR! WHAT MANNER OF CREATURE IS THIS WHICH ATTACKS ME?
EVEN AS HE ACTS TO SAVE HIMSELF, DR. STRANGE REALIZES...
THIS IS NO SIMPLE, UNTHINKING MONSTER FROM THE INFINITE VOID...
I CAN SENSE A HUMAN-LIKE INTELLIGENCE BEHIND ITS ABHORRENT APPEARANCE!
...THEREFORE, IT MUST BE MY MAGIC SPELLS WHICH WILL DEFEND ME--AS I BLOCK THE BEAST'S ADVANCES WITH MY CLOAK OF LEVITATION!
4

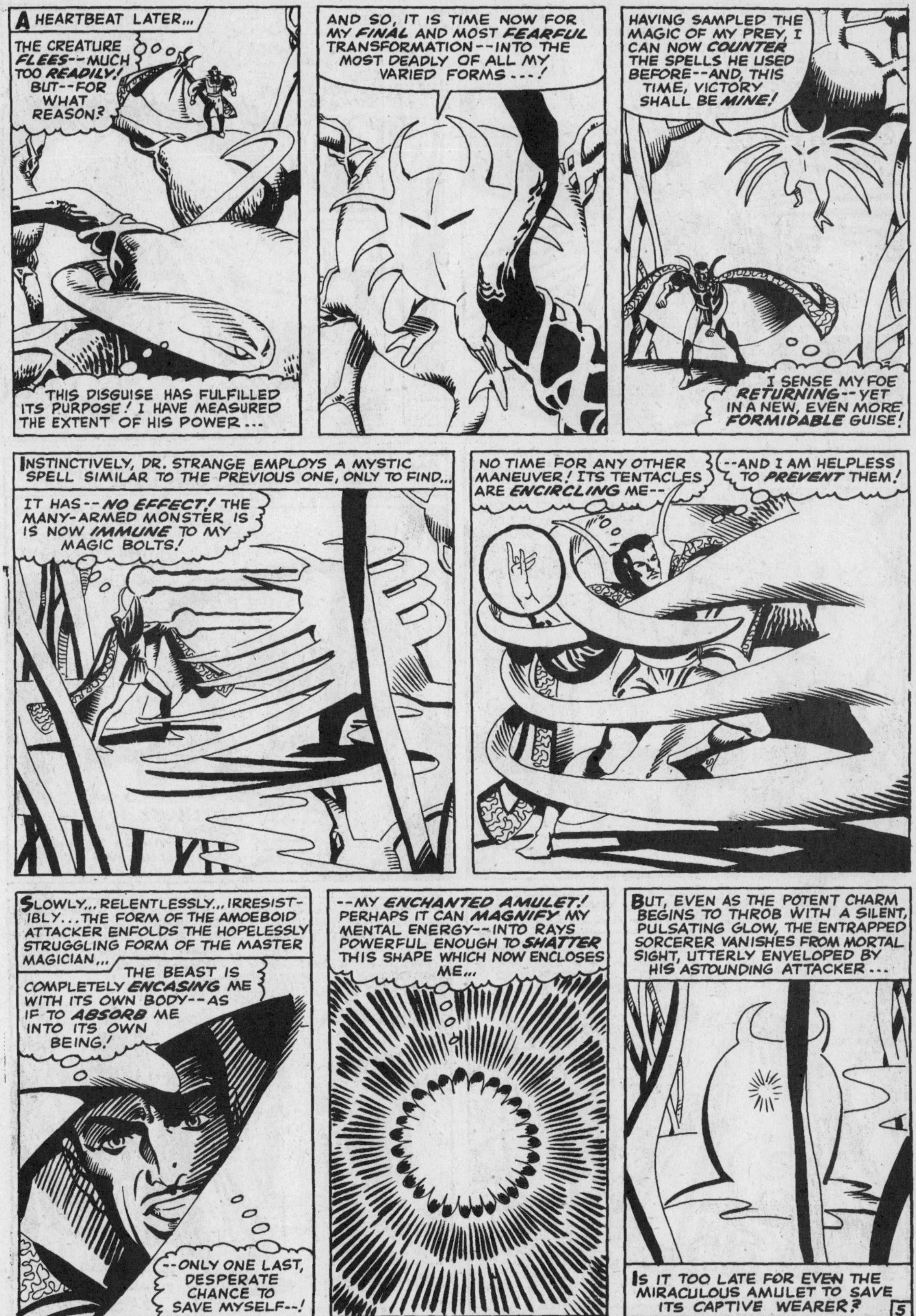
A HEARTBEAT LATER...
THE CREATURE FLEES--MUCH TOO READILY! BUT--FOR WHAT REASON?
THIS DISGUISE HAS FULFILLED ITS PURPOSE! I HAVE MEASURED THE EXTENT OF HIS POWER...
AND SO, IT IS TIME NOW FOR MY FINAL AND MOST FEARFUL TRANSFORMATION--INTO THE MOST DEADLY OF ALL MY VARIED FORMS...!
HAVING SAMPLED THE MAGIC OF MY PREY, I CAN NOW COUNTER THE SPELLS HE USED BEFORE--AND, THIS TIME, VICTORY SHALL BE MINE!
I SENSE MY FOE RETURNING--YET IN A NEW, EVEN MORE FORMIDABLE GUISE!
INSTINCTIVELY, DR. STRANGE EMPLOYS A MYSTIC SPELL SIMILAR TO THE PREVIOUS ONE, ONLY TO FIND...
IT HAS--NO EFFECT! THE MANY-ARMED MONSTER IS IS NOW IMMUNE TO MY MAGIC BOLTS!
NO TIME FOR ANY OTHER MANEUVER! ITS TENTACLES ARE ENCIRCLING ME--
--AND I AM HELPLESS TO PREVENT THEM!
SLOWLY... RELENTLESSLY... IRRESISTIBLY... THE FORM OF THE AMOEBOID ATTACKER ENFOLDS THE HOPELESSLY STRUGGLING FORM OF THE MASTER MAGICIAN...
THE BEAST IS COMPLETELY ENCASING ME WITH ITS OWN BODY--AS IF TO ABSORB ME INTO ITS OWN BEING!
--ONLY ONE LAST, DESPERATE CHANCE TO SAVE MYSELF--!
--MY ENCHANTED AMULET! PERHAPS IT CAN MAGNIFY MY MENTAL ENERGY--INTO RAYS POWERFUL ENOUGH TO SHATTER THIS SHAPE WHICH NOW ENCLOSES ME...
BUT, EVEN AS THE POTENT CHARM BEGINS TO THROB WITH A SILENT, PULSATING GLOW, THE ENTRAPPED SORCERER VANISHES FROM MORTAL SIGHT, UTTERLY ENVELOPED BY HIS ASTOUNDING ATTACKER...
IS IT TOO LATE FOR EVEN THE MIRACULOUS AMULET TO SAVE ITS CAPTIVE WEARER?
5

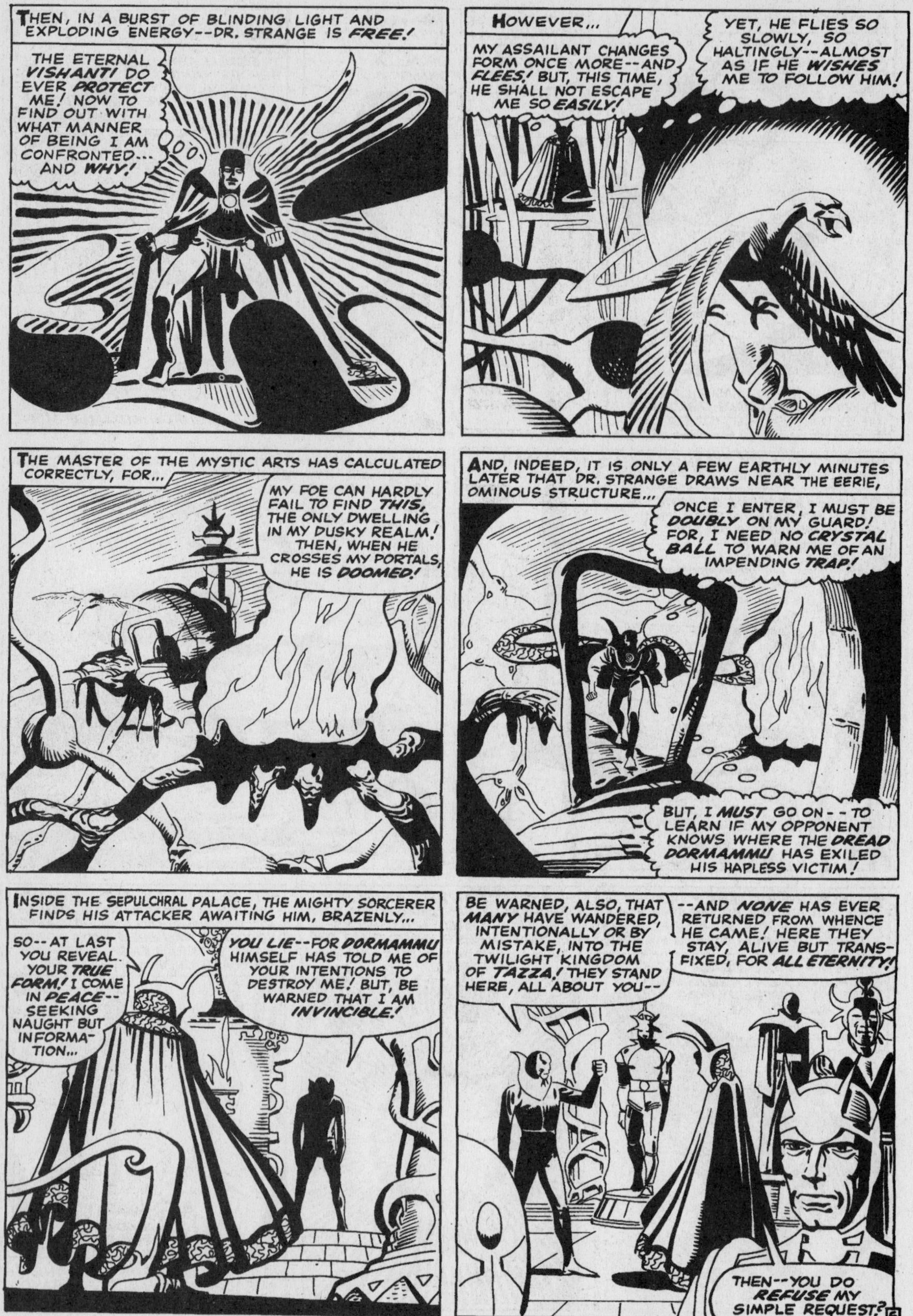
THEN, IN A BURST OF BLINDING LIGHT AND EXPLODING ENERGY--DR. STRANGE IS FREE!
THE ETERNAL VISHANTI DO EVER PROTECT ME! NOW TO FIND OUT WITH WHAT MANNER OF BEING I AM CONFRONTED... AND WHY!
HOWEVER...
MY ASSAILANT CHANGES FORM ONCE MORE--AND FLEES! BUT, THIS TIME, HE SHALL NOT ESCAPE ME SO EASILY!
YET, HE FLIES SO SLOWLY, SO HALTINGLY--ALMOST AS IF HE WISHES ME TO FOLLOW HIM!
THE MASTER OF THE MYSTIC ARTS HAS CALCULATED CORRECTLY, FOR...
MY FOE CAN HARDLY FAIL TO FIND THIS, THE ONLY DWELLING IN MY DUSKY REALM! THEN, WHEN HE CROSSES MY PORTALS, HE IS DOOMED!
AND, INDEED, IT IS ONLY A FEW EARTHLY MINUTES LATER THAT DR. STRANGE DRAWS NEAR THE EERIE, OMINOUS STRUCTURE...
ONCE I ENTER, I MUST BE DOUBLY ON MY GUARD! FOR, I NEED NO CRYSTAL BALL TO WARN ME OF AN IMPENDING TRAP!
BUT, I MUST GO ON--TO LEARN IF MY OPPONENT KNOWS WHERE THE DREAD DORMAMMU HAS EXILED HIS HAPLESS VICTIM!
INSIDE THE SEPULCHRAL PALACE, THE MIGHTY SORCERER FINDS HIS ATTACKER AWAITING HIM, BRAZENLY...
SO--AT LAST YOU REVEAL YOUR TRUE FORM! I COME IN PEACE--SEEKING NAUGHT BUT INFORMATION...
YOU LIE--FOR DORMAMMU HIMSELF HAS TOLD ME OF YOUR INTENTIONS TO DESTROY ME! BUT, BE WARNED THAT I AM INVINCIBLE!
BE WARNED, ALSO, THAT MANY HAVE WANDERED, INTENTIONALLY OR BY MISTAKE, INTO THE TWILIGHT KINGDOM OF TAZZA! THEY STAND HERE, ALL ABOUT YOU--
--AND NONE HAS EVER RETURNED FROM WHENCE HE CAME! HERE THEY STAY, ALIVE BUT TRANSFIXED, FOR ALL ETERNITY!
THEN--YOU DO REFUSE MY SIMPLE REQUEST?
6

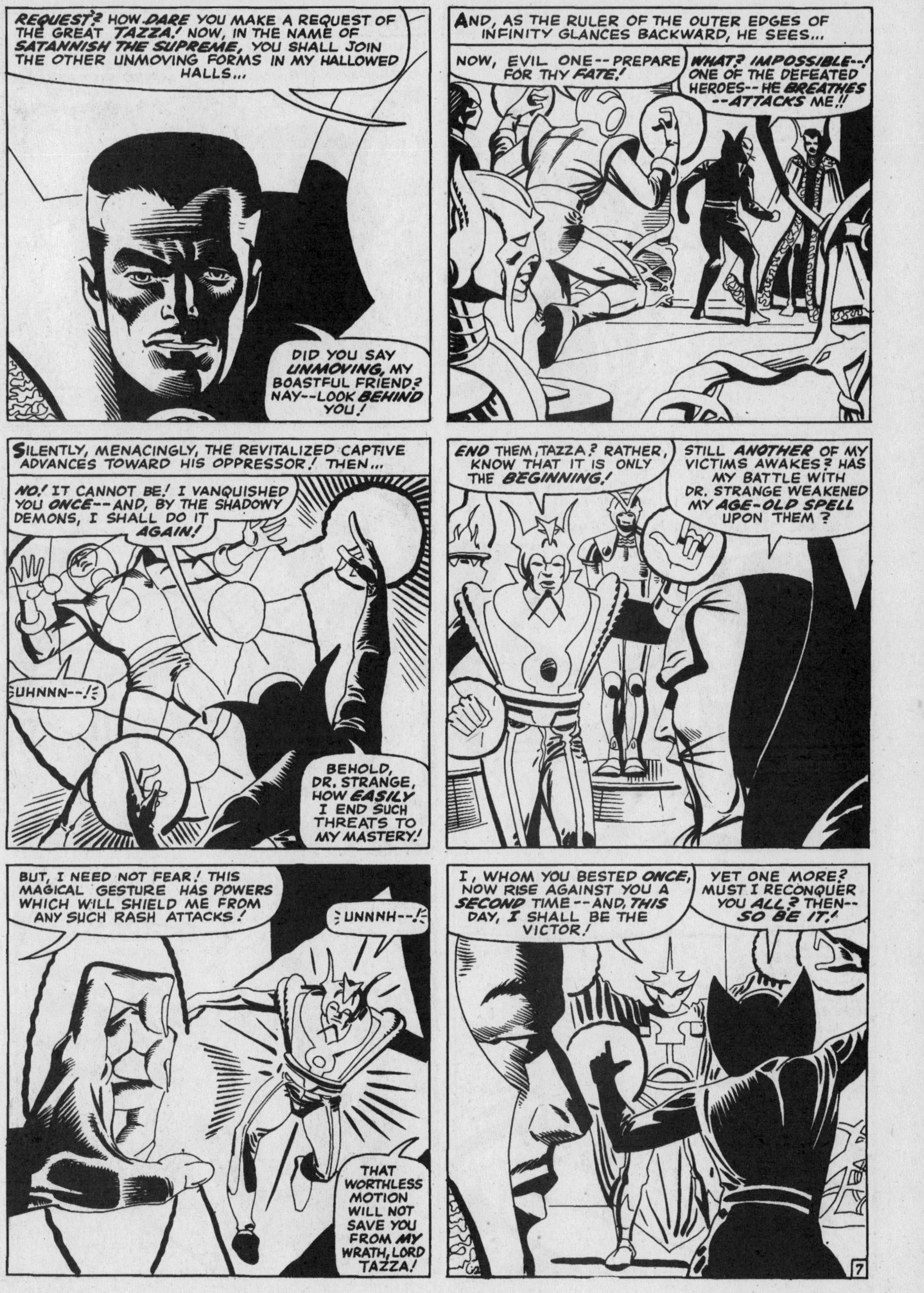
REQUEST? HOW DARE YOU MAKE A REQUEST OF THE GREAT TAZZA! NOW, IN THE NAME OF SATANNISH THE SUPREME, YOU SHALL JOIN THE OTHER UNMOVING FORMS IN MY HALLOWED HALLS...
DID YOU SAY UNMOVING, MY BOASTFUL FRIEND? NAY--LOOK BEHIND YOU!
AND, AS THE RULER OF THE OUTER EDGES OF INFINITY GLANCES BACKWARD, HE SEES...
NOW, EVIL ONE--PREPARE FOR THY FATE!
WHAT? IMPOSSIBLE--! ONE OF THE DEFEATED HEROES--HE BREATHES--ATTACKS ME!!
SILENTLY, MENACINGLY, THE REVITALIZED CAPTIVE ADVANCES TOWARD HIS OPPRESSOR! THEN...
NO! IT CANNOT BE! I VANQUISHED YOU ONCE--AND, BY THE SHADOWY DEMONS, I SHALL DO IT AGAIN!
UHNNN--!
BEHOLD, DR. STRANGE, HOW EASILY I END SUCH THREATS TO MY MASTERY!
END THEM, TAZZA? RATHER, KNOW THAT IT IS ONLY THE BEGINNING!
STILL ANOTHER OF MY VICTIMS AWAKES? HAS MY BATTLE WITH DR. STRANGE WEAKENED MY AGE-OLD SPELL UPON THEM?
BUT, I NEED NOT FEAR! THIS MAGICAL GESTURE HAS POWERS WHICH WILL SHIELD ME FROM ANY SUCH RASH ATTACKS!
UNNNH--!
THAT WORTHLESS MOTION WILL NOT SAVE YOU FROM MY WRATH, LORD TAZZA!
I, WHOM YOU BESTED ONCE, NOW RISE AGAINST YOU A SECOND TIME--AND, THIS DAY, I SHALL BE THE VICTOR!
YET ONE MORE? MUST I RECONQUER YOU ALL? THEN--SO BE IT!
7

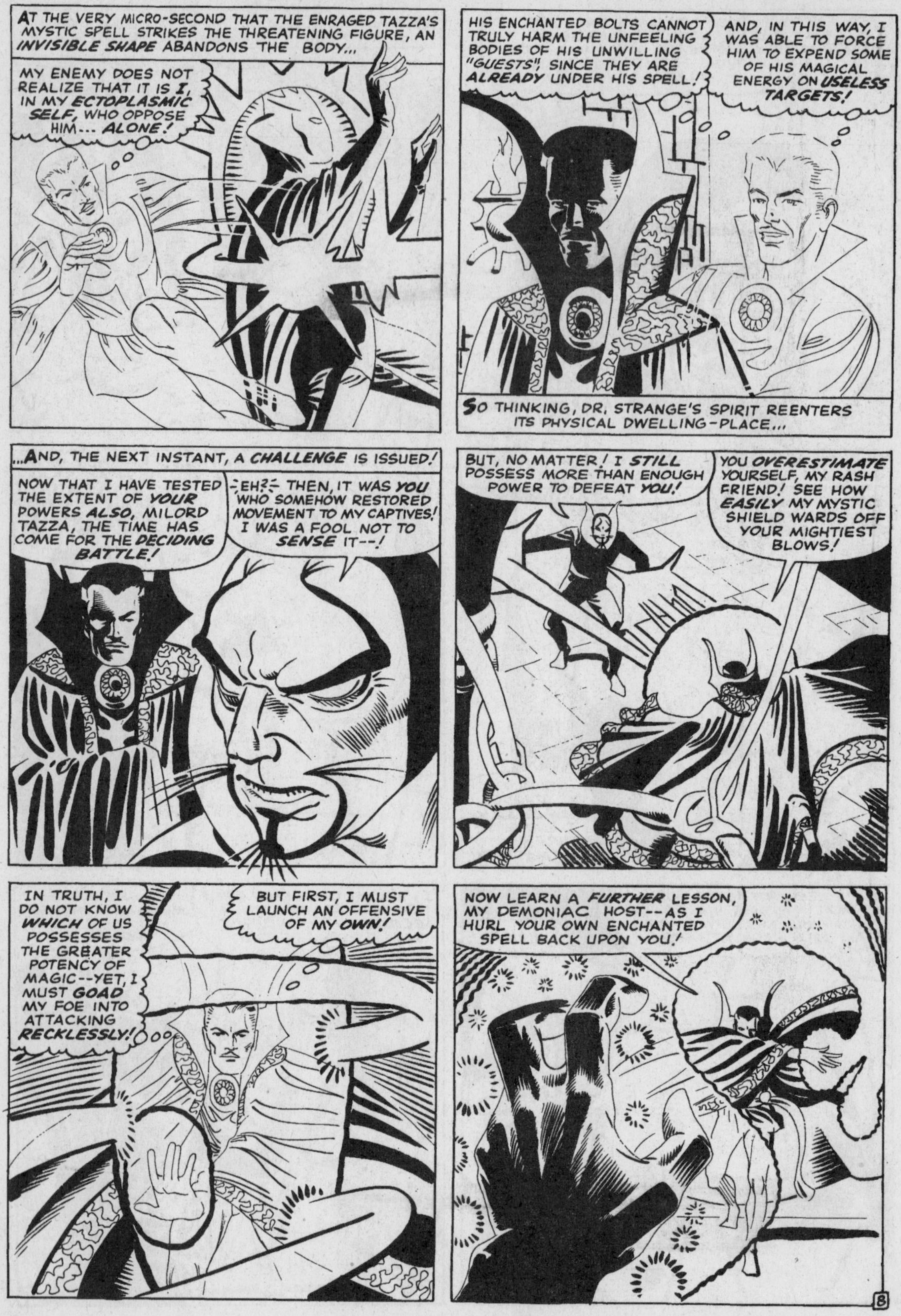
AT THE VERY MICRO-SECOND THAT THE ENRAGED TAZZA'S MYSTIC SPELL STRIKES THE THREATENING FIGURE, AN INVISIBLE SHAPE ABANDONS THE BODY...
MY ENEMY DOES NOT REALIZE THAT IT IS I, IN MY ECTOPLASMIC SELF, WHO OPPOSE HIM... ALONE!
HIS ENCHANTED BOLTS CANNOT TRULY HARM THE UNFEELING BODIES OF HIS UNWILLING "GUESTS", SINCE THEY ARE ALREADY UNDER HIS SPELL!
AND, IN THIS WAY, I WAS ABLE TO FORCE HIM TO EXPEND SOME OF HIS MAGICAL ENERGY ON USELESS TARGETS!
SO THINKING, DR. STRANGE'S SPIRIT REENTERS ITS PHYSICAL DWELLING-PLACE...
...AND, THE NEXT INSTANT, A CHALLENGE IS ISSUED!
NOW THAT I HAVE TESTED THE EXTENT OF YOUR POWERS ALSO, MILORD TAZZA, THE TIME HAS COME FOR THE DECIDING BATTLE!
EH?-- THEN, IT WAS YOU WHO SOMEHOW RESTORED MOVEMENT TO MY CAPTIVES! I WAS A FOOL NOT TO SENSE IT--!
BUT, NO MATTER! I STILL POSSESS MORE THAN ENOUGH POWER TO DEFEAT YOU!
YOU OVERESTIMATE YOURSELF, MY RASH FRIEND! SEE HOW EASILY MY MYSTIC SHIELD WARDS OFF YOUR MIGHTIEST BLOWS!
IN TRUTH, I DO NOT KNOW WHICH OF US POSSESSES THE GREATER POTENCY OF MAGIC--YET, I MUST GOAD MY FOE INTO ATTACKING RECKLESSLY!
BUT FIRST, I MUST LAUNCH AN OFFENSIVE OF MY OWN!
NOW LEARN A FURTHER LESSON, MY DEMONIAC HOST--AS I HURL YOUR OWN ENCHANTED SPELL BACK UPON YOU!
8

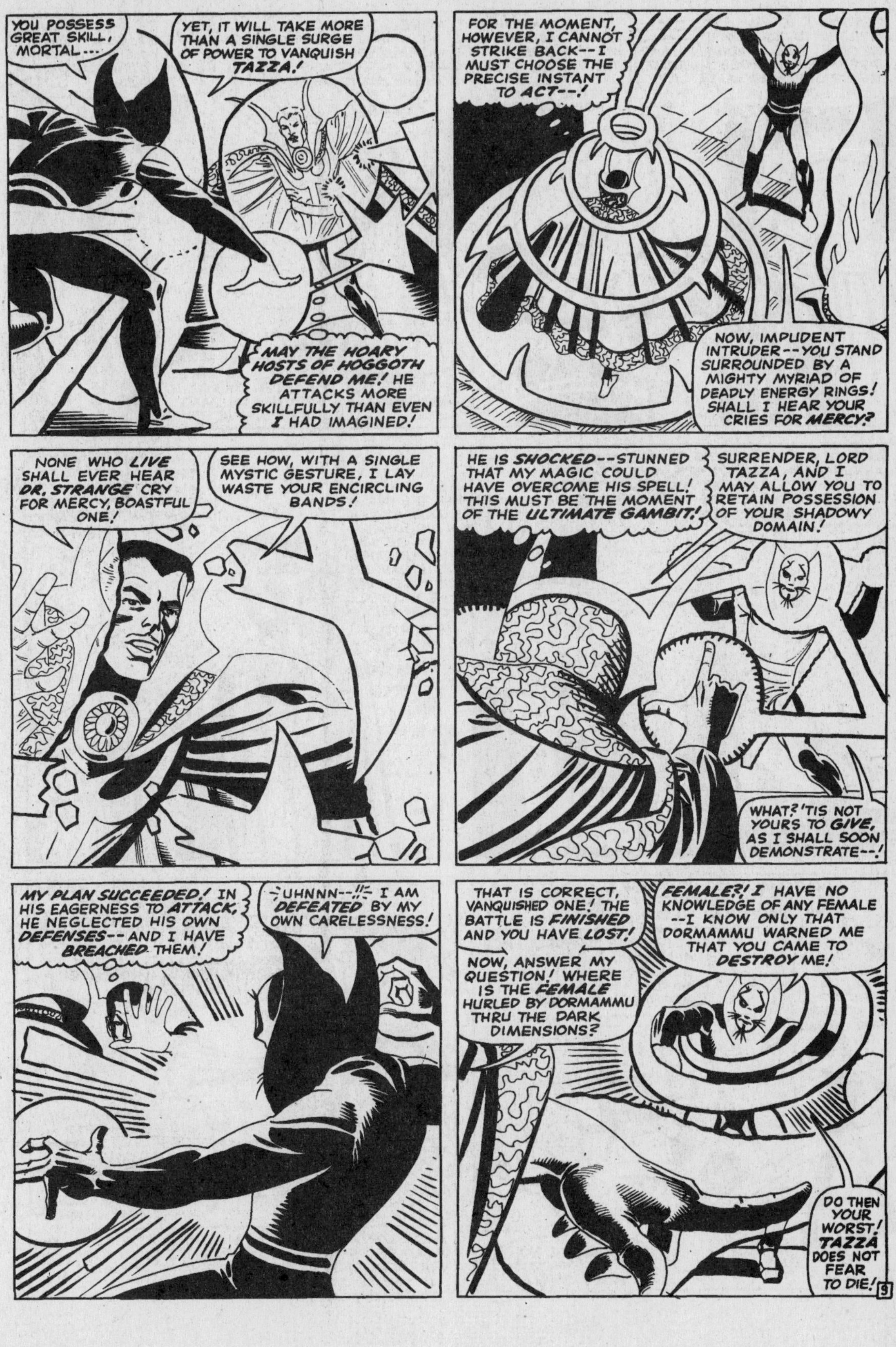

YOU POSSESS GREAT SKILL, MORTAL...
YET, IT WILL TAKE MORE THAN A SINGLE SURGE OF POWER TO VANQUISH TAZZA!
MAY THE HOARY HOSTS OF HOGGOTH DEFEND ME! HE ATTACKS MORE SKILLFULLY THAN EVEN I HAD IMAGINED!
FOR THE MOMENT, HOWEVER, I CANNOT STRIKE BACK--I MUST CHOOSE THE PRECISE INSTANT TO ACT--!
NOW, IMPUDENT INTRUDER--YOU STAND SURROUNDED BY A MIGHTY MYRIAD OF DEADLY ENERGY RINGS! SHALL I HEAR YOUR CRIES FOR MERCY?
NONE WHO LIVE SHALL EVER HEAR DR. STRANGE CRY FOR MERCY, BOASTFUL ONE!
SEE HOW, WITH A SINGLE MYSTIC GESTURE, I LAY WASTE YOUR ENCIRCLING BANDS!
HE IS SHOCKED--STUNNED THAT MY MAGIC COULD HAVE OVERCOME HIS SPELL! THIS MUST BE THE MOMENT OF THE ULTIMATE GAMBIT!
SURRENDER, LORD TAZZA, AND I MAY ALLOW YOU TO RETAIN POSSESSION OF YOUR SHADOWY DOMAIN!
WHAT? 'TIS NOT YOURS TO GIVE, AS I SHALL SOON DEMONSTRATE--!
MY PLAN SUCCEEDED! IN HIS EAGERNESS TO ATTACK, HE NEGLECTED HIS OWN DEFENSES--AND I HAVE BREACHED THEM!
UHNNN--!! I AM DEFEATED BY MY OWN CARELESSNESS!
THAT IS CORRECT, VANQUISHED ONE! THE BATTLE IS FINISHED AND YOU HAVE LOST!
NOW, ANSWER MY QUESTION! WHERE IS THE FEMALE HURLED BY DORMAMMU THRU THE DARK DIMENSIONS?
FEMALE?! I HAVE NO KNOWLEDGE OF ANY FEMALE--I KNOW ONLY THAT DORMAMMU WARNED ME THAT YOU CAME TO DESTROY ME!
DO THEN YOUR WORST! TAZZA DOES NOT FEAR TO DIE!
9

DESTROY? I AM PLEDGED TO DESTROY *NO ONE!* THUS, IF YOU HAVE NO KNOWLEDGE OF THE *GIRL* WHOM I SEEK--

I HAVE *SAID* IT!

AND MY OWN *HEART* SADLY TELLS ME YOU SPEAK THE *TRUTH!* THEN, I HAVE NO FURTHER CAUSE FOR *QUARREL* WITH YOU!

MERELY UNSHACKLE THE SPIRITS OF THOSE VICTIMS YOU HAVE HELD IN BONDAGE THESE MANY YEARS, AND I SHALL *RELEASE* YOU!

IT SHALL BE AS YOU HAVE COMMANDED! *LOOK*--EVEN NOW, THE WRAITHS COME TO REJOIN THEIR CAPTIVE BODIES!

PRAISES TO THEE, O MASTER OF MAGIC, FOR THY VALIANT VICTORY IN OUR BEHALF!

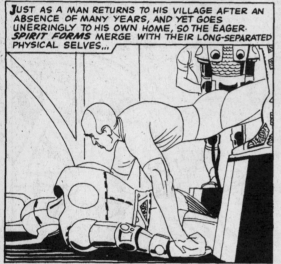

JUST AS A MAN RETURNS TO HIS VILLAGE AFTER AN ABSENCE OF MANY YEARS, AND YET GOES UNERRINGLY TO HIS OWN HOME, SO THE EAGER *SPIRIT FORMS* MERGE WITH THEIR LONG-SEPARATED PHYSICAL SELVES...

ALL OF YOU ARE FREE TO GO NOW! AND, IF THE BRASH *TAZZA* EVER CHOOSES TO BE SO INHOSPITABLE TO STRANGERS IN THE *FUTURE,* WE TWO SHALL CLASH *AGAIN!*

MAY THE *OMNIPOTENT OSHTUR* GUIDE THEE ALWAYS, DR. STRANGE! AND GRANT THAT WE MAY SOME DAY *REPAY* THEE FOR FREEING US!

IN ANOTHER DIMENSION--FURTHER THAN THE STARS, YET NEARER THAN A HEARTBEAT--A FEARFUL *ASTI* FACES HIS FIERCE OVERLORD...

...AND SO, OUR PLAN TO HAVE *TAZZA* DESTROY DR. STRANGE FOR US HAS *FAILED,* O MASTER!

IT IS OF NO CONSEQUENCE, ALL-SEEING ONE! I AM BUT *TOYING* WITH MY IMPLACABLE FOE, TILL I AM READY TO *CRUSH* HIM!

AND MAKE NO MISTAKE--CRUSH HIM I *SHALL!*

BUT, EVEN AS THE EVIL DORMAMMU SPEAKS, A WEARY, CLOAKED FIGURE DRIFTS HOMEWARD...

I MUST RETURN TO MY OWN WORLD FOR A TIME -- TO REST! BUT, I MUST SOON RETURN TO RESCUE HER WHO ONCE HELPED *ME!*

THEN, *DORMAMMU* AND I MAY FIND OURSELVES IN FINAL MORTAL COMBAT-- SO I MUST STRIVE TO *PREPARE* MYSELF FOR THAT DREAD DAY!

AND, *UNTIL* THAT DAY, MAY THE FURIOUS FLAMES OF THE FALTINE NEVER FIND THY FIREPLACE! PLAY WELL, STAY WELL-- AND WE'LL SEE THEE NEXT ISSUE!

THE END

10

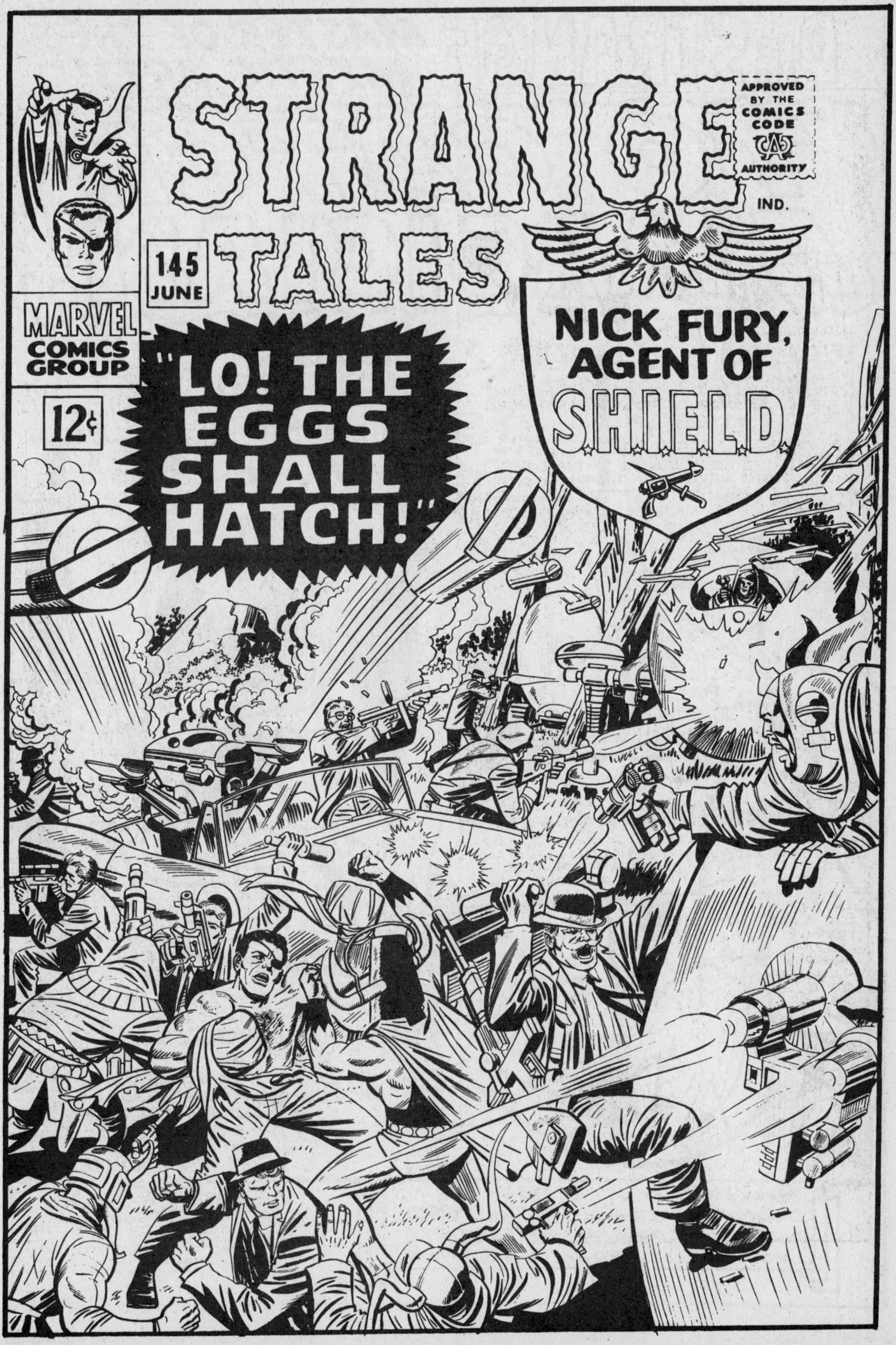
STRANGE TALES
145
JUNE
MARVEL COMICS GROUP
12¢
APPROVED BY THE COMICS CODE CA AUTHORITY
IND.
NICK FURY, AGENT OF S.H.I.E.L.D.
"LO! THE EGGS SHALL HATCH!"

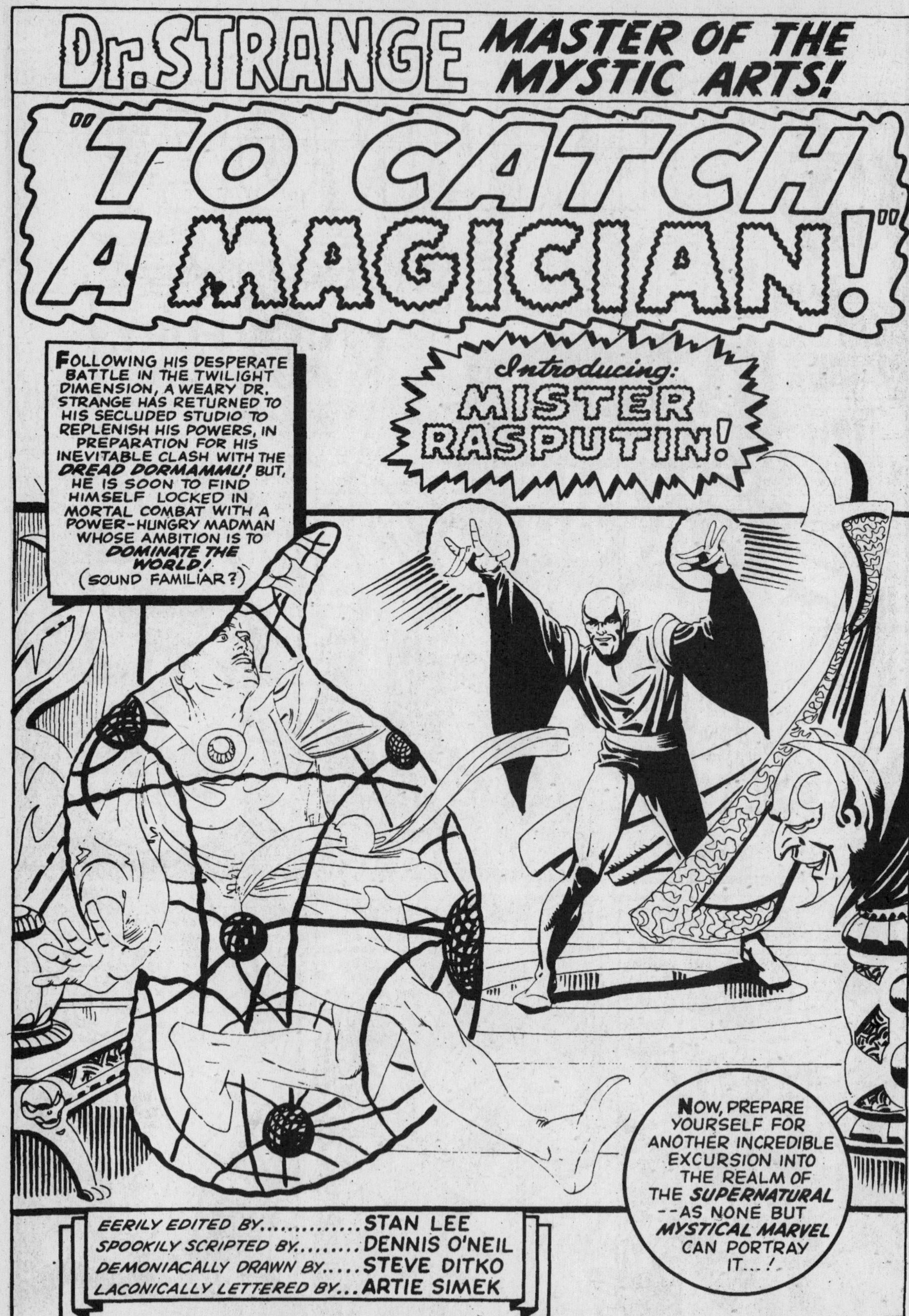

Dr. STRANGE MASTER OF THE MYSTIC ARTS!
"TO CATCH A MAGICIAN!"
FOLLOWING HIS DESPERATE BATTLE IN THE TWILIGHT DIMENSION, A WEARY DR. STRANGE HAS RETURNED TO HIS SECLUDED STUDIO TO REPLENISH HIS POWERS, IN PREPARATION FOR HIS INEVITABLE CLASH WITH THE DREAD DORMAMMU! BUT, HE IS SOON TO FIND HIMSELF LOCKED IN MORTAL COMBAT WITH A POWER-HUNGRY MADMAN WHOSE AMBITION IS TO DOMINATE THE WORLD! (SOUND FAMILIAR?)
Introducing: MISTER RASPUTIN!
NOW, PREPARE YOURSELF FOR ANOTHER INCREDIBLE EXCURSION INTO THE REALM OF THE SUPERNATURAL --AS NONE BUT MYSTICAL MARVEL CAN PORTRAY IT...!
EERILY EDITED BY............STAN LEE
SPOOKILY SCRIPTED BY........DENNIS O'NEIL
DEMONIACALLY DRAWN BY.....STEVE DITKO
LACONICALLY LETTERED BY...ARTIE SIMEK
1

Panel 1: LATE ONE NIGHT, IN THE CAPITAL OF A TINY EUROPEAN REPUBLIC, A HARRIED OFFICIAL IS STARTLED BY AN AWESOME VISITOR...

GOOD EVENING, MY DEAR *PRIME MINISTER!* SINCE YOU'VE REFUSED TO TURN OVER THE *STATE SECRETS* I REQUESTED, I AM COMPELLED TO HAVE MY *FRIEND,* HERE, ASK YOU FOR THEM!

A *GHOST!* IT...IT *CANNOT* BE! *NO!!*

Panel 2: HOW SAD! MY LITTLE ILLUSION CAUSED THE POOR SOUL TO *FAINT!* I AM FORCED TO *TAKE* WHAT I *WANT!*

YOU HAVE THE *MONEY* YOU PROMISED ME FOR MY COOPERATION?

AH, YES-- THE *MONEY!*

Panel 3: SUDDENLY, THE CLOAKED FIGURE SEEMS TO MELT AS...

I-- *CAN'T* MOVE!

I SHOULD BE MOST *ALARMED* IF YOU *COULD!* BUT, DON'T FRET-- THE SPELL WILL DISSOLVE WITH THE MORNING!

Panel 4: A DAY LATER, IN A GOVERNMENT OFFICE THOUSANDS OF MILES AWAY...

HOW INTERESTING! THIS DIARY INDICATES THAT TWO LONG-HOSTILE NATIONS HAVE JUST AGREED TO EXCHANGE DEFENSE SECRETS --SUCH *USEFUL* INFORMATION!

HOLD! NO ONE IS *PERMITTED* HERE!

Panel 5: WITH A SINGLE GESTURE, THE STRANGER PARALYZES THE GUARD...

WHEN YOU RECOVER, TELL YOUR SUPERIORS THAT *MR. RASPUTIN* THANKS THEM FOR THEIR HOSPITALITY!

Panel 6: ONE AFTER ANOTHER, THE MOST GUARDED SECRETS OF THE WORLD'S NATIONS ARE PILFERED BY THE ONE KNOWN ONLY AS... *MR. RASPUTIN!* NO ONE KNOWS *WHERE* HE WILL NEXT STRIKE --OR *WHEN!*

Panel 7: THEN, ON A CRISP DAY IN MARCH, A SINISTER FIGURE ARRIVES, UN-NOTICED IN GREENWICH VILLAGE...

I MUST FIND A PLACE WHERE I WILL NOT BE DISTURBED! LATER, I SHALL PAY A LITTLE CALL ON THE *UNITED NATIONS!*

SOON, THE DESTINY DENIED MY ILLUSTRIOUS ANCESTOR, THE *FIRST* RASPUTIN, WILL BE *MINE!*

Panel 8: RENTING A LONG-ABANDONED LOFT, THE MYSTERIOUS MAGICIAN TESTS HIS FANTASTIC POWERS...

AH! MY SKILL AT CREATING THE *ILLUSIONS OF IKONN* HAS NOT DIMINISHED! IF ANYTHING, IT IS IN-CREASING WITH CONTINUED USE!

Panel 9: WITH BOTH *MAGIC* AND STOLEN *SCIENTIFIC KNOWLEDGE* AT MY DISPOSAL, *NO ONE* WILL DARE REFUSE MY DEMANDS! I SHALL RULE MEN AS THEY *SHOULD* BE RULED --AS THEY *NEED* TO BE RULED---

--BY *TOTAL FEAR!*

2

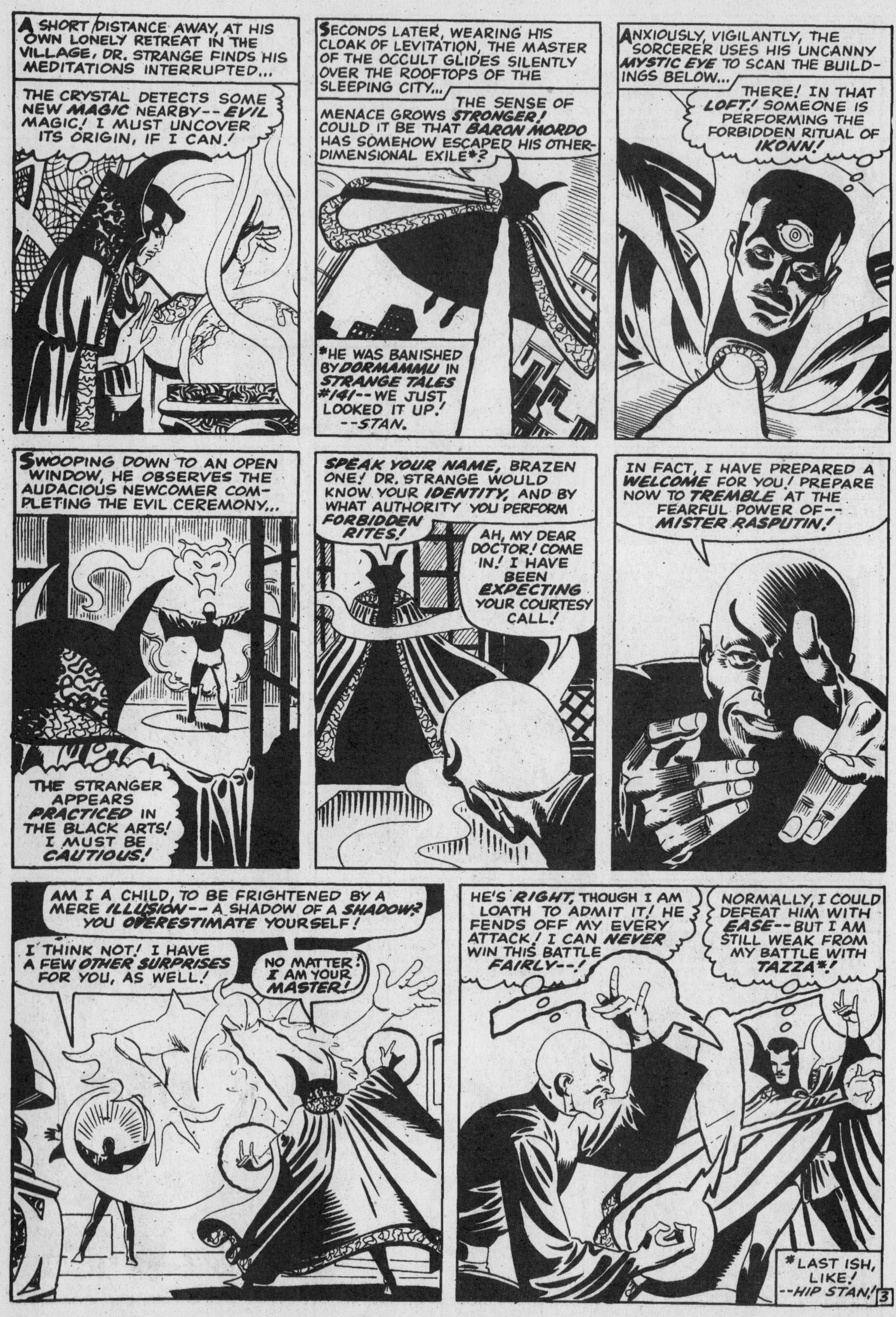

A SHORT DISTANCE AWAY, AT HIS OWN LONELY RETREAT IN THE VILLAGE, DR. STRANGE FINDS HIS MEDITATIONS INTERRUPTED...
THE CRYSTAL DETECTS SOME NEW MAGIC NEARBY-- EVIL MAGIC! I MUST UNCOVER ITS ORIGIN, IF I CAN!
SECONDS LATER, WEARING HIS CLOAK OF LEVITATION, THE MASTER OF THE OCCULT GLIDES SILENTLY OVER THE ROOFTOPS OF THE SLEEPING CITY...
THE SENSE OF MENACE GROWS STRONGER! COULD IT BE THAT BARON MORDO HAS SOMEHOW ESCAPED HIS OTHER-DIMENSIONAL EXILE*?
*HE WAS BANISHED BY DORMAMMU IN STRANGE TALES #141-- WE JUST LOOKED IT UP! --STAN.
ANXIOUSLY, VIGILANTLY, THE SORCERER USES HIS UNCANNY MYSTIC EYE TO SCAN THE BUILDINGS BELOW...
THERE! IN THAT LOFT! SOMEONE IS PERFORMING THE FORBIDDEN RITUAL OF IKONN!
SWOOPING DOWN TO AN OPEN WINDOW, HE OBSERVES THE AUDACIOUS NEWCOMER COMPLETING THE EVIL CEREMONY...
THE STRANGER APPEARS PRACTICED IN THE BLACK ARTS! I MUST BE CAUTIOUS!
SPEAK YOUR NAME, BRAZEN ONE! DR. STRANGE WOULD KNOW YOUR IDENTITY, AND BY WHAT AUTHORITY YOU PERFORM FORBIDDEN RITES!
AH, MY DEAR DOCTOR! COME IN! I HAVE BEEN EXPECTING YOUR COURTESY CALL!
IN FACT, I HAVE PREPARED A WELCOME FOR YOU! PREPARE NOW TO TREMBLE AT THE FEARFUL POWER OF-- MISTER RASPUTIN!
AM I A CHILD, TO BE FRIGHTENED BY A MERE ILLUSION-- A SHADOW OF A SHADOW? YOU OVERESTIMATE YOURSELF!
I THINK NOT! I HAVE A FEW OTHER SURPRISES FOR YOU, AS WELL!
NO MATTER! I AM YOUR MASTER!
HE'S RIGHT, THOUGH I AM LOATH TO ADMIT IT! HE FENDS OFF MY EVERY ATTACK! I CAN NEVER WIN THIS BATTLE FAIRLY--!
NORMALLY, I COULD DEFEAT HIM WITH EASE-- BUT I AM STILL WEAK FROM MY BATTLE WITH TAZZA*!
*LAST ISH, LIKE! --HIP STAN!
3

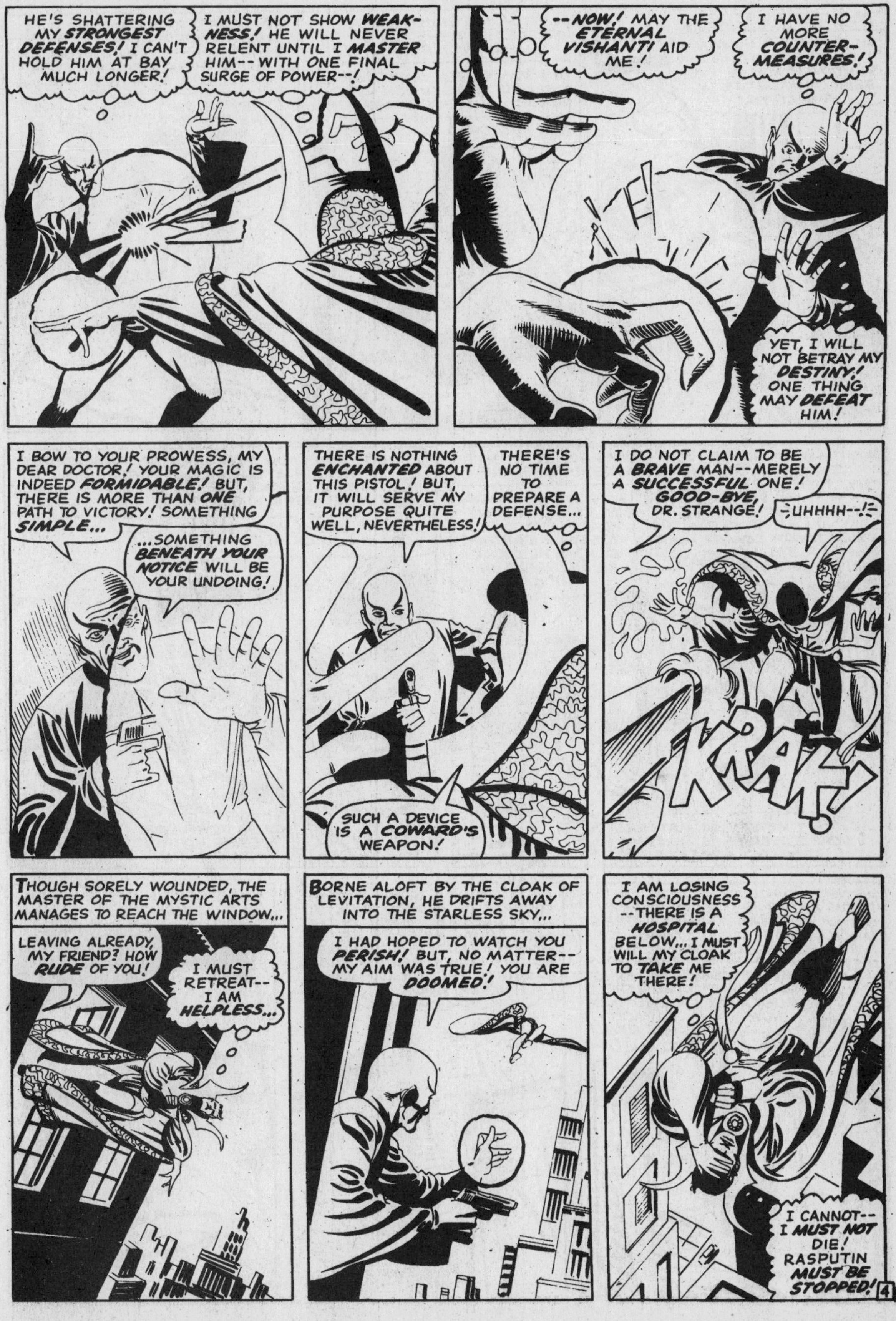
HE'S SHATTERING MY STRONGEST DEFENSES! I CAN'T HOLD HIM AT BAY MUCH LONGER!
I MUST NOT SHOW WEAKNESS! HE WILL NEVER RELENT UNTIL I MASTER HIM--WITH ONE FINAL SURGE OF POWER--!
--NOW! MAY THE ETERNAL VISHANTI AID ME!
I HAVE NO MORE COUNTER-MEASURES!
YET, I WILL NOT BETRAY MY DESTINY! ONE THING MAY DEFEAT HIM!
I BOW TO YOUR PROWESS, MY DEAR DOCTOR! YOUR MAGIC IS INDEED FORMIDABLE! BUT, THERE IS MORE THAN ONE PATH TO VICTORY! SOMETHING SIMPLE...
...SOMETHING BENEATH YOUR NOTICE WILL BE YOUR UNDOING!
THERE IS NOTHING ENCHANTED ABOUT THIS PISTOL! BUT, IT WILL SERVE MY PURPOSE QUITE WELL, NEVERTHELESS!
THERE'S NO TIME TO PREPARE A DEFENSE...
SUCH A DEVICE IS A COWARD'S WEAPON!
I DO NOT CLAIM TO BE A BRAVE MAN--MERELY A SUCCESSFUL ONE! GOOD-BYE, DR. STRANGE!
UHHHH--!
KRAK!
THOUGH SORELY WOUNDED, THE MASTER OF THE MYSTIC ARTS MANAGES TO REACH THE WINDOW...
LEAVING ALREADY, MY FRIEND? HOW RUDE OF YOU!
I MUST RETREAT--I AM HELPLESS...
BORNE ALOFT BY THE CLOAK OF LEVITATION, HE DRIFTS AWAY INTO THE STARLESS SKY...
I HAD HOPED TO WATCH YOU PERISH! BUT, NO MATTER--MY AIM WAS TRUE! YOU ARE DOOMED!
I AM LOSING CONSCIOUSNESS--THERE IS A HOSPITAL BELOW... I MUST WILL MY CLOAK TO TAKE ME THERE!
I CANNOT--I MUST NOT DIE! RASPUTIN MUST BE STOPPED!

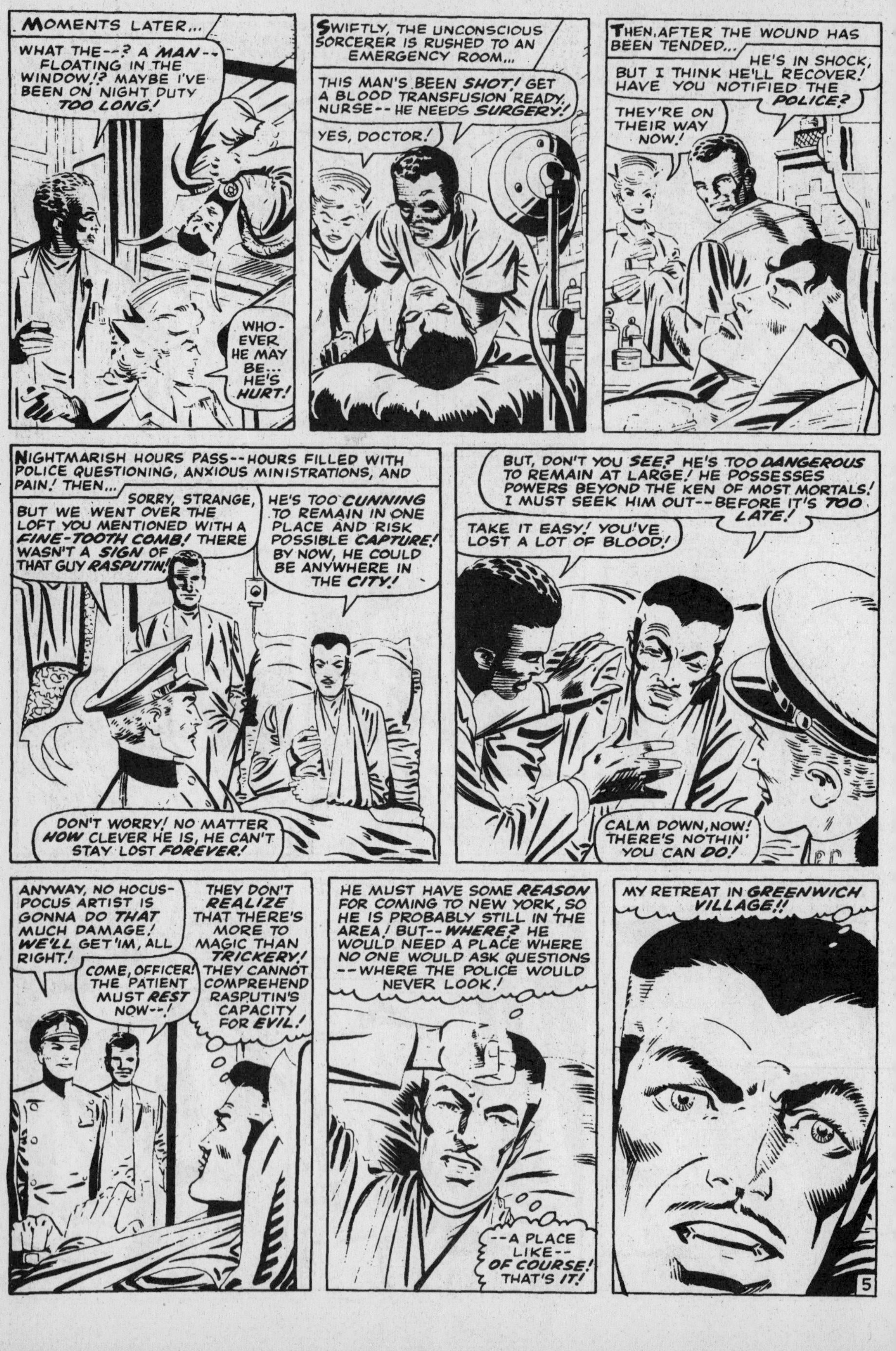
MOMENTS LATER...
WHAT THE--? A MAN--FLOATING IN THE WINDOW!? MAYBE I'VE BEEN ON NIGHT DUTY TOO LONG!
WHO-EVER HE MAY BE... HE'S HURT!
SWIFTLY, THE UNCONSCIOUS SORCERER IS RUSHED TO AN EMERGENCY ROOM...
THIS MAN'S BEEN SHOT! GET A BLOOD TRANSFUSION READY, NURSE--HE NEEDS SURGERY!
YES, DOCTOR!
THEN, AFTER THE WOUND HAS BEEN TENDED...
HE'S IN SHOCK, BUT I THINK HE'LL RECOVER! HAVE YOU NOTIFIED THE POLICE?
THEY'RE ON THEIR WAY NOW!
NIGHTMARISH HOURS PASS--HOURS FILLED WITH POLICE QUESTIONING, ANXIOUS MINISTRATIONS, AND PAIN! THEN...
SORRY, STRANGE, BUT WE WENT OVER THE LOFT YOU MENTIONED WITH A FINE-TOOTH COMB! THERE WASN'T A SIGN OF THAT GUY RASPUTIN!
HE'S TOO CUNNING TO REMAIN IN ONE PLACE AND RISK POSSIBLE CAPTURE! BY NOW, HE COULD BE ANYWHERE IN THE CITY!
DON'T WORRY! NO MATTER HOW CLEVER HE IS, HE CAN'T STAY LOST FOREVER!
BUT, DON'T YOU SEE? HE'S TOO DANGEROUS TO REMAIN AT LARGE! HE POSSESSES POWERS BEYOND THE KEN OF MOST MORTALS! I MUST SEEK HIM OUT--BEFORE IT'S TOO LATE!
TAKE IT EASY! YOU'VE LOST A LOT OF BLOOD!
CALM DOWN, NOW! THERE'S NOTHIN' YOU CAN DO!
ANYWAY, NO HOCUS-POCUS ARTIST IS GONNA DO THAT MUCH DAMAGE! WE'LL GET 'IM, ALL RIGHT!
COME, OFFICER! THE PATIENT MUST REST NOW--!
THEY DON'T REALIZE THAT THERE'S MORE TO MAGIC THAN TRICKERY! THEY CANNOT COMPREHEND RASPUTIN'S CAPACITY FOR EVIL!
HE MUST HAVE SOME REASON FOR COMING TO NEW YORK, SO HE IS PROBABLY STILL IN THE AREA! BUT--WHERE? HE WOULD NEED A PLACE WHERE NO ONE WOULD ASK QUESTIONS --WHERE THE POLICE WOULD NEVER LOOK!
--A PLACE LIKE--OF COURSE! THAT'S IT!
MY RETREAT IN GREENWICH VILLAGE!!
5

AND YET, I CAN'T BE CERTAIN-- SO I SHALL ASSUME MY *ECTOPLASMIC FORM* AND PAY MY SANCTUM SANCTORUM A *VISIT!* LUCKILY, MY *ETHEREAL SELF* CANNOT BE WEAKENED BY A PHYSICAL WOUND!

DR. STRANGE'S GUESS IS A GOOD ONE-- FOR MR. RASPUTIN IS AT THAT MOMENT IN THE MYSTIC MASTER'S STUDIO, SPEAKING TO A HARD-BITTEN THUG!

HE MAY HAVE *SURVIVED!* I WANT YOU TO CHECK THE HOSPITALS, AND IF STRANGE STILL LIVES ...*ELIMINATE HIM!*

IF YOU GOT MY PRICE, CHUM, I'LL DO YOUR LITTLE JOB!

I'LL BE IN TOUCH AS SOON AS I'VE *FINISHED* THE JOB! SO GET THE CASH *READY!*

EXCELLENT, MY FRIEND! YOU WILL BE GIVEN *EXACTLY* WHAT YOU *DESERVE*, I PROMISE YOU!

WITH DR. STRANGE GONE, I SHALL FINALLY ACHIEVE THE *DOMINATION* DENIED MY ILLUSTRIOUS ANCESTOR, THE FIRST *RASPUTIN*, WHEN THE FOOLISH RUSSIANS *KILLED* HIM!

BUT THE TIME TO GLOAT WILL COME *LATER!* NOW, I MUST STUDY THE INCANTATIONS CONTAINED IN THESE BOOKS, IN ORDER TO BECOME STILL *MORE* POWERFUL!

I WAS RIGHT! HE *IS* HERE!

HE IS STUDYING THE SACRED TEXTS OF THE ETERNAL *VISHANTI* AND OF THE *OMNIPOTENT OSHTUR!*

IF HE DECIPHERS THOSE SPELLS, I COULD BE *DOOMED!*

I CANNOT BATTLE RASPUTIN UNTIL I GAIN *PHYSICAL* AID-- AND THERE IS BUT ONE PLACE FROM WHICH THAT AID CAN *COME!*

SILENTLY, THE ALL-SEEING *EYE OF AGAMOTTO* PROJECTS AN INDOMITABLE WILL ACROSS THE DISTANCE TO THE HOSPITAL ROOM...

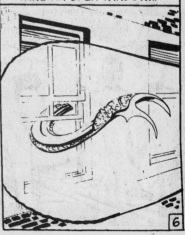

A HEARTBEAT LATER, AT AN UNSPOKEN COMMAND, THE MYSTIC *CLOAK OF LEVITATION* STIRS, THEN FLOATS EERILY THRU AN OPEN WINDOW...

6

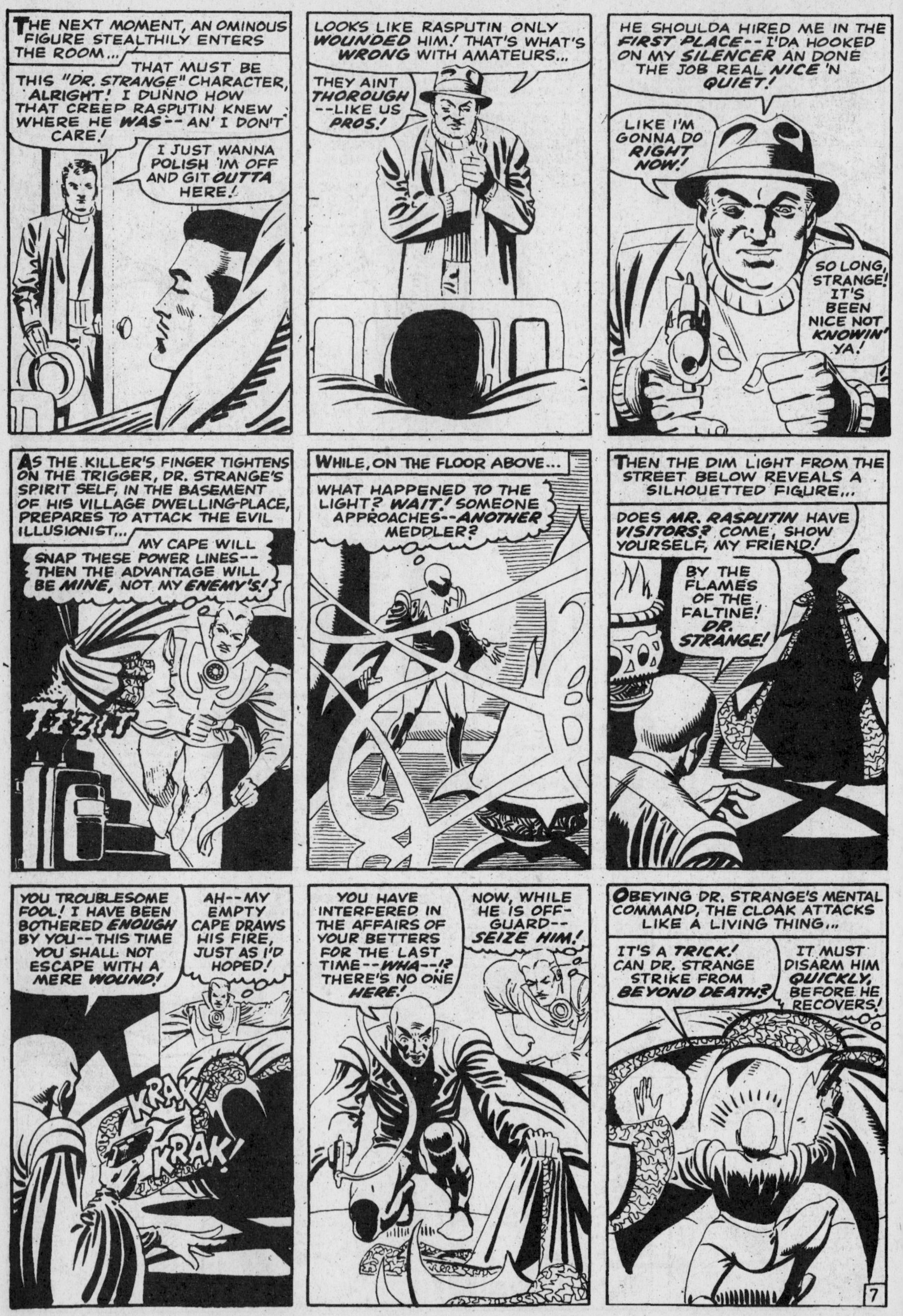
THE NEXT MOMENT, AN OMINOUS FIGURE STEALTHILY ENTERS THE ROOM...
THAT MUST BE THIS "DR. STRANGE" CHARACTER, ALRIGHT! I DUNNO HOW THAT CREEP RASPUTIN KNEW WHERE HE WAS-- AN' I DON'T CARE!
I JUST WANNA POLISH 'IM OFF AND GIT OUTTA HERE!
LOOKS LIKE RASPUTIN ONLY WOUNDED HIM! THAT'S WHAT'S WRONG WITH AMATEURS...
THEY AINT THOROUGH --LIKE US PROS!
HE SHOULDA HIRED ME IN THE FIRST PLACE-- I'DA HOOKED ON MY SILENCER AN DONE THE JOB REAL NICE 'N QUIET!
LIKE I'M GONNA DO RIGHT NOW!
SO LONG, STRANGE! IT'S BEEN NICE NOT KNOWIN' YA!
AS THE KILLER'S FINGER TIGHTENS ON THE TRIGGER, DR. STRANGE'S SPIRIT SELF, IN THE BASEMENT OF HIS VILLAGE DWELLING-PLACE, PREPARES TO ATTACK THE EVIL ILLUSIONIST...
MY CAPE WILL SNAP THESE POWER LINES-- THEN THE ADVANTAGE WILL BE MINE, NOT MY ENEMY'S!
TZZZTT
WHILE, ON THE FLOOR ABOVE...
WHAT HAPPENED TO THE LIGHT? WAIT! SOMEONE APPROACHES--ANOTHER MEDDLER?
THEN THE DIM LIGHT FROM THE STREET BELOW REVEALS A SILHOUETTED FIGURE...
DOES MR. RASPUTIN HAVE VISITORS? COME, SHOW YOURSELF, MY FRIEND!
BY THE FLAMES OF THE FALTINE! DR. STRANGE!
YOU TROUBLESOME FOOL! I HAVE BEEN BOTHERED ENOUGH BY YOU-- THIS TIME YOU SHALL NOT ESCAPE WITH A MERE WOUND!
AH--MY EMPTY CAPE DRAWS HIS FIRE, JUST AS I'D HOPED!
KRAK! KRAK!
YOU HAVE INTERFERED IN THE AFFAIRS OF YOUR BETTERS FOR THE LAST TIME--WHA--!? THERE'S NO ONE HERE!
NOW, WHILE HE IS OFF-GUARD-- SEIZE HIM!
OBEYING DR. STRANGE'S MENTAL COMMAND, THE CLOAK ATTACKS LIKE A LIVING THING...
IT'S A TRICK! CAN DR. STRANGE STRIKE FROM BEYOND DEATH?
IT MUST DISARM HIM QUICKLY, BEFORE HE RECOVERS!

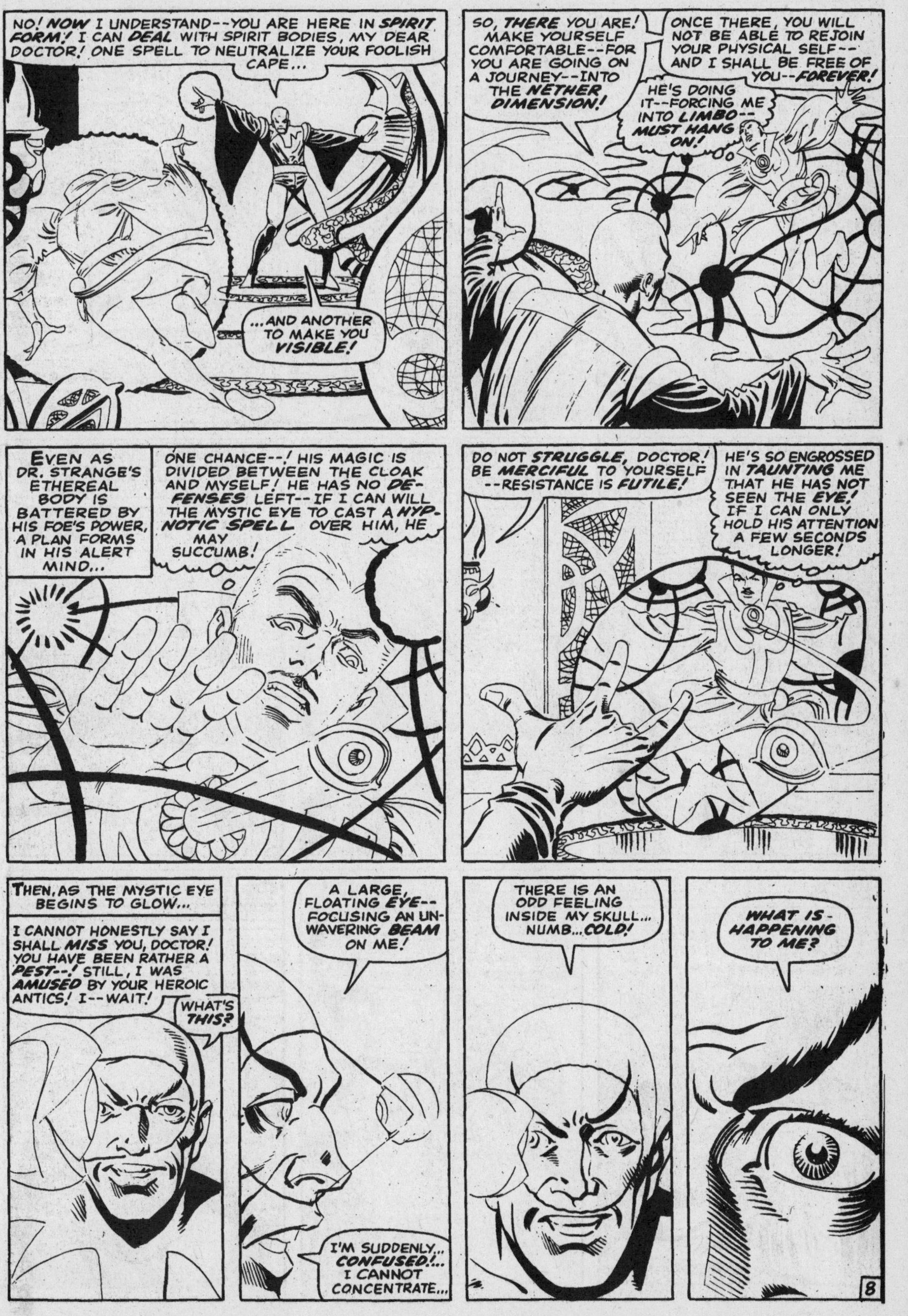

NO! NOW I UNDERSTAND--YOU ARE HERE IN SPIRIT FORM! I CAN DEAL WITH SPIRIT BODIES, MY DEAR DOCTOR! ONE SPELL TO NEUTRALIZE YOUR FOOLISH CAPE...
...AND ANOTHER TO MAKE YOU VISIBLE!
SO, THERE YOU ARE! MAKE YOURSELF COMFORTABLE--FOR YOU ARE GOING ON A JOURNEY--INTO THE NETHER DIMENSION!
ONCE THERE, YOU WILL NOT BE ABLE TO REJOIN YOUR PHYSICAL SELF--AND I SHALL BE FREE OF YOU--FOREVER!
HE'S DOING IT--FORCING ME INTO LIMBO--MUST HANG ON!
EVEN AS DR. STRANGE'S ETHEREAL BODY IS BATTERED BY HIS FOE'S POWER, A PLAN FORMS IN HIS ALERT MIND...
ONE CHANCE--! HIS MAGIC IS DIVIDED BETWEEN THE CLOAK AND MYSELF! HE HAS NO DEFENSES LEFT--IF I CAN WILL THE MYSTIC EYE TO CAST A HYPNOTIC SPELL OVER HIM, HE MAY SUCCUMB!
DO NOT STRUGGLE, DOCTOR! BE MERCIFUL TO YOURSELF--RESISTANCE IS FUTILE!
HE'S SO ENGROSSED IN TAUNTING ME THAT HE HAS NOT SEEN THE EYE! IF I CAN ONLY HOLD HIS ATTENTION A FEW SECONDS LONGER!
THEN, AS THE MYSTIC EYE BEGINS TO GLOW...
I CANNOT HONESTLY SAY I SHALL MISS YOU, DOCTOR! YOU HAVE BEEN RATHER A PEST--! STILL, I WAS AMUSED BY YOUR HEROIC ANTICS! I--WAIT!
WHAT'S THIS?
A LARGE, FLOATING EYE--FOCUSING AN UNWAVERING BEAM ON ME!
I'M SUDDENLY... CONFUSED!... I CANNOT CONCENTRATE...
THERE IS AN ODD FEELING INSIDE MY SKULL... NUMB... COLD!
WHAT IS HAPPENING TO ME?

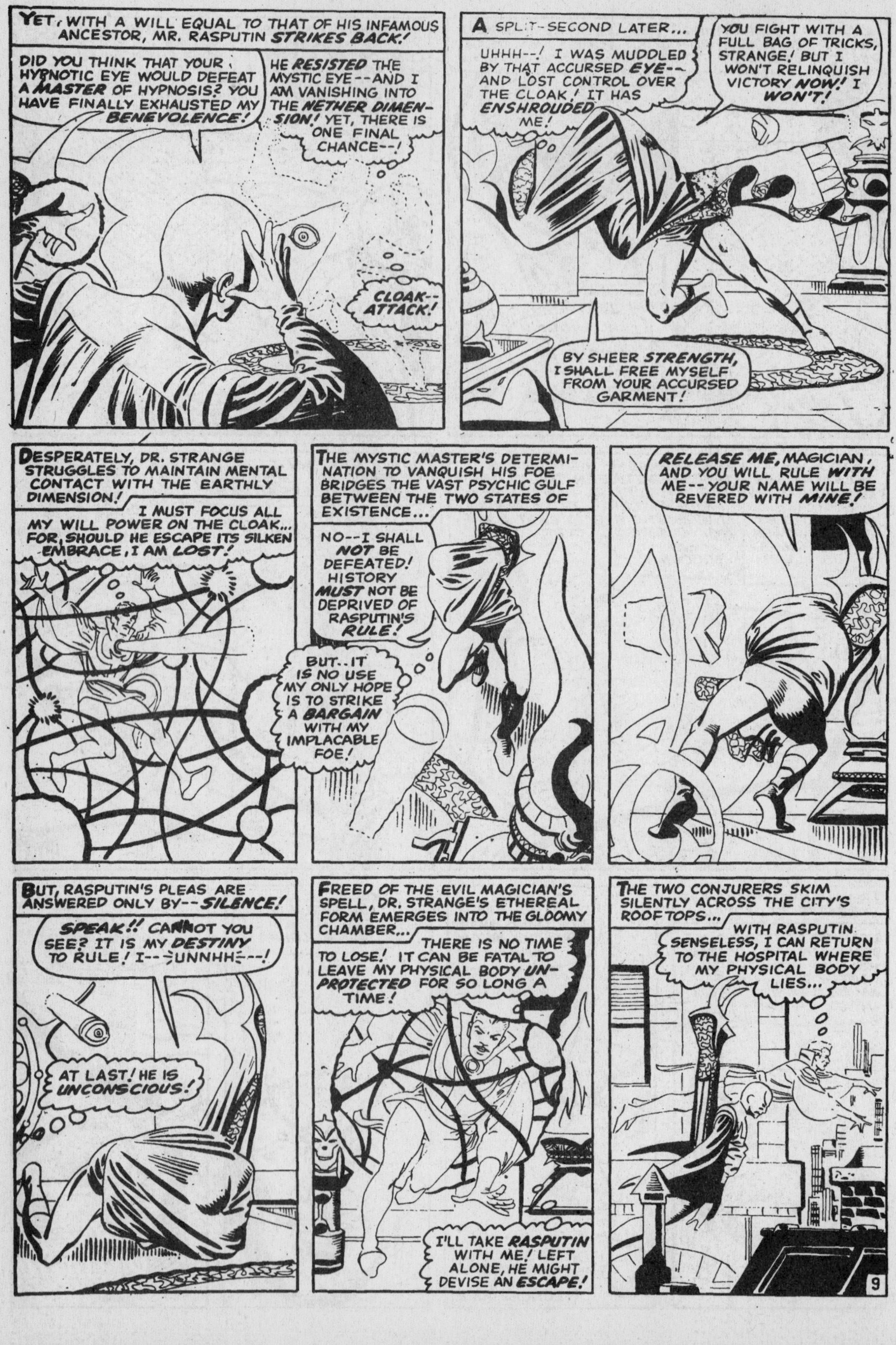
YET, WITH A WILL EQUAL TO THAT OF HIS INFAMOUS ANCESTOR, MR. RASPUTIN STRIKES BACK!
DID YOU THINK THAT YOUR HYPNOTIC EYE WOULD DEFEAT A MASTER OF HYPNOSIS? YOU HAVE FINALLY EXHAUSTED MY BENEVOLENCE!
HE RESISTED THE MYSTIC EYE--AND I AM VANISHING INTO THE NETHER DIMENSION! YET, THERE IS ONE FINAL CHANCE--!
CLOAK--ATTACK!
A SPLIT-SECOND LATER...
UHHH--! I WAS MUDDLED BY THAT ACCURSED EYE--AND LOST CONTROL OVER THE CLOAK! IT HAS ENSHROUDED ME!
YOU FIGHT WITH A FULL BAG OF TRICKS, STRANGE! BUT I WON'T RELINQUISH VICTORY NOW! I WON'T!
BY SHEER STRENGTH, I SHALL FREE MYSELF FROM YOUR ACCURSED GARMENT!
DESPERATELY, DR. STRANGE STRUGGLES TO MAINTAIN MENTAL CONTACT WITH THE EARTHLY DIMENSION!
I MUST FOCUS ALL MY WILL POWER ON THE CLOAK... FOR, SHOULD HE ESCAPE ITS SILKEN EMBRACE, I AM LOST!
THE MYSTIC MASTER'S DETERMINATION TO VANQUISH HIS FOE BRIDGES THE VAST PSYCHIC GULF BETWEEN THE TWO STATES OF EXISTENCE...
NO--I SHALL NOT BE DEFEATED! HISTORY MUST NOT BE DEPRIVED OF RASPUTIN'S RULE!
BUT..IT IS NO USE MY ONLY HOPE IS TO STRIKE A BARGAIN WITH MY IMPLACABLE FOE!
RELEASE ME, MAGICIAN, AND YOU WILL RULE WITH ME--YOUR NAME WILL BE REVERED WITH MINE!
BUT, RASPUTIN'S PLEAS ARE ANSWERED ONLY BY--SILENCE!
SPEAK!! CANNOT YOU SEE? IT IS MY DESTINY TO RULE! I--UNNHH--!
AT LAST! HE IS UNCONSCIOUS!
FREED OF THE EVIL MAGICIAN'S SPELL, DR. STRANGE'S ETHEREAL FORM EMERGES INTO THE GLOOMY CHAMBER...
THERE IS NO TIME TO LOSE! IT CAN BE FATAL TO LEAVE MY PHYSICAL BODY UNPROTECTED FOR SO LONG A TIME!
I'LL TAKE RASPUTIN WITH ME! LEFT ALONE, HE MIGHT DEVISE AN ESCAPE!
THE TWO CONJURERS SKIM SILENTLY ACROSS THE CITY'S ROOF TOPS...
WITH RASPUTIN SENSELESS, I CAN RETURN TO THE HOSPITAL WHERE MY PHYSICAL BODY LIES...
9

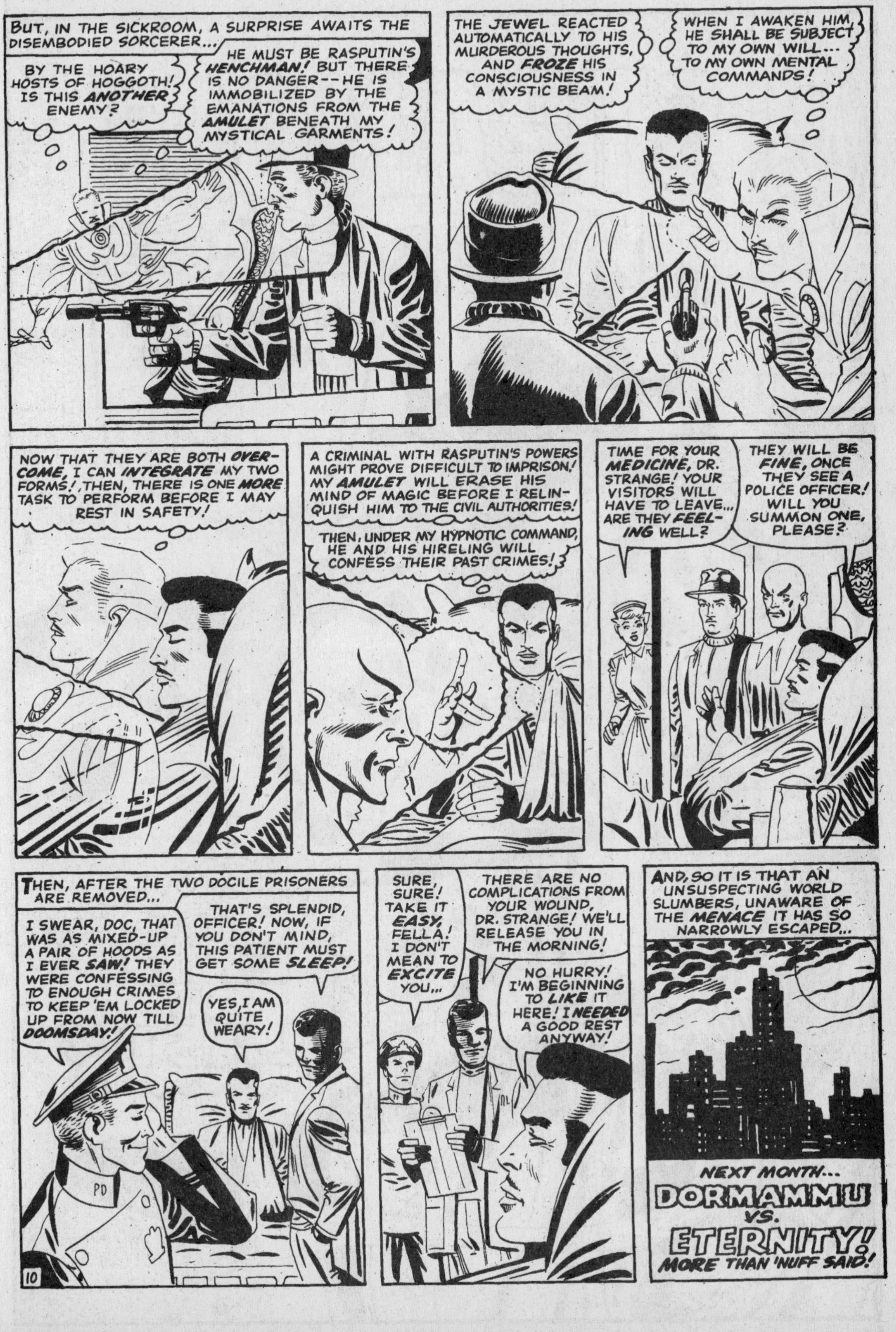

BUT, IN THE SICKROOM, A SURPRISE AWAITS THE DISEMBODIED SORCERER...
BY THE HOARY HOSTS OF HOGGOTH! IS THIS ANOTHER ENEMY?
HE MUST BE RASPUTIN'S HENCHMAN! BUT THERE IS NO DANGER--HE IS IMMOBILIZED BY THE EMANATIONS FROM THE AMULET BENEATH MY MYSTICAL GARMENTS!
THE JEWEL REACTED AUTOMATICALLY TO HIS MURDEROUS THOUGHTS, AND FROZE HIS CONSCIOUSNESS IN A MYSTIC BEAM!
WHEN I AWAKEN HIM, HE SHALL BE SUBJECT TO MY OWN WILL... TO MY OWN MENTAL COMMANDS!
NOW THAT THEY ARE BOTH OVERCOME, I CAN INTEGRATE MY TWO FORMS! THEN, THERE IS ONE MORE TASK TO PERFORM BEFORE I MAY REST IN SAFETY!
A CRIMINAL WITH RASPUTIN'S POWERS MIGHT PROVE DIFFICULT TO IMPRISON! MY AMULET WILL ERASE HIS MIND OF MAGIC BEFORE I RELINQUISH HIM TO THE CIVIL AUTHORITIES!
THEN, UNDER MY HYPNOTIC COMMAND, HE AND HIS HIRELING WILL CONFESS THEIR PAST CRIMES!
TIME FOR YOUR MEDICINE, DR. STRANGE! YOUR VISITORS WILL HAVE TO LEAVE... ARE THEY FEELING WELL?
THEY WILL BE FINE, ONCE THEY SEE A POLICE OFFICER! WILL YOU SUMMON ONE, PLEASE?
THEN, AFTER THE TWO DOCILE PRISONERS ARE REMOVED...
I SWEAR, DOC, THAT WAS AS MIXED-UP A PAIR OF HOODS AS I EVER SAW! THEY WERE CONFESSING TO ENOUGH CRIMES TO KEEP 'EM LOCKED UP FROM NOW TILL DOOMSDAY!
THAT'S SPLENDID, OFFICER! NOW, IF YOU DON'T MIND, THIS PATIENT MUST GET SOME SLEEP!
YES, I AM QUITE WEARY!
PD
SURE, SURE! TAKE IT EASY, FELLA! I DON'T MEAN TO EXCITE YOU...
THERE ARE NO COMPLICATIONS FROM YOUR WOUND, DR. STRANGE! WE'LL RELEASE YOU IN THE MORNING!
NO HURRY! I'M BEGINNING TO LIKE IT HERE! I NEEDED A GOOD REST ANYWAY!
AND, SO IT IS THAT AN UNSUSPECTING WORLD SLUMBERS, UNAWARE OF THE MENACE IT HAS SO NARROWLY ESCAPED...
NEXT MONTH...
DORMAMMU VS. ETERNITY!
MORE THAN 'NUFF SAID!
10

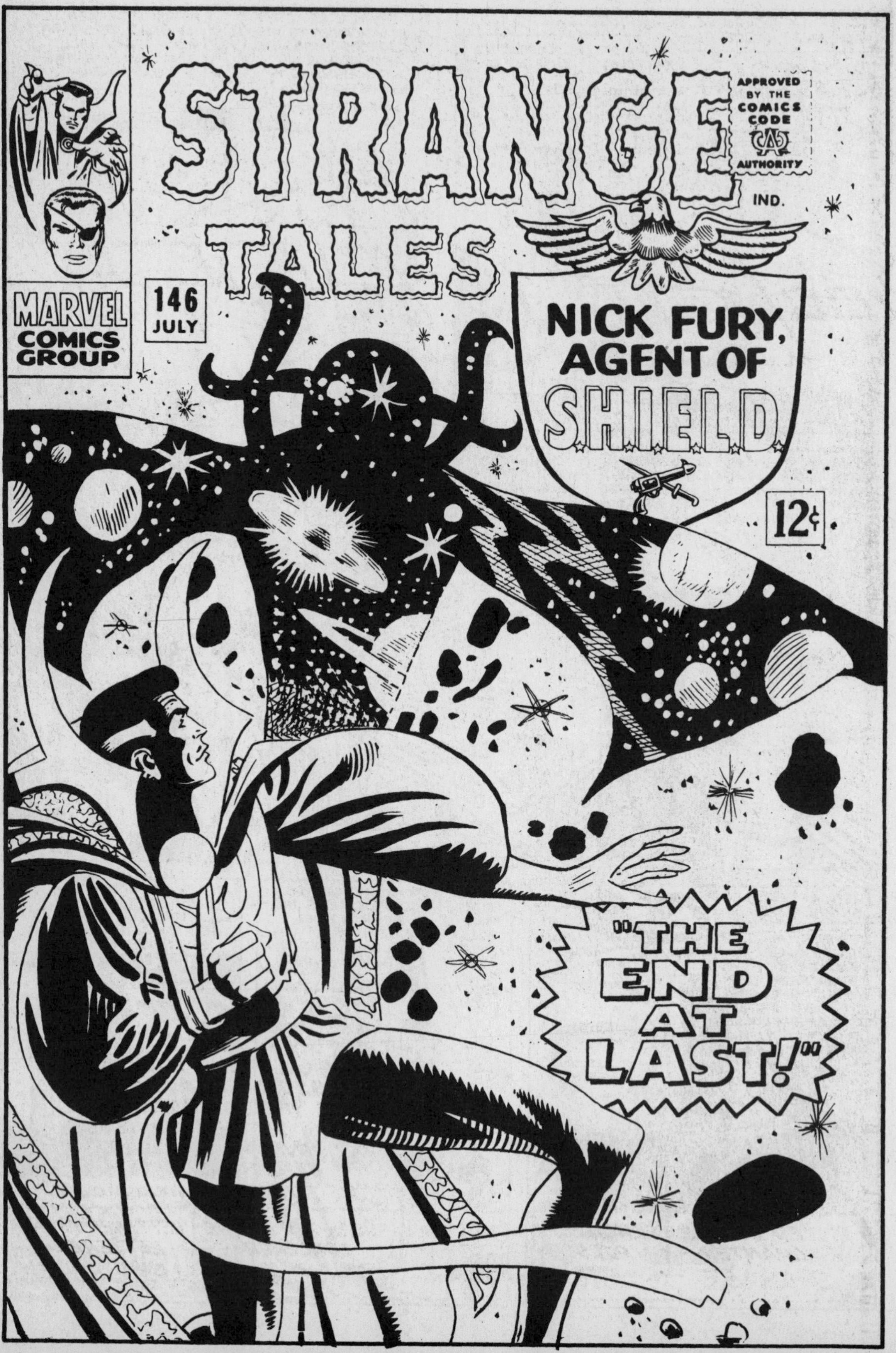
STRANGE TALES
APPROVED BY THE COMICS CODE AUTHORITY
IND.
MARVEL COMICS GROUP
146
JULY
NICK FURY, AGENT OF S.H.I.E.L.D.
12¢
"THE END AT LAST!"

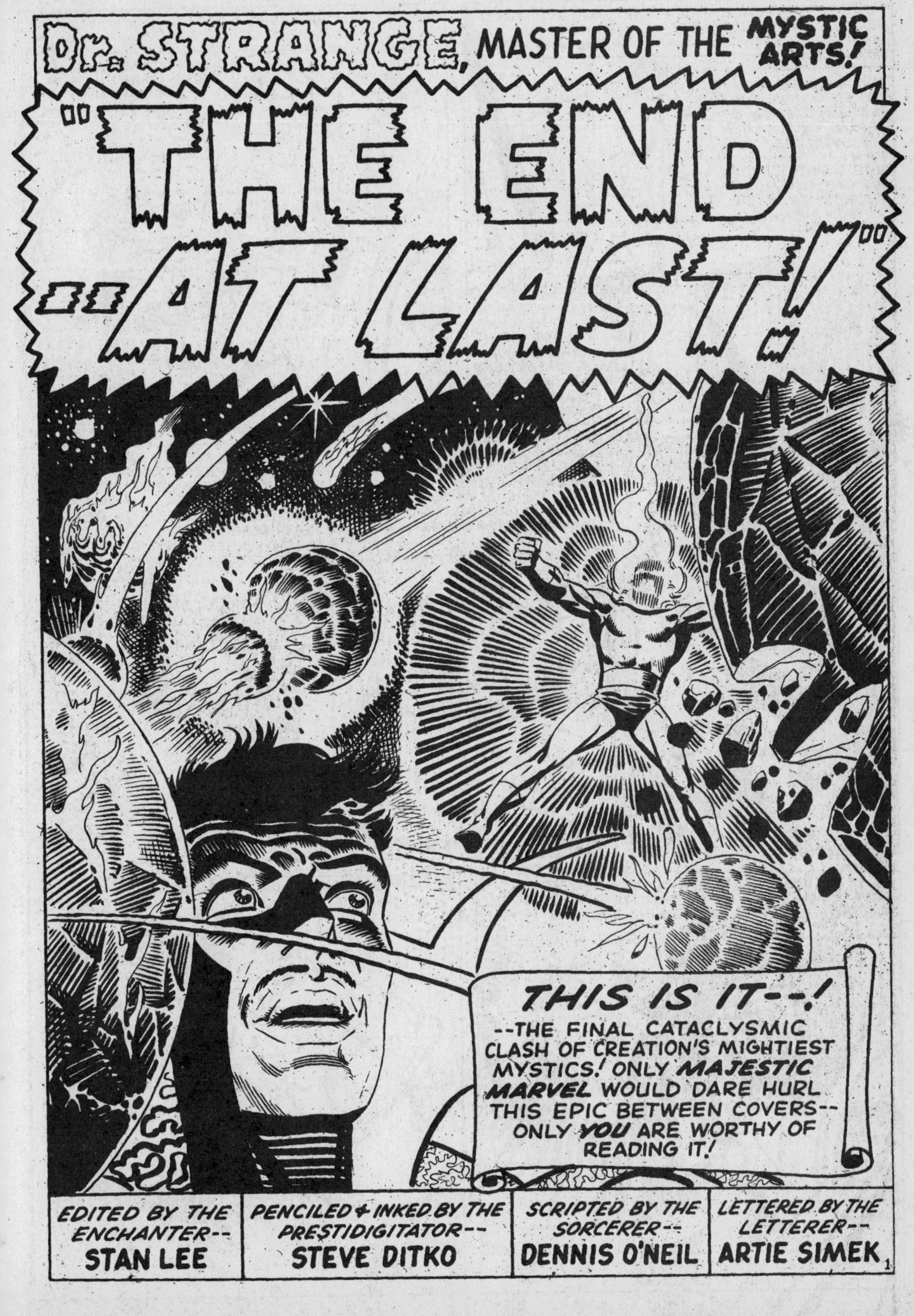
Dr. STRANGE, MASTER OF THE MYSTIC ARTS!
"THE END ..AT LAST!"
THIS IS IT--! --THE FINAL CATACLYSMIC CLASH OF CREATION'S MIGHTIEST MYSTICS! ONLY MAJESTIC MARVEL WOULD DARE HURL THIS EPIC BETWEEN COVERS-- ONLY YOU ARE WORTHY OF READING IT!
EDITED BY THE ENCHANTER-- STAN LEE
PENCILED & INKED BY THE PRESTIDIGITATOR-- STEVE DITKO
SCRIPTED BY THE SORCERER-- DENNIS O'NEIL
LETTERED BY THE LETTERER-- ARTIE SIMEK
1

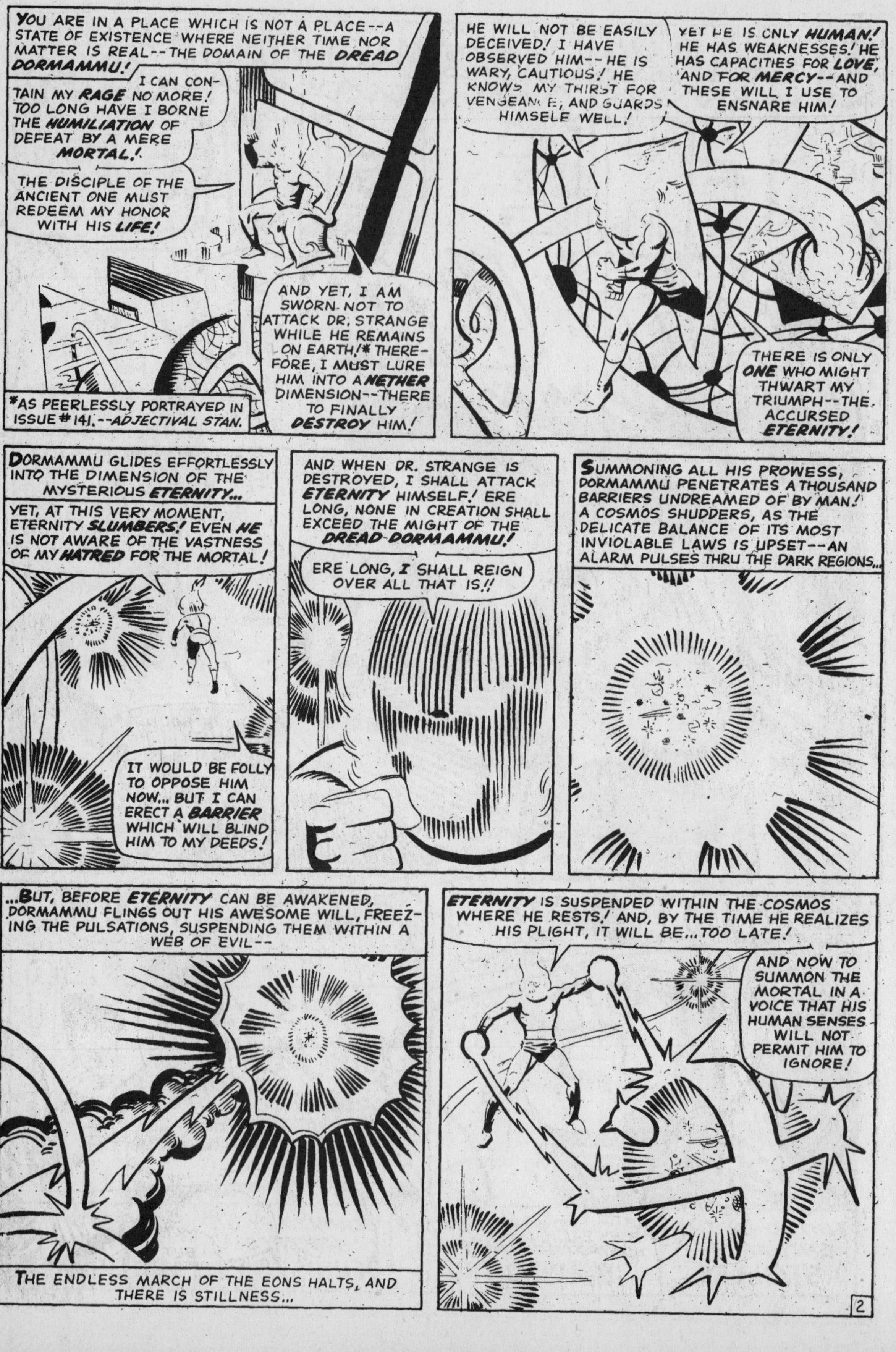
YOU ARE IN A PLACE WHICH IS NOT A PLACE--A STATE OF EXISTENCE WHERE NEITHER TIME NOR MATTER IS REAL--THE DOMAIN OF THE DREAD DORMAMMU!
I CAN CONTAIN MY RAGE NO MORE! TOO LONG HAVE I BORNE THE HUMILIATION OF DEFEAT BY A MERE MORTAL!
THE DISCIPLE OF THE ANCIENT ONE MUST REDEEM MY HONOR WITH HIS LIFE!
AND YET, I AM SWORN NOT TO ATTACK DR. STRANGE WHILE HE REMAINS ON EARTH!* THEREFORE, I MUST LURE HIM INTO A NETHER DIMENSION--THERE TO FINALLY DESTROY HIM!
*AS PEERLESSLY PORTRAYED IN ISSUE #141.--ADJECTIVAL STAN.
HE WILL NOT BE EASILY DECEIVED! I HAVE OBSERVED HIM--HE IS WARY, CAUTIOUS! HE KNOWS MY THIRST FOR VENGEANCE, AND GUARDS HIMSELF WELL!
YET HE IS ONLY HUMAN! HE HAS WEAKNESSES! HE HAS CAPACITIES FOR LOVE, AND FOR MERCY--AND THESE WILL I USE TO ENSNARE HIM!
THERE IS ONLY ONE WHO MIGHT THWART MY TRIUMPH--THE ACCURSED ETERNITY!
DORMAMMU GLIDES EFFORTLESSLY INTO THE DIMENSION OF THE MYSTERIOUS ETERNITY...
YET, AT THIS VERY MOMENT, ETERNITY SLUMBERS! EVEN HE IS NOT AWARE OF THE VASTNESS OF MY HATRED FOR THE MORTAL!
IT WOULD BE FOLLY TO OPPOSE HIM NOW... BUT I CAN ERECT A BARRIER WHICH WILL BLIND HIM TO MY DEEDS!
AND WHEN DR. STRANGE IS DESTROYED, I SHALL ATTACK ETERNITY HIMSELF! ERE LONG, NONE IN CREATION SHALL EXCEED THE MIGHT OF THE DREAD DORMAMMU!
ERE LONG, I SHALL REIGN OVER ALL THAT IS!!
SUMMONING ALL HIS PROWESS, DORMAMMU PENETRATES A THOUSAND BARRIERS UNDREAMED OF BY MAN! A COSMOS SHUDDERS, AS THE DELICATE BALANCE OF ITS MOST INVIOLABLE LAWS IS UPSET--AN ALARM PULSES THRU THE DARK REGIONS...
...BUT, BEFORE ETERNITY CAN BE AWAKENED, DORMAMMU FLINGS OUT HIS AWESOME WILL, FREEZING THE PULSATIONS, SUSPENDING THEM WITHIN A WEB OF EVIL--
THE ENDLESS MARCH OF THE EONS HALTS, AND THERE IS STILLNESS...
ETERNITY IS SUSPENDED WITHIN THE COSMOS WHERE HE RESTS! AND, BY THE TIME HE REALIZES HIS PLIGHT, IT WILL BE...TOO LATE!
AND NOW TO SUMMON THE MORTAL IN A VOICE THAT HIS HUMAN SENSES WILL NOT PERMIT HIM TO IGNORE!
2

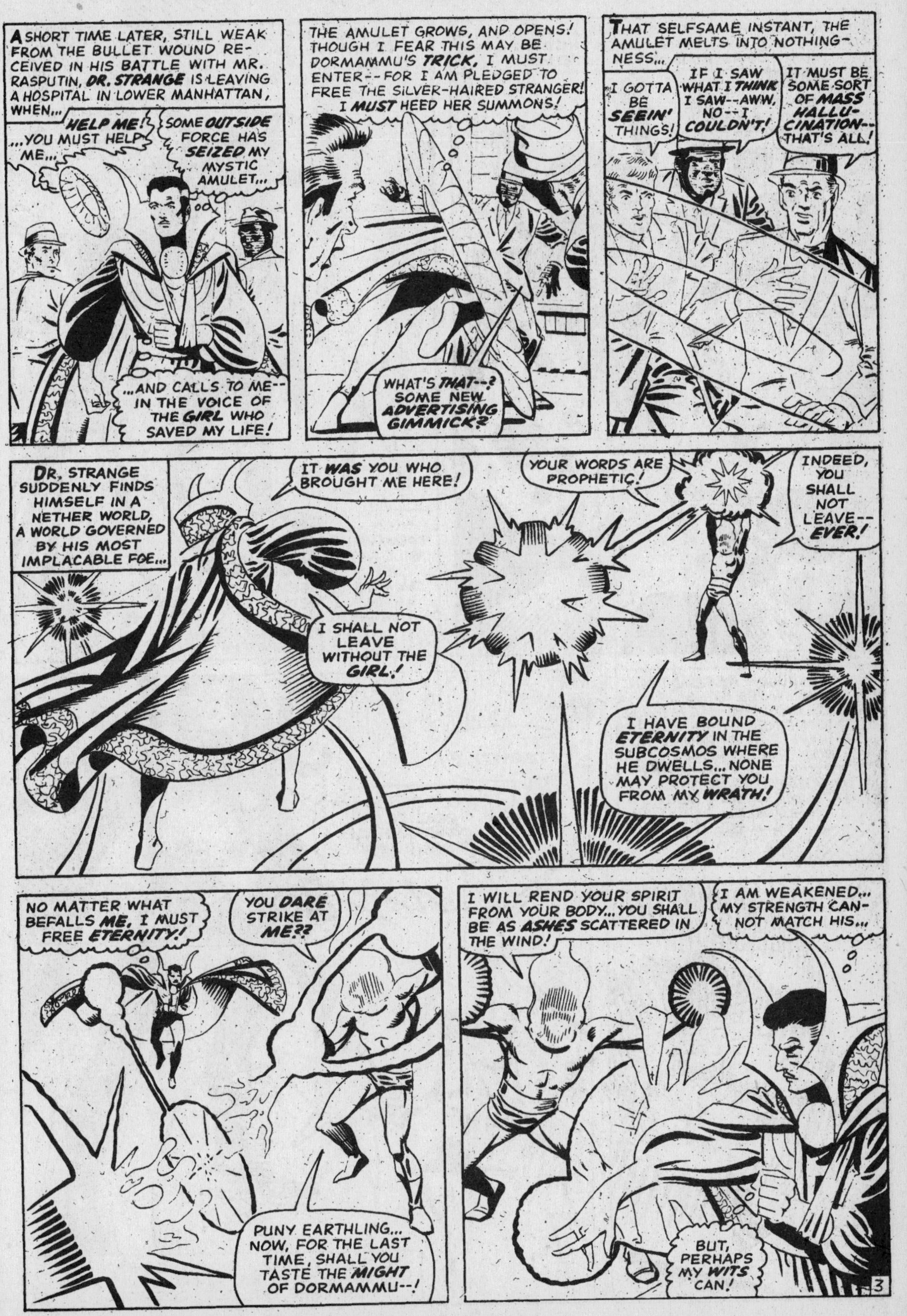

A SHORT TIME LATER, STILL WEAK FROM THE BULLET WOUND RECEIVED IN HIS BATTLE WITH MR. RASPUTIN, DR. STRANGE IS LEAVING A HOSPITAL IN LOWER MANHATTAN, WHEN...
HELP ME! ...YOU MUST HELP ME...
SOME OUTSIDE FORCE HAS SEIZED MY MYSTIC AMULET...
...AND CALLS TO ME-- IN THE VOICE OF THE GIRL WHO SAVED MY LIFE!
THE AMULET GROWS, AND OPENS! THOUGH I FEAR THIS MAY BE DORMAMMU'S TRICK, I MUST ENTER--FOR I AM PLEDGED TO FREE THE SILVER-HAIRED STRANGER! I MUST HEED HER SUMMONS!
WHAT'S THAT--? SOME NEW ADVERTISING GIMMICK?
THAT SELFSAME INSTANT, THE AMULET MELTS INTO NOTHINGNESS...
I GOTTA BE SEEIN' THINGS!
IF I SAW WHAT I THINK I SAW--AWW, NO--I COULDN'T!
IT MUST BE SOME SORT OF MASS HALLUCINATION-- THAT'S ALL!
DR. STRANGE SUDDENLY FINDS HIMSELF IN A NETHER WORLD, A WORLD GOVERNED BY HIS MOST IMPLACABLE FOE...
IT WAS YOU WHO BROUGHT ME HERE!
YOUR WORDS ARE PROPHETIC!
INDEED, YOU SHALL NOT LEAVE-- EVER!
I SHALL NOT LEAVE WITHOUT THE GIRL!
I HAVE BOUND ETERNITY IN THE SUBCOSMOS WHERE HE DWELLS... NONE MAY PROTECT YOU FROM MY WRATH!
NO MATTER WHAT BEFALLS ME, I MUST FREE ETERNITY!
YOU DARE STRIKE AT ME??
PUNY EARTHLING... NOW, FOR THE LAST TIME, SHALL YOU TASTE THE MIGHT OF DORMAMMU--!
I WILL REND YOUR SPIRIT FROM YOUR BODY... YOU SHALL BE AS ASHES SCATTERED IN THE WIND!
I AM WEAKENED... MY STRENGTH CANNOT MATCH HIS...
BUT, PERHAPS MY WITS CAN!
3

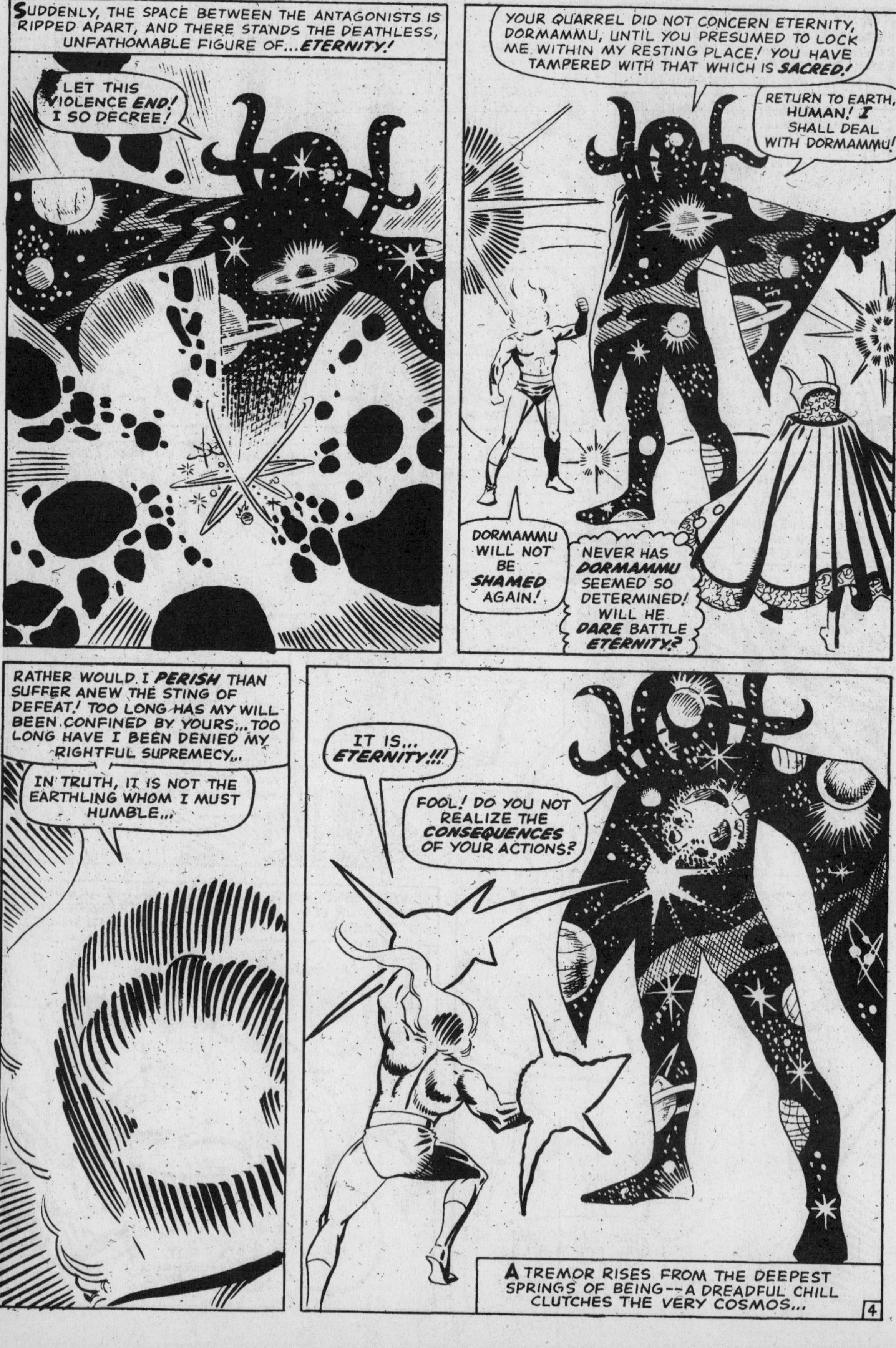
SUDDENLY, THE SPACE BETWEEN THE ANTAGONISTS IS RIPPED APART, AND THERE STANDS THE DEATHLESS, UNFATHOMABLE FIGURE OF... ETERNITY!
LET THIS VIOLENCE END! I SO DECREE!
YOUR QUARREL DID NOT CONCERN ETERNITY, DORMAMMU, UNTIL YOU PRESUMED TO LOCK ME WITHIN MY RESTING PLACE! YOU HAVE TAMPERED WITH THAT WHICH IS SACRED!
RETURN TO EARTH, HUMAN! I SHALL DEAL WITH DORMAMMU!
DORMAMMU WILL NOT BE SHAMED AGAIN!
NEVER HAS DORMAMMU SEEMED SO DETERMINED! WILL HE DARE BATTLE ETERNITY?
RATHER WOULD I PERISH THAN SUFFER ANEW THE STING OF DEFEAT! TOO LONG HAS MY WILL BEEN CONFINED BY YOURS... TOO LONG HAVE I BEEN DENIED MY RIGHTFUL SUPREMECY...
IN TRUTH, IT IS NOT THE EARTHLING WHOM I MUST HUMBLE...
IT IS... ETERNITY!!!
FOOL! DO YOU NOT REALIZE THE CONSEQUENCES OF YOUR ACTIONS?
A TREMOR RISES FROM THE DEEPEST SPRINGS OF BEING--A DREADFUL CHILL CLUTCHES THE VERY COSMOS...
4

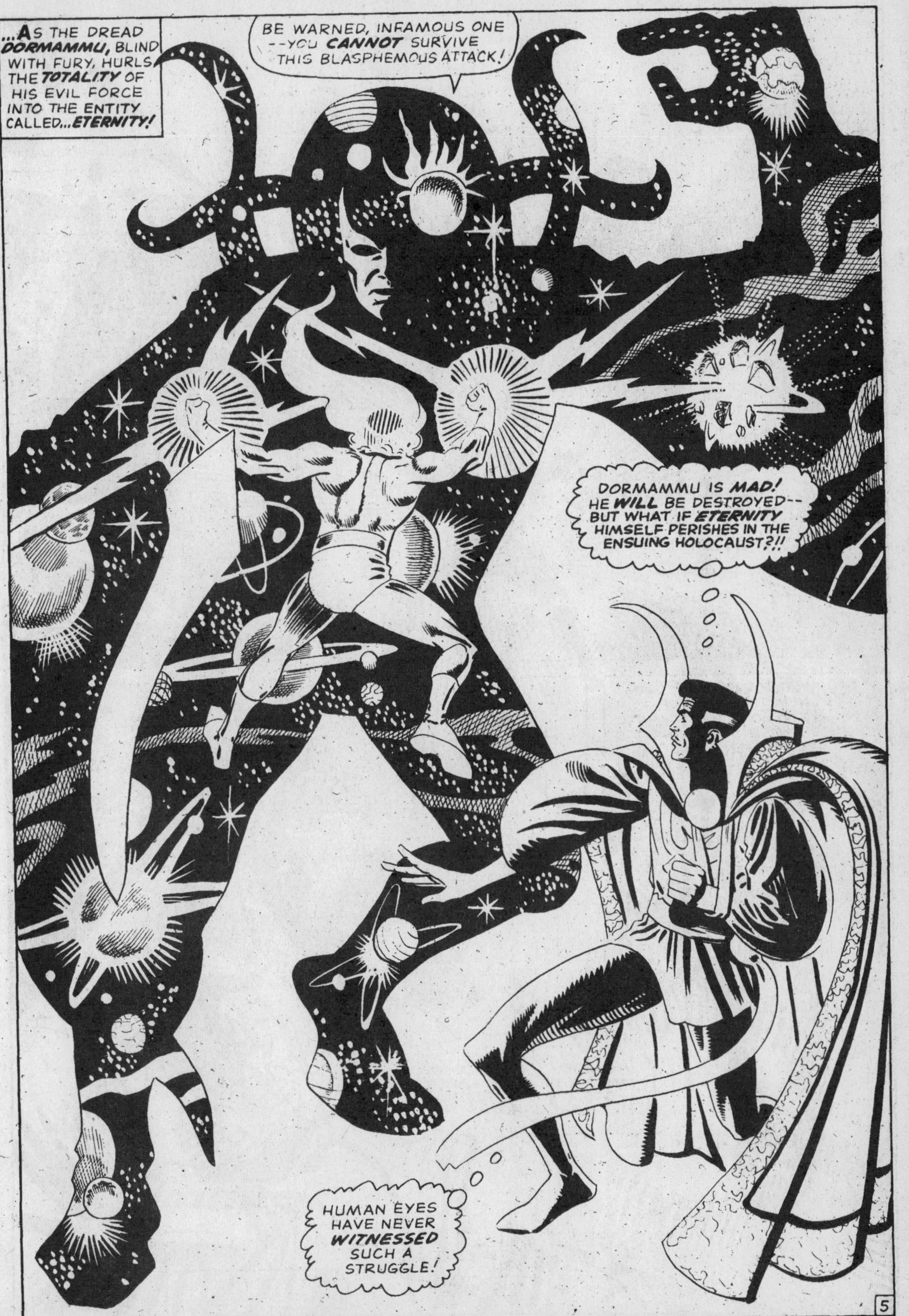
...AS THE DREAD DORMAMMU, BLIND WITH FURY, HURLS THE TOTALITY OF HIS EVIL FORCE INTO THE ENTITY CALLED...ETERNITY!
BE WARNED, INFAMOUS ONE --YOU CANNOT SURVIVE THIS BLASPHEMOUS ATTACK!
DORMAMMU IS MAD! HE WILL BE DESTROYED-- BUT WHAT IF ETERNITY HIMSELF PERISHES IN THE ENSUING HOLOCAUST?!!
HUMAN EYES HAVE NEVER WITNESSED SUCH A STRUGGLE!
5

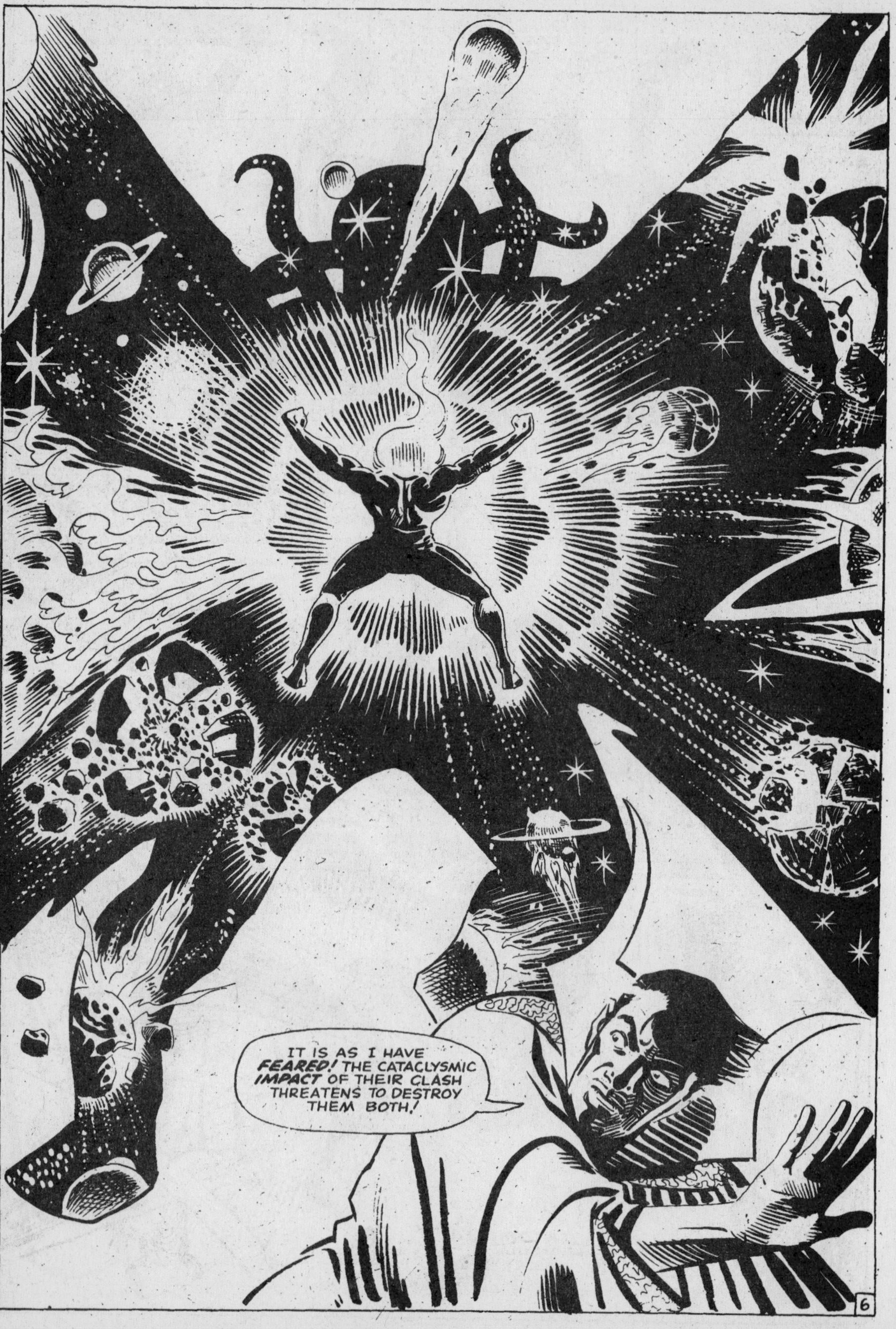
IT IS AS I HAVE FEARED! THE CATACLYSMIC IMPACT OF THEIR CLASH THREATENS TO DESTROY THEM BOTH!
6

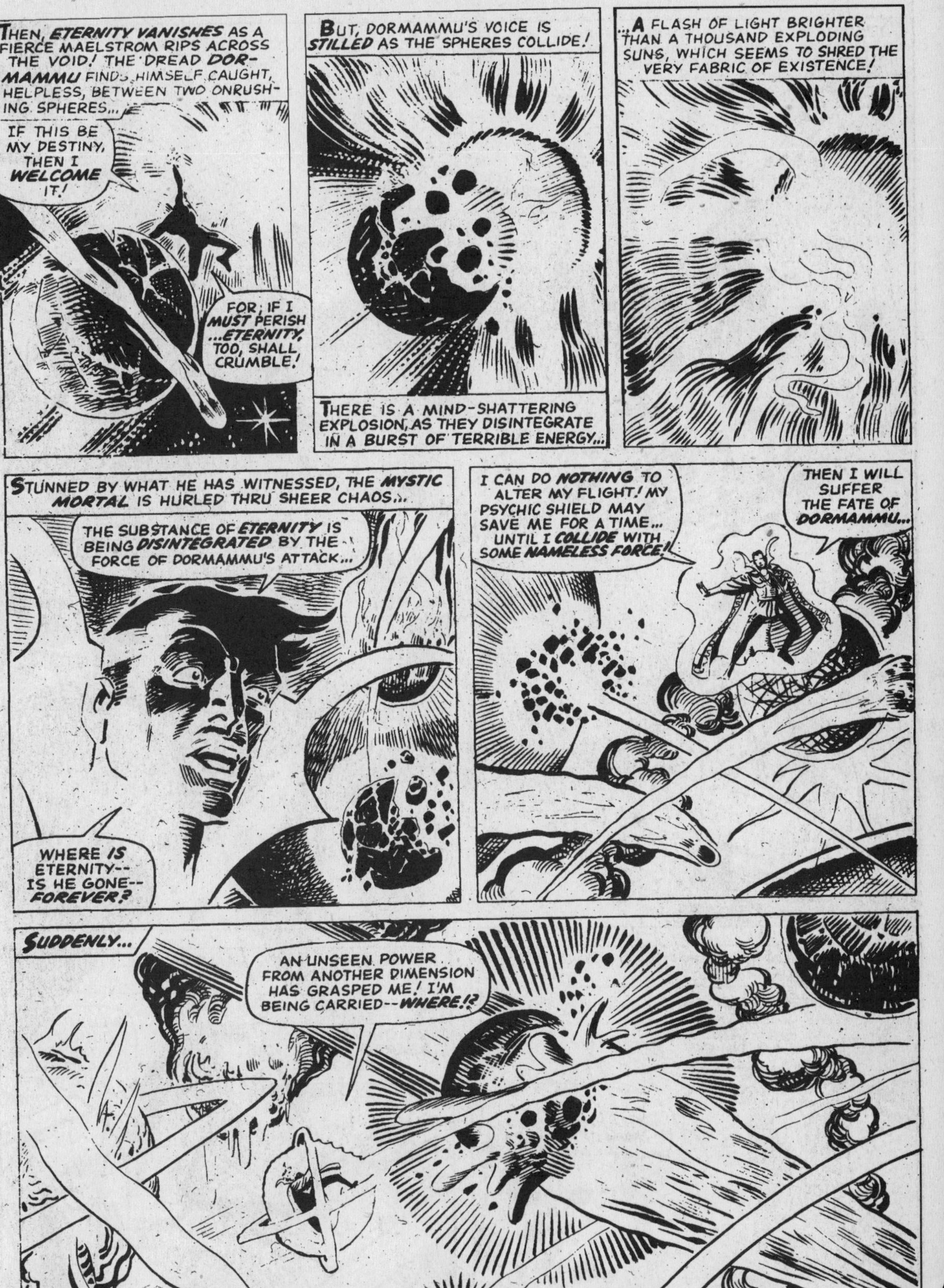
THEN, ETERNITY VANISHES AS A FIERCE MAELSTROM RIPS ACROSS THE VOID! THE DREAD DORMAMMU FINDS HIMSELF CAUGHT, HELPLESS, BETWEEN TWO ONRUSHING SPHERES...
IF THIS BE MY DESTINY, THEN I WELCOME IT!
FOR, IF I MUST PERISH ...ETERNITY, TOO, SHALL CRUMBLE!
BUT, DORMAMMU'S VOICE IS STILLED AS THE SPHERES COLLIDE!
THERE IS A MIND-SHATTERING EXPLOSION, AS THEY DISINTEGRATE IN A BURST OF TERRIBLE ENERGY...
...A FLASH OF LIGHT BRIGHTER THAN A THOUSAND EXPLODING SUNS, WHICH SEEMS TO SHRED THE VERY FABRIC OF EXISTENCE!
STUNNED BY WHAT HE HAS WITNESSED, THE MYSTIC MORTAL IS HURLED THRU SHEER CHAOS...
THE SUBSTANCE OF ETERNITY IS BEING DISINTEGRATED BY THE FORCE OF DORMAMMU'S ATTACK...
WHERE IS ETERNITY-- IS HE GONE-- FOREVER?
I CAN DO NOTHING TO ALTER MY FLIGHT! MY PSYCHIC SHIELD MAY SAVE ME FOR A TIME... UNTIL I COLLIDE WITH SOME NAMELESS FORCE!
THEN I WILL SUFFER THE FATE OF DORMAMMU...
SUDDENLY...
AN UNSEEN POWER FROM ANOTHER DIMENSION HAS GRASPED ME! I'M BEING CARRIED--WHERE!?

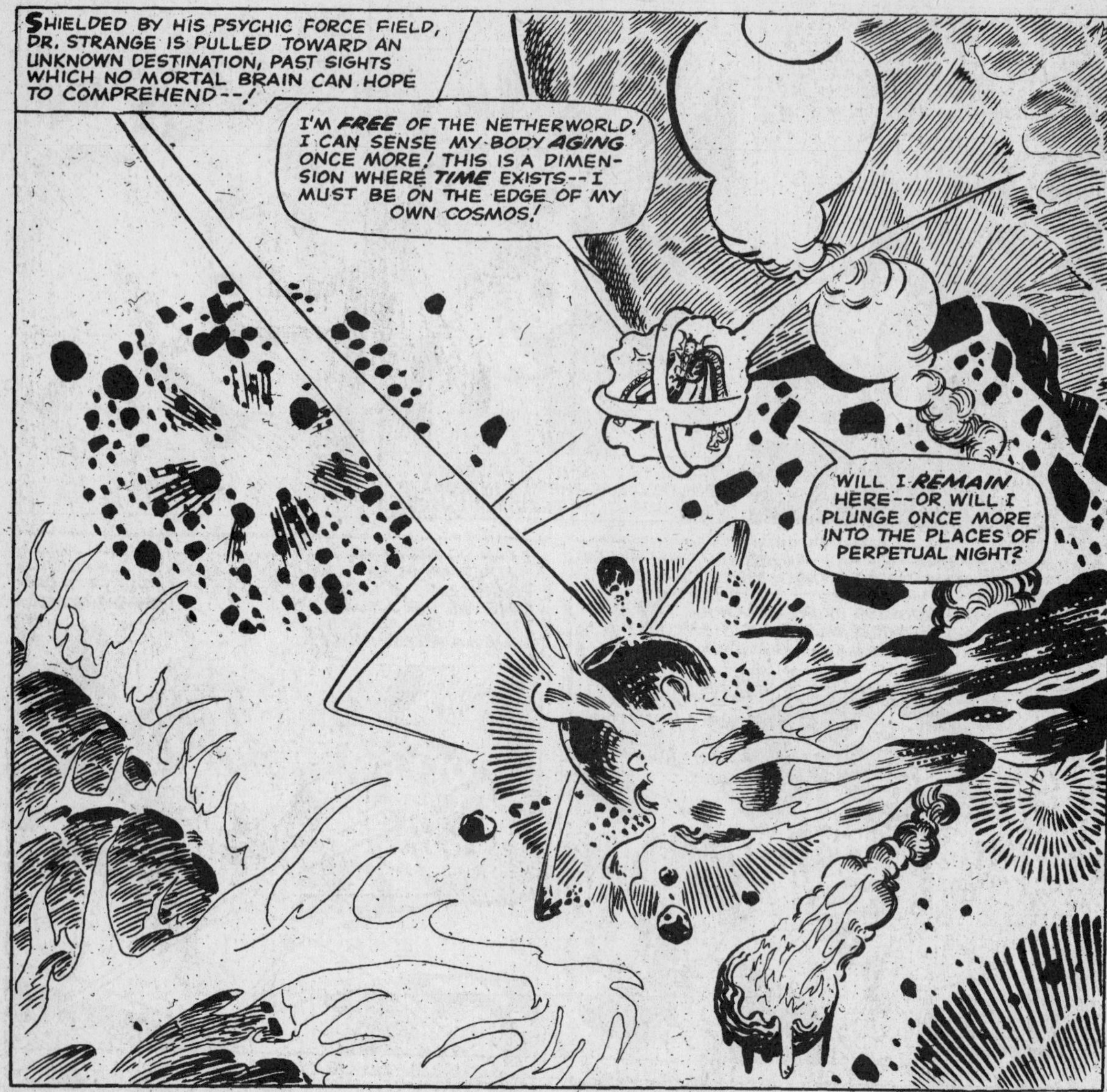
SHIELDED BY HIS PSYCHIC FORCE FIELD, DR. STRANGE IS PULLED TOWARD AN UNKNOWN DESTINATION, PAST SIGHTS WHICH NO MORTAL BRAIN CAN HOPE TO COMPREHEND--!
I'M FREE OF THE NETHERWORLD! I CAN SENSE MY BODY AGING ONCE MORE! THIS IS A DIMENSION WHERE TIME EXISTS--I MUST BE ON THE EDGE OF MY OWN COSMOS!
WILL I REMAIN HERE--OR WILL I PLUNGE ONCE MORE INTO THE PLACES OF PERPETUAL NIGHT?

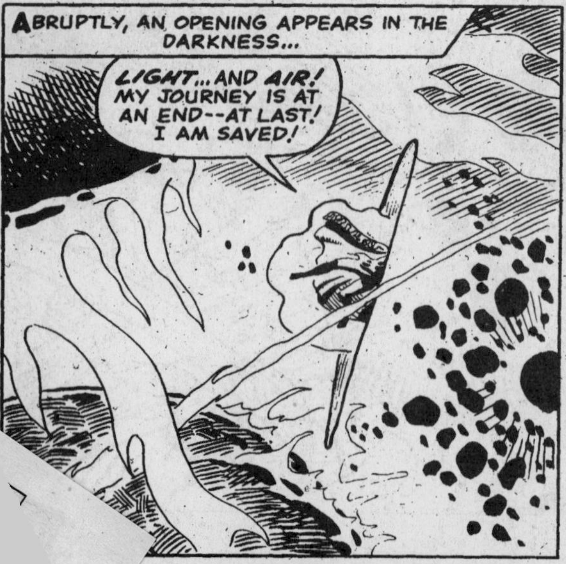
ABRUPTLY, AN OPENING APPEARS IN THE DARKNESS...
LIGHT...AND AIR! MY JOURNEY IS AT AN END--AT LAST! I AM SAVED!

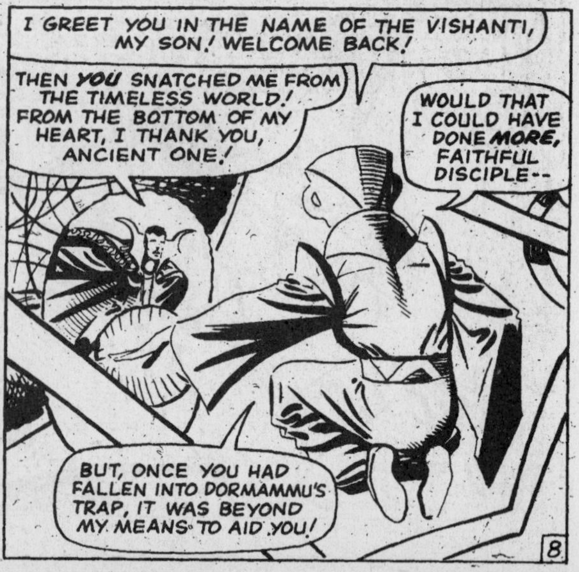
I GREET YOU IN THE NAME OF THE VISHANTI, MY SON! WELCOME BACK!
THEN YOU SNATCHED ME FROM THE TIMELESS WORLD! FROM THE BOTTOM OF MY HEART, I THANK YOU, ANCIENT ONE!
WOULD THAT I COULD HAVE DONE MORE, FAITHFUL DISCIPLE--
BUT, ONCE YOU HAD FALLEN INTO DORMAMMU'S TRAP, IT WAS BEYOND MY MEANS TO AID YOU!
8

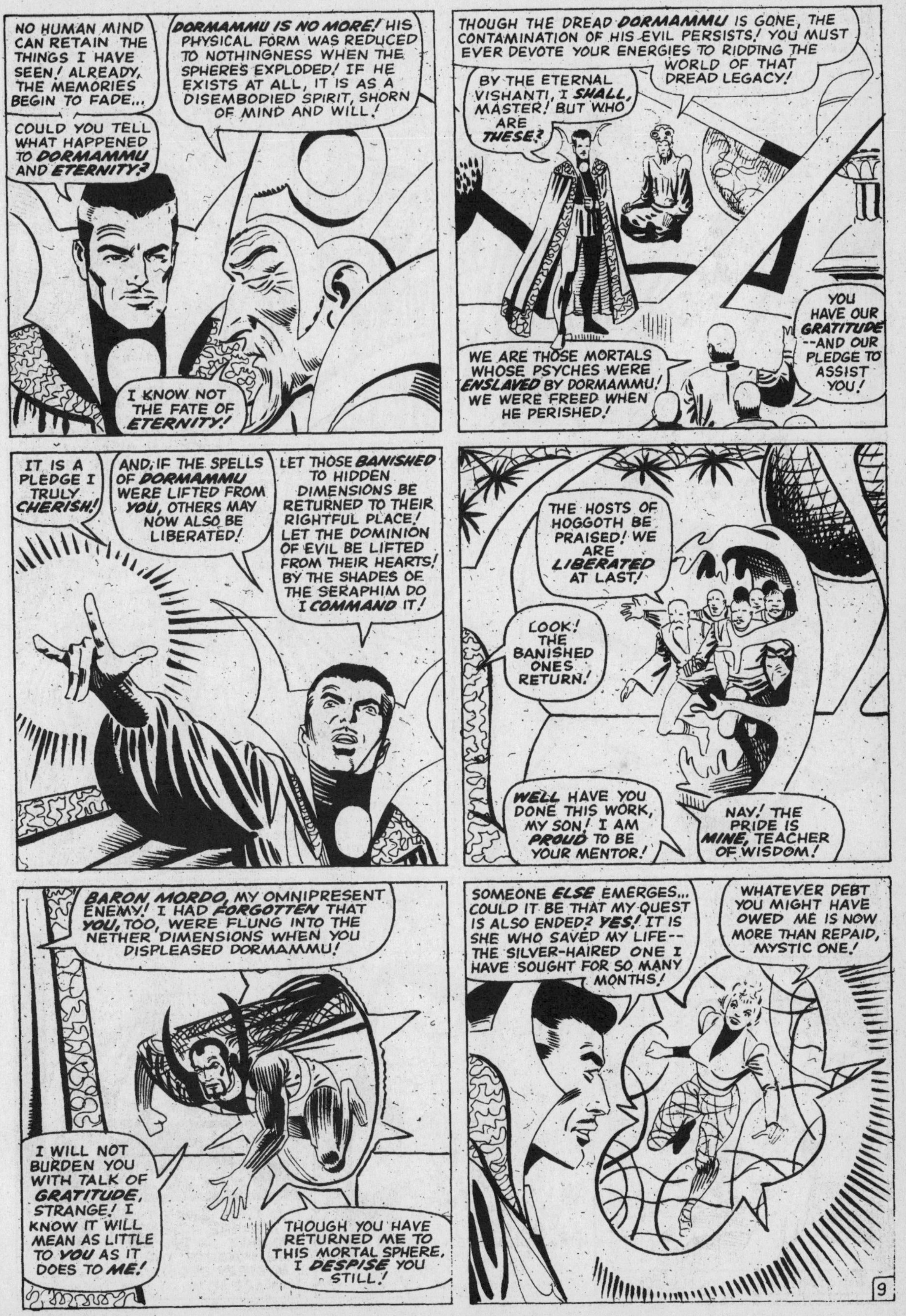
NO HUMAN MIND CAN RETAIN THE THINGS I HAVE SEEN! ALREADY, THE MEMORIES BEGIN TO FADE...
COULD YOU TELL WHAT HAPPENED TO DORMAMMU AND ETERNITY?
DORMAMMU IS NO MORE! HIS PHYSICAL FORM WAS REDUCED TO NOTHINGNESS WHEN THE SPHERES EXPLODED! IF HE EXISTS AT ALL, IT IS AS A DISEMBODIED SPIRIT, SHORN OF MIND AND WILL!
I KNOW NOT THE FATE OF ETERNITY!
THOUGH THE DREAD DORMAMMU IS GONE, THE CONTAMINATION OF HIS EVIL PERSISTS! YOU MUST EVER DEVOTE YOUR ENERGIES TO RIDDING THE WORLD OF THAT DREAD LEGACY!
BY THE ETERNAL VISHANTI, I SHALL, MASTER! BUT WHO ARE THESE?
WE ARE THOSE MORTALS WHOSE PSYCHES WERE ENSLAVED BY DORMAMMU! WE WERE FREED WHEN HE PERISHED!
YOU HAVE OUR GRATITUDE --AND OUR PLEDGE TO ASSIST YOU!
IT IS A PLEDGE I TRULY CHERISH!
AND, IF THE SPELLS OF DORMAMMU WERE LIFTED FROM YOU, OTHERS MAY NOW ALSO BE LIBERATED!
LET THOSE BANISHED TO HIDDEN DIMENSIONS BE RETURNED TO THEIR RIGHTFUL PLACE! LET THE DOMINION OF EVIL BE LIFTED FROM THEIR HEARTS! BY THE SHADES OF THE SERAPHIM DO I COMMAND IT!
THE HOSTS OF HOGGOTH BE PRAISED! WE ARE LIBERATED AT LAST!
LOOK! THE BANISHED ONES RETURN!
WELL HAVE YOU DONE THIS WORK, MY SON! I AM PROUD TO BE YOUR MENTOR!
NAY! THE PRIDE IS MINE, TEACHER OF WISDOM!
BARON MORDO, MY OMNIPRESENT ENEMY! I HAD FORGOTTEN THAT YOU, TOO, WERE FLUNG INTO THE NETHER DIMENSIONS WHEN YOU DISPLEASED DORMAMMU!
I WILL NOT BURDEN YOU WITH TALK OF GRATITUDE, STRANGE! I KNOW IT WILL MEAN AS LITTLE TO YOU AS IT DOES TO ME!
THOUGH YOU HAVE RETURNED ME TO THIS MORTAL SPHERE, I DESPISE YOU STILL!
SOMEONE ELSE EMERGES... COULD IT BE THAT MY QUEST IS ALSO ENDED? YES! IT IS SHE WHO SAVED MY LIFE-- THE SILVER-HAIRED ONE I HAVE SOUGHT FOR SO MANY MONTHS!
WHATEVER DEBT YOU MIGHT HAVE OWED ME IS NOW MORE THAN REPAID, MYSTIC ONE!
9

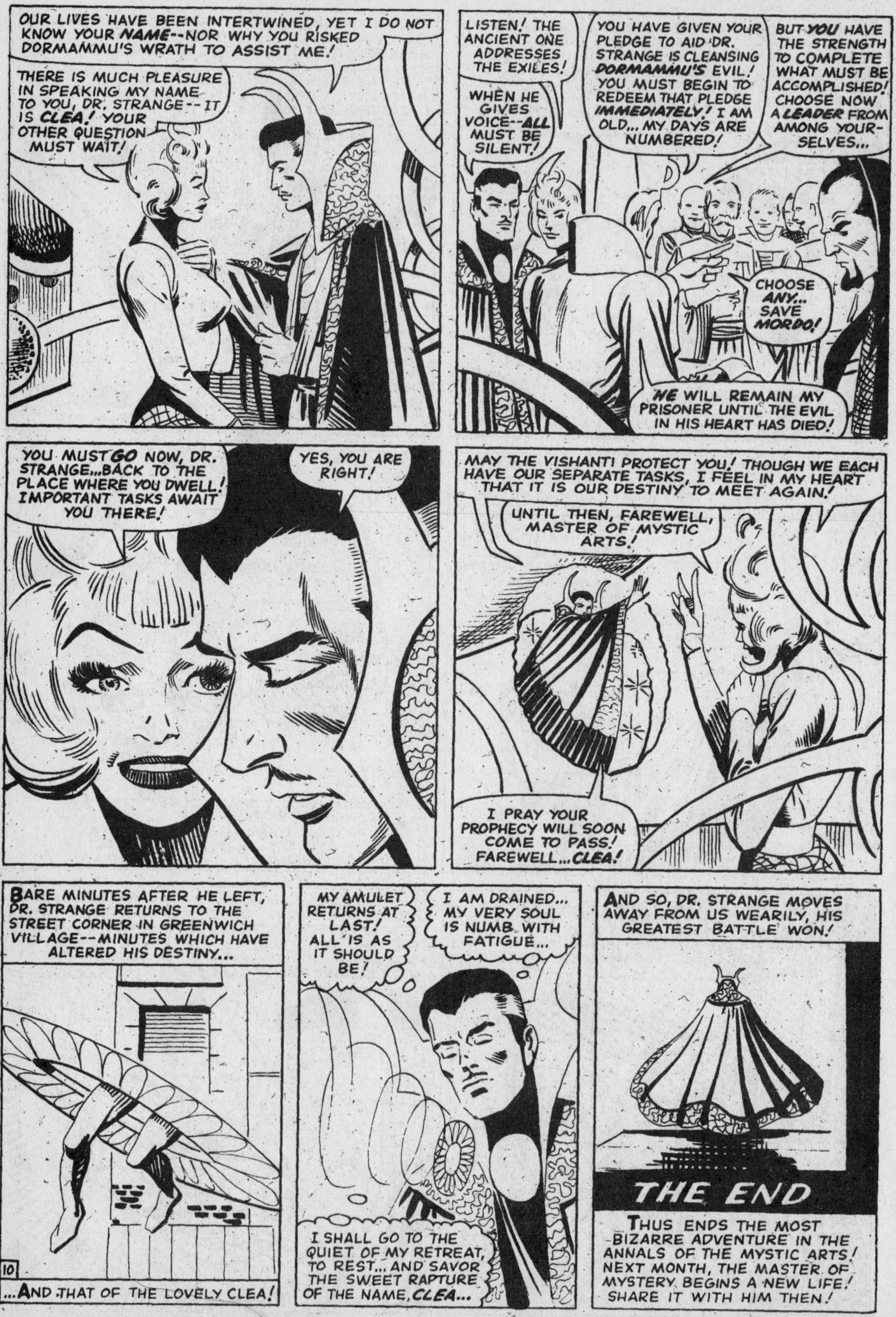
OUR LIVES HAVE BEEN INTERTWINED, YET I DO NOT KNOW YOUR NAME--NOR WHY YOU RISKED DORMAMMU'S WRATH TO ASSIST ME!
THERE IS MUCH PLEASURE IN SPEAKING MY NAME TO YOU, DR. STRANGE--IT IS CLEA! YOUR OTHER QUESTION MUST WAIT!
LISTEN! THE ANCIENT ONE ADDRESSES THE EXILES!
WHEN HE GIVES VOICE--ALL MUST BE SILENT!
YOU HAVE GIVEN YOUR PLEDGE TO AID DR. STRANGE IS CLEANSING DORMAMMU'S EVIL! YOU MUST BEGIN TO REDEEM THAT PLEDGE IMMEDIATELY! I AM OLD... MY DAYS ARE NUMBERED!
BUT YOU HAVE THE STRENGTH TO COMPLETE WHAT MUST BE ACCOMPLISHED! CHOOSE NOW A LEADER FROM AMONG YOURSELVES...
CHOOSE ANY... SAVE MORDO!
HE WILL REMAIN MY PRISONER UNTIL THE EVIL IN HIS HEART HAS DIED!
YOU MUST GO NOW, DR. STRANGE...BACK TO THE PLACE WHERE YOU DWELL! IMPORTANT TASKS AWAIT YOU THERE!
YES, YOU ARE RIGHT!
MAY THE VISHANTI PROTECT YOU! THOUGH WE EACH HAVE OUR SEPARATE TASKS, I FEEL IN MY HEART THAT IT IS OUR DESTINY TO MEET AGAIN!
UNTIL THEN, FAREWELL, MASTER OF MYSTIC ARTS!
I PRAY YOUR PROPHECY WILL SOON COME TO PASS! FAREWELL...CLEA!
BARE MINUTES AFTER HE LEFT, DR. STRANGE RETURNS TO THE STREET CORNER IN GREENWICH VILLAGE--MINUTES WHICH HAVE ALTERED HIS DESTINY...
10
...AND THAT OF THE LOVELY CLEA!
MY AMULET RETURNS AT LAST! ALL IS AS IT SHOULD BE!
I AM DRAINED... MY VERY SOUL IS NUMB WITH FATIGUE...
I SHALL GO TO THE QUIET OF MY RETREAT, TO REST... AND SAVOR THE SWEET RAPTURE OF THE NAME, CLEA...
AND SO, DR. STRANGE MOVES AWAY FROM US WEARILY, HIS GREATEST BATTLE WON!
THE END
THUS ENDS THE MOST BIZARRE ADVENTURE IN THE ANNALS OF THE MYSTIC ARTS! NEXT MONTH, THE MASTER OF MYSTERY BEGINS A NEW LIFE! SHARE IT WITH HIM THEN!

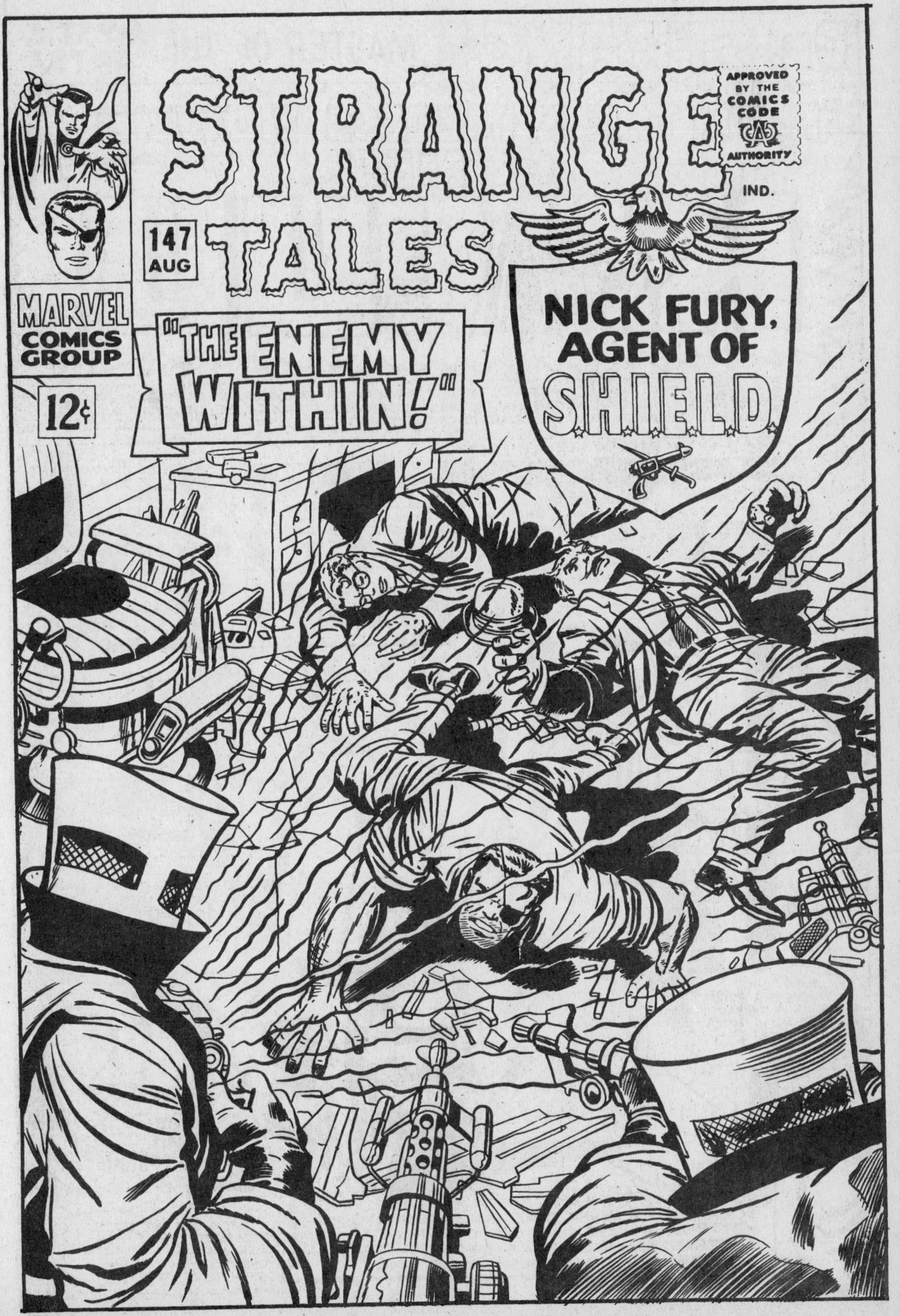
STRANGE TALES
147 AUG
MARVEL COMICS GROUP
12¢
APPROVED BY THE COMICS CODE AUTHORITY
IND.
"THE ENEMY WITHIN!"
NICK FURY, AGENT OF S.H.I.E.L.D.

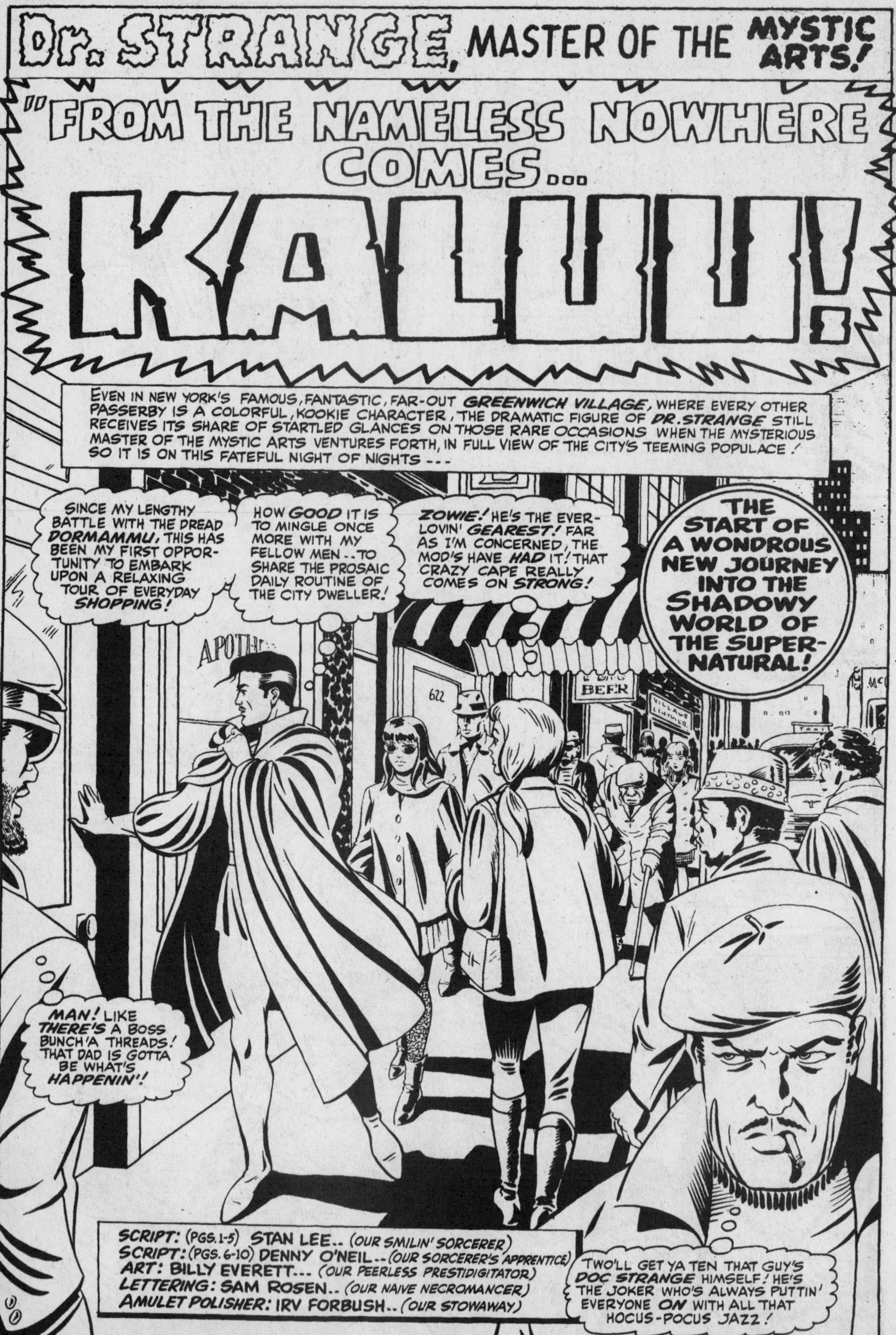

Dr. STRANGE, MASTER OF THE MYSTIC ARTS!
"FROM THE NAMELESS NOWHERE COMES... KALUU!
EVEN IN NEW YORK'S FAMOUS, FANTASTIC, FAR-OUT GREENWICH VILLAGE, WHERE EVERY OTHER PASSERBY IS A COLORFUL, KOOKIE CHARACTER, THE DRAMATIC FIGURE OF DR. STRANGE STILL RECEIVES ITS SHARE OF STARTLED GLANCES ON THOSE RARE OCCASIONS WHEN THE MYSTERIOUS MASTER OF THE MYSTIC ARTS VENTURES FORTH, IN FULL VIEW OF THE CITY'S TEEMING POPULACE! SO IT IS ON THIS FATEFUL NIGHT OF NIGHTS ---
SINCE MY LENGTHY BATTLE WITH THE DREAD DORMAMMU, THIS HAS BEEN MY FIRST OPPORTUNITY TO EMBARK UPON A RELAXING TOUR OF EVERYDAY SHOPPING!
HOW GOOD IT IS TO MINGLE ONCE MORE WITH MY FELLOW MEN -- TO SHARE THE PROSAIC DAILY ROUTINE OF THE CITY DWELLER!
ZOWIE! HE'S THE EVER-LOVIN' GEAREST! FAR AS I'M CONCERNED, THE MOD'S HAVE HAD IT! THAT CRAZY CAPE REALLY COMES ON STRONG!
THE START OF A WONDROUS NEW JOURNEY INTO THE SHADOWY WORLD OF THE SUPER-NATURAL!
BEER
622
MAN! LIKE THERE'S A BOSS BUNCH'A THREADS! THAT DAD IS GOTTA BE WHAT'S HAPPENIN'!
SCRIPT: (PGS. 1-5) STAN LEE.. (OUR SMILIN' SORCERER)
SCRIPT: (PGS. 6-10) DENNY O'NEIL--(OUR SORCERER'S APPRENTICE)
ART: BILLY EVERETT... (OUR PEERLESS PRESTIDIGITATOR)
LETTERING: SAM ROSEN.. (OUR NAIVE NECROMANCER)
AMULET POLISHER: IRV FORBUSH.. (OUR STOWAWAY)
TWO'LL GET YA TEN THAT GUY'S DOC STRANGE HIMSELF! HE'S THE JOKER WHO'S ALWAYS PUTTIN' EVERYONE ON WITH ALL THAT HOCUS-POCUS JAZZ!

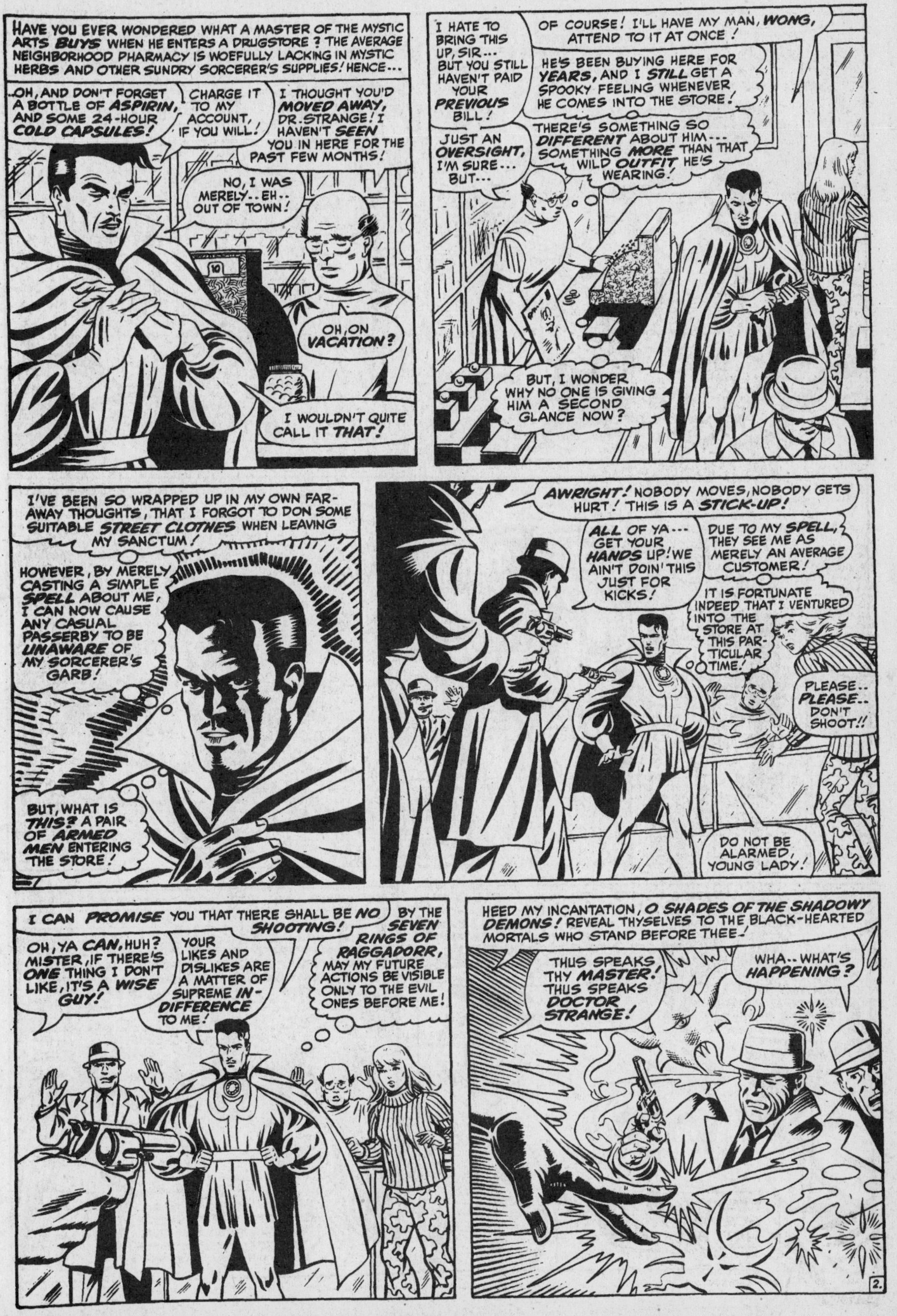

HAVE YOU EVER WONDERED WHAT A MASTER OF THE MYSTIC ARTS BUYS WHEN HE ENTERS A DRUGSTORE ? THE AVERAGE NEIGHBORHOOD PHARMACY IS WOEFULLY LACKING IN MYSTIC HERBS AND OTHER SUNDRY SORCERER'S SUPPLIES! HENCE...
..OH, AND DON'T FORGET A BOTTLE OF ASPIRIN, AND SOME 24-HOUR COLD CAPSULES!
CHARGE IT TO MY ACCOUNT, IF YOU WILL!
I THOUGHT YOU'D MOVED AWAY, DR. STRANGE! I HAVEN'T SEEN YOU IN HERE FOR THE PAST FEW MONTHS!
NO, I WAS MERELY.. EH.. OUT OF TOWN!
OH, ON VACATION?
I WOULDN'T QUITE CALL IT THAT!
I HATE TO BRING THIS UP, SIR... BUT YOU STILL HAVEN'T PAID YOUR PREVIOUS BILL!
OF COURSE! I'LL HAVE MY MAN, WONG, ATTEND TO IT AT ONCE!
JUST AN OVERSIGHT, I'M SURE... BUT...
HE'S BEEN BUYING HERE FOR YEARS, AND I STILL GET A SPOOKY FEELING WHENEVER HE COMES INTO THE STORE!
THERE'S SOMETHING SO DIFFERENT ABOUT HIM... SOMETHING MORE THAN THAT WILD OUTFIT HE'S WEARING!
BUT, I WONDER WHY NO ONE IS GIVING HIM A SECOND GLANCE NOW?
I'VE BEEN SO WRAPPED UP IN MY OWN FAR-AWAY THOUGHTS, THAT I FORGOT TO DON SOME SUITABLE STREET CLOTHES WHEN LEAVING MY SANCTUM!
HOWEVER, BY MERELY CASTING A SIMPLE SPELL ABOUT ME, I CAN NOW CAUSE ANY CASUAL PASSERBY TO BE UNAWARE OF MY SORCERER'S GARB!
BUT, WHAT IS THIS? A PAIR OF ARMED MEN ENTERING THE STORE!
AWRIGHT! NOBODY MOVES, NOBODY GETS HURT! THIS IS A STICK-UP!
ALL OF YA--- GET YOUR HANDS UP! WE AIN'T DOIN' THIS JUST FOR KICKS!
DUE TO MY SPELL, THEY SEE ME AS MERELY AN AVERAGE CUSTOMER!
IT IS FORTUNATE INDEED THAT I VENTURED INTO THE STORE AT THIS PARTICULAR TIME!
PLEASE.. PLEASE.. DON'T SHOOT!!
DO NOT BE ALARMED, YOUNG LADY!
I CAN PROMISE YOU THAT THERE SHALL BE NO SHOOTING!
OH, YA CAN, HUH? MISTER, IF THERE'S ONE THING I DON'T LIKE, IT'S A WISE GUY!
YOUR LIKES AND DISLIKES ARE A MATTER OF SUPREME INDIFFERENCE TO ME!
BY THE SEVEN RINGS OF RAGGADORR, MAY MY FUTURE ACTIONS BE VISIBLE ONLY TO THE EVIL ONES BEFORE ME!
HEED MY INCANTATION, O SHADES OF THE SHADOWY DEMONS! REVEAL THYSELVES TO THE BLACK-HEARTED MORTALS WHO STAND BEFORE THEE!
THUS SPEAKS THY MASTER! THUS SPEAKS DOCTOR STRANGE!
WHA.. WHAT'S HAPPENING?
2.

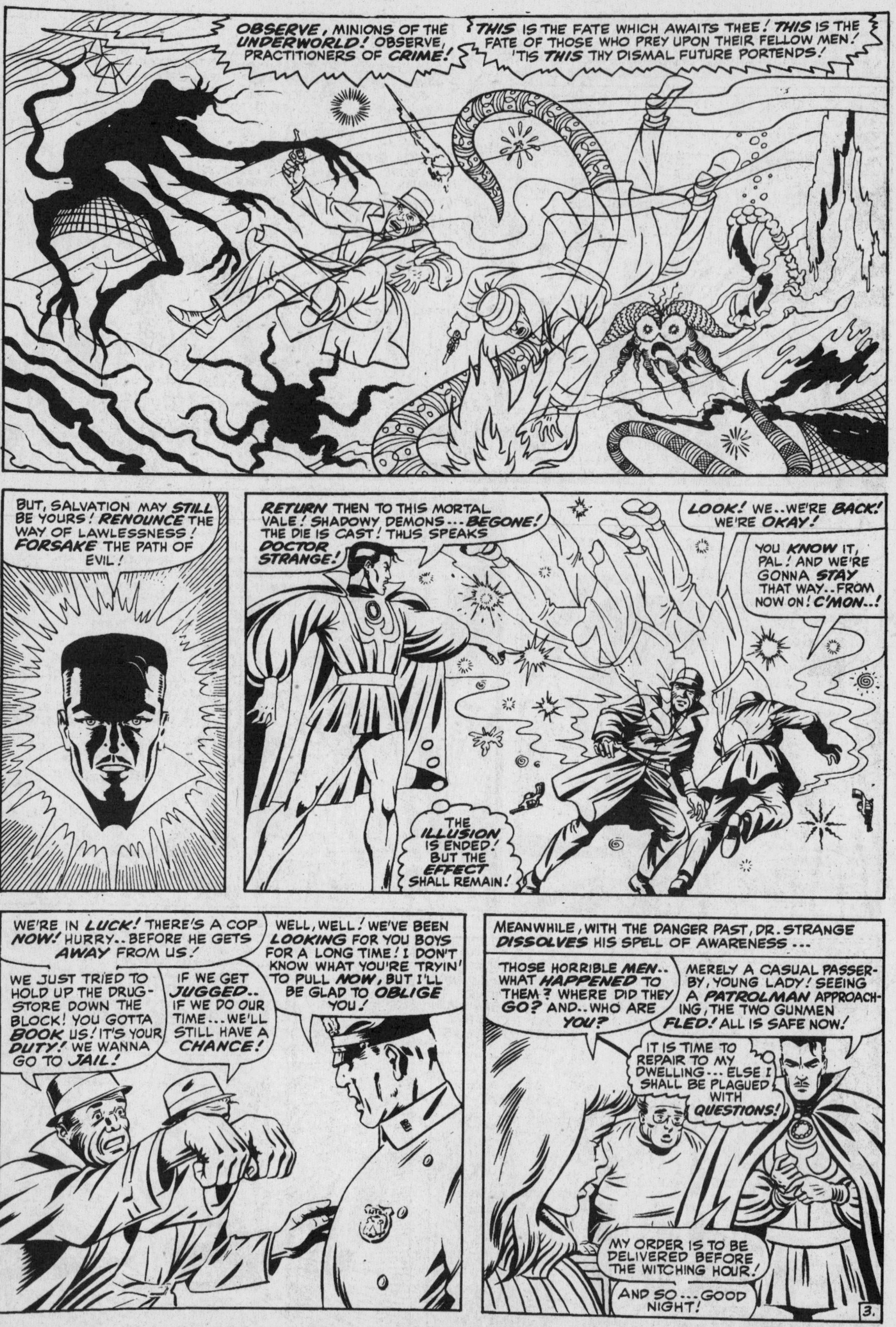

OBSERVE, MINIONS OF THE UNDERWORLD! OBSERVE, PRACTITIONERS OF CRIME!
THIS IS THE FATE WHICH AWAITS THEE! THIS IS THE FATE OF THOSE WHO PREY UPON THEIR FELLOW MEN! 'TIS THIS THY DISMAL FUTURE PORTENDS!
BUT, SALVATION MAY STILL BE YOURS! RENOUNCE THE WAY OF LAWLESSNESS! FORSAKE THE PATH OF EVIL!
RETURN THEN TO THIS MORTAL VALE! SHADOWY DEMONS... BEGONE! THE DIE IS CAST! THUS SPEAKS DOCTOR STRANGE!
LOOK! WE.. WE'RE BACK! WE'RE OKAY!
YOU KNOW IT, PAL! AND WE'RE GONNA STAY THAT WAY.. FROM NOW ON! C'MON..!
THE ILLUSION IS ENDED! BUT THE EFFECT SHALL REMAIN!
WE'RE IN LUCK! THERE'S A COP NOW! HURRY.. BEFORE HE GETS AWAY FROM US!
WE JUST TRIED TO HOLD UP THE DRUG-STORE DOWN THE BLOCK! YOU GOTTA BOOK US! IT'S YOUR DUTY! WE WANNA GO TO JAIL!
IF WE GET JUGGED.. IF WE DO OUR TIME... WE'LL STILL HAVE A CHANCE!
WELL, WELL! WE'VE BEEN LOOKING FOR YOU BOYS FOR A LONG TIME! I DON'T KNOW WHAT YOU'RE TRYIN' TO PULL NOW, BUT I'LL BE GLAD TO OBLIGE YOU!
MEANWHILE, WITH THE DANGER PAST, DR. STRANGE DISSOLVES HIS SPELL OF AWARENESS ...
THOSE HORRIBLE MEN.. WHAT HAPPENED TO THEM? WHERE DID THEY GO? AND.. WHO ARE YOU?
MERELY A CASUAL PASSER-BY, YOUNG LADY! SEEING A PATROLMAN APPROACHING, THE TWO GUNMEN FLED! ALL IS SAFE NOW!
IT IS TIME TO REPAIR TO MY DWELLING... ELSE I SHALL BE PLAGUED WITH QUESTIONS!
MY ORDER IS TO BE DELIVERED BEFORE THE WITCHING HOUR!
AND SO... GOOD NIGHT!
3.

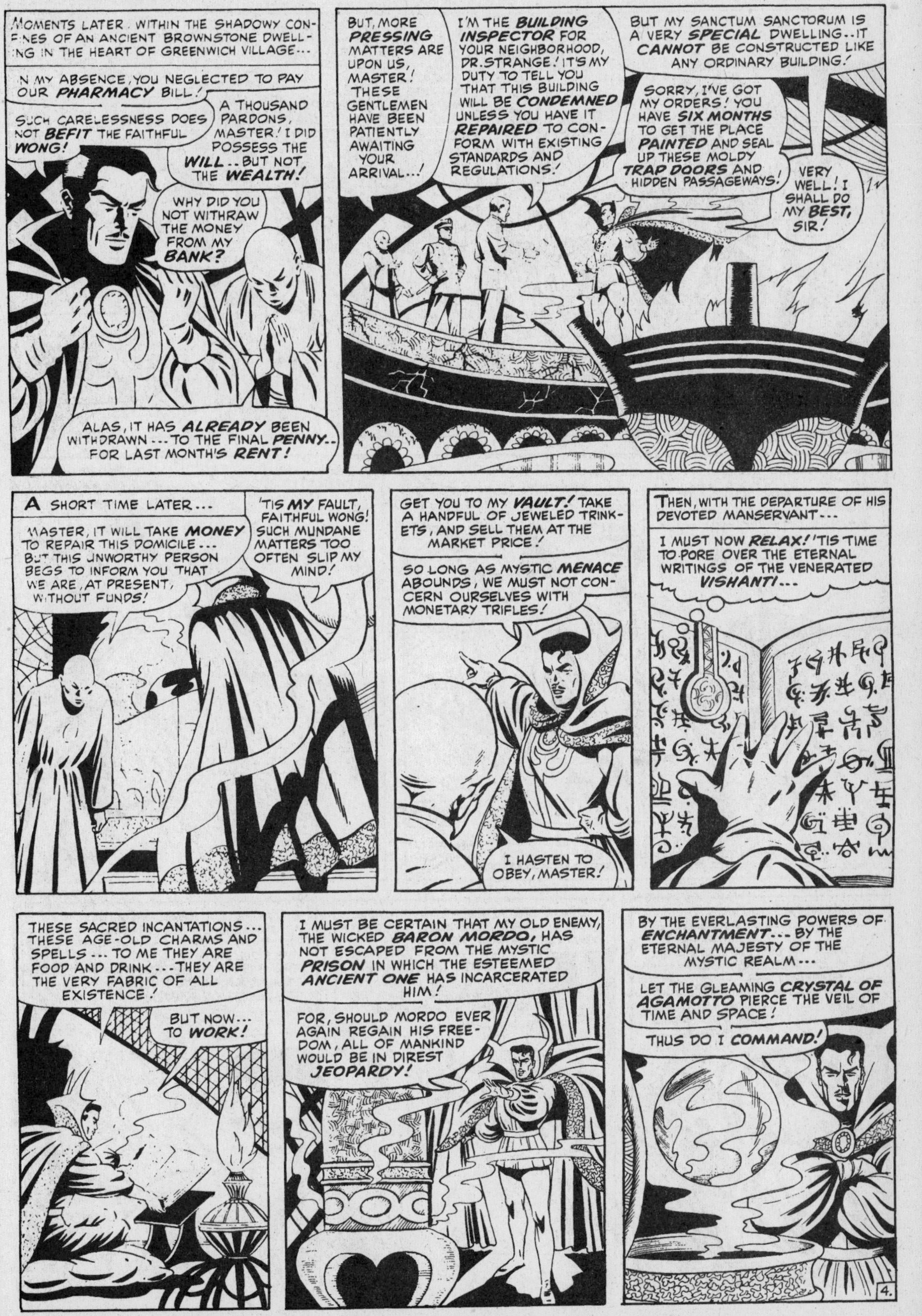
MOMENTS LATER WITHIN THE SHADOWY CONFINES OF AN ANCIENT BROWNSTONE DWELLING IN THE HEART OF GREENWICH VILLAGE...
IN MY ABSENCE, YOU NEGLECTED TO PAY OUR PHARMACY BILL!
SUCH CARELESSNESS DOES NOT BEFIT THE FAITHFUL WONG!
A THOUSAND PARDONS, MASTER! I DID POSSESS THE WILL.. BUT NOT THE WEALTH!
WHY DID YOU NOT WITHRAW THE MONEY FROM MY BANK?
ALAS, IT HAS ALREADY BEEN WITHDRAWN --- TO THE FINAL PENNY.. FOR LAST MONTH'S RENT!
BUT, MORE PRESSING MATTERS ARE UPON US, MASTER! THESE GENTLEMEN HAVE BEEN PATIENTLY AWAITING YOUR ARRIVAL...!
I'M THE BUILDING INSPECTOR FOR YOUR NEIGHBORHOOD, DR. STRANGE! IT'S MY DUTY TO TELL YOU THAT THIS BUILDING WILL BE CONDEMNED UNLESS YOU HAVE IT REPAIRED TO CONFORM WITH EXISTING STANDARDS AND REGULATIONS!
BUT MY SANCTUM SANCTORUM IS A VERY SPECIAL DWELLING..IT CANNOT BE CONSTRUCTED LIKE ANY ORDINARY BUILDING!
SORRY, I'VE GOT MY ORDERS! YOU HAVE SIX MONTHS TO GET THE PLACE PAINTED AND SEAL UP THESE MOLDY TRAP DOORS AND HIDDEN PASSAGEWAYS!
VERY WELL! I SHALL DO MY BEST, SIR!
A SHORT TIME LATER...
MASTER, IT WILL TAKE MONEY TO REPAIR THIS DOMICILE --- BUT THIS UNWORTHY PERSON BEGS TO INFORM YOU THAT WE ARE, AT PRESENT, WITHOUT FUNDS!
'TIS MY FAULT, FAITHFUL WONG! SUCH MUNDANE MATTERS TOO OFTEN SLIP MY MIND!
GET YOU TO MY VAULT! TAKE A HANDFUL OF JEWELED TRINKETS, AND SELL THEM AT THE MARKET PRICE!
SO LONG AS MYSTIC MENACE ABOUNDS, WE MUST NOT CONCERN OURSELVES WITH MONETARY TRIFLES!
I HASTEN TO OBEY, MASTER!
THEN, WITH THE DEPARTURE OF HIS DEVOTED MANSERVANT---
I MUST NOW RELAX! 'TIS TIME TO PORE OVER THE ETERNAL WRITINGS OF THE VENERATED VISHANTI...
THESE SACRED INCANTATIONS... THESE AGE-OLD CHARMS AND SPELLS... TO ME THEY ARE FOOD AND DRINK---THEY ARE THE VERY FABRIC OF ALL EXISTENCE!
BUT NOW... TO WORK!
I MUST BE CERTAIN THAT MY OLD ENEMY, THE WICKED BARON MORDO, HAS NOT ESCAPED FROM THE MYSTIC PRISON IN WHICH THE ESTEEMED ANCIENT ONE HAS INCARCERATED HIM!
FOR, SHOULD MORDO EVER AGAIN REGAIN HIS FREEDOM, ALL OF MANKIND WOULD BE IN DIREST JEOPARDY!
BY THE EVERLASTING POWERS OF ENCHANTMENT--- BY THE ETERNAL MAJESTY OF THE MYSTIC REALM---
LET THE GLEAMING CRYSTAL OF AGAMOTTO PIERCE THE VEIL OF TIME AND SPACE!
THUS DO I COMMAND!
4.

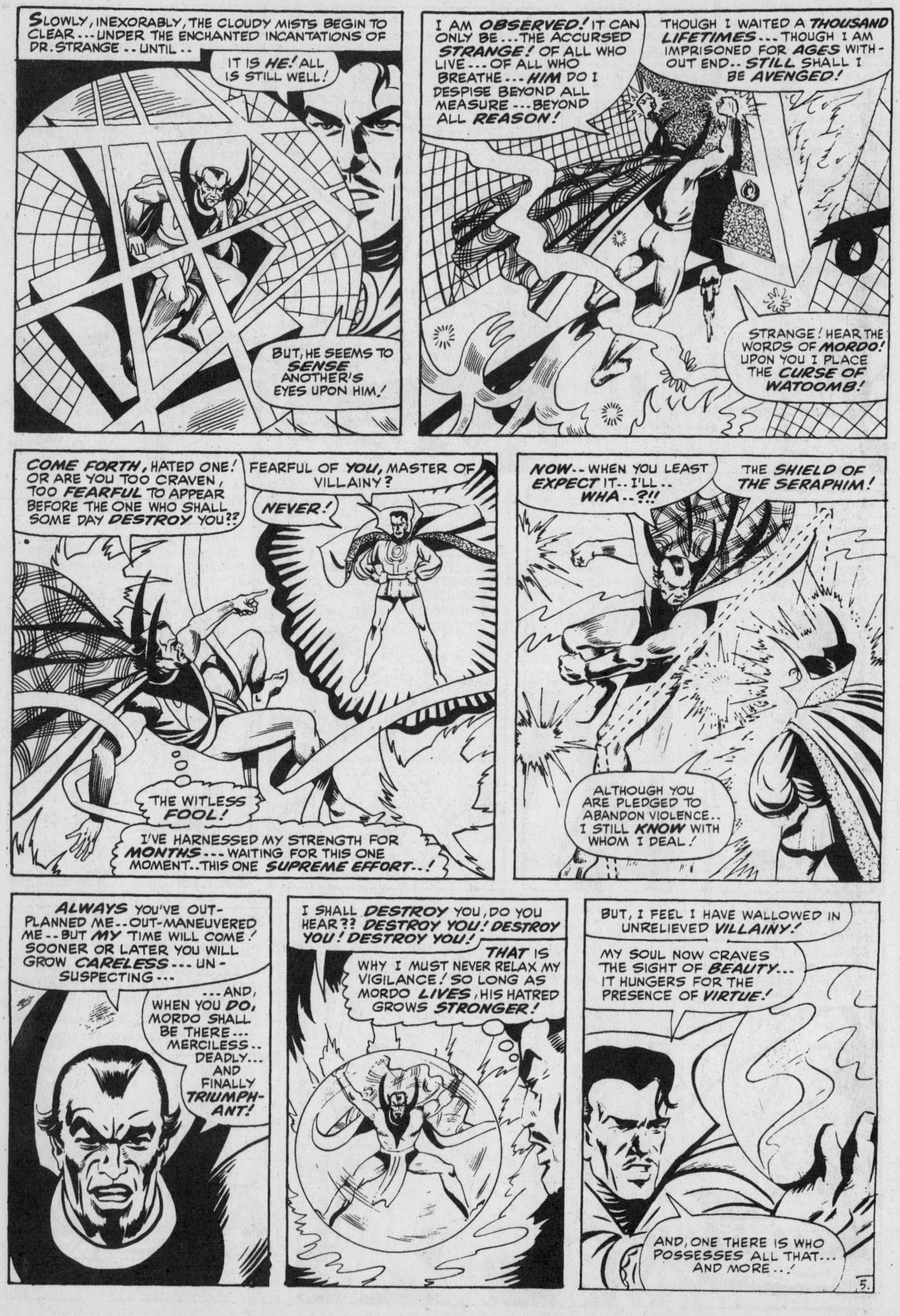
SLOWLY, INEXORABLY, THE CLOUDY MISTS BEGIN TO CLEAR... UNDER THE ENCHANTED INCANTATIONS OF DR. STRANGE.. UNTIL..
IT IS HE! ALL IS STILL WELL!
BUT, HE SEEMS TO SENSE ANOTHER'S EYES UPON HIM!
I AM OBSERVED! IT CAN ONLY BE... THE ACCURSED STRANGE! OF ALL WHO LIVE... OF ALL WHO BREATHE... HIM DO I DESPISE BEYOND ALL MEASURE... BEYOND ALL REASON!
THOUGH I WAITED A THOUSAND LIFETIMES... THOUGH I AM IMPRISONED FOR AGES WITH-OUT END.. STILL SHALL I BE AVENGED!
STRANGE! HEAR THE WORDS OF MORDO! UPON YOU I PLACE THE CURSE OF WATOOMB!
COME FORTH, HATED ONE! OR ARE YOU TOO CRAVEN, TOO FEARFUL TO APPEAR BEFORE THE ONE WHO SHALL SOME DAY DESTROY YOU??
FEARFUL OF YOU, MASTER OF VILLAINY?
NEVER!
THE WITLESS FOOL!
I'VE HARNESSED MY STRENGTH FOR MONTHS... WAITING FOR THIS ONE MOMENT.. THIS ONE SUPREME EFFORT..!
NOW.. WHEN YOU LEAST EXPECT IT.. I'LL.. WHA..?!!
THE SHIELD OF THE SERAPHIM!
ALTHOUGH YOU ARE PLEDGED TO ABANDON VIOLENCE.. I STILL KNOW WITH WHOM I DEAL!
ALWAYS YOU'VE OUT-PLANNED ME.. OUT-MANEUVERED ME.. BUT MY TIME WILL COME! SOONER OR LATER YOU WILL GROW CARELESS... UN-SUSPECTING...
...AND, WHEN YOU DO, MORDO SHALL BE THERE... MERCILESS.. DEADLY... AND FINALLY TRIUMPH-ANT!
I SHALL DESTROY YOU, DO YOU HEAR?? DESTROY YOU! DESTROY YOU! DESTROY YOU!
THAT IS WHY I MUST NEVER RELAX MY VIGILANCE! SO LONG AS MORDO LIVES, HIS HATRED GROWS STRONGER!
BUT, I FEEL I HAVE WALLOWED IN UNRELIEVED VILLAINY!
MY SOUL NOW CRAVES THE SIGHT OF BEAUTY... IT HUNGERS FOR THE PRESENCE OF VIRTUE!
AND, ONE THERE IS WHO POSSESSES ALL THAT... AND MORE..!
5.

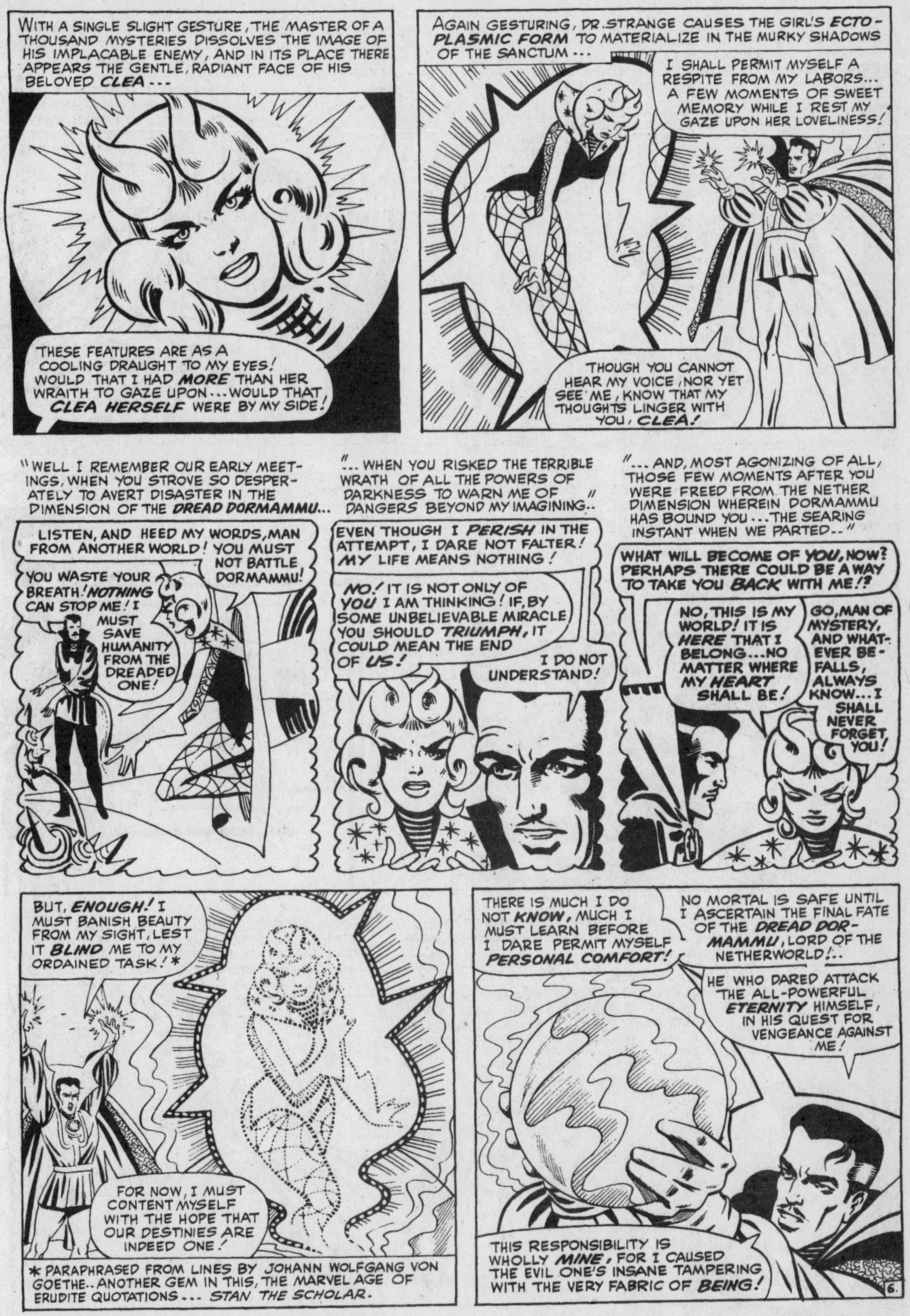
WITH A SINGLE SLIGHT GESTURE, THE MASTER OF A THOUSAND MYSTERIES DISSOLVES THE IMAGE OF HIS IMPLACABLE ENEMY, AND IN ITS PLACE THERE APPEARS THE GENTLE, RADIANT FACE OF HIS BELOVED CLEA...
THESE FEATURES ARE AS A COOLING DRAUGHT TO MY EYES! WOULD THAT I HAD MORE THAN HER WRAITH TO GAZE UPON... WOULD THAT CLEA HERSELF WERE BY MY SIDE!
AGAIN GESTURING, DR. STRANGE CAUSES THE GIRL'S ECTO-PLASMIC FORM TO MATERIALIZE IN THE MURKY SHADOWS OF THE SANCTUM...
I SHALL PERMIT MYSELF A RESPITE FROM MY LABORS... A FEW MOMENTS OF SWEET MEMORY WHILE I REST MY GAZE UPON HER LOVELINESS!
THOUGH YOU CANNOT HEAR MY VOICE, NOR YET SEE ME, KNOW THAT MY THOUGHTS LINGER WITH YOU, CLEA!
"WELL I REMEMBER OUR EARLY MEET-INGS, WHEN YOU STROVE SO DESPER-ATELY TO AVERT DISASTER IN THE DIMENSION OF THE DREAD DORMAMMU...
LISTEN, AND HEED MY WORDS, MAN FROM ANOTHER WORLD! YOU MUST NOT BATTLE DORMAMMU!
YOU WASTE YOUR BREATH! NOTHING CAN STOP ME! I MUST SAVE HUMANITY FROM THE DREADED ONE!
"... WHEN YOU RISKED THE TERRIBLE WRATH OF ALL THE POWERS OF DARKNESS TO WARN ME OF DANGERS BEYOND MY IMAGINING.."
EVEN THOUGH I PERISH IN THE ATTEMPT, I DARE NOT FALTER! MY LIFE MEANS NOTHING!
NO! IT IS NOT ONLY OF YOU I AM THINKING! IF, BY SOME UNBELIEVABLE MIRACLE YOU SHOULD TRIUMPH, IT COULD MEAN THE END OF US!
I DO NOT UNDERSTAND!
"... AND, MOST AGONIZING OF ALL, THOSE FEW MOMENTS AFTER YOU WERE FREED FROM THE NETHER DIMENSION WHEREIN DORMAMMU HAS BOUND YOU... THE SEARING INSTANT WHEN WE PARTED--"
WHAT WILL BECOME OF YOU, NOW? PERHAPS THERE COULD BE A WAY TO TAKE YOU BACK WITH ME!?
NO, THIS IS MY WORLD! IT IS HERE THAT I BELONG... NO MATTER WHERE MY HEART SHALL BE!
GO, MAN OF MYSTERY, AND WHAT-EVER BE-FALLS, ALWAYS KNOW... I SHALL NEVER FORGET YOU!
BUT, ENOUGH! I MUST BANISH BEAUTY FROM MY SIGHT, LEST IT BLIND ME TO MY ORDAINED TASK! *
FOR NOW, I MUST CONTENT MYSELF WITH THE HOPE THAT OUR DESTINIES ARE INDEED ONE!
* PARAPHRASED FROM LINES BY JOHANN WOLFGANG VON GOETHE.. ANOTHER GEM IN THIS, THE MARVEL AGE OF ERUDITE QUOTATIONS... STAN THE SCHOLAR.
THERE IS MUCH I DO NOT KNOW, MUCH I MUST LEARN BEFORE I DARE PERMIT MYSELF PERSONAL COMFORT!
NO MORTAL IS SAFE UNTIL I ASCERTAIN THE FINAL FATE OF THE DREAD DOR-MAMMU, LORD OF THE NETHERWORLD!..
HE WHO DARED ATTACK THE ALL-POWERFUL ETERNITY HIMSELF, IN HIS QUEST FOR VENGEANCE AGAINST ME!
THIS RESPONSIBILITY IS WHOLLY MINE, FOR I CAUSED THE EVIL ONE'S INSANE TAMPERING WITH THE VERY FABRIC OF BEING!
6.

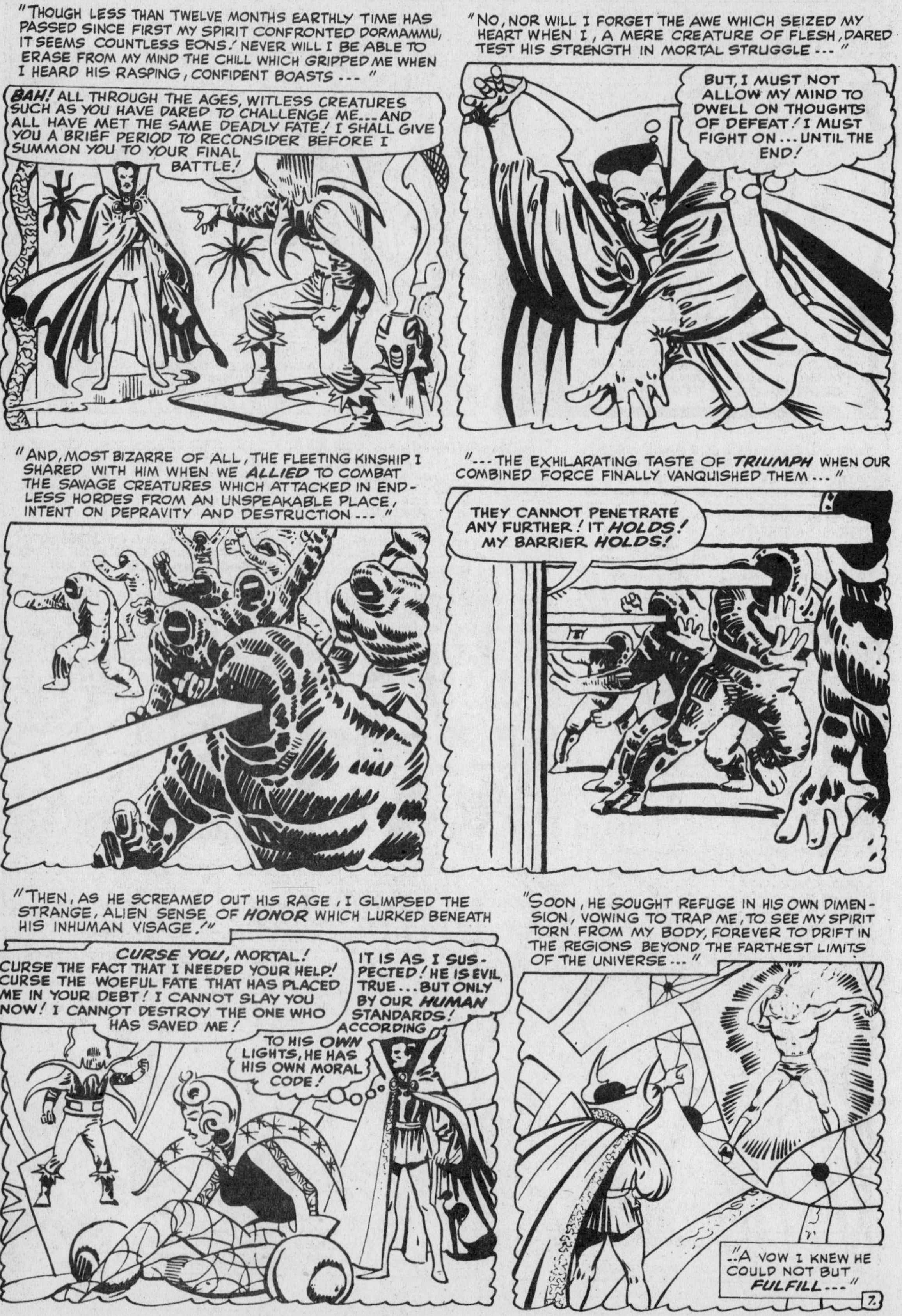
"THOUGH LESS THAN TWELVE MONTHS EARTHLY TIME HAS PASSED SINCE FIRST MY SPIRIT CONFRONTED DORMAMMU, IT SEEMS COUNTLESS EONS! NEVER WILL I BE ABLE TO ERASE FROM MY MIND THE CHILL WHICH GRIPPED ME WHEN I HEARD HIS RASPING, CONFIDENT BOASTS ---"
BAH! ALL THROUGH THE AGES, WITLESS CREATURES SUCH AS YOU HAVE DARED TO CHALLENGE ME... AND ALL HAVE MET THE SAME DEADLY FATE! I SHALL GIVE YOU A BRIEF PERIOD TO RECONSIDER BEFORE I SUMMON YOU TO YOUR FINAL BATTLE!
"NO, NOR WILL I FORGET THE AWE WHICH SEIZED MY HEART WHEN I, A MERE CREATURE OF FLESH, DARED TEST HIS STRENGTH IN MORTAL STRUGGLE ---"
BUT, I MUST NOT ALLOW MY MIND TO DWELL ON THOUGHTS OF DEFEAT! I MUST FIGHT ON... UNTIL THE END!
"AND, MOST BIZARRE OF ALL, THE FLEETING KINSHIP I SHARED WITH HIM WHEN WE ALLIED TO COMBAT THE SAVAGE CREATURES WHICH ATTACKED IN END-LESS HORDES FROM AN UNSPEAKABLE PLACE, INTENT ON DEPRAVITY AND DESTRUCTION ---"
"---THE EXHILARATING TASTE OF TRIUMPH WHEN OUR COMBINED FORCE FINALLY VANQUISHED THEM ..."
THEY CANNOT PENETRATE ANY FURTHER! IT HOLDS! MY BARRIER HOLDS!
"THEN, AS HE SCREAMED OUT HIS RAGE, I GLIMPSED THE STRANGE, ALIEN SENSE OF HONOR WHICH LURKED BENEATH HIS INHUMAN VISAGE!"
CURSE YOU, MORTAL! CURSE THE FACT THAT I NEEDED YOUR HELP! CURSE THE WOEFUL FATE THAT HAS PLACED ME IN YOUR DEBT! I CANNOT SLAY YOU NOW! I CANNOT DESTROY THE ONE WHO HAS SAVED ME!
IT IS AS I SUS-PECTED! HE IS EVIL, TRUE... BUT ONLY BY OUR HUMAN STANDARDS! ACCORDING TO HIS OWN LIGHTS, HE HAS HIS OWN MORAL CODE!
"SOON, HE SOUGHT REFUGE IN HIS OWN DIMEN-SION, VOWING TO TRAP ME, TO SEE MY SPIRIT TORN FROM MY BODY, FOREVER TO DRIFT IN THE REGIONS BEYOND THE FARTHEST LIMITS OF THE UNIVERSE ..."
..A VOW I KNEW HE COULD NOT BUT FULFILL ..."
7.

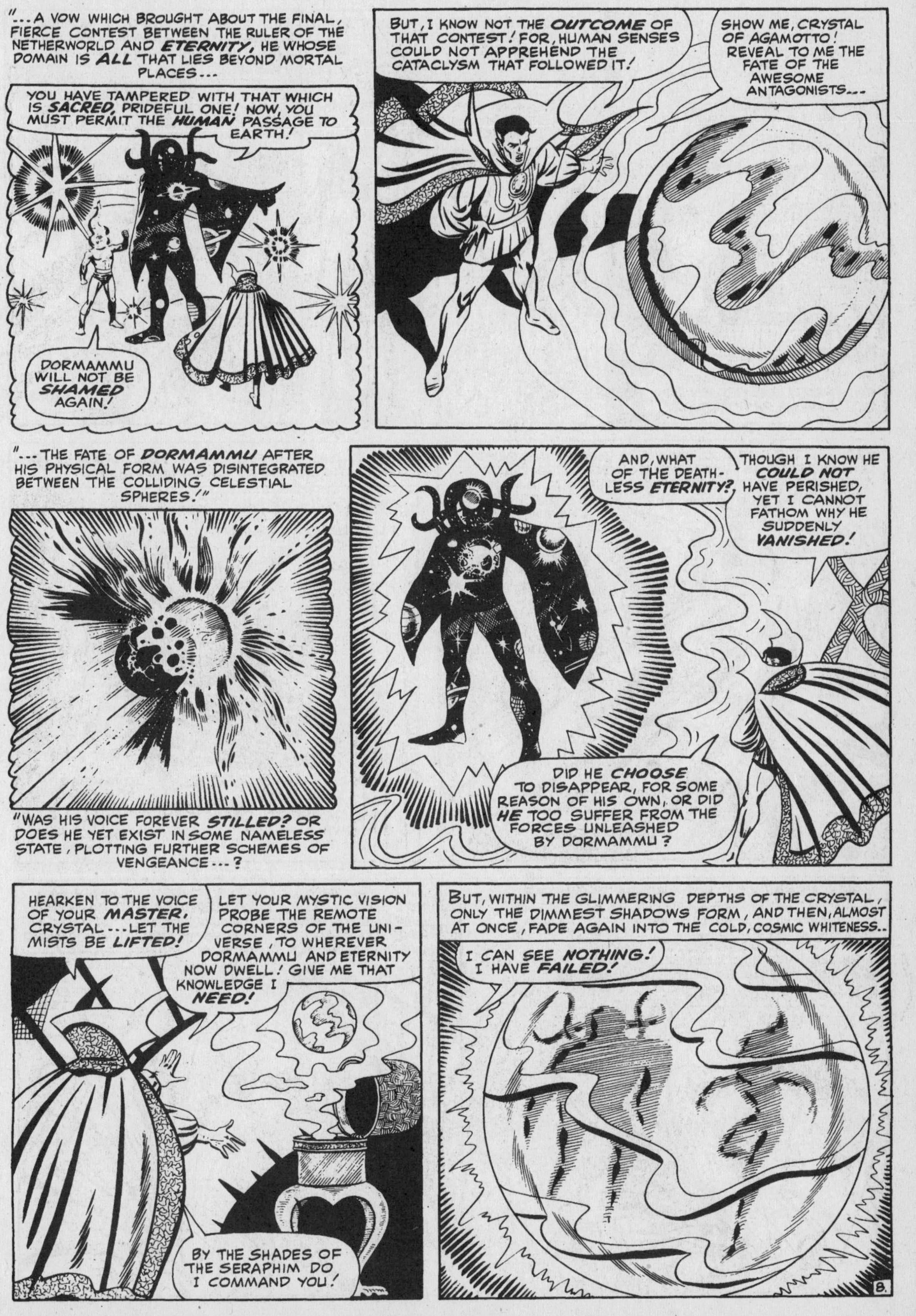
"...A VOW WHICH BROUGHT ABOUT THE FINAL, FIERCE CONTEST BETWEEN THE RULER OF THE NETHERWORLD AND ETERNITY, HE WHOSE DOMAIN IS ALL THAT LIES BEYOND MORTAL PLACES...
YOU HAVE TAMPERED WITH THAT WHICH IS SACRED, PRIDEFUL ONE! NOW, YOU MUST PERMIT THE HUMAN PASSAGE TO EARTH!
DORMAMMU WILL NOT BE SHAMED AGAIN!
BUT, I KNOW NOT THE OUTCOME OF THAT CONTEST! FOR, HUMAN SENSES COULD NOT APPREHEND THE CATACLYSM THAT FOLLOWED IT!
SHOW ME, CRYSTAL OF AGAMOTTO! REVEAL TO ME THE FATE OF THE AWESOME ANTAGONISTS...
"...THE FATE OF DORMAMMU AFTER HIS PHYSICAL FORM WAS DISINTEGRATED BETWEEN THE COLLIDING CELESTIAL SPHERES!"
"WAS HIS VOICE FOREVER STILLED? OR DOES HE YET EXIST IN SOME NAMELESS STATE, PLOTTING FURTHER SCHEMES OF VENGEANCE...?
AND, WHAT OF THE DEATHLESS ETERNITY?
THOUGH I KNOW HE COULD NOT HAVE PERISHED, YET I CANNOT FATHOM WHY HE SUDDENLY VANISHED!
DID HE CHOOSE TO DISAPPEAR, FOR SOME REASON OF HIS OWN, OR DID HE TOO SUFFER FROM THE FORCES UNLEASHED BY DORMAMMU?
HEARKEN TO THE VOICE OF YOUR MASTER, CRYSTAL...LET THE MISTS BE LIFTED!
LET YOUR MYSTIC VISION PROBE THE REMOTE CORNERS OF THE UNIVERSE, TO WHEREVER DORMAMMU AND ETERNITY NOW DWELL! GIVE ME THAT KNOWLEDGE I NEED!
BY THE SHADES OF THE SERAPHIM DO I COMMAND YOU!
BUT, WITHIN THE GLIMMERING DEPTHS OF THE CRYSTAL, ONLY THE DIMMEST SHADOWS FORM, AND THEN, ALMOST AT ONCE, FADE AGAIN INTO THE COLD, COSMIC WHITENESS..
I CAN SEE NOTHING! I HAVE FAILED!
8.

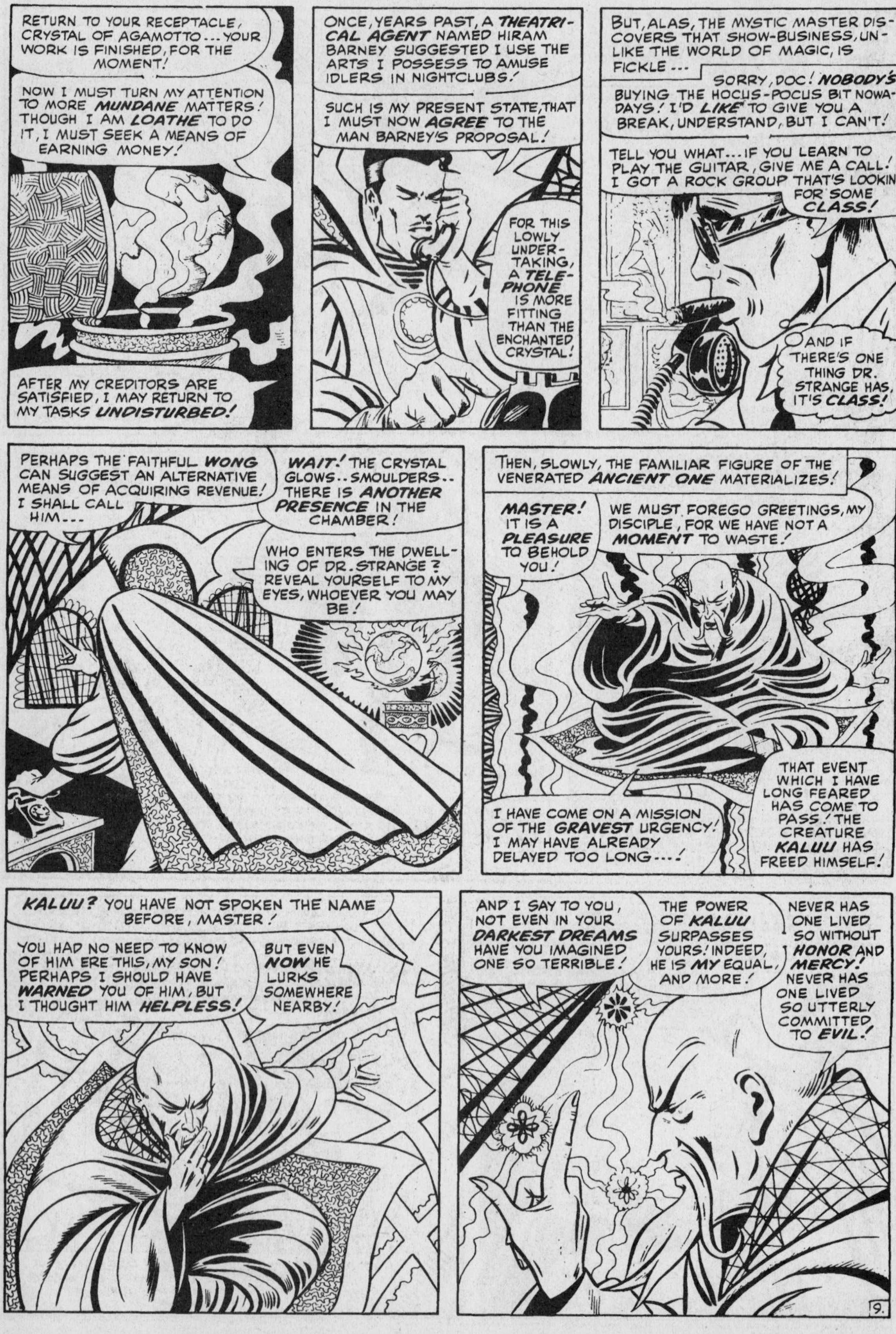
RETURN TO YOUR RECEPTACLE, CRYSTAL OF AGAMOTTO... YOUR WORK IS FINISHED, FOR THE MOMENT!
NOW I MUST TURN MY ATTENTION TO MORE MUNDANE MATTERS! THOUGH I AM LOATHE TO DO IT, I MUST SEEK A MEANS OF EARNING MONEY!
AFTER MY CREDITORS ARE SATISFIED, I MAY RETURN TO MY TASKS UNDISTURBED!
ONCE, YEARS PAST, A THEATRICAL AGENT NAMED HIRAM BARNEY SUGGESTED I USE THE ARTS I POSSESS TO AMUSE IDLERS IN NIGHTCLUBS!
SUCH IS MY PRESENT STATE, THAT I MUST NOW AGREE TO THE MAN BARNEY'S PROPOSAL!
FOR THIS LOWLY UNDERTAKING, A TELEPHONE IS MORE FITTING THAN THE ENCHANTED CRYSTAL!
BUT, ALAS, THE MYSTIC MASTER DISCOVERS THAT SHOW-BUSINESS, UNLIKE THE WORLD OF MAGIC, IS FICKLE ---
SORRY, DOC! NOBODY'S BUYING THE HOCUS-POCUS BIT NOWADAYS! I'D LIKE TO GIVE YOU A BREAK, UNDERSTAND, BUT I CAN'T!
TELL YOU WHAT... IF YOU LEARN TO PLAY THE GUITAR, GIVE ME A CALL! I GOT A ROCK GROUP THAT'S LOOKIN' FOR SOME CLASS!
AND IF THERE'S ONE THING DR. STRANGE HAS, IT'S CLASS!
PERHAPS THE FAITHFUL WONG CAN SUGGEST AN ALTERNATIVE MEANS OF ACQUIRING REVENUE! I SHALL CALL HIM---
WAIT! THE CRYSTAL GLOWS.. SMOULDERS.. THERE IS ANOTHER PRESENCE IN THE CHAMBER!
WHO ENTERS THE DWELLING OF DR. STRANGE? REVEAL YOURSELF TO MY EYES, WHOEVER YOU MAY BE!
THEN, SLOWLY, THE FAMILIAR FIGURE OF THE VENERATED ANCIENT ONE MATERIALIZES!
MASTER! IT IS A PLEASURE TO BEHOLD YOU!
WE MUST FOREGO GREETINGS, MY DISCIPLE, FOR WE HAVE NOT A MOMENT TO WASTE!
I HAVE COME ON A MISSION OF THE GRAVEST URGENCY! I MAY HAVE ALREADY DELAYED TOO LONG---!
THAT EVENT WHICH I HAVE LONG FEARED HAS COME TO PASS! THE CREATURE KALUU HAS FREED HIMSELF!
KALUU? YOU HAVE NOT SPOKEN THE NAME BEFORE, MASTER!
YOU HAD NO NEED TO KNOW OF HIM ERE THIS, MY SON! PERHAPS I SHOULD HAVE WARNED YOU OF HIM, BUT I THOUGHT HIM HELPLESS!
BUT EVEN NOW HE LURKS SOMEWHERE NEARBY!
AND I SAY TO YOU, NOT EVEN IN YOUR DARKEST DREAMS HAVE YOU IMAGINED ONE SO TERRIBLE!
THE POWER OF KALUU SURPASSES YOURS! INDEED, HE IS MY EQUAL, AND MORE!
NEVER HAS ONE LIVED SO WITHOUT HONOR AND MERCY! NEVER HAS ONE LIVED SO UTTERLY COMMITTED TO EVIL!
9.

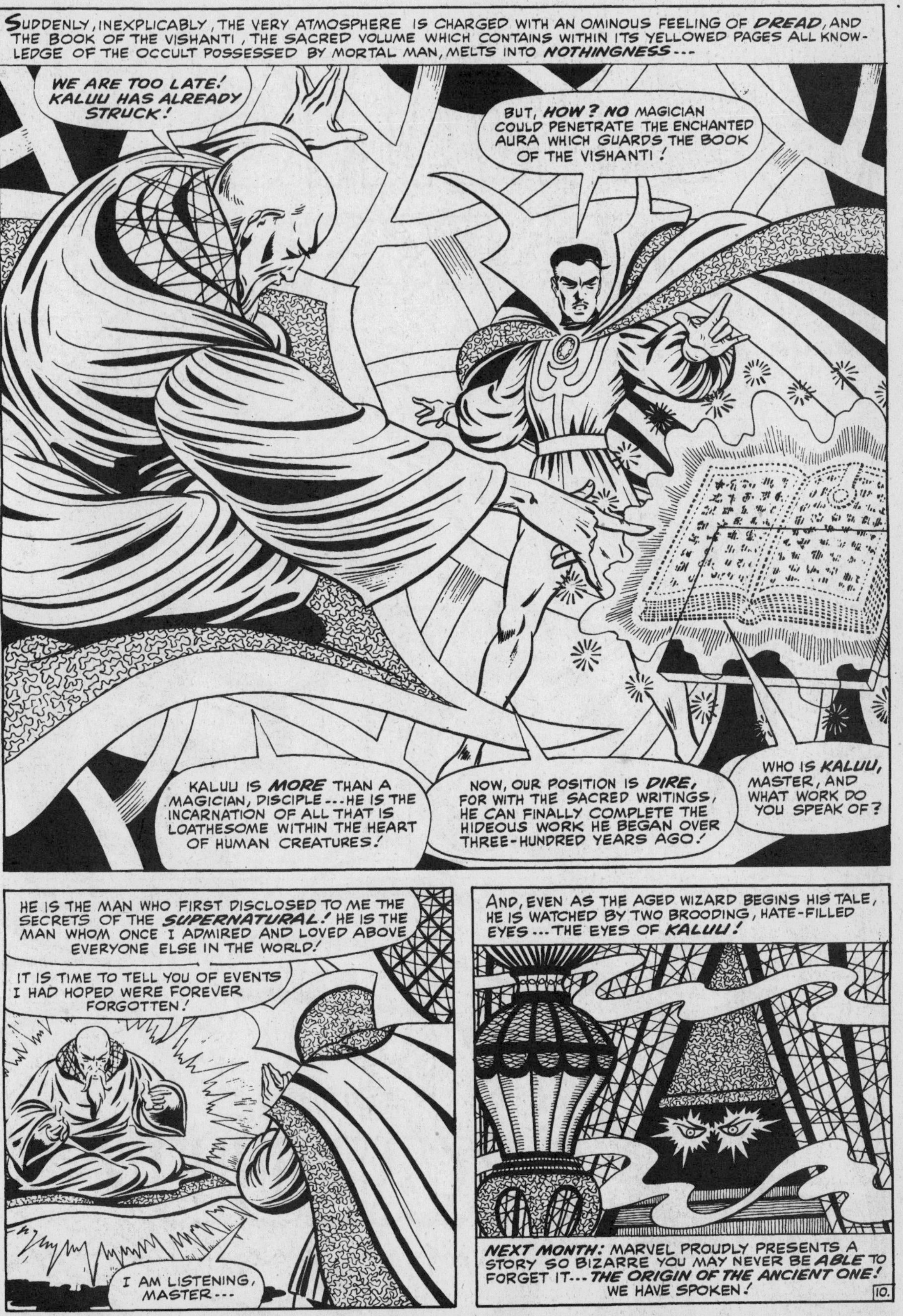

SUDDENLY, INEXPLICABLY, THE VERY ATMOSPHERE IS CHARGED WITH AN OMINOUS FEELING OF DREAD, AND THE BOOK OF THE VISHANTI, THE SACRED VOLUME WHICH CONTAINS WITHIN ITS YELLOWED PAGES ALL KNOWLEDGE OF THE OCCULT POSSESSED BY MORTAL MAN, MELTS INTO NOTHINGNESS---
WE ARE TOO LATE! KALUU HAS ALREADY STRUCK!
BUT, HOW? NO MAGICIAN COULD PENETRATE THE ENCHANTED AURA WHICH GUARDS THE BOOK OF THE VISHANTI!
KALUU IS MORE THAN A MAGICIAN, DISCIPLE---HE IS THE INCARNATION OF ALL THAT IS LOATHESOME WITHIN THE HEART OF HUMAN CREATURES!
NOW, OUR POSITION IS DIRE, FOR WITH THE SACRED WRITINGS, HE CAN FINALLY COMPLETE THE HIDEOUS WORK HE BEGAN OVER THREE-HUNDRED YEARS AGO!
WHO IS KALUU, MASTER, AND WHAT WORK DO YOU SPEAK OF?
HE IS THE MAN WHO FIRST DISCLOSED TO ME THE SECRETS OF THE SUPERNATURAL! HE IS THE MAN WHOM ONCE I ADMIRED AND LOVED ABOVE EVERYONE ELSE IN THE WORLD!
IT IS TIME TO TELL YOU OF EVENTS I HAD HOPED WERE FOREVER FORGOTTEN!
I AM LISTENING, MASTER---
AND, EVEN AS THE AGED WIZARD BEGINS HIS TALE, HE IS WATCHED BY TWO BROODING, HATE-FILLED EYES... THE EYES OF KALUU!
NEXT MONTH: MARVEL PROUDLY PRESENTS A STORY SO BIZARRE YOU MAY NEVER BE ABLE TO FORGET IT--- THE ORIGIN OF THE ANCIENT ONE! WE HAVE SPOKEN!
10.

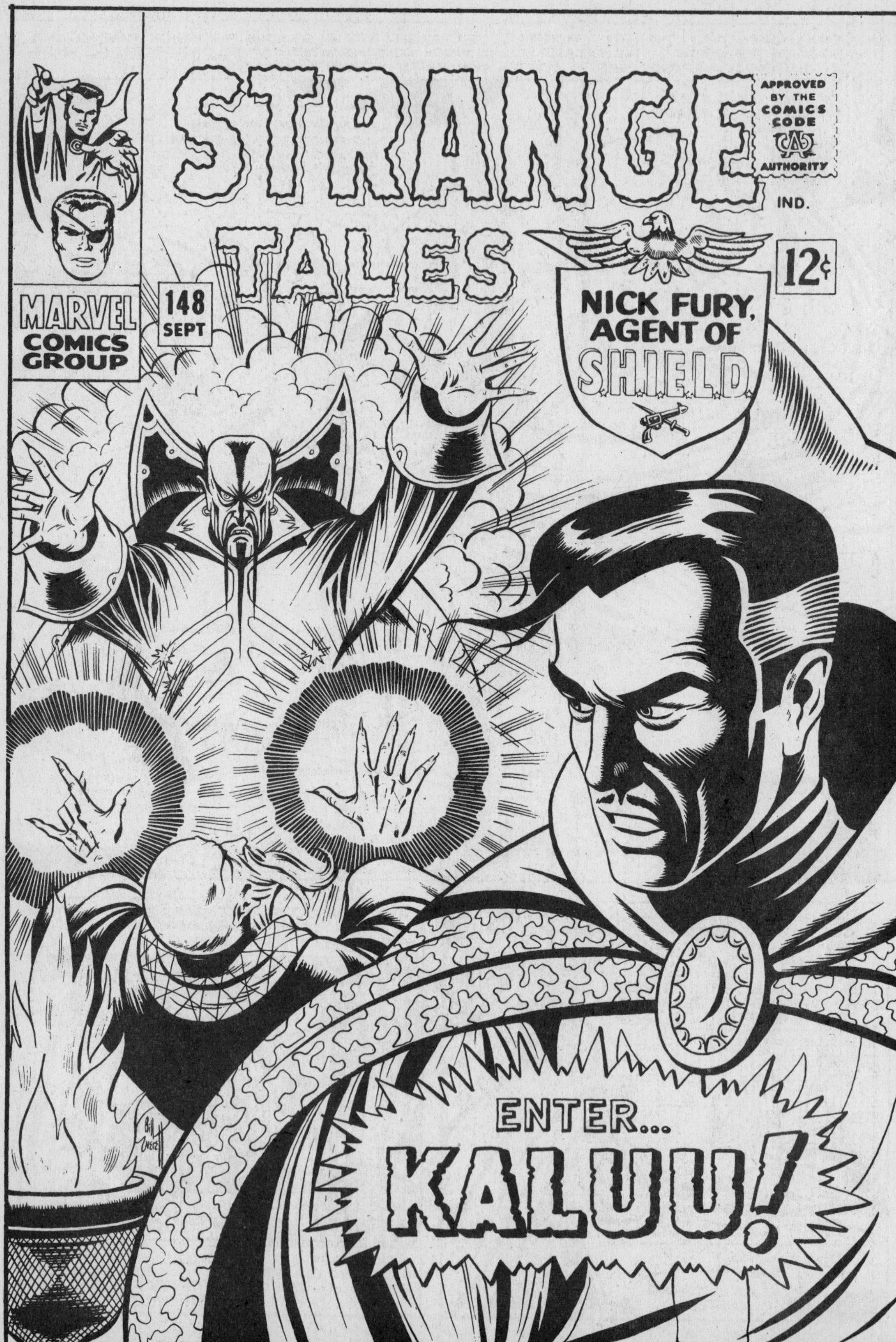

STRANGE TALES
APPROVED BY THE COMICS CODE AUTHORITY
IND.
12¢
MARVEL COMICS GROUP
148 SEPT
NICK FURY, AGENT OF S.H.I.E.L.D
ENTER... KALUU!

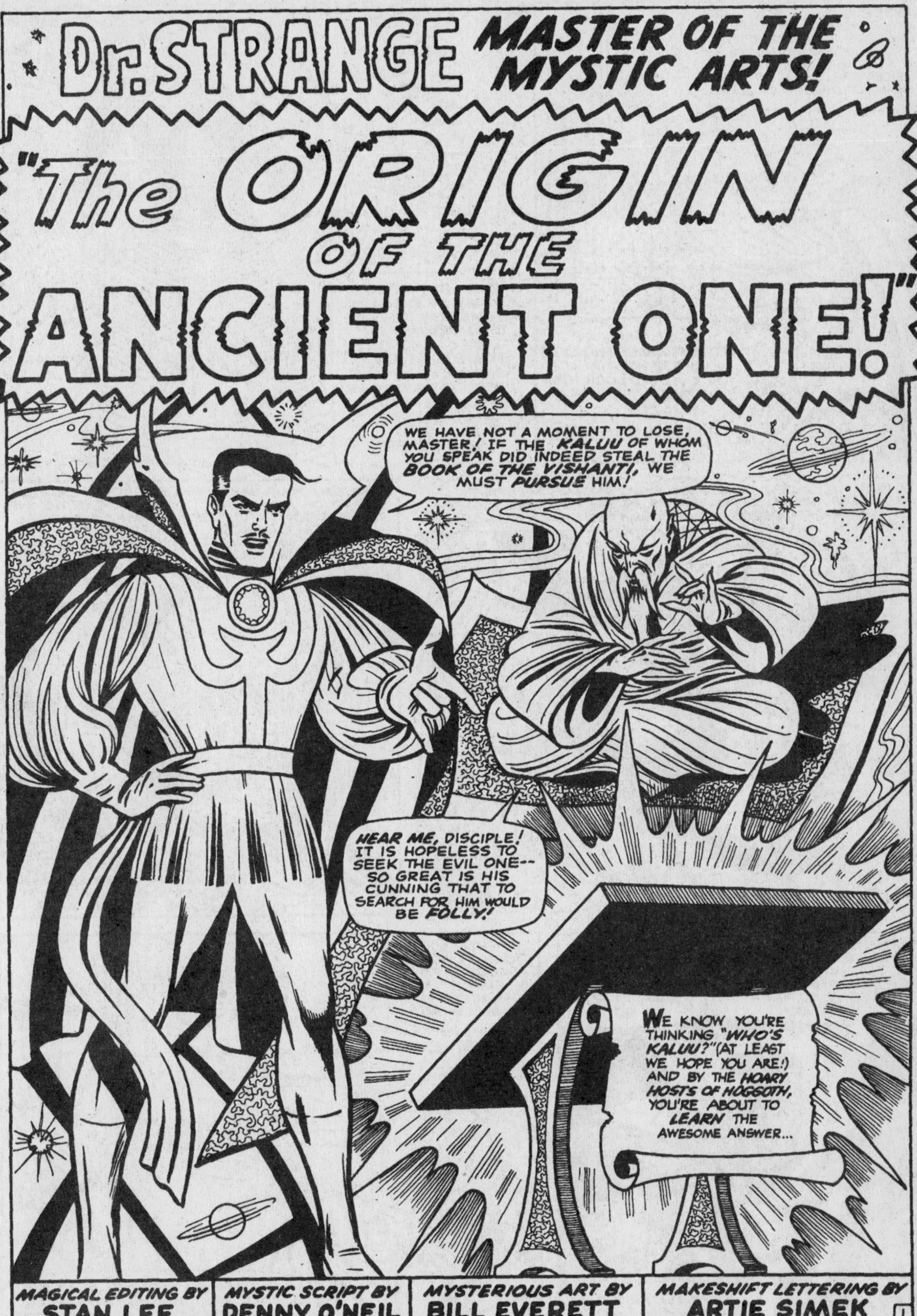
Dr. STRANGE MASTER OF THE MYSTIC ARTS!
"The ORIGIN OF THE ANCIENT ONE!"
WE HAVE NOT A MOMENT TO LOSE, MASTER! IF THE KALUU OF WHOM YOU SPEAK DID INDEED STEAL THE BOOK OF THE VISHANTI, WE MUST PURSUE HIM!
HEAR ME, DISCIPLE! IT IS HOPELESS TO SEEK THE EVIL ONE-- SO GREAT IS HIS CUNNING THAT TO SEARCH FOR HIM WOULD BE FOLLY!
WE KNOW YOU'RE THINKING "WHO'S KALUU?" (AT LEAST WE HOPE YOU ARE!) AND BY THE HOARY HOSTS OF HOGGOTH, YOU'RE ABOUT TO LEARN THE AWESOME ANSWER...
MAGICAL EDITING BY STAN LEE
MYSTIC SCRIPT BY DENNY O'NEIL
MYSTERIOUS ART BY BILL EVERETT
MAKESHIFT LETTERING BY ARTIE SIMEK
1

THERE IS AN AURA IN THE ATMOSPHERE AROUND THE LECTERN THAT HELD THE *BOOK OF THE VISHANTI* -- A FEELING OF GREAT STRENGTH TWISTED INTO AN INSTRUMENT OF *EVIL!*

I SHALL CAUSE AN *ECTOPLASMIC IMAGE* OF KALUU TO MATERIALIZE! FOR I WOULD LOOK UPON THE *FACE* OF ONE SO BRAZEN...

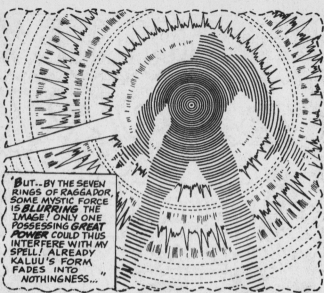

"BUT...BY THE SEVEN RINGS OF RAGGADOR, SOME MYSTIC FORCE IS *BLURRING* THE IMAGE! ONLY ONE POSSESSING *GREAT POWER* COULD THUS INTERFERE WITH MY SPELL! ALREADY KALUU'S FORM FADES INTO NOTHINGNESS..."

"AND, IN ITS PLACE, I BEHOLD EVIL SHAPES--MENACING SPIRITS! IF *THESE* ARE KALUU'S SERVANTS, HE WILL BE *PUNISHED* FOR WHATEVER DARK DEEDS HE HAS COMMITTED! I, DR. STRANGE, VOW IT!"

ENOUGH! YOUR BABBLING IS THAT OF A CALLOW *SCHOOLBOY,* DISCIPLE! SUCH TALK IS NOT *WORTHY* OF MY MOST ACCOMPLISHED FOLLOWER!

YOU SPEAK LIGHTLY OF DEFEATING ONE WHOSE MAGICAL PROWESS IS FAR SUPERIOR TO YOUR OWN--ONE WHOSE WILL IS *INDOMITABLE!*

FOR THOUGH THE BODY OF KALUU BE *ME* THROUGH SHEER WILL-POWER HE HAS MADE HIS SPIRIT *MORE* THAN HUMAN!

FORGIVE ME, WISE ONE, IF I HAVE OFFENDED YOU! YET, I DO NOT UNDERSTAND... HOW CAN ANY MORTAL MAN PRESENT SO GREAT A *THREAT!*

WHY DO *YOU,* THE SUPREME MASTER OF ENCHANTMENT, SEEM TO *FEAR* HIM SO?

TO ANSWER YOUR QUESTION, I MUST SPEAK OF EVENTS WHICH HAPPENED MORE THAN *FIVE HUNDRED YEARS AGO...*

...EVENTS WHICH TOOK PLACE IN *KAMAR-TAJ,* A HIDDEN LAND HIGH IN THE HIMALAYAS!

IT WAS POPULATED BY A RACE OF PEOPLE WHO, THOUGH NOT OUT-*WARDLY ADVANCED,* HAD DEVELOPED THE ARTS OF JOYOUS LIVING TO A DEGREE *UNDREAMED OF* BY MORE COMPLEX CIVILIZATIONS! IT WAS THE BIRTHPLACE OF BOTH *KALUU* AND *MYSELF...*

2

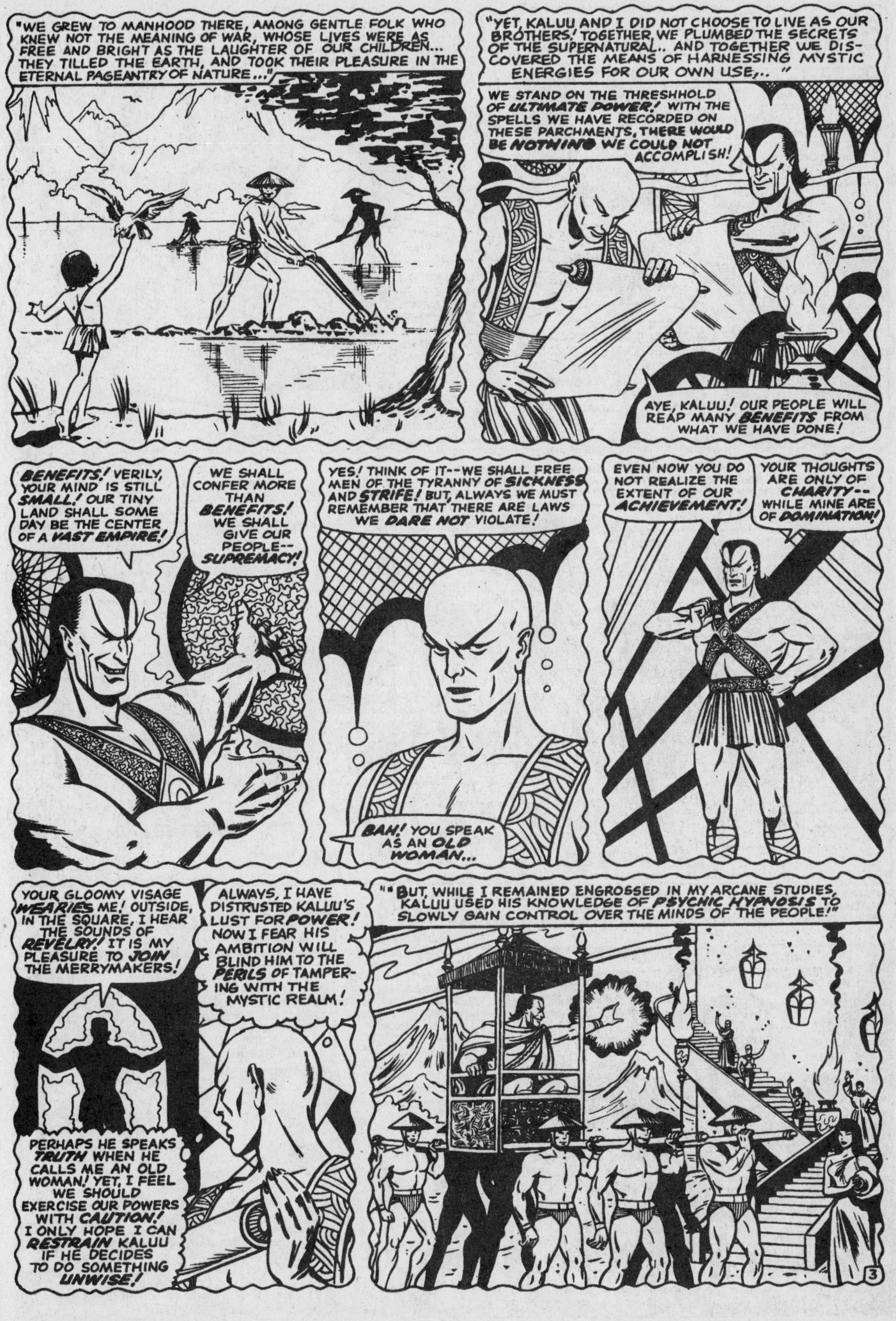
"WE GREW TO MANHOOD THERE, AMONG GENTLE FOLK WHO KNEW NOT THE MEANING OF WAR, WHOSE LIVES WERE AS FREE AND BRIGHT AS THE LAUGHTER OF OUR CHILDREN... THEY TILLED THE EARTH, AND TOOK THEIR PLEASURE IN THE ETERNAL PAGEANTRY OF NATURE..."
"YET, KALUU AND I DID NOT CHOOSE TO LIVE AS OUR BROTHERS! TOGETHER, WE PLUMBED THE SECRETS OF THE SUPERNATURAL.. AND TOGETHER WE DISCOVERED THE MEANS OF HARNESSING MYSTIC ENERGIES FOR OUR OWN USE,.. "
WE STAND ON THE THRESHHOLD OF ULTIMATE POWER! WITH THE SPELLS WE HAVE RECORDED ON THESE PARCHMENTS, THERE WOULD BE NOTHING WE COULD NOT ACCOMPLISH!
AYE, KALUU! OUR PEOPLE WILL REAP MANY BENEFITS FROM WHAT WE HAVE DONE!
BENEFITS! VERILY, YOUR MIND IS STILL SMALL! OUR TINY LAND SHALL SOME DAY BE THE CENTER OF A VAST EMPIRE!
WE SHALL CONFER MORE THAN BENEFITS! WE SHALL GIVE OUR PEOPLE-- SUPREMACY!
YES! THINK OF IT--WE SHALL FREE MEN OF THE TYRANNY OF SICKNESS AND STRIFE! BUT, ALWAYS WE MUST REMEMBER THAT THERE ARE LAWS WE DARE NOT VIOLATE!
BAH! YOU SPEAK AS AN OLD WOMAN...
EVEN NOW YOU DO NOT REALIZE THE EXTENT OF OUR ACHIEVEMENT!
YOUR THOUGHTS ARE ONLY OF CHARITY-- WHILE MINE ARE OF DOMINATION!
YOUR GLOOMY VISAGE WEARIES ME! OUTSIDE, IN THE SQUARE, I HEAR THE SOUNDS OF REVELRY! IT IS MY PLEASURE TO JOIN THE MERRYMAKERS!
ALWAYS, I HAVE DISTRUSTED KALUU'S LUST FOR POWER! NOW I FEAR HIS AMBITION WILL BLIND HIM TO THE PERILS OF TAMPERING WITH THE MYSTIC REALM!
PERHAPS HE SPEAKS TRUTH WHEN HE CALLS ME AN OLD WOMAN! YET, I FEEL WE SHOULD EXERCISE OUR POWERS WITH CAUTION! I ONLY HOPE I CAN RESTRAIN KALUU IF HE DECIDES TO DO SOMETHING UNWISE!
"" BUT, WHILE I REMAINED ENGROSSED IN MY ARCANE STUDIES, KALUU USED HIS KNOWLEDGE OF PSYCHIC HYPNOSIS TO SLOWLY GAIN CONTROL OVER THE MINDS OF THE PEOPLE!"
3

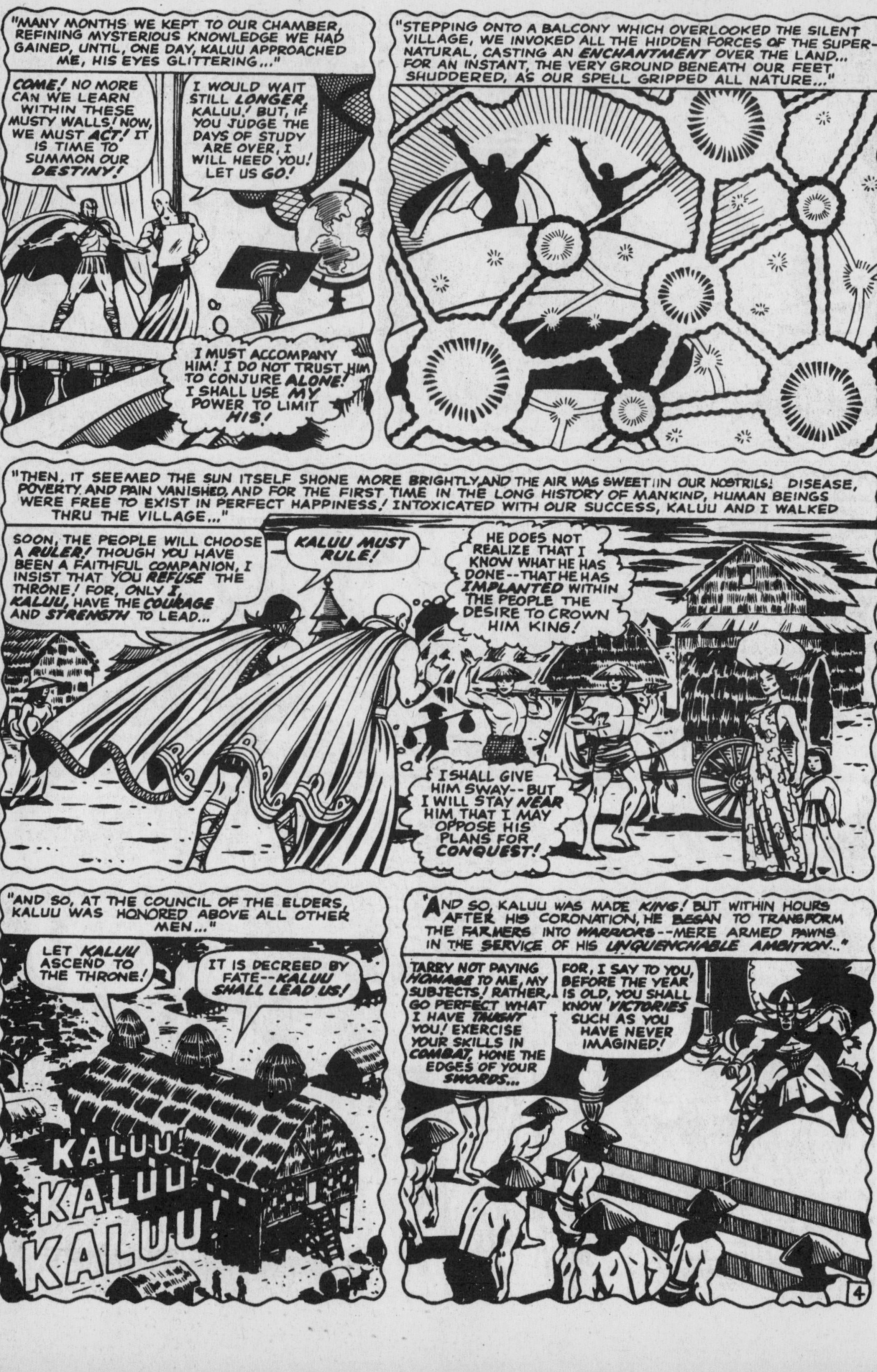

"MANY MONTHS WE KEPT TO OUR CHAMBER, REFINING MYSTERIOUS KNOWLEDGE WE HAD GAINED, UNTIL, ONE DAY, KALUU APPROACHED ME, HIS EYES GLITTERING..."
COME! NO MORE CAN WE LEARN WITHIN THESE MUSTY WALLS! NOW, WE MUST ACT! IT IS TIME TO SUMMON OUR DESTINY!
I WOULD WAIT STILL LONGER, KALUU! BUT, IF YOU JUDGE THE DAYS OF STUDY ARE OVER, I WILL HEED YOU! LET US GO!
I MUST ACCOMPANY HIM! I DO NOT TRUST HIM TO CONJURE ALONE! I SHALL USE MY POWER TO LIMIT HIS!
"STEPPING ONTO A BALCONY WHICH OVERLOOKED THE SILENT VILLAGE, WE INVOKED ALL THE HIDDEN FORCES OF THE SUPER-NATURAL, CASTING AN ENCHANTMENT OVER THE LAND... FOR AN INSTANT, THE VERY GROUND BENEATH OUR FEET SHUDDERED, AS OUR SPELL GRIPPED ALL NATURE..."
"THEN, IT SEEMED THE SUN ITSELF SHONE MORE BRIGHTLY AND THE AIR WAS SWEET IN OUR NOSTRILS! DISEASE, POVERTY AND PAIN VANISHED, AND FOR THE FIRST TIME IN THE LONG HISTORY OF MANKIND, HUMAN BEINGS WERE FREE TO EXIST IN PERFECT HAPPINESS! INTOXICATED WITH OUR SUCCESS, KALUU AND I WALKED THRU THE VILLAGE..."
SOON, THE PEOPLE WILL CHOOSE A RULER! THOUGH YOU HAVE BEEN A FAITHFUL COMPANION, I INSIST THAT YOU REFUSE THE THRONE! FOR, ONLY I, KALUU, HAVE THE COURAGE AND STRENGTH TO LEAD...
KALUU MUST RULE!
HE DOES NOT REALIZE THAT I KNOW WHAT HE HAS DONE--THAT HE HAS IMPLANTED WITHIN THE PEOPLE THE DESIRE TO CROWN HIM KING!
I SHALL GIVE HIM SWAY--BUT I WILL STAY NEAR HIM THAT I MAY OPPOSE HIS PLANS FOR CONQUEST!
"AND SO, AT THE COUNCIL OF THE ELDERS, KALUU WAS HONORED ABOVE ALL OTHER MEN..."
LET KALUU ASCEND TO THE THRONE!
IT IS DECREED BY FATE--KALUU SHALL LEAD US!
KALUU! KALUU!... KALUU!
"AND SO, KALUU WAS MADE KING! BUT WITHIN HOURS AFTER HIS CORONATION, HE BEGAN TO TRANSFORM THE FARMERS INTO WARRIORS--MERE ARMED PAWNS IN THE SERVICE OF HIS UNQUENCHABLE AMBITION..."
TARRY NOT PAYING HOMAGE TO ME, MY SUBJECTS! RATHER, GO PERFECT WHAT I HAVE TAUGHT YOU! EXERCISE YOUR SKILLS IN COMBAT, HONE THE EDGES OF YOUR SWORDS...
FOR, I SAY TO YOU, BEFORE THE YEAR IS OLD, YOU SHALL KNOW VICTORIES SUCH AS YOU HAVE NEVER IMAGINED!

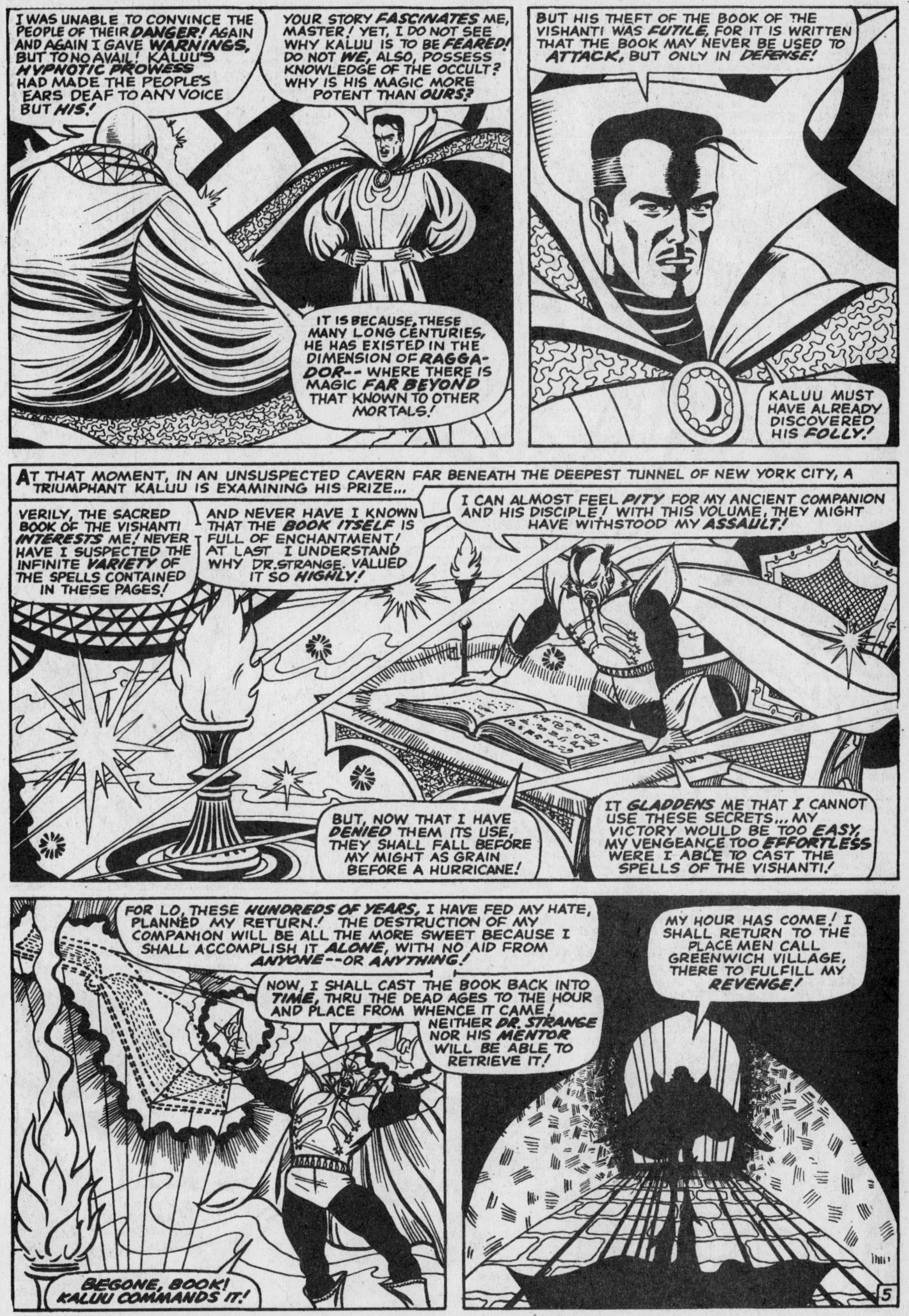
I WAS UNABLE TO CONVINCE THE PEOPLE OF THEIR DANGER! AGAIN AND AGAIN I GAVE WARNINGS, BUT TO NO AVAIL! KALUU'S HYPNOTIC PROWESS HAD MADE THE PEOPLE'S EARS DEAF TO ANY VOICE BUT HIS!
YOUR STORY FASCINATES ME, MASTER! YET, I DO NOT SEE WHY KALUU IS TO BE FEARED! DO NOT WE, ALSO, POSSESS KNOWLEDGE OF THE OCCULT? WHY IS HIS MAGIC MORE POTENT THAN OURS?
IT IS BECAUSE, THESE MANY LONG CENTURIES, HE HAS EXISTED IN THE DIMENSION OF RAGGADOR-- WHERE THERE IS MAGIC FAR BEYOND THAT KNOWN TO OTHER MORTALS!
BUT HIS THEFT OF THE BOOK OF THE VISHANTI WAS FUTILE, FOR IT IS WRITTEN THAT THE BOOK MAY NEVER BE USED TO ATTACK, BUT ONLY IN DEFENSE!
KALUU MUST HAVE ALREADY DISCOVERED HIS FOLLY!
AT THAT MOMENT, IN AN UNSUSPECTED CAVERN FAR BENEATH THE DEEPEST TUNNEL OF NEW YORK CITY, A TRIUMPHANT KALUU IS EXAMINING HIS PRIZE...
VERILY, THE SACRED BOOK OF THE VISHANTI INTERESTS ME! NEVER HAVE I SUSPECTED THE INFINITE VARIETY OF THE SPELLS CONTAINED IN THESE PAGES!
AND NEVER HAVE I KNOWN THAT THE BOOK ITSELF IS FULL OF ENCHANTMENT! AT LAST I UNDERSTAND WHY DR. STRANGE. VALUED IT SO HIGHLY!
I CAN ALMOST FEEL PITY FOR MY ANCIENT COMPANION AND HIS DISCIPLE! WITH THIS VOLUME, THEY MIGHT HAVE WITHSTOOD MY ASSAULT!
BUT, NOW THAT I HAVE DENIED THEM ITS USE, THEY SHALL FALL BEFORE MY MIGHT AS GRAIN BEFORE A HURRICANE!
IT GLADDENS ME THAT I CANNOT USE THESE SECRETS... MY VICTORY WOULD BE TOO EASY, MY VENGEANCE TOO EFFORTLESS WERE I ABLE TO CAST THE SPELLS OF THE VISHANTI!
FOR LO, THESE HUNDREDS OF YEARS, I HAVE FED MY HATE, PLANNED MY RETURN! THE DESTRUCTION OF MY COMPANION WILL BE ALL THE MORE SWEET BECAUSE I SHALL ACCOMPLISH IT ALONE, WITH NO AID FROM ANYONE--OR ANYTHING!
NOW, I SHALL CAST THE BOOK BACK INTO TIME, THRU THE DEAD AGES TO THE HOUR AND PLACE FROM WHENCE IT CAME!
NEITHER DR. STRANGE NOR HIS MENTOR WILL BE ABLE TO RETRIEVE IT!
BEGONE, BOOK! KALUU COMMANDS IT!
MY HOUR HAS COME! I SHALL RETURN TO THE PLACE MEN CALL GREENWICH VILLAGE, THERE TO FULFILL MY REVENGE!
5

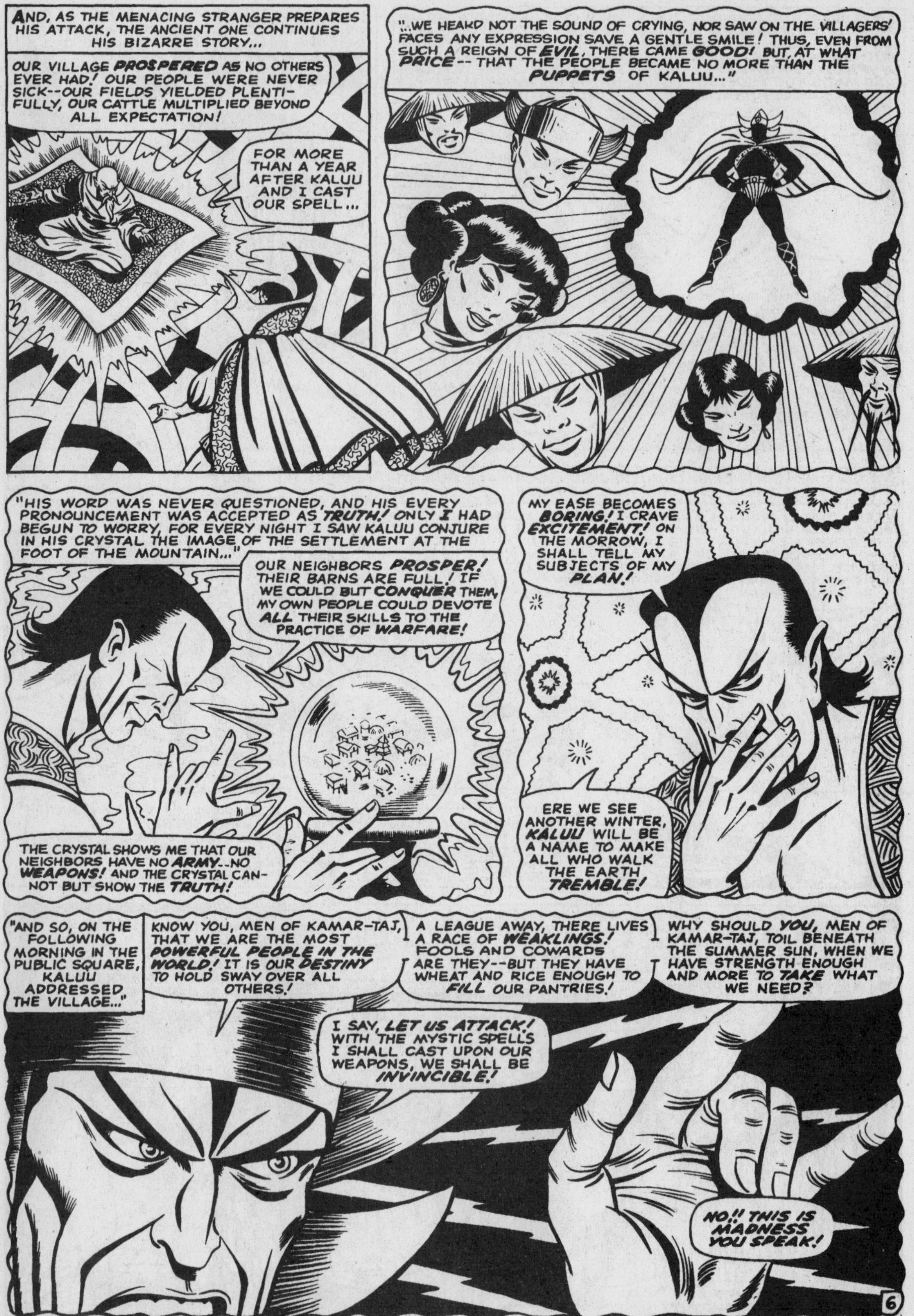
AND, AS THE MENACING STRANGER PREPARES HIS ATTACK, THE ANCIENT ONE CONTINUES HIS BIZARRE STORY...
OUR VILLAGE PROSPERED AS NO OTHERS EVER HAD! OUR PEOPLE WERE NEVER SICK--OUR FIELDS YIELDED PLENTIFULLY, OUR CATTLE MULTIPLIED BEYOND ALL EXPECTATION!
FOR MORE THAN A YEAR AFTER KALUU AND I CAST OUR SPELL...
"...WE HEARD NOT THE SOUND OF CRYING, NOR SAW ON THE VILLAGERS' FACES ANY EXPRESSION SAVE A GENTLE SMILE! THUS, EVEN FROM SUCH A REIGN OF EVIL, THERE CAME GOOD! BUT, AT WHAT PRICE -- THAT THE PEOPLE BECAME NO MORE THAN THE PUPPETS OF KALUU..."
"HIS WORD WAS NEVER QUESTIONED, AND HIS EVERY PRONOUNCEMENT WAS ACCEPTED AS TRUTH! ONLY I HAD BEGUN TO WORRY, FOR EVERY NIGHT I SAW KALUU CONJURE IN HIS CRYSTAL THE IMAGE OF THE SETTLEMENT AT THE FOOT OF THE MOUNTAIN..."
OUR NEIGHBORS PROSPER! THEIR BARNS ARE FULL! IF WE COULD BUT CONQUER THEM, MY OWN PEOPLE COULD DEVOTE ALL THEIR SKILLS TO THE PRACTICE OF WARFARE!
THE CRYSTAL SHOWS ME THAT OUR NEIGHBORS HAVE NO ARMY--NO WEAPONS! AND THE CRYSTAL CANNOT BUT SHOW THE TRUTH!
MY EASE BECOMES BORING! I CRAVE EXCITEMENT! ON THE MORROW, I SHALL TELL MY SUBJECTS OF MY PLAN!
ERE WE SEE ANOTHER WINTER, KALUU WILL BE A NAME TO MAKE ALL WHO WALK THE EARTH TREMBLE!
"AND SO, ON THE FOLLOWING MORNING IN THE PUBLIC SQUARE, KALUU ADDRESSED THE VILLAGE..."
KNOW YOU, MEN OF KAMAR-TAJ, THAT WE ARE THE MOST POWERFUL PEOPLE IN THE WORLD! IT IS OUR DESTINY TO HOLD SWAY OVER ALL OTHERS!
A LEAGUE AWAY, THERE LIVES A RACE OF WEAKLINGS! FOOLS AND COWARDS ARE THEY--BUT THEY HAVE WHEAT AND RICE ENOUGH TO FILL OUR PANTRIES!
WHY SHOULD YOU, MEN OF KAMAR-TAJ, TOIL BENEATH THE SUMMER SUN, WHEN WE HAVE STRENGTH ENOUGH AND MORE TO TAKE WHAT WE NEED?
I SAY, LET US ATTACK! WITH THE MYSTIC SPELLS I SHALL CAST UPON OUR WEAPONS, WE SHALL BE INVINCIBLE!
NO!! THIS IS MADNESS YOU SPEAK!
6

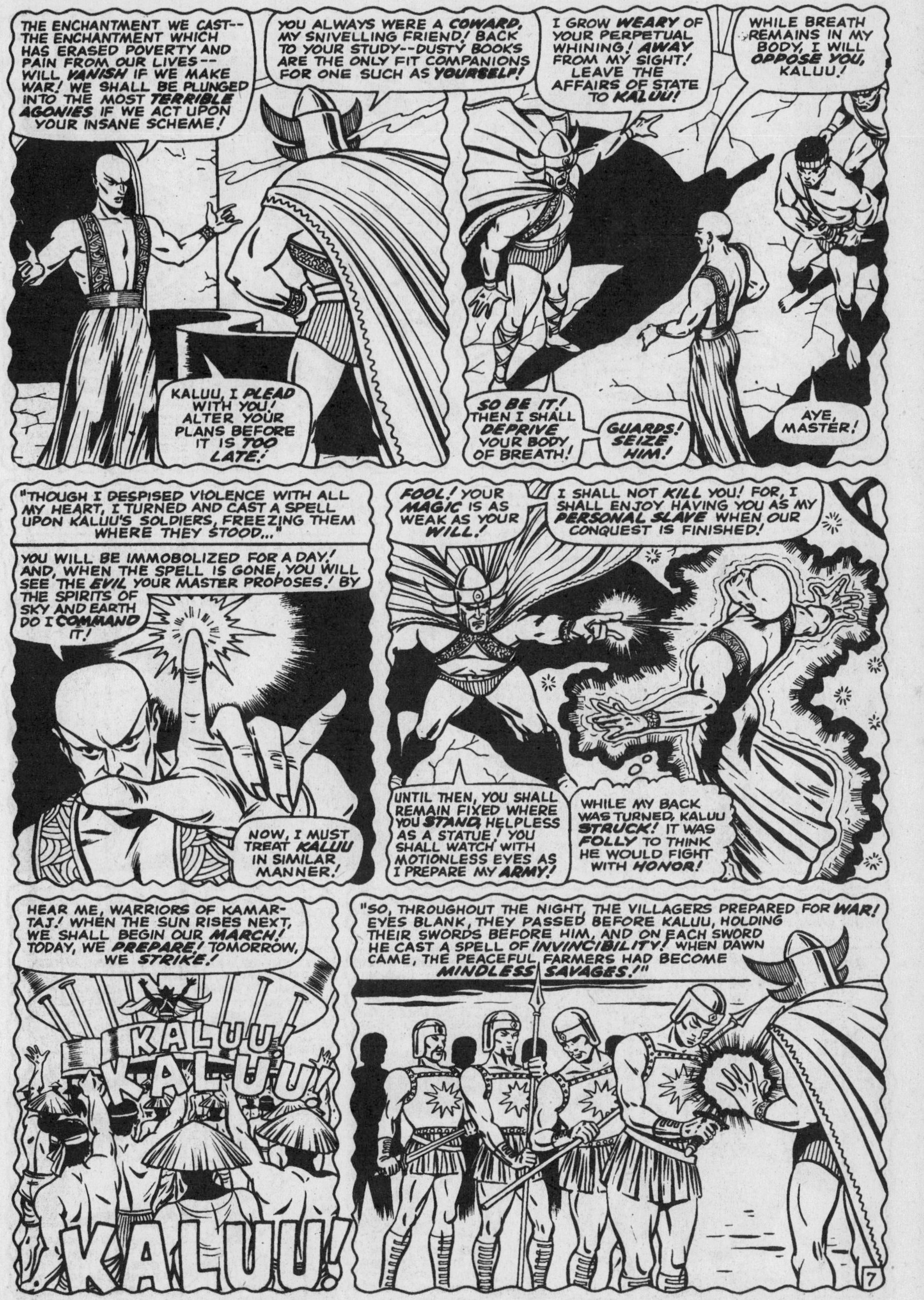

THE ENCHANTMENT WE CAST-- THE ENCHANTMENT WHICH HAS ERASED POVERTY AND PAIN FROM OUR LIVES-- WILL VANISH IF WE MAKE WAR! WE SHALL BE PLUNGED INTO THE MOST TERRIBLE AGONIES IF WE ACT UPON YOUR INSANE SCHEME!
YOU ALWAYS WERE A COWARD, MY SNIVELLING FRIEND! BACK TO YOUR STUDY--DUSTY BOOKS ARE THE ONLY FIT COMPANIONS FOR ONE SUCH AS YOURSELF!
KALUU, I PLEAD WITH YOU! ALTER YOUR PLANS BEFORE IT IS TOO LATE!
I GROW WEARY OF YOUR PERPETUAL WHINING! AWAY FROM MY SIGHT! LEAVE THE AFFAIRS OF STATE TO KALUU!
WHILE BREATH REMAINS IN MY BODY, I WILL OPPOSE YOU, KALUU!
SO BE IT! THEN I SHALL DEPRIVE YOUR BODY OF BREATH!
GUARDS! SEIZE HIM!
AYE, MASTER!
"THOUGH I DESPISED VIOLENCE WITH ALL MY HEART, I TURNED AND CAST A SPELL UPON KALUU'S SOLDIERS, FREEZING THEM WHERE THEY STOOD..."
YOU WILL BE IMMOBOLIZED FOR A DAY! AND, WHEN THE SPELL IS GONE, YOU WILL SEE THE EVIL YOUR MASTER PROPOSES! BY THE SPIRITS OF SKY AND EARTH DO I COMMAND IT!
NOW, I MUST TREAT KALUU IN SIMILAR MANNER!
FOOL! YOUR MAGIC IS AS WEAK AS YOUR WILL!
I SHALL NOT KILL YOU! FOR, I SHALL ENJOY HAVING YOU AS MY PERSONAL SLAVE WHEN OUR CONQUEST IS FINISHED!
UNTIL THEN, YOU SHALL REMAIN FIXED WHERE YOU STAND, HELPLESS AS A STATUE! YOU SHALL WATCH WITH MOTIONLESS EYES AS I PREPARE MY ARMY!
WHILE MY BACK WAS TURNED, KALUU STRUCK! IT WAS FOLLY TO THINK HE WOULD FIGHT WITH HONOR!
HEAR ME, WARRIORS OF KAMAR-TAJ! WHEN THE SUN RISES NEXT, WE SHALL BEGIN OUR MARCH! TODAY, WE PREPARE! TOMORROW, WE STRIKE!
KALUU! KALUU! KALUU!
"SO, THROUGHOUT THE NIGHT, THE VILLAGERS PREPARED FOR WAR! EYES BLANK, THEY PASSED BEFORE KALUU, HOLDING THEIR SWORDS BEFORE HIM, AND ON EACH SWORD HE CAST A SPELL OF INVINCIBILITY! WHEN DAWN CAME, THE PEACEFUL FARMERS HAD BECOME MINDLESS SAVAGES!"

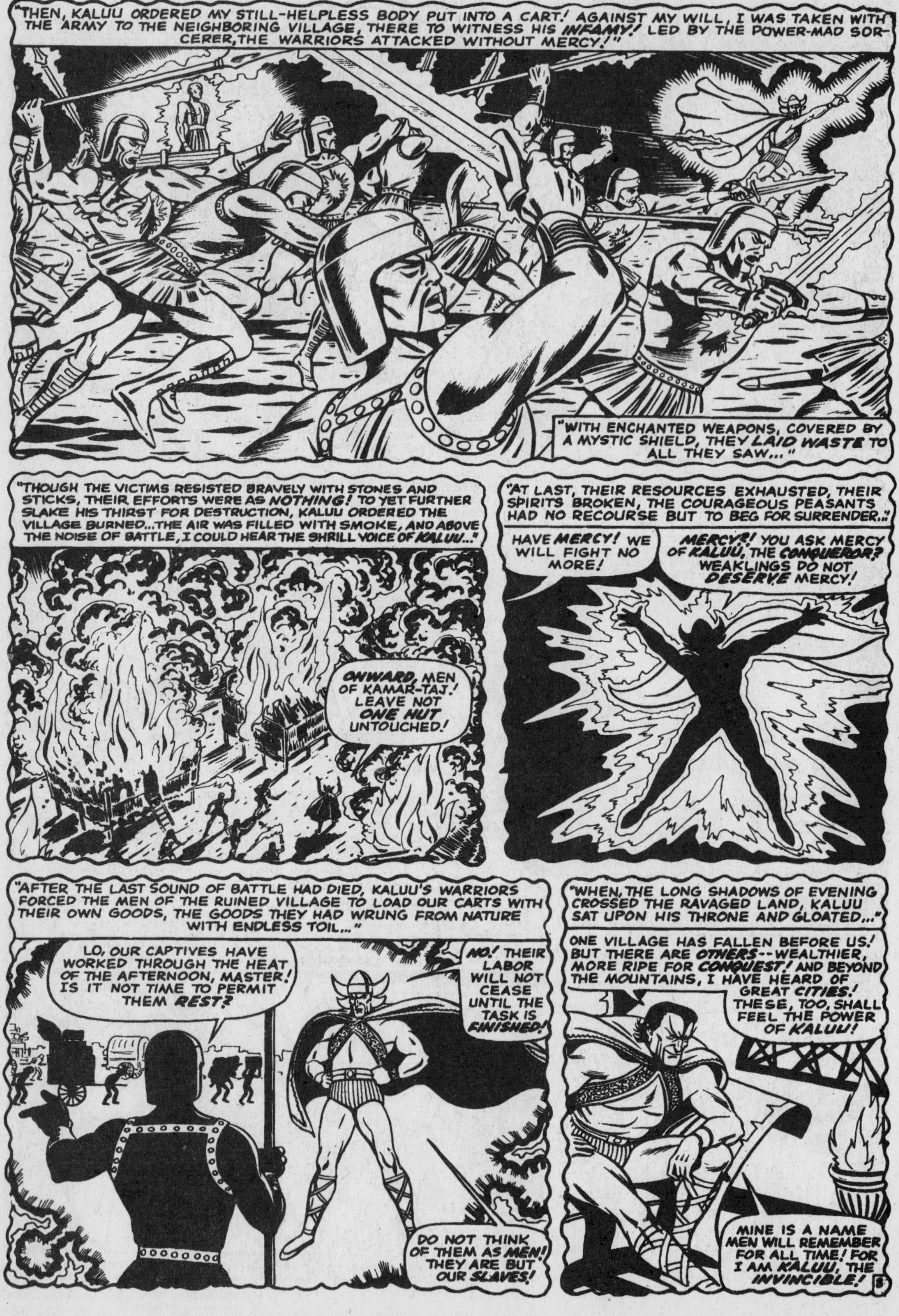
"THEN, KALUU ORDERED MY STILL-HELPLESS BODY PUT INTO A CART! AGAINST MY WILL, I WAS TAKEN WITH THE ARMY TO THE NEIGHBORING VILLAGE, THERE TO WITNESS HIS INFAMY! LED BY THE POWER-MAD SORCERER, THE WARRIORS ATTACKED WITHOUT MERCY!"
"WITH ENCHANTED WEAPONS, COVERED BY A MYSTIC SHIELD, THEY LAID WASTE TO ALL THEY SAW..."
"THOUGH THE VICTIMS RESISTED BRAVELY WITH STONES AND STICKS, THEIR EFFORTS WERE AS NOTHING! TO YET FURTHER SLAKE HIS THIRST FOR DESTRUCTION, KALUU ORDERED THE VILLAGE BURNED...THE AIR WAS FILLED WITH SMOKE, AND ABOVE THE NOISE OF BATTLE, I COULD HEAR THE SHRILL VOICE OF KALUU..."
ONWARD, MEN OF KAMAR-TAJ! LEAVE NOT ONE HUT UNTOUCHED!
"AT LAST, THEIR RESOURCES EXHAUSTED, THEIR SPIRITS BROKEN, THE COURAGEOUS PEASANTS HAD NO RECOURSE BUT TO BEG FOR SURRENDER..."
HAVE MERCY! WE WILL FIGHT NO MORE!
MERCY?! YOU ASK MERCY OF KALUU, THE CONQUEROR? WEAKLINGS DO NOT DESERVE MERCY!
"AFTER THE LAST SOUND OF BATTLE HAD DIED, KALUU'S WARRIORS FORCED THE MEN OF THE RUINED VILLAGE TO LOAD OUR CARTS WITH THEIR OWN GOODS, THE GOODS THEY HAD WRUNG FROM NATURE WITH ENDLESS TOIL..."
LO, OUR CAPTIVES HAVE WORKED THROUGH THE HEAT OF THE AFTERNOON, MASTER! IS IT NOT TIME TO PERMIT THEM REST?
NO! THEIR LABOR WILL NOT CEASE UNTIL THE TASK IS FINISHED!
DO NOT THINK OF THEM AS MEN! THEY ARE BUT OUR SLAVES!
"WHEN THE LONG SHADOWS OF EVENING CROSSED THE RAVAGED LAND, KALUU SAT UPON HIS THRONE AND GLOATED..."
ONE VILLAGE HAS FALLEN BEFORE US! BUT THERE ARE OTHERS--WEALTHIER, MORE RIPE FOR CONQUEST! AND BEYOND THE MOUNTAINS, I HAVE HEARD OF GREAT CITIES! THESE, TOO, SHALL FEEL THE POWER OF KALUU!
MINE IS A NAME MEN WILL REMEMBER FOR ALL TIME! FOR I AM KALUU, THE INVINCIBLE!
5

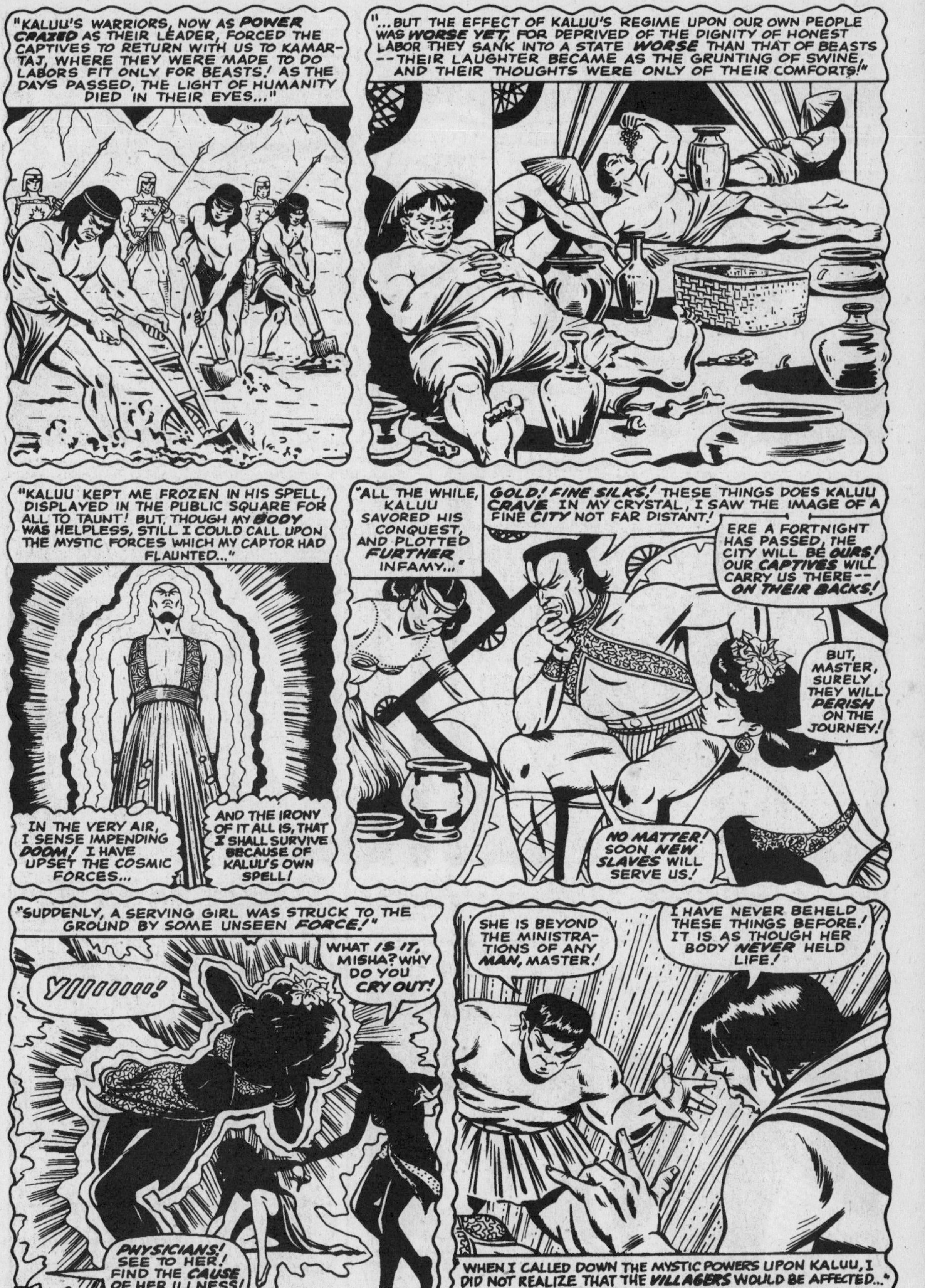
"KALUU'S WARRIORS, NOW AS POWER CRAZED AS THEIR LEADER, FORCED THE CAPTIVES TO RETURN WITH US TO KAMAR-TAJ, WHERE THEY WERE MADE TO DO LABORS FIT ONLY FOR BEASTS! AS THE DAYS PASSED, THE LIGHT OF HUMANITY DIED IN THEIR EYES..."
"...BUT THE EFFECT OF KALUU'S REGIME UPON OUR OWN PEOPLE WAS WORSE YET, FOR DEPRIVED OF THE DIGNITY OF HONEST LABOR THEY SANK INTO A STATE WORSE THAN THAT OF BEASTS --THEIR LAUGHTER BECAME AS THE GRUNTING OF SWINE, AND THEIR THOUGHTS WERE ONLY OF THEIR COMFORTS!"
"KALUU KEPT ME FROZEN IN HIS SPELL, DISPLAYED IN THE PUBLIC SQUARE FOR ALL TO TAUNT! BUT, THOUGH MY BODY WAS HELPLESS, STILL I COULD CALL UPON THE MYSTIC FORCES WHICH MY CAPTOR HAD FLAUNTED..."
IN THE VERY AIR, I SENSE IMPENDING DOOM! I HAVE UPSET THE COSMIC FORCES...
AND THE IRONY OF IT ALL IS, THAT I SHALL SURVIVE BECAUSE OF KALUU'S OWN SPELL!
"ALL THE WHILE, KALUU SAVORED HIS CONQUEST, AND PLOTTED FURTHER INFAMY..."
GOLD! FINE SILKS! THESE THINGS DOES KALUU CRAVE. IN MY CRYSTAL, I SAW THE IMAGE OF A FINE CITY NOT FAR DISTANT!
ERE A FORTNIGHT HAS PASSED, THE CITY WILL BE OURS! OUR CAPTIVES WILL CARRY US THERE-- ON THEIR BACKS!
BUT, MASTER, SURELY THEY WILL PERISH ON THE JOURNEY!
NO MATTER! SOON NEW SLAVES WILL SERVE US!
"SUDDENLY, A SERVING GIRL WAS STRUCK TO THE GROUND BY SOME UNSEEN FORCE!"
YIIIIIIII!
WHAT IS IT, MISHA? WHY DO YOU CRY OUT!
PHYSICIANS! SEE TO HER! FIND THE CAUSE OF HER ILLNESS!
SHE IS BEYOND THE MINISTRATIONS OF ANY MAN, MASTER!
I HAVE NEVER BEHELD THESE THINGS BEFORE! IT IS AS THOUGH HER BODY NEVER HELD LIFE!
"WHEN I CALLED DOWN THE MYSTIC POWERS UPON KALUU, I DID NOT REALIZE THAT THE VILLAGERS WOULD BE AFFECTED..."
9

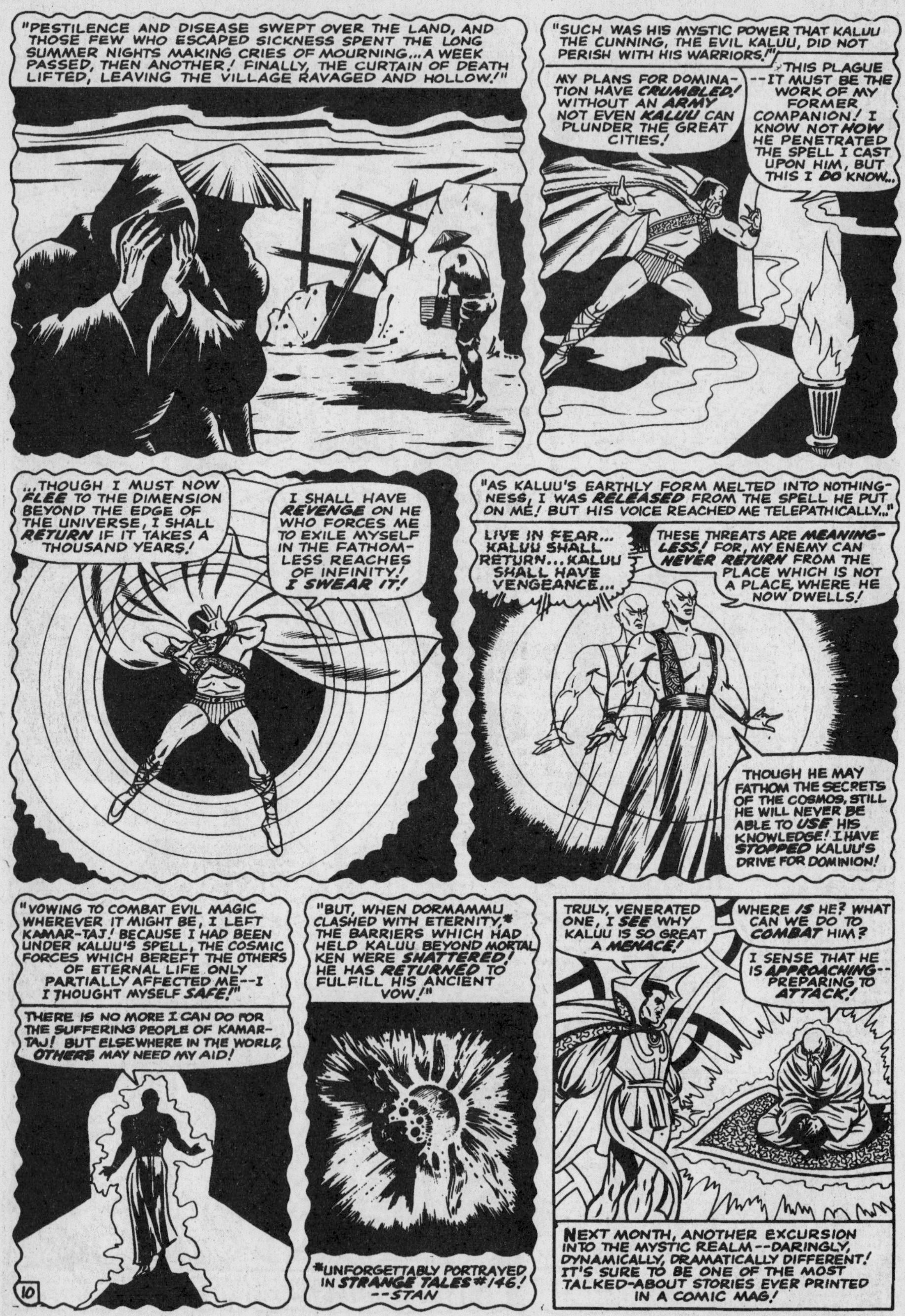
"PESTILENCE AND DISEASE SWEPT OVER THE LAND, AND THOSE FEW WHO ESCAPED SICKNESS SPENT THE LONG SUMMER NIGHTS MAKING CRIES OF MOURNING... A WEEK PASSED, THEN ANOTHER! FINALLY, THE CURTAIN OF DEATH LIFTED, LEAVING THE VILLAGE RAVAGED AND HOLLOW!"
"SUCH WAS HIS MYSTIC POWER THAT KALUU THE CUNNING, THE EVIL KALUU, DID NOT PERISH WITH HIS WARRIORS!"
MY PLANS FOR DOMINATION HAVE CRUMBLED! WITHOUT AN ARMY NOT EVEN KALUU CAN PLUNDER THE GREAT CITIES!
--THIS PLAGUE --IT MUST BE THE WORK OF MY FORMER COMPANION! I KNOW NOT HOW HE PENETRATED THE SPELL I CAST UPON HIM, BUT THIS I DO KNOW...
...THOUGH I MUST NOW FLEE TO THE DIMENSION BEYOND THE EDGE OF THE UNIVERSE, I SHALL RETURN IF IT TAKES A THOUSAND YEARS!
I SHALL HAVE REVENGE ON HE WHO FORCES ME TO EXILE MYSELF IN THE FATHOMLESS REACHES OF INFINITY! I SWEAR IT!
"AS KALUU'S EARTHLY FORM MELTED INTO NOTHINGNESS, I WAS RELEASED FROM THE SPELL HE PUT ON ME! BUT HIS VOICE REACHED ME TELEPATHICALLY..."
LIVE IN FEAR... KALUU SHALL RETURN... KALUU SHALL HAVE VENGEANCE...
THESE THREATS ARE MEANINGLESS! FOR, MY ENEMY CAN NEVER RETURN FROM THE PLACE WHICH IS NOT A PLACE, WHERE HE NOW DWELLS!
THOUGH HE MAY FATHOM THE SECRETS OF THE COSMOS, STILL HE WILL NEVER BE ABLE TO USE HIS KNOWLEDGE! I HAVE STOPPED KALUU'S DRIVE FOR DOMINION!
"VOWING TO COMBAT EVIL MAGIC WHEREVER IT MIGHT BE, I LEFT KAMAR-TAJ! BECAUSE I HAD BEEN UNDER KALUU'S SPELL, THE COSMIC FORCES WHICH BEREFT THE OTHERS OF ETERNAL LIFE ONLY PARTIALLY AFFECTED ME--I THOUGHT MYSELF SAFE!"
THERE IS NO MORE I CAN DO FOR THE SUFFERING PEOPLE OF KAMAR-TAJ! BUT ELSEWHERE IN THE WORLD, OTHERS MAY NEED MY AID!
"BUT, WHEN DORMAMMU CLASHED WITH ETERNITY,* THE BARRIERS WHICH HAD HELD KALUU BEYOND MORTAL KEN WERE SHATTERED! HE HAS RETURNED TO FULFILL HIS ANCIENT VOW!"
*UNFORGETTABLY PORTRAYED IN STRANGE TALES #146! --STAN
TRULY, VENERATED ONE, I SEE WHY KALUU IS SO GREAT A MENACE!
WHERE IS HE? WHAT CAN WE DO TO COMBAT HIM?
I SENSE THAT HE IS APPROACHING--PREPARING TO ATTACK!
NEXT MONTH, ANOTHER EXCURSION INTO THE MYSTIC REALM--DARINGLY, DYNAMICALLY, DRAMATICALLY DIFFERENT! IT'S SURE TO BE ONE OF THE MOST TALKED-ABOUT STORIES EVER PRINTED IN A COMIC MAG!
10

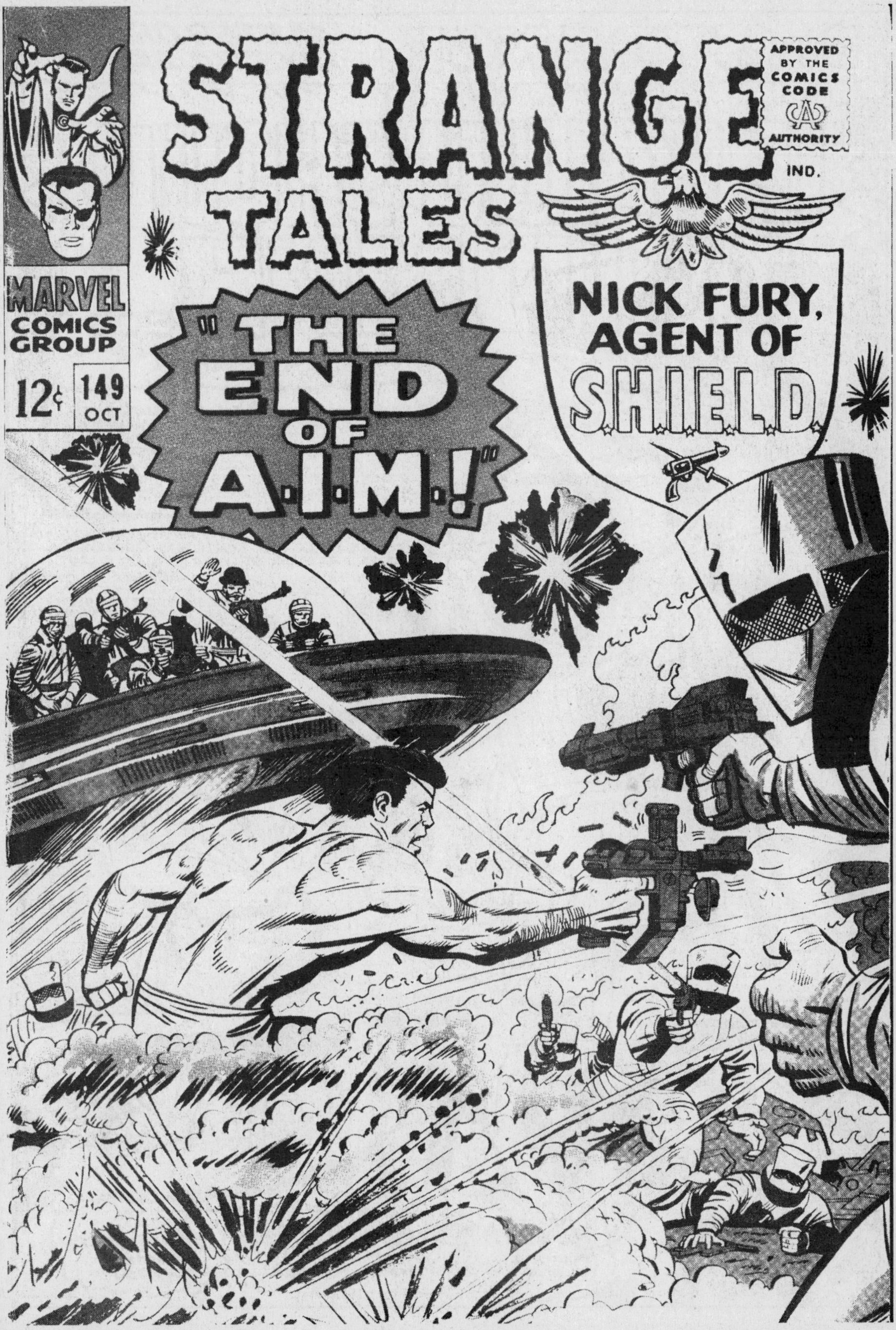
STRANGE TALES
MARVEL COMICS GROUP
12¢ 149 OCT
APPROVED BY THE COMICS CODE AUTHORITY
IND.
"THE END OF A.I.M.!"
NICK FURY, AGENT OF S.H.I.E.L.D.

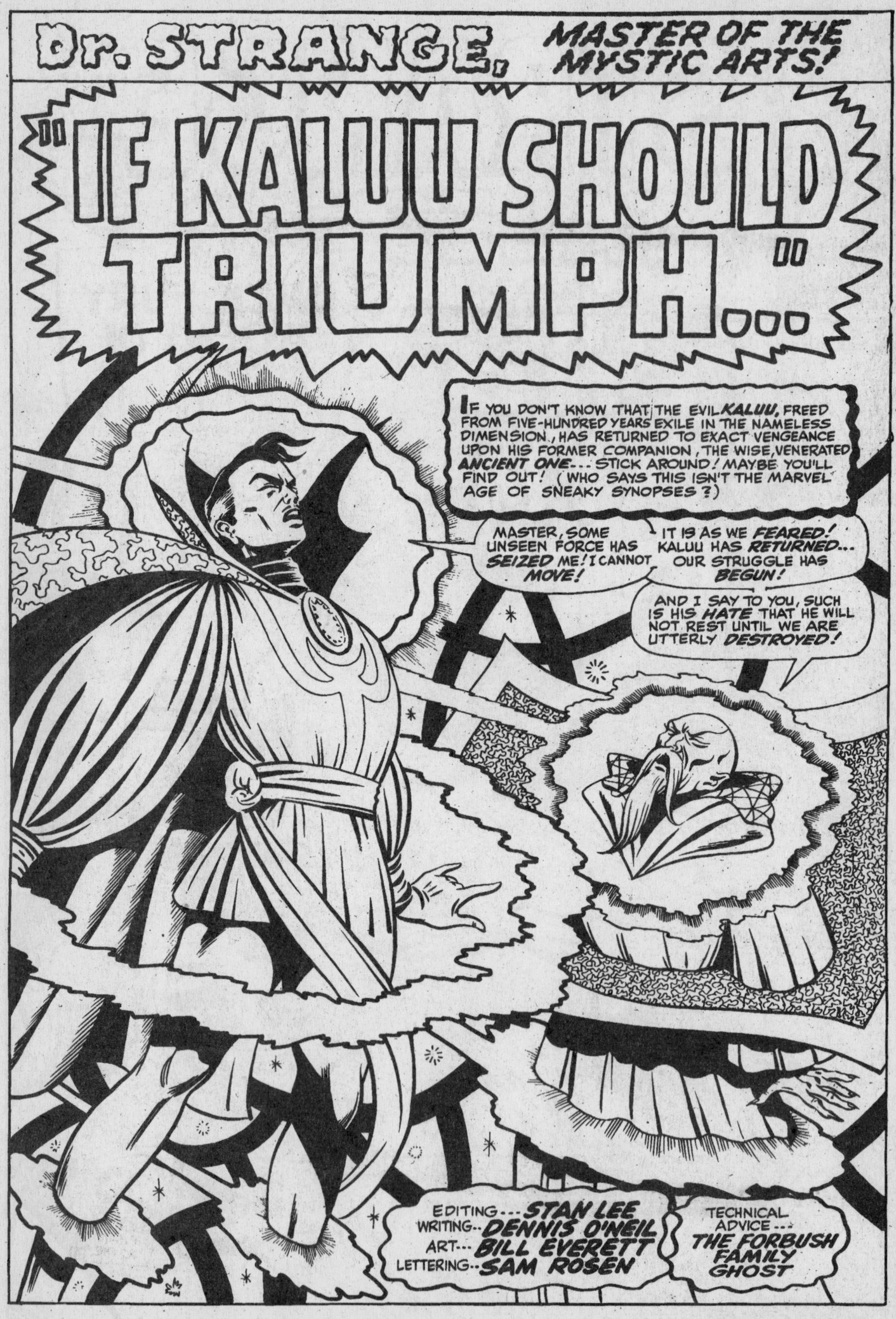

Dr. STRANGE, MASTER OF THE MYSTIC ARTS!
"IF KALUU SHOULD TRIUMPH..."
IF YOU DON'T KNOW THAT THE EVIL KALUU, FREED FROM FIVE-HUNDRED YEARS EXILE IN THE NAMELESS DIMENSION, HAS RETURNED TO EXACT VENGEANCE UPON HIS FORMER COMPANION, THE WISE, VENERATED ANCIENT ONE... STICK AROUND! MAYBE YOU'LL FIND OUT! (WHO SAYS THIS ISN'T THE MARVEL AGE OF SNEAKY SYNOPSES?)
MASTER, SOME UNSEEN FORCE HAS SEIZED ME! I CANNOT MOVE!
IT IS AS WE FEARED! KALUU HAS RETURNED... OUR STRUGGLE HAS BEGUN!
AND I SAY TO YOU, SUCH IS HIS HATE THAT HE WILL NOT REST UNTIL WE ARE UTTERLY DESTROYED!
EDITING... STAN LEE WRITING.. DENNIS O'NEIL ART... BILL EVERETT LETTERING.. SAM ROSEN
TECHNICAL ADVICE... THE FORBUSH FAMILY GHOST

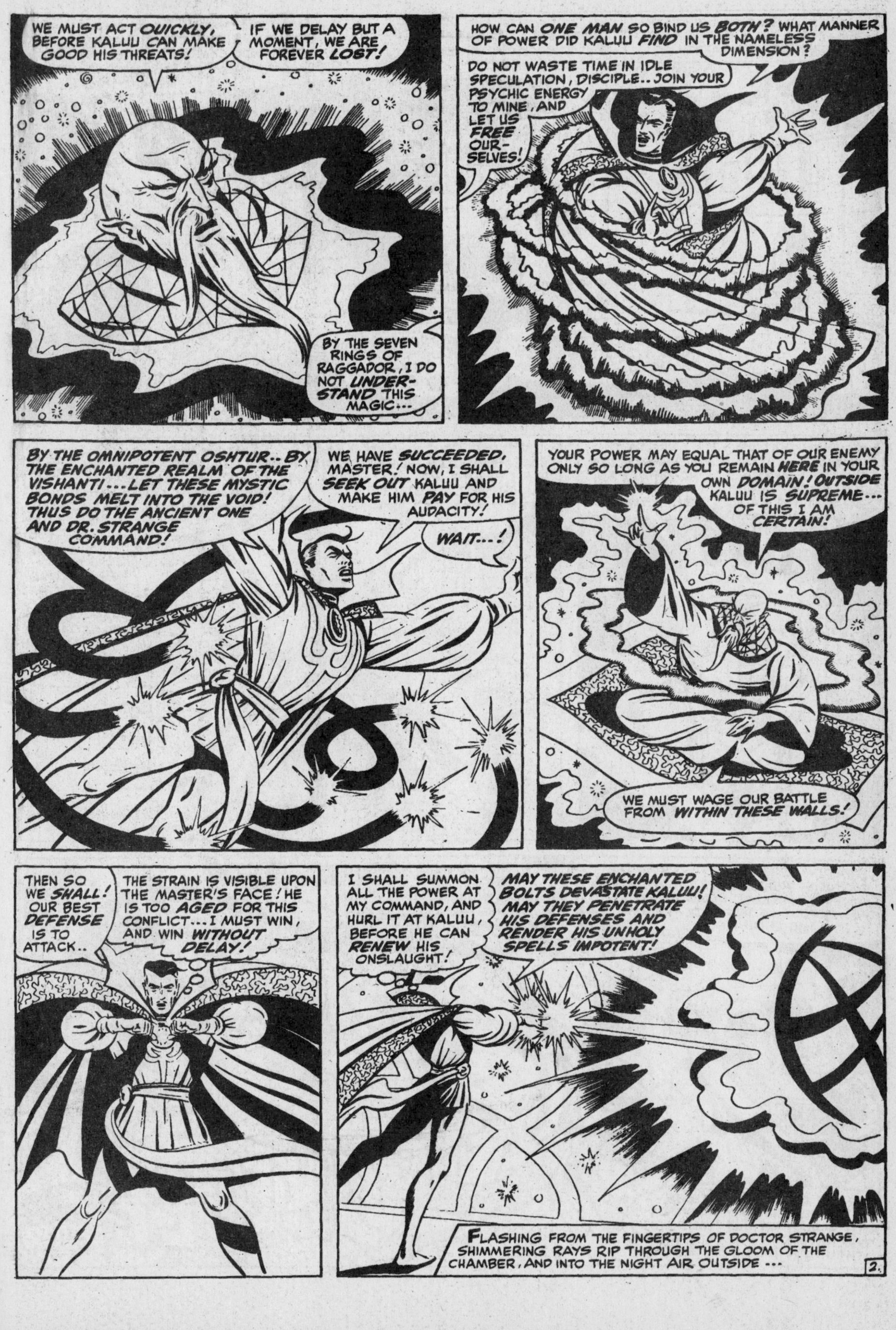
WE MUST ACT QUICKLY, BEFORE KALUU CAN MAKE GOOD HIS THREATS!
IF WE DELAY BUT A MOMENT, WE ARE FOREVER LOST!
BY THE SEVEN RINGS OF RAGGADOR, I DO NOT UNDERSTAND THIS MAGIC...
HOW CAN ONE MAN SO BIND US BOTH? WHAT MANNER OF POWER DID KALUU FIND IN THE NAMELESS DIMENSION?
DO NOT WASTE TIME IN IDLE SPECULATION, DISCIPLE... JOIN YOUR PSYCHIC ENERGY TO MINE, AND LET US FREE OURSELVES!
BY THE OMNIPOTENT OSHTUR.. BY THE ENCHANTED REALM OF THE VISHANTI... LET THESE MYSTIC BONDS MELT INTO THE VOID! THUS DO THE ANCIENT ONE AND DR. STRANGE COMMAND!
WE HAVE SUCCEEDED, MASTER! NOW, I SHALL SEEK OUT KALUU AND MAKE HIM PAY FOR HIS AUDACITY!
WAIT...!
YOUR POWER MAY EQUAL THAT OF OUR ENEMY ONLY SO LONG AS YOU REMAIN HERE IN YOUR OWN DOMAIN! OUTSIDE KALUU IS SUPREME... OF THIS I AM CERTAIN!
WE MUST WAGE OUR BATTLE FROM WITHIN THESE WALLS!
THEN SO WE SHALL! OUR BEST DEFENSE IS TO ATTACK..
THE STRAIN IS VISIBLE UPON THE MASTER'S FACE! HE IS TOO AGED FOR THIS CONFLICT... I MUST WIN, AND WIN WITHOUT DELAY!
I SHALL SUMMON ALL THE POWER AT MY COMMAND, AND HURL IT AT KALUU, BEFORE HE CAN RENEW HIS ONSLAUGHT!
MAY THESE ENCHANTED BOLTS DEVASTATE KALUU! MAY THEY PENETRATE HIS DEFENSES AND RENDER HIS UNHOLY SPELLS IMPOTENT!
FLASHING FROM THE FINGERTIPS OF DOCTOR STRANGE, SHIMMERING RAYS RIP THROUGH THE GLOOM OF THE CHAMBER, AND INTO THE NIGHT AIR OUTSIDE ---
2.

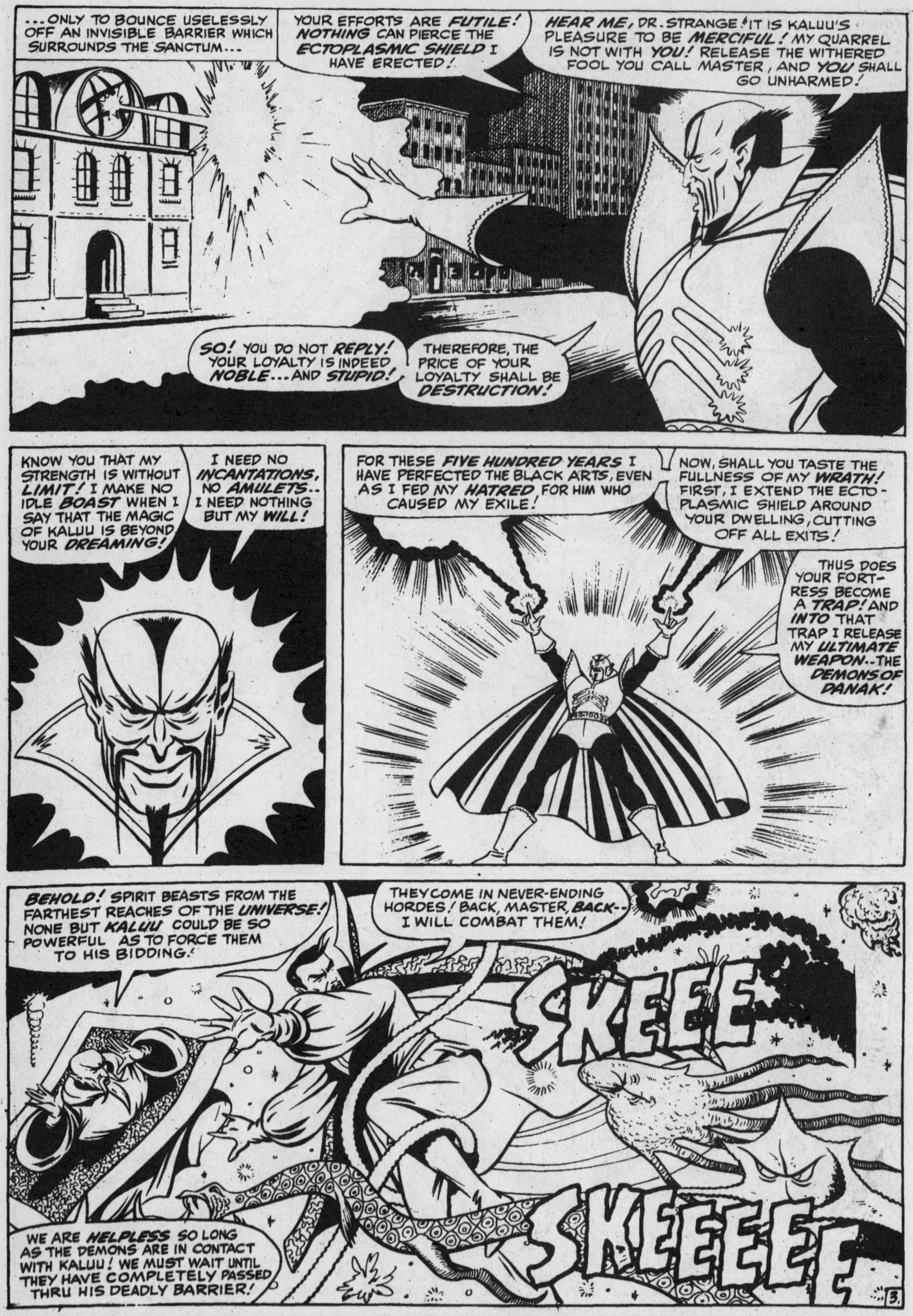
...ONLY TO BOUNCE USELESSLY OFF AN INVISIBLE BARRIER WHICH SURROUNDS THE SANCTUM...
YOUR EFFORTS ARE FUTILE! NOTHING CAN PIERCE THE ECTOPLASMIC SHIELD I HAVE ERECTED!
HEAR ME, DR. STRANGE! IT IS KALUU'S PLEASURE TO BE MERCIFUL! MY QUARREL IS NOT WITH YOU! RELEASE THE WITHERED FOOL YOU CALL MASTER, AND YOU SHALL GO UNHARMED!
SO! YOU DO NOT REPLY! YOUR LOYALTY IS INDEED NOBLE...AND STUPID!
THEREFORE, THE PRICE OF YOUR LOYALTY SHALL BE DESTRUCTION!
KNOW YOU THAT MY STRENGTH IS WITHOUT LIMIT! I MAKE NO IDLE BOAST WHEN I SAY THAT THE MAGIC OF KALUU IS BEYOND YOUR DREAMING!
I NEED NO INCANTATIONS, NO AMULETS.. I NEED NOTHING BUT MY WILL!
FOR THESE FIVE HUNDRED YEARS I HAVE PERFECTED THE BLACK ARTS, EVEN AS I FED MY HATRED FOR HIM WHO CAUSED MY EXILE!
NOW, SHALL YOU TASTE THE FULLNESS OF MY WRATH! FIRST, I EXTEND THE ECTO-PLASMIC SHIELD AROUND YOUR DWELLING, CUTTING OFF ALL EXITS!
THUS DOES YOUR FORT-RESS BECOME A TRAP! AND INTO THAT TRAP I RELEASE MY ULTIMATE WEAPON--THE DEMONS OF DANAK!
BEHOLD! SPIRIT BEASTS FROM THE FARTHEST REACHES OF THE UNIVERSE! NONE BUT KALUU COULD BE SO POWERFUL AS TO FORCE THEM TO HIS BIDDING!
THEY COME IN NEVER-ENDING HORDES! BACK, MASTER, BACK-- I WILL COMBAT THEM!
SKEEE
SKEEEEEE
WE ARE HELPLESS SO LONG AS THE DEMONS ARE IN CONTACT WITH KALUU! WE MUST WAIT UNTIL THEY HAVE COMPLETELY PASSED THRU HIS DEADLY BARRIER!
3

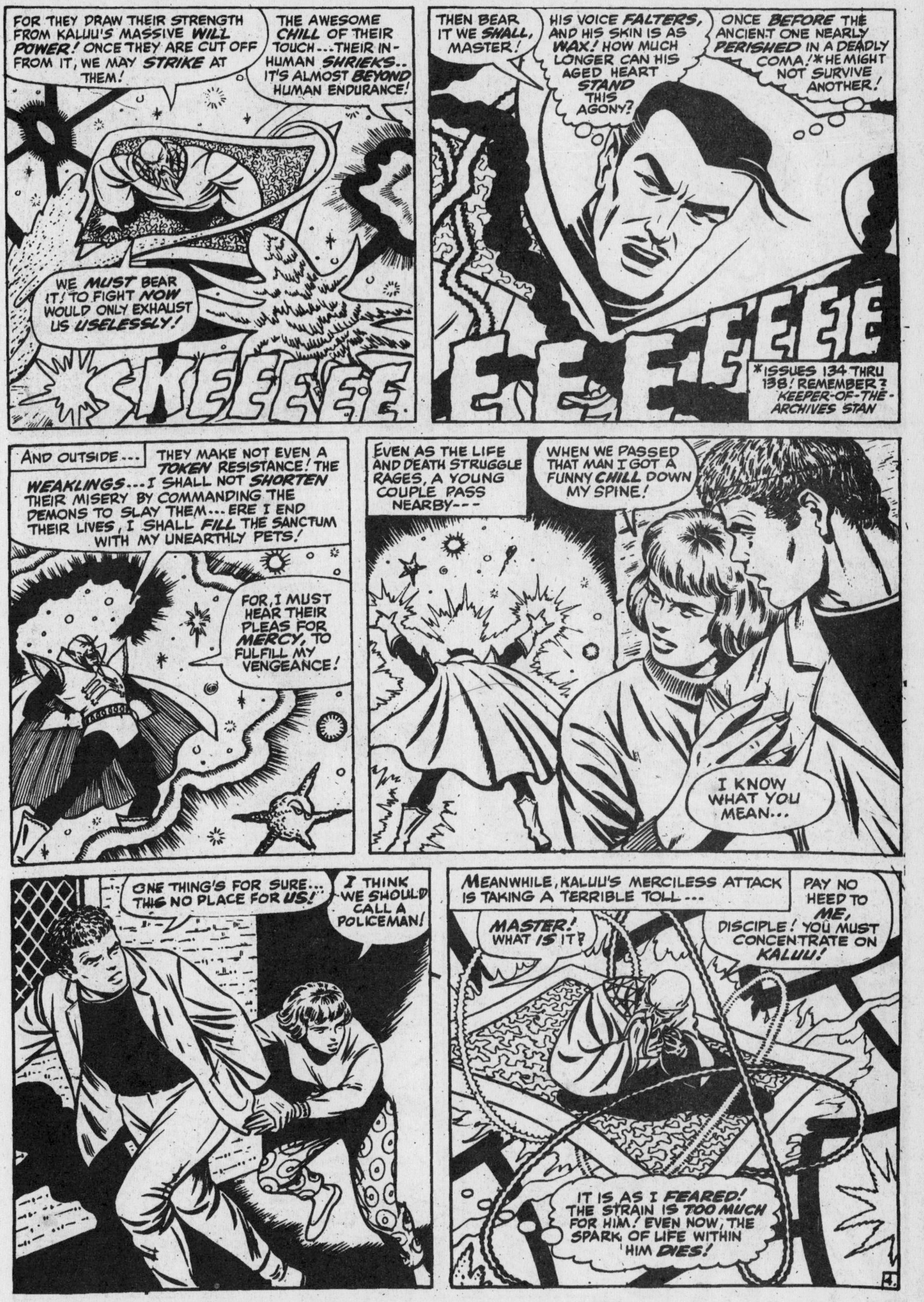

FOR THEY DRAW THEIR STRENGTH FROM KALUU'S MASSIVE WILL POWER! ONCE THEY ARE CUT OFF FROM IT, WE MAY STRIKE AT THEM!
THE AWESOME CHILL OF THEIR TOUCH... THEIR IN-HUMAN SHRIEKS.. IT'S ALMOST BEYOND HUMAN ENDURANCE!
WE MUST BEAR IT! TO FIGHT NOW WOULD ONLY EXHAUST US USELESSLY!
SKEEEEEE
THEN BEAR IT WE SHALL, MASTER!
HIS VOICE FALTERS, AND HIS SKIN IS AS WAX! HOW MUCH LONGER CAN HIS AGED HEART STAND THIS AGONY?
ONCE BEFORE THE ANCIENT ONE NEARLY PERISHED IN A DEADLY COMA!* HE MIGHT NOT SURVIVE ANOTHER!
EEEEEEE
*ISSUES 134 THRU 138! REMEMBER? KEEPER-OF-THE-ARCHIVES STAN
AND OUTSIDE...
THEY MAKE NOT EVEN A TOKEN RESISTANCE! THE WEAKLINGS... I SHALL NOT SHORTEN THEIR MISERY BY COMMANDING THE DEMONS TO SLAY THEM... ERE I END THEIR LIVES, I SHALL FILL THE SANCTUM WITH MY UNEARTHLY PETS!
FOR, I MUST HEAR THEIR PLEAS FOR MERCY, TO FULFILL MY VENGEANCE!
EVEN AS THE LIFE AND DEATH STRUGGLE RAGES, A YOUNG COUPLE PASS NEARBY---
WHEN WE PASSED THAT MAN I GOT A FUNNY CHILL DOWN MY SPINE!
I KNOW WHAT YOU MEAN...
ONE THING'S FOR SURE... THIS NO PLACE FOR US!
I THINK WE SHOULD CALL A POLICEMAN!
MEANWHILE, KALUU'S MERCILESS ATTACK IS TAKING A TERRIBLE TOLL...
MASTER! WHAT IS IT?
PAY NO HEED TO ME, DISCIPLE! YOU MUST CONCENTRATE ON KALUU!
IT IS AS I FEARED! THE STRAIN IS TOO MUCH FOR HIM! EVEN NOW, THE SPARK OF LIFE WITHIN HIM DIES!
4.

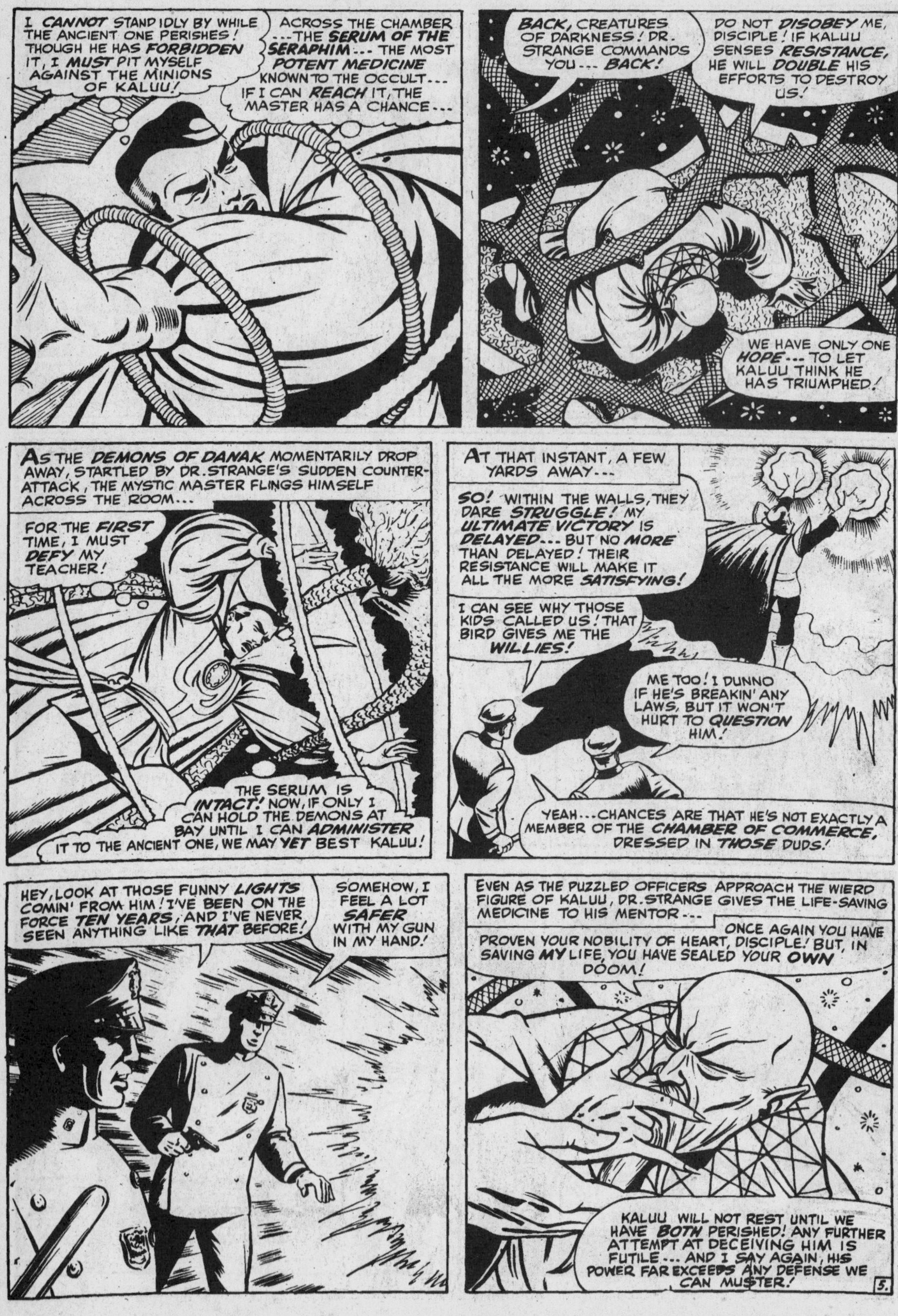
I CANNOT STAND IDLY BY WHILE THE ANCIENT ONE PERISHES! THOUGH HE HAS FORBIDDEN IT, I MUST PIT MYSELF AGAINST THE MINIONS OF KALUU!
ACROSS THE CHAMBER ---THE SERUM OF THE SERAPHIM--- THE MOST POTENT MEDICINE KNOWN TO THE OCCULT--- IF I CAN REACH IT, THE MASTER HAS A CHANCE---
BACK, CREATURES OF DARKNESS! DR. STRANGE COMMANDS YOU--- BACK!
DO NOT DISOBEY ME, DISCIPLE! IF KALUU SENSES RESISTANCE, HE WILL DOUBLE HIS EFFORTS TO DESTROY US!
WE HAVE ONLY ONE HOPE--- TO LET KALUU THINK HE HAS TRIUMPHED!
AS THE DEMONS OF DANAK MOMENTARILY DROP AWAY, STARTLED BY DR. STRANGE'S SUDDEN COUNTER-ATTACK, THE MYSTIC MASTER FLINGS HIMSELF ACROSS THE ROOM...
FOR THE FIRST TIME, I MUST DEFY MY TEACHER!
THE SERUM IS INTACT! NOW, IF ONLY I CAN HOLD THE DEMONS AT BAY UNTIL I CAN ADMINISTER IT TO THE ANCIENT ONE, WE MAY YET BEST KALUU!
AT THAT INSTANT, A FEW YARDS AWAY---
SO! WITHIN THE WALLS, THEY DARE STRUGGLE! MY ULTIMATE VICTORY IS DELAYED--- BUT NO MORE THAN DELAYED! THEIR RESISTANCE WILL MAKE IT ALL THE MORE SATISFYING!
I CAN SEE WHY THOSE KIDS CALLED US! THAT BIRD GIVES ME THE WILLIES!
ME TOO! I DUNNO IF HE'S BREAKIN' ANY LAWS, BUT IT WON'T HURT TO QUESTION HIM!
YEAH---CHANCES ARE THAT HE'S NOT EXACTLY A MEMBER OF THE CHAMBER OF COMMERCE, DRESSED IN THOSE DUDS!
HEY, LOOK AT THOSE FUNNY LIGHTS COMIN' FROM HIM! I'VE BEEN ON THE FORCE TEN YEARS, AND I'VE NEVER SEEN ANYTHING LIKE THAT BEFORE!
SOMEHOW, I FEEL A LOT SAFER WITH MY GUN IN MY HAND!
EVEN AS THE PUZZLED OFFICERS APPROACH THE WIERD FIGURE OF KALUU, DR. STRANGE GIVES THE LIFE-SAVING MEDICINE TO HIS MENTOR---
ONCE AGAIN YOU HAVE PROVEN YOUR NOBILITY OF HEART, DISCIPLE! BUT, IN SAVING MY LIFE, YOU HAVE SEALED YOUR OWN DOOM!
KALUU WILL NOT REST UNTIL WE HAVE BOTH PERISHED! ANY FURTHER ATTEMPT AT DECEIVING HIM IS FUTILE--- AND I SAY AGAIN, HIS POWER FAR EXCEEDS ANY DEFENSE WE CAN MUSTER!
5.

I MUST KEEP THE ATTENTION OF THE DEMONS UPON *MYSELF* UNTIL THE MASTER IS FULLY RECOVERED! THEY ARE *MINDLESS*---THEY WILL ATTACK WHERE THEY SENSE THE GREATEST *DANGER!*

BUT HOW LONG CAN I *STAND* THEIR INHUMAN TOUCH? ALREADY, MY BODY GROWS WEARY...MY MIND *NUMBED!* I AM *CONFUSED*...I CAN NOT THINK CLEARLY...

HEAR ME, DISCIPLE! IT IS *HOPELESS* TO CONTINUE YOUR STRUGGLE! UNLESS WE FIND *HELP*, OUR CAUSE IS *LOST!*

ABANDON YOUR PHYSICAL BODY! GO---IN YOUR *ECTOPLASMIC SELF*, SEEK AID OF THOSE YOU RESCUED FROM *DORMAMMU!**

IT IS THE HOUR FOR THEM TO *ACT* UPON THEIR PLEDGE OF LOYALTY TO YOU!

* ISH # 146, OLD BUDDIES! --CHUMMY STAN.

I SHALL DO AS YOU *WISH*, VENERATED ONE!

I HAVE MERE *SECONDS* TO FIND THE OTHERS AND RETURN, BEFORE THE DEMONS TURN UPON THE MASTER!

YET, IF THE FATES ARE WITH ME, SECONDS WILL BE *ENOUGH!*

BUT, EVEN *THAT* AVENUE OF ESCAPE IS DENIED ME!

KALUU'S BARRIER! NOT EVEN MY *SPIRIT FORM* CAN PENETRATE IT!

THEN WE ARE UTTERLY *TRAPPED!* WE MUST FACE THE MENACE OF KALUU *ALONE!*

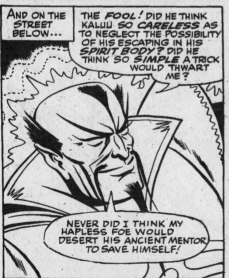

AND ON THE STREET BELOW...

THE *FOOL!* DID HE THINK KALUU SO *CARELESS* AS TO NEGLECT THE POSSIBILITY OF HIS ESCAPING IN HIS *SPIRIT BODY?* DID HE THINK SO *SIMPLE* A TRICK WOULD THWART ME?

NEVER DID I THINK MY *HAPLESS* FOE WOULD DESERT HIS ANCIENT MENTOR TO SAVE HIMSELF!

AT THAT INSTANT, A POLICE PATROL CAR ARRIVES ON THE SCENE...

I'M GLAD WE DOUBLED BACK! LOOKS LIKE WE'RE GONNA SEE SOME *REAL* ACTION!

I *STILL* THINK WE SHOULD HAVE GONE TO THE MOVIES! I PREFER *MY* ACTION ON THE SCREEN, WHERE IT CAN'T *HURT* ANYONE!

HEY, JACK, YOU GUYS HAVING *TROUBLE* HERE?

I DON'T KNOW! I THINK WE GOT A *NUT* ON OUR HANDS!

6.

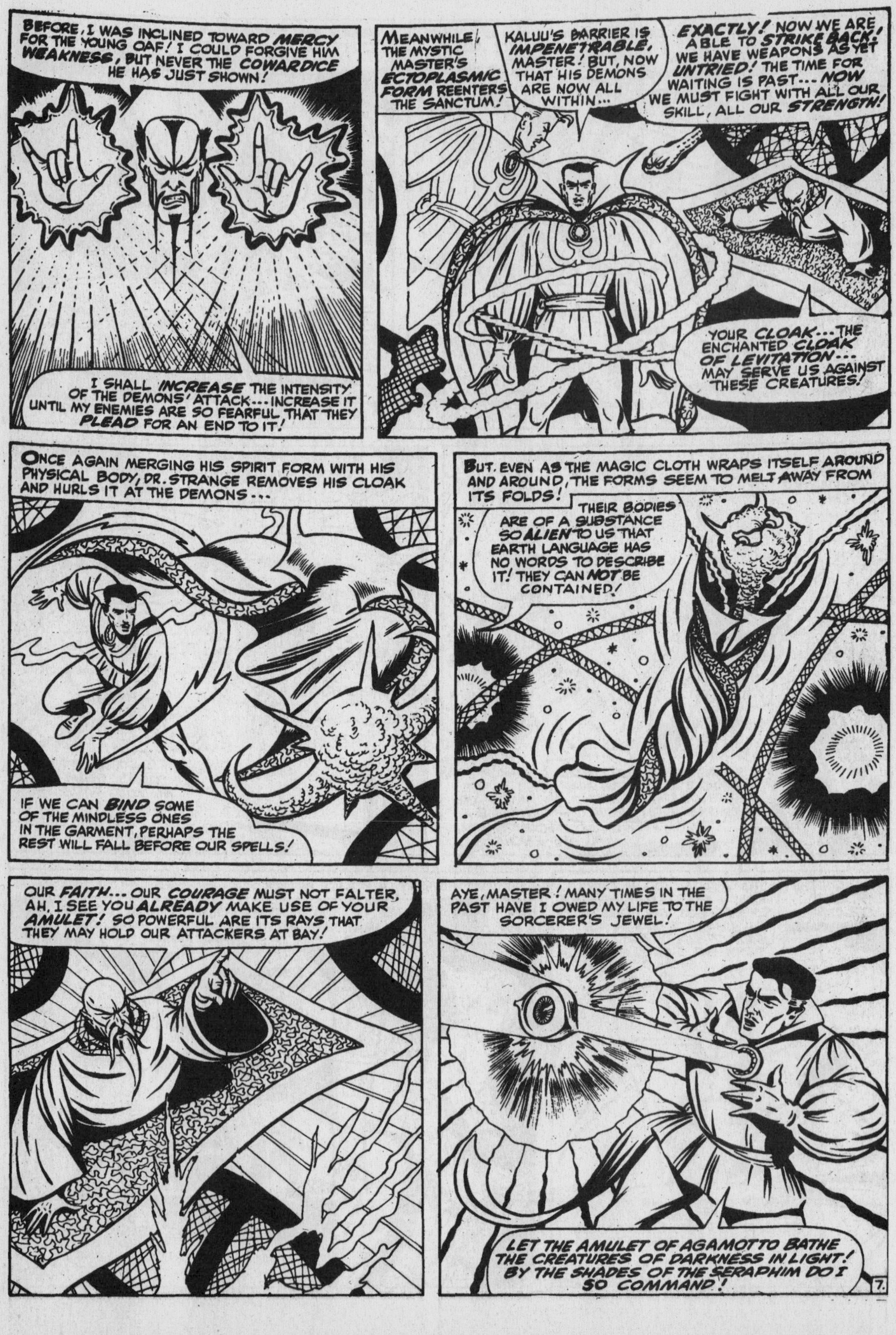
BEFORE, I WAS INCLINED TOWARD MERCY FOR THE YOUNG OAF! I COULD FORGIVE HIM WEAKNESS, BUT NEVER THE COWARDICE HE HAS JUST SHOWN!
I SHALL INCREASE THE INTENSITY OF THE DEMONS' ATTACK... INCREASE IT UNTIL MY ENEMIES ARE SO FEARFUL THAT THEY PLEAD FOR AN END TO IT!
MEANWHILE, THE MYSTIC MASTER'S ECTOPLASMIC FORM REENTERS THE SANCTUM!
KALUU'S BARRIER IS IMPENETRABLE, MASTER! BUT, NOW THAT HIS DEMONS ARE NOW ALL WITHIN...
EXACTLY! NOW WE ARE ABLE TO STRIKE BACK! WE HAVE WEAPONS AS YET UNTRIED! THE TIME FOR WAITING IS PAST... NOW WE MUST FIGHT WITH ALL OUR SKILL, ALL OUR STRENGTH!
YOUR CLOAK... THE ENCHANTED CLOAK OF LEVITATION... MAY SERVE US AGAINST THESE CREATURES!
ONCE AGAIN MERGING HIS SPIRIT FORM WITH HIS PHYSICAL BODY, DR. STRANGE REMOVES HIS CLOAK AND HURLS IT AT THE DEMONS...
IF WE CAN BIND SOME OF THE MINDLESS ONES IN THE GARMENT, PERHAPS THE REST WILL FALL BEFORE OUR SPELLS!
BUT, EVEN AS THE MAGIC CLOTH WRAPS ITSELF AROUND AND AROUND, THE FORMS SEEM TO MELT AWAY FROM ITS FOLDS!
THEIR BODIES ARE OF A SUBSTANCE SO ALIEN TO US THAT EARTH LANGUAGE HAS NO WORDS TO DESCRIBE IT! THEY CAN NOT BE CONTAINED!
OUR FAITH... OUR COURAGE MUST NOT FALTER. AH, I SEE YOU ALREADY MAKE USE OF YOUR AMULET! SO POWERFUL ARE ITS RAYS THAT THEY MAY HOLD OUR ATTACKERS AT BAY!
AYE, MASTER! MANY TIMES IN THE PAST HAVE I OWED MY LIFE TO THE SORCERER'S JEWEL!
LET THE AMULET OF AGAMOTTO BATHE THE CREATURES OF DARKNESS IN LIGHT! BY THE SHADES OF THE SERAPHIM DO I SO COMMAND!
7.

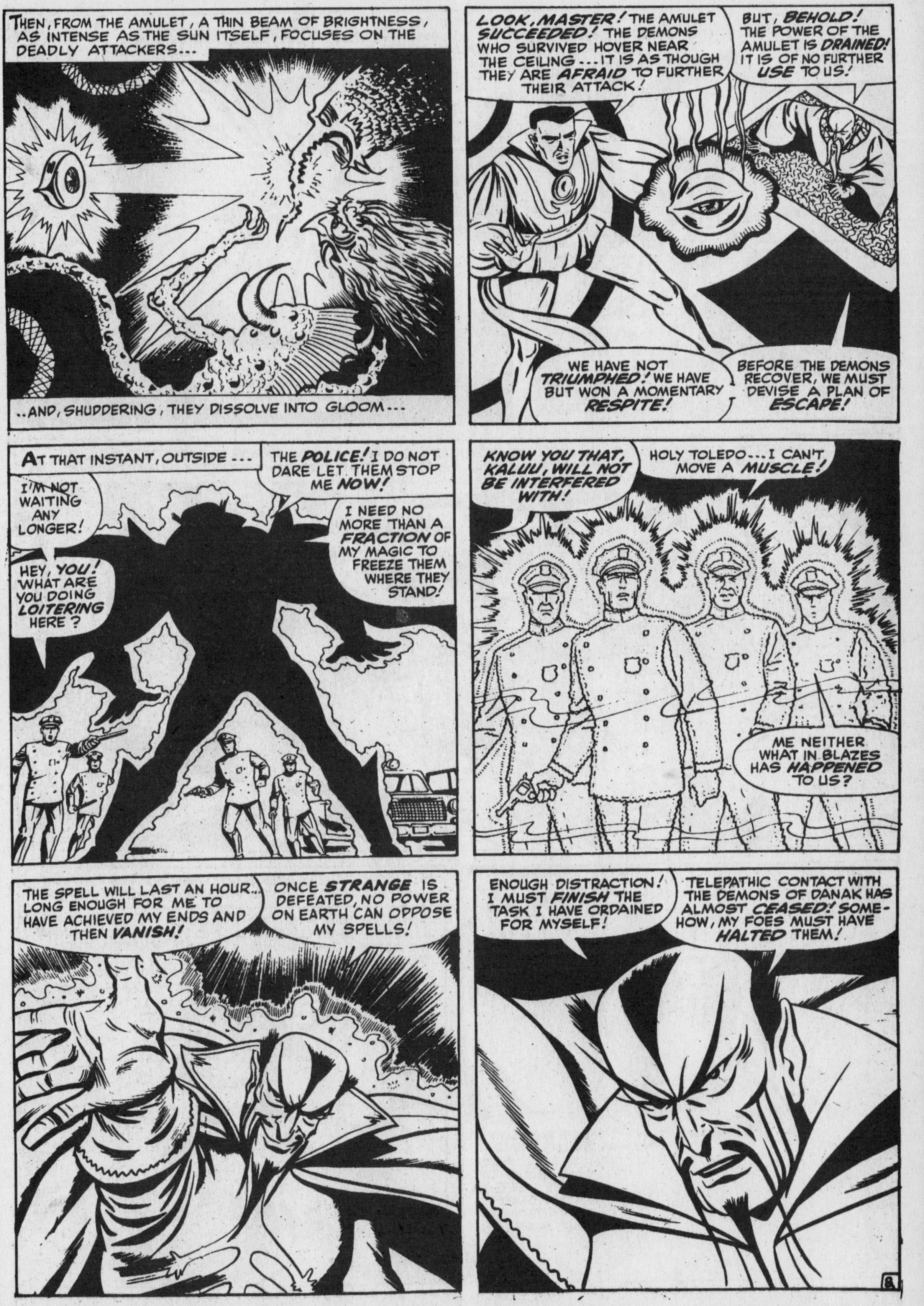
THEN, FROM THE AMULET, A THIN BEAM OF BRIGHTNESS, AS INTENSE AS THE SUN ITSELF, FOCUSES ON THE DEADLY ATTACKERS...
..AND, SHUDDERING, THEY DISSOLVE INTO GLOOM...
LOOK, MASTER! THE AMULET SUCCEEDED! THE DEMONS WHO SURVIVED HOVER NEAR THE CEILING... IT IS AS THOUGH THEY ARE AFRAID TO FURTHER THEIR ATTACK!
BUT, BEHOLD! THE POWER OF THE AMULET IS DRAINED! IT IS OF NO FURTHER USE TO US!
WE HAVE NOT TRIUMPHED! WE HAVE BUT WON A MOMENTARY RESPITE!
BEFORE THE DEMONS RECOVER, WE MUST DEVISE A PLAN OF ESCAPE!
AT THAT INSTANT, OUTSIDE ...
I'M NOT WAITING ANY LONGER!
HEY, YOU! WHAT ARE YOU DOING LOITERING HERE?
THE POLICE! I DO NOT DARE LET THEM STOP ME NOW!
I NEED NO MORE THAN A FRACTION OF MY MAGIC TO FREEZE THEM WHERE THEY STAND!
KNOW YOU THAT, KALUU, WILL NOT BE INTERFERED WITH!
HOLY TOLEDO...I CAN'T MOVE A MUSCLE!
ME NEITHER WHAT IN BLAZES HAS HAPPENED TO US?
THE SPELL WILL LAST AN HOUR... LONG ENOUGH FOR ME TO HAVE ACHIEVED MY ENDS AND THEN VANISH!
ONCE STRANGE IS DEFEATED, NO POWER ON EARTH CAN OPPOSE MY SPELLS!
ENOUGH DISTRACTION! I MUST FINISH THE TASK I HAVE ORDAINED FOR MYSELF!
TELEPATHIC CONTACT WITH THE DEMONS OF DANAK HAS ALMOST CEASED! SOMEHOW, MY FOES MUST HAVE HALTED THEM!
8

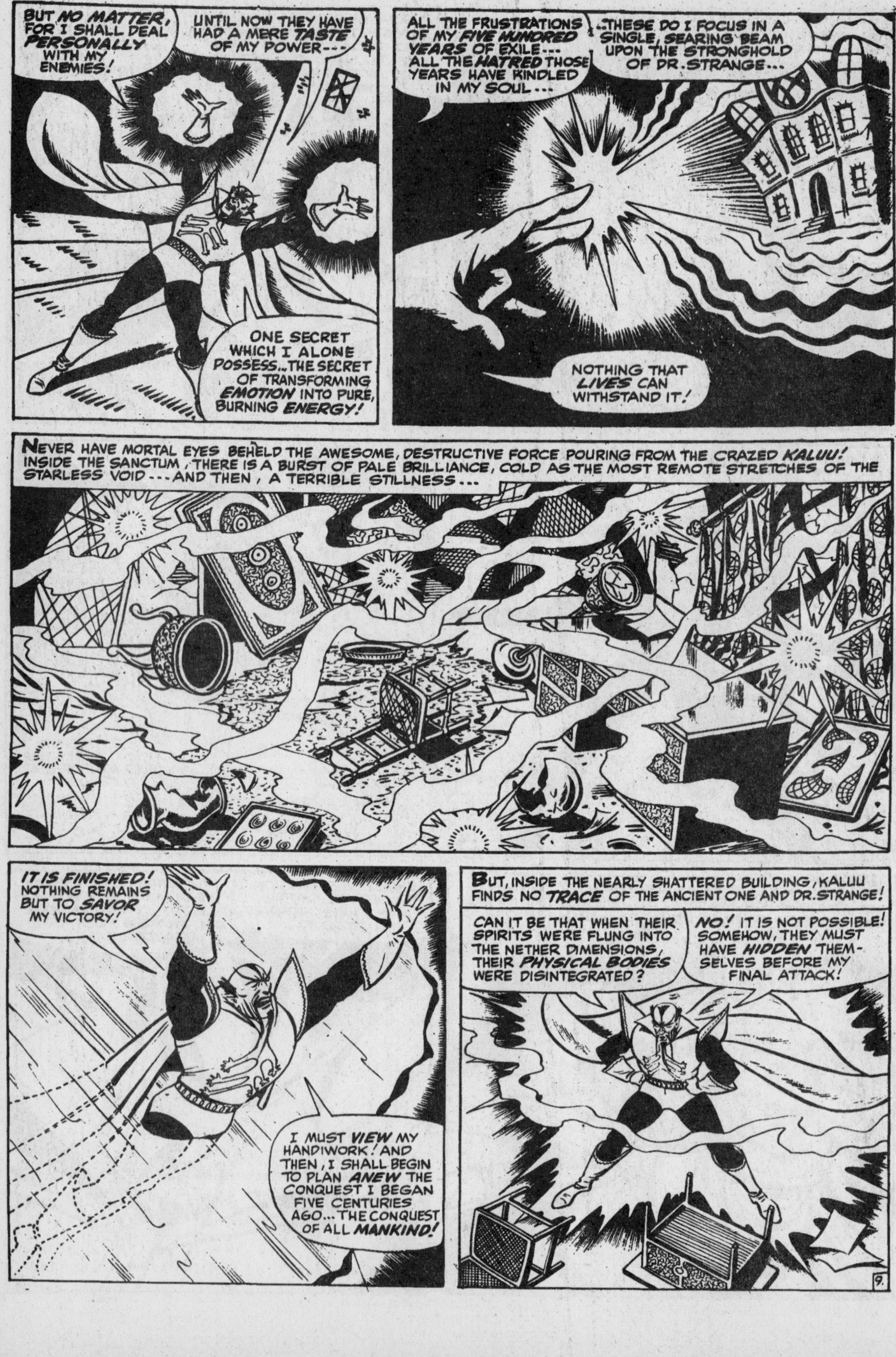
BUT NO MATTER, FOR I SHALL DEAL PERSONALLY WITH MY ENEMIES!
UNTIL NOW THEY HAVE HAD A MERE TASTE OF MY POWER---
ONE SECRET WHICH I ALONE POSSESS...THE SECRET OF TRANSFORMING EMOTION INTO PURE, BURNING ENERGY!
ALL THE FRUSTRATIONS OF MY FIVE HUNDRED YEARS OF EXILE--- ALL THE HATRED THOSE YEARS HAVE KINDLED IN MY SOUL...
...THESE DO I FOCUS IN A SINGLE, SEARING BEAM UPON THE STRONGHOLD OF DR. STRANGE...
NOTHING THAT LIVES CAN WITHSTAND IT!
NEVER HAVE MORTAL EYES BEHELD THE AWESOME, DESTRUCTIVE FORCE POURING FROM THE CRAZED KALUU! INSIDE THE SANCTUM, THERE IS A BURST OF PALE BRILLIANCE, COLD AS THE MOST REMOTE STRETCHES OF THE STARLESS VOID---AND THEN, A TERRIBLE STILLNESS...
IT IS FINISHED! NOTHING REMAINS BUT TO SAVOR MY VICTORY!
I MUST VIEW MY HANDIWORK! AND THEN, I SHALL BEGIN TO PLAN ANEW THE CONQUEST I BEGAN FIVE CENTURIES AGO... THE CONQUEST OF ALL MANKIND!
BUT, INSIDE THE NEARLY SHATTERED BUILDING, KALUU FINDS NO TRACE OF THE ANCIENT ONE AND DR. STRANGE!
CAN IT BE THAT WHEN THEIR SPIRITS WERE FLUNG INTO THE NETHER DIMENSIONS, THEIR PHYSICAL BODIES WERE DISINTEGRATED?
NO! IT IS NOT POSSIBLE! SOMEHOW, THEY MUST HAVE HIDDEN THEMSELVES BEFORE MY FINAL ATTACK!
9.

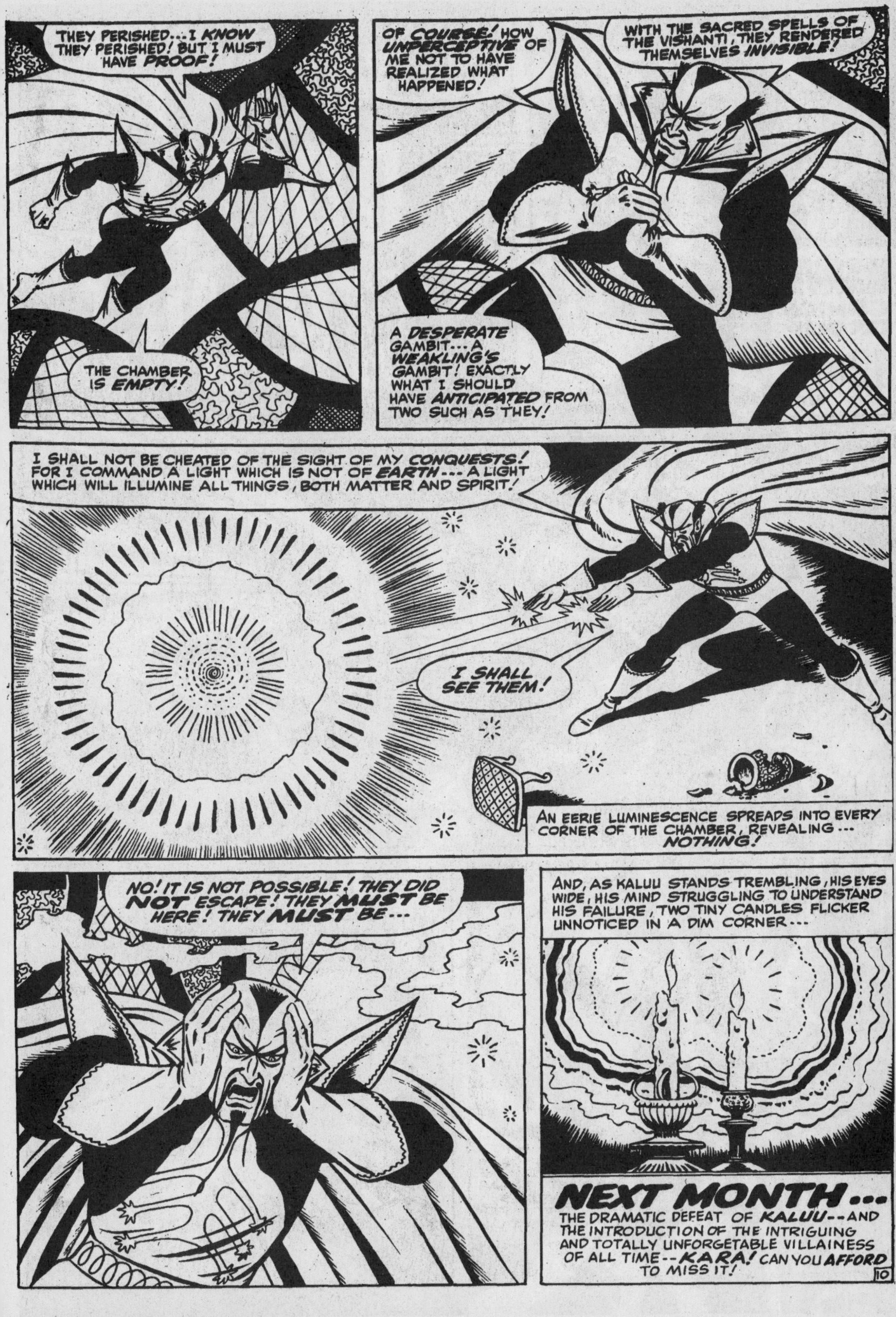
THEY PERISHED... I KNOW THEY PERISHED! BUT I MUST HAVE PROOF!
THE CHAMBER IS EMPTY!
OF COURSE! HOW UNPERCEPTIVE OF ME NOT TO HAVE REALIZED WHAT HAPPENED!
WITH THE SACRED SPELLS OF THE VISHANTI, THEY RENDERED THEMSELVES INVISIBLE!
A DESPERATE GAMBIT... A WEAKLING'S GAMBIT! EXACTLY WHAT I SHOULD HAVE ANTICIPATED FROM TWO SUCH AS THEY!
I SHALL NOT BE CHEATED OF THE SIGHT OF MY CONQUESTS! FOR I COMMAND A LIGHT WHICH IS NOT OF EARTH--- A LIGHT WHICH WILL ILLUMINE ALL THINGS, BOTH MATTER AND SPIRIT!
I SHALL SEE THEM!
AN EERIE LUMINESCENCE SPREADS INTO EVERY CORNER OF THE CHAMBER, REVEALING --- NOTHING!
NO! IT IS NOT POSSIBLE! THEY DID NOT ESCAPE! THEY MUST BE HERE! THEY MUST BE...
AND, AS KALUU STANDS TREMBLING, HIS EYES WIDE, HIS MIND STRUGGLING TO UNDERSTAND HIS FAILURE, TWO TINY CANDLES FLICKER UNNOTICED IN A DIM CORNER ---
NEXT MONTH...
THE DRAMATIC DEFEAT OF KALUU--AND THE INTRODUCTION OF THE INTRIGUING AND TOTALLY UNFORGETABLE VILLAINESS OF ALL TIME--KARA! CAN YOU AFFORD TO MISS IT!
10

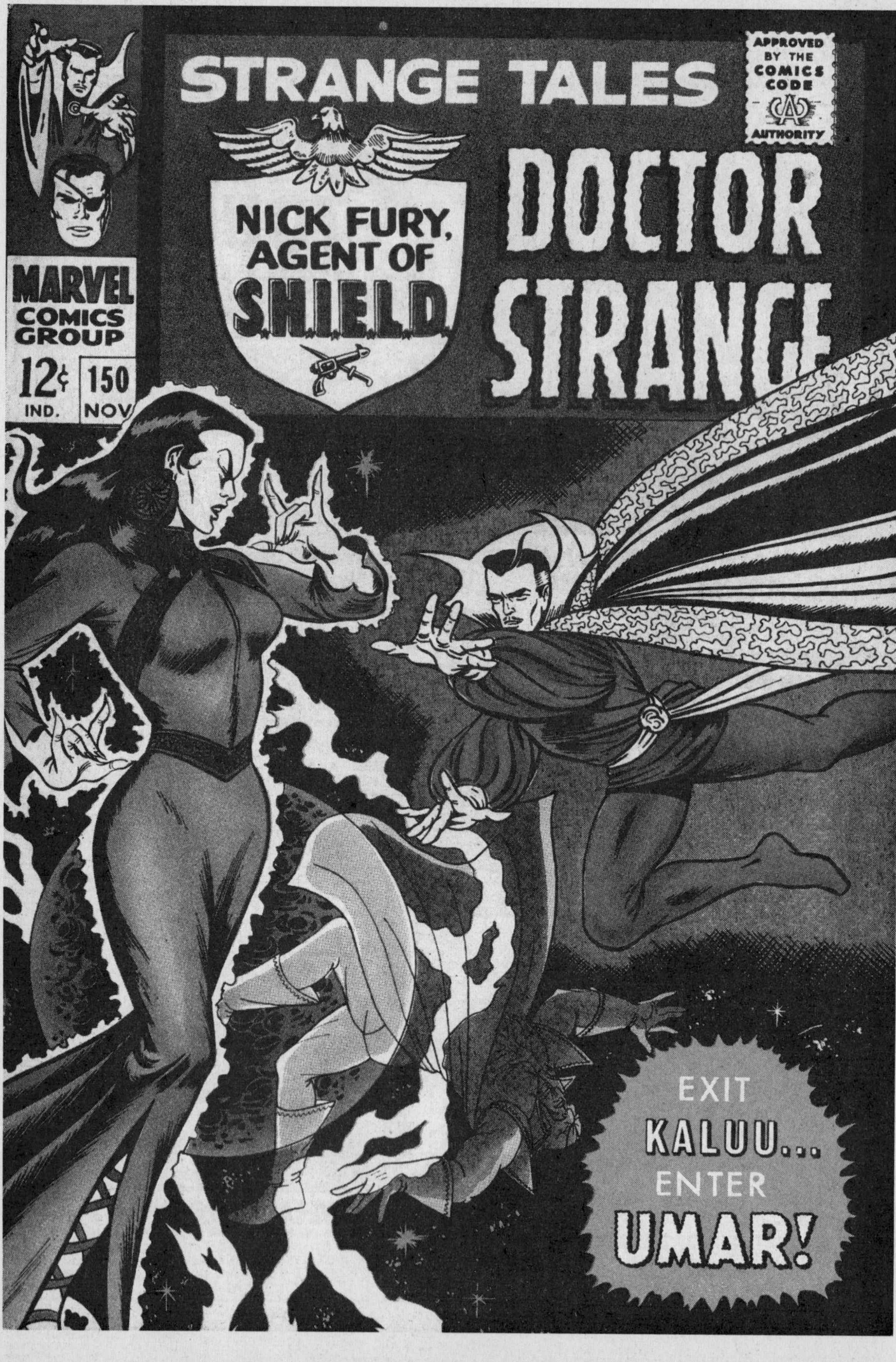
STRANGE TALES
APPROVED BY THE COMICS CODE AUTHORITY
NICK FURY, AGENT OF S.H.I.E.L.D.
DOCTOR STRANGE
MARVEL COMICS GROUP
12¢ IND.
150 NOV
EXIT KALUU... ENTER UMAR!

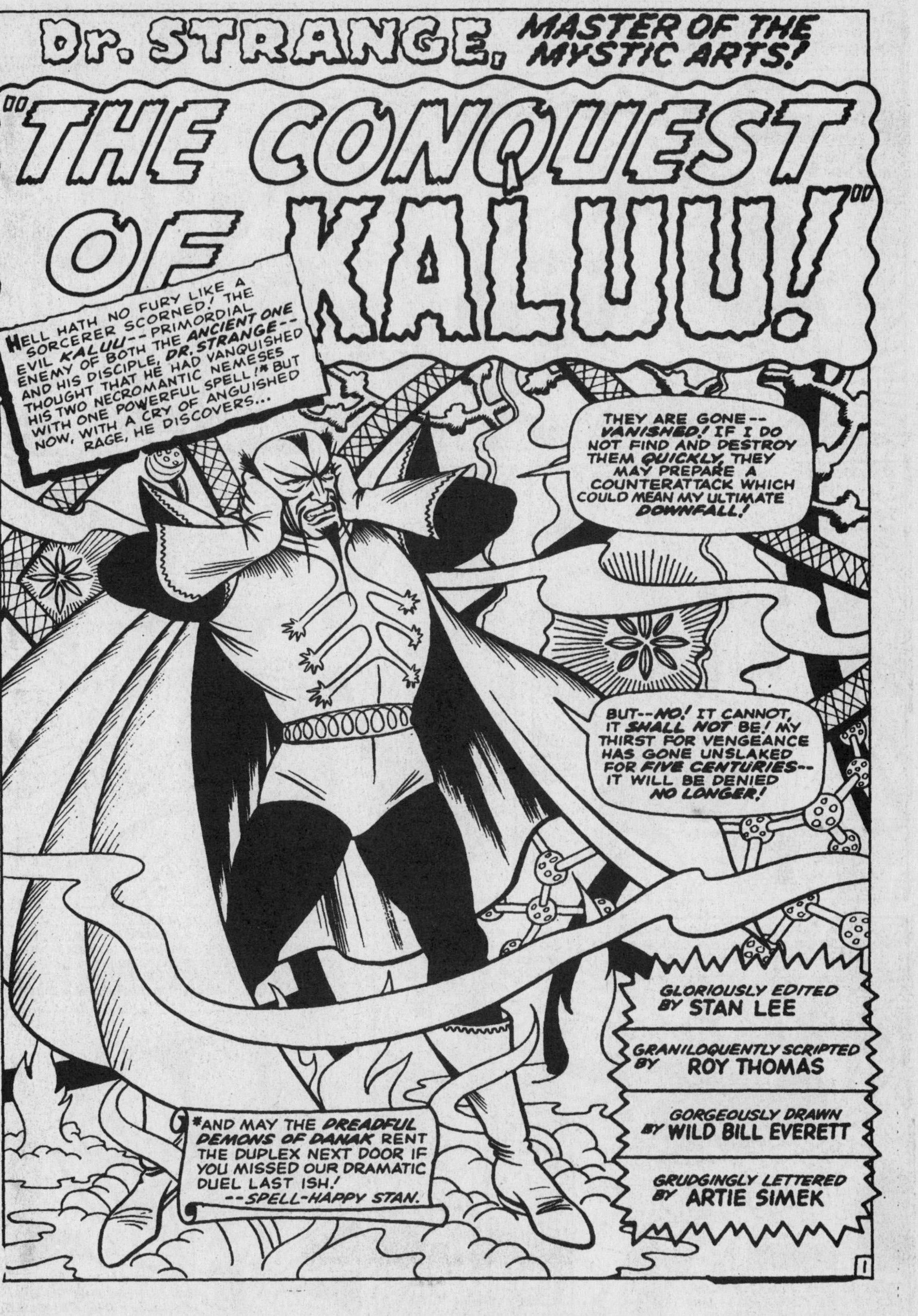

Dr. STRANGE, MASTER OF THE MYSTIC ARTS!
"THE CONQUEST OF KALUU!"
HELL HATH NO FURY LIKE A SORCERER SCORNED! THE EVIL KALUU--PRIMORDIAL ENEMY OF BOTH THE ANCIENT ONE AND HIS DISCIPLE, DR. STRANGE--THOUGHT THAT HE HAD VANQUISHED HIS TWO NECROMANTIC NEMESES WITH ONE POWERFUL SPELL!* BUT NOW, WITH A CRY OF ANGUISHED RAGE, HE DISCOVERS...
THEY ARE GONE--VANISHED! IF I DO NOT FIND AND DESTROY THEM QUICKLY, THEY MAY PREPARE A COUNTERATTACK WHICH COULD MEAN MY ULTIMATE DOWNFALL!
BUT--NO! IT CANNOT, IT SHALL NOT BE! MY THIRST FOR VENGEANCE HAS GONE UNSLAKED FOR FIVE CENTURIES--IT WILL BE DENIED NO LONGER!
GLORIOUSLY EDITED BY STAN LEE
GRANILOQUENTLY SCRIPTED BY ROY THOMAS
GORGEOUSLY DRAWN BY WILD BILL EVERETT
GRUDGINGLY LETTERED BY ARTIE SIMEK
*AND MAY THE DREADFUL DEMONS OF DANAK RENT THE DUPLEX NEXT DOOR IF YOU MISSED OUR DRAMATIC DUEL LAST ISH! --SPELL-HAPPY STAN.
1

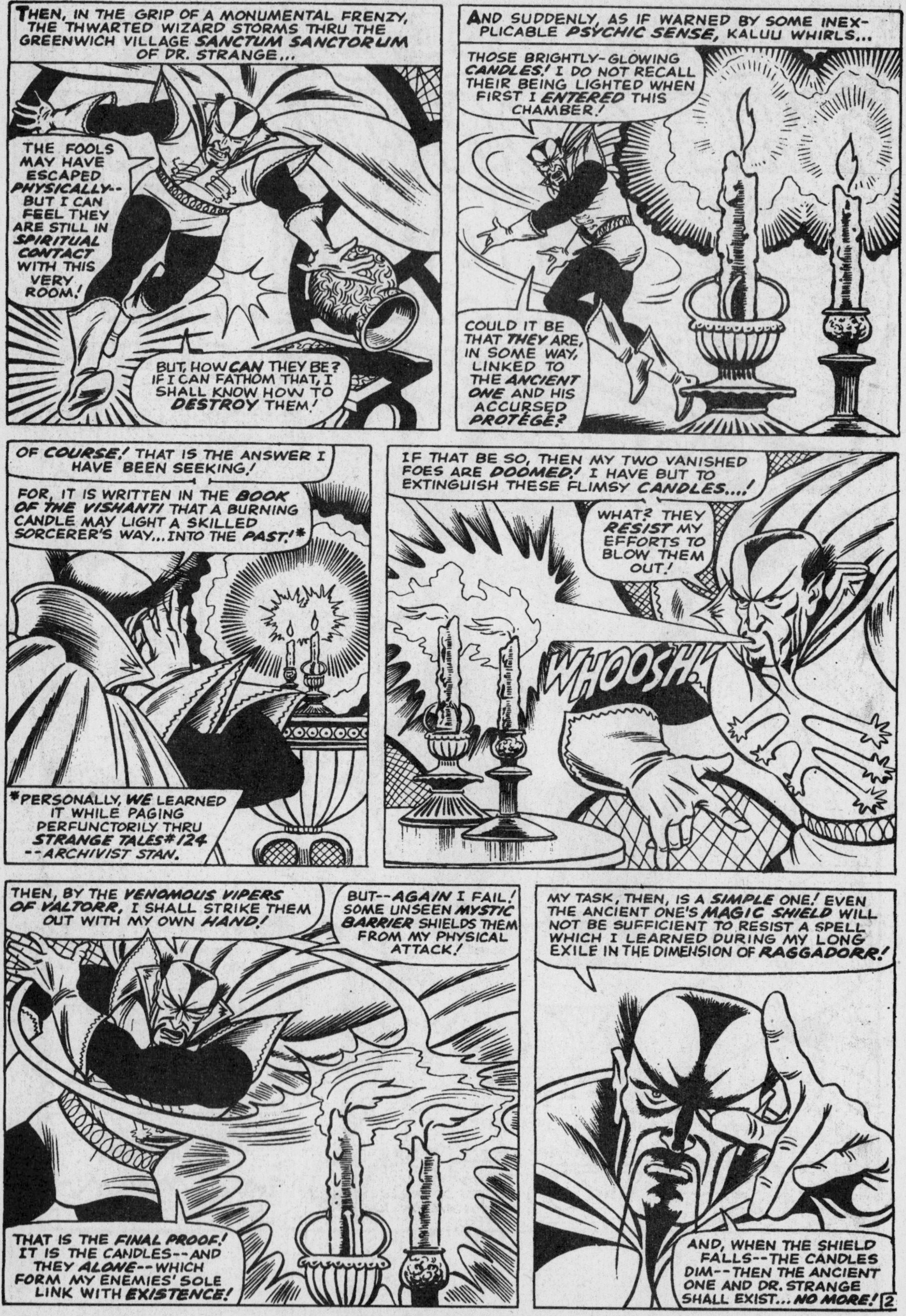
THEN, IN THE GRIP OF A MONUMENTAL FRENZY, THE THWARTED WIZARD STORMS THRU THE GREENWICH VILLAGE SANCTUM SANCTORUM OF DR. STRANGE...
THE FOOLS MAY HAVE ESCAPED PHYSICALLY-- BUT I CAN FEEL THEY ARE STILL IN SPIRITUAL CONTACT WITH THIS VERY ROOM!
BUT, HOW CAN THEY BE? IF I CAN FATHOM THAT, I SHALL KNOW HOW TO DESTROY THEM!
AND SUDDENLY, AS IF WARNED BY SOME INEXPLICABLE PSYCHIC SENSE, KALUU WHIRLS...
THOSE BRIGHTLY-GLOWING CANDLES! I DO NOT RECALL THEIR BEING LIGHTED WHEN FIRST I ENTERED THIS CHAMBER!
COULD IT BE THAT THEY ARE, IN SOME WAY, LINKED TO THE ANCIENT ONE AND HIS ACCURSED PROTÉGÉ?
OF COURSE! THAT IS THE ANSWER I HAVE BEEN SEEKING!
FOR, IT IS WRITTEN IN THE BOOK OF THE VISHANTI THAT A BURNING CANDLE MAY LIGHT A SKILLED SORCERER'S WAY...INTO THE PAST!*
*PERSONALLY, WE LEARNED IT WHILE PAGING PERFUNCTORILY THRU STRANGE TALES #124 --ARCHIVIST STAN.
IF THAT BE SO, THEN MY TWO VANISHED FOES ARE DOOMED! I HAVE BUT TO EXTINGUISH THESE FLIMSY CANDLES....!
WHAT? THEY RESIST MY EFFORTS TO BLOW THEM OUT!
WHOOSH!
THEN, BY THE VENOMOUS VIPERS OF VALTORR, I SHALL STRIKE THEM OUT WITH MY OWN HAND!
BUT--AGAIN I FAIL! SOME UNSEEN MYSTIC BARRIER SHIELDS THEM FROM MY PHYSICAL ATTACK!
THAT IS THE FINAL PROOF! IT IS THE CANDLES--AND THEY ALONE--WHICH FORM MY ENEMIES' SOLE LINK WITH EXISTENCE!
MY TASK, THEN, IS A SIMPLE ONE! EVEN THE ANCIENT ONE'S MAGIC SHIELD WILL NOT BE SUFFICIENT TO RESIST A SPELL WHICH I LEARNED DURING MY LONG EXILE IN THE DIMENSION OF RAGGADORR!
AND, WHEN THE SHIELD FALLS--THE CANDLES DIM--THEN THE ANCIENT ONE AND DR. STRANGE SHALL EXIST... NO MORE!
2

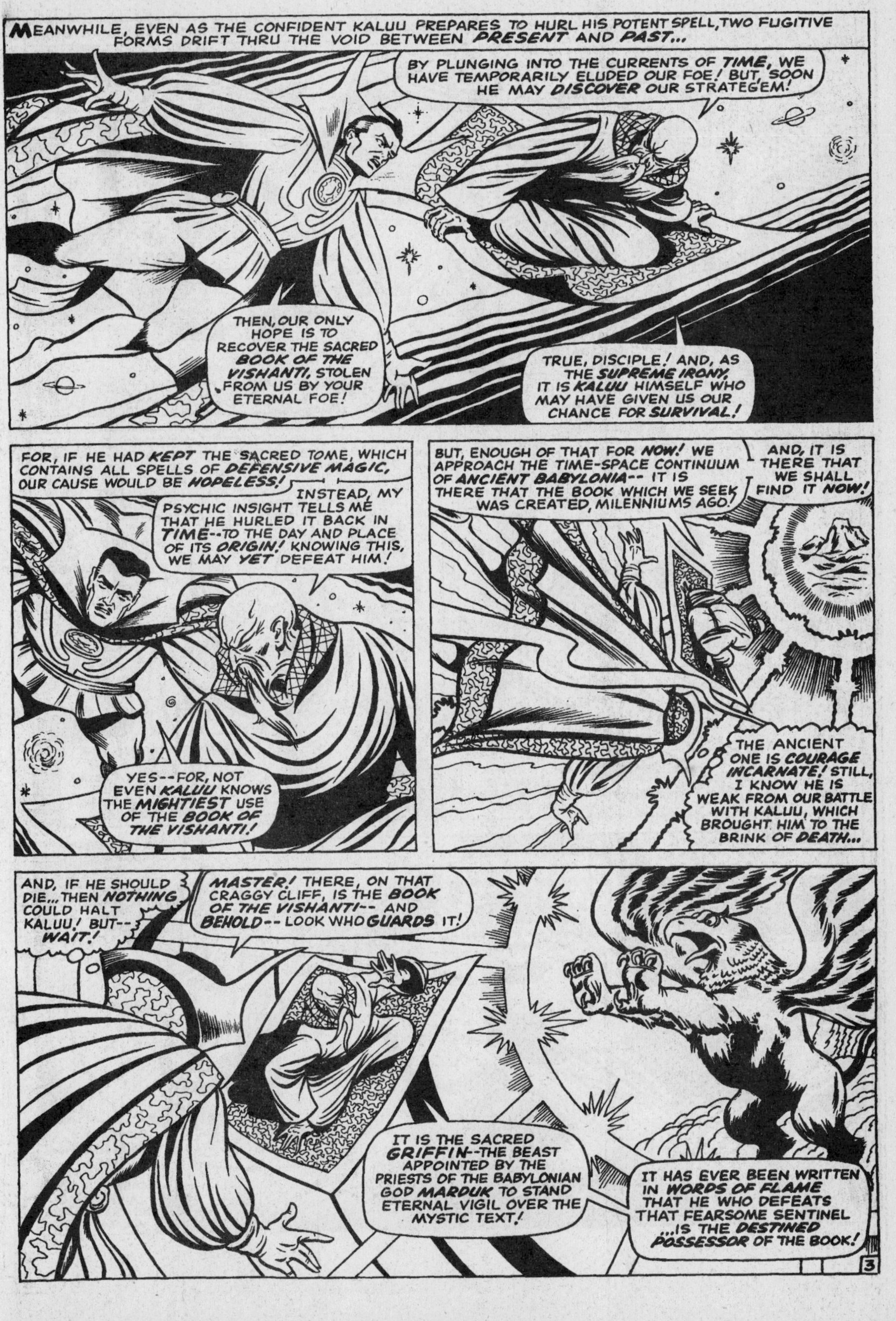
MEANWHILE, EVEN AS THE CONFIDENT KALUU PREPARES TO HURL HIS POTENT SPELL, TWO FUGITIVE FORMS DRIFT THRU THE VOID BETWEEN PRESENT AND PAST...
BY PLUNGING INTO THE CURRENTS OF TIME, WE HAVE TEMPORARILY ELUDED OUR FOE! BUT, SOON HE MAY DISCOVER OUR STRATEGEM!
THEN, OUR ONLY HOPE IS TO RECOVER THE SACRED BOOK OF THE VISHANTI, STOLEN FROM US BY YOUR ETERNAL FOE!
TRUE, DISCIPLE! AND, AS THE SUPREME IRONY, IT IS KALUU HIMSELF WHO MAY HAVE GIVEN US OUR CHANCE FOR SURVIVAL!
FOR, IF HE HAD KEPT THE SACRED TOME, WHICH CONTAINS ALL SPELLS OF DEFENSIVE MAGIC, OUR CAUSE WOULD BE HOPELESS!
INSTEAD, MY PSYCHIC INSIGHT TELLS ME THAT HE HURLED IT BACK IN TIME--TO THE DAY AND PLACE OF ITS ORIGIN! KNOWING THIS, WE MAY YET DEFEAT HIM!
YES--FOR, NOT EVEN KALUU KNOWS THE MIGHTIEST USE OF THE BOOK OF THE VISHANTI!
BUT, ENOUGH OF THAT FOR NOW! WE APPROACH THE TIME-SPACE CONTINUUM OF ANCIENT BABYLONIA-- IT IS THERE THAT THE BOOK WHICH WE SEEK WAS CREATED, MILENNIUMS AGO!
AND, IT IS THERE THAT WE SHALL FIND IT NOW!
THE ANCIENT ONE IS COURAGE INCARNATE! STILL, I KNOW HE IS WEAK FROM OUR BATTLE WITH KALUU, WHICH BROUGHT HIM TO THE BRINK OF DEATH...
AND, IF HE SHOULD DIE... THEN NOTHING COULD HALT KALUU! BUT-- WAIT!
MASTER! THERE, ON THAT CRAGGY CLIFF, IS THE BOOK OF THE VISHANTI-- AND BEHOLD-- LOOK WHO GUARDS IT!
IT IS THE SACRED GRIFFIN--THE BEAST APPOINTED BY THE PRIESTS OF THE BABYLONIAN GOD MARDUK TO STAND ETERNAL VIGIL OVER THE MYSTIC TEXT!
IT HAS EVER BEEN WRITTEN IN WORDS OF FLAME THAT HE WHO DEFEATS THAT FEARSOME SENTINEL ...IS THE DESTINED POSSESSOR OF THE BOOK!
3

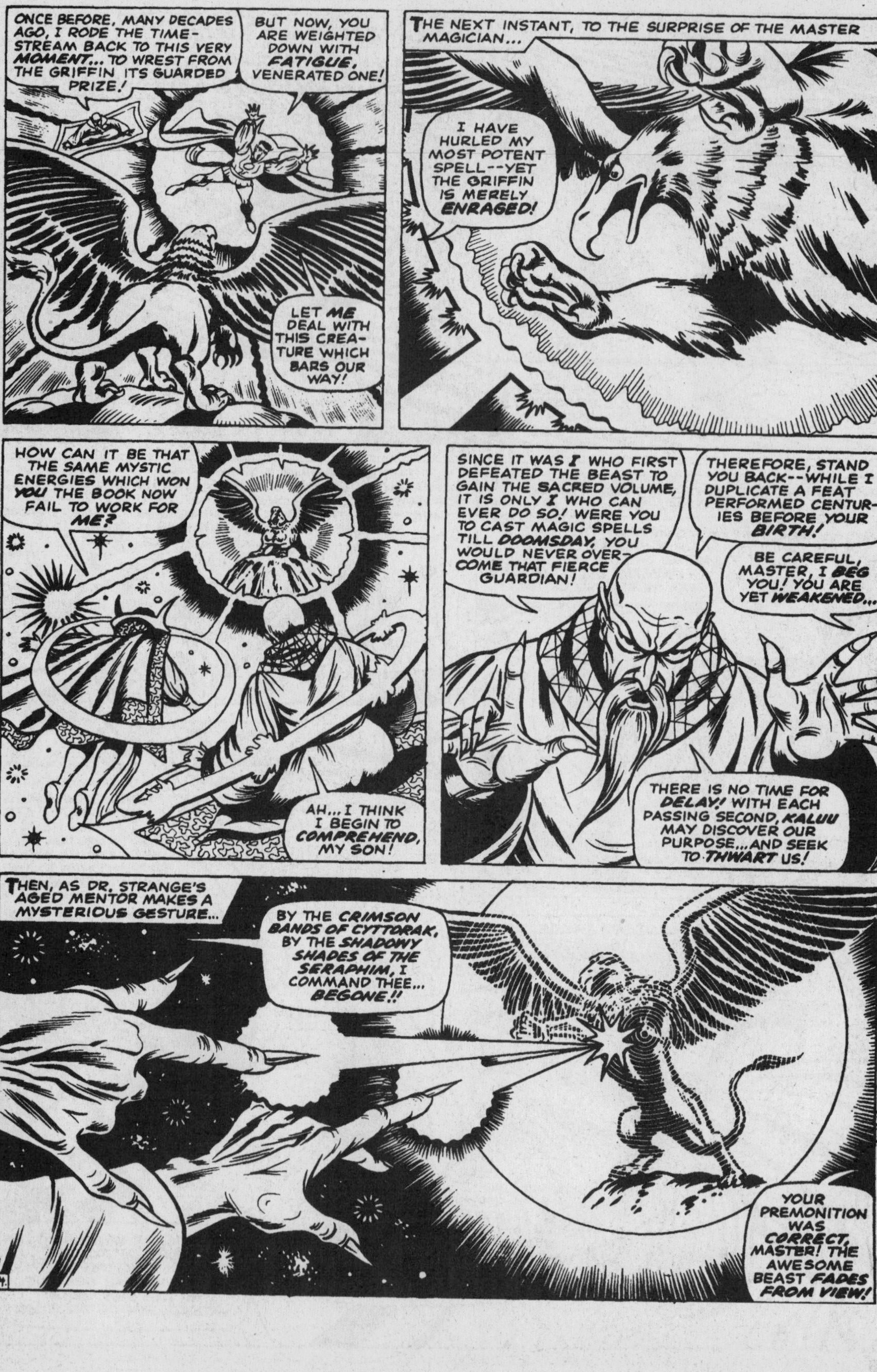

ONCE BEFORE, MANY DECADES AGO, I RODE THE TIME-STREAM BACK TO THIS VERY MOMENT... TO WREST FROM THE GRIFFIN ITS GUARDED PRIZE!
BUT NOW, YOU ARE WEIGHTED DOWN WITH FATIGUE, VENERATED ONE!
LET ME DEAL WITH THIS CREATURE WHICH BARS OUR WAY!
THE NEXT INSTANT, TO THE SURPRISE OF THE MASTER MAGICIAN...
I HAVE HURLED MY MOST POTENT SPELL--YET THE GRIFFIN IS MERELY ENRAGED!
HOW CAN IT BE THAT THE SAME MYSTIC ENERGIES WHICH WON YOU THE BOOK NOW FAIL TO WORK FOR ME?
AH... I THINK I BEGIN TO COMPREHEND, MY SON!
SINCE IT WAS I WHO FIRST DEFEATED THE BEAST TO GAIN THE SACRED VOLUME, IT IS ONLY I WHO CAN EVER DO SO! WERE YOU TO CAST MAGIC SPELLS TILL DOOMSDAY, YOU WOULD NEVER OVER-COME THAT FIERCE GUARDIAN!
THEREFORE, STAND YOU BACK--WHILE I DUPLICATE A FEAT PERFORMED CENTURIES BEFORE YOUR BIRTH!
BE CAREFUL, MASTER, I BEG YOU! YOU ARE YET WEAKENED...
THERE IS NO TIME FOR DELAY! WITH EACH PASSING SECOND, KALUU MAY DISCOVER OUR PURPOSE... AND SEEK TO THWART US!
THEN, AS DR. STRANGE'S AGED MENTOR MAKES A MYSTERIOUS GESTURE...
BY THE CRIMSON BANDS OF CYTTORAK, BY THE SHADOWY SHADES OF THE SERAPHIM, I COMMAND THEE... BEGONE!!
YOUR PREMONITION WAS CORRECT, MASTER! THE AWESOME BEAST FADES FROM VIEW!
4.

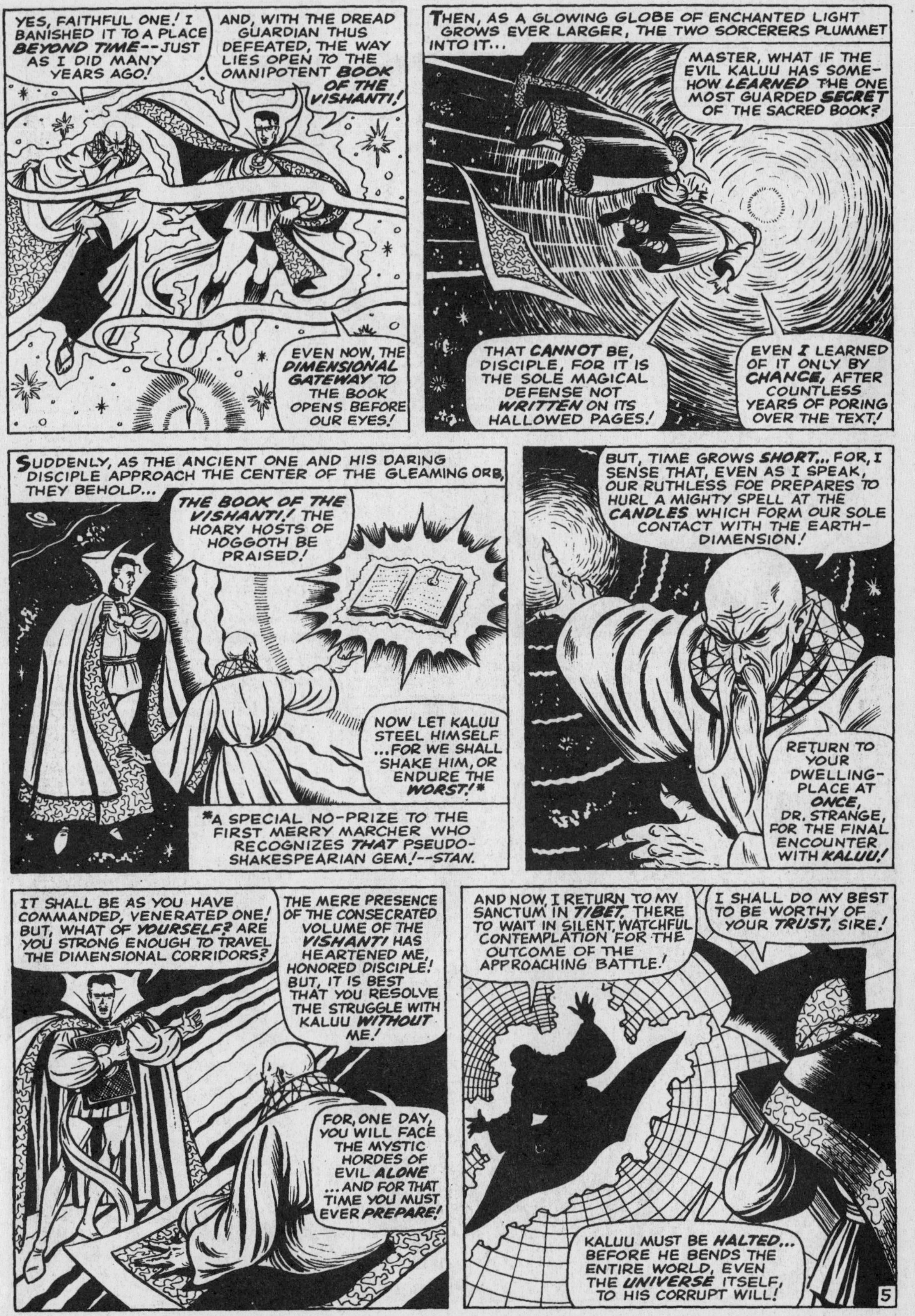
YES, FAITHFUL ONE! I BANISHED IT TO A PLACE BEYOND TIME--JUST AS I DID MANY YEARS AGO!
AND, WITH THE DREAD GUARDIAN THUS DEFEATED, THE WAY LIES OPEN TO THE OMNIPOTENT BOOK OF THE VISHANTI!
EVEN NOW, THE DIMENSIONAL GATEWAY TO THE BOOK OPENS BEFORE OUR EYES!
THEN, AS A GLOWING GLOBE OF ENCHANTED LIGHT GROWS EVER LARGER, THE TWO SORCERERS PLUMMET INTO IT...
MASTER, WHAT IF THE EVIL KALUU HAS SOME-HOW LEARNED THE ONE MOST GUARDED SECRET OF THE SACRED BOOK?
THAT CANNOT BE, DISCIPLE, FOR IT IS THE SOLE MAGICAL DEFENSE NOT WRITTEN ON ITS HALLOWED PAGES!
EVEN I LEARNED OF IT ONLY BY CHANCE, AFTER COUNTLESS YEARS OF PORING OVER THE TEXT!
SUDDENLY, AS THE ANCIENT ONE AND HIS DARING DISCIPLE APPROACH THE CENTER OF THE GLEAMING ORB, THEY BEHOLD...
THE BOOK OF THE VISHANTI! THE HOARY HOSTS OF HOGGOTH BE PRAISED!
NOW LET KALUU STEEL HIMSELF ...FOR WE SHALL SHAKE HIM, OR ENDURE THE WORST!*
*A SPECIAL NO-PRIZE TO THE FIRST MERRY MARCHER WHO RECOGNIZES THAT PSEUDO-SHAKESPEARIAN GEM!--STAN.
BUT, TIME GROWS SHORT... FOR, I SENSE THAT, EVEN AS I SPEAK, OUR RUTHLESS FOE PREPARES TO HURL A MIGHTY SPELL AT THE CANDLES WHICH FORM OUR SOLE CONTACT WITH THE EARTH-DIMENSION!
RETURN TO YOUR DWELLING-PLACE AT ONCE, DR. STRANGE, FOR THE FINAL ENCOUNTER WITH KALUU!
IT SHALL BE AS YOU HAVE COMMANDED, VENERATED ONE! BUT, WHAT OF YOURSELF? ARE YOU STRONG ENOUGH TO TRAVEL THE DIMENSIONAL CORRIDORS?
THE MERE PRESENCE OF THE CONSECRATED VOLUME OF THE VISHANTI HAS HEARTENED ME, HONORED DISCIPLE! BUT, IT IS BEST THAT YOU RESOLVE THE STRUGGLE WITH KALUU WITHOUT ME!
FOR, ONE DAY, YOU WILL FACE THE MYSTIC HORDES OF EVIL ALONE ...AND FOR THAT TIME YOU MUST EVER PREPARE!
AND NOW, I RETURN TO MY SANCTUM IN TIBET, THERE TO WAIT IN SILENT, WATCHFUL CONTEMPLATION FOR THE OUTCOME OF THE APPROACHING BATTLE!
I SHALL DO MY BEST TO BE WORTHY OF YOUR TRUST, SIRE!
KALUU MUST BE HALTED... BEFORE HE BENDS THE ENTIRE WORLD, EVEN THE UNIVERSE ITSELF, TO HIS CORRUPT WILL!
5

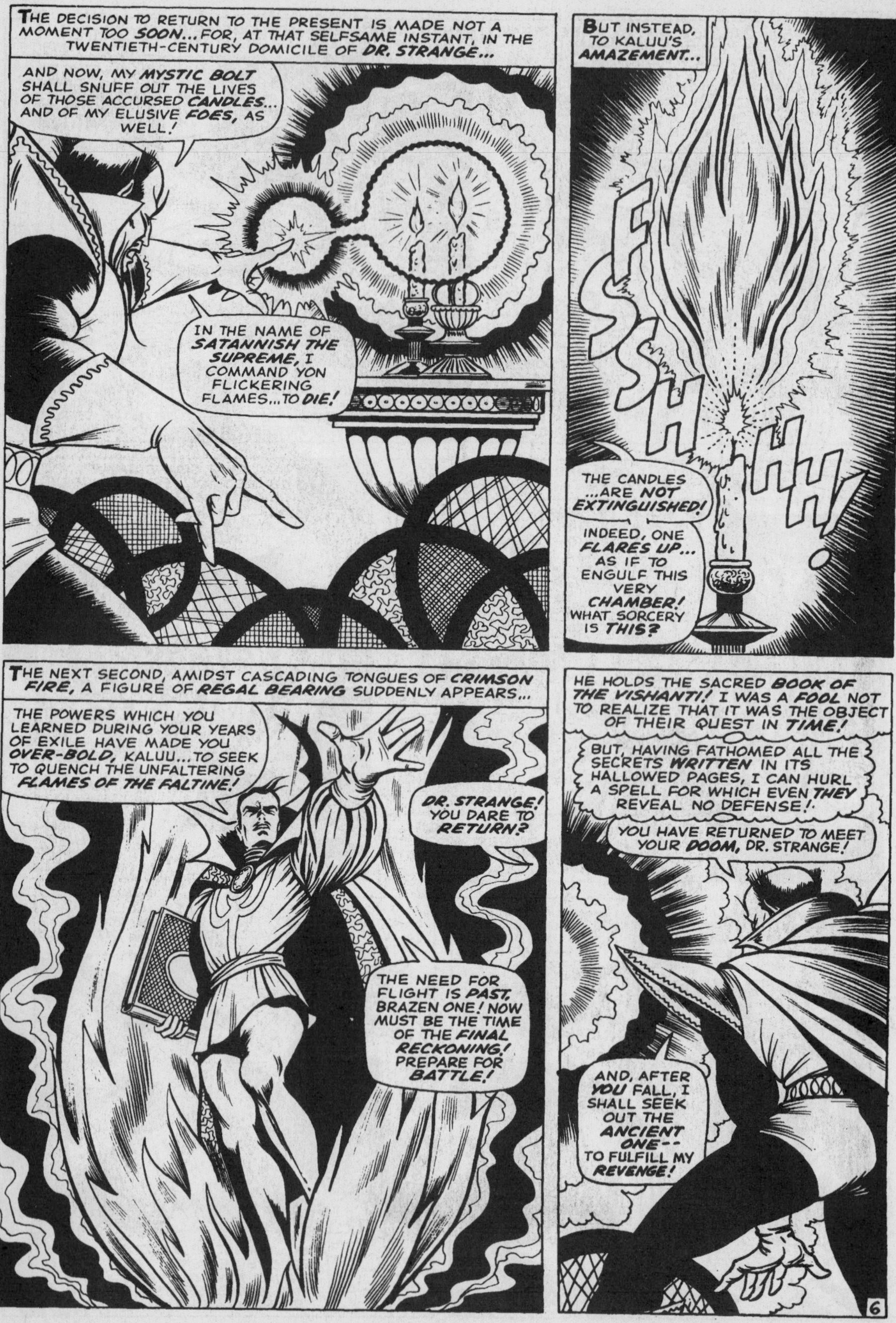
THE DECISION TO RETURN TO THE PRESENT IS MADE NOT A MOMENT TOO SOON... FOR, AT THAT SELFSAME INSTANT, IN THE TWENTIETH-CENTURY DOMICILE OF DR. STRANGE...
AND NOW, MY MYSTIC BOLT SHALL SNUFF OUT THE LIVES OF THOSE ACCURSED CANDLES... AND OF MY ELUSIVE FOES, AS WELL!
IN THE NAME OF SATANNISH THE SUPREME, I COMMAND YON FLICKERING FLAMES... TO DIE!
BUT INSTEAD, TO KALUU'S AMAZEMENT...
FSSHHHH!
THE CANDLES ...ARE NOT EXTINGUISHED!
INDEED, ONE FLARES UP... AS IF TO ENGULF THIS VERY CHAMBER! WHAT SORCERY IS THIS?
THE NEXT SECOND, AMIDST CASCADING TONGUES OF CRIMSON FIRE, A FIGURE OF REGAL BEARING SUDDENLY APPEARS...
THE POWERS WHICH YOU LEARNED DURING YOUR YEARS OF EXILE HAVE MADE YOU OVER-BOLD, KALUU... TO SEEK TO QUENCH THE UNFALTERING FLAMES OF THE FALTINE!
DR. STRANGE! YOU DARE TO RETURN?
THE NEED FOR FLIGHT IS PAST, BRAZEN ONE! NOW MUST BE THE TIME OF THE FINAL RECKONING! PREPARE FOR BATTLE!
HE HOLDS THE SACRED BOOK OF THE VISHANTI! I WAS A FOOL NOT TO REALIZE THAT IT WAS THE OBJECT OF THEIR QUEST IN TIME!
BUT, HAVING FATHOMED ALL THE SECRETS WRITTEN IN ITS HALLOWED PAGES, I CAN HURL A SPELL FOR WHICH EVEN THEY REVEAL NO DEFENSE!.
YOU HAVE RETURNED TO MEET YOUR DOOM, DR. STRANGE!
AND, AFTER YOU FALL, I SHALL SEEK OUT THE ANCIENT ONE-- TO FULFILL MY REVENGE!
6

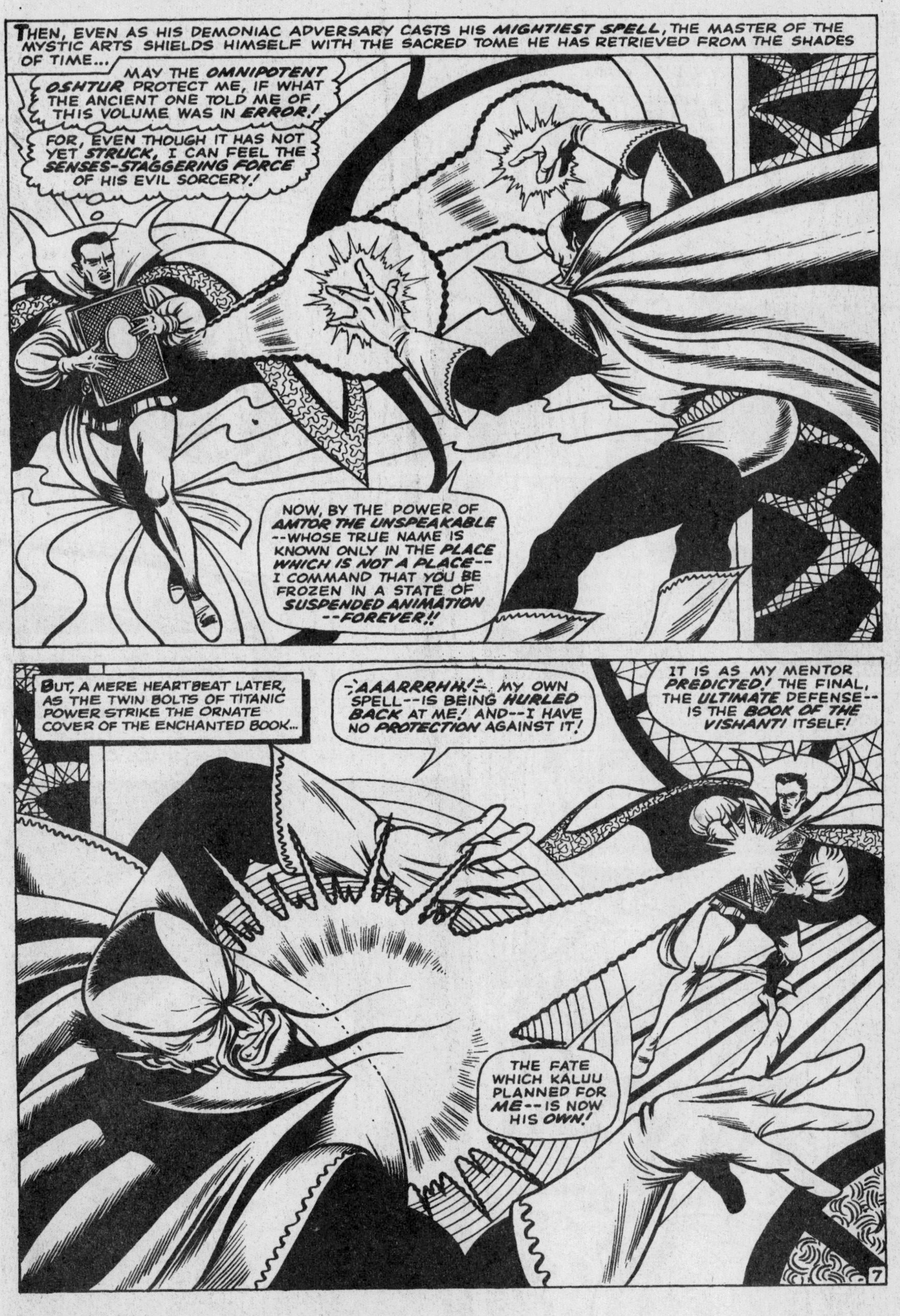
THEN, EVEN AS HIS DEMONIAC ADVERSARY CASTS HIS MIGHTIEST SPELL, THE MASTER OF THE MYSTIC ARTS SHIELDS HIMSELF WITH THE SACRED TOME HE HAS RETRIEVED FROM THE SHADES OF TIME...
MAY THE OMNIPOTENT OSHTUR PROTECT ME, IF WHAT THE ANCIENT ONE TOLD ME OF THIS VOLUME WAS IN ERROR!
FOR, EVEN THOUGH IT HAS NOT YET STRUCK, I CAN FEEL THE SENSES-STAGGERING FORCE OF HIS EVIL SORCERY!
NOW, BY THE POWER OF AMTOR THE UNSPEAKABLE --WHOSE TRUE NAME IS KNOWN ONLY IN THE PLACE WHICH IS NOT A PLACE-- I COMMAND THAT YOU BE FROZEN IN A STATE OF SUSPENDED ANIMATION --FOREVER!!
BUT, A MERE HEARTBEAT LATER, AS THE TWIN BOLTS OF TITANIC POWER STRIKE THE ORNATE COVER OF THE ENCHANTED BOOK...
AAARRRHH!-- MY OWN SPELL--IS BEING HURLED BACK AT ME! AND--I HAVE NO PROTECTION AGAINST IT!
IT IS AS MY MENTOR PREDICTED! THE FINAL, THE ULTIMATE DEFENSE-- IS THE BOOK OF THE VISHANTI ITSELF!
THE FATE WHICH KALUU PLANNED FOR ME--IS NOW HIS OWN!
7

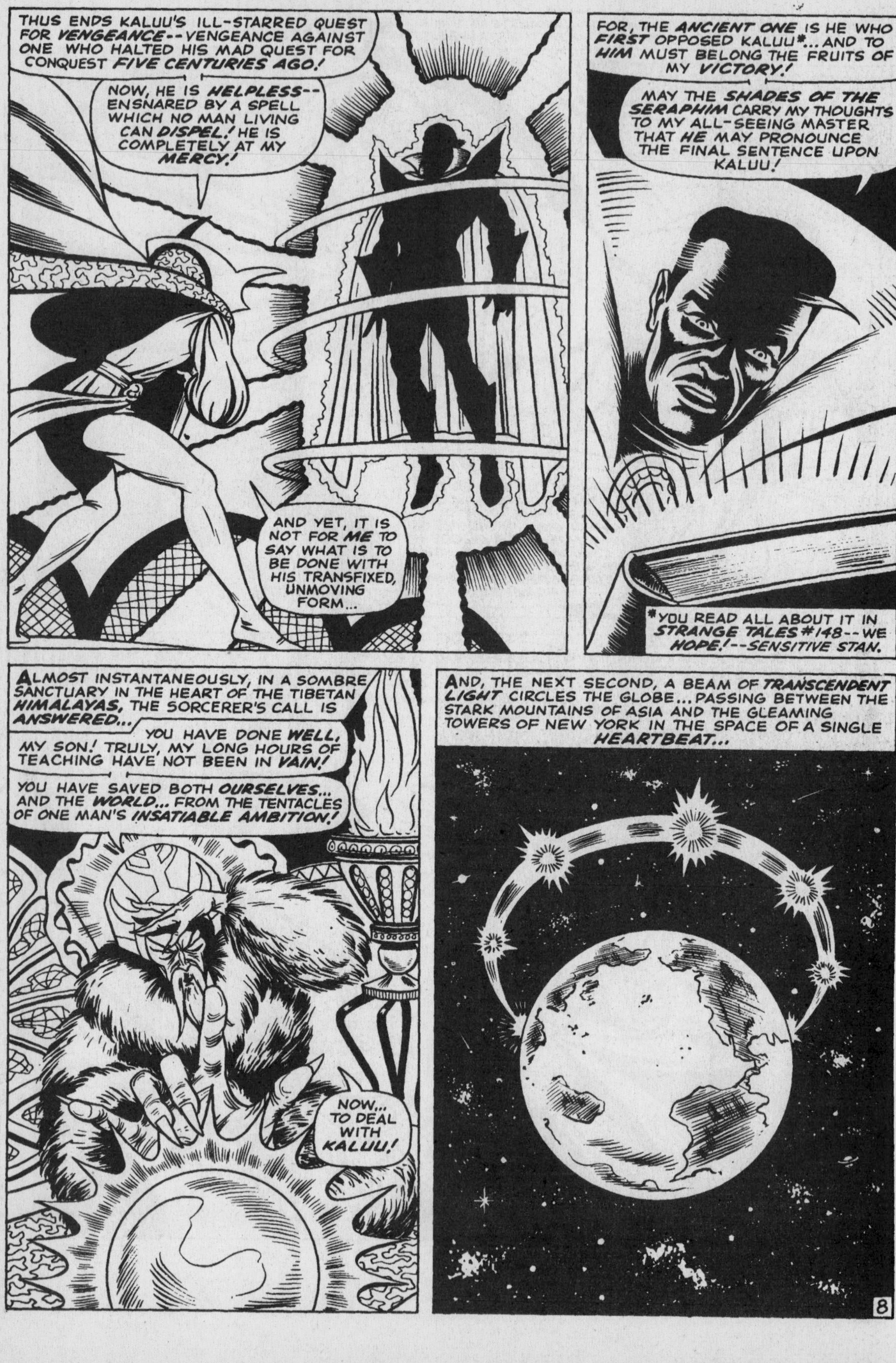
THUS ENDS KALUU'S ILL-STARRED QUEST FOR VENGEANCE--VENGEANCE AGAINST ONE WHO HALTED HIS MAD QUEST FOR CONQUEST FIVE CENTURIES AGO!
NOW, HE IS HELPLESS--ENSNARED BY A SPELL WHICH NO MAN LIVING CAN DISPEL! HE IS COMPLETELY AT MY MERCY!
AND YET, IT IS NOT FOR ME TO SAY WHAT IS TO BE DONE WITH HIS TRANSFIXED, UNMOVING FORM...
FOR, THE ANCIENT ONE IS HE WHO FIRST OPPOSED KALUU*... AND TO HIM MUST BELONG THE FRUITS OF MY VICTORY!
MAY THE SHADES OF THE SERAPHIM CARRY MY THOUGHTS TO MY ALL-SEEING MASTER THAT HE MAY PRONOUNCE THE FINAL SENTENCE UPON KALUU!
*YOU READ ALL ABOUT IT IN STRANGE TALES #148--WE HOPE!--SENSITIVE STAN.
ALMOST INSTANTANEOUSLY, IN A SOMBRE SANCTUARY IN THE HEART OF THE TIBETAN HIMALAYAS, THE SORCERER'S CALL IS ANSWERED...
YOU HAVE DONE WELL, MY SON! TRULY, MY LONG HOURS OF TEACHING HAVE NOT BEEN IN VAIN!
YOU HAVE SAVED BOTH OURSELVES... AND THE WORLD... FROM THE TENTACLES OF ONE MAN'S INSATIABLE AMBITION!
NOW... TO DEAL WITH KALUU!
AND, THE NEXT SECOND, A BEAM OF TRANSCENDENT LIGHT CIRCLES THE GLOBE... PASSING BETWEEN THE STARK MOUNTAINS OF ASIA AND THE GLEAMING TOWERS OF NEW YORK IN THE SPACE OF A SINGLE HEARTBEAT...
8

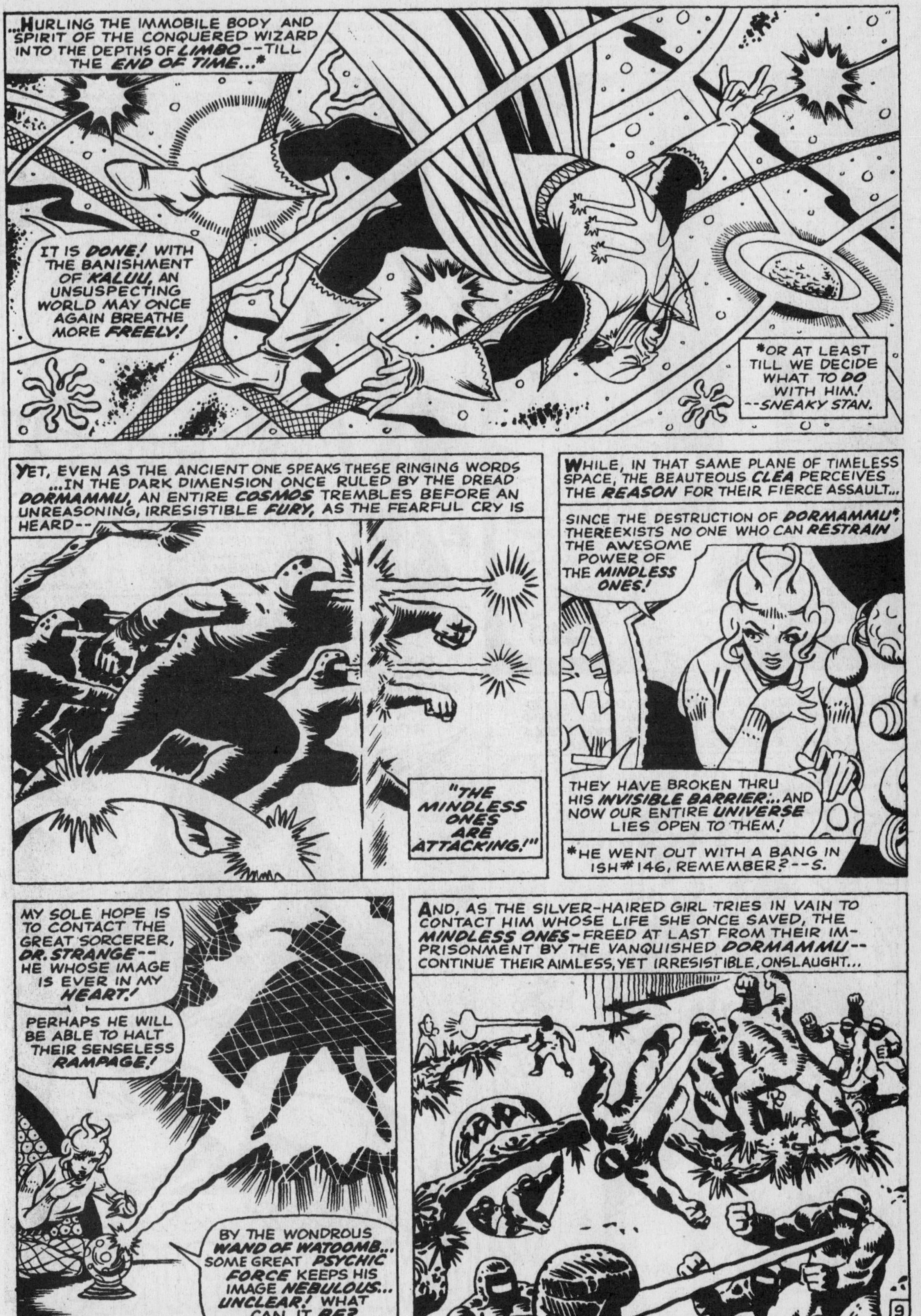
...HURLING THE IMMOBILE BODY AND SPIRIT OF THE CONQUERED WIZARD INTO THE DEPTHS OF LIMBO--TILL THE END OF TIME...*
IT IS DONE! WITH THE BANISHMENT OF KALUU, AN UNSUSPECTING WORLD MAY ONCE AGAIN BREATHE MORE FREELY!
*OR AT LEAST TILL WE DECIDE WHAT TO DO WITH HIM! --SNEAKY STAN.
YET, EVEN AS THE ANCIENT ONE SPEAKS THESE RINGING WORDS ...IN THE DARK DIMENSION ONCE RULED BY THE DREAD DORMAMMU, AN ENTIRE COSMOS TREMBLES BEFORE AN UNREASONING, IRRESISTIBLE FURY, AS THE FEARFUL CRY IS HEARD--
"THE MINDLESS ONES ARE ATTACKING!"
WHILE, IN THAT SAME PLANE OF TIMELESS SPACE, THE BEAUTEOUS CLEA PERCEIVES THE REASON FOR THEIR FIERCE ASSAULT...
SINCE THE DESTRUCTION OF DORMAMMU*, THEREEXISTS NO ONE WHO CAN RESTRAIN THE AWESOME POWER OF THE MINDLESS ONES!
THEY HAVE BROKEN THRU HIS INVISIBLE BARRIER!...AND NOW OUR ENTIRE UNIVERSE LIES OPEN TO THEM!
*HE WENT OUT WITH A BANG IN ISH#146, REMEMBER?--S.
MY SOLE HOPE IS TO CONTACT THE GREAT SORCERER, DR. STRANGE--HE WHOSE IMAGE IS EVER IN MY HEART!
PERHAPS HE WILL BE ABLE TO HALT THEIR SENSELESS RAMPAGE!
BY THE WONDROUS WAND OF WATOOMB... SOME GREAT PSYCHIC FORCE KEEPS HIS IMAGE NEBULOUS... UNCLEAR! WHAT CAN IT BE?
AND, AS THE SILVER-HAIRED GIRL TRIES IN VAIN TO CONTACT HIM WHOSE LIFE SHE ONCE SAVED, THE MINDLESS ONES-FREED AT LAST FROM THEIR IMPRISONMENT BY THE VANQUISHED DORMAMMU--CONTINUE THEIR AIMLESS, YET IRRESISTIBLE, ONSLAUGHT...
9

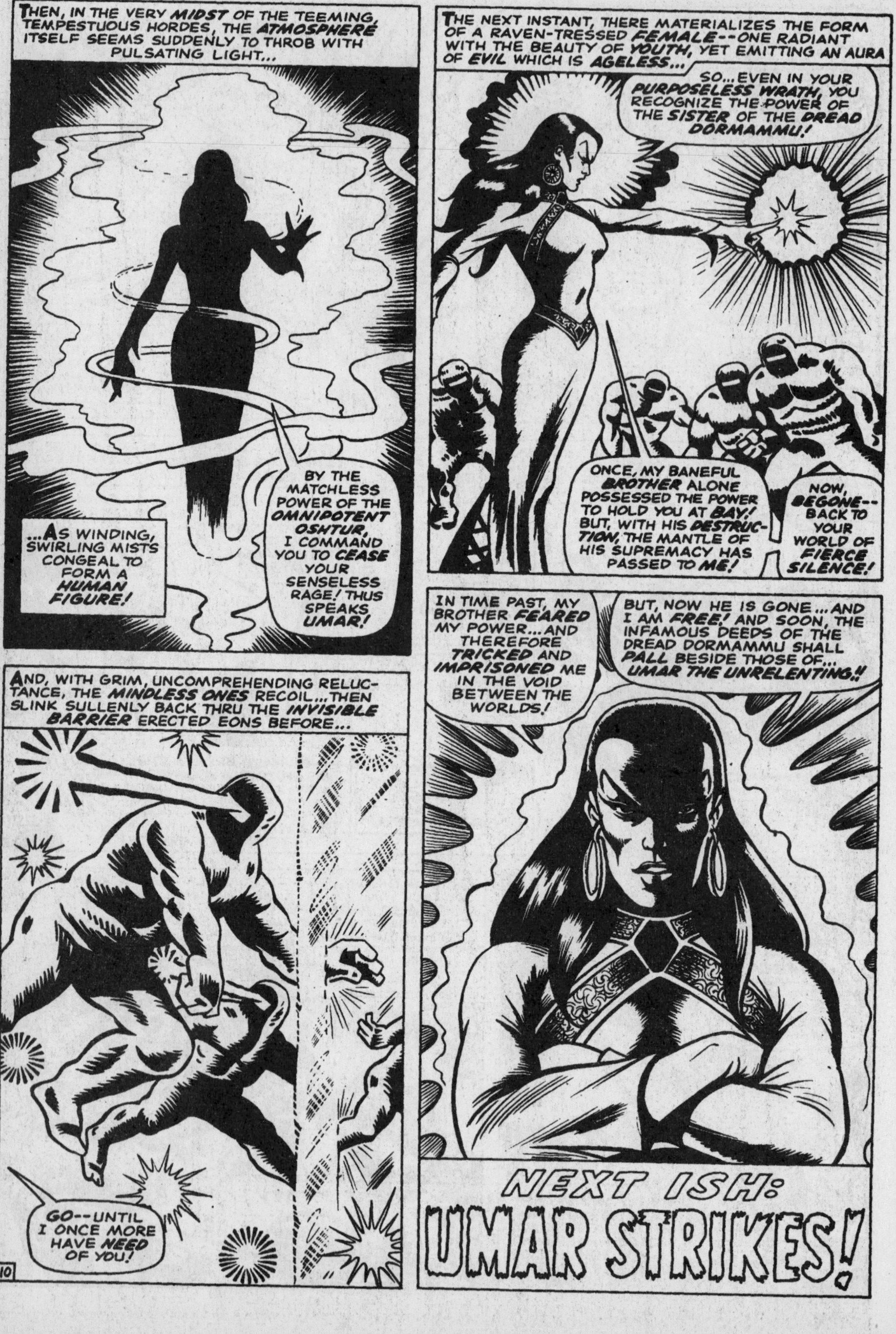

THEN, IN THE VERY MIDST OF THE TEEMING, TEMPESTUOUS HORDES, THE ATMOSPHERE ITSELF SEEMS SUDDENLY TO THROB WITH PULSATING LIGHT...
...AS WINDING, SWIRLING MISTS CONGEAL TO FORM A HUMAN FIGURE!
BY THE MATCHLESS POWER OF THE OMNIPOTENT OSHTUR, I COMMAND YOU TO CEASE YOUR SENSELESS RAGE! THUS SPEAKS UMAR!
THE NEXT INSTANT, THERE MATERIALIZES THE FORM OF A RAVEN-TRESSED FEMALE--ONE RADIANT WITH THE BEAUTY OF YOUTH, YET EMITTING AN AURA OF EVIL WHICH IS AGELESS...
SO...EVEN IN YOUR PURPOSELESS WRATH, YOU RECOGNIZE THE POWER OF THE SISTER OF THE DREAD DORMAMMU!
ONCE, MY BANEFUL BROTHER ALONE POSSESSED THE POWER TO HOLD YOU AT BAY! BUT, WITH HIS DESTRUCTION, THE MANTLE OF HIS SUPREMACY HAS PASSED TO ME!
NOW, BEGONE--BACK TO YOUR WORLD OF FIERCE SILENCE!
AND, WITH GRIM, UNCOMPREHENDING RELUCTANCE, THE MINDLESS ONES RECOIL...THEN SLINK SULLENLY BACK THRU THE INVISIBLE BARRIER ERECTED EONS BEFORE...
GO--UNTIL I ONCE MORE HAVE NEED OF YOU!
10
IN TIME PAST, MY BROTHER FEARED MY POWER...AND THEREFORE TRICKED AND IMPRISONED ME IN THE VOID BETWEEN THE WORLDS!
BUT, NOW HE IS GONE...AND I AM FREE! AND SOON, THE INFAMOUS DEEDS OF THE DREAD DORMAMMU SHALL PALL BESIDE THOSE OF... UMAR THE UNRELENTING!!
NEXT ISH:
UMAR STRIKES!

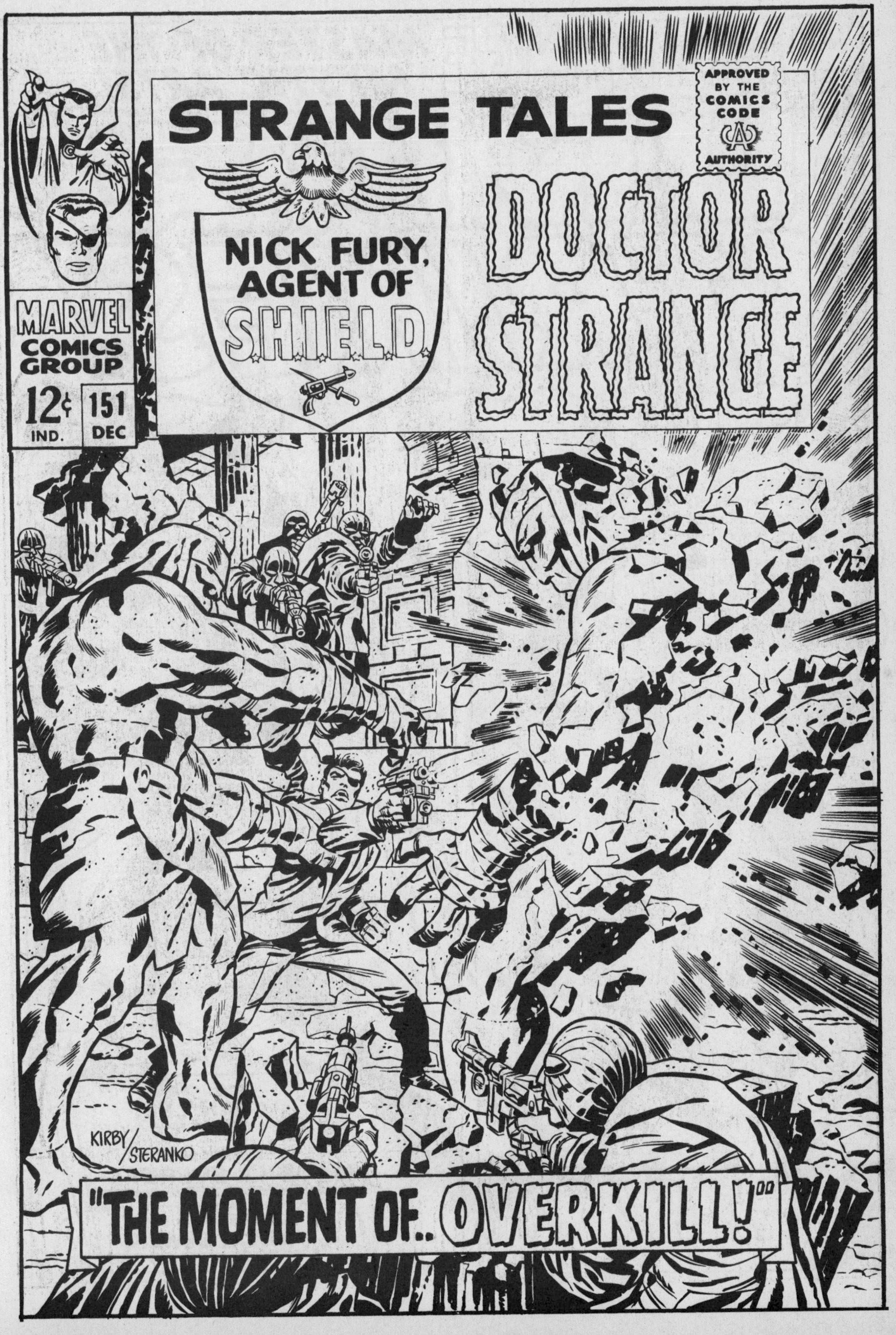
STRANGE TALES
APPROVED BY THE COMICS CODE AUTHORITY
NICK FURY, AGENT OF S.H.I.E.L.D.
DOCTOR STRANGE
MARVEL COMICS GROUP
12¢ IND.
151 DEC
KIRBY/STERANKO
"THE MOMENT OF.. OVERKILL!"

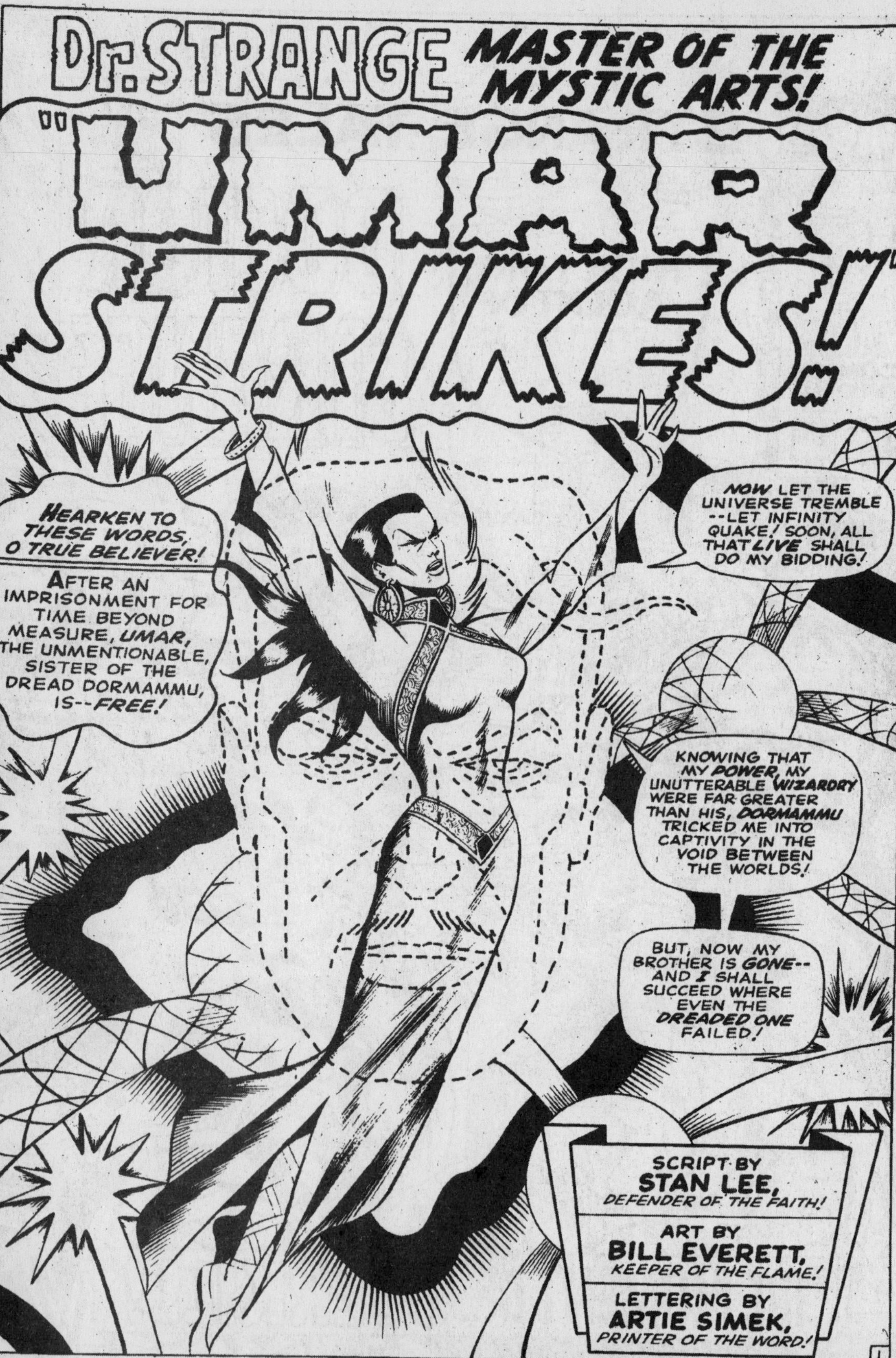

Dr. STRANGE MASTER OF THE MYSTIC ARTS!
"UMAR STRIKES!"
HEARKEN TO THESE WORDS, O TRUE BELIEVER!
AFTER AN IMPRISONMENT FOR TIME BEYOND MEASURE, UMAR, THE UNMENTIONABLE, SISTER OF THE DREAD DORMAMMU, IS--FREE!
NOW LET THE UNIVERSE TREMBLE --LET INFINITY QUAKE! SOON, ALL THAT LIVE SHALL DO MY BIDDING!
KNOWING THAT MY POWER, MY UNUTTERABLE WIZARDRY WERE FAR GREATER THAN HIS, DORMAMMU TRICKED ME INTO CAPTIVITY IN THE VOID BETWEEN THE WORLDS!
BUT, NOW MY BROTHER IS GONE-- AND I SHALL SUCCEED WHERE EVEN THE DREADED ONE FAILED!
SCRIPT BY STAN LEE, DEFENDER OF THE FAITH!
ART BY BILL EVERETT, KEEPER OF THE FLAME!
LETTERING BY ARTIE SIMEK, PRINTER OF THE WORD!
1

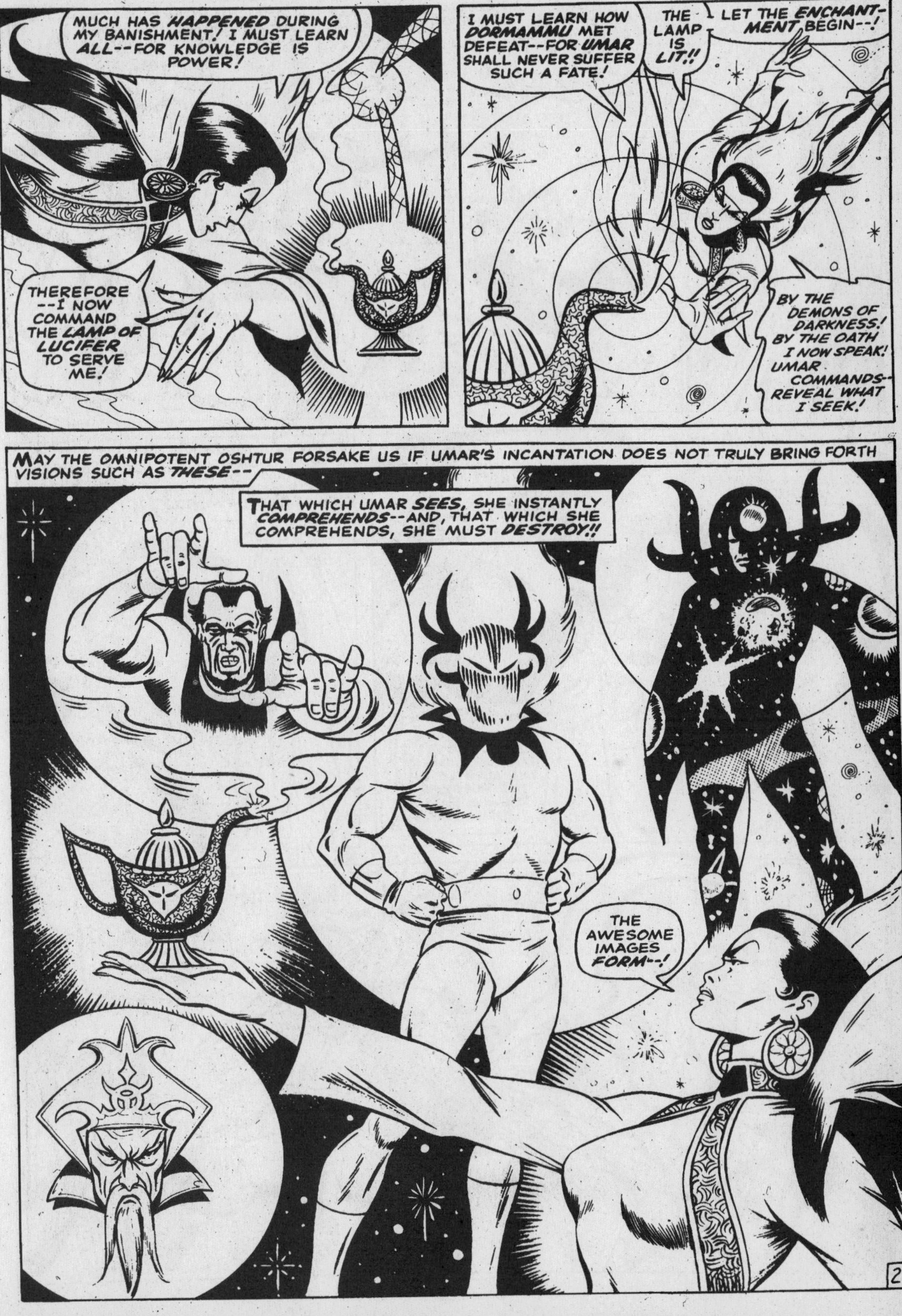
MUCH HAS HAPPENED DURING MY BANISHMENT! I MUST LEARN ALL--FOR KNOWLEDGE IS POWER!
THEREFORE--I NOW COMMAND THE LAMP OF LUCIFER TO SERVE ME!
I MUST LEARN HOW DORMAMMU MET DEFEAT--FOR UMAR SHALL NEVER SUFFER SUCH A FATE!
THE LAMP IS LIT!!
LET THE ENCHANTMENT BEGIN--!
BY THE DEMONS OF DARKNESS! BY THE OATH I NOW SPEAK! UMAR COMMANDS-- REVEAL WHAT I SEEK!
MAY THE OMNIPOTENT OSHTUR FORSAKE US IF UMAR'S INCANTATION DOES NOT TRULY BRING FORTH VISIONS SUCH AS THESE--
THAT WHICH UMAR SEES, SHE INSTANTLY COMPREHENDS--AND, THAT WHICH SHE COMPREHENDS, SHE MUST DESTROY!!
THE AWESOME IMAGES FORM--!
2

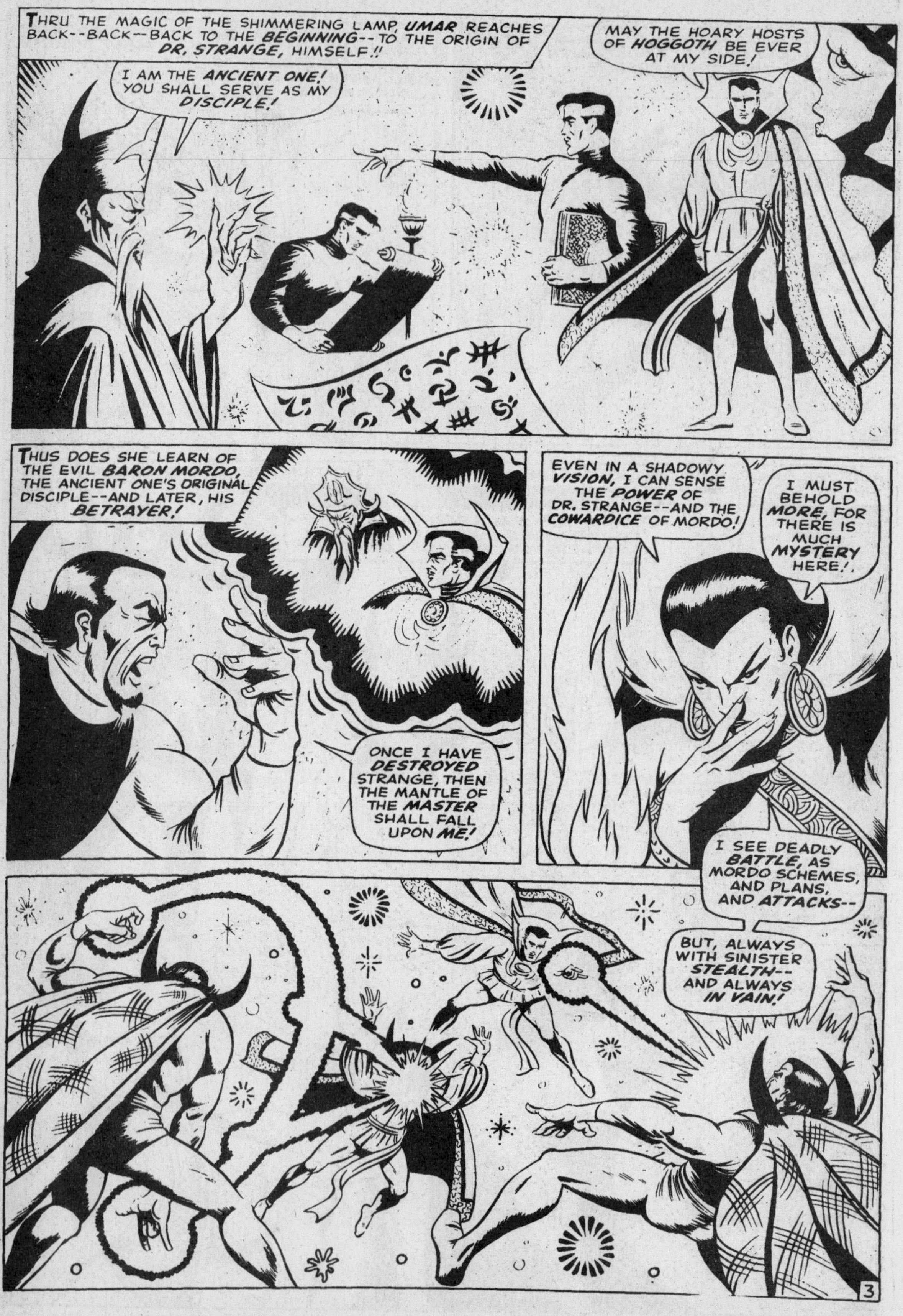
THRU THE MAGIC OF THE SHIMMERING LAMP, UMAR REACHES BACK--BACK--BACK TO THE BEGINNING--TO THE ORIGIN OF DR. STRANGE, HIMSELF!!
I AM THE ANCIENT ONE! YOU SHALL SERVE AS MY DISCIPLE!
MAY THE HOARY HOSTS OF HOGGOTH BE EVER AT MY SIDE!
THUS DOES SHE LEARN OF THE EVIL BARON MORDO, THE ANCIENT ONE'S ORIGINAL DISCIPLE--AND LATER, HIS BETRAYER!
ONCE I HAVE DESTROYED STRANGE, THEN THE MANTLE OF THE MASTER SHALL FALL UPON ME!
EVEN IN A SHADOWY VISION, I CAN SENSE THE POWER OF DR. STRANGE--AND THE COWARDICE OF MORDO!
I MUST BEHOLD MORE, FOR THERE IS MUCH MYSTERY HERE!
I SEE DEADLY BATTLE, AS MORDO SCHEMES, AND PLANS, AND ATTACKS--
BUT, ALWAYS WITH SINISTER STEALTH--AND ALWAYS IN VAIN!

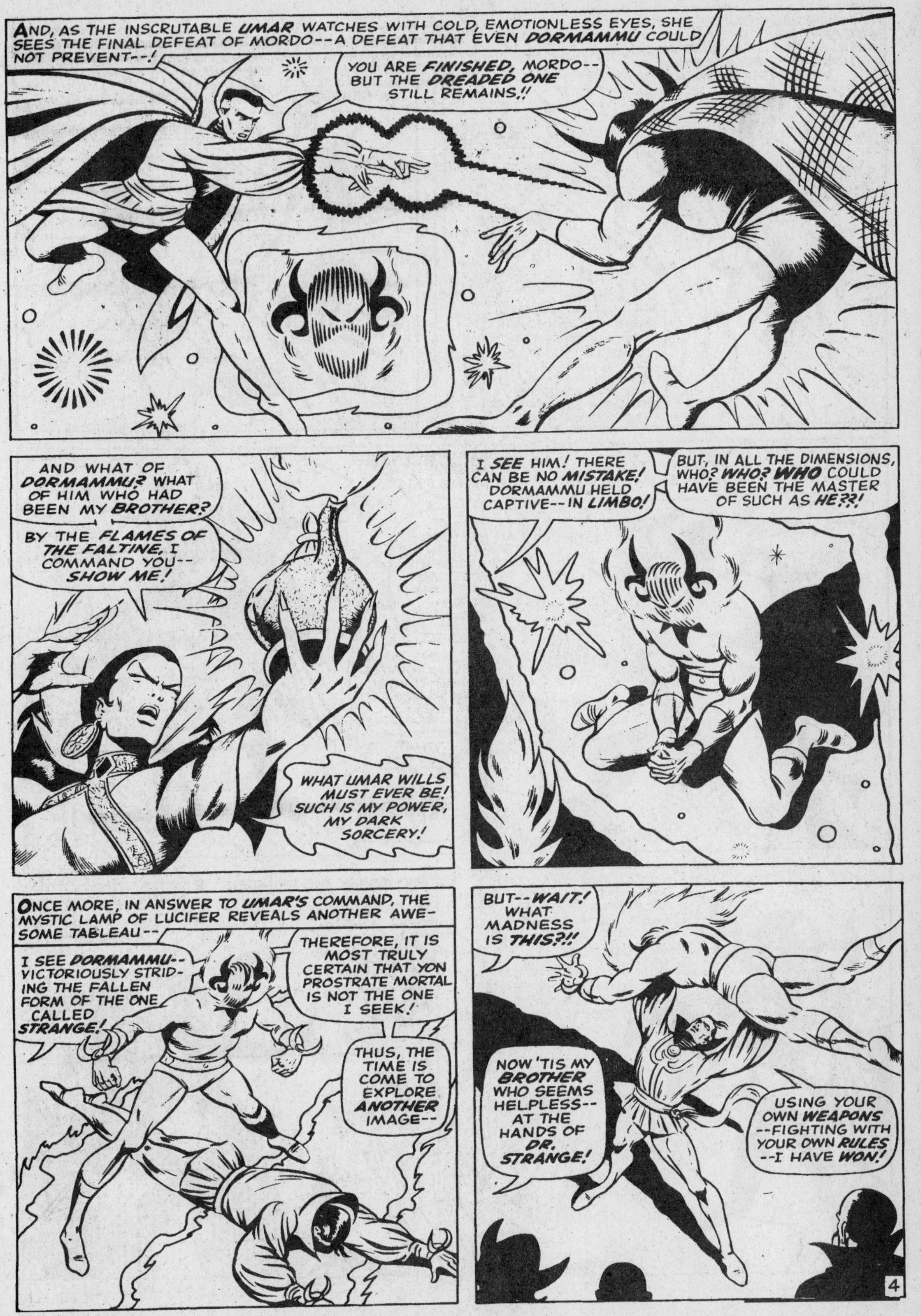
AND, AS THE INSCRUTABLE UMAR WATCHES WITH COLD, EMOTIONLESS EYES, SHE SEES THE FINAL DEFEAT OF MORDO--A DEFEAT THAT EVEN DORMAMMU COULD NOT PREVENT--!
YOU ARE FINISHED, MORDO-- BUT THE DREADED ONE STILL REMAINS.!!
AND WHAT OF DORMAMMU? WHAT OF HIM WHO HAD BEEN MY BROTHER?
BY THE FLAMES OF THE FALTINE, I COMMAND YOU-- SHOW ME!
WHAT UMAR WILLS MUST EVER BE! SUCH IS MY POWER, MY DARK SORCERY!
I SEE HIM! THERE CAN BE NO MISTAKE! DORMAMMU HELD CAPTIVE--IN LIMBO!
BUT, IN ALL THE DIMENSIONS, WHO? WHO? WHO COULD HAVE BEEN THE MASTER OF SUCH AS HE??!
ONCE MORE, IN ANSWER TO UMAR'S COMMAND, THE MYSTIC LAMP OF LUCIFER REVEALS ANOTHER AWESOME TABLEAU--
I SEE DORMAMMU--VICTORIOUSLY STRIDING THE FALLEN FORM OF THE ONE CALLED STRANGE!
THEREFORE, IT IS MOST TRULY CERTAIN THAT YON PROSTRATE MORTAL IS NOT THE ONE I SEEK!
THUS, THE TIME IS COME TO EXPLORE ANOTHER IMAGE--
BUT--WAIT! WHAT MADNESS IS THIS?!!
NOW 'TIS MY BROTHER WHO SEEMS HELPLESS--AT THE HANDS OF DR. STRANGE!
USING YOUR OWN WEAPONS --FIGHTING WITH YOUR OWN RULES --I HAVE WON!
4

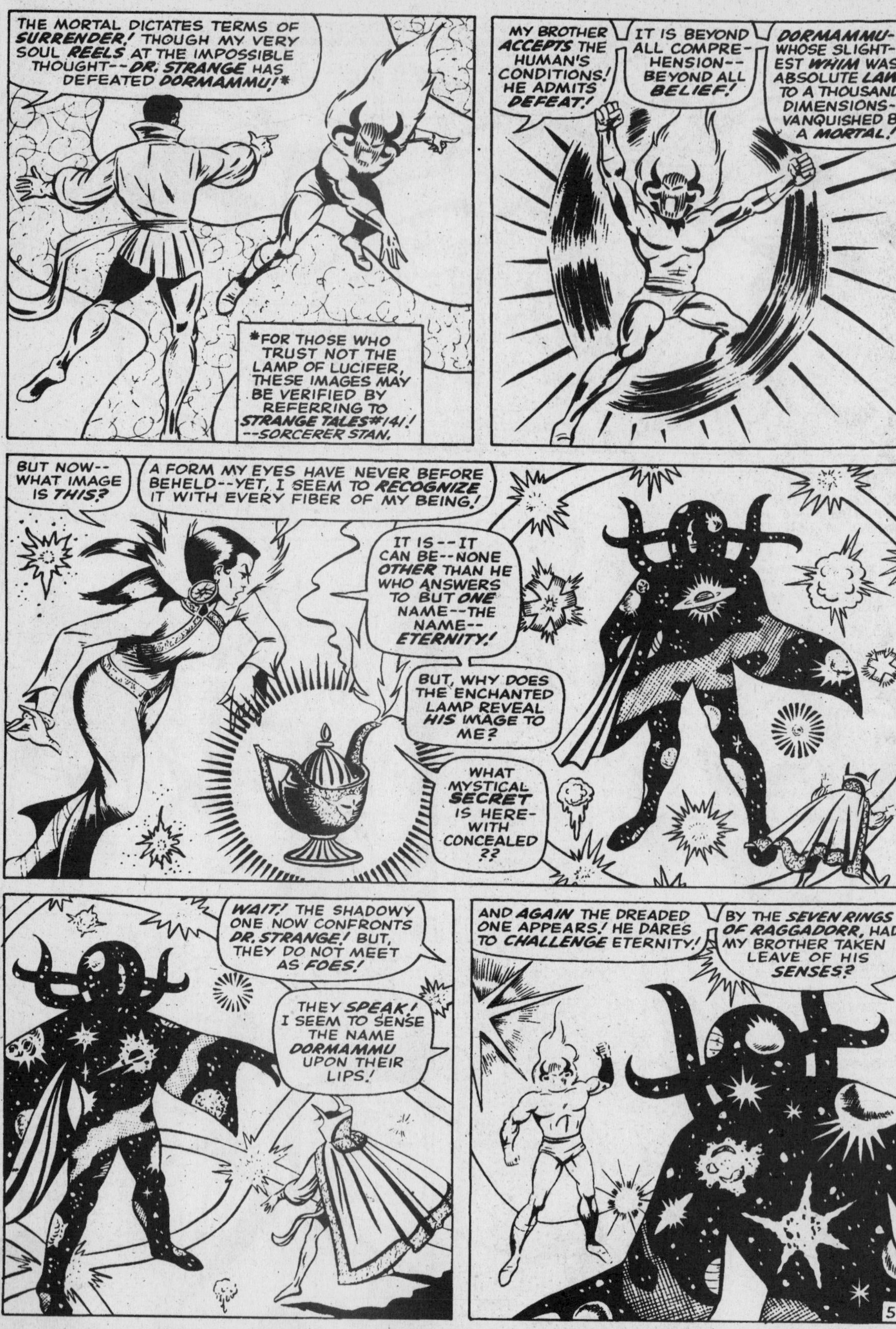

THE MORTAL DICTATES TERMS OF SURRENDER! THOUGH MY VERY SOUL REELS AT THE IMPOSSIBLE THOUGHT--DR. STRANGE HAS DEFEATED DORMAMMU!*
*FOR THOSE WHO TRUST NOT THE LAMP OF LUCIFER, THESE IMAGES MAY BE VERIFIED BY REFERRING TO STRANGE TALES #141! --SORCERER STAN.
MY BROTHER ACCEPTS THE HUMAN'S CONDITIONS! HE ADMITS DEFEAT!
IT IS BEYOND ALL COMPREHENSION--BEYOND ALL BELIEF!
DORMAMMU--WHOSE SLIGHTEST WHIM WAS ABSOLUTE LAW TO A THOUSAND DIMENSIONS--VANQUISHED BY A MORTAL!
BUT NOW--WHAT IMAGE IS THIS?
A FORM MY EYES HAVE NEVER BEFORE BEHELD--YET, I SEEM TO RECOGNIZE IT WITH EVERY FIBER OF MY BEING!
IT IS--IT CAN BE--NONE OTHER THAN HE WHO ANSWERS TO BUT ONE NAME--THE NAME--ETERNITY!
BUT, WHY DOES THE ENCHANTED LAMP REVEAL HIS IMAGE TO ME?
WHAT MYSTICAL SECRET IS HEREWITH CONCEALED??
WAIT! THE SHADOWY ONE NOW CONFRONTS DR. STRANGE! BUT, THEY DO NOT MEET AS FOES!
THEY SPEAK! I SEEM TO SENSE THE NAME DORMAMMU UPON THEIR LIPS!
AND AGAIN THE DREADED ONE APPEARS! HE DARES TO CHALLENGE ETERNITY!
BY THE SEVEN RINGS OF RAGGADORR, HAD MY BROTHER TAKEN LEAVE OF HIS SENSES?
5

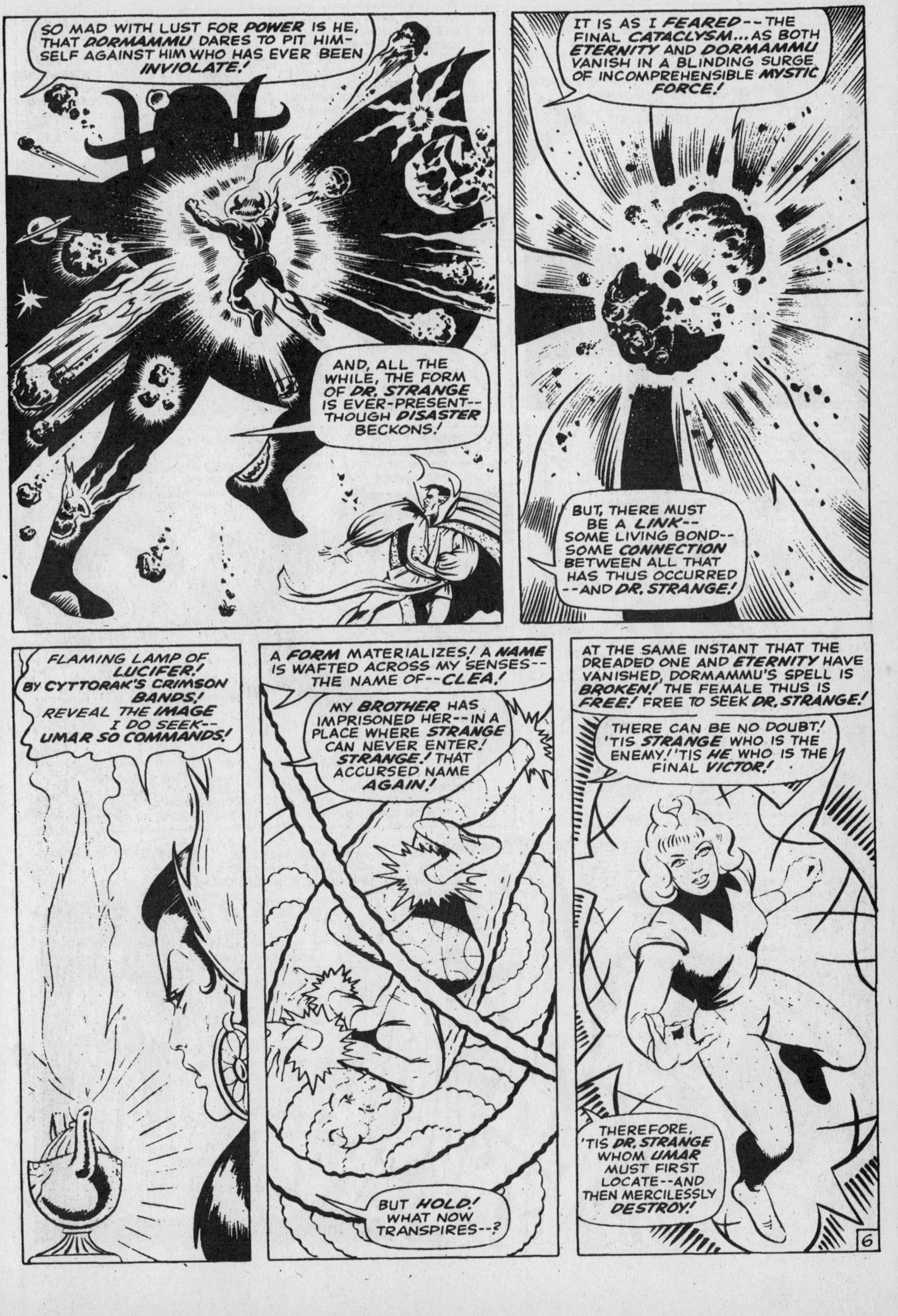
SO MAD WITH LUST FOR POWER IS HE, THAT DORMAMMU DARES TO PIT HIMSELF AGAINST HIM WHO HAS EVER BEEN INVIOLATE!
AND, ALL THE WHILE, THE FORM OF DR. STRANGE IS EVER-PRESENT-- THOUGH DISASTER BECKONS!
IT IS AS I FEARED-- THE FINAL CATACLYSM... AS BOTH ETERNITY AND DORMAMMU VANISH IN A BLINDING SURGE OF INCOMPREHENSIBLE MYSTIC FORCE!
BUT, THERE MUST BE A LINK-- SOME LIVING BOND-- SOME CONNECTION BETWEEN ALL THAT HAS THUS OCCURRED --AND DR. STRANGE!
FLAMING LAMP OF LUCIFER! BY CYTTORAK'S CRIMSON BANDS! REVEAL THE IMAGE I DO SEEK-- UMAR SO COMMANDS!
A FORM MATERIALIZES! A NAME IS WAFTED ACROSS MY SENSES-- THE NAME OF--CLEA!
MY BROTHER HAS IMPRISONED HER--IN A PLACE WHERE STRANGE CAN NEVER ENTER! STRANGE! THAT ACCURSED NAME AGAIN!
BUT HOLD! WHAT NOW TRANSPIRES--?
AT THE SAME INSTANT THAT THE DREADED ONE AND ETERNITY HAVE VANISHED, DORMAMMU'S SPELL IS BROKEN! THE FEMALE THUS IS FREE! FREE TO SEEK DR. STRANGE!
THERE CAN BE NO DOUBT! 'TIS STRANGE WHO IS THE ENEMY! 'TIS HE WHO IS THE FINAL VICTOR!
THEREFORE, 'TIS DR. STRANGE WHOM UMAR MUST FIRST LOCATE--AND THEN MERCILESSLY DESTROY!
6

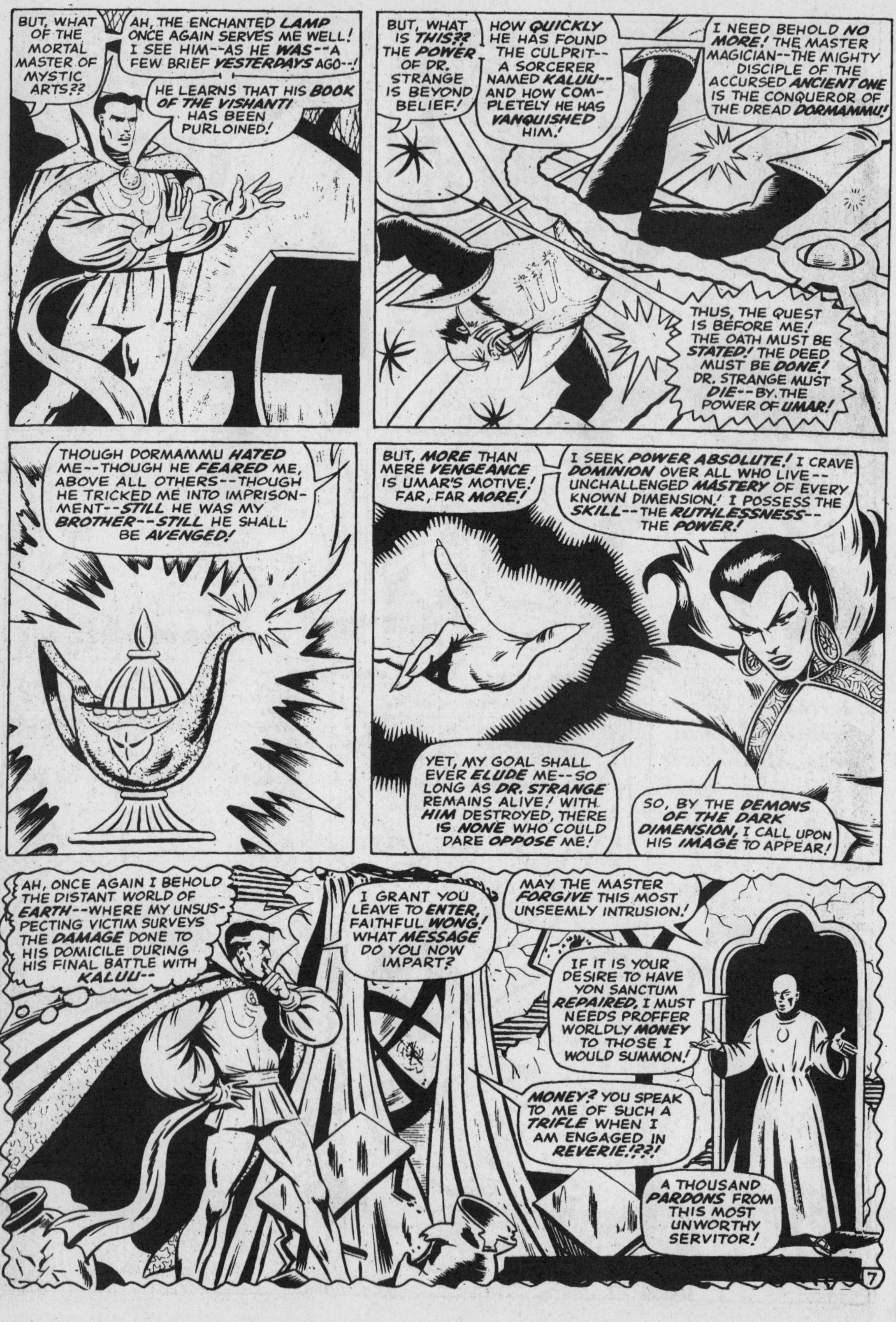
BUT, WHAT OF THE MORTAL MASTER OF MYSTIC ARTS??
AH, THE ENCHANTED LAMP ONCE AGAIN SERVES ME WELL! I SEE HIM--AS HE WAS--A FEW BRIEF YESTERDAYS AGO--!
HE LEARNS THAT HIS BOOK OF THE VISHANTI HAS BEEN PURLOINED!
BUT, WHAT IS THIS?? THE POWER OF DR. STRANGE IS BEYOND BELIEF!
HOW QUICKLY HE HAS FOUND THE CULPRIT--A SORCERER NAMED KALUU--AND HOW COMPLETELY HE HAS VANQUISHED HIM!
I NEED BEHOLD NO MORE! THE MASTER MAGICIAN--THE MIGHTY DISCIPLE OF THE ACCURSED ANCIENT ONE IS THE CONQUEROR OF THE DREAD DORMAMMU!
THUS, THE QUEST IS BEFORE ME! THE OATH MUST BE STATED! THE DEED MUST BE DONE! DR. STRANGE MUST DIE--BY THE POWER OF UMAR!
THOUGH DORMAMMU HATED ME--THOUGH HE FEARED ME, ABOVE ALL OTHERS--THOUGH HE TRICKED ME INTO IMPRISONMENT--STILL HE WAS MY BROTHER--STILL HE SHALL BE AVENGED!
BUT, MORE THAN MERE VENGEANCE IS UMAR'S MOTIVE! FAR, FAR MORE!
I SEEK POWER ABSOLUTE! I CRAVE DOMINION OVER ALL WHO LIVE--UNCHALLENGED MASTERY OF EVERY KNOWN DIMENSION! I POSSESS THE SKILL--THE RUTHLESSNESS--THE POWER!
YET, MY GOAL SHALL EVER ELUDE ME--SO LONG AS DR. STRANGE REMAINS ALIVE! WITH HIM DESTROYED, THERE IS NONE WHO COULD DARE OPPOSE ME!
SO, BY THE DEMONS OF THE DARK DIMENSION, I CALL UPON HIS IMAGE TO APPEAR!
AH, ONCE AGAIN I BEHOLD THE DISTANT WORLD OF EARTH--WHERE MY UNSUSPECTING VICTIM SURVEYS THE DAMAGE DONE TO HIS DOMICILE DURING HIS FINAL BATTLE WITH KALUU--
I GRANT YOU LEAVE TO ENTER, FAITHFUL WONG! WHAT MESSAGE DO YOU NOW IMPART?
MAY THE MASTER FORGIVE THIS MOST UNSEEMLY INTRUSION!
IF IT IS YOUR DESIRE TO HAVE YON SANCTUM REPAIRED, I MUST NEEDS PROFFER WORLDLY MONEY TO THOSE I WOULD SUMMON!
MONEY? YOU SPEAK TO ME OF SUCH A TRIFLE WHEN I AM ENGAGED IN REVERIE!??!
A THOUSAND PARDONS FROM THIS MOST UNWORTHY SERVITOR!
7

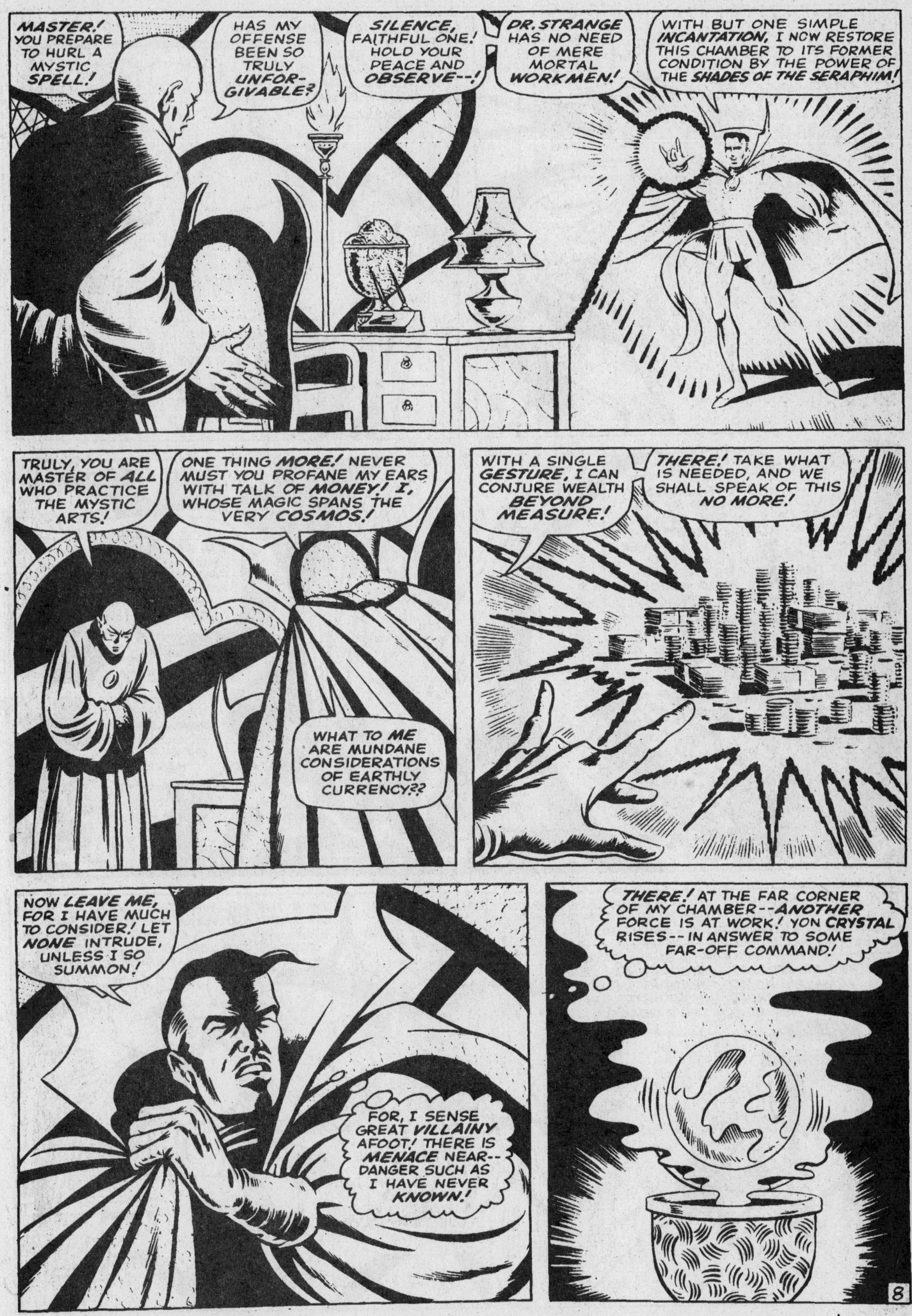

MASTER! YOU PREPARE TO HURL A MYSTIC SPELL!
HAS MY OFFENSE BEEN SO TRULY UNFORGIVABLE?
SILENCE, FAITHFUL ONE! HOLD YOUR PEACE AND OBSERVE--!
DR. STRANGE HAS NO NEED OF MERE MORTAL WORKMEN!
WITH BUT ONE SIMPLE INCANTATION, I NOW RESTORE THIS CHAMBER TO ITS FORMER CONDITION BY THE POWER OF THE SHADES OF THE SERAPHIM!
TRULY, YOU ARE MASTER OF ALL WHO PRACTICE THE MYSTIC ARTS!
ONE THING MORE! NEVER MUST YOU PROFANE MY EARS WITH TALK OF MONEY! I, WHOSE MAGIC SPANS THE VERY COSMOS!
WHAT TO ME ARE MUNDANE CONSIDERATIONS OF EARTHLY CURRENCY??
WITH A SINGLE GESTURE, I CAN CONJURE WEALTH BEYOND MEASURE!
THERE! TAKE WHAT IS NEEDED, AND WE SHALL SPEAK OF THIS NO MORE!
NOW LEAVE ME, FOR I HAVE MUCH TO CONSIDER! LET NONE INTRUDE, UNLESS I SO SUMMON!
FOR, I SENSE GREAT VILLAINY AFOOT! THERE IS MENACE NEAR-- DANGER SUCH AS I HAVE NEVER KNOWN!
THERE! AT THE FAR CORNER OF MY CHAMBER--ANOTHER FORCE IS AT WORK! YON CRYSTAL RISES-- IN ANSWER TO SOME FAR-OFF COMMAND!
8

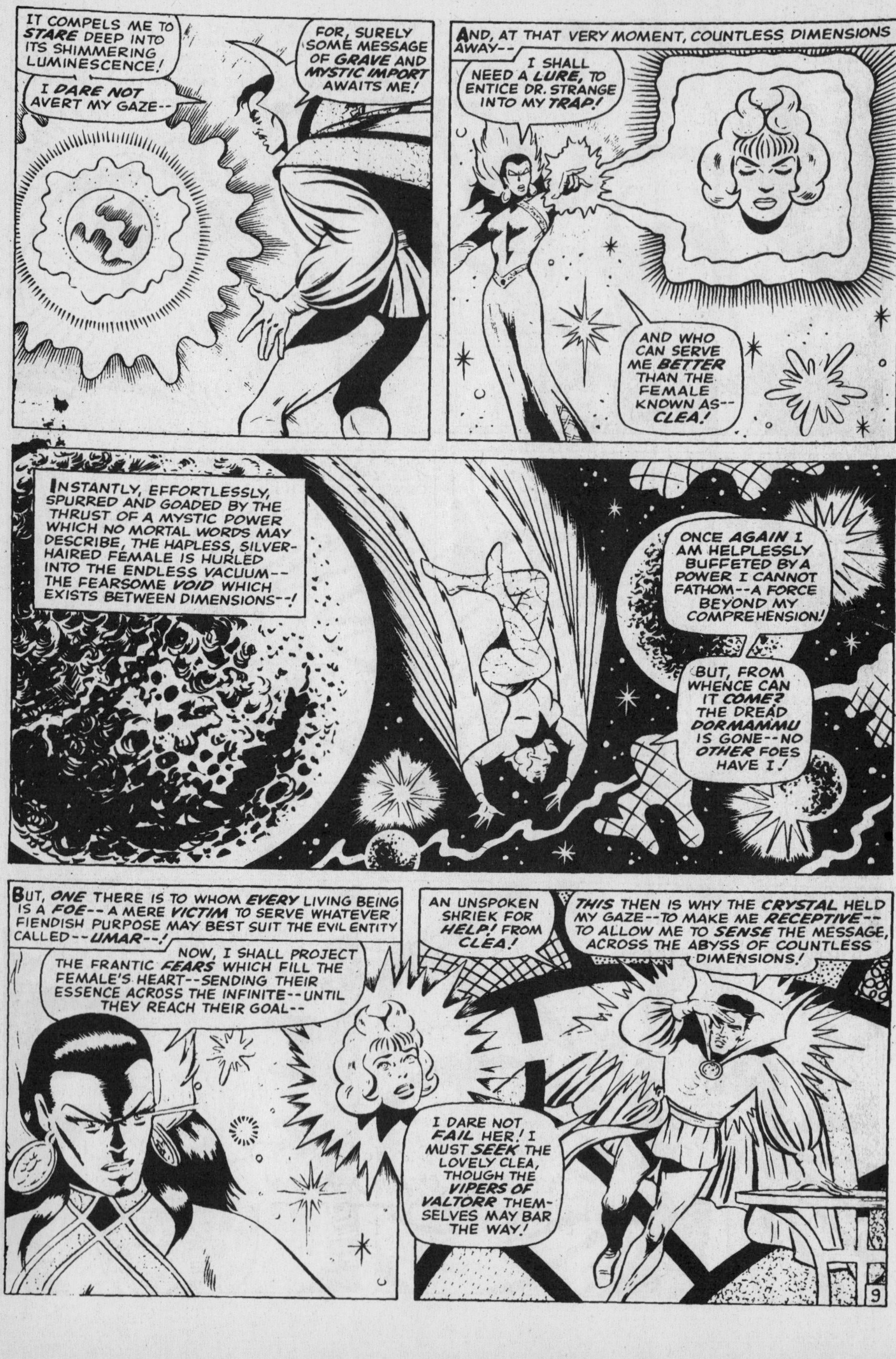
IT COMPELS ME TO STARE DEEP INTO ITS SHIMMERING LUMINESCENCE!
I DARE NOT AVERT MY GAZE--
FOR, SURELY SOME MESSAGE OF GRAVE AND MYSTIC IMPORT AWAITS ME!
AND, AT THAT VERY MOMENT, COUNTLESS DIMENSIONS AWAY--
I SHALL NEED A LURE, TO ENTICE DR. STRANGE INTO MY TRAP!
AND WHO CAN SERVE ME BETTER THAN THE FEMALE KNOWN AS-- CLEA!
INSTANTLY, EFFORTLESSLY, SPURRED AND GOADED BY THE THRUST OF A MYSTIC POWER WHICH NO MORTAL WORDS MAY DESCRIBE, THE HAPLESS, SILVER-HAIRED FEMALE IS HURLED INTO THE ENDLESS VACUUM-- THE FEARSOME VOID WHICH EXISTS BETWEEN DIMENSIONS--!
ONCE AGAIN I AM HELPLESSLY BUFFETED BY A POWER I CANNOT FATHOM--A FORCE BEYOND MY COMPREHENSION!
BUT, FROM WHENCE CAN IT COME? THE DREAD DORMAMMU IS GONE--NO OTHER FOES HAVE I!
BUT, ONE THERE IS TO WHOM EVERY LIVING BEING IS A FOE-- A MERE VICTIM TO SERVE WHATEVER FIENDISH PURPOSE MAY BEST SUIT THE EVIL ENTITY CALLED--UMAR--!
NOW, I SHALL PROJECT THE FRANTIC FEARS WHICH FILL THE FEMALE'S HEART--SENDING THEIR ESSENCE ACROSS THE INFINITE--UNTIL THEY REACH THEIR GOAL--
AN UNSPOKEN SHRIEK FOR HELP! FROM CLEA!
THIS THEN IS WHY THE CRYSTAL HELD MY GAZE--TO MAKE ME RECEPTIVE-- TO ALLOW ME TO SENSE THE MESSAGE, ACROSS THE ABYSS OF COUNTLESS DIMENSIONS!
I DARE NOT FAIL HER! I MUST SEEK THE LOVELY CLEA, THOUGH THE VIPERS OF VALTORR THEMSELVES MAY BAR THE WAY!
9

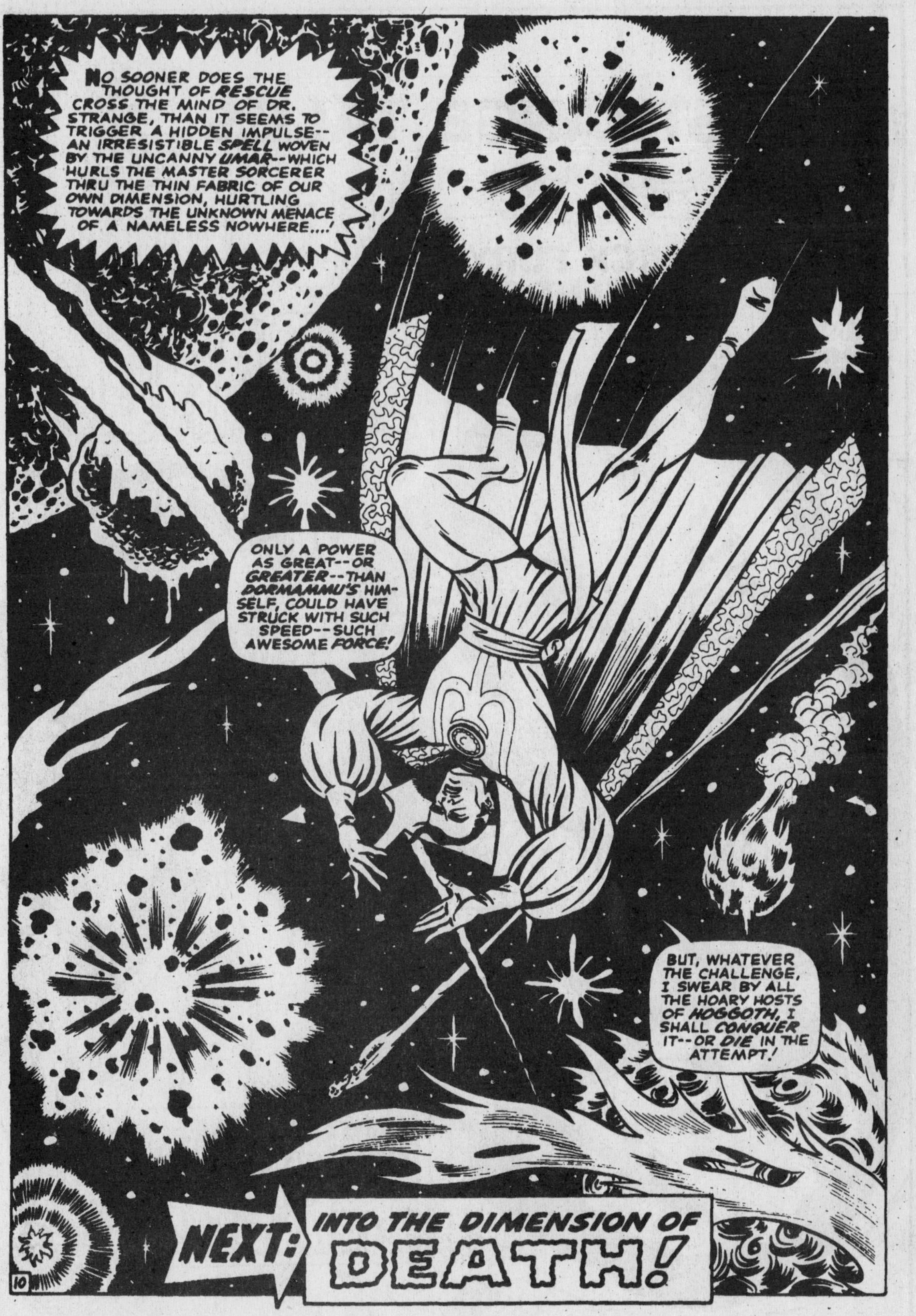
NO SOONER DOES THE THOUGHT OF RESCUE CROSS THE MIND OF DR. STRANGE, THAN IT SEEMS TO TRIGGER A HIDDEN IMPULSE--AN IRRESISTIBLE SPELL WOVEN BY THE UNCANNY UMAR--WHICH HURLS THE MASTER SORCERER THRU THE THIN FABRIC OF OUR OWN DIMENSION, HURTLING TOWARDS THE UNKNOWN MENACE OF A NAMELESS NOWHERE....!
ONLY A POWER AS GREAT--OR GREATER--THAN DORMAMMU'S HIMSELF, COULD HAVE STRUCK WITH SUCH SPEED--SUCH AWESOME FORCE!
BUT, WHATEVER THE CHALLENGE, I SWEAR BY ALL THE HOARY HOSTS OF HOGGOTH, I SHALL CONQUER IT--OR DIE IN THE ATTEMPT!
NEXT: INTO THE DIMENSION OF DEATH!
10

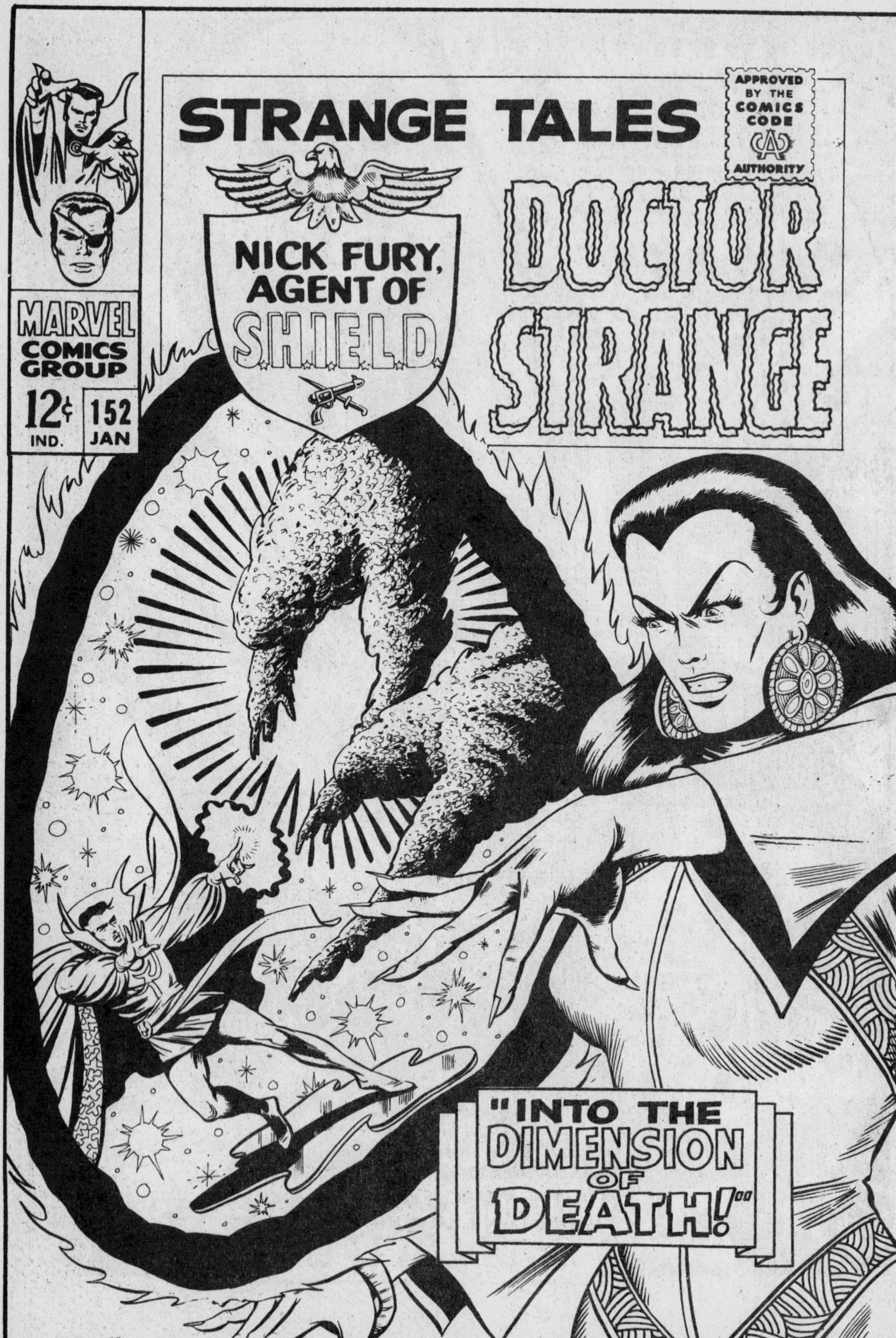
MARVEL
COMICS
GROUP
12¢
IND.
152
JAN
STRANGE TALES
APPROVED
BY THE
COMICS
CODE
AUTHORITY
NICK FURY, AGENT OF S.H.I.E.L.D.
DOCTOR STRANGE
"INTO THE DIMENSION OF DEATH!"

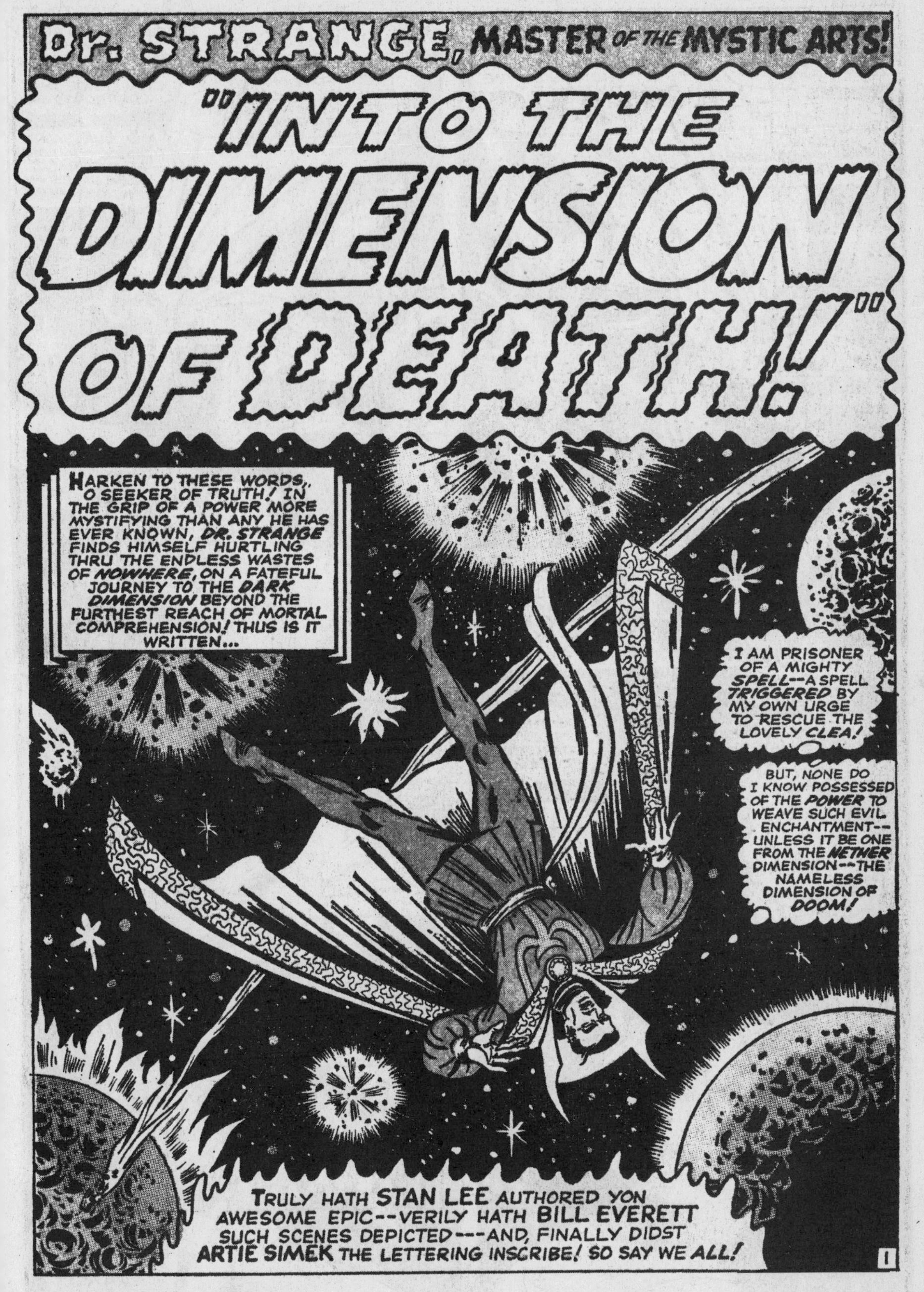

Dr. STRANGE, MASTER OF THE MYSTIC ARTS!
"INTO THE DIMENSION OF DEATH!"
HARKEN TO THESE WORDS, O SEEKER OF TRUTH! IN THE GRIP OF A POWER MORE MYSTIFYING THAN ANY HE HAS EVER KNOWN, DR. STRANGE FINDS HIMSELF HURTLING THRU THE ENDLESS WASTES OF NOWHERE, ON A FATEFUL JOURNEY TO THE DARK DIMENSION BEYOND THE FURTHEST REACH OF MORTAL COMPREHENSION! THUS IS IT WRITTEN...
I AM PRISONER OF A MIGHTY SPELL--A SPELL TRIGGERED BY MY OWN URGE TO RESCUE THE LOVELY CLEA!
BUT, NONE DO I KNOW POSSESSED OF THE POWER TO WEAVE SUCH EVIL ENCHANTMENT--UNLESS IT BE ONE FROM THE NETHER DIMENSION--THE NAMELESS DIMENSION OF DOOM!
TRULY HATH STAN LEE AUTHORED YON AWESOME EPIC--VERILY HATH BILL EVERETT SUCH SCENES DEPICTED---AND, FINALLY DIDST ARTIE SIMEK THE LETTERING INSCRIBE! SO SAY WE ALL!
1

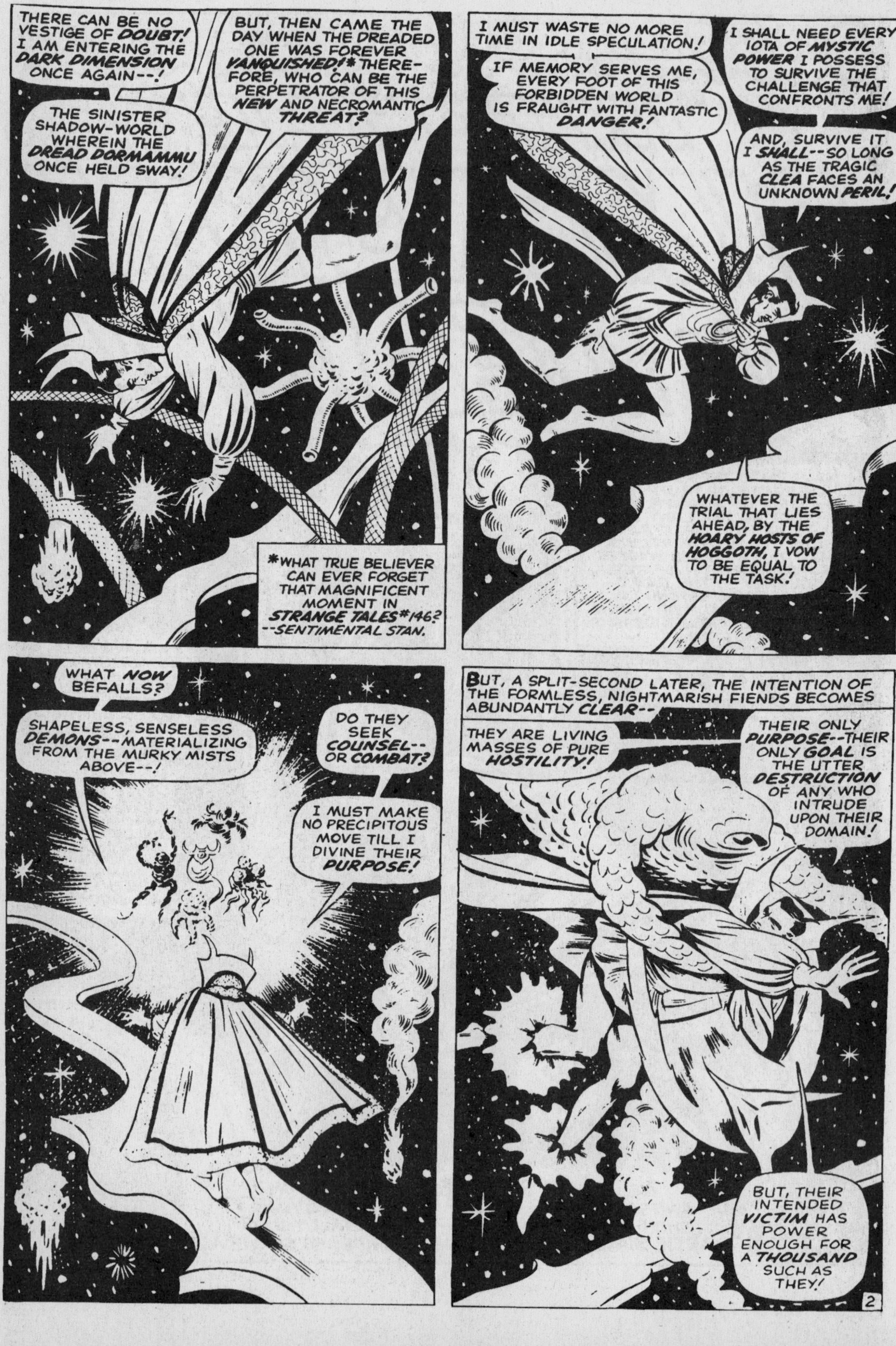

THERE CAN BE NO VESTIGE OF DOUBT! I AM ENTERING THE DARK DIMENSION ONCE AGAIN--!
THE SINISTER SHADOW-WORLD WHEREIN THE DREAD DORMAMMU ONCE HELD SWAY!
BUT, THEN CAME THE DAY WHEN THE DREADED ONE WAS FOREVER VANQUISHED!* THEREFORE, WHO CAN BE THE PERPETRATOR OF THIS NEW AND NECROMANTIC THREAT?
*WHAT TRUE BELIEVER CAN EVER FORGET THAT MAGNIFICENT MOMENT IN STRANGE TALES #146? --SENTIMENTAL STAN.
I MUST WASTE NO MORE TIME IN IDLE SPECULATION!
IF MEMORY SERVES ME, EVERY FOOT OF THIS FORBIDDEN WORLD IS FRAUGHT WITH FANTASTIC DANGER!
I SHALL NEED EVERY IOTA OF MYSTIC POWER I POSSESS TO SURVIVE THE CHALLENGE THAT CONFRONTS ME!
AND, SURVIVE IT I SHALL--SO LONG AS THE TRAGIC CLEA FACES AN UNKNOWN PERIL!
WHATEVER THE TRIAL THAT LIES AHEAD, BY THE HOARY HOSTS OF HOGGOTH, I VOW TO BE EQUAL TO THE TASK!
WHAT NOW BEFALLS?
SHAPELESS, SENSELESS DEMONS--MATERIALIZING FROM THE MURKY MISTS ABOVE--!
DO THEY SEEK COUNSEL--OR COMBAT?
I MUST MAKE NO PRECIPITOUS MOVE TILL I DIVINE THEIR PURPOSE!
BUT, A SPLIT-SECOND LATER, THE INTENTION OF THE FORMLESS, NIGHTMARISH FIENDS BECOMES ABUNDANTLY CLEAR--
THEY ARE LIVING MASSES OF PURE HOSTILITY!
THEIR ONLY PURPOSE--THEIR ONLY GOAL IS THE UTTER DESTRUCTION OF ANY WHO INTRUDE UPON THEIR DOMAIN!
BUT, THEIR INTENDED VICTIM HAS POWER ENOUGH FOR A THOUSAND SUCH AS THEY!
2

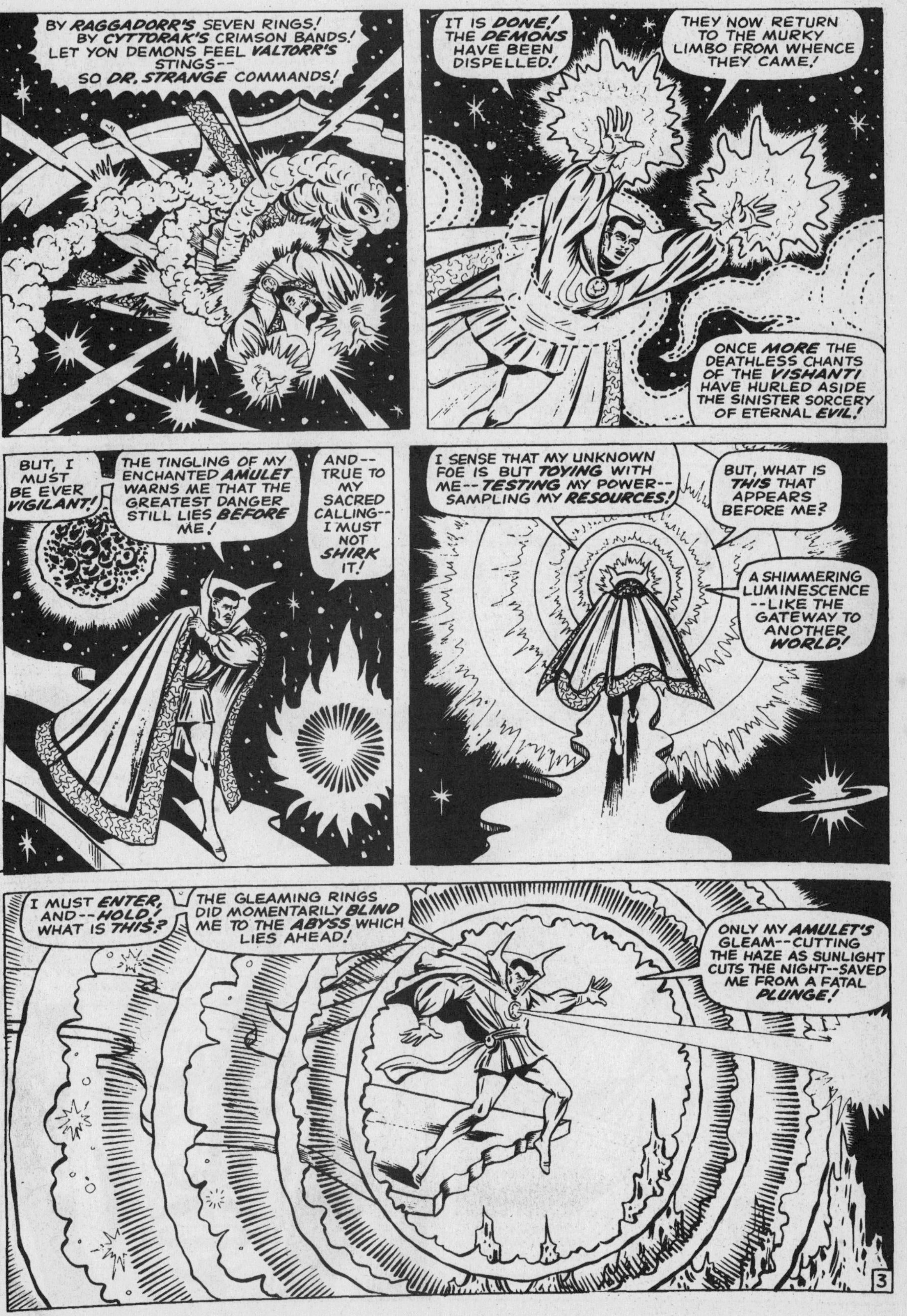
BY RAGGADORR'S SEVEN RINGS! BY CYTTORAK'S CRIMSON BANDS! LET YON DEMONS FEEL VALTORR'S STINGS-- SO DR. STRANGE COMMANDS!
IT IS DONE! THE DEMONS HAVE BEEN DISPELLED!
THEY NOW RETURN TO THE MURKY LIMBO FROM WHENCE THEY CAME!
ONCE MORE THE DEATHLESS CHANTS OF THE VISHANTI HAVE HURLED ASIDE THE SINISTER SORCERY OF ETERNAL EVIL!
BUT, I MUST BE EVER VIGILANT!
THE TINGLING OF MY ENCHANTED AMULET WARNS ME THAT THE GREATEST DANGER STILL LIES BEFORE ME!
AND--TRUE TO MY SACRED CALLING--I MUST NOT SHIRK IT!
I SENSE THAT MY UNKNOWN FOE IS BUT TOYING WITH ME--TESTING MY POWER--SAMPLING MY RESOURCES!
BUT, WHAT IS THIS THAT APPEARS BEFORE ME?
A SHIMMERING LUMINESCENCE --LIKE THE GATEWAY TO ANOTHER WORLD!
I MUST ENTER, AND--HOLD! WHAT IS THIS?
THE GLEAMING RINGS DID MOMENTARILY BLIND ME TO THE ABYSS WHICH LIES AHEAD!
ONLY MY AMULET'S GLEAM--CUTTING THE HAZE AS SUNLIGHT CUTS THE NIGHT--SAVED ME FROM A FATAL PLUNGE!
3

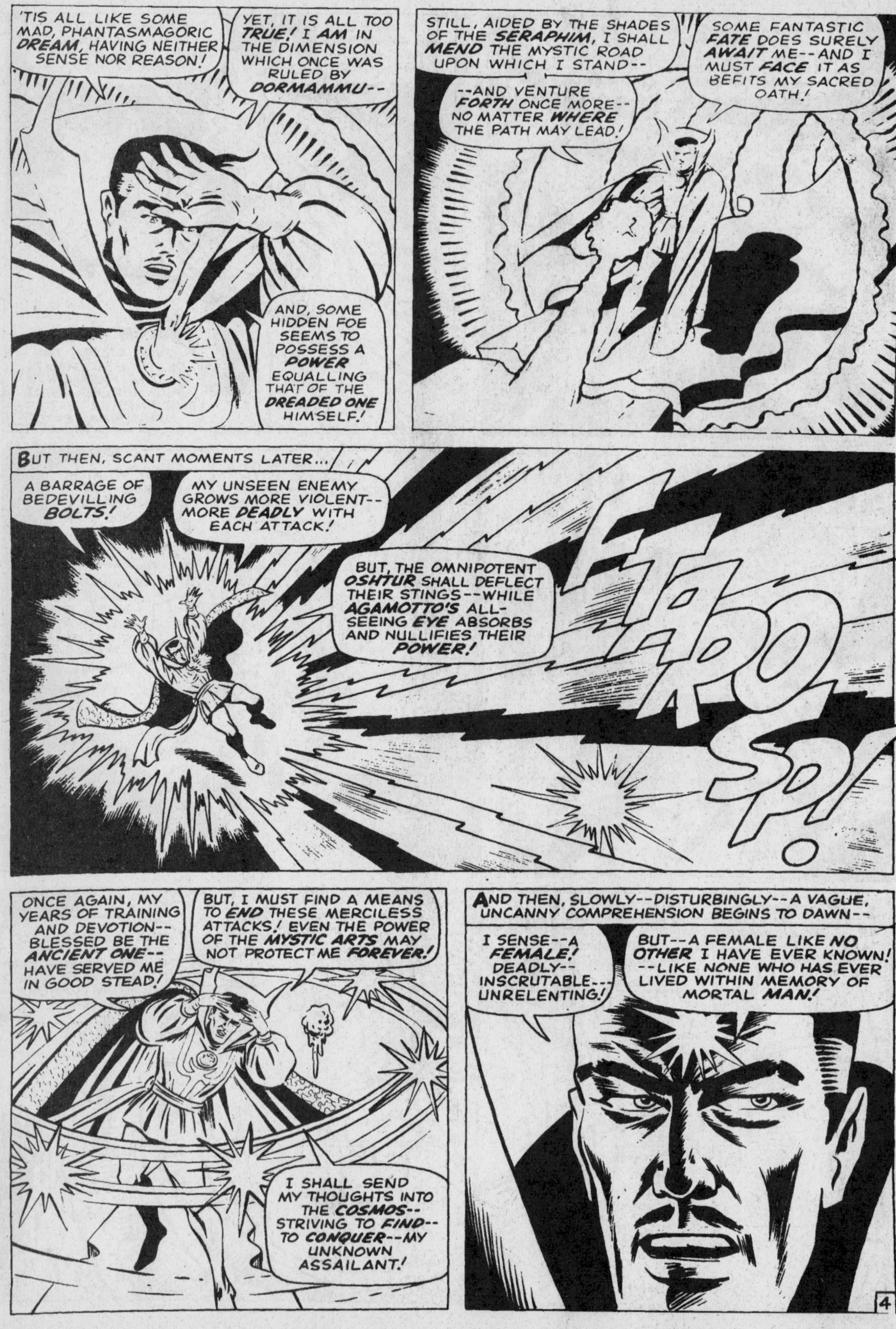
'TIS ALL LIKE SOME MAD, PHANTASMAGORIC DREAM, HAVING NEITHER SENSE NOR REASON!
YET, IT IS ALL TOO TRUE! I AM IN THE DIMENSION WHICH ONCE WAS RULED BY DORMAMMU--
AND, SOME HIDDEN FOE SEEMS TO POSSESS A POWER EQUALLING THAT OF THE DREADED ONE HIMSELF!
STILL, AIDED BY THE SHADES OF THE SERAPHIM, I SHALL MEND THE MYSTIC ROAD UPON WHICH I STAND--
--AND VENTURE FORTH ONCE MORE--NO MATTER WHERE THE PATH MAY LEAD!
SOME FANTASTIC FATE DOES SURELY AWAIT ME--AND I MUST FACE IT AS BEFITS MY SACRED OATH!
BUT THEN, SCANT MOMENTS LATER...
A BARRAGE OF BEDEVILLING BOLTS!
MY UNSEEN ENEMY GROWS MORE VIOLENT--MORE DEADLY WITH EACH ATTACK!
BUT, THE OMNIPOTENT OSHTUR SHALL DEFLECT THEIR STINGS--WHILE AGAMOTTO'S ALL-SEEING EYE ABSORBS AND NULLIFIES THEIR POWER!
FTAROOSP!
ONCE AGAIN, MY YEARS OF TRAINING AND DEVOTION--BLESSED BE THE ANCIENT ONE--HAVE SERVED ME IN GOOD STEAD!
BUT, I MUST FIND A MEANS TO END THESE MERCILESS ATTACKS! EVEN THE POWER OF THE MYSTIC ARTS MAY NOT PROTECT ME FOREVER!
I SHALL SEND MY THOUGHTS INTO THE COSMOS--STRIVING TO FIND--TO CONQUER--MY UNKNOWN ASSAILANT!
AND THEN, SLOWLY--DISTURBINGLY--A VAGUE, UNCANNY COMPREHENSION BEGINS TO DAWN--
I SENSE--A FEMALE! DEADLY--INSCRUTABLE--UNRELENTING!
BUT--A FEMALE LIKE NO OTHER I HAVE EVER KNOWN! --LIKE NONE WHO HAS EVER LIVED WITHIN MEMORY OF MORTAL MAN!
4

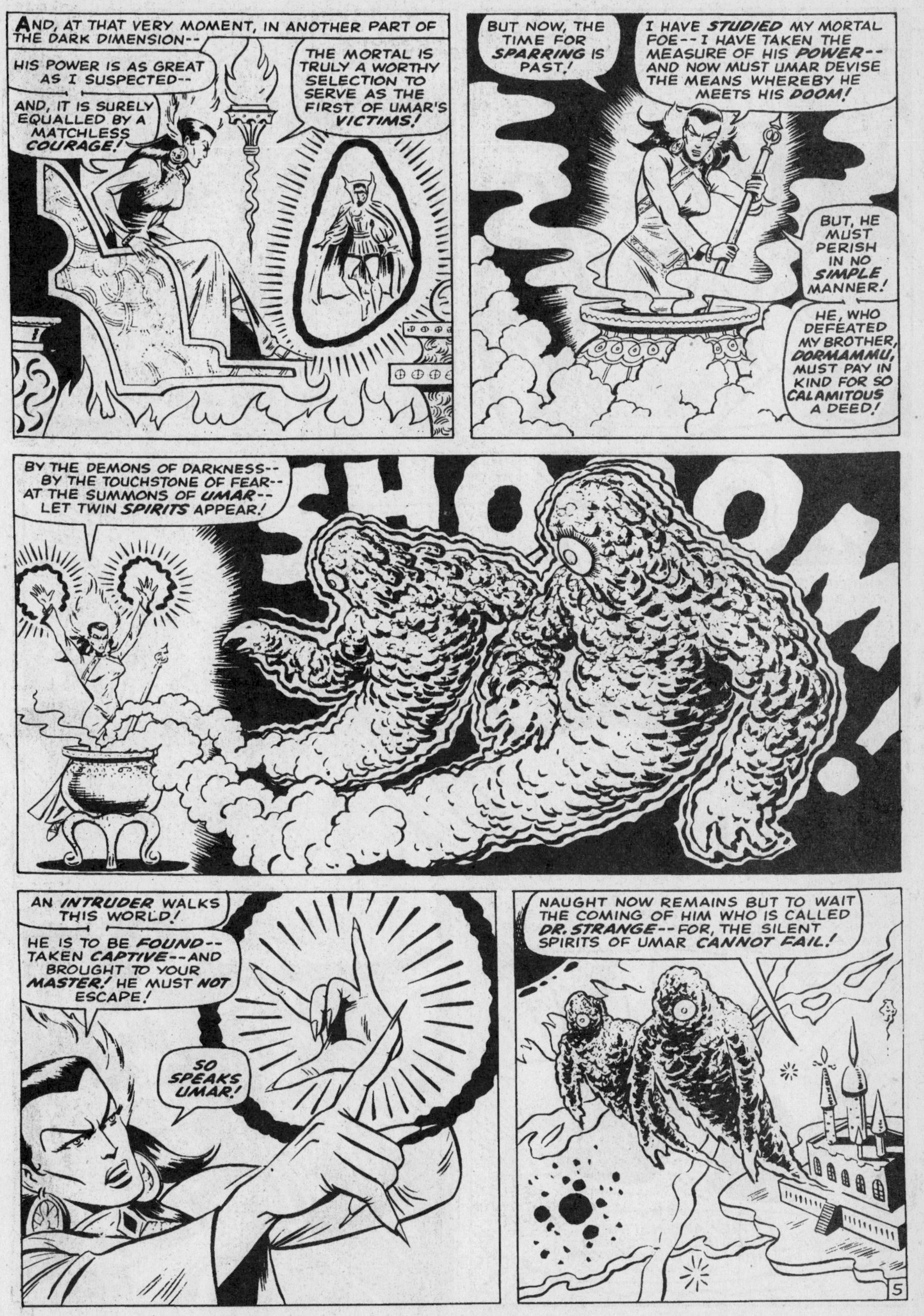
AND, AT THAT VERY MOMENT, IN ANOTHER PART OF THE DARK DIMENSION--
HIS POWER IS AS GREAT AS I SUSPECTED--
AND, IT IS SURELY EQUALLED BY A MATCHLESS COURAGE!
THE MORTAL IS TRULY A WORTHY SELECTION TO SERVE AS THE FIRST OF UMAR'S VICTIMS!
BUT NOW, THE TIME FOR SPARRING IS PAST!
I HAVE STUDIED MY MORTAL FOE--I HAVE TAKEN THE MEASURE OF HIS POWER--AND NOW MUST UMAR DEVISE THE MEANS WHEREBY HE MEETS HIS DOOM!
BUT, HE MUST PERISH IN NO SIMPLE MANNER!
HE, WHO DEFEATED MY BROTHER, DORMAMMU, MUST PAY IN KIND FOR SO CALAMITOUS A DEED!
BY THE DEMONS OF DARKNESS--BY THE TOUCHSTONE OF FEAR--AT THE SUMMONS OF UMAR--LET TWIN SPIRITS APPEAR!
SHOOOM!
AN INTRUDER WALKS THIS WORLD!
HE IS TO BE FOUND--TAKEN CAPTIVE--AND BROUGHT TO YOUR MASTER! HE MUST NOT ESCAPE!
SO SPEAKS UMAR!
NAUGHT NOW REMAINS BUT TO WAIT THE COMING OF HIM WHO IS CALLED DR. STRANGE--FOR, THE SILENT SPIRITS OF UMAR CANNOT FAIL!
5

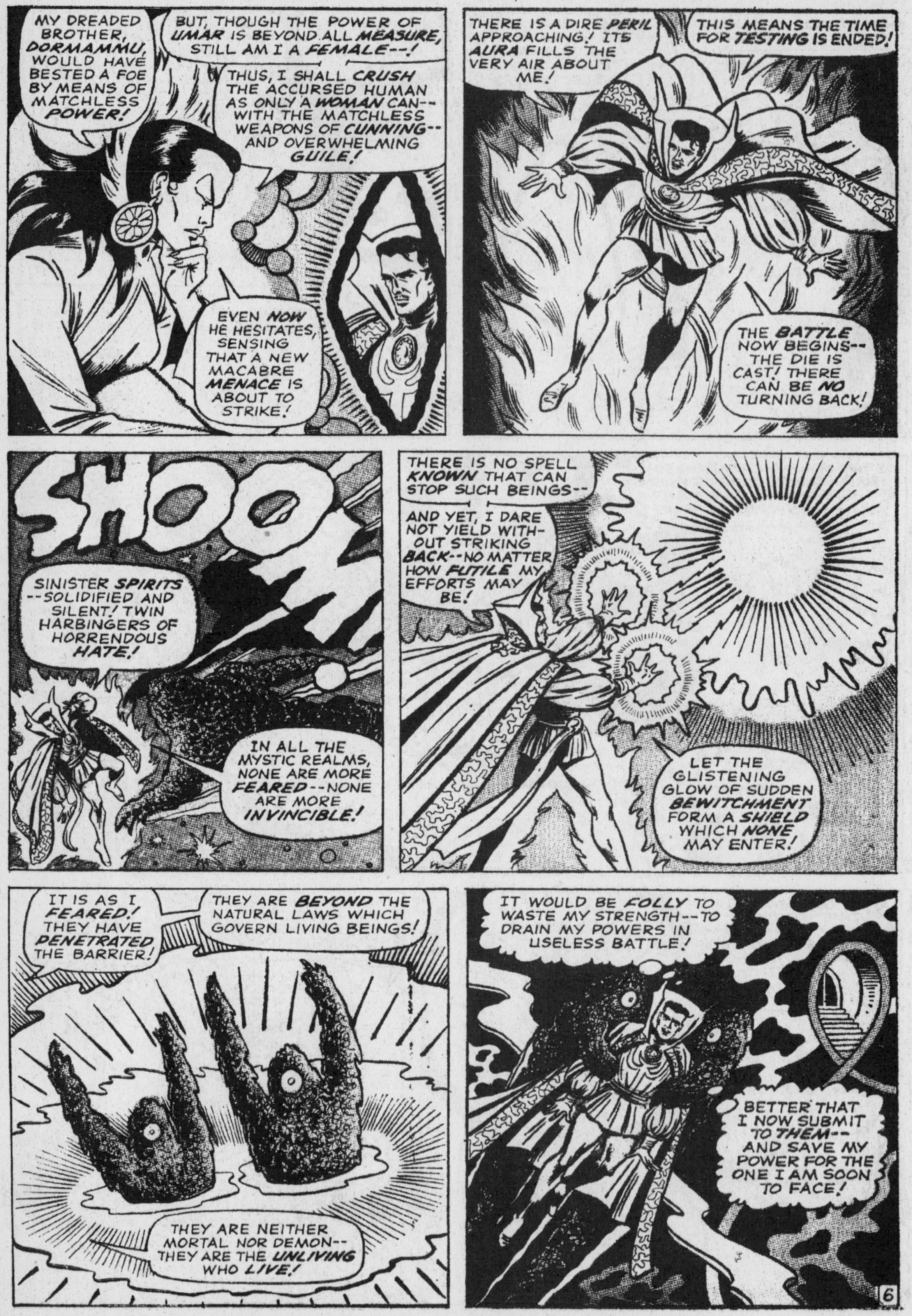
MY DREADED BROTHER, DORMAMMU, WOULD HAVE BESTED A FOE BY MEANS OF MATCHLESS POWER!
BUT, THOUGH THE POWER OF UMAR IS BEYOND ALL MEASURE, STILL AM I A FEMALE--!
THUS, I SHALL CRUSH THE ACCURSED HUMAN AS ONLY A WOMAN CAN--WITH THE MATCHLESS WEAPONS OF CUNNING--AND OVERWHELMING GUILE!
EVEN NOW HE HESITATES, SENSING THAT A NEW MACABRE MENACE IS ABOUT TO STRIKE!
THERE IS A DIRE PERIL APPROACHING! ITS AURA FILLS THE VERY AIR ABOUT ME!
THIS MEANS THE TIME FOR TESTING IS ENDED!
THE BATTLE NOW BEGINS--THE DIE IS CAST! THERE CAN BE NO TURNING BACK!
SHOOM
SINISTER SPIRITS--SOLIDIFIED AND SILENT! TWIN HARBINGERS OF HORRENDOUS HATE!
IN ALL THE MYSTIC REALMS, NONE ARE MORE FEARED--NONE ARE MORE INVINCIBLE!
THERE IS NO SPELL KNOWN THAT CAN STOP SUCH BEINGS--
AND YET, I DARE NOT YIELD WITHOUT STRIKING BACK--NO MATTER HOW FUTILE MY EFFORTS MAY BE!
LET THE GLISTENING GLOW OF SUDDEN BEWITCHMENT FORM A SHIELD WHICH NONE MAY ENTER!
IT IS AS I FEARED! THEY HAVE PENETRATED THE BARRIER!
THEY ARE BEYOND THE NATURAL LAWS WHICH GOVERN LIVING BEINGS!
THEY ARE NEITHER MORTAL NOR DEMON--THEY ARE THE UNLIVING WHO LIVE!
IT WOULD BE FOLLY TO WASTE MY STRENGTH--TO DRAIN MY POWERS IN USELESS BATTLE!
BETTER THAT I NOW SUBMIT TO THEM--AND SAVE MY POWER FOR THE ONE I AM SOON TO FACE!
6

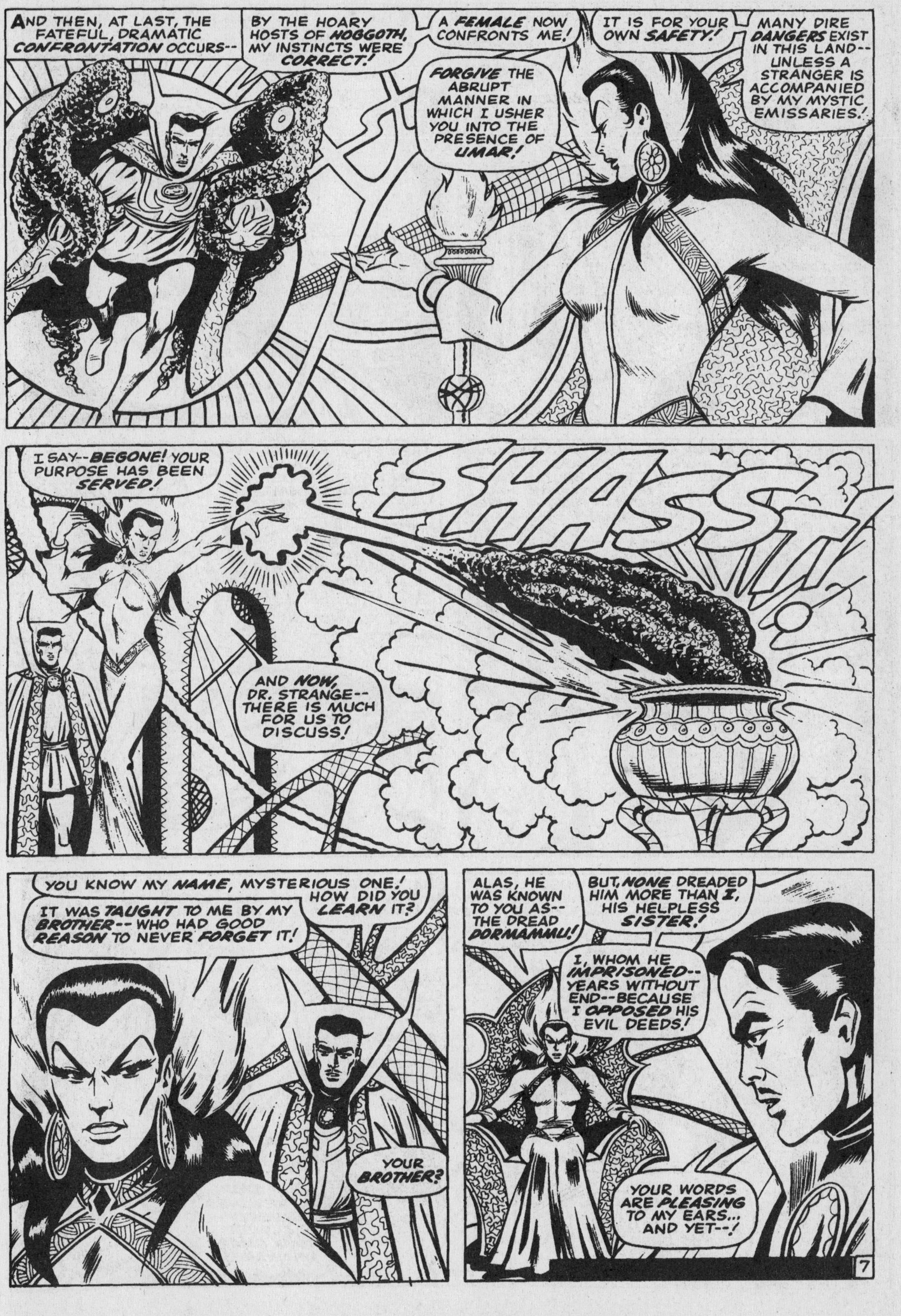
AND THEN, AT LAST, THE FATEFUL, DRAMATIC CONFRONTATION OCCURS--
BY THE HOARY HOSTS OF HOGGOTH, MY INSTINCTS WERE CORRECT!
A FEMALE NOW CONFRONTS ME!
FORGIVE THE ABRUPT MANNER IN WHICH I USHER YOU INTO THE PRESENCE OF UMAR!
IT IS FOR YOUR OWN SAFETY!
MANY DIRE DANGERS EXIST IN THIS LAND-- UNLESS A STRANGER IS ACCOMPANIED BY MY MYSTIC EMISSARIES!
I SAY--BEGONE! YOUR PURPOSE HAS BEEN SERVED!
SHASST!
AND NOW, DR. STRANGE-- THERE IS MUCH FOR US TO DISCUSS!
YOU KNOW MY NAME, MYSTERIOUS ONE! HOW DID YOU LEARN IT?
IT WAS TAUGHT TO ME BY MY BROTHER-- WHO HAD GOOD REASON TO NEVER FORGET IT!
YOUR BROTHER?
ALAS, HE WAS KNOWN TO YOU AS-- THE DREAD DORMAMMU!
BUT, NONE DREADED HIM MORE THAN I, HIS HELPLESS SISTER!
I, WHOM HE IMPRISONED-- YEARS WITHOUT END--BECAUSE I OPPOSED HIS EVIL DEEDS!
YOUR WORDS ARE PLEASING TO MY EARS... AND YET--!
7

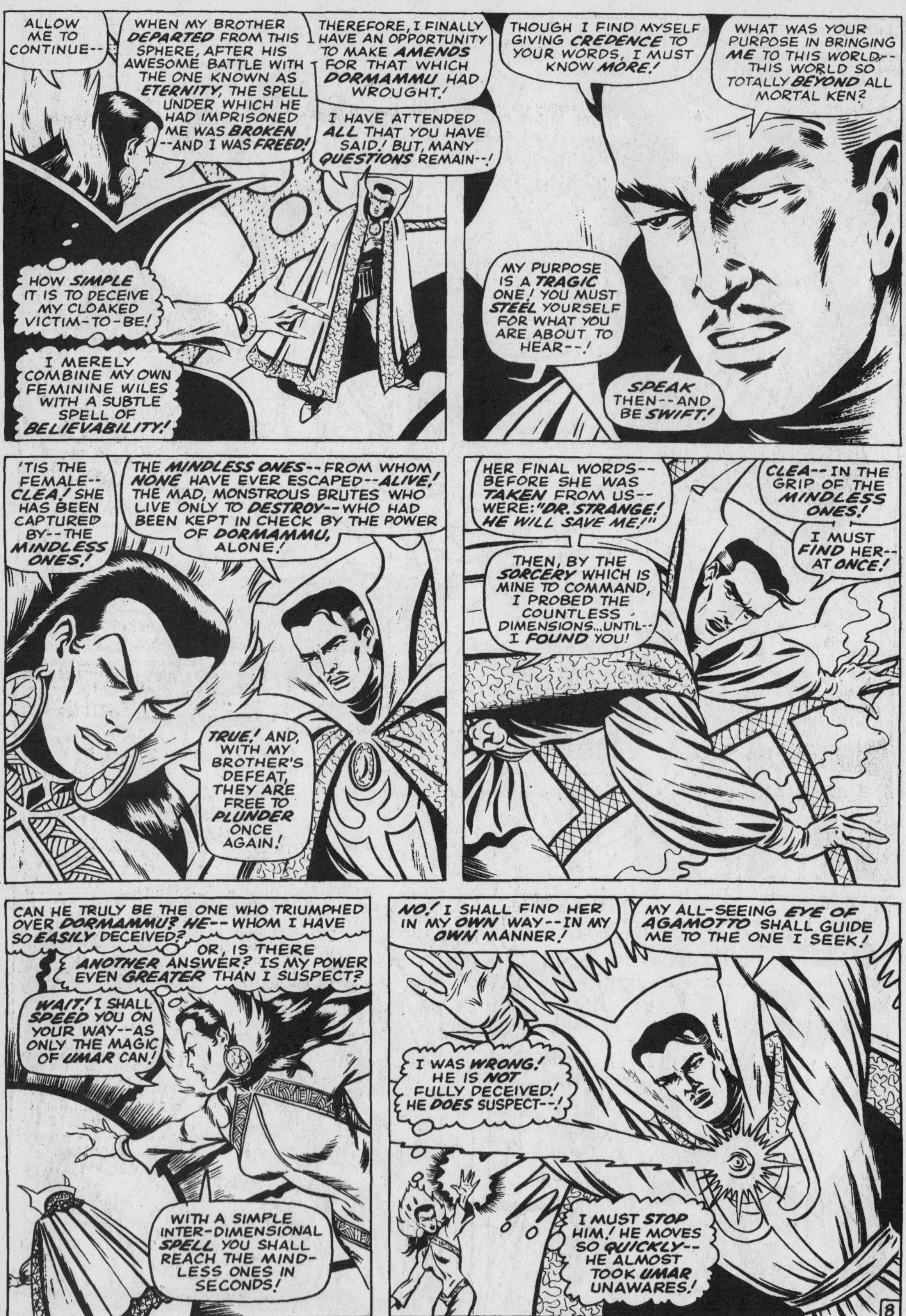
ALLOW ME TO CONTINUE--
WHEN MY BROTHER DEPARTED FROM THIS SPHERE, AFTER HIS AWESOME BATTLE WITH THE ONE KNOWN AS ETERNITY, THE SPELL UNDER WHICH HE HAD IMPRISONED ME WAS BROKEN --AND I WAS FREED!
THEREFORE, I FINALLY HAVE AN OPPORTUNITY TO MAKE AMENDS FOR THAT WHICH DORMAMMU HAD WROUGHT!
I HAVE ATTENDED ALL THAT YOU HAVE SAID! BUT, MANY QUESTIONS REMAIN--!
HOW SIMPLE IT IS TO DECEIVE MY CLOAKED VICTIM-TO-BE!
I MERELY COMBINE MY OWN FEMININE WILES WITH A SUBTLE SPELL OF BELIEVABILITY!
THOUGH I FIND MYSELF GIVING CREDENCE TO YOUR WORDS, I MUST KNOW MORE!
WHAT WAS YOUR PURPOSE IN BRINGING ME TO THIS WORLD-- THIS WORLD SO TOTALLY BEYOND ALL MORTAL KEN?
MY PURPOSE IS A TRAGIC ONE! YOU MUST STEEL YOURSELF FOR WHAT YOU ARE ABOUT TO HEAR--!
SPEAK THEN--AND BE SWIFT!
'TIS THE FEMALE-- CLEA! SHE HAS BEEN CAPTURED BY--THE MINDLESS ONES!
THE MINDLESS ONES--FROM WHOM NONE HAVE EVER ESCAPED--ALIVE! THE MAD, MONSTROUS BRUTES WHO LIVE ONLY TO DESTROY--WHO HAD BEEN KEPT IN CHECK BY THE POWER OF DORMAMMU, ALONE!
TRUE! AND, WITH MY BROTHER'S DEFEAT, THEY ARE FREE TO PLUNDER ONCE AGAIN!
HER FINAL WORDS-- BEFORE SHE WAS TAKEN FROM US-- WERE: "DR. STRANGE! HE WILL SAVE ME!"
THEN, BY THE SORCERY WHICH IS MINE TO COMMAND, I PROBED THE COUNTLESS DIMENSIONS...UNTIL-- I FOUND YOU!
CLEA--IN THE GRIP OF THE MINDLESS ONES!
I MUST FIND HER-- AT ONCE!
CAN HE TRULY BE THE ONE WHO TRIUMPHED OVER DORMAMMU? HE--WHOM I HAVE SO EASILY DECEIVED?
OR, IS THERE ANOTHER ANSWER? IS MY POWER EVEN GREATER THAN I SUSPECT?
WAIT! I SHALL SPEED YOU ON YOUR WAY--AS ONLY THE MAGIC OF UMAR CAN!
WITH A SIMPLE INTER-DIMENSIONAL SPELL YOU SHALL REACH THE MIND-LESS ONES IN SECONDS!
NO! I SHALL FIND HER IN MY OWN WAY--IN MY OWN MANNER!
MY ALL-SEEING EYE OF AGAMOTTO SHALL GUIDE ME TO THE ONE I SEEK!
I WAS WRONG! HE IS NOT FULLY DECEIVED! HE DOES SUSPECT--!
I MUST STOP HIM! HE MOVES SO QUICKLY-- HE ALMOST TOOK UMAR UNAWARES!
8

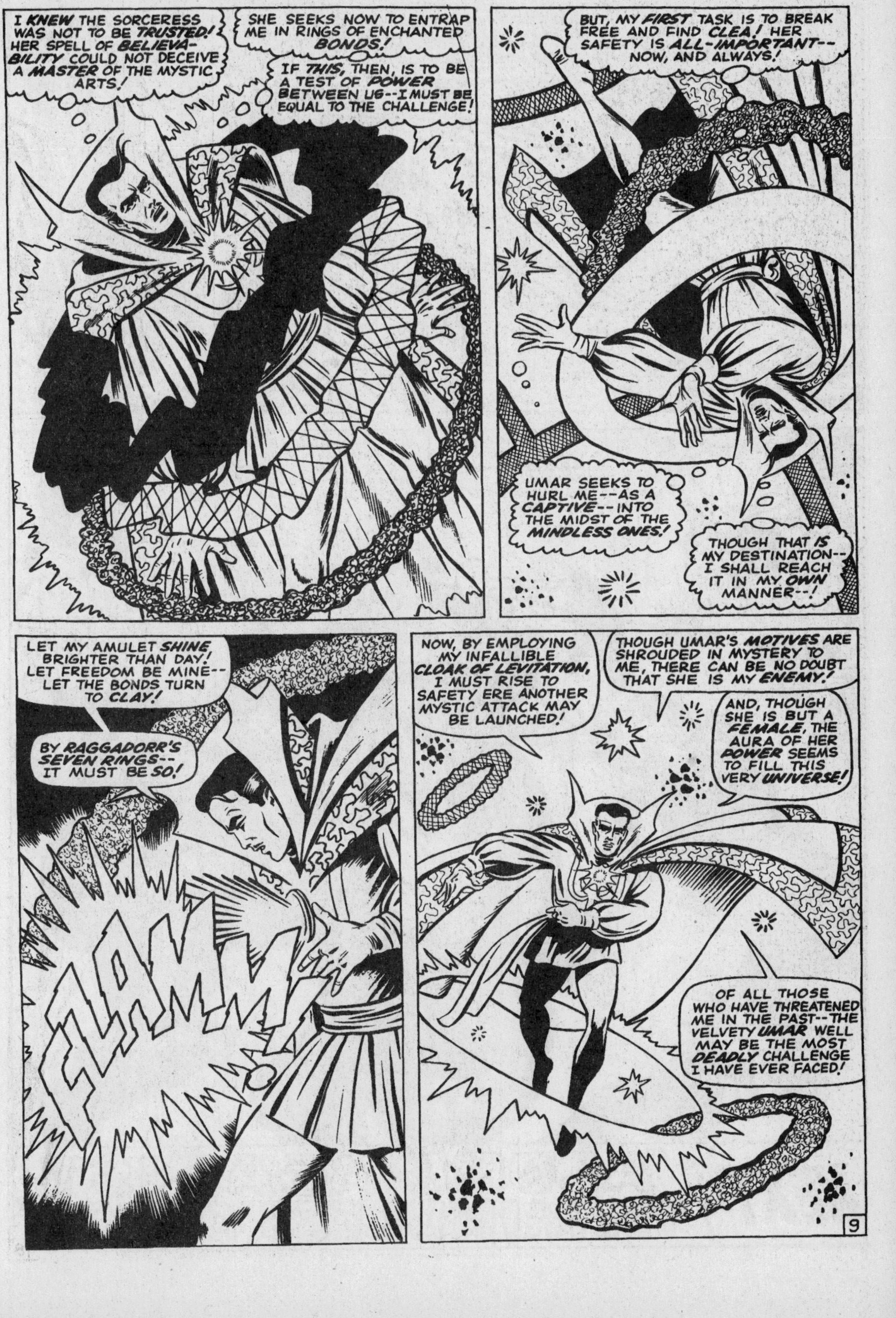
I KNEW THE SORCERESS WAS NOT TO BE TRUSTED! HER SPELL OF BELIEVA-BILITY COULD NOT DECEIVE A MASTER OF THE MYSTIC ARTS!
SHE SEEKS NOW TO ENTRAP ME IN RINGS OF ENCHANTED BONDS!
IF THIS, THEN, IS TO BE A TEST OF POWER BETWEEN US--I MUST BE EQUAL TO THE CHALLENGE!
BUT, MY FIRST TASK IS TO BREAK FREE AND FIND CLEA! HER SAFETY IS ALL-IMPORTANT--NOW, AND ALWAYS!
UMAR SEEKS TO HURL ME--AS A CAPTIVE--INTO THE MIDST OF THE MINDLESS ONES!
THOUGH THAT IS MY DESTINATION--I SHALL REACH IT IN MY OWN MANNER--!
LET MY AMULET SHINE BRIGHTER THAN DAY! LET FREEDOM BE MINE--LET THE BONDS TURN TO CLAY!
BY RAGGADORR'S SEVEN RINGS--IT MUST BE SO!
FLAM
NOW, BY EMPLOYING MY INFALLIBLE CLOAK OF LEVITATION, I MUST RISE TO SAFETY ERE ANOTHER MYSTIC ATTACK MAY BE LAUNCHED!
THOUGH UMAR'S MOTIVES ARE SHROUDED IN MYSTERY TO ME, THERE CAN BE NO DOUBT THAT SHE IS MY ENEMY!
AND, THOUGH SHE IS BUT A FEMALE, THE AURA OF HER POWER SEEMS TO FILL THIS VERY UNIVERSE!
OF ALL THOSE WHO HAVE THREATENED ME IN THE PAST--THE VELVETY UMAR WELL MAY BE THE MOST DEADLY CHALLENGE I HAVE EVER FACED!
9

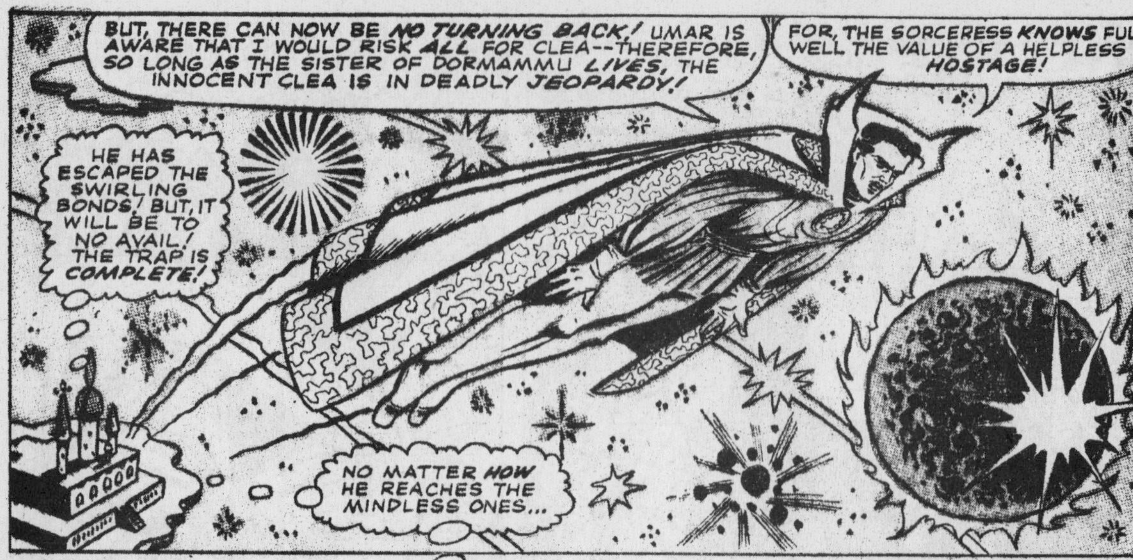
BUT, THERE CAN NOW BE NO TURNING BACK! UMAR IS AWARE THAT I WOULD RISK ALL FOR CLEA--THEREFORE, SO LONG AS THE SISTER OF DORMAMMU LIVES, THE INNOCENT CLEA IS IN DEADLY JEOPARDY!
FOR, THE SORCERESS KNOWS FULL WELL THE VALUE OF A HELPLESS HOSTAGE!
HE HAS ESCAPED THE SWIRLING BONDS! BUT, IT WILL BE TO NO AVAIL! THE TRAP IS COMPLETE!
NO MATTER HOW HE REACHES THE MINDLESS ONES...

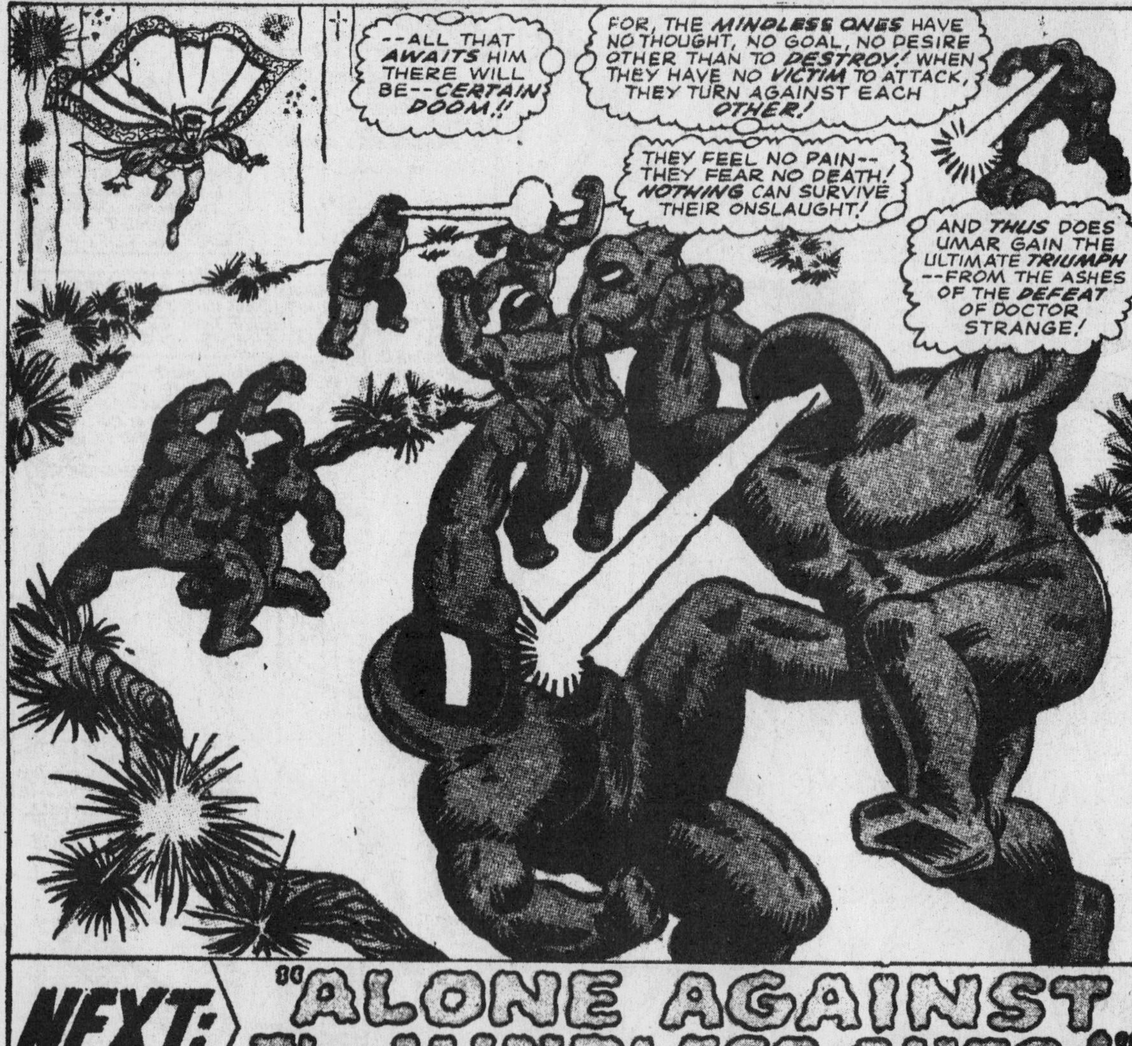
--ALL THAT AWAITS HIM THERE WILL BE--CERTAIN DOOM!!
FOR, THE MINDLESS ONES HAVE NO THOUGHT, NO GOAL, NO DESIRE OTHER THAN TO DESTROY! WHEN THEY HAVE NO VICTIM TO ATTACK, THEY TURN AGAINST EACH OTHER!
THEY FEEL NO PAIN--THEY FEAR NO DEATH! NOTHING CAN SURVIVE THEIR ONSLAUGHT!
AND THUS DOES UMAR GAIN THE ULTIMATE TRIUMPH --FROM THE ASHES OF THE DEFEAT OF DOCTOR STRANGE!

NEXT: "ALONE AGAINST The MINDLESS ONES!"

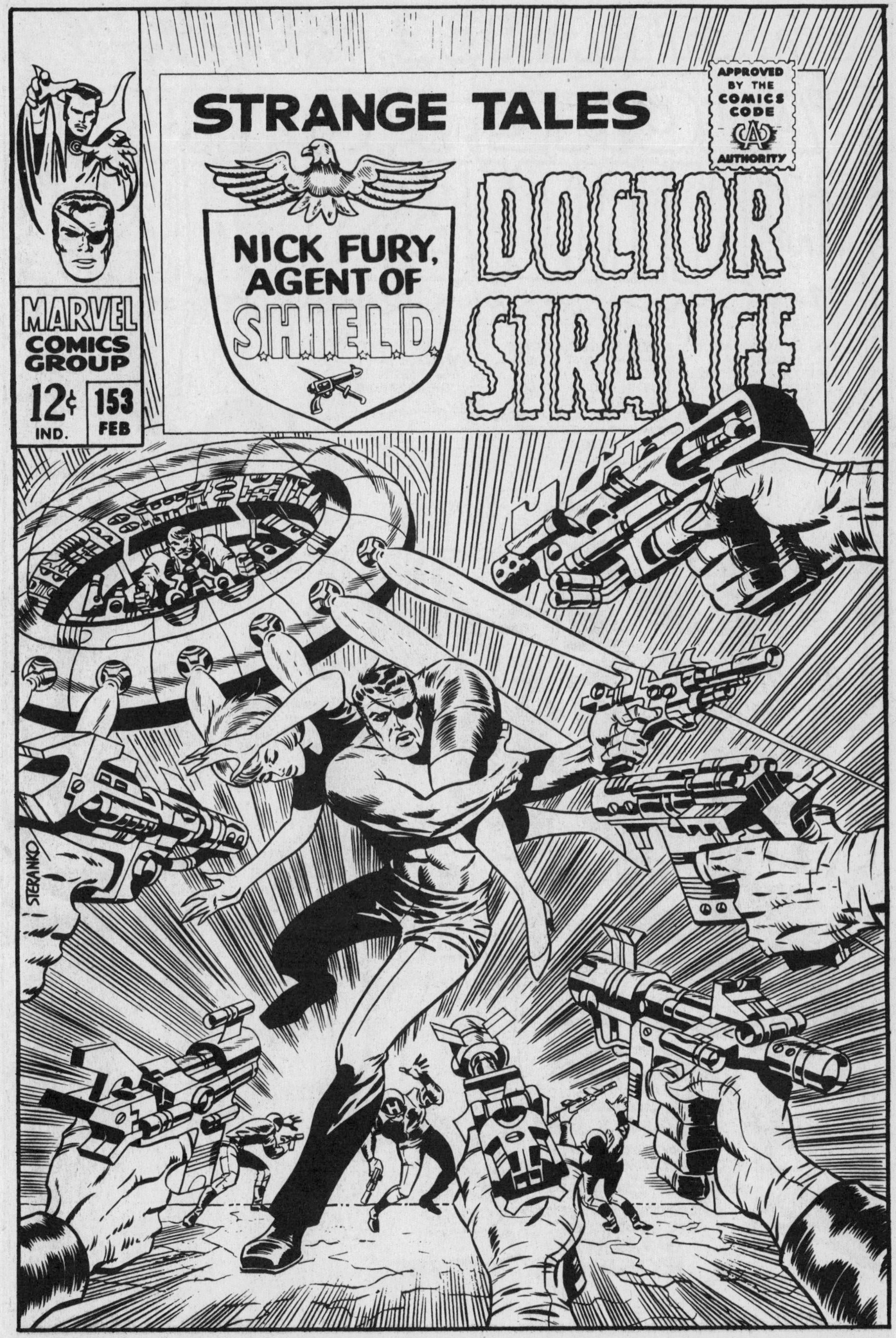
STRANGE TALES
APPROVED BY THE COMICS CODE AUTHORITY
NICK FURY, AGENT OF S.H.I.E.L.D.
DOCTOR STRANGE
MARVEL COMICS GROUP
12¢ IND.
153 FEB
STERANKO

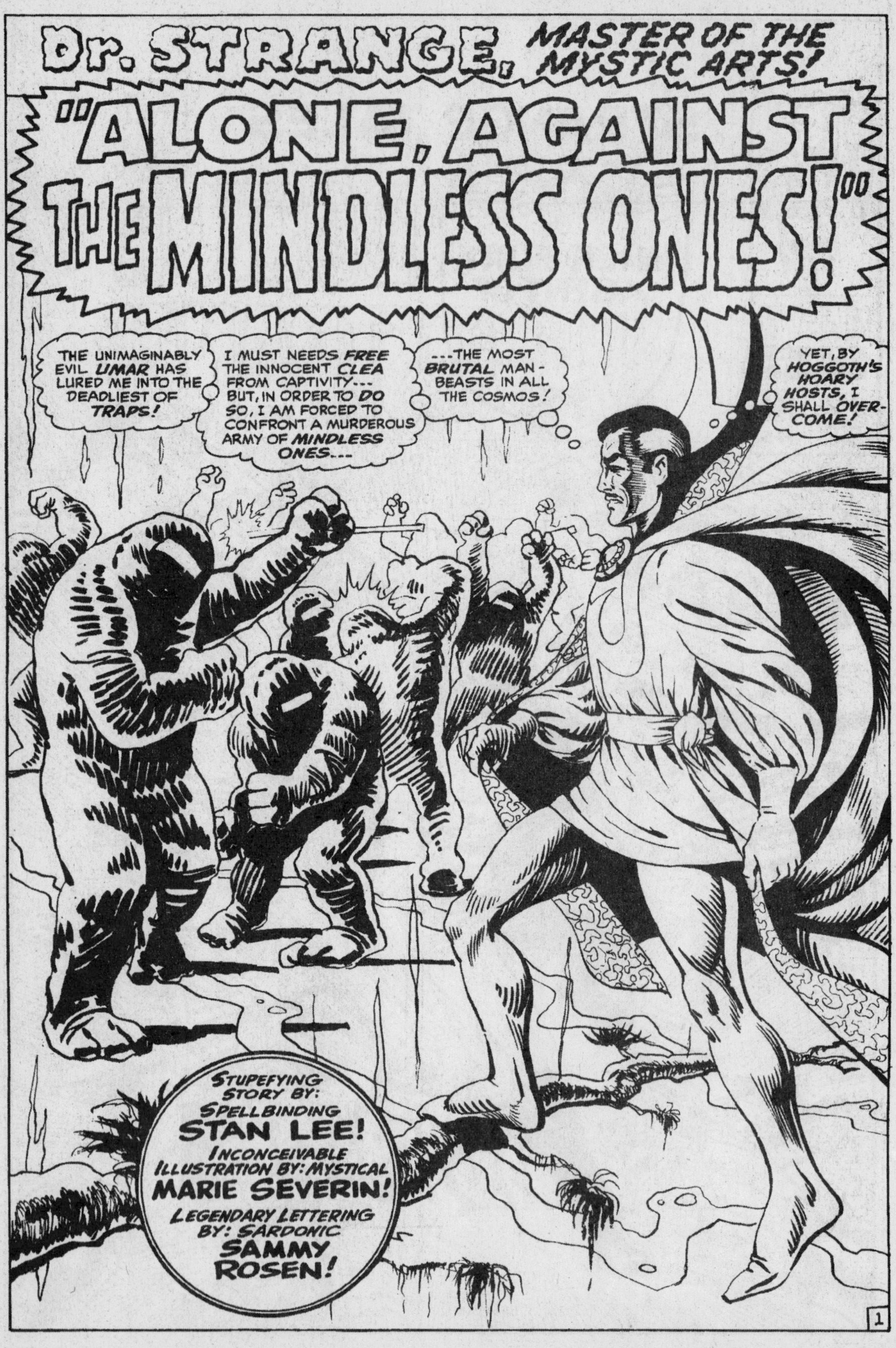
Dr. STRANGE, MASTER OF THE MYSTIC ARTS!
"ALONE, AGAINST THE MINDLESS ONES!"
THE UNIMAGINABLY EVIL UMAR HAS LURED ME INTO THE DEADLIEST OF TRAPS!
I MUST NEEDS FREE THE INNOCENT CLEA FROM CAPTIVITY--- BUT, IN ORDER TO DO SO, I AM FORCED TO CONFRONT A MURDEROUS ARMY OF MINDLESS ONES---
---THE MOST BRUTAL MAN-BEASTS IN ALL THE COSMOS!
YET, BY HOGGOTH'S HOARY HOSTS, I SHALL OVER-COME!
STUPEFYING STORY BY: SPELLBINDING STAN LEE! INCONCEIVABLE ILLUSTRATION BY: MYSTICAL MARIE SEVERIN! LEGENDARY LETTERING BY: SARDONIC SAMMY ROSEN!
1

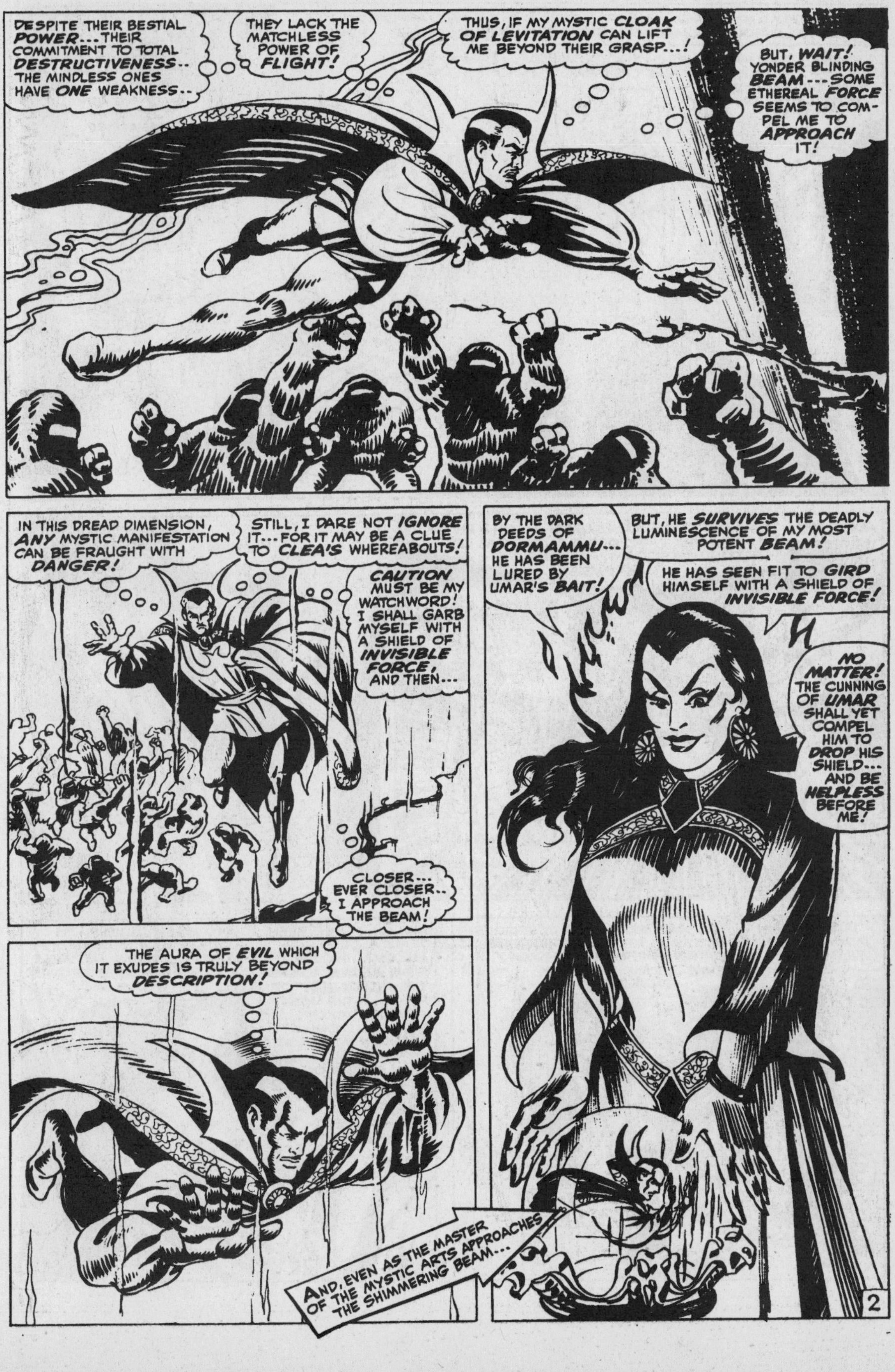
DESPITE THEIR BESTIAL POWER... THEIR COMMITMENT TO TOTAL DESTRUCTIVENESS.. THE MINDLESS ONES HAVE ONE WEAKNESS..
THEY LACK THE MATCHLESS POWER OF FLIGHT!
THUS, IF MY MYSTIC CLOAK OF LEVITATION CAN LIFT ME BEYOND THEIR GRASP...!
BUT, WAIT! YONDER BLINDING BEAM---SOME ETHEREAL FORCE SEEMS TO COMPEL ME TO APPROACH IT!
IN THIS DREAD DIMENSION, ANY MYSTIC MANIFESTATION CAN BE FRAUGHT WITH DANGER!
STILL, I DARE NOT IGNORE IT... FOR IT MAY BE A CLUE TO CLEA'S WHEREABOUTS!
CAUTION MUST BE MY WATCHWORD! I SHALL GARB MYSELF WITH A SHIELD OF INVISIBLE FORCE, AND THEN...
CLOSER... EVER CLOSER.. I APPROACH THE BEAM!
THE AURA OF EVIL WHICH IT EXUDES IS TRULY BEYOND DESCRIPTION!
AND, EVEN AS THE MASTER OF THE MYSTIC ARTS APPROACHES THE SHIMMERING BEAM...
BY THE DARK DEEDS OF DORMAMMU... HE HAS BEEN LURED BY UMAR'S BAIT!
BUT, HE SURVIVES THE DEADLY LUMINESCENCE OF MY MOST POTENT BEAM!
HE HAS SEEN FIT TO GIRD HIMSELF WITH A SHIELD OF INVISIBLE FORCE!
NO MATTER! THE CUNNING OF UMAR SHALL YET COMPEL HIM TO DROP HIS SHIELD... AND BE HELPLESS BEFORE ME!
2

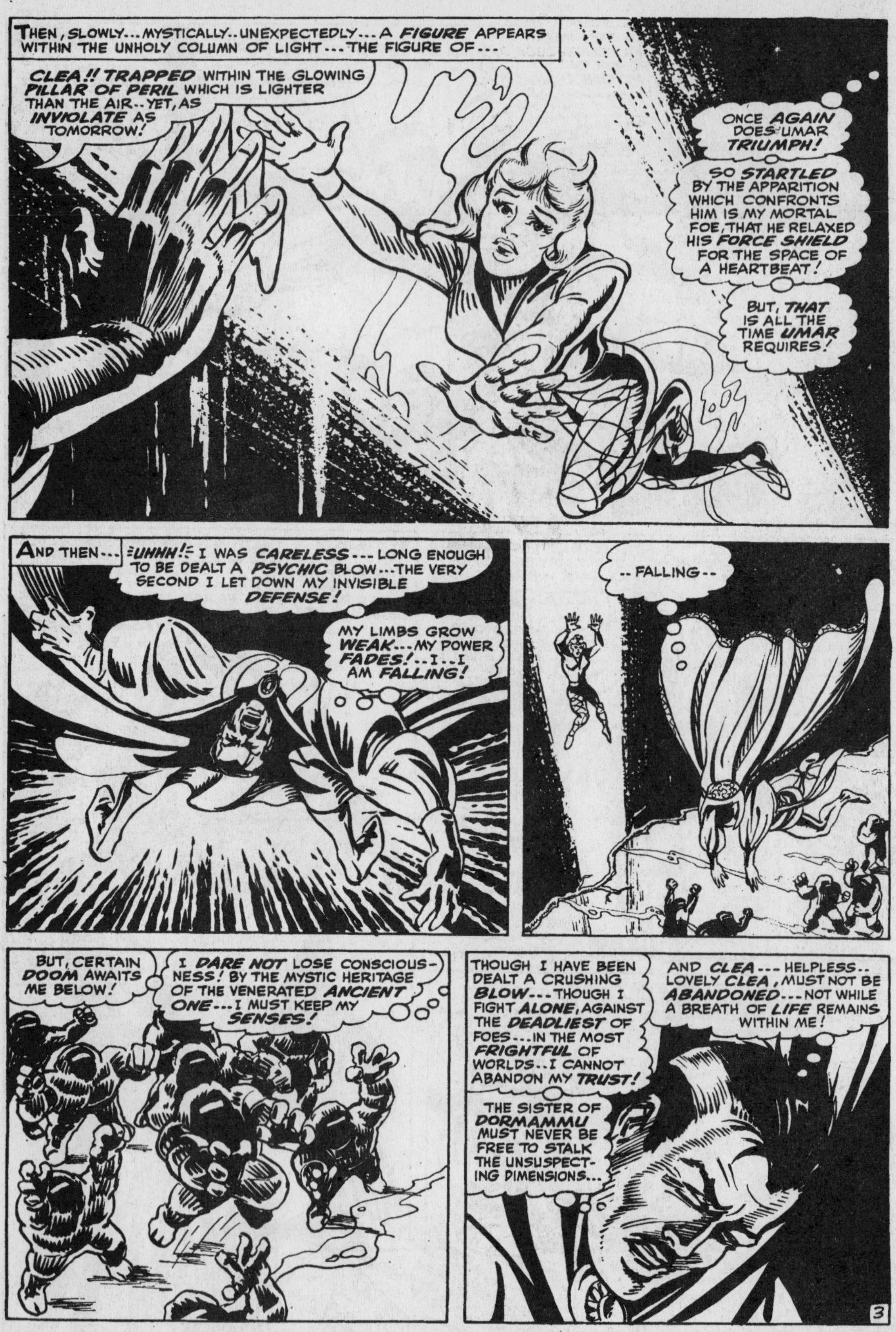
THEN, SLOWLY... MYSTICALLY.. UNEXPECTEDLY... A FIGURE APPEARS WITHIN THE UNHOLY COLUMN OF LIGHT... THE FIGURE OF...
CLEA!! TRAPPED WITHIN THE GLOWING PILLAR OF PERIL WHICH IS LIGHTER THAN THE AIR-- YET, AS INVIOLATE AS TOMORROW!
ONCE AGAIN DOES UMAR TRIUMPH!
SO STARTLED BY THE APPARITION WHICH CONFRONTS HIM IS MY MORTAL FOE, THAT HE RELAXED HIS FORCE SHIELD FOR THE SPACE OF A HEARTBEAT!
BUT, THAT IS ALL THE TIME UMAR REQUIRES!
AND THEN...
UHHH!-- I WAS CARELESS --- LONG ENOUGH TO BE DEALT A PSYCHIC BLOW---THE VERY SECOND I LET DOWN MY INVISIBLE DEFENSE!
MY LIMBS GROW WEAK---MY POWER FADES!.. I.. I AM FALLING!
-- FALLING --
BUT, CERTAIN DOOM AWAITS ME BELOW!
I DARE NOT LOSE CONSCIOUSNESS! BY THE MYSTIC HERITAGE OF THE VENERATED ANCIENT ONE--- I MUST KEEP MY SENSES!
THOUGH I HAVE BEEN DEALT A CRUSHING BLOW--- THOUGH I FIGHT ALONE, AGAINST THE DEADLIEST OF FOES... IN THE MOST FRIGHTFUL OF WORLDS.. I CANNOT ABANDON MY TRUST!
AND CLEA --- HELPLESS.. LOVELY CLEA, MUST NOT BE ABANDONED--- NOT WHILE A BREATH OF LIFE REMAINS WITHIN ME!
THE SISTER OF DORMAMMU MUST NEVER BE FREE TO STALK THE UNSUSPECTING DIMENSIONS...
3

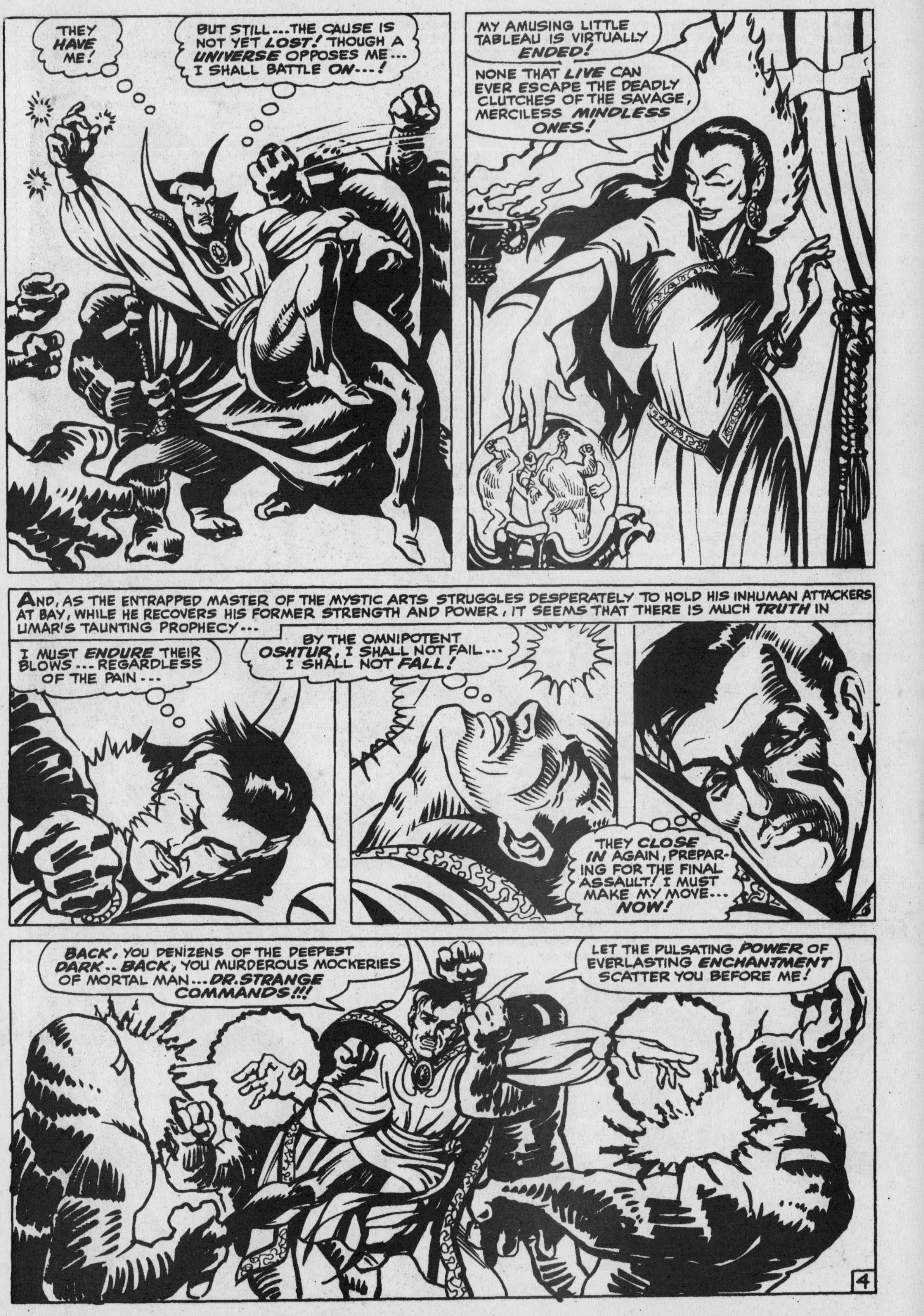
THEY HAVE ME!
BUT STILL... THE CAUSE IS NOT YET LOST! THOUGH A UNIVERSE OPPOSES ME... I SHALL BATTLE ON...!
MY AMUSING LITTLE TABLEAU IS VIRTUALLY ENDED!
NONE THAT LIVE CAN EVER ESCAPE THE DEADLY CLUTCHES OF THE SAVAGE, MERCILESS MINDLESS ONES!
AND, AS THE ENTRAPPED MASTER OF THE MYSTIC ARTS STRUGGLES DESPERATELY TO HOLD HIS INHUMAN ATTACKERS AT BAY, WHILE HE RECOVERS HIS FORMER STRENGTH AND POWER, IT SEEMS THAT THERE IS MUCH TRUTH IN UMAR'S TAUNTING PROPHECY...
I MUST ENDURE THEIR BLOWS... REGARDLESS OF THE PAIN...
BY THE OMNIPOTENT OSHTUR, I SHALL NOT FAIL... I SHALL NOT FALL!
THEY CLOSE IN AGAIN, PREPARING FOR THE FINAL ASSAULT! I MUST MAKE MY MOVE... NOW!
BACK, YOU DENIZENS OF THE DEEPEST DARK.. BACK, YOU MURDEROUS MOCKERIES OF MORTAL MAN... DR. STRANGE COMMANDS!!!
LET THE PULSATING POWER OF EVERLASTING ENCHANTMENT SCATTER YOU BEFORE ME!
4

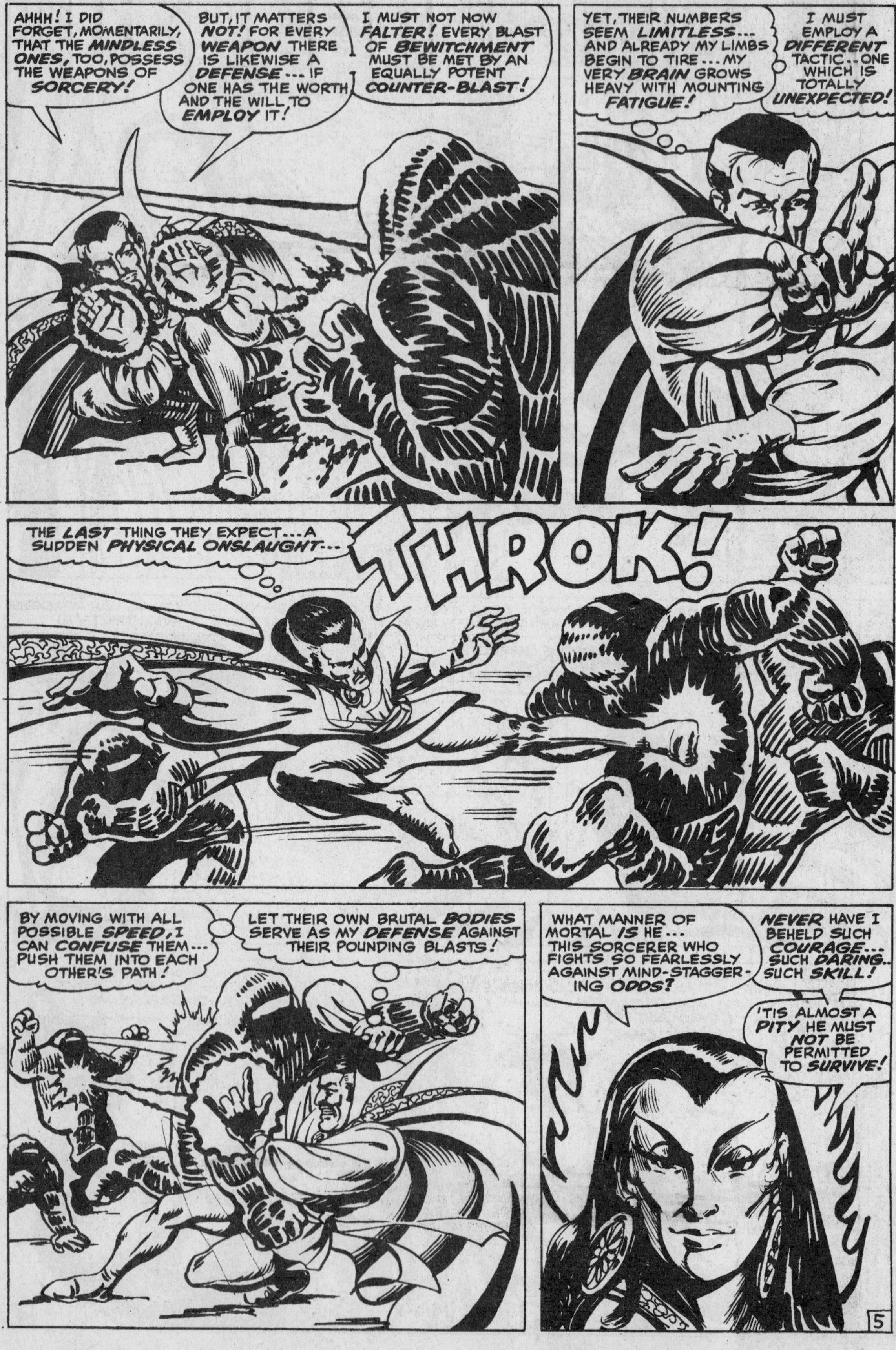
AHHH! I DID FORGET, MOMENTARILY, THAT THE MINDLESS ONES, TOO, POSSESS THE WEAPONS OF SORCERY!
BUT, IT MATTERS NOT! FOR EVERY WEAPON THERE IS LIKEWISE A DEFENSE... IF ONE HAS THE WORTH AND THE WILL TO EMPLOY IT!
I MUST NOT NOW FALTER! EVERY BLAST OF BEWITCHMENT MUST BE MET BY AN EQUALLY POTENT COUNTER-BLAST!
YET, THEIR NUMBERS SEEM LIMITLESS... AND ALREADY MY LIMBS BEGIN TO TIRE... MY VERY BRAIN GROWS HEAVY WITH MOUNTING FATIGUE!
I MUST EMPLOY A DIFFERENT TACTIC... ONE WHICH IS TOTALLY UNEXPECTED!
THE LAST THING THEY EXPECT... A SUDDEN PHYSICAL ONSLAUGHT...
THROK!
BY MOVING WITH ALL POSSIBLE SPEED, I CAN CONFUSE THEM... PUSH THEM INTO EACH OTHER'S PATH!
LET THEIR OWN BRUTAL BODIES SERVE AS MY DEFENSE AGAINST THEIR POUNDING BLASTS!
WHAT MANNER OF MORTAL IS HE... THIS SORCERER WHO FIGHTS SO FEARLESSLY AGAINST MIND-STAGGERING ODDS?
NEVER HAVE I BEHELD SUCH COURAGE... SUCH DARING.. SUCH SKILL!
'TIS ALMOST A PITY HE MUST NOT BE PERMITTED TO SURVIVE!
5

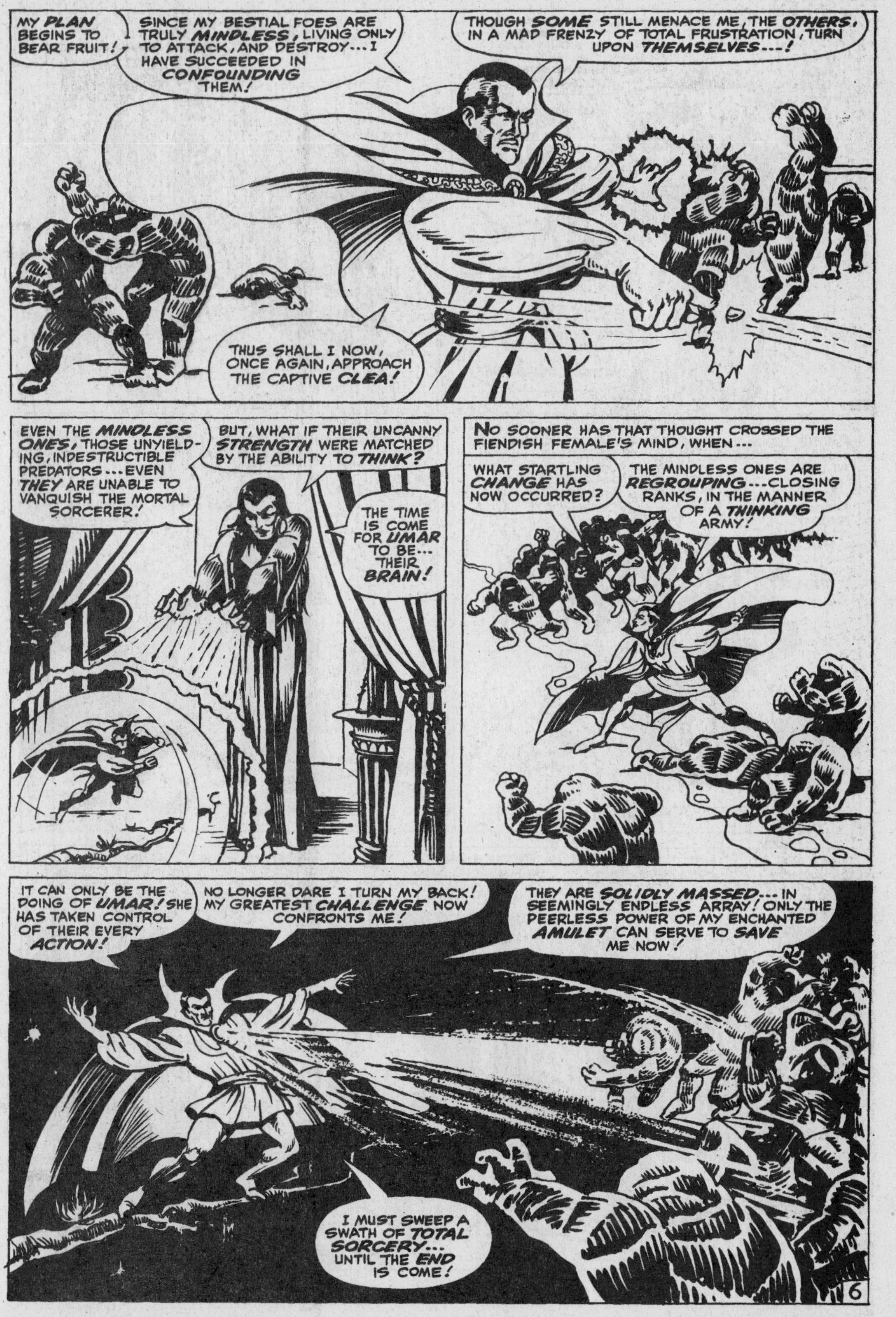

MY PLAN BEGINS TO BEAR FRUIT!
SINCE MY BESTIAL FOES ARE TRULY MINDLESS, LIVING ONLY TO ATTACK, AND DESTROY... I HAVE SUCCEEDED IN CONFOUNDING THEM!
THOUGH SOME STILL MENACE ME, THE OTHERS, IN A MAD FRENZY OF TOTAL FRUSTRATION, TURN UPON THEMSELVES---!
THUS SHALL I NOW, ONCE AGAIN, APPROACH THE CAPTIVE CLEA!
EVEN THE MINDLESS ONES, THOSE UNYIELDING, INDESTRUCTIBLE PREDATORS... EVEN THEY ARE UNABLE TO VANQUISH THE MORTAL SORCERER!
BUT, WHAT IF THEIR UNCANNY STRENGTH WERE MATCHED BY THE ABILITY TO THINK?
THE TIME IS COME FOR UMAR TO BE... THEIR BRAIN!
NO SOONER HAS THAT THOUGHT CROSSED THE FIENDISH FEMALE'S MIND, WHEN...
WHAT STARTLING CHANGE HAS NOW OCCURRED?
THE MINDLESS ONES ARE REGROUPING...CLOSING RANKS, IN THE MANNER OF A THINKING ARMY!
IT CAN ONLY BE THE DOING OF UMAR! SHE HAS TAKEN CONTROL OF THEIR EVERY ACTION!
NO LONGER DARE I TURN MY BACK! MY GREATEST CHALLENGE NOW CONFRONTS ME!
THEY ARE SOLIDLY MASSED... IN SEEMINGLY ENDLESS ARRAY! ONLY THE PEERLESS POWER OF MY ENCHANTED AMULET CAN SERVE TO SAVE ME NOW!
I MUST SWEEP A SWATH OF TOTAL SORCERY... UNTIL THE END IS COME!
6

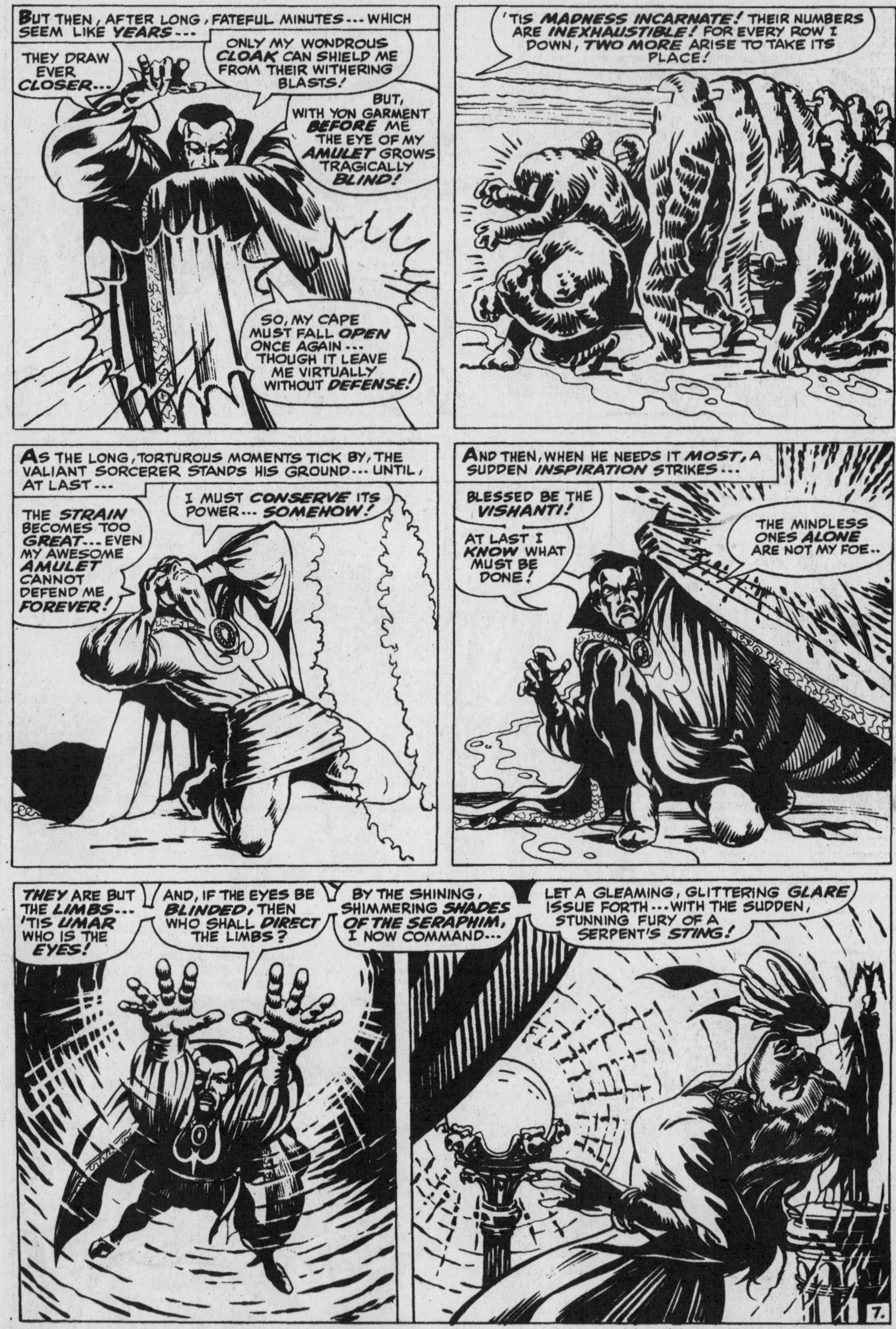

BUT THEN, AFTER LONG, FATEFUL MINUTES... WHICH SEEM LIKE YEARS...
THEY DRAW EVER CLOSER...
ONLY MY WONDROUS CLOAK CAN SHIELD ME FROM THEIR WITHERING BLASTS!
BUT, WITH YON GARMENT BEFORE ME THE EYE OF MY AMULET GROWS TRAGICALLY BLIND!
SO, MY CAPE MUST FALL OPEN ONCE AGAIN... THOUGH IT LEAVE ME VIRTUALLY WITHOUT DEFENSE!
'TIS MADNESS INCARNATE! THEIR NUMBERS ARE INEXHAUSTIBLE! FOR EVERY ROW I DOWN, TWO MORE ARISE TO TAKE ITS PLACE!
AS THE LONG, TORTUROUS MOMENTS TICK BY, THE VALIANT SORCERER STANDS HIS GROUND... UNTIL, AT LAST...
THE STRAIN BECOMES TOO GREAT... EVEN MY AWESOME AMULET CANNOT DEFEND ME FOREVER!
I MUST CONSERVE ITS POWER... SOMEHOW!
AND THEN, WHEN HE NEEDS IT MOST, A SUDDEN INSPIRATION STRIKES...
BLESSED BE THE VISHANTI!
AT LAST I KNOW WHAT MUST BE DONE!
THE MINDLESS ONES ALONE ARE NOT MY FOE..
THEY ARE BUT THE LIMBS... 'TIS UMAR WHO IS THE EYES!
AND, IF THE EYES BE BLINDED, THEN WHO SHALL DIRECT THE LIMBS?
BY THE SHINING, SHIMMERING SHADES OF THE SERAPHIM, I NOW COMMAND...
LET A GLEAMING, GLITTERING GLARE ISSUE FORTH... WITH THE SUDDEN, STUNNING FURY OF A SERPENT'S STING!

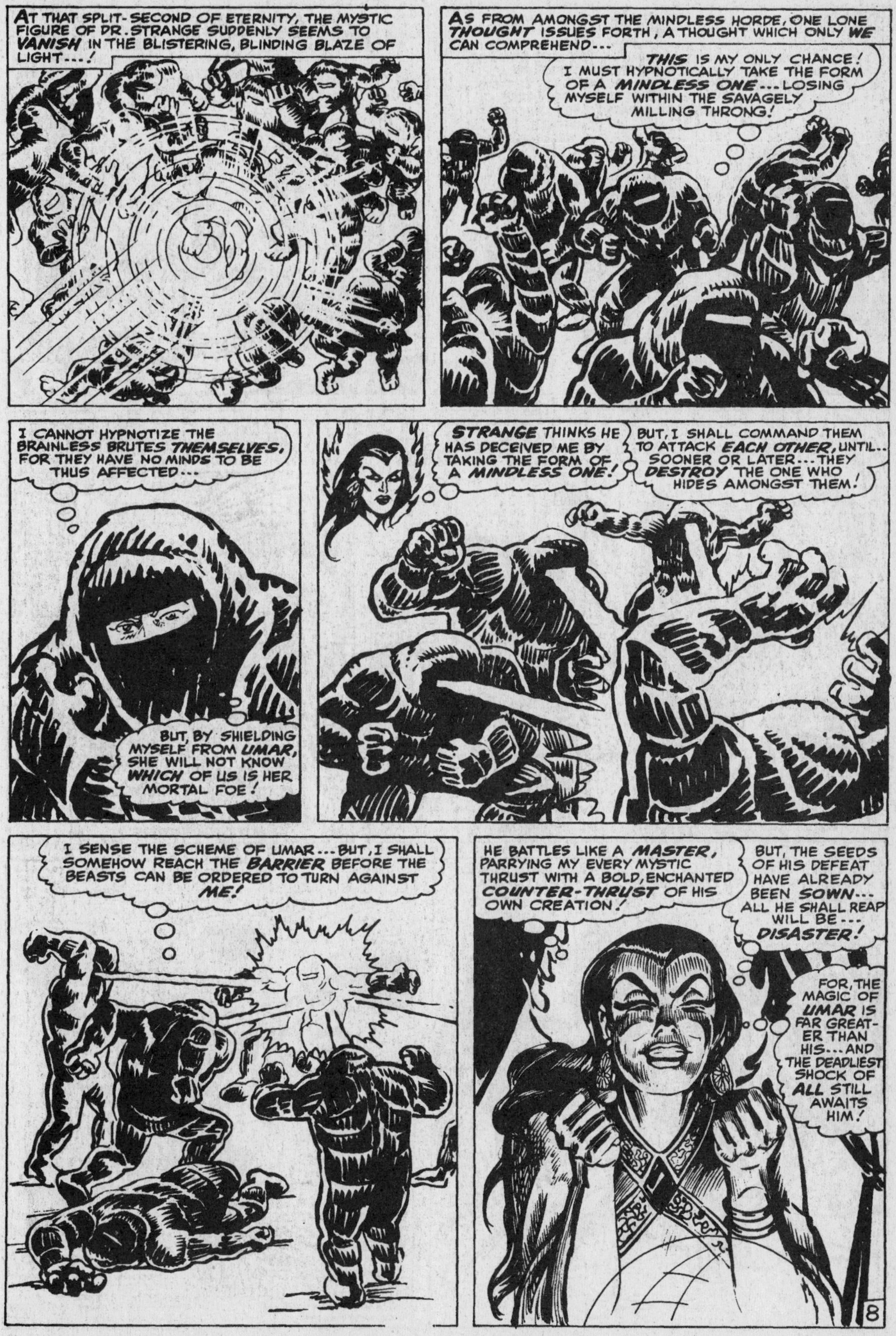
AT THAT SPLIT-SECOND OF ETERNITY, THE MYSTIC FIGURE OF DR. STRANGE SUDDENLY SEEMS TO VANISH IN THE BLISTERING, BLINDING BLAZE OF LIGHT...!
AS FROM AMONGST THE MINDLESS HORDE, ONE LONE THOUGHT ISSUES FORTH, A THOUGHT WHICH ONLY WE CAN COMPREHEND...
THIS IS MY ONLY CHANCE! I MUST HYPNOTICALLY TAKE THE FORM OF A MINDLESS ONE... LOSING MYSELF WITHIN THE SAVAGELY MILLING THRONG!
I CANNOT HYPNOTIZE THE BRAINLESS BRUTES THEMSELVES, FOR THEY HAVE NO MINDS TO BE THUS AFFECTED...
BUT, BY SHIELDING MYSELF FROM UMAR, SHE WILL NOT KNOW WHICH OF US IS HER MORTAL FOE!
STRANGE THINKS HE HAS DECEIVED ME BY TAKING THE FORM OF A MINDLESS ONE!
BUT, I SHALL COMMAND THEM TO ATTACK EACH OTHER, UNTIL... SOONER OR LATER... THEY DESTROY THE ONE WHO HIDES AMONGST THEM!
I SENSE THE SCHEME OF UMAR... BUT, I SHALL SOMEHOW REACH THE BARRIER BEFORE THE BEASTS CAN BE ORDERED TO TURN AGAINST ME!
HE BATTLES LIKE A MASTER, PARRYING MY EVERY MYSTIC THRUST WITH A BOLD, ENCHANTED COUNTER-THRUST OF HIS OWN CREATION!
BUT, THE SEEDS OF HIS DEFEAT HAVE ALREADY BEEN SOWN... ALL HE SHALL REAP WILL BE... DISASTER!
FOR, THE MAGIC OF UMAR IS FAR GREATER THAN HIS... AND THE DEADLIEST SHOCK OF ALL STILL AWAITS HIM!
8

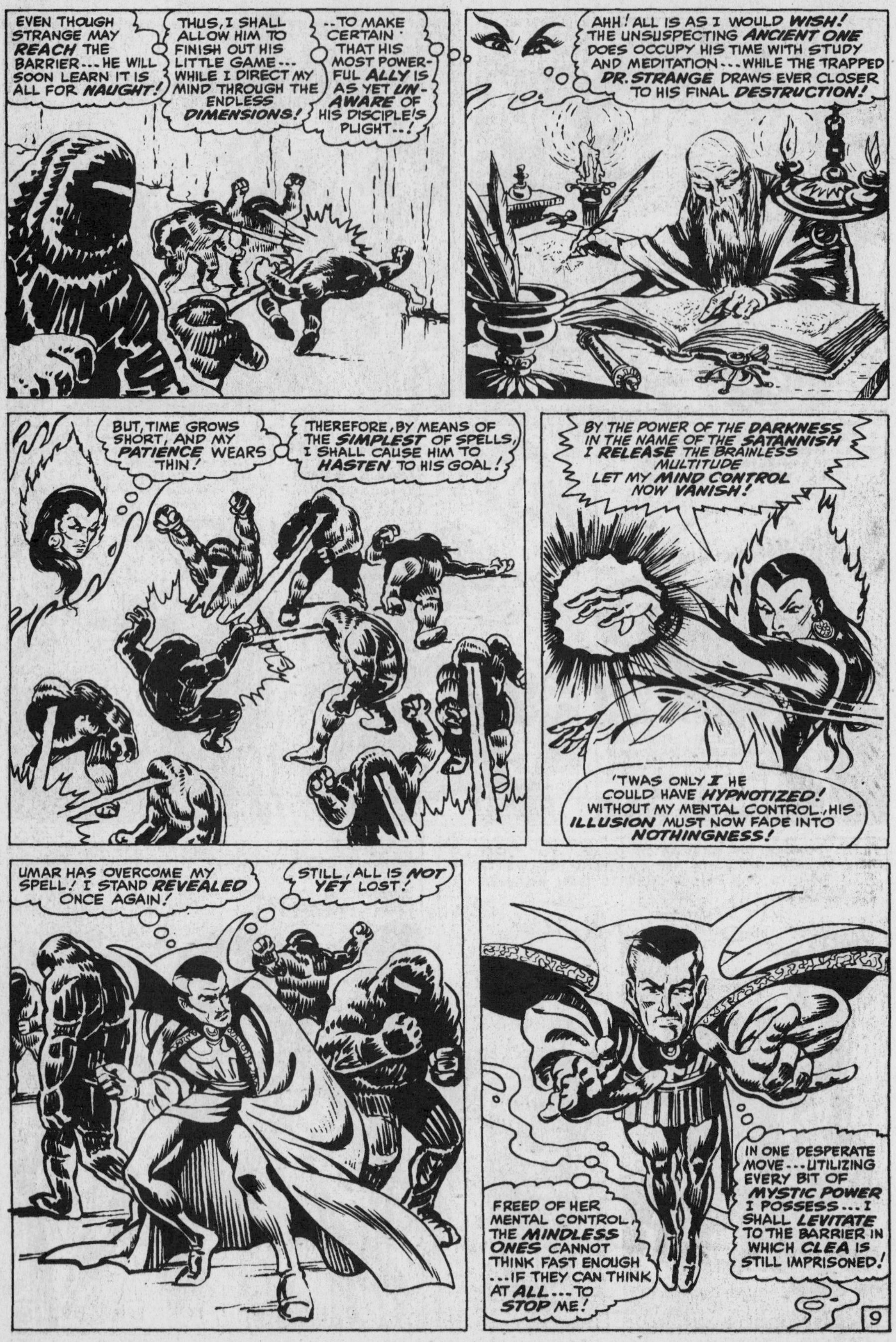
EVEN THOUGH STRANGE MAY REACH THE BARRIER... HE WILL SOON LEARN IT IS ALL FOR NAUGHT!
THUS, I SHALL ALLOW HIM TO FINISH OUT HIS LITTLE GAME... WHILE I DIRECT MY MIND THROUGH THE ENDLESS DIMENSIONS!
--TO MAKE CERTAIN THAT HIS MOST POWERFUL ALLY IS AS YET UNAWARE OF HIS DISCIPLE'S PLIGHT--!
AHH! ALL IS AS I WOULD WISH! THE UNSUSPECTING ANCIENT ONE DOES OCCUPY HIS TIME WITH STUDY AND MEDITATION... WHILE THE TRAPPED DR. STRANGE DRAWS EVER CLOSER TO HIS FINAL DESTRUCTION!
BUT, TIME GROWS SHORT, AND MY PATIENCE WEARS THIN!
THEREFORE, BY MEANS OF THE SIMPLEST OF SPELLS, I SHALL CAUSE HIM TO HASTEN TO HIS GOAL!
BY THE POWER OF THE DARKNESS IN THE NAME OF THE SATANNISH I RELEASE THE BRAINLESS MULTITUDE LET MY MIND CONTROL NOW VANISH!
'TWAS ONLY I HE COULD HAVE HYPNOTIZED! WITHOUT MY MENTAL CONTROL, HIS ILLUSION MUST NOW FADE INTO NOTHINGNESS!
UMAR HAS OVERCOME MY SPELL! I STAND REVEALED ONCE AGAIN!
STILL, ALL IS NOT YET LOST!
IN ONE DESPERATE MOVE... UTILIZING EVERY BIT OF MYSTIC POWER I POSSESS... I SHALL LEVITATE TO THE BARRIER IN WHICH CLEA IS STILL IMPRISONED!
FREED OF HER MENTAL CONTROL, THE MINDLESS ONES CANNOT THINK FAST ENOUGH ...IF THEY CAN THINK AT ALL... TO STOP ME!
9

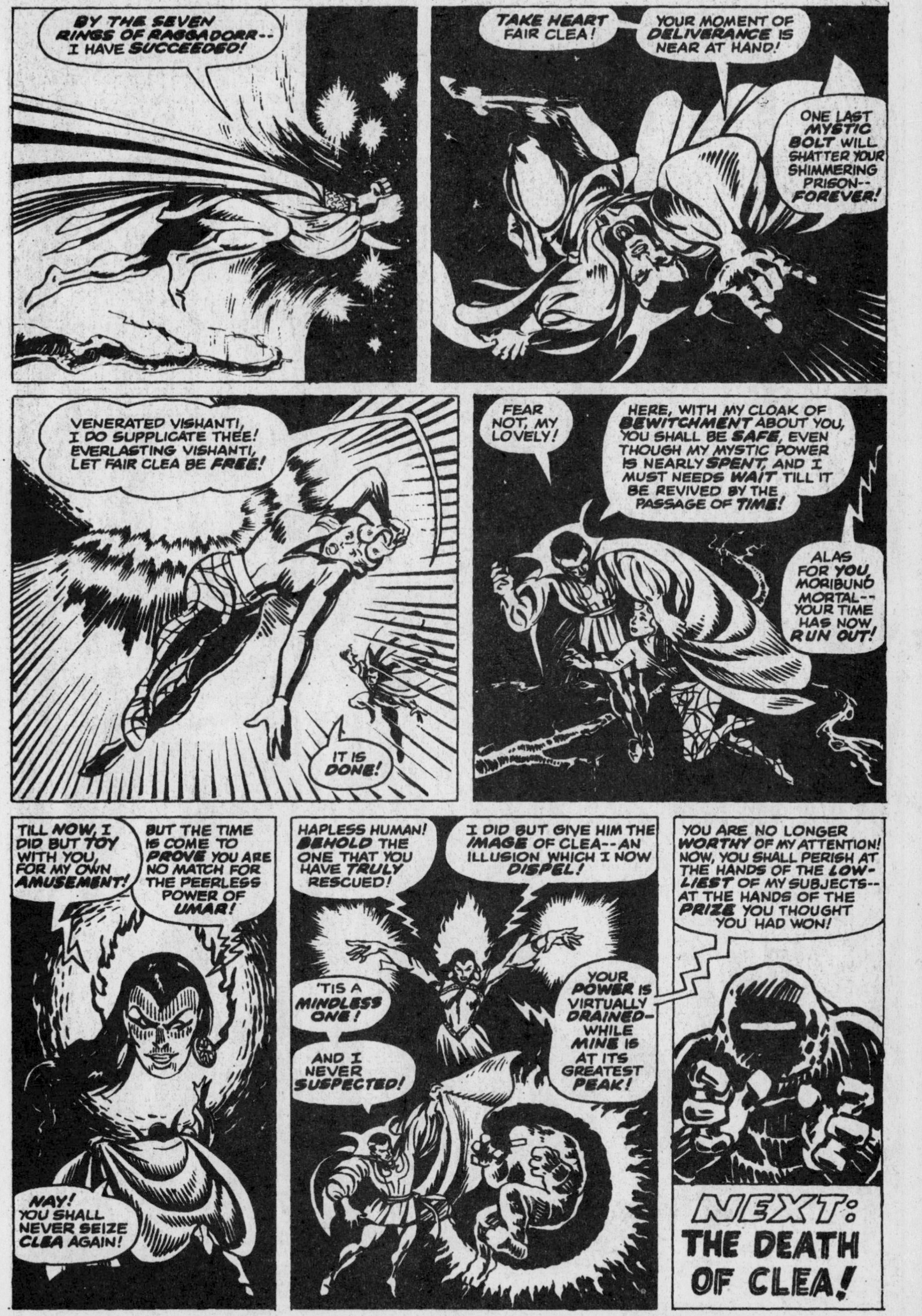
BY THE SEVEN RINGS OF RAGGADORR-- I HAVE SUCCEEDED!
TAKE HEART FAIR CLEA!
YOUR MOMENT OF DELIVERANCE IS NEAR AT HAND!
ONE LAST MYSTIC BOLT WILL SHATTER YOUR SHIMMERING PRISON-- FOREVER!
VENERATED VISHANTI, I DO SUPPLICATE THEE! EVERLASTING VISHANTI, LET FAIR CLEA BE FREE!
IT IS DONE!
FEAR NOT, MY LOVELY!
HERE, WITH MY CLOAK OF BEWITCHMENT ABOUT YOU, YOU SHALL BE SAFE, EVEN THOUGH MY MYSTIC POWER IS NEARLY SPENT, AND I MUST NEEDS WAIT TILL IT BE REVIVED BY THE PASSAGE OF TIME!
ALAS FOR YOU, MORIBUND MORTAL-- YOUR TIME HAS NOW RUN OUT!
TILL NOW, I DID BUT TOY WITH YOU, FOR MY OWN AMUSEMENT!
BUT THE TIME IS COME TO PROVE YOU ARE NO MATCH FOR THE PEERLESS POWER OF UMAR!
NAY! YOU SHALL NEVER SEIZE CLEA AGAIN!
HAPLESS HUMAN! BEHOLD THE ONE THAT YOU HAVE TRULY RESCUED!
I DID BUT GIVE HIM THE IMAGE OF CLEA--AN ILLUSION WHICH I NOW DISPEL!
'TIS A MINDLESS ONE!
AND I NEVER SUSPECTED!
YOUR POWER IS VIRTUALLY DRAINED-- WHILE MINE IS AT ITS GREATEST PEAK!
YOU ARE NO LONGER WORTHY OF MY ATTENTION! NOW, YOU SHALL PERISH AT THE HANDS OF THE LOWLIEST OF MY SUBJECTS-- AT THE HANDS OF THE PRIZE YOU THOUGHT YOU HAD WON!
NEXT: THE DEATH OF CLEA!

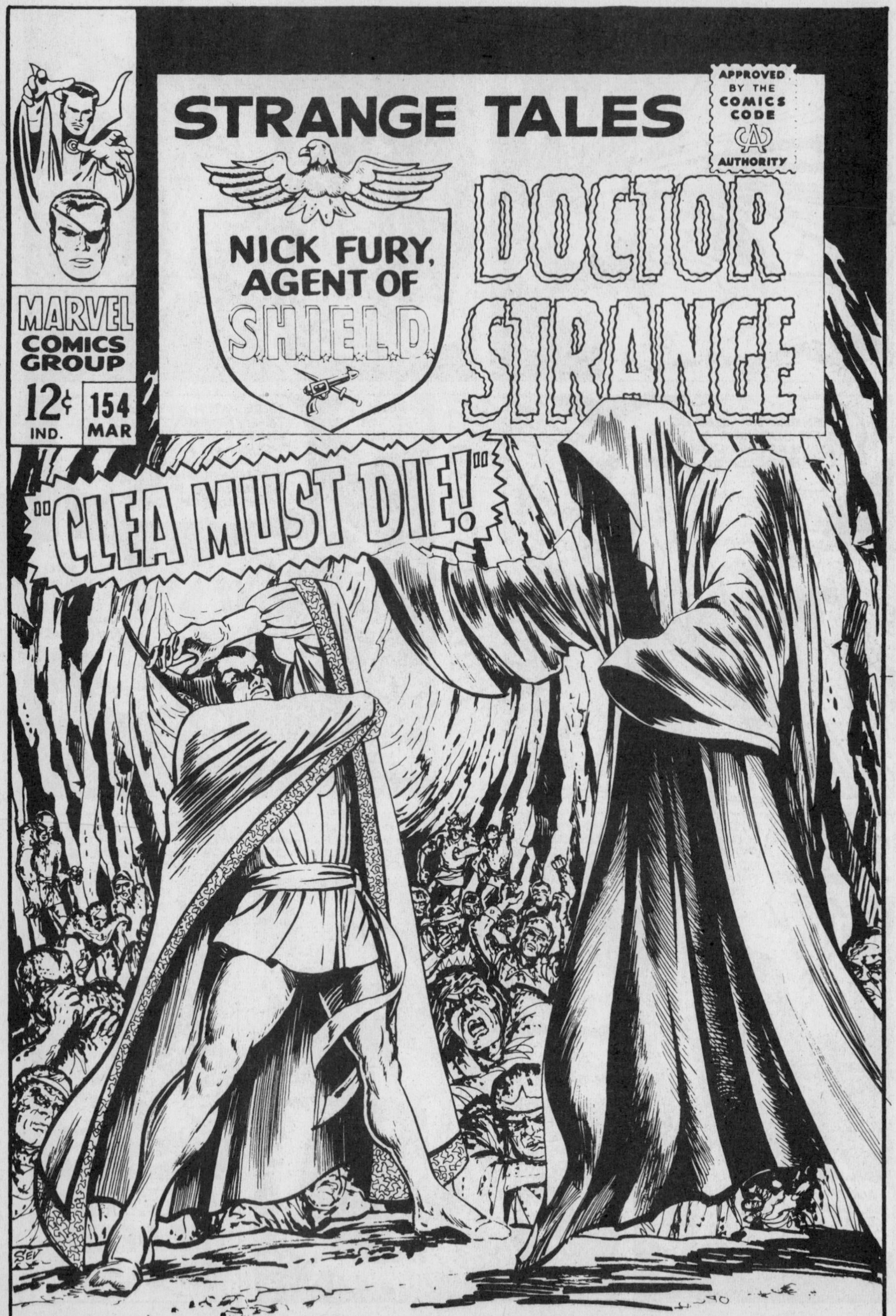

MARVEL COMICS GROUP
12¢ IND.
154 MAR
STRANGE TALES
APPROVED BY THE COMICS CODE AUTHORITY
NICK FURY, AGENT OF S.H.I.E.L.D.
DOCTOR STRANGE
"CLEA MUST DIE!"

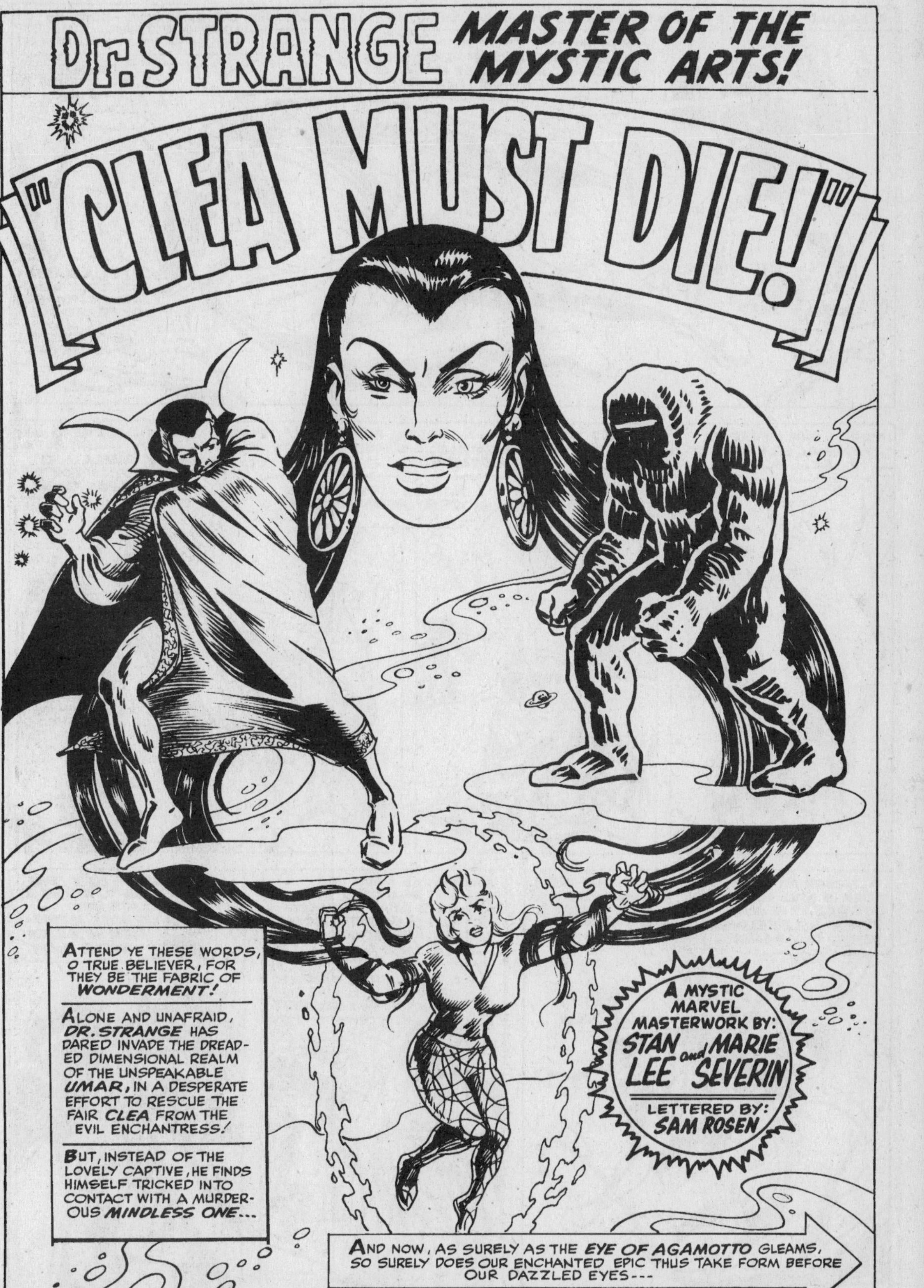

Dr. STRANGE MASTER OF THE MYSTIC ARTS!
"CLEA MUST DIE!"
ATTEND YE THESE WORDS, O TRUE BELIEVER, FOR THEY BE THE FABRIC OF WONDERMENT!
ALONE AND UNAFRAID, DR. STRANGE HAS DARED INVADE THE DREADED DIMENSIONAL REALM OF THE UNSPEAKABLE UMAR, IN A DESPERATE EFFORT TO RESCUE THE FAIR CLEA FROM THE EVIL ENCHANTRESS!
BUT, INSTEAD OF THE LOVELY CAPTIVE, HE FINDS HIMSELF TRICKED INTO CONTACT WITH A MURDEROUS MINDLESS ONE...
A MYSTIC MARVEL MASTERWORK BY: STAN LEE and MARIE SEVERIN
LETTERED BY: SAM ROSEN
AND NOW, AS SURELY AS THE EYE OF AGAMOTTO GLEAMS, SO SURELY DOES OUR ENCHANTED EPIC THUS TAKE FORM BEFORE OUR DAZZLED EYES---

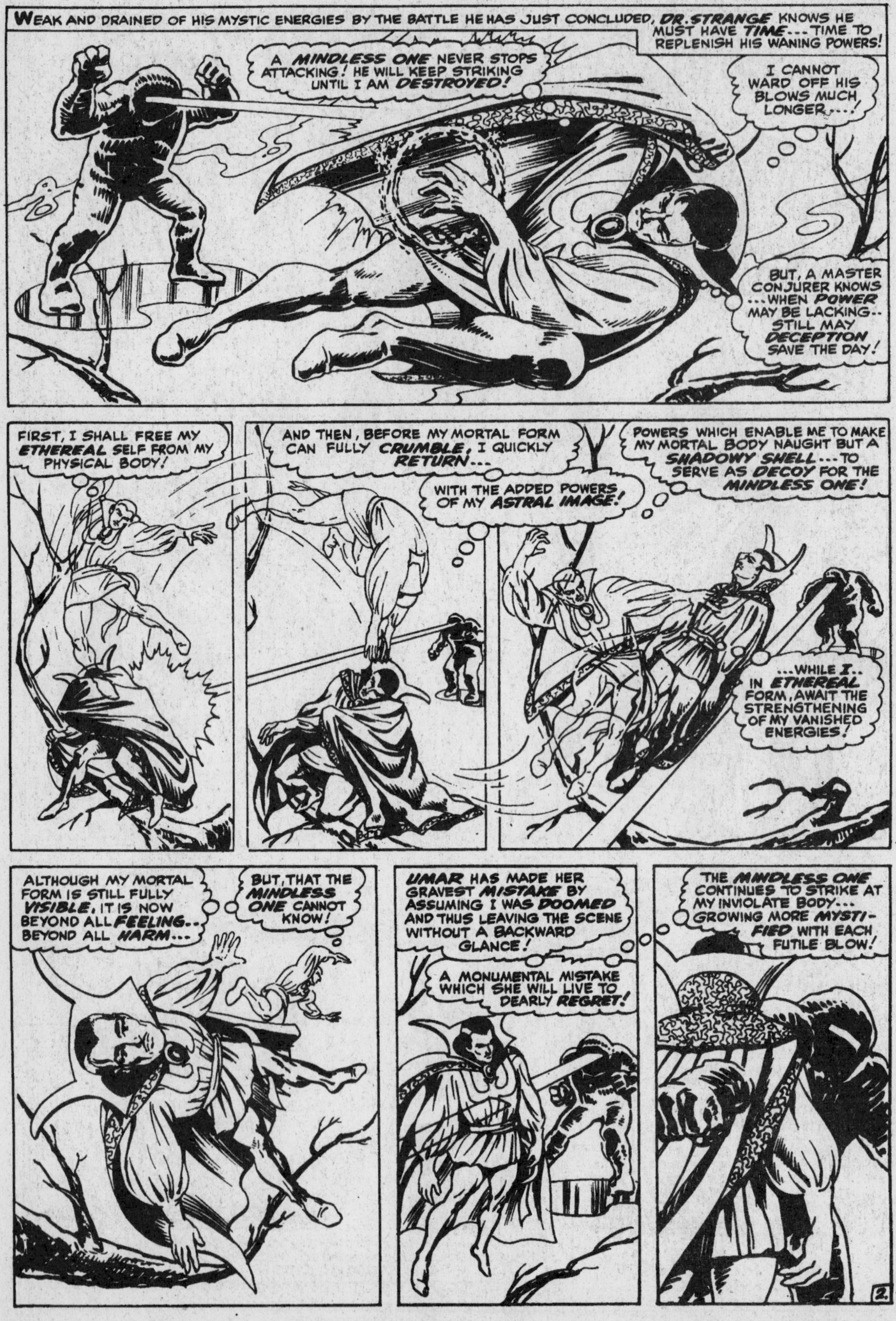
WEAK AND DRAINED OF HIS MYSTIC ENERGIES BY THE BATTLE HE HAS JUST CONCLUDED, DR. STRANGE KNOWS HE MUST HAVE TIME--- TIME TO REPLENISH HIS WANING POWERS!
A MINDLESS ONE NEVER STOPS ATTACKING! HE WILL KEEP STRIKING UNTIL I AM DESTROYED!
I CANNOT WARD OFF HIS BLOWS MUCH LONGER....!
BUT, A MASTER CONJURER KNOWS ...WHEN POWER MAY BE LACKING-- STILL MAY DECEPTION SAVE THE DAY!
FIRST, I SHALL FREE MY ETHEREAL SELF FROM MY PHYSICAL BODY!
AND THEN, BEFORE MY MORTAL FORM CAN FULLY CRUMBLE, I QUICKLY RETURN...
WITH THE ADDED POWERS OF MY ASTRAL IMAGE!
POWERS WHICH ENABLE ME TO MAKE MY MORTAL BODY NAUGHT BUT A SHADOWY SHELL--- TO SERVE AS DECOY FOR THE MINDLESS ONE!
...WHILE I.. IN ETHEREAL FORM, AWAIT THE STRENGTHENING OF MY VANISHED ENERGIES!
ALTHOUGH MY MORTAL FORM IS STILL FULLY VISIBLE, IT IS NOW BEYOND ALL FEELING.. BEYOND ALL HARM...
BUT, THAT THE MINDLESS ONE CANNOT KNOW!
UMAR HAS MADE HER GRAVEST MISTAKE BY ASSUMING I WAS DOOMED AND THUS LEAVING THE SCENE WITHOUT A BACKWARD GLANCE!
A MONUMENTAL MISTAKE WHICH SHE WILL LIVE TO DEARLY REGRET!
THE MINDLESS ONE CONTINUES TO STRIKE AT MY INVIOLATE BODY... GROWING MORE MYSTI-FIED WITH EACH FUTILE BLOW!
2.

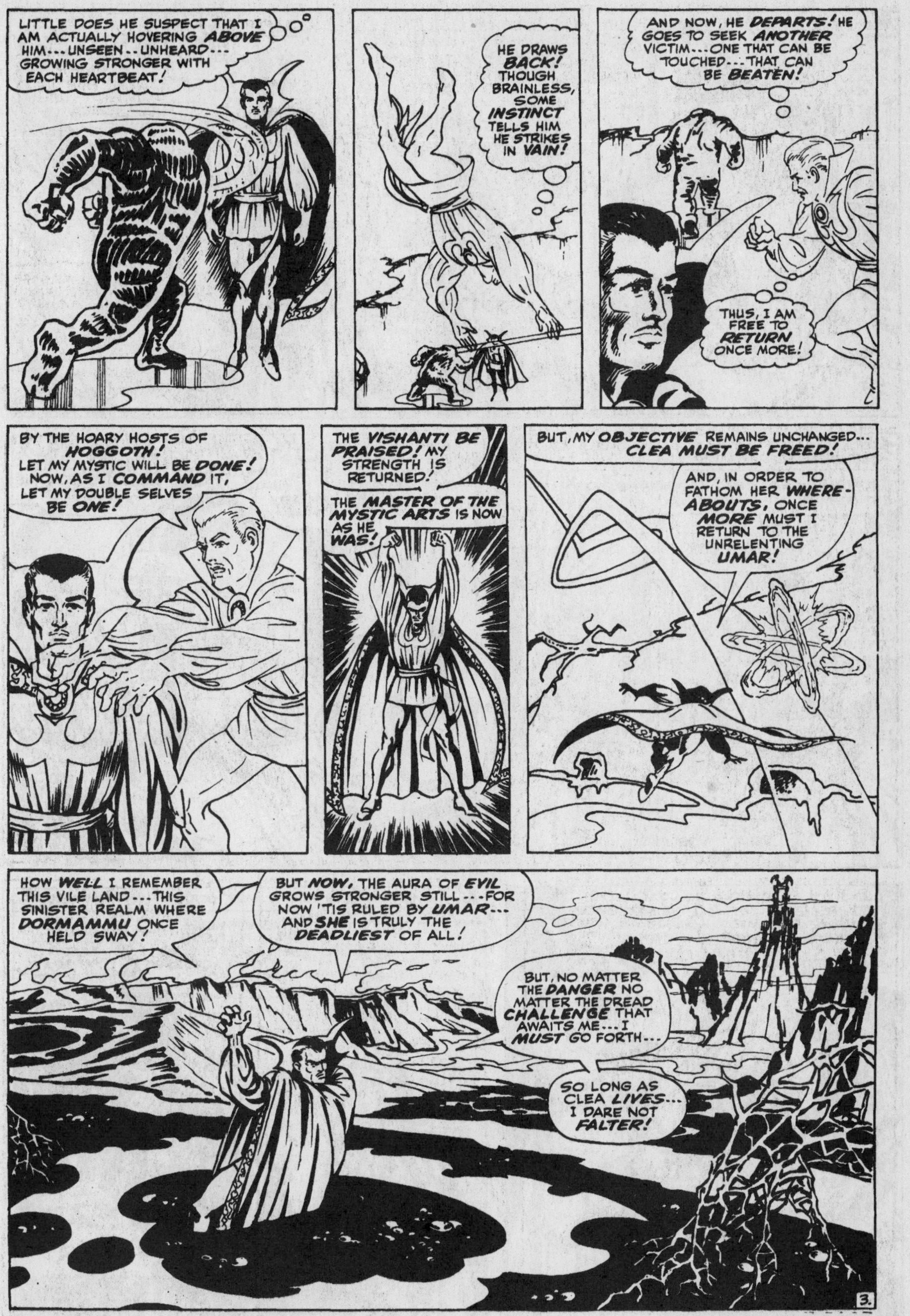
LITTLE DOES HE SUSPECT THAT I AM ACTUALLY HOVERING ABOVE HIM... UNSEEN.. UNHEARD... GROWING STRONGER WITH EACH HEARTBEAT!
HE DRAWS BACK! THOUGH BRAINLESS, SOME INSTINCT TELLS HIM HE STRIKES IN VAIN!
AND NOW, HE DEPARTS! HE GOES TO SEEK ANOTHER VICTIM... ONE THAT CAN BE TOUCHED... THAT CAN BE BEATEN!
THUS, I AM FREE TO RETURN ONCE MORE!
BY THE HOARY HOSTS OF HOGGOTH! LET MY MYSTIC WILL BE DONE! NOW, AS I COMMAND IT, LET MY DOUBLE SELVES BE ONE!
THE VISHANTI BE PRAISED! MY STRENGTH IS RETURNED!
THE MASTER OF THE MYSTIC ARTS IS NOW AS HE WAS!
BUT, MY OBJECTIVE REMAINS UNCHANGED... CLEA MUST BE FREED!
AND, IN ORDER TO FATHOM HER WHERE-ABOUTS, ONCE MORE MUST I RETURN TO THE UNRELENTING UMAR!
HOW WELL I REMEMBER THIS VILE LAND... THIS SINISTER REALM WHERE DORMAMMU ONCE HELD SWAY!
BUT NOW, THE AURA OF EVIL GROWS STRONGER STILL... FOR NOW 'TIS RULED BY UMAR... AND SHE IS TRULY THE DEADLIEST OF ALL!
BUT, NO MATTER THE DANGER NO MATTER THE DREAD CHALLENGE THAT AWAITS ME... I MUST GO FORTH...
SO LONG AS CLEA LIVES... I DARE NOT FALTER!

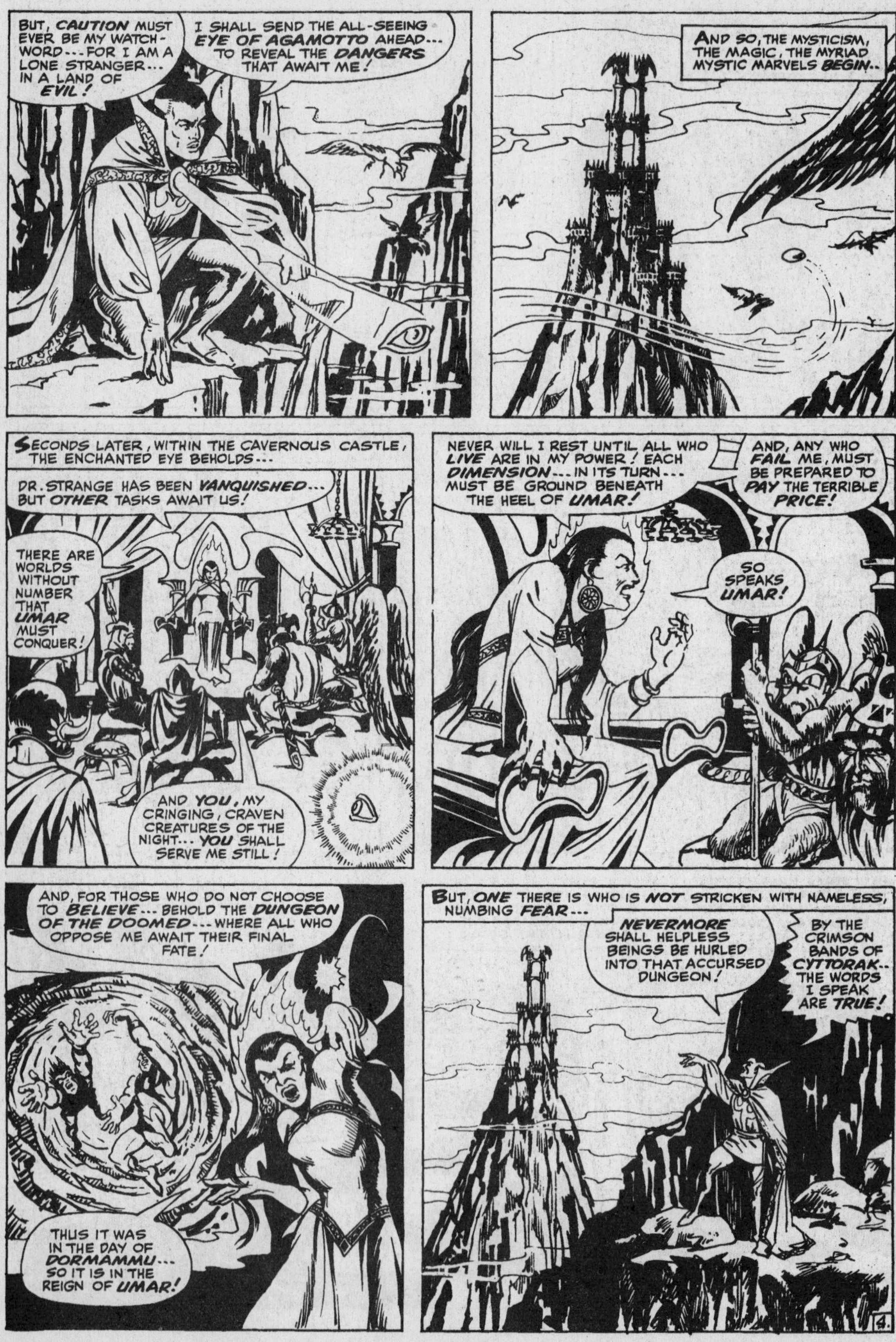
BUT, CAUTION MUST EVER BE MY WATCH-WORD--- FOR I AM A LONE STRANGER... IN A LAND OF EVIL!
I SHALL SEND THE ALL-SEEING EYE OF AGAMOTTO AHEAD... TO REVEAL THE DANGERS THAT AWAIT ME!
AND SO, THE MYSTICISM, THE MAGIC, THE MYRIAD MYSTIC MARVELS BEGIN..
SECONDS LATER, WITHIN THE CAVERNOUS CASTLE, THE ENCHANTED EYE BEHOLDS---
DR. STRANGE HAS BEEN VANQUISHED--- BUT OTHER TASKS AWAIT US!
THERE ARE WORLDS WITHOUT NUMBER THAT UMAR MUST CONQUER!
AND YOU, MY CRINGING, CRAVEN CREATURES OF THE NIGHT--- YOU SHALL SERVE ME STILL!
NEVER WILL I REST UNTIL ALL WHO LIVE ARE IN MY POWER! EACH DIMENSION--- IN ITS TURN--- MUST BE GROUND BENEATH THE HEEL OF UMAR!
AND, ANY WHO FAIL ME, MUST BE PREPARED TO PAY THE TERRIBLE PRICE!
SO SPEAKS UMAR!
AND, FOR THOSE WHO DO NOT CHOOSE TO BELIEVE--- BEHOLD THE DUNGEON OF THE DOOMED--- WHERE ALL WHO OPPOSE ME AWAIT THEIR FINAL FATE!
THUS IT WAS IN THE DAY OF DORMAMMU--- SO IT IS IN THE REIGN OF UMAR!
BUT, ONE THERE IS WHO IS NOT STRICKEN WITH NAMELESS, NUMBING FEAR---
NEVERMORE SHALL HELPLESS BEINGS BE HURLED INTO THAT ACCURSED DUNGEON!
BY THE CRIMSON BANDS OF CYTTORAK.. THE WORDS I SPEAK ARE TRUE!
4.

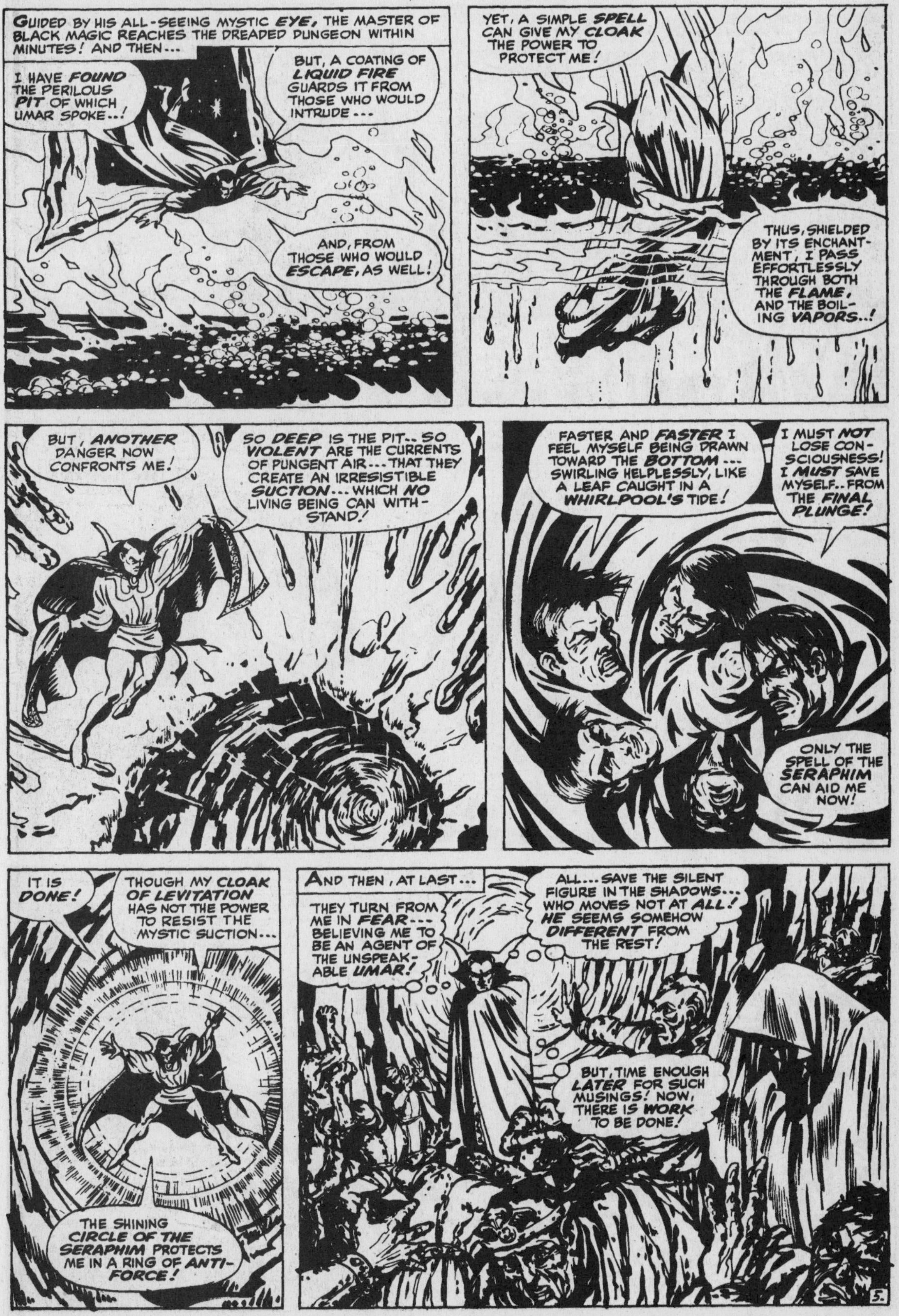
GUIDED BY HIS ALL-SEEING MYSTIC EYE, THE MASTER OF BLACK MAGIC REACHES THE DREADED DUNGEON WITHIN MINUTES! AND THEN...
I HAVE FOUND THE PERILOUS PIT OF WHICH UMAR SPOKE..!
BUT, A COATING OF LIQUID FIRE GUARDS IT FROM THOSE WHO WOULD INTRUDE ---
AND, FROM THOSE WHO WOULD ESCAPE, AS WELL!
YET, A SIMPLE SPELL CAN GIVE MY CLOAK THE POWER TO PROTECT ME!
THUS, SHIELDED BY ITS ENCHANTMENT, I PASS EFFORTLESSLY THROUGH BOTH THE FLAME, AND THE BOILING VAPORS..!
BUT, ANOTHER DANGER NOW CONFRONTS ME!
SO DEEP IS THE PIT.. SO VIOLENT ARE THE CURRENTS OF PUNGENT AIR --- THAT THEY CREATE AN IRRESISTIBLE SUCTION ... WHICH NO LIVING BEING CAN WITHSTAND!
FASTER AND FASTER I FEEL MYSELF BEING DRAWN TOWARD THE BOTTOM --- SWIRLING HELPLESSLY, LIKE A LEAF CAUGHT IN A WHIRLPOOL'S TIDE!
I MUST NOT LOSE CONSCIOUSNESS! I MUST SAVE MYSELF.. FROM THE FINAL PLUNGE!
ONLY THE SPELL OF THE SERAPHIM CAN AID ME NOW!
IT IS DONE!
THOUGH MY CLOAK OF LEVITATION HAS NOT THE POWER TO RESIST THE MYSTIC SUCTION...
THE SHINING CIRCLE OF THE SERAPHIM PROTECTS ME IN A RING OF ANTI-FORCE!
AND THEN, AT LAST...
THEY TURN FROM ME IN FEAR --- BELIEVING ME TO BE AN AGENT OF THE UNSPEAKABLE UMAR!
ALL... SAVE THE SILENT FIGURE IN THE SHADOWS... WHO MOVES NOT AT ALL! HE SEEMS SOMEHOW DIFFERENT FROM THE REST!
BUT, TIME ENOUGH LATER FOR SUCH MUSINGS! NOW, THERE IS WORK TO BE DONE!
5.

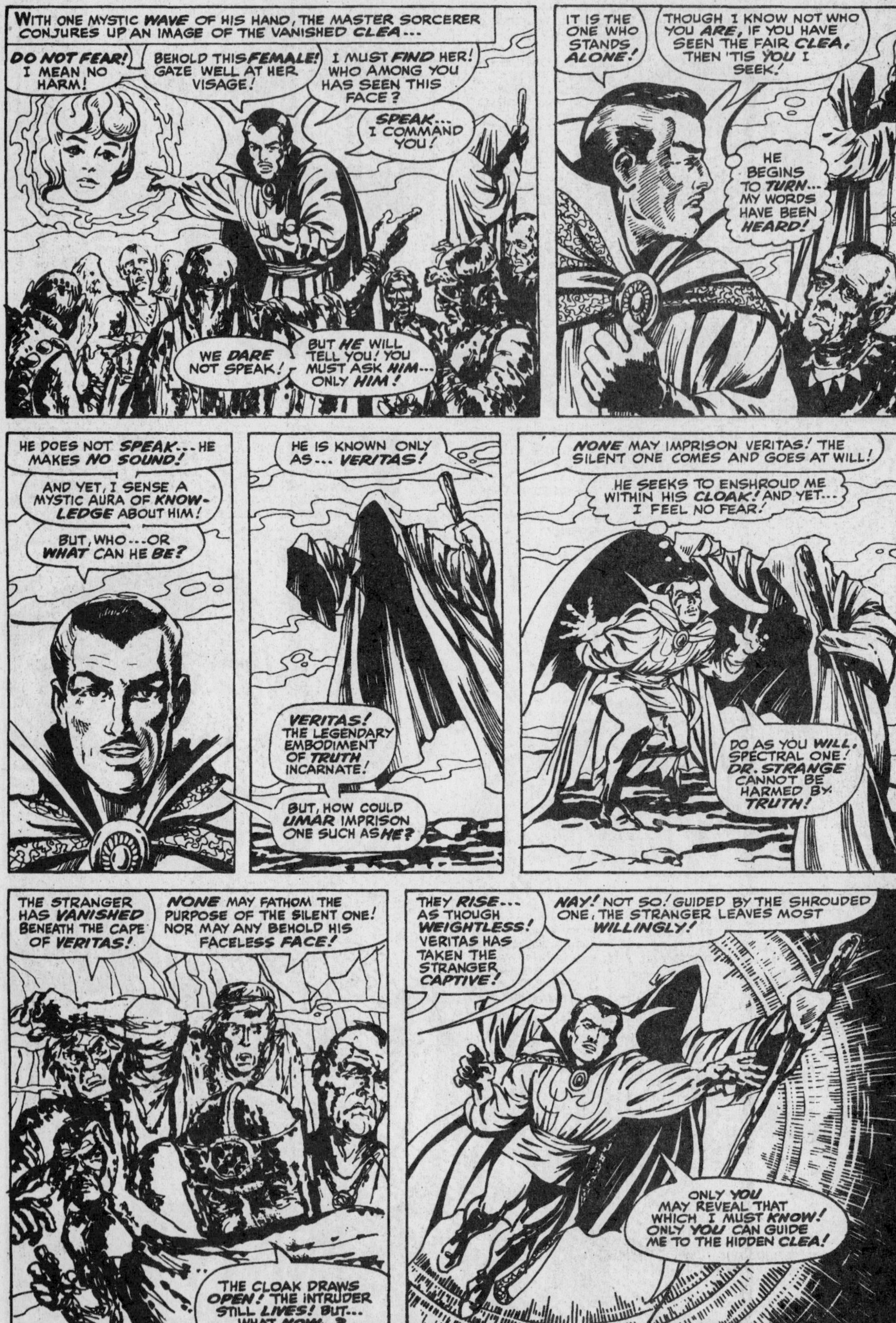
WITH ONE MYSTIC WAVE OF HIS HAND, THE MASTER SORCERER CONJURES UP AN IMAGE OF THE VANISHED CLEA...
DO NOT FEAR! I MEAN NO HARM!
BEHOLD THIS FEMALE! GAZE WELL AT HER VISAGE!
I MUST FIND HER! WHO AMONG YOU HAS SEEN THIS FACE?
SPEAK... I COMMAND YOU!
WE DARE NOT SPEAK!
BUT HE WILL TELL YOU! YOU MUST ASK HIM... ONLY HIM!
IT IS THE ONE WHO STANDS ALONE!
THOUGH I KNOW NOT WHO YOU ARE, IF YOU HAVE SEEN THE FAIR CLEA, THEN 'TIS YOU I SEEK!
HE BEGINS TO TURN... MY WORDS HAVE BEEN HEARD!
HE DOES NOT SPEAK... HE MAKES NO SOUND!
AND YET, I SENSE A MYSTIC AURA OF KNOW-LEDGE ABOUT HIM!
BUT, WHO... OR WHAT CAN HE BE?
HE IS KNOWN ONLY AS... VERITAS!
VERITAS! THE LEGENDARY EMBODIMENT OF TRUTH INCARNATE!
BUT, HOW COULD UMAR IMPRISON ONE SUCH AS HE?
NONE MAY IMPRISON VERITAS! THE SILENT ONE COMES AND GOES AT WILL!
HE SEEKS TO ENSHROUD ME WITHIN HIS CLOAK! AND YET... I FEEL NO FEAR!
DO AS YOU WILL, SPECTRAL ONE! DR. STRANGE CANNOT BE HARMED BY TRUTH!
THE STRANGER HAS VANISHED BENEATH THE CAPE OF VERITAS!
NONE MAY FATHOM THE PURPOSE OF THE SILENT ONE! NOR MAY ANY BEHOLD HIS FACELESS FACE!
THE CLOAK DRAWS OPEN! THE INTRUDER STILL LIVES! BUT... WHAT NOW...?
THEY RISE... AS THOUGH WEIGHTLESS! VERITAS HAS TAKEN THE STRANGER CAPTIVE!
NAY! NOT SO! GUIDED BY THE SHROUDED ONE, THE STRANGER LEAVES MOST WILLINGLY!
ONLY YOU MAY REVEAL THAT WHICH I MUST KNOW! ONLY YOU CAN GUIDE ME TO THE HIDDEN CLEA!
6.

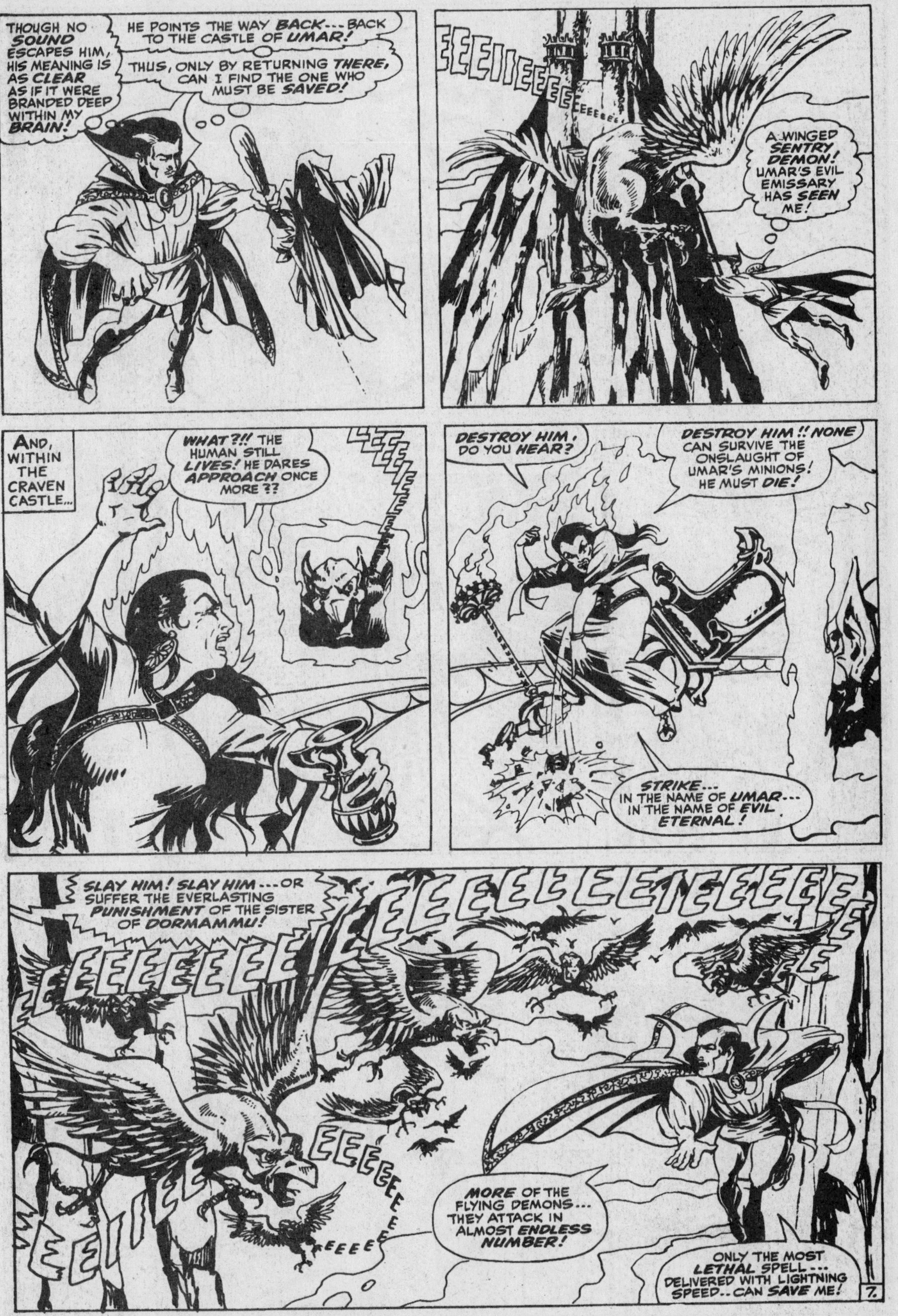
THOUGH NO SOUND ESCAPES HIM, HIS MEANING IS AS CLEAR AS IF IT WERE BRANDED DEEP WITHIN MY BRAIN!
HE POINTS THE WAY BACK--- BACK TO THE CASTLE OF UMAR!
THUS, ONLY BY RETURNING THERE, CAN I FIND THE ONE WHO MUST BE SAVED!
EEEIIIEEEEEeeeeeee
A WINGED SENTRY DEMON! UMAR'S EVIL EMISSARY HAS SEEN ME!
AND, WITHIN THE CRAVEN CASTLE...
WHAT?!! THE HUMAN STILL LIVES! HE DARES APPROACH ONCE MORE??
DESTROY HIM, DO YOU HEAR?
DESTROY HIM!! NONE CAN SURVIVE THE ONSLAUGHT OF UMAR'S MINIONS! HE MUST DIE!
STRIKE... IN THE NAME OF UMAR--- IN THE NAME OF EVIL ETERNAL!
SLAY HIM! SLAY HIM ....OR SUFFER THE EVERLASTING PUNISHMENT OF THE SISTER OF DORMAMMU!
EEEEEEEEEEEEEIEEEEEEE
MORE OF THE FLYING DEMONS... THEY ATTACK IN ALMOST ENDLESS NUMBER!
ONLY THE MOST LETHAL SPELL... DELIVERED WITH LIGHTNING SPEED.. CAN SAVE ME!
7.

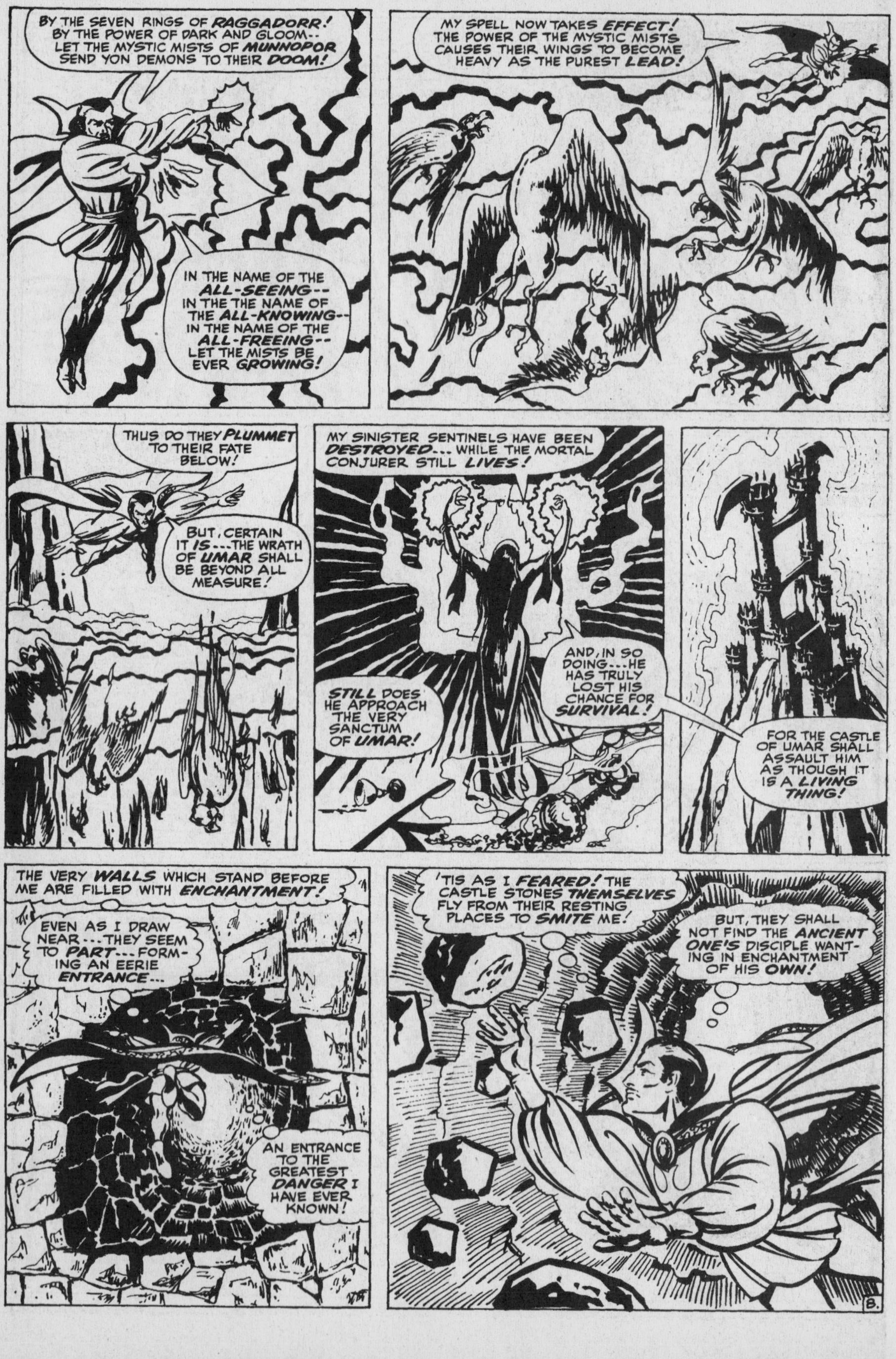
BY THE SEVEN RINGS OF RAGGADORR! BY THE POWER OF DARK AND GLOOM-- LET THE MYSTIC MISTS OF MUNNOPOR SEND YON DEMONS TO THEIR DOOM!
IN THE NAME OF THE ALL-SEEING-- IN THE THE NAME OF THE ALL-KNOWING-- IN THE NAME OF THE ALL-FREEING-- LET THE MISTS BE EVER GROWING!
MY SPELL NOW TAKES EFFECT! THE POWER OF THE MYSTIC MISTS CAUSES THEIR WINGS TO BECOME HEAVY AS THE PUREST LEAD!
THUS DO THEY PLUMMET TO THEIR FATE BELOW!
BUT, CERTAIN IT IS---THE WRATH OF UMAR SHALL BE BEYOND ALL MEASURE!
MY SINISTER SENTINELS HAVE BEEN DESTROYED... WHILE THE MORTAL CONJURER STILL LIVES!
STILL DOES HE APPROACH THE VERY SANCTUM OF UMAR!
AND, IN SO DOING...HE HAS TRULY LOST HIS CHANCE FOR SURVIVAL!
FOR THE CASTLE OF UMAR SHALL ASSAULT HIM AS THOUGH IT IS A LIVING THING!
THE VERY WALLS WHICH STAND BEFORE ME ARE FILLED WITH ENCHANTMENT!
EVEN AS I DRAW NEAR---THEY SEEM TO PART---FORMING AN EERIE ENTRANCE...
AN ENTRANCE TO THE GREATEST DANGER I HAVE EVER KNOWN!
'TIS AS I FEARED! THE CASTLE STONES THEMSELVES FLY FROM THEIR RESTING PLACES TO SMITE ME!
BUT, THEY SHALL NOT FIND THE ANCIENT ONE'S DISCIPLE WANTING IN ENCHANTMENT OF HIS OWN!
8.

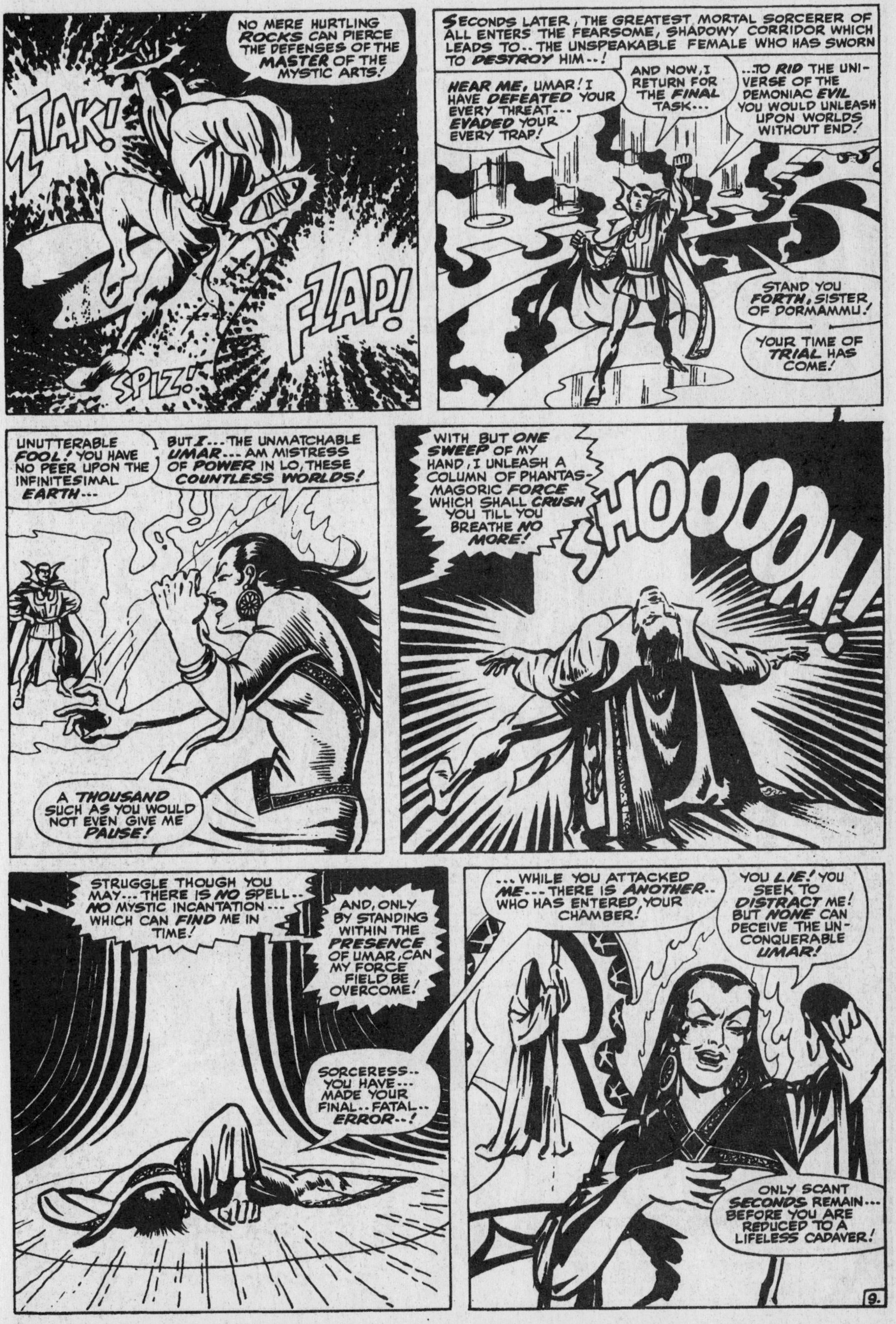

NO MERE HURTLING ROCKS CAN PIERCE THE DEFENSES OF THE MASTER OF THE MYSTIC ARTS!
TAK!
FZAP!
SPIZ!
SECONDS LATER, THE GREATEST MORTAL SORCERER OF ALL ENTERS THE FEARSOME, SHADOWY CORRIDOR WHICH LEADS TO.. THE UNSPEAKABLE FEMALE WHO HAS SWORN TO DESTROY HIM--!
HEAR ME, UMAR! I HAVE DEFEATED YOUR EVERY THREAT--- EVADED YOUR EVERY TRAP!
AND NOW, I RETURN FOR THE FINAL TASK...
...TO RID THE UNIVERSE OF THE DEMONIAC EVIL YOU WOULD UNLEASH UPON WORLDS WITHOUT END!
STAND YOU FORTH, SISTER OF DORMAMMU!
YOUR TIME OF TRIAL HAS COME!
UNUTTERABLE FOOL! YOU HAVE NO PEER UPON THE INFINITESIMAL EARTH---
BUT I... THE UNMATCHABLE UMAR... AM MISTRESS OF POWER IN LO, THESE COUNTLESS WORLDS!
A THOUSAND SUCH AS YOU WOULD NOT EVEN GIVE ME PAUSE!
WITH BUT ONE SWEEP OF MY HAND, I UNLEASH A COLUMN OF PHANTASMAGORIC FORCE WHICH SHALL CRUSH YOU TILL YOU BREATHE NO MORE!
SHOOOOM!
STRUGGLE THOUGH YOU MAY... THERE IS NO SPELL.. NO MYSTIC INCANTATION--- WHICH CAN FIND ME IN TIME!
AND, ONLY BY STANDING WITHIN THE PRESENCE OF UMAR, CAN MY FORCE FIELD BE OVERCOME!
SORCERESS.. YOU HAVE--- MADE YOUR FINAL.. FATAL.. ERROR--!
...WHILE YOU ATTACKED ME--- THERE IS ANOTHER.. WHO HAS ENTERED YOUR CHAMBER!
YOU LIE! YOU SEEK TO DISTRACT ME! BUT NONE CAN DECEIVE THE UNCONQUERABLE UMAR!
ONLY SCANT SECONDS REMAIN--- BEFORE YOU ARE REDUCED TO A LIFELESS CADAVER!
9.

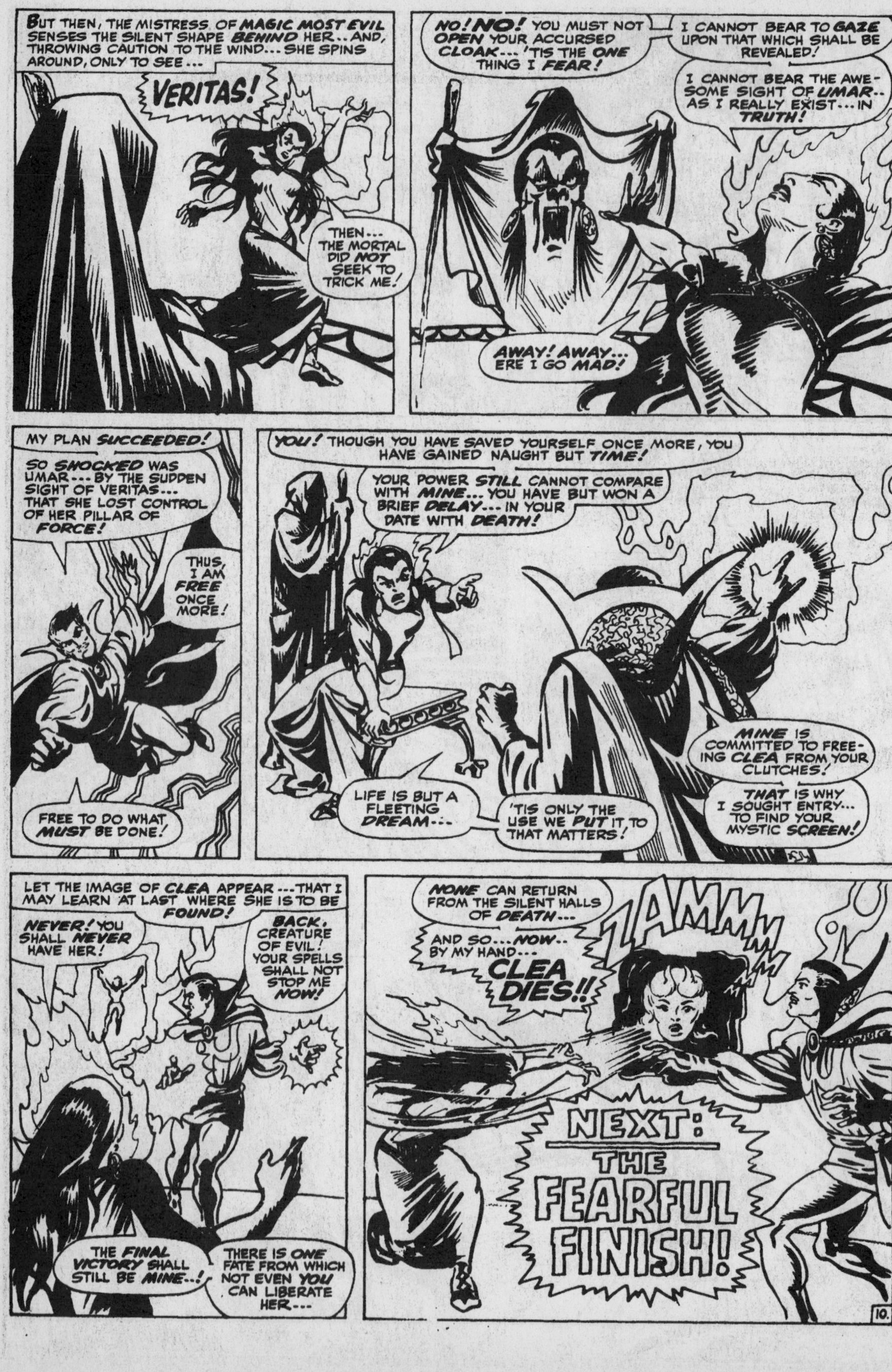

But then, the mistress of MAGIC MOST EVIL senses the silent shape BEHIND her.. And, throwing caution to the wind... she spins around, only to see...
VERITAS!
THEN... THE MORTAL DID NOT SEEK TO TRICK ME!
NO! NO! YOU MUST NOT OPEN YOUR ACCURSED CLOAK... 'TIS THE ONE THING I FEAR!
I CANNOT BEAR TO GAZE UPON THAT WHICH SHALL BE REVEALED!
I CANNOT BEAR THE AWE-SOME SIGHT OF UMAR.. AS I REALLY EXIST... IN TRUTH!
AWAY! AWAY... ERE I GO MAD!
MY PLAN SUCCEEDED!
SO SHOCKED WAS UMAR... BY THE SUDDEN SIGHT OF VERITAS... THAT SHE LOST CONTROL OF HER PILLAR OF FORCE!
THUS, I AM FREE ONCE MORE!
FREE TO DO WHAT MUST BE DONE!
YOU! THOUGH YOU HAVE SAVED YOURSELF ONCE MORE, YOU HAVE GAINED NAUGHT BUT TIME!
YOUR POWER STILL CANNOT COMPARE WITH MINE... YOU HAVE BUT WON A BRIEF DELAY... IN YOUR DATE WITH DEATH!
LIFE IS BUT A FLEETING DREAM...
'TIS ONLY THE USE WE PUT IT, TO THAT MATTERS!
MINE IS COMMITTED TO FREEING CLEA FROM YOUR CLUTCHES!
THAT IS WHY I SOUGHT ENTRY... TO FIND YOUR MYSTIC SCREEN!
LET THE IMAGE OF CLEA APPEAR ---THAT I MAY LEARN AT LAST WHERE SHE IS TO BE FOUND!
NEVER! YOU SHALL NEVER HAVE HER!
BACK, CREATURE OF EVIL! YOUR SPELLS SHALL NOT STOP ME NOW!
THE FINAL VICTORY SHALL STILL BE MINE..!
THERE IS ONE FATE FROM WHICH NOT EVEN YOU CAN LIBERATE HER---
NONE CAN RETURN FROM THE SILENT HALLS OF DEATH---
AND SO... NOW.. BY MY HAND--- CLEA DIES!!
ZAMMMM
NEXT: THE FEARFUL FINISH!
10.

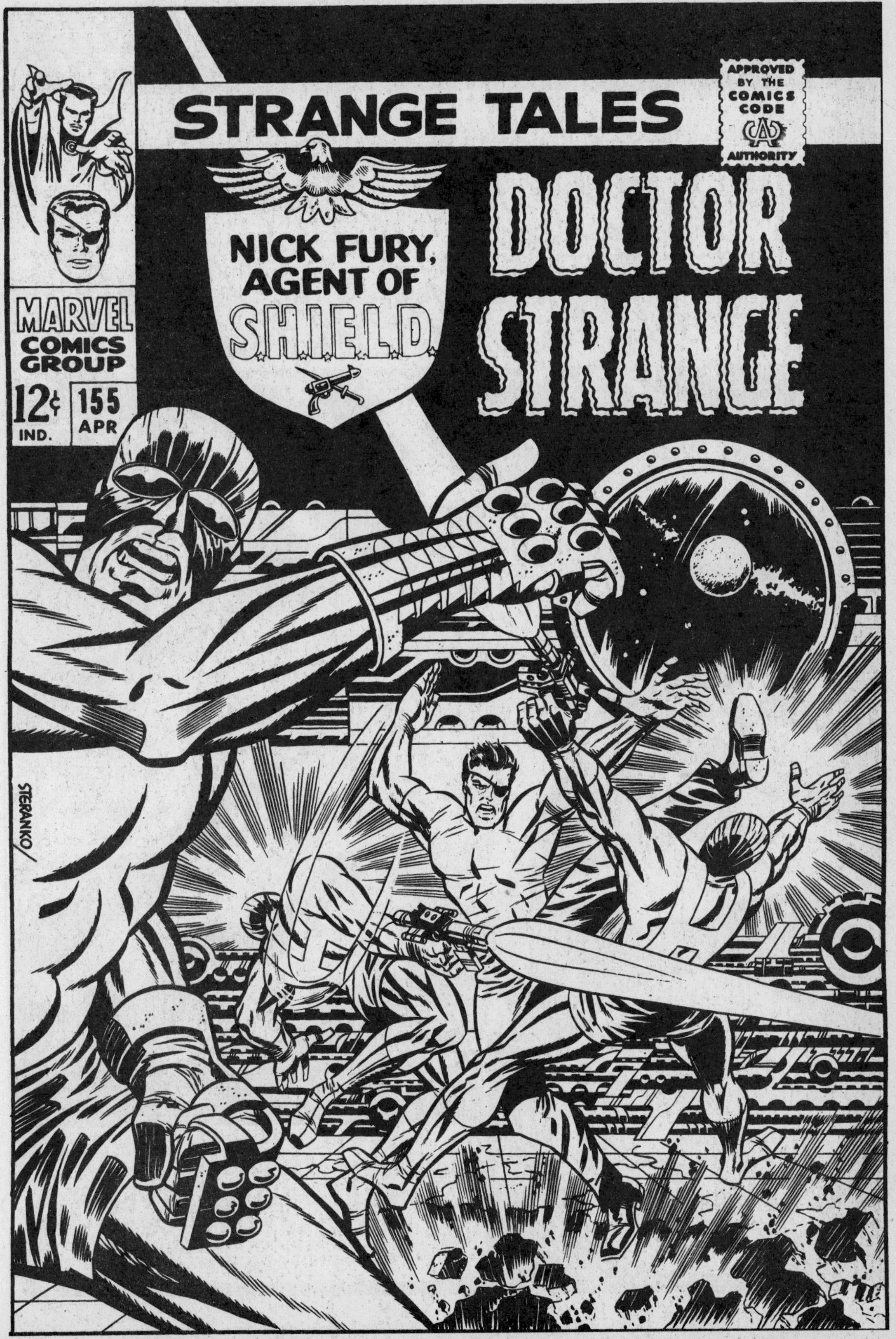
STRANGE TALES
APPROVED BY THE COMICS CODE AUTHORITY
NICK FURY, AGENT OF S.H.I.E.L.D.
DOCTOR STRANGE
MARVEL COMICS GROUP
12¢ IND.
155 APR
STERANKO

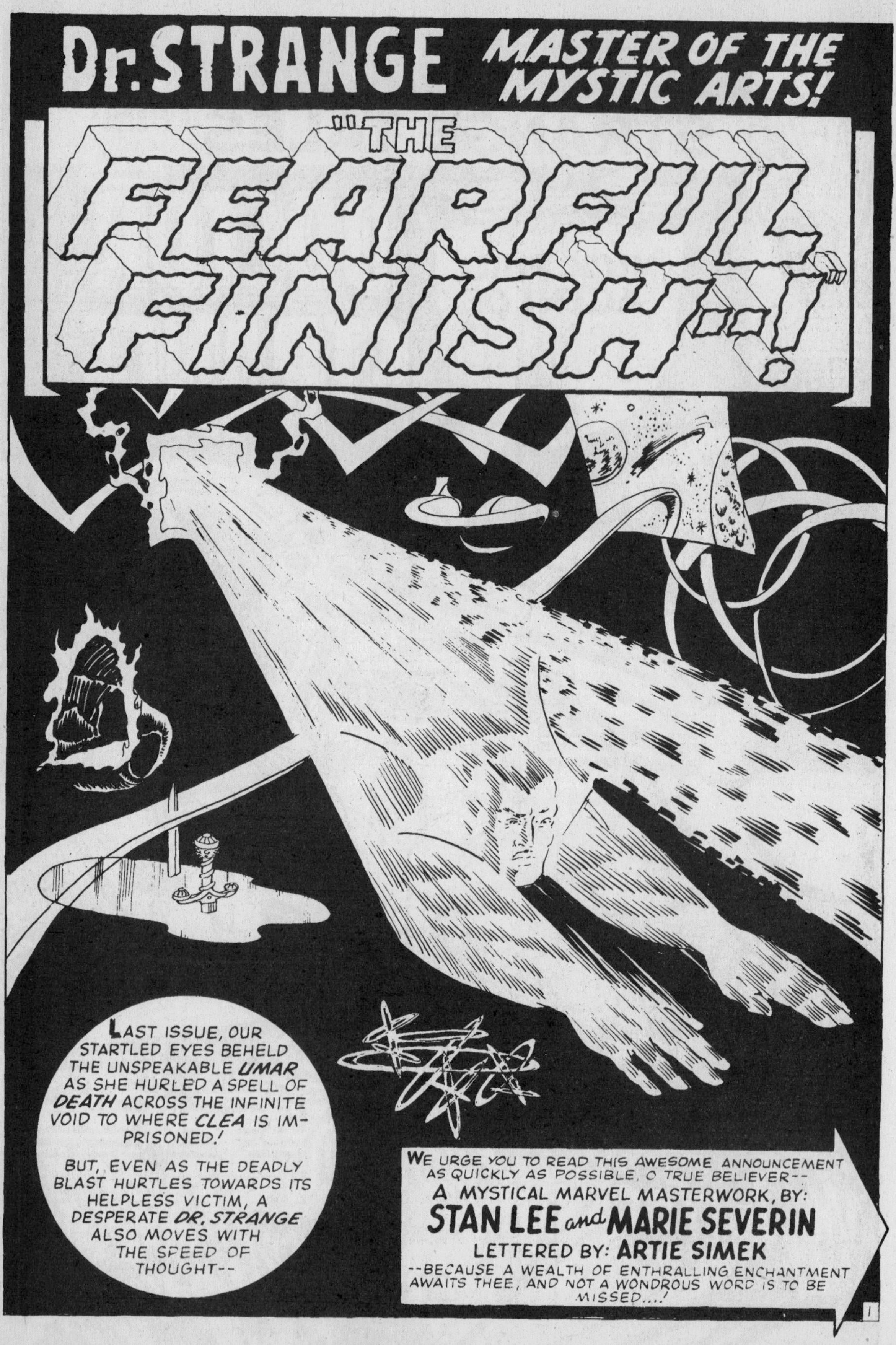

Dr. STRANGE
MASTER OF THE MYSTIC ARTS!
"THE FEARFUL FINISH--!
LAST ISSUE, OUR STARTLED EYES BEHELD THE UNSPEAKABLE UMAR AS SHE HURLED A SPELL OF DEATH ACROSS THE INFINITE VOID TO WHERE CLEA IS IMPRISONED!
BUT, EVEN AS THE DEADLY BLAST HURTLES TOWARDS ITS HELPLESS VICTIM, A DESPERATE DR. STRANGE ALSO MOVES WITH THE SPEED OF THOUGHT--
WE URGE YOU TO READ THIS AWESOME ANNOUNCEMENT AS QUICKLY AS POSSIBLE, O TRUE BELIEVER--
A MYSTICAL MARVEL MASTERWORK, BY:
STAN LEE and MARIE SEVERIN
LETTERED BY: ARTIE SIMEK
--BECAUSE A WEALTH OF ENTHRALLING ENCHANTMENT AWAITS THEE, AND NOT A WONDROUS WORD IS TO BE MISSED...!
1

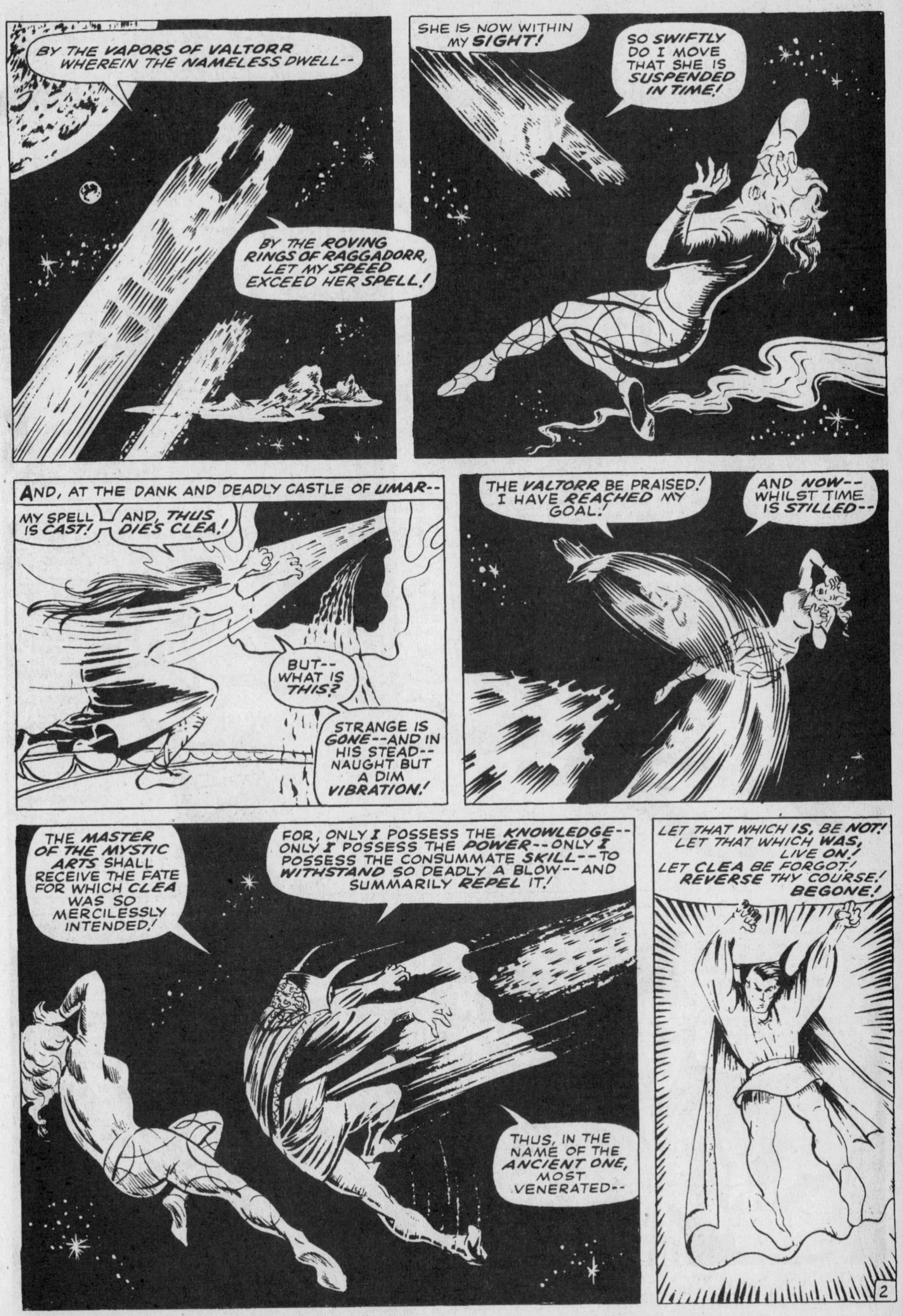
BY THE VAPORS OF VALTORR WHEREIN THE NAMELESS DWELL--
BY THE ROVING RINGS OF RAGGADORR, LET MY SPEED EXCEED HER SPELL!
SHE IS NOW WITHIN MY SIGHT!
SO SWIFTLY DO I MOVE THAT SHE IS SUSPENDED IN TIME!
AND, AT THE DANK AND DEADLY CASTLE OF UMAR--
MY SPELL IS CAST!
AND, THUS DIES CLEA!
BUT-- WHAT IS THIS?
STRANGE IS GONE--AND IN HIS STEAD-- NAUGHT BUT A DIM VIBRATION!
THE VALTORR BE PRAISED! I HAVE REACHED MY GOAL!
AND NOW-- WHILST TIME IS STILLED--
THE MASTER OF THE MYSTIC ARTS SHALL RECEIVE THE FATE FOR WHICH CLEA WAS SO MERCILESSLY INTENDED!
FOR, ONLY I POSSESS THE KNOWLEDGE-- ONLY I POSSESS THE POWER--ONLY I POSSESS THE CONSUMMATE SKILL--TO WITHSTAND SO DEADLY A BLOW--AND SUMMARILY REPEL IT!
THUS, IN THE NAME OF THE ANCIENT ONE, MOST VENERATED--
LET THAT WHICH IS, BE NOT! LET THAT WHICH WAS, LIVE ON! LET CLEA BE FORGOT! REVERSE THY COURSE! BEGONE!
2

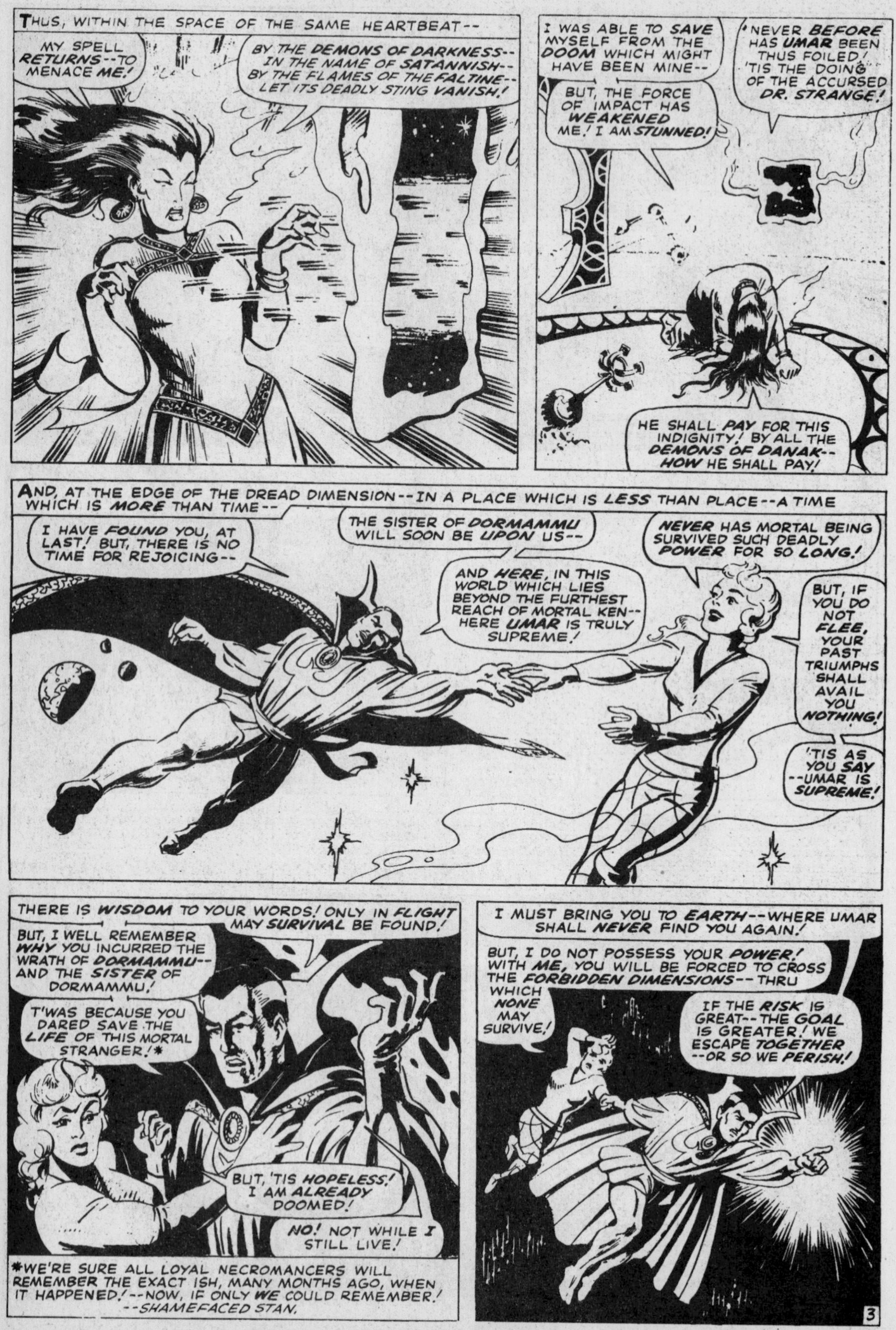

THUS, WITHIN THE SPACE OF THE SAME HEARTBEAT--
MY SPELL RETURNS--TO MENACE ME!
BY THE DEMONS OF DARKNESS--IN THE NAME OF SATANNISH--BY THE FLAMES OF THE FALTINE--LET ITS DEADLY STING VANISH!
I WAS ABLE TO SAVE MYSELF FROM THE DOOM WHICH MIGHT HAVE BEEN MINE--
BUT, THE FORCE OF IMPACT HAS WEAKENED ME! I AM STUNNED!
NEVER BEFORE HAS UMAR BEEN THUS FOILED! 'TIS THE DOING OF THE ACCURSED DR. STRANGE!
HE SHALL PAY FOR THIS INDIGNITY! BY ALL THE DEMONS OF DANAK--HOW HE SHALL PAY!
AND, AT THE EDGE OF THE DREAD DIMENSION--IN A PLACE WHICH IS LESS THAN PLACE--A TIME WHICH IS MORE THAN TIME--
I HAVE FOUND YOU, AT LAST! BUT, THERE IS NO TIME FOR REJOICING--
THE SISTER OF DORMAMMU WILL SOON BE UPON US--
AND HERE, IN THIS WORLD WHICH LIES BEYOND THE FURTHEST REACH OF MORTAL KEN--HERE UMAR IS TRULY SUPREME!
NEVER HAS MORTAL BEING SURVIVED SUCH DEADLY POWER FOR SO LONG!
BUT, IF YOU DO NOT FLEE, YOUR PAST TRIUMPHS SHALL AVAIL YOU NOTHING!
'TIS AS YOU SAY--UMAR IS SUPREME!
THERE IS WISDOM TO YOUR WORDS! ONLY IN FLIGHT MAY SURVIVAL BE FOUND!
BUT, I WELL REMEMBER WHY YOU INCURRED THE WRATH OF DORMAMMU--AND THE SISTER OF DORMAMMU!
T'WAS BECAUSE YOU DARED SAVE THE LIFE OF THIS MORTAL STRANGER!*
BUT, 'TIS HOPELESS! I AM ALREADY DOOMED!
NO! NOT WHILE I STILL LIVE!
*WE'RE SURE ALL LOYAL NECROMANCERS WILL REMEMBER THE EXACT ISH, MANY MONTHS AGO, WHEN IT HAPPENED!--NOW, IF ONLY WE COULD REMEMBER! --SHAMEFACED STAN.
I MUST BRING YOU TO EARTH--WHERE UMAR SHALL NEVER FIND YOU AGAIN!
BUT, I DO NOT POSSESS YOUR POWER! WITH ME, YOU WILL BE FORCED TO CROSS THE FORBIDDEN DIMENSIONS--THRU WHICH NONE MAY SURVIVE!
IF THE RISK IS GREAT--THE GOAL IS GREATER! WE ESCAPE TOGETHER--OR SO WE PERISH!
3

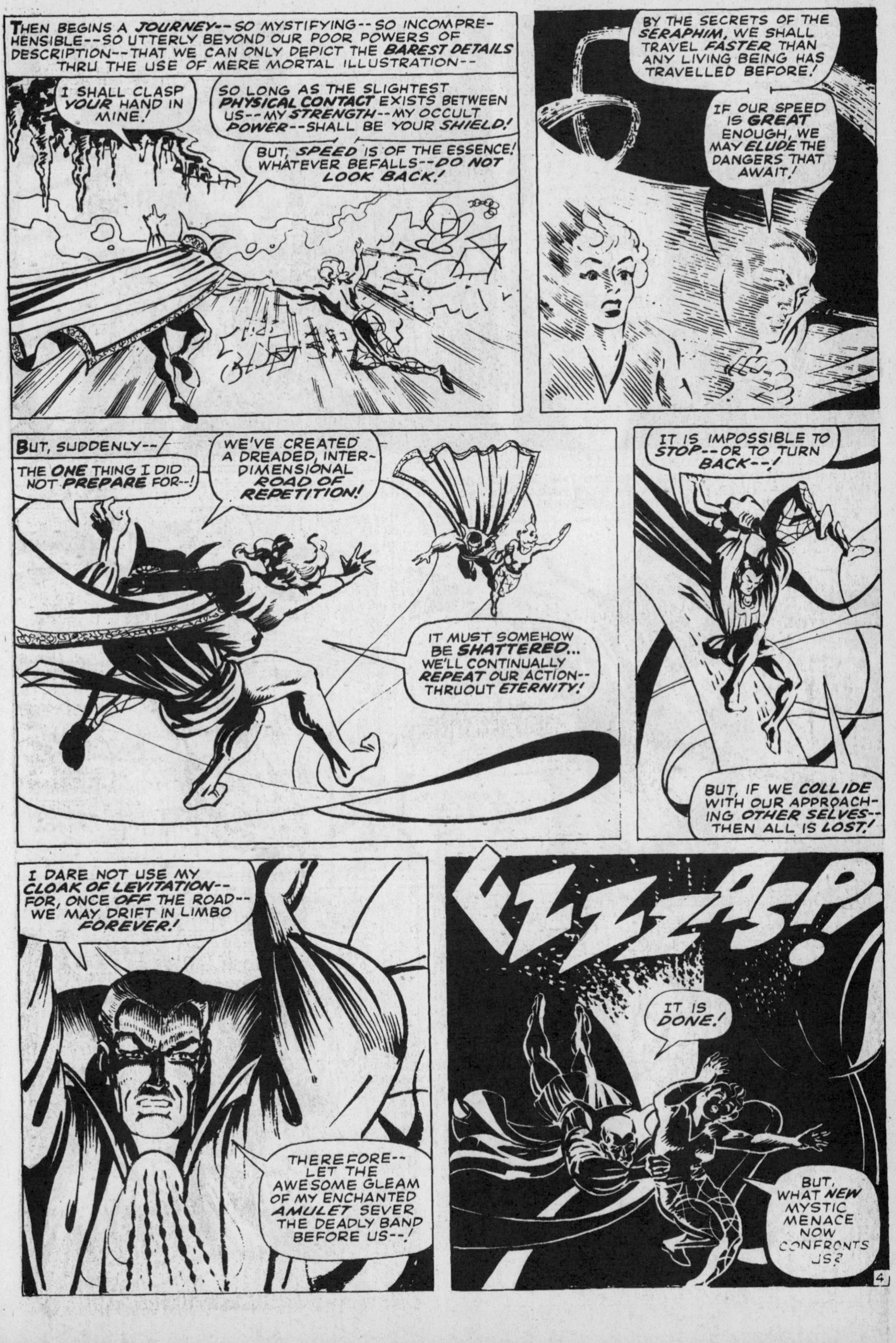
THEN BEGINS A JOURNEY-- SO MYSTIFYING-- SO INCOMPREHENSIBLE--SO UTTERLY BEYOND OUR POOR POWERS OF DESCRIPTION--THAT WE CAN ONLY DEPICT THE BAREST DETAILS THRU THE USE OF MERE MORTAL ILLUSTRATION--
I SHALL CLASP YOUR HAND IN MINE!
SO LONG AS THE SLIGHTEST PHYSICAL CONTACT EXISTS BETWEEN US--MY STRENGTH--MY OCCULT POWER--SHALL BE YOUR SHIELD!
BUT, SPEED IS OF THE ESSENCE! WHATEVER BEFALLS--DO NOT LOOK BACK!
BY THE SECRETS OF THE SERAPHIM, WE SHALL TRAVEL FASTER THAN ANY LIVING BEING HAS TRAVELLED BEFORE!
IF OUR SPEED IS GREAT ENOUGH, WE MAY ELUDE THE DANGERS THAT AWAIT!
BUT, SUDDENLY--
THE ONE THING I DID NOT PREPARE FOR--!
WE'VE CREATED A DREADED, INTER-DIMENSIONAL ROAD OF REPETITION!
IT MUST SOMEHOW BE SHATTERED... WE'LL CONTINUALLY REPEAT OUR ACTION--THRUOUT ETERNITY!
IT IS IMPOSSIBLE TO STOP--OR TO TURN BACK--!
BUT, IF WE COLLIDE WITH OUR APPROACHING OTHER SELVES--THEN ALL IS LOST!
I DARE NOT USE MY CLOAK OF LEVITATION--FOR, ONCE OFF THE ROAD--WE MAY DRIFT IN LIMBO FOREVER!
THEREFORE--LET THE AWESOME GLEAM OF MY ENCHANTED AMULET SEVER THE DEADLY BAND BEFORE US--!
ZZZZASP!
IT IS DONE!
BUT, WHAT NEW MYSTIC MENACE NOW CONFRONTS US?
4

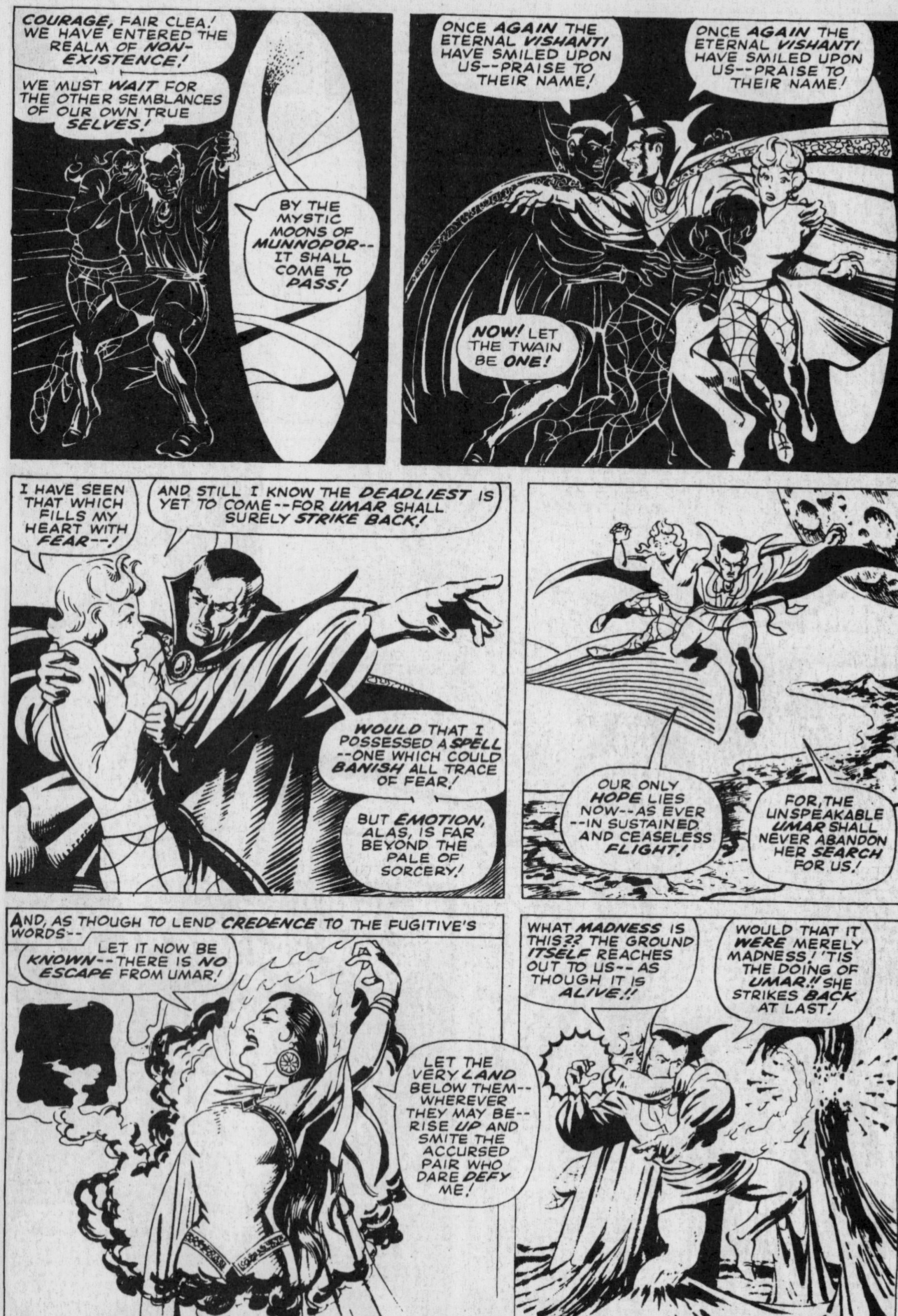
COURAGE, FAIR CLEA! WE HAVE ENTERED THE REALM OF NON-EXISTENCE!
WE MUST WAIT FOR THE OTHER SEMBLANCES OF OUR OWN TRUE SELVES!
BY THE MYSTIC MOONS OF MUNNOPOR-- IT SHALL COME TO PASS!
ONCE AGAIN THE ETERNAL VISHANTI HAVE SMILED UPON US--PRAISE TO THEIR NAME!
ONCE AGAIN THE ETERNAL VISHANTI HAVE SMILED UPON US--PRAISE TO THEIR NAME!
NOW! LET THE TWAIN BE ONE!
I HAVE SEEN THAT WHICH FILLS MY HEART WITH FEAR--!
AND STILL I KNOW THE DEADLIEST IS YET TO COME--FOR UMAR SHALL SURELY STRIKE BACK!
WOULD THAT I POSSESSED A SPELL --ONE WHICH COULD BANISH ALL TRACE OF FEAR!
BUT EMOTION, ALAS, IS FAR BEYOND THE PALE OF SORCERY!
OUR ONLY HOPE LIES NOW--AS EVER --IN SUSTAINED AND CEASELESS FLIGHT!
FOR, THE UNSPEAKABLE UMAR SHALL NEVER ABANDON HER SEARCH FOR US!
AND, AS THOUGH TO LEND CREDENCE TO THE FUGITIVE'S WORDS--
LET IT NOW BE KNOWN--THERE IS NO ESCAPE FROM UMAR!
LET THE VERY LAND BELOW THEM-- WHEREVER THEY MAY BE-- RISE UP AND SMITE THE ACCURSED PAIR WHO DARE DEFY ME!
WHAT MADNESS IS THIS?? THE GROUND ITSELF REACHES OUT TO US-- AS THOUGH IT IS ALIVE!!
WOULD THAT IT WERE MERELY MADNESS! 'TIS THE DOING OF UMAR!! SHE STRIKES BACK AT LAST!
5

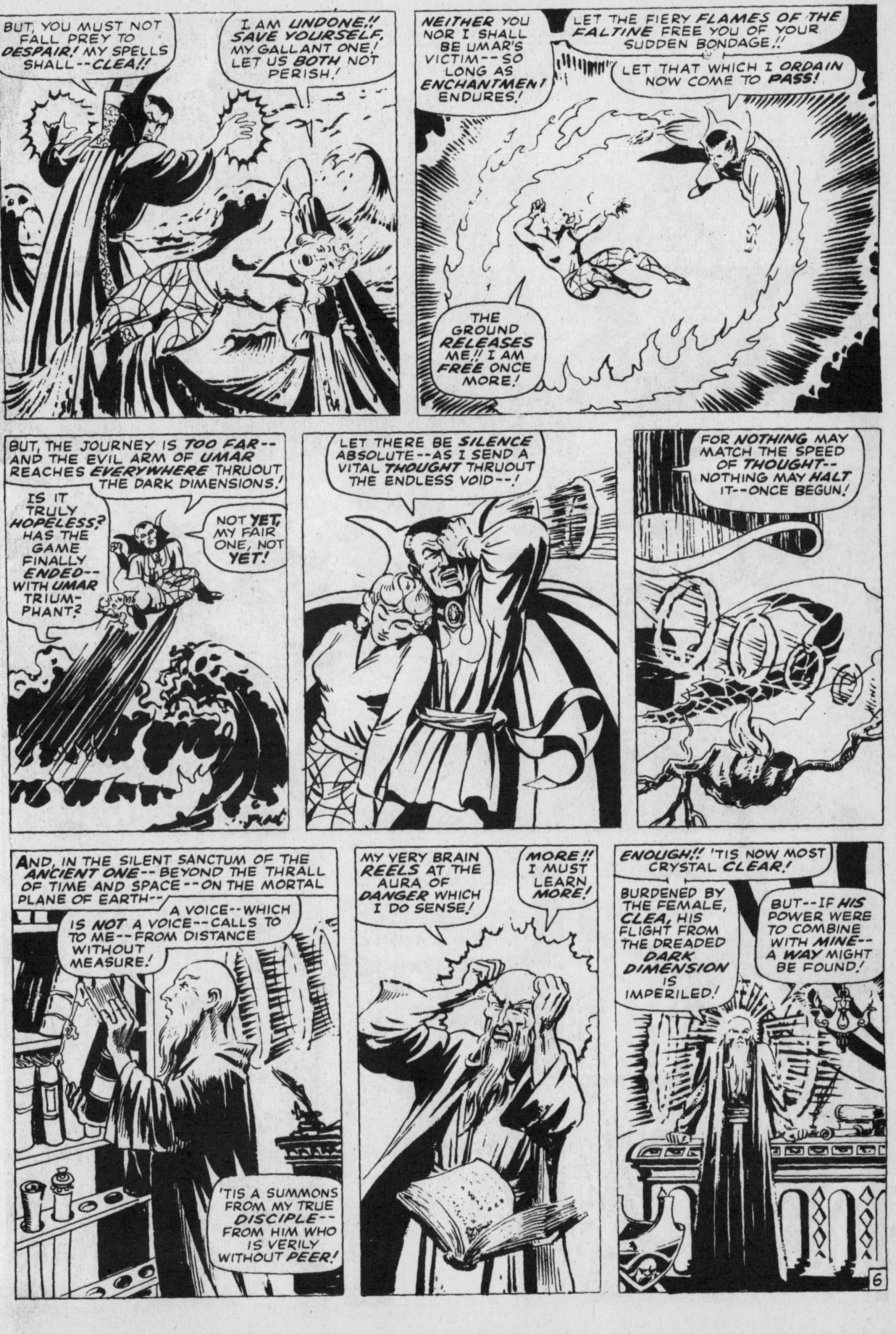
BUT, YOU MUST NOT FALL PREY TO DESPAIR! MY SPELLS SHALL--CLEA!!
I AM UNDONE!! SAVE YOURSELF, MY GALLANT ONE! LET US BOTH NOT PERISH!
NEITHER YOU NOR I SHALL BE UMAR'S VICTIM--SO LONG AS ENCHANTMENT ENDURES!
LET THE FIERY FLAMES OF THE FALTINE FREE YOU OF YOUR SUDDEN BONDAGE!!
LET THAT WHICH I ORDAIN NOW COME TO PASS!
THE GROUND RELEASES ME!! I AM FREE ONCE MORE!
BUT, THE JOURNEY IS TOO FAR--AND THE EVIL ARM OF UMAR REACHES EVERYWHERE THRUOUT THE DARK DIMENSIONS!
IS IT TRULY HOPELESS? HAS THE GAME FINALLY ENDED--WITH UMAR TRIUMPHANT?
NOT YET, MY FAIR ONE, NOT YET!
LET THERE BE SILENCE ABSOLUTE--AS I SEND A VITAL THOUGHT THRUOUT THE ENDLESS VOID--!
FOR NOTHING MAY MATCH THE SPEED OF THOUGHT--NOTHING MAY HALT IT--ONCE BEGUN!
AND, IN THE SILENT SANCTUM OF THE ANCIENT ONE--BEYOND THE THRALL OF TIME AND SPACE--ON THE MORTAL PLANE OF EARTH--
A VOICE--WHICH IS NOT A VOICE--CALLS TO TO ME--FROM DISTANCE WITHOUT MEASURE!
'TIS A SUMMONS FROM MY TRUE DISCIPLE--FROM HIM WHO IS VERILY WITHOUT PEER!
MY VERY BRAIN REELS AT THE AURA OF DANGER WHICH I DO SENSE!
MORE!! I MUST LEARN MORE!
ENOUGH!! 'TIS NOW MOST CRYSTAL CLEAR!
BURDENED BY THE FEMALE, CLEA, HIS FLIGHT FROM THE DREADED DARK DIMENSION IS IMPERILED!
BUT--IF HIS POWER WERE TO COMBINE WITH MINE--A WAY MIGHT BE FOUND!
6

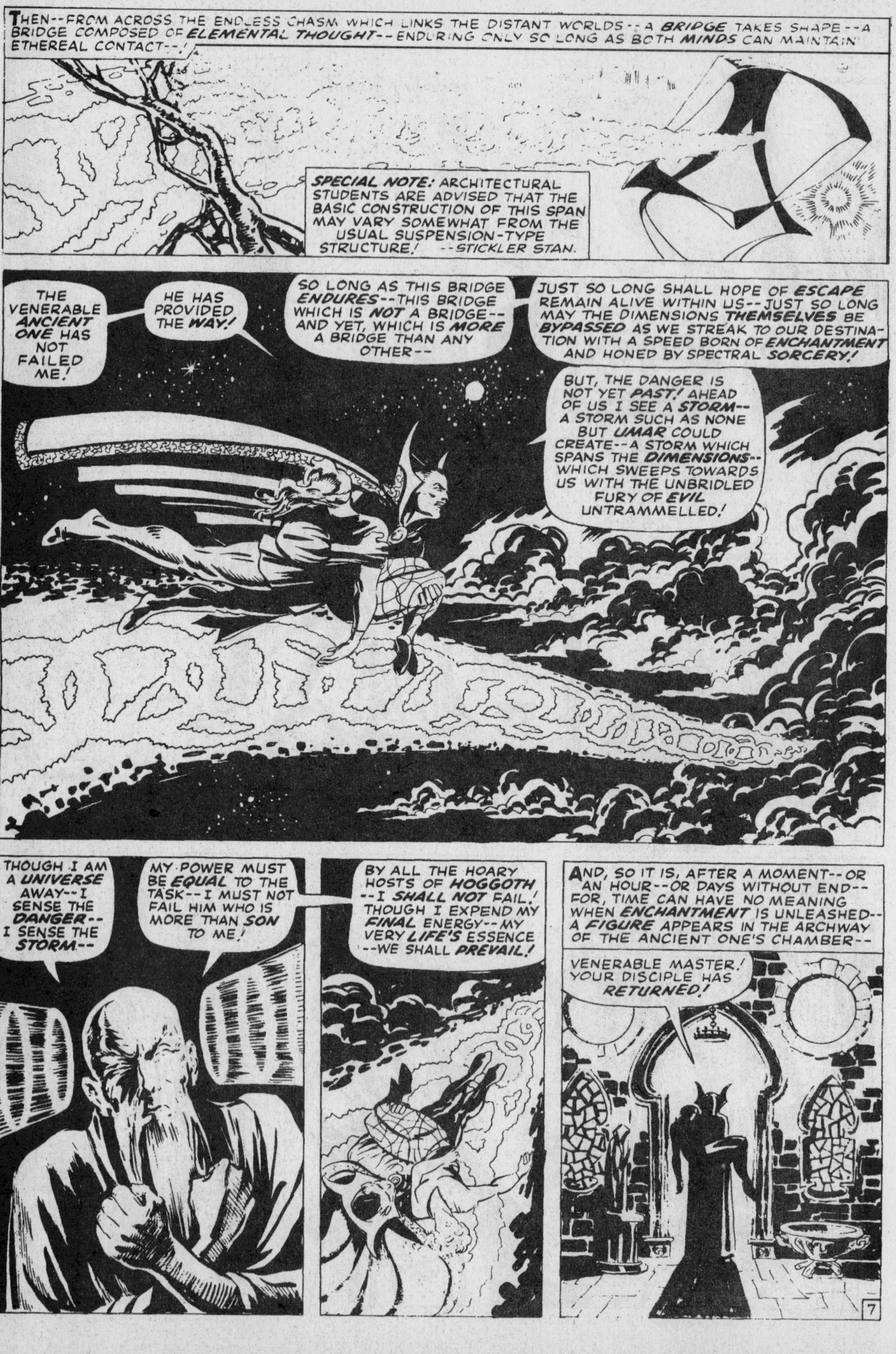
THEN--FROM ACROSS THE ENDLESS CHASM WHICH LINKS THE DISTANT WORLDS--A BRIDGE TAKES SHAPE--A BRIDGE COMPOSED OF ELEMENTAL THOUGHT--ENDURING ONLY SO LONG AS BOTH MINDS CAN MAINTAIN ETHEREAL CONTACT--!
SPECIAL NOTE: ARCHITECTURAL STUDENTS ARE ADVISED THAT THE BASIC CONSTRUCTION OF THIS SPAN MAY VARY SOMEWHAT FROM THE USUAL SUSPENSION-TYPE STRUCTURE! --STICKLER STAN.
THE VENERABLE ANCIENT ONE HAS NOT FAILED ME!
HE HAS PROVIDED THE WAY!
SO LONG AS THIS BRIDGE ENDURES--THIS BRIDGE WHICH IS NOT A BRIDGE--AND YET, WHICH IS MORE A BRIDGE THAN ANY OTHER--
JUST SO LONG SHALL HOPE OF ESCAPE REMAIN ALIVE WITHIN US--JUST SO LONG MAY THE DIMENSIONS THEMSELVES BE BYPASSED AS WE STREAK TO OUR DESTINATION WITH A SPEED BORN OF ENCHANTMENT AND HONED BY SPECTRAL SORCERY!
BUT, THE DANGER IS NOT YET PAST! AHEAD OF US I SEE A STORM--A STORM SUCH AS NONE BUT UMAR COULD CREATE--A STORM WHICH SPANS THE DIMENSIONS--WHICH SWEEPS TOWARDS US WITH THE UNBRIDLED FURY OF EVIL UNTRAMMELLED!
THOUGH I AM A UNIVERSE AWAY--I SENSE THE DANGER--I SENSE THE STORM--
MY POWER MUST BE EQUAL TO THE TASK--I MUST NOT FAIL HIM WHO IS MORE THAN SON TO ME!
BY ALL THE HOARY HOSTS OF HOGGOTH--I SHALL NOT FAIL! THOUGH I EXPEND MY FINAL ENERGY--MY VERY LIFE'S ESSENCE--WE SHALL PREVAIL!
AND, SO IT IS, AFTER A MOMENT--OR AN HOUR--OR DAYS WITHOUT END--FOR, TIME CAN HAVE NO MEANING WHEN ENCHANTMENT IS UNLEASHED--A FIGURE APPEARS IN THE ARCHWAY OF THE ANCIENT ONE'S CHAMBER--
VENERABLE MASTER! YOUR DISCIPLE HAS RETURNED!
7

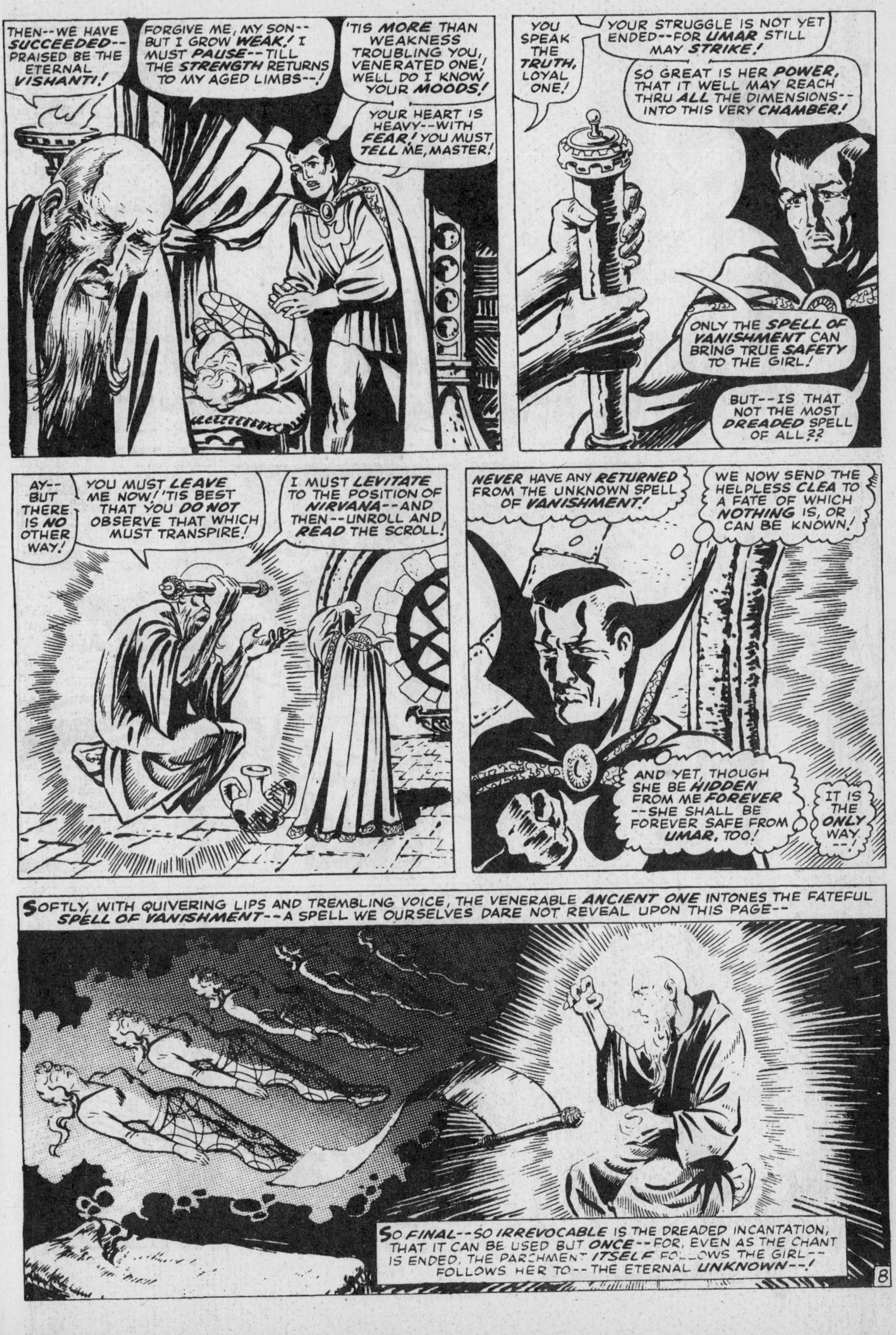
THEN--WE HAVE SUCCEEDED--PRAISED BE THE ETERNAL VISHANTI!
FORGIVE ME, MY SON--BUT I GROW WEAK! I MUST PAUSE--TILL THE STRENGTH RETURNS TO MY AGED LIMBS--!
'TIS MORE THAN WEAKNESS TROUBLING YOU, VENERATED ONE! WELL DO I KNOW YOUR MOODS!
YOUR HEART IS HEAVY--WITH FEAR! YOU MUST TELL ME, MASTER!
YOU SPEAK THE TRUTH, LOYAL ONE!
YOUR STRUGGLE IS NOT YET ENDED--FOR UMAR STILL MAY STRIKE!
SO GREAT IS HER POWER, THAT IT WELL MAY REACH THRU ALL THE DIMENSIONS--INTO THIS VERY CHAMBER!
ONLY THE SPELL OF VANISHMENT CAN BRING TRUE SAFETY TO THE GIRL!
BUT--IS THAT NOT THE MOST DREADED SPELL OF ALL??
AY--BUT THERE IS NO OTHER WAY!
YOU MUST LEAVE ME NOW! 'TIS BEST THAT YOU DO NOT OBSERVE THAT WHICH MUST TRANSPIRE!
I MUST LEVITATE TO THE POSITION OF NIRVANA--AND THEN--UNROLL AND READ THE SCROLL!
NEVER HAVE ANY RETURNED FROM THE UNKNOWN SPELL OF VANISHMENT!
WE NOW SEND THE HELPLESS CLEA TO A FATE OF WHICH NOTHING IS, OR CAN BE KNOWN!
AND YET, THOUGH SHE BE HIDDEN FROM ME FOREVER--SHE SHALL BE FOREVER SAFE FROM UMAR, TOO!
IT IS THE ONLY WAY--!
SOFTLY, WITH QUIVERING LIPS AND TREMBLING VOICE, THE VENERABLE ANCIENT ONE INTONES THE FATEFUL SPELL OF VANISHMENT--A SPELL WE OURSELVES DARE NOT REVEAL UPON THIS PAGE--
SO FINAL--SO IRREVOCABLE IS THE DREADED INCANTATION, THAT IT CAN BE USED BUT ONCE--FOR, EVEN AS THE CHANT IS ENDED, THE PARCHMENT ITSELF FOLLOWS THE GIRL--FOLLOWS HER TO--THE ETERNAL UNKNOWN--!
8

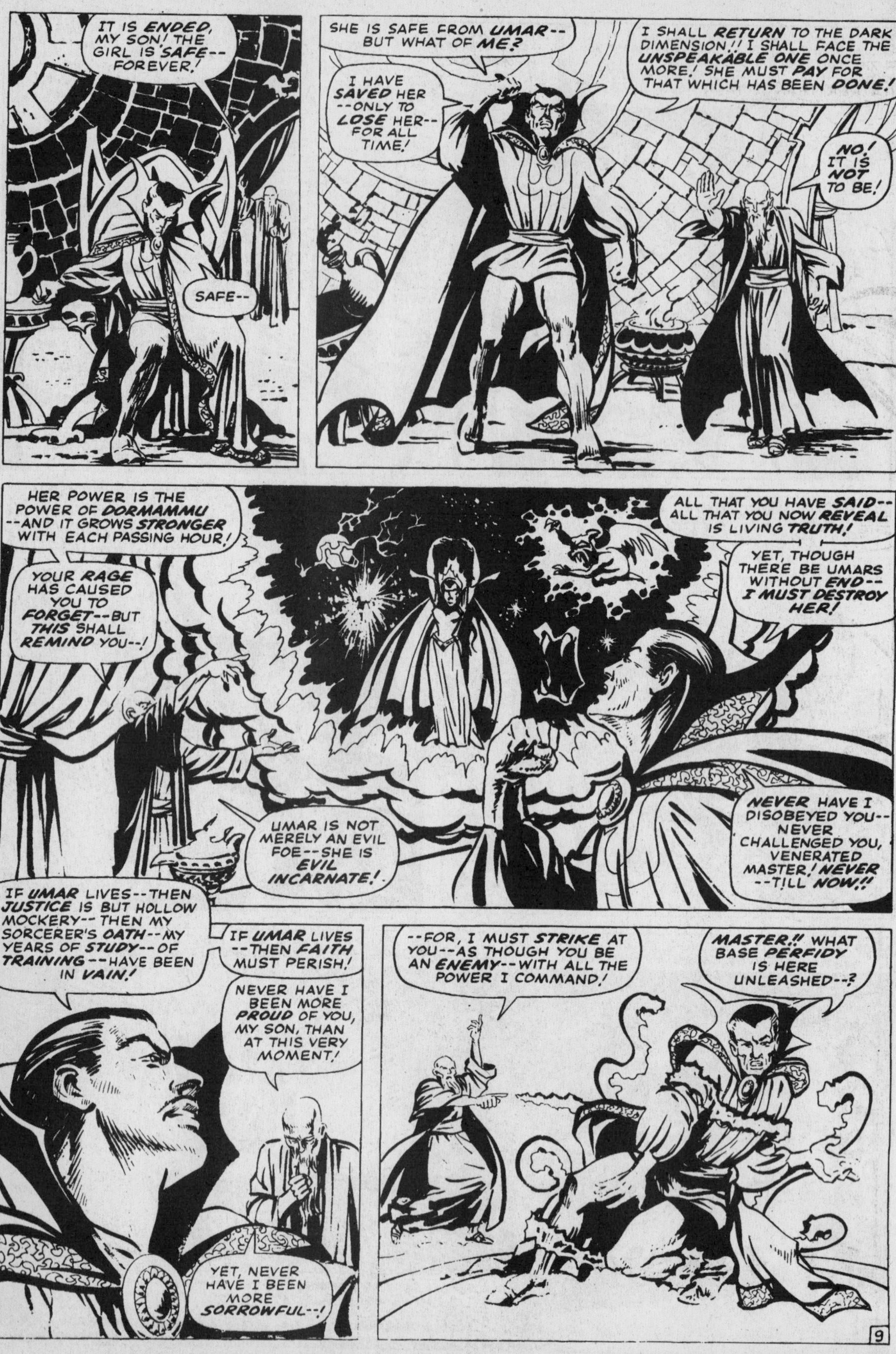
IT IS ENDED, MY SON! THE GIRL IS 'SAFE'--FOREVER!
SAFE--
SHE IS SAFE FROM UMAR--BUT WHAT OF ME?
I HAVE SAVED HER--ONLY TO LOSE HER--FOR ALL TIME!
I SHALL RETURN TO THE DARK DIMENSION!! I SHALL FACE THE UNSPEAKABLE ONE ONCE MORE! SHE MUST PAY FOR THAT WHICH HAS BEEN DONE!
NO! IT IS NOT TO BE!
HER POWER IS THE POWER OF DORMAMMU--AND IT GROWS STRONGER WITH EACH PASSING HOUR!
YOUR RAGE HAS CAUSED YOU TO FORGET--BUT THIS SHALL REMIND YOU--!
ALL THAT YOU HAVE SAID--ALL THAT YOU NOW REVEAL IS LIVING TRUTH!
YET, THOUGH THERE BE UMARS WITHOUT END--I MUST DESTROY HER!
UMAR IS NOT MERELY AN EVIL FOE--SHE IS EVIL INCARNATE!
NEVER HAVE I DISOBEYED YOU--NEVER CHALLENGED YOU, VENERATED MASTER! NEVER--TILL NOW!!
IF UMAR LIVES--THEN JUSTICE IS BUT HOLLOW MOCKERY--THEN MY SORCERER'S OATH--MY YEARS OF STUDY--OF TRAINING--HAVE BEEN IN VAIN!
IF UMAR LIVES--THEN FAITH MUST PERISH!
NEVER HAVE I BEEN MORE PROUD OF YOU, MY SON, THAN AT THIS VERY MOMENT!
YET, NEVER HAVE I BEEN MORE SORROWFUL--!
--FOR, I MUST STRIKE AT YOU--AS THOUGH YOU BE AN ENEMY--WITH ALL THE POWER I COMMAND!
MASTER!! WHAT BASE PERFIDY IS HERE UNLEASHED--?
9

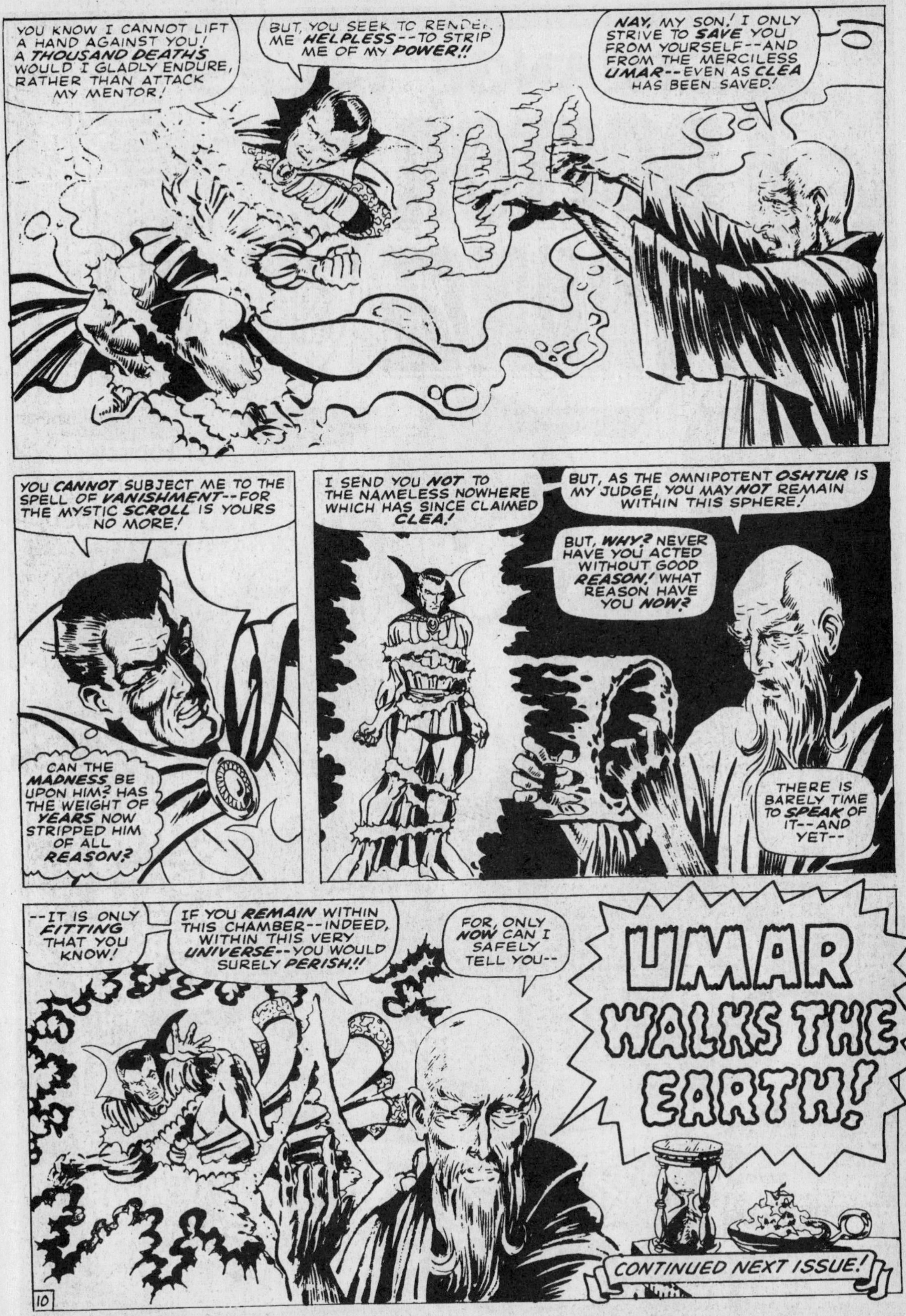
YOU KNOW I CANNOT LIFT A HAND AGAINST YOU! A THOUSAND DEATHS WOULD I GLADLY ENDURE, RATHER THAN ATTACK MY MENTOR!
BUT, YOU SEEK TO RENDER ME HELPLESS--TO STRIP ME OF MY POWER!!
NAY, MY SON! I ONLY STRIVE TO SAVE YOU FROM YOURSELF--AND FROM THE MERCILESS UMAR--EVEN AS CLEA HAS BEEN SAVED!
YOU CANNOT SUBJECT ME TO THE SPELL OF VANISHMENT--FOR THE MYSTIC SCROLL IS YOURS NO MORE!
CAN THE MADNESS BE UPON HIM? HAS THE WEIGHT OF YEARS NOW STRIPPED HIM OF ALL REASON?
I SEND YOU NOT TO THE NAMELESS NOWHERE WHICH HAS SINCE CLAIMED CLEA!
BUT, AS THE OMNIPOTENT OSHTUR IS MY JUDGE, YOU MAY NOT REMAIN WITHIN THIS SPHERE!
BUT, WHY? NEVER HAVE YOU ACTED WITHOUT GOOD REASON! WHAT REASON HAVE YOU NOW?
THERE IS BARELY TIME TO SPEAK OF IT--AND YET--
--IT IS ONLY FITTING THAT YOU KNOW!
IF YOU REMAIN WITHIN THIS CHAMBER--INDEED, WITHIN THIS VERY UNIVERSE--YOU WOULD SURELY PERISH!!
FOR, ONLY NOW CAN I SAFELY TELL YOU--
UMAR WALKS THE EARTH!
CONTINUED NEXT ISSUE!
10

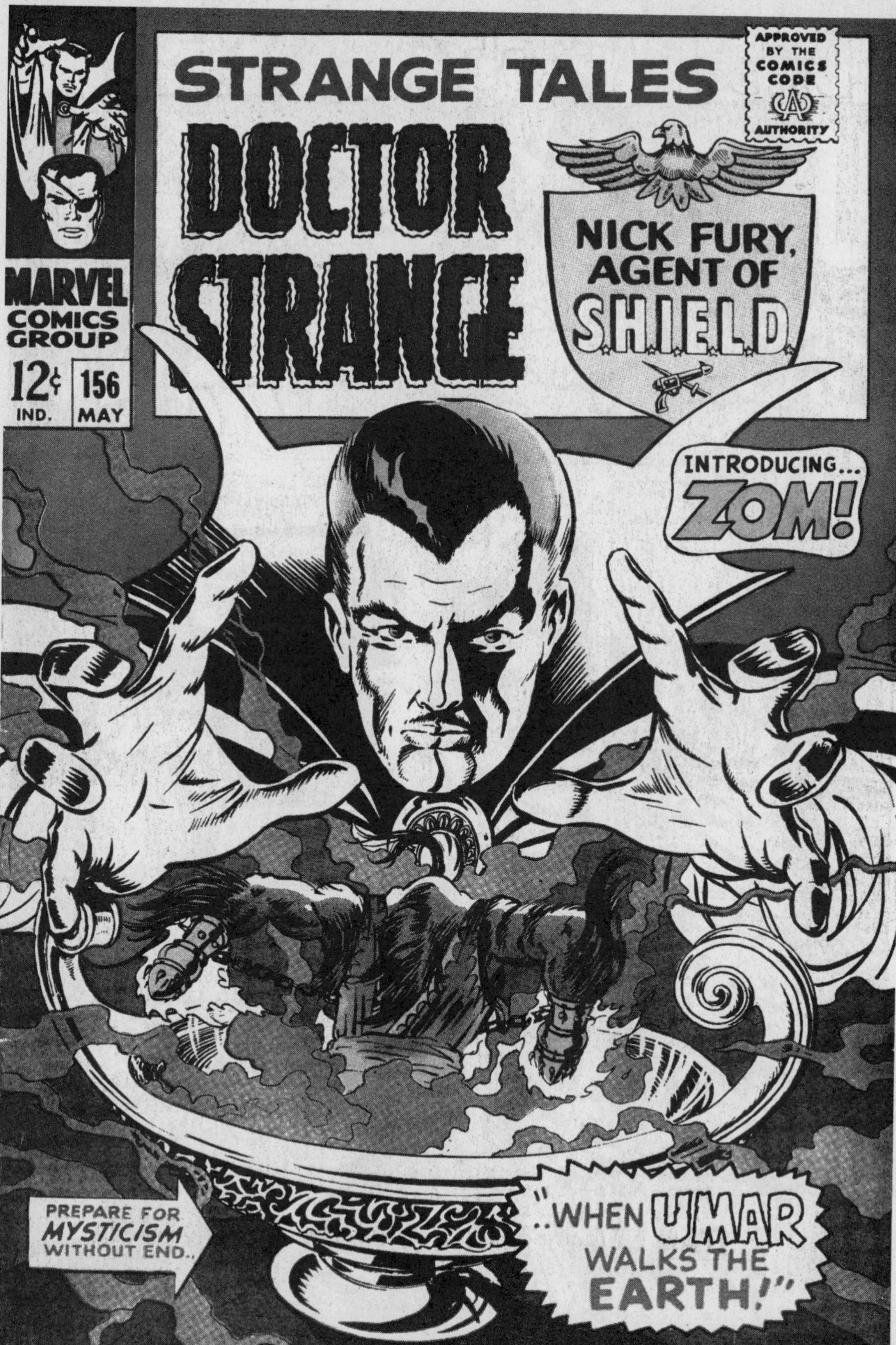
STRANGE TALES
DOCTOR STRANGE
APPROVED BY THE COMICS CODE AUTHORITY
NICK FURY, AGENT OF S.H.I.E.L.D.
MARVEL COMICS GROUP
12¢ IND.
156 MAY
INTRODUCING... ZOM!
PREPARE FOR MYSTICISM WITHOUT END..
"..WHEN UMAR WALKS THE EARTH!"

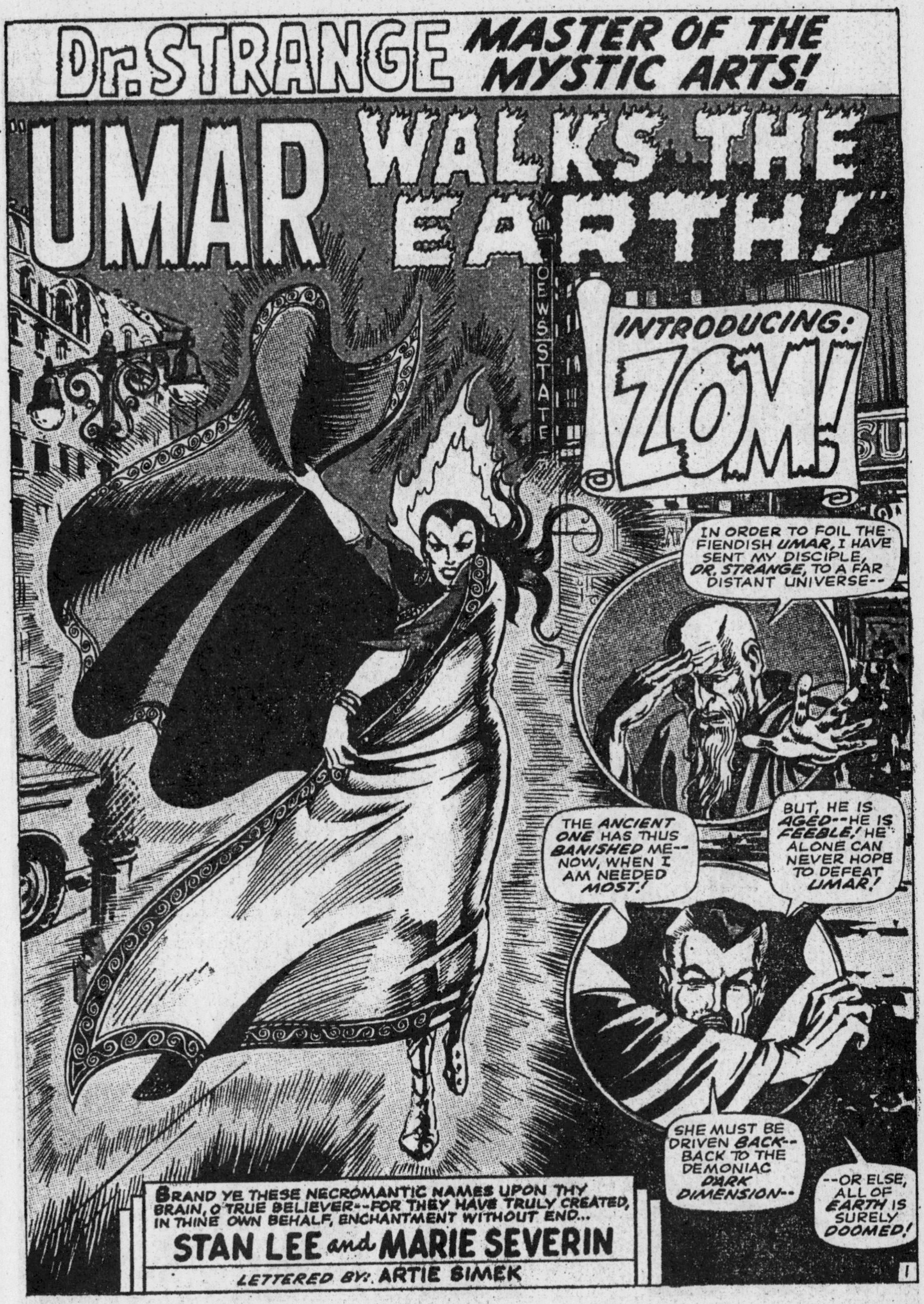

Dr. STRANGE MASTER OF THE MYSTIC ARTS!
"UMAR WALKS THE EARTH!"
INTRODUCING: ZOM!
LOEWS STATE
IN ORDER TO FOIL THE FIENDISH UMAR, I HAVE SENT MY DISCIPLE, DR. STRANGE, TO A FAR DISTANT UNIVERSE--
BUT, HE IS AGED--HE IS FEEBLE! HE ALONE CAN NEVER HOPE TO DEFEAT UMAR!
THE ANCIENT ONE HAS THUS BANISHED ME--NOW, WHEN I AM NEEDED MOST!
SHE MUST BE DRIVEN BACK--BACK TO THE DEMONIAC DARK DIMENSION--
--OR ELSE, ALL OF EARTH IS SURELY DOOMED!
BRAND YE THESE NECROMANTIC NAMES UPON THY BRAIN, O TRUE BELIEVER--FOR THEY HAVE TRULY CREATED, IN THINE OWN BEHALF, ENCHANTMENT WITHOUT END...
STAN LEE and MARIE SEVERIN
LETTERED BY: ARTIE SIMEK
1

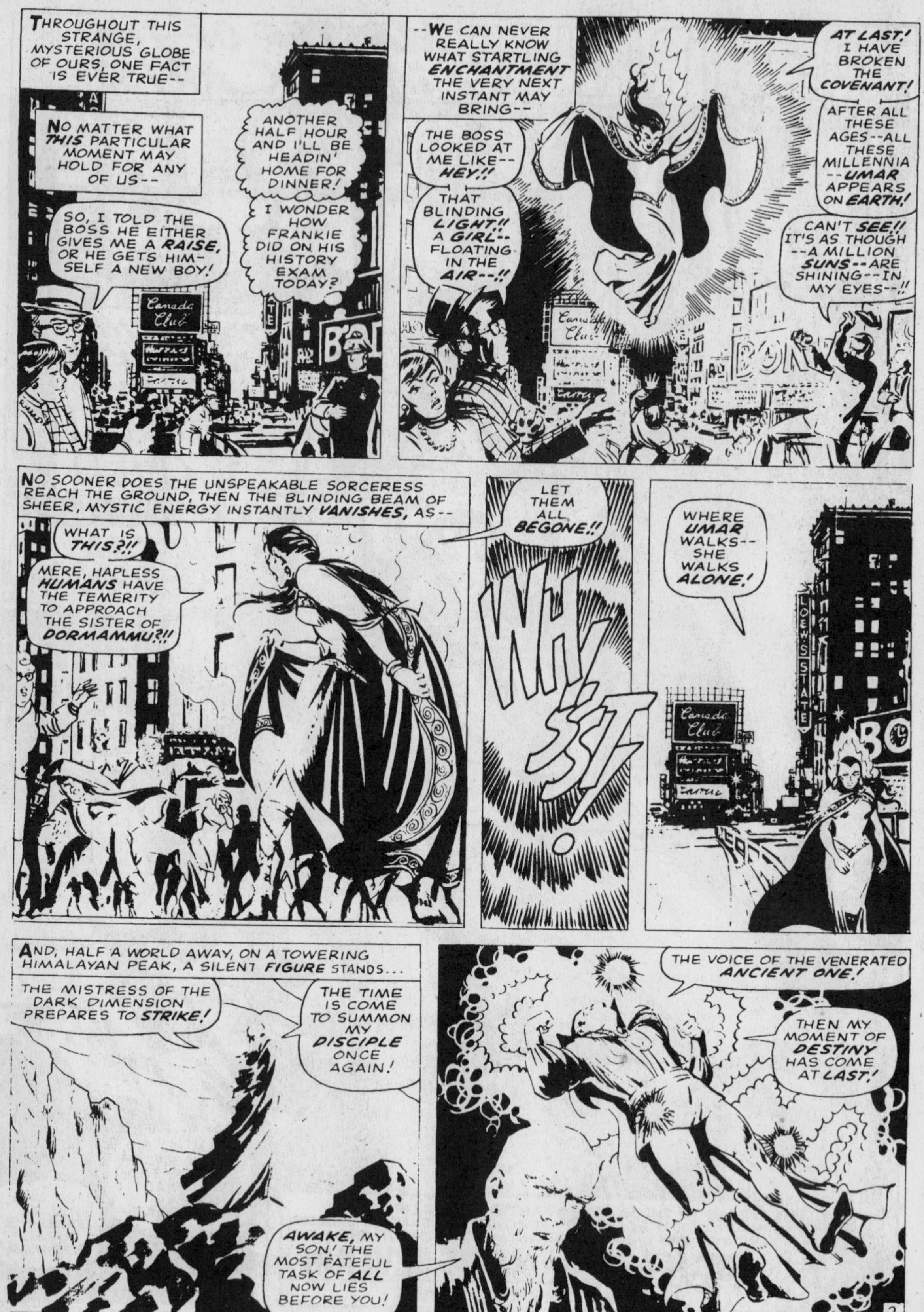

THROUGHOUT THIS STRANGE, MYSTERIOUS GLOBE OF OURS, ONE FACT IS EVER TRUE--
NO MATTER WHAT THIS PARTICULAR MOMENT MAY HOLD FOR ANY OF US--
SO, I TOLD THE BOSS HE EITHER GIVES ME A RAISE, OR HE GETS HIMSELF A NEW BOY!
ANOTHER HALF HOUR AND I'LL BE HEADIN' HOME FOR DINNER!
I WONDER HOW FRANKIE DID ON HIS HISTORY EXAM TODAY?
Canada Club
--WE CAN NEVER REALLY KNOW WHAT STARTLING ENCHANTMENT THE VERY NEXT INSTANT MAY BRING--
THE BOSS LOOKED AT ME LIKE--HEY!!
THAT BLINDING LIGHT!! A GIRL--FLOATING IN THE AIR--!!
AT LAST! I HAVE BROKEN THE COVENANT!
AFTER ALL THESE AGES--ALL THESE MILLENNIA--UMAR APPEARS ON EARTH!
CAN'T SEE!! IT'S AS THOUGH--A MILLION SUNS--ARE SHINING--IN MY EYES--!!
NO SOONER DOES THE UNSPEAKABLE SORCERESS REACH THE GROUND, THEN THE BLINDING BEAM OF SHEER, MYSTIC ENERGY INSTANTLY VANISHES, AS--
WHAT IS THIS?!!
MERE, HAPLESS HUMANS HAVE THE TEMERITY TO APPROACH THE SISTER OF DORMAMMU?!!
LET THEM ALL BEGONE!!
WHSSST!
WHERE UMAR WALKS--SHE WALKS ALONE!
Canada Club
LOEWS STATE
AND, HALF A WORLD AWAY, ON A TOWERING HIMALAYAN PEAK, A SILENT FIGURE STANDS...
THE MISTRESS OF THE DARK DIMENSION PREPARES TO STRIKE!
THE TIME IS COME TO SUMMON MY DISCIPLE ONCE AGAIN!
AWAKE, MY SON! THE MOST FATEFUL TASK OF ALL NOW LIES BEFORE YOU!
THE VOICE OF THE VENERATED ANCIENT ONE!
THEN MY MOMENT OF DESTINY HAS COME AT LAST!
2

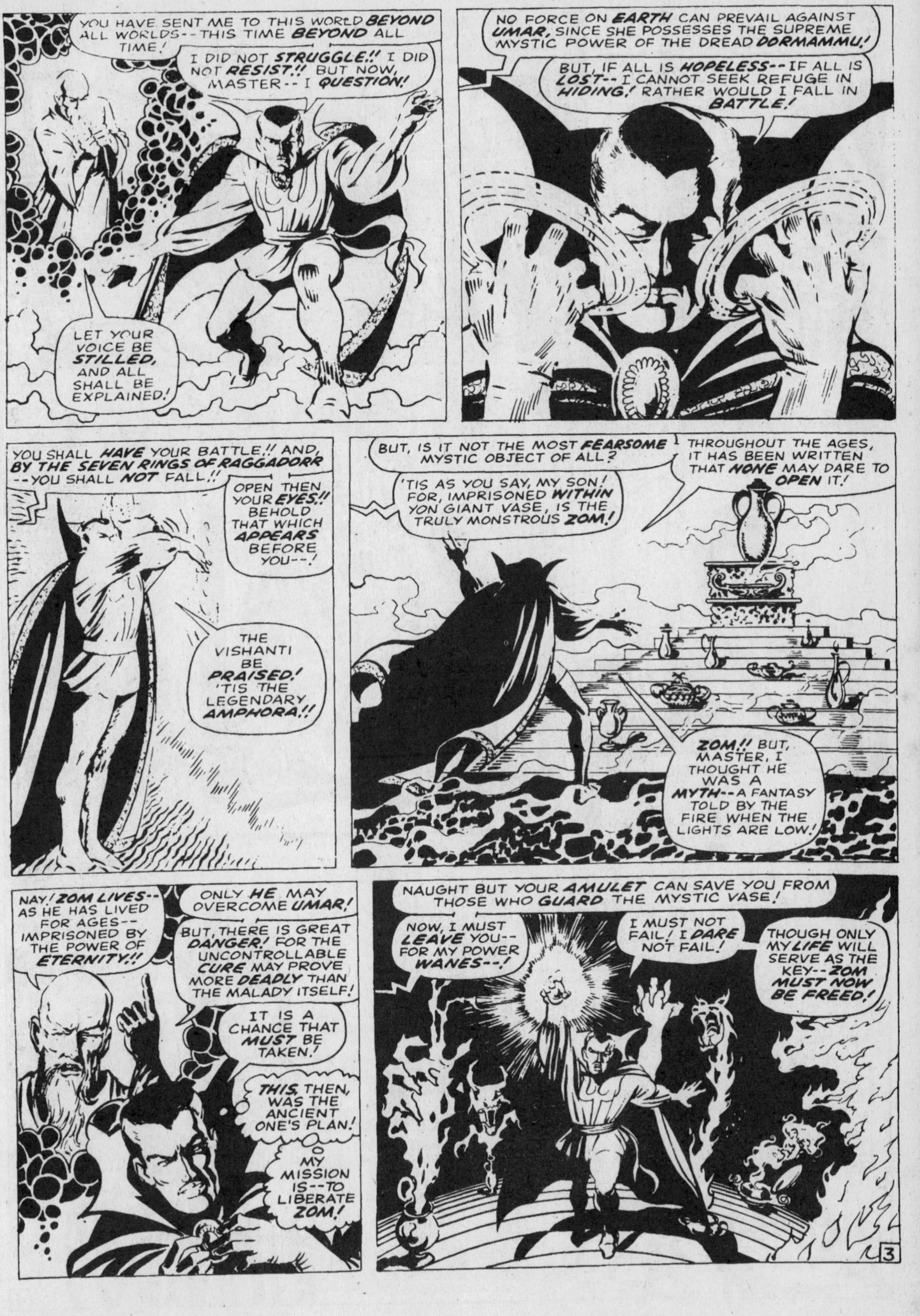
YOU HAVE SENT ME TO THIS WORLD BEYOND ALL WORLDS--THIS TIME BEYOND ALL TIME!
I DID NOT STRUGGLE!! I DID NOT RESIST!! BUT NOW, MASTER--I QUESTION!
LET YOUR VOICE BE STILLED, AND ALL SHALL BE EXPLAINED!
NO FORCE ON EARTH CAN PREVAIL AGAINST UMAR, SINCE SHE POSSESSES THE SUPREME MYSTIC POWER OF THE DREAD DORMAMMU!
BUT, IF ALL IS HOPELESS--IF ALL IS LOST--I CANNOT SEEK REFUGE IN HIDING! RATHER WOULD I FALL IN BATTLE!
YOU SHALL HAVE YOUR BATTLE!! AND, BY THE SEVEN RINGS OF RAGGADORR--YOU SHALL NOT FALL!!
OPEN THEN YOUR EYES!! BEHOLD THAT WHICH APPEARS BEFORE YOU--!
THE VISHANTI BE PRAISED! 'TIS THE LEGENDARY AMPHORA!!
BUT, IS IT NOT THE MOST FEARSOME MYSTIC OBJECT OF ALL?
THROUGHOUT THE AGES, IT HAS BEEN WRITTEN THAT NONE MAY DARE TO OPEN IT!
'TIS AS YOU SAY, MY SON! FOR, IMPRISONED WITHIN YON GIANT VASE, IS THE TRULY MONSTROUS ZOM!
ZOM!! BUT, MASTER, I THOUGHT HE WAS A MYTH--A FANTASY TOLD BY THE FIRE WHEN THE LIGHTS ARE LOW!
NAY! ZOM LIVES--AS HE HAS LIVED FOR AGES--IMPRISONED BY THE POWER OF ETERNITY!!
ONLY HE MAY OVERCOME UMAR!
BUT, THERE IS GREAT DANGER! FOR THE UNCONTROLLABLE CURE MAY PROVE MORE DEADLY THAN THE MALADY ITSELF!
IT IS A CHANCE THAT MUST BE TAKEN!
THIS, THEN, WAS THE ANCIENT ONE'S PLAN!
MY MISSION IS--TO LIBERATE ZOM!
NAUGHT BUT YOUR AMULET CAN SAVE YOU FROM THOSE WHO GUARD THE MYSTIC VASE!
NOW, I MUST LEAVE YOU--FOR MY POWER WANES--!
I MUST NOT FAIL! I DARE NOT FAIL!
THOUGH ONLY MY LIFE WILL SERVE AS THE KEY--ZOM MUST NOW BE FREED!
3

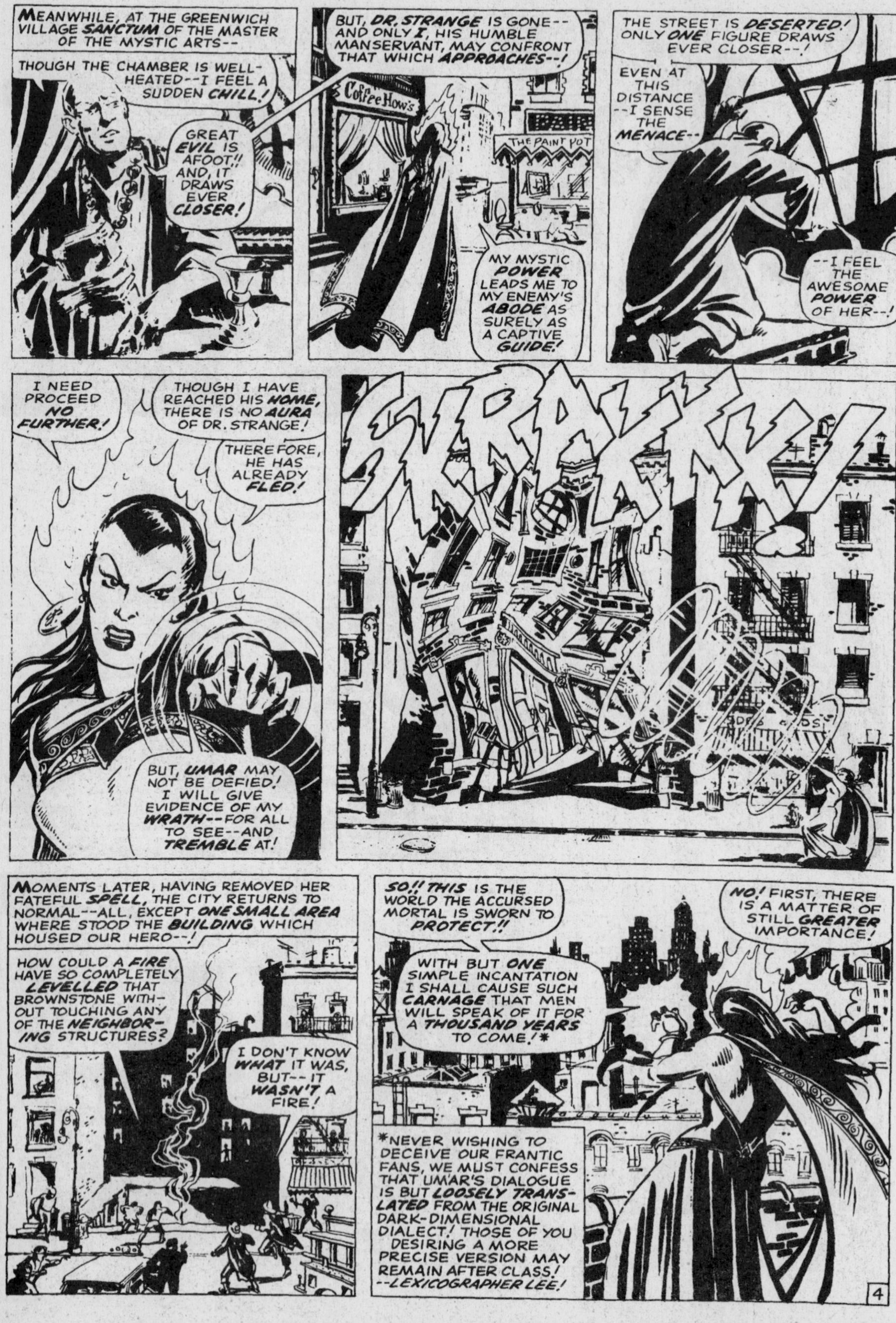
MEANWHILE, AT THE GREENWICH VILLAGE SANCTUM OF THE MASTER OF THE MYSTIC ARTS--
THOUGH THE CHAMBER IS WELL-HEATED--I FEEL A SUDDEN CHILL!
GREAT EVIL IS AFOOT!! AND, IT DRAWS EVER CLOSER!
BUT, DR. STRANGE IS GONE--AND ONLY I, HIS HUMBLE MANSERVANT, MAY CONFRONT THAT WHICH APPROACHES--!
Coffee How's
THE PAINT POT
MY MYSTIC POWER LEADS ME TO MY ENEMY'S ABODE AS SURELY AS A CAPTIVE GUIDE!
THE STREET IS DESERTED! ONLY ONE FIGURE DRAWS EVER CLOSER--!
EVEN AT THIS DISTANCE --I SENSE THE MENACE--
--I FEEL THE AWESOME POWER OF HER--!
I NEED PROCEED NO FURTHER!
THOUGH I HAVE REACHED HIS HOME, THERE IS NO AURA OF DR. STRANGE!
THERE FORE, HE HAS ALREADY FLED!
BUT, UMAR MAY NOT BE DEFIED! I WILL GIVE EVIDENCE OF MY WRATH--FOR ALL TO SEE--AND TREMBLE AT!
SKRAKK!
MOMENTS LATER, HAVING REMOVED HER FATEFUL SPELL, THE CITY RETURNS TO NORMAL--ALL, EXCEPT ONE SMALL AREA WHERE STOOD THE BUILDING WHICH HOUSED OUR HERO--!
HOW COULD A FIRE HAVE SO COMPLETELY LEVELLED THAT BROWNSTONE WITHOUT TOUCHING ANY OF THE NEIGHBORING STRUCTURES?
I DON'T KNOW WHAT IT WAS, BUT-- IT WASN'T A FIRE!
SO!! THIS IS THE WORLD THE ACCURSED MORTAL IS SWORN TO PROTECT!!
WITH BUT ONE SIMPLE INCANTATION I SHALL CAUSE SUCH CARNAGE THAT MEN WILL SPEAK OF IT FOR A THOUSAND YEARS TO COME!*
NO! FIRST, THERE IS A MATTER OF STILL GREATER IMPORTANCE!
*NEVER WISHING TO DECEIVE OUR FRANTIC FANS, WE MUST CONFESS THAT UMAR'S DIALOGUE IS BUT LOOSELY TRANSLATED FROM THE ORIGINAL DARK-DIMENSIONAL DIALECT! THOSE OF YOU DESIRING A MORE PRECISE VERSION MAY REMAIN AFTER CLASS! --LEXICOGRAPHER LEE!
4

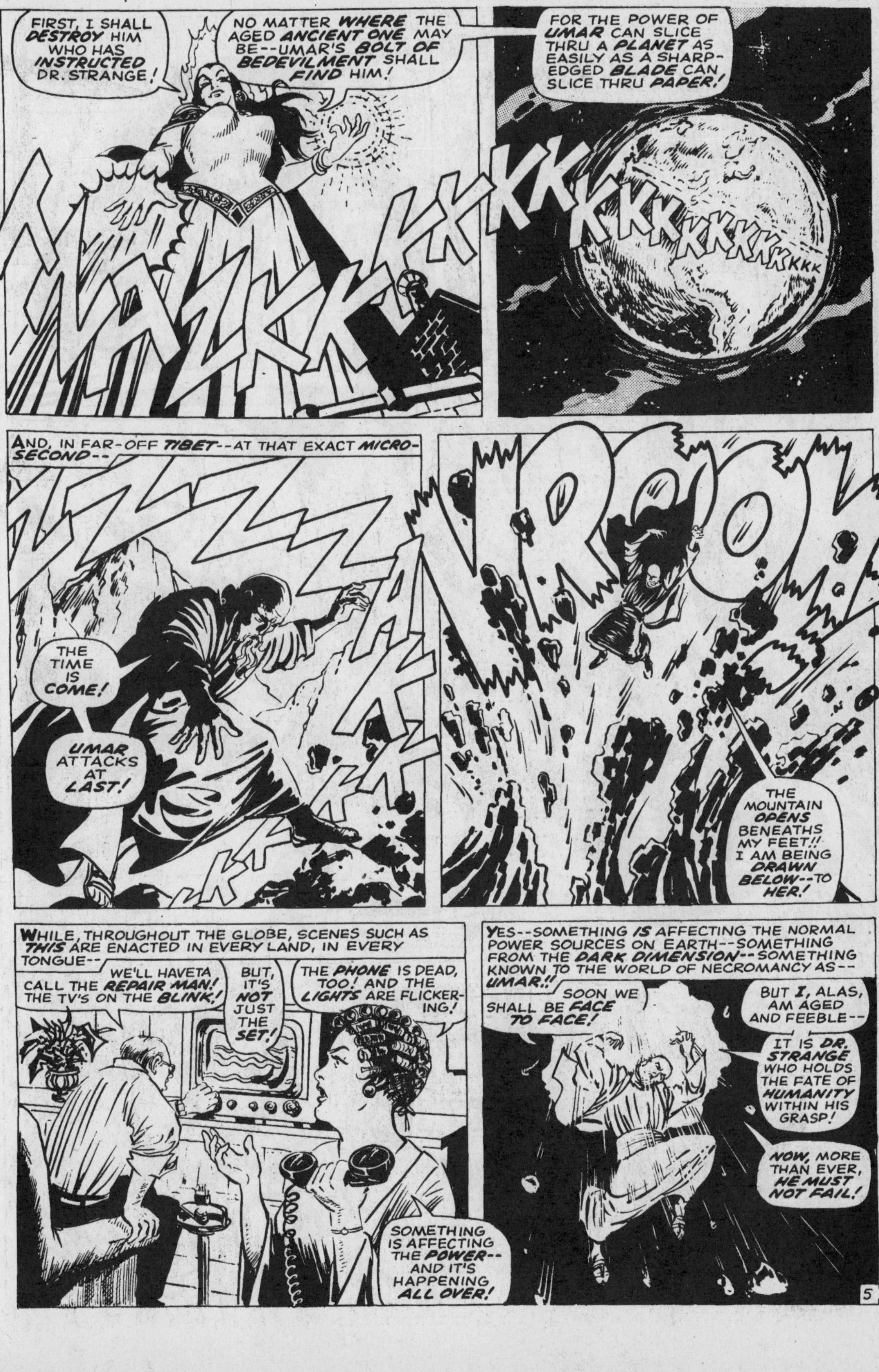
FIRST, I SHALL DESTROY HIM WHO HAS INSTRUCTED DR. STRANGE!
NO MATTER WHERE THE AGED ANCIENT ONE MAY BE--UMAR'S BOLT OF BEDEVILMENT SHALL FIND HIM!
FOR THE POWER OF UMAR CAN SLICE THRU A PLANET AS EASILY AS A SHARP-EDGED BLADE CAN SLICE THRU PAPER!
ZAZKKKKKKKKKKKKKKKKKKKK
AND, IN FAR-OFF TIBET--AT THAT EXACT MICRO-SECOND--
THE TIME IS COME!
UMAR ATTACKS AT LAST!
VROOOM
THE MOUNTAIN OPENS BENEATHS MY FEET!! I AM BEING DRAWN BELOW--TO HER!
WHILE, THROUGHOUT THE GLOBE, SCENES SUCH AS THIS ARE ENACTED IN EVERY LAND, IN EVERY TONGUE--
WE'LL HAVETA CALL THE REPAIR MAN! THE TV'S ON THE BLINK!
BUT, IT'S NOT JUST THE SET!
THE PHONE IS DEAD, TOO! AND THE LIGHTS ARE FLICKERING!
SOMETHING IS AFFECTING THE POWER-- AND IT'S HAPPENING ALL OVER!
YES--SOMETHING IS AFFECTING THE NORMAL POWER SOURCES ON EARTH--SOMETHING FROM THE DARK DIMENSION--SOMETHING KNOWN TO THE WORLD OF NECROMANCY AS--UMAR!!
SOON WE SHALL BE FACE TO FACE!
BUT I, ALAS, AM AGED AND FEEBLE--
IT IS DR. STRANGE WHO HOLDS THE FATE OF HUMANITY WITHIN HIS GRASP!
NOW, MORE THAN EVER, HE MUST NOT FAIL!

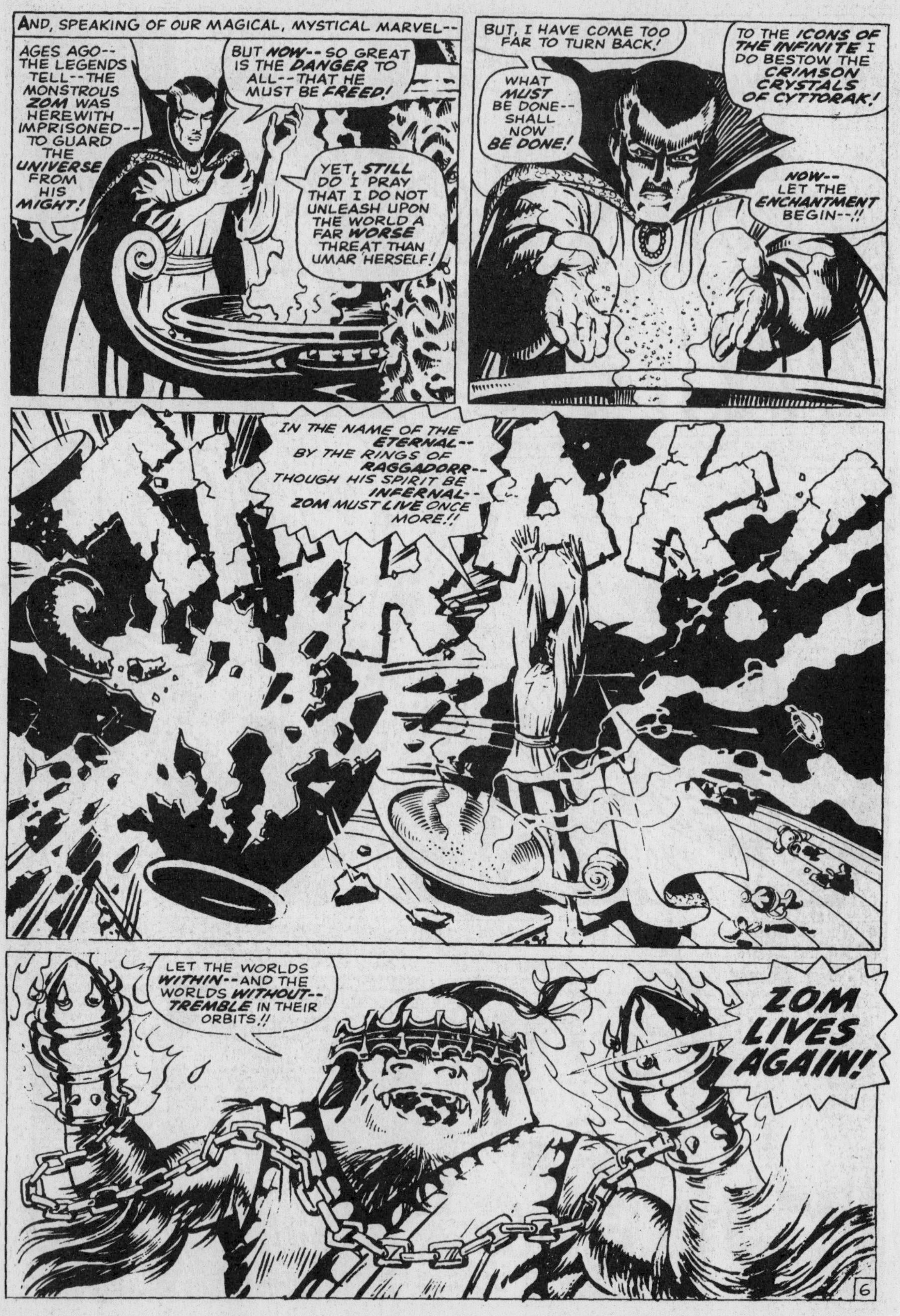
AND, SPEAKING OF OUR MAGICAL, MYSTICAL MARVEL--
AGES AGO-- THE LEGENDS TELL--THE MONSTROUS ZOM WAS HEREWITH IMPRISONED-- TO GUARD THE UNIVERSE FROM HIS MIGHT!
BUT NOW-- SO GREAT IS THE DANGER TO ALL--THAT HE MUST BE FREED!
YET, STILL DO I PRAY THAT I DO NOT UNLEASH UPON THE WORLD A FAR WORSE THREAT THAN UMAR HERSELF!
BUT, I HAVE COME TOO FAR TO TURN BACK!
WHAT MUST BE DONE-- SHALL NOW BE DONE!
TO THE ICONS OF THE INFINITE I DO BESTOW THE CRIMSON CRYSTALS OF CYTTORAK!
NOW-- LET THE ENCHANTMENT BEGIN--!!
IN THE NAME OF THE ETERNAL-- BY THE RINGS OF RAGGADORR-- THOUGH HIS SPIRIT BE INFERNAL-- ZOM MUST LIVE ONCE MORE!!
LET THE WORLDS WITHIN--AND THE WORLDS WITHOUT-- TREMBLE IN THEIR ORBITS!!
ZOM LIVES AGAIN!
6

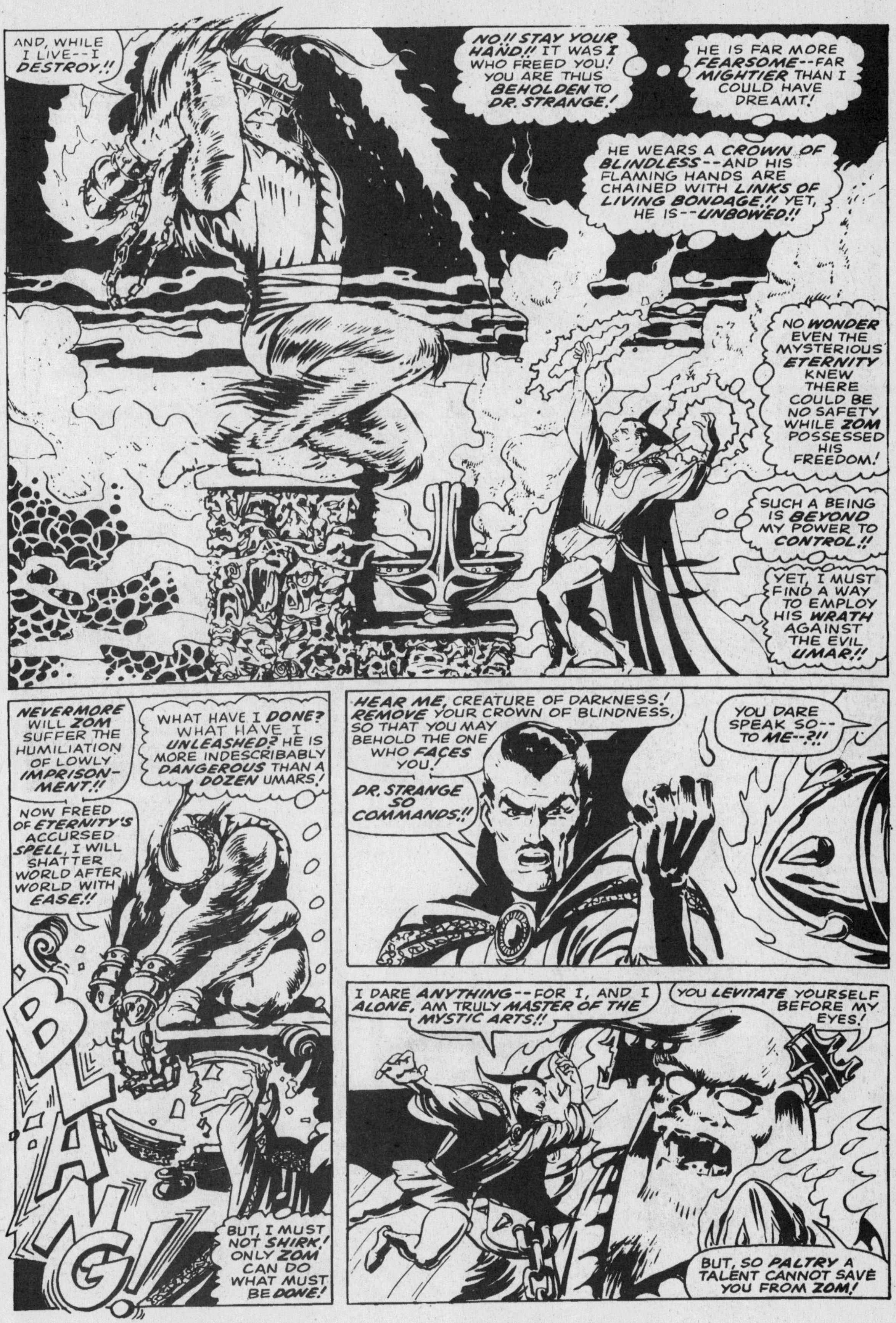

AND, WHILE I LIVE--I DESTROY.!!
NO!! STAY YOUR HAND!! IT WAS I WHO FREED YOU! YOU ARE THUS BEHOLDEN TO DR. STRANGE!
HE IS FAR MORE FEARSOME--FAR MIGHTIER THAN I COULD HAVE DREAMT!
HE WEARS A CROWN OF BLINDLESS--AND HIS FLAMING HANDS ARE CHAINED WITH LINKS OF LIVING BONDAGE!! YET, HE IS--UNBOWED!!
NO WONDER EVEN THE MYSTERIOUS ETERNITY KNEW THERE COULD BE NO SAFETY WHILE ZOM POSSESSED HIS FREEDOM!
SUCH A BEING IS BEYOND MY POWER TO CONTROL!!
YET, I MUST FIND A WAY TO EMPLOY HIS WRATH AGAINST THE EVIL UMAR!!
NEVERMORE WILL ZOM SUFFER THE HUMILIATION OF LOWLY IMPRISONMENT!!
WHAT HAVE I DONE? WHAT HAVE I UNLEASHED? HE IS MORE INDESCRIBABLY DANGEROUS THAN A DOZEN UMARS!
NOW FREED OF ETERNITY'S ACCURSED SPELL, I WILL SHATTER WORLD AFTER WORLD WITH EASE!!
BLANG!
BUT, I MUST NOT SHIRK! ONLY ZOM CAN DO WHAT MUST BE DONE!
HEAR ME, CREATURE OF DARKNESS! REMOVE YOUR CROWN OF BLINDNESS, SO THAT YOU MAY BEHOLD THE ONE WHO FACES YOU!
DR. STRANGE SO COMMANDS!!
YOU DARE SPEAK SO--TO ME--?!!
I DARE ANYTHING--FOR I, AND I ALONE, AM TRULY MASTER OF THE MYSTIC ARTS!!
YOU LEVITATE YOURSELF BEFORE MY EYES!
BUT, SO PALTRY A TALENT CANNOT SAVE YOU FROM ZOM!

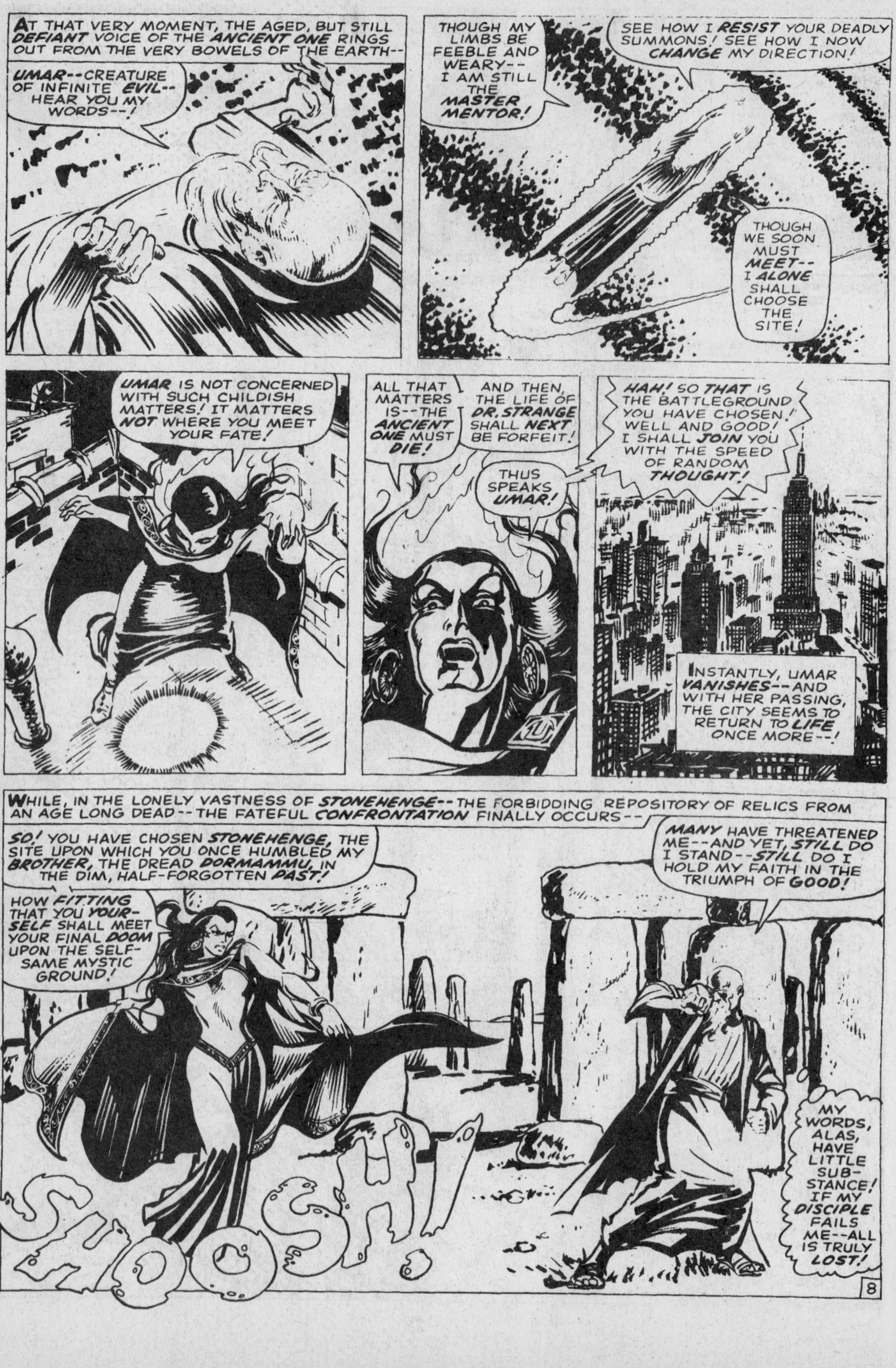
AT THAT VERY MOMENT, THE AGED, BUT STILL DEFIANT VOICE OF THE ANCIENT ONE RINGS OUT FROM THE VERY BOWELS OF THE EARTH--
UMAR--CREATURE OF INFINITE EVIL--HEAR YOU MY WORDS--!
THOUGH MY LIMBS BE FEEBLE AND WEARY--I AM STILL THE MASTER MENTOR!
SEE HOW I RESIST YOUR DEADLY SUMMONS! SEE HOW I NOW CHANGE MY DIRECTION!
THOUGH WE SOON MUST MEET--I ALONE SHALL CHOOSE THE SITE!
UMAR IS NOT CONCERNED WITH SUCH CHILDISH MATTERS! IT MATTERS NOT WHERE YOU MEET YOUR FATE!
ALL THAT MATTERS IS--THE ANCIENT ONE MUST DIE!
AND THEN, THE LIFE OF DR. STRANGE SHALL NEXT BE FORFEIT!
THUS SPEAKS UMAR!
HAH! SO THAT IS THE BATTLEGROUND YOU HAVE CHOSEN! WELL AND GOOD! I SHALL JOIN YOU WITH THE SPEED OF RANDOM THOUGHT!
INSTANTLY, UMAR VANISHES--AND WITH HER PASSING, THE CITY SEEMS TO RETURN TO LIFE ONCE MORE--!
WHILE, IN THE LONELY VASTNESS OF STONEHENGE--THE FORBIDDING REPOSITORY OF RELICS FROM AN AGE LONG DEAD--THE FATEFUL CONFRONTATION FINALLY OCCURS--
SO! YOU HAVE CHOSEN STONEHENGE, THE SITE UPON WHICH YOU ONCE HUMBLED MY BROTHER, THE DREAD DORMAMMU, IN THE DIM, HALF-FORGOTTEN PAST!
HOW FITTING THAT YOU YOURSELF SHALL MEET YOUR FINAL DOOM UPON THE SELF-SAME MYSTIC GROUND!
MANY HAVE THREATENED ME--AND YET, STILL DO I STAND--STILL DO I HOLD MY FAITH IN THE TRIUMPH OF GOOD!
SHOOSH!
MY WORDS, ALAS, HAVE LITTLE SUBSTANCE! IF MY DISCIPLE FAILS ME--ALL IS TRULY LOST!

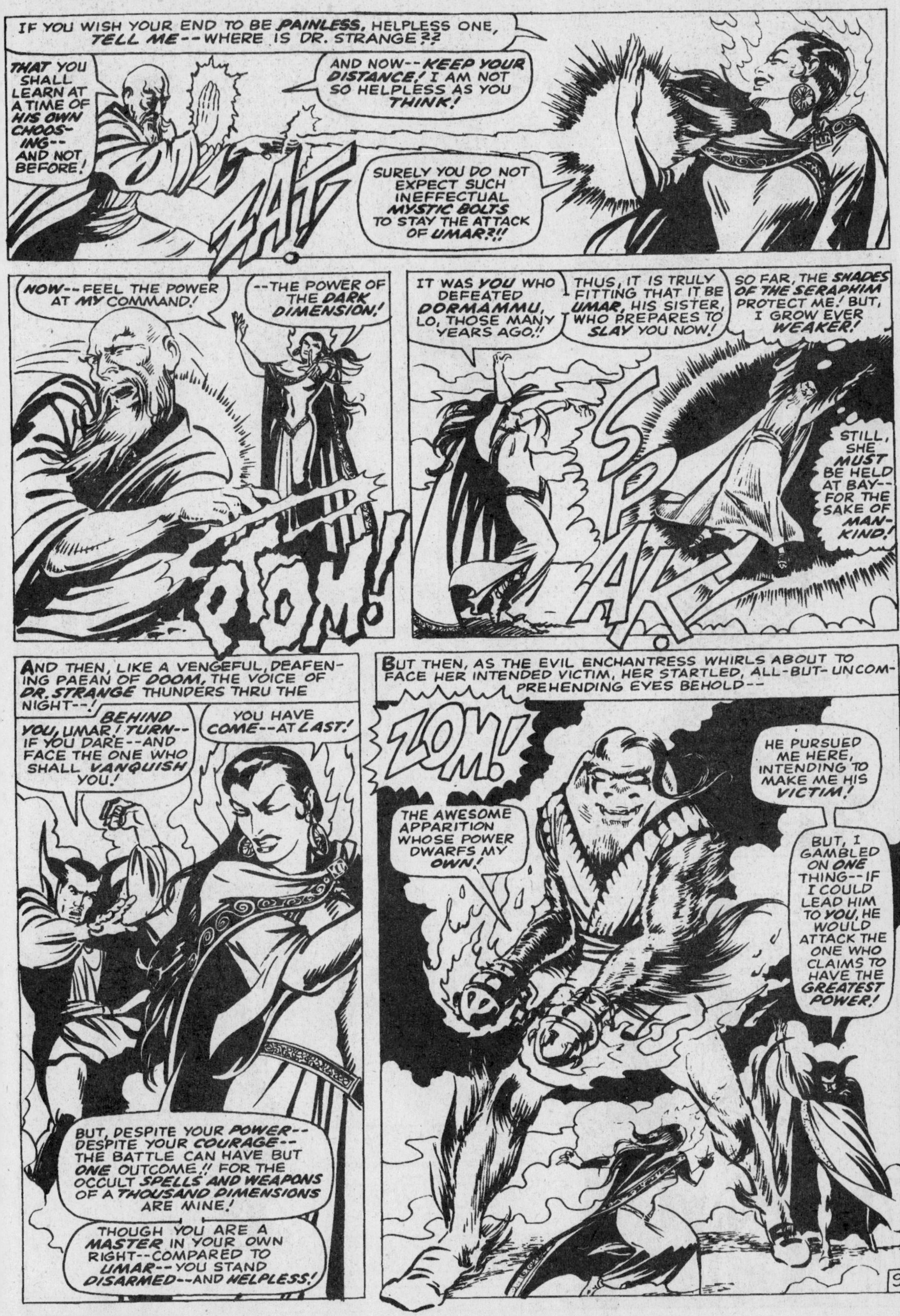
IF YOU WISH YOUR END TO BE PAINLESS, HELPLESS ONE, TELL ME--WHERE IS DR. STRANGE??
THAT YOU SHALL LEARN AT A TIME OF HIS OWN CHOOSING--AND NOT BEFORE!
AND NOW--KEEP YOUR DISTANCE! I AM NOT SO HELPLESS AS YOU THINK!
ZAT!
SURELY YOU DO NOT EXPECT SUCH INEFFECTUAL MYSTIC BOLTS TO STAY THE ATTACK OF UMAR?!!
NOW--FEEL THE POWER AT MY COMMAND!
--THE POWER OF THE DARK DIMENSION!
POOM!
IT WAS YOU WHO DEFEATED DORMAMMU, LO, THOSE MANY YEARS AGO!!
THUS, IT IS TRULY FITTING THAT IT BE UMAR, HIS SISTER, WHO PREPARES TO SLAY YOU NOW!
SO FAR, THE SHADES OF THE SERAPHIM PROTECT ME! BUT, I GROW EVER WEAKER!
STILL, SHE MUST BE HELD AT BAY--FOR THE SAKE OF MANKIND!
SPAK!
AND THEN, LIKE A VENGEFUL, DEAFENING PAEAN OF DOOM, THE VOICE OF DR. STRANGE THUNDERS THRU THE NIGHT--!
BEHIND YOU, UMAR! TURN--IF YOU DARE--AND FACE THE ONE WHO SHALL VANQUISH YOU!
YOU HAVE COME--AT LAST!
BUT, DESPITE YOUR POWER--DESPITE YOUR COURAGE--THE BATTLE CAN HAVE BUT ONE OUTCOME!! FOR THE OCCULT SPELLS AND WEAPONS OF A THOUSAND DIMENSIONS ARE MINE!
THOUGH YOU ARE A MASTER IN YOUR OWN RIGHT--COMPARED TO UMAR--YOU STAND DISARMED--AND HELPLESS!
BUT THEN, AS THE EVIL ENCHANTRESS WHIRLS ABOUT TO FACE HER INTENDED VICTIM, HER STARTLED, ALL-BUT-UNCOMPREHENDING EYES BEHOLD--
ZOM!
THE AWESOME APPARITION WHOSE POWER DWARFS MY OWN!
HE PURSUED ME HERE, INTENDING TO MAKE ME HIS VICTIM!
BUT, I GAMBLED ON ONE THING--IF I COULD LEAD HIM TO YOU, HE WOULD ATTACK THE ONE WHO CLAIMS TO HAVE THE GREATEST POWER!
9

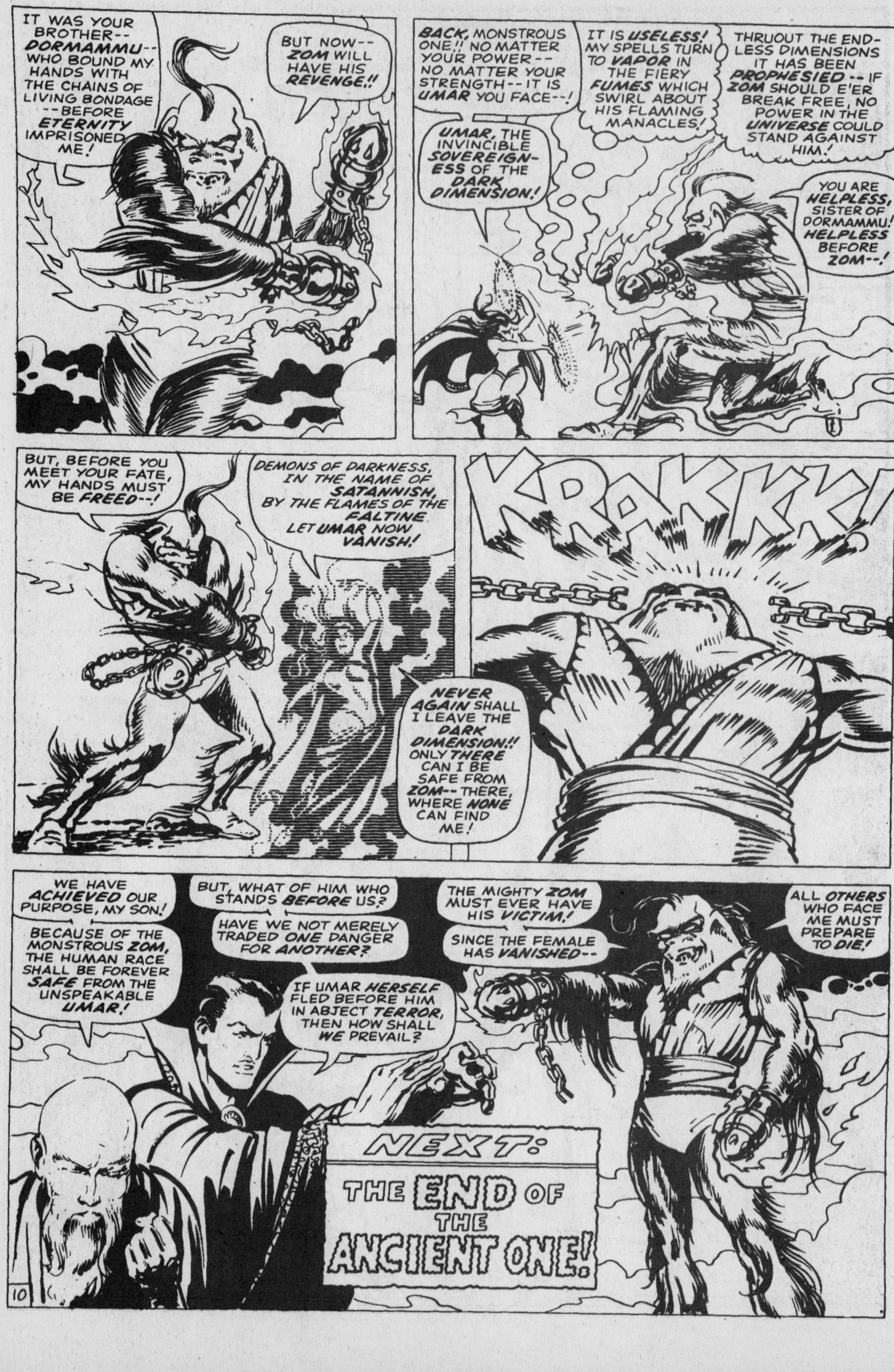
IT WAS YOUR BROTHER-- DORMAMMU-- WHO BOUND MY HANDS WITH THE CHAINS OF LIVING BONDAGE --BEFORE ETERNITY IMPRISONED ME!
BUT NOW-- ZOM WILL HAVE HIS REVENGE!!
BACK, MONSTROUS ONE!! NO MATTER YOUR POWER-- NO MATTER YOUR STRENGTH-- IT IS UMAR YOU FACE--!
UMAR, THE INVINCIBLE SOVEREIGNESS OF THE DARK DIMENSION!
IT IS USELESS! MY SPELLS TURN TO VAPOR IN THE FIERY FUMES WHICH SWIRL ABOUT HIS FLAMING MANACLES!
THRUOUT THE ENDLESS DIMENSIONS IT HAS BEEN PROPHESIED-- IF ZOM SHOULD E'ER BREAK FREE, NO POWER IN THE UNIVERSE COULD STAND AGAINST HIM!
YOU ARE HELPLESS, SISTER OF DORMAMMU! HELPLESS BEFORE ZOM--!
BUT, BEFORE YOU MEET YOUR FATE, MY HANDS MUST BE FREED--!
DEMONS OF DARKNESS, IN THE NAME OF SATANNISH, BY THE FLAMES OF THE FALTINE, LET UMAR NOW VANISH!
NEVER AGAIN SHALL I LEAVE THE DARK DIMENSION!! ONLY THERE CAN I BE SAFE FROM ZOM-- THERE, WHERE NONE CAN FIND ME!
KRAKKK!
WE HAVE ACHIEVED OUR PURPOSE, MY SON!
BECAUSE OF THE MONSTROUS ZOM, THE HUMAN RACE SHALL BE FOREVER SAFE FROM THE UNSPEAKABLE UMAR!
BUT, WHAT OF HIM WHO STANDS BEFORE US?
HAVE WE NOT MERELY TRADED ONE DANGER FOR ANOTHER?
IF UMAR HERSELF FLED BEFORE HIM IN ABJECT TERROR, THEN HOW SHALL WE PREVAIL?
THE MIGHTY ZOM MUST EVER HAVE HIS VICTIM!
SINCE THE FEMALE HAS VANISHED--
ALL OTHERS WHO FACE ME MUST PREPARE TO DIE!
NEXT:
THE END OF THE ANCIENT ONE!
10

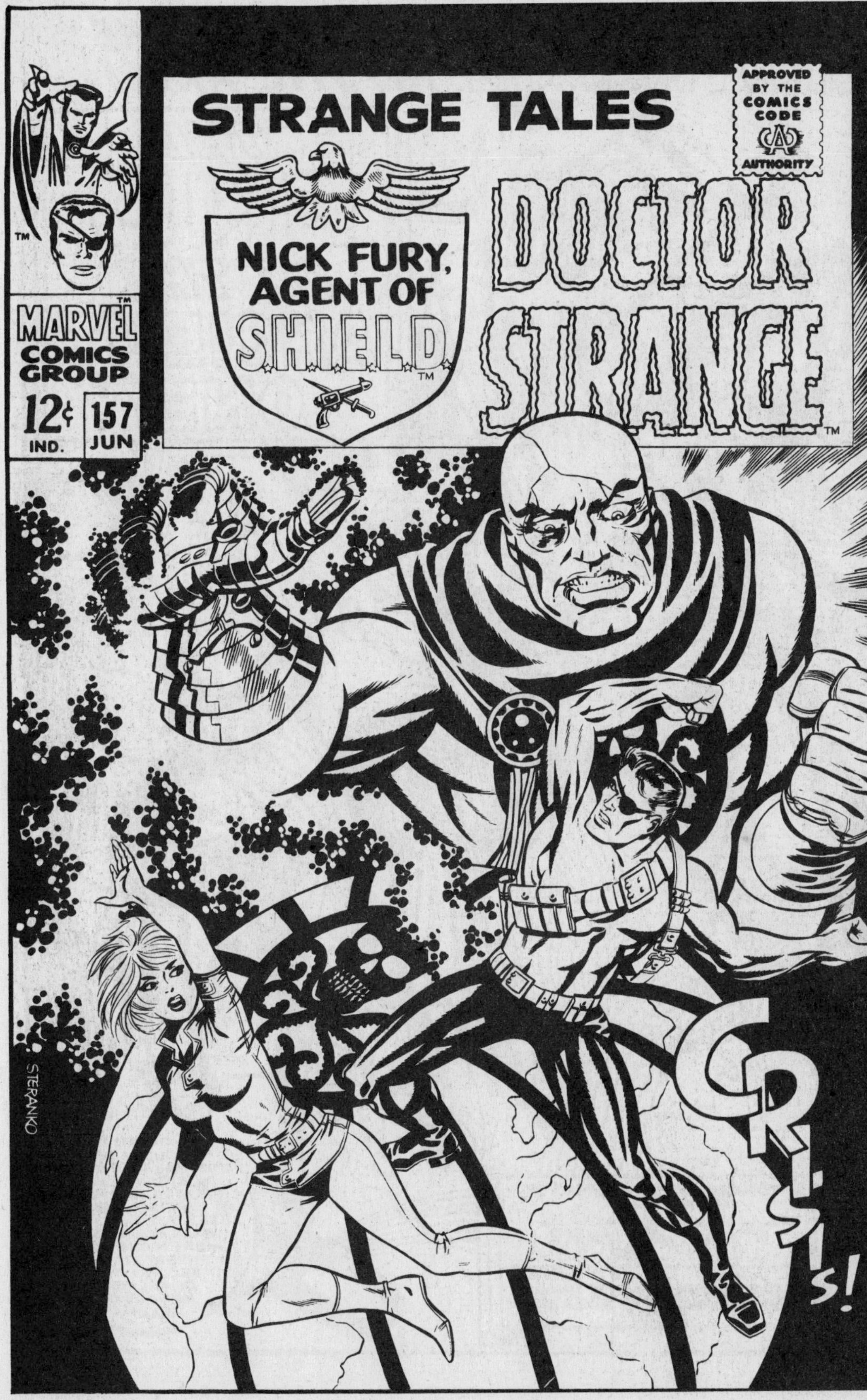

STRANGE TALES
APPROVED BY THE COMICS CODE AUTHORITY
NICK FURY, AGENT OF S.H.I.E.L.D.
DOCTOR STRANGE
MARVEL COMICS GROUP
12¢ IND.
157 JUN
STERANKO
CRISIS!

Dr. STRANGE MASTER OF THE MYSTIC ARTS!

"THE END OF THE ANCIENT ONE!"

PRODUCED BY THE MASTERS OF MYTHOPOEIA:

SPELLBINDING STAN LEE and MAGICAL MARIE SEVERIN

INKING: HERB TRIMPE OF THEM AMULETS

LETTERING: ARTIE SIMEK OF SKULL KNOW THEM

IN ORDER TO VANQUISH THE UNSPEAKABLE *UMAR*, DR. STRANGE HAS LIBERATED *ZOM* FROM AN IMPRISONMENT OF AGES! BUT NOW, WITH UMAR GONE, THE MONSTROUS ZOM THREATENS TO BECOME THE DEADLIEST MENACE OF ALL--!

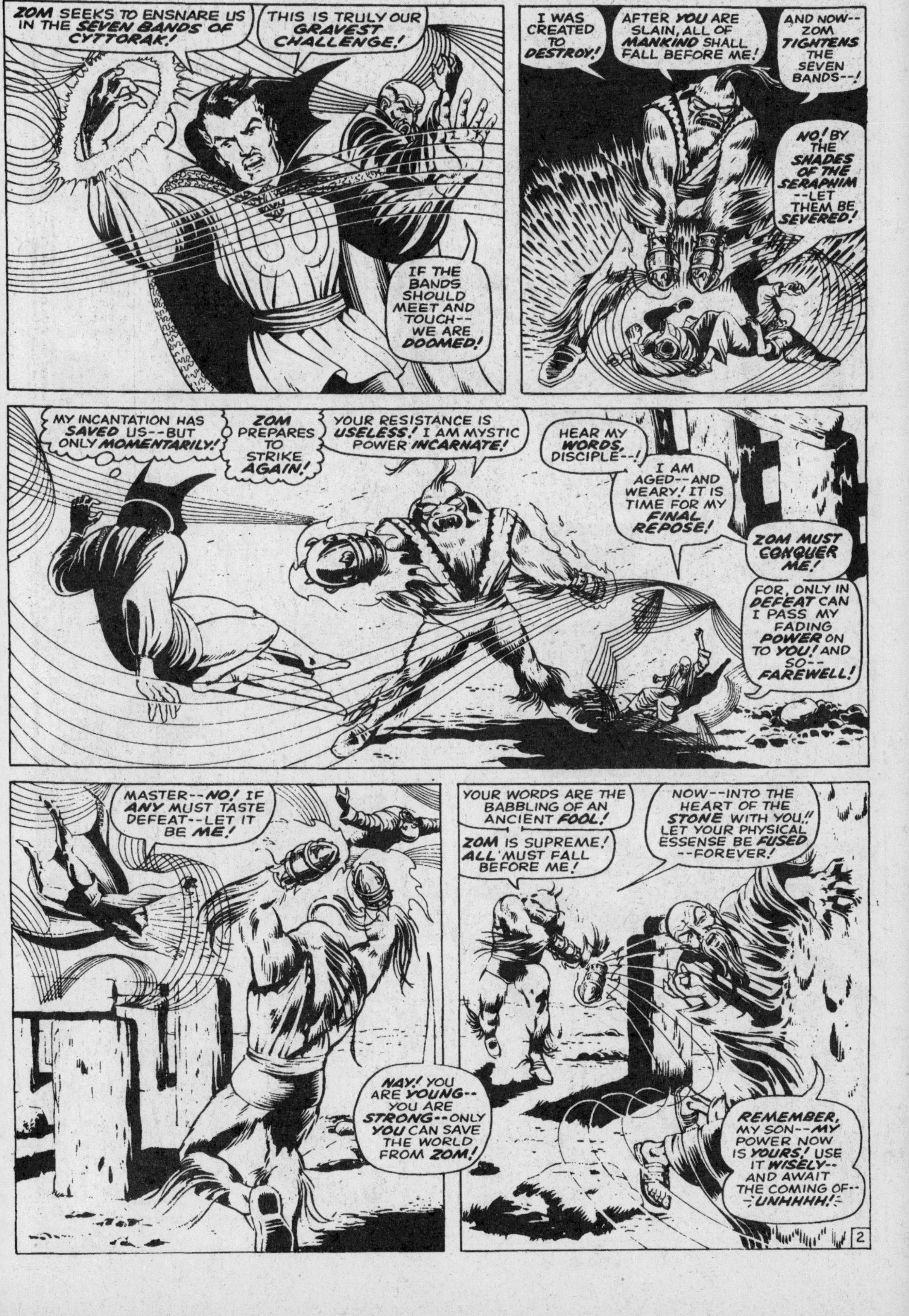
ZOM SEEKS TO ENSNARE US IN THE SEVEN BANDS OF CYTTORAK!
THIS IS TRULY OUR GRAVEST CHALLENGE!
IF THE BANDS SHOULD MEET AND TOUCH--WE ARE DOOMED!
I WAS CREATED TO DESTROY!
AFTER YOU ARE SLAIN, ALL OF MANKIND SHALL FALL BEFORE ME!
AND NOW--ZOM TIGHTENS THE SEVEN BANDS--!
NO! BY THE SHADES OF THE SERAPHIM--LET THEM BE SEVERED!
MY INCANTATION HAS SAVED US--BUT ONLY MOMENTARILY!
ZOM PREPARES TO STRIKE AGAIN!
YOUR RESISTANCE IS USELESS! I AM MYSTIC POWER INCARNATE!
HEAR MY WORDS, DISCIPLE--!
I AM AGED--AND WEARY! IT IS TIME FOR MY FINAL REPOSE!
ZOM MUST CONQUER ME!
FOR, ONLY IN DEFEAT CAN I PASS MY FADING POWER ON TO YOU! AND SO--FAREWELL!
MASTER--NO! IF ANY MUST TASTE DEFEAT--LET IT BE ME!
NAY! YOU ARE YOUNG--YOU ARE STRONG--ONLY YOU CAN SAVE THE WORLD FROM ZOM!
YOUR WORDS ARE THE BABBLING OF AN ANCIENT FOOL!
ZOM IS SUPREME! ALL MUST FALL BEFORE ME!
NOW--INTO THE HEART OF THE STONE WITH YOU!! LET YOUR PHYSICAL ESSENSE BE FUSED--FOREVER!
REMEMBER, MY SON--MY POWER NOW IS YOURS! USE IT WISELY--AND AWAIT THE COMING OF--UNHHHH!
2

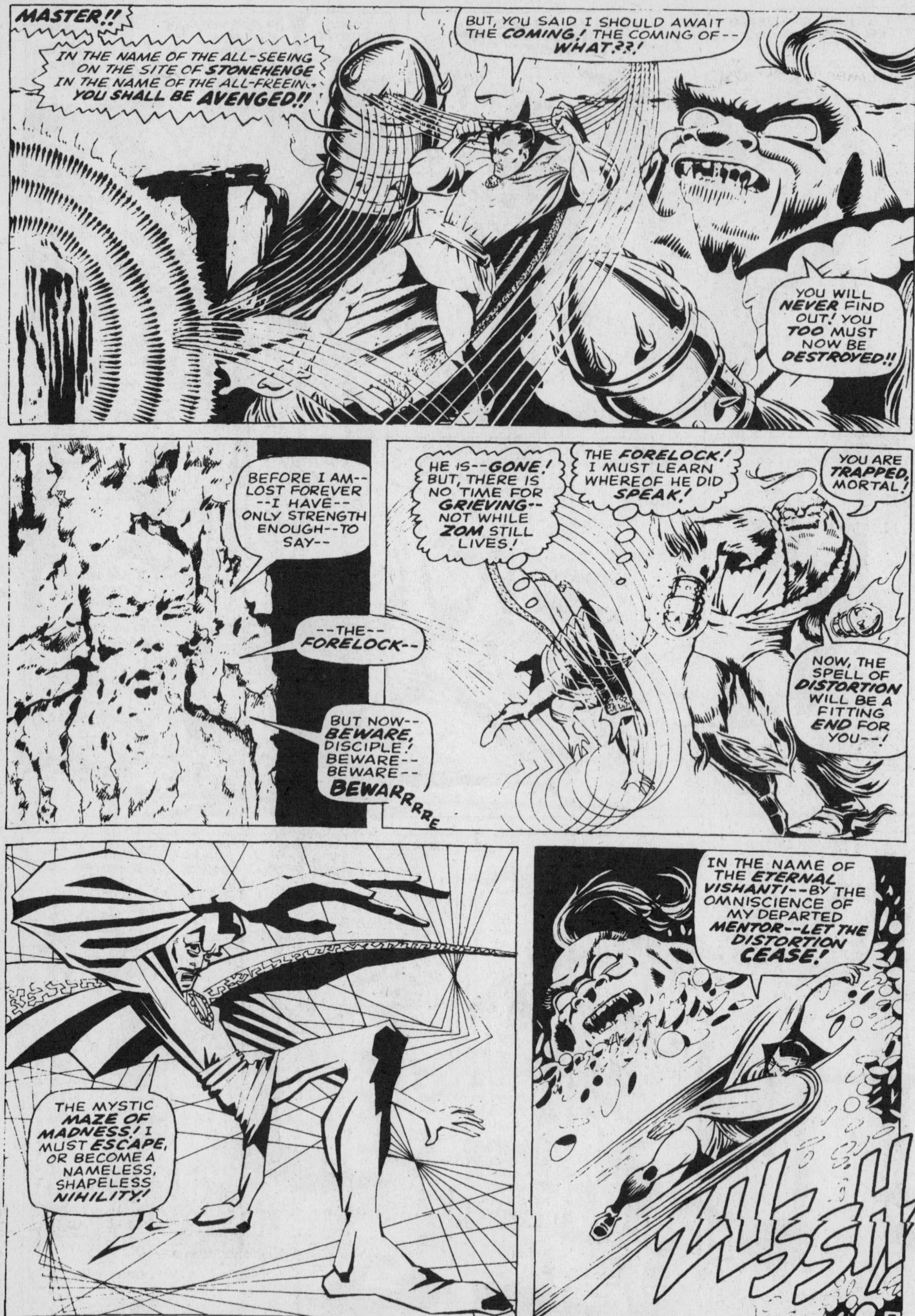
MASTER!!
IN THE NAME OF THE ALL-SEEING ON THE SITE OF STONEHENGE IN THE NAME OF THE ALL-FREEING YOU SHALL BE AVENGED!!
BUT, YOU SAID I SHOULD AWAIT THE COMING! THE COMING OF -- WHAT??!
YOU WILL NEVER FIND OUT! YOU TOO MUST NOW BE DESTROYED!!
BEFORE I AM-- LOST FOREVER --I HAVE-- ONLY STRENGTH ENOUGH--TO SAY--
--THE-- FORELOCK--
BUT NOW-- BEWARE, DISCIPLE! BEWARE-- BEWARE-- BEWARRRRE
HE IS--GONE! BUT, THERE IS NO TIME FOR GRIEVING-- NOT WHILE ZOM STILL LIVES!
THE FORELOCK! I MUST LEARN WHEREOF HE DID SPEAK!
YOU ARE TRAPPED, MORTAL!
NOW, THE SPELL OF DISTORTION WILL BE A FITTING END FOR YOU--!
THE MYSTIC MAZE OF MADNESS! I MUST ESCAPE, OR BECOME A NAMELESS, SHAPELESS NIHILITY!
IN THE NAME OF THE ETERNAL VISHANTI--BY THE OMNISCIENCE OF MY DEPARTED MENTOR--LET THE DISTORTION CEASE!
ZUSSH
3

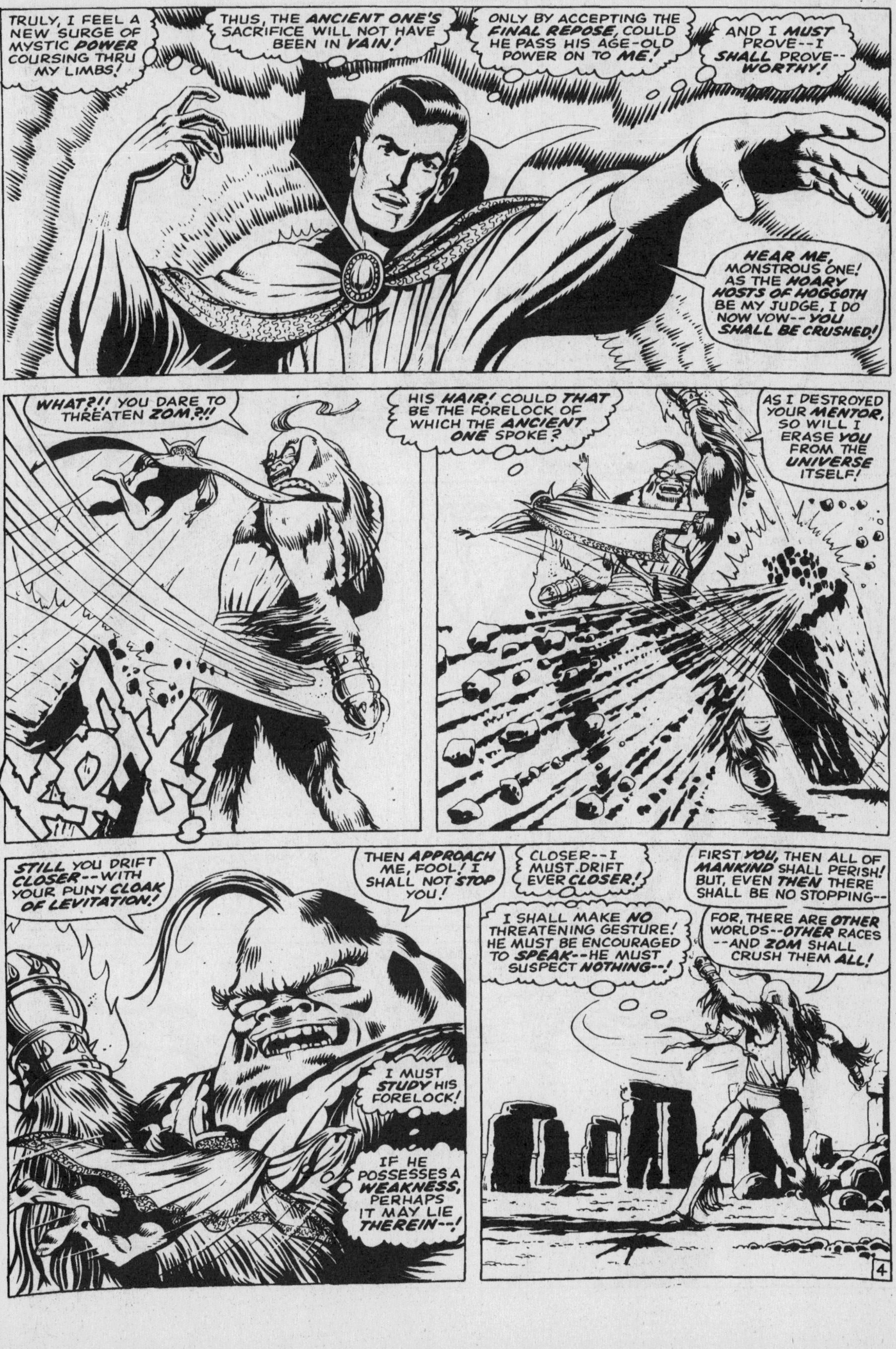
TRULY, I FEEL A NEW SURGE OF MYSTIC POWER COURSING THRU MY LIMBS!
THUS, THE ANCIENT ONE'S SACRIFICE WILL NOT HAVE BEEN IN VAIN!
ONLY BY ACCEPTING THE FINAL REPOSE, COULD HE PASS HIS AGE-OLD POWER ON TO ME!
AND I MUST PROVE--I SHALL PROVE--WORTHY!
HEAR ME, MONSTROUS ONE! AS THE HOARY HOSTS OF HOGGOTH BE MY JUDGE, I DO NOW VOW--YOU SHALL BE CRUSHED!
WHAT?!! YOU DARE TO THREATEN ZOM?!!
HIS HAIR! COULD THAT BE THE FORELOCK OF WHICH THE ANCIENT ONE SPOKE?
AS I DESTROYED YOUR MENTOR, SO WILL I ERASE YOU FROM THE UNIVERSE ITSELF!
STILL YOU DRIFT CLOSER--WITH YOUR PUNY CLOAK OF LEVITATION!
THEN APPROACH ME, FOOL! I SHALL NOT STOP YOU!
I MUST STUDY HIS FORELOCK!
IF HE POSSESSES A WEAKNESS, PERHAPS IT MAY LIE THEREIN--!
CLOSER--I MUST DRIFT EVER CLOSER!
I SHALL MAKE NO THREATENING GESTURE! HE MUST BE ENCOURAGED TO SPEAK--HE MUST SUSPECT NOTHING--!
FIRST YOU, THEN ALL OF MANKIND SHALL PERISH! BUT, EVEN THEN THERE SHALL BE NO STOPPING--
FOR, THERE ARE OTHER WORLDS--OTHER RACES--AND ZOM SHALL CRUSH THEM ALL!
4

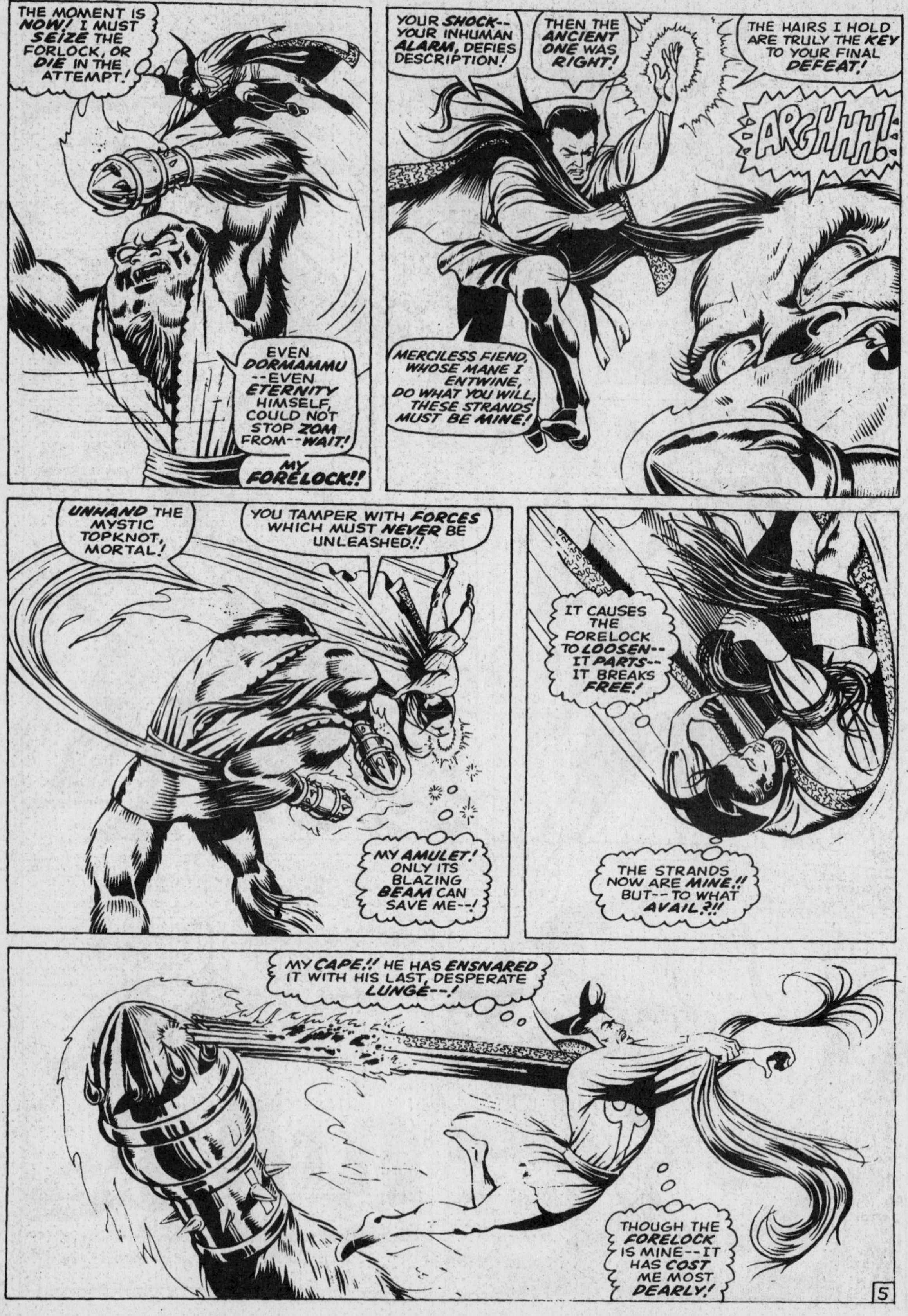
THE MOMENT IS NOW! I MUST SEIZE THE FORLOCK, OR DIE IN THE ATTEMPT!
EVEN DORMAMMU --EVEN ETERNITY HIMSELF, COULD NOT STOP ZOM FROM--WAIT!
MY FORELOCK!!
YOUR SHOCK--YOUR INHUMAN ALARM, DEFIES DESCRIPTION!
THEN THE ANCIENT ONE WAS RIGHT!
THE HAIRS I HOLD ARE TRULY THE KEY TO YOUR FINAL DEFEAT!
ARGHHH!
MERCILESS FIEND, WHOSE MANE I ENTWINE, DO WHAT YOU WILL, THESE STRANDS MUST BE MINE!
UNHAND THE MYSTIC TOPKNOT, MORTAL!
YOU TAMPER WITH FORCES WHICH MUST NEVER BE UNLEASHED!!
MY AMULET! ONLY ITS BLAZING BEAM CAN SAVE ME--!
IT CAUSES THE FORELOCK TO LOOSEN--IT PARTS--IT BREAKS FREE!
THE STRANDS NOW ARE MINE!! BUT--TO WHAT AVAIL?!!
MY CAPE!! HE HAS ENSNARED IT WITH HIS LAST, DESPERATE LUNGE--!
THOUGH THE FORELOCK IS MINE--IT HAS COST ME MOST DEARLY!
5

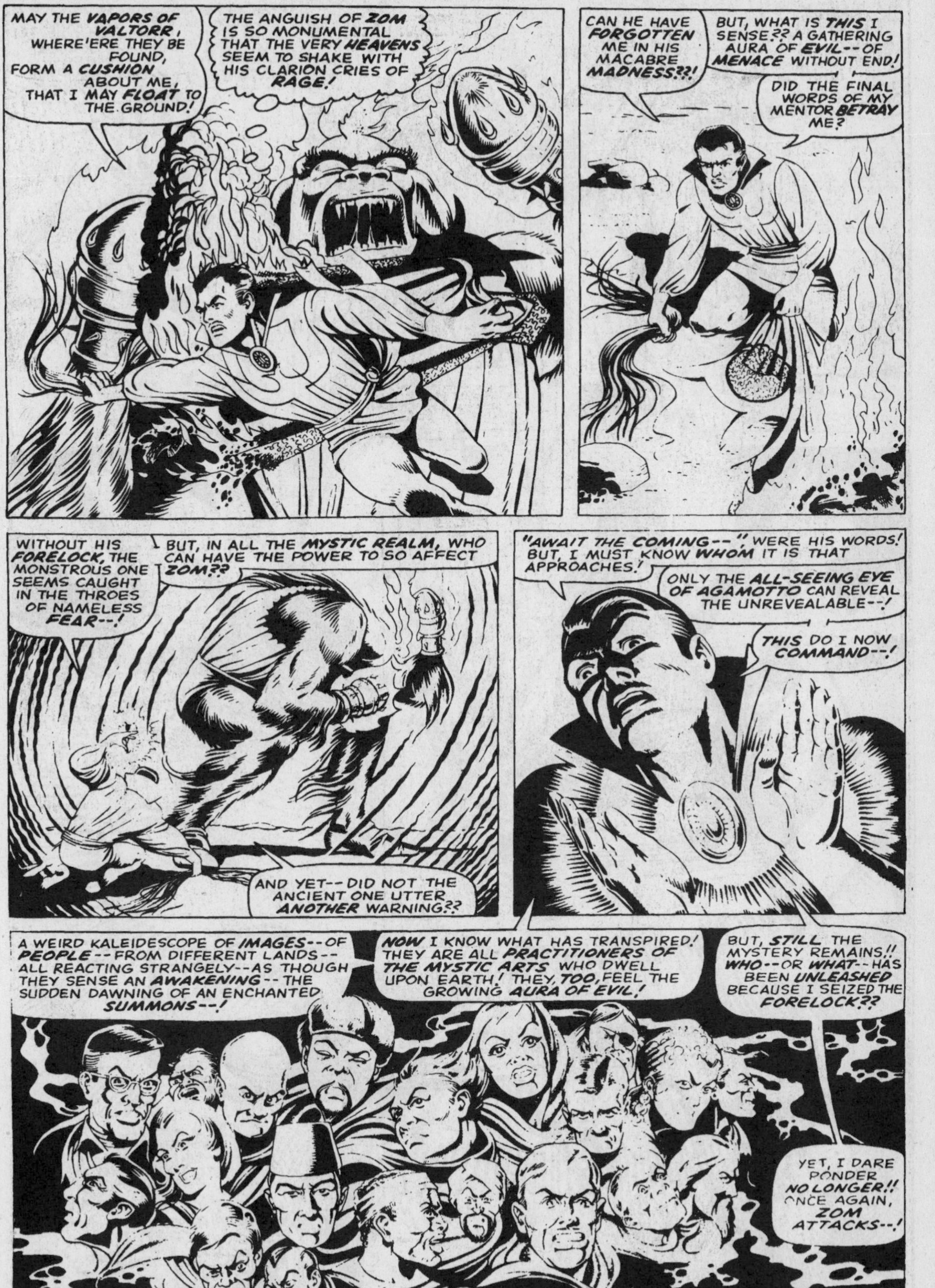
MAY THE VAPORS OF VALTORR, WHERE'ERE THEY BE FOUND, FORM A CUSHION ABOUT ME, THAT I MAY FLOAT TO THE GROUND!
THE ANGUISH OF ZOM IS SO MONUMENTAL THAT THE VERY HEAVENS SEEM TO SHAKE WITH HIS CLARION CRIES OF RAGE!
CAN HE HAVE FORGOTTEN ME IN HIS MACABRE MADNESS??!
BUT, WHAT IS THIS I SENSE?? A GATHERING AURA OF EVIL--OF MENACE WITHOUT END!
DID THE FINAL WORDS OF MY MENTOR BETRAY ME?
WITHOUT HIS FORELOCK, THE MONSTROUS ONE SEEMS CAUGHT IN THE THROES OF NAMELESS FEAR--!
BUT, IN ALL THE MYSTIC REALM, WHO CAN HAVE THE POWER TO SO AFFECT ZOM??
AND YET--DID NOT THE ANCIENT ONE UTTER ANOTHER WARNING??
"AWAIT THE COMING--" WERE HIS WORDS! BUT, I MUST KNOW WHOM IT IS THAT APPROACHES!
ONLY THE ALL-SEEING EYE OF AGAMOTTO CAN REVEAL THE UNREVEALABLE--!
THIS DO I NOW COMMAND--!
A WEIRD KALEIDESCOPE OF IMAGES--OF PEOPLE--FROM DIFFERENT LANDS--ALL REACTING STRANGELY--AS THOUGH THEY SENSE AN AWAKENING--THE SUDDEN DAWNING OF AN ENCHANTED SUMMONS--!
NOW I KNOW WHAT HAS TRANSPIRED! THEY ARE ALL PRACTITIONERS OF THE MYSTIC ARTS WHO DWELL UPON EARTH! THEY, TOO, FEEL THE GROWING AURA OF EVIL!
BUT, STILL THE MYSTERY REMAINS!! WHO--OR WHAT--HAS BEEN UNLEASHED BECAUSE I SEIZED THE FORELOCK??
YET, I DARE PONDER NO LONGER!! ONCE AGAIN, ZOM ATTACKS--!

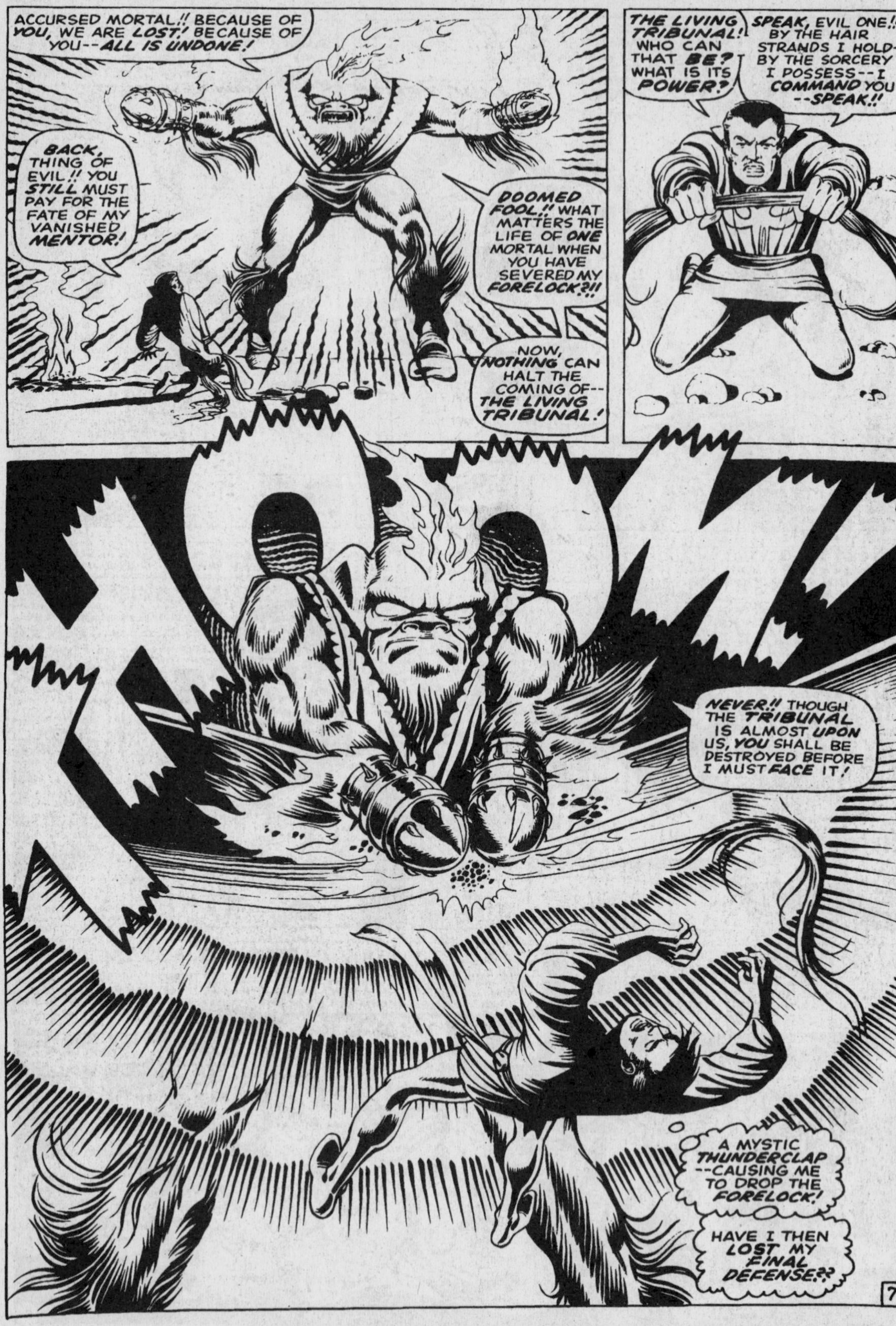

ACCURSED MORTAL!! BECAUSE OF YOU, WE ARE LOST! BECAUSE OF YOU--ALL IS UNDONE!
BACK, THING OF EVIL!! YOU STILL MUST PAY FOR THE FATE OF MY VANISHED MENTOR!
DOOMED FOOL!! WHAT MATTERS THE LIFE OF ONE MORTAL WHEN YOU HAVE SEVERED MY FORELOCK?!!
NOW, NOTHING CAN HALT THE COMING OF--THE LIVING TRIBUNAL!
THE LIVING TRIBUNAL! WHO CAN THAT BE? WHAT IS ITS POWER?
SPEAK, EVIL ONE!! BY THE HAIR STRANDS I HOLD--BY THE SORCERY I POSSESS--I COMMAND YOU--SPEAK!!
NEVER!! THOUGH THE TRIBUNAL IS ALMOST UPON US, YOU SHALL BE DESTROYED BEFORE I MUST FACE IT!
A MYSTIC THUNDERCLAP--CAUSING ME TO DROP THE FORELOCK!
HAVE I THEN LOST MY FINAL DEFENSE??
7

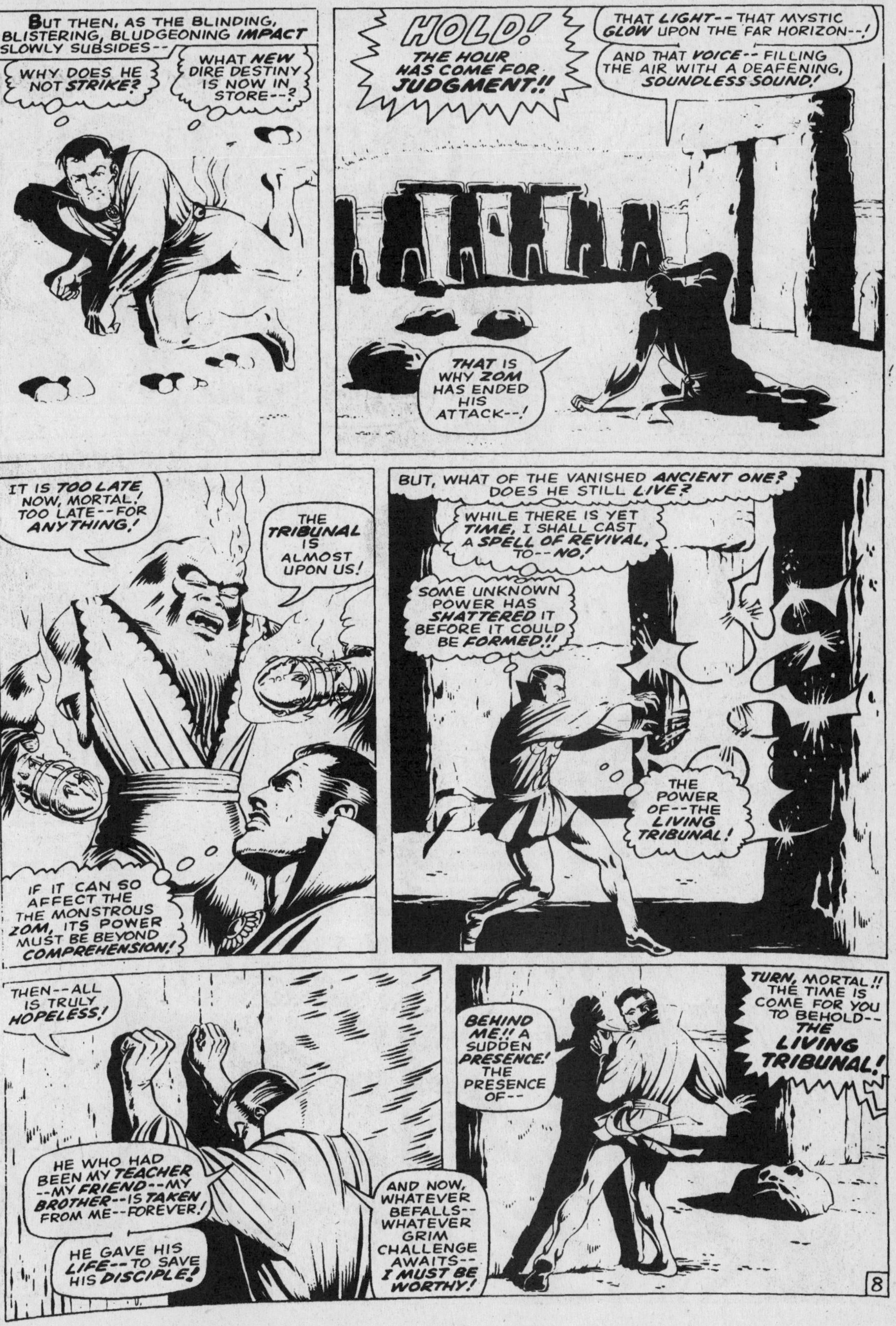
BUT THEN, AS THE BLINDING, BLISTERING, BLUDGEONING IMPACT SLOWLY SUBSIDES--
WHY DOES HE NOT STRIKE?
WHAT NEW DIRE DESTINY IS NOW IN STORE--?
HOLD! THE HOUR HAS COME FOR JUDGMENT!!
THAT LIGHT--THAT MYSTIC GLOW UPON THE FAR HORIZON--!
AND THAT VOICE--FILLING THE AIR WITH A DEAFENING, SOUNDLESS SOUND!
THAT IS WHY ZOM HAS ENDED HIS ATTACK--!
IT IS TOO LATE NOW, MORTAL! TOO LATE--FOR ANYTHING!
THE TRIBUNAL IS ALMOST UPON US!
IF IT CAN SO AFFECT THE THE MONSTROUS ZOM, ITS POWER MUST BE BEYOND COMPREHENSION!
BUT, WHAT OF THE VANISHED ANCIENT ONE? DOES HE STILL LIVE?
WHILE THERE IS YET TIME, I SHALL CAST A SPELL OF REVIVAL, TO--NO!
SOME UNKNOWN POWER HAS SHATTERED IT BEFORE IT COULD BE FORMED!!
THE POWER OF--THE LIVING TRIBUNAL!
THEN--ALL IS TRULY HOPELESS!
HE WHO HAD BEEN MY TEACHER--MY FRIEND--MY BROTHER--IS TAKEN FROM ME--FOREVER!
HE GAVE HIS LIFE--TO SAVE HIS DISCIPLE!
AND NOW, WHATEVER BEFALLS--WHATEVER GRIM CHALLENGE AWAITS--I MUST BE WORTHY!
BEHIND ME!! A SUDDEN PRESENCE! THE PRESENCE OF--
TURN, MORTAL!! THE TIME IS COME FOR YOU TO BEHOLD--THE LIVING TRIBUNAL!
8

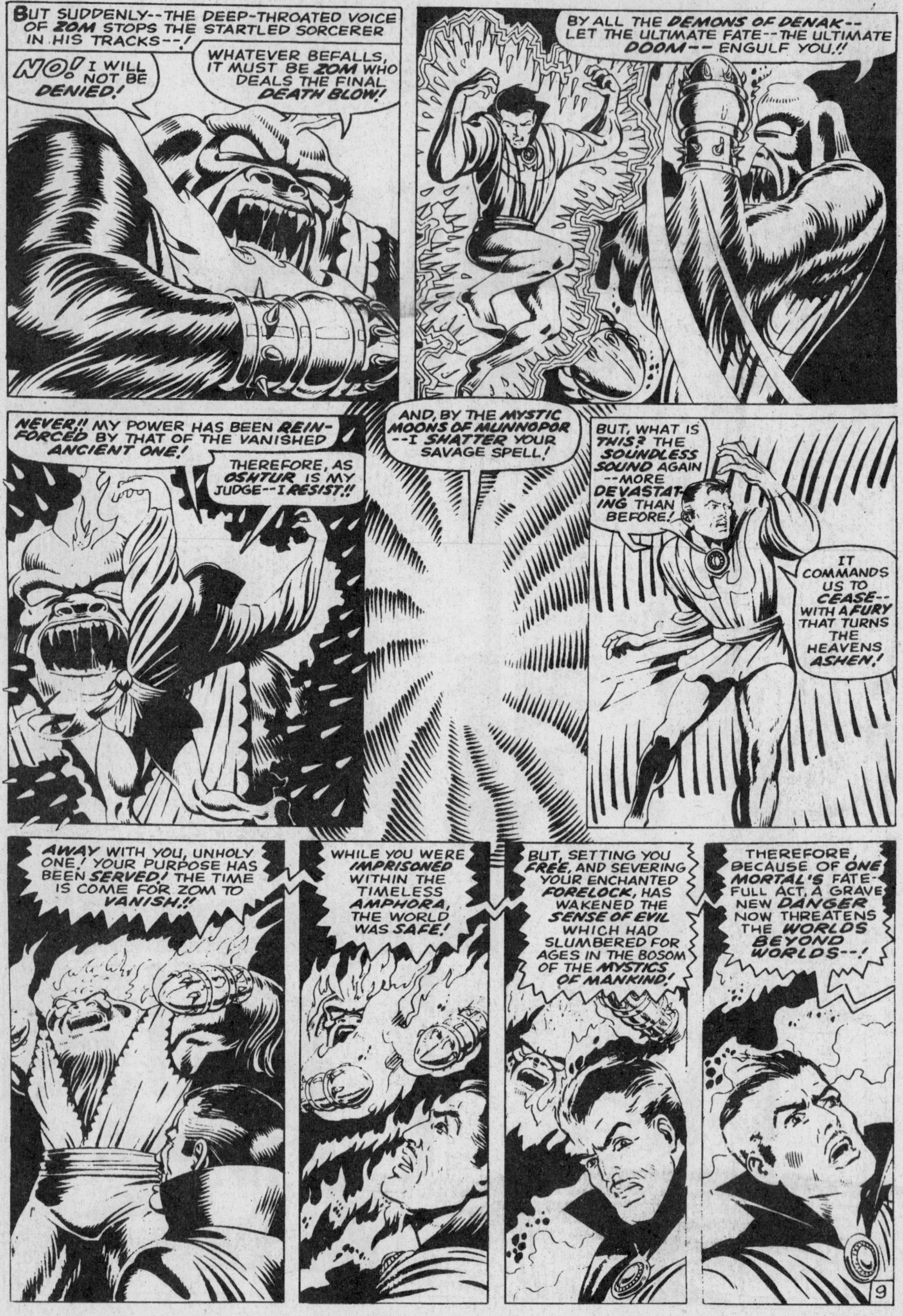

BUT SUDDENLY--THE DEEP-THROATED VOICE OF ZOM STOPS THE STARTLED SORCERER IN HIS TRACKS--!
NO! I WILL NOT BE DENIED!
WHATEVER BEFALLS, IT MUST BE ZOM WHO DEALS THE FINAL DEATH BLOW!
BY ALL THE DEMONS OF DENAK--LET THE ULTIMATE FATE--THE ULTIMATE DOOM--ENGULF YOU!!
NEVER!! MY POWER HAS BEEN REIN-FORCED BY THAT OF THE VANISHED ANCIENT ONE!
THEREFORE, AS OSHTUR IS MY JUDGE--I RESIST!!
AND, BY THE MYSTIC MOONS OF MUNNOPOR--I SHATTER YOUR SAVAGE SPELL!
BUT, WHAT IS THIS? THE SOUNDLESS SOUND AGAIN--MORE DEVASTATING THAN BEFORE!
IT COMMANDS US TO CEASE--WITH A FURY THAT TURNS THE HEAVENS ASHEN!
AWAY WITH YOU, UNHOLY ONE! YOUR PURPOSE HAS BEEN SERVED! THE TIME IS COME FOR ZOM TO VANISH!!
WHILE YOU WERE IMPRISONED WITHIN THE TIMELESS AMPHORA, THE WORLD WAS SAFE!
BUT, SETTING YOU FREE, AND SEVERING YOUR ENCHANTED FORELOCK, HAS WAKENED THE SENSE OF EVIL WHICH HAD SLUMBERED FOR AGES IN THE BOSOM OF THE MYSTICS OF MANKIND!
THEREFORE, BECAUSE OF ONE MORTAL'S FATE-FULL ACT, A GRAVE NEW DANGER NOW THREATENS THE WORLDS BEYOND WORLDS--!
9

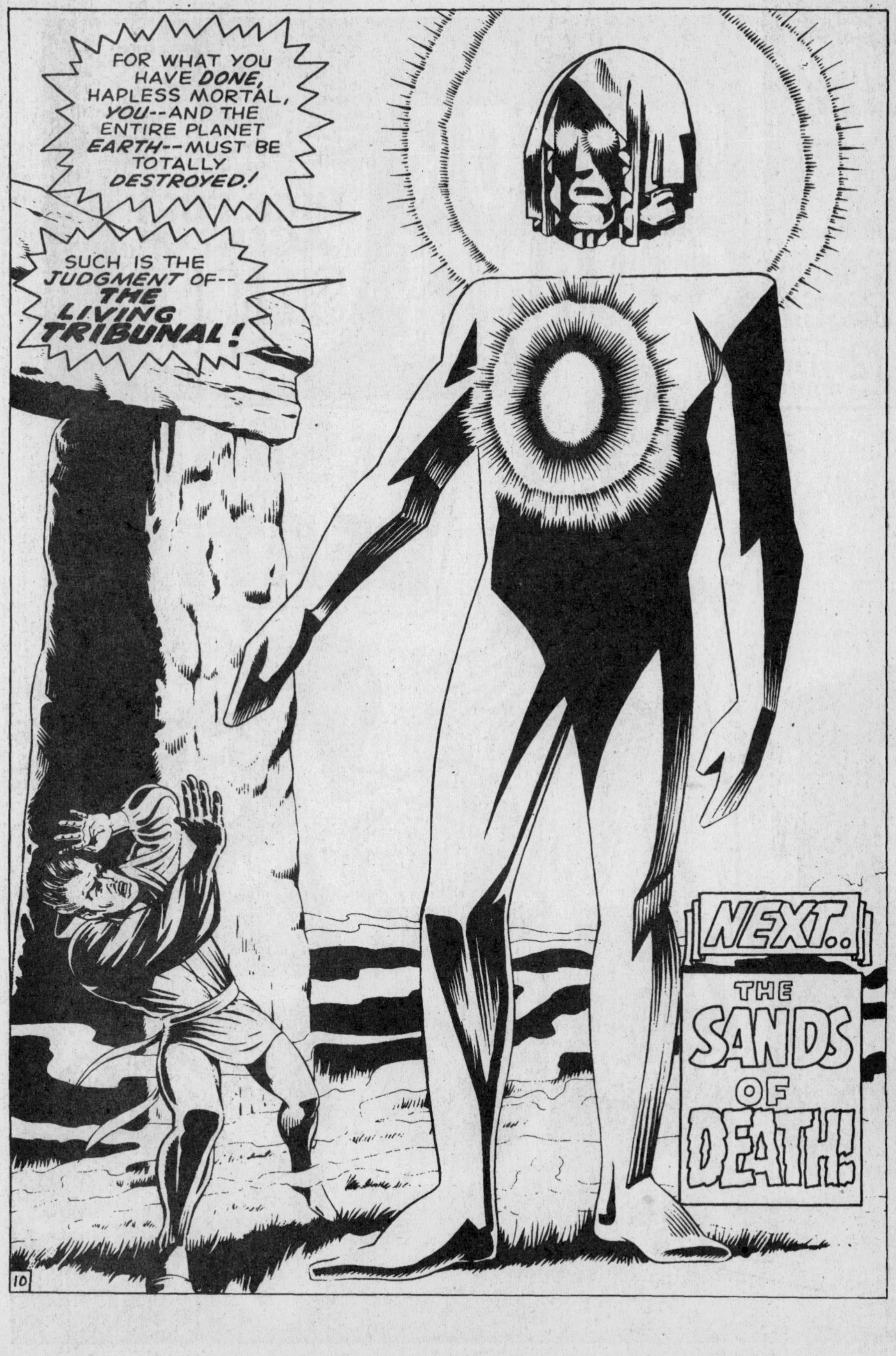
FOR WHAT YOU HAVE DONE, HAPLESS MORTAL, YOU--AND THE ENTIRE PLANET EARTH--MUST BE TOTALLY DESTROYED!
SUCH IS THE JUDGMENT OF-- THE LIVING TRIBUNAL!
NEXT..
THE SANDS OF DEATH!
10

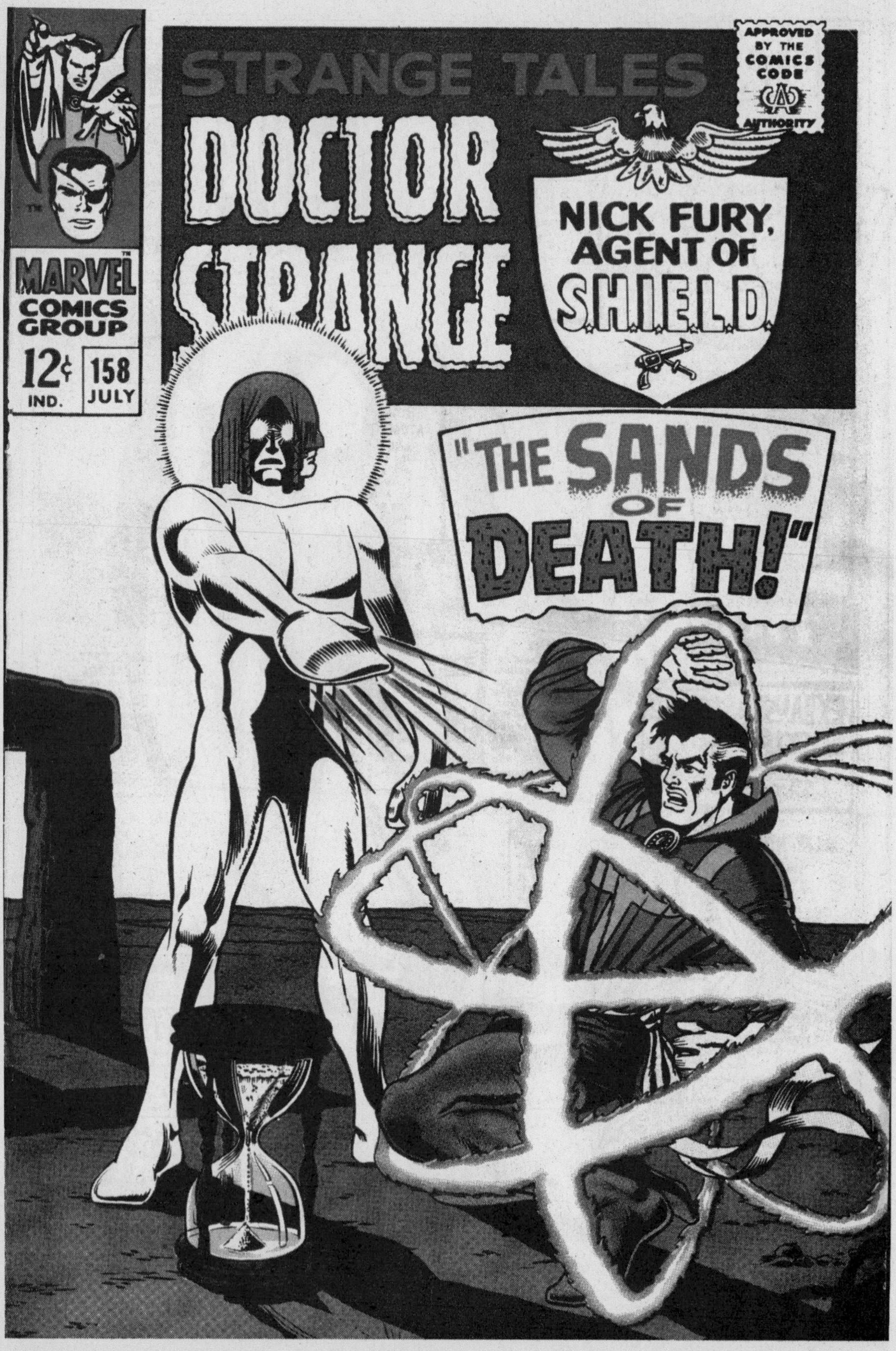
STRANGE TALES
DOCTOR STRANGE
NICK FURY, AGENT OF S.H.I.E.L.D.
APPROVED BY THE COMICS CODE AUTHORITY
MARVEL COMICS GROUP
12¢ IND.
158 JULY
"THE SANDS OF DEATH!"

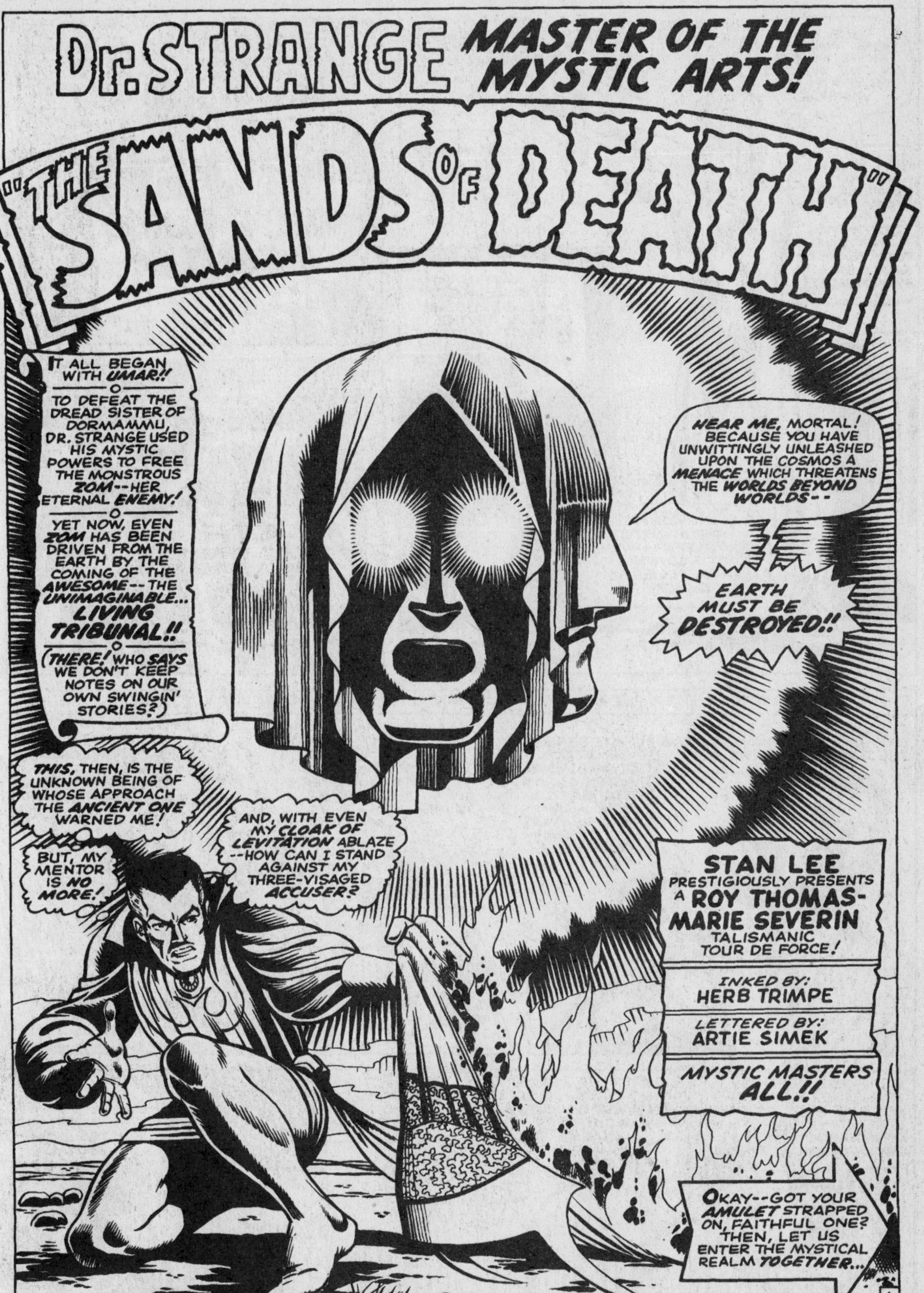

Dr. STRANGE MASTER OF THE MYSTIC ARTS!
"THE SANDS OF DEATH"
IT ALL BEGAN WITH UMAR!! TO DEFEAT THE DREAD SISTER OF DORMAMMU, DR. STRANGE USED HIS MYSTIC POWERS TO FREE THE MONSTROUS ZOM--HER ETERNAL ENEMY! YET NOW, EVEN ZOM HAS BEEN DRIVEN FROM THE EARTH BY THE COMING OF THE AWESOME--THE UNIMAGINABLE... LIVING TRIBUNAL!! (THERE! WHO SAYS WE DON'T KEEP NOTES ON OUR OWN SWINGIN' STORIES?)
HEAR ME, MORTAL! BECAUSE YOU HAVE UNWITTINGLY UNLEASHED UPON THE COSMOS A MENACE WHICH THREATENS THE WORLDS BEYOND WORLDS--
EARTH MUST BE DESTROYED!!
THIS, THEN, IS THE UNKNOWN BEING OF WHOSE APPROACH THE ANCIENT ONE WARNED ME!
BUT, MY MENTOR IS NO MORE!
AND, WITH EVEN MY CLOAK OF LEVITATION ABLAZE--HOW CAN I STAND AGAINST MY THREE-VISAGED ACCUSER?
STAN LEE PRESTIGIOUSLY PRESENTS A ROY THOMAS-MARIE SEVERIN TALISMANIC TOUR DE FORCE!
INKED BY: HERB TRIMPE
LETTERED BY: ARTIE SIMEK
MYSTIC MASTERS ALL!!
OKAY--GOT YOUR AMULET STRAPPED ON, FAITHFUL ONE? THEN, LET US ENTER THE MYSTICAL REALM TOGETHER...
1

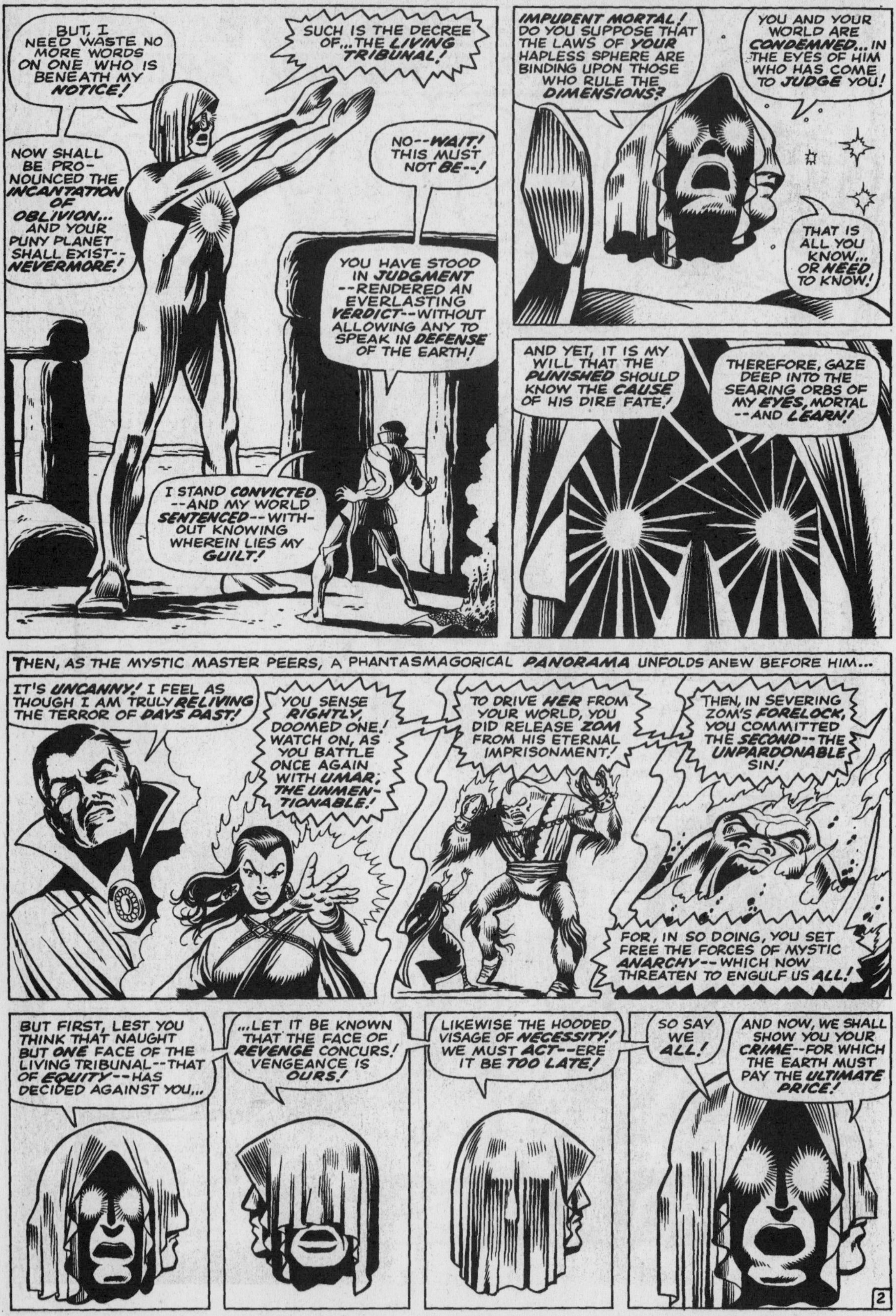

BUT, I NEED WASTE NO MORE WORDS ON ONE WHO IS BENEATH MY NOTICE!
NOW SHALL BE PRO-NOUNCED THE INCANTATION OF OBLIVION... AND YOUR PUNY PLANET SHALL EXIST--NEVERMORE!
SUCH IS THE DECREE OF... THE LIVING TRIBUNAL!
NO--WAIT! THIS MUST NOT BE--!
YOU HAVE STOOD IN JUDGMENT --RENDERED AN EVERLASTING VERDICT--WITHOUT ALLOWING ANY TO SPEAK IN DEFENSE OF THE EARTH!
I STAND CONVICTED --AND MY WORLD SENTENCED--WITH-OUT KNOWING WHEREIN LIES MY GUILT!
IMPUDENT MORTAL! DO YOU SUPPOSE THAT THE LAWS OF YOUR HAPLESS SPHERE ARE BINDING UPON THOSE WHO RULE THE DIMENSIONS?
YOU AND YOUR WORLD ARE CONDEMNED... IN THE EYES OF HIM WHO HAS COME TO JUDGE YOU!
THAT IS ALL YOU KNOW... OR NEED TO KNOW!
AND YET, IT IS MY WILL THAT THE PUNISHED SHOULD KNOW THE CAUSE OF HIS DIRE FATE!
THEREFORE, GAZE DEEP INTO THE SEARING ORBS OF MY EYES, MORTAL --AND LEARN!
THEN, AS THE MYSTIC MASTER PEERS, A PHANTASMAGORICAL PANORAMA UNFOLDS ANEW BEFORE HIM...
IT'S UNCANNY! I FEEL AS THOUGH I AM TRULY RELIVING THE TERROR OF DAYS PAST!
YOU SENSE RIGHTLY, DOOMED ONE! WATCH ON, AS YOU BATTLE ONCE AGAIN WITH UMAR, THE UNMEN-TIONABLE!
TO DRIVE HER FROM YOUR WORLD, YOU DID RELEASE ZOM FROM HIS ETERNAL IMPRISONMENT!
THEN, IN SEVERING ZOM'S FORELOCK, YOU COMMITTED THE SECOND--THE UNPARDONABLE SIN!
FOR, IN SO DOING, YOU SET FREE THE FORCES OF MYSTIC ANARCHY--WHICH NOW THREATEN TO ENGULF US ALL!
BUT FIRST, LEST YOU THINK THAT NAUGHT BUT ONE FACE OF THE LIVING TRIBUNAL--THAT OF EQUITY--HAS DECIDED AGAINST YOU...
...LET IT BE KNOWN THAT THE FACE OF REVENGE CONCURS! VENGEANCE IS OURS!
LIKEWISE THE HOODED VISAGE OF NECESSITY! WE MUST ACT--ERE IT BE TOO LATE!
SO SAY WE ALL!
AND NOW, WE SHALL SHOW YOU YOUR CRIME--FOR WHICH THE EARTH MUST PAY THE ULTIMATE PRICE!
2

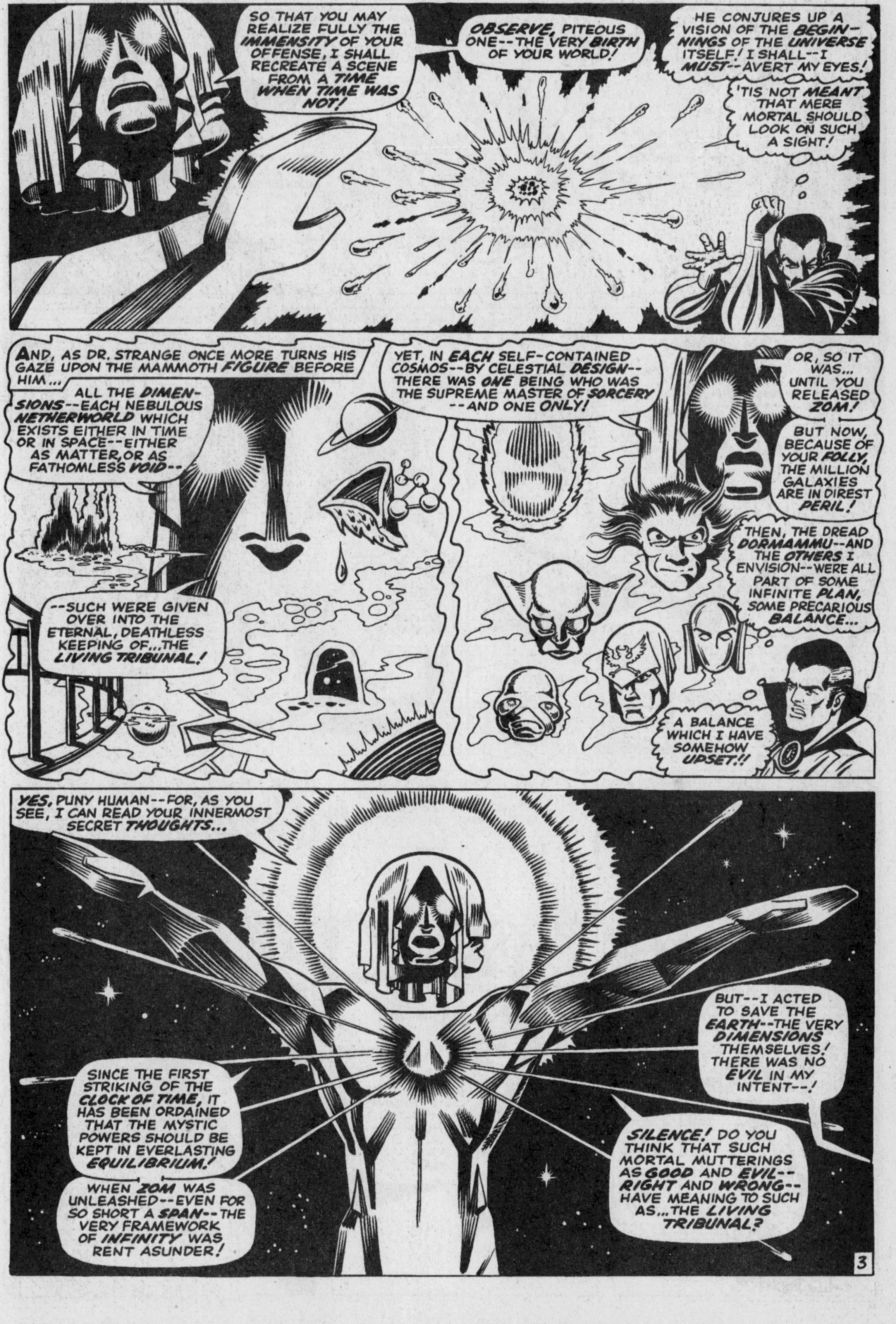
SO THAT YOU MAY REALIZE FULLY THE IMMENSITY OF YOUR OFFENSE, I SHALL RECREATE A SCENE FROM A TIME WHEN TIME WAS NOT!
OBSERVE, PITEOUS ONE--THE VERY BIRTH OF YOUR WORLD!
HE CONJURES UP A VISION OF THE BEGINNINGS OF THE UNIVERSE ITSELF! I SHALL--I MUST--AVERT MY EYES!
'TIS NOT MEANT THAT MERE MORTAL SHOULD LOOK ON SUCH A SIGHT!
AND, AS DR. STRANGE ONCE MORE TURNS HIS GAZE UPON THE MAMMOTH FIGURE BEFORE HIM...
ALL THE DIMENSIONS--EACH NEBULOUS NETHERWORLD WHICH EXISTS EITHER IN TIME OR IN SPACE--EITHER AS MATTER, OR AS FATHOMLESS VOID--
--SUCH WERE GIVEN OVER INTO THE ETERNAL, DEATHLESS KEEPING OF...THE LIVING TRIBUNAL!
YET, IN EACH SELF-CONTAINED COSMOS--BY CELESTIAL DESIGN--THERE WAS ONE BEING WHO WAS THE SUPREME MASTER OF SORCERY--AND ONE ONLY!
OR, SO IT WAS... UNTIL YOU RELEASED ZOM!
BUT NOW, BECAUSE OF YOUR FOLLY, THE MILLION GALAXIES ARE IN DIREST PERIL!
THEN, THE DREAD DORMAMMU--AND THE OTHERS I ENVISION--WERE ALL PART OF SOME INFINITE PLAN, SOME PRECARIOUS BALANCE...
A BALANCE WHICH I HAVE SOMEHOW UPSET!!
YES, PUNY HUMAN--FOR, AS YOU SEE, I CAN READ YOUR INNERMOST SECRET THOUGHTS...
SINCE THE FIRST STRIKING OF THE CLOCK OF TIME, IT HAS BEEN ORDAINED THAT THE MYSTIC POWERS SHOULD BE KEPT IN EVERLASTING EQUILIBRIUM!
WHEN ZOM WAS UNLEASHED--EVEN FOR SO SHORT A SPAN--THE VERY FRAMEWORK OF INFINITY WAS RENT ASUNDER!
BUT--I ACTED TO SAVE THE EARTH--THE VERY DIMENSIONS THEMSELVES! THERE WAS NO EVIL IN MY INTENT--!
SILENCE! DO YOU THINK THAT SUCH MORTAL MUTTERINGS AS GOOD AND EVIL--RIGHT AND WRONG--HAVE MEANING TO SUCH AS...THE LIVING TRIBUNAL?
3

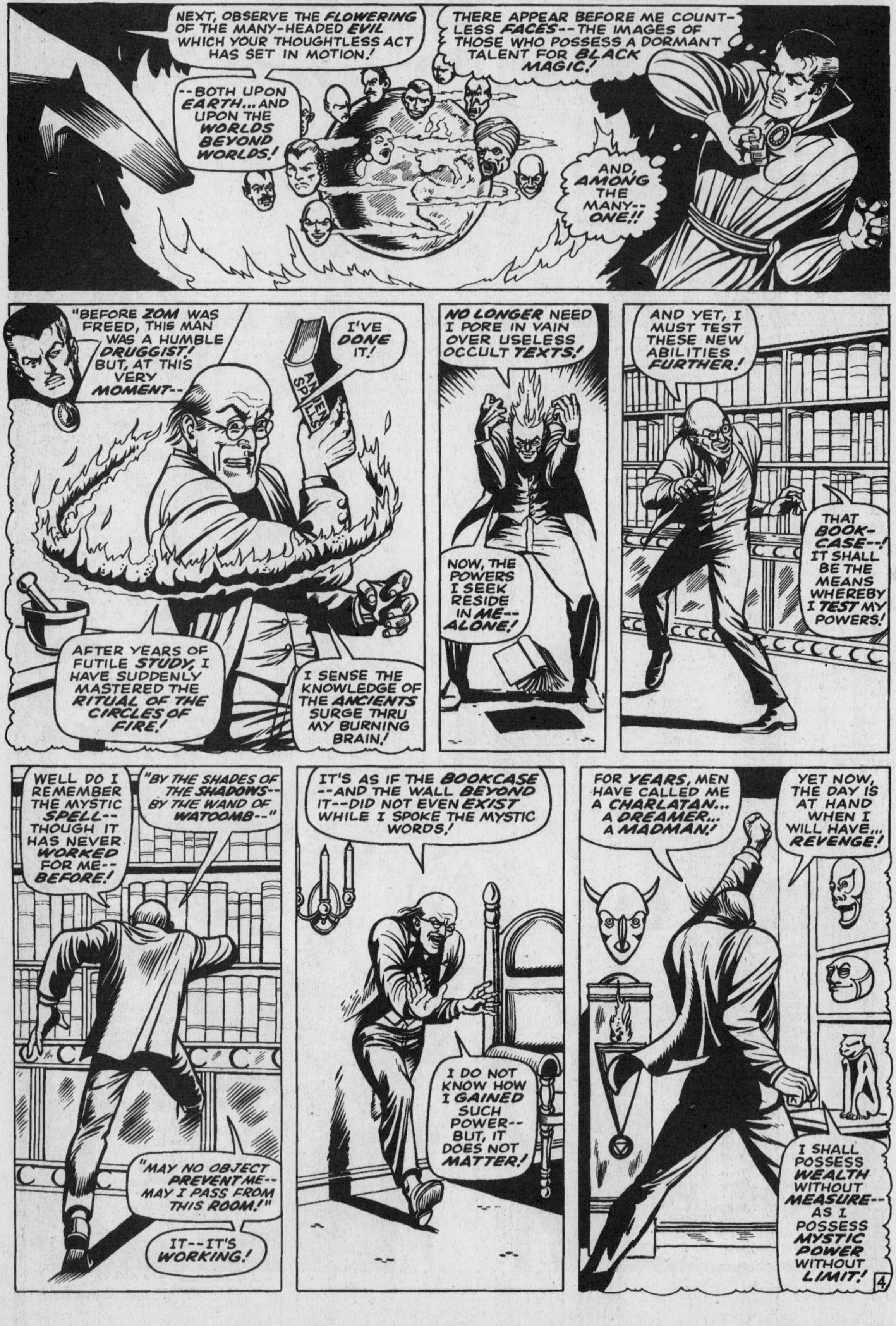
NEXT, OBSERVE THE FLOWERING OF THE MANY-HEADED EVIL WHICH YOUR THOUGHTLESS ACT HAS SET IN MOTION!
--BOTH UPON EARTH... AND UPON THE WORLDS BEYOND WORLDS!
THERE APPEAR BEFORE ME COUNTLESS FACES--THE IMAGES OF THOSE WHO POSSESS A DORMANT TALENT FOR BLACK MAGIC!
AND, AMONG THE MANY-- ONE!!
"BEFORE ZOM WAS FREED, THIS MAN WAS A HUMBLE DRUGGIST! BUT, AT THIS VERY MOMENT--
I'VE DONE IT!
ANCIENT SPELLS
AFTER YEARS OF FUTILE STUDY, I HAVE SUDDENLY MASTERED THE RITUAL OF THE CIRCLES OF FIRE!
I SENSE THE KNOWLEDGE OF THE ANCIENTS SURGE THRU MY BURNING BRAIN!
NO LONGER NEED I PORE IN VAIN OVER USELESS OCCULT TEXTS!
NOW, THE POWERS I SEEK RESIDE IN ME--ALONE!
AND YET, I MUST TEST THESE NEW ABILITIES FURTHER!
THAT BOOK-CASE--! IT SHALL BE THE MEANS WHEREBY I TEST MY POWERS!
WELL DO I REMEMBER THE MYSTIC SPELL--THOUGH IT HAS NEVER WORKED FOR ME--BEFORE!
"BY THE SHADES OF THE SHADOWS--BY THE WAND OF WATOOMB--"
"MAY NO OBJECT PREVENT ME--MAY I PASS FROM THIS ROOM!"
IT--IT'S WORKING!
IT'S AS IF THE BOOKCASE--AND THE WALL BEYOND IT--DID NOT EVEN EXIST WHILE I SPOKE THE MYSTIC WORDS!
I DO NOT KNOW HOW I GAINED SUCH POWER--BUT, IT DOES NOT MATTER!
FOR YEARS, MEN HAVE CALLED ME A CHARLATAN... A DREAMER... A MADMAN!
YET NOW, THE DAY IS AT HAND WHEN I WILL HAVE... REVENGE!
I SHALL POSSESS WEALTH WITHOUT MEASURE--AS I POSSESS MYSTIC POWER WITHOUT LIMIT!
4

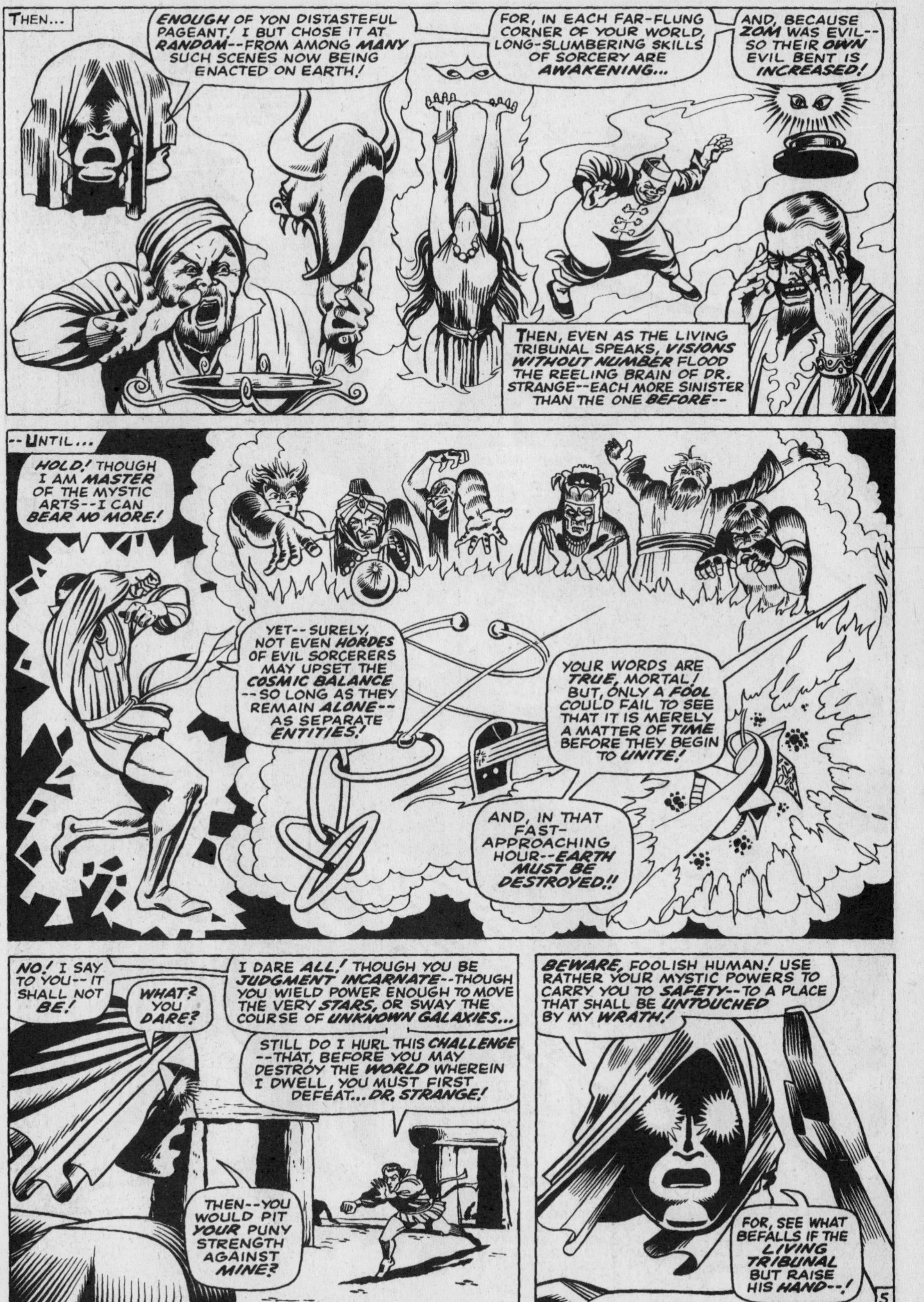
THEN...
ENOUGH OF YON DISTASTEFUL PAGEANT! I BUT CHOSE IT AT RANDOM--FROM AMONG MANY SUCH SCENES NOW BEING ENACTED ON EARTH!
FOR, IN EACH FAR-FLUNG CORNER OF YOUR WORLD, LONG-SLUMBERING SKILLS OF SORCERY ARE AWAKENING...
AND, BECAUSE ZOM WAS EVIL-- SO THEIR OWN EVIL BENT IS INCREASED!
THEN, EVEN AS THE LIVING TRIBUNAL SPEAKS, VISIONS WITHOUT NUMBER FLOOD THE REELING BRAIN OF DR. STRANGE--EACH MORE SINISTER THAN THE ONE BEFORE--
--UNTIL...
HOLD! THOUGH I AM MASTER OF THE MYSTIC ARTS--I CAN BEAR NO MORE!
YET--SURELY, NOT EVEN HORDES OF EVIL SORCERERS MAY UPSET THE COSMIC BALANCE --SO LONG AS THEY REMAIN ALONE-- AS SEPARATE ENTITIES!
YOUR WORDS ARE TRUE, MORTAL! BUT, ONLY A FOOL COULD FAIL TO SEE THAT IT IS MERELY A MATTER OF TIME BEFORE THEY BEGIN TO UNITE!
AND, IN THAT FAST-APPROACHING HOUR--EARTH MUST BE DESTROYED!!
NO! I SAY TO YOU--IT SHALL NOT BE!
WHAT? YOU DARE?
I DARE ALL! THOUGH YOU BE JUDGMENT INCARNATE--THOUGH YOU WIELD POWER ENOUGH TO MOVE THE VERY STARS, OR SWAY THE COURSE OF UNKNOWN GALAXIES...
STILL DO I HURL THIS CHALLENGE --THAT, BEFORE YOU MAY DESTROY THE WORLD WHEREIN I DWELL, YOU MUST FIRST DEFEAT... DR. STRANGE!
THEN--YOU WOULD PIT YOUR PUNY STRENGTH AGAINST MINE?
BEWARE, FOOLISH HUMAN! USE RATHER YOUR MYSTIC POWERS TO CARRY YOU TO SAFETY--TO A PLACE THAT SHALL BE UNTOUCHED BY MY WRATH!
FOR, SEE WHAT BEFALLS IF THE LIVING TRIBUNAL BUT RAISE HIS HAND--!
5

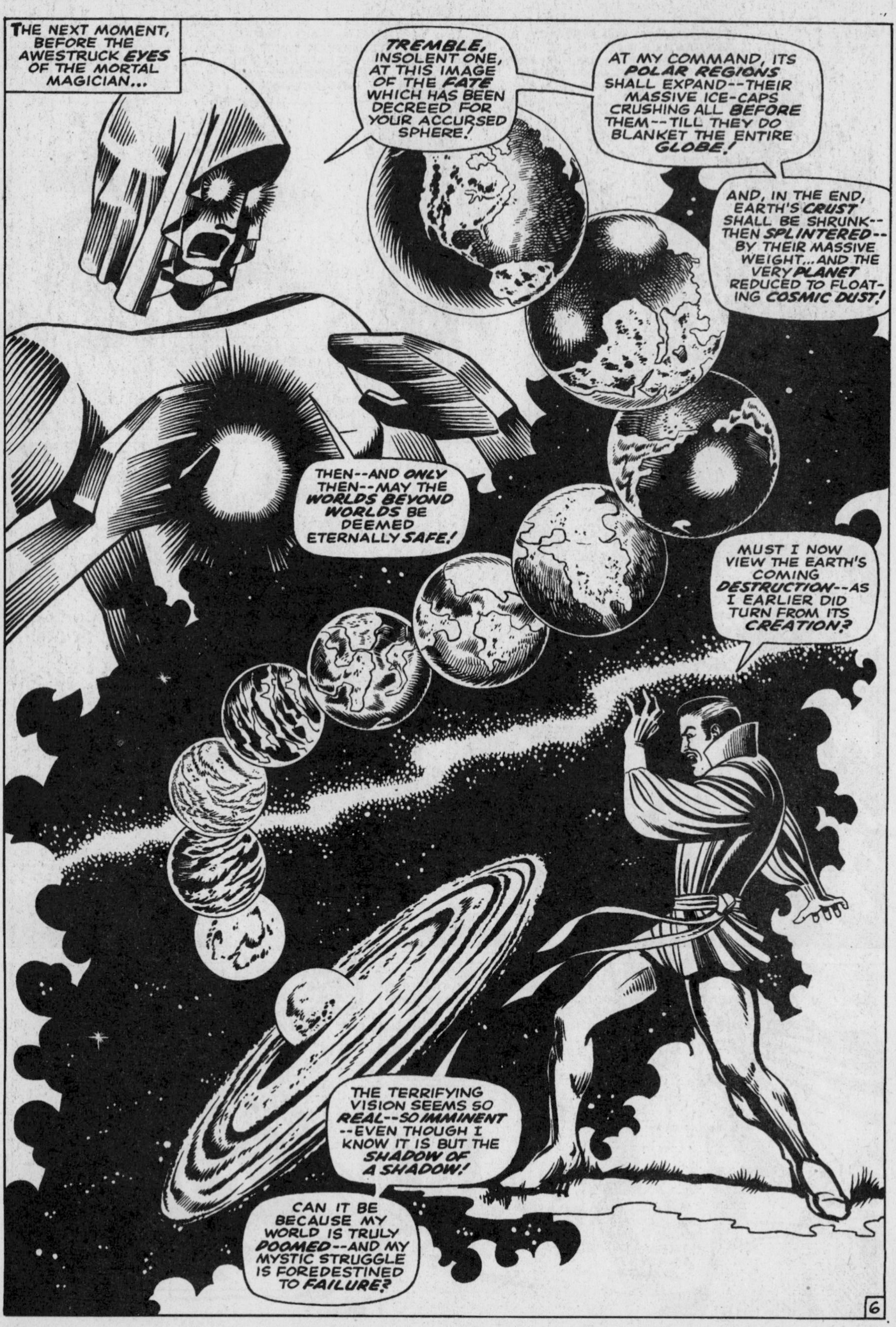
THE NEXT MOMENT, BEFORE THE AWESTRUCK EYES OF THE MORTAL MAGICIAN...
TREMBLE, INSOLENT ONE, AT THIS IMAGE OF THE FATE WHICH HAS BEEN DECREED FOR YOUR ACCURSED SPHERE!
AT MY COMMAND, ITS POLAR REGIONS SHALL EXPAND--THEIR MASSIVE ICE-CAPS CRUSHING ALL BEFORE THEM--TILL THEY DO BLANKET THE ENTIRE GLOBE!
AND, IN THE END, EARTH'S CRUST SHALL BE SHRUNK--THEN SPLINTERED--BY THEIR MASSIVE WEIGHT...AND THE VERY PLANET REDUCED TO FLOATING COSMIC DUST!
THEN--AND ONLY THEN--MAY THE WORLDS BEYOND WORLDS BE DEEMED ETERNALLY SAFE!
MUST I NOW VIEW THE EARTH'S COMING DESTRUCTION--AS I EARLIER DID TURN FROM ITS CREATION?
THE TERRIFYING VISION SEEMS SO REAL--SO IMMINENT--EVEN THOUGH I KNOW IT IS BUT THE SHADOW OF A SHADOW!
CAN IT BE BECAUSE MY WORLD IS TRULY DOOMED--AND MY MYSTIC STRUGGLE IS FOREDESTINED TO FAILURE?
6

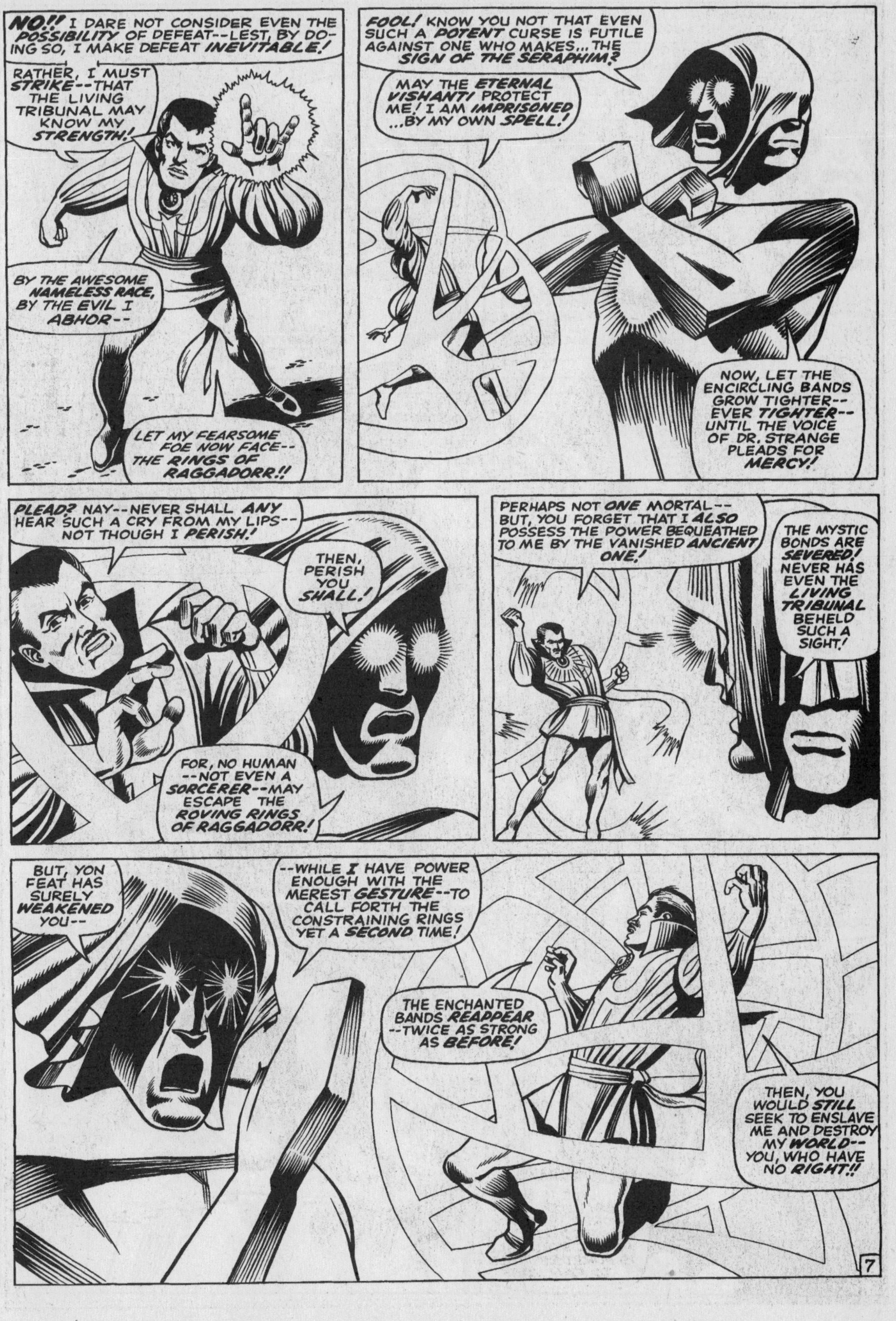
NO!! I DARE NOT CONSIDER EVEN THE POSSIBILITY OF DEFEAT--LEST, BY DOING SO, I MAKE DEFEAT INEVITABLE!
RATHER, I MUST STRIKE--THAT THE LIVING TRIBUNAL MAY KNOW MY STRENGTH!
BY THE AWESOME NAMELESS RACE, BY THE EVIL I ABHOR--
LET MY FEARSOME FOE NOW FACE--THE RINGS OF RAGGADORR!!
FOOL! KNOW YOU NOT THAT EVEN SUCH A POTENT CURSE IS FUTILE AGAINST ONE WHO MAKES... THE SIGN OF THE SERAPHIM?
MAY THE ETERNAL VISHANTI PROTECT ME! I AM IMPRISONED ...BY MY OWN SPELL!
NOW, LET THE ENCIRCLING BANDS GROW TIGHTER--EVER TIGHTER--UNTIL THE VOICE OF DR. STRANGE PLEADS FOR MERCY!
PLEAD? NAY--NEVER SHALL ANY HEAR SUCH A CRY FROM MY LIPS--NOT THOUGH I PERISH!
THEN, PERISH YOU SHALL!
FOR, NO HUMAN --NOT EVEN A SORCERER--MAY ESCAPE THE ROVING RINGS OF RAGGADORR!
PERHAPS NOT ONE MORTAL--BUT, YOU FORGET THAT I ALSO POSSESS THE POWER BEQUEATHED TO ME BY THE VANISHED ANCIENT ONE!
THE MYSTIC BONDS ARE SEVERED! NEVER HAS EVEN THE LIVING TRIBUNAL BEHELD SUCH A SIGHT!
BUT, YON FEAT HAS SURELY WEAKENED YOU--
--WHILE I HAVE POWER ENOUGH WITH THE MEREST GESTURE--TO CALL FORTH THE CONSTRAINING RINGS YET A SECOND TIME!
THE ENCHANTED BANDS REAPPEAR --TWICE AS STRONG AS BEFORE!
THEN, YOU WOULD STILL SEEK TO ENSLAVE ME AND DESTROY MY WORLD--YOU, WHO HAVE NO RIGHT!!
7

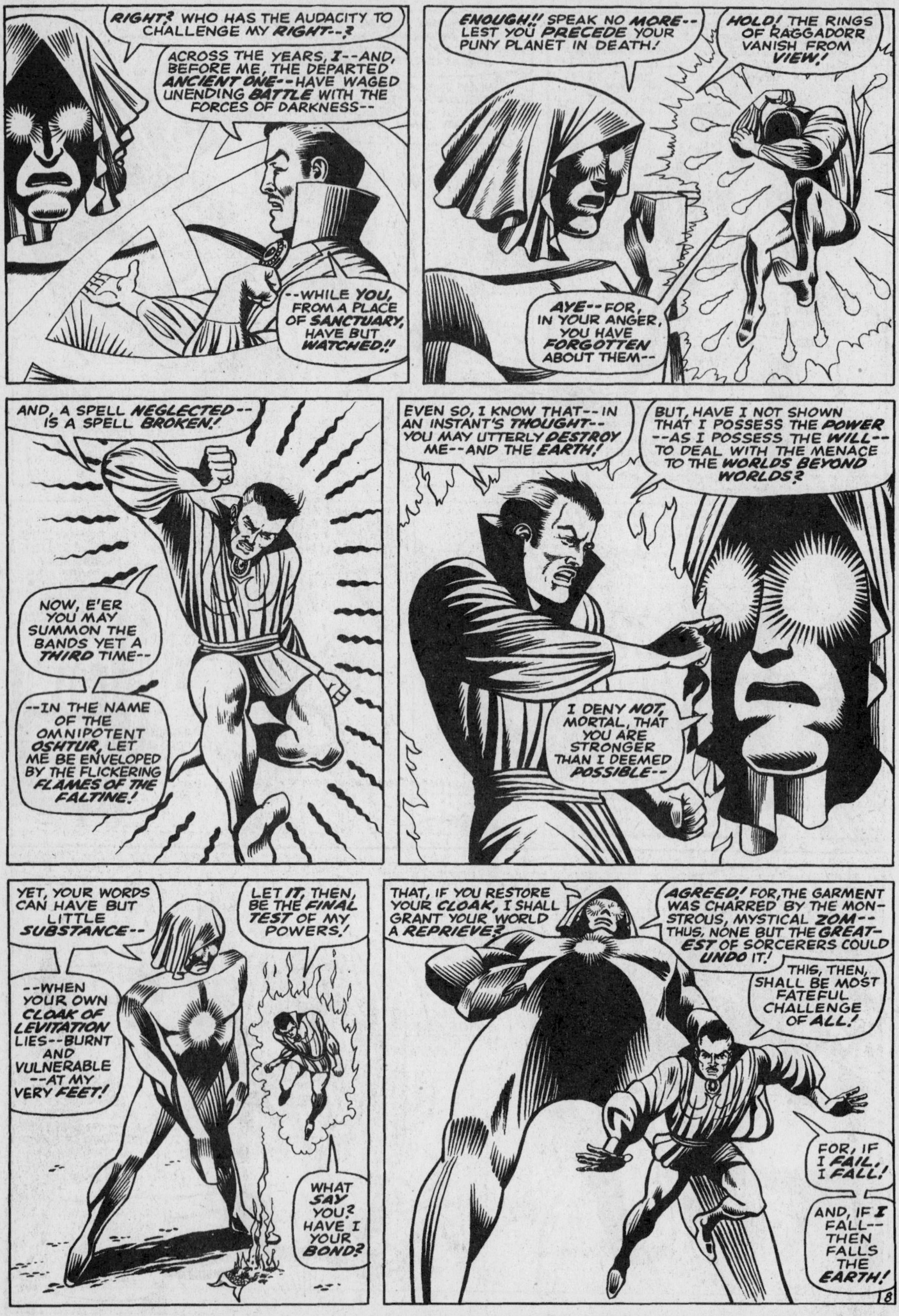

RIGHT? WHO HAS THE AUDACITY TO CHALLENGE MY RIGHT--?
ACROSS THE YEARS, I--AND, BEFORE ME, THE DEPARTED ANCIENT ONE--HAVE WAGED UNENDING BATTLE WITH THE FORCES OF DARKNESS--
--WHILE YOU, FROM A PLACE OF SANCTUARY, HAVE BUT WATCHED!!
ENOUGH!! SPEAK NO MORE--LEST YOU PRECEDE YOUR PUNY PLANET IN DEATH!
HOLD! THE RINGS OF RAGGADORR VANISH FROM VIEW!
AYE--FOR, IN YOUR ANGER, YOU HAVE FORGOTTEN ABOUT THEM--
AND, A SPELL NEGLECTED--IS A SPELL BROKEN!
NOW, E'ER YOU MAY SUMMON THE BANDS YET A THIRD TIME--
--IN THE NAME OF THE OMNIPOTENT OSHTUR, LET ME BE ENVELOPED BY THE FLICKERING FLAMES OF THE FALTINE!
EVEN SO, I KNOW THAT--IN AN INSTANT'S THOUGHT--YOU MAY UTTERLY DESTROY ME--AND THE EARTH!
BUT, HAVE I NOT SHOWN THAT I POSSESS THE POWER--AS I POSSESS THE WILL--TO DEAL WITH THE MENACE TO THE WORLDS BEYOND WORLDS?
I DENY NOT, MORTAL, THAT YOU ARE STRONGER THAN I DEEMED POSSIBLE--
YET, YOUR WORDS CAN HAVE BUT LITTLE SUBSTANCE--
--WHEN YOUR OWN CLOAK OF LEVITATION LIES--BURNT AND VULNERABLE--AT MY VERY FEET!
LET IT, THEN, BE THE FINAL TEST OF MY POWERS!
WHAT SAY YOU? HAVE I YOUR BOND?
THAT, IF YOU RESTORE YOUR CLOAK, I SHALL GRANT YOUR WORLD A REPRIEVE?
AGREED! FOR, THE GARMENT WAS CHARRED BY THE MONSTROUS, MYSTICAL ZOM--THUS, NONE BUT THE GREATEST OF SORCERERS COULD UNDO IT!
THIS, THEN, SHALL BE MOST FATEFUL CHALLENGE OF ALL!
FOR, IF I FAIL, I FALL!
AND, IF I FALL--THEN FALLS THE EARTH!
8

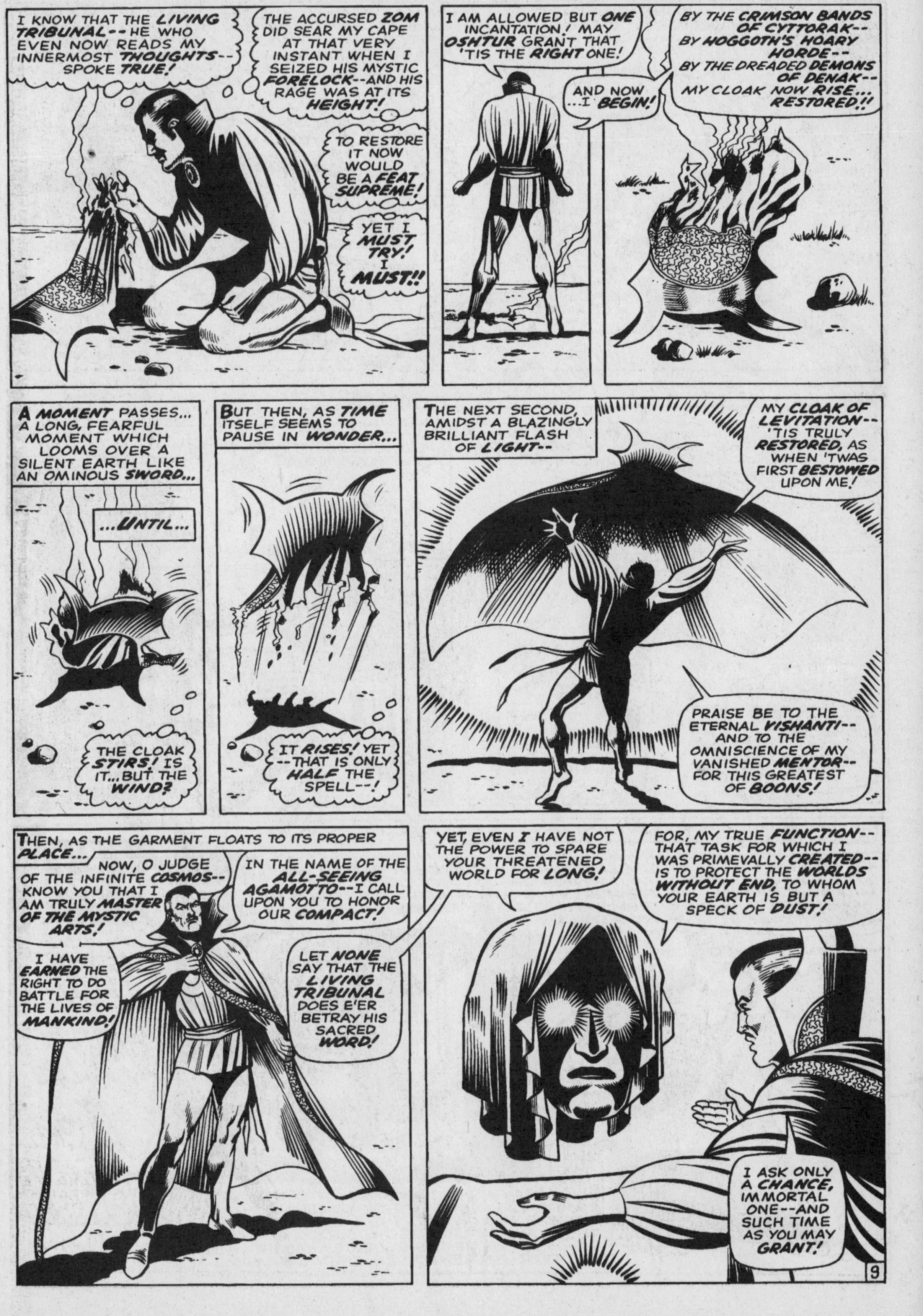
I KNOW THAT THE LIVING TRIBUNAL--HE WHO EVEN NOW READS MY INNERMOST THOUGHTS--SPOKE TRUE!
THE ACCURSED ZOM DID SEAR MY CAPE AT THAT VERY INSTANT WHEN I SEIZED HIS MYSTIC FORELOCK--AND HIS RAGE WAS AT ITS HEIGHT!
TO RESTORE IT NOW WOULD BE A FEAT SUPREME!
YET I MUST TRY! I MUST!!
I AM ALLOWED BUT ONE INCANTATION! MAY OSHTUR GRANT THAT 'TIS THE RIGHT ONE!
AND NOW ...I BEGIN!
BY THE CRIMSON BANDS OF CYTTORAK--BY HOGGOTH'S HOARY HORDE--BY THE DREADED DEMONS OF DENAK--MY CLOAK NOW RISE...RESTORED!!
A MOMENT PASSES... A LONG, FEARFUL MOMENT WHICH LOOMS OVER A SILENT EARTH LIKE AN OMINOUS SWORD...
...UNTIL...
THE CLOAK STIRS! IS IT...BUT THE WIND?
BUT THEN, AS TIME ITSELF SEEMS TO PAUSE IN WONDER...
IT RISES! YET --THAT IS ONLY HALF THE SPELL--!
THE NEXT SECOND, AMIDST A BLAZINGLY BRILLIANT FLASH OF LIGHT--
MY CLOAK OF LEVITATION--'TIS TRULY RESTORED, AS WHEN 'TWAS FIRST BESTOWED UPON ME!
PRAISE BE TO THE ETERNAL VISHANTI--AND TO THE OMNISCIENCE OF MY VANISHED MENTOR--FOR THIS GREATEST OF BOONS!
THEN, AS THE GARMENT FLOATS TO ITS PROPER PLACE...
NOW, O JUDGE OF THE INFINITE COSMOS--KNOW YOU THAT I AM TRULY MASTER OF THE MYSTIC ARTS!
I HAVE EARNED THE RIGHT TO DO BATTLE FOR THE LIVES OF MANKIND!
IN THE NAME OF THE ALL-SEEING AGAMOTTO--I CALL UPON YOU TO HONOR OUR COMPACT!
LET NONE SAY THAT THE LIVING TRIBUNAL DOES E'ER BETRAY HIS SACRED WORD!
YET, EVEN I HAVE NOT THE POWER TO SPARE YOUR THREATENED WORLD FOR LONG!
FOR, MY TRUE FUNCTION--THAT TASK FOR WHICH I WAS PRIMEVALLY CREATED--IS TO PROTECT THE WORLDS WITHOUT END, TO WHOM YOUR EARTH IS BUT A SPECK OF DUST!
I ASK ONLY A CHANCE, IMMORTAL ONE--AND SUCH TIME AS YOU MAY GRANT!
9

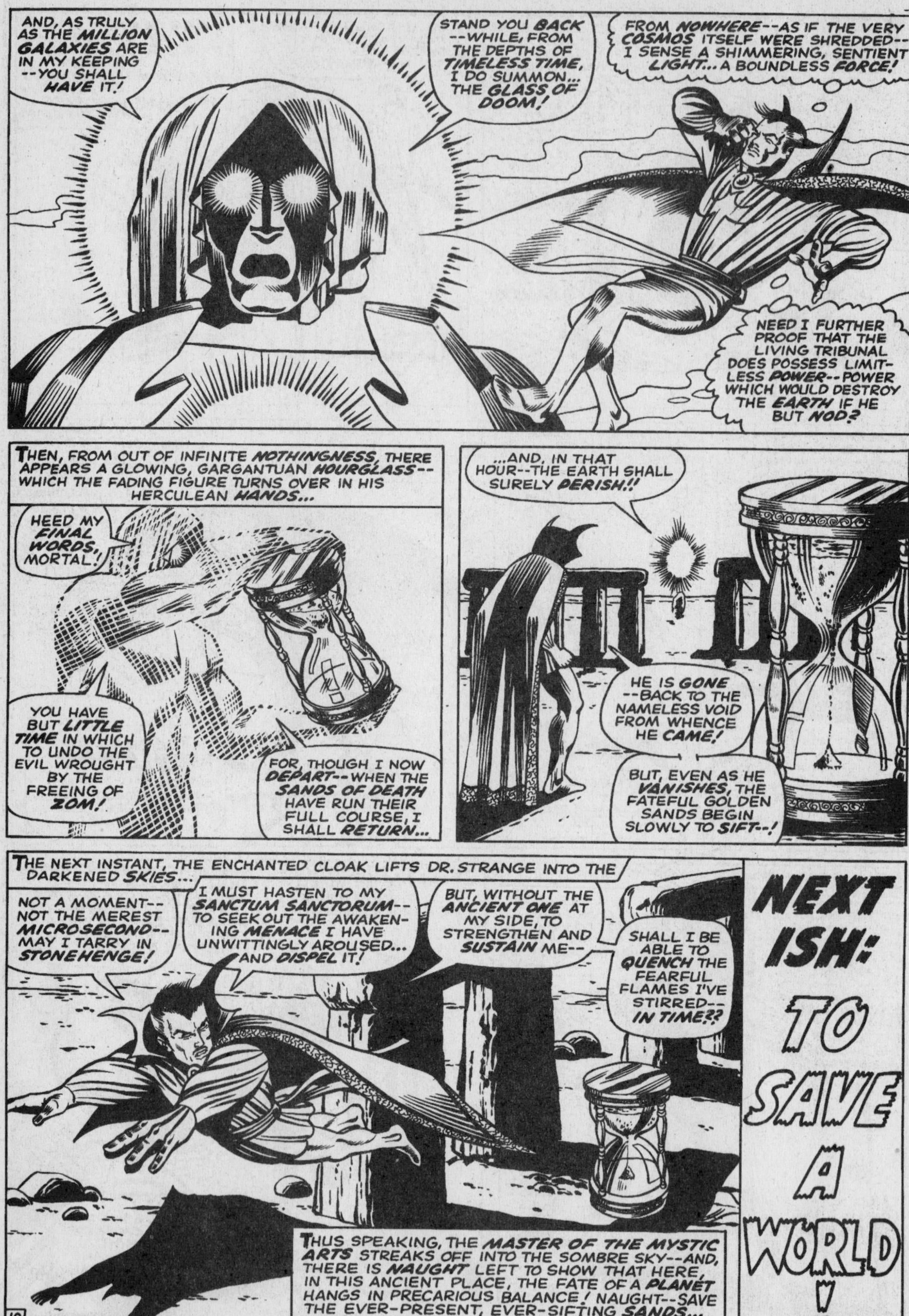

AND, AS TRULY AS THE MILLION GALAXIES ARE IN MY KEEPING --YOU SHALL HAVE IT!
STAND YOU BACK --WHILE, FROM THE DEPTHS OF TIMELESS TIME, I DO SUMMON... THE GLASS OF DOOM!
FROM NOWHERE--AS IF THE VERY COSMOS ITSELF WERE SHREDDED-- I SENSE A SHIMMERING, SENTIENT LIGHT... A BOUNDLESS FORCE!
NEED I FURTHER PROOF THAT THE LIVING TRIBUNAL DOES POSSESS LIMITLESS POWER--POWER WHICH WOULD DESTROY THE EARTH IF HE BUT NOD?
THEN, FROM OUT OF INFINITE NOTHINGNESS, THERE APPEARS A GLOWING, GARGANTUAN HOURGLASS-- WHICH THE FADING FIGURE TURNS OVER IN HIS HERCULEAN HANDS...
HEED MY FINAL WORDS, MORTAL!
YOU HAVE BUT LITTLE TIME IN WHICH TO UNDO THE EVIL WROUGHT BY THE FREEING OF ZOM!
FOR, THOUGH I NOW DEPART--WHEN THE SANDS OF DEATH HAVE RUN THEIR FULL COURSE, I SHALL RETURN...
...AND, IN THAT HOUR--THE EARTH SHALL SURELY PERISH!!
HE IS GONE --BACK TO THE NAMELESS VOID FROM WHENCE HE CAME!
BUT, EVEN AS HE VANISHES, THE FATEFUL GOLDEN SANDS BEGIN SLOWLY TO SIFT--!
THE NEXT INSTANT, THE ENCHANTED CLOAK LIFTS DR. STRANGE INTO THE DARKENED SKIES...
NOT A MOMENT-- NOT THE MEREST MICROSECOND-- MAY I TARRY IN STONEHENGE!
I MUST HASTEN TO MY SANCTUM SANCTORUM-- TO SEEK OUT THE AWAKENING MENACE I HAVE UNWITTINGLY AROUSED... AND DISPEL IT!
BUT, WITHOUT THE ANCIENT ONE AT MY SIDE, TO STRENGTHEN AND SUSTAIN ME--
SHALL I BE ABLE TO QUENCH THE FEARFUL FLAMES I'VE STIRRED-- IN TIME??
THUS SPEAKING, THE MASTER OF THE MYSTIC ARTS STREAKS OFF INTO THE SOMBRE SKY--AND, THERE IS NAUGHT LEFT TO SHOW THAT HERE, IN THIS ANCIENT PLACE, THE FATE OF A PLANET HANGS IN PRECARIOUS BALANCE! NAUGHT--SAVE THE EVER-PRESENT, EVER-SIFTING SANDS...
NEXT ISH: TO SAVE A WORLD!
10

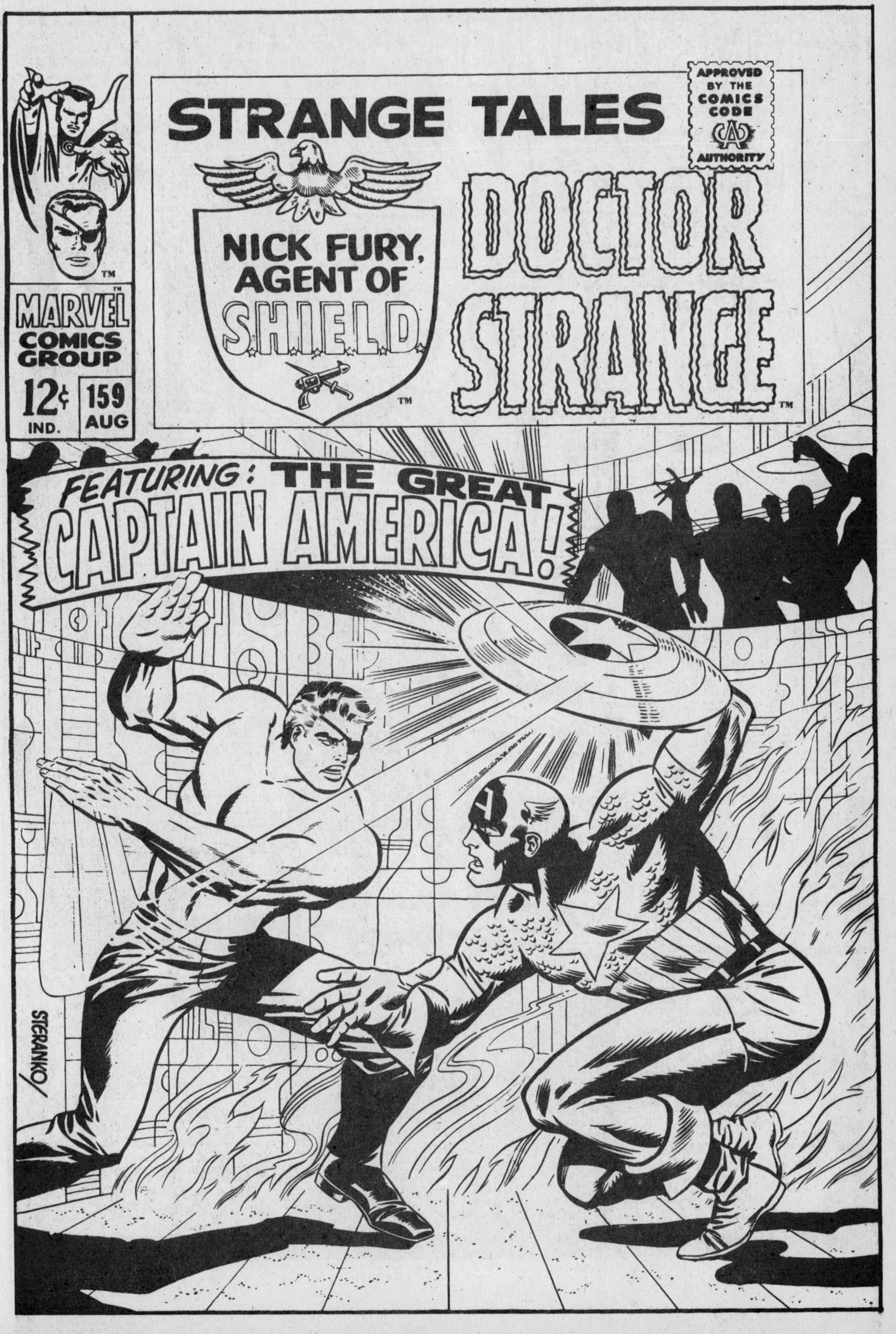
MARVEL COMICS GROUP
12¢ IND.
159 AUG
STRANGE TALES
APPROVED BY THE COMICS CODE AUTHORITY
NICK FURY, AGENT OF S.H.I.E.L.D.
DOCTOR STRANGE
FEATURING: THE GREAT CAPTAIN AMERICA!
STERANKO

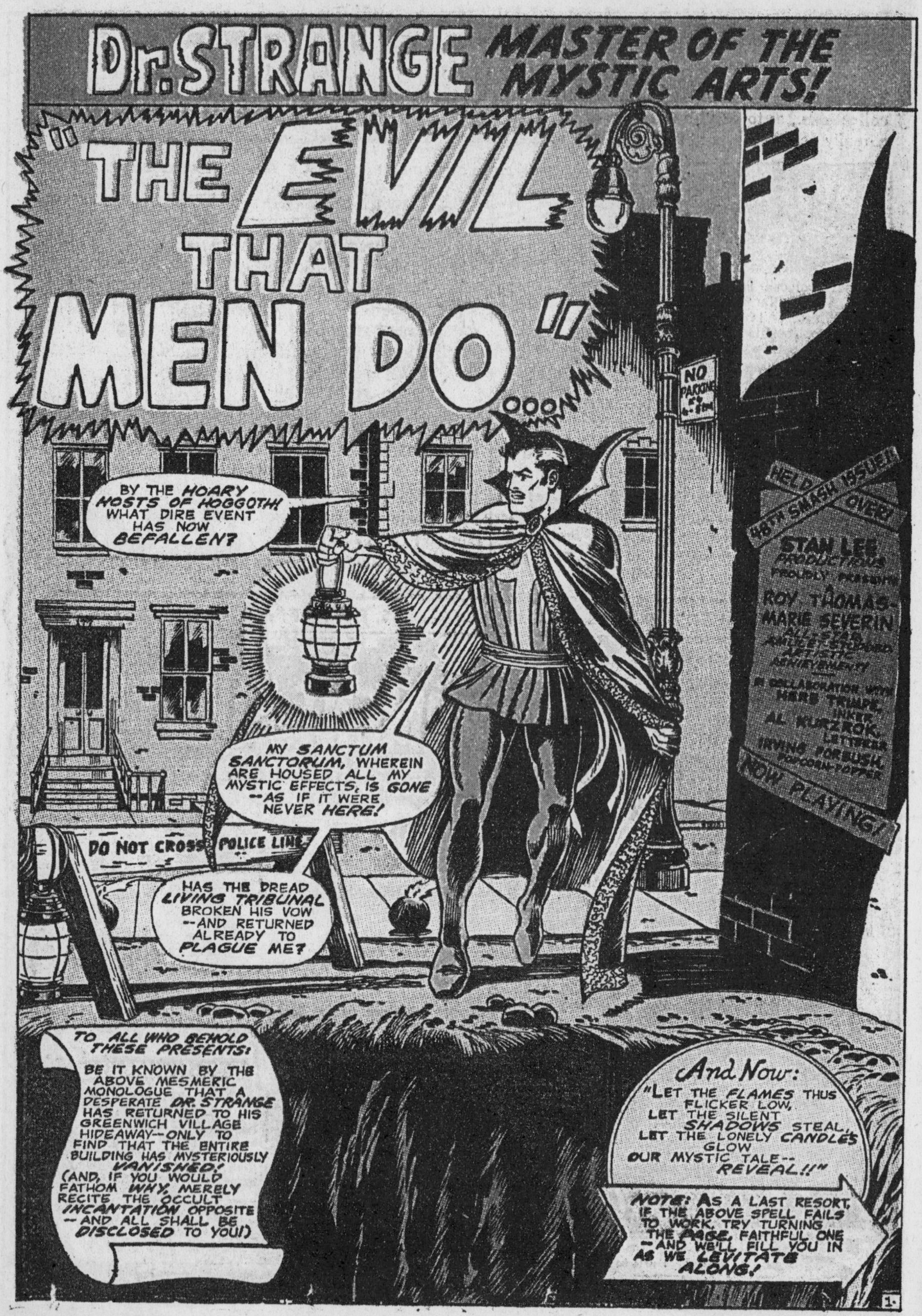

Dr. STRANGE MASTER OF THE MYSTIC ARTS!
"THE EVIL THAT MEN DO" ...
BY THE HOARY HOSTS OF HOGGOTH! WHAT DIRE EVENT HAS NOW BEFALLEN?
MY SANCTUM SANCTORUM, WHEREIN ARE HOUSED ALL MY MYSTIC EFFECTS, IS GONE --AS IF IT WERE NEVER HERE!
HAS THE DREAD LIVING TRIBUNAL BROKEN HIS VOW --AND RETURNED ALREADY TO PLAGUE ME?
NO PARKING
DO NOT CROSS POLICE LINE
HELD OVER!
48TH SMASH ISSUE!!
STAN LEE PRODUCTIONS
ROY THOMAS-MARIE SEVERIN
MARIE SEVERIN
IN COLLABORATION WITH HERB TRIMPE, INKER
AL KURZROK, LETTERER
IRVING FORBUSH, POPCORN-POPPER
NOW PLAYING!
TO ALL WHO BEHOLD THESE PRESENTS: BE IT KNOWN BY THE ABOVE MESMERIC MONOLOGUE THAT A DESPERATE DR. STRANGE HAS RETURNED TO HIS GREENWICH VILLAGE HIDEAWAY--ONLY TO FIND THAT THE ENTIRE BUILDING HAS MYSTERIOUSLY VANISHED! (AND, IF YOU WOULD FATHOM WHY, MERELY RECITE THE OCCULT INCANTATION OPPOSITE --AND ALL SHALL BE DISCLOSED TO YOU!)
And Now: "LET THE FLAMES THUS FLICKER LOW, LET THE SILENT SHADOWS STEAL, LET THE LONELY CANDLES GLOW OUR MYSTIC TALE-- REVEAL!!"
NOTE: AS A LAST RESORT, IF THE ABOVE SPELL FAILS TO WORK, TRY TURNING THE PAGE, FAITHFUL ONE --AND WE'LL FILL YOU IN AS WE LEVITATE ALONG!
1

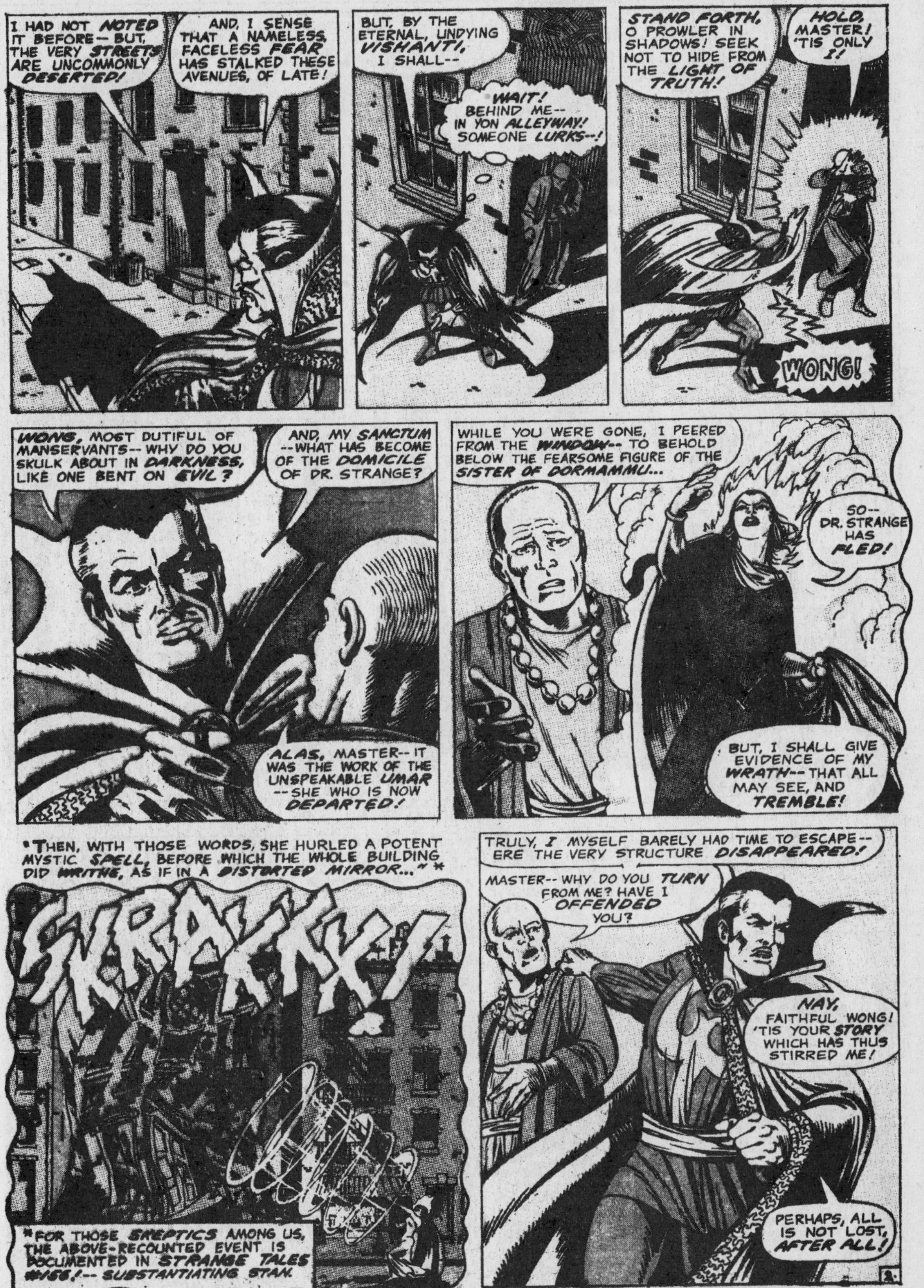
I HAD NOT NOTED IT BEFORE-- BUT, THE VERY STREETS ARE UNCOMMONLY DESERTED!
AND, I SENSE THAT A NAMELESS, FACELESS FEAR HAS STALKED THESE AVENUES, OF LATE!
BUT, BY THE ETERNAL, UNDYING VISHANTI, I SHALL--
WAIT! BEHIND ME-- IN YON ALLEYWAY! SOMEONE LURKS--!
STAND FORTH, O PROWLER IN SHADOWS! SEEK NOT TO HIDE FROM THE LIGHT OF TRUTH!
HOLD, MASTER! 'TIS ONLY I!
WONG!
WONG, MOST DUTIFUL OF MANSERVANTS-- WHY DO YOU SKULK ABOUT IN DARKNESS, LIKE ONE BENT ON EVIL?
AND, MY SANCTUM --WHAT HAS BECOME OF THE DOMICILE OF DR. STRANGE?
ALAS, MASTER-- IT WAS THE WORK OF THE UNSPEAKABLE UMAR --SHE WHO IS NOW DEPARTED!
WHILE YOU WERE GONE, I PEERED FROM THE WINDOW-- TO BEHOLD BELOW THE FEARSOME FIGURE OF THE SISTER OF DORMAMMU...
SO-- DR. STRANGE HAS FLED!
BUT, I SHALL GIVE EVIDENCE OF MY WRATH-- THAT ALL MAY SEE, AND TREMBLE!
"THEN, WITH THOSE WORDS, SHE HURLED A POTENT MYSTIC SPELL, BEFORE WHICH THE WHOLE BUILDING DID WRITHE, AS IF IN A DISTORTED MIRROR..." *
SKRAKKK!
*FOR THOSE SKEPTICS AMONG US, THE ABOVE-RECOUNTED EVENT IS DOCUMENTED IN STRANGE TALES #155!-- SUBSTANTIATING STAN.
TRULY, I MYSELF BARELY HAD TIME TO ESCAPE-- ERE THE VERY STRUCTURE DISAPPEARED!
MASTER-- WHY DO YOU TURN FROM ME? HAVE I OFFENDED YOU?
NAY, FAITHFUL WONG! 'TIS YOUR STORY WHICH HAS THUS STIRRED ME!
PERHAPS, ALL IS NOT LOST, AFTER ALL!
2.

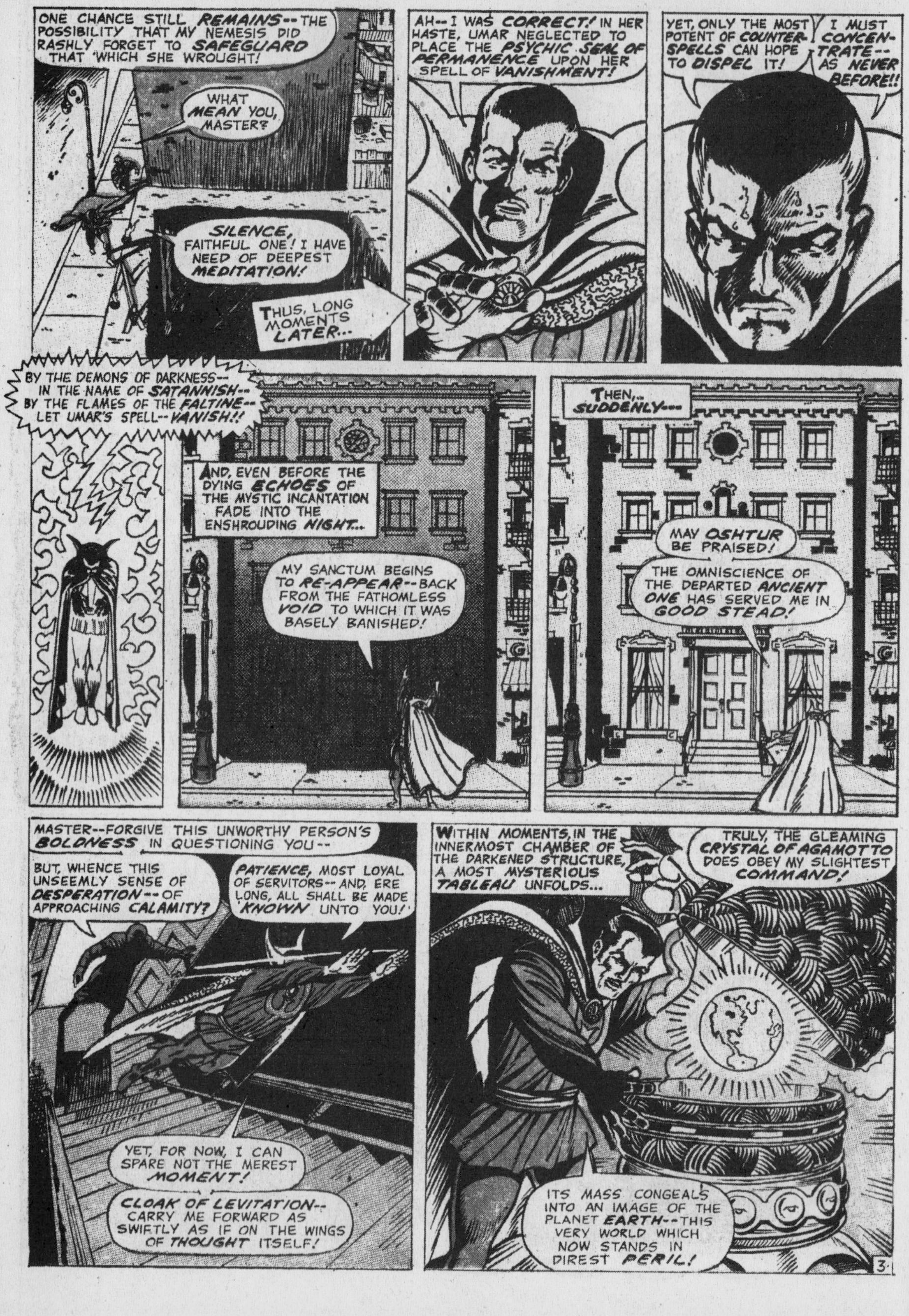

ONE CHANCE STILL REMAINS-- THE POSSIBILITY THAT MY NEMESIS DID RASHLY FORGET TO SAFEGUARD THAT WHICH SHE WROUGHT!
WHAT MEAN YOU, MASTER?
SILENCE, FAITHFUL ONE! I HAVE NEED OF DEEPEST MEDITATION!
THUS, LONG MOMENTS LATER...
AH-- I WAS CORRECT! IN HER HASTE, UMAR NEGLECTED TO PLACE THE PSYCHIC SEAL OF PERMANENCE UPON HER SPELL OF VANISHMENT!
YET, ONLY THE MOST POTENT OF COUNTER-SPELLS CAN HOPE TO DISPEL IT!
I MUST CONCEN-TRATE-- AS NEVER BEFORE!!
BY THE DEMONS OF DARKNESS-- IN THE NAME OF SATANNISH-- BY THE FLAMES OF THE FALTINE-- LET UMAR'S SPELL--VANISH!!
AND, EVEN BEFORE THE DYING ECHOES OF THE MYSTIC INCANTATION FADE INTO THE ENSHROUDING NIGHT...
MY SANCTUM BEGINS TO RE-APPEAR-- BACK FROM THE FATHOMLESS VOID TO WHICH IT WAS BASELY BANISHED!
THEN,.. SUDDENLY---
MAY OSHTUR BE PRAISED!
THE OMNISCIENCE OF THE DEPARTED ANCIENT ONE HAS SERVED ME IN GOOD STEAD!
MASTER--FORGIVE THIS UNWORTHY PERSON'S BOLDNESS IN QUESTIONING YOU--
BUT, WHENCE THIS UNSEEMLY SENSE OF DESPERATION-- OF APPROACHING CALAMITY?
PATIENCE, MOST LOYAL OF SERVITORS-- AND, ERE LONG, ALL SHALL BE MADE KNOWN UNTO YOU!
YET, FOR NOW, I CAN SPARE NOT THE MEREST MOMENT!
CLOAK OF LEVITATION-- CARRY ME FORWARD AS SWIFTLY AS IF ON THE WINGS OF THOUGHT ITSELF!
WITHIN MOMENTS, IN THE INNERMOST CHAMBER OF THE DARKENED STRUCTURE, A MOST MYSTERIOUS TABLEAU UNFOLDS...
TRULY, THE GLEAMING CRYSTAL OF AGAMOTTO DOES OBEY MY SLIGHTEST COMMAND!
ITS MASS CONGEALS INTO AN IMAGE OF THE PLANET EARTH-- THIS VERY WORLD WHICH NOW STANDS IN DIREST PERIL!
3

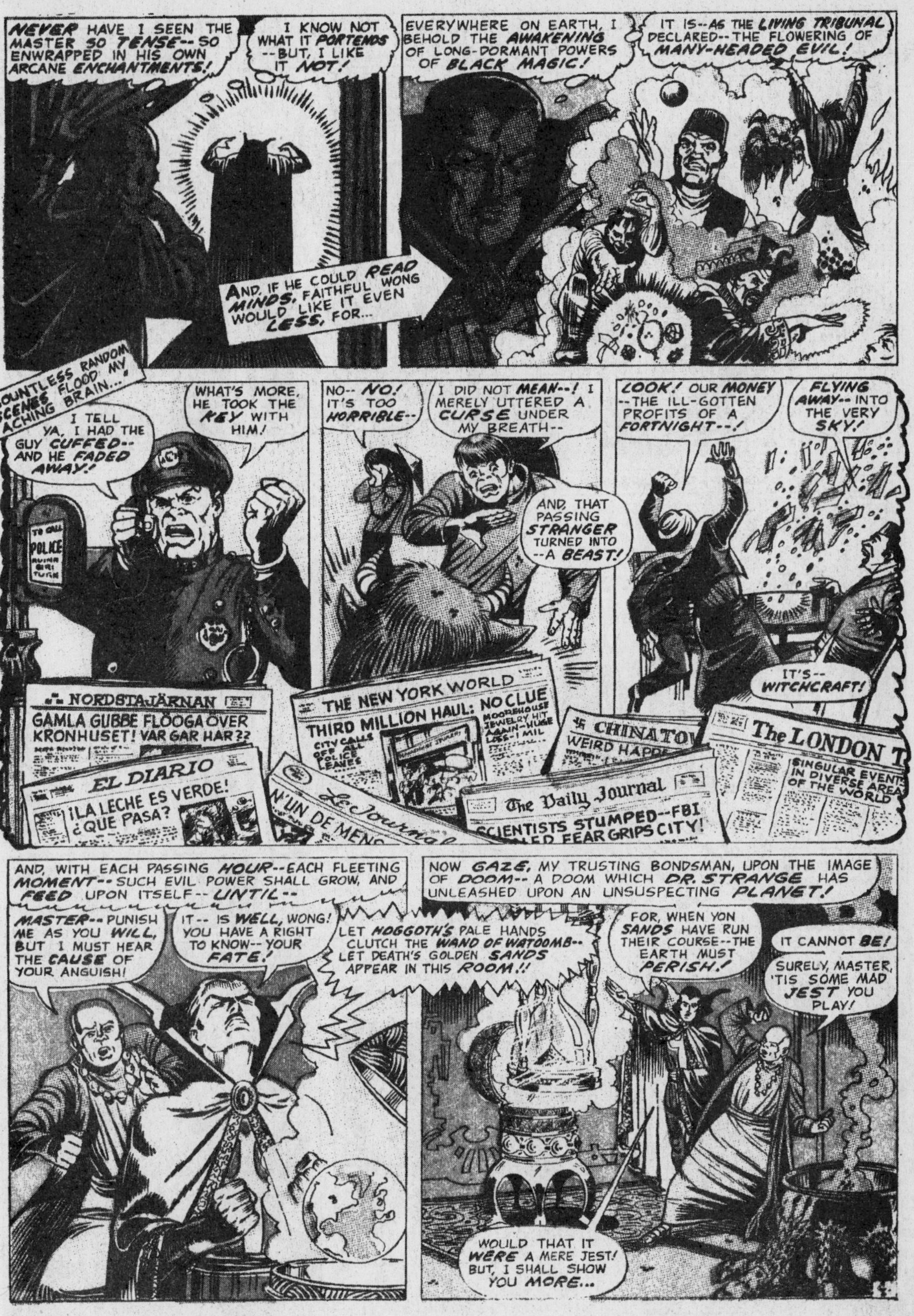
NEVER HAVE I SEEN THE MASTER SO TENSE-- SO ENWRAPPED IN HIS OWN ARCANE ENCHANTMENTS!
I KNOW NOT WHAT IT PORTENDS --BUT, I LIKE IT NOT!
AND, IF HE COULD READ MINDS, FAITHFUL WONG WOULD LIKE IT EVEN LESS, FOR...
EVERYWHERE ON EARTH, I BEHOLD THE AWAKENING OF LONG-DORMANT POWERS OF BLACK MAGIC!
IT IS--AS THE LIVING TRIBUNAL DECLARED--THE FLOWERING OF MANY-HEADED EVIL!
"COUNTLESS RANDOM SCENES FLOOD MY ACHING BRAIN..."
YA, I TELL YA, I HAD THE GUY CUFFED-- AND HE FADED AWAY!
WHAT'S MORE, HE TOOK THE KEY WITH HIM!
TO CALL POLICE
NO-- NO! IT'S TOO HORRIBLE--
I DID NOT MEAN--! I MERELY UTTERED A CURSE UNDER MY BREATH--
AND, THAT PASSING STRANGER TURNED INTO --A BEAST!
LOOK! OUR MONEY --THE ILL-GOTTEN PROFITS OF A FORTNIGHT--!
FLYING AWAY-- INTO THE VERY SKY!
IT'S-- WITCHCRAFT!
NORDSTAJÄRNAN
GAMLA GUBBE FLÖOGA OVER KRONHUSET! VAR GAR HAR??
THE NEW YORK WORLD
THIRD MILLION HAUL: NO CLUE
MOORHOUSE JEWELRY HIT AGAIN-HUGE LOSS-1 MIL
CITY CALLS OFF ALL POLICE LEAVES
EL DIARIO
¡LA LECHE ES VERDE!
¿QUE PASA?
Le Journal
CHINATO
WEIRD HAPPE
The LONDON T
SINGULAR EVENT IN DIVERSE AREA OF THE WORLD
The Daily Journal
SCIENTISTS STUMPED--FBI
FEAR GRIPS CITY!
AND, WITH EACH PASSING HOUR--EACH FLEETING MOMENT-- SUCH EVIL POWER SHALL GROW, AND FEED UPON ITSELF-- UNTIL--
MASTER-- PUNISH ME AS YOU WILL, BUT I MUST HEAR THE CAUSE OF YOUR ANGUISH!
IT-- IS WELL, WONG! YOU HAVE A RIGHT TO KNOW-- YOUR FATE!
LET HOGGOTH'S PALE HANDS CLUTCH THE WAND OF WATOOMB-- LET DEATH'S GOLDEN SANDS APPEAR IN THIS ROOM!!
NOW GAZE, MY TRUSTING BONDSMAN, UPON THE IMAGE OF DOOM-- A DOOM WHICH DR. STRANGE HAS UNLEASHED UPON AN UNSUSPECTING PLANET!
FOR, WHEN YON SANDS HAVE RUN THEIR COURSE--THE EARTH MUST PERISH!
IT CANNOT BE!
SURELY, MASTER, 'TIS SOME MAD JEST YOU PLAY!
WOULD THAT IT WERE A MERE JEST! BUT, I SHALL SHOW YOU MORE...

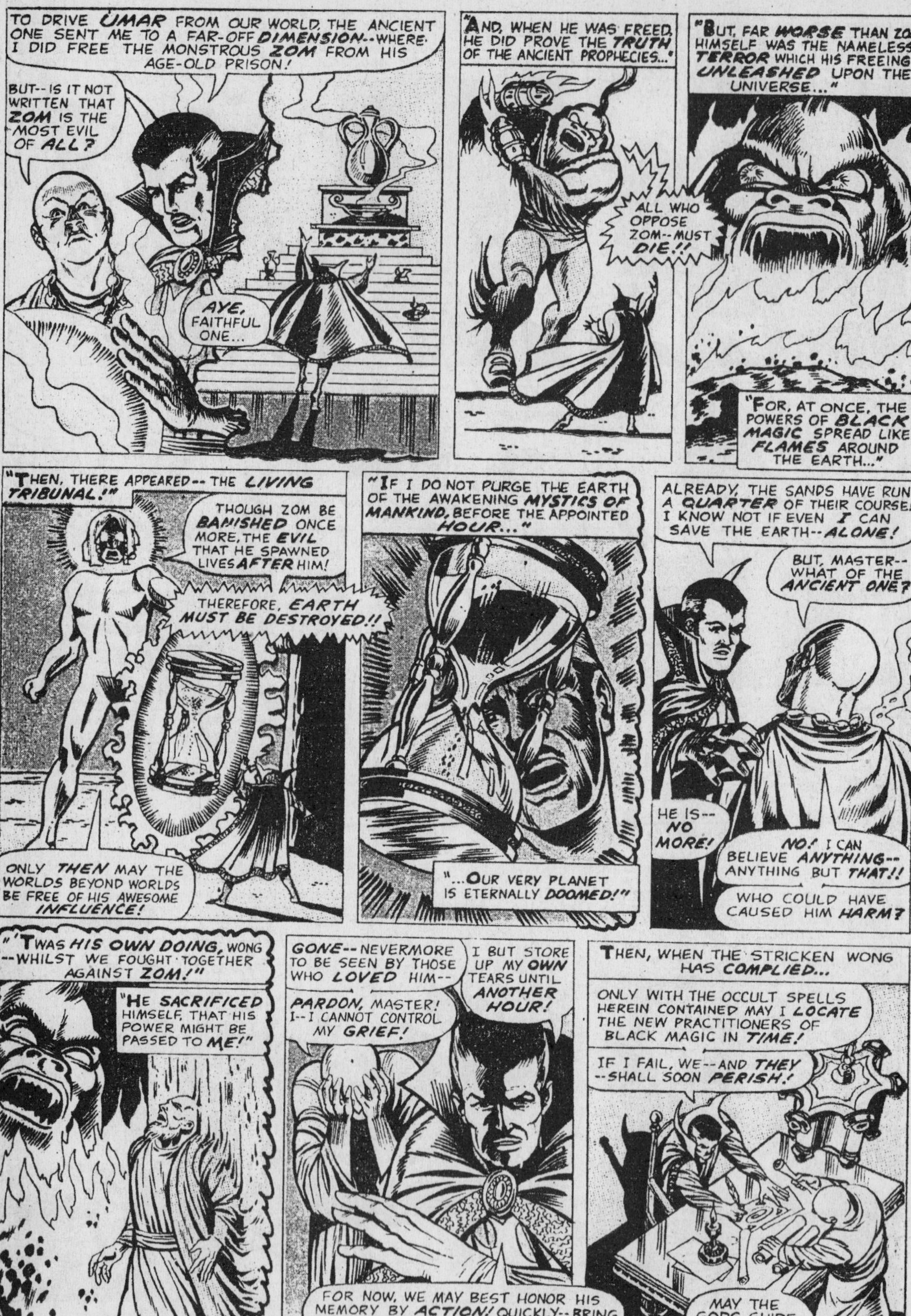
TO DRIVE UMAR FROM OUR WORLD, THE ANCIENT ONE SENT ME TO A FAR-OFF DIMENSION--WHERE I DID FREE THE MONSTROUS ZOM FROM HIS AGE-OLD PRISON!
BUT--IS IT NOT WRITTEN THAT ZOM IS THE MOST EVIL OF ALL?
AYE, FAITHFUL ONE...
"AND, WHEN HE WAS FREED, HE DID PROVE THE TRUTH OF THE ANCIENT PROPHECIES..."
ALL WHO OPPOSE ZOM--MUST DIE!!
"BUT, FAR WORSE THAN ZOM HIMSELF WAS THE NAMELESS TERROR WHICH HIS FREEING UNLEASHED UPON THE UNIVERSE..."
"FOR, AT ONCE, THE POWERS OF BLACK MAGIC SPREAD LIKE FLAMES AROUND THE EARTH..."
"THEN, THERE APPEARED--THE LIVING TRIBUNAL!"
THOUGH ZOM BE BANISHED ONCE MORE, THE EVIL THAT HE SPAWNED LIVES AFTER HIM!
THEREFORE, EARTH MUST BE DESTROYED!!
ONLY THEN MAY THE WORLDS BEYOND WORLDS BE FREE OF HIS AWESOME INFLUENCE!
"IF I DO NOT PURGE THE EARTH OF THE AWAKENING MYSTICS OF MANKIND, BEFORE THE APPOINTED HOUR..."
"...OUR VERY PLANET IS ETERNALLY DOOMED!"
ALREADY, THE SANDS HAVE RUN A QUARTER OF THEIR COURSE! I KNOW NOT IF EVEN I CAN SAVE THE EARTH--ALONE!
BUT, MASTER--WHAT OF THE ANCIENT ONE?
HE IS--NO MORE!
NO! I CAN BELIEVE ANYTHING--ANYTHING BUT THAT!!
WHO COULD HAVE CAUSED HIM HARM?
"'TWAS HIS OWN DOING, WONG--WHILST WE FOUGHT TOGETHER AGAINST ZOM!"
"HE SACRIFICED HIMSELF, THAT HIS POWER MIGHT BE PASSED TO ME!"
GONE--NEVERMORE TO BE SEEN BY THOSE WHO LOVED HIM--
I BUT STORE UP MY OWN TEARS UNTIL ANOTHER HOUR!
PARDON, MASTER! I--I CANNOT CONTROL MY GRIEF!
FOR NOW, WE MAY BEST HONOR HIS MEMORY BY ACTION! QUICKLY--BRING ME YON SACROSANCT SCROLLS...
THEN, WHEN THE STRICKEN WONG HAS COMPLIED...
ONLY WITH THE OCCULT SPELLS HEREIN CONTAINED MAY I LOCATE THE NEW PRACTITIONERS OF BLACK MAGIC IN TIME!
IF I FAIL, WE--AND THEY--SHALL SOON PERISH!
MAY THE GODS GUIDE YOUR HAND!
5

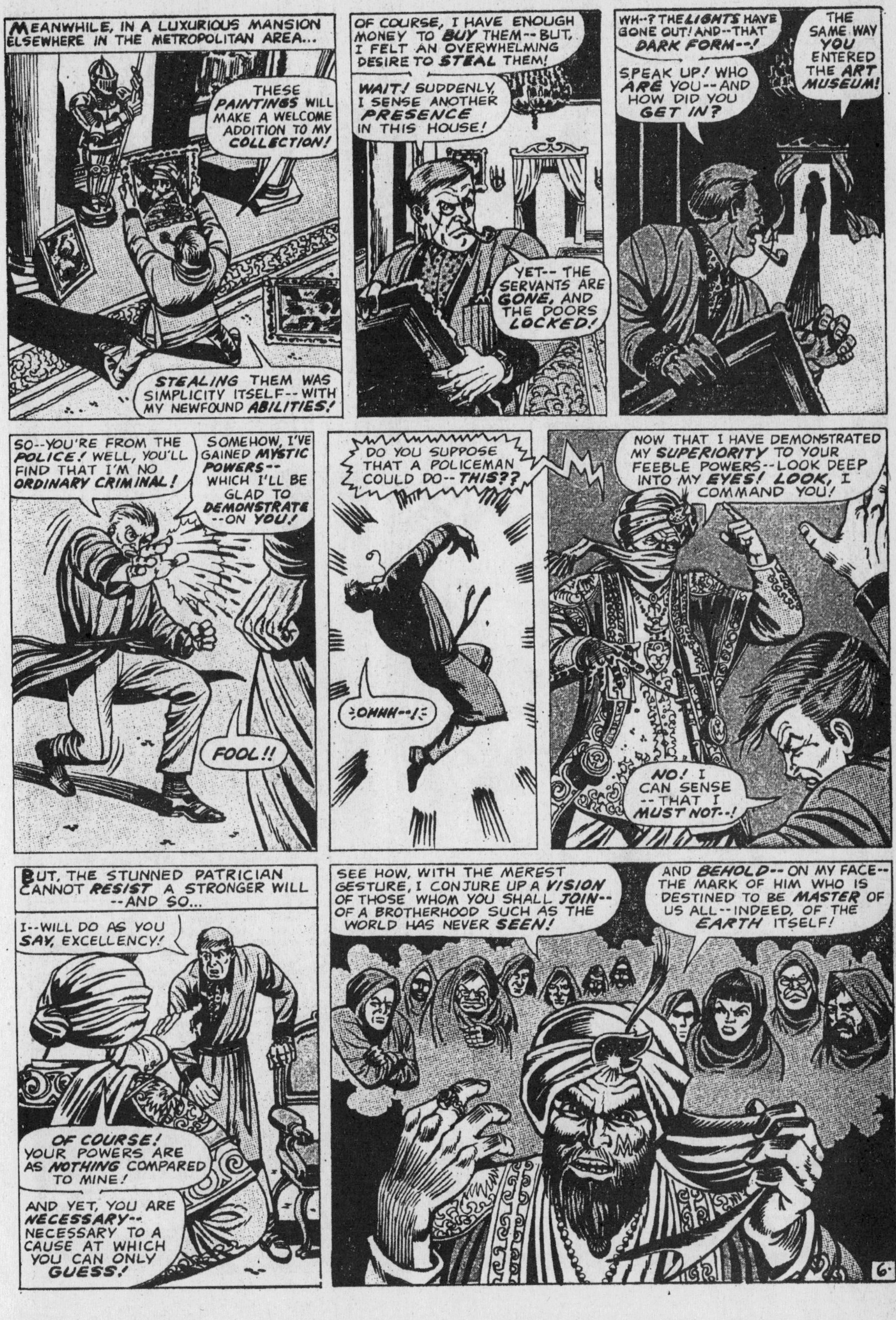
MEANWHILE, IN A LUXURIOUS MANSION ELSEWHERE IN THE METROPOLITAN AREA...
THESE PAINTINGS WILL MAKE A WELCOME ADDITION TO MY COLLECTION!
STEALING THEM WAS SIMPLICITY ITSELF--WITH MY NEWFOUND ABILITIES!
OF COURSE, I HAVE ENOUGH MONEY TO BUY THEM--BUT, I FELT AN OVERWHELMING DESIRE TO STEAL THEM!
WAIT! SUDDENLY, I SENSE ANOTHER PRESENCE IN THIS HOUSE!
YET--THE SERVANTS ARE GONE, AND THE DOORS LOCKED!
WH--? THE LIGHTS HAVE GONE OUT! AND--THAT DARK FORM--!
SPEAK UP! WHO ARE YOU--AND HOW DID YOU GET IN?
THE SAME WAY YOU ENTERED THE ART MUSEUM!
SO--YOU'RE FROM THE POLICE! WELL, YOU'LL FIND THAT I'M NO ORDINARY CRIMINAL!
SOMEHOW, I'VE GAINED MYSTIC POWERS--WHICH I'LL BE GLAD TO DEMONSTRATE--ON YOU!
FOOL!!
DO YOU SUPPOSE THAT A POLICEMAN COULD DO--THIS??
OHHH--!
NOW THAT I HAVE DEMONSTRATED MY SUPERIORITY TO YOUR FEEBLE POWERS--LOOK DEEP INTO MY EYES! LOOK, I COMMAND YOU!
NO! I CAN SENSE--THAT I MUST NOT--!
BUT, THE STUNNED PATRICIAN CANNOT RESIST A STRONGER WILL--AND SO...
I--WILL DO AS YOU SAY, EXCELLENCY!
OF COURSE! YOUR POWERS ARE AS NOTHING COMPARED TO MINE!
AND YET, YOU ARE NECESSARY--NECESSARY TO A CAUSE AT WHICH YOU CAN ONLY GUESS!
SEE HOW, WITH THE MEREST GESTURE, I CONJURE UP A VISION OF THOSE WHOM YOU SHALL JOIN--OF A BROTHERHOOD SUCH AS THE WORLD HAS NEVER SEEN!
AND BEHOLD--ON MY FACE--THE MARK OF HIM WHO IS DESTINED TO BE MASTER OF US ALL--INDEED, OF THE EARTH ITSELF!
6

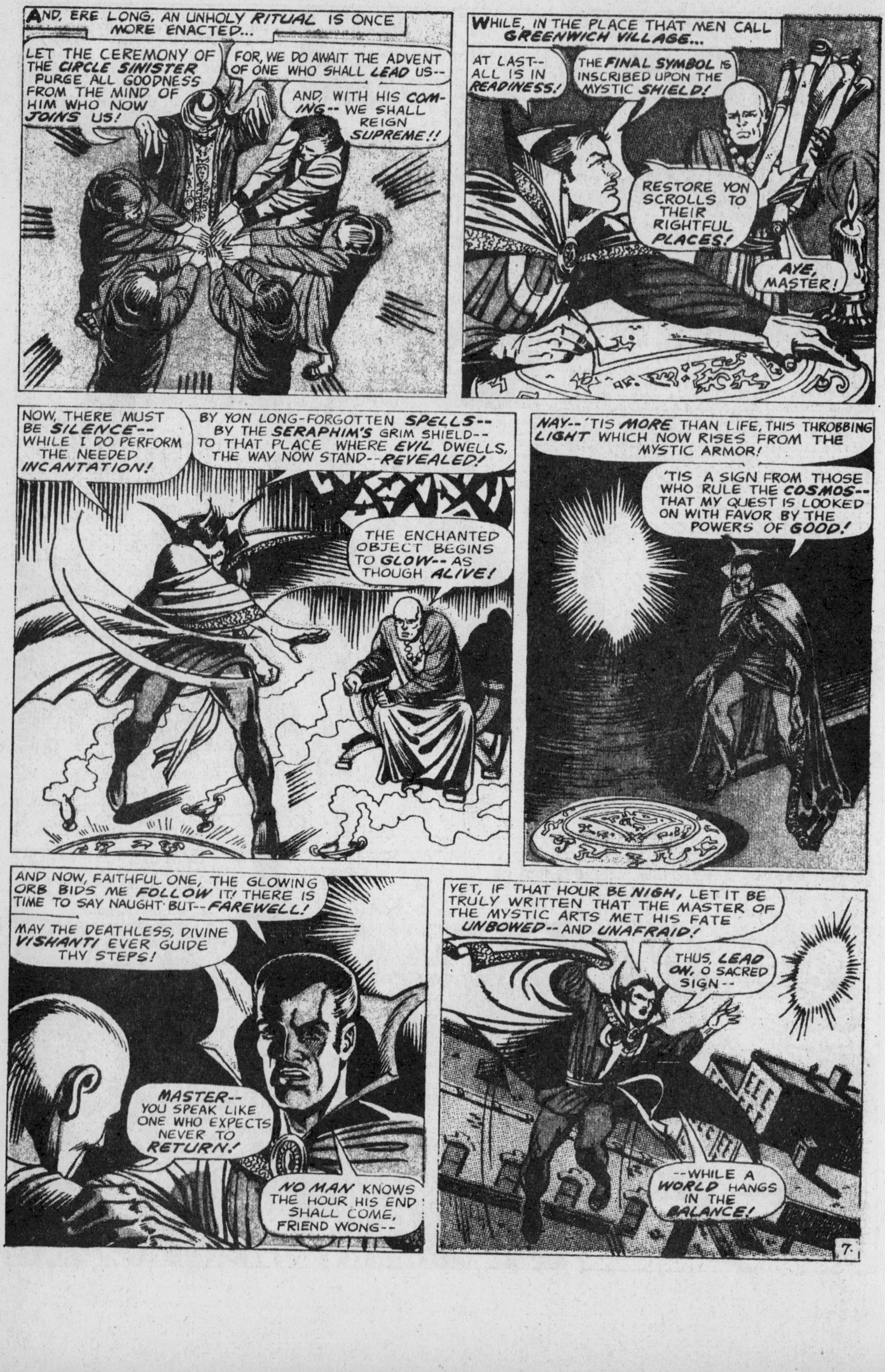

AND, ERE LONG, AN UNHOLY RITUAL IS ONCE MORE ENACTED...
LET THE CEREMONY OF THE CIRCLE SINISTER PURGE ALL GOODNESS FROM THE MIND OF HIM WHO NOW JOINS US!
FOR, WE DO AWAIT THE ADVENT OF ONE WHO SHALL LEAD US--
AND, WITH HIS COMING-- WE SHALL REIGN SUPREME!!
WHILE, IN THE PLACE THAT MEN CALL GREENWICH VILLAGE...
AT LAST-- ALL IS IN READINESS!
THE FINAL SYMBOL IS INSCRIBED UPON THE MYSTIC SHIELD!
RESTORE YON SCROLLS TO THEIR RIGHTFUL PLACES!
AYE, MASTER!
NOW, THERE MUST BE SILENCE-- WHILE I DO PERFORM THE NEEDED INCANTATION!
BY YON LONG-FORGOTTEN SPELLS-- BY THE SERAPHIM'S GRIM SHIELD-- TO THAT PLACE WHERE EVIL DWELLS, THE WAY NOW STAND--REVEALED!
THE ENCHANTED OBJECT BEGINS TO GLOW-- AS THOUGH ALIVE!
NAY--'TIS MORE THAN LIFE, THIS THROBBING LIGHT WHICH NOW RISES FROM THE MYSTIC ARMOR!
'TIS A SIGN FROM THOSE WHO RULE THE COSMOS-- THAT MY QUEST IS LOOKED ON WITH FAVOR BY THE POWERS OF GOOD!
AND NOW, FAITHFUL ONE, THE GLOWING ORB BIDS ME FOLLOW IT! THERE IS TIME TO SAY NAUGHT BUT--FAREWELL!
MAY THE DEATHLESS, DIVINE VISHANTI EVER GUIDE THY STEPS!
MASTER-- YOU SPEAK LIKE ONE WHO EXPECTS NEVER TO RETURN!
NO MAN KNOWS THE HOUR HIS END SHALL COME, FRIEND WONG--
YET, IF THAT HOUR BE NIGH, LET IT BE TRULY WRITTEN THAT THE MASTER OF THE MYSTIC ARTS MET HIS FATE UNBOWED-- AND UNAFRAID!
THUS, LEAD ON, O SACRED SIGN--
--WHILE A WORLD HANGS IN THE BALANCE!

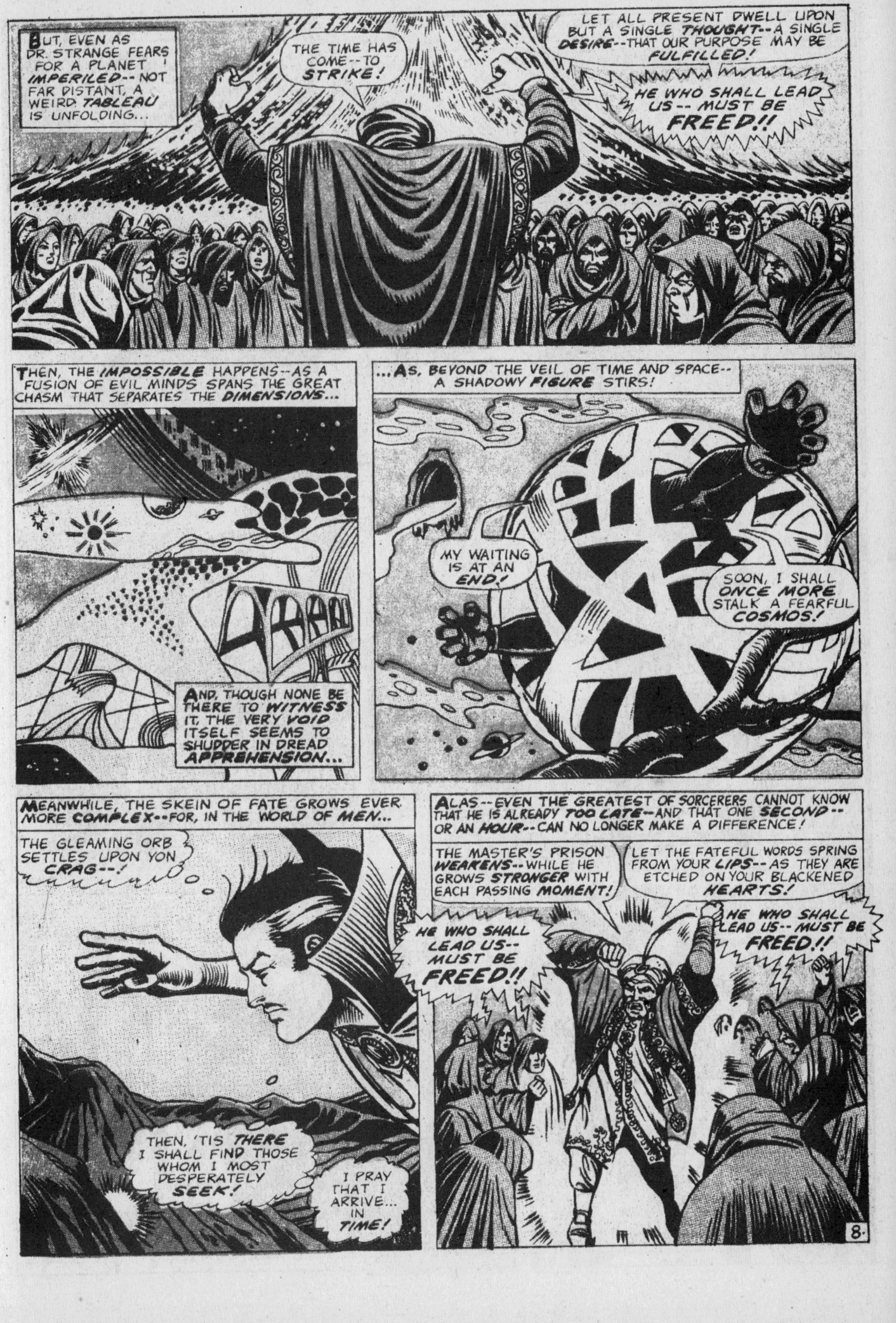

BUT, EVEN AS DR. STRANGE FEARS FOR A PLANET IMPERILED--NOT FAR DISTANT, A WEIRD TABLEAU IS UNFOLDING...
THE TIME HAS COME--TO STRIKE!
LET ALL PRESENT DWELL UPON BUT A SINGLE THOUGHT--A SINGLE DESIRE--THAT OUR PURPOSE MAY BE FULFILLED!
HE WHO SHALL LEAD US--MUST BE FREED!!
THEN, THE IMPOSSIBLE HAPPENS--AS A FUSION OF EVIL MINDS SPANS THE GREAT CHASM THAT SEPARATES THE DIMENSIONS...
AND, THOUGH NONE BE THERE TO WITNESS IT, THE VERY VOID ITSELF SEEMS TO SHUDDER IN DREAD APPREHENSION...
...AS, BEYOND THE VEIL OF TIME AND SPACE--A SHADOWY FIGURE STIRS!
MY WAITING IS AT AN END!
SOON, I SHALL ONCE MORE STALK A FEARFUL COSMOS!
MEANWHILE, THE SKEIN OF FATE GROWS EVER MORE COMPLEX--FOR, IN THE WORLD OF MEN...
THE GLEAMING ORB SETTLES UPON YON CRAG--!
THEN, 'TIS THERE I SHALL FIND THOSE WHOM I MOST DESPERATELY SEEK!
I PRAY THAT I ARRIVE... IN TIME!
ALAS--EVEN THE GREATEST OF SORCERERS CANNOT KNOW THAT HE IS ALREADY TOO LATE--AND THAT ONE SECOND--OR AN HOUR--CAN NO LONGER MAKE A DIFFERENCE!
THE MASTER'S PRISON WEAKENS--WHILE HE GROWS STRONGER WITH EACH PASSING MOMENT!
LET THE FATEFUL WORDS SPRING FROM YOUR LIPS--AS THEY ARE ETCHED ON YOUR BLACKENED HEARTS!
HE WHO SHALL LEAD US--MUST BE FREED!!
HE WHO SHALL LEAD US--MUST BE FREED!!
8

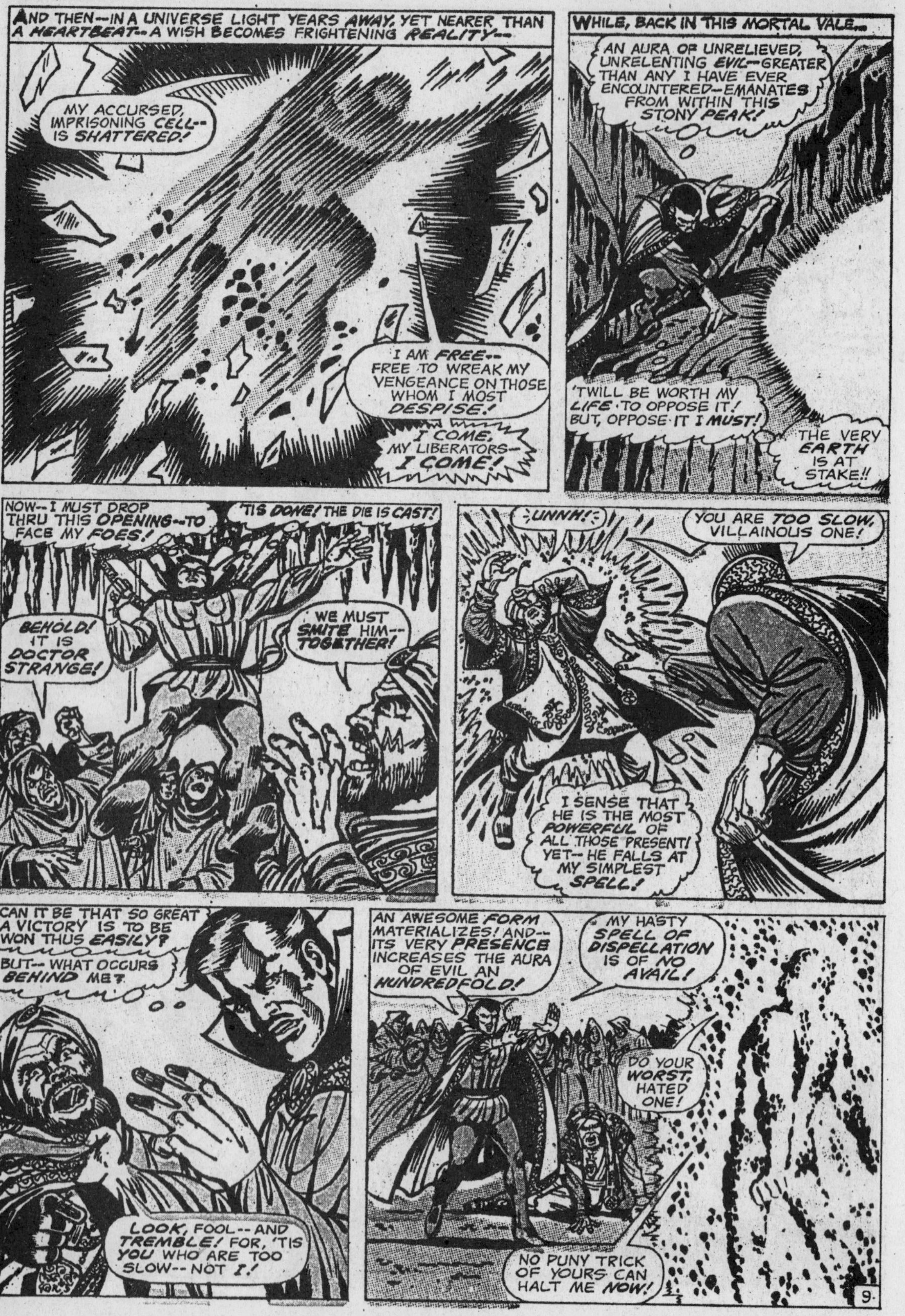
AND THEN--IN A UNIVERSE LIGHT YEARS AWAY, YET NEARER THAN A HEARTBEAT--A WISH BECOMES FRIGHTENING REALITY--
MY ACCURSED, IMPRISONING CELL--IS SHATTERED!
I AM FREE--FREE TO WREAK MY VENGEANCE ON THOSE WHOM I MOST DESPISE!
I COME, MY LIBERATORS--I COME!
WHILE, BACK IN THIS MORTAL VALE...
AN AURA OF UNRELIEVED, UNRELENTING EVIL--GREATER THAN ANY I HAVE EVER ENCOUNTERED--EMANATES FROM WITHIN THIS STONY PEAK!
'TWILL BE WORTH MY LIFE TO OPPOSE IT! BUT, OPPOSE IT I MUST!
THE VERY EARTH IS AT STAKE!!
NOW--I MUST DROP THRU THIS OPENING--TO FACE MY FOES!
'TIS DONE! THE DIE IS CAST!
BEHOLD! IT IS DOCTOR STRANGE!
WE MUST SMITE HIM--TOGETHER!
UNNH!
YOU ARE TOO SLOW, VILLAINOUS ONE!
I SENSE THAT HE IS THE MOST POWERFUL OF ALL THOSE PRESENT! YET--HE FALLS AT MY SIMPLEST SPELL!
CAN IT BE THAT SO GREAT A VICTORY IS TO BE WON THUS EASILY?
BUT--WHAT OCCURS BEHIND ME?
LOOK, FOOL--AND TREMBLE! FOR, 'TIS YOU WHO ARE TOO SLOW--NOT I!
AN AWESOME FORM MATERIALIZES! AND--ITS VERY PRESENCE INCREASES THE AURA OF EVIL AN HUNDREDFOLD!
MY HASTY SPELL OF DISPELLATION IS OF NO AVAIL!
DO YOUR WORST, HATED ONE!
NO PUNY TRICK OF YOURS CAN HALT ME NOW!

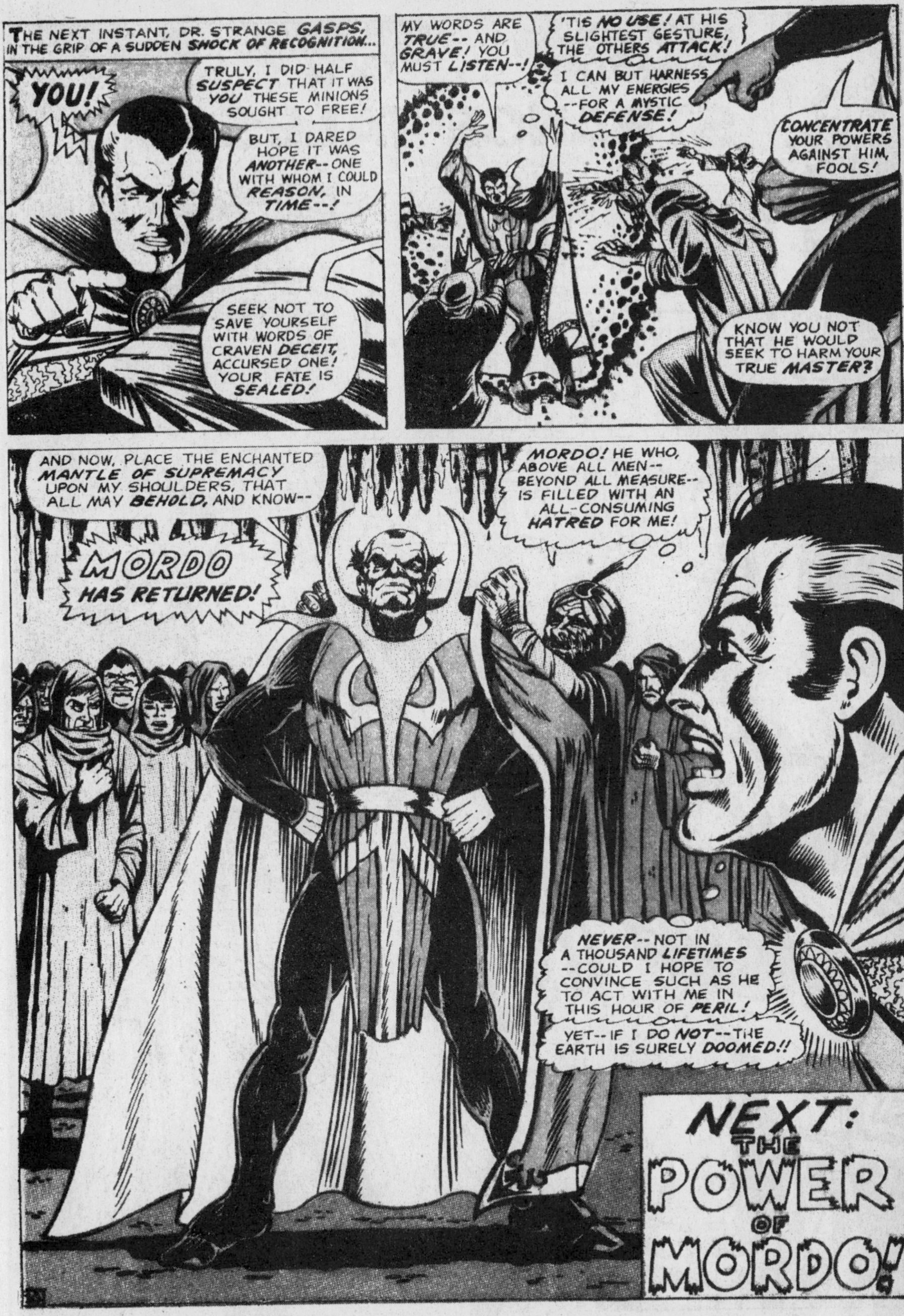
THE NEXT INSTANT, DR. STRANGE GASPS, IN THE GRIP OF A SUDDEN SHOCK OF RECOGNITION...
YOU!
TRULY, I DID HALF SUSPECT THAT IT WAS YOU THESE MINIONS SOUGHT TO FREE!
BUT, I DARED HOPE IT WAS ANOTHER--ONE WITH WHOM I COULD REASON, IN TIME--!
SEEK NOT TO SAVE YOURSELF WITH WORDS OF CRAVEN DECEIT, ACCURSED ONE! YOUR FATE IS SEALED!
MY WORDS ARE TRUE-- AND GRAVE! YOU MUST LISTEN--!
'TIS NO USE! AT HIS SLIGHTEST GESTURE, THE OTHERS ATTACK!
I CAN BUT HARNESS ALL MY ENERGIES --FOR A MYSTIC DEFENSE!
CONCENTRATE YOUR POWERS AGAINST HIM, FOOLS!
KNOW YOU NOT THAT HE WOULD SEEK TO HARM YOUR TRUE MASTER?
AND NOW, PLACE THE ENCHANTED MANTLE OF SUPREMACY UPON MY SHOULDERS, THAT ALL MAY BEHOLD, AND KNOW--
MORDO HAS RETURNED!
MORDO! HE WHO, ABOVE ALL MEN-- BEYOND ALL MEASURE-- IS FILLED WITH AN ALL-CONSUMING HATRED FOR ME!
NEVER--NOT IN A THOUSAND LIFETIMES --COULD I HOPE TO CONVINCE SUCH AS HE TO ACT WITH ME IN THIS HOUR OF PERIL!
YET--IF I DO NOT--THE EARTH IS SURELY DOOMED!!
NEXT: THE POWER OF MORDO!

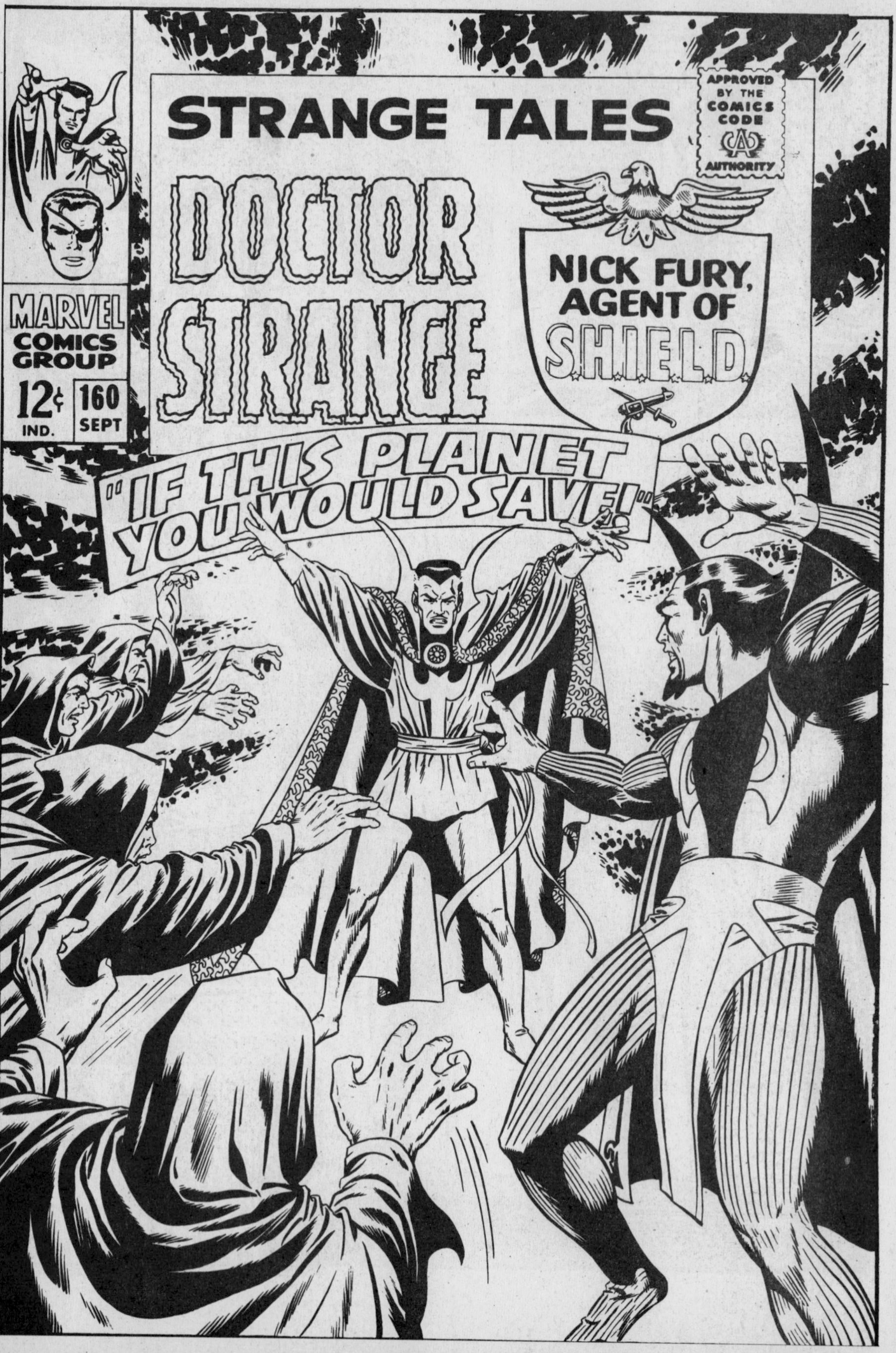

APPROVED BY THE COMICS CODE AUTHORITY
STRANGE TALES
DOCTOR STRANGE
NICK FURY, AGENT OF S.H.I.E.L.D.
MARVEL COMICS GROUP
12¢ IND.
160 SEPT
"IF THIS PLANET YOU WOULD SAVE!"

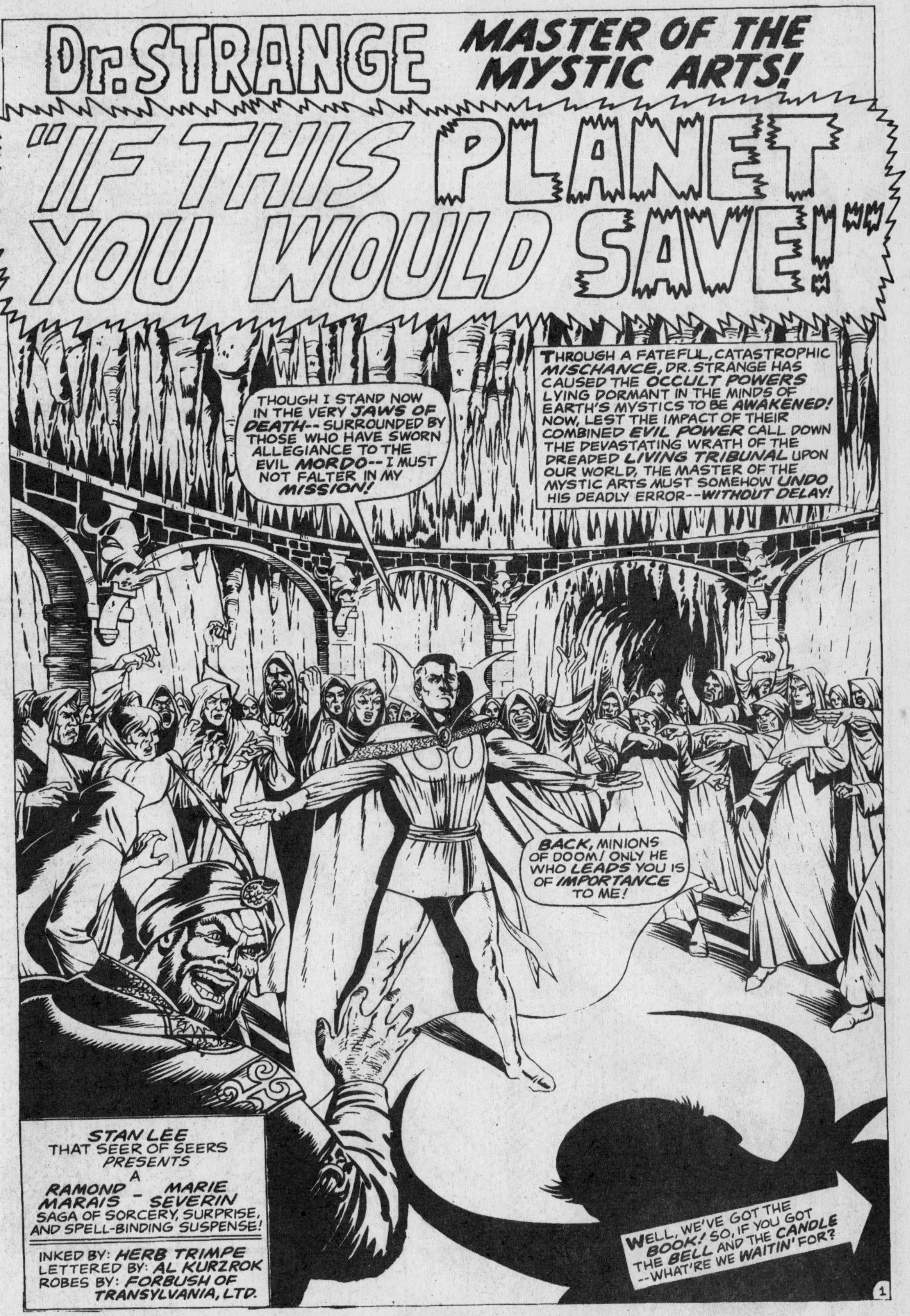
Dr. STRANGE
MASTER OF THE MYSTIC ARTS!
"IF THIS PLANET YOU WOULD SAVE!"
THROUGH A FATEFUL, CATASTROPHIC MISCHANCE, DR. STRANGE HAS CAUSED THE OCCULT POWERS LYING DORMANT IN THE MINDS OF EARTH'S MYSTICS TO BE AWAKENED! NOW, LEST THE IMPACT OF THEIR COMBINED EVIL POWER CALL DOWN THE DEVASTATING WRATH OF THE DREADED LIVING TRIBUNAL UPON OUR WORLD, THE MASTER OF THE MYSTIC ARTS MUST SOMEHOW UNDO HIS DEADLY ERROR--WITHOUT DELAY!
THOUGH I STAND NOW IN THE VERY JAWS OF DEATH-- SURROUNDED BY THOSE WHO HAVE SWORN ALLEGIANCE TO THE EVIL MORDO-- I MUST NOT FALTER IN MY MISSION!
BACK, MINIONS OF DOOM! ONLY HE WHO LEADS YOU IS OF IMPORTANCE TO ME!
STAN LEE THAT SEER OF SEERS PRESENTS A RAMOND MARAIS - MARIE SEVERIN SAGA OF SORCERY, SURPRISE, AND SPELL-BINDING SUSPENSE!
INKED BY: HERB TRIMPE
LETTERED BY: AL KURZROK
ROBES BY: FORBUSH OF TRANSYLVANIA, LTD.
WELL, WE'VE GOT THE BOOK! SO, IF YOU GOT THE BELL AND THE CANDLE --WHAT'RE WE WAITIN' FOR?
1

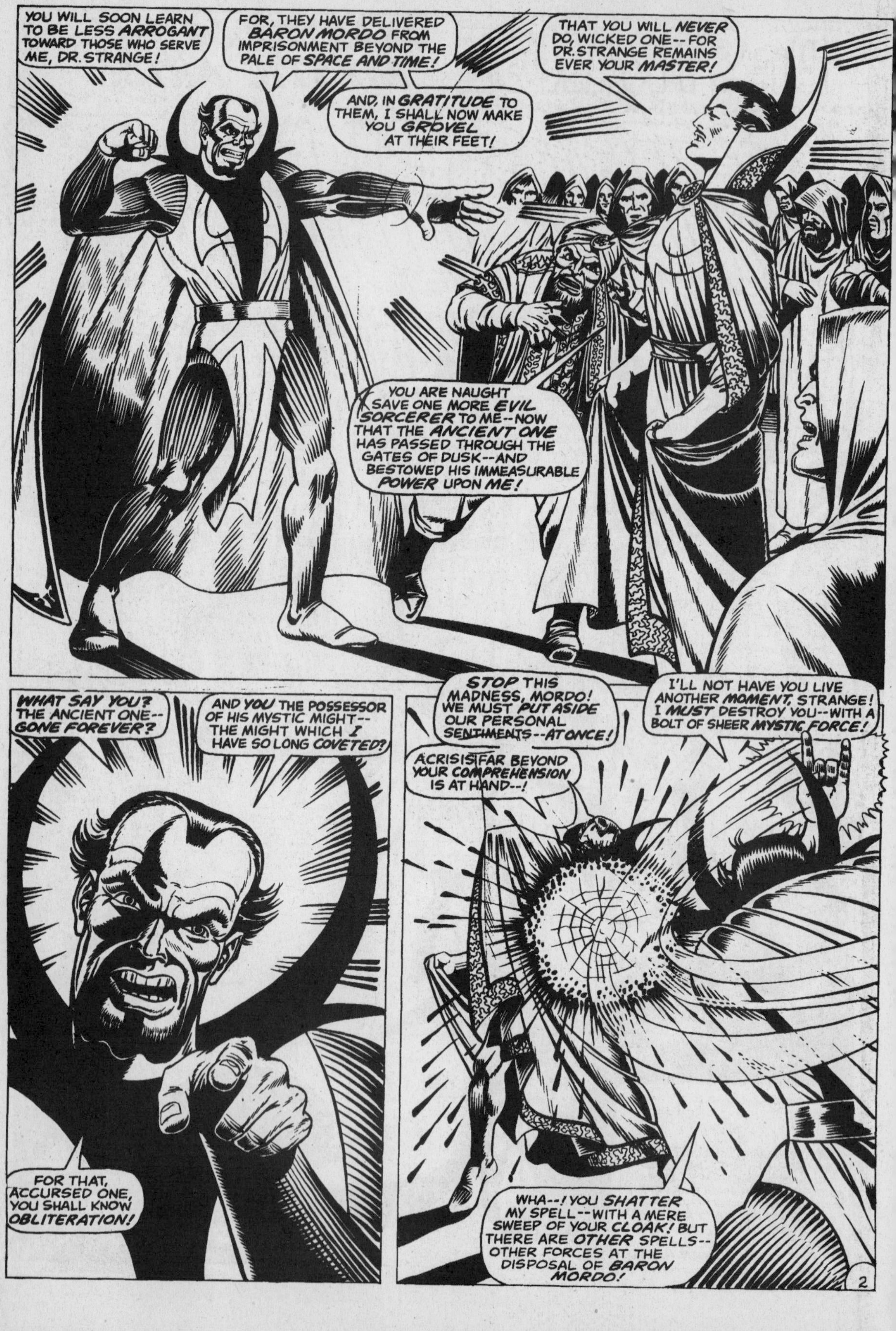
YOU WILL SOON LEARN TO BE LESS ARROGANT TOWARD THOSE WHO SERVE ME, DR. STRANGE!
FOR, THEY HAVE DELIVERED BARON MORDO FROM IMPRISONMENT BEYOND THE PALE OF SPACE AND TIME!
AND, IN GRATITUDE TO THEM, I SHALL NOW MAKE YOU GROVEL AT THEIR FEET!
THAT YOU WILL NEVER DO, WICKED ONE-- FOR DR. STRANGE REMAINS EVER YOUR MASTER!
YOU ARE NAUGHT SAVE ONE MORE EVIL SORCERER TO ME--NOW THAT THE ANCIENT ONE HAS PASSED THROUGH THE GATES OF DUSK--AND BESTOWED HIS IMMEASURABLE POWER UPON ME!
WHAT SAY YOU? THE ANCIENT ONE-- GONE FOREVER?
AND YOU THE POSSESSOR OF HIS MYSTIC MIGHT-- THE MIGHT WHICH I HAVE SO LONG COVETED?
FOR THAT, ACCURSED ONE, YOU SHALL KNOW OBLITERATION!
STOP THIS MADNESS, MORDO! WE MUST PUT ASIDE OUR PERSONAL SENTIMENTS--AT ONCE!
A CRISIS FAR BEYOND YOUR COMPREHENSION IS AT HAND--!
I'LL NOT HAVE YOU LIVE ANOTHER MOMENT, STRANGE! I MUST DESTROY YOU--WITH A BOLT OF SHEER MYSTIC FORCE!
WHA--! YOU SHATTER MY SPELL--WITH A MERE SWEEP OF YOUR CLOAK! BUT THERE ARE OTHER SPELLS-- OTHER FORCES AT THE DISPOSAL OF BARON MORDO!
2

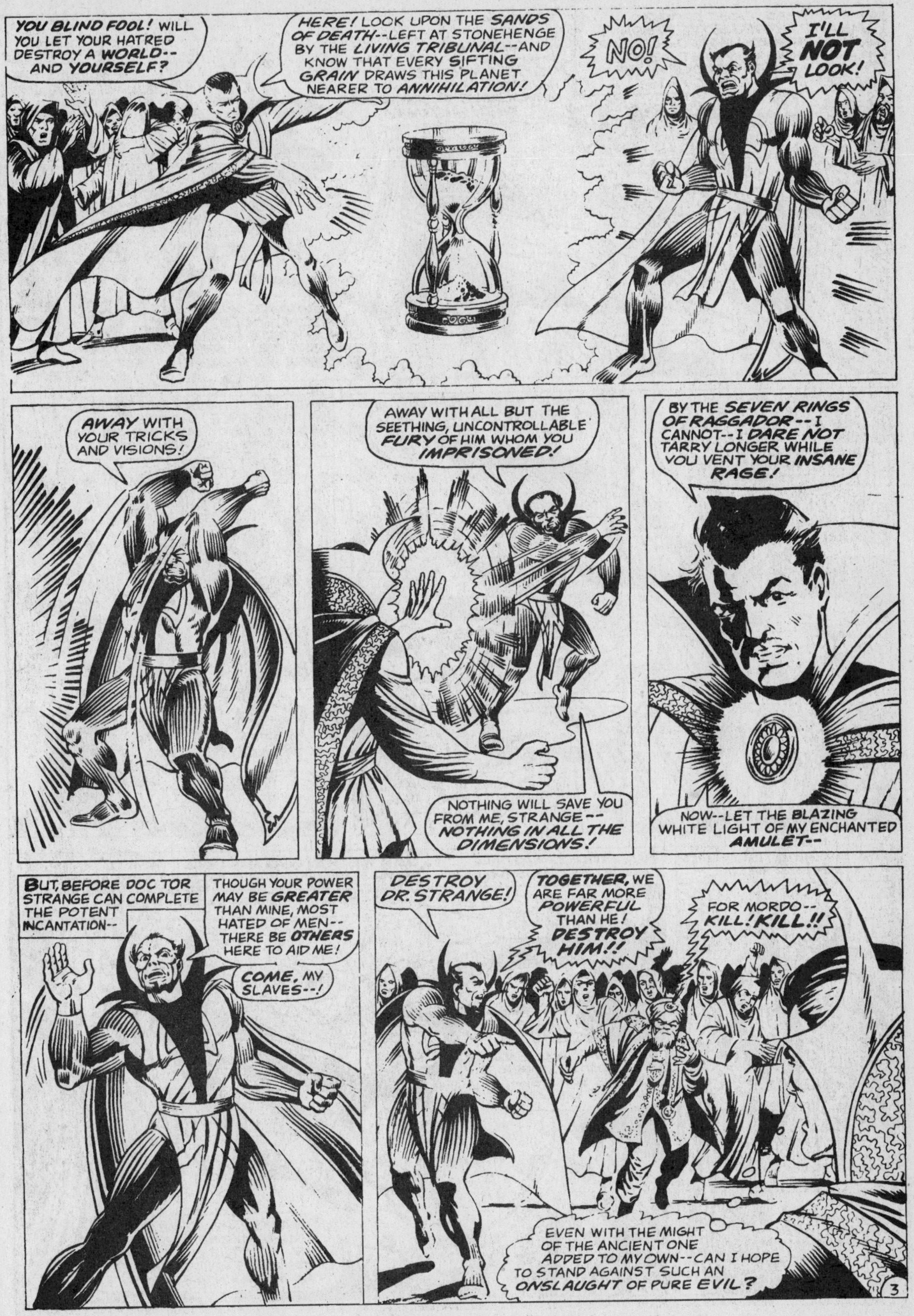
YOU BLIND FOOL! WILL YOU LET YOUR HATRED DESTROY A WORLD-- AND YOURSELF?
HERE! LOOK UPON THE SANDS OF DEATH--LEFT AT STONEHENGE BY THE LIVING TRIBUNAL--AND KNOW THAT EVERY SIFTING GRAIN DRAWS THIS PLANET NEARER TO ANNIHILATION!
NO!
I'LL NOT LOOK!
AWAY WITH YOUR TRICKS AND VISIONS!
AWAY WITH ALL BUT THE SEETHING, UNCONTROLLABLE FURY OF HIM WHOM YOU IMPRISONED!
NOTHING WILL SAVE YOU FROM ME, STRANGE-- NOTHING IN ALL THE DIMENSIONS!
BY THE SEVEN RINGS OF RAGGADOR--I CANNOT--I DARE NOT TARRY LONGER WHILE YOU VENT YOUR INSANE RAGE!
NOW--LET THE BLAZING WHITE LIGHT OF MY ENCHANTED AMULET--
BUT, BEFORE DOC TOR STRANGE CAN COMPLETE THE POTENT INCANTATION--
THOUGH YOUR POWER MAY BE GREATER THAN MINE, MOST HATED OF MEN-- THERE BE OTHERS HERE TO AID ME!
COME, MY SLAVES--!
DESTROY DR. STRANGE!
TOGETHER, WE ARE FAR MORE POWERFUL THAN HE! DESTROY HIM!!
FOR MORDO-- KILL! KILL!!
EVEN WITH THE MIGHT OF THE ANCIENT ONE ADDED TO MY OWN--CAN I HOPE TO STAND AGAINST SUCH AN ONSLAUGHT OF PURE EVIL?
3

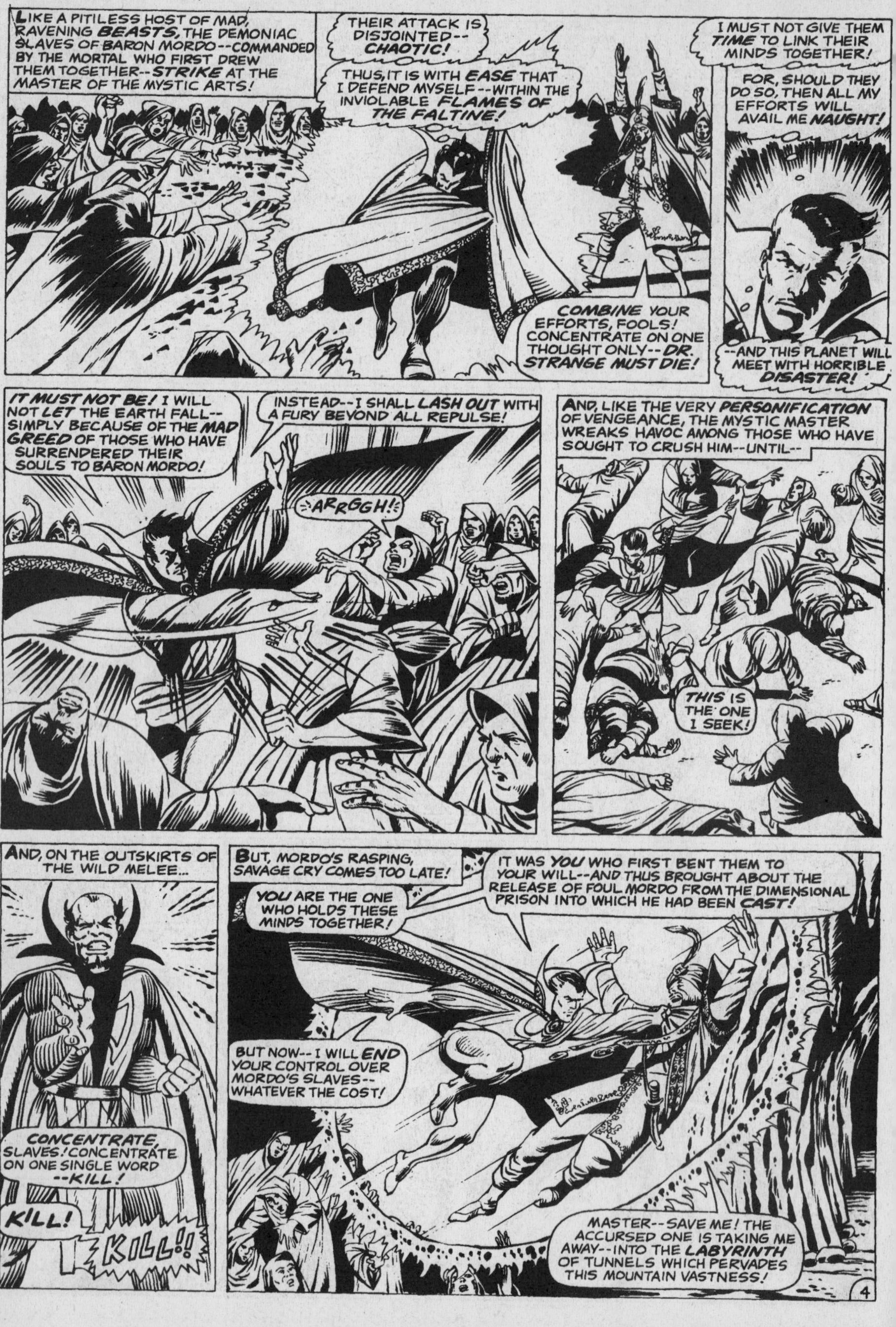
LIKE A PITILESS HOST OF MAD, RAVENING BEASTS, THE DEMONIAC SLAVES OF BARON MORDO--COMMANDED BY THE MORTAL WHO FIRST DREW THEM TOGETHER--STRIKE AT THE MASTER OF THE MYSTIC ARTS!
THEIR ATTACK IS DISJOINTED--CHAOTIC!
THUS, IT IS WITH EASE THAT I DEFEND MYSELF--WITHIN THE INVIOLABLE FLAMES OF THE FALTINE!
COMBINE YOUR EFFORTS, FOOLS! CONCENTRATE ON ONE THOUGHT ONLY--DR. STRANGE MUST DIE!
I MUST NOT GIVE THEM TIME TO LINK THEIR MINDS TOGETHER!
FOR, SHOULD THEY DO SO, THEN ALL MY EFFORTS WILL AVAIL ME NAUGHT!
--AND THIS PLANET WILL MEET WITH HORRIBLE DISASTER!
IT MUST NOT BE! I WILL NOT LET THE EARTH FALL--SIMPLY BECAUSE OF THE MAD GREED OF THOSE WHO HAVE SURRENDERED THEIR SOULS TO BARON MORDO!
INSTEAD--I SHALL LASH OUT WITH A FURY BEYOND ALL REPULSE!
ARRGGH!
AND, LIKE THE VERY PERSONIFICATION OF VENGEANCE, THE MYSTIC MASTER WREAKS HAVOC AMONG THOSE WHO HAVE SOUGHT TO CRUSH HIM--UNTIL--
THIS IS THE ONE I SEEK!
AND, ON THE OUTSKIRTS OF THE WILD MELEE...
CONCENTRATE, SLAVES! CONCENTRATE ON ONE SINGLE WORD --KILL!
KILL!
KILL!
BUT, MORDO'S RASPING, SAVAGE CRY COMES TOO LATE!
YOU ARE THE ONE WHO HOLDS THESE MINDS TOGETHER!
IT WAS YOU WHO FIRST BENT THEM TO YOUR WILL--AND THUS BROUGHT ABOUT THE RELEASE OF FOUL MORDO FROM THE DIMENSIONAL PRISON INTO WHICH HE HAD BEEN CAST!
BUT NOW--I WILL END YOUR CONTROL OVER MORDO'S SLAVES--WHATEVER THE COST!
MASTER--SAVE ME! THE ACCURSED ONE IS TAKING ME AWAY--INTO THE LABYRINTH OF TUNNELS WHICH PERVADES THIS MOUNTAIN VASTNESS!
4

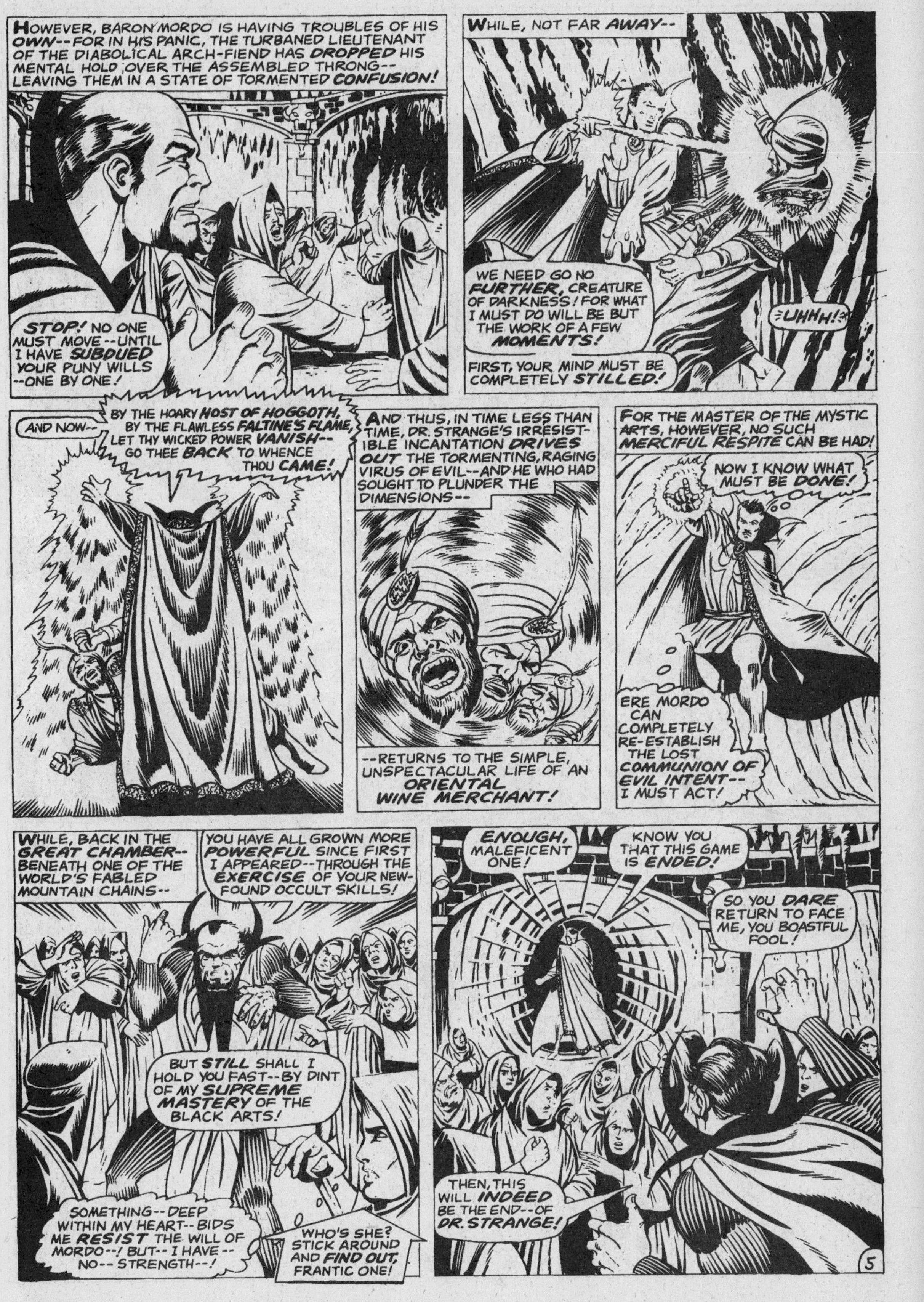
HOWEVER, BARON MORDO IS HAVING TROUBLES OF HIS OWN--FOR IN HIS PANIC, THE TURBANED LIEUTENANT OF THE DIABOLICAL ARCH-FIEND HAS DROPPED HIS MENTAL HOLD OVER THE ASSEMBLED THRONG--LEAVING THEM IN A STATE OF TORMENTED CONFUSION!
STOP! NO ONE MUST MOVE--UNTIL I HAVE SUBDUED YOUR PUNY WILLS--ONE BY ONE!
WHILE, NOT FAR AWAY--
WE NEED GO NO FURTHER, CREATURE OF DARKNESS! FOR WHAT I MUST DO WILL BE BUT THE WORK OF A FEW MOMENTS!
FIRST, YOUR MIND MUST BE COMPLETELY STILLED!
UHHH!
AND NOW--
BY THE HOARY HOST OF HOGGOTH, BY THE FLAWLESS FALTINE'S FLAME, LET THY WICKED POWER VANISH--GO THEE BACK TO WHENCE THOU CAME!
AND THUS, IN TIME LESS THAN TIME, DR. STRANGE'S IRRESISTIBLE INCANTATION DRIVES OUT THE TORMENTING, RAGING VIRUS OF EVIL--AND HE WHO HAD SOUGHT TO PLUNDER THE DIMENSIONS--
--RETURNS TO THE SIMPLE, UNSPECTACULAR LIFE OF AN ORIENTAL WINE MERCHANT!
FOR THE MASTER OF THE MYSTIC ARTS, HOWEVER, NO SUCH MERCIFUL RESPITE CAN BE HAD!
NOW I KNOW WHAT MUST BE DONE!
ERE MORDO CAN COMPLETELY RE-ESTABLISH THE LOST COMMUNION OF EVIL INTENT--I MUST ACT!
WHILE, BACK IN THE GREAT CHAMBER--BENEATH ONE OF THE WORLD'S FABLED MOUNTAIN CHAINS--
YOU HAVE ALL GROWN MORE POWERFUL SINCE FIRST I APPEARED--THROUGH THE EXERCISE OF YOUR NEW-FOUND OCCULT SKILLS!
BUT STILL SHALL I HOLD YOU FAST--BY DINT OF MY SUPREME MASTERY OF THE BLACK ARTS!
SOMETHING--DEEP WITHIN MY HEART--BIDS ME RESIST THE WILL OF MORDO--! BUT--I HAVE--NO--STRENGTH--!
WHO'S SHE? STICK AROUND AND FIND OUT, FRANTIC ONE!
ENOUGH, MALEFICENT ONE!
KNOW YOU THAT THIS GAME IS ENDED!
SO YOU DARE RETURN TO FACE ME, YOU BOASTFUL FOOL!
THEN, THIS WILL INDEED BE THE END--OF DR. STRANGE!

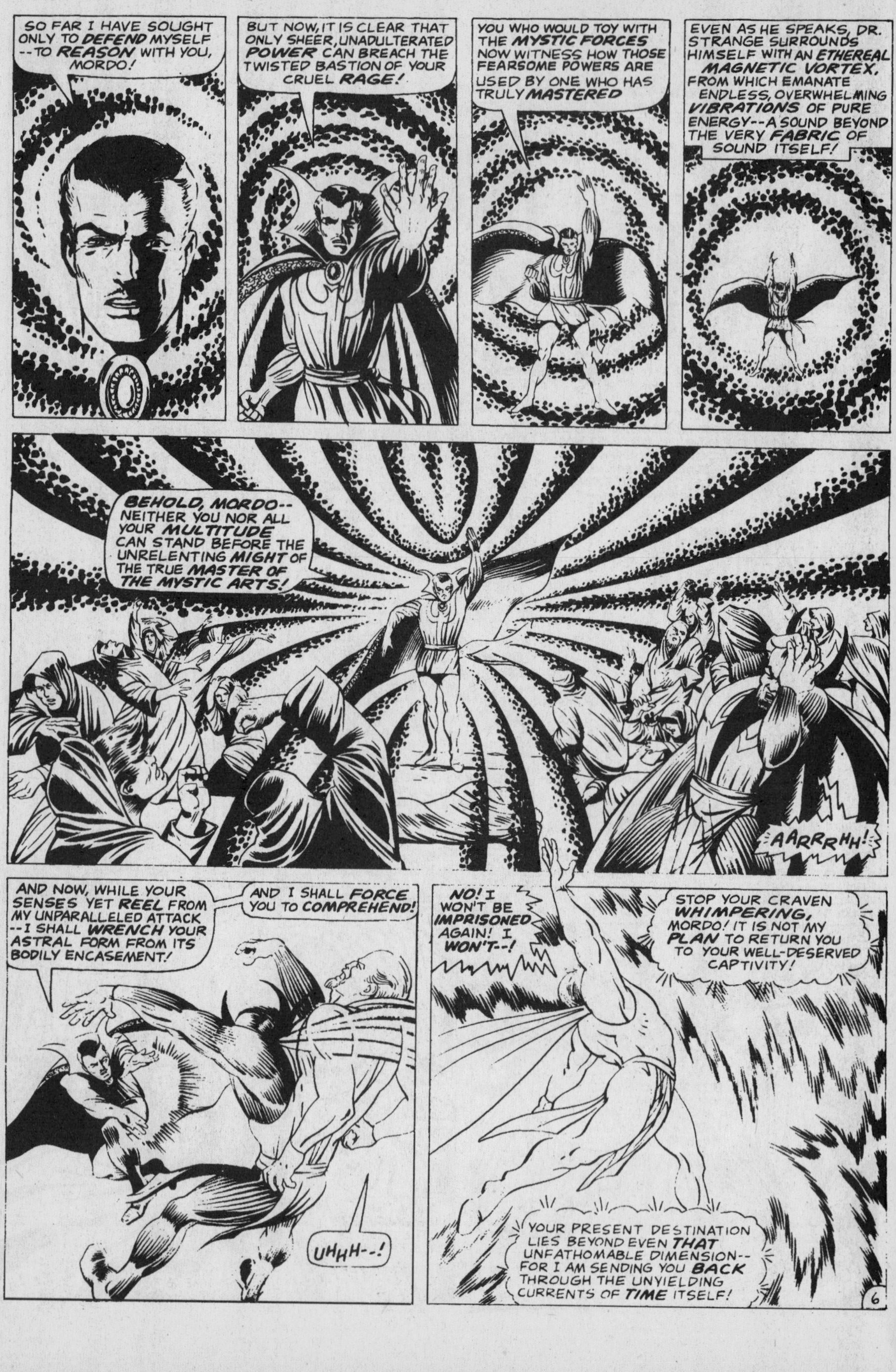

SO FAR I HAVE SOUGHT ONLY TO DEFEND MYSELF --TO REASON WITH YOU, MORDO!
BUT NOW, IT IS CLEAR THAT ONLY SHEER, UNADULTERATED POWER CAN BREACH THE TWISTED BASTION OF YOUR CRUEL RAGE!
YOU WHO WOULD TOY WITH THE MYSTIC FORCES NOW WITNESS HOW THOSE FEARSOME POWERS ARE USED BY ONE WHO HAS TRULY MASTERED
EVEN AS HE SPEAKS, DR. STRANGE SURROUNDS HIMSELF WITH AN ETHEREAL MAGNETIC VORTEX, FROM WHICH EMANATE ENDLESS, OVERWHELMING VIBRATIONS OF PURE ENERGY--A SOUND BEYOND THE VERY FABRIC OF SOUND ITSELF!
BEHOLD, MORDO-- NEITHER YOU NOR ALL YOUR MULTITUDE CAN STAND BEFORE THE UNRELENTING MIGHT OF THE TRUE MASTER OF THE MYSTIC ARTS!
AARRRHH!
AND NOW, WHILE YOUR SENSES YET REEL FROM MY UNPARALLELED ATTACK --I SHALL WRENCH YOUR ASTRAL FORM FROM ITS BODILY ENCASEMENT!
AND I SHALL FORCE YOU TO COMPREHEND!
UHHH--!
NO! I WON'T BE IMPRISONED AGAIN! I WON'T--!
STOP YOUR CRAVEN WHIMPERING, MORDO! IT IS NOT MY PLAN TO RETURN YOU TO YOUR WELL-DESERVED CAPTIVITY!
YOUR PRESENT DESTINATION LIES BEYOND EVEN THAT UNFATHOMABLE DIMENSION-- FOR I AM SENDING YOU BACK THROUGH THE UNYIELDING CURRENTS OF TIME ITSELF!

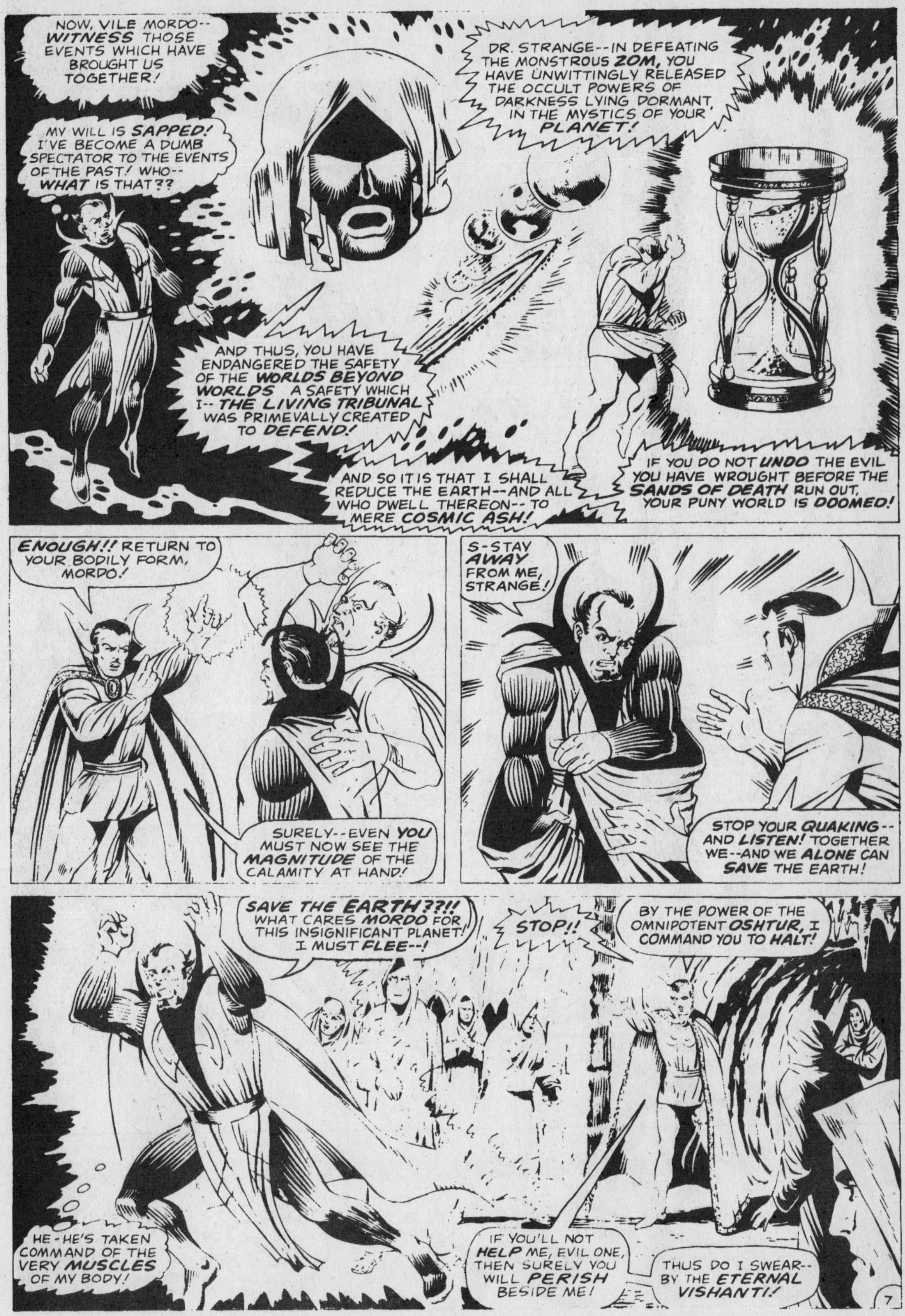
NOW, VILE MORDO-- WITNESS THOSE EVENTS WHICH HAVE BROUGHT US TOGETHER!
MY WILL IS SAPPED! I'VE BECOME A DUMB SPECTATOR TO THE EVENTS OF THE PAST! WHO-- WHAT IS THAT??
DR. STRANGE--IN DEFEATING THE MONSTROUS ZOM, YOU HAVE UNWITTINGLY RELEASED THE OCCULT POWERS OF DARKNESS LYING DORMANT IN THE MYSTICS OF YOUR PLANET!
AND THUS, YOU HAVE ENDANGERED THE SAFETY OF THE WORLDS BEYOND WORLDS A SAFETY WHICH I-- THE LIVING TRIBUNAL WAS PRIMEVALLY CREATED TO DEFEND!
AND SO IT IS THAT I SHALL REDUCE THE EARTH--AND ALL WHO DWELL THEREON-- TO MERE COSMIC ASH!
IF YOU DO NOT UNDO THE EVIL YOU HAVE WROUGHT BEFORE THE SANDS OF DEATH RUN OUT, YOUR PUNY WORLD IS DOOMED!
ENOUGH!! RETURN TO YOUR BODILY FORM, MORDO!
SURELY--EVEN YOU MUST NOW SEE THE MAGNITUDE OF THE CALAMITY AT HAND!
S-STAY AWAY FROM ME, STRANGE!
STOP YOUR QUAKING-- AND LISTEN! TOGETHER WE--AND WE ALONE CAN SAVE THE EARTH!
SAVE THE EARTH??!! WHAT CARES MORDO FOR THIS INSIGNIFICANT PLANET! I MUST FLEE--!
STOP!!
BY THE POWER OF THE OMNIPOTENT OSHTUR, I COMMAND YOU TO HALT!
HE-HE'S TAKEN COMMAND OF THE VERY MUSCLES OF MY BODY!
IF YOU'LL NOT HELP ME, EVIL ONE, THEN SURELY YOU WILL PERISH BESIDE ME!
THUS DO I SWEAR-- BY THE ETERNAL VISHANTI!
7

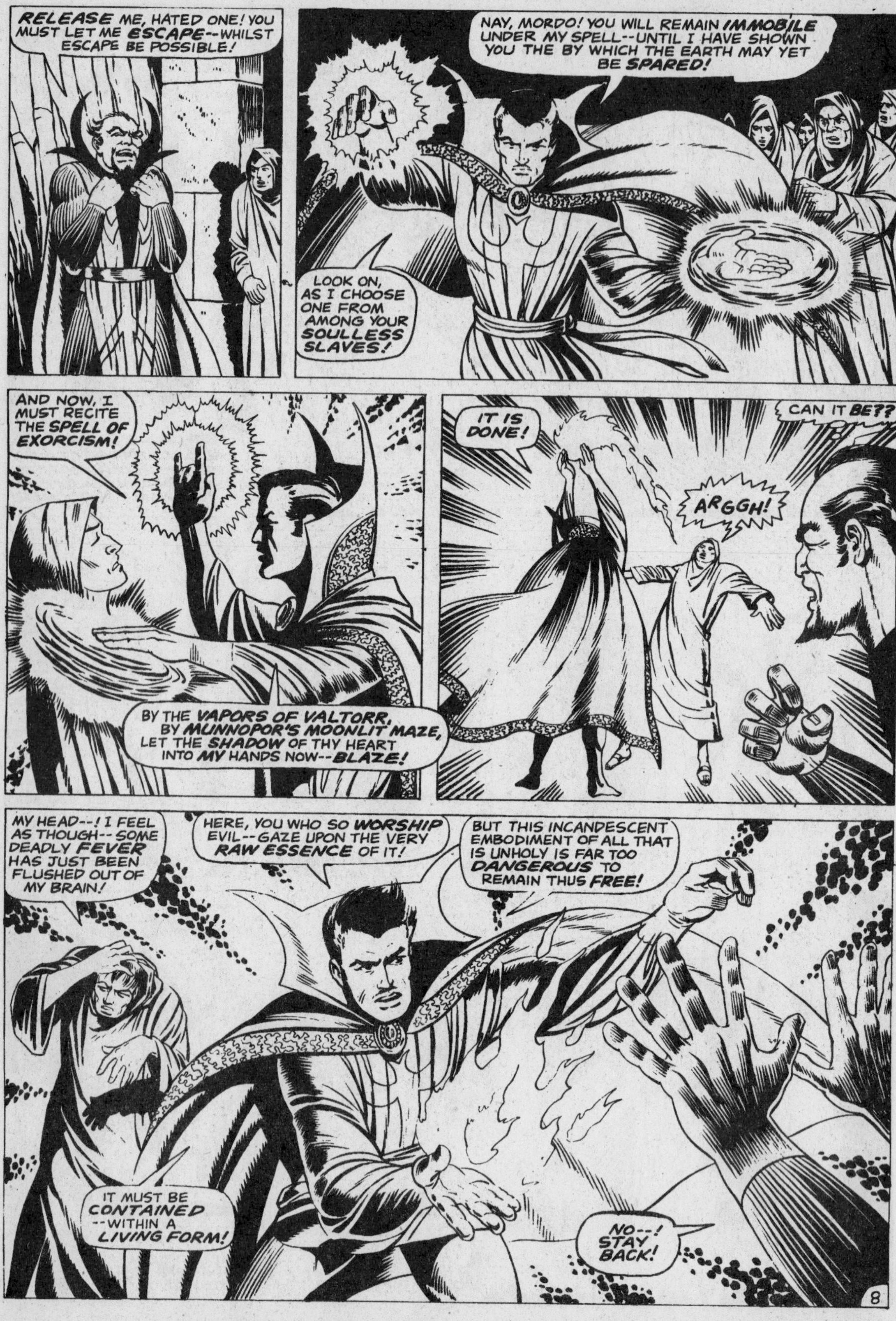
RELEASE ME, HATED ONE! YOU MUST LET ME ESCAPE--WHILST ESCAPE BE POSSIBLE!
NAY, MORDO! YOU WILL REMAIN IMMOBILE UNDER MY SPELL--UNTIL I HAVE SHOWN YOU THE BY WHICH THE EARTH MAY YET BE SPARED!
LOOK ON, AS I CHOOSE ONE FROM AMONG YOUR SOULLESS SLAVES!
AND NOW, I MUST RECITE THE SPELL OF EXORCISM!
BY THE VAPORS OF VALTORR, BY MUNNOPOR'S MOONLIT MAZE, LET THE SHADOW OF THY HEART INTO MY HANDS NOW--BLAZE!
IT IS DONE!
CAN IT BE??
ARGGH!
MY HEAD--! I FEEL AS THOUGH--SOME DEADLY FEVER HAS JUST BEEN FLUSHED OUT OF MY BRAIN!
HERE, YOU WHO SO WORSHIP EVIL--GAZE UPON THE VERY RAW ESSENCE OF IT!
BUT THIS INCANDESCENT EMBODIMENT OF ALL THAT IS UNHOLY IS FAR TOO DANGEROUS TO REMAIN THUS FREE!
IT MUST BE CONTAINED --WITHIN A LIVING FORM!
NO--! STAY BACK!
8

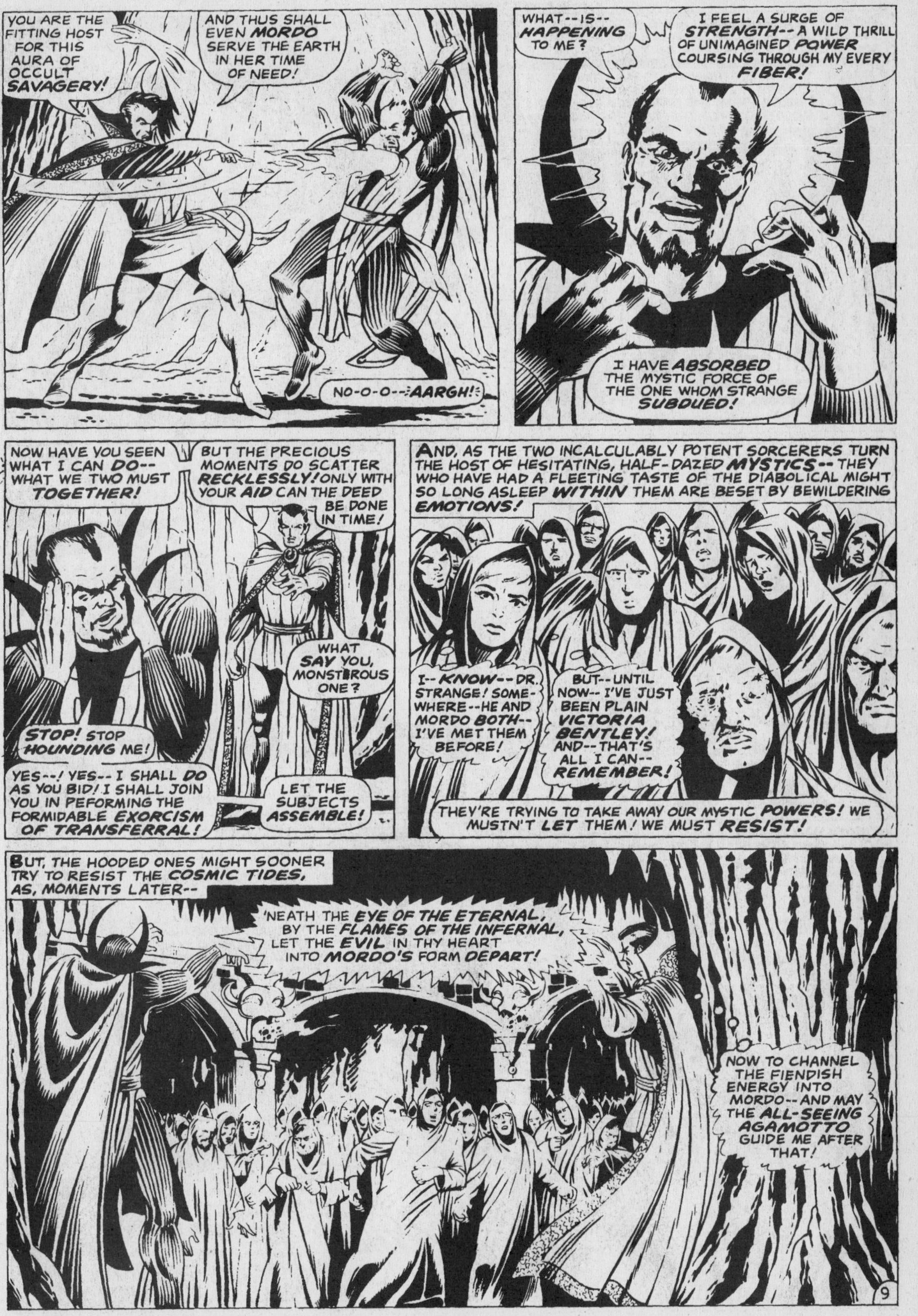
YOU ARE THE FITTING HOST FOR THIS AURA OF OCCULT SAVAGERY!
AND THUS SHALL EVEN MORDO SERVE THE EARTH IN HER TIME OF NEED!
NO-O-O--AARGH!
WHAT--IS--HAPPENING TO ME?
I FEEL A SURGE OF STRENGTH--A WILD THRILL OF UNIMAGINED POWER COURSING THROUGH MY EVERY FIBER!
I HAVE ABSORBED THE MYSTIC FORCE OF THE ONE WHOM STRANGE SUBDUED!
NOW HAVE YOU SEEN WHAT I CAN DO--WHAT WE TWO MUST TOGETHER!
BUT THE PRECIOUS MOMENTS DO SCATTER RECKLESSLY! ONLY WITH YOUR AID CAN THE DEED BE DONE IN TIME!
WHAT SAY YOU, MONSTROUS ONE?
STOP! STOP HOUNDING ME!
YES--! YES--I SHALL DO AS YOU BID! I SHALL JOIN YOU IN PEFORMING THE FORMIDABLE EXORCISM OF TRANSFERRAL!
LET THE SUBJECTS ASSEMBLE!
AND, AS THE TWO INCALCULABLY POTENT SORCERERS TURN THE HOST OF HESITATING, HALF-DAZED MYSTICS--THEY WHO HAVE HAD A FLEETING TASTE OF THE DIABOLICAL MIGHT SO LONG ASLEEP WITHIN THEM ARE BESET BY BEWILDERING EMOTIONS!
I--KNOW--DR. STRANGE! SOMEWHERE--HE AND MORDO BOTH--I'VE MET THEM BEFORE!
BUT--UNTIL NOW--I'VE JUST BEEN PLAIN VICTORIA BENTLEY! AND--THAT'S ALL I CAN--REMEMBER!
THEY'RE TRYING TO TAKE AWAY OUR MYSTIC POWERS! WE MUSTN'T LET THEM! WE MUST RESIST!
BUT, THE HOODED ONES MIGHT SOONER TRY TO RESIST THE COSMIC TIDES, AS, MOMENTS LATER--
'NEATH THE EYE OF THE ETERNAL, BY THE FLAMES OF THE INFERNAL, LET THE EVIL IN THY HEART INTO MORDO'S FORM DEPART!
NOW TO CHANNEL THE FIENDISH ENERGY INTO MORDO--AND MAY THE ALL-SEEING AGAMOTTO GUIDE ME AFTER THAT!

THUS, O TRUE BELIEVER, HAVE WE COME TO WITNESS THE MOST MIND-STAGGERING DISPLAY OF PURE MYSTIC SKILL IN ALL THE ANNALS OF *NECROMANCY* (AS FAR AS *THIS* ISH GOES, ANYWAY)!

FOR, DR. STRANGE, STRAINING TO THE UTMOST HIS MIGHTY POWERS--*DRAINS* THE DEADLY OCCULT FORCE FROM THE GATHERED FIGURES--AND *DRIVES* IT INTO THE WILLING FORM OF BARON MORDO!

THE SPELL IS A COMPLETE SUCCESS! BUT WHAT OF *MORDO--?*

IS HE WRAPT BY AGONY--OR ENWRAPT IN A SHUDDERING *ECSTASY OF EVIL?*

ARRGG!

'TIS ACCOMPLISHED!

AND LONG SHALL MANKIND *RUE* THE DAY!

MANKIND? *HAH!* THE VERY UNIVERSE *ITSELF* WOULD TREMBLE IN A PAROXYSM OF *FEAR* COULD IT NOW BEHOLD MY AWESOME RESOLVE! FOR I AM BECOME--

--POWER INCARNATE!!

AND FIRST TO KNOW MY PITILESS FURY SHALL BE HE WHOM I DO *LOATHE* ABOVE ALL *CREATURES!*

MORDO, YOU FOOL--! WAIT! THE *LIVING TRIBUNAL--!*

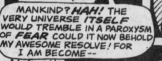

FALL, STRANGE! FALL HELPLESS AT MY *FEET*--THAT YOU MAY MEET YOUR ULTIMATE *FATE!*

THUS, YOUR *PHYSICAL FORM* SHALL LIE HERE FOREVER--WHILE YOUR *ASTRAL* BODY SHALL BE ETERNALLY CONSIGNED TO THE *WORLD OF THE MILLION PERILS!*

AND NOW-- BY THE GHASTLY VISAGE OF *DORMAMMU*--I SHALL GRASP ALL INFINITY IN MY HAND--AND *CRUSH* IT!!

NEXT ISH: "--AND A *SCOURGE* SHALL COME UPON YOU!"

10

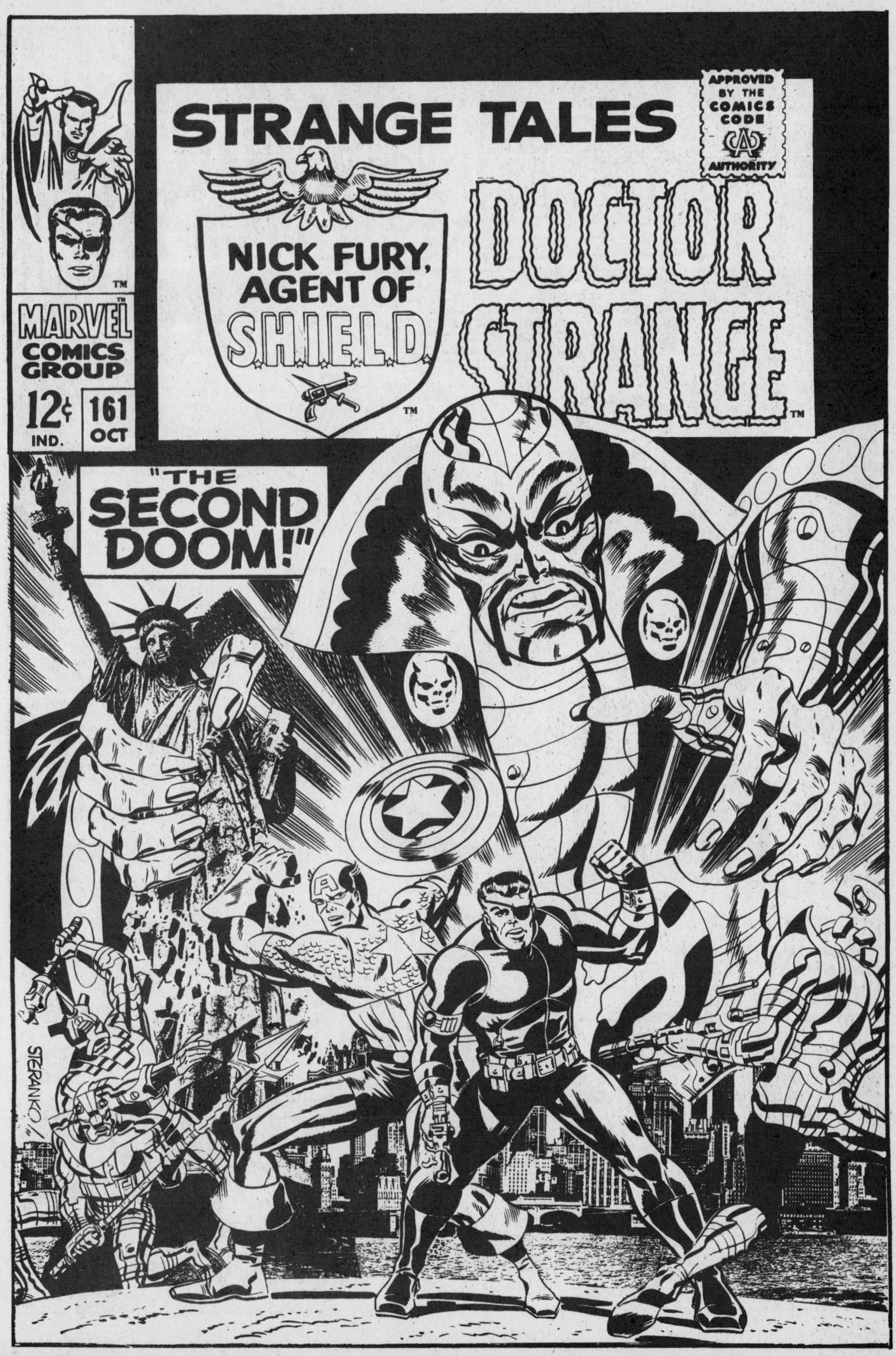

MARVEL COMICS GROUP
12¢ IND.
161 OCT
STRANGE TALES
APPROVED BY THE COMICS CODE AUTHORITY
NICK FURY, AGENT OF S.H.I.E.L.D.
DOCTOR STRANGE
"THE SECOND DOOM!"
STERANKO

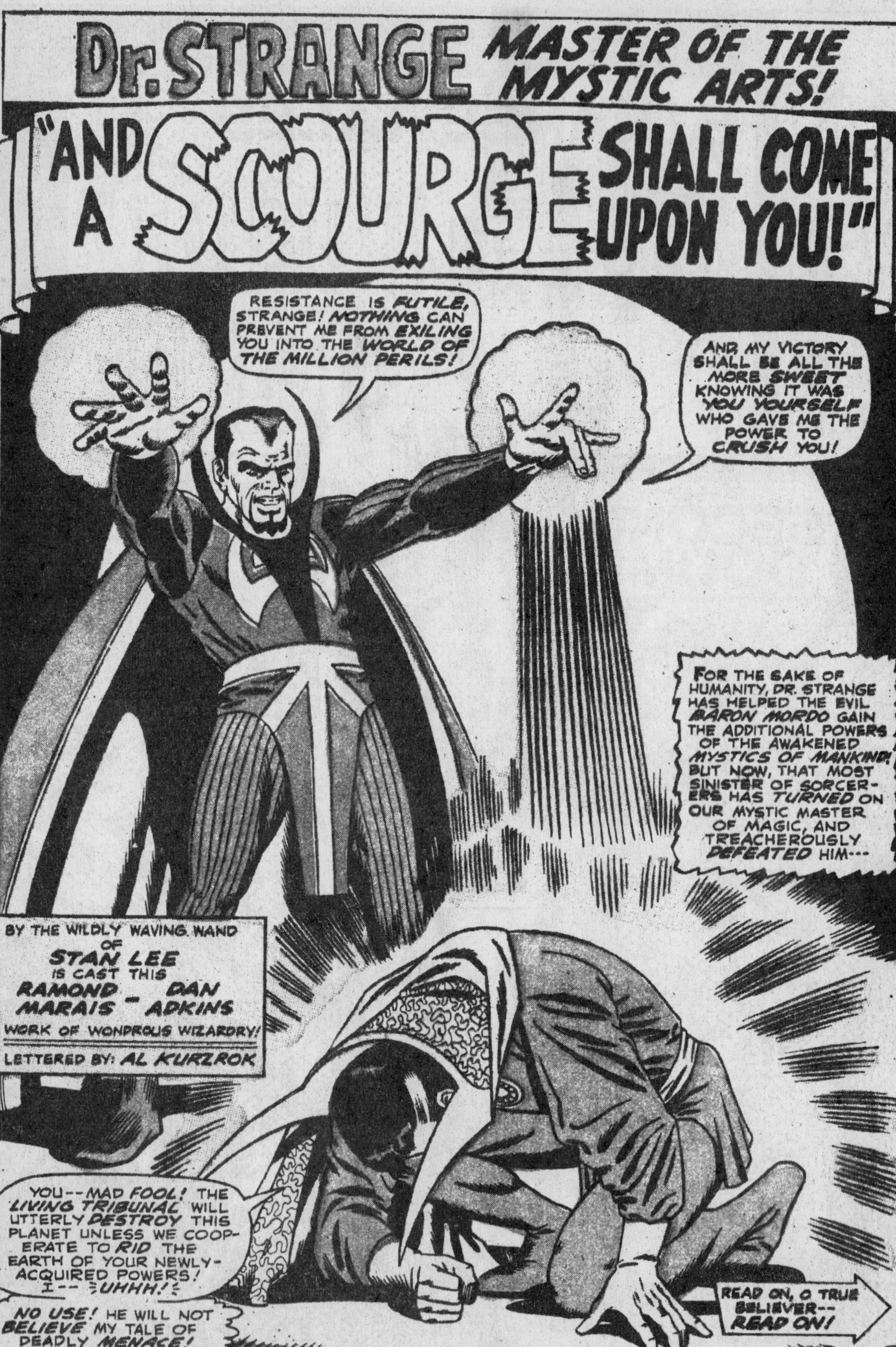
DR. STRANGE MASTER OF THE MYSTIC ARTS!
"AND A SCOURGE SHALL COME UPON YOU!"
RESISTANCE IS FUTILE, STRANGE! NOTHING CAN PREVENT ME FROM EXILING YOU INTO THE WORLD OF THE MILLION PERILS!
AND MY VICTORY SHALL BE ALL THE MORE SWEET KNOWING IT WAS YOU YOURSELF WHO GAVE ME THE POWER TO CRUSH YOU!
FOR THE SAKE OF HUMANITY, DR. STRANGE HAS HELPED THE EVIL BARON MORDO GAIN THE ADDITIONAL POWERS OF THE AWAKENED MYSTICS OF MANKIND! BUT NOW, THAT MOST SINISTER OF SORCERERS HAS TURNED ON OUR MYSTIC MASTER OF MAGIC, AND TREACHEROUSLY DEFEATED HIM---
BY THE WILDLY WAVING WAND OF STAN LEE IS CAST THIS RAMOND MARAIS - DAN ADKINS WORK OF WONDROUS WIZARDRY!
LETTERED BY: AL KURZROK
YOU--MAD FOOL! THE LIVING TRIBUNAL WILL UTTERLY DESTROY THIS PLANET UNLESS WE COOPERATE TO RID THE EARTH OF YOUR NEWLY-ACQUIRED POWERS! I-- UHHH!
NO USE! HE WILL NOT BELIEVE MY TALE OF DEADLY MENACE!
READ ON, O TRUE BELIEVER-- READ ON!
1

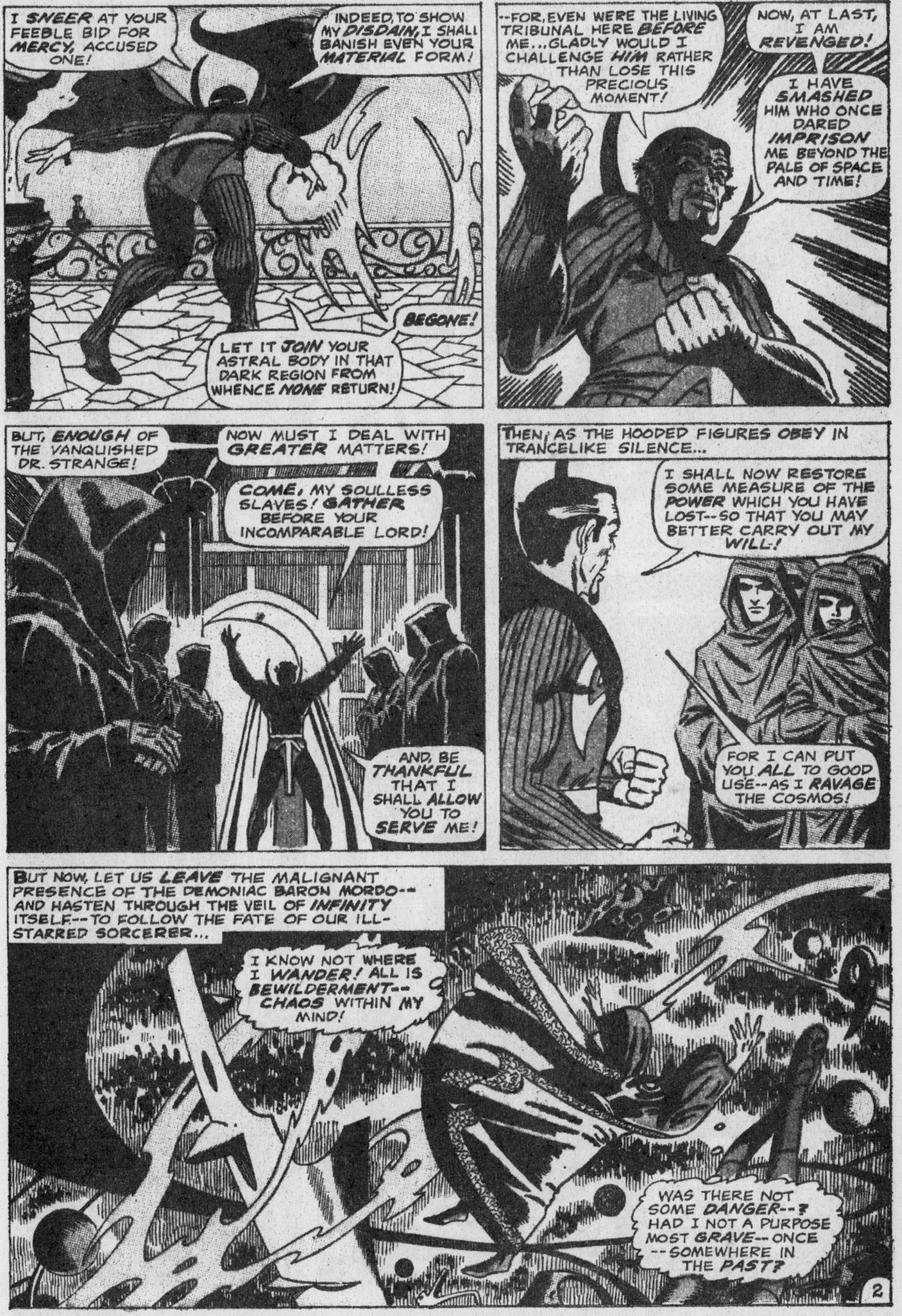
I SNEER AT YOUR FEEBLE BID FOR MERCY, ACCUSED ONE!
INDEED, TO SHOW MY DISDAIN, I SHALL BANISH EVEN YOUR MATERIAL FORM!
BEGONE!
LET IT JOIN YOUR ASTRAL BODY IN THAT DARK REGION FROM WHENCE NONE RETURN!
--FOR, EVEN WERE THE LIVING TRIBUNAL HERE BEFORE ME...GLADLY WOULD I CHALLENGE HIM RATHER THAN LOSE THIS PRECIOUS MOMENT!
NOW, AT LAST, I AM REVENGED!
I HAVE SMASHED HIM WHO ONCE DARED IMPRISON ME BEYOND THE PALE OF SPACE AND TIME!
BUT, ENOUGH OF THE VANQUISHED DR. STRANGE!
NOW MUST I DEAL WITH GREATER MATTERS!
COME, MY SOULLESS SLAVES! GATHER BEFORE YOUR INCOMPARABLE LORD!
AND, BE THANKFUL THAT I SHALL ALLOW YOU TO SERVE ME!
THEN, AS THE HOODED FIGURES OBEY IN TRANCELIKE SILENCE...
I SHALL NOW RESTORE SOME MEASURE OF THE POWER WHICH YOU HAVE LOST--SO THAT YOU MAY BETTER CARRY OUT MY WILL!
FOR I CAN PUT YOU ALL TO GOOD USE--AS I RAVAGE THE COSMOS!
BUT NOW, LET US LEAVE THE MALIGNANT PRESENCE OF THE DEMONIAC BARON MORDO-- AND HASTEN THROUGH THE VEIL OF INFINITY ITSELF--TO FOLLOW THE FATE OF OUR ILL-STARRED SORCERER...
I KNOW NOT WHERE I WANDER! ALL IS BEWILDERMENT-- CHAOS WITHIN MY MIND!
WAS THERE NOT SOME DANGER--? HAD I NOT A PURPOSE MOST GRAVE--ONCE --SOMEWHERE IN THE PAST?
2

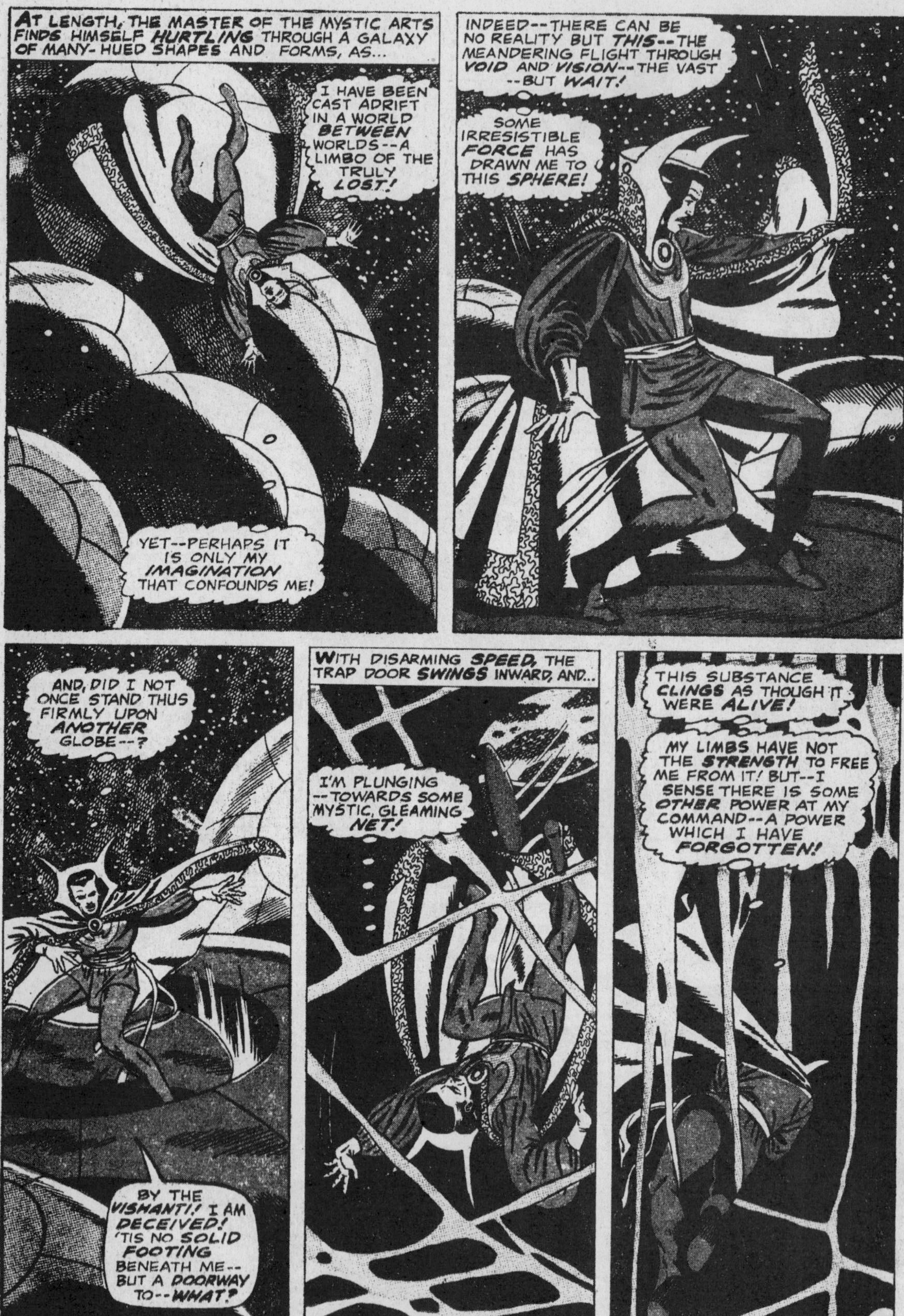
AT LENGTH, THE MASTER OF THE MYSTIC ARTS FINDS HIMSELF HURTLING THROUGH A GALAXY OF MANY-HUED SHAPES AND FORMS, AS...
I HAVE BEEN CAST ADRIFT IN A WORLD BETWEEN WORLDS--A LIMBO OF THE TRULY LOST!
YET--PERHAPS IT IS ONLY MY IMAGINATION THAT CONFOUNDS ME!
INDEED--THERE CAN BE NO REALITY BUT THIS--THE MEANDERING FLIGHT THROUGH VOID AND VISION--THE VAST --BUT WAIT!
SOME IRRESISTIBLE FORCE HAS DRAWN ME TO THIS SPHERE!
AND, DID I NOT ONCE STAND THUS FIRMLY UPON ANOTHER GLOBE--?
BY THE VISHANTI! I AM DECEIVED! 'TIS NO SOLID FOOTING BENEATH ME--BUT A DOORWAY TO--WHAT?
WITH DISARMING SPEED, THE TRAP DOOR SWINGS INWARD, AND...
I'M PLUNGING --TOWARDS SOME MYSTIC, GLEAMING NET!
THIS SUBSTANCE CLINGS AS THOUGH IT WERE ALIVE!
MY LIMBS HAVE NOT THE STRENGTH TO FREE ME FROM IT! BUT--I SENSE THERE IS SOME OTHER POWER AT MY COMMAND--A POWER WHICH I HAVE FORGOTTEN!
3

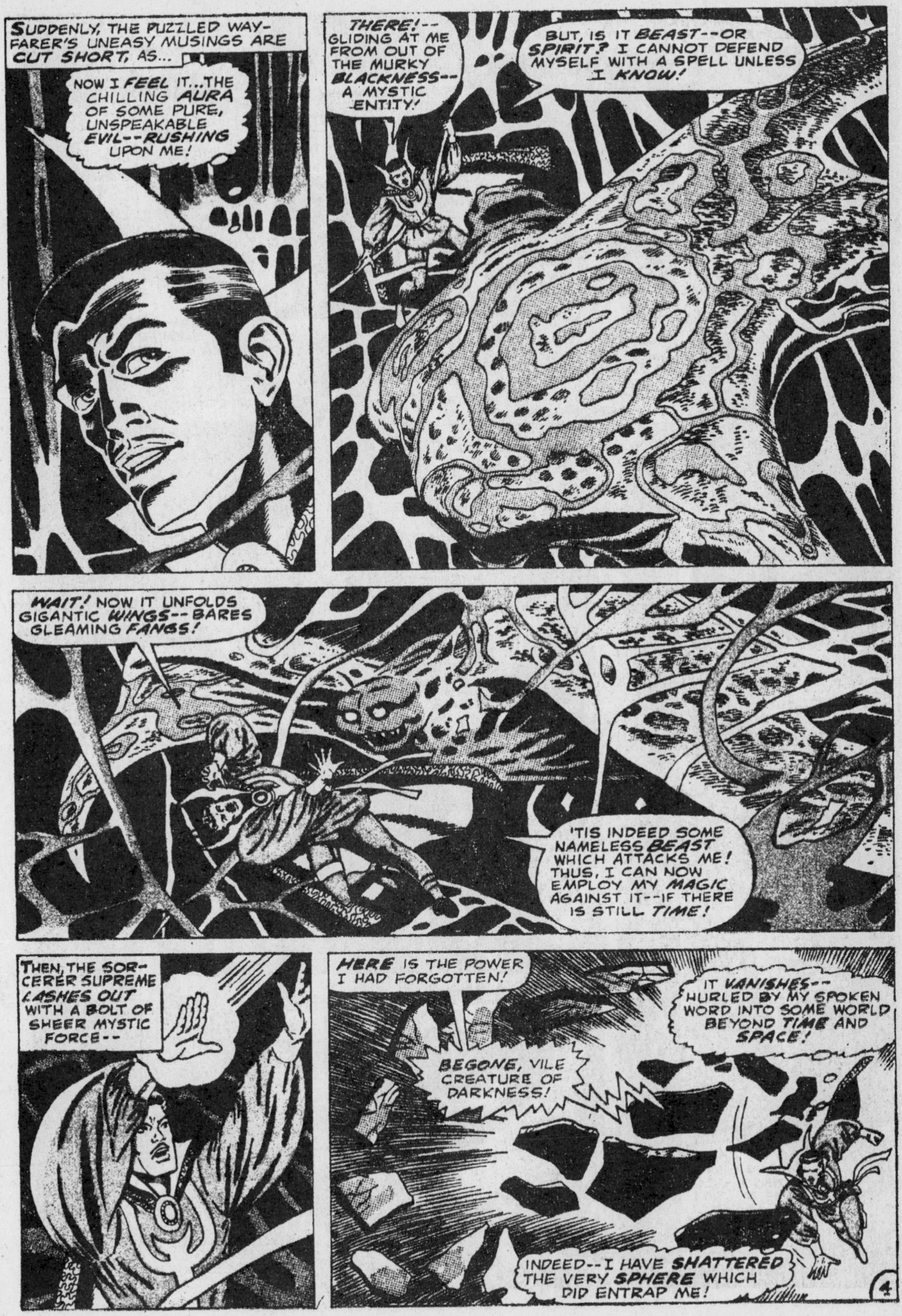
SUDDENLY, THE PUZZLED WAY-FARER'S UNEASY MUSINGS ARE CUT SHORT, AS...
NOW I FEEL IT...THE CHILLING AURA OF SOME PURE, UNSPEAKABLE EVIL--RUSHING UPON ME!
THERE!--GLIDING AT ME FROM OUT OF THE MURKY BLACKNESS--A MYSTIC ENTITY!
BUT, IS IT BEAST--OR SPIRIT? I CANNOT DEFEND MYSELF WITH A SPELL UNLESS I KNOW!
WAIT! NOW IT UNFOLDS GIGANTIC WINGS--BARES GLEAMING FANGS!
'TIS INDEED SOME NAMELESS BEAST WHICH ATTACKS ME! THUS, I CAN NOW EMPLOY MY MAGIC AGAINST IT--IF THERE IS STILL TIME!
THEN, THE SORCERER SUPREME LASHES OUT WITH A BOLT OF SHEER MYSTIC FORCE--
HERE IS THE POWER I HAD FORGOTTEN!
BEGONE, VILE CREATURE OF DARKNESS!
IT VANISHES--HURLED BY MY SPOKEN WORD INTO SOME WORLD BEYOND TIME AND SPACE!
INDEED--I HAVE SHATTERED THE VERY SPHERE WHICH DID ENTRAP ME!
4

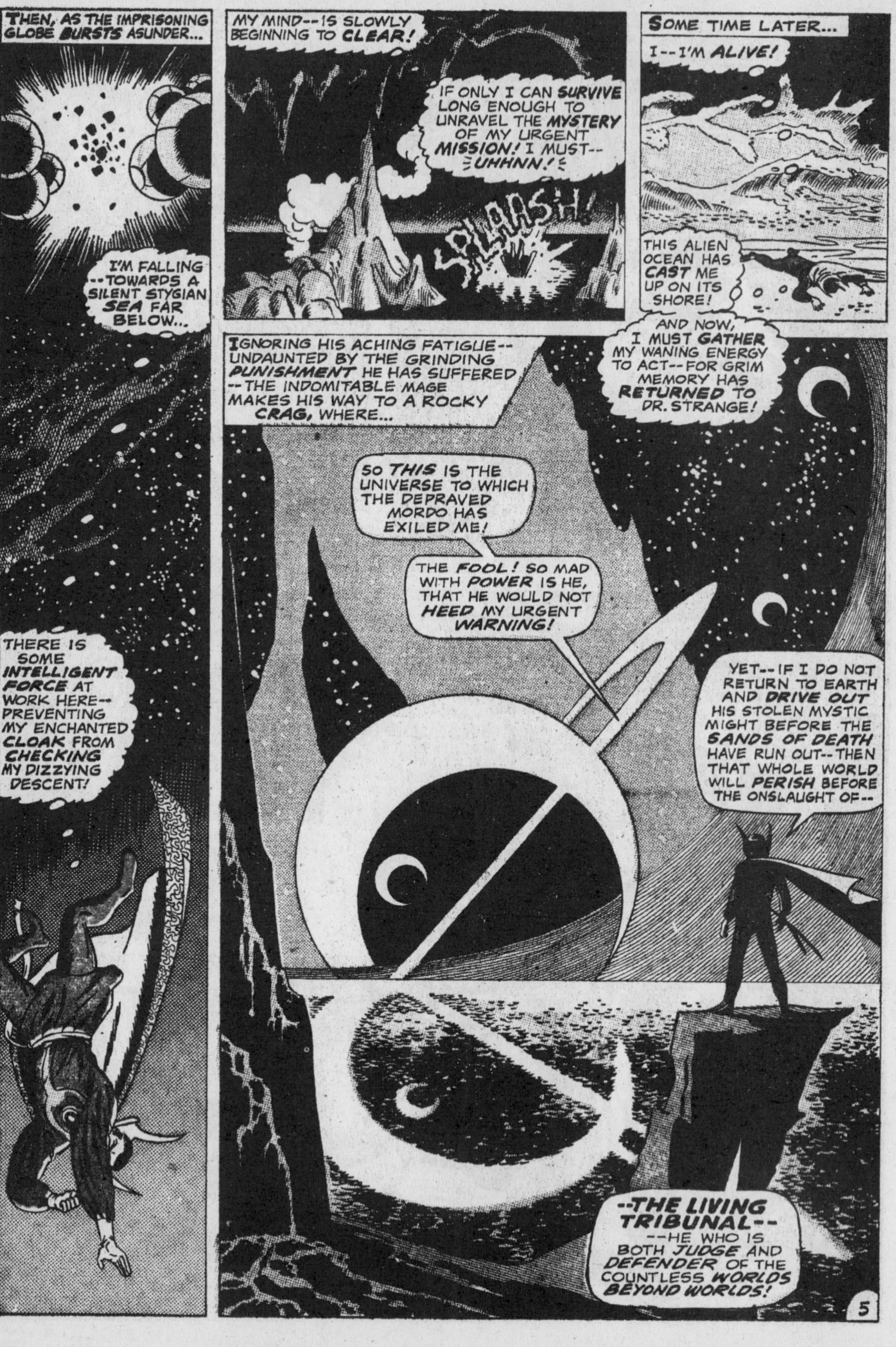

THEN, AS THE IMPRISONING GLOBE BURSTS ASUNDER...
I'M FALLING --TOWARDS A SILENT STYGIAN SEA FAR BELOW...
THERE IS SOME INTELLIGENT FORCE AT WORK HERE--PREVENTING MY ENCHANTED CLOAK FROM CHECKING MY DIZZYING DESCENT!
MY MIND--IS SLOWLY BEGINNING TO CLEAR!
IF ONLY I CAN SURVIVE LONG ENOUGH TO UNRAVEL THE MYSTERY OF MY URGENT MISSION! I MUST-- UHHNN!
SPLAASH!
SOME TIME LATER...
I--I'M ALIVE!
THIS ALIEN OCEAN HAS CAST ME UP ON ITS SHORE!
AND NOW, I MUST GATHER MY WANING ENERGY TO ACT--FOR GRIM MEMORY HAS RETURNED TO DR. STRANGE!
IGNORING HIS ACHING FATIGUE--UNDAUNTED BY THE GRINDING PUNISHMENT HE HAS SUFFERED --THE INDOMITABLE MAGE MAKES HIS WAY TO A ROCKY CRAG, WHERE...
SO THIS IS THE UNIVERSE TO WHICH THE DEPRAVED MORDO HAS EXILED ME!
THE FOOL! SO MAD WITH POWER IS HE, THAT HE WOULD NOT HEED MY URGENT WARNING!
YET--IF I DO NOT RETURN TO EARTH AND DRIVE OUT HIS STOLEN MYSTIC MIGHT BEFORE THE SANDS OF DEATH HAVE RUN OUT--THEN THAT WHOLE WORLD WILL PERISH BEFORE THE ONSLAUGHT OF--
--THE LIVING TRIBUNAL--
--HE WHO IS BOTH JUDGE AND DEFENDER OF THE COUNTLESS WORLDS BEYOND WORLDS!
5

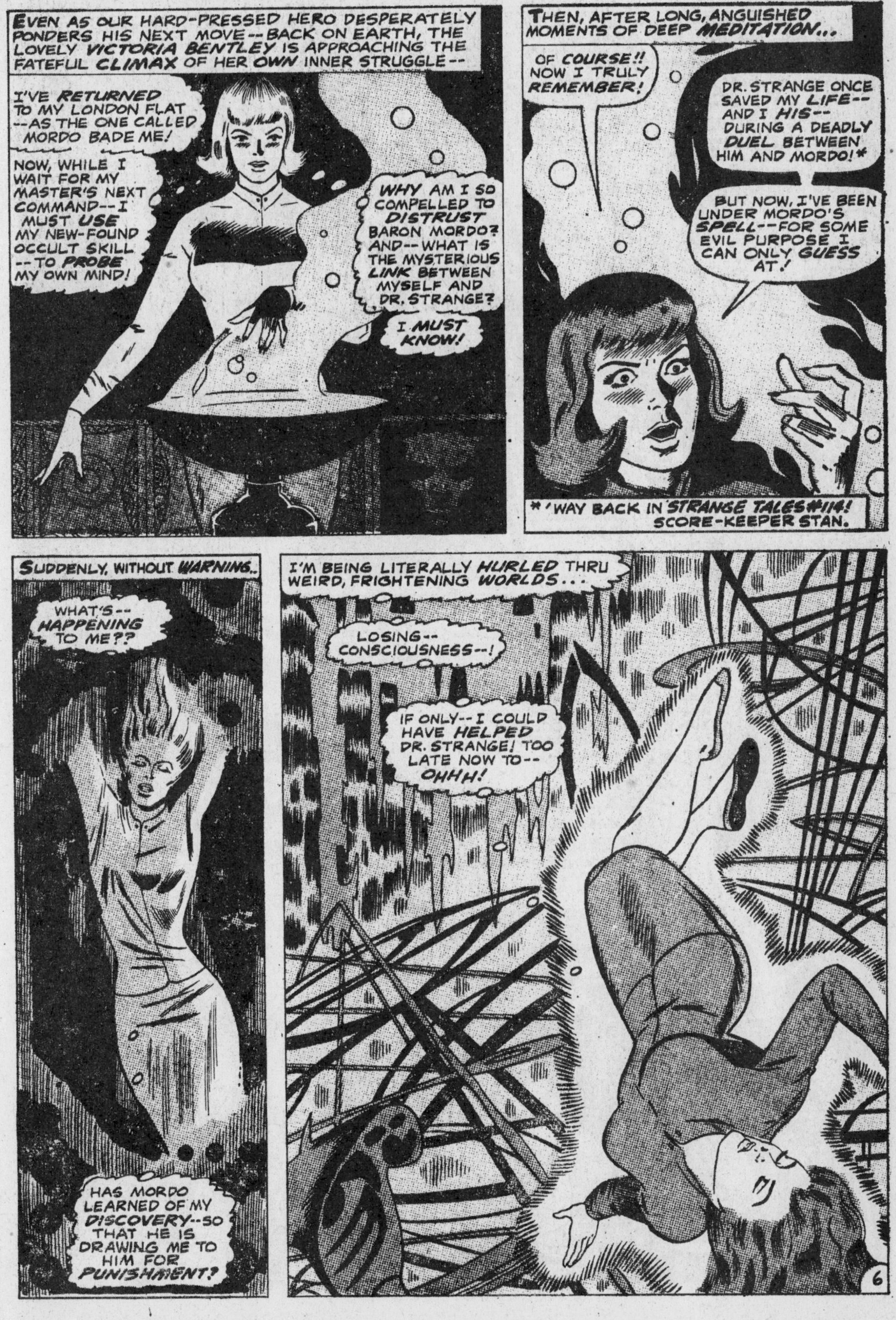
EVEN AS OUR HARD-PRESSED HERO DESPERATELY PONDERS HIS NEXT MOVE--BACK ON EARTH, THE LOVELY VICTORIA BENTLEY IS APPROACHING THE FATEFUL CLIMAX OF HER OWN INNER STRUGGLE--
I'VE RETURNED TO MY LONDON FLAT--AS THE ONE CALLED MORDO BADE ME!
NOW, WHILE I WAIT FOR MY MASTER'S NEXT COMMAND--I MUST USE MY NEW-FOUND OCCULT SKILL--TO PROBE MY OWN MIND!
WHY AM I SO COMPELLED TO DISTRUST BARON MORDO? AND--WHAT IS THE MYSTERIOUS LINK BETWEEN MYSELF AND DR. STRANGE?
I MUST KNOW!
THEN, AFTER LONG, ANGUISHED MOMENTS OF DEEP MEDITATION...
OF COURSE!! NOW I TRULY REMEMBER!
DR. STRANGE ONCE SAVED MY LIFE--AND I HIS--DURING A DEADLY DUEL BETWEEN HIM AND MORDO!*
BUT NOW, I'VE BEEN UNDER MORDO'S SPELL--FOR SOME EVIL PURPOSE I CAN ONLY GUESS AT!
*'WAY BACK IN STRANGE TALES #114! SCORE-KEEPER STAN.
SUDDENLY, WITHOUT WARNING..
WHAT'S--HAPPENING TO ME??
HAS MORDO LEARNED OF MY DISCOVERY--SO THAT HE IS DRAWING ME TO HIM FOR PUNISHMENT?
I'M BEING LITERALLY HURLED THRU WEIRD, FRIGHTENING WORLDS...
LOSING--CONSCIOUSNESS--!
IF ONLY--I COULD HAVE HELPED DR. STRANGE! TOO LATE NOW TO--OHHH!
6

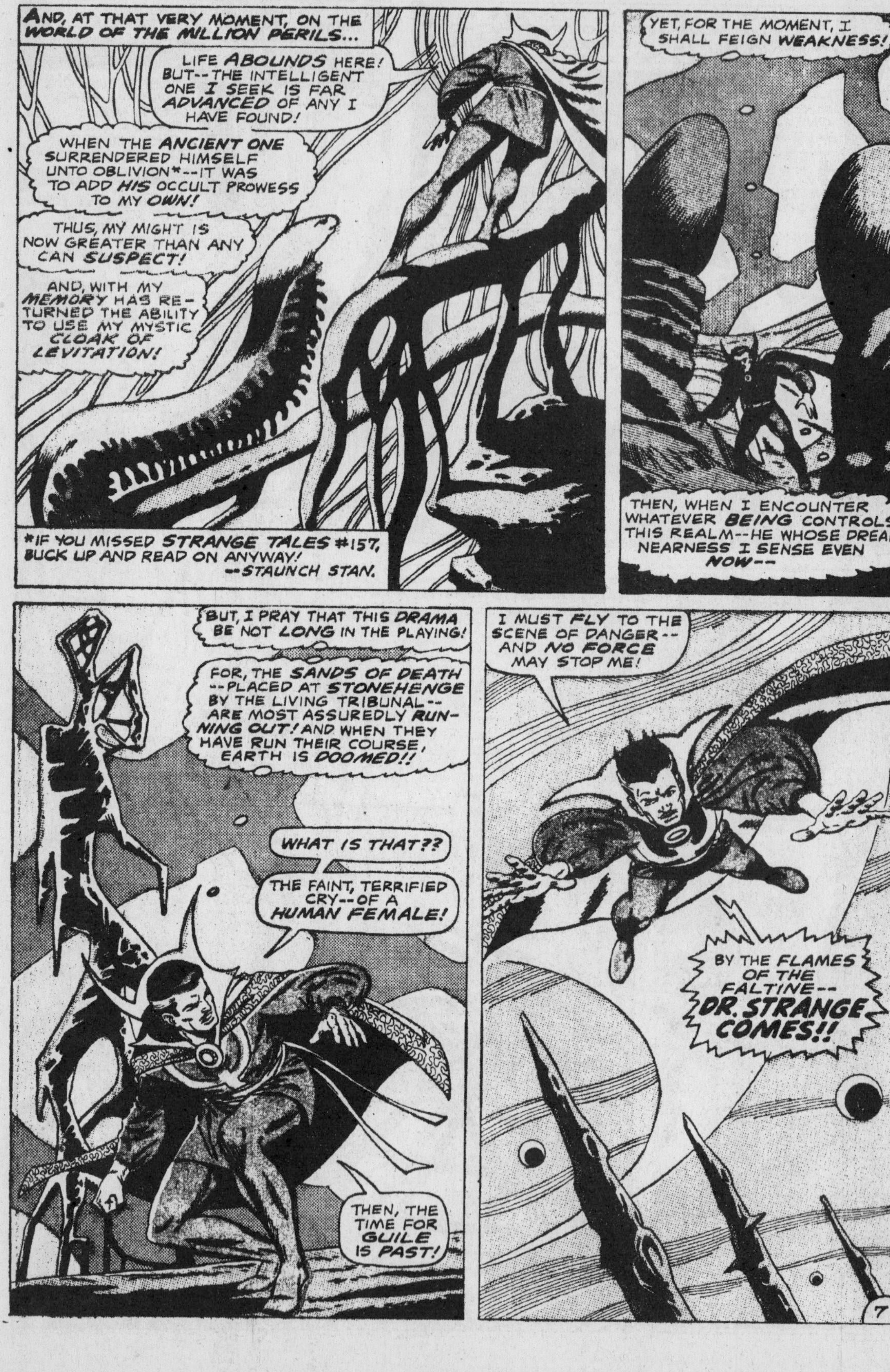
AND, AT THAT VERY MOMENT, ON THE WORLD OF THE MILLION PERILS...
LIFE ABOUNDS HERE! BUT--THE INTELLIGENT ONE I SEEK IS FAR ADVANCED OF ANY I HAVE FOUND!
WHEN THE ANCIENT ONE SURRENDERED HIMSELF UNTO OBLIVION*--IT WAS TO ADD HIS OCCULT PROWESS TO MY OWN!
THUS, MY MIGHT IS NOW GREATER THAN ANY CAN SUSPECT!
AND, WITH MY MEMORY HAS RETURNED THE ABILITY TO USE MY MYSTIC CLOAK OF LEVITATION!
*IF YOU MISSED STRANGE TALES #157, BUCK UP AND READ ON ANYWAY! --STAUNCH STAN.
YET, FOR THE MOMENT, I SHALL FEIGN WEAKNESS!
THEN, WHEN I ENCOUNTER WHATEVER BEING CONTROLS THIS REALM--HE WHOSE DREAD NEARNESS I SENSE EVEN NOW--
BUT, I PRAY THAT THIS DRAMA BE NOT LONG IN THE PLAYING!
FOR, THE SANDS OF DEATH --PLACED AT STONEHENGE BY THE LIVING TRIBUNAL-- ARE MOST ASSUREDLY RUNNING OUT! AND WHEN THEY HAVE RUN THEIR COURSE, EARTH IS DOOMED!!
WHAT IS THAT??
THE FAINT, TERRIFIED CRY--OF A HUMAN FEMALE!
THEN, THE TIME FOR GUILE IS PAST!
I MUST FLY TO THE SCENE OF DANGER-- AND NO FORCE MAY STOP ME!
BY THE FLAMES OF THE FALTINE-- DR. STRANGE COMES!!
7

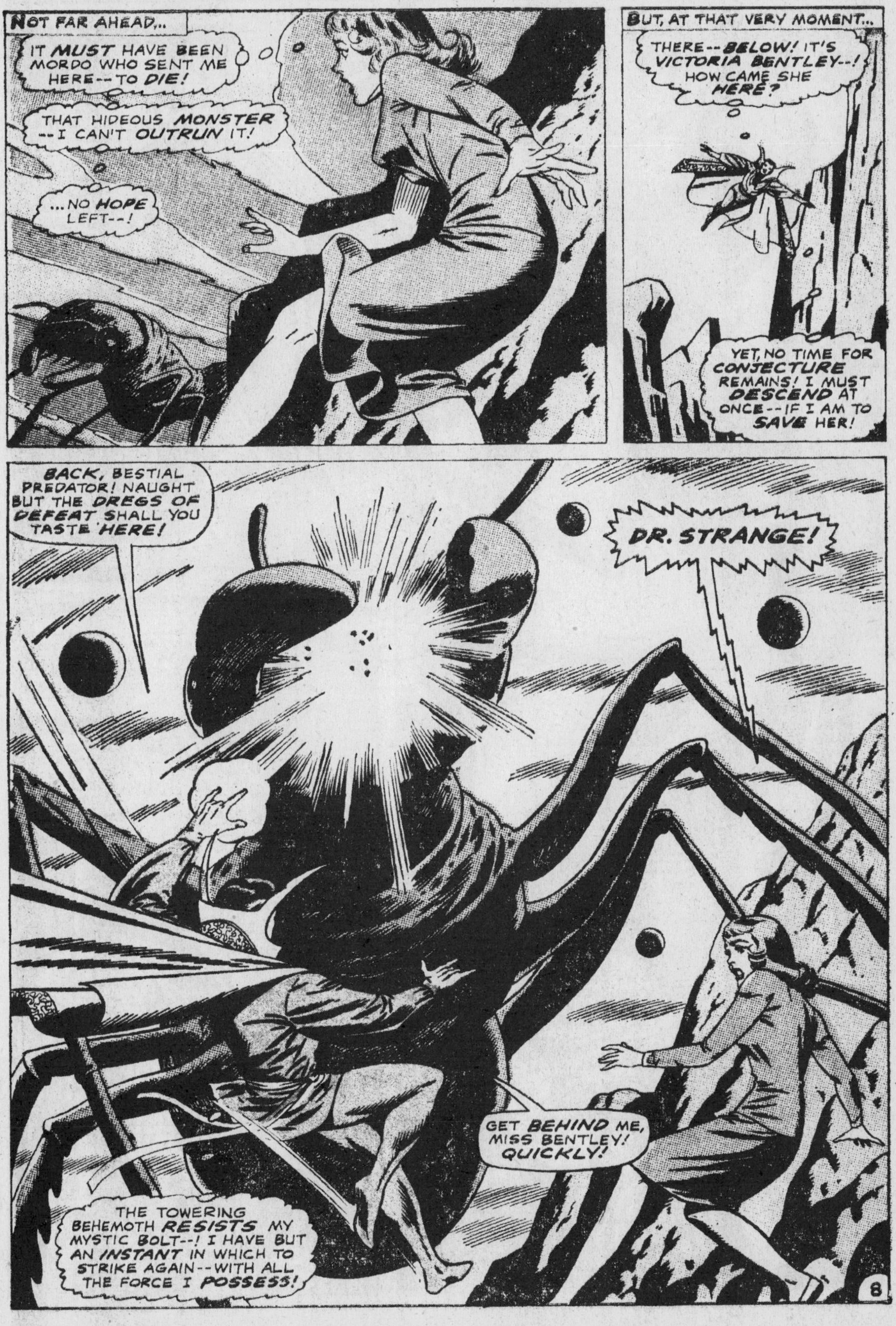
NOT FAR AHEAD...
IT MUST HAVE BEEN MORDO WHO SENT ME HERE--TO DIE!
THAT HIDEOUS MONSTER --I CAN'T OUTRUN IT!
...NO HOPE LEFT--!
BUT, AT THAT VERY MOMENT...
THERE--BELOW! IT'S VICTORIA BENTLEY--! HOW CAME SHE HERE?
YET, NO TIME FOR CONJECTURE REMAINS! I MUST DESCEND AT ONCE--IF I AM TO SAVE HER!
BACK, BESTIAL PREDATOR! NAUGHT BUT THE DREGS OF DEFEAT SHALL YOU TASTE HERE!
DR. STRANGE!
GET BEHIND ME, MISS BENTLEY! QUICKLY!
THE TOWERING BEHEMOTH RESISTS MY MYSTIC BOLT--! I HAVE BUT AN INSTANT IN WHICH TO STRIKE AGAIN--WITH ALL THE FORCE I POSSESS!
8

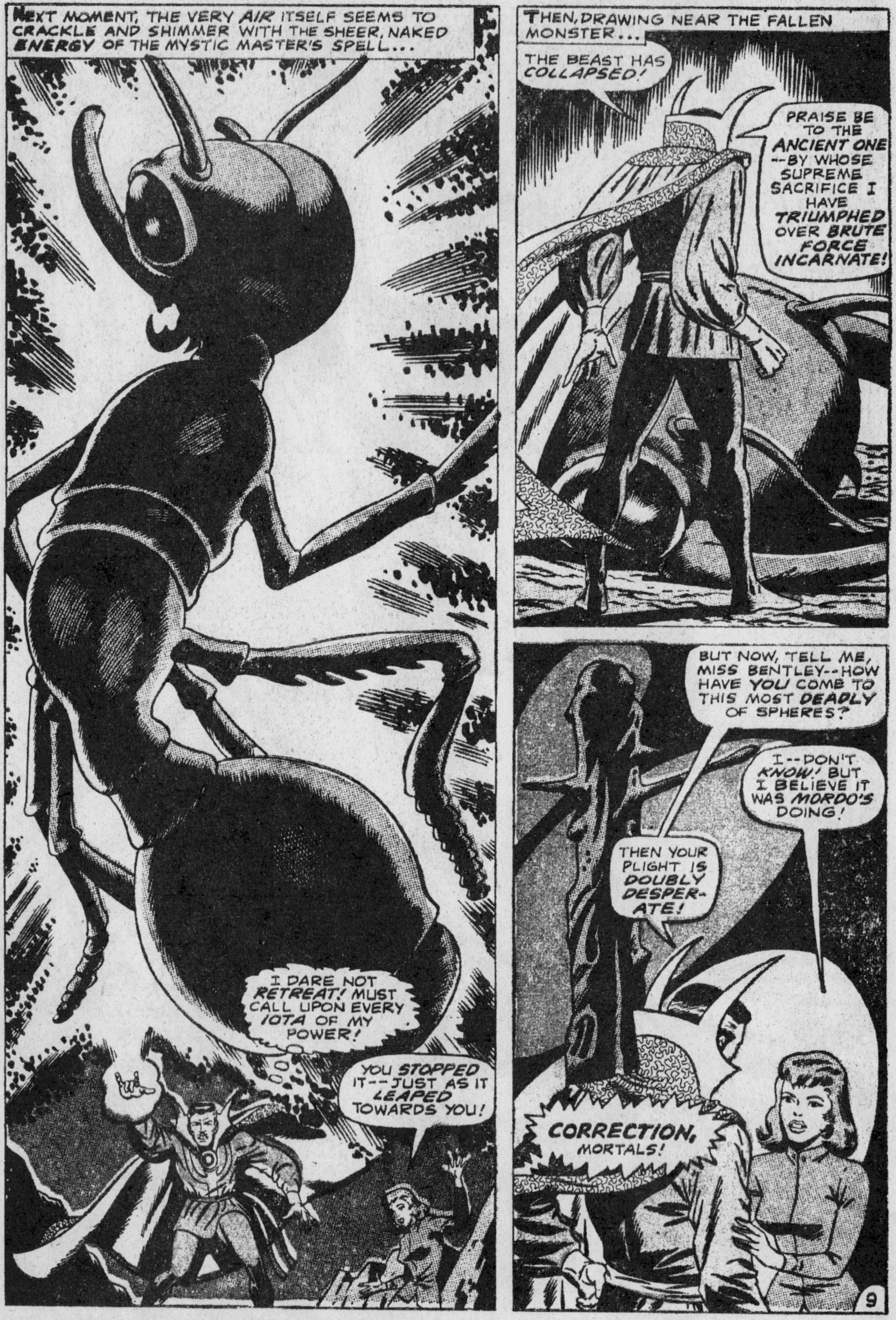
NEXT MOMENT, THE VERY AIR ITSELF SEEMS TO CRACKLE AND SHIMMER WITH THE SHEER, NAKED ENERGY OF THE MYSTIC MASTER'S SPELL...
I DARE NOT RETREAT! MUST CALL UPON EVERY IOTA OF MY POWER!
YOU STOPPED IT--JUST AS IT LEAPED TOWARDS YOU!
THEN, DRAWING NEAR THE FALLEN MONSTER...
THE BEAST HAS COLLAPSED!
PRAISE BE TO THE ANCIENT ONE --BY WHOSE SUPREME SACRIFICE I HAVE TRIUMPHED OVER BRUTE FORCE INCARNATE!
BUT NOW, TELL ME, MISS BENTLEY--HOW HAVE YOU COME TO THIS MOST DEADLY OF SPHERES?
I--DON'T KNOW! BUT I BELIEVE IT WAS MORDO'S DOING!
THEN YOUR PLIGHT IS DOUBLY DESPERATE!
CORRECTION, MORTALS!
9

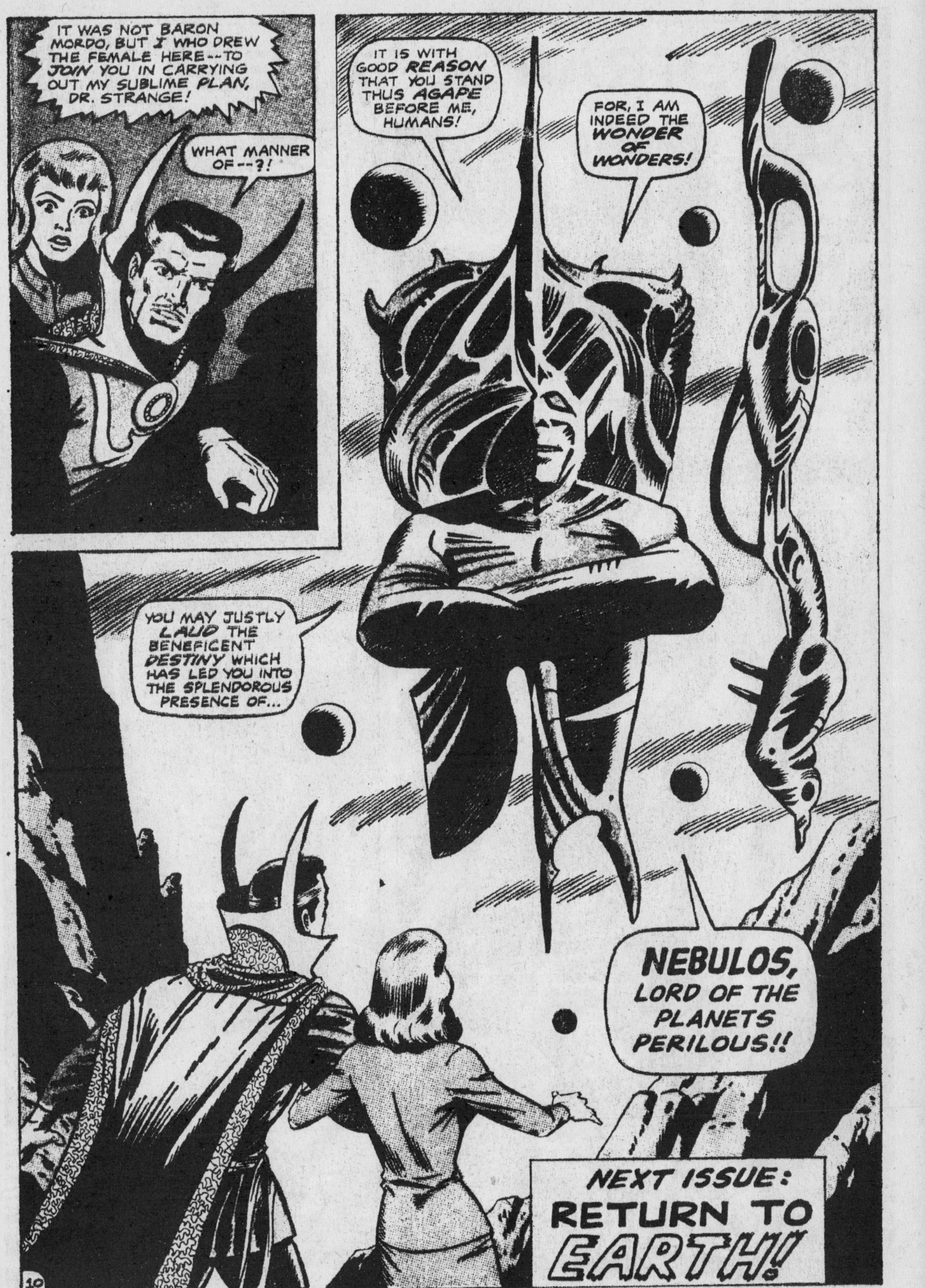

IT WAS NOT BARON MORDO, BUT I WHO DREW THE FEMALE HERE--TO JOIN YOU IN CARRYING OUT MY SUBLIME PLAN, DR. STRANGE!
WHAT MANNER OF--?!
IT IS WITH GOOD REASON THAT YOU STAND THUS AGAPE BEFORE ME, HUMANS!
FOR, I AM INDEED THE WONDER OF WONDERS!
YOU MAY JUSTLY LAUD THE BENEFICENT DESTINY WHICH HAS LED YOU INTO THE SPLENDOROUS PRESENCE OF...
NEBULOS, LORD OF THE PLANETS PERILOUS!!
NEXT ISSUE: RETURN TO EARTH!
10

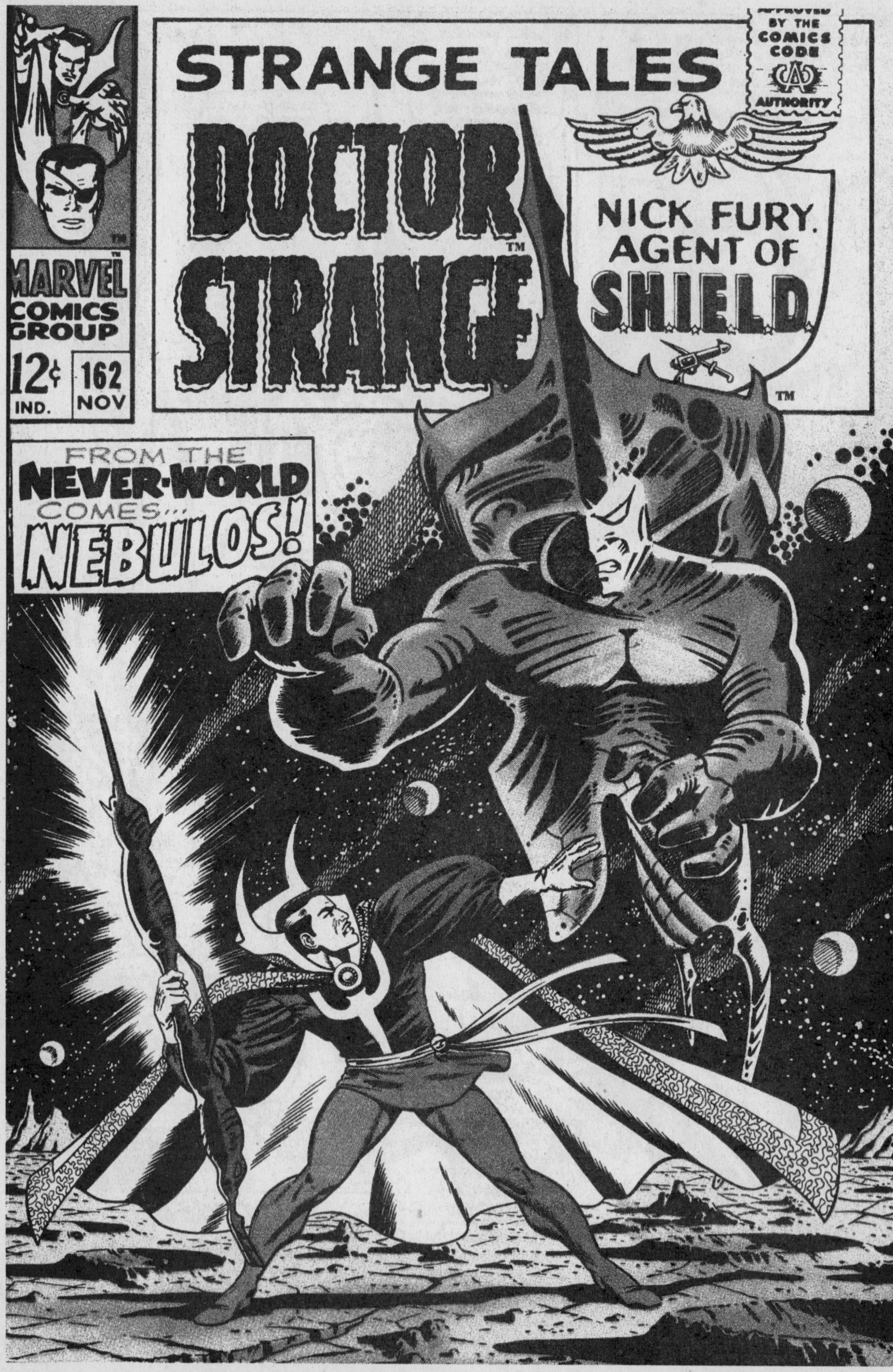
STRANGE TALES
DOCTOR STRANGE™
NICK FURY, AGENT OF SHIELD™
APPROVED BY THE COMICS CODE AUTHORITY
MARVEL COMICS GROUP
12¢ IND.
162 NOV
FROM THE NEVER-WORLD COMES... NEBULOS!

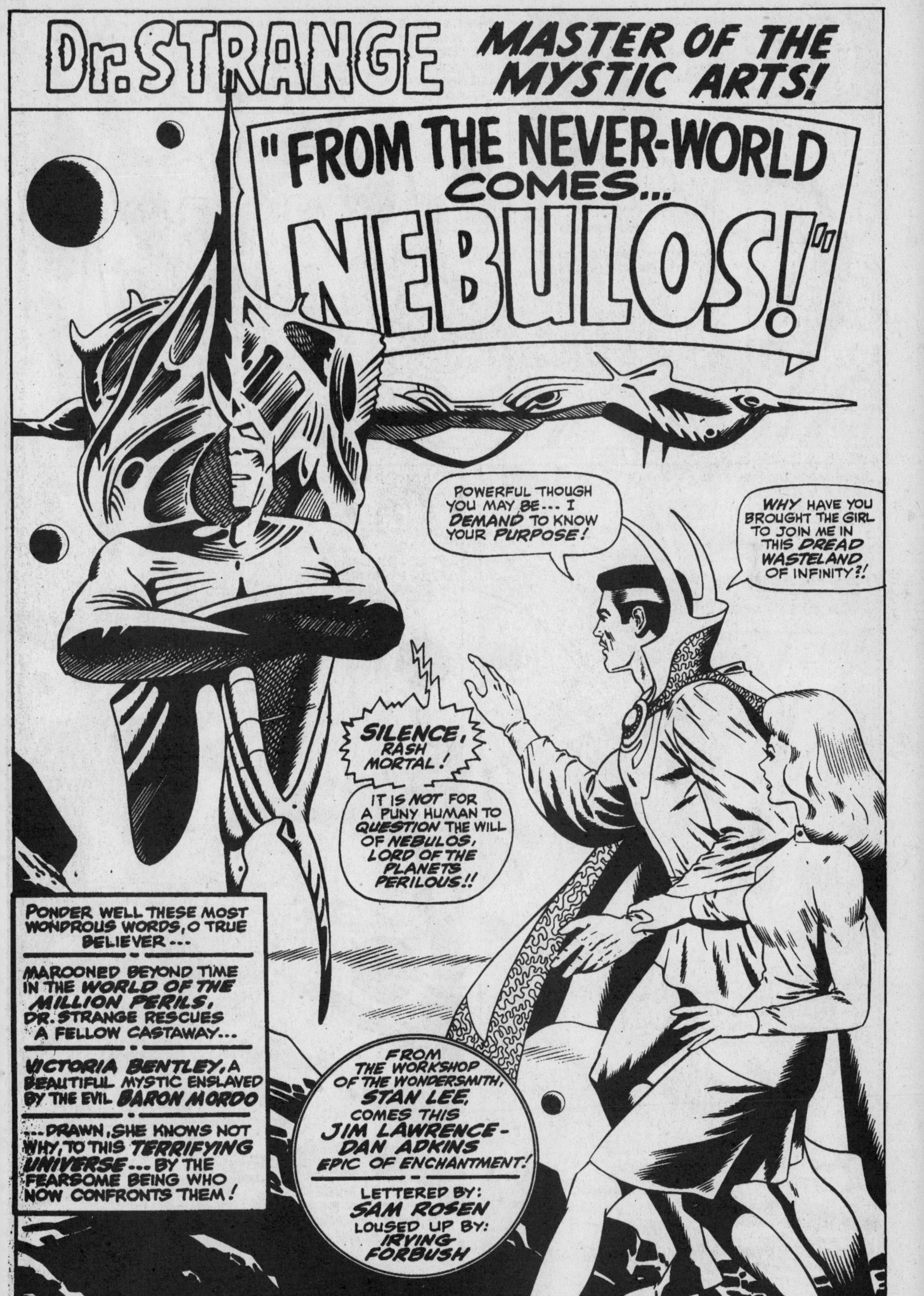

Dr. STRANGE
MASTER OF THE MYSTIC ARTS!
"FROM THE NEVER-WORLD COMES... NEBULOS!"
POWERFUL THOUGH YOU MAY BE... I DEMAND TO KNOW YOUR PURPOSE!
WHY HAVE YOU BROUGHT THE GIRL TO JOIN ME IN THIS DREAD WASTELAND OF INFINITY?!
SILENCE, RASH MORTAL!
IT IS NOT FOR A PUNY HUMAN TO QUESTION THE WILL OF NEBULOS, LORD OF THE PLANETS PERILOUS!!
PONDER WELL THESE MOST WONDROUS WORDS, O TRUE BELIEVER...
MAROONED BEYOND TIME IN THE WORLD OF THE MILLION PERILS, DR. STRANGE RESCUES A FELLOW CASTAWAY...
VICTORIA BENTLEY, A BEAUTIFUL MYSTIC ENSLAVED BY THE EVIL BARON MORDO
...DRAWN, SHE KNOWS NOT WHY, TO THIS TERRIFYING UNIVERSE... BY THE FEARSOME BEING WHO NOW CONFRONTS THEM!
FROM THE WORKSHOP OF THE WONDERSMITH, STAN LEE, COMES THIS JIM LAWRENCE-DAN ADKINS EPIC OF ENCHANTMENT!
LETTERED BY: SAM ROSEN
LOUSED UP BY: IRVING FORBUSH

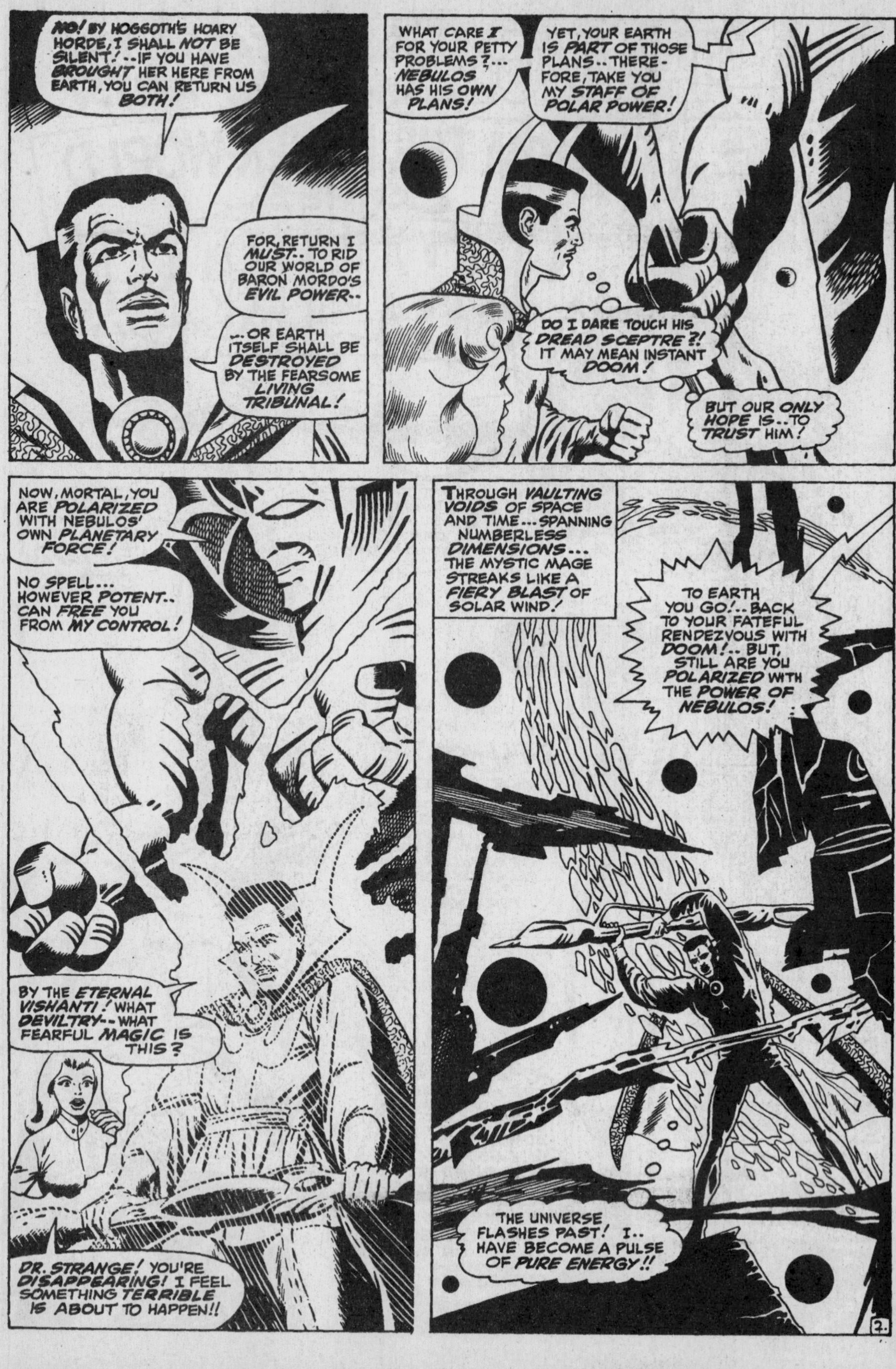
NO! BY HOGGOTH'S HOARY HORDE, I SHALL NOT BE SILENT! --IF YOU HAVE BROUGHT HER HERE FROM EARTH, YOU CAN RETURN US BOTH!
FOR, RETURN I MUST-- TO RID OUR WORLD OF BARON MORDO'S EVIL POWER--
...OR EARTH ITSELF SHALL BE DESTROYED BY THE FEARSOME LIVING TRIBUNAL!
WHAT CARE I FOR YOUR PETTY PROBLEMS?... NEBULOS HAS HIS OWN PLANS!
YET, YOUR EARTH IS PART OF THOSE PLANS.. THERE-FORE, TAKE YOU MY STAFF OF POLAR POWER!
DO I DARE TOUCH HIS DREAD SCEPTRE?! IT MAY MEAN INSTANT DOOM!
BUT OUR ONLY HOPE IS..TO TRUST HIM!
NOW, MORTAL, YOU ARE POLARIZED WITH NEBULOS' OWN PLANETARY FORCE!
NO SPELL... HOWEVER POTENT.. CAN FREE YOU FROM MY CONTROL!
BY THE ETERNAL VISHANTI! WHAT DEVILTRY-- WHAT FEARFUL MAGIC IS THIS?
DR. STRANGE! YOU'RE DISAPPEARING! I FEEL SOMETHING TERRIBLE IS ABOUT TO HAPPEN!!
THROUGH VAULTING VOIDS OF SPACE AND TIME... SPANNING NUMBERLESS DIMENSIONS... THE MYSTIC MAGE STREAKS LIKE A FIERY BLAST OF SOLAR WIND!
TO EARTH YOU GO!.. BACK TO YOUR FATEFUL RENDEZVOUS WITH DOOM!.. BUT, STILL ARE YOU POLARIZED WITH THE POWER OF NEBULOS!
THE UNIVERSE FLASHES PAST! I.. HAVE BECOME A PULSE OF PURE ENERGY!!
2.

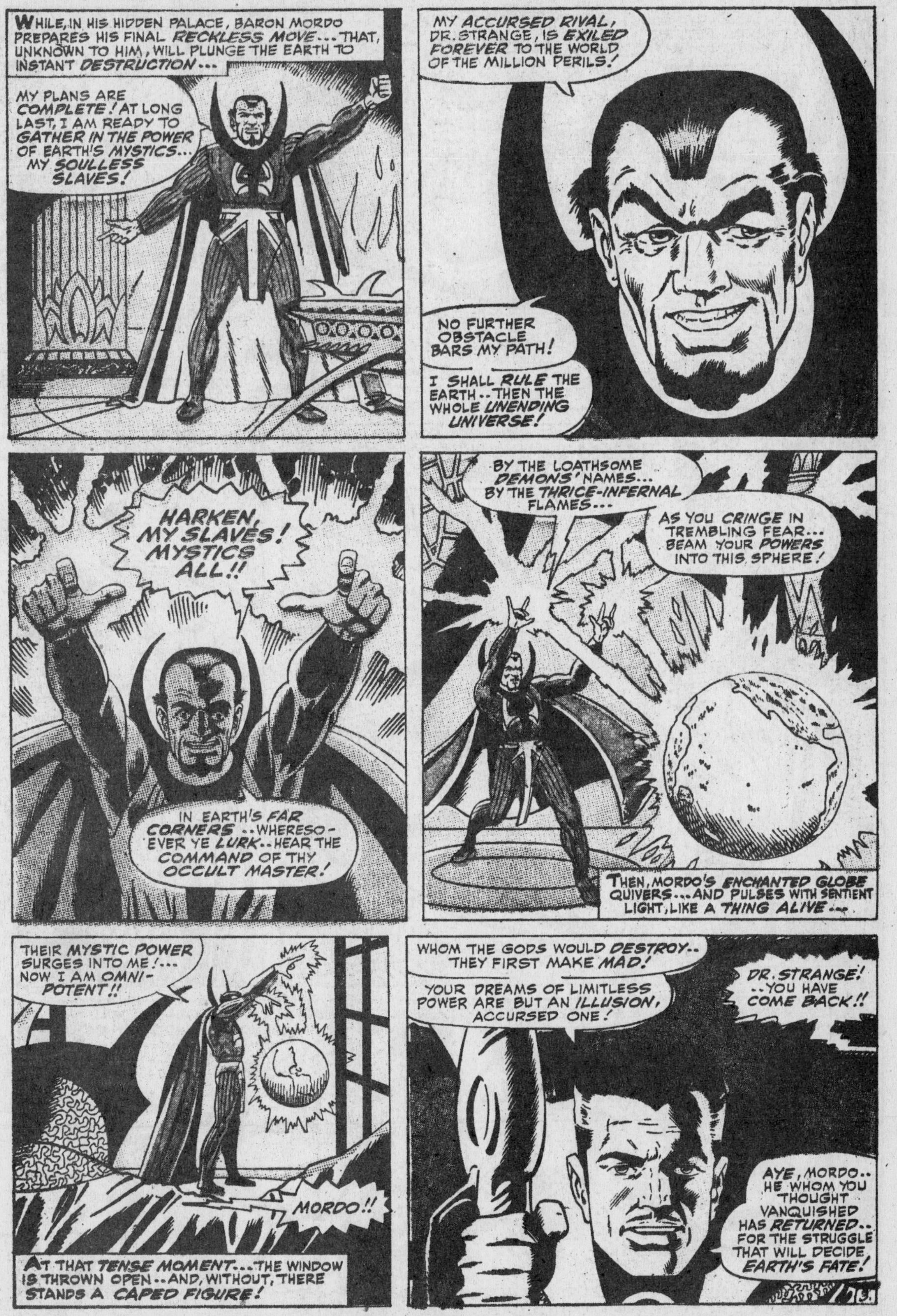
WHILE, IN HIS HIDDEN PALACE, BARON MORDO PREPARES HIS FINAL RECKLESS MOVE... THAT, UNKNOWN TO HIM, WILL PLUNGE THE EARTH TO INSTANT DESTRUCTION...
MY PLANS ARE COMPLETE! AT LONG LAST, I AM READY TO GATHER IN THE POWER OF EARTH'S MYSTICS... MY SOULLESS SLAVES!
MY ACCURSED RIVAL, DR. STRANGE, IS EXILED FOREVER TO THE WORLD OF THE MILLION PERILS!
NO FURTHER OBSTACLE BARS MY PATH!
I SHALL RULE THE EARTH.. THEN THE WHOLE UNENDING UNIVERSE!
HARKEN, MY SLAVES! MYSTICS ALL!!
IN EARTH'S FAR CORNERS.. WHERESO-EVER YE LURK.. HEAR THE COMMAND OF THY OCCULT MASTER!
BY THE LOATHSOME DEMONS' NAMES... BY THE THRICE-INFERNAL FLAMES...
AS YOU CRINGE IN TREMBLING FEAR... BEAM YOUR POWERS INTO THIS SPHERE!
THEN, MORDO'S ENCHANTED GLOBE QUIVERS... AND PULSES WITH SENTIENT LIGHT, LIKE A THING ALIVE...
THEIR MYSTIC POWER SURGES INTO ME!... NOW I AM OMNI-POTENT!!
MORDO!!
AT THAT TENSE MOMENT... THE WINDOW IS THROWN OPEN.. AND, WITHOUT, THERE STANDS A CAPED FIGURE!
WHOM THE GODS WOULD DESTROY.. THEY FIRST MAKE MAD!
YOUR DREAMS OF LIMITLESS POWER ARE BUT AN ILLUSION, ACCURSED ONE!
DR. STRANGE! ..YOU HAVE COME BACK!!
AYE, MORDO.. HE WHOM YOU THOUGHT VANQUISHED HAS RETURNED.. FOR THE STRUGGLE THAT WILL DECIDE EARTH'S FATE!
3.

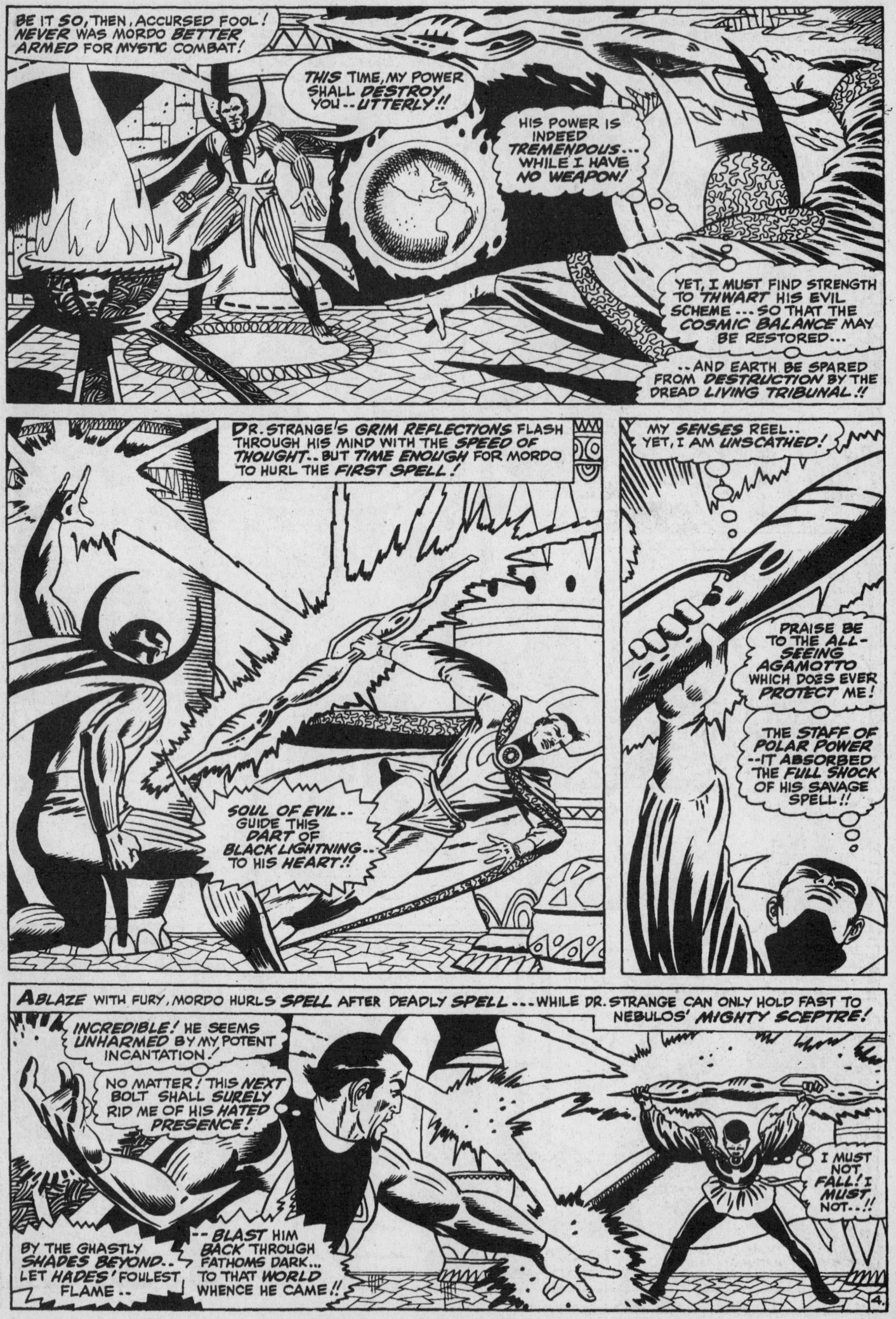
BE IT SO, THEN, ACCURSED FOOL! NEVER WAS MORDO BETTER ARMED FOR MYSTIC COMBAT!
THIS TIME, MY POWER SHALL DESTROY YOU--UTTERLY!!
HIS POWER IS INDEED TREMENDOUS... WHILE I HAVE NO WEAPON!
YET, I MUST FIND STRENGTH TO THWART HIS EVIL SCHEME... SO THAT THE COSMIC BALANCE MAY BE RESTORED...
..AND EARTH BE SPARED FROM DESTRUCTION BY THE DREAD LIVING TRIBUNAL!!
DR. STRANGE'S GRIM REFLECTIONS FLASH THROUGH HIS MIND WITH THE SPEED OF THOUGHT.. BUT TIME ENOUGH FOR MORDO TO HURL THE FIRST SPELL!
SOUL OF EVIL-- GUIDE THIS DART OF BLACK LIGHTNING.. TO HIS HEART!!
MY SENSES REEL.. YET, I AM UNSCATHED!
PRAISE BE TO THE ALL-SEEING AGAMOTTO WHICH DOES EVER PROTECT ME!
THE STAFF OF POLAR POWER --IT ABSORBED THE FULL SHOCK OF HIS SAVAGE SPELL!!
ABLAZE WITH FURY, MORDO HURLS SPELL AFTER DEADLY SPELL... WHILE DR. STRANGE CAN ONLY HOLD FAST TO NEBULOS' MIGHTY SCEPTRE!
INCREDIBLE! HE SEEMS UNHARMED BY MY POTENT INCANTATION!
NO MATTER! THIS NEXT BOLT SHALL SURELY RID ME OF HIS HATED PRESENCE!
BY THE GHASTLY SHADES BEYOND.. LET HADES' FOULEST FLAME..
--BLAST HIM BACK THROUGH FATHOMS DARK... TO THAT WORLD WHENCE HE CAME!!
I MUST NOT FALL! I MUST NOT..!!
4.

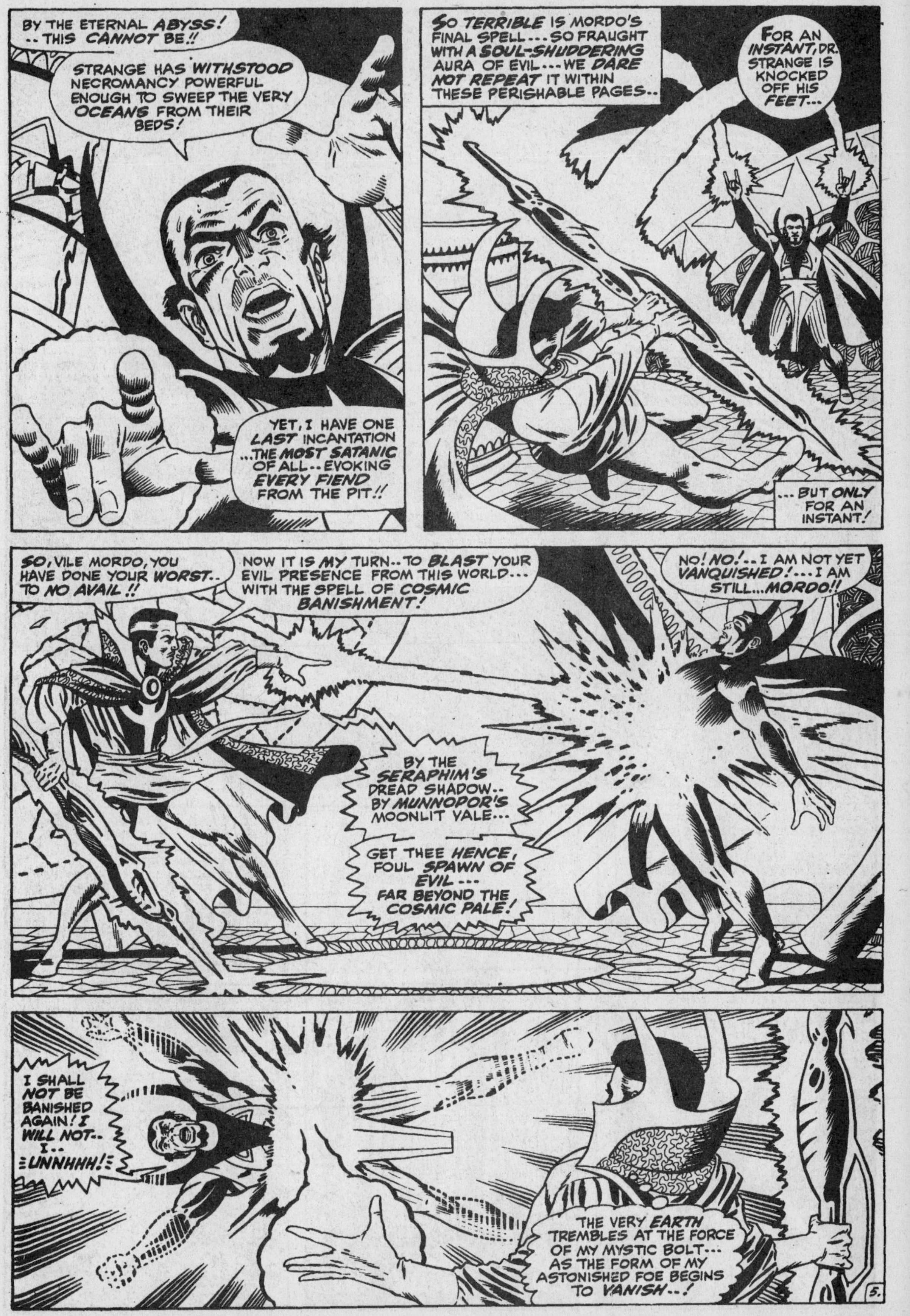

BY THE ETERNAL ABYSS! ..THIS CANNOT BE!!
STRANGE HAS WITHSTOOD NECROMANCY POWERFUL ENOUGH TO SWEEP THE VERY OCEANS FROM THEIR BEDS!
YET, I HAVE ONE LAST INCANTATION ...THE MOST SATANIC OF ALL..EVOKING EVERY FIEND FROM THE PIT!!
SO TERRIBLE IS MORDO'S FINAL SPELL...SO FRAUGHT WITH A SOUL-SHUDDERING AURA OF EVIL...WE DARE NOT REPEAT IT WITHIN THESE PERISHABLE PAGES..
FOR AN INSTANT, DR. STRANGE IS KNOCKED OFF HIS FEET...
...BUT ONLY FOR AN INSTANT!
SO, VILE MORDO, YOU HAVE DONE YOUR WORST.. TO NO AVAIL!!
NOW IT IS MY TURN..TO BLAST YOUR EVIL PRESENCE FROM THIS WORLD... WITH THE SPELL OF COSMIC BANISHMENT!
NO! NO!..I AM NOT YET VANQUISHED!...I AM STILL...MORDO!!
BY THE SERAPHIM'S DREAD SHADOW.. BY MUNNOPOR'S MOONLIT VALE...
GET THEE HENCE, FOUL SPAWN OF EVIL... FAR BEYOND THE COSMIC PALE!
I SHALL NOT BE BANISHED AGAIN! I WILL NOT.. I.. UNNHHH!
THE VERY EARTH TREMBLES AT THE FORCE OF MY MYSTIC BOLT... AS THE FORM OF MY ASTONISHED FOE BEGINS TO VANISH..!
5.

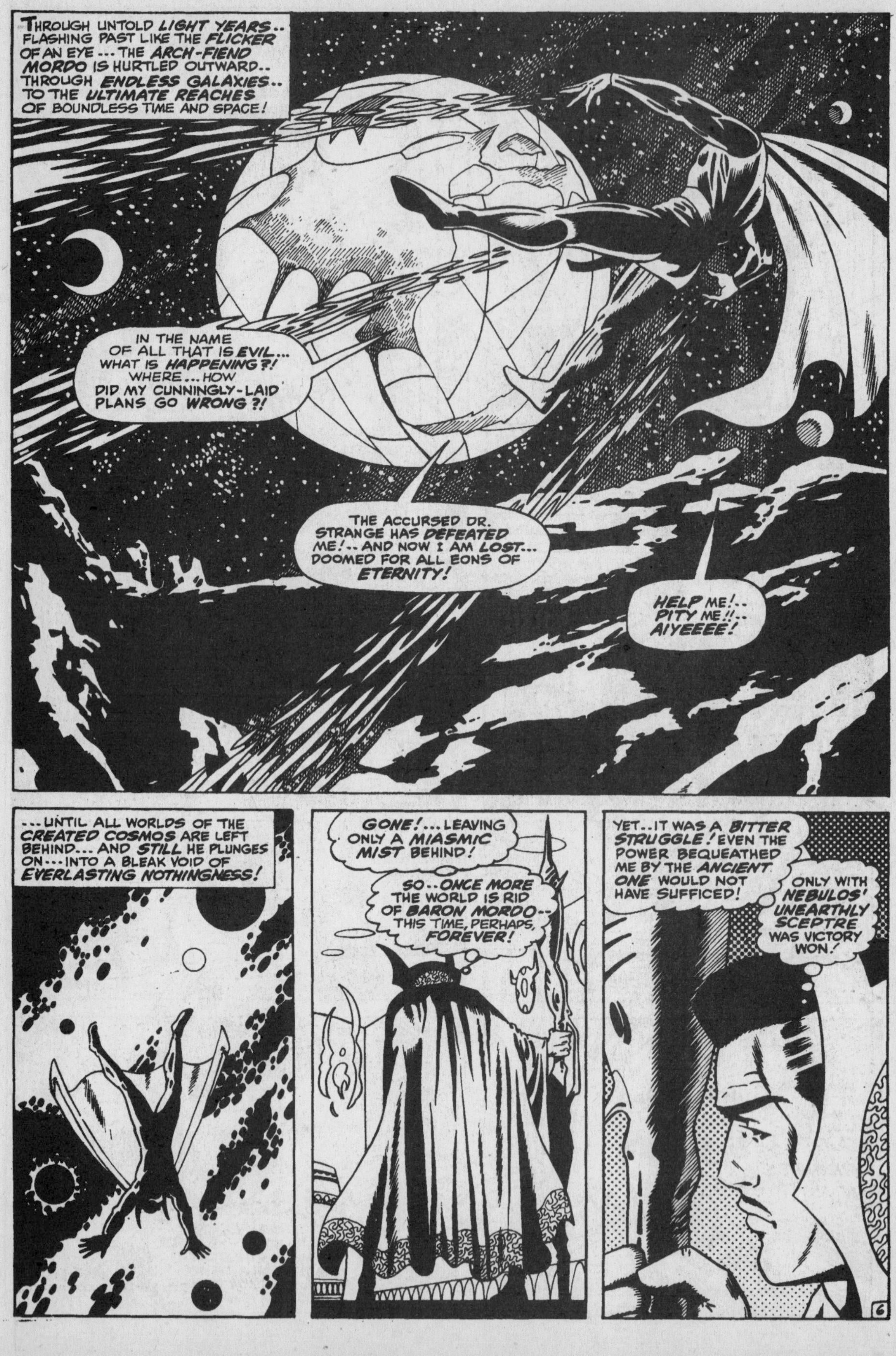
THROUGH UNTOLD LIGHT YEARS.. FLASHING PAST LIKE THE FLICKER OF AN EYE --- THE ARCH-FIEND MORDO IS HURTLED OUTWARD.. THROUGH ENDLESS GALAXIES.. TO THE ULTIMATE REACHES OF BOUNDLESS TIME AND SPACE!
IN THE NAME OF ALL THAT IS EVIL... WHAT IS HAPPENING?! WHERE... HOW DID MY CUNNINGLY-LAID PLANS GO WRONG?!
THE ACCURSED DR. STRANGE HAS DEFEATED ME!-- AND NOW I AM LOST... DOOMED FOR ALL EONS OF ETERNITY!
HELP ME!.. PITY ME!!.. AIYEEEE!
...UNTIL ALL WORLDS OF THE CREATED COSMOS ARE LEFT BEHIND... AND STILL HE PLUNGES ON--- INTO A BLEAK VOID OF EVERLASTING NOTHINGNESS!
GONE!... LEAVING ONLY A MIASMIC MIST BEHIND!
SO.. ONCE MORE THE WORLD IS RID OF BARON MORDO-- THIS TIME, PERHAPS, FOREVER!
YET... IT WAS A BITTER STRUGGLE! EVEN THE POWER BEQUEATHED ME BY THE ANCIENT ONE WOULD NOT HAVE SUFFICED!
ONLY WITH NEBULOS' UNEARTHLY SCEPTRE WAS VICTORY WON!
6

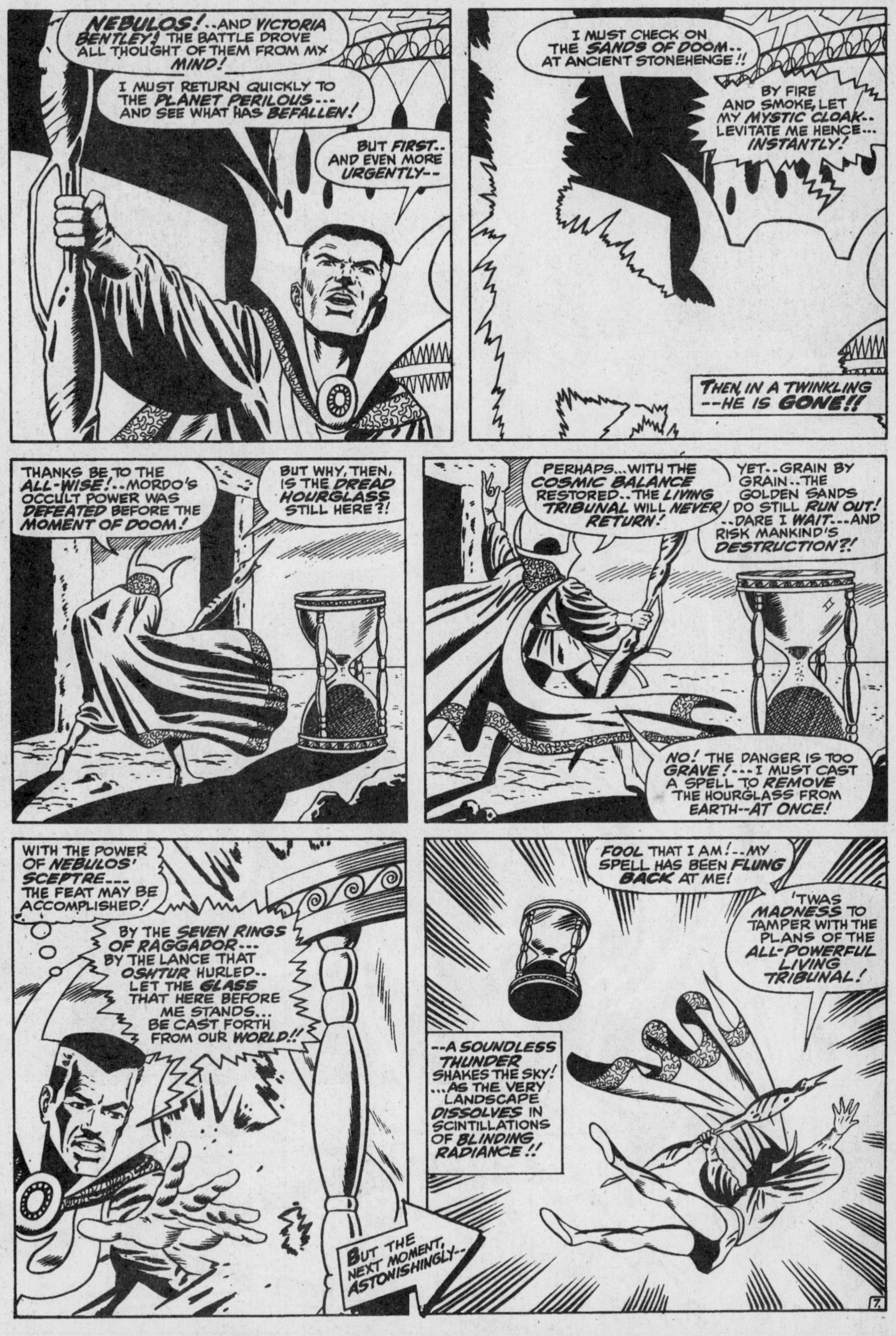
NEBULOS!..AND VICTORIA BENTLEY! THE BATTLE DROVE ALL THOUGHT OF THEM FROM MY MIND!
I MUST RETURN QUICKLY TO THE PLANET PERILOUS... AND SEE WHAT HAS BEFALLEN!
BUT FIRST.. AND EVEN MORE URGENTLY--
I MUST CHECK ON THE SANDS OF DOOM.. AT ANCIENT STONEHENGE!!
BY FIRE AND SMOKE, LET MY MYSTIC CLOAK.. LEVITATE ME HENCE... INSTANTLY!
THEN, IN A TWINKLING --HE IS GONE!!
THANKS BE TO THE ALL-WISE!..MORDO'S OCCULT POWER WAS DEFEATED BEFORE THE MOMENT OF DOOM!
BUT WHY, THEN, IS THE DREAD HOURGLASS STILL HERE?!
PERHAPS...WITH THE COSMIC BALANCE RESTORED..THE LIVING TRIBUNAL WILL NEVER RETURN!
YET..GRAIN BY GRAIN..THE GOLDEN SANDS DO STILL RUN OUT! ..DARE I WAIT...AND RISK MANKIND'S DESTRUCTION?!
NO! THE DANGER IS TOO GRAVE!...I MUST CAST A SPELL TO REMOVE THE HOURGLASS FROM EARTH--AT ONCE!
WITH THE POWER OF NEBULOS' SCEPTRE... THE FEAT MAY BE ACCOMPLISHED!
BY THE SEVEN RINGS OF RAGGADOR... BY THE LANCE THAT OSHTUR HURLED.. LET THE GLASS THAT HERE BEFORE ME STANDS... BE CAST FORTH FROM OUR WORLD!!
BUT THE NEXT MOMENT, ASTONISHINGLY--
--A SOUNDLESS THUNDER SHAKES THE SKY! ...AS THE VERY LANDSCAPE DISSOLVES IN SCINTILLATIONS OF BLINDING RADIANCE!!
FOOL THAT I AM!--MY SPELL HAS BEEN FLUNG BACK AT ME!
'TWAS MADNESS TO TAMPER WITH THE PLANS OF THE ALL-POWERFUL LIVING TRIBUNAL!
7.

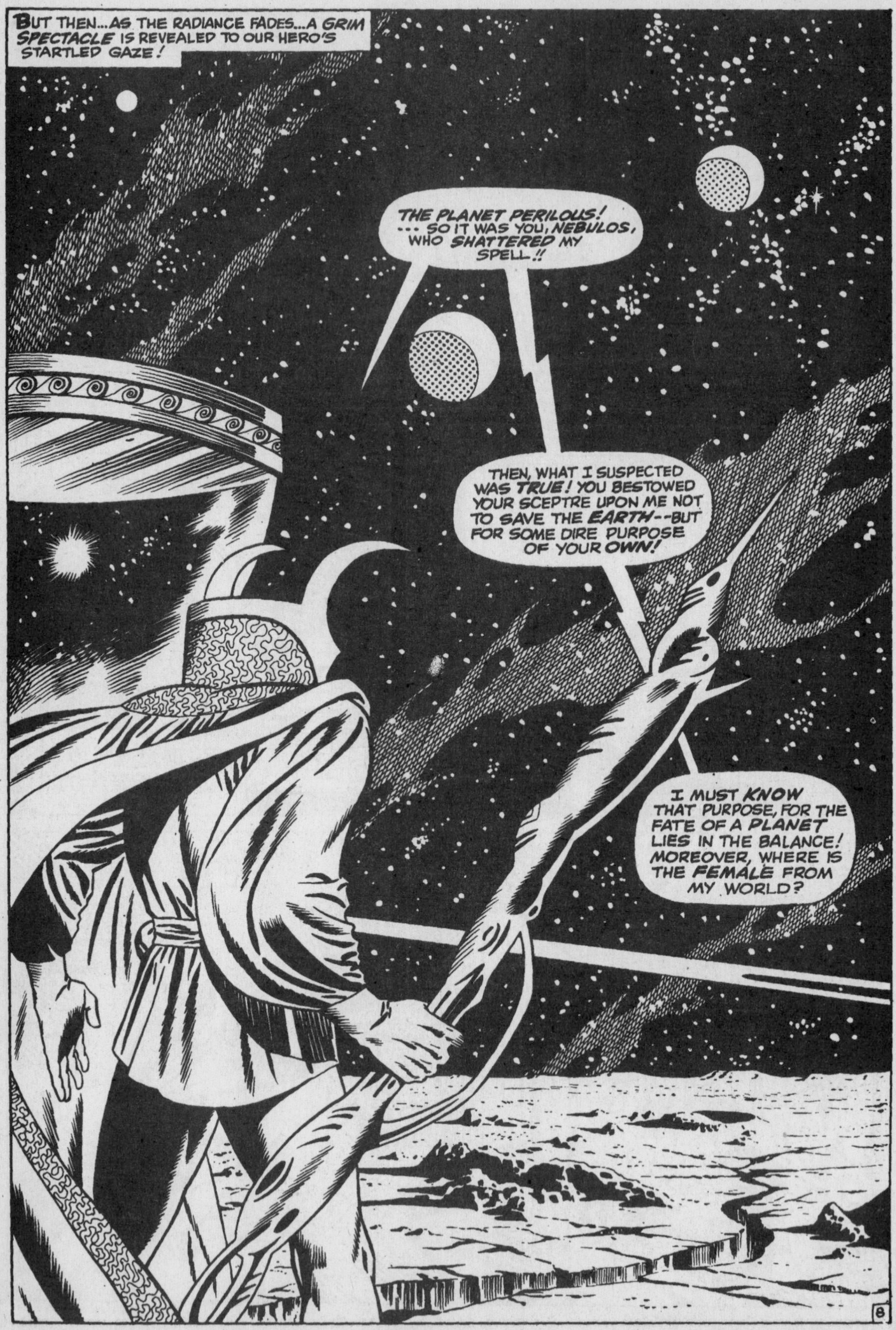
BUT THEN...AS THE RADIANCE FADES...A GRIM SPECTACLE IS REVEALED TO OUR HERO'S STARTLED GAZE!
THE PLANET PERILOUS! --- SO IT WAS YOU, NEBULOS, WHO SHATTERED MY SPELL!!
THEN, WHAT I SUSPECTED WAS TRUE! YOU BESTOWED YOUR SCEPTRE UPON ME NOT TO SAVE THE EARTH--BUT FOR SOME DIRE PURPOSE OF YOUR OWN!
I MUST KNOW THAT PURPOSE, FOR THE FATE OF A PLANET LIES IN THE BALANCE! MOREOVER, WHERE IS THE FEMALE FROM MY WORLD?
8

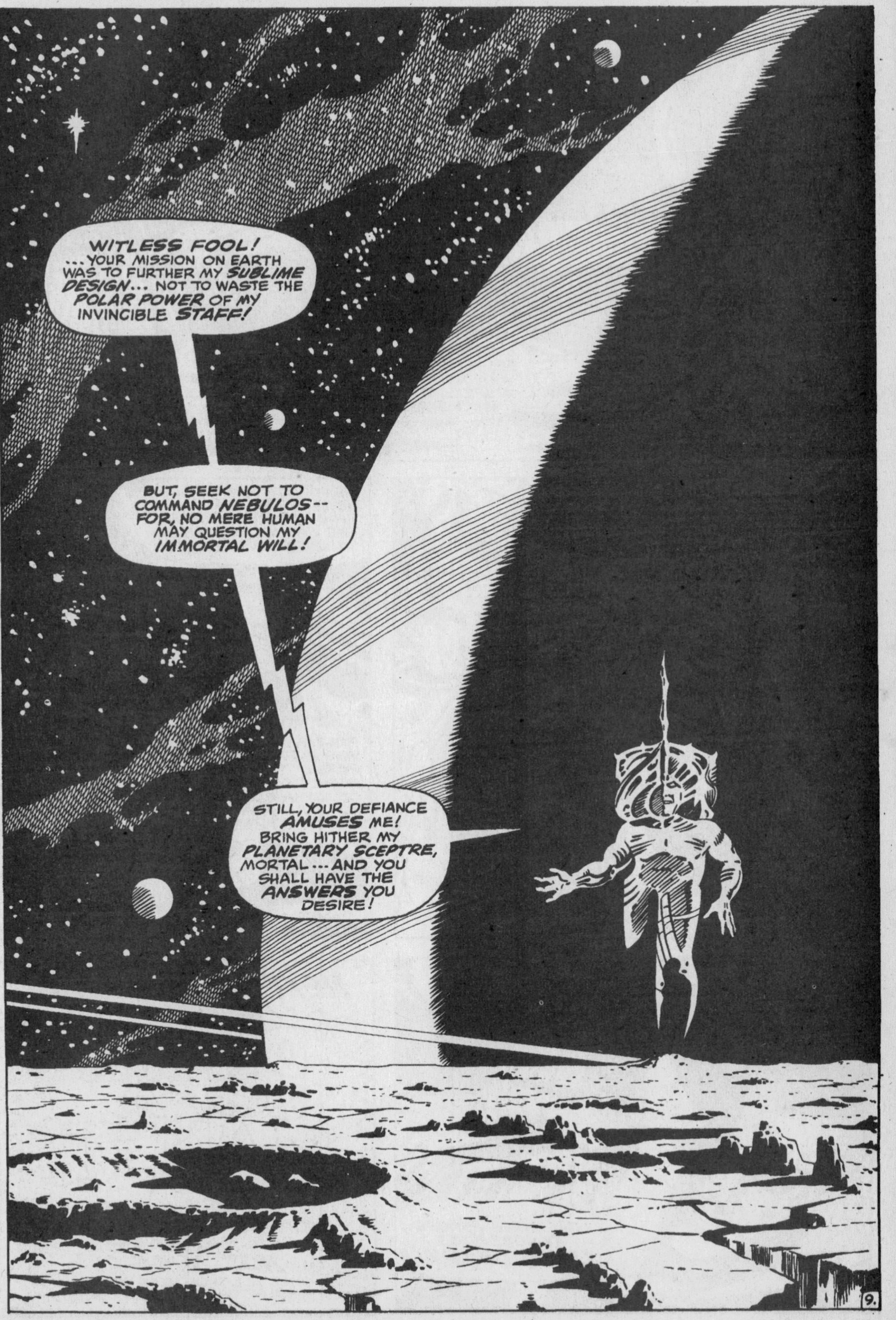

WITLESS FOOL! ...YOUR MISSION ON EARTH WAS TO FURTHER MY SUBLIME DESIGN... NOT TO WASTE THE POLAR POWER OF MY INVINCIBLE STAFF!
BUT, SEEK NOT TO COMMAND NEBULOS-- FOR, NO MERE HUMAN MAY QUESTION MY IMMORTAL WILL!
STILL, YOUR DEFIANCE AMUSES ME! BRING HITHER MY PLANETARY SCEPTRE, MORTAL... AND YOU SHALL HAVE THE ANSWERS YOU DESIRE!
9.

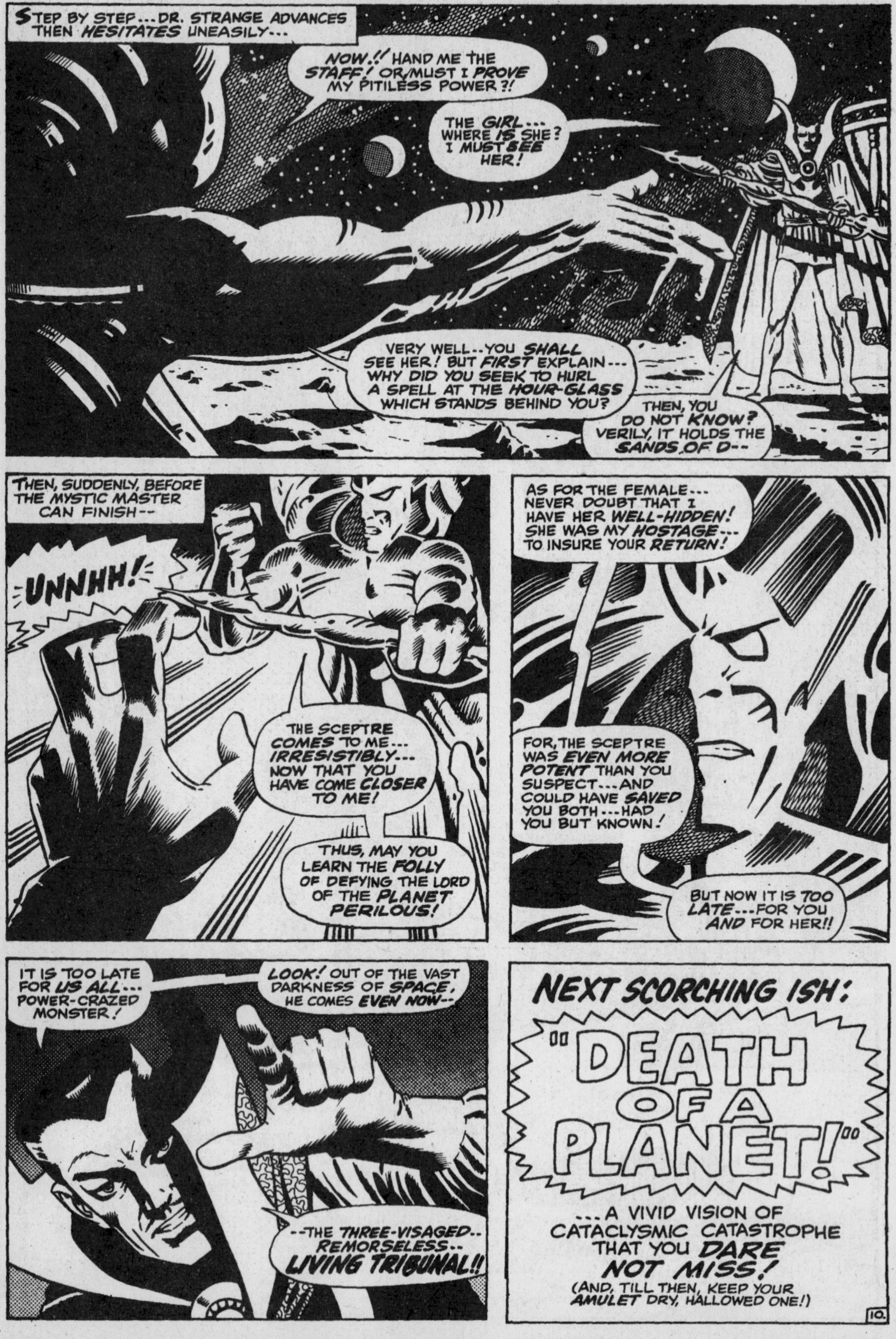
STEP BY STEP... DR. STRANGE ADVANCES THEN HESITATES UNEASILY...
NOW.!! HAND ME THE STAFF! OR/MUST I PROVE MY PITILESS POWER?!
THE GIRL... WHERE IS SHE? I MUST SEE HER!
VERY WELL--YOU SHALL SEE HER! BUT FIRST EXPLAIN--- WHY DID YOU SEEK TO HURL A SPELL AT THE HOUR-GLASS WHICH STANDS BEHIND YOU?
THEN, YOU DO NOT KNOW? VERILY, IT HOLDS THE SANDS OF D--
THEN, SUDDENLY, BEFORE THE MYSTIC MASTER CAN FINISH--
UNNHH!
THE SCEPTRE COMES TO ME... IRRESISTIBLY--- NOW THAT YOU HAVE COME CLOSER TO ME!
THUS, MAY YOU LEARN THE FOLLY OF DEFYING THE LORD OF THE PLANET PERILOUS!
AS FOR THE FEMALE... NEVER DOUBT THAT I HAVE HER WELL-HIDDEN! SHE WAS MY HOSTAGE--- TO INSURE YOUR RETURN!
FOR, THE SCEPTRE WAS EVEN MORE POTENT THAN YOU SUSPECT... AND COULD HAVE SAVED YOU BOTH---HAD YOU BUT KNOWN!
BUT NOW IT IS TOO LATE...FOR YOU AND FOR HER!!
IT IS TOO LATE FOR US ALL... POWER-CRAZED MONSTER!
LOOK! OUT OF THE VAST DARKNESS OF SPACE, HE COMES EVEN NOW--
--THE THREE-VISAGED.. REMORSELESS.. LIVING TRIBUNAL!!
NEXT SCORCHING ISH:
"DEATH OF A PLANET!"
...A VIVID VISION OF CATACLYSMIC CATASTROPHE THAT YOU DARE NOT MISS!
(AND, TILL THEN, KEEP YOUR AMULET DRY, HALLOWED ONE!)
10.

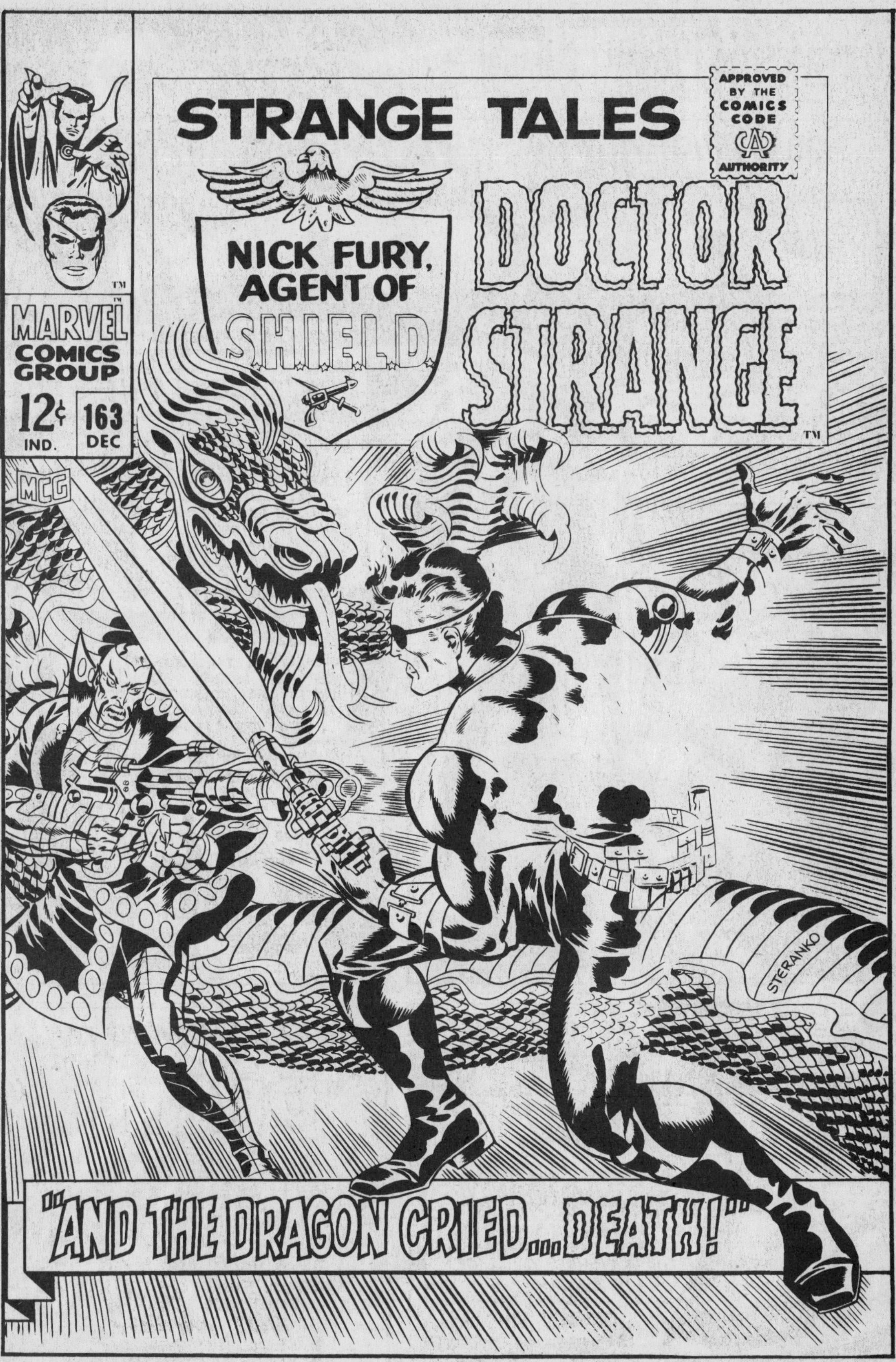

STRANGE TALES
APPROVED BY THE COMICS CODE AUTHORITY
NICK FURY, AGENT OF S.H.I.E.L.D.
DOCTOR STRANGE
MARVEL COMICS GROUP
12¢ IND.
163 DEC
MCG
STERANKO
"AND THE DRAGON CRIED... DEATH!"

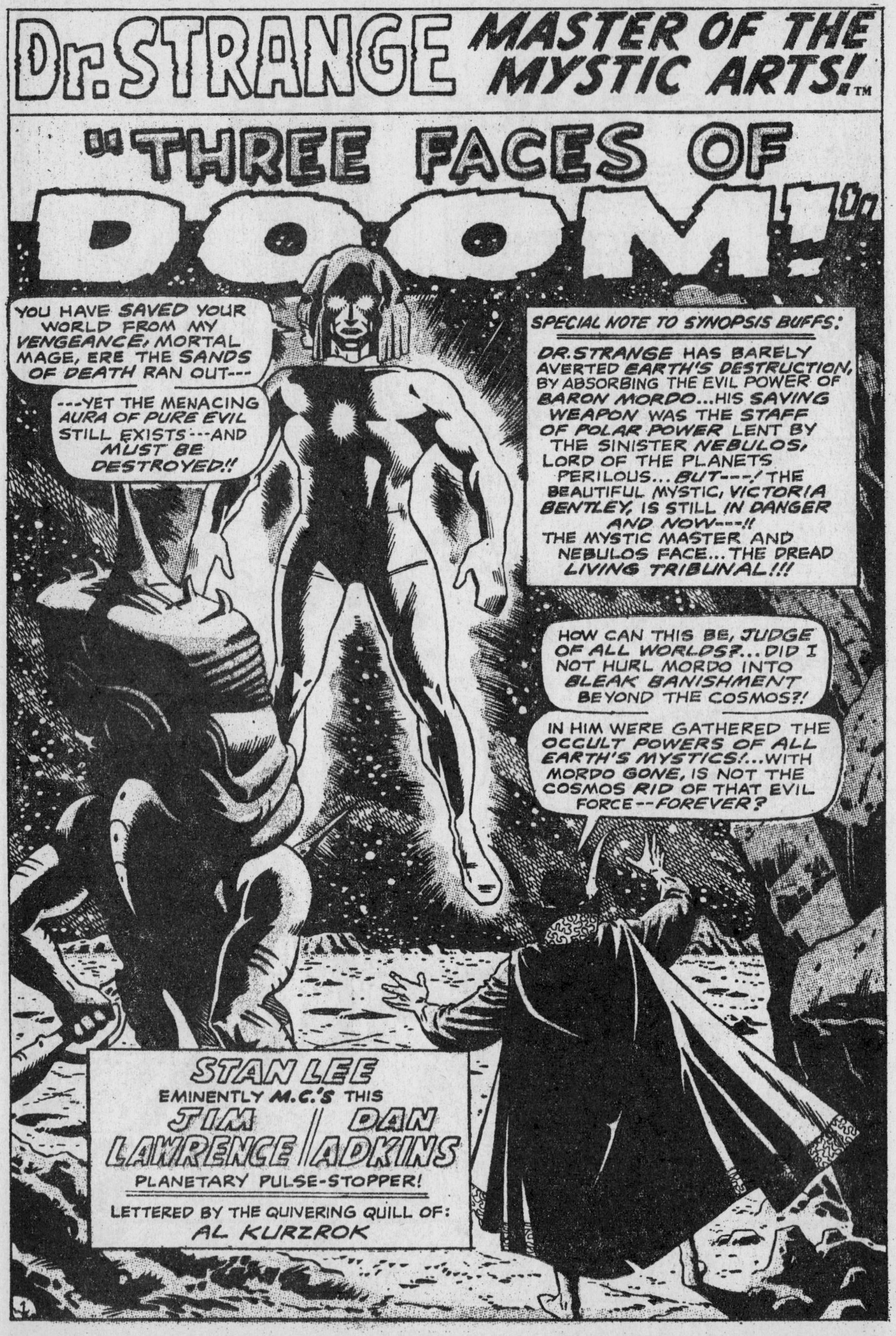
Dr. STRANGE MASTER OF THE MYSTIC ARTS!™
"THREE FACES OF DOOM!"
YOU HAVE SAVED YOUR WORLD FROM MY VENGEANCE, MORTAL MAGE, ERE THE SANDS OF DEATH RAN OUT---
---YET THE MENACING AURA OF PURE EVIL STILL EXISTS---AND MUST BE DESTROYED!!
SPECIAL NOTE TO SYNOPSIS BUFFS:
DR. STRANGE HAS BARELY AVERTED EARTH'S DESTRUCTION, BY ABSORBING THE EVIL POWER OF BARON MORDO...HIS SAVING WEAPON WAS THE STAFF OF POLAR POWER LENT BY THE SINISTER NEBULOS, LORD OF THE PLANETS PERILOUS... BUT---! THE BEAUTIFUL MYSTIC, VICTORIA BENTLEY, IS STILL IN DANGER AND NOW---!! THE MYSTIC MASTER AND NEBULOS FACE... THE DREAD LIVING TRIBUNAL!!!
HOW CAN THIS BE, JUDGE OF ALL WORLDS?...DID I NOT HURL MORDO INTO BLEAK BANISHMENT BEYOND THE COSMOS?!
IN HIM WERE GATHERED THE OCCULT POWERS OF ALL EARTH'S MYSTICS!...WITH MORDO GONE, IS NOT THE COSMOS RID OF THAT EVIL FORCE--FOREVER?
STAN LEE EMINENTLY M.C.'S THIS JIM LAWRENCE / DAN ADKINS PLANETARY PULSE-STOPPER!
LETTERED BY THE QUIVERING QUILL OF: AL KURZROK
1

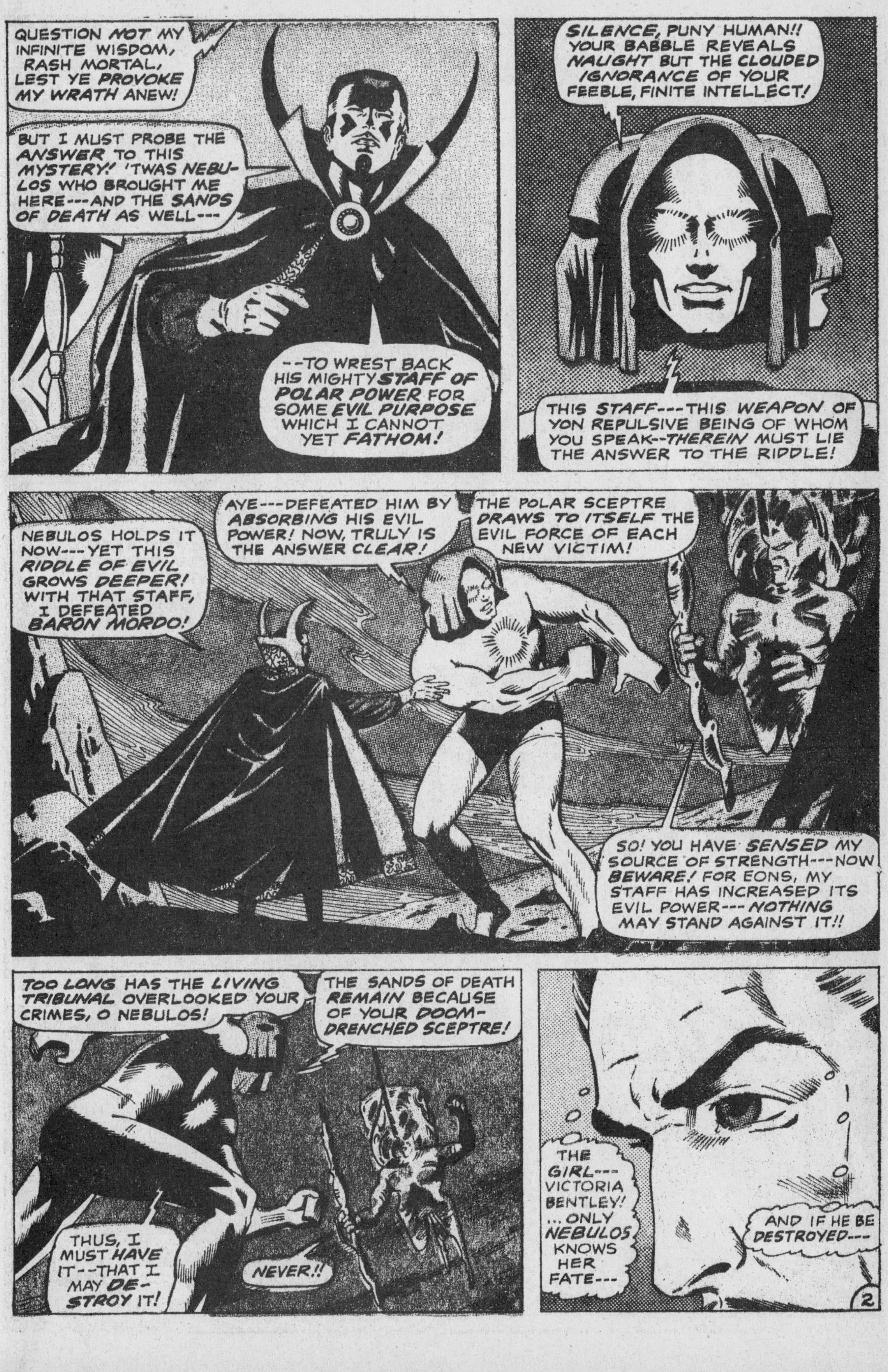
QUESTION NOT MY INFINITE WISDOM, RASH MORTAL, LEST YE PROVOKE MY WRATH ANEW!
BUT I MUST PROBE THE ANSWER TO THIS MYSTERY! 'TWAS NEBULOS WHO BROUGHT ME HERE---AND THE SANDS OF DEATH AS WELL---
--TO WREST BACK HIS MIGHTY STAFF OF POLAR POWER FOR SOME EVIL PURPOSE WHICH I CANNOT YET FATHOM!
SILENCE, PUNY HUMAN!! YOUR BABBLE REVEALS NAUGHT BUT THE CLOUDED IGNORANCE OF YOUR FEEBLE, FINITE INTELLECT!
THIS STAFF---THIS WEAPON OF YON REPULSIVE BEING OF WHOM YOU SPEAK--THEREIN MUST LIE THE ANSWER TO THE RIDDLE!
NEBULOS HOLDS IT NOW---YET THIS RIDDLE OF EVIL GROWS DEEPER! WITH THAT STAFF, I DEFEATED BARON MORDO!
AYE---DEFEATED HIM BY ABSORBING HIS EVIL POWER! NOW, TRULY IS THE ANSWER CLEAR!
THE POLAR SCEPTRE DRAWS TO ITSELF THE EVIL FORCE OF EACH NEW VICTIM!
SO! YOU HAVE SENSED MY SOURCE OF STRENGTH---NOW BEWARE! FOR EONS, MY STAFF HAS INCREASED ITS EVIL POWER---NOTHING MAY STAND AGAINST IT!!
TOO LONG HAS THE LIVING TRIBUNAL OVERLOOKED YOUR CRIMES, O NEBULOS!
THE SANDS OF DEATH REMAIN BECAUSE OF YOUR DOOM-DRENCHED SCEPTRE!
THUS, I MUST HAVE IT--THAT I MAY DESTROY IT!
NEVER!!
THE GIRL---VICTORIA BENTLEY! ...ONLY NEBULOS KNOWS HER FATE---
AND IF HE BE DESTROYED---
2

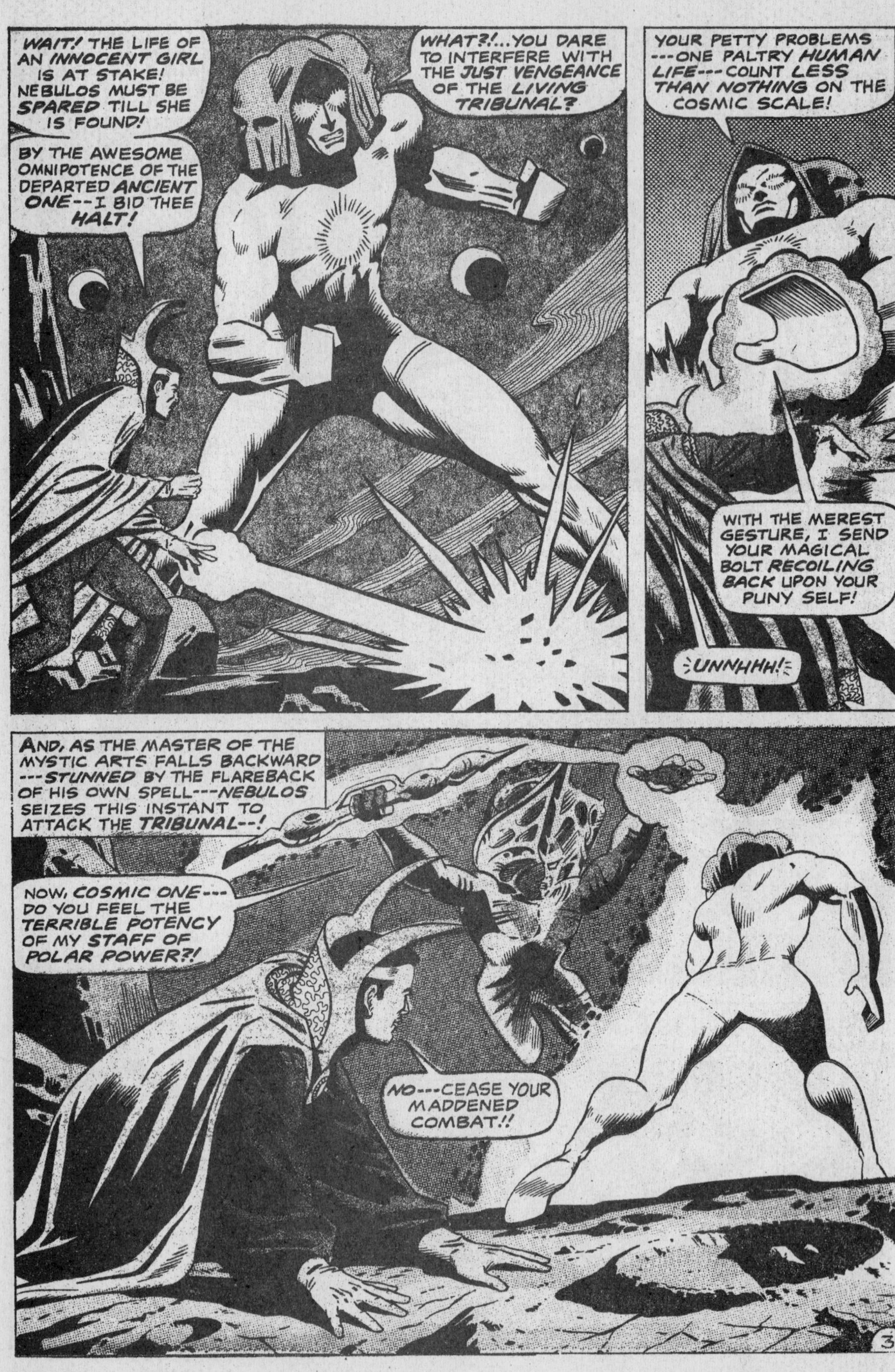
WAIT! THE LIFE OF AN INNOCENT GIRL IS AT STAKE! NEBULOS MUST BE SPARED TILL SHE IS FOUND!
BY THE AWESOME OMNIPOTENCE OF THE DEPARTED ANCIENT ONE--I BID THEE HALT!
WHAT?!...YOU DARE TO INTERFERE WITH THE JUST VENGEANCE OF THE LIVING TRIBUNAL?
YOUR PETTY PROBLEMS---ONE PALTRY HUMAN LIFE---COUNT LESS THAN NOTHING ON THE COSMIC SCALE!
WITH THE MEREST GESTURE, I SEND YOUR MAGICAL BOLT RECOILING BACK UPON YOUR PUNY SELF!
UNNHHH!
AND, AS THE MASTER OF THE MYSTIC ARTS FALLS BACKWARD---STUNNED BY THE FLAREBACK OF HIS OWN SPELL---NEBULOS SEIZES THIS INSTANT TO ATTACK THE TRIBUNAL--!
NOW, COSMIC ONE---DO YOU FEEL THE TERRIBLE POTENCY OF MY STAFF OF POLAR POWER?!
NO---CEASE YOUR MADDENED COMBAT!!

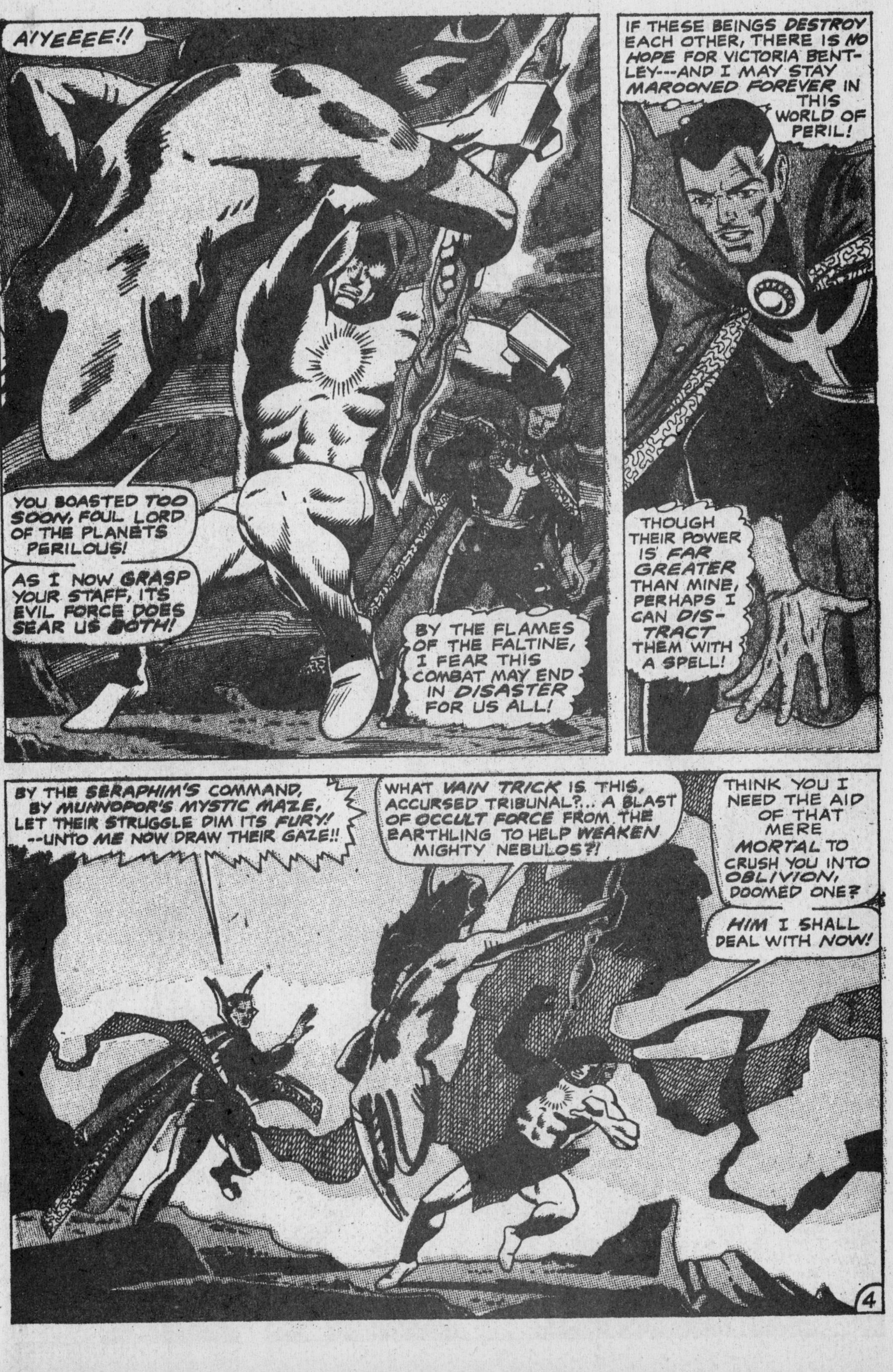
AIYEEEE!!
YOU BOASTED TOO SOON, FOUL LORD OF THE PLANETS PERILOUS!
AS I NOW GRASP YOUR STAFF, ITS EVIL FORCE DOES SEAR US BOTH!
BY THE FLAMES OF THE FALTINE, I FEAR THIS COMBAT MAY END IN DISASTER FOR US ALL!
IF THESE BEINGS DESTROY EACH OTHER, THERE IS NO HOPE FOR VICTORIA BENTLEY---AND I MAY STAY MAROONED FOREVER IN THIS WORLD OF PERIL!
THOUGH THEIR POWER IS FAR GREATER THAN MINE, PERHAPS I CAN DISTRACT THEM WITH A SPELL!
BY THE SERAPHIM'S COMMAND, BY MUNNOPOR'S MYSTIC MAZE, LET THEIR STRUGGLE DIM ITS FURY! --UNTO ME NOW DRAW THEIR GAZE!!
WHAT VAIN TRICK IS THIS, ACCURSED TRIBUNAL?... A BLAST OF OCCULT FORCE FROM THE EARTHLING TO HELP WEAKEN MIGHTY NEBULOS?!
THINK YOU I NEED THE AID OF THAT MERE MORTAL TO CRUSH YOU INTO OBLIVION, DOOMED ONE?
HIM I SHALL DEAL WITH NOW!
4

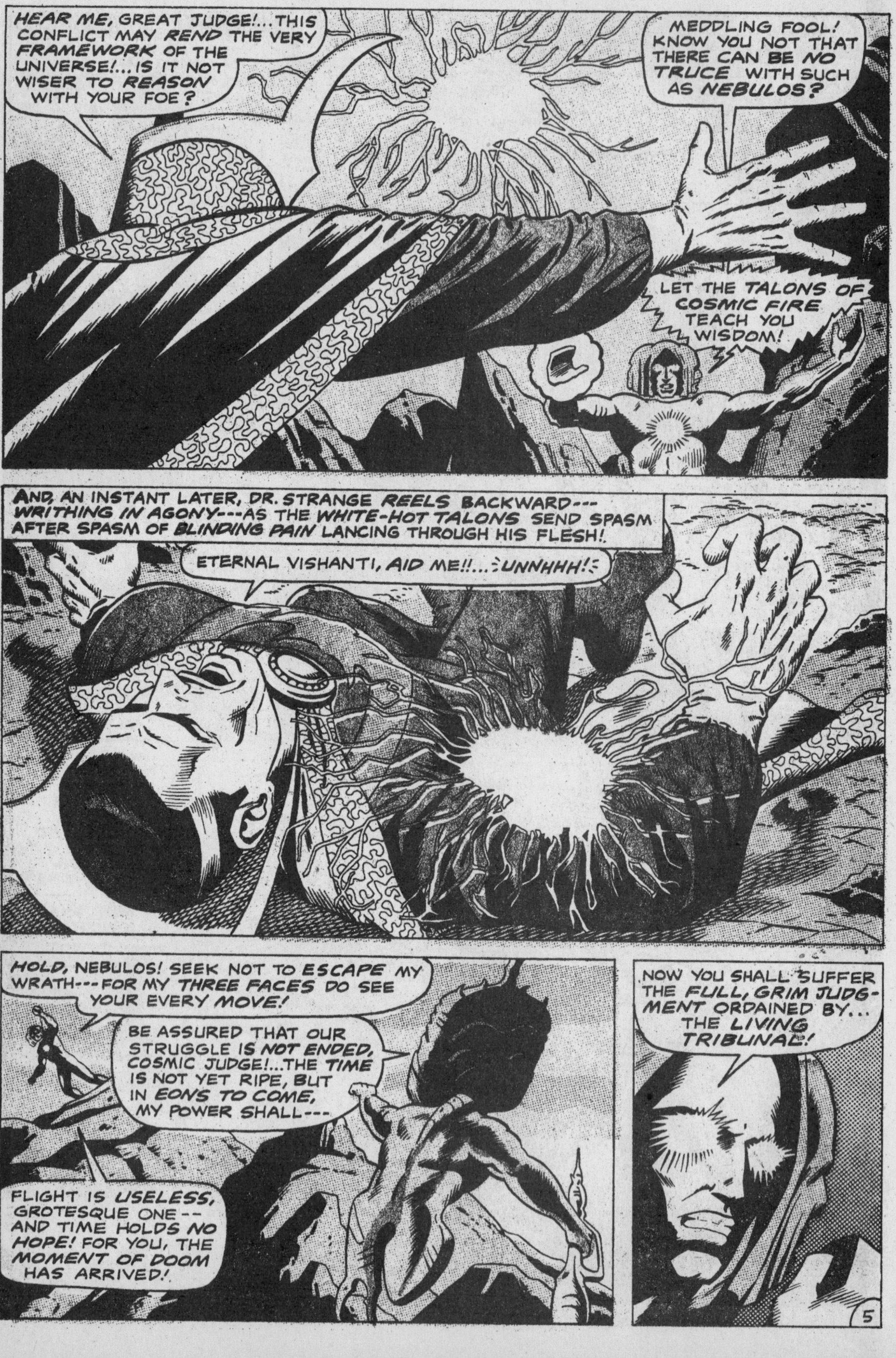
HEAR ME, GREAT JUDGE!...THIS CONFLICT MAY REND THE VERY FRAMEWORK OF THE UNIVERSE!...IS IT NOT WISER TO REASON WITH YOUR FOE?
MEDDLING FOOL! KNOW YOU NOT THAT THERE CAN BE NO TRUCE WITH SUCH AS NEBULOS?
LET THE TALONS OF COSMIC FIRE TEACH YOU WISDOM!
AND AN INSTANT LATER, DR. STRANGE REELS BACKWARD---WRITHING IN AGONY---AS THE WHITE-HOT TALONS SEND SPASM AFTER SPASM OF BLINDING PAIN LANCING THROUGH HIS FLESH!
ETERNAL VISHANTI, AID ME!!...UNNHHH!
HOLD, NEBULOS! SEEK NOT TO ESCAPE MY WRATH---FOR MY THREE FACES DO SEE YOUR EVERY MOVE!
BE ASSURED THAT OUR STRUGGLE IS NOT ENDED, COSMIC JUDGE!...THE TIME IS NOT YET RIPE, BUT IN EONS TO COME, MY POWER SHALL---
FLIGHT IS USELESS, GROTESQUE ONE--AND TIME HOLDS NO HOPE! FOR YOU, THE MOMENT OF DOOM HAS ARRIVED!
NOW YOU SHALL SUFFER THE FULL, GRIM JUDGMENT ORDAINED BY... THE LIVING TRIBUNAL!
5

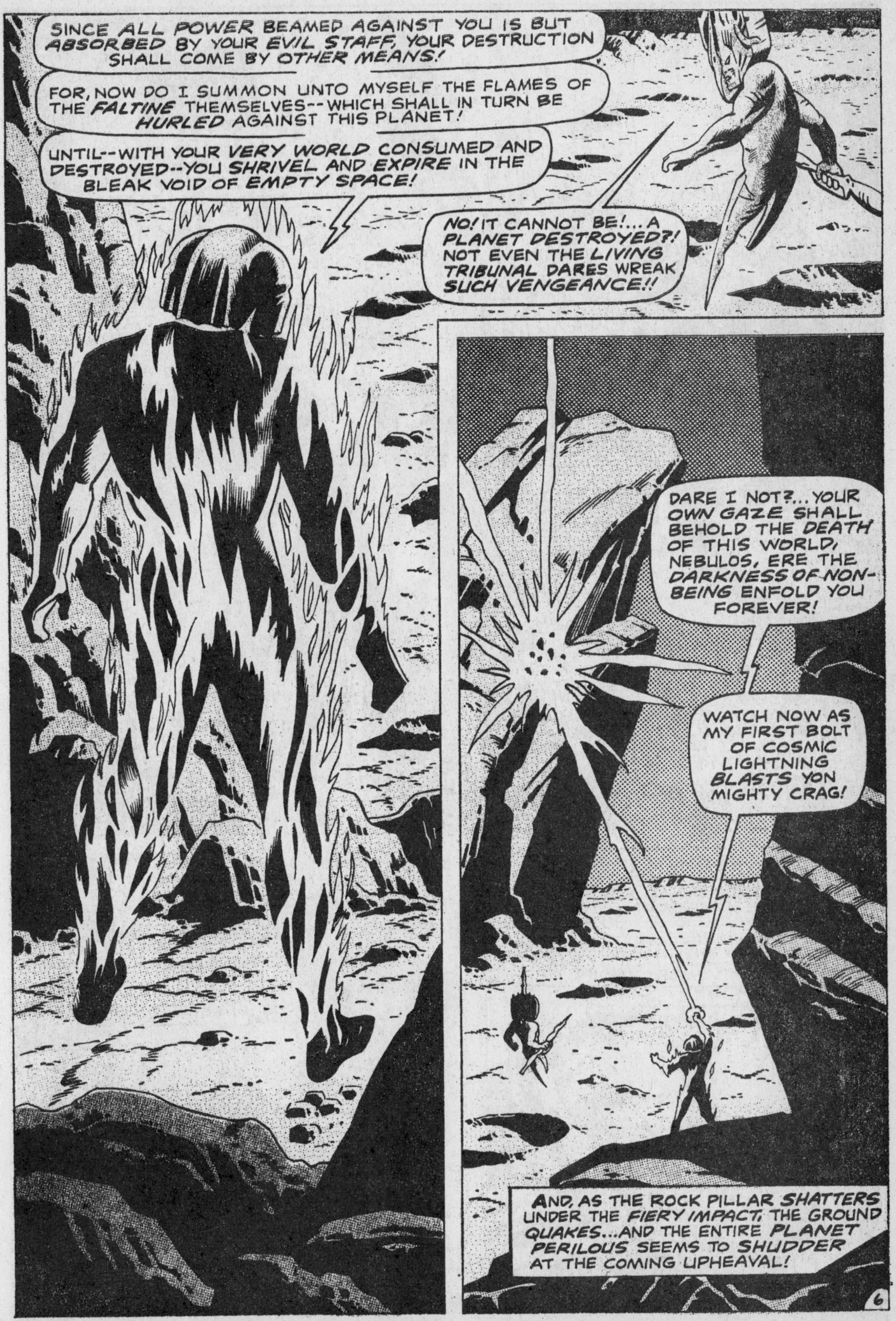
SINCE ALL POWER BEAMED AGAINST YOU IS BUT ABSORBED BY YOUR EVIL STAFF, YOUR DESTRUCTION SHALL COME BY OTHER MEANS!
FOR, NOW DO I SUMMON UNTO MYSELF THE FLAMES OF THE FALTINE THEMSELVES--WHICH SHALL IN TURN BE HURLED AGAINST THIS PLANET!
UNTIL--WITH YOUR VERY WORLD CONSUMED AND DESTROYED--YOU SHRIVEL AND EXPIRE IN THE BLEAK VOID OF EMPTY SPACE!
NO! IT CANNOT BE!... A PLANET DESTROYED?! NOT EVEN THE LIVING TRIBUNAL DARES WREAK SUCH VENGEANCE!!
DARE I NOT?... YOUR OWN GAZE SHALL BEHOLD THE DEATH OF THIS WORLD, NEBULOS, ERE THE DARKNESS OF NON-BEING ENFOLD YOU FOREVER!
WATCH NOW AS MY FIRST BOLT OF COSMIC LIGHTNING BLASTS YON MIGHTY CRAG!
AND, AS THE ROCK PILLAR SHATTERS UNDER THE FIERY IMPACT, THE GROUND QUAKES...AND THE ENTIRE PLANET PERILOUS SEEMS TO SHUDDER AT THE COMING UPHEAVAL!

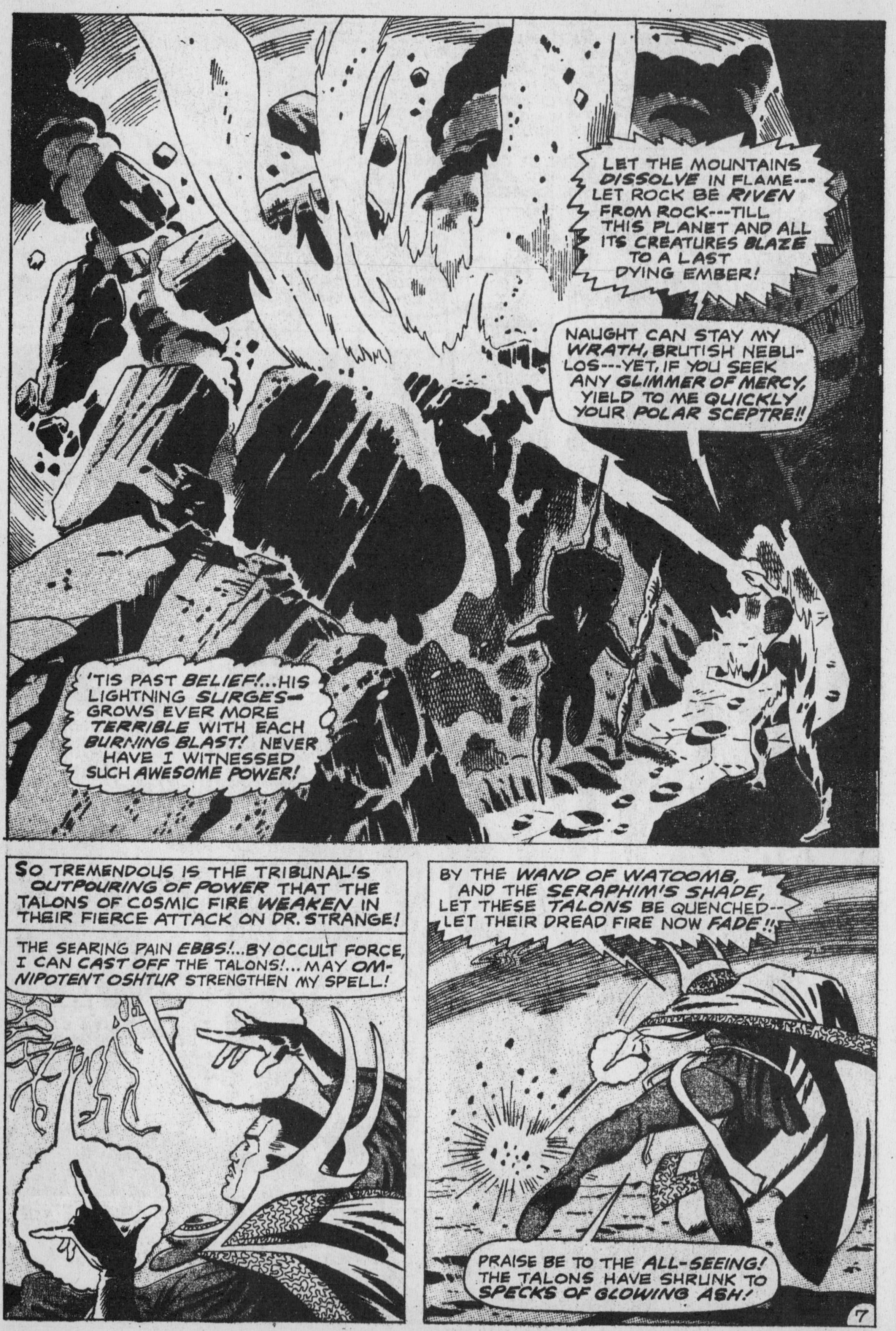
LET THE MOUNTAINS DISSOLVE IN FLAME--- LET ROCK BE RIVEN FROM ROCK---TILL THIS PLANET AND ALL ITS CREATURES BLAZE TO A LAST DYING EMBER!
NAUGHT CAN STAY MY WRATH, BRUTISH NEBULOS---YET, IF YOU SEEK ANY GLIMMER OF MERCY, YIELD TO ME QUICKLY YOUR POLAR SCEPTRE!!
'TIS PAST BELIEF!...HIS LIGHTNING SURGES-- GROWS EVER MORE TERRIBLE WITH EACH BURNING BLAST! NEVER HAVE I WITNESSED SUCH AWESOME POWER!
SO TREMENDOUS IS THE TRIBUNAL'S OUTPOURING OF POWER THAT THE TALONS OF COSMIC FIRE WEAKEN IN THEIR FIERCE ATTACK ON DR. STRANGE!
THE SEARING PAIN EBBS!...BY OCCULT FORCE, I CAN CAST OFF THE TALONS!... MAY OMNIPOTENT OSHTUR STRENGTHEN MY SPELL!
BY THE WAND OF WATOOMB, AND THE SERAPHIM'S SHADE, LET THESE TALONS BE QUENCHED-- LET THEIR DREAD FIRE NOW FADE!!
PRAISE BE TO THE ALL-SEEING! THE TALONS HAVE SHRUNK TO SPECKS OF GLOWING ASH!

BY THE HOARY HOSTS OF *HOGGOTH!* AN *AVALANCHE* OF FALLING ROCKS!

THE *TITANIC* STRUGGLE BETWEEN NEBULOS AND THE TRIBUNAL MUST BE *SHAKING* THE VERY MOUNTAINS!

CLOAK OF LEVITATION-- LIFT ME *INSTANTLY* TO THE HIGHEST PEAK OF THIS *DOOMED* WORLD --WHERE I MAY SEE THE CAUSE OF *SUCH UPHEAVAL!*

NOT A MOMENT MUST BE *LOST* --OR VICTORIA BENTLEY'S FATE AND MY OWN MAY BE SEALED *FOREVER!*

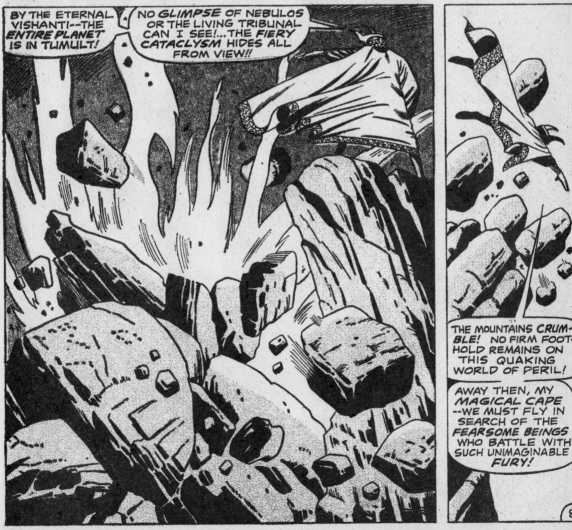

BY THE ETERNAL VISHANTI--THE *ENTIRE* PLANET IS IN TUMULT!

NO *GLIMPSE* OF NEBULOS OR THE LIVING TRIBUNAL CAN I SEE!...THE *FIERY* CATACLYSM HIDES ALL FROM VIEW!!

THE MOUNTAINS *CRUMBLE!* NO FIRM FOOT-HOLD REMAINS ON THIS QUAKING WORLD OF PERIL!

AWAY THEN, MY *MAGICAL CAPE* --WE MUST FLY IN SEARCH OF THE *FEARSOME BEINGS* WHO BATTLE WITH SUCH UNIMAGINABLE *FURY!*

8

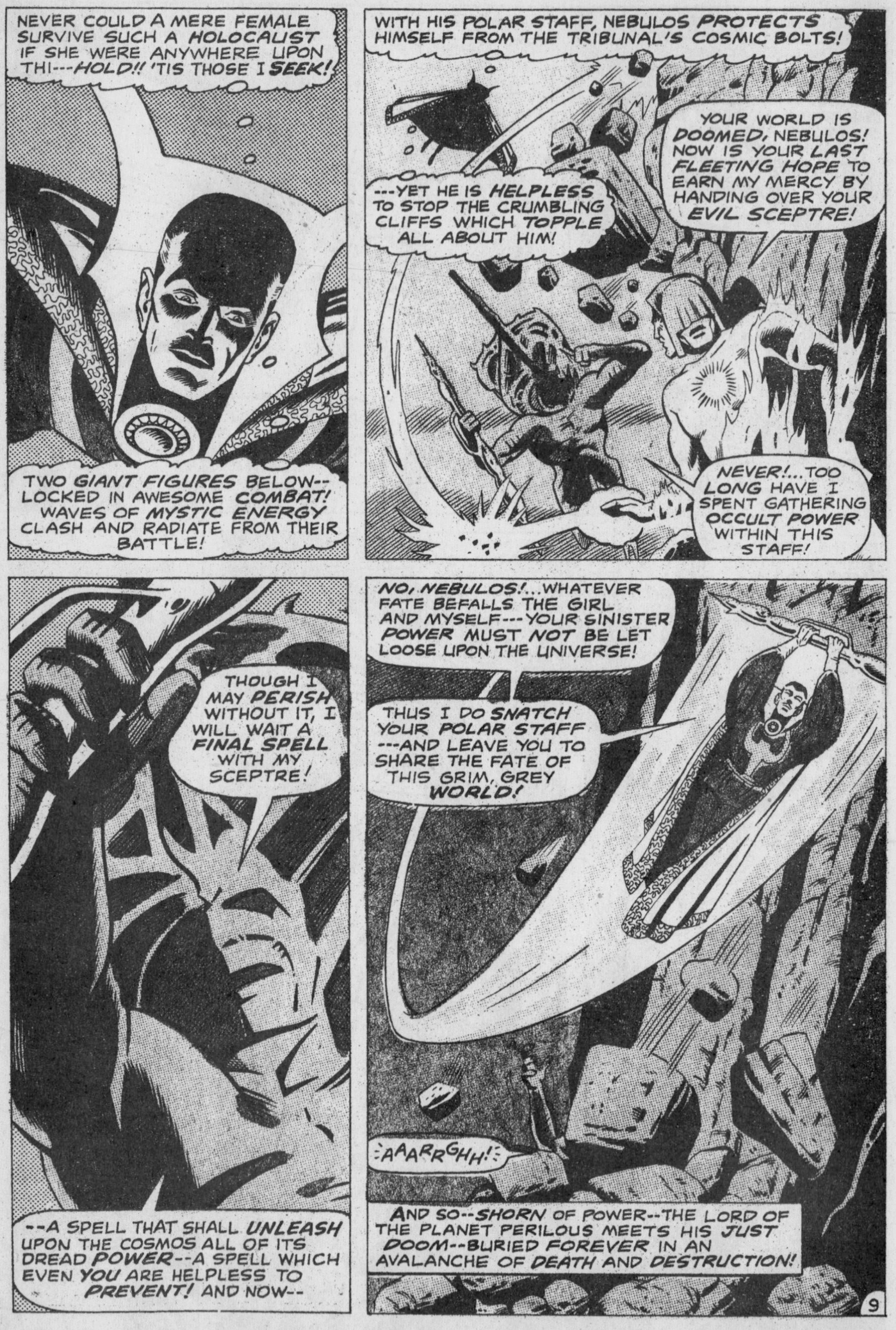
NEVER COULD A MERE FEMALE SURVIVE SUCH A HOLOCAUST IF SHE WERE ANYWHERE UPON THI---HOLD!! 'TIS THOSE I SEEK!
TWO GIANT FIGURES BELOW--LOCKED IN AWESOME COMBAT! WAVES OF MYSTIC ENERGY CLASH AND RADIATE FROM THEIR BATTLE!
WITH HIS POLAR STAFF, NEBULOS PROTECTS HIMSELF FROM THE TRIBUNAL'S COSMIC BOLTS!
---YET HE IS HELPLESS TO STOP THE CRUMBLING CLIFFS WHICH TOPPLE ALL ABOUT HIM!
YOUR WORLD IS DOOMED, NEBULOS! NOW IS YOUR LAST FLEETING HOPE TO EARN MY MERCY BY HANDING OVER YOUR EVIL SCEPTRE!
NEVER!...TOO LONG HAVE I SPENT GATHERING OCCULT POWER WITHIN THIS STAFF!
THOUGH I MAY PERISH WITHOUT IT, I WILL WAIT A FINAL SPELL WITH MY SCEPTRE!
--A SPELL THAT SHALL UNLEASH UPON THE COSMOS ALL OF ITS DREAD POWER--A SPELL WHICH EVEN YOU ARE HELPLESS TO PREVENT! AND NOW--
NO, NEBULOS!...WHATEVER FATE BEFALLS THE GIRL AND MYSELF---YOUR SINISTER POWER MUST NOT BE LET LOOSE UPON THE UNIVERSE!
THUS I DO SNATCH YOUR POLAR STAFF ---AND LEAVE YOU TO SHARE THE FATE OF THIS GRIM, GREY WORLD!
AAARRGHH!
AND SO--SHORN OF POWER--THE LORD OF THE PLANET PERILOUS MEETS HIS JUST DOOM--BURIED FOREVER IN AN AVALANCHE OF DEATH AND DESTRUCTION!
9

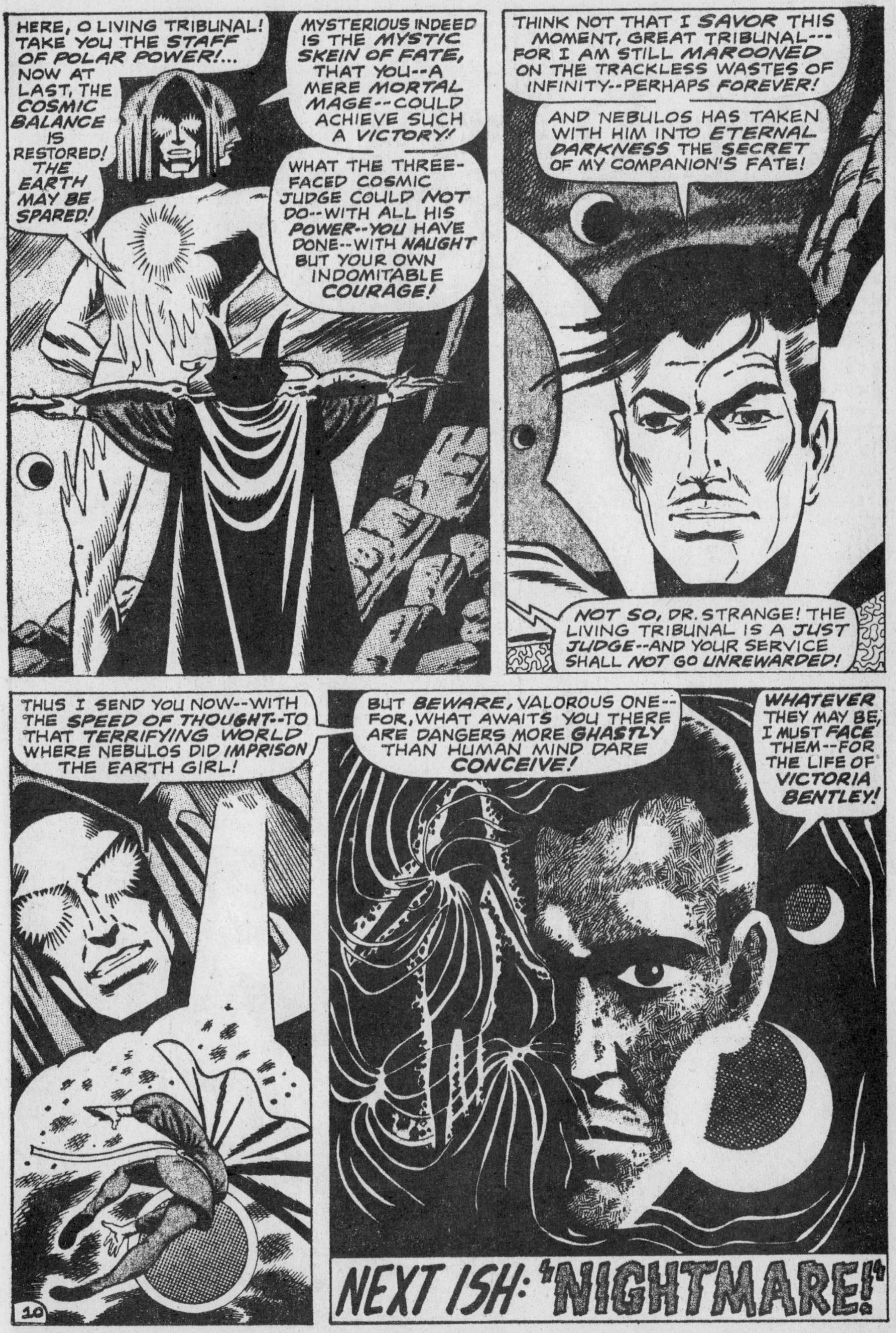
HERE, O LIVING TRIBUNAL! TAKE YOU THE STAFF OF POLAR POWER!... NOW AT LAST, THE COSMIC BALANCE IS RESTORED! THE EARTH MAY BE SPARED!
MYSTERIOUS INDEED IS THE MYSTIC SKEIN OF FATE, THAT YOU--A MERE MORTAL MAGE--COULD ACHIEVE SUCH A VICTORY!
WHAT THE THREE-FACED COSMIC JUDGE COULD NOT DO--WITH ALL HIS POWER--YOU HAVE DONE--WITH NAUGHT BUT YOUR OWN INDOMITABLE COURAGE!
THINK NOT THAT I SAVOR THIS MOMENT, GREAT TRIBUNAL---FOR I AM STILL MAROONED ON THE TRACKLESS WASTES OF INFINITY--PERHAPS FOREVER!
AND NEBULOS HAS TAKEN WITH HIM INTO ETERNAL DARKNESS THE SECRET OF MY COMPANION'S FATE!
NOT SO, DR. STRANGE! THE LIVING TRIBUNAL IS A JUST JUDGE--AND YOUR SERVICE SHALL NOT GO UNREWARDED!
THUS I SEND YOU NOW--WITH THE SPEED OF THOUGHT--TO THAT TERRIFYING WORLD WHERE NEBULOS DID IMPRISON THE EARTH GIRL!
BUT BEWARE, VALOROUS ONE--FOR, WHAT AWAITS YOU THERE ARE DANGERS MORE GHASTLY THAN HUMAN MIND DARE CONCEIVE!
WHATEVER THEY MAY BE, I MUST FACE THEM--FOR THE LIFE OF VICTORIA BENTLEY!
NEXT ISH: "NIGHTMARE!"
10

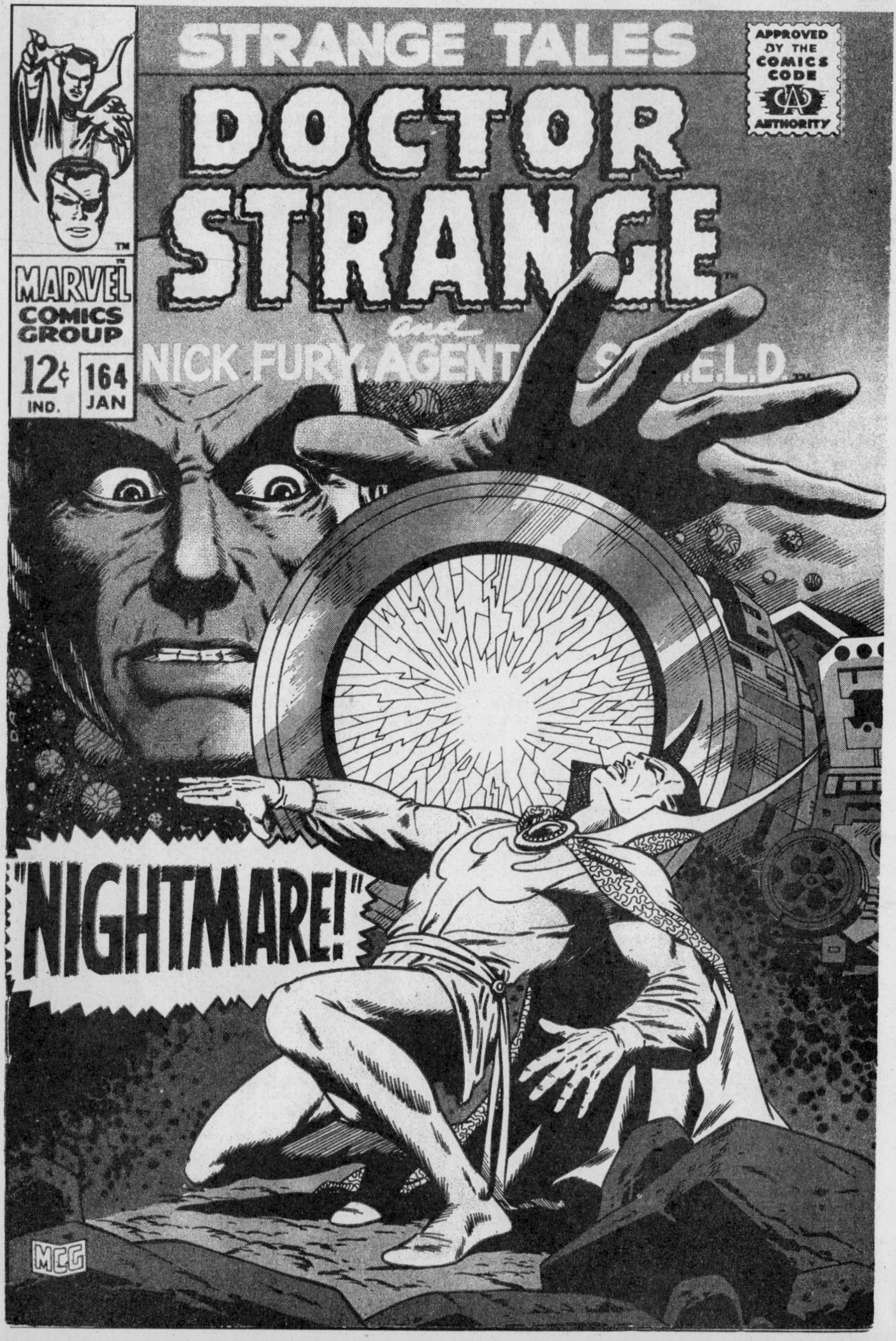

STRANGE TALES
DOCTOR STRANGE
and
NICK FURY, AGENT
MARVEL COMICS GROUP
12¢ IND.
164 JAN
APPROVED BY THE COMICS CODE AUTHORITY
"NIGHTMARE!"
MCG

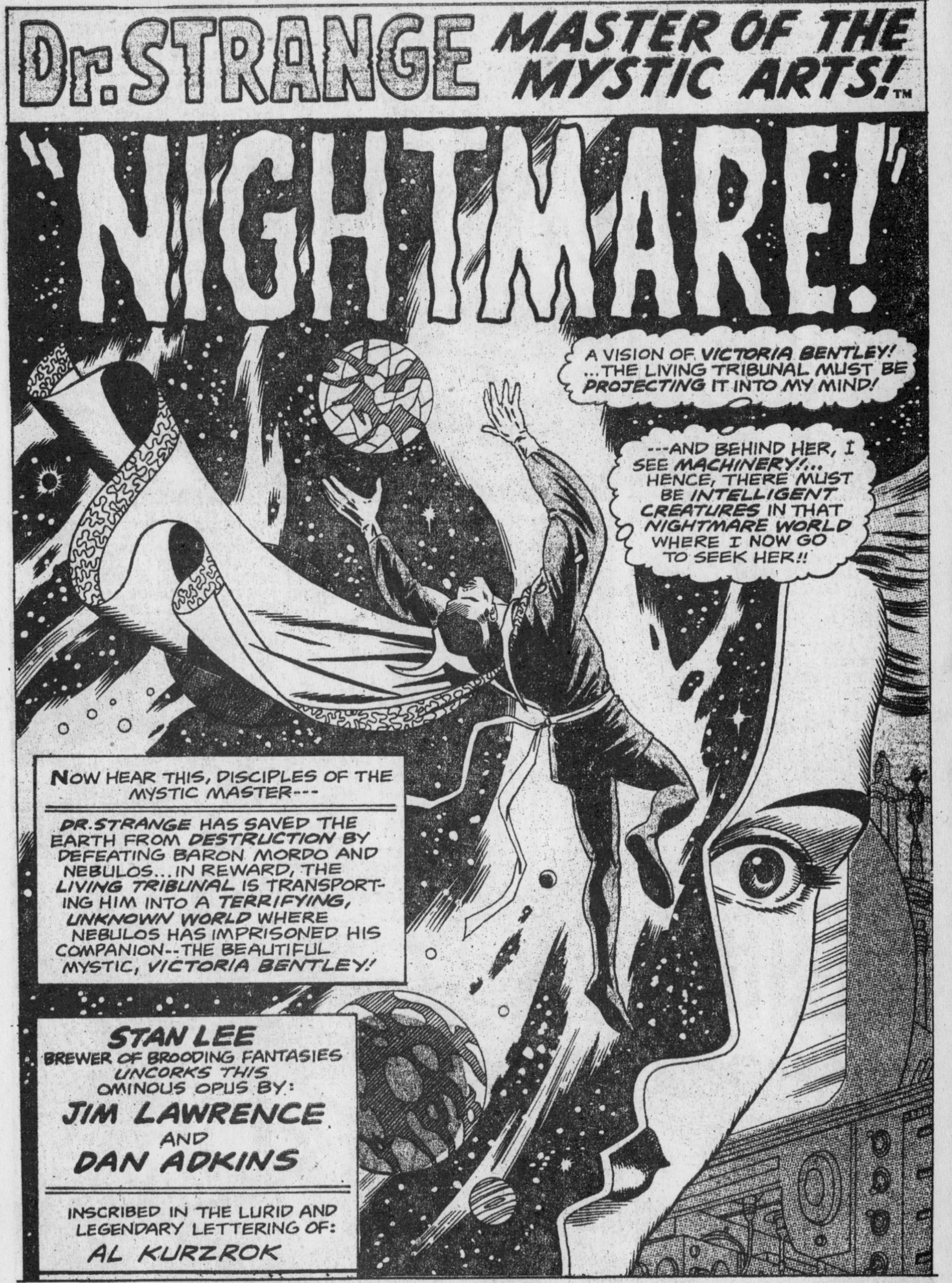
Dr. STRANGE MASTER OF THE MYSTIC ARTS!™
"NIGHTMARE!"
A VISION OF VICTORIA BENTLEY! ...THE LIVING TRIBUNAL MUST BE PROJECTING IT INTO MY MIND!
---AND BEHIND HER, I SEE MACHINERY!... HENCE, THERE MUST BE INTELLIGENT CREATURES IN THAT NIGHTMARE WORLD WHERE I NOW GO TO SEEK HER!!
NOW HEAR THIS, DISCIPLES OF THE MYSTIC MASTER---
DR. STRANGE HAS SAVED THE EARTH FROM DESTRUCTION BY DEFEATING BARON MORDO AND NEBULOS...IN REWARD, THE LIVING TRIBUNAL IS TRANSPORTING HIM INTO A TERRIFYING, UNKNOWN WORLD WHERE NEBULOS HAS IMPRISONED HIS COMPANION--THE BEAUTIFUL MYSTIC, VICTORIA BENTLEY!
STAN LEE BREWER OF BROODING FANTASIES UNCORKS THIS OMINOUS OPUS BY: JIM LAWRENCE AND DAN ADKINS
INSCRIBED IN THE LURID AND LEGENDARY LETTERING OF: AL KURZROK

AND NOW THE VISION *FADES* AND IS GONE!... ONCE MORE THE *DARK* VOID OF *TIMELESS* SPACE ENFOLDS ME!

UNTIL, SUDDENLY...

PRAISE BE TO THE *ALL-SEEING* AGAMOTTO--MY TRIP IS *DONE!*... I AM BEING DRAWN TO THAT *BECKONING* PLANET BELOW!

MY FEELING OF *WEIGHT* IS RETURNING AS I BUFFET INTO ITS *OUTER* ATMOSPHERE!

BY THE *VAPORS OF VALTOR* --LET THE MAGIC CLOAK OF LEVITATION *SLOW* MY DESCENT!

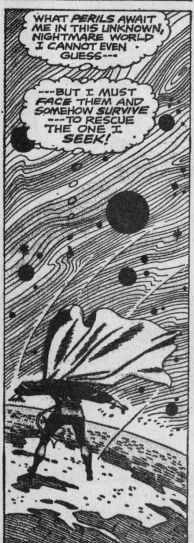

WHAT *PERILS* AWAIT ME IN THIS UNKNOWN, NIGHTMARE WORLD I CANNOT EVEN GUESS---

---BUT I MUST *FACE* THEM AND SOMEHOW *SURVIVE* ---TO RESCUE THE ONE I *SEEK!*

MOMENTS LATER, DR. STRANGE LANDS--AMID A FANTASTIC LANDSCAPE OF TWINING, LUXURIANT PLANT GROWTH--ON A *WEIRDLY* POCK-MARKED TERRAIN OF RIOTOUS COLORS!

BY THE HOARY HOSTS OF HOGGOTH, IT IS MORE LIKE A *JUNGLE* THAN ANY WORLD WHERE *CIVILIZATION* MAY BE SPAWNED!

NOT A *TRACE* DO I SEE OF THE *GIRL*--NOR ANY SIGN OF *MACHINERY,* SUCH AS I GLIMPSED IN MY *VISION!*

2

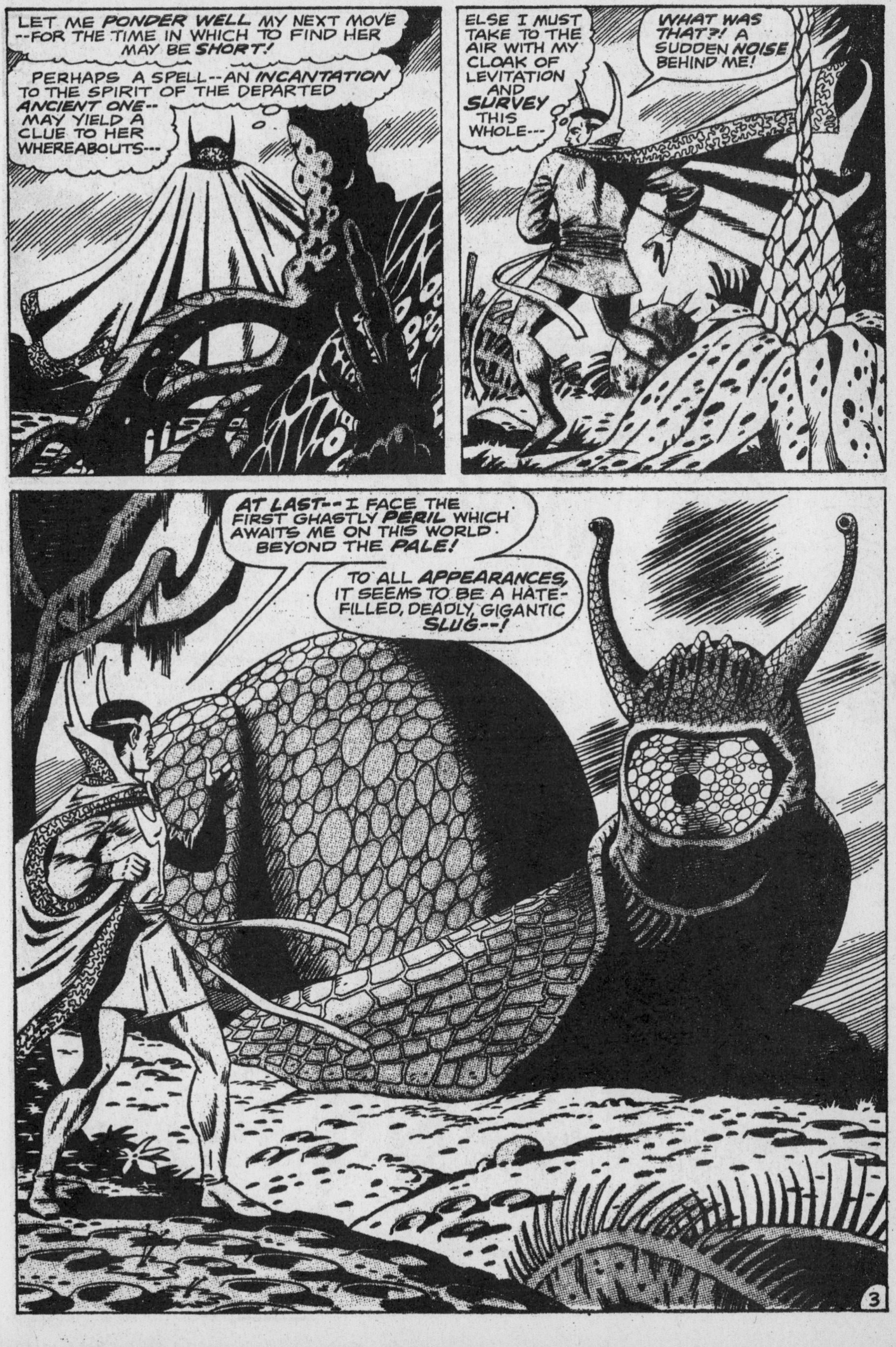

LET ME PONDER WELL MY NEXT MOVE --FOR THE TIME IN WHICH TO FIND HER MAY BE SHORT!
PERHAPS A SPELL--AN INCANTATION TO THE SPIRIT OF THE DEPARTED ANCIENT ONE-- MAY YIELD A CLUE TO HER WHEREABOUTS---
ELSE I MUST TAKE TO THE AIR WITH MY CLOAK OF LEVITATION AND SURVEY THIS WHOLE---
WHAT WAS THAT?! A SUDDEN NOISE BEHIND ME!
AT LAST--I FACE THE FIRST GHASTLY PERIL WHICH AWAITS ME ON THIS WORLD BEYOND THE PALE!
TO ALL APPEARANCES, IT SEEMS TO BE A HATE-FILLED, DEADLY, GIGANTIC SLUG--!
3

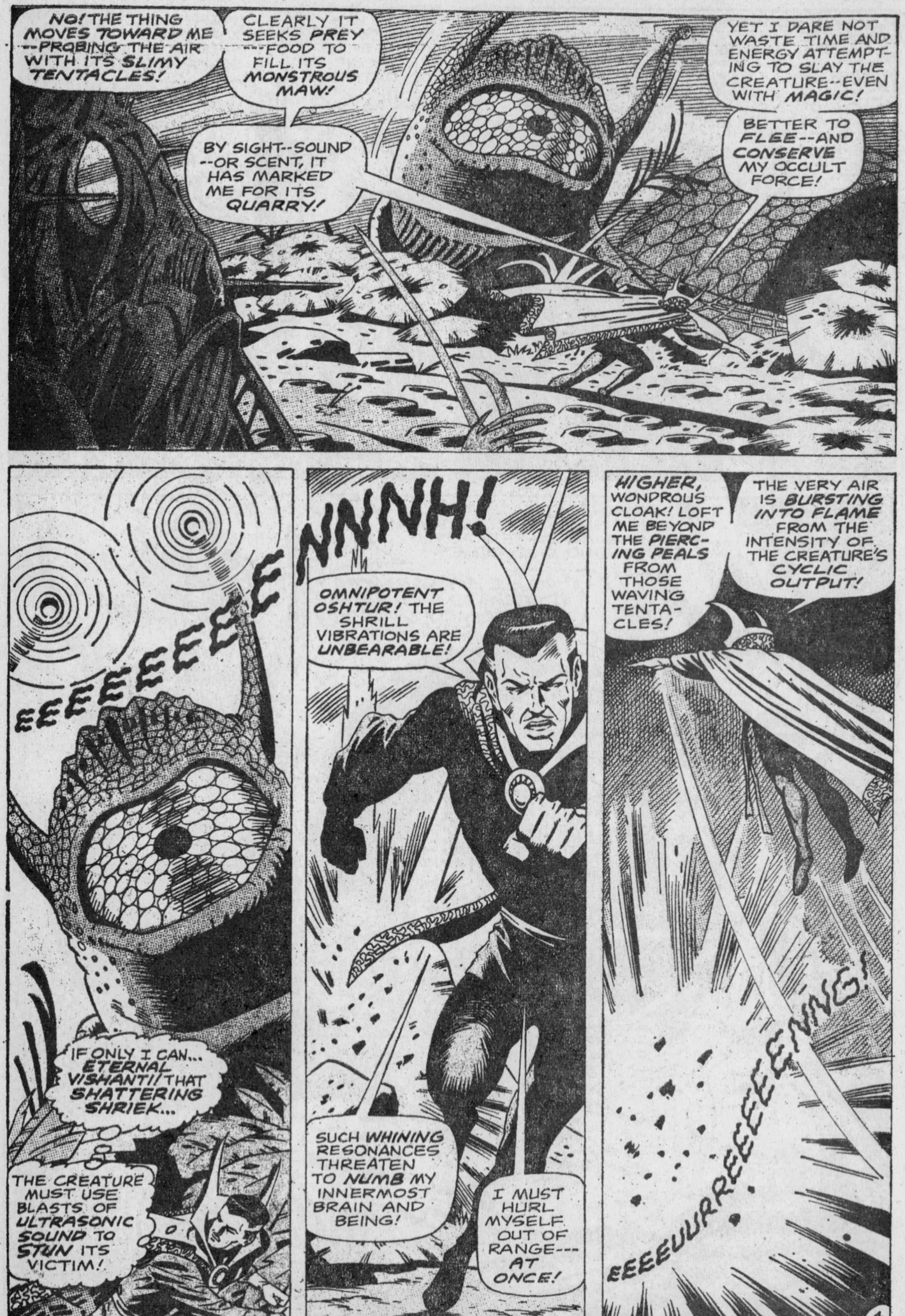
NO! THE THING MOVES TOWARD ME --PROBING THE AIR WITH ITS SLIMY TENTACLES!
CLEARLY IT SEEKS PREY --FOOD TO FILL ITS MONSTROUS MAW!
BY SIGHT--SOUND --OR SCENT, IT HAS MARKED ME FOR ITS QUARRY!
YET I DARE NOT WASTE TIME AND ENERGY ATTEMPTING TO SLAY THE CREATURE--EVEN WITH MAGIC!
BETTER TO FLEE--AND CONSERVE MY OCCULT FORCE!
EEEEEEEEEENNNH!
IF ONLY I CAN... ETERNAL VISHANTI!! THAT SHATTERING SHRIEK...
THE CREATURE MUST USE BLASTS OF ULTRASONIC SOUND TO STUN ITS VICTIM!
OMNIPOTENT OSHTUR! THE SHRILL VIBRATIONS ARE UNBEARABLE!
SUCH WHINING RESONANCES THREATEN TO NUMB MY INNERMOST BRAIN AND BEING!
I MUST HURL MYSELF OUT OF RANGE--- AT ONCE!
HIGHER, WONDROUS CLOAK! LOFT ME BEYOND THE PIERCING PEALS FROM THOSE WAVING TENTACLES!
THE VERY AIR IS BURSTING INTO FLAME FROM THE INTENSITY OF THE CREATURE'S CYCLIC OUTPUT!
EEEEUURREEEEENNG!

BY THE TWIN HORNS OF BELIAL, *STILL* THE DREAD CREATURE *PURSUES* ME!

A MICROSECOND LATER AND ITS *SONIC BEAMS* WOULD HAVE REDUCED ME TO A MASS OF *QUIVERING FLESH!*

THERE IS NO *ESCAPING* THE SLUG'S MINDLESS FURY--- I MUST *ATTACK!*

KRRZEEEEENNN

BACK--MONSTROUS SPAWN OF THIS PERILOUS PLANET! LET MY MYSTIC BOLT QUELL YOUR SAVAGE ONSLAUGHT!

WIZZZAPP!

YAAAWRRRGH!

BY THE *FLAMES OF THE FALTINE*--THE SLUG HALTS IN HIS *TRACKS*--

AND NOW IT SPRAWLS MOTIONLESS--TEMPORARILY *STUNNED!* FOR A WHILE AT LEAST, IT PRESENTS NO FURTHER *DANGER!*

BUT I MUST MOVE ON--*QUICKLY*--BEFORE ITS DEADLY TENTACLES *RESUME* THEIR ULTRASONIC HUNTING BLASTS!

FOR THE ALL-SEEING *ALONE* KNOWS WHAT OTHER *NIGHTMARISH* CREATURES MAY LURK IN THIS JUNGLED WILDERNESS!

THEN, AS THE MASTER OF THE MYSTIC ARTS PRESSES *ONWARD*...

A FEELING OF *GRIM FOREBODING* GRIPS ME--

--ALREADY I SUSPECT THAT THE TASK OF RESCUING MISS BENTLEY MAY BE EVEN *MORE HOPELESS* THAN I HAD GUESSED!

AND IF I *DO* SUCCEED, WILL I BE IN TIME TO *SAVE* HER--WITH SUCH MONSTERS AS THE GIANT SLUG LYING IN *WAIT* FOR ME--IN EVERY *SHADOW!*

5

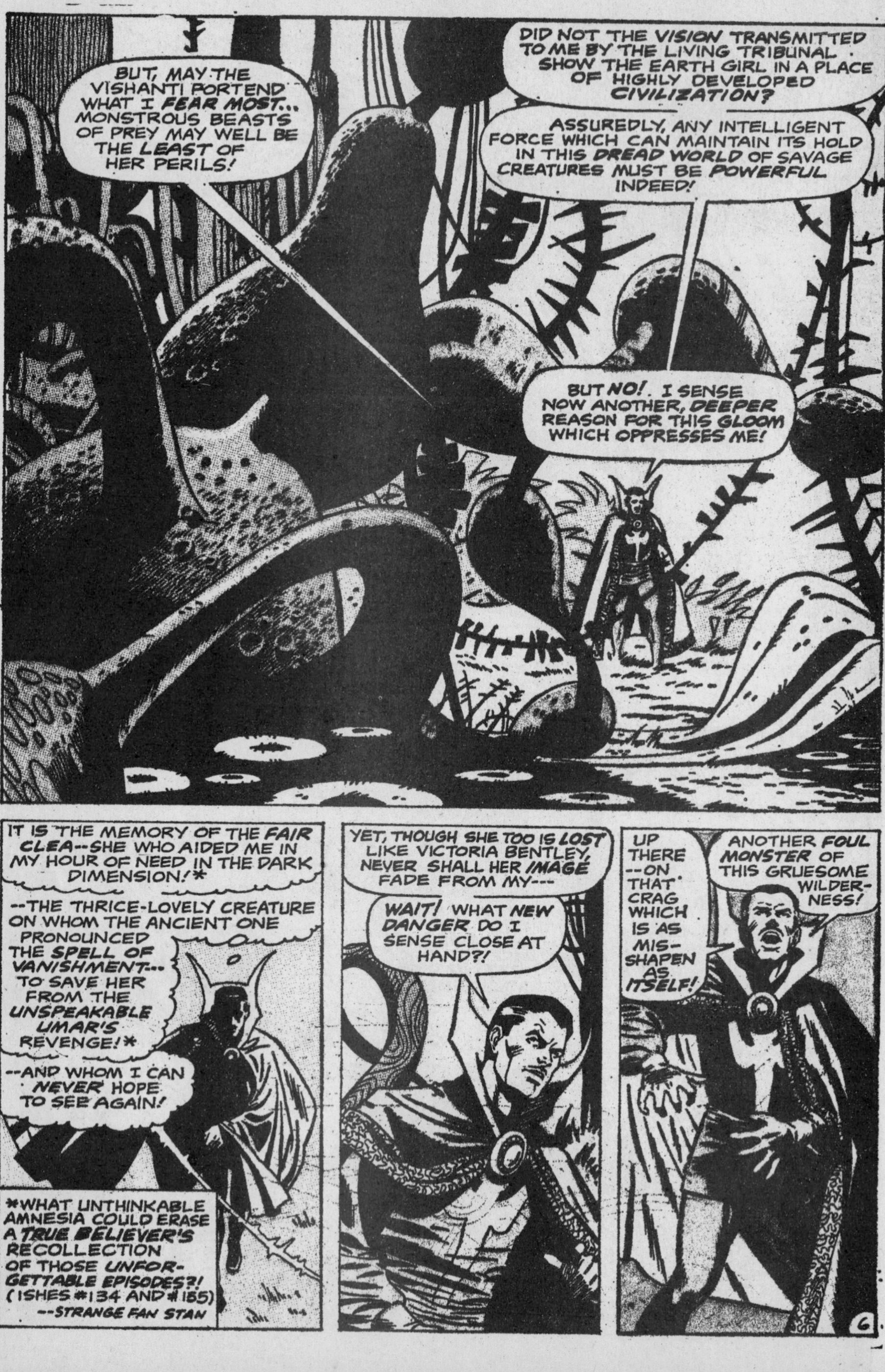

BUT, MAY THE VISHANTI PORTEND WHAT I FEAR MOST... MONSTROUS BEASTS OF PREY MAY WELL BE THE LEAST OF HER PERILS!
DID NOT THE VISION TRANSMITTED TO ME BY THE LIVING TRIBUNAL SHOW THE EARTH GIRL IN A PLACE OF HIGHLY DEVELOPED CIVILIZATION?
ASSUREDLY, ANY INTELLIGENT FORCE WHICH CAN MAINTAIN ITS HOLD IN THIS DREAD WORLD OF SAVAGE CREATURES MUST BE POWERFUL INDEED!
BUT NO! I SENSE NOW ANOTHER, DEEPER REASON FOR THIS GLOOM WHICH OPPRESSES ME!
IT IS THE MEMORY OF THE FAIR CLEA--SHE WHO AIDED ME IN MY HOUR OF NEED IN THE DARK DIMENSION!*
--THE THRICE-LOVELY CREATURE ON WHOM THE ANCIENT ONE PRONOUNCED THE SPELL OF VANISHMENT... TO SAVE HER FROM THE UNSPEAKABLE UMAR'S REVENGE!*
--AND WHOM I CAN NEVER HOPE TO SEE AGAIN!
*WHAT UNTHINKABLE AMNESIA COULD ERASE A TRUE BELIEVER'S RECOLLECTION OF THOSE UNFORGETTABLE EPISODES?! (ISHES #134 AND #135) --STRANGE FAN STAN
YET, THOUGH SHE TOO IS LOST LIKE VICTORIA BENTLEY, NEVER SHALL HER IMAGE FADE FROM MY---
WAIT! WHAT NEW DANGER DO I SENSE CLOSE AT HAND?!
UP THERE --ON THAT CRAG WHICH IS AS MIS-SHAPEN AS ITSELF!
ANOTHER FOUL MONSTER OF THIS GRUESOME WILDER-NESS!
6

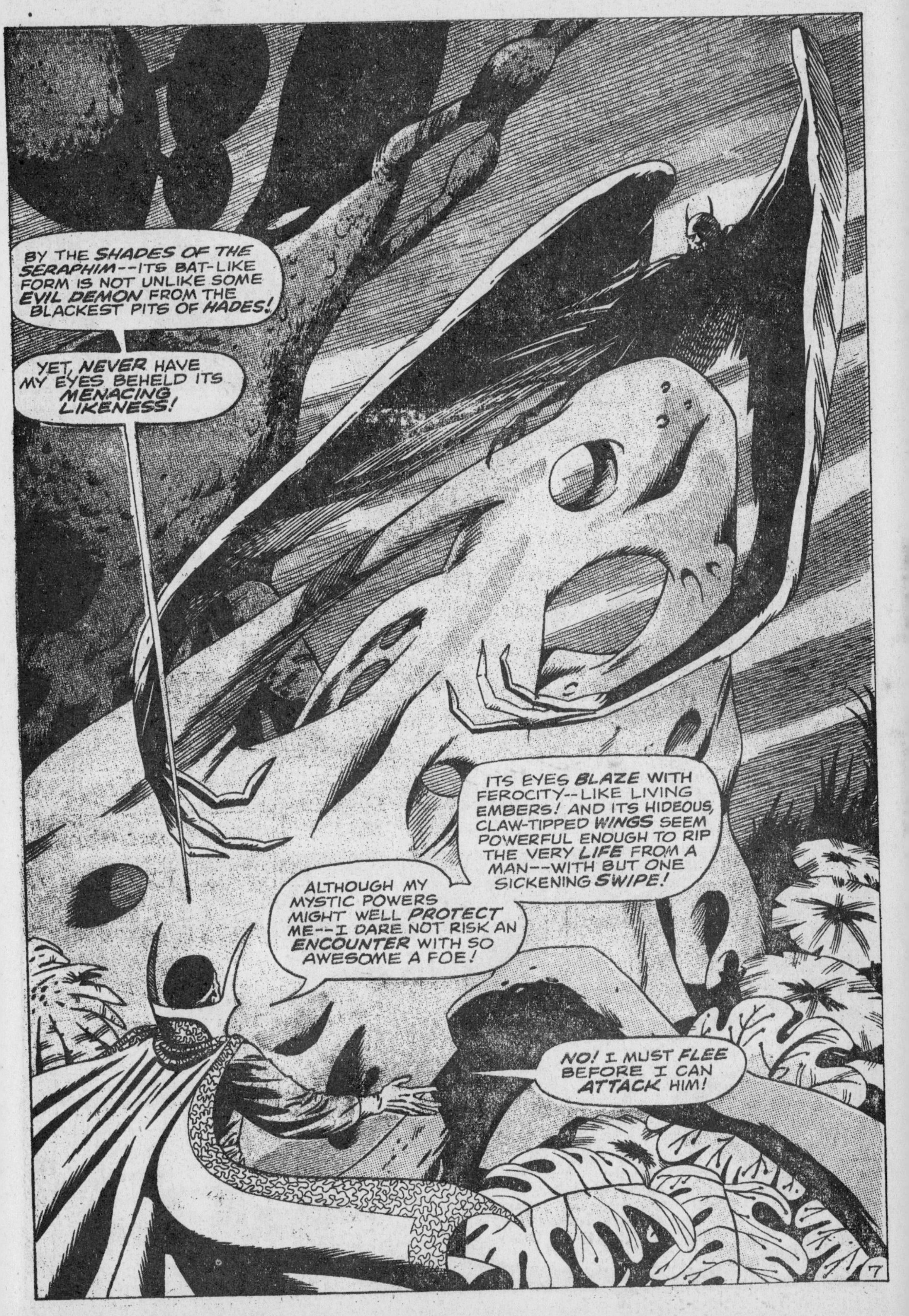
BY THE SHADES OF THE SERAPHIM--ITS BAT-LIKE FORM IS NOT UNLIKE SOME EVIL DEMON FROM THE BLACKEST PITS OF HADES!
YET, NEVER HAVE MY EYES BEHELD ITS MENACING LIKENESS!
ITS EYES BLAZE WITH FEROCITY--LIKE LIVING EMBERS! AND ITS HIDEOUS, CLAW-TIPPED WINGS SEEM POWERFUL ENOUGH TO RIP THE VERY LIFE FROM A MAN--WITH BUT ONE SICKENING SWIPE!
ALTHOUGH MY MYSTIC POWERS MIGHT WELL PROTECT ME--I DARE NOT RISK AN ENCOUNTER WITH SO AWESOME A FOE!
NO! I MUST FLEE BEFORE I CAN ATTACK HIM!
7

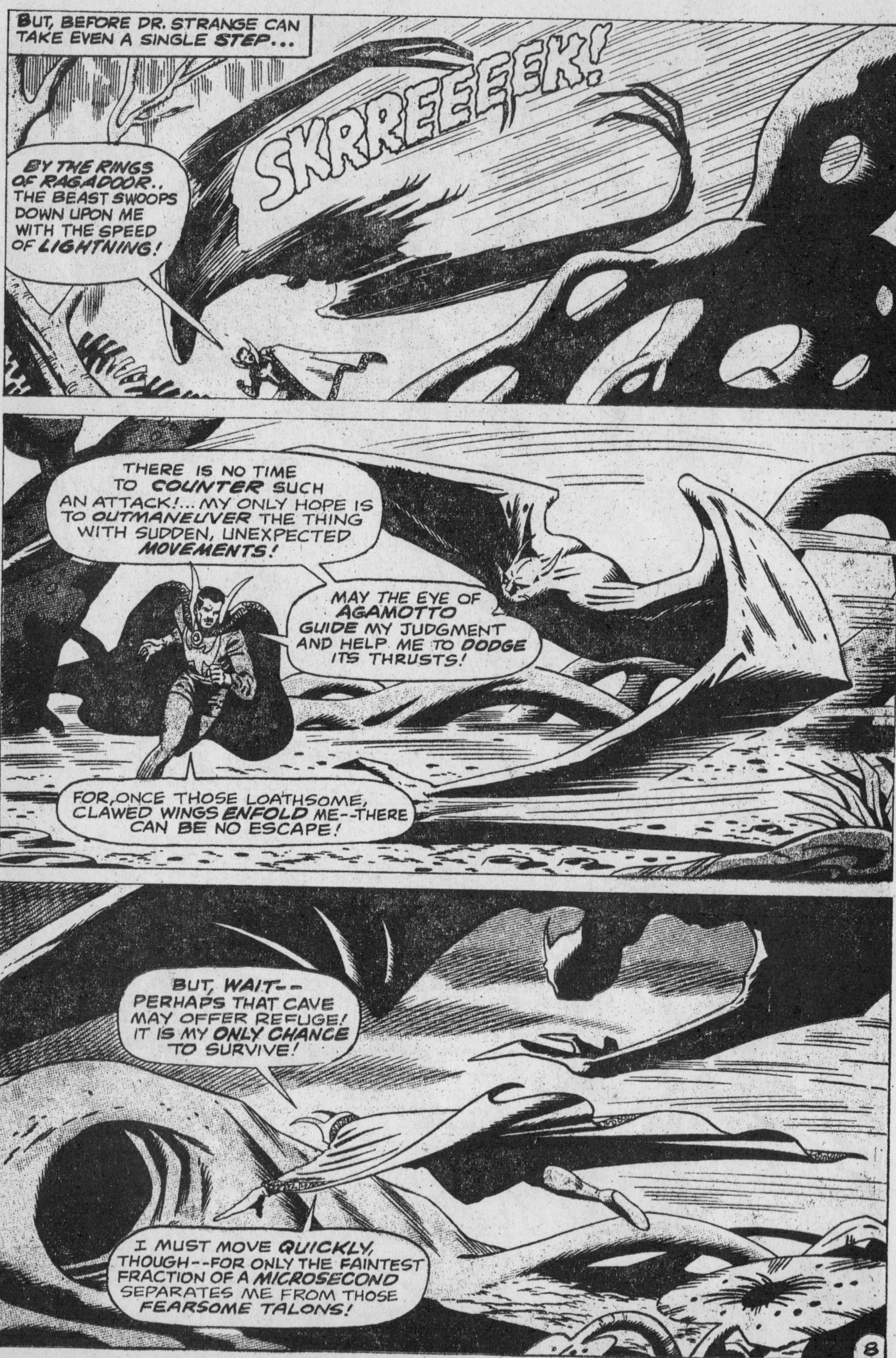
BUT, BEFORE DR. STRANGE CAN TAKE EVEN A SINGLE STEP...
SKRREEEEK!
BY THE RINGS OF RAGADOOR.. THE BEAST SWOOPS DOWN UPON ME WITH THE SPEED OF LIGHTNING!
THERE IS NO TIME TO COUNTER SUCH AN ATTACK!... MY ONLY HOPE IS TO OUTMANEUVER THE THING WITH SUDDEN, UNEXPECTED MOVEMENTS!
MAY THE EYE OF AGAMOTTO GUIDE MY JUDGMENT AND HELP ME TO DODGE ITS THRUSTS!
FOR, ONCE THOSE LOATHSOME, CLAWED WINGS ENFOLD ME--THERE CAN BE NO ESCAPE!
BUT, WAIT-- PERHAPS THAT CAVE MAY OFFER REFUGE! IT IS MY ONLY CHANCE TO SURVIVE!
I MUST MOVE QUICKLY, THOUGH--FOR ONLY THE FAINTEST FRACTION OF A MICROSECOND SEPARATES ME FROM THOSE FEARSOME TALONS!
8

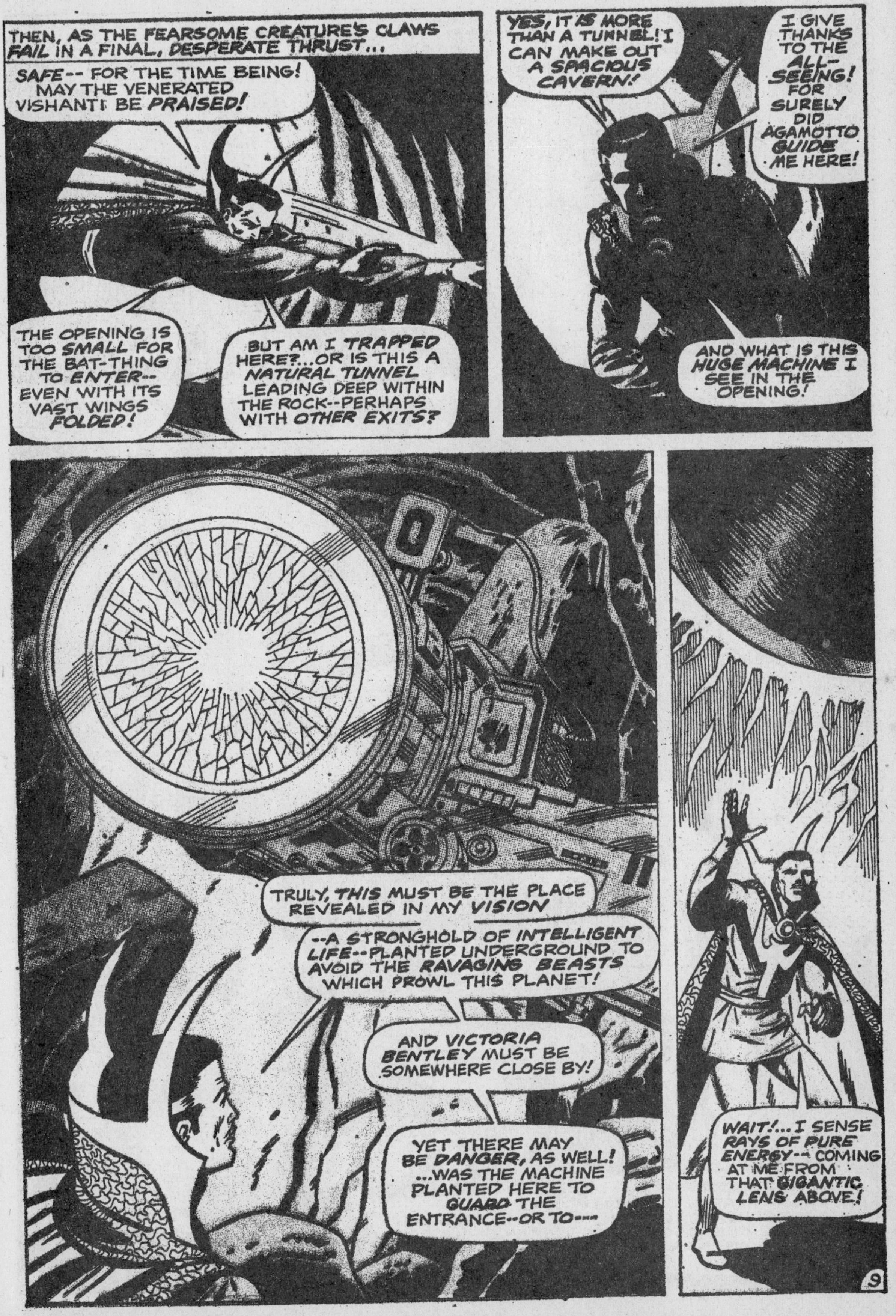
THEN, AS THE FEARSOME CREATURE'S CLAWS FAIL IN A FINAL, DESPERATE THRUST...
SAFE-- FOR THE TIME BEING! MAY THE VENERATED VISHANTI BE PRAISED!
THE OPENING IS TOO SMALL FOR THE BAT-THING TO ENTER-- EVEN WITH ITS VAST WINGS FOLDED!
BUT AM I TRAPPED HERE?...OR IS THIS A NATURAL TUNNEL LEADING DEEP WITHIN THE ROCK--PERHAPS WITH OTHER EXITS?
YES, IT IS MORE THAN A TUNNEL! I CAN MAKE OUT A SPACIOUS CAVERN!
I GIVE THANKS TO THE ALL-SEEING! FOR SURELY DID AGAMOTTO GUIDE ME HERE!
AND WHAT IS THIS HUGE MACHINE I SEE IN THE OPENING!
TRULY, THIS MUST BE THE PLACE REVEALED IN MY VISION
--A STRONGHOLD OF INTELLIGENT LIFE--PLANTED UNDERGROUND TO AVOID THE RAVAGING BEASTS WHICH PROWL THIS PLANET!
AND VICTORIA BENTLEY MUST BE SOMEWHERE CLOSE BY!
YET THERE MAY BE DANGER, AS WELL! ...WAS THE MACHINE PLANTED HERE TO GUARD THE ENTRANCE--OR TO---
WAIT!...I SENSE RAYS OF PURE ENERGY-- COMING AT ME FROM THAT GIGANTIC LENS ABOVE!
9

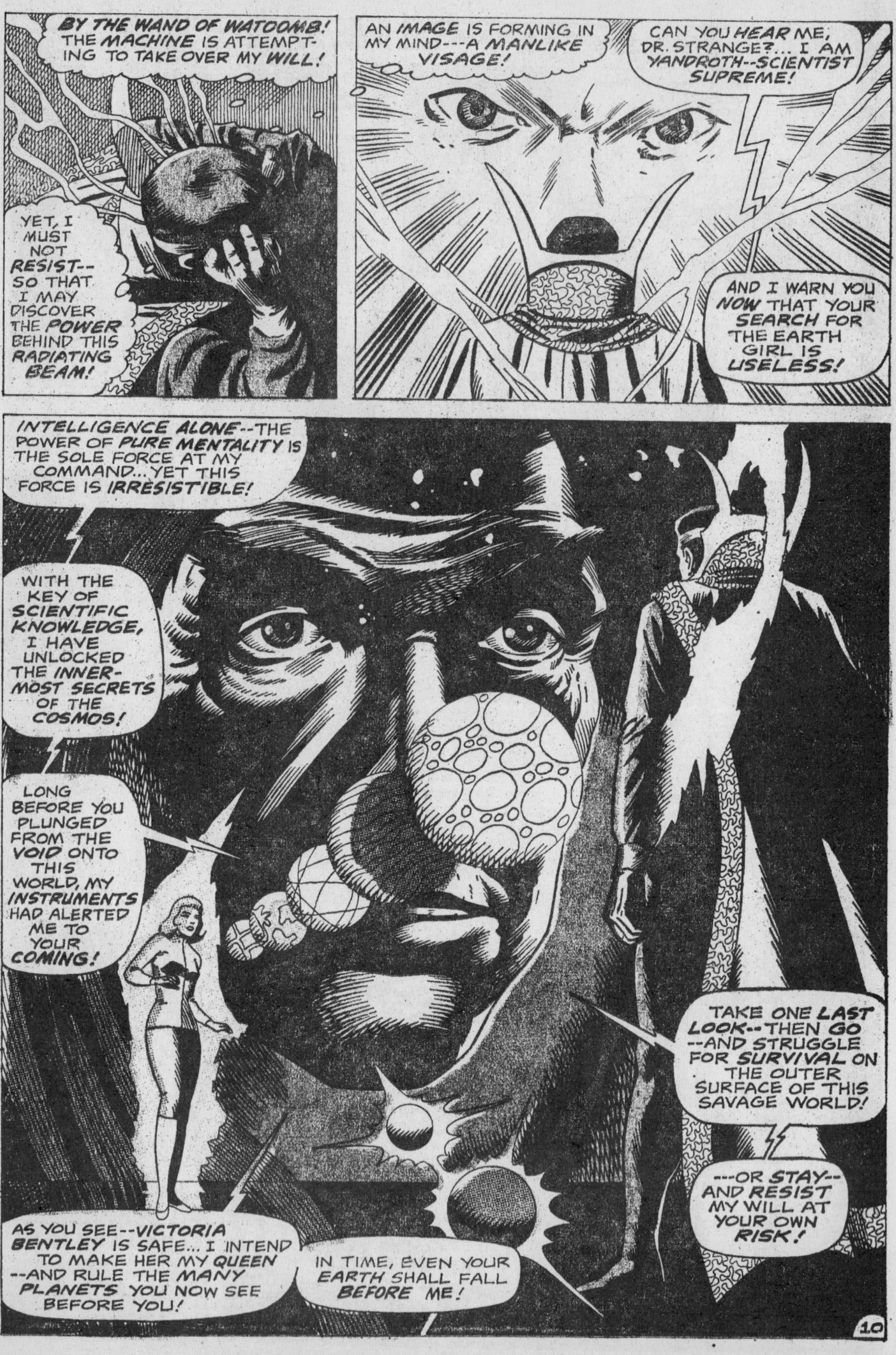
BY THE WAND OF WATOOMB! THE MACHINE IS ATTEMPTING TO TAKE OVER MY WILL!
YET, I MUST NOT RESIST-- SO THAT I MAY DISCOVER THE POWER BEHIND THIS RADIATING BEAM!
AN IMAGE IS FORMING IN MY MIND---A MANLIKE VISAGE!
CAN YOU HEAR ME, DR. STRANGE?... I AM YANDROTH--SCIENTIST SUPREME!
AND I WARN YOU NOW THAT YOUR SEARCH FOR THE EARTH GIRL IS USELESS!
INTELLIGENCE ALONE--THE POWER OF PURE MENTALITY IS THE SOLE FORCE AT MY COMMAND...YET THIS FORCE IS IRRESISTIBLE!
WITH THE KEY OF SCIENTIFIC KNOWLEDGE, I HAVE UNLOCKED THE INNER-MOST SECRETS OF THE COSMOS!
LONG BEFORE YOU PLUNGED FROM THE VOID ONTO THIS WORLD, MY INSTRUMENTS HAD ALERTED ME TO YOUR COMING!
AS YOU SEE--VICTORIA BENTLEY IS SAFE... I INTEND TO MAKE HER MY QUEEN --AND RULE THE MANY PLANETS YOU NOW SEE BEFORE YOU!
IN TIME, EVEN YOUR EARTH SHALL FALL BEFORE ME!
TAKE ONE LAST LOOK--THEN GO --AND STRUGGLE FOR SURVIVAL ON THE OUTER SURFACE OF THIS SAVAGE WORLD!
---OR STAY-- AND RESIST MY WILL AT YOUR OWN RISK!
10

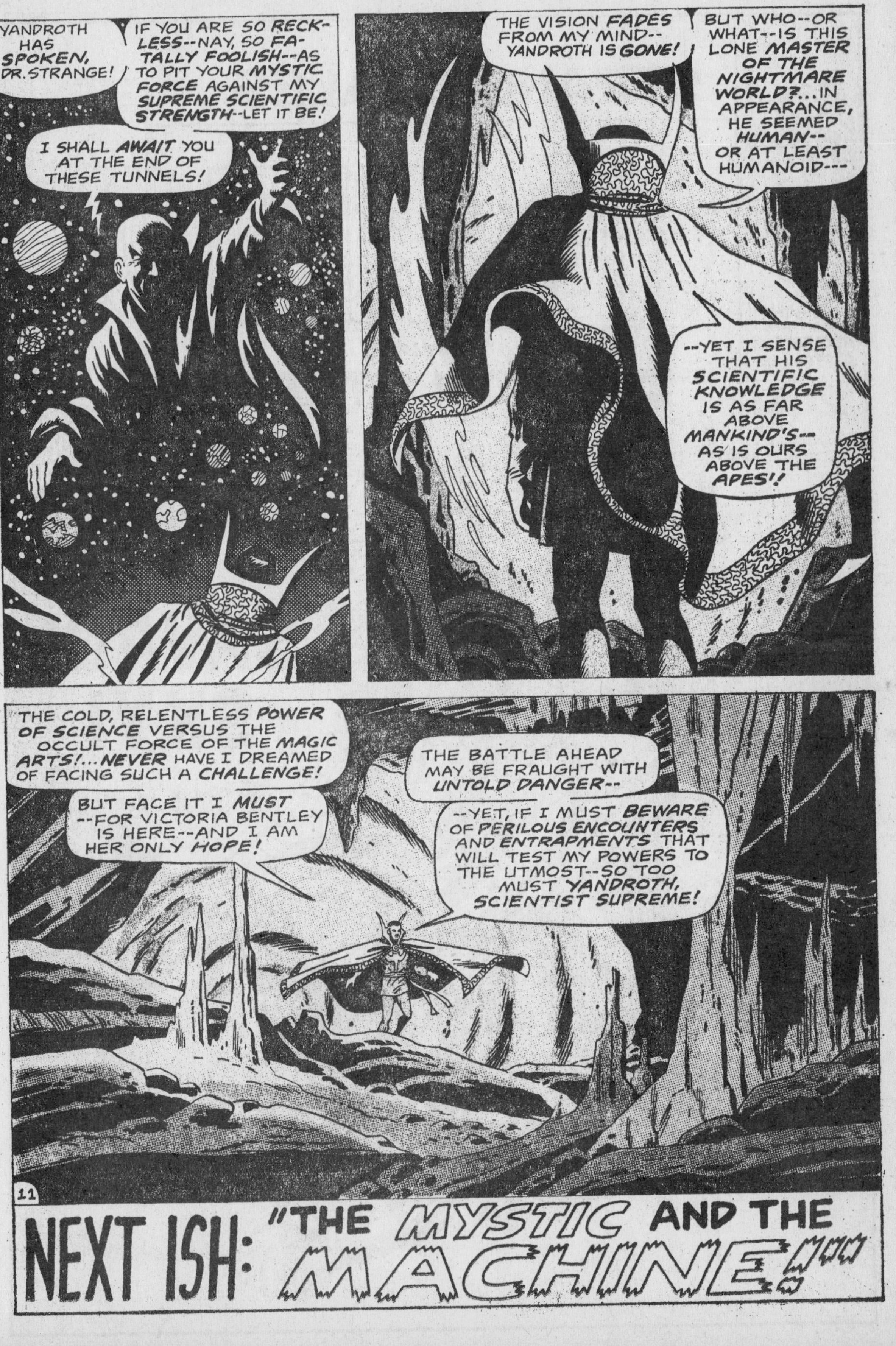
YANDROTH HAS SPOKEN, DR. STRANGE!
IF YOU ARE SO RECKLESS--NAY, SO FATALLY FOOLISH--AS TO PIT YOUR MYSTIC FORCE AGAINST MY SUPREME SCIENTIFIC STRENGTH--LET IT BE!
I SHALL AWAIT YOU AT THE END OF THESE TUNNELS!
THE VISION FADES FROM MY MIND--YANDROTH IS GONE!
BUT WHO--OR WHAT--IS THIS LONE MASTER OF THE NIGHTMARE WORLD?...IN APPEARANCE, HE SEEMED HUMAN--OR AT LEAST HUMANOID---
--YET I SENSE THAT HIS SCIENTIFIC KNOWLEDGE IS AS FAR ABOVE MANKIND'S--AS IS OURS ABOVE THE APES!!
THE COLD, RELENTLESS POWER OF SCIENCE VERSUS THE OCCULT FORCE OF THE MAGIC ARTS!...NEVER HAVE I DREAMED OF FACING SUCH A CHALLENGE!
BUT FACE IT I MUST--FOR VICTORIA BENTLEY IS HERE--AND I AM HER ONLY HOPE!
THE BATTLE AHEAD MAY BE FRAUGHT WITH UNTOLD DANGER--
--YET, IF I MUST BEWARE OF PERILOUS ENCOUNTERS AND ENTRAPMENTS THAT WILL TEST MY POWERS TO THE UTMOST--SO TOO MUST YANDROTH, SCIENTIST SUPREME!
11
NEXT ISH: "THE MYSTIC AND THE MACHINE!"

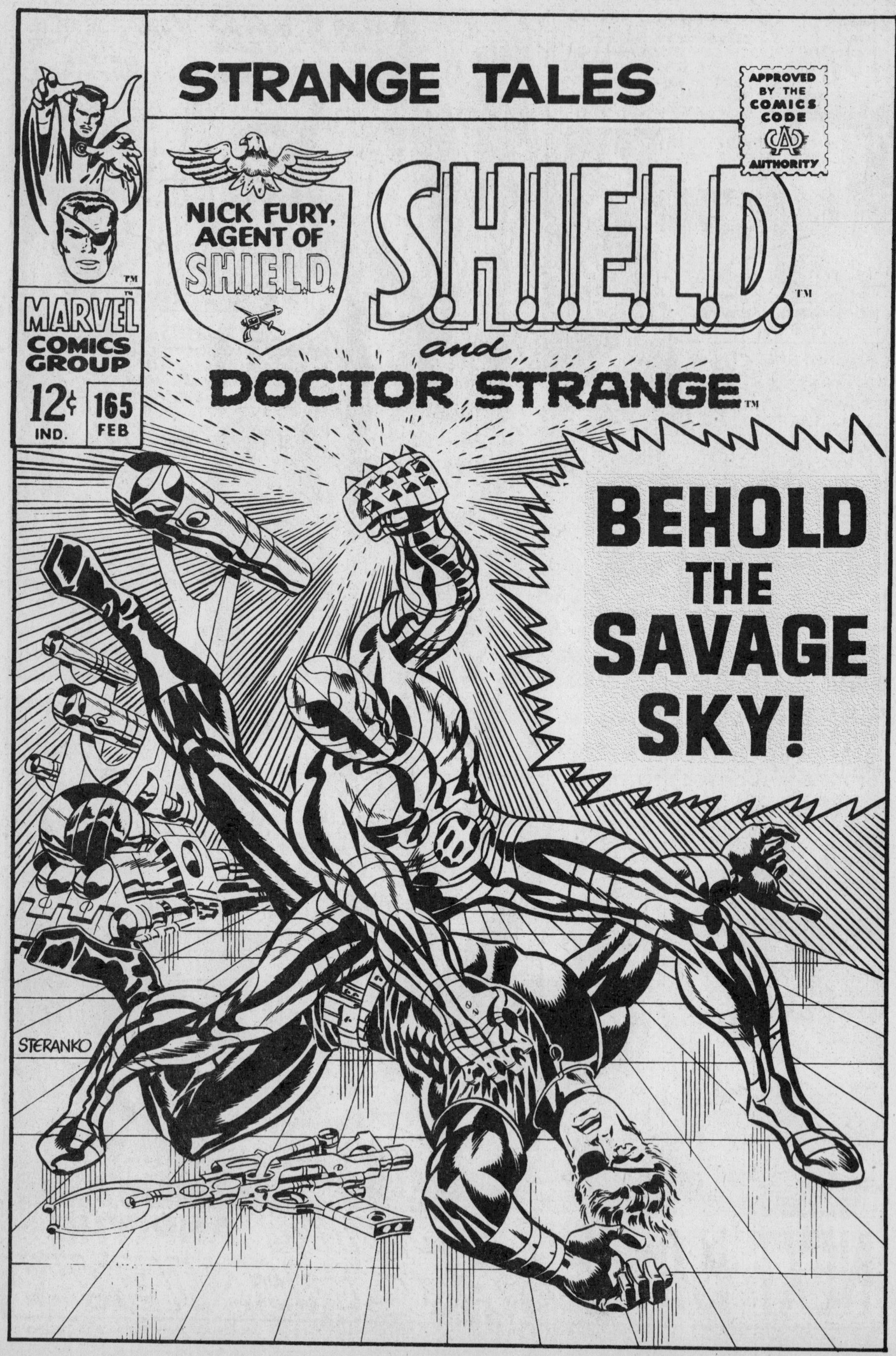
STRANGE TALES
APPROVED BY THE COMICS CODE AUTHORITY
NICK FURY, AGENT OF S.H.I.E.L.D.
S.H.I.E.L.D.™
and
DOCTOR STRANGE™
MARVEL™ COMICS GROUP
12¢ IND.
165 FEB
BEHOLD THE SAVAGE SKY!
STERANKO

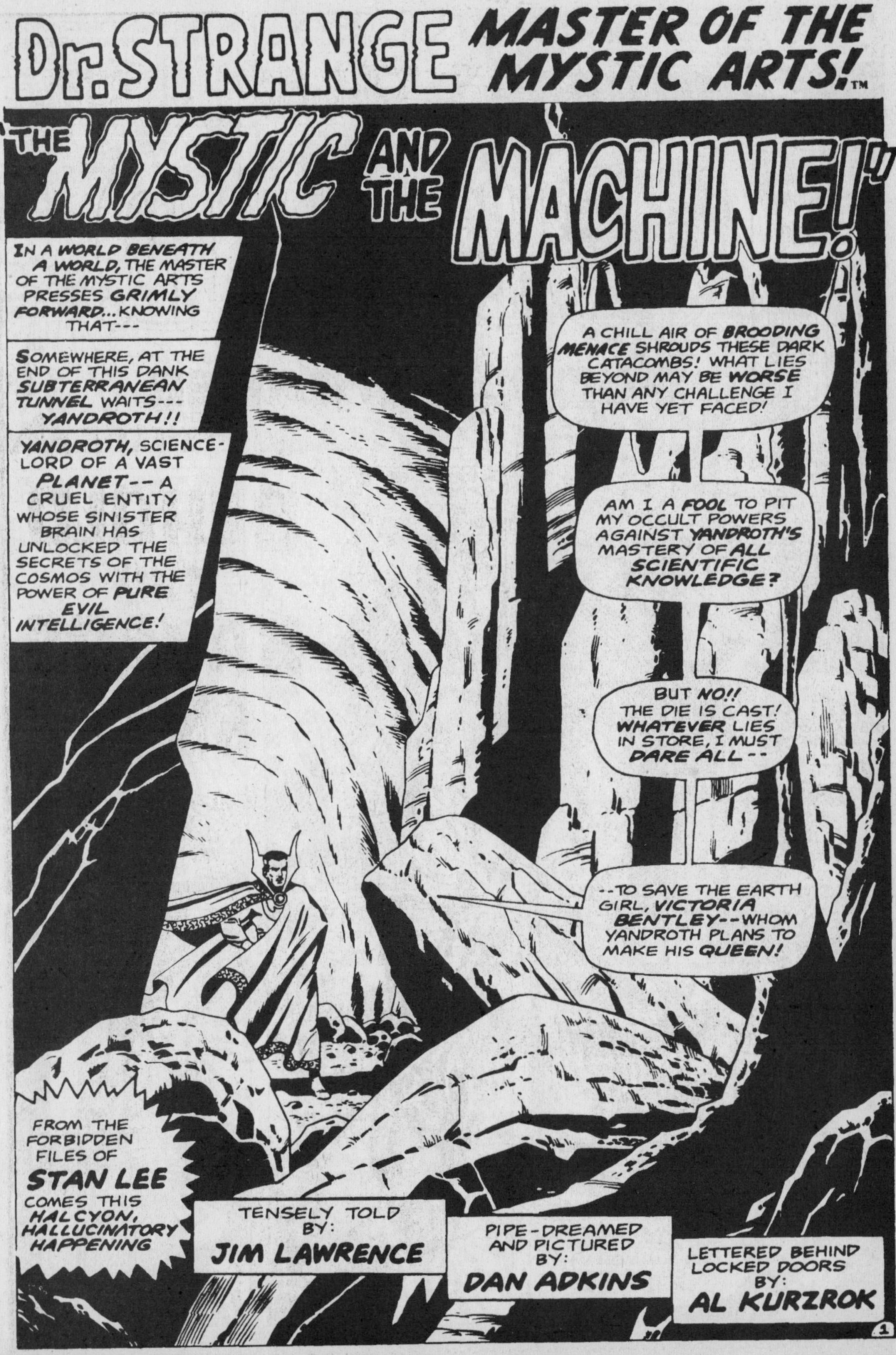

Dr. STRANGE MASTER OF THE MYSTIC ARTS!™
"THE MYSTIC AND THE MACHINE!"
IN A WORLD BENEATH A WORLD, THE MASTER OF THE MYSTIC ARTS PRESSES GRIMLY FORWARD... KNOWING THAT---
SOMEWHERE, AT THE END OF THIS DANK SUBTERRANEAN TUNNEL WAITS--- YANDROTH!!
YANDROTH, SCIENCE-LORD OF A VAST PLANET-- A CRUEL ENTITY WHOSE SINISTER BRAIN HAS UNLOCKED THE SECRETS OF THE COSMOS WITH THE POWER OF PURE EVIL INTELLIGENCE!
A CHILL AIR OF BROODING MENACE SHROUDS THESE DARK CATACOMBS! WHAT LIES BEYOND MAY BE WORSE THAN ANY CHALLENGE I HAVE YET FACED!
AM I A FOOL TO PIT MY OCCULT POWERS AGAINST YANDROTH'S MASTERY OF ALL SCIENTIFIC KNOWLEDGE?
BUT NO!! THE DIE IS CAST! WHATEVER LIES IN STORE, I MUST DARE ALL--
--TO SAVE THE EARTH GIRL, VICTORIA BENTLEY--WHOM YANDROTH PLANS TO MAKE HIS QUEEN!
FROM THE FORBIDDEN FILES OF STAN LEE COMES THIS HALCYON, HALLUCINATORY HAPPENING
TENSELY TOLD BY: JIM LAWRENCE
PIPE-DREAMED AND PICTURED BY: DAN ADKINS
LETTERED BEHIND LOCKED DOORS BY: AL KURZROK
1

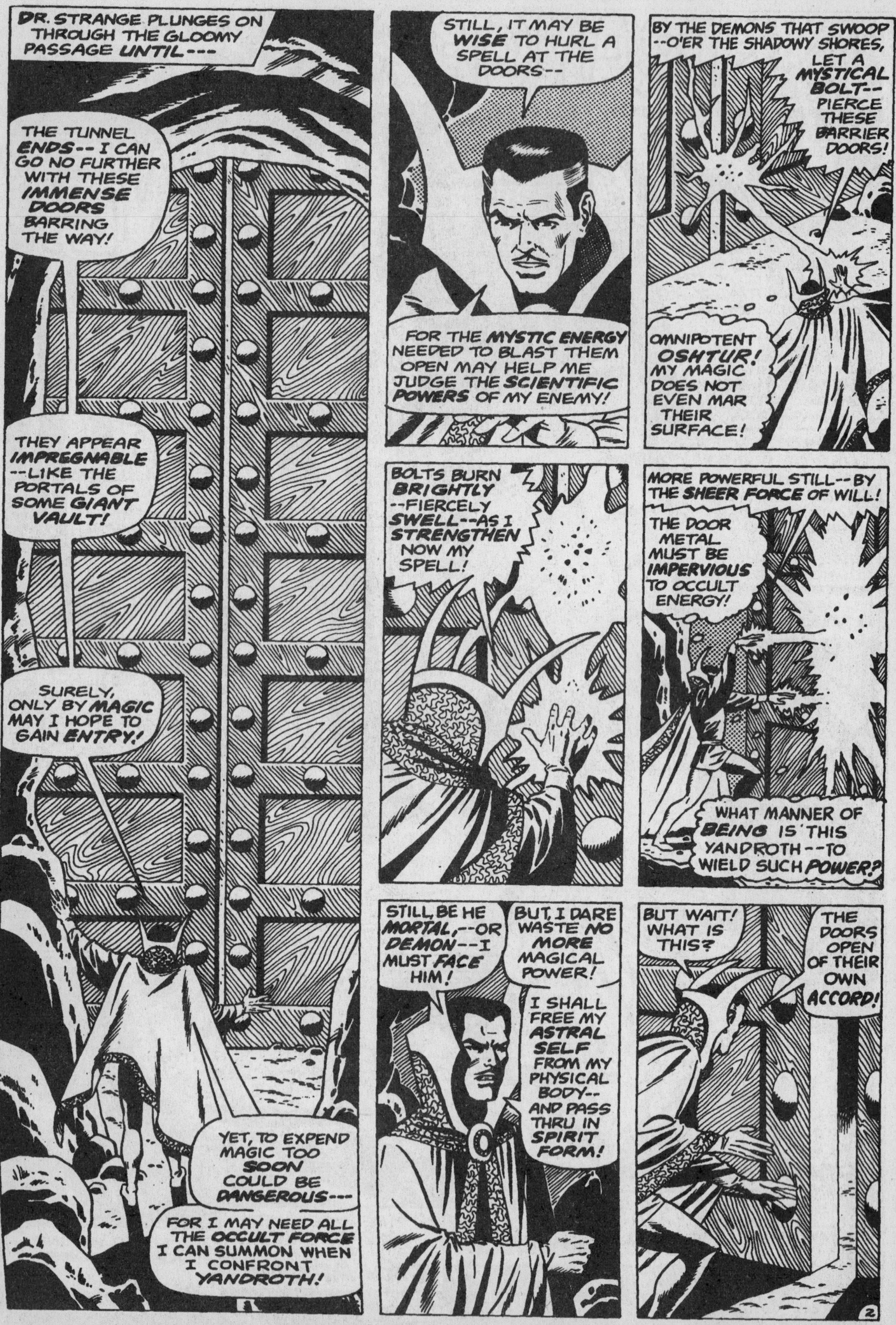
DR. STRANGE PLUNGES ON THROUGH THE GLOOMY PASSAGE UNTIL---
THE TUNNEL ENDS-- I CAN GO NO FURTHER WITH THESE IMMENSE DOORS BARRING THE WAY!
THEY APPEAR IMPREGNABLE --LIKE THE PORTALS OF SOME GIANT VAULT!
SURELY, ONLY BY MAGIC MAY I HOPE TO GAIN ENTRY!
YET, TO EXPEND MAGIC TOO SOON COULD BE DANGEROUS---
FOR I MAY NEED ALL THE OCCULT FORCE I CAN SUMMON WHEN I CONFRONT YANDROTH!
STILL, IT MAY BE WISE TO HURL A SPELL AT THE DOORS--
FOR THE MYSTIC ENERGY NEEDED TO BLAST THEM OPEN MAY HELP ME JUDGE THE SCIENTIFIC POWERS OF MY ENEMY!
BY THE DEMONS THAT SWOOP --O'ER THE SHADOWY SHORES, LET A MYSTICAL BOLT-- PIERCE THESE BARRIER DOORS!
OMNIPOTENT OSHTUR! MY MAGIC DOES NOT EVEN MAR THEIR SURFACE!
BOLTS BURN BRIGHTLY --FIERCELY SWELL--AS I STRENGTHEN NOW MY SPELL!
MORE POWERFUL STILL--BY THE SHEER FORCE OF WILL!
THE DOOR METAL MUST BE IMPERVIOUS TO OCCULT ENERGY!
WHAT MANNER OF BEING IS THIS YANDROTH--TO WIELD SUCH POWER?
STILL, BE HE MORTAL,--OR DEMON--I MUST FACE HIM!
BUT, I DARE WASTE NO MORE MAGICAL POWER!
I SHALL FREE MY ASTRAL SELF FROM MY PHYSICAL BODY-- AND PASS THRU IN SPIRIT FORM!
BUT WAIT! WHAT IS THIS?
THE DOORS OPEN OF THEIR OWN ACCORD!
2

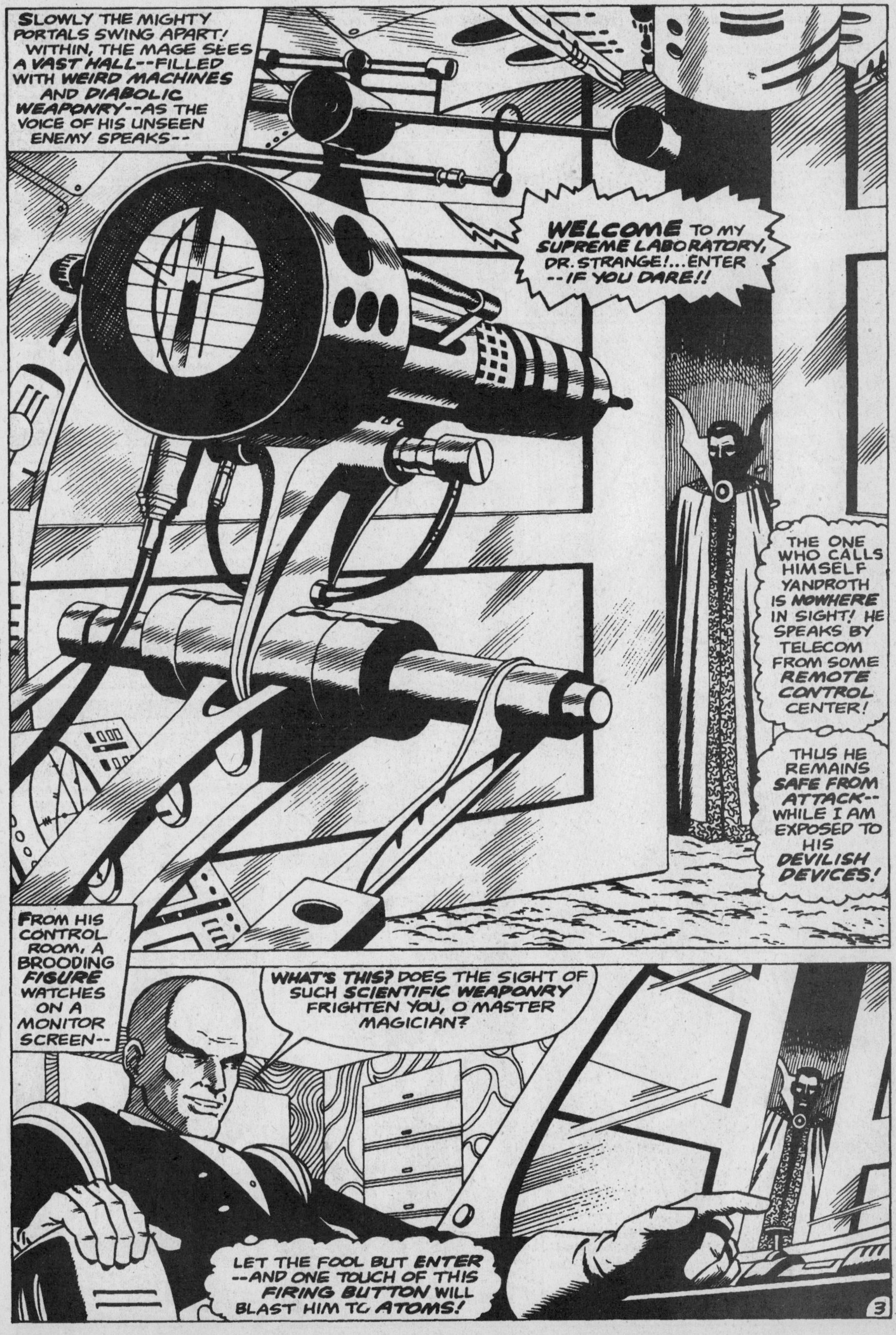
SLOWLY THE MIGHTY PORTALS SWING APART! WITHIN, THE MAGE SEES A VAST HALL--FILLED WITH WEIRD MACHINES AND DIABOLIC WEAPONRY--AS THE VOICE OF HIS UNSEEN ENEMY SPEAKS--
WELCOME TO MY SUPREME LABORATORY, DR. STRANGE!... ENTER --IF YOU DARE!!
THE ONE WHO CALLS HIMSELF YANDROTH IS NOWHERE IN SIGHT! HE SPEAKS BY TELECOM FROM SOME REMOTE CONTROL CENTER!
THUS HE REMAINS SAFE FROM ATTACK-- WHILE I AM EXPOSED TO HIS DEVILISH DEVICES!
FROM HIS CONTROL ROOM, A BROODING FIGURE WATCHES ON A MONITOR SCREEN--
WHAT'S THIS? DOES THE SIGHT OF SUCH SCIENTIFIC WEAPONRY FRIGHTEN YOU, O MASTER MAGICIAN?
LET THE FOOL BUT ENTER --AND ONE TOUCH OF THIS FIRING BUTTON WILL BLAST HIM TO ATOMS!
3

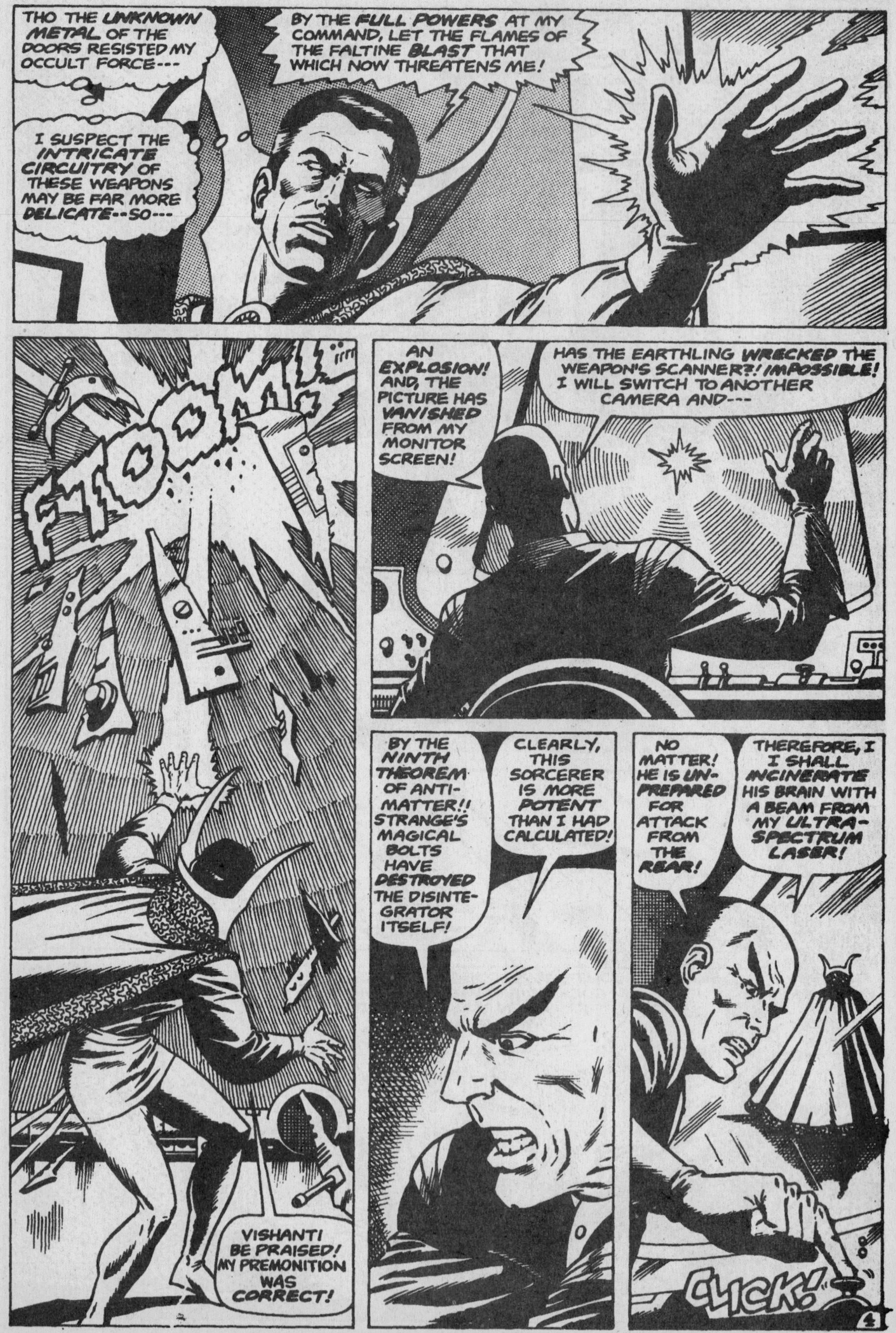
THO THE UNKNOWN METAL OF THE DOORS RESISTED MY OCCULT FORCE---
I SUSPECT THE INTRICATE CIRCUITRY OF THESE WEAPONS MAY BE FAR MORE DELICATE--SO---
BY THE FULL POWERS AT MY COMMAND, LET THE FLAMES OF THE FALTINE BLAST THAT WHICH NOW THREATENS ME!
FTOOM!!
VISHANTI BE PRAISED! MY PREMONITION WAS CORRECT!
AN EXPLOSION! AND, THE PICTURE HAS VANISHED FROM MY MONITOR SCREEN!
HAS THE EARTHLING WRECKED THE WEAPON'S SCANNER?! IMPOSSIBLE! I WILL SWITCH TO ANOTHER CAMERA AND---
BY THE NINTH THEOREM OF ANTI-MATTER!! STRANGE'S MAGICAL BOLTS HAVE DESTROYED THE DISINTEGRATOR ITSELF!
CLEARLY, THIS SORCERER IS MORE POTENT THAN I HAD CALCULATED!
NO MATTER! HE IS UNPREPARED FOR ATTACK FROM THE REAR!
THEREFORE, I I SHALL INCINERATE HIS BRAIN WITH A BEAM FROM MY ULTRA-SPECTRUM LASER!
CLICK!

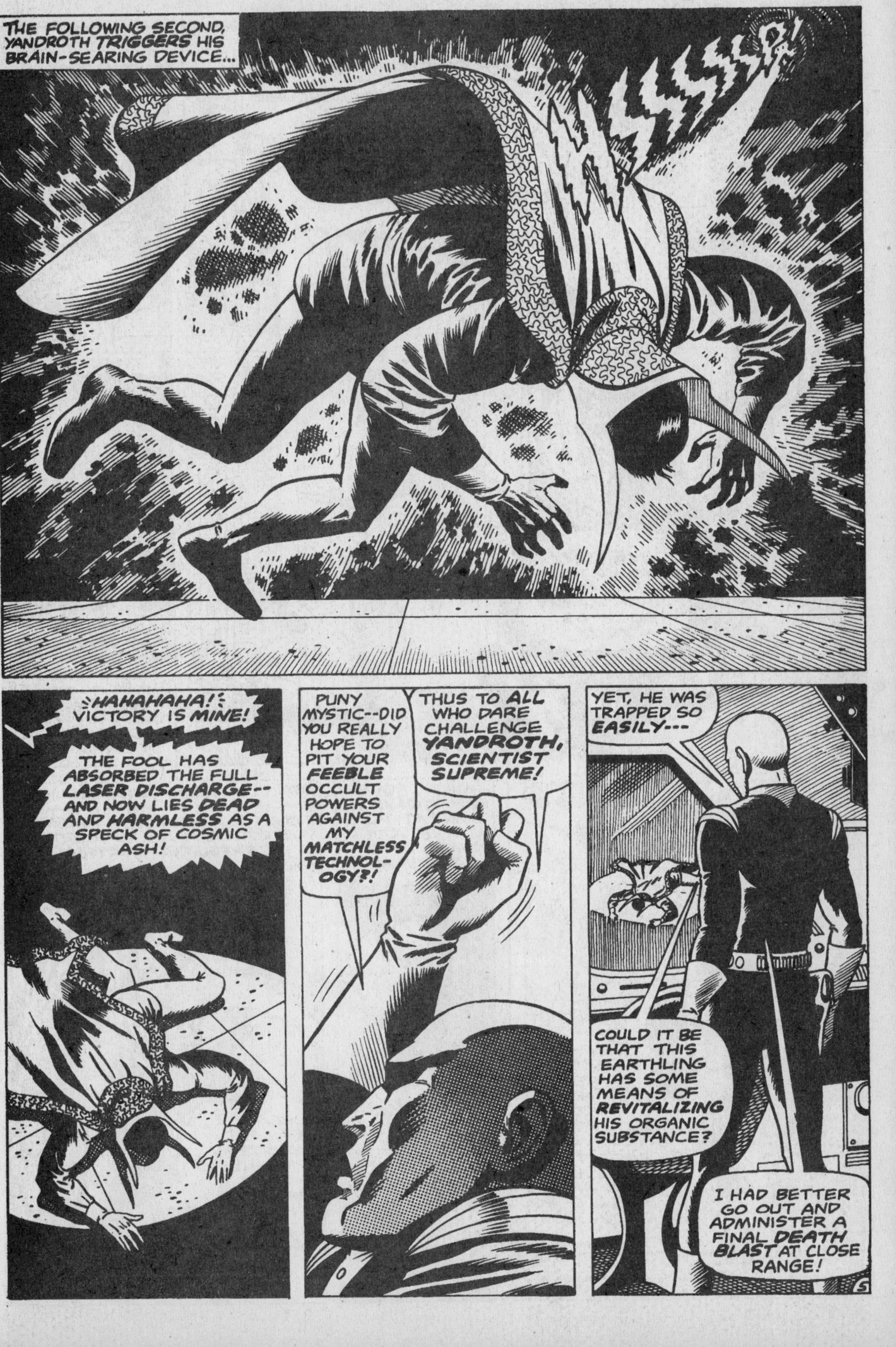
THE FOLLOWING SECOND, YANDROTH TRIGGERS HIS BRAIN-SEARING DEVICE...
HAHAHAHA! VICTORY IS MINE!
THE FOOL HAS ABSORBED THE FULL LASER DISCHARGE-- AND NOW LIES DEAD AND HARMLESS AS A SPECK OF COSMIC ASH!
PUNY MYSTIC--DID YOU REALLY HOPE TO PIT YOUR FEEBLE OCCULT POWERS AGAINST MY MATCHLESS TECHNOL-OGY?!
THUS TO ALL WHO DARE CHALLENGE YANDROTH, SCIENTIST SUPREME!
YET, HE WAS TRAPPED SO EASILY---
COULD IT BE THAT THIS EARTHLING HAS SOME MEANS OF REVITALIZING HIS ORGANIC SUBSTANCE?
I HAD BETTER GO OUT AND ADMINISTER A FINAL DEATH BLAST AT CLOSE RANGE!
5

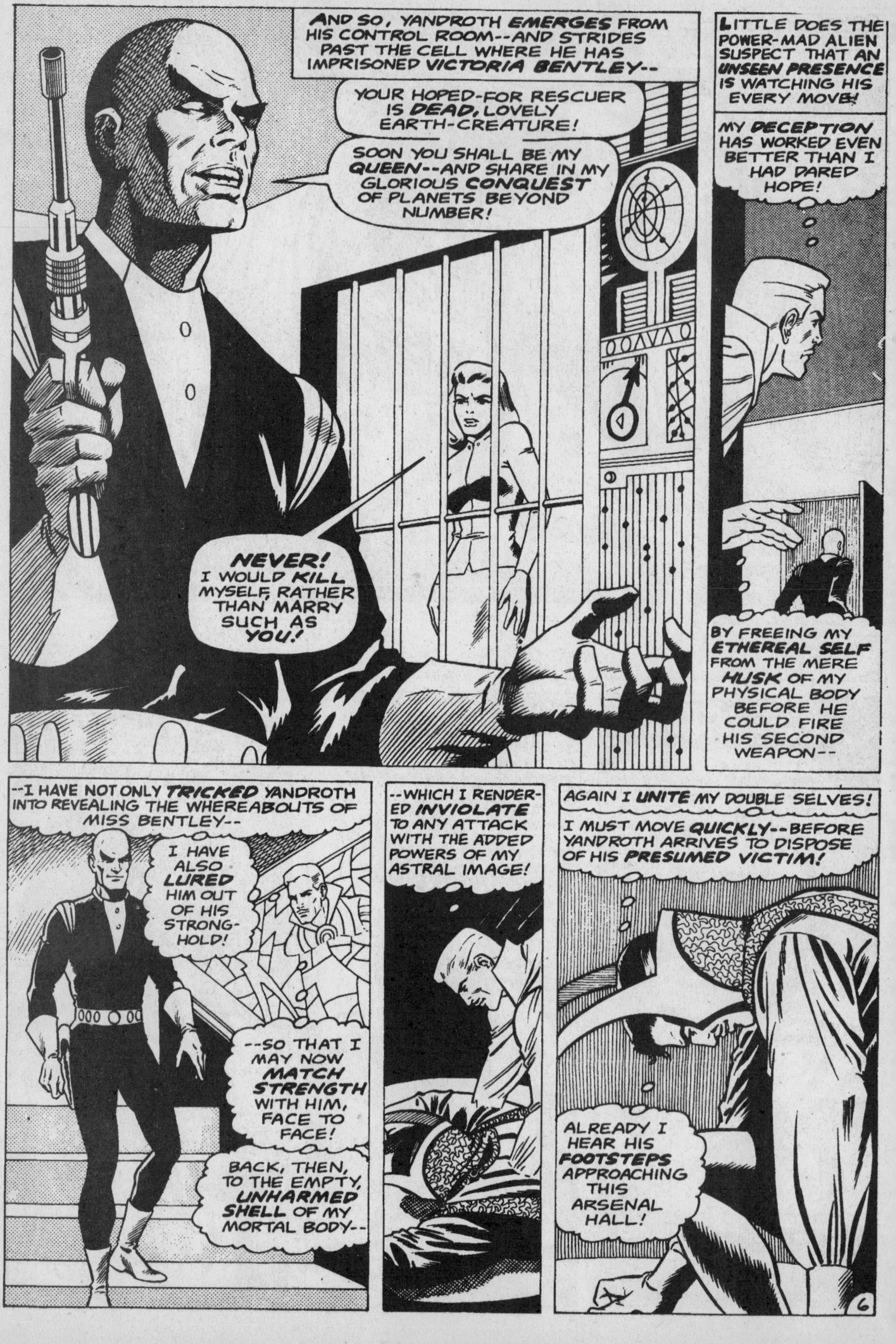

AND SO, YANDROTH EMERGES FROM HIS CONTROL ROOM--AND STRIDES PAST THE CELL WHERE HE HAS IMPRISONED VICTORIA BENTLEY--
YOUR HOPED-FOR RESCUER IS DEAD, LOVELY EARTH-CREATURE!
SOON YOU SHALL BE MY QUEEN--AND SHARE IN MY GLORIOUS CONQUEST OF PLANETS BEYOND NUMBER!
NEVER! I WOULD KILL MYSELF, RATHER THAN MARRY SUCH AS YOU!
LITTLE DOES THE POWER-MAD ALIEN SUSPECT THAT AN UNSEEN PRESENCE IS WATCHING HIS EVERY MOVE!
MY DECEPTION HAS WORKED EVEN BETTER THAN I HAD DARED HOPE!
BY FREEING MY ETHEREAL SELF FROM THE MERE HUSK OF MY PHYSICAL BODY BEFORE HE COULD FIRE HIS SECOND WEAPON--
--I HAVE NOT ONLY TRICKED YANDROTH INTO REVEALING THE WHEREABOUTS OF MISS BENTLEY--
I HAVE ALSO LURED HIM OUT OF HIS STRONG-HOLD!
--SO THAT I MAY NOW MATCH STRENGTH WITH HIM, FACE TO FACE!
BACK, THEN, TO THE EMPTY, UNHARMED SHELL OF MY MORTAL BODY--
--WHICH I RENDER-ED INVIOLATE TO ANY ATTACK WITH THE ADDED POWERS OF MY ASTRAL IMAGE!
AGAIN I UNITE MY DOUBLE SELVES!
I MUST MOVE QUICKLY--BEFORE YANDROTH ARRIVES TO DISPOSE OF HIS PRESUMED VICTIM!
ALREADY I HEAR HIS FOOTSTEPS APPROACHING THIS ARSENAL HALL!
6

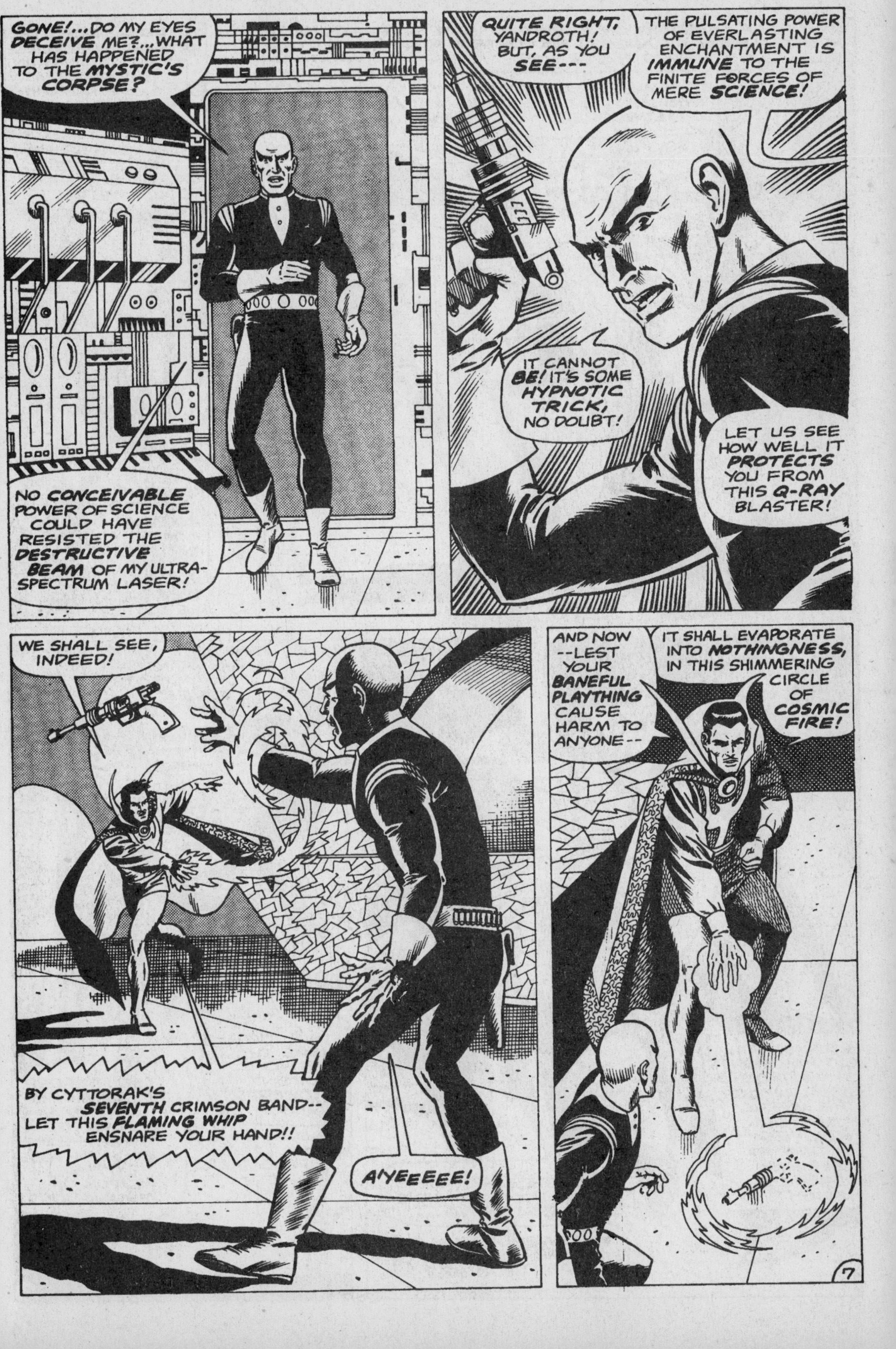
GONE!...DO MY EYES DECEIVE ME?...WHAT HAS HAPPENED TO THE MYSTIC'S CORPSE?
NO CONCEIVABLE POWER OF SCIENCE COULD HAVE RESISTED THE DESTRUCTIVE BEAM OF MY ULTRA-SPECTRUM LASER!
QUITE RIGHT, YANDROTH! BUT, AS YOU SEE---
THE PULSATING POWER OF EVERLASTING ENCHANTMENT IS IMMUNE TO THE FINITE FORCES OF MERE SCIENCE!
IT CANNOT BE! IT'S SOME HYPNOTIC TRICK, NO DOUBT!
LET US SEE HOW WELL IT PROTECTS YOU FROM THIS Q-RAY BLASTER!
WE SHALL SEE, INDEED!
BY CYTTORAK'S SEVENTH CRIMSON BAND-- LET THIS FLAMING WHIP ENSNARE YOUR HAND!!
AIYEEEEE!
AND NOW --LEST YOUR BANEFUL PLAYTHING CAUSE HARM TO ANYONE--
IT SHALL EVAPORATE INTO NOTHINGNESS, IN THIS SHIMMERING CIRCLE OF COSMIC FIRE!
7

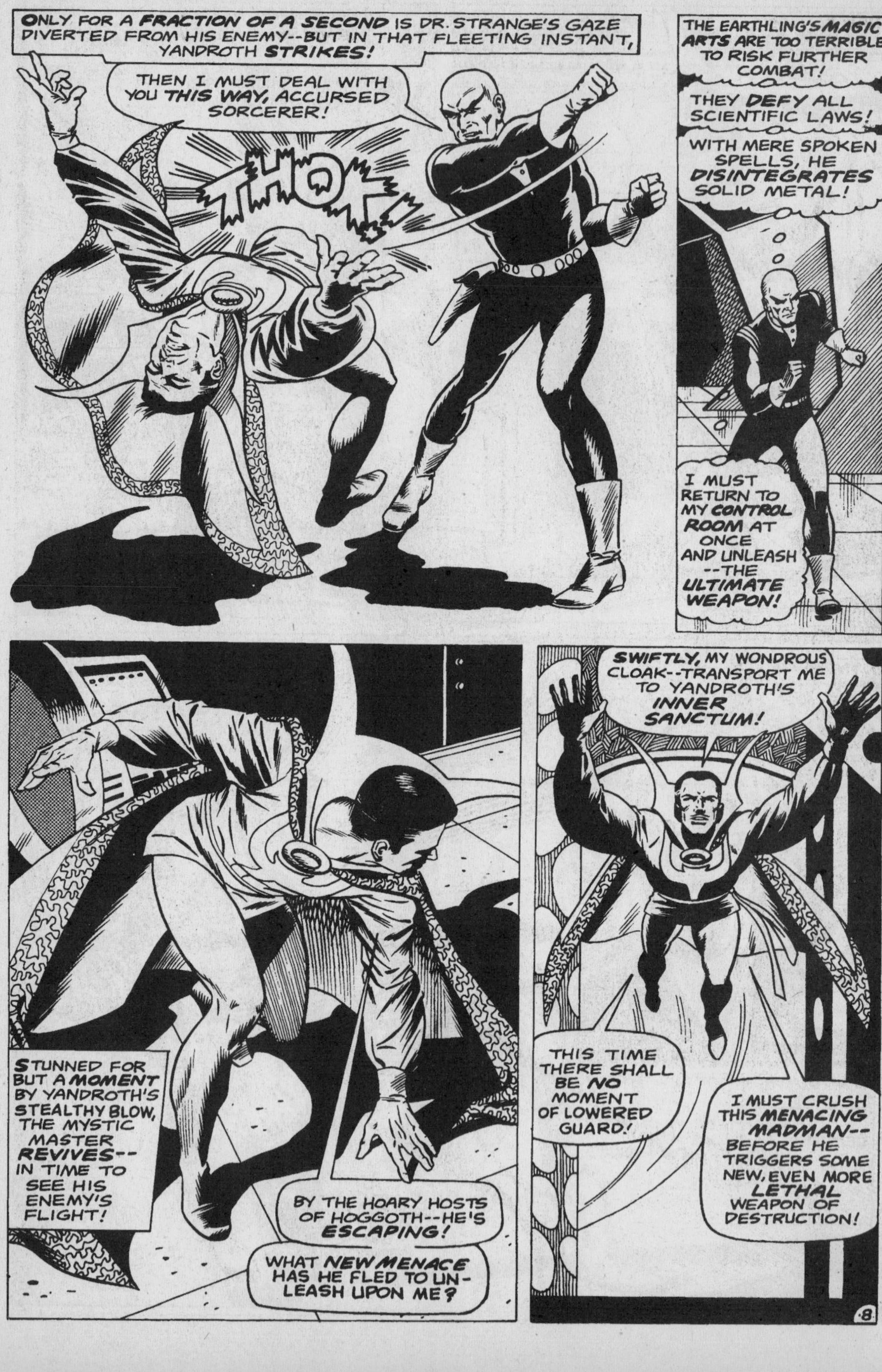

ONLY FOR A FRACTION OF A SECOND IS DR. STRANGE'S GAZE DIVERTED FROM HIS ENEMY--BUT IN THAT FLEETING INSTANT, YANDROTH STRIKES!
THEN I MUST DEAL WITH YOU THIS WAY, ACCURSED SORCERER!
THOK!
THE EARTHLING'S MAGIC ARTS ARE TOO TERRIBLE TO RISK FURTHER COMBAT!
THEY DEFY ALL SCIENTIFIC LAWS!
WITH MERE SPOKEN SPELLS, HE DISINTEGRATES SOLID METAL!
I MUST RETURN TO MY CONTROL ROOM AT ONCE AND UNLEASH --THE ULTIMATE WEAPON!
STUNNED FOR BUT A MOMENT BY YANDROTH'S STEALTHY BLOW, THE MYSTIC MASTER REVIVES-- IN TIME TO SEE HIS ENEMY'S FLIGHT!
BY THE HOARY HOSTS OF HOGGOTH--HE'S ESCAPING!
WHAT NEW MENACE HAS HE FLED TO UNLEASH UPON ME?
SWIFTLY, MY WONDROUS CLOAK--TRANSPORT ME TO YANDROTH'S INNER SANCTUM!
THIS TIME THERE SHALL BE NO MOMENT OF LOWERED GUARD!
I MUST CRUSH THIS MENACING MADMAN-- BEFORE HE TRIGGERS SOME NEW, EVEN MORE LETHAL WEAPON OF DESTRUCTION!

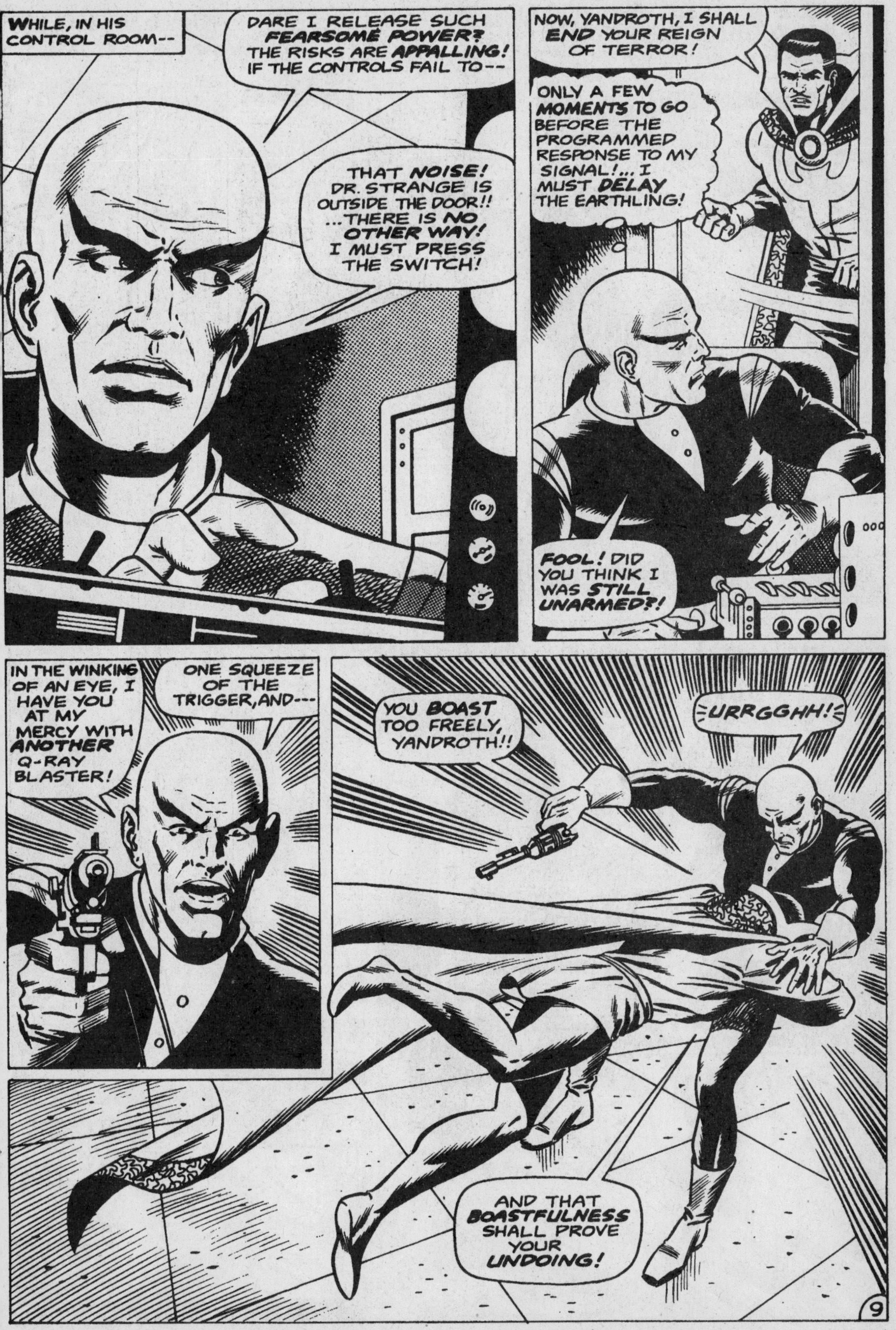
WHILE, IN HIS CONTROL ROOM--
DARE I RELEASE SUCH FEARSOME POWER? THE RISKS ARE APPALLING! IF THE CONTROLS FAIL TO--
THAT NOISE! DR. STRANGE IS OUTSIDE THE DOOR!! ...THERE IS NO OTHER WAY! I MUST PRESS THE SWITCH!
NOW, YANDROTH, I SHALL END YOUR REIGN OF TERROR!
ONLY A FEW MOMENTS TO GO BEFORE THE PROGRAMMED RESPONSE TO MY SIGNAL!... I MUST DELAY THE EARTHLING!
FOOL! DID YOU THINK I WAS STILL UNARMED?!
IN THE WINKING OF AN EYE, I HAVE YOU AT MY MERCY WITH ANOTHER Q-RAY BLASTER!
ONE SQUEEZE OF THE TRIGGER, AND---
YOU BOAST TOO FREELY, YANDROTH!!
URRGGHH!
AND THAT BOASTFULNESS SHALL PROVE YOUR UNDOING!
9

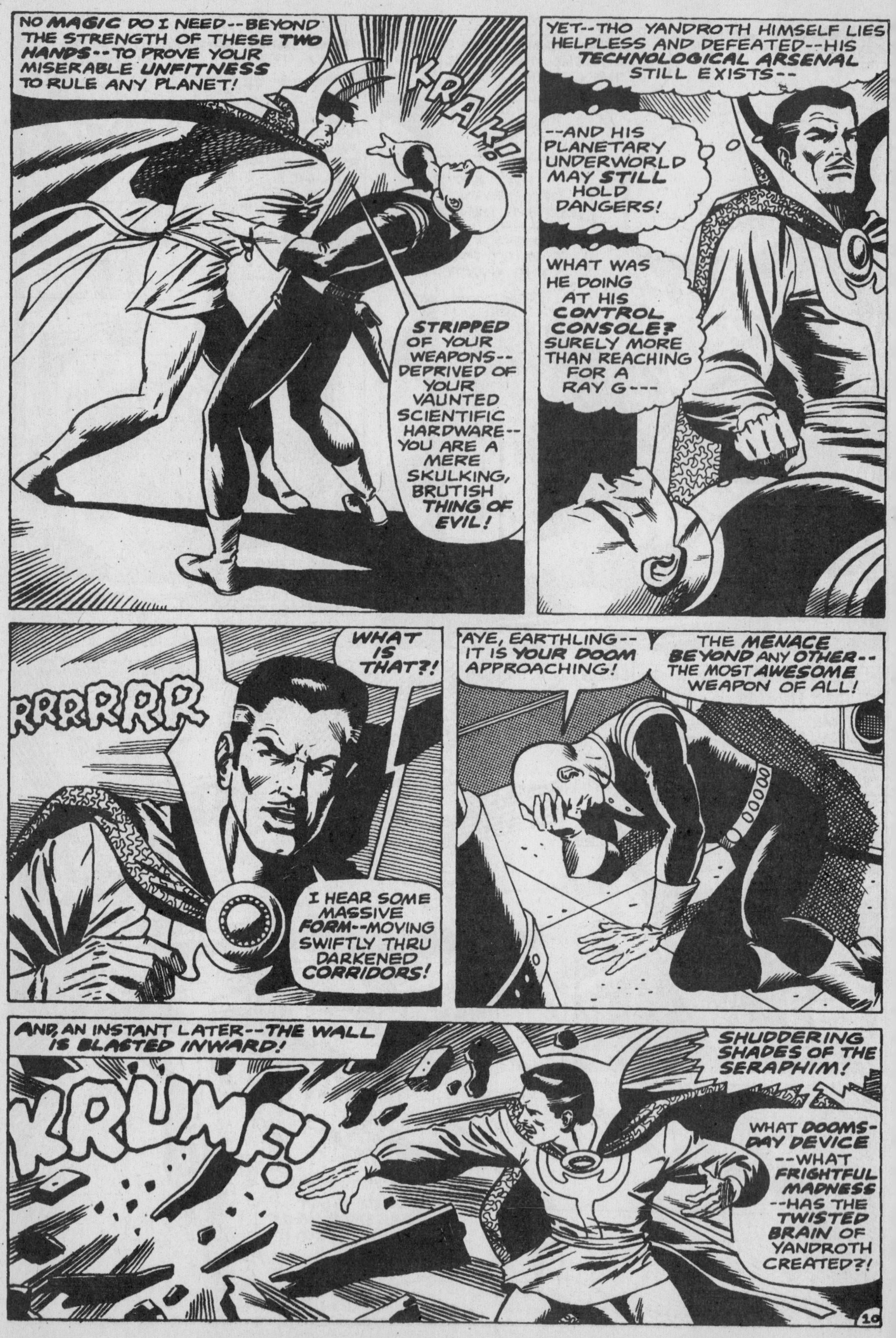
NO MAGIC DO I NEED--BEYOND THE STRENGTH OF THESE TWO HANDS--TO PROVE YOUR MISERABLE UNFITNESS TO RULE ANY PLANET!
KRAKK!
STRIPPED OF YOUR WEAPONS--DEPRIVED OF YOUR VAUNTED SCIENTIFIC HARDWARE--YOU ARE A MERE SKULKING, BRUTISH THING OF EVIL!
YET--THO YANDROTH HIMSELF LIES HELPLESS AND DEFEATED--HIS TECHNOLOGICAL ARSENAL STILL EXISTS--
--AND HIS PLANETARY UNDERWORLD MAY STILL HOLD DANGERS!
WHAT WAS HE DOING AT HIS CONTROL CONSOLE? SURELY MORE THAN REACHING FOR A RAY G---
RRRRRR
WHAT IS THAT?!
I HEAR SOME MASSIVE FORM--MOVING SWIFTLY THRU DARKENED CORRIDORS!
AYE, EARTHLING--IT IS YOUR DOOM APPROACHING!
THE MENACE BEYOND ANY OTHER--THE MOST AWESOME WEAPON OF ALL!
AND, AN INSTANT LATER--THE WALL IS BLASTED INWARD!
KRUMF!
SHUDDERING SHADES OF THE SERAPHIM!
WHAT DOOMS-DAY DEVICE--WHAT FRIGHTFUL MADNESS--HAS THE TWISTED BRAIN OF YANDROTH CREATED?!
10

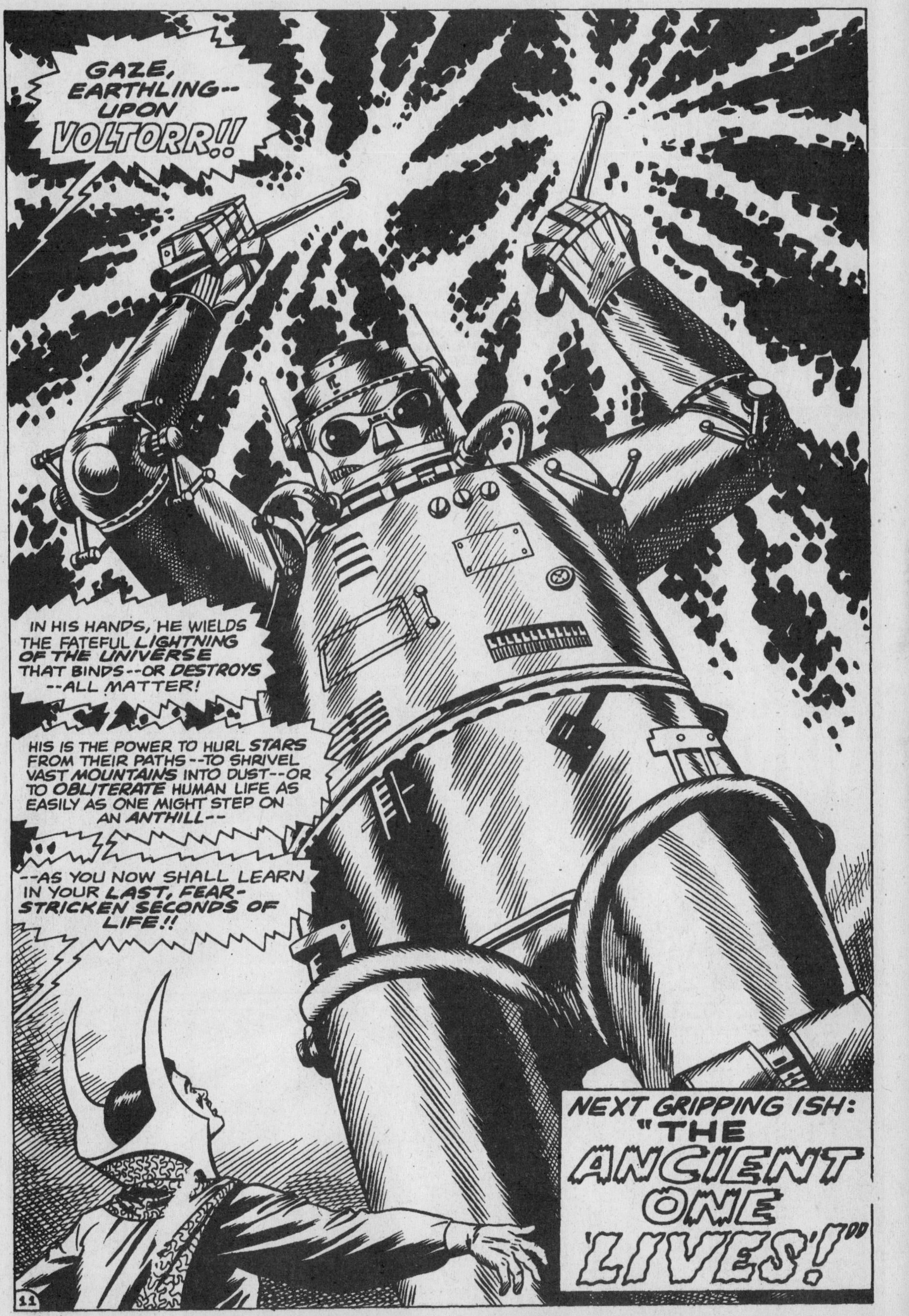
GAZE, EARTHLING-- UPON VOLTORR!!
IN HIS HANDS, HE WIELDS THE FATEFUL LIGHTNING OF THE UNIVERSE THAT BINDS--OR DESTROYS --ALL MATTER!
HIS IS THE POWER TO HURL STARS FROM THEIR PATHS--TO SHRIVEL VAST MOUNTAINS INTO DUST--OR TO OBLITERATE HUMAN LIFE AS EASILY AS ONE MIGHT STEP ON AN ANTHILL--
--AS YOU NOW SHALL LEARN IN YOUR LAST, FEAR-STRICKEN SECONDS OF LIFE!!
NEXT GRIPPING ISH: "THE ANCIENT ONE LIVES!"
11

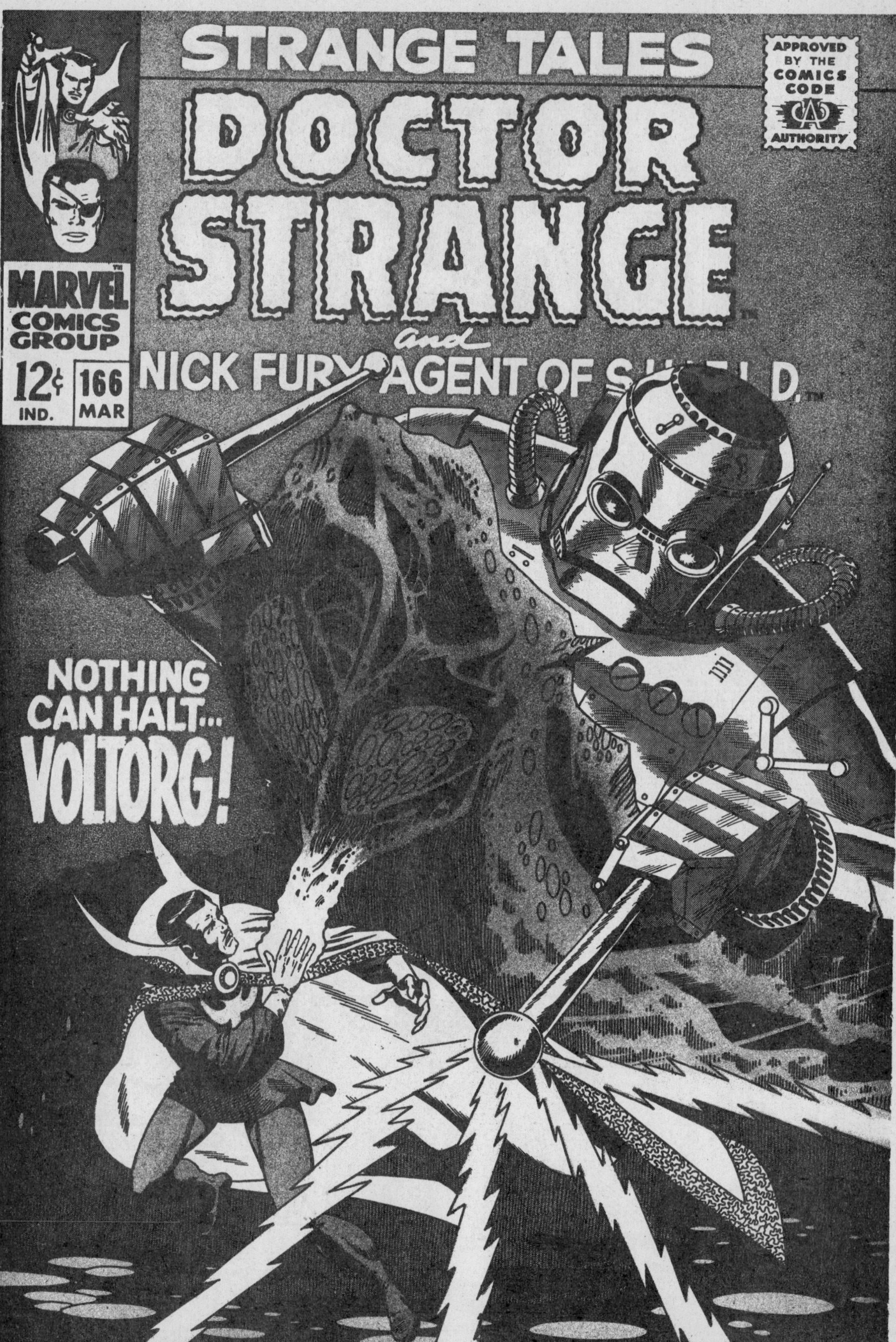
STRANGE TALES
APPROVED BY THE COMICS CODE AUTHORITY
DOCTOR STRANGE
MARVEL COMICS GROUP
12¢ IND.
166 MAR
and
NICK FURY AGENT OF S.H.I.E.L.D.
NOTHING CAN HALT... VOLTORG!

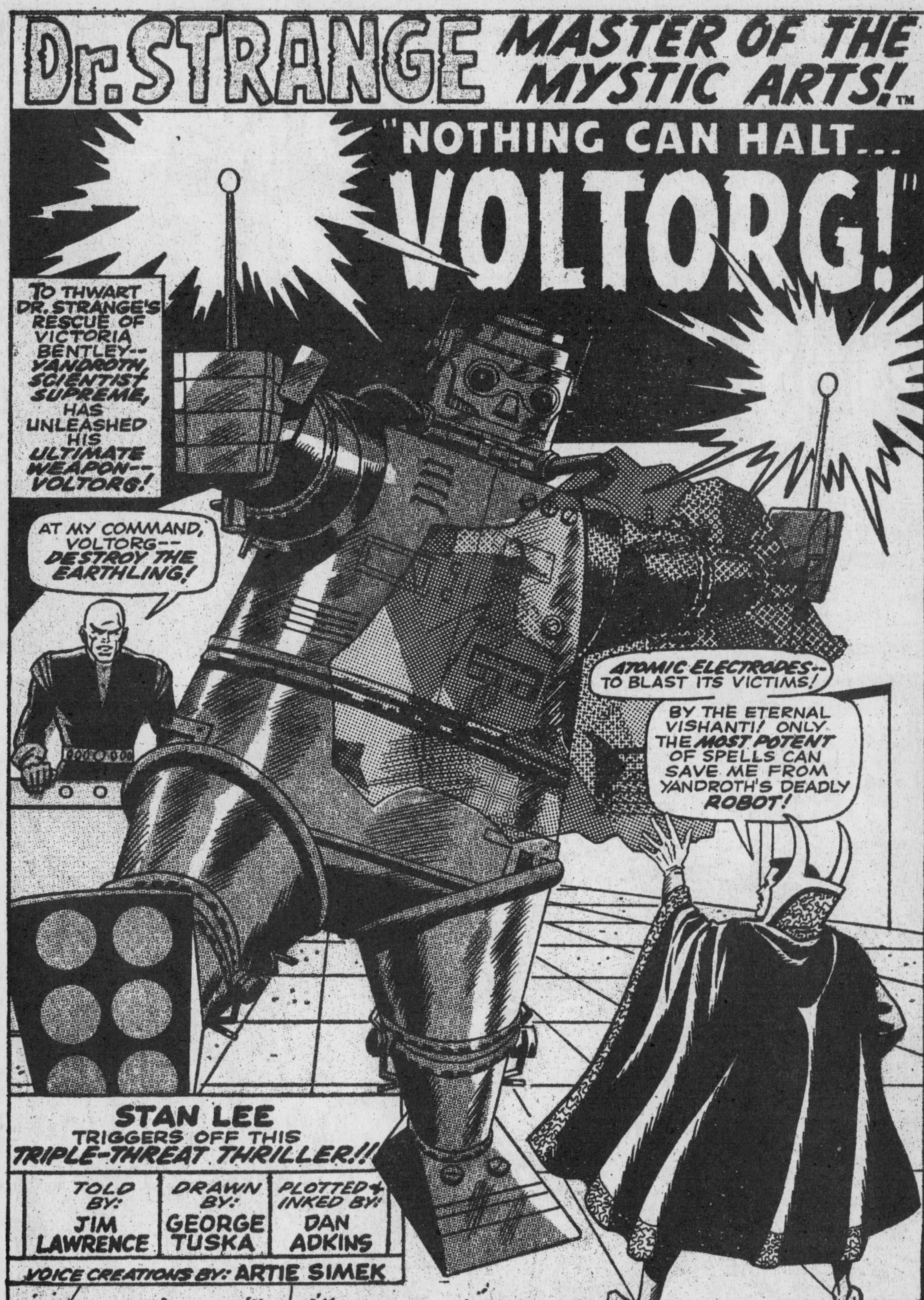
Dr. STRANGE MASTER OF THE MYSTIC ARTS!™
"NOTHING CAN HALT... VOLTORG!"
TO THWART DR. STRANGE'S RESCUE OF VICTORIA BENTLEY-- YANDROTH, SCIENTIST SUPREME, HAS UNLEASHED HIS ULTIMATE WEAPON-- VOLTORG!
AT MY COMMAND, VOLTORG-- DESTROY THE EARTHLING!
ATOMIC ELECTRODES-- TO BLAST ITS VICTIMS!
BY THE ETERNAL VISHANTI! ONLY THE MOST POTENT OF SPELLS CAN SAVE ME FROM YANDROTH'S DEADLY ROBOT!
STAN LEE TRIGGERS OFF THIS TRIPLE-THREAT THRILLER!!
TOLD BY: JIM LAWRENCE
DRAWN BY: GEORGE TUSKA
PLOTTED & INKED BY: DAN ADKINS
VOICE CREATIONS BY: ARTIE SIMEK

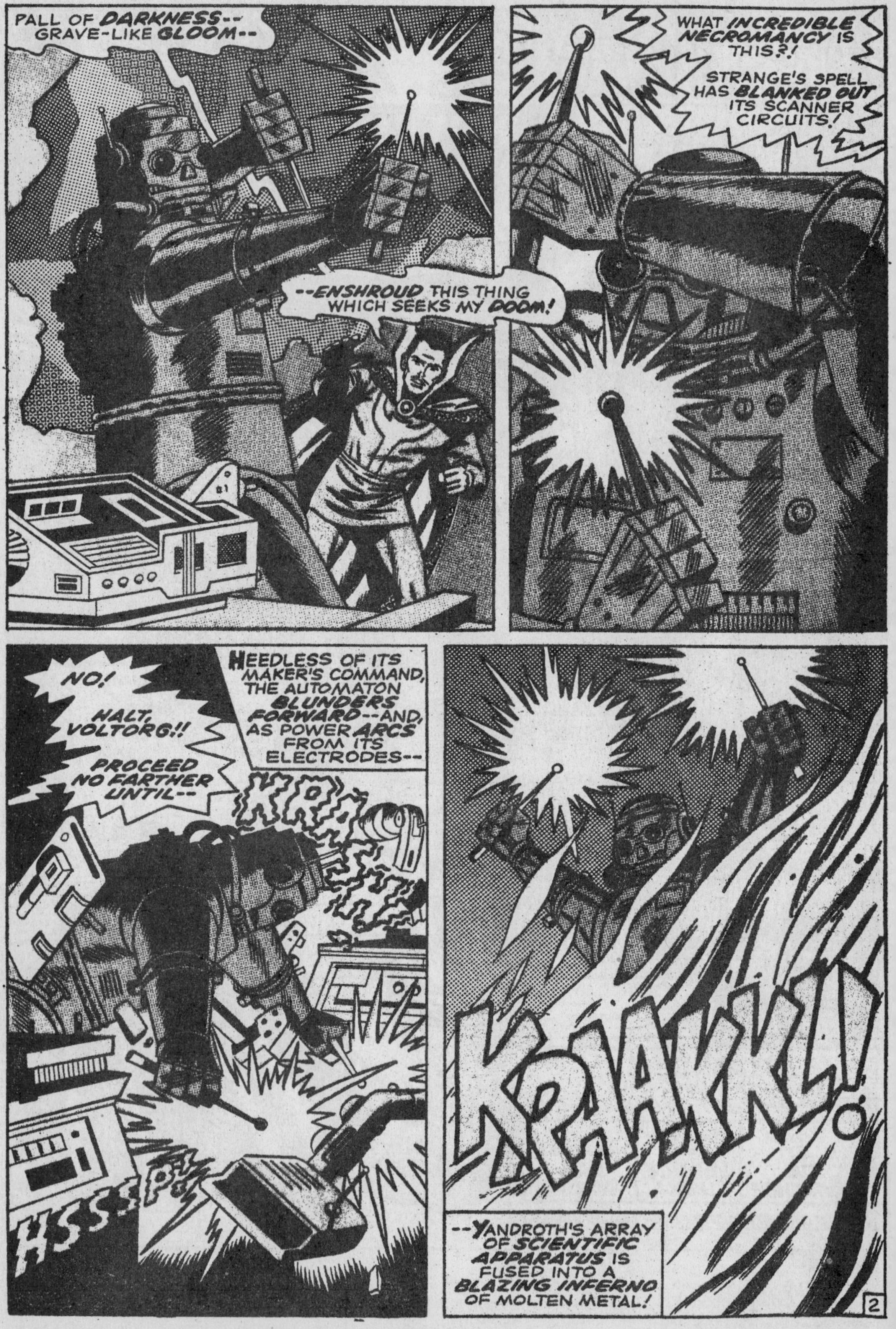
PALL OF DARKNESS-- GRAVE-LIKE GLOOM--
--ENSHROUD THIS THING WHICH SEEKS MY DOOM!
WHAT INCREDIBLE NECROMANCY IS THIS?!
STRANGE'S SPELL HAS BLANKED OUT ITS SCANNER CIRCUITS!
NO!
HALT, VOLTORG!!
PROCEED NO FARTHER UNTIL--
HEEDLESS OF ITS MAKER'S COMMAND, THE AUTOMATON BLUNDERS FORWARD--AND, AS POWER ARCS FROM ITS ELECTRODES--
HSSSP!
KRAAKL!
--YANDROTH'S ARRAY OF SCIENTIFIC APPARATUS IS FUSED INTO A BLAZING INFERNO OF MOLTEN METAL!

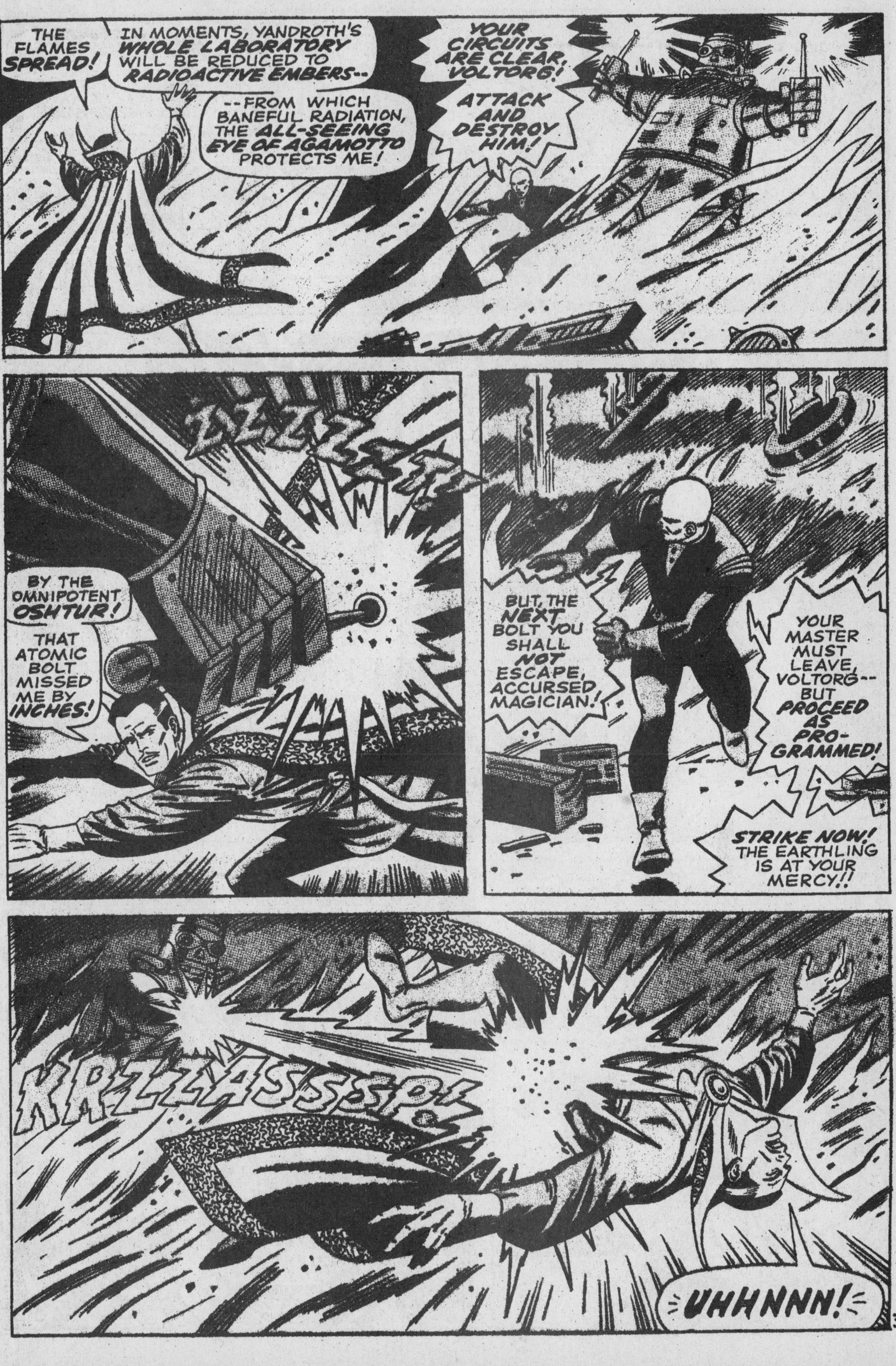

THE FLAMES SPREAD!
IN MOMENTS, YANDROTH'S WHOLE LABORATORY WILL BE REDUCED TO RADIOACTIVE EMBERS--
--FROM WHICH BANEFUL RADIATION, THE ALL-SEEING EYE OF AGAMOTTO PROTECTS ME!
YOUR CIRCUITS ARE CLEAR, VOLTORG!
ATTACK AND DESTROY HIM!
ZZZZZZZAT
BY THE OMNIPOTENT OSHTUR!
THAT ATOMIC BOLT MISSED ME BY INCHES!
BUT, THE NEXT BOLT YOU SHALL NOT ESCAPE, ACCURSED MAGICIAN!
YOUR MASTER MUST LEAVE, VOLTORG-- BUT PROCEED AS PRO-GRAMMED!
STRIKE NOW! THE EARTHLING IS AT YOUR MERCY!!
KRZZASSSP!
UHHNNN!

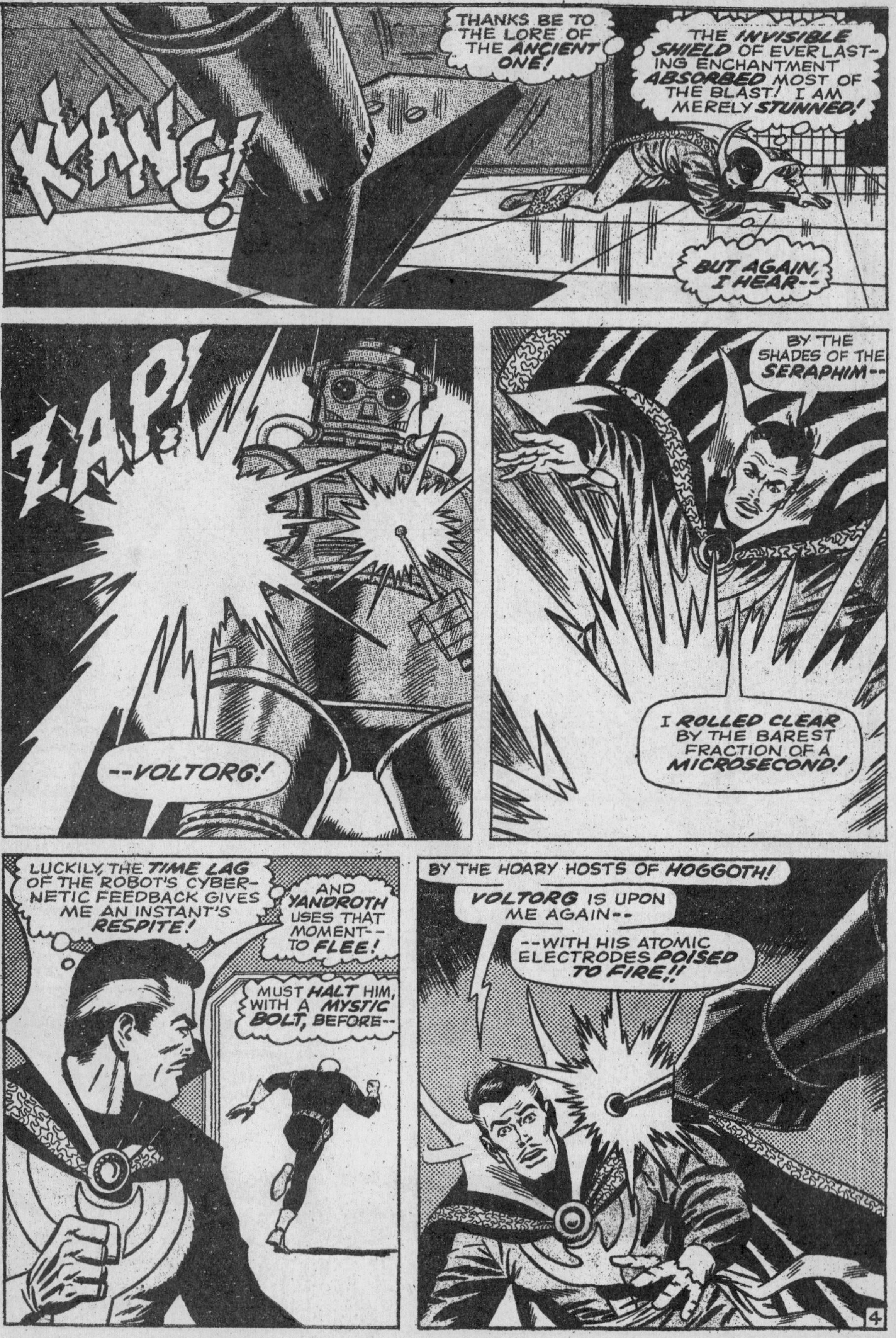

KLANG!
THANKS BE TO THE LORE OF THE ANCIENT ONE!
THE INVISIBLE SHIELD OF EVERLASTING ENCHANTMENT ABSORBED MOST OF THE BLAST! I AM MERELY STUNNED!
BUT AGAIN, I HEAR--
ZAP!
--VOLTORG!
BY THE SHADES OF THE SERAPHIM--
I ROLLED CLEAR BY THE BAREST FRACTION OF A MICROSECOND!
LUCKILY, THE TIME LAG OF THE ROBOT'S CYBERNETIC FEEDBACK GIVES ME AN INSTANT'S RESPITE!
AND YANDROTH USES THAT MOMENT--TO FLEE!
MUST HALT HIM, WITH A MYSTIC BOLT, BEFORE--
BY THE HOARY HOSTS OF HOGGOTH!
VOLTORG IS UPON ME AGAIN--
--WITH HIS ATOMIC ELECTRODES POISED TO FIRE!!
4

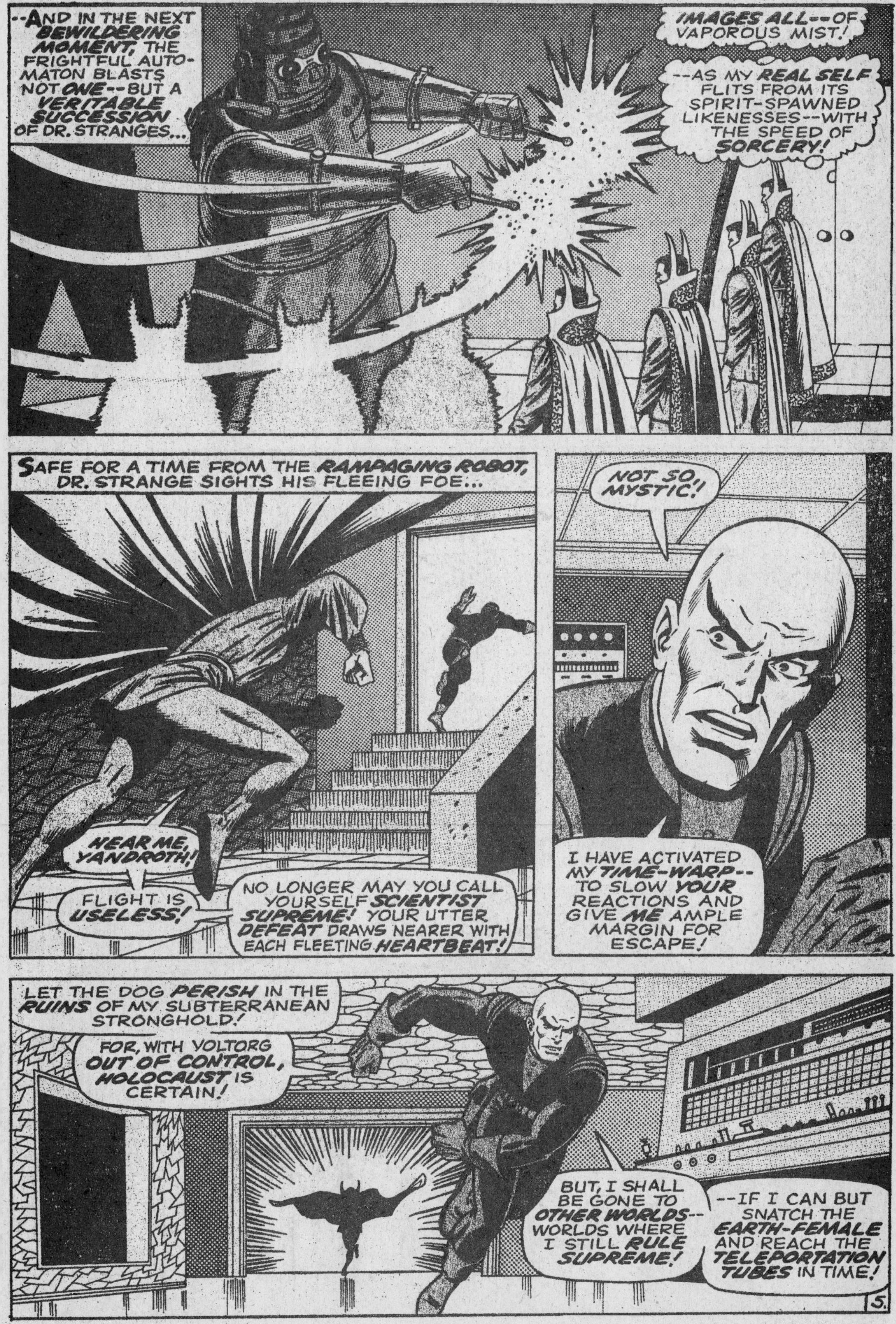
--AND IN THE NEXT BEWILDERING MOMENT, THE FRIGHTFUL AUTOMATON BLASTS NOT ONE--BUT A VERITABLE SUCCESSION OF DR. STRANGES...
IMAGES ALL--OF VAPOROUS MIST!
--AS MY REAL SELF FLITS FROM ITS SPIRIT-SPAWNED LIKENESSES--WITH THE SPEED OF SORCERY!
SAFE FOR A TIME FROM THE RAMPAGING ROBOT, DR. STRANGE SIGHTS HIS FLEEING FOE...
HEAR ME, YANDROTH!
FLIGHT IS USELESS!
NO LONGER MAY YOU CALL YOURSELF SCIENTIST SUPREME! YOUR UTTER DEFEAT DRAWS NEARER WITH EACH FLEETING HEARTBEAT!
NOT SO, MYSTIC!
I HAVE ACTIVATED MY TIME-WARP--TO SLOW YOUR REACTIONS AND GIVE ME AMPLE MARGIN FOR ESCAPE!
LET THE DOG PERISH IN THE RUINS OF MY SUBTERRANEAN STRONGHOLD!
FOR, WITH VOLTORG OUT OF CONTROL, HOLOCAUST IS CERTAIN!
BUT, I SHALL BE GONE TO OTHER WORLDS--WORLDS WHERE I STILL RULE SUPREME!
--IF I CAN BUT SNATCH THE EARTH-FEMALE AND REACH THE TELEPORTATION TUBES IN TIME!
5.

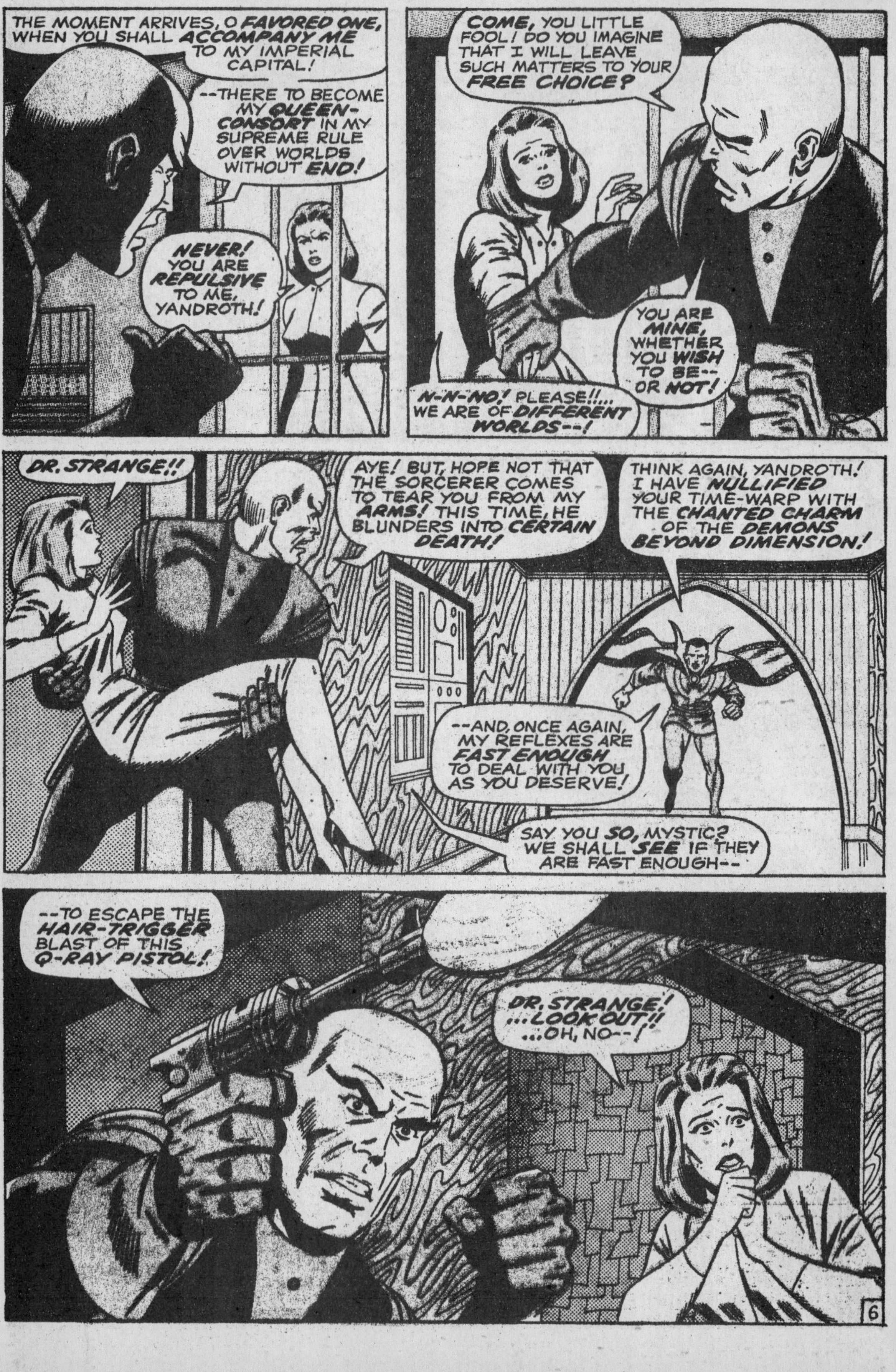
THE MOMENT ARRIVES, O FAVORED ONE, WHEN YOU SHALL ACCOMPANY ME TO MY IMPERIAL CAPITAL!
--THERE TO BECOME MY QUEEN-CONSORT IN MY SUPREME RULE OVER WORLDS WITHOUT END!
NEVER! YOU ARE REPULSIVE TO ME, YANDROTH!
COME, YOU LITTLE FOOL! DO YOU IMAGINE THAT I WILL LEAVE SUCH MATTERS TO YOUR FREE CHOICE?
YOU ARE MINE, WHETHER YOU WISH TO BE-- OR NOT!
N-N-NO! PLEASE!!... WE ARE OF DIFFERENT WORLDS--!
DR. STRANGE!!
AYE! BUT, HOPE NOT THAT THE SORCERER COMES TO TEAR YOU FROM MY ARMS! THIS TIME, HE BLUNDERS INTO CERTAIN DEATH!
THINK AGAIN, YANDROTH! I HAVE NULLIFIED YOUR TIME-WARP WITH THE CHANTED CHARM OF THE DEMONS BEYOND DIMENSION!
--AND, ONCE AGAIN, MY REFLEXES ARE FAST ENOUGH TO DEAL WITH YOU AS YOU DESERVE!
SAY YOU SO, MYSTIC? WE SHALL SEE IF THEY ARE FAST ENOUGH--
--TO ESCAPE THE HAIR-TRIGGER BLAST OF THIS Q-RAY PISTOL!
DR. STRANGE! ...LOOK OUT!! ...OH, NO--!
6

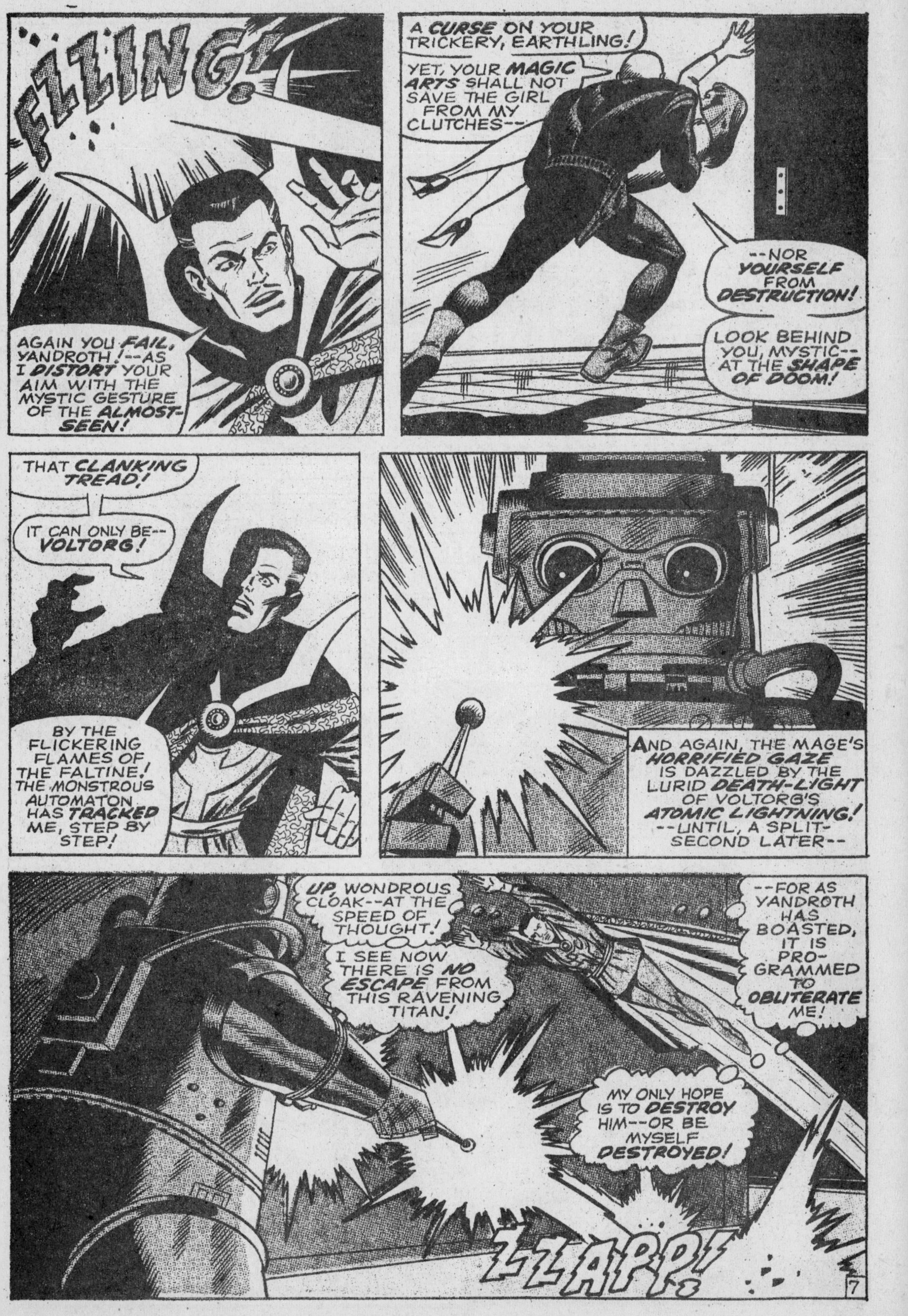
FZZING!
AGAIN YOU FAIL, YANDROTH!--AS I DISTORT YOUR AIM WITH THE MYSTIC GESTURE OF THE ALMOST-SEEN!
A CURSE ON YOUR TRICKERY, EARTHLING!
YET, YOUR MAGIC ARTS SHALL NOT SAVE THE GIRL FROM MY CLUTCHES--
--NOR YOURSELF FROM DESTRUCTION!
LOOK BEHIND YOU, MYSTIC--AT THE SHAPE OF DOOM!
THAT CLANKING TREAD!
IT CAN ONLY BE--VOLTORG!
BY THE FLICKERING FLAMES OF THE FALTINE! THE MONSTROUS AUTOMATON HAS TRACKED ME, STEP BY STEP!
AND AGAIN, THE MAGE'S HORRIFIED GAZE IS DAZZLED BY THE LURID DEATH-LIGHT OF VOLTORG'S ATOMIC LIGHTNING! --UNTIL, A SPLIT-SECOND LATER--
UP, WONDROUS CLOAK--AT THE SPEED OF THOUGHT!
I SEE NOW THERE IS NO ESCAPE FROM THIS RAVENING TITAN!
--FOR AS YANDROTH HAS BOASTED, IT IS PRO-GRAMMED TO OBLITERATE ME!
MY ONLY HOPE IS TO DESTROY HIM--OR BE MYSELF DESTROYED!
ZZAPP!
7

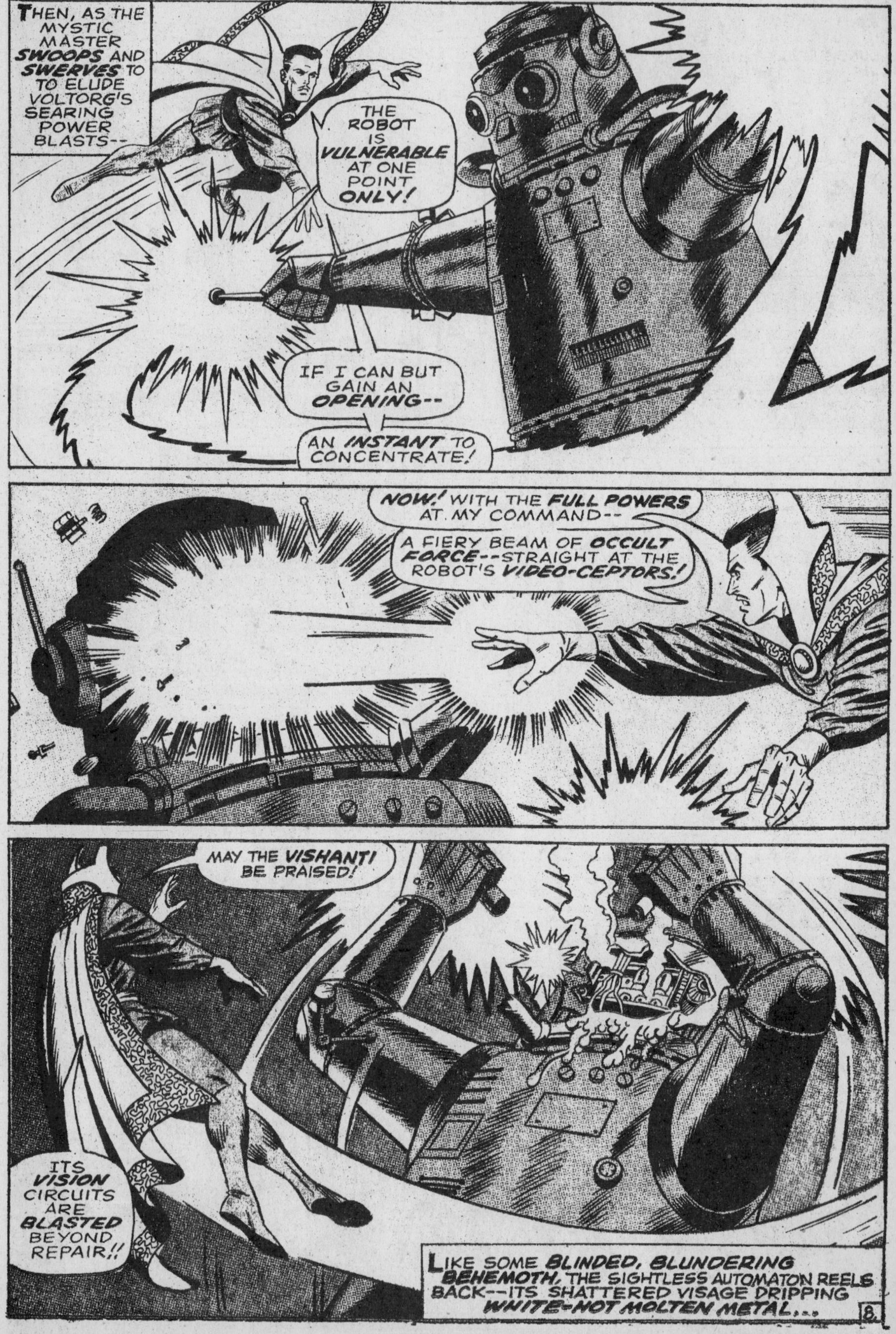
THEN, AS THE MYSTIC MASTER SWOOPS AND SWERVES TO TO ELUDE VOLTORG'S SEARING POWER BLASTS--
THE ROBOT IS VULNERABLE AT ONE POINT ONLY!
IF I CAN BUT GAIN AN OPENING--
AN INSTANT TO CONCENTRATE!
NOW! WITH THE FULL POWERS AT MY COMMAND--
A FIERY BEAM OF OCCULT FORCE--STRAIGHT AT THE ROBOT'S VIDEO-CEPTORS!
MAY THE VISHANTI BE PRAISED!
ITS VISION CIRCUITS ARE BLASTED BEYOND REPAIR!!
LIKE SOME BLINDED, BLUNDERING BEHEMOTH, THE SIGHTLESS AUTOMATON REELS BACK--ITS SHATTERED VISAGE DRIPPING WHITE-HOT MOLTEN METAL...
8

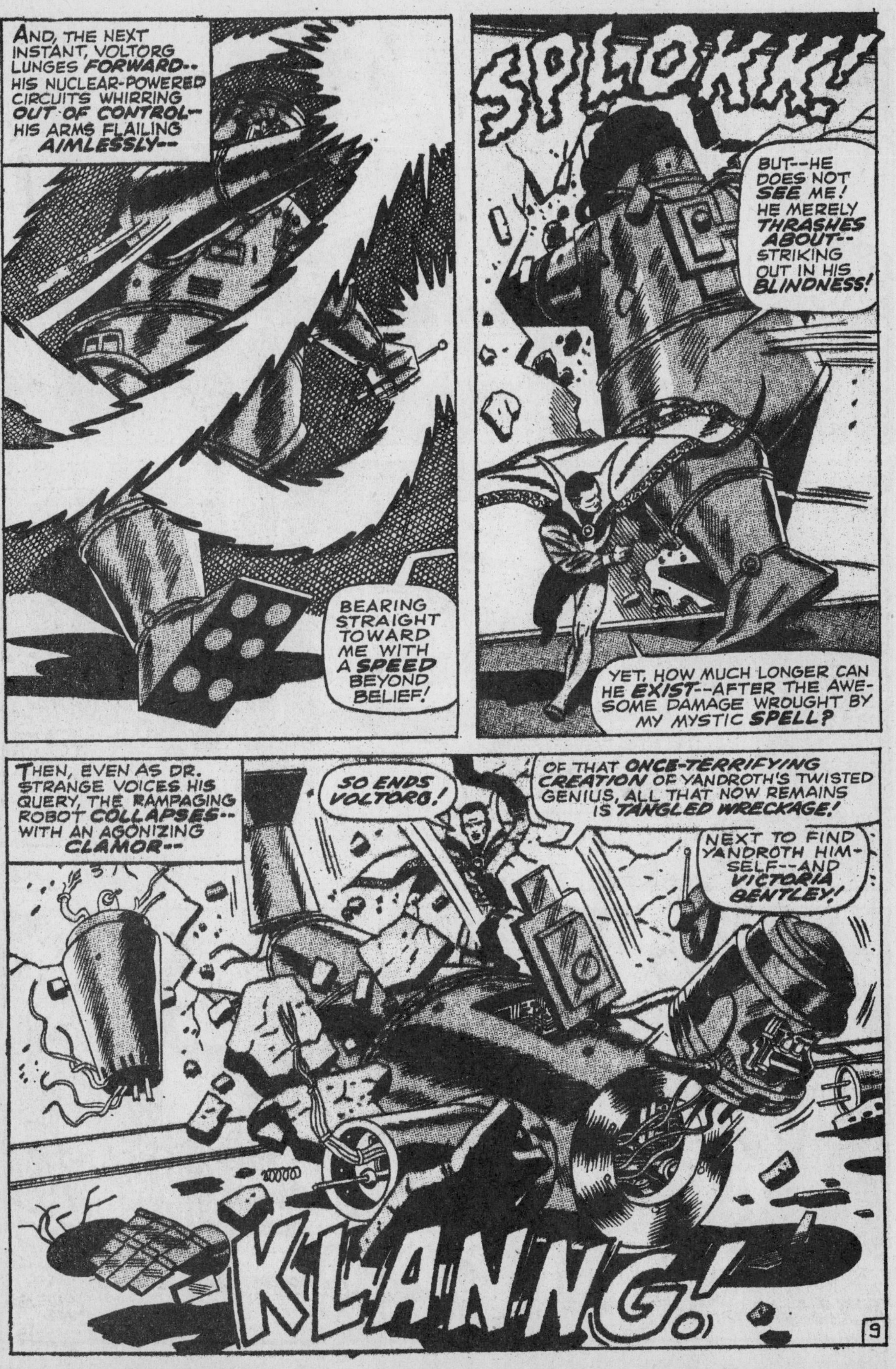

AND, THE NEXT INSTANT, VOLTORG LUNGES FORWARD-- HIS NUCLEAR-POWERED CIRCUITS WHIRRING OUT OF CONTROL-- HIS ARMS FLAILING AIMLESSLY--
BEARING STRAIGHT TOWARD ME WITH A SPEED BEYOND BELIEF!
SPLOKK!
BUT--HE DOES NOT SEE ME! HE MERELY THRASHES ABOUT-- STRIKING OUT IN HIS BLINDNESS!
YET, HOW MUCH LONGER CAN HE EXIST--AFTER THE AWE-SOME DAMAGE WROUGHT BY MY MYSTIC SPELL?
THEN, EVEN AS DR. STRANGE VOICES HIS QUERY, THE RAMPAGING ROBOT COLLAPSES-- WITH AN AGONIZING CLAMOR--
SO ENDS VOLTORG!
OF THAT ONCE-TERRIFYING CREATION OF YANDROTH'S TWISTED GENIUS, ALL THAT NOW REMAINS IS TANGLED WRECKAGE!
NEXT TO FIND YANDROTH HIM-SELF--AND VICTORIA BENTLEY!
KLANNG!
9

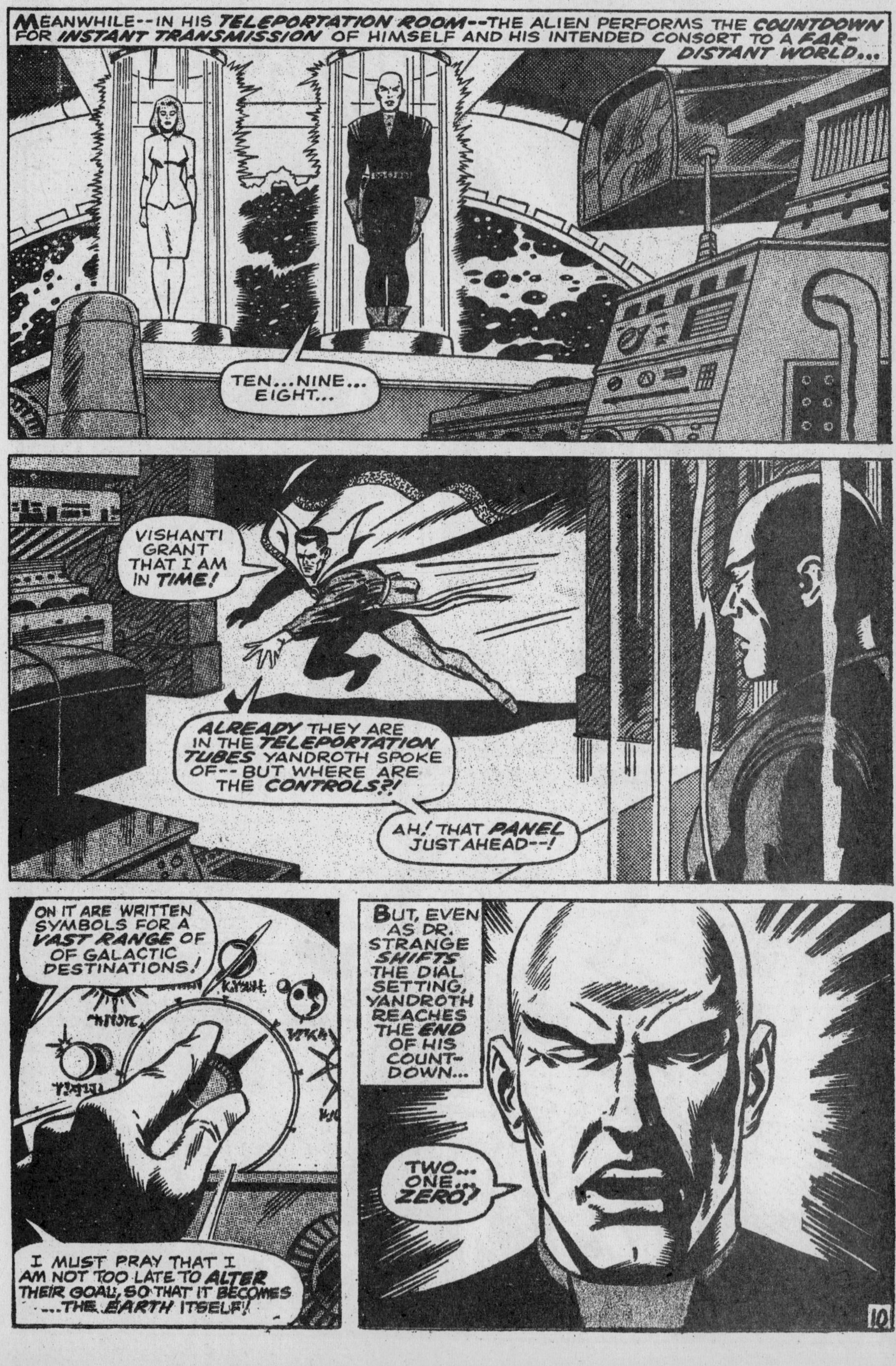
MEANWHILE--IN HIS TELEPORTATION ROOM--THE ALIEN PERFORMS THE COUNTDOWN FOR INSTANT TRANSMISSION OF HIMSELF AND HIS INTENDED CONSORT TO A FAR-DISTANT WORLD...
TEN...NINE... EIGHT...
VISHANTI GRANT THAT I AM IN TIME!
ALREADY THEY ARE IN THE TELEPORTATION TUBES YANDROTH SPOKE OF-- BUT WHERE ARE THE CONTROLS?!
AH! THAT PANEL JUST AHEAD--!
ON IT ARE WRITTEN SYMBOLS FOR A VAST RANGE OF OF GALACTIC DESTINATIONS!
I MUST PRAY THAT I AM NOT TOO LATE TO ALTER THEIR GOAL, SO THAT IT BECOMES ...THE EARTH ITSELF!
BUT, EVEN AS DR. STRANGE SHIFTS THE DIAL SETTING, YANDROTH REACHES THE END OF HIS COUNT-DOWN...
TWO... ONE... ZERO!
10

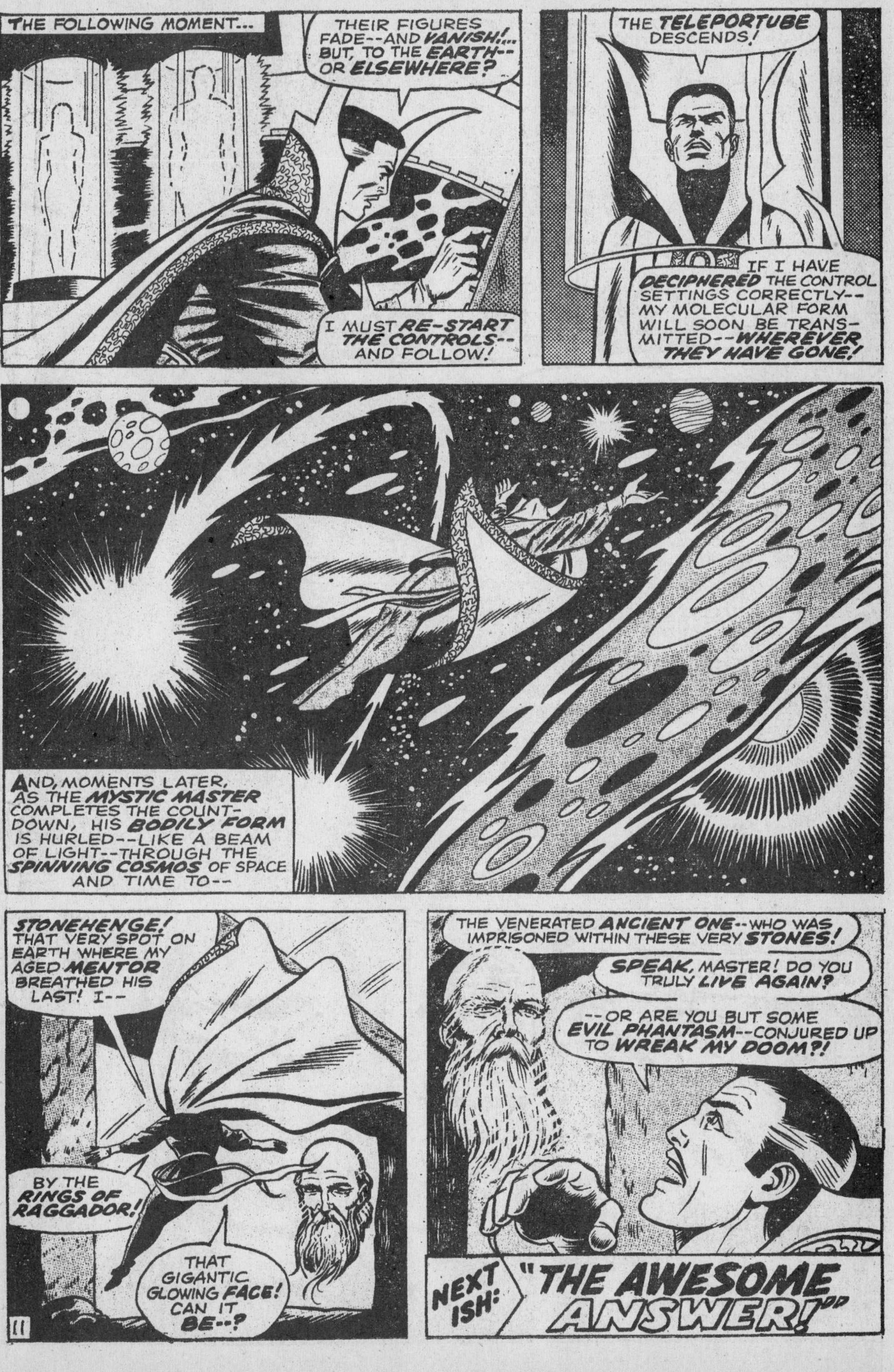
THE FOLLOWING MOMENT...
THEIR FIGURES FADE--AND VANISH!... BUT, TO THE EARTH-- OR ELSEWHERE?
I MUST RE-START THE CONTROLS-- AND FOLLOW!
THE TELEPORTUBE DESCENDS!
IF I HAVE DECIPHERED THE CONTROL SETTINGS CORRECTLY-- MY MOLECULAR FORM WILL SOON BE TRANS-MITTED--WHEREVER THEY HAVE GONE!
AND, MOMENTS LATER, AS THE MYSTIC MASTER COMPLETES THE COUNT-DOWN, HIS BODILY FORM IS HURLED--LIKE A BEAM OF LIGHT--THROUGH THE SPINNING COSMOS OF SPACE AND TIME TO--
STONEHENGE! THAT VERY SPOT ON EARTH WHERE MY AGED MENTOR BREATHED HIS LAST! I--
BY THE RINGS OF RAGGADOR!
THAT GIGANTIC GLOWING FACE! CAN IT BE--?
11
THE VENERATED ANCIENT ONE--WHO WAS IMPRISONED WITHIN THESE VERY STONES!
SPEAK, MASTER! DO YOU TRULY LIVE AGAIN?
--OR ARE YOU BUT SOME EVIL PHANTASM--CONJURED UP TO WREAK MY DOOM?!
NEXT ISH: "THE AWESOME ANSWER!"

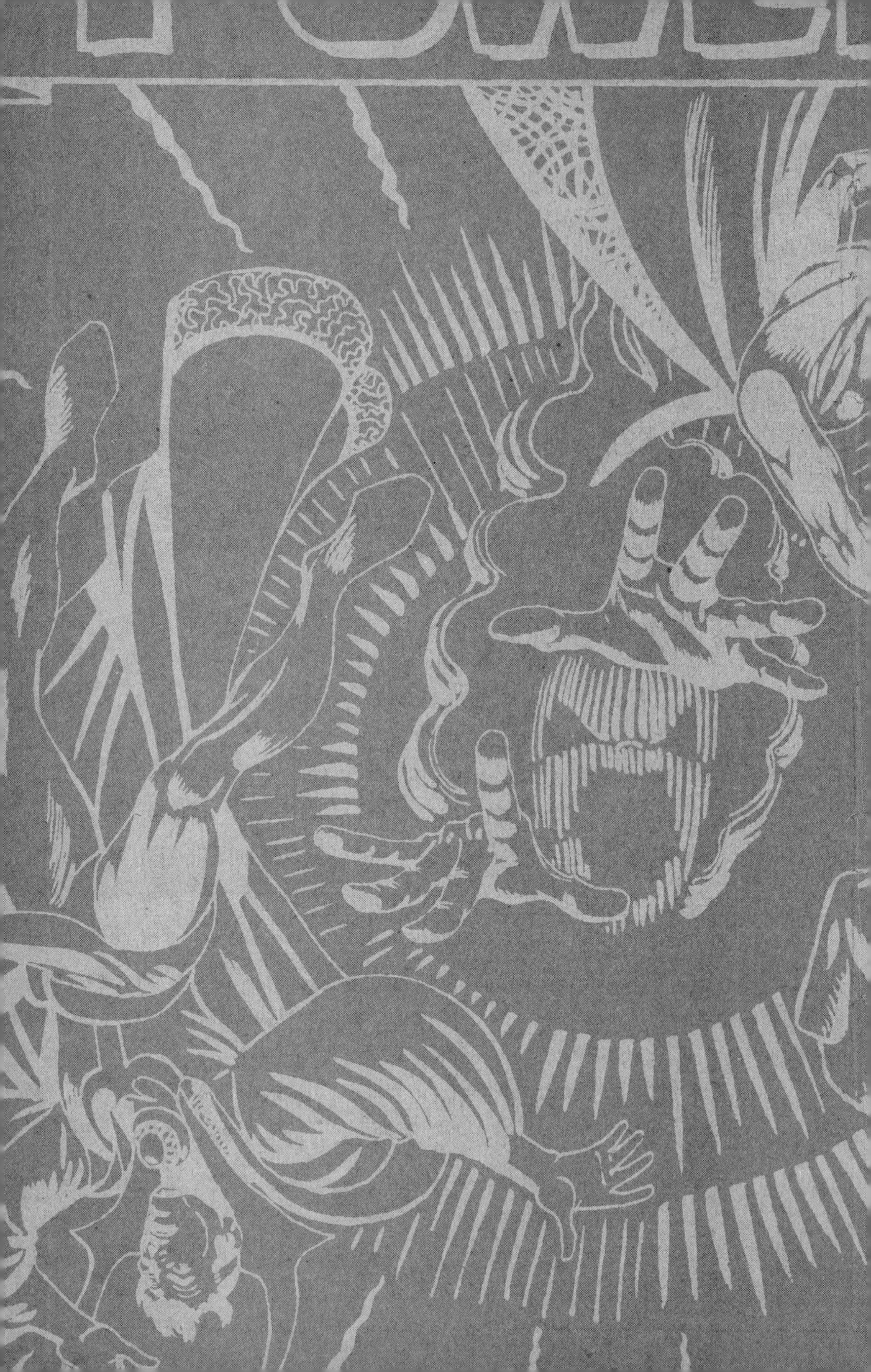

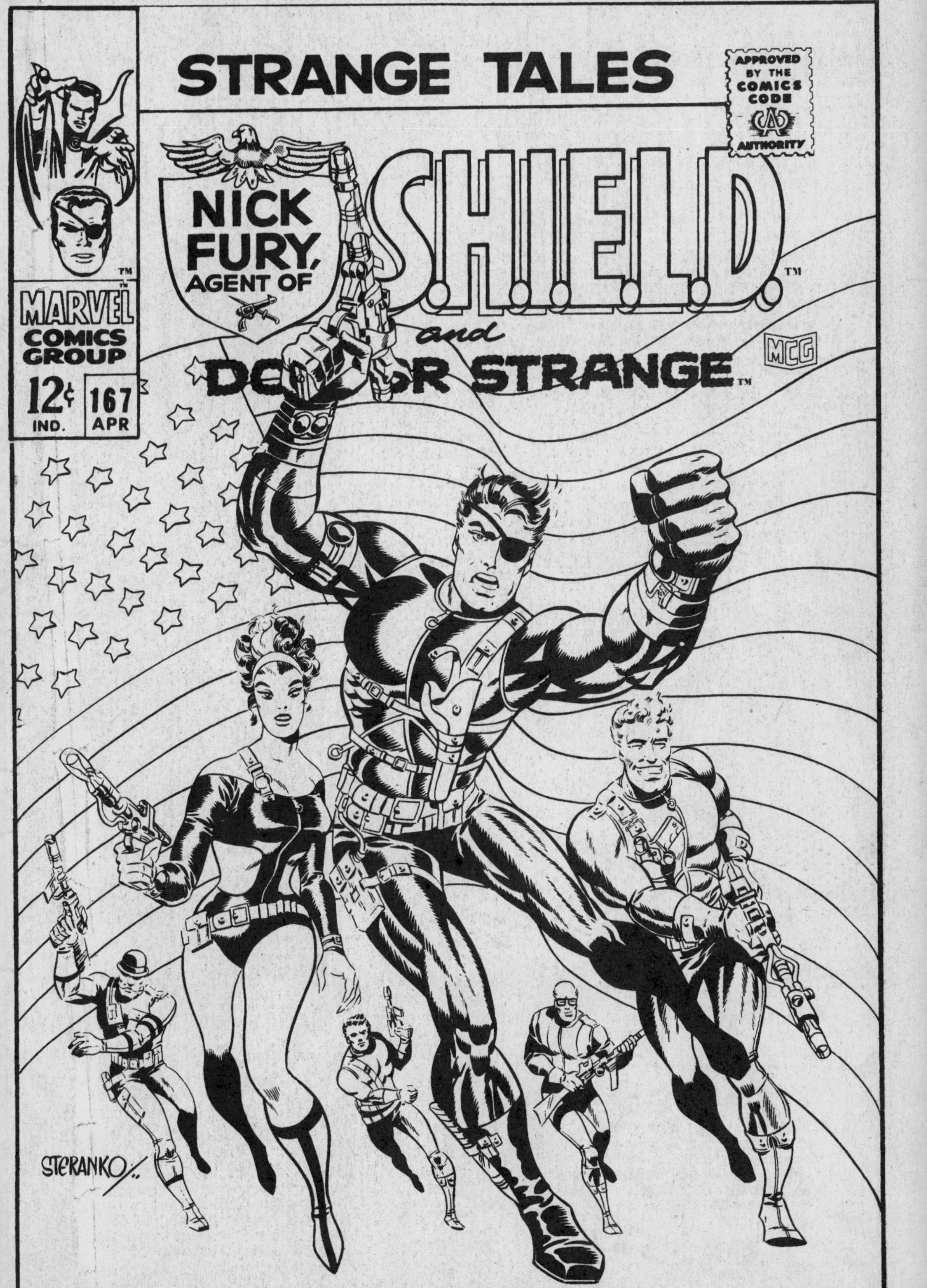
STRANGE TALES
APPROVED BY THE COMICS CODE AUTHORITY
NICK FURY, AGENT OF
S.H.I.E.L.D.
and
STRANGE
MARVEL COMICS GROUP
12¢ IND.
167 APR
MCG
STERANKO

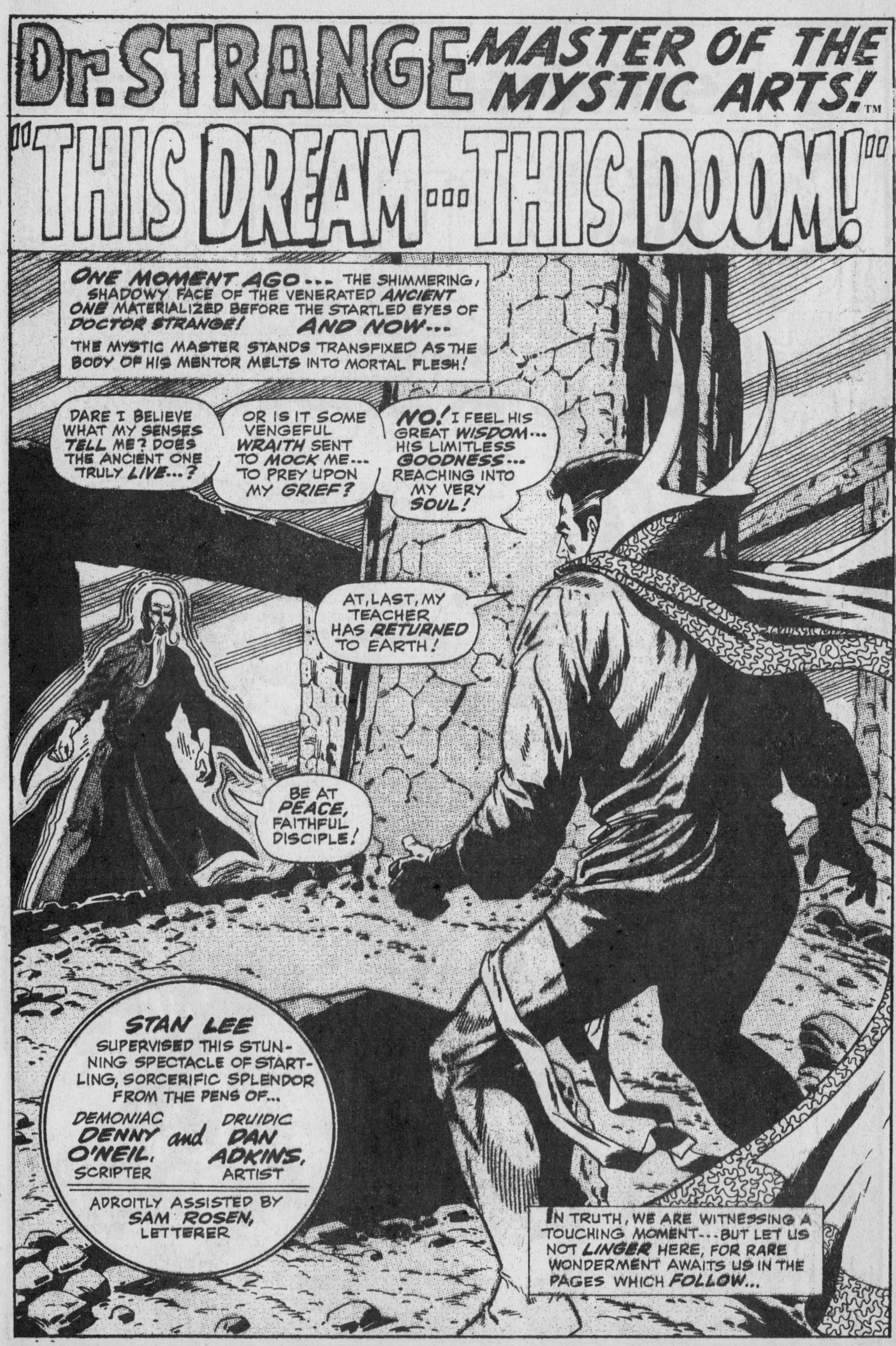

Dr. STRANGE MASTER OF THE MYSTIC ARTS!™
"THIS DREAM... THIS DOOM!"
ONE MOMENT AGO... THE SHIMMERING, SHADOWY FACE OF THE VENERATED ANCIENT ONE MATERIALIZED BEFORE THE STARTLED EYES OF DOCTOR STRANGE! AND NOW... THE MYSTIC MASTER STANDS TRANSFIXED AS THE BODY OF HIS MENTOR MELTS INTO MORTAL FLESH!
DARE I BELIEVE WHAT MY SENSES TELL ME? DOES THE ANCIENT ONE TRULY LIVE...?
OR IS IT SOME VENGEFUL WRAITH SENT TO MOCK ME... TO PREY UPON MY GRIEF?
NO! I FEEL HIS GREAT WISDOM... HIS LIMITLESS GOODNESS... REACHING INTO MY VERY SOUL!
AT LAST, MY TEACHER HAS RETURNED TO EARTH!
BE AT PEACE, FAITHFUL DISCIPLE!
STAN LEE SUPERVISED THIS STUNNING SPECTACLE OF STARTLING, SORCERIFIC SPLENDOR FROM THE PENS OF... DEMONIAC DENNY O'NEIL, SCRIPTER and DRUIDIC DAN ADKINS, ARTIST
ADROITLY ASSISTED BY SAM ROSEN, LETTERER
IN TRUTH, WE ARE WITNESSING A TOUCHING MOMENT... BUT LET US NOT LINGER HERE, FOR RARE WONDERMENT AWAITS US IN THE PAGES WHICH FOLLOW...

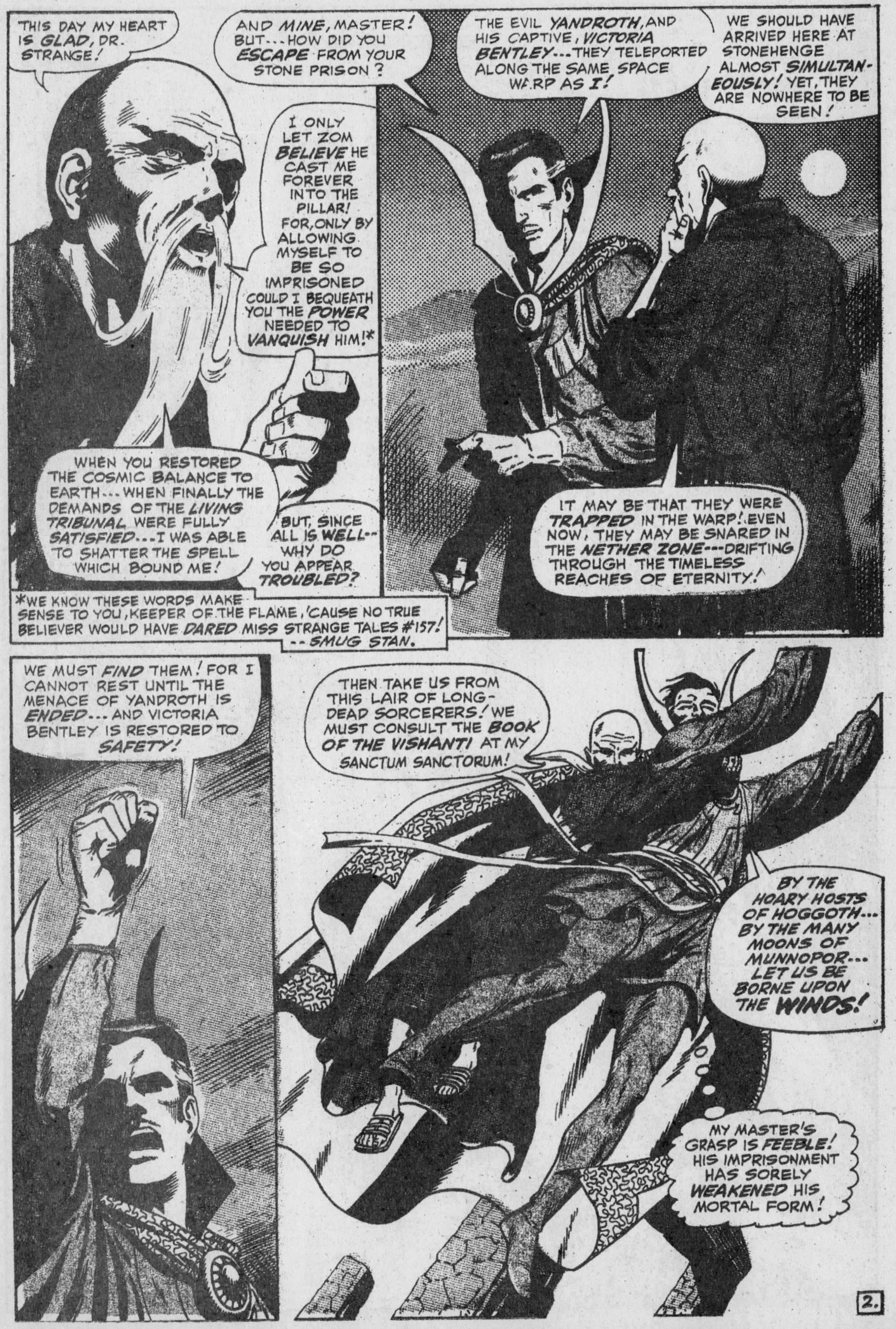
THIS DAY MY HEART IS GLAD, DR. STRANGE!
AND MINE, MASTER! BUT... HOW DID YOU ESCAPE FROM YOUR STONE PRISON?
I ONLY LET ZOM BELIEVE HE CAST ME FOREVER INTO THE PILLAR! FOR, ONLY BY ALLOWING MYSELF TO BE SO IMPRISONED COULD I BEQUEATH YOU THE POWER NEEDED TO VANQUISH HIM!*
WHEN YOU RESTORED THE COSMIC BALANCE TO EARTH... WHEN FINALLY THE DEMANDS OF THE LIVING TRIBUNAL WERE FULLY SATISFIED... I WAS ABLE TO SHATTER THE SPELL WHICH BOUND ME!
BUT, SINCE ALL IS WELL-- WHY DO YOU APPEAR TROUBLED?
*WE KNOW THESE WORDS MAKE SENSE TO YOU, KEEPER OF THE FLAME, 'CAUSE NO TRUE BELIEVER WOULD HAVE DARED MISS STRANGE TALES #157! --SMUG STAN.
THE EVIL YANDROTH, AND HIS CAPTIVE, VICTORIA BENTLEY... THEY TELEPORTED ALONG THE SAME SPACE WARP AS I!
WE SHOULD HAVE ARRIVED HERE AT STONEHENGE ALMOST SIMULTANEOUSLY! YET, THEY ARE NOWHERE TO BE SEEN!
IT MAY BE THAT THEY WERE TRAPPED IN THE WARP! EVEN NOW, THEY MAY BE SNARED IN THE NETHER ZONE---DRIFTING THROUGH THE TIMELESS REACHES OF ETERNITY!
WE MUST FIND THEM! FOR I CANNOT REST UNTIL THE MENACE OF YANDROTH IS ENDED... AND VICTORIA BENTLEY IS RESTORED TO SAFETY!
THEN TAKE US FROM THIS LAIR OF LONG-DEAD SORCERERS! WE MUST CONSULT THE BOOK OF THE VISHANTI AT MY SANCTUM SANCTORUM!
BY THE HOARY HOSTS OF HOGGOTH... BY THE MANY MOONS OF MUNNOPOR... LET US BE BORNE UPON THE WINDS!
MY MASTER'S GRASP IS FEEBLE! HIS IMPRISONMENT HAS SORELY WEAKENED HIS MORTAL FORM!
2.

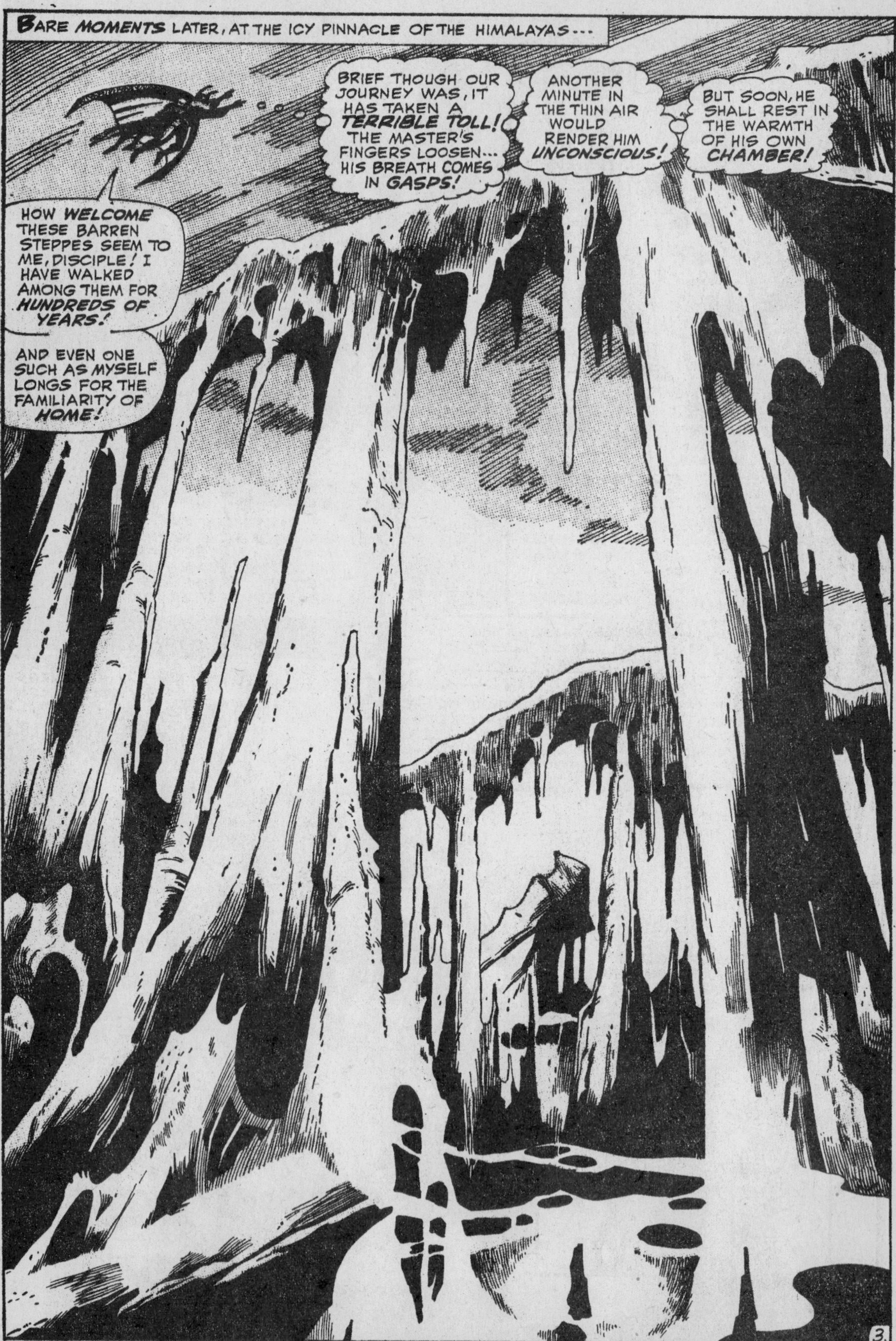
BARE MOMENTS LATER, AT THE ICY PINNACLE OF THE HIMALAYAS...
HOW WELCOME THESE BARREN STEPPES SEEM TO ME, DISCIPLE! I HAVE WALKED AMONG THEM FOR HUNDREDS OF YEARS!
AND EVEN ONE SUCH AS MYSELF LONGS FOR THE FAMILIARITY OF HOME!
BRIEF THOUGH OUR JOURNEY WAS, IT HAS TAKEN A TERRIBLE TOLL! THE MASTER'S FINGERS LOOSEN... HIS BREATH COMES IN GASPS!
ANOTHER MINUTE IN THE THIN AIR WOULD RENDER HIM UNCONSCIOUS!
BUT SOON, HE SHALL REST IN THE WARMTH OF HIS OWN CHAMBER!
3.

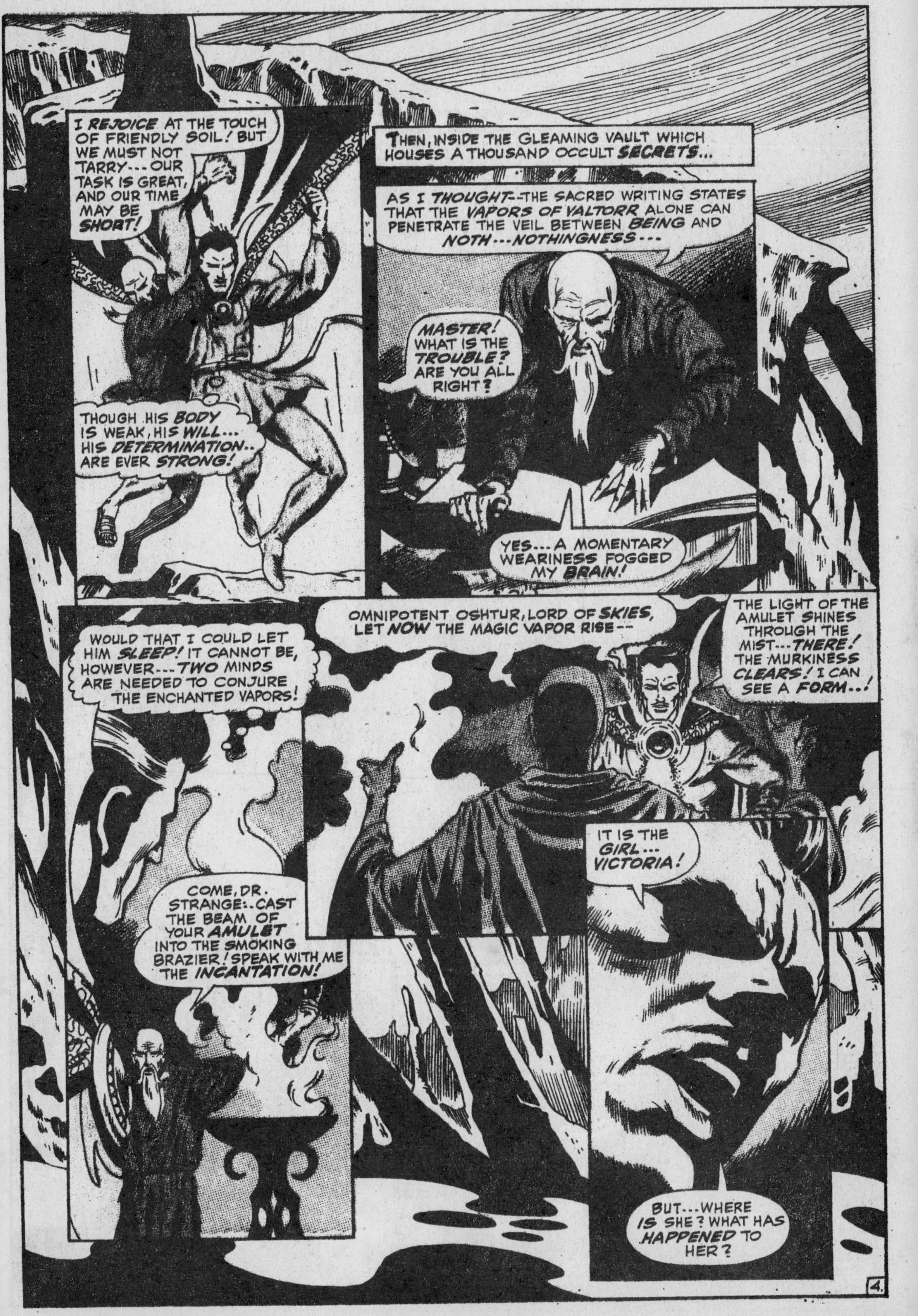
I REJOICE AT THE TOUCH OF FRIENDLY SOIL! BUT WE MUST NOT TARRY... OUR TASK IS GREAT, AND OUR TIME MAY BE SHORT!
THOUGH HIS BODY IS WEAK, HIS WILL... HIS DETERMINATION.. ARE EVER STRONG!
THEN, INSIDE THE GLEAMING VAULT WHICH HOUSES A THOUSAND OCCULT SECRETS...
AS I THOUGHT--THE SACRED WRITING STATES THAT THE VAPORS OF VALTORR ALONE CAN PENETRATE THE VEIL BETWEEN BEING AND NOTH---NOTHINGNESS---
MASTER! WHAT IS THE TROUBLE? ARE YOU ALL RIGHT?
YES... A MOMENTARY WEARINESS FOGGED MY BRAIN!
WOULD THAT I COULD LET HIM SLEEP! IT CANNOT BE, HOWEVER---TWO MINDS ARE NEEDED TO CONJURE THE ENCHANTED VAPORS!
COME, DR. STRANGE:.CAST THE BEAM OF YOUR AMULET INTO THE SMOKING BRAZIER! SPEAK WITH ME THE INCANTATION!
OMNIPOTENT OSHTUR, LORD OF SKIES, LET NOW THE MAGIC VAPOR RISE--
THE LIGHT OF THE AMULET SHINES THROUGH THE MIST---THERE! THE MURKINESS CLEARS! I CAN SEE A FORM..!
IT IS THE GIRL... VICTORIA!
BUT...WHERE IS SHE? WHAT HAS HAPPENED TO HER?
4

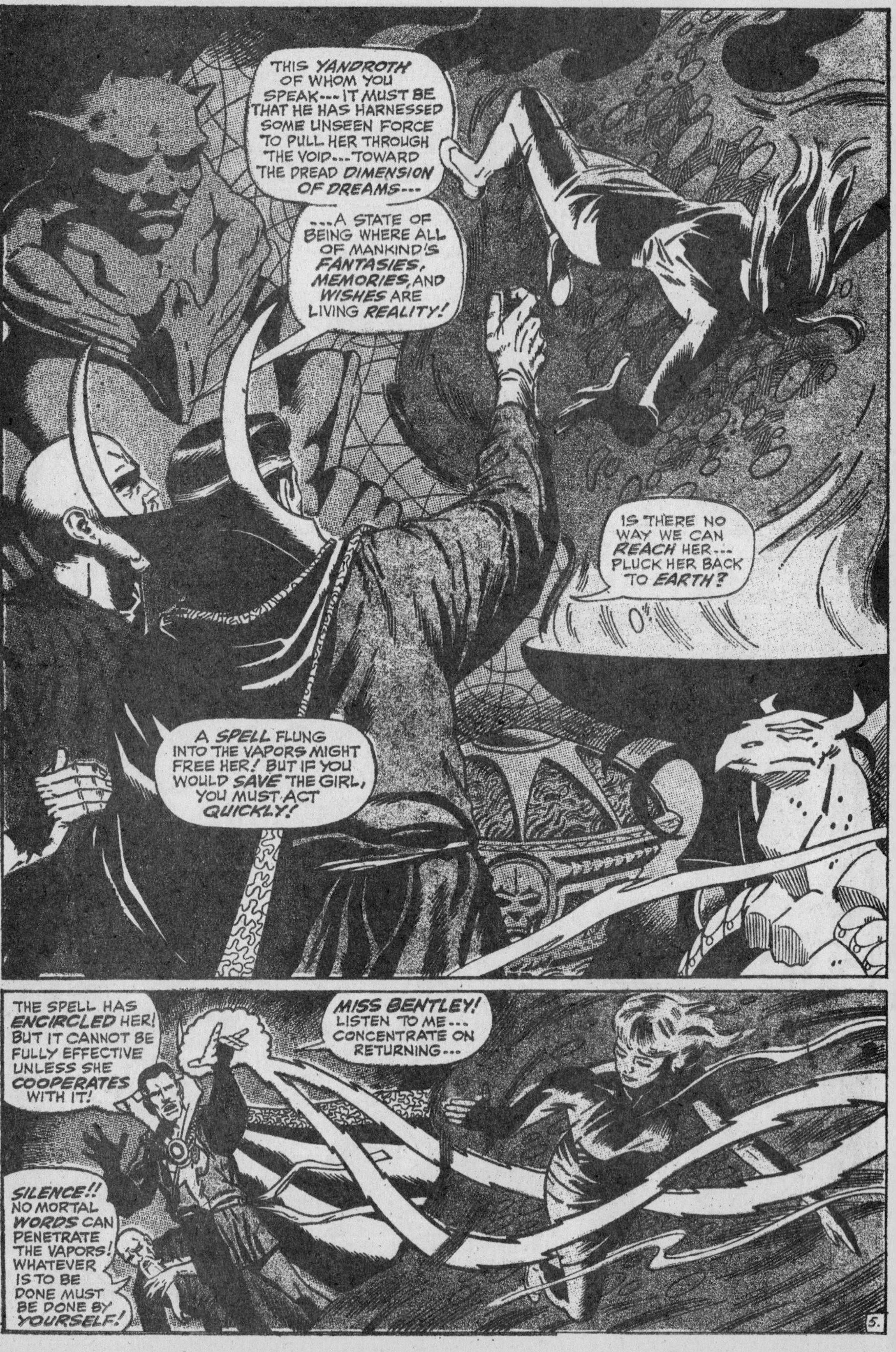
THIS YANDROTH OF WHOM YOU SPEAK--- IT MUST BE THAT HE HAS HARNESSED SOME UNSEEN FORCE TO PULL HER THROUGH THE VOID--- TOWARD THE DREAD DIMENSION OF DREAMS---
---A STATE OF BEING WHERE ALL OF MANKIND'S FANTASIES, MEMORIES, AND WISHES ARE LIVING REALITY!
IS THERE NO WAY WE CAN REACH HER--- PLUCK HER BACK TO EARTH?
A SPELL FLUNG INTO THE VAPORS MIGHT FREE HER! BUT IF YOU WOULD SAVE THE GIRL, YOU MUST ACT QUICKLY!
THE SPELL HAS ENCIRCLED HER! BUT IT CANNOT BE FULLY EFFECTIVE UNLESS SHE COOPERATES WITH IT!
MISS BENTLEY! LISTEN TO ME--- CONCENTRATE ON RETURNING---
SILENCE!! NO MORTAL WORDS CAN PENETRATE THE VAPORS! WHATEVER IS TO BE DONE MUST BE DONE BY YOURSELF!
5.

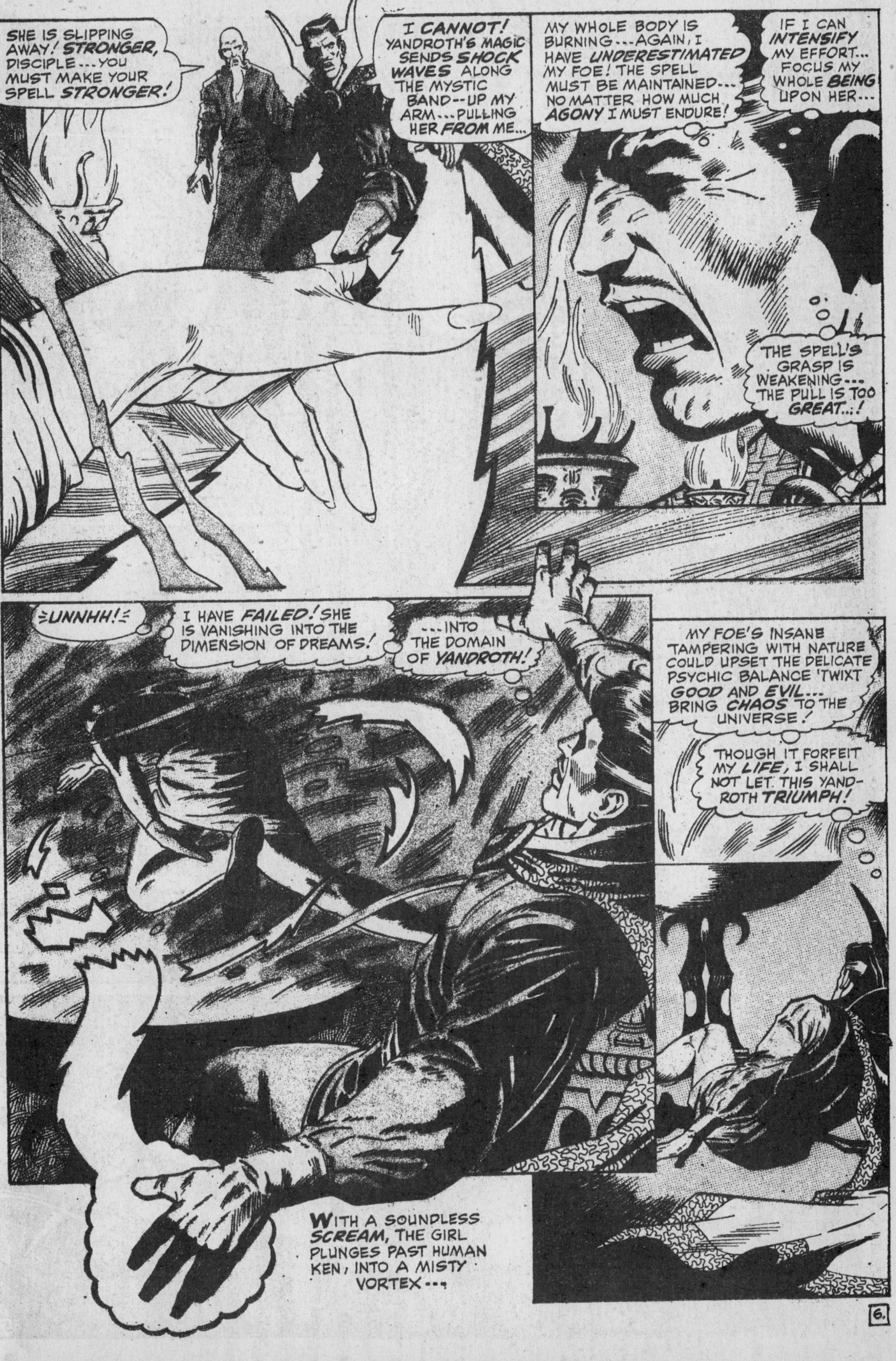
SHE IS SLIPPING AWAY! STRONGER, DISCIPLE--- YOU MUST MAKE YOUR SPELL STRONGER!
I CANNOT! YANDROTH'S MAGIC SENDS SHOCK WAVES ALONG THE MYSTIC BAND--UP MY ARM---PULLING HER FROM ME...
MY WHOLE BODY IS BURNING---AGAIN, I HAVE UNDERESTIMATED MY FOE! THE SPELL MUST BE MAINTAINED--- NO MATTER HOW MUCH AGONY I MUST ENDURE!
IF I CAN INTENSIFY MY EFFORT... FOCUS MY WHOLE BEING UPON HER...
THE SPELL'S GRASP IS WEAKENING--- THE PULL IS TOO GREAT...!
UNNHH!
I HAVE FAILED! SHE IS VANISHING INTO THE DIMENSION OF DREAMS!
---INTO THE DOMAIN OF YANDROTH!
MY FOE'S INSANE TAMPERING WITH NATURE COULD UPSET THE DELICATE PSYCHIC BALANCE 'TWIXT GOOD AND EVIL... BRING CHAOS TO THE UNIVERSE!
THOUGH IT FORFEIT MY LIFE, I SHALL NOT LET. THIS YANDROTH TRIUMPH!
WITH A SOUNDLESS SCREAM, THE GIRL PLUNGES PAST HUMAN KEN, INTO A MISTY VORTEX---
6.

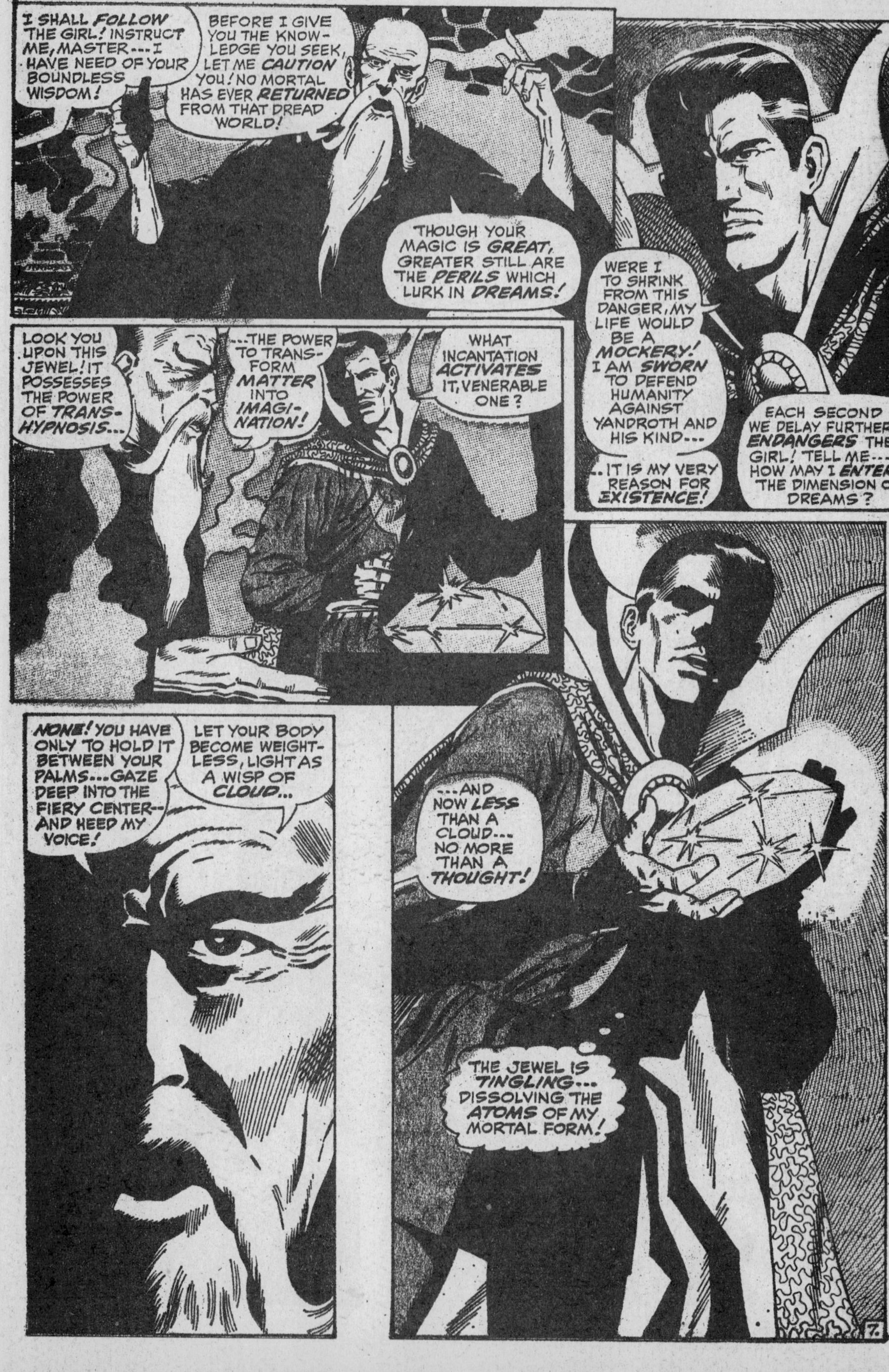
I SHALL FOLLOW THE GIRL! INSTRUCT ME, MASTER--- I HAVE NEED OF YOUR BOUNDLESS WISDOM!
BEFORE I GIVE YOU THE KNOWLEDGE YOU SEEK, LET ME CAUTION YOU! NO MORTAL HAS EVER RETURNED FROM THAT DREAD WORLD!
THOUGH YOUR MAGIC IS GREAT, GREATER STILL ARE THE PERILS WHICH LURK IN DREAMS!
WERE I TO SHRINK FROM THIS DANGER, MY LIFE WOULD BE A MOCKERY! I AM SWORN TO DEFEND HUMANITY AGAINST YANDROTH AND HIS KIND---
...IT IS MY VERY REASON FOR EXISTENCE!
EACH SECOND WE DELAY FURTHER ENDANGERS THE GIRL! TELL ME--- HOW MAY I ENTER THE DIMENSION OF DREAMS?
LOOK YOU UPON THIS JEWEL! IT POSSESSES THE POWER OF TRANS-HYPNOSIS...
...THE POWER TO TRANSFORM MATTER INTO IMAGINATION!
WHAT INCANTATION ACTIVATES IT, VENERABLE ONE?
NONE! YOU HAVE ONLY TO HOLD IT BETWEEN YOUR PALMS... GAZE DEEP INTO THE FIERY CENTER-- AND HEED MY VOICE!
LET YOUR BODY BECOME WEIGHTLESS, LIGHT AS A WISP OF CLOUD...
...AND NOW LESS THAN A CLOUD... NO MORE THAN A THOUGHT!
THE JEWEL IS TINGLING... DISSOLVING THE ATOMS OF MY MORTAL FORM!
7.

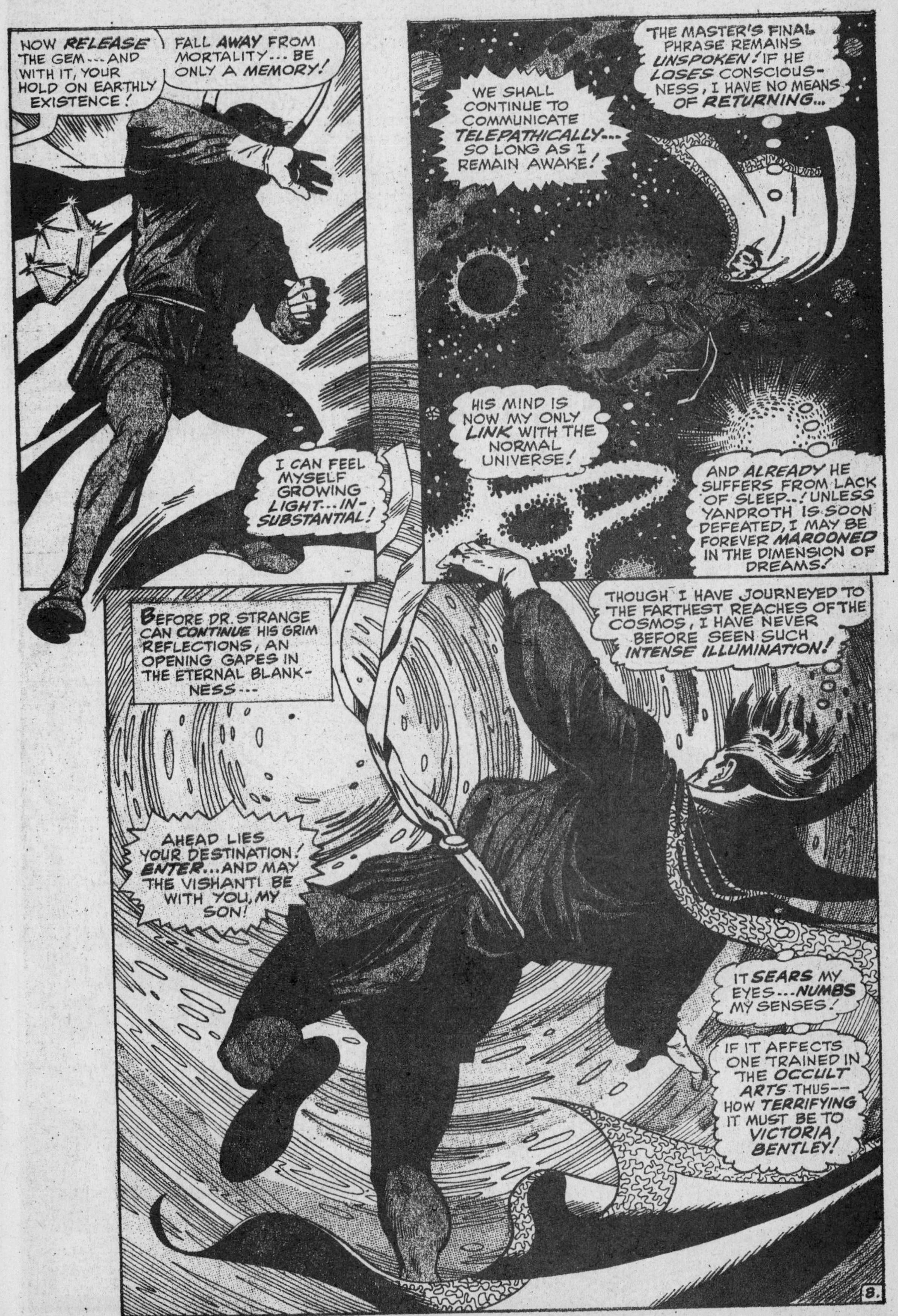
NOW RELEASE THE GEM--- AND WITH IT, YOUR HOLD ON EARTHLY EXISTENCE!
FALL AWAY FROM MORTALITY... BE ONLY A MEMORY!
I CAN FEEL MYSELF GROWING LIGHT... IN-SUBSTANTIAL!
WE SHALL CONTINUE TO COMMUNICATE TELEPATHICALLY... SO LONG AS I REMAIN AWAKE!
THE MASTER'S FINAL PHRASE REMAINS UNSPOKEN! IF HE LOSES CONSCIOUS-NESS, I HAVE NO MEANS OF RETURNING...
HIS MIND IS NOW MY ONLY LINK WITH THE NORMAL UNIVERSE!
AND ALREADY HE SUFFERS FROM LACK OF SLEEP..! UNLESS YANDROTH IS SOON DEFEATED, I MAY BE FOREVER MAROONED IN THE DIMENSION OF DREAMS!
BEFORE DR. STRANGE CAN CONTINUE HIS GRIM REFLECTIONS, AN OPENING GAPES IN THE ETERNAL BLANK-NESS---
THOUGH I HAVE JOURNEYED TO THE FARTHEST REACHES OF THE COSMOS, I HAVE NEVER BEFORE SEEN SUCH INTENSE ILLUMINATION!
AHEAD LIES YOUR DESTINATION! ENTER... AND MAY THE VISHANTI BE WITH YOU, MY SON!
IT SEARS MY EYES... NUMBS MY SENSES!
IF IT AFFECTS ONE TRAINED IN THE OCCULT ARTS THUS-- HOW TERRIFYING IT MUST BE TO VICTORIA BENTLEY!

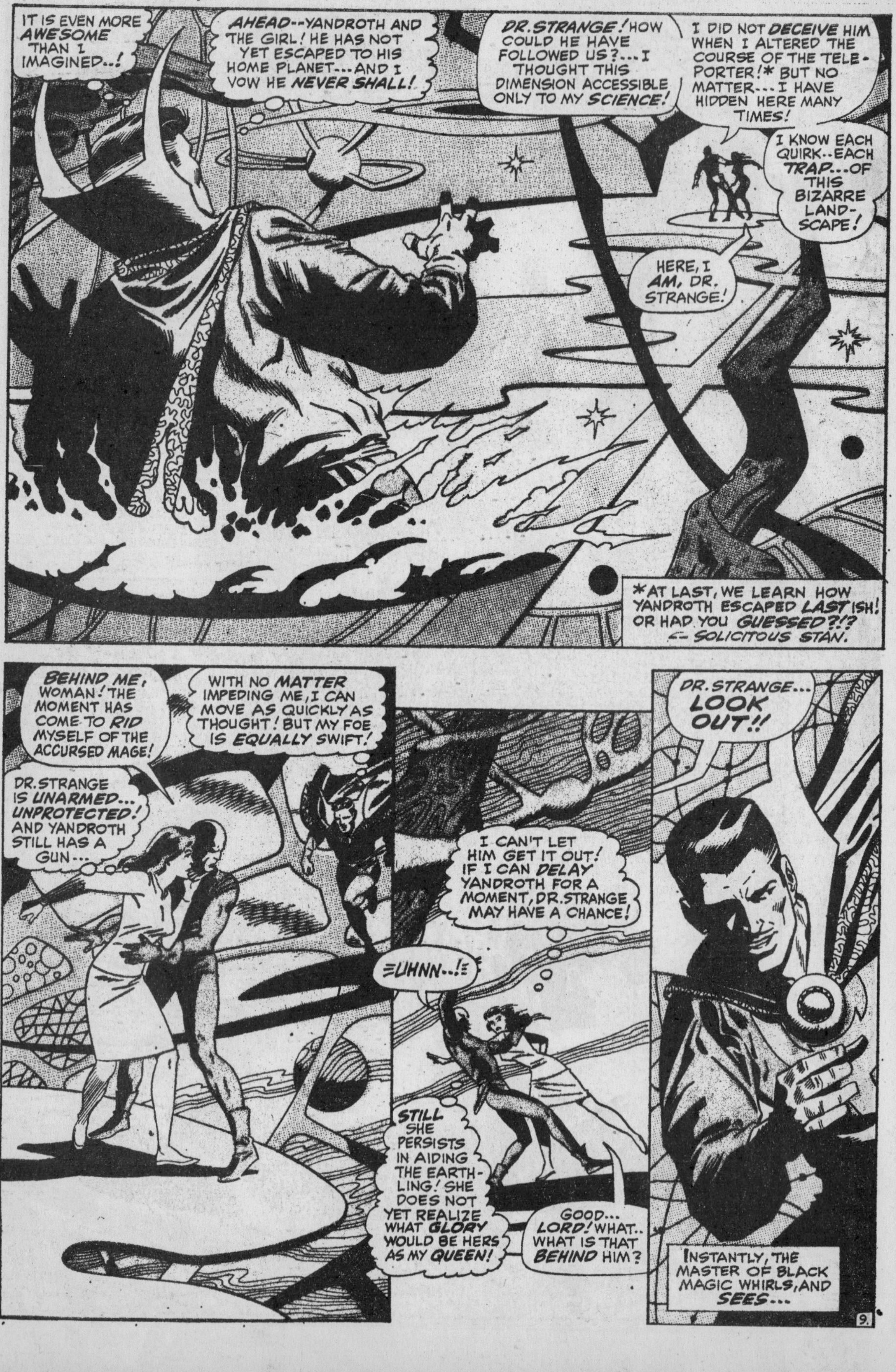
IT IS EVEN MORE AWESOME THAN I IMAGINED..!
AHEAD--YANDROTH AND THE GIRL! HE HAS NOT YET ESCAPED TO HIS HOME PLANET---AND I VOW HE NEVER SHALL!
DR. STRANGE! HOW COULD HE HAVE FOLLOWED US?...I THOUGHT THIS DIMENSION ACCESSIBLE ONLY TO MY SCIENCE!
I DID NOT DECEIVE HIM WHEN I ALTERED THE COURSE OF THE TELE-PORTER!* BUT NO MATTER---I HAVE HIDDEN HERE MANY TIMES!
I KNOW EACH QUIRK--EACH TRAP...OF THIS BIZARRE LAND-SCAPE!
HERE, I AM, DR. STRANGE!
*AT LAST, WE LEARN HOW YANDROTH ESCAPED LAST ISH! OR HAD YOU GUESSED?!? <-- SOLICITOUS STAN.
BEHIND ME, WOMAN! THE MOMENT HAS COME TO RID MYSELF OF THE ACCURSED MAGE!
WITH NO MATTER IMPEDING ME, I CAN MOVE AS QUICKLY AS THOUGHT! BUT MY FOE IS EQUALLY SWIFT!
DR. STRANGE IS UNARMED... UNPROTECTED! AND YANDROTH STILL HAS A GUN...
I CAN'T LET HIM GET IT OUT! IF I CAN DELAY YANDROTH FOR A MOMENT, DR. STRANGE MAY HAVE A CHANCE!
UHNN..!
STILL SHE PERSISTS IN AIDING THE EARTH-LING! SHE DOES NOT YET REALIZE WHAT GLORY WOULD BE HERS AS MY QUEEN!
GOOD... LORD! WHAT.. WHAT IS THAT BEHIND HIM?
DR. STRANGE... LOOK OUT!!
INSTANTLY, THE MASTER OF BLACK MAGIC WHIRLS, AND SEES...

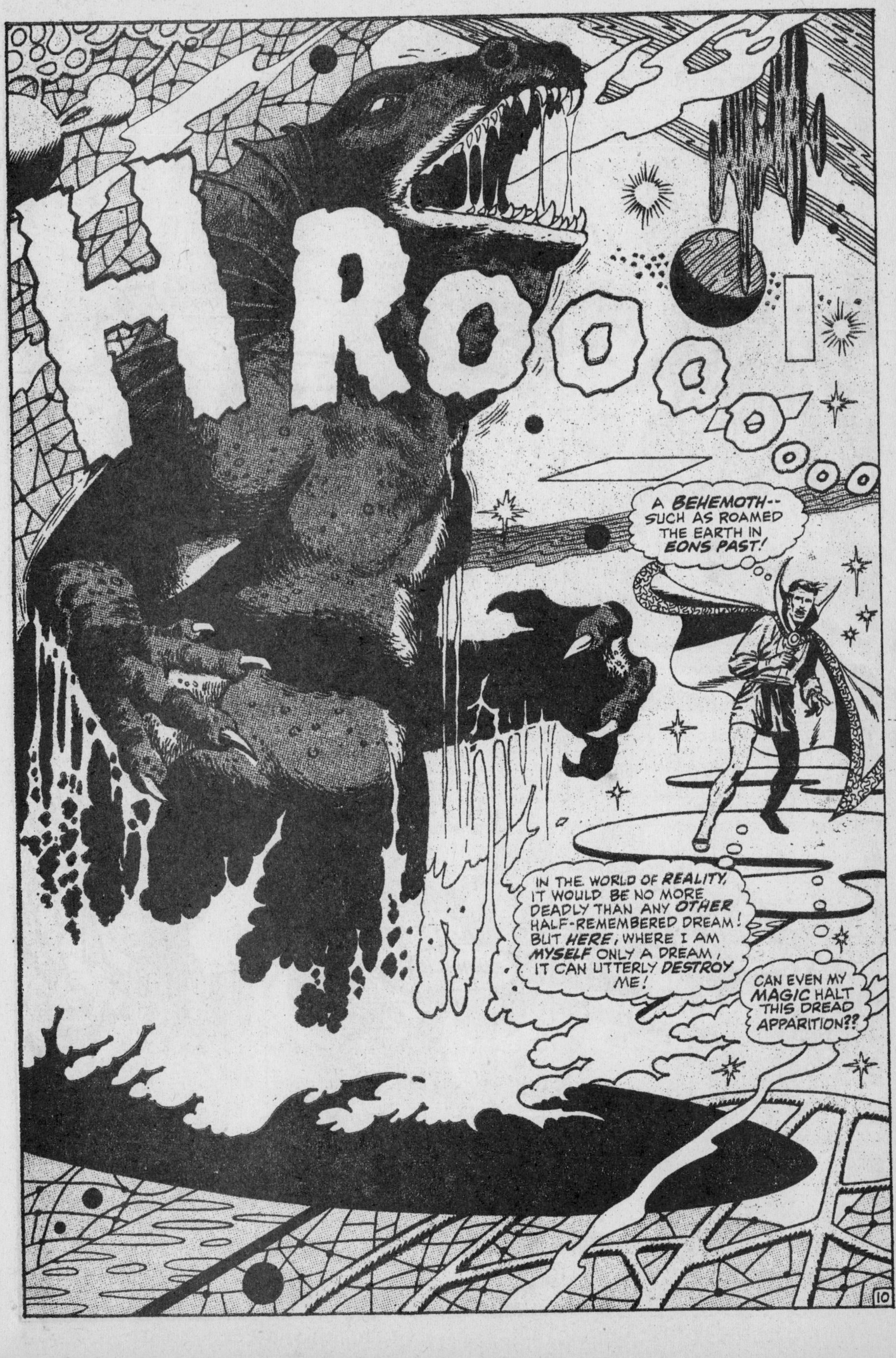
HROOOOOOOO!
A BEHEMOTH-- SUCH AS ROAMED THE EARTH IN EONS PAST!
IN THE WORLD OF REALITY, IT WOULD BE NO MORE DEADLY THAN ANY OTHER HALF-REMEMBERED DREAM! BUT HERE, WHERE I AM MYSELF ONLY A DREAM, IT CAN UTTERLY DESTROY ME!
CAN EVEN MY MAGIC HALT THIS DREAD APPARITION??
10

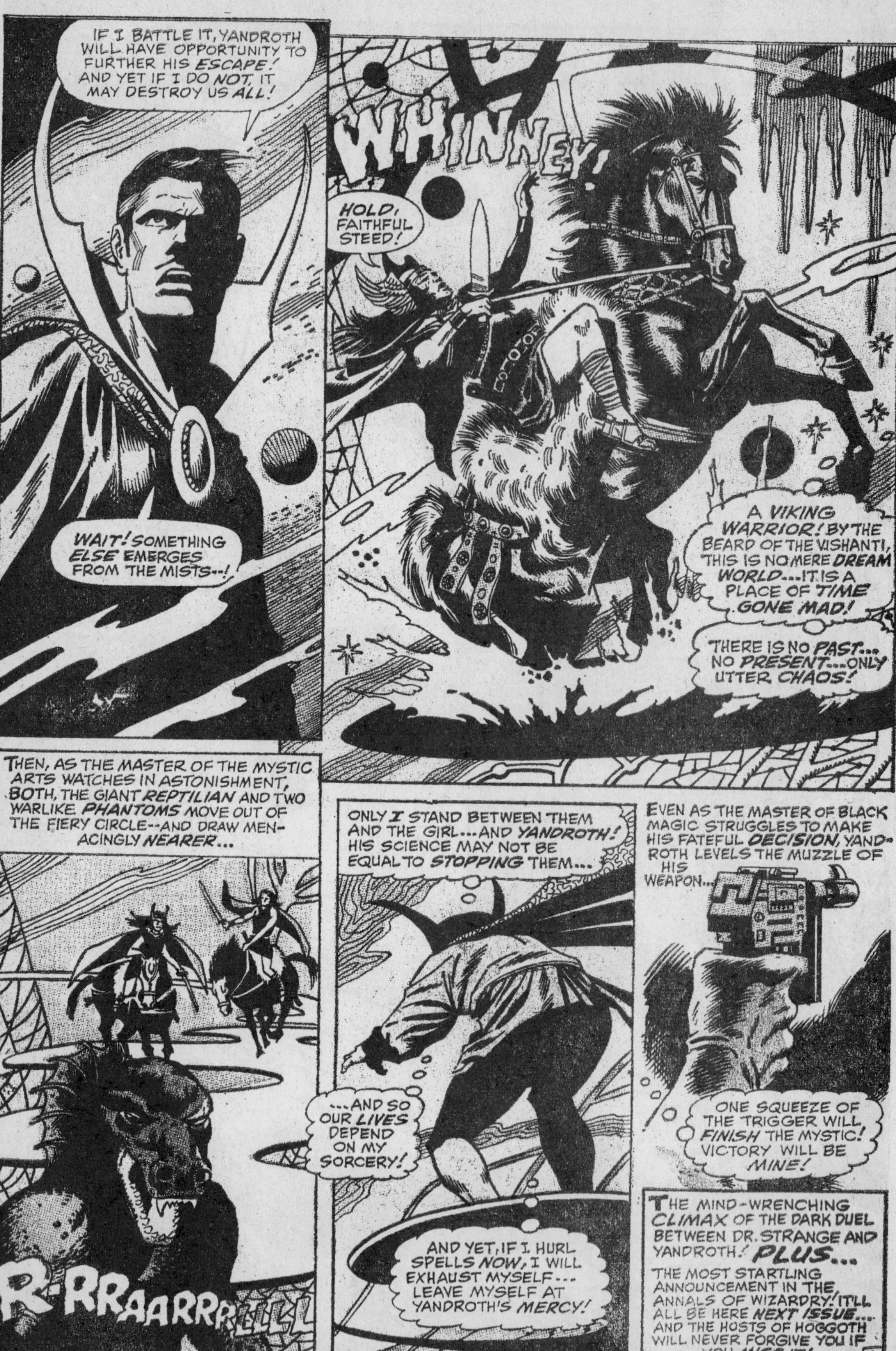
IF I BATTLE IT, YANDROTH WILL HAVE OPPORTUNITY TO FURTHER HIS ESCAPE! AND YET IF I DO NOT, IT MAY DESTROY US ALL!
WAIT! SOMETHING ELSE EMERGES FROM THE MISTS--!
WHINNEY!
HOLD, FAITHFUL STEED!
A VIKING WARRIOR! BY THE BEARD OF THE VISHANTI, THIS IS NO MERE DREAM WORLD...IT IS A PLACE OF TIME GONE MAD!
THERE IS NO PAST... NO PRESENT...ONLY UTTER CHAOS!
THEN, AS THE MASTER OF THE MYSTIC ARTS WATCHES IN ASTONISHMENT, BOTH, THE GIANT REPTILIAN AND TWO WARLIKE PHANTOMS MOVE OUT OF THE FIERY CIRCLE--AND DRAW MEN-ACINGLY NEARER...
R-RRAARRRRLLL
ONLY I STAND BETWEEN THEM AND THE GIRL...AND YANDROTH! HIS SCIENCE MAY NOT BE EQUAL TO STOPPING THEM...
...AND SO OUR LIVES DEPEND ON MY SORCERY!
AND YET, IF I HURL SPELLS NOW, I WILL EXHAUST MYSELF... LEAVE MYSELF AT YANDROTH'S MERCY!
EVEN AS THE MASTER OF BLACK MAGIC STRUGGLES TO MAKE HIS FATEFUL DECISION, YANDROTH LEVELS THE MUZZLE OF HIS WEAPON...
ONE SQUEEZE OF THE TRIGGER WILL FINISH THE MYSTIC! VICTORY WILL BE MINE!
THE MIND-WRENCHING CLIMAX OF THE DARK DUEL BETWEEN DR. STRANGE AND YANDROTH! PLUS...
THE MOST STARTLING ANNOUNCEMENT IN THE ANNALS OF WIZARDRY! IT'LL ALL BE HERE NEXT ISSUE... AND THE HOSTS OF HOGGOTH WILL NEVER FORGIVE YOU IF YOU MISS IT!
11.

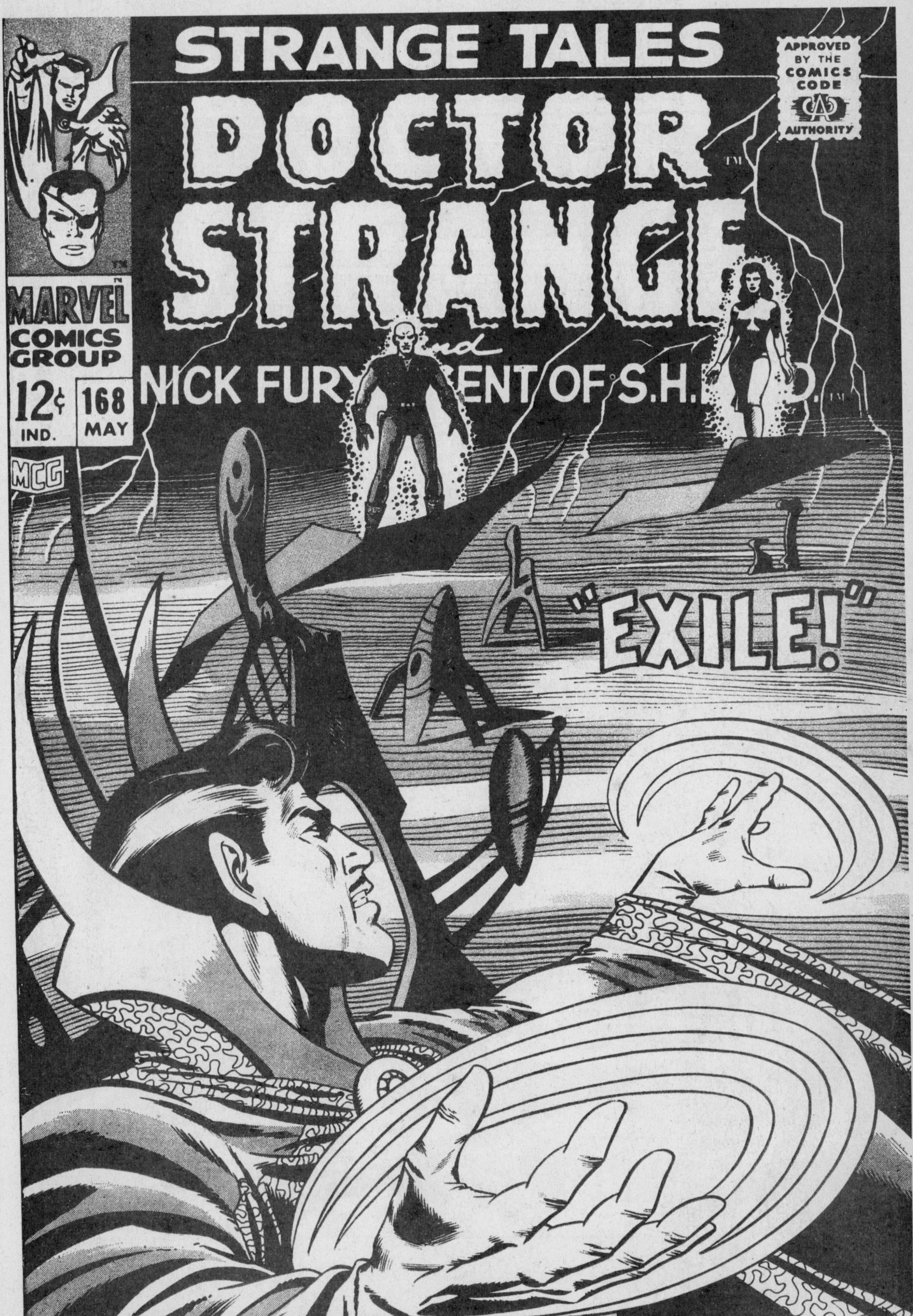
STRANGE TALES
DOCTOR STRANGE
and
NICK FURY AGENT OF S.H.I.E.L.D.
APPROVED BY THE COMICS CODE AUTHORITY
MARVEL COMICS GROUP
12¢ IND.
168 MAY
MCG
"EXILE!"

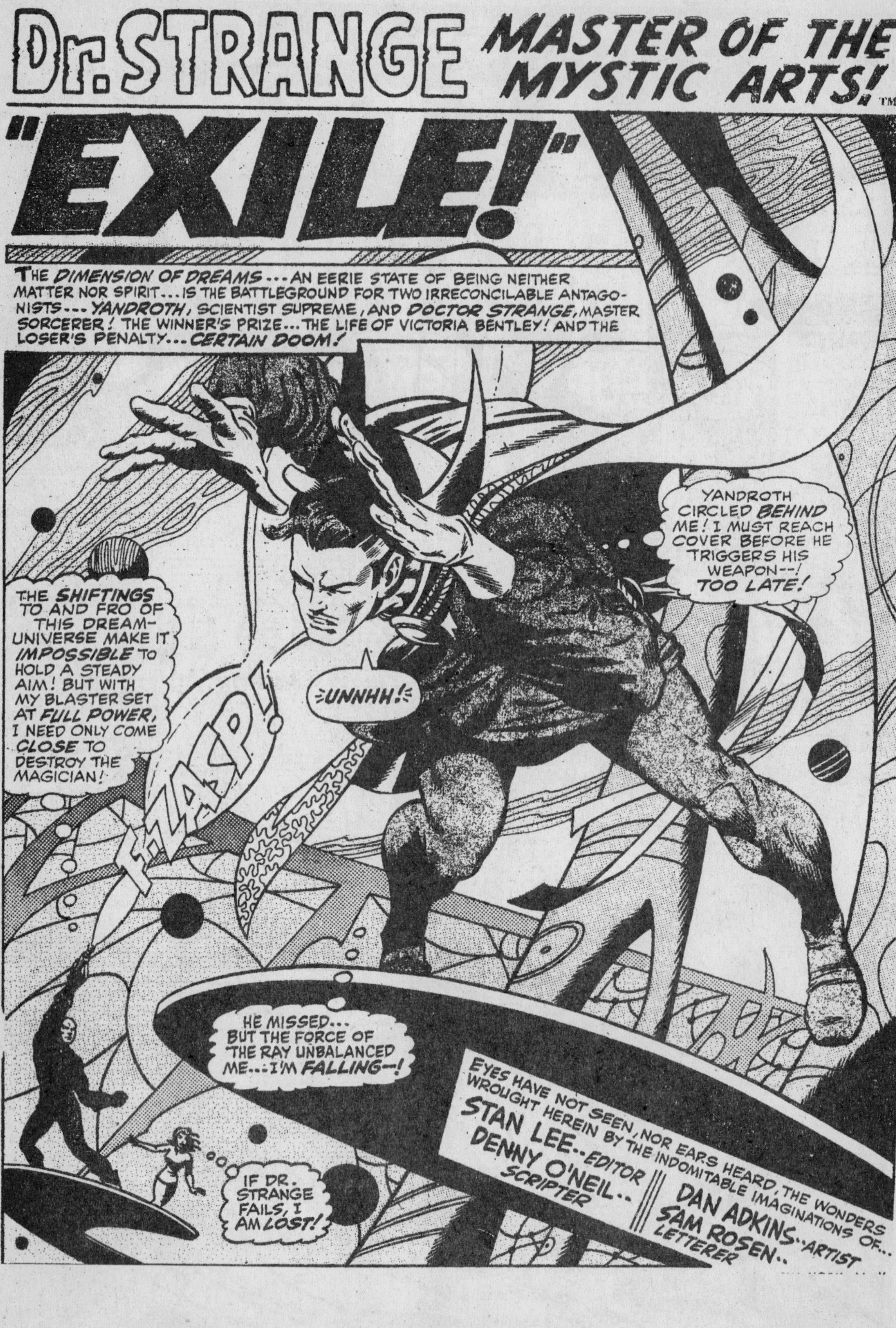

Dr. STRANGE MASTER OF THE MYSTIC ARTS! ™
"EXILE!"
THE DIMENSION OF DREAMS... AN EERIE STATE OF BEING NEITHER MATTER NOR SPIRIT... IS THE BATTLEGROUND FOR TWO IRRECONCILABLE ANTAGONISTS... YANDROTH, SCIENTIST SUPREME, AND DOCTOR STRANGE, MASTER SORCERER! THE WINNER'S PRIZE... THE LIFE OF VICTORIA BENTLEY! AND THE LOSER'S PENALTY... CERTAIN DOOM!
YANDROTH CIRCLED BEHIND ME! I MUST REACH COVER BEFORE HE TRIGGERS HIS WEAPON--! TOO LATE!
THE SHIFTINGS TO AND FRO OF THIS DREAM-UNIVERSE MAKE IT IMPOSSIBLE TO HOLD A STEADY AIM! BUT WITH MY BLASTER SET AT FULL POWER, I NEED ONLY COME CLOSE TO DESTROY THE MAGICIAN!
UNNHH!
F-ZAKP!
HE MISSED... BUT THE FORCE OF THE RAY UNBALANCED ME... I'M FALLING--!
IF DR. STRANGE FAILS, I AM LOST!
EYES HAVE NOT SEEN, NOR EARS HEARD, THE WONDERS WROUGHT HEREIN BY THE INDOMITABLE IMAGINATIONS OF...
STAN LEE.. EDITOR
DENNY O'NEIL.. SCRIPTER
DAN ADKINS.. ARTIST
SAM ROSEN.. LETTERER

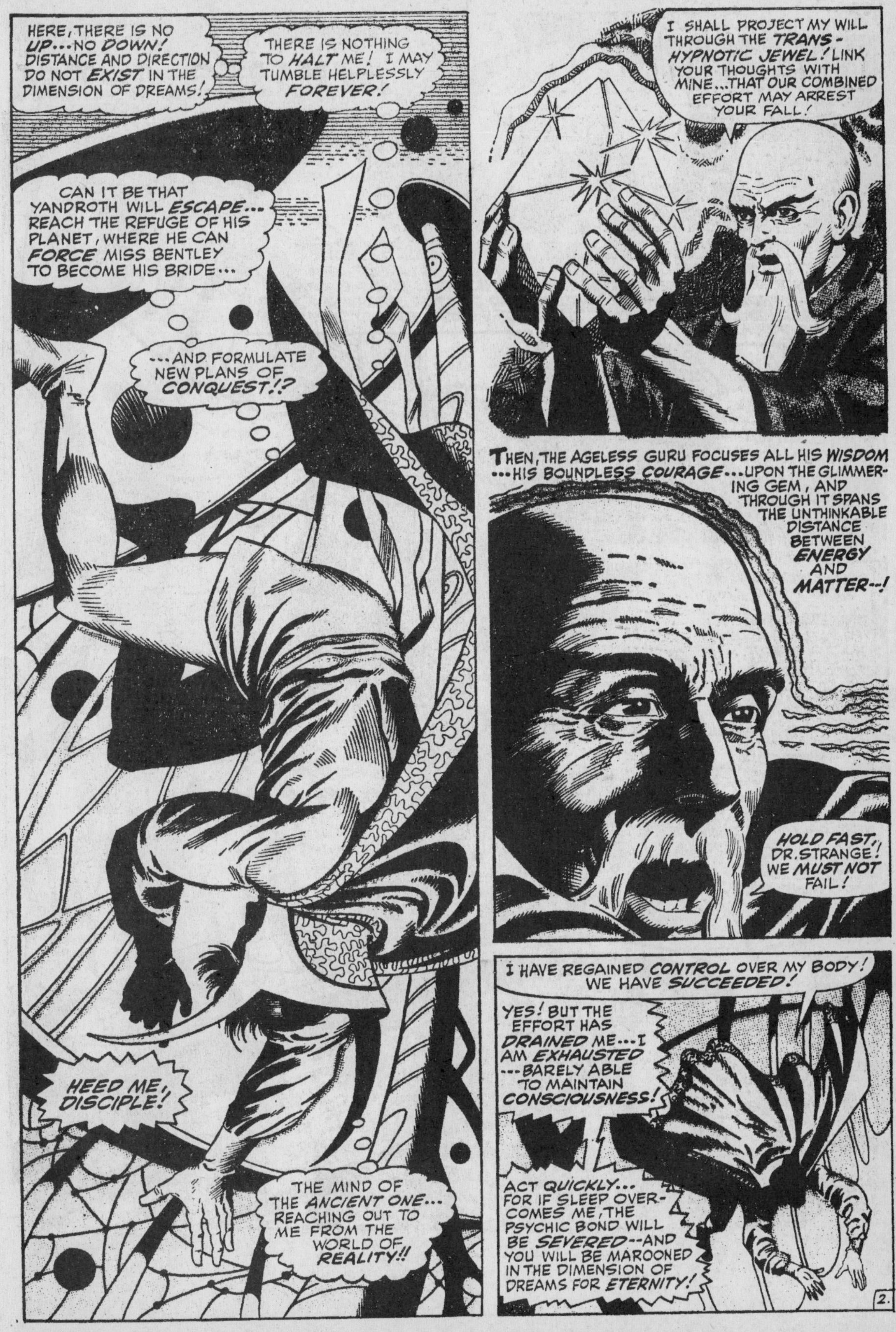
HERE, THERE IS NO UP...NO DOWN! DISTANCE AND DIRECTION DO NOT EXIST IN THE DIMENSION OF DREAMS!
THERE IS NOTHING TO HALT ME! I MAY TUMBLE HELPLESSLY FOREVER!
CAN IT BE THAT YANDROTH WILL ESCAPE... REACH THE REFUGE OF HIS PLANET, WHERE HE CAN FORCE MISS BENTLEY TO BECOME HIS BRIDE...
...AND FORMULATE NEW PLANS OF CONQUEST!?
HEED ME, DISCIPLE!
THE MIND OF THE ANCIENT ONE... REACHING OUT TO ME FROM THE WORLD OF REALITY!!
I SHALL PROJECT MY WILL THROUGH THE TRANS-HYPNOTIC JEWEL! LINK YOUR THOUGHTS WITH MINE...THAT OUR COMBINED EFFORT MAY ARREST YOUR FALL!
THEN, THE AGELESS GURU FOCUSES ALL HIS WISDOM ...HIS BOUNDLESS COURAGE...UPON THE GLIMMERING GEM, AND THROUGH IT SPANS THE UNTHINKABLE DISTANCE BETWEEN ENERGY AND MATTER--!
HOLD FAST, DR. STRANGE! WE MUST NOT FAIL!
I HAVE REGAINED CONTROL OVER MY BODY! WE HAVE SUCCEEDED!
YES! BUT THE EFFORT HAS DRAINED ME...I AM EXHAUSTED ...BARELY ABLE TO MAINTAIN CONSCIOUSNESS!
ACT QUICKLY... FOR IF SLEEP OVERCOMES ME, THE PSYCHIC BOND WILL BE SEVERED--AND YOU WILL BE MAROONED IN THE DIMENSION OF DREAMS FOR ETERNITY!
2.

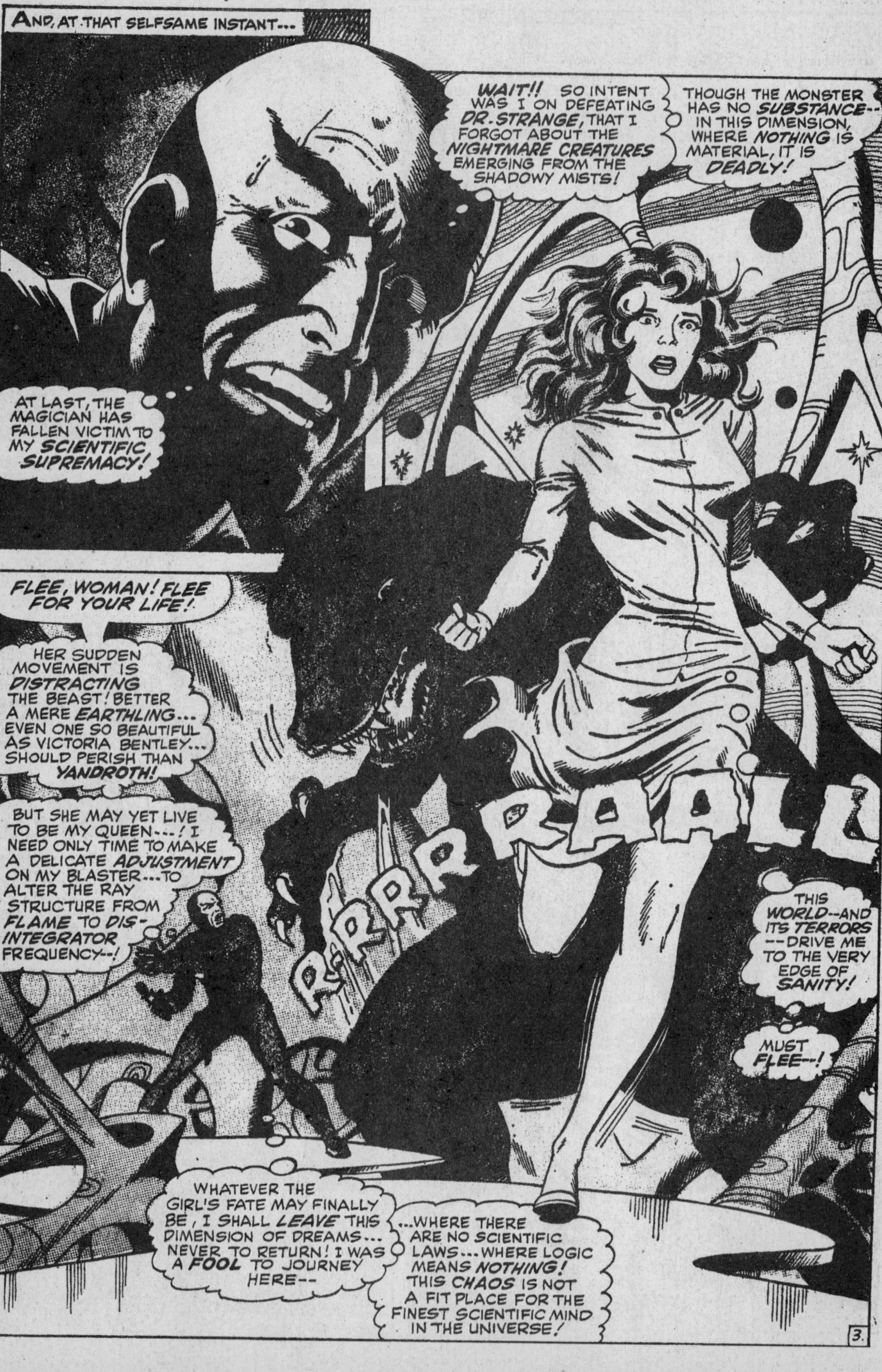

AND, AT THAT SELFSAME INSTANT...
WAIT!! SO INTENT WAS I ON DEFEATING DR. STRANGE, THAT I FORGOT ABOUT THE NIGHTMARE CREATURES EMERGING FROM THE SHADOWY MISTS!
THOUGH THE MONSTER HAS NO SUBSTANCE-- IN THIS DIMENSION, WHERE NOTHING IS MATERIAL, IT IS DEADLY!
AT LAST, THE MAGICIAN HAS FALLEN VICTIM TO MY SCIENTIFIC SUPREMACY!
FLEE, WOMAN! FLEE FOR YOUR LIFE!
HER SUDDEN MOVEMENT IS DISTRACTING THE BEAST! BETTER A MERE EARTHLING... EVEN ONE SO BEAUTIFUL AS VICTORIA BENTLEY... SHOULD PERISH THAN YANDROTH!
BUT SHE MAY YET LIVE TO BE MY QUEEN...! I NEED ONLY TIME TO MAKE A DELICATE ADJUSTMENT ON MY BLASTER...TO ALTER THE RAY STRUCTURE FROM FLAME TO DIS-INTEGRATOR FREQUENCY--!
RRRRRAALL
THIS WORLD--AND ITS TERRORS --DRIVE ME TO THE VERY EDGE OF SANITY!
MUST FLEE--!
WHATEVER THE GIRL'S FATE MAY FINALLY BE, I SHALL LEAVE THIS DIMENSION OF DREAMS... NEVER TO RETURN! I WAS A FOOL TO JOURNEY HERE--
...WHERE THERE ARE NO SCIENTIFIC LAWS...WHERE LOGIC MEANS NOTHING! THIS CHAOS IS NOT A FIT PLACE FOR THE FINEST SCIENTIFIC MIND IN THE UNIVERSE!

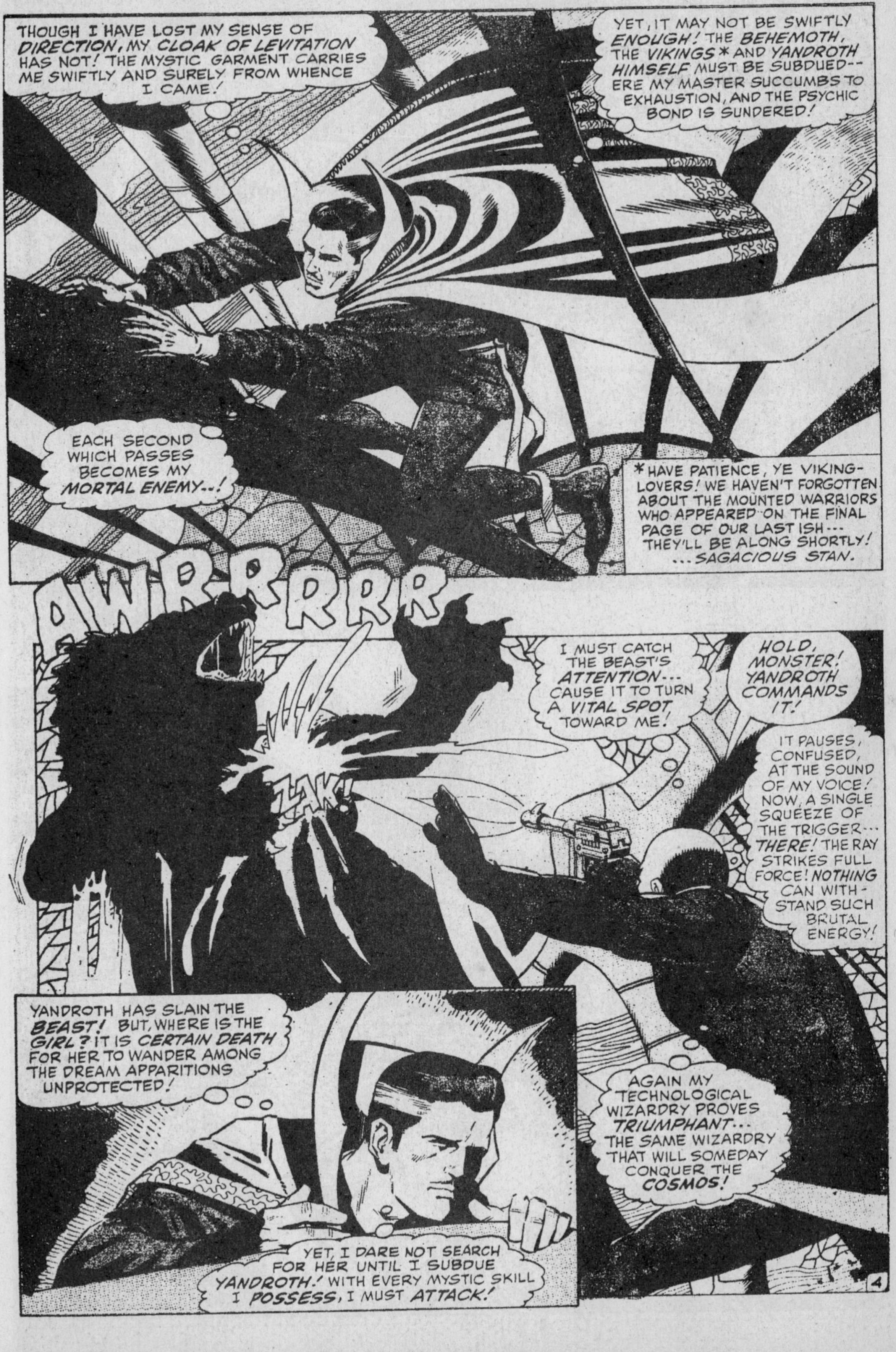
THOUGH I HAVE LOST MY SENSE OF DIRECTION, MY CLOAK OF LEVITATION HAS NOT! THE MYSTIC GARMENT CARRIES ME SWIFTLY AND SURELY FROM WHENCE I CAME!
YET, IT MAY NOT BE SWIFTLY ENOUGH! THE BEHEMOTH, THE VIKINGS* AND YANDROTH HIMSELF MUST BE SUBDUED-- ERE MY MASTER SUCCUMBS TO EXHAUSTION, AND THE PSYCHIC BOND IS SUNDERED!
EACH SECOND WHICH PASSES BECOMES MY MORTAL ENEMY..!
*HAVE PATIENCE, YE VIKING-LOVERS! WE HAVEN'T FORGOTTEN ABOUT THE MOUNTED WARRIORS WHO APPEARED ON THE FINAL PAGE OF OUR LAST ISH--- THEY'LL BE ALONG SHORTLY! ...SAGACIOUS STAN.
AWRRRRR
I MUST CATCH THE BEAST'S ATTENTION... CAUSE IT TO TURN A VITAL SPOT TOWARD ME!
HOLD, MONSTER! YANDROTH COMMANDS IT!
IT PAUSES, CONFUSED, AT THE SOUND OF MY VOICE! NOW, A SINGLE SQUEEZE OF THE TRIGGER--- THERE! THE RAY STRIKES FULL FORCE! NOTHING CAN WITHSTAND SUCH BRUTAL ENERGY!
ZAK!
YANDROTH HAS SLAIN THE BEAST! BUT, WHERE IS THE GIRL? IT IS CERTAIN DEATH FOR HER TO WANDER AMONG THE DREAM APPARITIONS UNPROTECTED!
AGAIN MY TECHNOLOGICAL WIZARDRY PROVES TRIUMPHANT... THE SAME WIZARDRY THAT WILL SOMEDAY CONQUER THE COSMOS!
YET, I DARE NOT SEARCH FOR HER UNTIL I SUBDUE YANDROTH! WITH EVERY MYSTIC SKILL I POSSESS, I MUST ATTACK!
4

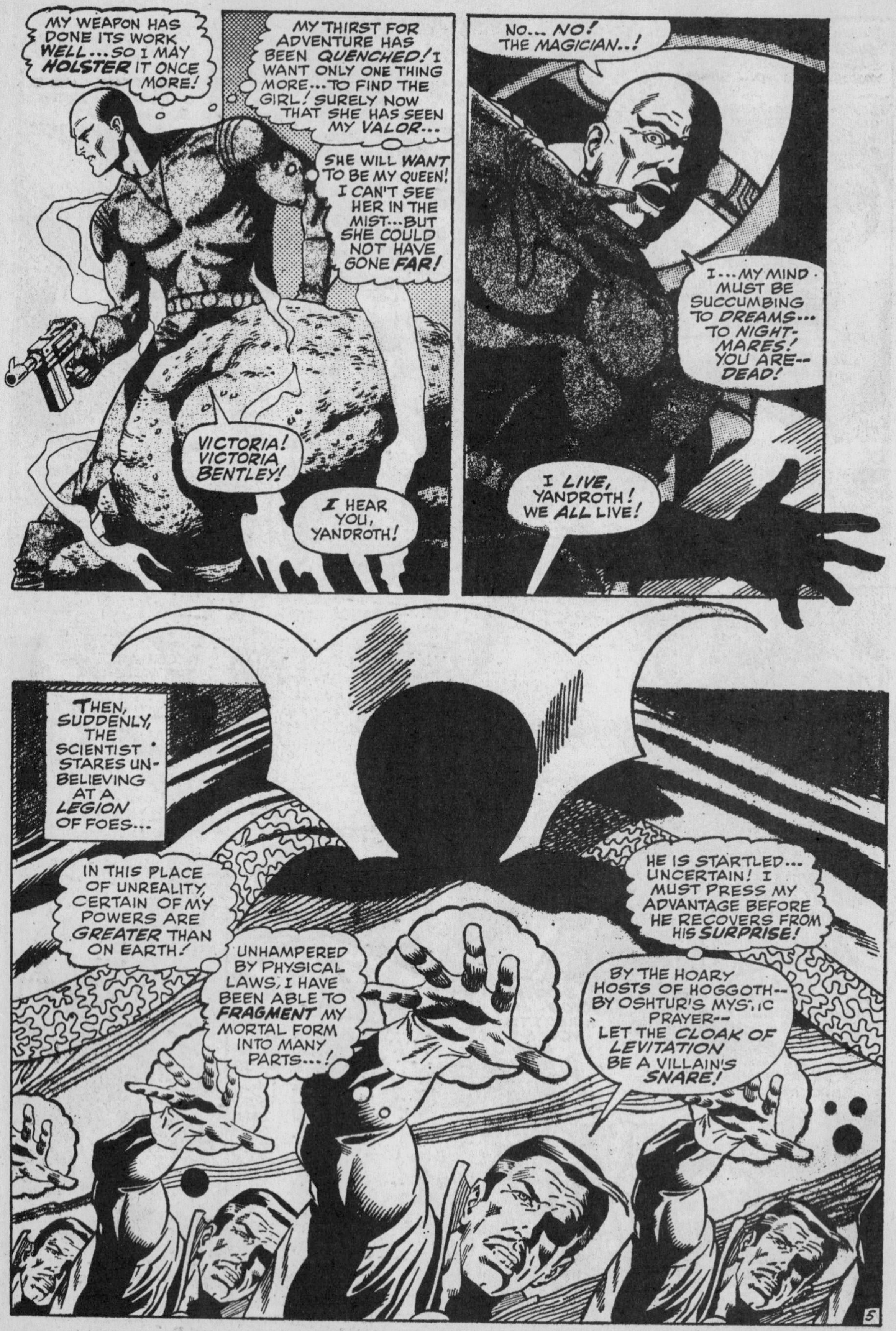

MY WEAPON HAS DONE ITS WORK WELL... SO I MAY HOLSTER IT ONCE MORE!
MY THIRST FOR ADVENTURE HAS BEEN QUENCHED! I WANT ONLY ONE THING MORE... TO FIND THE GIRL! SURELY NOW THAT SHE HAS SEEN MY VALOR...
SHE WILL WANT TO BE MY QUEEN! I CAN'T SEE HER IN THE MIST... BUT SHE COULD NOT HAVE GONE FAR!
VICTORIA! VICTORIA BENTLEY!
I HEAR YOU, YANDROTH!
NO... NO! THE MAGICIAN..!
I... MY MIND MUST BE SUCCUMBING TO DREAMS... TO NIGHT-MARES! YOU ARE-- DEAD!
I LIVE, YANDROTH! WE ALL LIVE!
THEN, SUDDENLY, THE SCIENTIST STARES UN-BELIEVING AT A LEGION OF FOES...
IN THIS PLACE OF UNREALITY, CERTAIN OF MY POWERS ARE GREATER THAN ON EARTH!
UNHAMPERED BY PHYSICAL LAWS, I HAVE BEEN ABLE TO FRAGMENT MY MORTAL FORM INTO MANY PARTS...!
HE IS STARTLED... UNCERTAIN! I MUST PRESS MY ADVANTAGE BEFORE HE RECOVERS FROM HIS SURPRISE!
BY THE HOARY HOSTS OF HOGGOTH-- BY OSHTUR'S MYSTIC PRAYER-- LET THE CLOAK OF LEVITATION BE A VILLAIN'S SNARE!
5

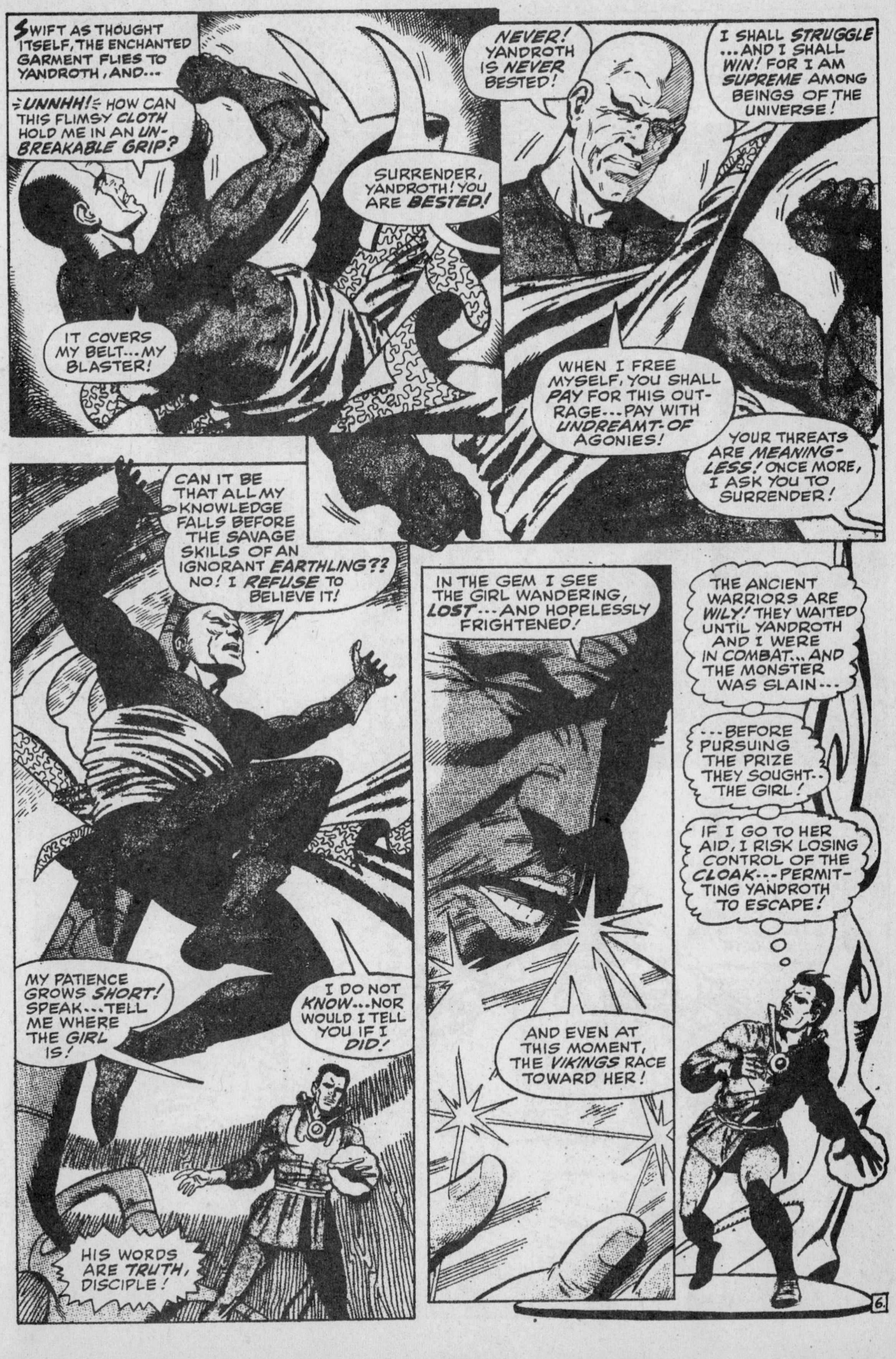
SWIFT AS THOUGHT ITSELF, THE ENCHANTED GARMENT FLIES TO YANDROTH, AND...
UNNHH! HOW CAN THIS FLIMSY CLOTH HOLD ME IN AN UN-BREAKABLE GRIP?
SURRENDER, YANDROTH! YOU ARE BESTED!
IT COVERS MY BELT...MY BLASTER!
NEVER! YANDROTH IS NEVER BESTED!
I SHALL STRUGGLE ...AND I SHALL WIN! FOR I AM SUPREME AMONG BEINGS OF THE UNIVERSE!
WHEN I FREE MYSELF, YOU SHALL PAY FOR THIS OUT-RAGE...PAY WITH UNDREAMT-OF AGONIES!
YOUR THREATS ARE MEANING-LESS! ONCE MORE, I ASK YOU TO SURRENDER!
CAN IT BE THAT ALL MY KNOWLEDGE FALLS BEFORE THE SAVAGE SKILLS OF AN IGNORANT EARTHLING?? NO! I REFUSE TO BELIEVE IT!
MY PATIENCE GROWS SHORT! SPEAK...TELL ME WHERE THE GIRL IS!
I DO NOT KNOW...NOR WOULD I TELL YOU IF I DID!
HIS WORDS ARE TRUTH, DISCIPLE!
IN THE GEM I SEE THE GIRL WANDERING, LOST...AND HOPELESSLY FRIGHTENED!
AND EVEN AT THIS MOMENT, THE VIKINGS RACE TOWARD HER!
THE ANCIENT WARRIORS ARE WILY! THEY WAITED UNTIL YANDROTH AND I WERE IN COMBAT...AND THE MONSTER WAS SLAIN...
...BEFORE PURSUING THE PRIZE THEY SOUGHT.. THE GIRL!
IF I GO TO HER AID, I RISK LOSING CONTROL OF THE CLOAK...PERMIT-TING YANDROTH TO ESCAPE!
6.

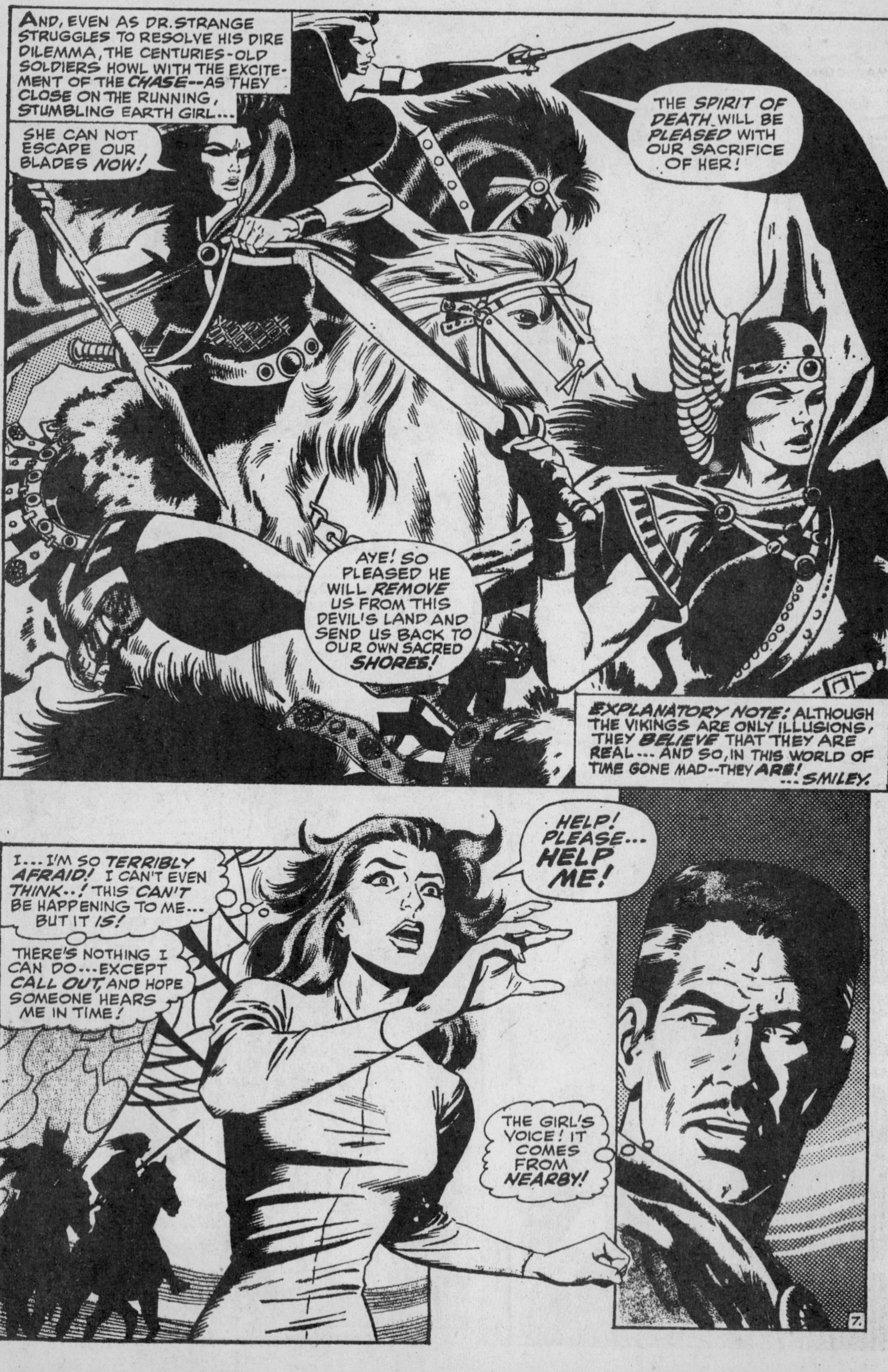
AND, EVEN AS DR. STRANGE STRUGGLES TO RESOLVE HIS DIRE DILEMMA, THE CENTURIES-OLD SOLDIERS HOWL WITH THE EXCITEMENT OF THE CHASE--AS THEY CLOSE ON THE RUNNING, STUMBLING EARTH GIRL...
SHE CAN NOT ESCAPE OUR BLADES NOW!
THE SPIRIT OF DEATH WILL BE PLEASED WITH OUR SACRIFICE OF HER!
AYE! SO PLEASED HE WILL REMOVE US FROM THIS DEVIL'S LAND AND SEND US BACK TO OUR OWN SACRED SHORES!
EXPLANATORY NOTE: ALTHOUGH THE VIKINGS ARE ONLY ILLUSIONS, THEY BELIEVE THAT THEY ARE REAL... AND SO, IN THIS WORLD OF TIME GONE MAD--THEY ARE! ...SMILEY.
I... I'M SO TERRIBLY AFRAID! I CAN'T EVEN THINK..! THIS CAN'T BE HAPPENING TO ME... BUT IT IS!
THERE'S NOTHING I CAN DO... EXCEPT CALL OUT, AND HOPE SOMEONE HEARS ME IN TIME!
HELP! PLEASE... HELP ME!
THE GIRL'S VOICE! IT COMES FROM NEARBY!
7.

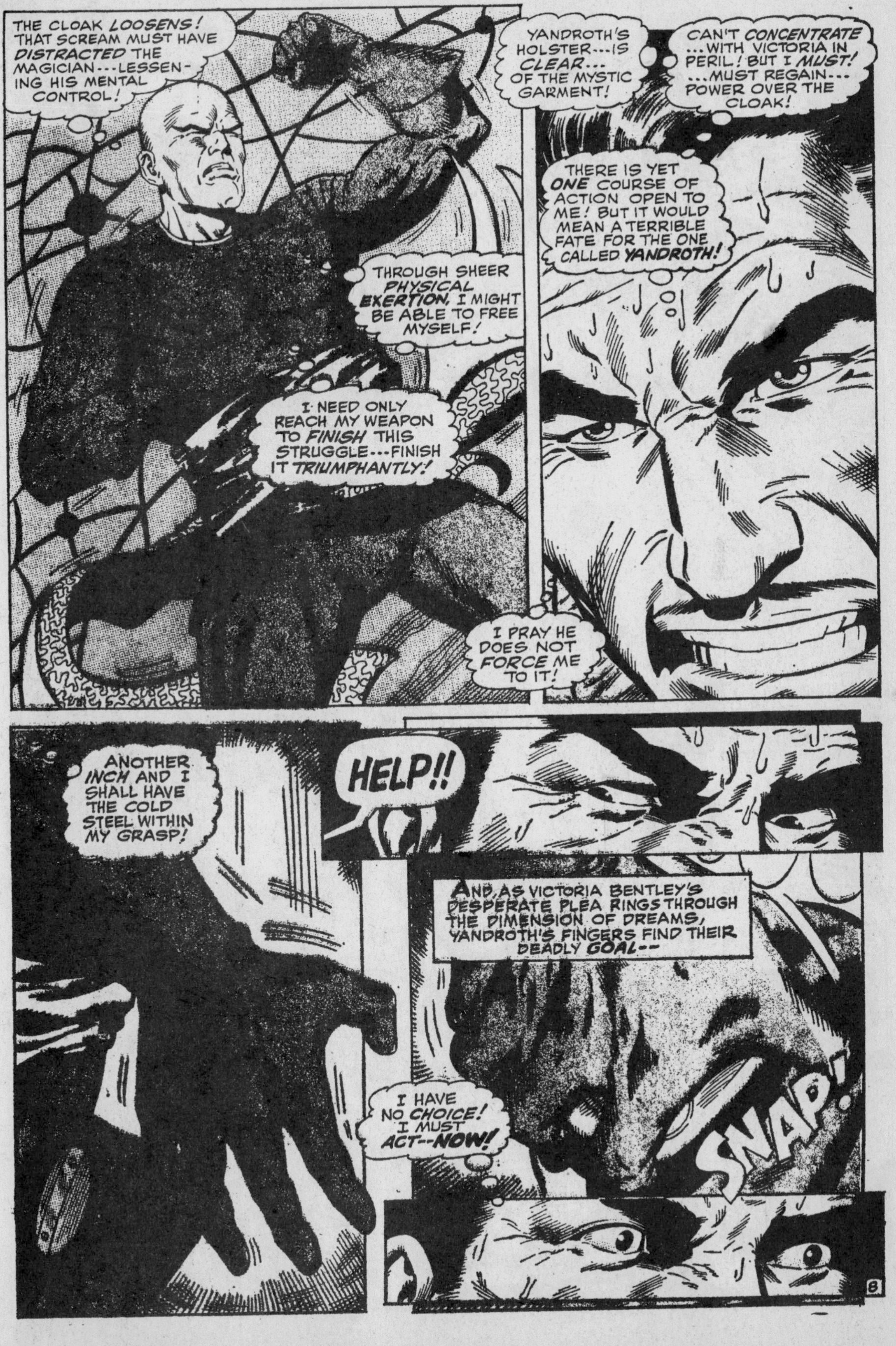
THE CLOAK LOOSENS! THAT SCREAM MUST HAVE DISTRACTED THE MAGICIAN---LESSENING HIS MENTAL CONTROL!
THROUGH SHEER PHYSICAL EXERTION, I MIGHT BE ABLE TO FREE MYSELF!
I NEED ONLY REACH MY WEAPON TO FINISH THIS STRUGGLE---FINISH IT TRIUMPHANTLY!
YANDROTH'S HOLSTER---IS CLEAR--- OF THE MYSTIC GARMENT!
CAN'T CONCENTRATE ...WITH VICTORIA IN PERIL! BUT I MUST! ...MUST REGAIN--- POWER OVER THE CLOAK!
THERE IS YET ONE COURSE OF ACTION OPEN TO ME! BUT IT WOULD MEAN A TERRIBLE FATE FOR THE ONE CALLED YANDROTH!
I PRAY HE DOES NOT FORCE ME TO IT!
ANOTHER INCH AND I SHALL HAVE THE COLD STEEL WITHIN MY GRASP!
HELP!!
AND, AS VICTORIA BENTLEY'S DESPERATE PLEA RINGS THROUGH THE DIMENSION OF DREAMS, YANDROTH'S FINGERS FIND THEIR DEADLY GOAL--
I HAVE NO CHOICE! I MUST ACT--NOW!
SNAP!
8

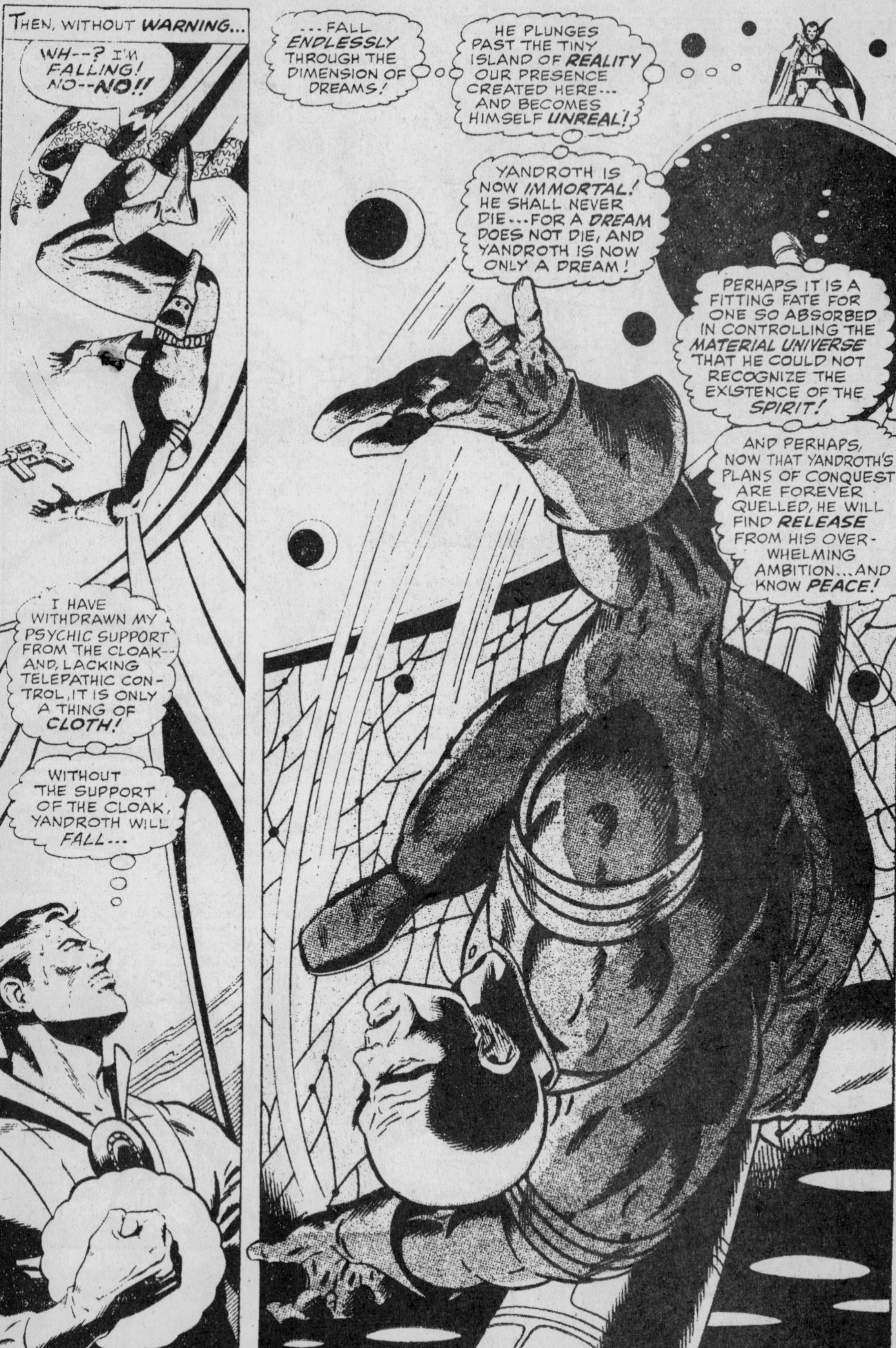

THEN, WITHOUT WARNING...
WH--? I'M FALLING! NO--NO!!
I HAVE WITHDRAWN MY PSYCHIC SUPPORT FROM THE CLOAK--AND, LACKING TELEPATHIC CONTROL, IT IS ONLY A THING OF CLOTH!
WITHOUT THE SUPPORT OF THE CLOAK, YANDROTH WILL FALL...
...FALL ENDLESSLY THROUGH THE DIMENSION OF DREAMS!
HE PLUNGES PAST THE TINY ISLAND OF REALITY OUR PRESENCE CREATED HERE... AND BECOMES HIMSELF UNREAL!
YANDROTH IS NOW IMMORTAL! HE SHALL NEVER DIE...FOR A DREAM DOES NOT DIE, AND YANDROTH IS NOW ONLY A DREAM!
PERHAPS IT IS A FITTING FATE FOR ONE SO ABSORBED IN CONTROLLING THE MATERIAL UNIVERSE THAT HE COULD NOT RECOGNIZE THE EXISTENCE OF THE SPIRIT!
AND PERHAPS, NOW THAT YANDROTH'S PLANS OF CONQUEST ARE FOREVER QUELLED, HE WILL FIND RELEASE FROM HIS OVERWHELMING AMBITION...AND KNOW PEACE!
9.

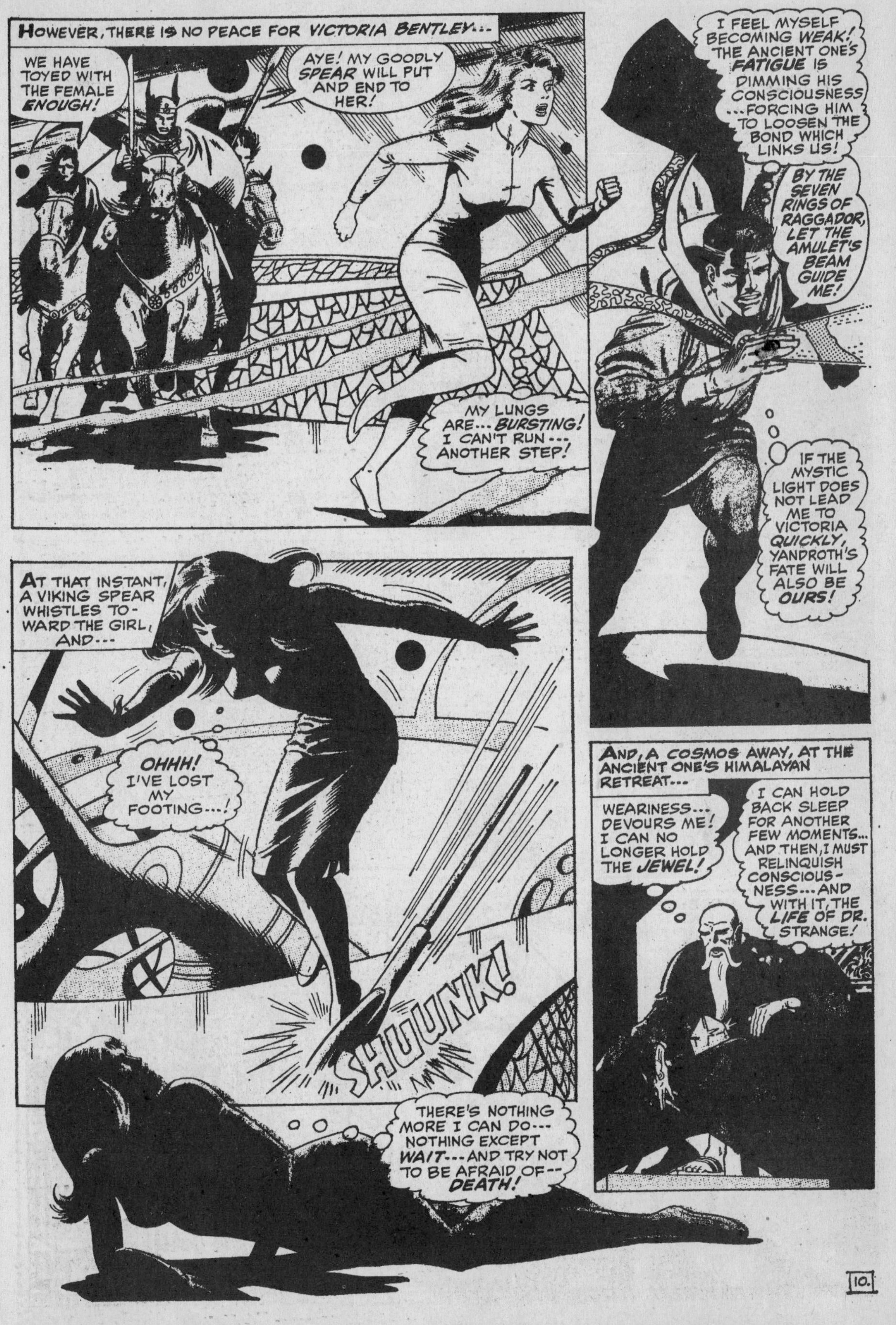

HOWEVER, THERE IS NO PEACE FOR VICTORIA BENTLEY...
WE HAVE TOYED WITH THE FEMALE ENOUGH!
AYE! MY GOODLY SPEAR WILL PUT AND END TO HER!
MY LUNGS ARE... BURSTING! I CAN'T RUN--- ANOTHER STEP!
I FEEL MYSELF BECOMING WEAK! THE ANCIENT ONE'S FATIGUE IS DIMMING HIS CONSCIOUSNESS ...FORCING HIM TO LOOSEN THE BOND WHICH LINKS US!
BY THE SEVEN RINGS OF RAGGADOR, LET THE AMULET'S BEAM GUIDE ME!
IF THE MYSTIC LIGHT DOES NOT LEAD ME TO VICTORIA QUICKLY, YANDROTH'S FATE WILL ALSO BE OURS!
AT THAT INSTANT, A VIKING SPEAR WHISTLES TOWARD THE GIRL, AND---
OHHH! I'VE LOST MY FOOTING---!
SHUUNK!
THERE'S NOTHING MORE I CAN DO--- NOTHING EXCEPT WAIT--- AND TRY NOT TO BE AFRAID OF-- DEATH!
AND, A COSMOS AWAY, AT THE ANCIENT ONE'S HIMALAYAN RETREAT...
WEARINESS... DEVOURS ME! I CAN NO LONGER HOLD THE JEWEL!
I CAN HOLD BACK SLEEP FOR ANOTHER FEW MOMENTS... AND THEN, I MUST RELINQUISH CONSCIOUSNESS... AND WITH IT, THE LIFE OF DR. STRANGE!
10.

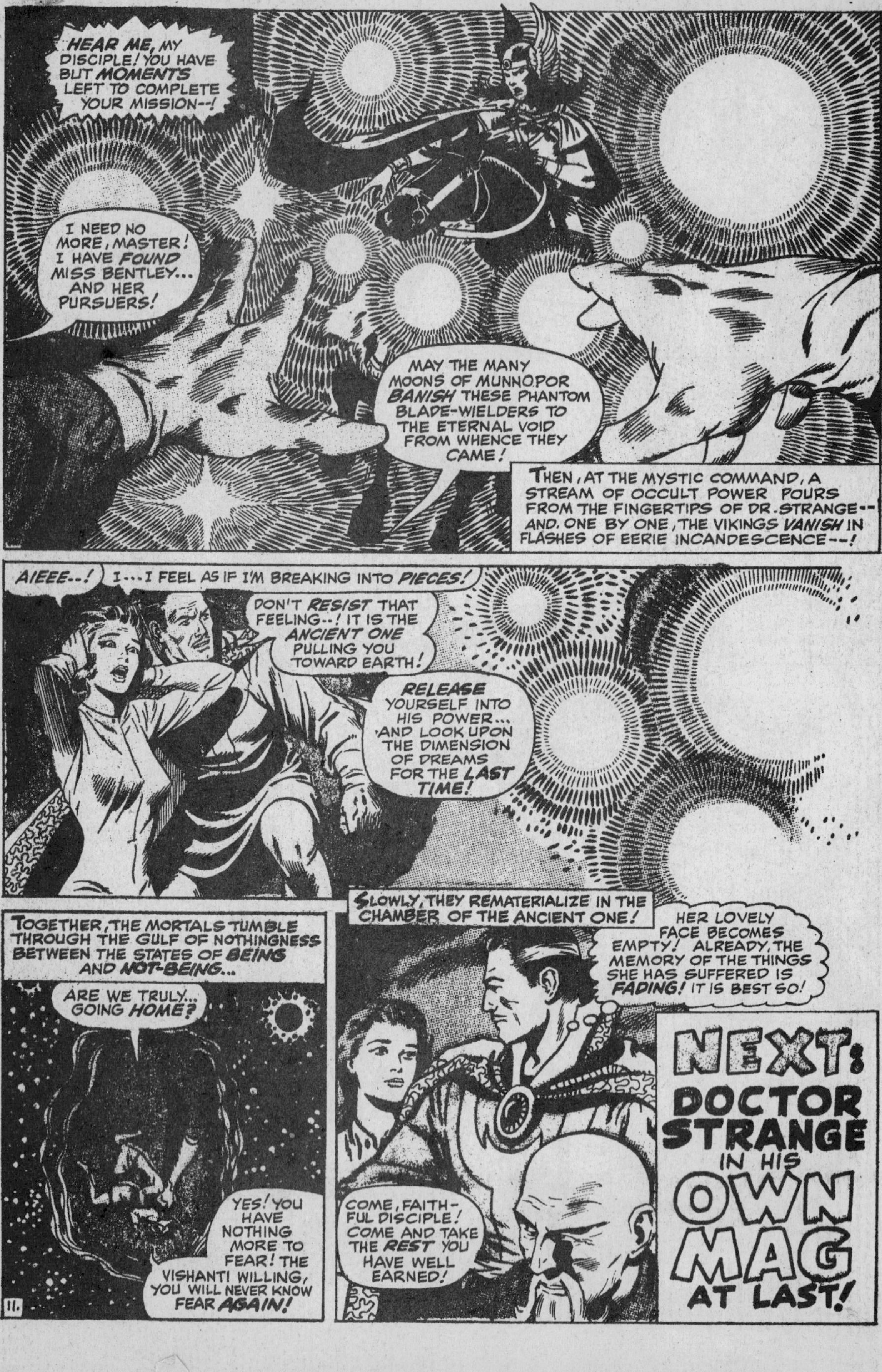
HEAR ME, MY DISCIPLE! YOU HAVE BUT MOMENTS LEFT TO COMPLETE YOUR MISSION--!
I NEED NO MORE, MASTER! I HAVE FOUND MISS BENTLEY... AND HER PURSUERS!
MAY THE MANY MOONS OF MUNNOPOR BANISH THESE PHANTOM BLADE-WIELDERS TO THE ETERNAL VOID FROM WHENCE THEY CAME!
THEN, AT THE MYSTIC COMMAND, A STREAM OF OCCULT POWER POURS FROM THE FINGERTIPS OF DR. STRANGE--AND, ONE BY ONE, THE VIKINGS VANISH IN FLASHES OF EERIE INCANDESCENCE--!
AIEEE--!
I--- I FEEL AS IF I'M BREAKING INTO PIECES!
DON'T RESIST THAT FEELING--! IT IS THE ANCIENT ONE PULLING YOU TOWARD EARTH!
RELEASE YOURSELF INTO HIS POWER... AND LOOK UPON THE DIMENSION OF DREAMS FOR THE LAST TIME!
TOGETHER, THE MORTALS TUMBLE THROUGH THE GULF OF NOTHINGNESS BETWEEN THE STATES OF BEING AND NOT-BEING...
ARE WE TRULY... GOING HOME?
YES! YOU HAVE NOTHING MORE TO FEAR! THE VISHANTI WILLING, YOU WILL NEVER KNOW FEAR AGAIN!
11.
SLOWLY, THEY REMATERIALIZE IN THE CHAMBER OF THE ANCIENT ONE!
HER LOVELY FACE BECOMES EMPTY! ALREADY, THE MEMORY OF THE THINGS SHE HAS SUFFERED IS FADING! IT IS BEST SO!
COME, FAITHFUL DISCIPLE! COME AND TAKE THE REST YOU HAVE WELL EARNED!
NEXT: DOCTOR STRANGE IN HIS OWN MAG AT LAST!